Admiralty Record®

Volume 3

PUBLISHED ADMIRALTY OPINIONS OF
THE SUPREME COURT OF THE UNITED STATES AND
THE UNITED STATES COURTS OF APPEALS ISSUED DURING
THE CALENDAR YEAR

2015

Cite as: 3 Adm. R. _____

REPORTED BY KIRK N. AURANDT, ESQ.
MEMBER OF THE BAR IN LOUISIANA AND PENNSYLVANIA

ADMIRALTY RECORD PUBLISHING COMPANY, L.L.C.
MANDEVILLE, LOUISIANA, U.S.A.

ISSN 2334-5411
ISBN 978-0-9983853-3-4

Admiralty record : published
admiralty opinions of the Supreme
Court of the United States and the
United States Courts of Appeals
issued during the calendar
year ... Mandeville, Louisiana,
U.S.A. : Admiralty Record
Publishing Company, LLC, 2014-

    KF1104 .A75
    ISSN: 2334-5411

https://lccn.loc.gov/2014200303

PREFACE

Volume 3—the third annual edition of the Admiralty Record®—reports the published admiralty opinions of the Supreme Court of the United States and the United States Courts of Appeals that were issued during the calendar year 2015. The opinions reported are the original majority, concurring, and dissenting opinions of the Court, with only minor changes in formatting to better suit a dual-column presentation. The pagination found in the original opinion is indicated by the number contained inside of black brackets. Also, where applicable, I have added parallel citations to opinions reported in Volumes 1, 2, and 3 of the Admiralty Record®.

The decision to select an opinion to appear in Volume 3 of the Admiralty Record® was made solely by me following an examination of those opinions that each of the above-named courts designated for publication in 2015. Every effort has been made to ensure inclusion of all 2015 federal appellate court admiralty opinions that were designated for publication; however, to the extent that a relevant admiralty opinion has been inadvertently overlooked or otherwise mistakenly omitted, the error is regretted and is solely my own. A few opinions from appeals in civil cases that technically may not have fallen under a federal district court's admiralty or maritime jurisdiction have been reported if they touched upon admiralty matters, or were otherwise deemed to be of potential interest to the admiralty practitioner. Additionally, several opinions from criminal cases involving maritime crimes and civil cases arising under the Federal Employers' Liability Act have been included.

To assist the reader in locating those opinions from 2015 involving subject matters of interest, I have prepared an Index to the opinions. I have also prepared Tables of Authority, which supply page references to the cases, statutes, and rules cited in each opinion. Prior to relying upon any of the opinions reported herein, the reader is reminded to verify the current status of any particular case as valid precedent by checking the case with a reliable citator.

Additional copies of Volume 1 (covering 2013), Volume 2 (covering 2014), Volume 3 (covering 2015), and succeeding-year volumes may be ordered at www.admiraltyrecord.com. I hope that the Admiralty Record® will become a valuable and ready reference source for not only the admiralty practitioner, but for anyone who is interested in reading the published admiralty opinions of the federal appellate courts.

KIRK N. AURANDT, ESQ.

This page intentionally left blank

TABLE OF CONTENTS [1]

(CASES ARRANGED CHRONOLOGICALLY BY COURT)

PAGE

---

[1] In 2015, there were no published admiralty opinions from the United States Court of Appeals for the Federal Circuit.

Supreme Court of the United States

Supreme Court of the United States

No. 13-7451

YATES
vs.
UNITED STATES

On Writ of Certiorari to the United States Court of Appeals for the Eleventh Circuit

Decided: February 25, 2015

Citation: 574 U.S. __, 135 S.Ct. 1074, 3 Adm. R. 2 (2015).

GINSBURG, J., announced the judgment of the Court and delivered an opinion, in which ROBERTS, C.J., and BREYER and SOTOMAYOR, J.J., join.

[—1—] GINSBURG, J.:

John Yates, a commercial fisherman, caught undersized red grouper in federal waters in the Gulf of Mexico. To prevent federal authorities from confirming that he had harvested undersized fish, Yates ordered a crew member to toss the suspect catch into the sea. For this offense, he was charged with, and convicted of, violating 18 U. S. C. §1519, which provides:

> "Whoever knowingly alters, destroys, mutilates, conceals, covers up, falsifies, or makes a false entry in any record, document, or tangible object with the intent to impede, obstruct, or influence the investigation or proper administration of any matter within the jurisdiction of any department or agency of the United States or any case filed under title 11, or in relation to or contemplation of any such matter or case, shall be fined under this title, imprisoned not more than 20 years, or both."

Yates was also indicted and convicted under §2232(a), which provides: [—2—]

> "DESTRUCTION OR REMOVAL OF PROPERTY TO PREVENT SEIZURE.— Whoever, before, during, or after any search for or seizure of property by any person authorized to make such search or seizure, knowingly destroys, damages, wastes, disposes of, transfers, or otherwise takes any action, or knowingly attempts to destroy, damage, waste, dispose of, transfer, or otherwise take any action, for the purpose of preventing or impairing the Government's lawful authority to take such property into its custody or control or to continue holding such property under its lawful custody and control, shall be fined under this title or imprisoned not more than 5 years, or both."

Yates does not contest his conviction for violating §2232(a), but he maintains that fish are not trapped within the term "tangible object," as that term is used in §1519.

Section 1519 was enacted as part of the Sarbanes-Oxley Act of 2002, 116 Stat. 745, legislation designed to protect investors and restore trust in financial markets following the collapse of Enron Corporation. A fish is no doubt an object that is tangible; fish can be seen, caught, and handled, and a catch, as this case illustrates, is vulnerable to destruction. But it would cut §1519 loose from its financial-fraud mooring to hold that it encompasses any and all objects, whatever their size or significance, destroyed with obstructive intent. Mindful that in Sarbanes-Oxley, Congress trained its attention on corporate and accounting deception and cover-ups, we conclude that a matching construction of §1519 is in order: A tangible object captured by §1519, we hold, must be one used to record or preserve information.

I

On August 23, 2007, the *Miss Katie*, a commercial fishing boat, was six days into an expedition in the Gulf of [—3—] Mexico. Her crew numbered three, including Yates, the captain. Engaged in a routine offshore patrol to inspect both recreational and commercial vessels, Officer John Jones of the Florida Fish and Wildlife Conservation Commission decided to board the *Miss Katie* to check on the vessel's compliance with fishing rules. Although the *Miss Katie* was far enough from the Florida coast to be in exclusively federal waters, she was nevertheless within Officer

Jones's jurisdiction. Because he had been deputized as a federal agent by the National Marine Fisheries Service, Officer Jones had authority to enforce federal, as well as state, fishing laws.

Upon boarding the *Miss Katie*, Officer Jones noticed three red grouper that appeared to be undersized hanging from a hook on the deck. At the time, federal conservation regulations required immediate release of red grouper less than 20 inches long. 50 CFR §622.37(d)(2)(ii) (effective April 2, 2007). Violation of those regulations is a civil offense punishable by a fine or fishing license suspension. See 16 U. S. C. §§1857(1)(A), (G), 1858(a), (g).

Suspecting that other undersized fish might be on board, Officer Jones proceeded to inspect the ship's catch, setting aside and measuring only fish that appeared to him to be shorter than 20 inches. Officer Jones ultimately determined that 72 fish fell short of the 20-inch mark. A fellow officer recorded the length of each of the undersized fish on a catch measurement verification form. With few exceptions, the measured fish were between 19 and 20 inches; three were less than 19 inches; none were less than 18.75 inches. After separating the fish measuring below 20 inches from the rest of the catch by placing them in wooden crates, Officer Jones directed Yates to leave the fish, thus segregated, in the crates until the *Miss Katie* returned to port. Before departing, Officer Jones issued Yates a citation for possession of undersized fish.

Four days later, after the *Miss Katie* had docked in [—4—] Cortez, Florida, Officer Jones measured the fish contained in the wooden crates. This time, however, the measured fish, although still less than 20 inches, slightly exceeded the lengths recorded on board. Jones surmised that the fish brought to port were not the same as those he had detected during his initial inspection. Under questioning, one of the crew members admitted that, at Yates's direction, he had thrown overboard the fish Officer Jones had measured at sea, and that he and Yates had replaced the tossed grouper with fish from the rest of the catch.

For reasons not disclosed in the record before us, more than 32 months passed before criminal charges were lodged against Yates. On May 5, 2010, he was indicted for destroying property to prevent a federal seizure, in violation of §2232(a), and for destroying, concealing, and covering up undersized fish to impede a federal investigation, in violation of §1519.[1] By the time of the indictment, the minimum legal length for Gulf red grouper had been lowered from 20 inches to 18 inches. See 50 CFR §622.37(d)(2)(iv) (effective May 18, 2009). No measured fish in Yates's catch fell below that limit. The record does not reveal what civil penalty, if any, Yates received for his possession of fish undersized under the 2007 regulation. See 16 U. S. C. §1858(a).

Yates was tried on the criminal charges in August 2011. At the end of the Government's case in chief, he moved for a judgment of acquittal on the §1519 charge. Pointing to §1519's title and its origin as a provision of the Sarbanes-Oxley Act, Yates argued that the section sets forth "a documents offense" and that its reference to "tangible object[s]" subsumes "computer hard drives, logbooks, [and] things of that nature," not fish. App. 91–92. Yates [—5—] acknowledged that the Criminal Code contains "sections that would have been appropriate for the [G]overnment to pursue" if it wished to prosecute him for tampering with evidence. App. 91. Section 2232(a), set out *supra*, at 1–2, fit that description. But §1519, Yates insisted, did not.

The Government countered that a "tangible object" within §1519's compass is "simply something other than a document or record." App. 93. The trial judge expressed misgivings about reading "tangible object" as broadly as the Government urged: "Isn't there a Latin phrase [about] construction of a statute . . . . The gist of it is . . . you take a look at [a] line

---

[1] Yates was also charged with making a false statement to federal law enforcement officers, in violation of 18 U. S. C. §1001(a)(2). That charge, on which Yates was acquitted, is not relevant to our analysis.

of words, and you interpret the words consistently. So if you're talking about documents, and records, tangible objects are tangible objects in the nature of a document or a record, as opposed to a fish." *Ibid.* The first-instance judge nonetheless followed controlling Eleventh Circuit precedent. While recognizing that §1519 was passed as part of legislation targeting corporate fraud, the Court of Appeals had instructed that "the broad language of §1519 is not limited to corporate fraud cases, and 'Congress is free to pass laws with language covering areas well beyond the particular crisis *du jour* that initially prompted legislative action.'" No. 2:10–cr–66–FtM–29SPC (MD Fla., Aug. 8, 2011), App. 116 (quoting *United States* v. *Hunt,* 526 F. 3d 739, 744 (CA11 2008)). Accordingly, the trial court read "tangible object" as a term "independent" of "record" or "document." App. 116. For violating §1519 and §2232(a), the court sentenced Yates to imprisonment for 30 days, followed by supervised release for three years. App. 118–120. For life, he will bear the stigma of having a federal felony conviction.

On appeal, the Eleventh Circuit found the text of §1519 "plain." 733 F. 3d 1059, 1064 (2013). Because "tangible object" was "undefined" in the statute, the Court of Appeals gave the term its "ordinary or natural meaning," *i.e.,* its dictionary definition, "[h]aving or possessing physical [—6—] form." *Ibid.* (quoting Black's Law Dictionary 1592 (9th ed. 2009)).

We granted certiorari, 572 U. S. ___ (2014), and now reverse the Eleventh Circuit's judgment.

II

The Sarbanes-Oxley Act, all agree, was prompted by the exposure of Enron's massive accounting fraud and revelations that the company's outside auditor, Arthur Andersen LLP, had systematically destroyed potentially incriminating documents. The Government acknowledges that §1519 was intended to prohibit, in particular, corporate document-shredding to hide evidence of financial wrong-doing. Brief for United States 46. Prior law

made it an offense to "intimidat[e], threate[n], or corruptly persuad[e] *another person*" to shred documents. §1512(b) (emphasis added). Section 1519 cured a conspicuous omission by imposing liability on a person who destroys records himself. See S. Rep. No. 107–146, p. 14 (2002) (describing §1519 as "a new general anti shredding provision" and explaining that "certain current provisions make it a crime to persuade another person to destroy documents, but not a crime to actually destroy the same documents yourself"). The new section also expanded prior law by including within the provision's reach "any matter within the jurisdiction of any department or agency of the United States." *Id.,* at 14–15.

In the Government's view, §1519 extends beyond the principal evil motivating its passage. The words of §1519, the Government argues, support reading the provision as a general ban on the spoliation of evidence, covering all physical items that might be relevant to any matter under federal investigation.

Yates urges a contextual reading of §1519, tying "tangible object" to the surrounding words, the placement of the provision within the Sarbanes-Oxley Act, and related [—7—] provisions enacted at the same time, in particular §1520 and §1512(c)(1), see *infra,* at 10, 12–13. Section 1519, he maintains, targets not all manner of evidence, but records, documents, and tangible objects used to preserve them, *e.g.,* computers, servers, and other media on which information is stored.

We agree with Yates and reject the Government's unrestrained reading. "Tangible object" in §1519, we conclude, is better read to cover only objects one can use to record or preserve information, not all objects in the physical world.

A

The ordinary meaning of an "object" that is "tangible," as stated in dictionary definitions, is "a discrete . . . thing," Webster's Third New International Dictionary 1555 (2002), that "possess[es] physical form," Black's Law Dictionary 1683 (10th ed. 2014). From this premise, the Government concludes that "tangible object," as that term appears in §1519, covers the waterfront, including fish from the sea.

Whether a statutory term is unambiguous, however, does not turn solely on dictionary definitions of its component words. Rather, "[t]he plainness or ambiguity of statutory language is determined [not only] by reference to the language itself, [but as well by] the specific context in which that language is used, and the broader context of the statute as a whole." *Robinson* v. *Shell Oil Co.*, 519 U. S. 337, 341 (1997). See also *Deal* v. *United States*, 508 U. S. 129, 132 (1993) (it is a "fundamental principle of statutory construction (and, indeed, of language itself) that the meaning of a word cannot be determined in isolation, but must be drawn from the context in which it is used"). Ordinarily, a word's usage accords with its dictionary definition. In law as in life, however, the same words, placed in different contexts, sometimes mean different things. [—8—]

We have several times affirmed that identical language may convey varying content when used in different statutes, sometimes even in different provisions of the same statute. See, *e.g., FAA* v. *Cooper*, 566 U. S. ___, ___–___ (2012), (slip op., at 6–7) ("actual damages" has different meanings in different statutes); *Wachovia Bank, N. A.* v. *Schmidt*, 546 U. S. 303, 313–314 (2006) ("located" has different meanings in different provisions of the National Bank Act); *General Dynamics Land Systems, Inc.* v. *Cline*, 540 U. S. 581, 595–597 (2004) ("age" has different meanings in different provisions of the Age Discrimination in Employment Act of 1967); *United States* v. *Cleveland Indians Baseball Co.*, 532 U. S. 200, 213 (2001) ("wages paid" has different meanings in different provisions of Title 26 U. S. C.); *Robinson*, 519 U. S., at 342–344 ("employee" has different meanings in different sections of Title VII of the Civil Rights Act of 1964); *Merrell Dow Pharmaceuticals Inc.* v. *Thompson*, 478 U. S. 804, 807–808 (1986) ("arising under" has different meanings in U. S. Const., Art. III, §2, and 28 U. S. C. §1331); *District of Columbia* v.

Carter, 409 U. S. 418, 420–421 (1973) ("State or Territory" has different meanings in 42 U. S. C. §1982 and §1983); *Atlantic Cleaners & Dyers, Inc.* v. *United States*, 286 U. S. 427, 433–437 (1932) ("trade or commerce" has different meanings in different sections of the Sherman Act). As the Court observed in *Atlantic Cleaners & Dyers*, 286 U. S., at 433:

"Most words have different shades of meaning and consequently may be variously construed . . . . Where the subject matter to which the words refer is not the same in the several places where [the words] are used, or the conditions are different, or the scope of the legislative power exercised in one case is broader than that exercised in another, the meaning well may vary to meet the purposes of the law, to be arrived at by a [—9—] consideration of the language in which those purposes are expressed, and of the circumstances under which the language was employed."[2]

In short, although dictionary definitions of the words "tangible" and "object" bear consideration, they are not dispositive of the meaning of "tangible object" in §1519.

Supporting a reading of "tangible object," as used in §1519, in accord with dictionary definitions, the Government points to the appearance of that term in Federal Rule of Criminal Procedure 16. That Rule requires the prosecution to grant a defendant's request to inspect "tangible objects" within the Government's control that have utility for the defense. See Fed. Rule Crim. Proc. 16(a)(1)(E).

Rule 16's reference to "tangible objects" has been interpreted to include any physical evidence. See 5 W. LaFave, J. Israel, N. King, & O. Kerr, Criminal Procedure §20.3(g), pp. 405–406, and n. 120 (3d ed. 2007). Rule 16 is a discovery rule designed to protect defendants by compelling the prosecution to turn over to the defense evidence material to the charges

---

[2] The dissent assiduously ignores all this, *post,* at 11–12, in insisting that Congress wrote §1519 to cover, along with shredded corporate documents, red grouper slightly smaller than the legal limit.

at issue. In that context, a comprehensive construction of "tangible objects" is fitting. In contrast, §1519 is a penal provision that refers to "tangible object" not in relation to a request for information relevant to a specific court proceeding, but rather in relation to federal investigations or proceedings of every kind, including those not yet begun.[3] See *Commissioner* v. *National Carbide Corp.*, 167 F. 2d 304, 306 (CA2 1948) (Hand, J.) **[—10—]** ("words are chameleons, which reflect the color of their environment"). Just as the context of Rule 16 supports giving "tangible object" a meaning as broad as its dictionary definition, the context of §1519 tugs strongly in favor of a narrower reading.

B

Familiar interpretive guides aid our construction of the words "tangible object" as they appear in §1519.

We note first §1519's caption: "Destruction, alteration, or falsification of records in Federal investigations and bankruptcy." That heading conveys no suggestion that the section prohibits spoliation of any and all physical evidence, however remote from records. Neither does the title of the section of the Sarbanes-Oxley Act in which §1519 was placed, §802: "Criminal penalties for altering documents." 116 Stat. 800. Furthermore, §1520, the only other provision passed as part of §802, is titled "Destruction of corporate audit records" and addresses only that specific subset of records and documents. While these headings are not commanding, they supply cues that Congress did not intend "tangible object" in §1519 to sweep within its reach physical objects of every kind, including things no one would describe as records, documents, or devices closely associated with them. See *Almendarez-Torres* v. *United States*, 523 U. S. 224, 234 (1998) ("[T]he title of a statute and the heading of a section are tools

available for the resolution of a doubt about the meaning of a statute." (internal quotation marks omitted)). If Congress indeed meant to make §1519 an all-encompassing ban on the spoliation of evidence, as the dissent believes Congress did, one would have expected a clearer indication of that intent.

Section 1519's position within Chapter 73 of Title 18 further signals that §1519 was not intended to serve as a cross-the-board ban on the destruction of physical evi- **[—11—]** dence of every kind. Congress placed §1519 (and its companion provision §1520) at the end of the chapter, following immediately after the pre-existing §1516, §1517, and §1518, each of them prohibiting obstructive acts in specific contexts. See §1516 (audits of recipients of federal funds); §1517 (federal examinations of financial institutions); §1518 (criminal investigations of federal health care offenses). See also S. Rep. No. 107–146, at 7 (observing that §1517 and §1518 "apply to obstruction in certain limited types of cases, such as bankruptcy fraud, examinations of financial institutions, and healthcare fraud").

But Congress did not direct codification of the Sarbanes-Oxley Act's other additions to Chapter 73 adjacent to these specialized provisions. Instead, Congress directed placement of those additions within or alongside retained provisions that address obstructive acts relating broadly to official proceedings and criminal trials: Section 806, "Civil Action to protect against retaliation in fraud cases," was codified as §1514A and inserted between the pre-existing §1514, which addresses civil actions to restrain harassment of victims and witnesses in criminal cases, and §1515, which defines terms used in §1512 and §1513. Section 1102, "Tampering with a record or otherwise impeding an official proceeding," was codified as §1512(c) and inserted within the pre-existing §1512, which addresses tampering with a victim, witness, or informant to impede any official proceeding. Section 1107, "Retaliation against informants," was codified as §1513(e) and inserted within the pre-existing §1513, which addresses retaliation against a victim, witness, or informant in any official proceeding. Congress thus ranked §1519, not

---

[3] For the same reason, we do not think the meaning of "tangible objects" (or "tangible things," see Fed. Rule Civ. Proc. 26(b)) in other discovery prescriptions cited by the Government leads to the conclusion that "tangible object" in §1519 encompasses any and all physical evidence existing on land or in the sea.

among the broad proscriptions, but together with specialized provisions expressly aimed at corporate fraud and financial audits. This placement accords with the view that Congress' conception of §1519's coverage was considerably [—12—] more limited than the Government's.[4]

The contemporaneous passage of §1512(c)(1), which was contained in a section of the Sarbanes-Oxley Act discrete from the section embracing §1519 and §1520, is also instructive. Section 1512(c)(1) provides:

"(c) Whoever corruptly—

"(1) alters, destroys, mutilates, or conceals a record, document, or other object, or attempts to do so, with the intent to impair the object's integrity or availability for use in an official proceeding

.   .   .   .   .   .

"shall be fined under this title or imprisoned not more than 20 years, or both."

The legislative history reveals that §1512(c)(1) was drafted and proposed after §1519. See 148 Cong. Rec. 12518, 13088–13089 (2002). The Government argues, and Yates does not dispute, that §1512(c)(1)'s reference to "other object" includes any and every physical object. But if §1519's reference to "tangible object" already included all physical objects, as the

Government and the dissent contend, then Congress had no reason to enact §1512(c)(1): Virtually any act that would violate §1512(c)(1) no doubt would violate §1519 as well, for §1519 applies to "the [—13—] investigation or proper administration of any matter within the jurisdiction of any department or agency of the United States . . . or in relation to or contemplation of any such matter," not just to "an official proceeding."[5]

The Government acknowledges that, under its reading, §1519 and §1512(c)(1) "significantly overlap." Brief for United States 49. Nowhere does the Government explain what independent function §1512(c)(1) would serve if the Government is right about the sweeping scope of §1519. We resist a reading of §1519 that would render superfluous an entire provision passed in proximity as part of the same Act.[6] See *Marx* v. *General Revenue Corp.*, 568 U. S. ___, ___ (2013) (slip op., at 14) ("[T]he canon against surplusage is strongest

---

[4] The dissent contends that nothing can be drawn from the placement of §1519 because, before and after Sarbanes-Oxley, "all of Chapter 73 was ordered chronologically." *Post*, at 9. The argument might have some force if the factual premise were correct. In Sarbanes-Oxley, Congress directed insertion of §1514A *before* §1518, then the last section in Chapter 73. If, as the dissent argues, Congress adopted §1519 to fill out §1512, *post*, at 6–7, it would have made more sense for Congress to codify the substance of §1519 within §1512 or in a new §1512A, rather than placing §1519 among specialized provisions. Notably, in Sarbanes-Oxley, Congress added §1512(c)(1), "a broad ban on evidence-spoliation," cf. *post*, at 9, n. 2, to §1512, even though §1512's preexisting title and provisions all related to witness-tampering.

[5] Despite this sweeping "in relation to" language, the dissent remarkably suggests that §1519 does not "ordinarily operate in th[e] context [of] federal court[s]," for those courts are not "department[s] or agenc[ies]." *Post*, at 10. That suggestion, which, as one would expect, lacks the Government's endorsement, does not withstand examination. The Senate Committee Report on §1519, on which the dissent elsewhere relies, see *post*, at 6, explained that an obstructive act is within §1519's scope if "done 'in contemplation' of or in relation to a matter or investigation." S. Rep. 107–146, at 15. The Report further informed that §1519 "is . . . meant to do away with the distinctions, which some courts have read into obstruction statutes, between court proceedings, investigations, regulatory or administrative proceedings (whether formal or not), and less formal government inquiries, regardless of their title." *Ibid.* If any doubt remained about the multiplicity of contexts in which §1519 was designed to apply, the Report added, "[t]he intent of the provision is simple; people should not be destroying, altering, or falsifying documents to obstruct any government function." *Ibid.*

[6] Furthermore, if "tangible object" in §1519 is read to include any physical object, §1519 would prohibit all of the conduct proscribed by §2232(a), which imposes a maximum penalty of five years in prison for destroying or removing "property" to prevent its seizure by the Government. See *supra*, at 1–2.

when an interpretation would render superfluous another part of the same statutory scheme.").

The words immediately surrounding "tangible object" in §1519—"falsifies, or makes a false entry in any record [or] [—14—] document"—also cabin the contextual meaning of that term. As explained in *Gustafson* v. *Alloyd Co.*, 513 U. S. 561, 575 (1995), we rely on the principle of *noscitur a sociis*—a word is known by the company it keeps—to "avoid ascribing to one word a meaning so broad that it is inconsistent with its accompanying words, thus giving unintended breadth to the Acts of Congress." (internal quotation marks omitted). See also *United States* v. *Williams*, 553 U. S. 285, 294 (2008) ("a word is given more precise content by the neighboring words with which it is associated"). In *Gustafson*, we interpreted the word "communication" in §2(10) of the Securities Act of 1933 to refer to a public communication, rather than any communication, because the word appeared in a list with other words, notably "notice, circular, [and] advertisement," making it "apparent that the list refer[red] to documents of wide dissemination." 513 U. S., at 575–576. And we did so even though the list began with the word "any."

The *noscitur a sociis* canon operates in a similar manner here. "Tangible object" is the last in a list of terms that begins "any record [or] document." The term is therefore appropriately read to refer, not to any tangible object, but specifically to the subset of tangible objects involving records and documents, *i.e.*, objects used to record or preserve information. See United States Sentencing Commission, Guidelines Manual §2J1.2, comment., n. 1 (Nov. 2014) ("'Records, documents, or tangible objects' includes (A) records, documents, or tangible objects that are stored on, or that are, magnetic, optical, digital, other electronic, or other storage mediums or devices; and (B) wire or electronic communications.").

This moderate interpretation of "tangible object" accords with the list of actions §1519 proscribes. The section applies to anyone who "alters, destroys, mutilates, conceals, covers up, *falsifies*, or *makes a false entry in* any record, document, or tangible object" with the requisite [—15—] obstructive intent. (Emphasis added.) The last two verbs, "falsif[y]" and "mak[e] a false entry in," typically take as grammatical objects records, documents, or things used to record or preserve information, such as logbooks or hard drives. See, *e.g.*, Black's Law Dictionary 720 (10th ed. 2014) (defining "falsify" as "[t]o make deceptive; to counterfeit, forge, or misrepresent; esp., to tamper with (a document, record, etc.)"). It would be unnatural, for example, to describe a killer's act of wiping his fingerprints from a gun as "falsifying" the murder weapon. But it would not be strange to refer to "falsifying" data stored on a hard drive as simply "falsifying" a hard drive. Furthermore, Congress did not include on §1512(c)(1)'s list of prohibited actions "falsifies" or "makes a false entry in." See §1512(c)(1) (making it unlawful to "alte[r], destro[y], mutilat[e], or concea[l] a record, document, or other object" with the requisite obstructive intent). That contemporaneous omission also suggests that Congress intended "tangible object" in §1519 to have a narrower scope than "other object" in §1512(c)(1).[7]

A canon related to *noscitur a sociis*, *ejusdem generis*, counsels: "Where general words follow specific words in a [—16—] statutory enumeration, the general words are

---

[7] The dissent contends that "record, document, or tangible object" in §1519 should be construed in conformity with "record, document, or other object" in §1512(c)(1) because both provisions address "the same basic problem." *Post*, at 11–12. But why should that be so when Congress prohibited in §1519 additional actions, specific to paper and electronic documents and records, actions it did not prohibit in §1512(c)(1)? When Congress passed Sarbanes-Oxley in 2002, courts had already interpreted the phrase "alter, destroy, mutilate, or conceal an object" in §1512(b)(2)(B) to apply to all types of physical evidence. See, *e.g.*, *United States* v. *Applewhaite*, 195 F. 3d 679, 688 (CA3 1999) (affirming conviction under §1512(b)(2)(B) for persuading another person to paint over blood spatter). Congress' use of a formulation in §1519 that did not track the one used in §1512(b)(2)(B) (and repeated in §1512(c)(1)) suggests that Congress designed §1519 to be interpreted apart from §1512, not in lockstep with it.

[usually] construed to embrace only objects similar in nature to those objects enumerated by the preceding specific words." *Washington State Dept. of Social and Health Servs.* v. *Guardianship Estate of Keffeler*, 537 U. S. 371, 384 (2003) (internal quotation marks omitted). In *Begay* v. *United States*, 553 U. S. 137, 142–143 (2008), for example, we relied on this principle to determine what crimes were covered by the statutory phrase "any crime . . . that . . . is burglary, arson, or extortion, involves use of explosives, or otherwise involves conduct that presents a serious potential risk of physical injury to another," 18 U. S. C. §924(e)(2)(B)(ii). The enumeration of specific crimes, we explained, indicates that the "otherwise involves" provision covers "only *similar* crimes, rather than *every* crime that 'presents a serious potential risk of physical injury to another.'" 553 U. S., at 142. Had Congress intended the latter "all encompassing" meaning, we observed, "it is hard to see why it would have needed to include the examples at all." *Ibid.* See also *CSX Transp., Inc.* v. *Alabama Dept. of Revenue*, 562 U. S. 277, ___ (2011) (slip op., at 16) ("We typically use *ejusdem generis* to ensure that a general word will not render specific words meaningless."). Just so here. Had Congress intended "tangible object" in §1519 to be interpreted so generically as to capture physical objects as dissimilar as documents and fish, Congress would have had no reason to refer specifically to "record" or "document." The Government's unbounded reading of "tangible object" would render those words misleading surplusage.

Having used traditional tools of statutory interpretation to examine markers of congressional intent within the Sarbanes-Oxley Act and §1519 itself, we are persuaded that an aggressive interpretation of "tangible object" must be rejected. It is highly improbable that Congress would have buried a general spoliation statute covering objects of [—17—] any and every kind in a provision targeting fraud in financial record-keeping.

The Government argues, however, that our inquiry would be incomplete if we failed to consider the origins of the phrase "record, document, or tangible object." Congress drew that phrase, the Government says, from a 1962 Model Penal Code (MPC) provision, and reform proposals based on that provision. The MPC provision and proposals prompted by it would have imposed liability on anyone who "alters, destroys, mutilates, conceals, or removes a record, document or thing." See ALI, MPC §241.7(1), p. 175 (1962). Those proscriptions were understood to refer to all physical evidence. See MPC §241.7, Comment 3, at 179 (1980) (provision "applies to any physical object"). Accordingly, the Government reasons, and the dissent exuberantly agrees, *post*, at 4–5, Congress must have intended §1519 to apply to the universe of physical evidence.

The inference is unwarranted. True, the 1962 MPC provision prohibited tampering with any kind of physical evidence. But unlike §1519, the MPC provision did not prohibit actions that specifically relate to records, documents, and objects used to record or preserve information. The MPC provision also ranked the offense as a misdemeanor and limited liability to instances in which the actor "believ[es] that an official proceeding or investigation is pending or about to be instituted." MPC §241.7(1), at 175. Yates would have had scant reason to anticipate a felony prosecution, and certainly not one instituted at a time when even the smallest of the fish he caught came within the legal limit. See *supra*, at 4; cf. *Bond* v. *United States*, 572 U. S. ___, ___ (2014), (slip op., at 14) (rejecting "boundless reading" of a statutory term given "deeply serious consequences" that reading would entail). A proposed federal offense in line with the MPC provision, advanced by a federal commission in 1971, was similarly [—18—] qualified. See Final Report of the National Commission on Reform of Federal Criminal Laws §1323, pp. 116–117 (1971).

Section 1519 conspicuously lacks the limits built into the MPC provision and the federal proposal. It describes not a misdemeanor, but a felony punishable by up to 20 years in prison. And the section covers conduct intended to impede any federal investigation or proceeding, including one not even on the verge of commencement. Given these significant differences, the meaning of "record, document, or thing" in the MPC provision and a kindred proposal is not a reliable indicator of the meaning Congress assigned to "record, document, or tangible object" in §1519. The MPC provision, in short, tells us neither "what Congress wrote [nor] what Congress wanted," cf. *post*, at 15, concerning Yates's small fish as the subject of a federal felony prosecution.

C

Finally, if our recourse to traditional tools of statutory construction leaves any doubt about the meaning of "tangible object," as that term is used in §1519, we would invoke the rule that "ambiguity concerning the ambit of criminal statutes should be resolved in favor of lenity." *Cleveland* v. *United States*, 531 U.S. 12, 25 (2000) (quoting *Rewis* v. *United States*, 401 U. S. 808, 812 (1971)). That interpretative principle is relevant here, where the Government urges a reading of §1519 that exposes individuals to 20-year prison sentences for tampering with *any* physical object that *might* have evidentiary value in *any* federal investigation into *any* offense, no matter whether the investigation is pending or merely contemplated, or whether the offense subject to investigation is criminal or civil. See *Liparota* v. *United States*, 471 U.S. 419, 427 (1985) ("Application of the rule of lenity ensures that criminal statutes will provide fair warning concerning [—19—] conduct rendered illegal and strikes the appropriate balance between the legislature, the prosecutor, and the court in defining criminal liability."). In determining the meaning of "tangible object" in §1519, "it is appropriate, before we choose the harsher alternative, to require that Congress should have spoken in language that is clear and definite." See *Cleveland*, 531 U.S., at 25 (quoting *United States* v. *Universal C. I. T. Credit Corp.*, 344 U.S. 218, 222 (1952)). See also *Jones* v. *United States*, 529 U. S. 848, 858–859 (2000) (rule of lenity "reinforces" the conclusion that arson of an owner-occupied residence is not subject to federal prosecution under 18 U. S. C. §844(i) because such a residence does not qualify as property "used

in" commerce or commerce-affecting activity).[8]
[—20—]

* * *

For the reasons stated, we resist reading §1519 expansively to create a coverall spoliation of evidence statute, advisable as such a measure might be. Leaving that important decision to Congress, we hold that a "tangible object" within §1519's compass is one used to record or preserve information. The judgment of the U. S. Court of Appeals for the Eleventh Circuit is therefore reversed, and the case is remanded for further proceedings.

It is so ordered.

(Reporter's Note: Concurring opinion follows on p. 11).

---

[8] The dissent cites *United States* v. *McRae*, 702 F. 3d 806, 834–838 (CA5 2012), *United States* v. *Maury*, 695 F. 3d 227, 243–244 (CA3 2012), and *United States* v. *Natal*, 2014 U. S. Dist. LEXIS 108852, *24–*26 (Conn., Aug. 7, 2014), as cases that would not be covered by §1519 as we read it. *Post*, at 18–19. Those cases supply no cause for concern that persons who commit "major" obstructive acts, *id.* at 18, will go unpunished. The defendant in *McRae*, a police officer who seized a car containing a corpse and then set it on fire, was also convicted for that conduct under 18 U. S. C. §844(h) and sentenced to a term of 120 months' imprisonment for that offense. See 702 F. 3d, at 817–818, 839–840. The defendant in *Natal*, who repainted a van to cover up evidence of a fatal arson, was also convicted of three counts of violating 18 U. S. C. §3 and sentenced to concurrent terms of 174 months' imprisonment. See Judgment in *United States* v. *Morales*, No. 3:12–cr–164 (Conn., Jan. 12, 2015). And the defendant in *Maury*, a company convicted under §1519 of concealing evidence that a cement mixer's safety lock was disabled when a worker's fingers were amputated, was also convicted of numerous other violations, including three counts of violating 18 U. S. C. §1505 for concealing evidence of other worker safety violations. See 695 F. 3d, at 244–245. See also *United States* v. *Atlantic States Cast Iron Pipe Co.*, 2007 WL 2282514, *70 (NJ, Aug. 2, 2007) (setting forth charges against the company). For those violations, the company was fined millions of dollars and ordered to operate under the supervision of a court-appointed monitor. See 695 F. 3d, at 246.

[—1—] **ALITO, J.**, concurring in the judgment:

This case can and should be resolved on narrow grounds. And though the question is close, traditional tools of statutory construction confirm that John Yates has the better of the argument. Three features of 18 U. S. C. §1519 stand out to me: the statute's list of nouns, its list of verbs, and its title. Although perhaps none of these features by itself would tip the case in favor of Yates, the three combined do so.

Start with the nouns. Section 1519 refers to "any record, document, or tangible object." The *noscitur a sociis* canon instructs that when a statute contains a list, each word in that list presumptively has a "similar" meaning. See, *e.g., Gustafson* v. *Alloyd Co.*, 513 U. S. 561, 576 (1995). A related canon, *ejusdem generis* teaches that general words following a list of specific words should usually be read in light of those specific words to mean something "similar." See, *e.g., Christopher* v. *SmithKline Beecham Corp.*, 567 U. S. ___, ___ (2012) (slip op., at 18). Applying these canons to §1519's list of nouns, the term "tangible object" should refer to something similar to records or documents. A fish does not spring to mind— nor does an antelope, a colonial farmhouse, a hydrofoil, or an oil derrick. All are "objects" that are "tangible." But who wouldn't raise an eyebrow if a neighbor, when asked to identify something similar to a "record" or "document," [—2—] said "crocodile"?

This reading, of course, has its shortcomings. For instance, this is an imperfect *ejusdem generis* case because "record" and "document" are themselves quite general. And there is a risk that "tangible object" may be made superfluous—what is similar to a "record" or "document" but yet is not one? An e-mail, however, could be such a thing. See United States Sentencing Commission, Guidelines Manual §2J1.2 and comment. (Nov. 2003) (reading "records, documents, or tangible objects" to "includ[e]" what is found on "magnetic, optical, digital, other electronic, or other storage mediums or devices"). An e-mail, after all, might not be a "document" if, as was "traditionally" so, a document was a "piece of paper with information on it," not "information stored on a computer, electronic storage device, or any other medium." Black's Law Dictionary 587– 588 (10th ed. 2014). E-mails might also not be "records" if records are limited to "minutes" or other formal writings "designed to memorialize [past] events." *Id.*, at 1465. A hard drive, however, is tangible and can contain files that are precisely akin to even these narrow definitions. Both "record" and "document" can be read more expansively, but adding "tangible object" to §1519 would ensure beyond question that electronic files are included. To be sure, "tangible object" presumably can capture more than just e-mails; Congress enacts "catchall[s]" for "known unknowns." *Republic of Iraq* v. *Beaty*, 556 U. S. 848, 860 (2009). But where *noscitur a sociis* and *ejusdem generis* apply, "known unknowns" should be similar to known knowns, *i.e.*, here, records and documents. This is especially true because reading "tangible object" too broadly could render "record" and "document" superfluous.

Next, consider §1519's list of verbs: "alters, destroys, mutilates, conceals, covers up, falsifies, or makes a false entry in." Although many of those verbs could apply to nouns as far-flung as salamanders, satellites, or sand [—3—] dunes, the last phrase in the list— "makes a false entry in"—makes no sense outside of filekeeping. How does one make a false entry in a fish? "Alters" and especially "falsifies" are also closely associated with filekeeping. Not one of the verbs, moreover, *cannot* be applied to filekeeping—certainly not in the way that "makes a false entry in" is always inconsistent with the aquatic.

Again, the Government is not without a response. One can imagine Congress trying to write a law so broadly that not every verb lines up with every noun. But failure to "line up" may suggest that something has gone awry in one's interpretation of a text. Where, as here, each of a statute's verbs applies to a certain category of nouns, there is some reason to think that Congress had that category in mind. Categories, of course, are often underinclusive or overinclusive—§1519, for instance, applies to a bomb-threatening letter but not a bomb. But this does not mean that categories are not useful or that Congress does not enact them. See, *e.g., Vance* v. *Bradley*, 440 U. S. 93, 108–109 (1979). Here, focusing on the verbs, the category of nouns appears to be filekeeping. This observation is not dispositive, but neither is it nothing. The Government also contends that §1519's verbs cut both ways because it is unnatural to apply "falsifies" to tangible objects, and that is certainly true. One does not falsify the outside casing of a hard drive, but one could falsify or alter data physically recorded on that hard drive.

Finally, my analysis is influenced by §1519's title: "Destruction, alteration, or falsification of *records* in Federal investigations and bankruptcy." (Emphasis added.) This too points toward filekeeping, not fish. Titles can be useful devices to resolve "'doubt about the meaning of a statute.'" *Porter* v. *Nussle*, 534 U. S. 516, 527–528 (2002) (quoting *Almendarez-Torres* v. *United States*, 523 U. S. 224, 234 (1998)); see also *Lawson* v. *FMR LLC*, 571 U. S. ___, ___–___ (2014) (SOTOMAYOR, J., dissenting) (slip op., [—4—] at 4–6). The title is especially valuable here because it reinforces what the text's nouns and verbs independently suggest—that no matter how other statutes might be read, this particular one does not cover every noun in the universe with tangible form.

Titles, of course, are also not dispositive. Here, if the list of nouns did not already suggest that "tangible object" should mean something similar to records or documents, especially when read in conjunction with §1519's peculiar list of verbs with their focus on filekeeping, then the title would not be enough on its own. In conjunction with those other two textual features, however, the Government's argument, though colorable, becomes too implausible to accept. See, *e.g., Washington State Dept. of Social and Health Servs.* v. *Guardianship Estate of Keffeler*, 537 U.S. 371, 384–385 (2003) (focusing on the "product of [two] canons of construction" which was "confirmed" by other interpretative evidence); cf. *Al-Adahi* v. *Obama*, 613 F. 3d 1102, 1105–1106 (CADC 2010) (aggregating evidence).

(Reporter's Note: Dissenting opinion follows on p. 13).

KAGAN, J., with whom SCALIA, KENNEDY, and THOMAS, J.J., join, dissenting.

[—1—] KAGAN, J,:

A criminal law, 18 U. S. C. §1519, prohibits tampering with "any record, document, or tangible object" in an attempt to obstruct a federal investigation. This case raises the question whether the term "tangible object" means the same thing in §1519 as it means in everyday language—any object capable of being touched. The answer should be easy: Yes. The term "tangible object" is broad, but clear. Throughout the U. S. Code and many States' laws, it invariably covers physical objects of all kinds. And in §1519, context confirms what bare text says: All the words surrounding "tangible object" show that Congress meant the term to have a wide range. That fits with Congress's evident purpose in enacting §1519: to punish those who alter or destroy physical evidence—*any* physical evidence—with the intent of thwarting federal law enforcement.

The plurality instead interprets "tangible object" to cover "only objects one can use to record or preserve information." *Ante*, at 7. The concurring opinion similarly, if more vaguely, contends that "tangible object" should refer to "something similar to records or documents"—and shouldn't include colonial farmhouses, crocodiles, or fish. *Ante*, at 1 (ALITO, J., concurring in judgment). In my view, conventional tools of statutory construction all lead to a [—2—] more conventional result: A "tangible object" is an object that's tangible. I would apply the statute that Congress enacted and affirm the judgment below.

I

While the plurality starts its analysis with §1519's heading, see *ante*, at 10 ("We note first §1519's caption"), I would begin with §1519's text. When Congress has not supplied a definition, we generally give a statutory term its ordinary meaning. See, *e.g.*, *Schindler Elevator Corp.* v. *United States ex rel. Kirk*, 563 U. S. ___, ___ (2011) (slip op., at 5). As the plurality must acknowledge, the ordinary meaning of "tangible object" is "a discrete thing that possesses physical form." *Ante*, at 7 (punctuation and citation omitted). A fish is, of course, a discrete thing that possesses physical form. See generally Dr. Seuss, One Fish Two Fish Red Fish Blue Fish (1960). So the ordinary meaning of the term "tangible object" in §1519, as no one here disputes, covers fish (including too-small red grouper).

That interpretation accords with endless uses of the term in statute and rule books as construed by courts. Dozens of federal laws and rules of procedure (and hundreds of state enactments) include the term "tangible object" or its first cousin "tangible thing"—some in association with documents, others not. See, *e.g.*, 7 U. S. C. §8302(2) (referring to "any material or tangible object that could harbor a pest or disease"); 15 U. S. C. §57b–1(c) (authorizing investigative demands for "documentary material or tangible things"); 18 U. S. C. §668(a)(1)(D) (defining "museum" as entity that owns "tangible objects that are exhibited to the public"); 28 U. S. C. §2507(b) (allowing discovery of "relevant facts, books, papers, documents or tangible things").[1] To my knowledge, no court [—3—] has ever read any such provision to exclude things that don't record or preserve data; rather, all courts have adhered to the statutory language's ordinary (*i.e.*, expansive) meaning. For example, courts have understood the phrases "tangible objects" and "tangible things" in the Federal Rules of Criminal and Civil Procedure to cover everything from guns to drugs to machinery to . . . . animals. See, *e.g.*, *United States* v. *Obiukwu*, 17 F. 3d 816, 819 (CA6 1994) (*per curiam*) (handgun); *United States* v. *Acarino*,

---

[1] From Alabama and Alaska through Wisconsin and Wyoming (and [—3—] trust me—in all that come between), States similarly use the terms "tangible objects" and "tangible things" in statutes and rules of all sorts. See, *e.g.* , Ala. Code §34–17–1(3) (2010) (defining "landscape architecture" to include the design of certain "tangible objects and features"); Alaska Rule Civ. Proc. 34(a)(1) (2014) (allowing litigants to "inspect, copy, test, or sample any tangible things" that constitute or contain discoverable material); Wis. Stat. §804.09(1) (2014) (requiring the production of "designated tangible things" in civil proceedings); Wyo. Rule Crim. Proc. 41(h) (2014) (defining "property" for purposes of a search-and-seizure statute to include "documents, books, papers and any other tangible objects").

270 F. Supp. 526, 527–528 (EDNY 1967) (heroin); *In re Newman*, 782 F. 2d 971, 972–975 (CA Fed. 1986) (energy generation system); *Martin* v. *Reynolds Metals Corp.*, 297 F. 2d 49, 56–57 (CA9 1961) (cattle). No surprise, then, that—until today—courts have uniformly applied the term "tangible object" in §1519 in the same way. See, *e.g.*, *United States* v. *McRae*, 702 F. 3d 806, 834–838 (CA5 2012) (corpse); *United States* v. *Maury*, 695 F. 3d 227, 243–244 (CA3 2012) (cement mixer).

That is not necessarily the end of the matter; I agree with the plurality (really, who does not?) that context matters in interpreting statutes. We do not "construe the meaning of statutory terms in a vacuum." *Tyler* v. *Cain*, 533 U. S. 656, 662 (2001). Rather, we interpret particular words "in their context and with a view to their place in the overall statutory scheme." *Davis* v. *Michigan Dept. of Treasury*, 489 U. S. 803, 809 (1989). And sometimes that [—4—] means, as the plurality says, that the dictionary definition of a disputed term cannot control. See, *e.g.*, *Bloate* v. *United States*, 559 U. S. 196, 205, n. 9 (2010). But this is not such an occasion, for here the text and its context point the same way. Stepping back from the words "tangible object" provides only further evidence that Congress said what it meant and meant what it said.

Begin with the way the surrounding words in §1519 reinforce the breadth of the term at issue. Section 1519 refers to "any" tangible object, thus indicating (in line with *that* word's plain meaning) a tangible object "of whatever kind." Webster's Third New International Dictionary 97 (2002). This Court has time and again recognized that "any" has "an expansive meaning," bringing within a statute's reach *all* types of the item (here, "tangible object") to which the law refers. *Department of Housing and Urban Development* v. *Rucker*, 535 U. S. 125, 131 (2002); see, *e.g.*, *Republic of Iraq* v. *Beaty*, 556 U. S. 848, 856 (2009); *Ali* v. *Federal Bureau of Prisons*, 552 U. S. 214, 219–220 (2008). And the adjacent laundry list of verbs in §1519 ("alters, destroys, mutilates, conceals, covers up, falsifies, or makes a false entry") further shows that Congress wrote a statute with a wide scope. Those words are

supposed to ensure—just as "tangible object" is meant to—that §1519 covers the whole world of evidence-tampering, in all its prodigious variety. See *United States* v. *Rodgers*, 466 U. S. 475, 480 (1984) (rejecting a "narrow, technical definition" of a statutory term when it "clashes strongly" with "sweeping" language in the same sentence).

Still more, "tangible object" appears as part of a three-noun phrase (including also "records" and "documents") common to evidence-tampering laws and always understood to embrace things of all kinds. The Model Penal Code's evidence-tampering section, drafted more than 50 years ago, similarly prohibits a person from "alter[ing], destroy[ing], conceal[ing] or remov[ing]" any *record, docu-* [—5—] *ment or thing*" in an effort to thwart an official investigation or proceeding. ALI, Model Penal Code §241.7(1), p. 175 (1962) (emphasis added). The Code's commentary emphasizes that the offense described in that provision is "not limited to conduct that [alters] a written instrument." *Id.*, §241.7, Comment 3, at 179. Rather, the language extends to "any physical object." *Ibid.* Consistent with that statement—and, of course, with ordinary meaning—courts in the more than 15 States that have laws based on the Model Code's tampering provision apply them to all tangible objects, including drugs, guns, vehicles and . . . yes, animals. See, *e.g.*, *State* v. *Majors*, 318 S. W. 3d 850, 859–861 (Tenn. 2010) (cocaine); *Puckett* v. *State*, 328 Ark. 355, 357–360, 944 S. W. 2d 111, 113–114 (1997) (gun); *State* v. *Bruno*, 236 Conn. 514, 519–520, 673 A. 2d 1117, 1122–1123 (1996) (bicycle, skeleton, blood stains); *State* v. *Crites*, 2007 Mont. Dist. LEXIS 615, *5–*7 (Dec. 21, 2007) (deer antlers). Not a one has limited the phrase's scope to objects that record or preserve information.

The words "record, document, or tangible object" in §1519 also track language in 18 U. S. C. §1512, the federal witness-tampering law covering (as even the plurality accepts, see *ante*, at 12) physical evidence in all its forms. Section 1512, both in its original version (preceding §1519) and today, repeatedly uses the phrase "record, document, or other object"—most notably, in a provision prohibiting the use of force or threat to induce another person to withhold any of those materials from an official proceeding. §4(a) of the Victim and Witness Protection Act of 1982, 96 Stat. 1249, as amended, 18 U. S. C. §1512(b)(2). That language, which itself likely derived from the Model Penal Code, encompasses no less the bloody knife than the incriminating letter, as all courts have for decades agreed. See, *e.g.*, *United States* v. *Kellington*, 217 F. 3d 1084, 1088 (CA9 2000) (boat); *United States* v. *Applewhaite*, 195 F. 3d 679, 688 (CA3 1999) (stone wall). And typically "only the [—6—] most compelling evidence" will persuade this Court that Congress intended "nearly identical language" in provisions dealing with related subjects to bear different meanings. *Communication Workers* v. *Beck*, 487 U. S. 735, 754 (1988); see A. Scalia & B. Garner, Reading Law: The Interpretation of Legal Texts 252 (2012). Context thus again confirms what text indicates.

And legislative history, for those who care about it, puts extra icing on a cake already frosted. Section 1519, as the plurality notes, see *ante*, at 2, 6, was enacted after the Enron Corporation's collapse, as part of the Sarbanes-Oxley Act of 2002, 116 Stat. 745. But the provision began its life in a separate bill, and the drafters emphasized that Enron was "only a case study exposing the shortcomings in our current laws" relating to both "corporate and criminal" fraud. S. Rep. No. 107–146, pp. 2, 11 (2002). The primary "loophole[]" Congress identified, see *id.*, at 14, arose from limits in the part of §1512 just described: That provision, as uniformly construed, prohibited a person from inducing another to destroy "record[s], document[s], or other object[s]"—of every type—but not from doing so himself. §1512(b)(2); see *supra*, at 5. Congress (as even the plurality agrees, see *ante*, at 6) enacted §1519 to close that yawning gap. But §1519 could fully achieve that goal only if it covered all the records, documents, and objects §1512 did, as well as all the means of tampering with them. And so §1519 was written to do exactly that—"to apply broadly to any acts to destroy or fabricate physical evidence," as long as performed with the requisite intent. S. Rep.

No. 107–146, at 14. "When a person destroys evidence," the drafters explained, "overly technical legal distinctions should neither hinder nor prevent prosecution." *Id.*, at 7. Ah well: Congress, meet today's Court, which here invents just such a distinction with just such an effect. See *United States* v. *Philadelphia Nat. Bank*, 374 U. S. 321, 343 (1963) ("[C]reat[ing] a large loophole in [—7—] a statute designed to close a loophole" is "illogical and disrespectful of . . . congressional purpose").

As Congress recognized in using a broad term, giving immunity to those who destroy non-documentary evidence has no sensible basis in penal policy. A person who hides a murder victim's body is no less culpable than one who burns the victim's diary. A fisherman, like John Yates, who dumps undersized fish to avoid a fine is no less blameworthy than one who shreds his vessel's catch log for the same reason. Congress thus treated both offenders in the same way. It understood, in enacting §1519, that destroying evidence is destroying evidence, whether or not that evidence takes documentary form.

II

A

The plurality searches far and wide for anything—*anything*—to support its interpretation of §1519. But its fishing expedition comes up empty.

The plurality's analysis starts with §1519's title: "Destruction, alteration, or falsification of records in Federal investigations and bankruptcy." See *ante*, at 10; see also *ante*, at 3–4 (opinion of ALITO, J.). That's already a sign something is amiss. I know of no other case in which we have *begun* our interpretation of a statute with the title, or relied on a title to override the law's clear terms. Instead, we have followed "the wise rule that the title of a statute and the heading of a section cannot limit the plain meaning of the text." *Trainmen* v. *Baltimore & Ohio R. Co.*, 331 U. S. 519, 528–529 (1947).

The reason for that "wise rule" is easy to see: A title is, almost necessarily, an abridgment. Attempting to mention every term in a statute "would often be ungainly as well as useless"; accordingly, "matters in the text . . . are frequently unreflected in the headings." *Id.*, at 528. Just last year, this Court observed that two titles in a nearby [—8—] section of Sarbanes-Oxley serve as "but a short-hand reference to the general subject matter" of the provision at issue, "not meant to take the place of the detailed provisions of the text." *Lawson* v. *FMR LLC*, 571 U. S. ___, ___ (2014) (slip op., at 16) (quoting *Trainmen*, 331 U. S., at 528). The "under-inclusiveness" of the headings, we stated, was "apparent." *Lawson*, 571 U. S., at ___ (slip op., at 16). So too for §1519's title, which refers to "destruction, alteration, or falsification" but *not* to mutilation, concealment, or covering up, and likewise mentions "records" but *not* other documents or objects. Presumably, the plurality would not refuse to apply §1519 when a person only conceals evidence rather than destroying, altering, or falsifying it; instead, the plurality would say that a title is just a title, which cannot "undo or limit" more specific statutory text. *Ibid.* (quoting *Trainmen*, 331 U. S., at 529). The same holds true when the evidence in question is not a "record" but something else whose destruction, alteration, etc., is intended to obstruct justice.

The plurality next tries to divine meaning from §1519's "position within Chapter 73 of Title 18." *Ante*, at 10. But that move is yet odder than the last. As far as I can tell, this Court has never once suggested that the section number assigned to a law bears upon its meaning. Cf. Scalia, *supra*, at xi–xvi (listing more than 50 interpretive principles and canons without mentioning the plurality's new number-in-the-Code theory). And even on its own terms, the plurality's argument is hard to fathom. The plurality claims that if §1519 applied to objects generally, Congress would not have placed it "after the pre-existing §1516, §1517, and §1518" because those are "specialized provisions." *Ante*, at 11. But search me if I can find a better place for a broad ban on evidence-tampering. The plurality seems to agree that the law properly goes in Chapter 73—the criminal code's chapter on "obstruction of justice." But the provision does not logically fit into any of that [—9—] chapter's pre-existing sections. And with the first 18 numbers of the chapter already taken (starting with §1501 and continuing through §1518), the law naturally took the 19th place. That is standard operating procedure. Prior to the Sarbanes-Oxley Act of 2002, all of Chapter 73 was ordered chronologically: Section 1518 was later enacted than §1517, which was later enacted than §1516, which was . . . well, you get the idea. And after Sarbanes-Oxley, Congress has continued in the same vein. Section 1519 is thus right where you would expect it (as is the contemporaneously passed §1520)—between §1518 (added in 1996) and §1521 (added in 2008).[2]

The plurality's third argument, relying on the surplusage canon, at least invokes a known tool of statutory construction—but it too comes to nothing. Says the plurality: If read naturally, §1519 "would render superfluous" §1512(c)(1), which Congress passed "as part of the same act." *Ante*, at 13. But that is not so: Although the two provisions significantly overlap, each applies to conduct the other does not. The key difference between the two is that §1519 protects the integrity of "matter[s] within the jurisdiction of any [federal] department or agency" whereas §1512(c)(1) safeguards "official proceeding[s]" as defined in §1515(a)(1)(A). Section 1519's language often applies more broadly than §1512(c)(1)'s, as the plurality notes. [—10—]

---

[2] The lonesome exception to Chapter 73's chronological order is §1514A, added in Sarbanes-Oxley to create a civil action to protect whistleblowers. Congress decided to place that provision right after the only other section in Chapter 73 to authorize a civil action (that one to protect victims and witnesses). The plurality, seizing on the §1514 example, says it likewise "would have made more sense for Congress to codify the substance of §1519 within §1512 or in a new §1512A." *Ante*, at 12, n. 4. But §1512 is titled "Tampering with a witness, victim, or an informant," and its provisions almost all protect witnesses from intimidation and harassment. It makes perfect sense that Congress wanted a broad ban on evidence-spoliation to stand on its own rather than as part of—or an appendage to—a witness-tampering provision.

For example, an FBI investigation counts as a matter within a federal department's jurisdiction, but falls outside the statutory definition of "official proceeding" as construed by courts. See, *e.g.*, *United States* v. *Gabriel*, 125 F. 3d 89, 105, n. 13 (CA2 1997). But conversely, §1512(c)(1) sometimes reaches more widely than §1519. For example, because an "official proceeding" includes any "proceeding before a judge or court of the United States," §1512(c)(1) prohibits tampering with evidence in federal litigation between private parties. See §1515(a)(1)(A); *United States* v. *Burge*, 711 F. 3d 803, 808–810 (CA7 2013); *United States* v. *Reich*, 479 F. 3d 179, 185–187 (CA2 2007) (Sotomayor, J.). By contrast, §1519 wouldn't ordinarily operate in that context because a federal court isn't a "department or agency." See *Hubbard* v. *United States*, 514 U. S. 695, 715 (1995).[3] So the surplusage canon doesn't come into play.[4] Overlap—even significant overlap—abounds in the criminal law. See *Loughrin* v. *United* **[—11—]** *States*, 573 U. S. ___, ___ – ___, n. 4 (2014) (slip op., at 6–7, n. 4). This Court has never thought that of such ordinary stuff surplusage is made. See *ibid.*; *Connecticut*

---

[3] The plurality's objection to this statement is difficult to understand. It cannot take issue with *Hubbard*'s holding that "a federal court is neither a 'department' nor an 'agency'" in a statute referring, just as §1519 does, to "any matter within the jurisdiction of any department or agency of the United States." 514 U. S., at 698, 715. So the plurality suggests that the phrase "in relation to . . . any such matter" in §1519 somehow changes *Hubbard*'s result. See *ante*, at 12–13, and n. 5. But that phrase still demands that evidence-tampering relate to a "matter within the jurisdiction of any department or agency"—excluding courts, as *Hubbard* commands. That is why the federal government, as far as I can tell, has never once brought a prosecution under §1519 for evidence-tampering in litigation between private parties. It instead uses §1512(c)(1) for that purpose.

[4] Section 1512(c)(1) also applies more broadly than §1519 in proceedings relating to insurance regulation. The term "official proceeding" in §1512(c)(1) is defined to include "proceeding[s] involving the business of insurance whose activities affect interstate commerce before any insurance regulatory official or agency." §1515(a)(1)(D). But §1519 wouldn't usually apply in that context because state, not federal, agencies handle most insurance regulation.

Nat. Bank v. *Germain*, 503 U. S. 249, 253 (1992).

And the legislative history to which the plurality appeals, see *ante*, at 6, only cuts against it because those materials show that lawmakers knew that §1519 and §1512(c)(1) share much common ground. Minority Leader Lott introduced the amendment that included §1512(c)(1) (along with other criminal and corporate fraud provisions) late in the legislative process, explaining that he did so at the specific request of the President. See 148 Cong. Rec. 12509, 12512 (2002) (remarks of Sen. Lott). Not only Lott but several other Senators noted the overlap between the President's package and provisions already in the bill, most notably §1519. See *id.*, at 12512 (remarks of Sen. Lott); *id.*, at 12513 (remarks of Sen. Biden); *id.*, at 12517 (remarks of Sens. Hatch and Gramm). The presence of both §1519 and §1512(c)(1) in the final Act may have reflected belt-and-suspenders caution: If §1519 contained some flaw, §1512(c)(1) would serve as a backstop. Or the addition of §1512(c)(1) may have derived solely from legislators' wish "to satisfy audiences other than courts"—that is, the President and his Justice Department. Gluck & Bressman, Statutory Interpretation from the Inside, 65 Stan. L. Rev. 901, 935 (2013) (emphasis deleted). Whichever the case, Congress's consciousness of overlap between the two provisions removes any conceivable reason to cast aside §1519's ordinary meaning in service of preventing some statutory repetition.

Indeed, the inclusion of §1512(c)(1) in Sarbanes-Oxley creates a far worse problem for the plurality's construction of §1519 than for mine. Section 1512(c)(1) criminalizes the destruction of any "record, document, or other object"; §1519 of any "record, document, or tangible object." On the plurality's view, one "object" is really an object, where- **[—12—]** as the other is only an object that preserves or stores information. But "[t]he normal rule of statutory construction assumes that identical words used in different parts of the same act," passed at the same time, "are intended to have the same meaning." *Sorenson* v. *Secretary of Treasury*, 475 U. S. 851, 860 (1986) (internal quotation marks omitted).

And that is especially true when the different provisions pertain to the same subject. See *supra*, at 5–6. The plurality doesn't—really, can't—explain why it instead interprets the same words used in two provisions of the same Act addressing the same basic problem to mean fundamentally different things.

Getting nowhere with surplusage, the plurality switches canons, hoping that *noscitur a sociis* and *ejusdem generis* will save it. See *ante*, at 13–16; see also *ante*, at 1–2 (opinion of ALITO, J.). The first of those related canons advises that words grouped in a list be given similar meanings. The second counsels that a general term following specific words embraces only things of a similar kind. According to the plurality, those Latin maxims change the English meaning of "tangible object" to only things, like records and documents, "used to record or preserve information." *Ante*, at 14.[5] But understood as this Court always has, the canons have no such transformative effect on the worka- [—13—] day language Congress chose.

As an initial matter, this Court uses *noscitur a sociis* and *ejusdem generis* to resolve ambiguity, not create it. Those principles are "useful rule[s] of construction where words are of obscure or doubtful meaning." *Russell Motor Car Co.* v. *United States*, 261 U. S. 514, 520 (1923). But when words have a clear definition, and all other contextual clues support that meaning, the canons cannot properly defeat Congress's

---

[5] The plurality seeks support for this argument in the Sentencing Commission's construction of the phrase "records, documents, or tangible objects," *ante*, at 14, but to no avail. The plurality cites a note in the Commission's Manual clarifying that this phrase, as used in the Sentencing Guidelines, "includes" various electronic information, communications, and storage devices. United States Sentencing Commission, Guidelines Manual §2J1.2, comment., n. 1 (Nov. 2014) (USSG). But "includes" (following its ordinary definition) "is not exhaustive," as the Commission's commentary makes explicit. USSG §1B1.1, comment., n. 2. Otherwise, the Commission's construction wouldn't encompass *paper* documents. All the note does is to make plain that "records, documents, or tangible objects" embraces stuff relating to the digital (as well as the material) world.

decision to draft broad legislation. See, *e.g.*, *Ali*, 552 U. S., at 227 (rejecting the invocation of these canons as an "attempt to create ambiguity where the statute's text and structure suggest none").

Anyway, assigning "tangible object" its ordinary meaning comports with *noscitur a sociis* and *ejusdem generis* when applied, as they should be, with attention to §1519's subject and purpose. Those canons require identifying a common trait that links all the words in a statutory phrase. See, *e.g.*, *Graham County Soil and Water Conservation Dist.* v. *United States ex rel. Wilson*, 559 U. S. 280, 289, n. 7 (2010); *Ali*, 552 U. S., at 224–226. In responding to that demand, the plurality characterizes records and documents as things that preserve information—and so they are. But just as much, they are things that provide information, and thus potentially serve as evidence relevant to matters under review. And in a statute pertaining to obstruction of federal investigations, that evidentiary function comes to the fore. The destruction of records and documents prevents law enforcement agents from gathering facts relevant to official inquiries. And so too does the destruction of tangible objects—of whatever kind. Whether the item is a fisherman's ledger or an undersized fish, throwing it overboard has the identical effect on the administration of justice. See *supra*, at 7. For purposes of §1519, records, documents, and (all) tangible objects are therefore alike.

Indeed, even the plurality can't fully credit its *nosci-* [—14—] *tur/ejusdem* argument. The same reasoning would apply to *every* law placing the word "object" (or "thing") after "record" and "document." But as noted earlier, such statutes are common: The phrase appears (among other places) in many state laws based on the Model Penal Code, as well as in multiple provisions of §1512. See *supra*, at 4–5. The plurality accepts that in those laws "object" means object; its argument about superfluity positively *depends* on giving §1512(c)(1) that broader reading. See *ante*, at 13, 16. What, then, is the difference here? The plurality proposes that some of those statutes describe less serious offenses than §1519. See *ante*, at 17. How and why that distinction affects application of the *noscitur a sociis* and *ejusdem generis* canons is left obscure: Count it as one more of the plurality's never-before-propounded, not-readily-explained interpretive theories. See *supra*, at 7, 8–9, 11–12. But in any event, that rationale cannot support the plurality's willingness to give "object" its natural meaning in §1512, which (like §1519) sets out felonies with penalties of up to 20 years. See §§1512(a)(3)(C), (b), (c). The canons, in the plurality's interpretive world, apparently switch on and off whenever convenient.

And the plurality's invocation of §1519's verbs does nothing to buttress its canon-based argument. See *ante*, at 14–15; *ante*, at 2–3 (opinion of ALITO, J.). The plurality observes that §1519 prohibits "falsif[ying]" or "mak[ing] a false entry in" a tangible object, and no one can do those things to, say, a murder weapon (or a fish). *Ante*, at 14. But of course someone can alter, destroy, mutilate, conceal, or cover up such a tangible object, and §1519 prohibits those actions too. The Court has never before suggested that all the verbs in a statute need to match up with all the nouns. See *Robers* v. *United States*, 572 U. S. ___, ___ (2014) (slip op., at 4) ("[T]he law does not require legislators to write extra language specifically exempting, phrase by phrase, applications in respect to which a portion of a [—15—] phrase is not needed"). And for good reason. It is exactly when Congress sets out to draft a statute broadly—to include every imaginable variation on a theme—that such mismatches will arise. To respond by narrowing the law, as the plurality does, is thus to flout both what Congress wrote and what Congress wanted.

Finally, when all else fails, the plurality invokes the rule of lenity. See *ante*, at 18. But even in its most robust form, that rule only kicks in when, "after all legitimate tools of interpretation have been exhausted, 'a reasonable doubt persists' regarding whether Congress has made the defendant's conduct a federal crime." *Abramski* v. *United States*, 573 U. S. ___, ___ (2014) (SCALIA, J., dissenting) (slip op., at 12) (quoting *Moskal* v. *United States*, 498 U. S. 103, 108 (1990)). No such doubt lingers here. The plurality points to the breadth of §1519, see *ante*, at 18, as though breadth were equivalent to ambiguity. It is not. Section 1519 *is* very broad. It is also very clear. Every traditional tool of statutory interpretation points in the same direction, toward "object" meaning object. Lenity offers no proper refuge from that straightforward (even though capacious) construction.[6] [—16—]

B

The concurring opinion is a shorter, vaguer version of the plurality's. It relies primarily on the *noscitur a sociis* and *ejusdem generis* canons, tries to bolster them with §1519's "list of verbs," and concludes with the section's title. See *supra*, at 7–8, 12–13, 14–15 (addressing each of those arguments). (Notably, even the concurrence puts no stock in the plurality's section-number and superfluity claims.) From those familiar materials, the concurrence arrives at the following definition: "'tangible object' should mean something similar to records or documents." *Ante*, at 4 (opinion of ALITO, J.). In amplifying that purported guidance, the concurrence suggests applying the term "tangible object" in keeping with what "a neighbor, when asked to identify something similar to record or document," might answer. *Ante*, at 1. "[W]ho wouldn't raise an eyebrow," the concurrence wonders, if the neighbor said "crocodile"? *Ante*, at 1–2. Courts sometimes say, when explaining the Latin maxims, that the "words of a statute should be interpreted

---

[6] As part of its lenity argument, the plurality asserts that Yates did not have "fair warning" that his conduct amounted to a felony. *Ante*, at 18; see *ante*, at 17 (stating that "Yates would have had scant reason to anticipate a felony prosecution" when throwing fish overboard). But even under the plurality's view, the dumping of fish is potentially a federal felony—just under §1512(c)(1), rather than §1519. See *ante*, at 12–13. In any event, the plurality itself acknowledges that the ordinary meaning of §1519 covers Yates's conduct, see *ante*, at 7: That provision, no less than §1512(c)(1), announces its broad scope in the clearest possible terms. And when an ordinary citizen seeks notice of a statute's scope, he is more likely to focus on the plain text than (as the plurality would have it) on the section number, the superfluity principle, and the *noscitur* and *ejusdem* canons.

consistent with their neighbors." See, *e.g.*, *United States* v. *Locke*, 529 U. S. 89, 105 (2000). The concurrence takes that expression literally.

But §1519's meaning should not hinge on the odd game of Mad Libs the concurrence proposes. No one reading §1519 needs to fill in a blank after the words "records" and "documents." That is because Congress, quite helpfully, already did so—adding the term "tangible object." The issue in this case is what that term means. So if the concurrence wishes to ask its neighbor a question, I'd recommend a more pertinent one: Do you think a fish (or, if the concurrence prefers, a crocodile) is a "tangible object"? As to that query, "who wouldn't raise an eyebrow" if the neighbor said "no"?

In insisting on its different question, the concurrence neglects the proper function of catchall phrases like "or tangible object." The reason Congress uses such terms is [—17—] precisely to reach things that, in the concurrence's words, "do[] not spring to mind"—to my mind, to my neighbor's, or (most important) to Congress's. *Ante*, at 1 (opinion of ALITO, J.). As this Court recently explained: "[T]he whole value of a generally phrased residual [term] is that it serves as a catchall for matters not specifically contemplated—known unknowns." *Beaty*, 556 U. S., at 860. Congress realizes that in a game of free association with "record" and "document," it will never think of all the other things—including crocodiles and fish—whose destruction or alteration can (less frequently but just as effectively) thwart law enforcement. Cf. *United States* v. *Stubbs*, 11 F. 3d 632, 637–638 (CA6 1993) (dead crocodiles used as evidence to support smuggling conviction). And so Congress adds the general term "or tangible object"—again, exactly because such things "do[] not spring to mind."[7]

---

[7] The concurrence contends that when the *noscitur* and *ejusdem* canons are in play, "'known unknowns' should be similar to known knowns, *i.e.*, here, records and documents." *Ante*, at 2. But as noted above, records and documents *are* similar to crocodiles and fish as far as §1519 is concerned: All are potentially useful as evidence in an investigation. See *supra*, at 13. The concurrence

The concurrence suggests that the term "tangible object" serves not as a catchall for physical evidence but to "ensure beyond question" that e-mails and other electronic files fall within §1519's compass. *Ante*, at 2. But that claim is eyebrow-raising in its own right. Would a Congress wishing to make certain that §1519 applies to e-mails add the phrase "tangible object" (as opposed, say, to "electronic communications")? Would a judge or jury member predictably find that "tangible object" encompasses something as virtual as e-mail (as compared, say, [—18—] with something as real as a fish)? If not (and the answer is not), then that term cannot function as a failsafe for e-mails.

The concurrence acknowledges that no one of its arguments can carry the day; rather, it takes the Latin canons plus §1519's verbs plus §1519's title to "tip the case" for Yates. *Ante*, at 1. But the sum total of three mistaken arguments is . . . three mistaken arguments. They do not get better in the combining. And so the concurrence ends up right where the plurality does, except that the concurrence, eschewing the rule of lenity, has nothing to fall back on.

III

If none of the traditional tools of statutory interpretation can produce today's result, then what accounts for it? The plurality offers a clue when it emphasizes the disproportionate penalties §1519 imposes if the law is read broadly. See *ante*, at 17–18. Section 1519, the plurality objects, would then "expose[] individuals to 20-year prison sentences for tampering with *any* physical object that *might* have evidentiary value in *any* federal investigation into *any* offense." *Ante*, at 18. That brings to the surface the real issue: overcriminalization and excessive punishment in the U. S. Code.

Now as to this statute, I think the plurality somewhat—though only somewhat—exaggerates the matter. The plurality omits from its description of §1519 the requirement that a

---

never explains why *that* similarity isn't the relevant one in a statute aimed at evidence-tampering.

person act "knowingly" and with "the intent to impede, obstruct, or influence" federal law enforcement. And in highlighting §1519's maximum penalty, the plurality glosses over the absence of any prescribed minimum. (Let's not forget that Yates's sentence was not 20 years, but 30 days.) Congress presumably enacts laws with high maximums and no minimums when it thinks the prohibited conduct may run the gamut from major to minor. That [—19—] is assuredly true of acts obstructing justice. Compare this case with the following, all of which properly come within, but now fall outside, §1519: *McRae*, 702 F. 3d, at 834–838 (burning human body to thwart murder investigation); *Maury*, 695 F. 3d, at 243–244 (altering cement mixer to impede inquiry into amputation of employee's fingers); *United States* v. *Natal*, 2014 U. S. Dist. LEXIS 108852, *24–*26 (D Conn., Aug. 7, 2014) (repainting van to cover up evidence of fatal arson). Most district judges, as Congress knows, will recognize differences between such cases and prosecutions like this one, and will try to make the punishment fit the crime. Still and all, I tend to think, for the reasons the plurality gives, that §1519 is a bad law— too broad and undifferentiated, with too-high maximum penalties, which give prosecutors too much leverage and sentencers too much discretion. And I'd go further: In those ways, §1519 is unfortunately not an outlier, but an emblem of a deeper pathology in the federal criminal code.

But whatever the wisdom or folly of §1519, this Court does not get to rewrite the law. "Resolution of the pros and cons of whether a statute should sweep broadly or narrowly is for Congress." *Rodgers*, 466 U. S., at 484. If judges disagree with Congress's choice, we are perfectly entitled to say so—in lectures, in law review articles, and even in dicta. But we are not entitled to replace the statute Congress enacted with an alternative of our own design.

I respectfully dissent.

This page intentionally left blank

United States Court of Appeals for the First Circuit

United States Court of Appeals
for the First Circuit

No. 13-2491

CATLIN (SYNDICATE 2003) AT LLOYD'S
VS.
SAN JUAN TOWING & MARINE SERVS., INC.

Appeal from the United States District Court for the
District of Puerto Rico

Decided: February 6, 2015

Citation: 778 F.3d 69, 3 Adm. R. 24 (1st Cir. 2015).

Before **TORRUELLA**, **THOMPSON**, and **KAYATTA**,
Circuit Judges.

[—2—] **TORRUELLA**, Circuit Judge:

This is an appeal from a decision of the United States District Court for the District of Puerto Rico sitting in admiralty. The trial involved a maritime insurance policy issued by Appellee Catlin (Syndicate 2003) at Lloyd's ("Catlin"), to cover the floating drydock[1] PERSEVERANCE owned by Appellant San

---

[1] A "floating drydock" is a floating structure that can be partially submerged to a predetermined depth by flooding its ballast tanks. After a ship to be repaired is docked into position on the partially submerged structure, the structure, with the ship aboard, is refloated by pumping the water out of the ballast tanks until the pontoon deck is clear of water, and then the repairs can be performed on the ship. This is distinguishable from what is commonly referred to as a *graving drydock*, which is a permanently fixed, land-based basin with entrance enclosures constructed at or near the water's edge, into which, when the basin is filled with water, a ship enters. After the entrance enclosures are closed, the basin is pumped dry of water, exposing the underwater portions of the vessel's hull to be repaired or worked on. *See O'Leary v. Puget Sound Bridge & Dry Dock Co.*, 349 F.2d 571, 573 (9th Cir. 1965)(quoting the Department of the Navy, Bureau of Yards and Docks); *see also JML Trading Corp. v. Marine Salvage Corp.*, 501 F. Supp. 323, 325 n.2 (E.D.N.Y. 1980); *Md. Cas. Co. v. Lawson*, 101 F.2d 732, 733 (5th Cir. 1939) ("A floating dock receives a vessel when the dock is submerged, after which the watertight compartments of the dock are pumped out and the buoyancy of the dock raises the vessel.")

Juan Towing and Marine Services ("SJT"), a ship repair company based in San Juan, Puerto Rico. At trial, the district court concluded that the insurance policy was void *ab initio* by reason of SJT's violation of the doctrine of *uberrimae fidei* in its application for the policy.[2] *See Catlin (Syndicate* [—3—] *2003) at Lloyd's v. San Juan Towing & Marine Servs., Inc.*, 979 F. Supp. 2d 181, 186 (D.P.R. 2013) ("*Catlin IV*"). The district court erred in deeming the contract void *ab initio*; rather, we find that it was voidable. We therefore affirm, albeit with a minor modification of the lower court's holding to reflect this correction.

I. *Background*

A. Factual History

In 2006, SJT retained the services of Marine Consultants, Inc. ("Marine Consultants") to perform a condition and valuation survey of the floating drydock PERSEVERANCE. In that survey, which was dated April 17, 2006, the PERSEVERANCE was valued at $1,500,000. Thereafter, on August 27, 2006, SJT purchased the PERSEVERANCE for $1,050,000. Subsequently, SJT made improvements to the floating drydock, modifying it so that it could be towed from Louisiana to Puerto Rico. Marine Consultants then issued another condition and valuation report on November 21, 2006, in which it valued the floating drydock at $1,750,000. This $250,000 increase in value from the first report to the second was the result of the value added to the

---

[2] *Uberrimae fidei* means roughly "utmost good faith." *See Black's Law Dictionary* 1754 (10th ed. 2014); *see also Grande v. St. Paul Fire & Marine Ins. Co.*, 436 F.3d 277, 282 (1st Cir. 2006). Under this doctrine, the insured in a maritime insurance contract is required "to disclose to the insurer all known circumstances that [—3—] materially affect the insurer's risk, the default of which . . . renders the insurance contract voidable by the insurer." *Windsor Mount Joy Mut. Ins. Co. v. Giragosian*, 57 F.3d 50, 54-55 (1st Cir. 1995); *accord Black's Law Dictionary* (10th ed. 2014) 808 (defining utmost good faith as "[t]he state of mind of a party to a contract who will freely and candidly disclose any information that might influence the other party's decision to enter into the contract").

floating drydock due to the [—4—] improvements and modifications that allowed the PERSEVERANCE to be towed to Puerto Rico.

By 2009, and as late as 2011, due to declining business and increasing financial distress, SJT was actively trying to sell the PERSEVERANCE. SJT had initially advertised the sale price in 2009 as $1,350,000. In February 2010, SJT advertised the floating drydock for sale in *Boats & Harbors*—a marine industry publication—for $1,350,000. During January 2011, SJT continued to advertise the PERSEVERANCE for sale at $1,350,000. On January 3, 2011, a potential buyer offered to purchase the floating drydock for $700,000. As negotiations progressed throughout the month, SJT lowered the PERSEVERANCE's purchase price to $850,000, and eventually, on January 29, 2011, to $800,000. That potential buyer ultimately did not consummate the purchase.

In April 2011, SJT again advertised the PERSEVERANCE for sale in *Boats & Harbors*. This time the asking price was $800,000. Five months later, on September 4, 2011, SJT agreed to sell the PERSEVERANCE to Leevac Shipyards ("Leevac"), a Louisiana-based company, and on September 19, 2011, SJT signed a purchase-and-sale agreement in which it accepted Leevac's offer to purchase the floating drydock for $700,000. The deal later fell through.

Between August 2006 and February 2011, SJT insured the PERSEVERANCE with the RLI Insurance Company ("RLI"), with a declared hull value of the PERSEVERANCE under this policy of [—5—] $1,750,000, presumably based on the second Marine Consultants condition and valuation report dated on November 21, 2006. In February 2011, RLI cancelled the drydock's insurance policy, cryptically stating "Loss History"[3] as the reason for said action.

Thereafter, at SJT's request, SJT's insurance broker, John Toscani ("Toscani"), who was located in New York, approached Catlin seeking, through Lloyd's, a *marine* insurance policy "consisting of *hull*, [protection and indemnity], ship repairs, general liability and contractor's equipment" (emphasis added). SJT's broker represented that the PERSEVERANCE's prior insurance coverage was for $1,750,000, but did not provide Catlin with a copy of RLI's notice of cancellation. The parties agree that SJT did not provide additional representations suggesting that this was the actual value of the PERSEVERANCE, and Catlin's representative, Mr. Kirchhofer, testified that he did not ask for more information on the floating drydock's value or condition, but rather assumed that the value was in line with that number. Most importantly, SJT also did not disclose information regarding substantial, preexisting damage to the PERSEVERANCE's hull, which had been evident since at least April 2010. [—6—]

Thereafter, the Catlin policy—the Ocean Marine Insurance Policy (the "Policy")—became effective in April 2011, with a total insurable value of $1,840,000. The Policy, however, contained an endorsement that modified its terms to list the insured value at $1,750,000, the same stated amount in the previous RLI policy. Additionally, the total limit of liability for each loss occurrence was set at $1,000,000.

On September 28, 2011, the PERSEVERANCE was berthed at Pier 15, in San Juan, Puerto Rico. At the direction of Mark Payne ("Payne"), one of SJT's principals, the floating drydock was ballasted[4] for the purpose of performing maintenance on parts of the hull. Payne instructed the repairmen to add ballast water to the floating drydock's

---

[3] A loss history reflects the decline in value of an asset due to some kind of adverse event (e.g., vandalism or a natural disaster). Loss histories are often included in loss history reports or similar

documentation, allowing insurers to verify the condition of the property more efficiently.

[4] *See supra* note 1. The act of ballasting involves pumping water into the floating drydock's "ballast tanks," which are empty when the boat is fully afloat and thus keep the drydock buoyant. Pumping water into the tanks reduces the buoyancy of the drydock, causing it to ride lower in the water.

stern compartments to allow access to the forward sections to be repaired. Thereafter, Payne left the PERSEVERANCE'S berthing area on personal business. At approximately 3:30 p.m., before he left for the day, SJT foreman José Monge gave instructions to the repairmen to pick up and shut off the water hose that was still filling at least one of the floating drydock's ballast tanks.

Late that evening, SJT tug Captain Padilla ("Padilla") returned to Pier 15 after a towing assignment and found the [—7—] PERSEVERANCE with its aft section completely underwater and its forward part awash. Padilla proceeded to call Payne on his cell phone to inform him of the dire situation the PERSEVERANCE was in, but ten minutes later, at about midnight, called him again to inform him of the total sinking of the PERSEVERANCE. Payne arrived shortly thereafter and, together with Padilla, observed that a fire hose connected to a water main on the dock was still pumping water into the sunken drydock, with the valve on shore still in an open position. Payne proceeded to shut the valve, which was easily seen and accessible to anyone who wished to turn off the flow of water.

Refloating the PERSEVERANCE turned out to be a challenging process, taking nearly one month to complete. After being refloated, the PERSEVERANCE was inspected and the damage assessed by expert marine surveyors. The surveyors found the underside of the floating drydock to be substantially rusted and decayed, the existence of which SJT had known about but failed to disclose to Catlin when it sought coverage under the Policy. This damage explained why refloating the PERSEVERANCE—a drydock that was designed specifically to be able to submerge and refloat using its ballast tanks—had been so difficult. During the month of December 2012, the drydock was sold for scrap for $40,000.00.

SJT proceeded to file a claim with Catlin, alleging the total loss of the PERSEVERANCE, in the amount of $1,750,000. Catlin denied this claim, relying on the discrepancy between the [—8—]

amount the PERSEVERANCE was insured for according to the Endorsement ($1,750,000) and its actual market value (approximately $700,000 to $800,000), as evidenced by the sale price advertised to potential buyers around the time when SJT sought the quote for the Policy.

B. Procedural History

To afford a better understanding of the final resolution of this appeal, we deem it appropriate to include a résumé of the procedural history of this case before the district court. On November 8, 2011, Catlin filed a declaratory judgement complaint against SJT, invoking both admiralty (28 U.S.C. § 1333) and diversity (28 U.S.C. § 1332) jurisdiction. Catlin alleged eight admiralty or maritime claims and sought to void the Policy pursuant to the doctrine of *uberrimae fidei*. In turn, SJT filed a separate diversity suit against Catlin, demanding recovery for the full insured value of $1,750,000 under the Policy for the loss of the PERSEVERANCE. Catlin counterclaimed and the cases were consolidated.

1. *Catlin I*

On April 8, 2013, the district court granted SJT's motion for partial summary judgment and dismissed without prejudice the claim brought by Catlin, concluding that under the recently decided case of *Lozman v. City of Riviera Beach*, 133 S. Ct. 735, 1 Adm. R. 2 (2013), the court lacked admiralty jurisdiction over this controversy because [—9—] the PERSEVERANCE was not a "vessel."[5] *See Catlin (Syndicate 2003) at Lloyd's v. San Juan Towing & Marine Servs, Inc.*, Civil Nos. 11-2093 (FAB); 11-2116 (FAB), 2013 U.S. Dist. LEXIS 52307, at *37-38 (D.P.R. Apr. 8, 2013) ("*Catlin I*"). This ruling was based on the court's determination that the PERSEVERANCE did not meet the *Lozman* test for determining whether a floating structure was a "vessel" for admiralty

_____

[5] In so ruling, the district court rejected the Report and Recommendation issued by the magistrate judge, who had found (prior to the announcement of the new *Lozman* test) that the PERSEVERANCE was a "vessel."

jurisdiction purposes because "a reasonable observer, looking to the PERSEVERANCE's physical characteristics and activities, would not consider it to be designed to any practical degree for carrying people or things on water." *Id*. at *37.

2. *Catlin II*

On May 13, 2013, the district court entertained a motion for reconsideration of its ruling in *Catlin I*. Although the court continued to adhere to its finding that the PERSEVERANCE failed to meet the *Lozman* standard as to what constitutes a vessel for the purposes of admiralty jurisdiction, it nevertheless concluded that admiralty jurisdiction was present because the central issue of the controversy concerned a maritime contract—i.e., the Policy—the "primary objective" of which was "essentially maritime [in] nature" and "relates to navigation, business or commerce of the sea." *Catlin (Syndicate 2003) at Lloyd's v. San Juan Towing & [—10—] Marine Servs., Inc.*, 946 F. Supp. 2d 256, 260 (D.P.R. 2013)("*Catlin II*"); *see also Norfolk S. Ry. Co. v. James N. Kirby, Pty Ltd.*, 543 U.S. 14, 24-25 (2004). It also ruled that Catlin's complaint properly pleaded diversity jurisdiction and found diversity to be an alternate ground for the exercise of federal jurisdiction, even if not in admiralty. *See Catlin II*, 946 F. Supp. 2d at 267.

3. *Catlin III*

On July 30, 2013, the district court once again opined on the dispute, this time regarding the outstanding motions for summary judgment filed by Catlin and SJT, respectively. *Catlin (Syndicate 2003) at Lloyd's v. San Juan Towing & Marine Servs., Inc.*, 974 F. Supp. 2d 64 (D.P.R. 2013) ("*Catlin III*"). In substance, the court concluded that notwithstanding its finding that the PERSEVERANCE was not a "vessel," federal admiralty jurisdiction and law did attach to this controversy because the interpretation of a maritime contract was at issue (as per *Catlin II*). *Id*. at 74-76. Furthermore, the district court held that the doctrine of *uberrimae fidei*'s representation and disclosure requirements together constituted

an "entrenched federal precedent" that would apply to this case if the facts alleged by Catlin were proven to be correct. *Id*. at 75-76. The court, however, was unable to decide the merits of these contentions because there were factual matters in dispute that needed to be resolved in a trial [—11—] and not via summary judgment. *Id*. at 79-80. In ruling on the question as to the risks covered by the Policy, an alternate issue raised by Catlin's denial of coverage, the district court found that the Policy was an "all risk insurance policy," as contended by SJT. *Id*. at 83. Summary judgment, however, could not be entered on behalf of SJT on this issue because there were factual issues in dispute as to whether the PERSEVERANCE sank due to "fortuitous circumstance[s] or casualty . . . covered under the all risk policy." *Id*. at 84. These outstanding factual issues needed to be resolved through a trial.

4. *Catlin IV*

On October 8, 2013, after a bench trial, the district court resolved the merits of this controversy. *See Catlin (Syndicate 2003) at Lloyd's v. San Juan Towing & Marine Servs., Inc.*, 979 F. Supp. 2d 181, 191 (D.P.R. 2013) ("*Catlin IV*"). Having already ruled in *Catlin III* that *uberrimae fidei* was an entrenched doctrine governing maritime insurance contracts, the court made findings of fact in support of its eventual conclusion that SJT had failed to comply with the doctrine of *uberrimae fidei* in its application for the Policy, and was therefore barred from recovery thereunder. *Id*. at 186-191.

II. *Discussion*

The application of the doctrine of *uberrimae fidei* to this controversy (as decided in *Catlin III*), which in modern [—12—] American jurisprudence is extant only in the context of maritime insurance,[6] depends on

---

[6] *See Giragosian*, 57 F.3d at 54 n.3 ("The sole remaining vestige of the doctrine is in maritime insurance."); Thomas J. Schoenbaum, *The Duty of Utmost Good Faith in Marine Insurance Law: A Comparative Analysis of American and English Law,* 29 J. Mar. L. & Com. 1, 39 (1998). At one time, good faith was a requirement of general

the outcome of the central issue raised by SJT both here and below: whether Puerto Rico's Insurance Code, P.R. Laws Ann. tit. 26, §§ 1101 et seq. ("the Code"), is the controlling substantive law in this controversy rather than general federal maritime law. SJT contends that Section 1110 of the Code contains specific provisions that address the issue of whether representations made during negotiations to obtain insurance coverage affect an insured's ability to collect on a policy. SJT alleges that these statutory provisions contravene and prevail over the doctrine of *uberrimae fidei* pursuant to the Jones Act of 1917 ("Jones Act"), 48 U.S.C. § 749,[7] and our holding in *Guerrido v. Alcoa S.S. Co.*, 234 F.2d 349, 355 (1st Cir. 1956). We conclude, based on our de novo review, that it does not. **[—13—]**

A. Does Federal Admiralty Law Apply to this Controversy?

As a general rule, in the absence of established and governing federal admiralty law, the states have largely unfettered power to regulate matters related to marine insurance. *See Wilburn Boat Co. v. Fireman's Fund Ins. Co.*, 348 U.S. 310, 321 (1955) ("We, like Congress, leave the regulation of marine insurance where it has been—with the States."); *Commercial Union Ins. Co. v. Pesante*, 459 F.3d 34, 37 (1st Cir. 2006) ("Generally, in cases involving a marine insurance contract, we will apply state law . . . .").

Under Sections 7 and 8 of the Jones Act, now codified at 48 U.S.C. §§ 747-749, because Puerto Rico has control over its harbors and navigable waters, we are required to treat Puerto Rico like a state. However, in the absence of a federal statute expressly made applicable to Puerto Rico, Sections 8, 9, and 37[8] of the Jones Act grant Puerto Rico more power to legislate in the admiralty and maritime field than if it were a state, insofar as the act authorizes inconsistent Puerto Rico laws. 48 U.S.C. § 749, 821.[9] Moreover, this Court has held that: **[—14—]**

[T]he rules of admiralty and maritime law of the United States are presently in force in the navigable waters of the United States in and around the island of Puerto Rico to the extent that they are not locally inapplicable either because they were not designed to apply to Puerto Rican waters or because they have been rendered inapplicable to these waters by inconsistent Puerto Rican legislation.

Guerrido, 234 F.2d at 355. The exercise of that power by Puerto Rico can have the effect of rendering conflicting *non-statutory* federal maritime law "locally inapplicable." *Id.*

SJT contends that Section 1110 of the Code should be deemed to be the kind of conflicting local legislation that can render inapplicable non-statutory admiralty law, including the doctrine of *uberrimae fidei*. Section 1110 states:

All statements and descriptions in any application for an insurance policy or in

---

contract law. *See generally* Eric M. Holmes, *A Contextual Study of Commercial Code Faith: Good-Faith Disclosure in Contract Formation*, 39 U. Pitt. L. Rev. 381 (1978) (providing an analysis of the historical development of the concept of good faith).

[7] The Jones Act granted U.S. citizenship to the people of Puerto Rico and established a "civil government" with a locally-elected legislative branch. 39 Stat. 951. Various statutory provisions of the Jones Act were repealed or amended with the enactment of the Puerto Rican Federal Relations Act of 1950 ("PRFRA"), which remains extant law today. *See* 48 U.S.C. §§ 731-916. Furthermore, the PRFRA authorized the people of Puerto Rico to organize a government pursuant to a constitution of their own adoption, but subject to Congressional approval. *Id.* § 731(a)-(d).

[8] The PRFRA repealed the last paragraph of Section 37 of the Jones Act, which dealt with local legislative authority to create executive departments

[9] Section 8 of the Jones Act, 48 U.S.C. § 749 states in relevant part:

All laws of the United States for the protection and improvement of the navigable waters of the United States and the preservation of the interests of navigation and **[—14—]** commerce, except as so far as the same may be locally inapplicable, shall apply to said island and waters and to its adjacent islands and waters.

negotiations therefor, by or in behalf of the insured, shall be deemed to be representations and not warranties. Misrepresentations, omissions, concealment of acts, and incorrect statements shall not prevent a recovery under the policy unless:

(1) Fraudulent; or
(2) material either to the acceptance of the risk, or to the hazard assumed by the insurer; or
(3) the insurer in good faith would either not have issued the policy, or would not have issued a policy in as large an amount, or would not have provided coverage with respect to the hazard resulting in the loss, if the true facts had been made known to the [—15—] insurer as required either by application for the policy or otherwise.

When the applicant incurs in any of the actions enumerated in subsections (1), (2), and (3) of this section, recovery shall only be prevented if such actions or omissions contributed to the loss that gave rise to the action.

P.R. Laws Ann. tit. 26, § 1110. Therefore, SJT urges us to apply the more favorable Section 1110, in lieu of the stricter *uberrimae fidei* doctrine.

We disagree with SJT's contention. This provision is not relevant to the present case because the applicability provision of the Code, Section 1101, expressly excludes ocean marine insurance from the ambit of the Code. Section 1101 states:

(1) The applicable provisions of this chapter [i.e. Chapter 11] shall apply to insurances *other than ocean marine . . . insurance*[] *as defined in subsection (2)* . . . .
(2) For the purposes of subsection (1) of this section and this title, *'ocean marine . . . insurance*[]*' shall include only:*
   (a) Insurances upon vessels, *crafts, hulls,* and of interests therein or with relation thereto.

(b) Insurance of *marine builders' risks*
. . . .

See P.R. Laws Ann. tit. 26, § 1101 (emphasis added). This Court has previously ruled that in enacting this provision, Puerto Rico intended "to exclude maritime insurance contracts from [the] statutory provisions [in the Code] governing the interpretation and construction of insurance contracts." *Lloyd's of London v. Pagán-* [—16—] *Sánchez*, 539 F.3d 19, 25 (1st Cir. 2008); *see also Reifer-Mapp v. 7 Maris, Inc.*, 830 F. Supp. 72, 76 (D.P.R. 1993).

It is exactly the kind of coverage described in Section 1101 of the Code that was provided to SJT by Catlin in the Policy:

Coverage: *Hull, Protection & Indemnity* including Collision & Towers Liability, *Marine General Liability* including *Ship Repairers Liability*, Equipment . . . .

(emphasis added). Therefore, there can be no doubt that the Policy is an ocean marine insurance policy within the meaning of Section 1101, because the PERSEVERANCE is a "craft" and/or a "hull," and the Policy covers maritime interests and risks. As previously stated, the Policy was procured for SJT by Toscani, who "placed a package policy consisting of *hull*, P&I, *ship repairs*, legal, general liability and contractors equipment" (emphasis added), with Catlin. Indeed, Toscani admitted that he considered the Policy to be a marine insurance policy. It contained Endorsement 5 ("Drydock"), which provided coverage for the PERSEVERANCE, and specifically identified the perils insured against as principally those related to the seas and related maritime risks:

TOUCHING THE ADVENTURES AND PERILS which we, the said Assurers, are contended to bear and take upon us, they are of the Seas, Rivers, Lakes, Harbours, . . . or other causes of whatsoever nature arising either on shore or otherwise, causing Loss of or injury to the Property hereby insured, and of all other Perils, Losses, and Misfortunes that have or shall have come to the Hurt, Detriment, or Damage of the said Dock . . . or any part thereof. [—17—]

The district court's findings regarding the PERSEVERANCE support the conclusion that the Policy covered a structure within the ocean marine insurance exception to the Code:

The *Perseverance* consisted of a horizontal platform called a pontoon, which measured 150 feet long, 70 feet wide, and 5 feet tall. It had a superstructure—its "wingwalls"—which consisted of two vertical elements 120 feet long, four feet wide, and sixteen feet tall. The top of the port wingwall was fitted with one semi-sheltered steel control room. The *Perseverance* had a raked bow and two tow pads to connect it to a towing vessel, and according to Payne [SJT's marine manager], "[t]he drydock was specially outfitted and prepared for the voyage to San Juan [from Louisiana, of approximately 2000 miles]. Upon arrival in San Juan, most of the *Perseverance*'s temporary modifications [including wire towing cable, towing chains, emergency retrieving line, emergency drag rope, emergency tow wire, and all emergency tow wire attachment clips] required for navigation, except for the raked bow, were removed and were not replaced. Additional modifications of the dry dock were then made, including the "installation of two steel gangways, shore power cable, a pneumatic manifold and an electrical distribution panel."

Catlin I, 2013 U.S. Dist. LEXIS 52307, at *6-8.[10] Further factual findings by the court help to support this conclusion:

The *Perseverance* was secured and attached to the southwestern end of the outfitting Pier 15 in Miramar, a location that was adjacent to an apron designed by the Puerto Rico Ports Authority

("Ports Authority") for rental [—18—] to . . . SJT. The area occupied by . . . SJT contained mooring lines, support equipment and machinery, grounding connection, electricity, and compressed air. At the pier, the *Perseverance* received electrical power from generators located on shore . . . when needed. A shoreside pneumatic line fed compressed air to the dry dock, and the wing wall was connected directly to a grounding lug on the pier with a three-quarter-inch grounding wire. At least one gangway—chained both to the dry dock and the pier—provided access to the *Perseverance*, which was tied to the dock with more than ten three-inch-diameter mooring lines and numerous spring lines. . . .

At the time that it sank, the *Perseverance* . . . had been non-operational for almost a year. Between the time it arrived in 2007 and when it sank in 2011, the dry dock was occasionally moved ten or fifteen feet within its assigned area at the pier. The movement [was] done for the purpose of returning the dry dock back to its original position after raising and repairing a vessel, and was accomplished by the use of ropes pulled by either harbor workers or a pickup truck.

Id. at 8-9.

Finally, based on the evidence presented, the district court found as follows: "The *Perseverance* was designed, constructed, and used to provide marine maintenance and repair services to vessels," and "[i]ts intended use [was] to lift floating equipment for inspection and repair." *Id.*

We again note that the Policy expressly included "hull" coverage for the PERSEVERANCE. At a minimum, the description of the PERSEVERANCE adopted by the trial court, and previously described, is undoubtedly encompassed within the term "hull" as [—19—] used in Section 1101's definition of ocean marine insurance under

---

[10] These findings were adopted by the district court as part of its findings in *Catlin IV*; they are not challenged on appeal. *See Catlin IV*, 979 F. Supp. 2d at 182 n.1.

the Code. *See* David Auburn et al., *Oxford American Writer's Thesaurus* 442 (1st ed. 2004) (listing "structure" as one synonym of "hull").[11]

Not to be ignored is the obvious fact that we are dealing with a floating structure, at least one that should be floating [—20—] under normal conditions, even when partly flooded to take on a ship in need of repairs. It is difficult to countenance the existence of a structure that not only floats on pontoons, performs essential maritime repair work on the water, and is capable of being towed (and

---

[11] The question of whether a maritime structure is a vessel, craft or hull under section 1101 of the Code is, of course, a question of Puerto Rico law, not federal law. However, in the only case in which the Puerto Rico Supreme Court has interpreted the relevant sections of the insurance code, to which SJT points in support of their argument, the court turned to federal law in general, and the federal law of admiralty in particular, as a source of guidance. *See Quiñones v. G. Amer. Ins. Co.*, 97 D.P.R. 368 (1969); *see also Hernández v. S.S. Mut. Underwriting Ass'n, Ltd.*, 388 F. Supp. 312 (D.P.R. 1974) (interpreting the Puerto Rico Insurance Code solely via federal law). Accordingly, we do likewise.

While the term "hull" is ill-defined in federal admiralty law, in contrast to "vessel," which has been the subject of extensive and ongoing discussion, it is nonetheless clear that the term is applicable to a structure such as the PERSEVERENCE. *See* Eric Sullivan, *The Marine Encyclopaedic Dictionary* 209 (5th ed. 1996) (defining a hull as the "[s]hell or body of a ship"). Interestingly, the origin of this nautical term appears to be botanical:

> **hull** [OE] The notion underlying the word *hull* is of 'covering' or 'concealing.' It originally meant 'peapod'—etymologically, the 'covering' of peas—and comes ultimately from the same Indo-European source as produced English *cell, clandestine, conceal, hall, hell,* and possibly *colour* and *holster*. It is generally assumed that *hull* 'main body of a ship,' which first appeared in the 15th century, is the same word (a ship's hull resembling an open peapod), although some etymologists have suggested that it may be connected with *hollow*.

John Ayoto, *Dictionary of Word Origins* 289 (1990). As a floating drydock unquestionably has the form of a shell afloat in the water, it can be aptly described as a hull.

in fact has been towed thousands of miles on the open ocean) without concluding that it is a "hull" or a "craft."

We need to discuss one final argument raised by SJT before entering into a discussion of the merits of whether the *uberrimae fidei* doctrine applies to this controversy: namely, SJT's contention that the controlling definition for what constitutes "marine and transportation insurance" is contained in Section 405 of Code, and not Section 1101. *See* P.R. Laws Ann. tit. 26 § 405. According to SJT, because Section 405(d) "includ[es] dry docks" as one of the structures covered by Section 405's definition of "marine insurance," the Policy in this case, which covers a floating drydock, is not within the ocean marine insurance exclusion contained in Section 1101. *See id.* Thus, SJT alleges Section 405 bars application of *uberrimae fidei*.

There are at least two fundamental reasons why SJT's argument on this issue is flawed. The first is that a plain reading of Section 1101 clearly establishes that the controlling definition for the *entire* Code as to what is marine insurance is found in that section of the Code. Section 1101(2) specifically states that for "purposes of subsection (1) of this section [which [—21—] establishes the exclusion of ocean marine insurance from application of the Code] *and this title*, 'ocean marine . . . insurances' shall include only: (a) Insurances upon vessels, *crafts, hulls*, and of interests therein or with relation thereto." P.R. Laws Ann. tit. 26, § 1101 (emphasis added). That definition supercedes all other conflicting language in Title 26, of which Section 405 is a part, even assuming there is such a conflict.

The second point is that there is no such conflict because the "dry docks" referred to in Section 405(1)(d) are totally different structures than the *floating* drydock involved in the present case. All the utilities referred to in Section 405(1)(d) are fixed, land-based structures, *e.g.*, "piers, wharves, docks and slips, and other aids to navigation and transportation, including dry dock and marine railways, dams and appurtenant facilities for the control of waterways." No legislative intent is discernible from this language to support the conclusion that we should include a movable, floating structure within that fixed, land-based conglomerate. Thus, Section 405 does not have any bearing on *floating* drydocks.[12]

In the present case, there is no local legislation that is "inconsistent" with federal admiralty law. Thus, based on the meaning of the terms craft and hull, the factual findings of the [—22—] district court as to the PERSEVERANCE's structure and function, the language of the Policy and the circumstances surrounding its procurement, and the clear dictate of Section 1101, the Policy is expressly excluded from the ambit of the Code by the "carve out" delimited in Section 1101.

B. Is *Uberrimae Fidei* an Entrenched Precept of Federal Admiralty Law Applicable to this Controversy?

Presented twice with this issue previously, we have not yet taken an authoritative stance on whether *uberrimae fidei* is an established rule of maritime law. *See Pesante*, 459 F.3d at 38 ("While we have never actually decided the issue, it is true that we have questioned whether *uberrimae fidei* is an established rule of maritime law."); *Giragosian*, 57 F.3d at 54 n.3 ("[I]t is debatable whether the doctrine can still be deemed an 'entrenched' rule of law."). The question of whether a doctrine is an established rule of maritime law, though seemingly abstruse, is of vital importance in admiralty cases as it can prove to be dispositive in controversies such as the dispute at hand. This is because for marine insurance contract cases, we only apply federal maritime rules that are established and settled; otherwise we would look to state law. *See Pesante*, 459 F.3d at 37; *Giragosian*, 57 F.3d at 54.

Marine insurance is vital to the adequate flow of commerce. The nature of the risks that are covered by maritime insurance is such

---

[12] *See* note 1, *supra*, for the distinction between floating and fixed dry docks.

that, given the urgent necessity for the [—23—] placement of this type of insurance coverage that is often present in the business of maritime commerce, as well as the extreme distances that often separate the insurance seeker and the insurer, it is imperative that the insurer be provided with truthful and valid information about the risk the insurer is asked to undertake by the party most able to provide such data: the insured.

Although this court had not yet held definitively that *uberrimae fidei* is an established rule of maritime law, we do so now, thus joining the near-unanimous consensus of our sister circuits,[13] ruling without further equivocation that the doctrine of *uberrimae fidei* is an established rule of maritime law in this Circuit.[14] This ruling

---

[13] *See, e.g., N.Y. Marine & Gen. Ins. Co. v. Cont'l Cement Co., LLC,* 761 F.3d 830, 839, 2 Adm. R. 468, 473 (8th Cir. 2014) (recognizing that *uberrimae fidei* is "established federal precedent"); *AGF Marine Aviation & Transp. v. Cassin,* 544 F.3d 255, 263 (3d Cir. 2008) (same); *Certain Underwriters at Lloyd's, London v. Inlet Fisheries Inc.,* 518 F.3d 645, 650-54 (9th Cir. 2008) (same); *HIH Marine Servs., Inc. v. Fraser,* 211 F.3d 1359, 1362 (11th Cir. 2000) (same); *Puritan Ins. Co. v. Eagle S.S. Co. S.A.,* 779 F.2d 866, 870 (2d Cir. 1985) (same). The Fifth Circuit is alone in holding that *uberrimae fidei* is "not entrenched federal precedent." *Albany Ins. Co. v. Anh Thi Kieu,* 927 F.2d 882, 889 (5th Cir. 1991) (internal quotation marks omitted). This view, however, has been heavily criticized. *See, e.g., Inlet Fisheries Inc.,* 518 F.3d at 652-54 (disparaging the *Anh Thi Kieu* decision as logically flawed and concluding that it "does violence" to established law).

[14] Our adoption of *uberrimae fidei* does not violate the Supreme Court's warning in *Wilburn Boat Co.,* 348 U.S. at 316, not to create new admiralty rules that govern marine insurance policies. *See Inlet Fisheries Inc.,* 518 F.3d at 650-51 ("[T]he Supreme Court in *Wilburn Boat* expressed a reluctance for federal courts to fashion *new* admiralty rules, not a desire to do away with existing ones."). *Uberrimae fidei* is a judicially created admiralty rule that [—24—] substantially predates *Wilburn Boat Co.* and has been reapplied time and time again even after the *Wilburn Boat Co.* decision. *See, e.g., Inlet Fisheries Inc.,* 518 F.3d at 653 (observing that *uberrimae fidei* is a 200-year-old rule); *see also McLanahan v. Universal Ins. Co.,* 26 U.S. 170, 185 (1828) (discussing *uberrimae fidei* in the context of insurance).

should hardly be surprising. As early as [—24—] 1828, the Supreme Court characterized an insurance contract as "a contract *uberrimae fidei*." *McLanahan v. Universal Ins. Co.*, 26 U.S. 170, 185 (1828). In fact, 100 years later, "the doctrine was referred to as a 'traditional' aspect of insurance law."[15] *N.Y. Marine & Gen. Ins. Co.*, 761 F.3d at 839, 2 Adm. R. at 473 (quoting *Stipcich v. Metro. Life Ins. Co.*, 277 U.S. 311, 316 (1928)). Even following the Supreme Court's *Wilburn Boat Co.* decision in 1955, which held that states should have the primary say in matters of marine insurance, 348 U.S. at 321, the circuit courts—including the Fifth Circuit prior to its *Anh Thi Kieu* decision in 1991—routinely applied *uberrimae fidei* as a federal admiralty rule to marine insurance contracts because it was so well-established. *See Inlet Fisheries Inc.*, 518 F.3d at 651-52 (citing, *e.g.*, *Ingersoll Milling Mach. Co. v. M/V Bodena*, 829 F.2d 293, 308 (2d Cir. 1987); *Fireman's Fund Ins. Co. v. Wilburn Boat Co.*, 300 F.2d 631, 646 (5th Cir. 1962) (on remand from the Supreme Court)). [—25—]

Then, in 1991, the Fifth Circuit held in *Anh Thi Kieu* that *uberrimae fidei* was not established maritime law, a decision that the Ninth Circuit has characterized as an "abrupt[] change[] [in] course". *Id.* at 652 (referencing *Anh Thi Kieu*, 927 F.2d at 889-90). "Ironically, were it not for the *Anh Thi Kieu* decision itself, there would be little cause at all to doubt that *uberrimae fidei* is indeed firmly entrenched maritime law." *Id.*

We find it instructive that following our 2006 decision in *Pesante*, in which we questioned whether *uberrimae fidei* was an established rule of maritime law, 459 F.3d at 38, three of our sister circuits—the Third Circuit in 2008, the Ninth Circuit in 2008, and the Eighth Circuit in 2014—formally recognized the doctrine as established admiralty law. *See N.Y. Marine & Gen. Ins. Co.*, 761 F.3d at 839, 2 Adm. R. at 473; *AGF Marine Aviation & Transp.*, 544 F.3d at 263; *Inlet Fisheries Inc.*, 518 F.3d at 654. Moreover, the Second and Eleventh Circuits—courts that have recognized *uberrimae fidei* as an established maritime rule since at least the 1980s[16]—have recently reaffirmed the vitality of *uberrimae fidei* within their respective jurisdictions. *See, e.g.*, *St. Paul Fire & Marine Ins. Co. v. Matrix Posh, LLC*, 507 F. App'x 94, 95 (2d Cir. 2013); *I.T.N. Consolidators, Inc. v. N. Marine Underwriters Ltd.*, 464 F. App'x 788, 790 n.3 (11th Cir. 2012) (per curiam). Therefore, based [—26—] on both the policy rationales supporting *uberrimae fidei* and the longstanding history and consistent application of the doctrine by most of the circuits, we formally recognize *uberrimae fidei* as an established admiralty rule within this Circuit.

C. Did SJT Violate *Uberrimae Fidei*?

We finally proceed to an analysis of the application of *uberrimae fidei* to this case.[17] At the bench trial, Richard Thompson ("Thompson"), a hull inspector who surveyed the PERSEVERANCE, testified that he found "heavy wastage" in the drydock's hull during an April 2010 inspection. After Thompson notified SJT of the rust and deterioration problems, SJT admitted that "those damages were pre-existing." Because the PERSEVERANCE was not in prime condition and business was slow, SJT offered to sell the floating drydock to potential buyers at a price between $700,000 to $800,000, which presumably approximated its actual value at the time. Indeed, in April 2011—the same month that the Catlin Policy took effect—SJT advertised the PERSEVERANCE for sale at a price of $800,000. Yet, SJT, in its request for marine insurance coverage from Catlin, represented to Catlin that the PERSEVERANCE had been previously insured by

---

[15] As one commentator has put it, "'no rule of marine insurance is better established tha[n] the utmost good faith rule.'" *Inlet Fisheries Inc.*, 518 F.3d at 653-54 (alteration in original) (quoting Thomas J. Schoenbaum, *The Duty of Utmost Good Faith in Marine Insurance Law: A Comparative Analysis of American and English Law*, 29 J. Mar. L. & Com. 1, 11 (1998)).

[16] *See Knight v. U.S. Fire Ins. Co.*, 804 F.2d 9, 13 (2d Cir. 1986); *Steelmet, Inc. v. Caribe Towing Corp.*, 747 F.2d 689, 695 (11th Cir. 1984).

[17] Our standards of review for a bench trial are well known; the district court's factual findings are protected by clear error review. *Giragosian*, 57 F.3d at 53.

RLI for $1,750,000 [—27—] —$700,000 *more* than what SJT paid for the drydock originally.[18] We agree with the district court that Catlin could have reasonably assumed the value presented to it in the previous insurance policy from RLI as the actual value and evaluated its risks based on the conditions it would have reasonably expected from a drydock of that value. SJT's failure to disclose the true value of the PERSEVERANCE, what SJT paid for the PERSEVERENCE, and the PERSEVER-ANCE's level of deterioration, therefore, are all material facts, the nondisclosure of which violates *uberrimae fidei*. *See N.H. Ins. Co. v. C'Est Moi, Inc.*, 519 F.3d 937, 939 (9th Cir. 2008) ("The purchase price of a vessel is unquestionably a fact material to the risk, as it provides an objective measure of the vessel's worth and the corresponding risk of insuring the vessel." (internal quotation marks and citation omitted)); *Pesante*, 459 F.3d at 38 (explaining that a material fact is "that which can possibly influence the mind of a prudent and intelligent insurer in determining whether it will accept [a] risk" (internal quotation marks omitted)); *Grande*, 436 F.3d at 283 ("[T]he strict maritime [—28—] rule of *uberrimae fidei* [provides that] an insured must make full disclosure of all material facts of which the insured has, or ought to have, knowledge . . . even though no inquiry be made." (last alteration in original) (internal quotation marks omitted)).

Under *uberrimae fidei*, when the marine insured fails to disclose to the marine insurer *all* circumstances known to it and unknown to the insurer which "materially affect the insurer's risk," the insurer may void the marine insurance policy at its option. *Giragosian*, 57 F.3d at 55. In other words, the policy becomes voidable.[19] *See id.* at 54-55. As discussed above, the evidence conclusively shows that SJT failed to disclose material information about the PERSEVERENCE's actual value and preexisting [—29—] deteriorated condition prior to Catlin determining whether it would accept the risk. Catlin was free, therefore, to void the policy.[20]

---

[18] It is true that the second Marine Consultants report valued the PERSEVERANCE at $1,750,000 in November 2006, due to the value added by the improvements made to the ship to prepare it for towing. Yet continuing to represent this amount as the drydock's actual value more than four years later fails to account for subsequent depreciation, damage, and decay, particularly in the absence of further major improvements to the vessel. Moreover, we find no error in drawing an inference that the drydock's advertised sale price of $800,000 in April 2011 better approximated the actual value of the PERSEVERENCE than an outdated valuation report from four years earlier.

[19] The district court concluded that under *uberrimae fidei*, the Policy was void *ab initio*, meaning that there was never an enforceable contract to begin with. *See Black's Law Dictionary* 1805 (10th ed. 2014). However, as the Supreme Court has described it, and as we conclude now, *uberrimae fidei* renders a marine insurance contract *voidable*—the contract is deemed valid until being voided at the election of the insurer. *See, e.g., Stipcich*, 277 U.S. at 316 ("Insurance policies are traditionally contracts uberrimae fidei and a failure by the insured to disclose conditions affecting the risk, of which he is aware, makes the contract voidable at the insurer's option."). Moreover, our prior cases that did not adopt *uberrimae fidei* as well-established law also describe the doctrine as one that renders an insurance contract voidable, not void *ab initio*. *See, e.g., Pesante*, 459 F.3d at 38 ("[I]f we were to find that the doctrine of *uberrimae fidei* is an established rule of maritime law, we would hold that the policy was voidable as a matter of law.").

[20] One might argue that there is a distinction between an insurance policy that pays the insured amount versus an insurance policy that pays the actual value in the event of a total loss of the drydock, and the facts in this case are not clear as to whether Catlin would have paid up to the liability limit ($1,000,000) or the market value (approximately $700,000 to $800,000, based on the prices at which SJT was willing to sell the vessel). However, this question is immaterial, as *uberrimae fidei* looks solely to whether SJT satisfied its duty of disclosing all material facts known to it. Regardless of the factual uncertainty in this respect, we find that SJT violated *uberrimae fidei* under either set of circumstances. Clearly, in the first scenario, in which Catlin owed the full liability limit of $1,000,000 in the event of total loss, then the actual value of the PERSEVERANCE would be a material fact, the nondisclosure of which would violate *uberrimae fidei*. *See Cassin*, 544 F.3d at 265; *N.H. Ins. Co.*, 519 F.3d at 939. As to the second scenario, had Catlin known that the PERSEVERANCE was being offered for sale at less than forty-six percent of its insured value, it, like any reasonable insurer, likely would not have

III. *Conclusion*

SJT violated the doctrine of *uberrimae fidei* in its procurement of the Policy. Thus, Catlin was entitled to void the Policy. The decision of the district court is affirmed, however, its holding is modified to reflect that the contract was voidable, not void *ab initio*.

Affirmed.

---

agreed to issue the $1,750,000 insurance policy in the first place. *See, e.g., Pesante*, 459 F.3d at 38.

United States Court of Appeals
for the First Circuit

No. 12-1991

UNITED STATES
vs.
REVEROL-RIVERA

Appeal from the United States District Court for the
District of Puerto Rico

Decided: February 20, 2015

Citation: 778 F.3d 363, 3 Adm. R. 36 (1st Cir. 2015).

Before **HOWARD**, **STAHL**, and **BARRON**, Circuit
Judges.

[—2—] **BARRON**, Circuit Judge:

Jorge Reverol-Rivera and an accomplice both pled guilty to importing cocaine to the United States. In this appeal, Reverol challenges the District Court's decision to give him a much longer sentence than his accomplice, even though both piloted the boat used to import the cocaine. Because the sentencing disparity between these co-defendants was reasonably justified by the difference in culpability that the District Court expressly found, we affirm the sentence.

I.

Reverol and an accomplice piloted a small boat to a rendezvous with another boat in international waters and then back towards Puerto Rico. After the two men entered United States territorial waters, law enforcement agents boarded the boat and discovered what was later confirmed to be 148.5 kilograms of cocaine.[1]

Pursuant to an agreement, *see* Fed. R. Crim. P. 11(c)(1)(A), (B), Reverol pled guilty to importing (and aiding and abetting his accomplice in importing) into the United

States at least five kilograms of a substance containing cocaine. 21 U.S.C. §§ 952(a), 960(a)(1), 960(b)(1)(B); 18 U.S.C. § 2. The government [—3—] and Reverol agreed to "recommend a sentence at the lower end of the applicable advisory guideline range."[2]

The Sentencing Guidelines recommend a range of sentences based on two variables. *See* U.S.S.G. § 5A. The first variable is the offense level, expressed as a point value determined initially by the seriousness of the offense and then adjusted upward or downward to account for aggravating or mitigating factors. *See id.* § 2 introductory cmt. The second variable is the defendant's criminal history. *See id.* § 4A1.1.

The statement of facts that accompanied the plea agreement stipulated that Reverol "captained the vessel" that transported the cocaine. The plea agreement's recommended guidelines calculation, however, did not apply the guideline that enhances a defendant's offense level by two points "[i]f the defendant unlawfully imported or exported a controlled substance under circumstances in which . . . the defendant acted as a pilot, copilot, captain, navigator, flight officer, or any other operation officer aboard any craft or vessel carrying a controlled substance." U.S.S.G. § 2D1.1(b)(3)(C). The government also promised not to seek further enhancements. [—4—]

The pre-sentence report, independently prepared by a probation officer, contained its own recommended guidelines calculation. *See* Fed. R. Crim. P. 32(d). The report took a different approach and applied the captain enhancement. The report based the enhancement on the factual stipulation in the plea agreement regarding Reverol's duties on the boat.

---

[1] "Since this appeal trails in the wake of a guilty plea, we draw the facts from the plea agreement, the change-of-plea colloquy, the undisputed portions of the presentence investigation report . . ., and the transcript of the disposition hearing." *United States v. Rivera-González*, __ F.3d __, 2015 WL 234774, at *1 (1st Cir. 2015).

[2] The agreement also contained a clause waiving Reverol's appeal rights if the District Court sentenced Reverol "according to [the agreement's] terms, conditions and recommendations." Because the District Court departed from the agreement's recommended calculation under the Sentencing Guidelines, this waiver does not preclude our review of this case. *See Rivera-González*, __ F.3d __, 2015 WL 234774, at *2.

At the sentencing hearing, the government, like Reverol, "st[oo]d by th[e] plea agreement." That approach led the government to inform the District Court at sentencing that 108 months in prison—the lower bound of the 108- to 135-month guidelines range for Reverol that the government, based on the plea agreement, calculated without using the captain enhancement—"would be sufficient punishment for this defendant even though he did undertake duties of captaining the boat." The government also argued that any sentence higher than 108 months would create an unjustified disparity with his accomplice's already-imposed sentence.

Reverol's accomplice, who the record indicates shared the same criminal history category as Reverol, had pled guilty in a straight plea without a formal agreement. The accomplice had then received a sentence of 63 months in prison. That sentence was at the lower end of the accomplice's guidelines sentencing range of 63 to 78 months. In calculating that range, the district court did not apply the captain enhancement but did apply a deduction for the [—5—] accomplice's having played a minor role in the crime. U.S.S.G. § 3B1.2(b).

At sentencing, both the government and Reverol stated that the accomplice shared some piloting duties on the boat and thus could have received the same captain enhancement. The government explained, however, that the government's version of the facts in the accomplice's plea colloquy did not mention that the accomplice shared captaining duties. The government also explained that the plea agreement with Reverol did include the description of Reverol's duties as captain "because he in fact was the ultimate person responsible for captaining the vessel" even if, in practice, the duties were shared. The government argued, however, that a sentence of 108 months for Reverol, compared to one of 63 months for his accomplice, would be about the right punishment differential and that a higher sentence for Reverol would be unjustified. For his part, Reverol also argued that he should receive a two-point deduction to cancel out the effects of the captain enhancement, though he conceded that he did not meet the requirements for a substantial assistance deduction, *see id.* § 5K1.1, and he did not identify any other guideline that would permit such a deduction.[3] [—6—]

The District Court followed the lead of the pre-sentence report rather than the plea agreement and included the two-point captain enhancement in calculating Reverol's guidelines sentencing range. The District Court then sentenced Reverol to 135 months in prison, which was the lower end of the 135- to 168-month guidelines range that the District Court calculated.

The District Court explained that the sentence was "sufficient but not greater than necessary." Addressing the disparity argument, the District Court concluded that Reverol's higher sentence was justified by his greater culpability. The District Court found that the accomplice was "a last minute replacement recruited by . . . Reverol . . . the day before the scheduled pickup," and that Reverol transported the accomplice to the boat, had primary responsibility for captaining the vessel, read the geolocation system, and "knew the pickup location." The District Court also explained that neither the government nor Reverol "provided any concrete information to the Court regarding the extent of Reverol[-]Rivera's assistance to the United States, or its contents" to qualify for a substantial-assistance deduction.

Reverol then brought this appeal.

II.

Reverol challenges the procedural and substantive reasonableness of his sentence. Because Reverol preserved these challenges, we review the discretionary sentence determinations for [—7—] abuse of discretion, findings of fact for clear error, and conclusions of law de novo. *United States v. Rivera-González*, __ F.3d __, 2015 WL 234774, at *2 (1st Cir. 2015).

---

[3] Reverol thus mischaracterizes the record when he states in his opening brief on appeal that he argued to the District Court that he deserved "a two-level departure for substantial assistance."

Reverol first argues that the District Court imposed a procedurally unreasonable sentence because it "failed to adequately consider" his arguments, including the disparity argument, in favor of a 108-month sentence. But the record clearly reveals the opposite. *See United States v. Ayala-Vazquez*, 751 F.3d 1, 31-32 (1st Cir. 2014) (concluding that district court adequately considered disparity argument by noting that disparate sentences were justified where co-defendants pled guilty and were thus not similarly situated to defendant who went to trial).

And so we turn to Reverol's substantive challenge. Reverol argues that the District Court's 135-month sentence, though within the guidelines range, was substantively unreasonable in light of the accomplice's 63-month sentence. Reverol concedes that he was more culpable than his accomplice. He argues, however, that his greater culpability would merit only a 108-month sentence, and that any sentence above that would create too much of a disparity with the sentence his accomplice received.

When imposing a sentence, a district court must consider "the need to avoid unwarranted sentence disparities among defendants with similar records who have been found guilty of similar conduct." 18 U.S.C. § 3553(a)(6). We have said that [—8—] § 3553(a)(6) is primarily concerned with national disparities. *See, e.g., United States v. Dávila-González*, 595 F.3d 42, 49 (1st Cir. 2010). But we have also examined arguments, like Reverol's, that a sentence was substantively unreasonable because of the disparity with the sentence given to a co-defendant. *See, e.g., id.* at 49-50 (contrasting co-defendant who pled to defendant who did not); *United States v. Mateo-Espejo*, 426 F.3d 508, 514 (1st Cir. 2005) (contrasting co-defendant's "prompt and full cooperation" with defendant's "belated and grudging cooperation").[4]

In performing such review, we have made clear that differences in culpability can justify disparate sentences among co-defendants. *United States v. Rivera-Maldonado*, 194 F.3d 224, 236 (1st Cir. 1999). And here, the District Court expressly found that Reverol was significantly more culpable than his accomplice, pointing to his accomplice's last-minute addition to the operation and subordinate role at sea, Reverol's arrangement for the accomplice's participation, and Reverol's ultimate responsibility for captaining the ship (including, unlike the accomplice, knowing the rendezvous location and guiding the boat using geolocation technology). [—9—]

Reverol asserts that 108 months was the highest sentence that could be justified given the lower sentence the accomplice received. But given that the record supports the District Court's determination that Reverol and the accomplice were not equally culpable, we find nothing in this record to indicate that the District Court abused its discretion in concluding that the 135-month sentence was justified by Reverol's individual level of culpability. *See Rivera-González*, __ F.3d __, 2015 WL 234774, at *6 ("In most cases, there is not a single appropriate sentence but, rather, a universe of reasonable sentences."); *United States v. Martin*, 520 F.3d 87, 96 (1st Cir. 2008) ("[T]he linchpin of a reasonable sentence is a plausible sentencing rationale and a defensible result.").

Our conclusion is not disturbed by the fact that the government and Reverol recommended 108 months as the highest sentence that could be justified by Reverol's greater culpability. The District Court was not bound by the jointly recommended sentence, *see Rivera-González*, __ F.3d __, 2015 WL 234774, at *5-6, and the District Court identified in some detail aspects of the role Reverol played that reasonably support its conclusion that his actions warranted a sentence of the length imposed.

We thus *affirm* the District Court's sentence.

---

[4] The government argues that we held in *Ayala-Vazquez*, 751 F.3d at 32, that co-defendant disparity need not be considered at all. But *Ayala-Vazquez* established only that the fact that one co-defendant pled guilty while the other went to trial may justify a disparity in their sentences. *Id.*

United States Court of Appeals
for the First Circuit

No. 13-1593

UNITED STATES
vs.
DE LA CRUZ-FELICIANO

Appeal from the United States District Court for the
District of Puerto Rico

Decided: May 13, 2015

Citation: 786 F.3d 78, 3 Adm. R. 39 (1st Cir. 2015).

Before **LYNCH**, Chief Judge, and **TORRUELLA** and
RIPPLE,* Circuit Judges.

*Of the Seventh Circuit, sitting by designation.

[—3—] **RIPPLE**, Circuit Judge:

Junior H. De La Cruz-Feliciano ("De La Cruz") and Sandri Rijo were charged with, and convicted of, conspiring to possess with intent to distribute five kilograms of cocaine and aiding and abetting others to do the same. They now appeal their convictions, alleging various procedural and evidentiary errors. For the reasons set forth in this opinion, we affirm the judgments of the district court.

I

BACKGROUND

This case involves a conspiracy to smuggle over 900 kilograms of cocaine into Santa Isabel, Puerto Rico. Eduardo Ubiera and Juan Baltazar orchestrated the operation. They recruited Francisco "Sandy" Navarro-Reyes ("Navarro") and Gary Brito-González ("Brito") to transport the cocaine, via a motorboat, from a "mother ship" at sea to Puerto Rico. The operation, however, did not run smoothly. While at sea, Navarro and Brito ran out of fuel and were unable to make it back to shore. At that point, according to government witnesses, Mr. De La Cruz was recruited to take another craft out to rendezvous with and refuel the stranded motorboat.

Mr. De La Cruz successfully delivered the fuel to the stranded motorboat. While still at sea, however, his own craft developed mechanical problems. Stranded at sea, Mr. De La Cruz and another individual aboard the vessel used a satellite phone [—4—] to call for help. According to Freddy Altagracia-Medina ("Altagracia"), a codefendant, Mr. De La Cruz had requested the satellite phone before departing in order to communicate with the stranded motorboat. The United States Coast Guard found Mr. De La Cruz's vessel adrift approximately sixty miles from shore and rescued its crew. Coast Guard agents questioned the men about their satellite phone. According to Agent Christopher David Xirau, the men claimed to have tossed the phone overboard because it had become wet.

Meanwhile, traveling in their refueled motorboat, Navarro and Brito reached the shore with the drugs on January 26, 2012, three days after the planned delivery date. Awaiting their arrival were several individuals recruited to help unload the motorboat. Mr. Rijo was among this group. According to government witnesses, he originally planned to serve only as a lookout; however, due to the motorboat's late arrival, he instead ended up helping to unload the cocaine from the motorboat into a Nissan Armada for transport to San Juan.

Following a tip from a confidential informant, law enforcement anticipated the January 26 delivery and were surveilling the area throughout the night. They observed several individuals unloading the drugs from the motorboat into a vehicle, but were unable to visually identify any of those involved in the operation. Two other vehicles were present at [—5—] the scene. Officers stopped the motorboat and three vehicles as they departed the beach. Ubiera and two other individuals were stopped in the Nissan Armada. Officers found over 900 kilograms of cocaine and three firearms in the vehicle. Navarro, Brito, and two other individuals were stopped in a second vehicle. Baltazar, Mr. Rijo, and one other person were stopped in a third vehicle. Three individuals were stopped in the motorboat. All thirteen men were arrested immediately. Officers arrested Mr. De La Cruz six days later.

On February 1, 2012, a grand jury returned an indictment, charging Mr. Rijo, Mr. De La Cruz, and their twelve codefendants with conspiring to possess with intent to distribute five kilograms of cocaine, in violation of 21 U.S.C. §§ 841(a)(1), (b)(1)(A)(ii), and 846, and aiding and abetting the same, in violation of 21 U.S.C. §§ 841(a)(1), (b)(1)(A)(ii) and 18 U.S.C. § 2.[1] Everyone except Mr. Rijo and Mr. De La Cruz accepted plea agreements. After a trial, the jury found both Mr. Rijo and Mr. De La Cruz guilty as to all charges.[2] After sentencing, the defendants timely appealed.[3] [—6—]

II

DISCUSSION

A. Mr. De La Cruz

On appeal, Mr. De La Cruz raises only one argument. It concerns the district court's questioning of Agent Xirau of the United States Coast Guard. At trial, the agent testified about the rescue of Mr. De La Cruz aboard the vessel that had gone adrift. Agent Xirau stated that he had asked Mr. De La Cruz and the other individual aboard the vessel about the satellite phone that they had used to call the Coast Guard. During the agent's testimony, on the fourth day of a six-day trial, the following exchange took place:

THE GOVERNMENT: I will ask you to clarify, when you refer to one of the two individuals on the boat, what specifically as to each individual they said, if anything?

AGENT XIRAU: Roger that.

THE GOVERNMENT: I was asking you about Junior De la Cruz, if upon you questioning him did he answer anything to you?

AGENT XIRAU: That was the only question that I remember him specifically giving me an answer.

THE GOVERNMENT: What about the other individual? [—7—]

AGENT XIRAU: I don't remember his name. When I say they, I could mean either one or the other, I don't remember who at time who was the one that gave answers to the several questions we asked.

THE COURT: But were questions generally answered?

AGENT XIRAU: Yes, ma'am.

THE COURT: Any of them express a disagreement with what the other was saying at the time?

AGENT XIRAU: No, ma'am.[4]

Defense counsel objected to the district court's questioning. In particular, counsel asserted that the questions conveyed that the district court was commenting on Mr. De La Cruz's silence when speaking with Coast Guard officials. The district court disagreed, stating that the witness "is not saying that [Mr. De La Cruz] did not answer, he says he does not remember who answered what."[5] Nevertheless, despite its disagreement with defense counsel's characterization of the exchange, the district court gave a cautionary instruction, stating that the jury was "not to draw any inferences from the [—8—] questions that [the court] posed."[6] "My only intent here," the district court explained, "was to assist in clarifying the situation. But once again I instruct you that there is no intent

---

[1] The indictment also charged Ubiera and two other defendants with possession of a firearm in furtherance of a drug trafficking crime, in violation of 18 U.S.C. § 924(c)(1)(A).

[2] The district court's jurisdiction was premised on 18 U.S.C. § 3231.

[3] Our jurisdiction is secure under 28 U.S.C. § 1291.

[4] R. 401 at 69–70. We have added the names of the speakers for the convenience of the reader.

[5] *Id.* at 71.

[6] *Id.* at 72.

and . . . no inference [should be] drawn from any type of question I have posed."[7]

Following the district court's cautionary instruction, Agent Xirau then testified that Mr. De La Cruz and the other individual aboard the vessel had offered a strange explanation for no longer possessing the satellite phone that they had used to call for help. According to the agent, the men had told him that they threw the satellite phone overboard because it had become wet. The agent described this explanation as "odd."[8]

Mr. De La Cruz now contends that the district court's questioning of Agent Xirau evinces judicial bias in violation of his right to due process of law. "When addressing allegations of judicial bias, we consider whether the comments were improper and, if so, whether the complaining party can show serious prejudice." *United States v. Ayala-Vazquez*, 751 F.3d 1, 24 (1st Cir. 2014) (internal quotation marks omitted). We assess statements in light of the record as a whole, not in isolation. *Id.* [—9—]

In assessing this claim of judicial bias, our starting point is the basic principle that "there is nothing inherently improper about a judge posing questions at trial." *Id.* Indeed, as we have previously observed, a court "has the prerogative, and at times the duty, of eliciting facts [it] deems necessary to the clear presentation of issues." *United States v. Rivera-Rodríguez*, 761 F.3d 105, 111 (1st Cir. 2014) (quoting *United States v. Paz Uribe*, 891 F.2d 396, 400 (1st Cir. 1989)); *see also* Fed. R. Evid. 614(b) ("The court may examine a witness regardless of who calls the witness."). Such questioning is permissible "so long as [the court] preserves an attitude of impartiality and guards against giving the jury an impression that the court believes the defendant is guilty." *Rivera-Rodríguez*, 761 F.3d at 111 (quoting *Paz Uribe*, 891 F.2d at 400–01). Notably, a question is not improper simply because it clarifies evidence to the disadvantage of the defendant. *See United States v. Montas*, 41 F.3d 775, 781 (1st Cir. 1994). "[T]he rule concerning judicial interrogation is designed to prevent judges from conveying prejudicial messages to the jury. It is not concerned with the damaging truth that the questions might uncover." *United States v. Martin*, 189 F.3d 547, 554 (7th Cir. 1999).

Even if a comment is improper, however, a defendant also must show that the judicial intervention resulted in [—10—] "serious prejudice." *Rivera-Rodríguez*, 761 F.3d at 112. As we recently have observed, this burden is comparable to demonstrating prejudice under plain error review. *See id.* In other words, "improper judicial intervention 'seriously prejudice[s]' a defendant's case when we find that there is a reasonable probability that, but for the error, the verdict would have been different." *Id.* The burden of establishing serious prejudice is more difficult where, as here, a court follows its comments with an appropriate cautionary instruction. *See Ayala-Vazquez*, 751 F.3d at 26 (noting that "within wide margins, the potential for prejudice stemming from improper testimony or comments can be satisfactorily dispelled by appropriate curative instructions" (quoting *United States v. Pagán-Ferrer*, 736 F.3d 573, 582 (1st Cir. 2013))).

Here, Agent Xirau testified that he could not remember who, between Mr. De La Cruz and the other individual aboard the vessel, had answered his questions regarding the satellite phone. The district court then asked whether either of the men "express[ed] a disagreement with what the other was saying at the time."[9] This question, Mr. De La Cruz contends, "conveyed to the jury that the defendant" was "in tacit agreement with any answers to the question about the satellite phone," thus [—11—] "creat[ing] 'cover' for the government to attribute the satellite phone to" him.[10]

We perceive no error in the district court's remarks. The court's inquiry was neither tinged with partiality nor suggestive of the court's stance on Mr. De La Cruz's guilt.

---

[7] *Id.*
[8] *Id.* at 74–75.

[9] *Id.* at 70.
[10] Appellant's Br. 28.

Rather, this inquiry merely clarified an ambiguity in Agent Xirau's testimony. That the resulting clarification was adverse to Mr. De La Cruz's case is not, without more, indicative of judicial bias. *See Martin*, 189 F.3d at 554. In any event, the court's remarks, which came on the fourth day of a six-day trial and were followed by an appropriate cautionary instruction, did not seriously prejudice Mr. De La Cruz's case. *See Ayala-Vazquez*, 751 F.3d at 25–26.

B. Mr. Rijo

Mr. Rijo raises three arguments on appeal. First, he contends that the Government violated its duty under *Brady v. Maryland*, 373 U.S. 83 (1963), by failing to disclose errors in an investigative report prior to his counsel's opening statement. Second, he submits that the district court erred in admitting evidence of his prior bad acts. Finally, he contends that the Government's closing argument inaccurately described [—12—] his role in the offense, thus resulting in prejudice that warrants a new trial.[11] We address these issues in turn.

1.

Mr. Rijo first submits that the Government committed a *Brady* violation by failing to disclose errors in a DEA Report of Investigation—known as a "DEA 6"—prior to defense counsel's opening statement. The DEA 6 at issue was prepared by Agent William Rosario and summarized statements made by Altagracia. The DEA 6 contained several erroneous statements due to the agent's confusion of Sandri Rijo, the defendant, with Sandy Navarro. In particular, the report erroneously stated that Mr. Rijo, rather than Navarro, was on the motorboat with Brito and had helped to transport the drugs from the "mother ship" to shore. Agent Rosario also created handwritten notes before preparing

the DEA 6. Those notes, however, were partially in Spanish and contained at least one instance where the agent again confused Mr. Rijo with Navarro.

The Government turned over the DEA 6 and the agent's handwritten notes to defense counsel during pretrial discovery. The Government also disclosed its plans to call Altagracia as a [—13—] witness to testify that Mr. Rijo was on the shore during the delivery and helped to unload the drugs.

Before opening statements, defense counsel informed the district court and the Government of his intent to attack Altagracia's credibility, in part by claiming that Altagracia had offered three different accounts of the relevant events. One of those accounts was premised on the erroneous statements in Agent Rosario's DEA 6. Defense counsel never explicitly told the Government of his intent to rely on those statements.

During opening statements, Mr. Rijo's counsel presented a defense premised in large part on impeaching the Government's three main witnesses, one of whom was Altagracia. Defense counsel presented his attack on Altagracia's credibility as follows:

> [Altagracia] has given the government at least three different versions as to what happened. The first time he gave a version to the government when he was originally caught, he said that he had been fishing since January 23. Now, that same witness did not mention anyone else at that time, he said I was fishing since January 23, three days before they were caught. Then, in April when he is already negotiating with the government and trying to get them to give him a good deal, he says that on January 22, I took Sandri Rijo to Fajardo, my client, to Fajardo to get on a boat to meet the mother boat, or the boat bringing in the drugs closer to Puerto Rico, to go there. And he also says that he did not see Sandri Rijo again until dawn on January 26 [—14—] when he came in piloting the boat that brought the drugs in.

---

[11] Originally, Mr. Rijo also appealed his sentence on procedural and substantive grounds. Following oral argument, however, Mr. Rijo, through his attorney, filed a signed letter asking to withdraw his sentencing challenge. We grant Mr. Rijo's request and thus do not consider this issue further.

Now, the third version that he gave, you just heard from the prosecutor. Notably when he gave the version of April he did not place Sandri Rijo anywhere else between the 22 to the 26, because Sandri Rijo was out on the boat, the mother boat. What do we say here, as I said you already heard the government give us a preview as to that.[12]

After opening statements, the Government informed defense counsel about the mistakes in its DEA 6. Defense counsel in turn moved for a mistrial, claiming that his "client['s] right to a fair trial ha[d] been compromised."[13] In particular, defense counsel expressed concern that the Government's late disclosure undermined the defense strategy that he had presented to the jury during opening statements.

The district court denied Mr. Rijo's motion. It concluded that defense counsel's ability to present Mr. Rijo's defense before the jury had not been impaired because he still could attack Altagracia's credibility at trial and could call Agent Rosario to testify about the DEA 6. Further, the court held that Agent Rosario's handwritten notes made clear that "the person identified was Sandy N[a]varro," and that the "inaccuracy in the DEA 6 . . . could be gathered by reviewing the [agent's] [—15—] rough notes."[14] Defense counsel did not call Agent Rosario as a witness at trial.

Mr. Rijo now contends that the Government violated its duty under *Brady* by failing to disclose, in a timely manner, the errors in its DEA 6. Specifically, Mr. Rijo submits that those errors are exculpatory because they provide evidence of a sloppy police investigation. Although Mr. Rijo's motion for a mistrial did not explicitly allege a *Brady* violation, both parties assume on appeal that the motion was based on *Brady*. Indeed, the Government has not argued that the claim was forfeited or waived. For this reason, we assume that a *Brady* claim was properly raised before the district court, *see*

United States v. Gonyer, 761 F.3d 157, 166 n.4 (1st Cir. 2014), and we review the district court's determination for abuse of discretion, *see United States v. Celestin*, 612 F.3d 14, 22 (1st Cir. 2010).

Brady requires that the Government disclose "evidence favorable to an accused" that is "material either to guilt or to punishment." 373 U.S. at 87. In order to prevail on a *Brady* claim, a defendant must show that: (1) evidence was suppressed; (2) the evidence was favorable to the accused; and (3) the evidence was material to either guilt or punishment. *See Strickler v. Greene*, 527 U.S. 263, 281–82 (1999). With regard [—16—] to the first prong, we do not consider favorable evidence suppressed "if the defendant either knew, or should have known[,] of the essential facts permitting him to take advantage of any exculpatory evidence." *Ellsworth v. Warden*, 333 F.3d 1, 6 (1st Cir. 2003) (quoting *United States v. LeRoy*, 687 F.2d 610, 618 (2d Cir. 1982)). As for the second and third prongs, "[e]vidence is 'favorable to the accused' if it is either exculpatory or impeaching in nature and 'material' if there is a reasonable probability that, had it been disclosed, the result of the proceeding would have been different." *United States v. Prochilo*, 629 F.3d 264, 268 (1st Cir. 2011).

Brady also applies in cases where the Government delays disclosure of relevant evidence. In such cases, the defendant further must show "that the delay prevented defense counsel from using the disclosed material effectively in preparing and presenting the defendant's case." *United States v. Van Anh*, 523 F.3d 43, 51 (1st Cir. 2008). To carry this burden, "[t]he defendant must at a minimum make a 'prima facie' showing of a plausible strategic option which the delay foreclosed." *Id.*

The parties' dispute largely centers on the timing of the Government's disclosure. Ruling for the Government, the district court determined that Agent Rosario's handwritten notes, disclosed along with the DEA 6, adequately informed [—17—] Mr. Rijo of the errors in the DEA 6. Further, the court held that, even if the Government's disclosure was

---

[12] R.385 at 12–13.

[13] R.394 at 5.

[14] *Id.* at 12, 16.

late, Mr. Rijo was not prejudiced by the delay because he still could call Agent Rosario as a witness to testify about the errors at trial. We are troubled by the district court's first rationale, but do agree that the second has merit.

As we noted earlier, evidence is not suppressed within the meaning of *Brady* "if the defendant either knew, or *should have known*[,] of the essential facts permitting him to take advantage of" the evidence. *Ellsworth*, 333 F.3d at 6 (emphasis added) (quoting *LeRoy*, 687 F.2d at 618). "The 'should have known' standard refers to trial preparation," and will generally impute to the defendant knowledge which he otherwise would have possessed from a diligent review of the evidence in his control. *See id.* at 7; *see also United States v. Pandozzi*, 878 F.2d 1526, 1529 (1st Cir. 1989) ("*Brady* does not require the government to turn over information which, with any reasonable diligence, the defendant can obtain himself." (alterations omitted) (quoting *Jarrell v. Balkcom*, 735 F.2d 1242, 1258 (11th Cir. 1984))). Here, the district court faulted Mr. Rijo for failing to notice incongruities between Agent Rosario's rough notes and the DEA 6, which, according to the district court, would have (or at least should have) alerted him to the errors in the DEA 6. Although we agree that a defendant *ordinarily* should notice errors in an [—18—] investigative report when such incongruities are clearly present,[15] we have significant reservations, in this instance, about the district court's conclusion. Agent Rosario's notes are of poor quality. The agent's rough handwriting, combined with the fact that the notes were disclosed in the form of a darkened photocopy, rendered the material that Mr. Rijo received almost entirely illegible. Moreover, the agent's notes were partially in Spanish and contained at least one instance in which the agent further confused Mr. Rijo with Navarro.

We agree with the district court, however, that the Government's late disclosure of this evidence did not prevent defense counsel from effectively using it at trial. The Government disclosed these errors after opening statements on the first day of trial, Monday, September 10, 2012. The Government rested its case at the end of the day on Friday, September 14. The defense rested on Tuesday, September 18, without calling a single witness. Neither party called Agent Rosario to testify even though the district court, in denying Mr. Rijo's motion for a mistrial, explicitly had advised Mr. Rijo that he could do so. Defense counsel thus had seven [—19—] days—three of which were unencumbered by trial—to use this evidence in preparing and presenting Mr. Rijo's case.

Mr. Rijo has offered no reason why this interval was not enough time for defense counsel to make effective use of the disclosed material, nor could he. *See United States v. Peters*, 732 F.2d 1004, 1009 (1st Cir. 1984) (holding that the Government's belated disclosure of impeachment evidence, which was "short, uncomplicated, and fairly predictable," did not violate *Brady* where the defendants had "two full days, including one nontrial day, in which to prepare to cross-examine" the witness). To the extent that this evidence was exculpatory, its relevance to Mr. Rijo's case was straightforward: it undermined the thoroughness and good faith of the Government's investigation. This defense is neither complicated nor inconsistent with the defense strategy pursued by Mr. Rijo. Seven days afforded ample time for its preparation. *See id.* On these facts, we cannot conclude that the Government's belated disclosure of this evidence prevented defense counsel from using it in preparing and presenting Mr. Rijo's case.

2.

Mr. Rijo next submits that the district court erred, under Federal Rules of Evidence 403 and 404(b), in admitting (1) testimony by Altagracia that Mr. Rijo had threatened him while in prison and (2) testimony by Agent Jesus Marrero that drug- [—20—] trafficking organizations would look for "experienced

---

[15] *Cf. Ellsworth v. Warden*, 333 F.3d 1, 7 (1st Cir. 2003) (noting that a defendant's *Brady* claim could be barred if he "knew of [potentially exculpatory evidence] at the time of his trial and failed to pursue the lead").

people" to handle a shipment of the size involved in this case. We review for abuse of discretion a district court's decision regarding the admissibility of evidence under Rules 403 and 404(b). *United States v. Lugo Guerrero*, 524 F.3d 5, 14 (1st Cir. 2008).

Rule 404(b) provides that "[e]vidence of a crime, wrong, or other act is not admissible to prove a person's character in order to show that on a particular occasion the person acted in accordance with the character." Fed. R. Evid. 404(b)(1). However, this rule permits the admission of prior acts evidence having "special" relevance—that is, evidence relevant for a non-propensity-based purpose, "such as proving motive, opportunity, intent, preparation, plan, knowledge, identity, absence of mistake, or lack of accident." *Id.* 404(b)(2).[16] In assessing whether prior acts evidence is admissible for such a purpose, we apply a two-step test. *United States v. Landry*, 631 F.3d 597, 601–02 (1st Cir. 2011). First, we ask whether the proffered evidence truly possesses "special" relevance. *Id.* at 602. If it does, we then apply Rule 403, admitting the evidence so long as its probative value is not substantially outweighed by the risk of unfair prejudice. *Id.* [—21—]

We start with the admission of Altagracia's testimony. At trial, Mr. Rijo's defense counsel cross-examined Altagracia about his limited relationship with Mr. Rijo. In particular, defense counsel asked when, if ever, he had spoken with Mr. Rijo. After first describing how they had spoken "in the field" during their criminal activities, Altagracia then responded that Mr. Rijo had threatened him while in prison:

> When I was at the 2B unit, Mr. Sandri Rijo yelled at me through the—in other words I was playing basketball out in the yard and he yelled at me and said that if I turned around with the authorities he was going to have my family kidnaped [sic], that he was going to also have me beat up and that he had

already given orders to have my family kidnaped [sic].[17]

Defense counsel objected to this unexpected testimony, but the district court overruled his objection, noting that defense counsel "had plenty of time to stop th[e] witness."[18]

The Government contends that the district court did not err in admitting evidence of Mr. Rijo's threat, given that defense counsel was the one who elicited this testimony. We agree. As we have acknowledged previously, a defendant cannot complain about the admission of testimony directly responsive to a question posed by defense counsel. *See United States v. Rivera-Rivera*, 477 F.3d 17, 20 (1st Cir. 2007) ("Rivera cannot [—22—] persuasively complain about the admission of this evidence, given that it was the defense—not the government—which elicited it in the course of its cross-examination. . . ."); *United States v. Lizardo*, 445 F.3d 73, 84 (1st Cir. 2006) (noting that where a defendant elicited challenged testimony on cross-examination, he could not "contest his own invited error" on appeal); *United States v. Cresta*, 825 F.2d 538, 552 (1st Cir. 1987) ("It is apparent from the record that defense counsel did elicit the response, although perhaps inadvertently, and cannot now complain of the alleged error."). Here, defense counsel asked Altagracia whether he ever had spoken with Mr. Rijo. In response, Altagracia stated that Mr. Rijo verbally had threatened him while in prison. Because this answer was directly responsive to defense counsel's open-ended question, Mr. Rijo cannot now complain of its admission on appeal.

In any event, Altagracia's testimony would have been admissible even if elicited by the Government. As the Government correctly notes, evidence that Mr. Rijo threatened a government witness is probative of his "consciousness of guilt." *United States v. Burnett*, 579 F.3d 129, 133 (1st Cir. 2009). "Such threats may imply that the defendant has something to hide or a desire to cover something up." *United States v. Rosa*, 705

---

[16] As we have noted on previous occasions, Rule 404(b)(2)'s listing of permissible purposes is illustrative rather than exhaustive. *United States v. Landry*, 631 F.3d 597, 602 (1st Cir. 2011).

[17] R.401 at 21.
[18] *Id.* at 22.

F.2d 1375, 1377 (1st Cir. 1983) (internal quotation marks omitted). This use of prior acts evidence is entirely [—23—] permissible under Rule 404(b). *See Burnett*, 579 F.3d at 133. Thus, because Mr. Rijo's threat is probative in this regard, Rule 404(b) does not require its exclusion.

Mr. Rijo's Rule 403 challenge is equally unavailing. In prior cases involving the application of Rule 403 to evidence of a defendant's threats against a government witness, we have considered a variety of factors, including "whether the jury heard graphic details of how the threat would be carried out, whether the threat was made as an emotional or impulsive reaction, and how important the evidence about the threat was to the Government's case."[19] *Id.* at 134 (citations omitted). Here, the district court certainly did not abuse its discretion in admitting the evidence. Altagracia's testimony did not involve graphic or sensational details of the content of Mr. Rijo's threat. Further, as we noted earlier, this evidence is probative of Mr. Rijo's consciousness of guilt, which, given his defense that he was essentially in the wrong place at the wrong time, was highly relevant to the Government's case. For these reasons, we cannot conclude that the probative value of Altagracia's testimony was outweighed, much less substantially so, by the risk of unfair prejudice. [—24—]

Turning to Agent Marrero's testimony, at trial the agent offered testimony about cocaine sales in Puerto Rico and the practices of drug smugglers. In particular, he testified that a drug-trafficking organization would look for "experienced people" to handle a shipment of the size involved in this case.[20] Mr. Rijo contends that this testimony ran afoul of Rules 404(b) and 403 by implying that he had prior experience in drug trafficking. Because Mr. Rijo did not raise these objections before the district court, our review is for plain error. *See United States v. Rodríguez-Adorno*, 695 F.3d 32, 38 (1st Cir. 2012).

With respect to his Rule 404(b) objection, Mr. Rijo's argument fails at its first step. Rule 404(b) only applies to "[e]vidence of a crime, wrong, or other act." Fed. R. Evid. 404(b)(1). Agent Marrero's testimony did not reveal a crime, wrong, or other act committed by Mr. Rijo. Rather, he merely described the way in which drug-trafficking organizations generally operate. As such, his testimony does not fall within the ambit of Rule 404(b).

In his Rule 403 objection, Mr. Rijo contends that Agent Marrero's testimony suggests that Mr. Rijo was an experienced drug trafficker, thus giving the impression that he [—25—] had participated in such acts in the past and was likely to do so in the future. This argument falls wide of the mark. The agent's testimony simply stated that drug dealers who undertake sea-to-shore delivery operations realize the high risk of such an undertaking. Consequently, they employ only individuals who are committed to the success of the operation and who have the experience necessary to bring the venture to a successful conclusion. This testimony was both relevant and probative; it rebutted Mr. Rijo's claim that he was not a member of the conspiracy but rather a mere tag-along or innocent bystander. The importance of this evidence outweighed any possible unfair prejudice that may have resulted from the implication that experience in the drug trade necessarily indicates a prior criminal history. The district court did not abuse its discretion in admitting this testimony and certainly did not commit plain error.

3.

Finally, Mr. Rijo contends that the Government's closing argument inaccurately described his role in the offense, thus resulting in prejudice warranting a new trial. Mr. Rijo's argument is premised on the original transcript filed in this case. That transcript shows four instances in which the Government incorrectly referred to Sandy Navarro as either "Sandi Rijo" or "Sandri Rijo" during its closing argument. [—26—] These misstatements, assuming they occurred, portrayed Mr. Rijo as considerably more

---

[19] This list of relevant factors is by no means exhaustive.

[20] R.405 at 147.

involved in the conspiracy than the evidence would otherwise show.

During the pendency of this appeal, the district court, acting pursuant to Federal Rule of Appellate Procedure 10(e), granted a motion by the Government to supplement the record on appeal with a revised transcript. This revised transcript, which the court reporter had certified and filed with the district court nearly nine months earlier, indicates that the Government did not in fact confuse Navarro with Mr. Rijo during its closing argument. The district court granted the Government's Rule 10(e) motion on the same day that it was filed, without giving Mr. Rijo an opportunity to respond.

Following the district court's order, Mr. Rijo filed a supplemental brief in this court asking us to reject the revised transcript. He also filed a motion for reconsideration in the district court. In both filings, Mr. Rijo raised several significant arguments attacking the reliability of the revised transcript.

Federal Rule of Appellate Procedure 10(e) governs the modification or correction of the record on appeal. In particular, Rule 10(e)(1) provides that, "[i]f any difference arises about whether the record truly discloses what occurred in the district court, the difference must be submitted to and [—27—] settled by that court and the record conformed accordingly." Fed. R. App. P. 10(e)(1). A district court's determination under Rule 10(e)(1) "is conclusive absent a showing of intentional falsification or plain unreasonableness." *Pagán-Ferrer*, 736 F.3d at 582 (quoting *United States v. Serrano*, 870 F.2d 1, 12 (1st Cir. 1989)).

Because Mr. Rijo was not afforded an opportunity to respond to the Government's Rule 10(e) motion, the district court never heard or considered any of his arguments before certifying the revised transcript as part of our record on appeal. In order to remedy this deficiency, we stayed Mr. Rijo's appeal following oral argument and, while retaining jurisdiction, remanded the case for the limited purpose of obtaining a ruling from the district court on Mr. Rijo's objection. In particular, we

ordered the district court to address Mr. Rijo's then-pending motion for reconsideration.

On remand, the district court ordered its court reporter to submit a certified copy of her stenographer's notes from the Government's closing argument as well as an affidavit explaining how those notes support the revised transcript. The court reporter did so, explaining in her affidavit that her stenographer's notes showed that the Government had not confused Navarro with Mr. Rijo during its closing. Rather, as the court reporter explained, she had simply mistyped "Rijo" instead of [—28—]

"Navarro" when transcribing her notes several months after the trial.

After receiving the court reporter's notes and accompanying affidavit, the district court held a hearing on Mr. Rijo's motion and, shortly thereafter, denied the motion in a written order. The court based its decision on the court reporter's filings, the parties' pleadings and exhibits, and the court's "own recollection and notes of [Mr. Rijo's] criminal trial."[21] Based on this evidence, the court concluded that it was "100 percent certain that the revised transcript [was] correct."[22]

The district court's order thoroughly and persuasively addressed each of Mr. Rijo's arguments. In light of the court's careful consideration of this issue, we cannot conclude that its decision to certify the revised transcript as part of the record on appeal was plainly unreasonable. *See id.* Accordingly, we accept the revised transcript as part of our record, and thus conclude that the Government did not confuse Sandy Navarro with Mr. Rijo during its closing argument.

III

CONCLUSION

The judgments of the district court are affirmed.

---

[21] R.635 at 9.
[22] *Id.* at 15.

AFFIRMED

United States Court of Appeals
for the First Circuit

No. 14-1903

FARNSWORTH

vs.

TOWBOAT NANTUCKET SOUND, INC.

Appeal from the United States District Court for the
District of Massachusetts

Decided: June 17, 2015

Citation: 790 F.3d 90, 3 Adm. R. 49 (1st Cir. 2015).

Before **HOWARD,** Chief Judge, and **SELYA** and **LYNCH,**
Circuit Judges.

[—2—] **LYNCH,** Circuit Judge:

Out of this maritime case come useful lessons for those who seek to challenge the validity of arbitration clauses in contracts they have signed.

Plaintiff Rodney Farnsworth, III, entered into a salvage contract with defendant Towboat Nantucket Sound, Inc. ("TNS"), to obtain help when Farnsworth's boat went aground on rocks one night near the Weepeckett Islands in Buzzards Bay. Farnsworth later tried to rescind the whole contract, claiming that he had signed it under duress, and disputed the sum owed to TNS.

The chronology of events is important. The parties by agreement submitted the dispute to a panel of three arbitrators pursuant to a binding arbitration clause in the salvage contract. After the arbitration proceeding had started, Farnsworth chose to file this lawsuit, seeking a preliminary injunction against the arbitration and a declaration that the salvage contract was unenforceable because Farnsworth had entered into it under duress. His complaint drew no distinction between the obligation to arbitrate and the merits issue of what payment was owed to TNS. The district court denied the motion for injunctive relief and stayed the case pending the outcome of the arbitration. The arbitration panel found in favor of TNS and ordered Farnsworth to pay a salvage award of $60,306.85. The district court confirmed [—3—] that award over Farnsworth's objection.

Farnsworth appeals, arguing that the district court erred in confirming the arbitration award without first addressing his duress claim as to the arbitration clause. We hold that, because Farnsworth did not challenge the validity of the arbitration clause specifically in his complaint (or indeed at any time before the conclusion of the arbitration proceedings),[1] the district court correctly found that the duress claim in all its aspects was for the arbitrator to resolve. Essentially, Farnsworth did too little, too late. We *affirm.*

I.

On the evening of July 28, 2012, Farnsworth was anchoring his boat, the M/Y AURORA, in the Weepecket Island anchorage in Buzzards Bay. The boat's depth sounder malfunctioned and Farnsworth inadvertently allowed the vessel to drift aground. [—4—] Farnsworth requested a tow over his marine radio, and TNS's vessel the NORTHPOINT responded to his call. Farnsworth also made contact with the Coast Guard, which instructed him that, if he had any problems, he should "make the appropriate hail" and the Coast Guard would assist.

The merits issue in this case turns on whether the contract which ensued was a towage or a salvage contract. The difference between the two is important under maritime law because towage is compensated at a

---

[1] Even if Farnsworth had specifically challenged the validity of the arbitration clause in his verified complaint, he might still be vulnerable to the argument that he waived his right to judicial review by first consenting to and participating in arbitration. *See Opals on Ice Lingerie v. Bodylines Inc.*, 320 F.3d 362, 368 (2d Cir. 2003) ("[I]f a party participates in arbitration proceedings without making a timely objection to the submission of the dispute to arbitration, that party may be found to have waived its right to object to the arbitration."); *ConnTech Dev. Co. v. Univ. of Conn. Educ. Props., Inc.*, 102 F.3d 677, 685 (2d Cir. 1996) (collecting cases). However, TNS has not pressed a waiver argument, and so we do not address the issue.

contract rate, whereas a salvor is entitled to an equitable award equal to a portion of the value of the salvaged property. 2 T.J. Schoenbaum, *Admiralty and Maritime Law* § 16-1 (5th ed. 2014); *see also Faneuil Advisors, Inc. v. O/S Sea Hawk*, 50 F.3d 88, 92 (1st Cir. 1995) (describing the law of salvage). Salvage service generally "commands a larger award," and a salvage contract creates a preferred maritime lien. *Evanow v. M/V Neptune*, 163 F.3d 1108, 1114 (9th Cir. 1998).[2]

The parties sharply differ over what happened in the [—5—] hours after Farnsworth made contact with the NORTHPOINT. Farnsworth's complaint alleges that the NORTHPOINT crew members "attempt[ed] to create a salvage" by taking various actions designed to make the AURORA's situation appear worse than it actually was. The complaint maintains that the "AURORA was undamaged, completely buoyant, and watertight," and needed only a tow, rather than a salvage. The complaint alleges that when Farnsworth resisted TNS's efforts to create a salvage, the NORTHPOINT intentionally pulled the AURORA onto charted rocks, damaging her hull; next ordered Farnsworth to drop anchor in dangerous, unprotected waters; and then sent two large men on board the AURORA to coerce Farnsworth to sign a contract giving TNS the rights to a salvage award for towing the AURORA. The complaint alleges that Farnsworth "attempted to refuse to sign the salvage contract three times," but finally relented "because he was alone aboard the vessel with two [TNS] employees, in a remote location, without hope of assistance, at a late hour (03:30 A.M.)," and because "[t]he employees indicated that they would not leave

without the signed contract."

During arbitration, John Mark Brown, one of the "large [TNS] employees" who Farnsworth says coerced him to sign the salvage contract, gave a starkly different account of the [—6—] encounter. Brown recounted that the AURORA was in serious danger. The area in which the AURORA was stranded, Brown said, was "littered with rocks," a danger compounded by the severe weather conditions in the area that night. Brown called Farnsworth on his cell phone and told him that, in light of those circumstances, TNS's services would not be covered under Farnsworth's towing policy; instead, Farnsworth would have to sign a "no cure, no pay" salvage contract.[3] Brown said Farnsworth initially agreed to accept salvage services during the phone conversation, but later balked at the arrangement when Brown boarded the AURORA, and then relented when Brown reminded him of his earlier agreement to a salvage contract. Brown also vigorously disputed Farnsworth's allegations that he and his partner threatened Farnsworth. Brown noted that Farnsworth had earlier spoken to the Coast Guard but "never attempted to contact the Coast Guard after we left."

The contract executed by the parties is a standard form "no cure, no pay" marine salvage agreement. Farnsworth wrote by hand the following addendum to the form contract: "Aurora was hard aground, Tow Boat prevented the Boat from going further aground, [—7—] and towed the boat when the Tide floated it off."[4]

The contract contains an arbitration clause:

---

[2] "The existence of a marine peril distinguishes a salvage contract from one for towage." *Evanow*, 163 F.3d at 1114; *accord* Schoenbaum, *supra*, § 16-1. That is, towage is undertaken "from considerations of convenience," whereas salvage is aimed at saving a vessel that is "disabled, and in need of assistance." *Evanow*, 163 F.3d at 1114 (quoting *The Flottbeck*, 118 F. 954, 960 (9th Cir. 1902)); *see also Lloyd's Syndicate 1861 v. Crosby Tugs, L.L.C.*, No. 13-5551, 2014 WL 3587375, at *3 (E.D. La. July 21, 2014) (collecting authorities).

[3] Under the "no cure, no pay" principle, "a prerequisite of a salvage award is that at least some of the property must be saved." Schoenbaum, *supra*, § 16-1 (noting that the policy underlying this principle "is that in 'pure' salvage, the reward is made out of the property that is spared from destruction").

[4] Farnsworth contends that he wanted to "include handwritten language on the form to indicate his objection to signing it" but that "Brown refused to let [him] write what [he] wanted and insisted that the additional language include a reference to being 'hard aground.'"

Read Carefully—Arbitration Provision—
In the event of any dispute arising out of this Contract including any dispute regarding this salvage or concerning the reasonableness of any fees or charges due hereunder, all parties agree to binding arbitration in the United States in accordance with the Rules for Recreational and Small Commercial Vessel Salvage Arbitration of the Society of Maritime Arbitrators, Inc. Arbitrators shall be familiar with maritime salvage. Any award hereunder shall include interest, attorneys' fees and costs, and arbitration administration expenses and shall be final and binding. For the purpose of enforcement, the Award may be entered for judgment in any court of competent jurisdiction.

Farnsworth's buyers' remorse set in quickly. Approximately five days later, on August 3, 2012, Farnsworth sent a letter to TNS purporting to rescind the salvage contract, demanding that TNS preserve evidence relating to "the prospective litigation," and intimating that TNS had engaged in illegal business practices. Farnsworth sent another letter to TNS on August 11 advising TNS of his belief that TNS had no salvage claim [—8—] and threatening to "fight to preserve [his] family tradition of venerable maritime activities."

He sent yet another letter on August 20, this time to TNS's counsel, again demanding the preservation of evidence and stating his belief that Dan Carpenter, a TNS representative, had engaged in "spoliation of evidence" by selectively editing the recordings of Farnsworth's radio conversations on the night of the incident.

On August 24, TNS's counsel wrote to Farnsworth with an invoice for payment of $95,546 due under the salvage contract. That amount represented TNS's estimate of a fair salvage award given the value of the salvaged property and principles of salvage law. Farnsworth did not pay the invoice.

Approximately a month later, TNS's counsel again wrote to Farnsworth, this time

demanding arbitration pursuant to the arbitration clause of the salvage contract and nominating an arbitrator. Farnsworth replied on October 5, alleging that TNS had violated Massachusetts' unfair trade practices statute and yet again demanding the preservation of evidence. Although Farnsworth initially made a passing suggestion that the arbitration clause was void, he subsequently nominated, through his counsel, an arbitrator a little over a month later, in November 2012. After [—9—] a period of discussions, the parties agreed that "all issues arising out of the events that took place on the evening in question must be heard by arbitrators."

The parties submitted their respective claims to the arbitration panel in April 2013. Farnsworth's statement of his counterclaims included allegations that he had signed the salvage contract "under duress, . . . alone, without hope of assistance, in the middle of the night."

On May 15, 2013, Farnsworth filed a verified complaint in federal court, seeking a declaratory judgment that (1) the salvage contract was void because it was procured by duress; (2) the parties were not required to arbitrate the dispute; and (3) TNS was entitled to compensation only for towage, not for salvage. He also sought a preliminary injunction to stop the arbitration proceedings. Farnsworth's purported justification for filing the lawsuit after he had already agreed to and commenced arbitration was that, after he reviewed recordings of his radio conversations produced by TNS, he "believe[d] [TNS] withheld, edited, or deleted unfavorable conversations pertaining to towing."

On May 17, 2013, the district court denied Farnsworth's request for a preliminary injunction after a hearing and granted TNS's motion to stay the case pending the outcome of the [—10—] arbitration proceeding. The arbitration went forward.

On November 15, 2013, the arbitration panel issued a decision rejecting Farnsworth's duress defense and finding that the salvage contract was valid. The panel ordered Farnsworth to pay $60,306.85 (a $50,000 salvage award plus interest) to TNS and dismissed Farnsworth's counterclaims.[5] This was a unanimous decision, with Farnsworth's arbitrator joining.

TNS then filed a motion in the district court to confirm the panel's award and dismiss Farnsworth's lawsuit. Farnsworth filed a lengthy opposition brief, requesting that the court vacate the arbitration award because the arbitrators lacked the authority to decide the dispute. In that brief, Farnsworth for the first time argued to the court that he had been coerced to agree to the arbitration clause specifically, as opposed to the contract as a whole.

The district court granted TNS's motion to confirm the arbitration award, rejecting Farnsworth's argument that the court, rather than the arbitrators, should have decided the duress as to arbitration issue. The court reasoned that Farnsworth had failed [—11—] to challenge the validity of the arbitration clause specifically in his complaint, as he was required to do in order to obtain court review of his duress challenge, and that the arbitration clause in the salvage contract was sufficiently broad to encompass the dispute about the validity of the contract.[6] This appeal followed.

II.

A. *Legal Principles*

The Federal Arbitration Act (FAA), 9 U.S.C. § 1 *et seq.*, "reflects the fundamental principle that arbitration is a matter of contract." *Rent-A-Center, W., Inc. v. Jackson*, 561 U.S. 63, 67 (2010). Under the FAA, courts must treat arbitration agreements in the same way as other contracts and "enforce them according to their terms." *Id.* Section 2 of the Act provides in relevant part as follows:

A written provision in any maritime transaction or a contract . . . to settle by arbitration a controversy thereafter arising out of such contract or transaction, . . . shall be valid, irrevocable, and enforceable, save upon such grounds as exist at law or in equity for the revocation of any contract.

9 U.S.C. § 2.

The Supreme Court has differentiated between two types [—12—] of challenges to the validity of arbitration agreements: (1) challenges to the validity of an entire contract which contains an arbitration clause, and (2) challenges to the validity of the specific agreement to resolve the dispute through arbitration. *Rent-A-Center*, 561 U.S. at 70; *Buckeye Check Cashing, Inc. v. Cardegna*, 546 U.S. 440, 444 (2006). In a line of cases beginning with *Prima Paint Corp. v. Flood & Conklin Manufacturing Co.*, 388 U.S. 395 (1967), the Court has held that challenges of the first type are for the arbitrator to decide, whereas challenges of the second type are for the courts to decide, if timely and properly made. *See, e.g., Rent-A-Center*, 561 U.S. at 70-71; *Buckeye Check*, 546 U.S. at 444-45; *Prima Paint*, 388 U.S. at 402-04; *see also Dialysis Access Ctr., LLC v. RMS Lifeline, Inc.*, 638 F.3d 367, 376-77, 383 (1st Cir. 2011).

This rule reflects two basic principles of arbitration law. The first is that, because "arbitration is a matter of contract[,] . . . a party cannot be required to submit to arbitration any dispute which he has not agreed so to submit." *Howsam v. Dean Witter Reynolds, Inc.*, 537 U.S. 79, 83 (2002) (citation and internal quotation marks omitted). The second is that, under § 2, a written arbitration agreement "is 'valid, irrevocable, and enforceable' *without mention* of the validity of [—13—] the contract in which it is contained." *Rent-A-Center*, 561 U.S. at 70 (quoting 9 U.S.C. § 2). The first principle means that if a party challenges the validity of the arbitration clause itself, a court must determine the challenge, "[f]or one must enter into the system *somewhere*." A.S. Rau, *Everything You Really Need to Know About "Separability" in Seventeen Simple Propositions*, 14 Am. Rev.

---

[5] The arbitration panel did "not award attorneys' fees to either side as it consider[ed] that both parties needlessly engaged in a war of attrition over what should have been a relatively simple salvage dispute."

[6] Farnsworth does not dispute this latter holding on appeal.

Int'l Arb. 1, 5 (2003). The second principle means that, if a party fails to challenge the validity of the arbitration clause itself, the agreement to arbitrate is enforceable and any dispute about the validity of the contract as a whole goes to the arbitrator. *Rent-A-Center*, 561 U.S. at 70-72.

Another way to frame this analysis is to say, as the Supreme Court has, that "an arbitration provision is severable from the remainder of the contract." *Buckeye Check*, 546 U.S. at 445; *see also Dialysis Access Ctr.*, 638 F.3d at 383. That severability is an issue of federal law. As the Supreme Court said in *Buckeye Check*, its cases establish that "as a matter of substantive federal arbitration law, an arbitration provision is severable from the remainder of the contract" and that, "unless the challenge is to the arbitration clause itself, the issue of the contract's validity is considered by the arbitrator in the first instance." 546 U.S. at 445-46. Or, as the Court put it in [—14—] *Rent-A-Center*, "even where . . . the alleged fraud that induced the whole contract equally induced the agreement to arbitrate which was part of that contract[,] we nonetheless require the basis of challenge to be directed specifically to the agreement to arbitrate before the court will intervene." 561 U.S. at 71.

It is also important in this analysis to distinguish between the issue of whether a contract containing an arbitration clause is *valid* and the issue of whether the contract *was ever actually formed*. *See Buckeye Check*, 546 U.S. at 444 n.1. The severability doctrine addresses only the former circumstance. *See Rent-A-Center*, 561 U.S. at 70 n.2.[7]

---

[7] Our case does not implicate the latter circumstance. As to that circumstance, some courts have held that, if a party argues that no contract was consummated, a court must resolve that issue, since the party is claiming that there is no agreement as to anything at all, arbitration included. *See, e.g., Sphere Drake Ins. Ltd. v. All Am. Ins. Co.*, 256 F.3d 587, 590-91 (7th Cir. 2001) (Easterbrook, J.) (collecting cases); see also *Buckeye Check*, 546 U.S. at 444 n.1 (collecting cases); Rau, *supra*, at 14-15.

B. *Application*

This case does implicate the severability doctrine because, as the district court correctly held (and Farnsworth does not now dispute), the issue here is the contract's validity, not its formation. *Cf.* 28 Williston on Contracts § 71:8 (4th ed.) (noting that duress usually renders a contract voidable by the [—15—] victim, rather than void, but that "in the relatively rare case where one person physically compels another to give apparent assent" there is no acceptance and hence no contract).[8] Farnsworth alleges that he was induced to sign the contract by an improper threat on the part of TNS. That duress allegation, if true, would make the contract invalid, but it would not mean that no contract was ever formed. *See SBRMCOA, LLC v. Bayside Resort, Inc.*, 707 F.3d 267, 273-74 (3d Cir. 2013); *see also Simula, Inc. v. Autoliv, Inc.*, 175 F.3d 716, 726 (9th Cir. 1999) (holding that duress challenge to a contract was for the arbitrator).

Farnsworth nevertheless argues that the district court erred in confirming the arbitration award for two reasons. First, he notes that he specifically challenged the arbitration clause in the salvage contract in his opposition to TNS's motion to confirm the arbitration award, and contends that the district court should have resolved that challenge under *Prima Paint* and its progeny. Second, he argues that his allegation of duress in the complaint logically went to the validity both of the salvage contract as a whole and of the arbitration clause contained within the salvage [—16—] contract, and so the district court should have resolved the duress issue even had Farnsworth not raised the validity of the arbitration clause specifically in his opposition brief.

The second argument is a nonstarter under Supreme Court precedent. Under the *Prima Paint* line of cases, a party must claim that

---

[8] To the extent Farnsworth does make an argument that no contract was formed because his signature was the product of "physical duress," the argument is entirely cursory and so waived. *See United States v. Zannino*, 895 F.2d 1, 17 (1st Cir. 1990).

the arbitration clause itself is invalid in order to obtain court resolution of the duress issue. Farnsworth protests that this "analytical framework does not facilitate precision when analyzing a contractual defense such as physical duress . . . where the defense cannot easily be applied to some clauses at the exclusion of others." The Supreme Court has unequivocally rejected this argument, explaining that even where the claimed basis for invalidity of the contract is logically applicable to the entire contract, courts "nonetheless require the basis of challenge to be directed specifically to the agreement to arbitrate before the court will intervene." *Rent-A-Center*, 561 U.S. at 71. Thus, Farnsworth's general claim of duress in his complaint—even if it did, as he asserts, "naturally appl[y] to every clause in the Salvage Contract specifically as well as the Salvage Contract as a whole"—was not used to support a direct challenge to the arbitration provision and so was not specific enough to permit court adjudication of the duress as to arbitration clause claim. [—17—]

This brings us to Farnsworth's challenge to the validity of the arbitration clause in his opposition brief to TNS's motion to confirm the arbitration award. On appeal, Farnsworth, relying on the general principle that a party has the right to "refine and clarify general allegations made in a complaint," argues that the district court erred in "ignor[ing]" that challenge.

That general principle does not help Farnsworth here. Farnsworth had ample opportunity to refine and clarify the general allegations made in his complaint so as to comply with the severability principle. He simply failed to avail himself of it. Indeed, TNS pointed out in its opposition to Farnsworth's motion for a preliminary injunction staying the arbitration proceedings that the complaint alleged only a general challenge to the validity of the Salvage Contract, not a specific challenge to the validity of the arbitration clause. The district court then held a hearing on the motion, and there is no indication in the record that Farnsworth sought to amend his complaint or contest TNS's position regarding that

proposition. Farnsworth's challenge to the validity of the arbitration clause itself came only after TNS moved to confirm the panel's award, which went against him. That was [—18—] far too late.[9]

"Under the FAA, courts may vacate an arbitrator's decision 'only in very unusual circumstances.'" *Oxford Health Plans LLC v. Sutter*, 133 S. Ct. 2064, 2068 (2013) (quoting *First Options of Chi., Inc. v. Kaplan*, 514 U.S. 938, 942 (1995)). Judicial review of binding arbitration awards is necessarily limited so as to "'maintain[] arbitration's essential virtue of resolving disputes straightaway.'" *Id.* (quoting *Hall Street Assocs., L.L.C. v. Mattel, Inc.*, 552 U.S. 576, 588 (2008)); *see also Booth v. Hume Pub., Inc.*, 902 F.2d 925, 932 (11th Cir. 1990) (characterizing § 9 confirmation proceedings as "summary" and noting that the FAA "expresses a presumption that arbitration [—19—] awards will be confirmed"). After the arbitration panel renders its decision, upon application by one party to a court to confirm the award, "the court *must* grant such an order unless the award is vacated, modified, or corrected as prescribed in" 9 U.S.C. § 10 and § 11. *See* 9 U.S.C. § 9 (emphasis added); *accord Hall Street*, 552 U.S. at 590 ("[Sections] 10 and 11 provide exclusive regimes for the review provided by the statute . . . ."); *FleetBoston Fin. Corp. v. Alt*, 638 F.3d 70, 78

---

[9] This case is readily distinguishable from *Bridge Fund Capital Corp. v. Fastbucks Franchise Corp.*, 622 F.3d 996 (9th Cir. 2010), the case upon which Farnsworth primarily relies. There, the plaintiff filed a lawsuit before arbitration was even contemplated, and the defendant, wishing to go to an arbitral forum instead, filed a motion to stay the lawsuit pending arbitration. The plaintiff contested the validity of the arbitration clause in motion papers opposing the defendant's motion. *See id.* at 999, 1001-02. The challenge to the arbitration clause thus came before arbitration started.

Because Farnsworth's challenge to the validity of the arbitration clause simply came too late, we need not decide the extent to which courts may (or must) take into account timely allegations outside the complaint in determining whether a given dispute is subject to arbitration. *Cf. Escobar-Noble v. Luxury Hotels Int'l of P.R., Inc.*, 680 F.3d 118, 121-22 (1st Cir. 2012) (noting that a court's review "centers on the factual allegations of the complaint" (citing *Dialysis Access Ctr.*, 638 F.3d at 378)).

n.8 (1st Cir. 2011) (noting that the Supreme Court has "made clear that, absent vacating or modifying an award under those provisions, an arbitral award must be enforced"). None of the circumstances listed in § 10 or § 11 is present here, and Farnsworth does not argue otherwise. Accordingly, the district court had no proper basis on which to refuse to confirm the arbitration panel's award. Farnsworth's belated attempt to press his duress claim in another forum by advancing allegations that he should have made when he sought to enjoin the arbitration provided no reason not to confirm.[10] *Cf.* [—20—] *Rent-A-Center*, 561 U.S. at 75-76 (declining to consider challenge to validity of specific arbitration clause that had not been raised below).

III.

We *affirm* the judgment of the district court. Costs are awarded against Farnsworth.

---

[10] Farnsworth argues in his reply brief that his challenge to the validity of the arbitration clause should have been resolved "regardless of the restrictions in section 10." But the cases he cites in support do not support his argument. In *Seacoast Motors of Salisbury, Inc. v. DaimlerChrysler Motors Corp.*, 271 F.3d 6 (1st Cir. 2001), we expressly declined to decide whether a party could move to vacate under § 10 on non-enumerated grounds. *See id.* at 8-9. In *MCI Telecommunications Corp. v. Exalon Industries, Inc.*, 138 F.3d 426 (1st Cir. 1998), we held only that the [—20—] "enforcement provisions of the FAA[] do not come into play unless there is a written agreement to arbitrate." *Id.* at 430. There was concededly an agreement to arbitrate here; the question is whether it was valid.

United States Court of Appeals
for the First Circuit

No. 13-2518

INDUSTRIA Y DISTRIBUCTION DE ALIMENTOS
VS.
TRAILER BRIDGE

Appeal from the United States District Court for the District of Puerto Rico

Decided: August 17, 2015

Citation: 797 F.3d 141, 3 Adm. R. 56 (1st Cir. 2015).

Before **HOWARD,** Chief Judge, and **LYNCH** and **KAYATTA,** Circuit Judges.

[—3—] **HOWARD,** Chief Judge:

The appellants are three shipping operators who pay a fee to Puerto Rico to conduct business out of the Port of San Juan. The Commonwealth supplied each company with cargo-scanning technology, required them to scan all of their inbound cargo, and then charged each an additional fee. The question on appeal is whether the dormant Commerce Clause bars Puerto Rico from charging the additional fee to defray the costs of the scanning. Because the operators have failed to establish that the additional fee violates the Constitution, we affirm the magistrate judge's decision holding the same.

I.

We draw the facts from the magistrate judge's findings following a bench trial. *See McDermott v. Marcus, Errico, Emmer & Brooks, P.C.,* 775 F.3d 109, 113 (1st Cir. 2014).

This matter stems from the aftermath of the terrorist attacks of September 11, 2001, and the concomitant need to augment port security. Until 2008, Puerto Rico's port security was predominantly limited to random and manual searches of cargo. To bolster this piecemeal approach, the Legislative Assembly of Puerto Rico passed a law calling for improved safety procedures. P.R. Laws Ann. tit. 23, §§ 3221 *et. seq.* The following year, the Puerto Rico Ports Authority ("PRPA") solicited proposals to implement that law with respect to its busiest port, the Port of San Juan. In particular, it sought to craft a system where it [—4—] would be able to scan all inbound cargo at the port. In due course, PRPA reached an agreement with Rapiscan Systems, Inc., which assumed responsibility for the scanning. In turn, Rapiscan Systems transferred its rights and obligations to a subsidiary, S2 Services Puerto Rico, LLC ("S2 Services").

In late 2011, PRPA promulgated Regulation No. 8067, which required the scanning of all inbound cargo at the Port of San Juan. The regulation permitted PRPA personnel, in the event of undue delay, to reduce the amount of cargo scanned at a given time. Through these requirements, PRPA aimed to increase the identification of unreported taxable goods and to improve security and safety at the port. S2 Services and the Puerto Rico Treasury Department were responsible for carrying out this directive.

As of 2013, Puerto Rico installed scanning technology at the facilities of three shipping operators at the port of San Juan: Crowley, Horizon Lines, and Sea Star Lines. Except during particularly busy times, these three operators were required to scan all containerized cargo (though not their bulk cargo) and then have two S2 Service employees and one Treasury agent review those scans. In total, 313,383 containers have been electronically scanned, an amount substantially higher than the 7,142 containers manually searched during a prior, analogous time period.

To pay for the scanning, PRPA charged all vessels carrying cargo into the Port of San Juan (including cargo carried [—5—] by operators who did not have access to the scanning facilities) an "Enhanced Security Fee" ("ESF"). PRPA assessed the ESF on top of the existing fees that it already charged operators to utilize the port. The amount of the ESF varied based on the weight and type of the vessel's cargo. Since implementing the ESF, PRPA billed Crowley, Horizon Lines, and Sea Star Lines with 63% of all costs arising from the scanning procedure. In total, PRPA has collected $20,412,371.34 through the ESF, and it has used that money to pay: $17,136,894 to S2 Services, $2 million to Treasury employees, $1.4 million to the General Security Office, and $300,000 to the Office of Maritime Security.

In response to Regulation 8067 and the ESF, thirty-two businesses and organizations involved in importing cargo at the Port of San Juan (along with associated trade groups) sued the heads of PRPA and Puerto Rico's Treasury Department; they attacked both the regulation and the fee. The parties consented to proceed before a magistrate judge, and the court conducted a bench trial. The bulk of the evidence at trial centered on the constitutionality of the scanning regulation and the permissibility of the ESF as applied to *all* of the operators (as opposed to just the three with access to the scanning technology).

Following those proceedings, the court ruled that the scanning procedure implemented by Regulation 8067 was constitutional but that the ESF, as applied to the operators who [—6—] did not have access to the scanning facilities, violated the dormant Commerce Clause. The court thus entered an injunction prohibiting the government from collecting the ESF from those shipping operators. Neither the government nor the plaintiffs appealed those decisions.

The magistrate judge next turned to the constitutionality of the ESF as applied to the three shipping operators equipped with the scanning technology. As to these three companies, the court concluded that the ESF was constitutional. The three operators timely appealed that decision; they continue to argue that the ESF violates the dormant Commerce Clause.[1]

---

[1] We pause to highlight the fact that some of the lines PRPA has drawn—e.g., that only three shipping operators are required to scan their cargo—do strike us as odd. Perhaps, as the Commonwealth claims, this is simply the first step of many to come in implementing the regulation. Perhaps not. Either way, we need not dwell on such oddities. The three shipping operators have brought this appeal solely under the dormant

II.

We review the lower court's factual findings following a bench trial for clear error and its legal conclusions *de novo. See Allstate Interiors & Exteriors, Inc. v. Stonestreet Constr., LLC*, 730 F.3d 67, 74 (1st Cir. 2013).

The Constitution's Commerce Clause serves as both an affirmative grant of power to Congress, U.S. Const. art. I, § 8, [—7—] cl. 3, and "a further, negative command, known as the dormant Commerce Clause." *Comptroller of Treasury of Md. v. Wynne*, 135 S. Ct. 1787, 1794 (2015). This latter doctrine "precludes States 'from discriminat[ing] between transactions on the basis of some interstate element,'" *id.*, and inhibits "economic protectionism" between the states, *New Energy Co. of Ind. v. Limbach*, 486 U.S. 269, 273-74 (1988).

A litigant can wield the dormant Commerce Clause to attack the propriety of a "user fee," i.e. a charge assessed for the use of a government facility or service. In such cases, we apply a three-pronged test. *See Evansville-Vanderburgh Airport Auth. Dist. v. Delta Airlines, Inc.*, 405 U.S. 707, 716-17 (1972). A user fee is constitutional if it: "(1) is based on some fair approximation of use of the facilities, (2) is not excessive in relation to the benefits conferred, and (3) does not discriminate against interstate commerce." *Nw. Airlines, Inc. v. Cty. of Kent*, 510 U.S. 355, 368-69 (1994). Those challenging the government action carry the burden of persuasion. *See N.H. Motor Transp. Ass'n v. Flynn*, 751 F.2d 43, 47 (1st Cir. 1984).

i.

Turning to *Evansville* in the context of this case, we first consider whether the user fee "is based on some fair approximation of use of the facilities." *Nw. Airlines*, 510 U.S. at 369; *cf. Capitol Greyhound Lines v. Brice*, 339 U.S. 542, 546 [—8—] (1950) (noting that a "rough approximation" is sufficient). This is essentially a question of allocation; we ask

---

Commerce Clause, and have only targeted the ESF as applied to them. Our analysis is therefore limited exclusively to that claim.

whether the government is charging each individual entity a fee that is reasonably proportional to the entity's use, and whether the government has reasonably drawn a line between those it is charging and those it is not. *See Nw. Airlines*, 510 U.S. at 368.

PRPA attempts to assess a fee to these three operators in an amount that is reasonably proportional to their use of the scanning services. PRPA requires the operators to scan nearly all of their containerized cargo (though their bulk cargo is not scanned), and then charges them an amount corresponding to the total cargo they import (comprising both containerized and bulk cargo). While not perfect, the fee was intentionally designed to approximate the operators' use of the scanning service. Moreover, these three operators are the only ones with access to the scanning service and, given the unchallenged injunction entered by the lower court, the only three that have to pay for it.[2]

Despite this conceptually sound approach, we see two potential flaws. First, the operators could be importing so much bulk cargo that the total amount of imports—and thus the fee [—9—] charged—is grossly disproportionate to the containerized cargo that is actually scanned. Likewise, during particularly busy times, PRPA exempts some containerized cargo from the scanning procedures; if this occurs with significant frequency, then the fee may not match the operators' use of the scanning service. Ultimately, though, the burden lies with the three operators to prove that either of these concerns renders the fee improper. *See Flynn*, 751 F.2d at 47. This they have failed to do. Specifically, the operators have not produced evidence contrasting the total amount of cargo imported with the amount of cargo actually scanned for these three operators, nor have they provided specific evidence that the

bypassing of containerized cargo occurs with such frequency that the ESF does not roughly correspond to their use of the scanning technology. While this record leaves us unable to definitively hold that the fee *is* a fair approximation of the operators' use of the scanning service, the operators' failure to prove the converse requires us to rule against them on this first *Evansville* factor.

The second *Evansville* query is whether the fee that the government charges is excessive when weighed against the benefits conferred. Though the case law utilizes the term "benefits" in characterizing this factor, this label is somewhat of a misnomer. Our task is actually fairly limited; we compare the fee with the "costs incurred in connection with . . . [the] facilities." *Am.* [—10—] *Airlines*, 560 F.2d at 1038. In other words, a fee is unconstitutional only insofar as it is "excessive in relation to *costs* incurred by the taxing authorities." *Evansville*, 405 U.S. at 719 (emphasis added).

The shipping operators again fail to satisfy their burden. PRPA charged these three operators roughly $ 18,617,449. It then spent over $ 20 million to implement the scanning procedure (specifically on the personnel necessary to conduct the scanning which, despite the operators' contention, is clearly a necessary expense related to the scanning service). If we add the revenue that PRPA collected from other operators, then PRPA brought in $20,412,371.34, and spent 97% of that money on costs related to the scanning service. Admittedly, these numbers may not reflect the entire picture. But, the operators have failed to provide other evidence establishing that PRPA collects an excessive amount compared to what it spends on the scanning service. Since it was the operators' burden to establish that proposition with "a record sufficiently specific and detailed," their failure to do so defeats their claim on this prong. *Flynn*, 751 F.2d at 48.[3] [—11—]

---

[2] As noted previously, the plaintiffs succeeded below in establishing that the Commonwealth improperly assessed the ESF to operators without access to the scanning facilities. This likely explains why, on appeal, the three shipping operators *do not* argue that the other entities should also be required to pay the fee.

---

[3] The operators emphasize that a small portion of the ESF is used to pay security fees that were previously paid for by another tariff (which is still being charged), and that said money is not used to directly pay for the scanning services. The operators do not challenge the continued validity of

The final move in the *Evansville* three-step is to determine whether the regulation discriminates against interstate commerce. Where we have a facially neutral regulation, as we do here (i.e., a Commonwealth corporation bringing cargo into the port, just like an out-of-Commonwealth company, would also pay the ESF), the law "will be upheld unless the burden imposed on such commerce is clearly excessive in relation to the putative local benefits." *Pike v. Bruce Church, Inc.*, 397 U.S. 137, 142 (1970). Notably, a party cannot satisfy its burden simply by showing that a government action affects an out-of-state company or manufacturer. *See Exxon Corp. v. Governor of Md.*, 437 U.S. 117, 126 (1978). Instead, the evidence must illustrate that the government action interferes with interstate commerce by, for example, dissuading competition from out-of-state corporations. *See, e.g., Family Winemakers of Cal. v. Jenkins*, 592 F.3d 1, 10-11 (1st Cir. 2010).

On this point, not much need be said. The shipping operators contend that because only out-of-Commonwealth companies utilize the Port of San Juan, and therefore only out-of-Commonwealth entities will pay the ESF, the fee interferes with commerce. Fair enough. But, as noted above, just because a [—12—] facially neutral policy has an impact on an out-of-state company (even exclusively so), it does not necessarily follow that the policy burdens *commerce*. *Id.* While the shipping operators make some rumblings that the *scanning requirement* interferes with commerce, they do not even attempt to fill the logical gap with any argumentation respecting the fee. Nor, we note, have we found evidence in this record which could sustain such an argument. The shipping operators therefore fall far short of their burden on this final *Evansville* factor.

_____

that other tariff, so our concern is solely with the ESF. To the extent that certain payments are made to general security-related items, the operators have not established that this payment is anything more than de [—11—] minimis. Indeed, even without such payments, the government would still have collected less from these three operators than it paid out on scanning-related costs.

ii.

Though the shipping operators take a few swings at the *Evansville* analysis above, their central argument really takes place on a different playing field. They attack the ESF by claiming that they (and the Commonwealth more generally) receive no benefit from the scanning procedure and that it is "wholly ineffective." They home in on the magistrate judge's statement that the operators received a "reputational benefit" from the scanning—a finding that they insist was clearly erroneous—and then go to great lengths to argue that the scanning is in fact detrimental to their business. Thus, they conclude: no user fee was ever appropriate; any fee is necessarily excessive given the lack of any benefit; and, any burden on interstate commerce necessarily outweighs the benefit created by this government service. [—13—]

This argument misses the point; our decision in *American Airlines* explains why. In that case, a number of airlines paid a "landing fee" at Logan Airport in exchange for use of the runways. The airport (through MassPort) increased the fee it charged in order to pay for three new projects at the airport which were "deemed by the airlines of little or no use to them." *Am. Airlines*, 560 F.2d at 1037. Over a dormant Commerce Clause challenge, we sided with MassPort and emphatically rejected the idea that "customer judgments of benefits received" form any part of the constitutional analysis. *Id.* at 1038. Instead, the service must merely be "relevant to the operation of the [entity]." *Id.* at 1039. Thus, so long as the expenditures "were made for legitimate . . . objectives," and so long as the state does not run "wild and tax users for all extravagances," the actual service that the government provides is immaterial when considering the constitutionality of a user fee. *Id.*

Therefore, whether the shipping operators here obtain a reputational benefit from the scanning, whether they approve of the scanning from a business perspective, or whether it is the optimal way for PRPA to secure its ports, are not dispositive. Indeed, these questions all boil down to whether the scanning procedure is sound public policy, not whether the user fee is constitutionally valid. But, the Commerce Clause inquiry for user fees has never been, and is not now, whether the government service [—14—] or facility is ideal or advantageous. For good reason. If the heart of the dormant Commerce Clause beats to protect interstate commerce, then it is irrelevant whether a government service is beneficial. That is, the success or failure of the service or facility itself has little bearing on whether the *user fee* restricts the flow of commerce. Ultimately then, since PRPA has done nothing more than increase its fee to pay for a new, legitimate service—one which, despite any shortcomings, is clearly relevant to the operation of the port—and since said fee satisfies *Evansville* (which is essentially a short-hand test for determining whether a user fee infects interstate commerce), we reject the operators' policy-based contention.[4]

III.

The three shipping operators have failed to prove that the ESF, as applied to them, violates the dormant Commerce Clause. Accordingly, we ***affirm***.

---

[4] The operators also argue that they are involuntary subjects of the scanning requirement and thus cannot be "users" required to pay a user fee. The shipping operators provide no case law for this proposition, nor do they provide any theoretical argument that would support their position. In any event, the operators can hardly be said to be "involuntary" users for dormant Commerce Clause purposes. The scanning is simply a service provided for using the port; a port that the operators voluntarily operate out of. In choosing to do so, they have tacitly agreed to "share both the benefits and the costs of [PRPA's] decisions, including the imprudent ones." *Am. Airlines*, 560 F.2d at 1039.

United States Court of Appeals
for the First Circuit

No. 13-2098

UNITED STATES

vs.

PAZ-ALVAREZ

Appeal from the United States District Court for the
District of Puerto Rico

Decided: August 21, 2015

Citation: 799 F.3d 12, 3 Adm. R. 61 (1st Cir. 2015).

Before **SELYA**, Circuit Judge, **SOUTER**,* Associate
Justice, and **LIPEZ**, Circuit Judge.

*Hon. David H. Souter, Associate Justice (Ret.) of the
Supreme Court of the United States, sitting by
designation.

[—2—] **LIPEZ**, Circuit Judge:

Appellants Angel Paz-Alvarez ("Paz")
and Luis Marrero-Marrero ("Marrero")
were convicted for their roles in a drug
trafficking conspiracy. Together, they built
sophisticated secret compartments ("clavos")
in boats designed to smuggle hundreds of
kilograms of cocaine into the United States.
They argue that their convictions should be
vacated because of errors in the jury
instructions. In addition, Paz challenges the
sufficiency of the evidence and the two-level
sentence enhancement he received for using a
"special skill," while Marrero argues that the
conspiracy statutes are unconstitutional as
applied to him, that the admission of hearsay
evidence gave rise to a prejudicial variance,
and that there was cumulative error. Finding
no errors and the evidence sufficient, we
affirm.

I. Background

A. Facts

Since one of the claims addressed in this
opinion is a challenge to the sufficiency of the
evidence, we recount the facts in the light
most favorable to the verdict. *See United
States v. Rodríguez-Soler*, 773 F.3d 289, 290
(1st Cir. 2014).[1] In 2009, Nick Irizarry-
Rosado ("Irizarry") and Edwin Retamar-Oriol
("Retamar") went into business together
smuggling cocaine into Puerto Rico. [—3—]
They had met while in the mutual employ of a
Puerto Rico drug trafficker, but Irizarry and
Retamar had grown dissatisfied with their
employer's way of doing business. Using one of
their former employer's boats and Irizarry's
contacts in the Dominican Republic, they
embarked on an independent venture and
successfully smuggled twenty kilograms of
cocaine into Puerto Rico.

With the profits from their first solo
smuggling job, they purchased a vessel of
their own, the *Sheymarie*. They quickly put
the *Sheymarie* to use, successfully smuggling
another 100 kilograms of cocaine into Puerto
Rico. Encouraged by the success of that
undertaking, their contacts in the Dominican
Republic then proposed smuggling a larger
quantity of cocaine, specifically, 500
kilograms. Irizarry and Retamar agreed that
they would take on the larger load and, to
accomplish the task, purchased a second
vessel, the *Such Is Life*.

Problematically, the *Such Is Life* was not
already outfitted with a clavo large enough to
smuggle 500 kilograms of cocaine.
Consequently, Irizarry and Retamar asked
drug dealers with whom they were in contact
to recommend individuals with the skills
necessary to build hidden compartments in
their boat. Paz and his assistant, Marrero,
came highly recommended. They had built
"several" clavos in the past for the drug
dealers Irizarry and Retamar consulted and
had reportedly done "a good job." [—4—]

After Paz and Marrero were assured that
Irizarry and Retamar could be trusted, Paz,
Marrero, and a third clavo builder, Jonathan
Delgado-Flores ("Delgado"), met with Irizarry
and Retamar in Puerto Rico. At the meeting,
Irizarry and Retamar told the clavo builders

---

[1] Paz challenges the sufficiency of the evidence.
We do not think that Marrero is prejudiced by the
application of this standard because the
substantive argument for one of his claims is, in
essence, a sufficiency challenge. *See* footnote 16,
infra.

that they needed a secret compartment built in the *Such Is Life* large enough to hold 500 kilograms of cocaine. Paz promised that "it would be done." Paz, Marrero, Irizarry, and Retamar then met several more times to plan the clavo.

In September 2009, Irizarry, Retamar, Paz, Marrero, and Delgado met inside the *Such Is Life* to discuss the completed clavo's operation. A sixth individual was also present at that meeting: Ramon Alvarado-Ignacio, who went by the moniker "Moncho" and administered the marina where the *Such Is Life* was harbored. Moncho was secretly a government informant, wired to record the meeting. Paz, however, was suspicious of Moncho and refused to discuss the clavo's operation in front of him. Moncho left the room, leaving the door open, and Paz instructed another person in the room to close the door so Moncho could not hear how to operate the secret compartment. Several minutes later, when that portion of the conversation was concluded, Moncho was permitted to reenter.

At the close of the meeting, Retamar told Paz that they needed a clavo built in their other boat, the *Sheymarie*. Soon, Paz and Marrero were at work on two secret compartments in that vessel: they enlarged an existing clavo and built a second one. [—5—] Within a month, however, law enforcement officials detected controlled substances onboard the *Sheymarie* and seized her.

On November 10, 2009, Irizarry, Retamar, Paz, and Marrero again met in Puerto Rico, this time to discuss building an additional compartment in the *Such Is Life*. A second compartment was needed because 500 kilograms of cocaine would not comfortably fit in the first clavo.[2]

---

[2] The first clavo had been built in a space that had a small motor and two rods that held the propellers. After "reinvestigat[ing]" that site, Retamar and his cohorts "found out it was too uncomfortable to do it [i.e, to store the cocaine] there. And we changed it." In other words, since putting the cocaine in the first clavo was "too difficult," the first clavo was "cancelled" (Paz contends this means "dismantled") and a second

Two days later, Retamar, Paz, Marrero, and others met in Puerto Rico to discuss the new clavo. They also discussed the upcoming trip, which was being coordinated with the Dominican contacts, to smuggle 500 kilograms of cocaine from Venezuela into Puerto Rico by way of a rendezvous point on the open sea near St. Croix. Retamar invited Paz, Marrero, and Delgado to join him on the voyage, and Marrero and Delgado agreed to go. Later, however, Marrero changed his mind; hence, neither he nor Paz accompanied Retamar on the drug-smuggling excursion. In December 2009, with the new clavo completed, Delgado and Retamar took the *Such Is Life* [—6—] to the rendezvous point.[3] The mission was unsuccessful, though, because the supplier never arrived.

At some point after that, Irizarry and Retamar parted ways. Retamar launched an independent operation using a new vessel. However, federal authorities soon arrested Retamar, seizing his new boat and the drugs onboard. Retamar then began cooperating with the authorities.

Under the direction of federal agents, Retamar reached out to Irizarry, ostensibly to resume business together. Retamar was actually helping to set up a sting operation: a voyage on which Irizarry and other conspirators would be caught smuggling drugs. As planned, Irizarry took the *Such Is Life* on a drug-smuggling mission and loaded it with cocaine. On its way back to Puerto Rico, however, the *Such Is Life* encountered mechanical trouble and stalled in the water. Federal agents rushed in, seizing the boat.

Agents from U.S. Customs and Border Protection, including Agent Rafael Reyes ("Reyes"), searched the *Such Is Life* for contraband. Reyes had ten years of experience on the anti-smuggling team, but he nevertheless struggled to find the sophisticated clavos that Paz and Marrero had constructed. Reyes and his team ultimately

---

clavo was constructed elsewhere on the boat. Trial Tr. Day 2 at 95-99, May 9, 2013.

[3] Delgado's job was to operate the complicated mechanism for opening and closing the clavo.

uncovered the clavos and found 150 kilograms of cocaine within. [—7—]

B. Procedure

In September 2012, a grand jury returned an indictment charging the appellants and nine others with: one count of conspiring to possess with intent to distribute controlled substances, in violation of 21 U.S.C. §§ 846, 841(a)(1), and 841(b)(1)(A)(ii); and one count of conspiring to import a controlled substance, in violation of 21 U.S.C. §§ 963, 952, 960(a)(1), and 960(b)(1)(B).[4]

Paz and Marrero were tried together.[5] The government's case relied heavily on cooperating witness Retamar, whose testimony comprised most of the first two days of the three-day trial. The jury returned a verdict of guilty on both counts as to both Paz and Marrero. On the same verdict sheet, the jury was asked whether "more than 5kg of cocaine" or "less than 5kg of cocaine" were involved in the conspiracy. The jury found that "more than 5kg of cocaine" were involved.

At sentencing, the district court determined that Paz's base offense level ("BOL") under the Sentencing Guidelines was 38 because, by a preponderance of the evidence, over 150 kilograms of [—8—] cocaine were involved in the conspiracy. Two levels were added to the BOL because Paz used a special skill, resulting in a total offense level of 40, with a corresponding Guidelines range of 292 to 365 months. The court sentenced Paz to 292 months' imprisonment.

The court also set Marrero's BOL at 38 based on its finding that the conspiracy involved more than 150 kilograms of cocaine. The court then reduced his BOL to 28 for, among other factors, minimal participation, yielding a Guidelines range of 78 to 97

months' imprisonment. However, the jury's finding that more than five kilograms of cocaine were involved in the conspiracy triggered a 120-month statutory minimum sentence. Hence, Marrero was sentenced to 120 months' imprisonment.

Paz and Marrero each appeal their sentences and convictions on multiple grounds, some overlapping.

II. Joint Issues

Appellants make two challenges to the jury instructions. First, they contend that the court did not properly charge the jury with the mens rea required for conspiracy. Second, they argue that the court did not properly instruct the jury to apply the reasonable doubt standard to its finding that more than five kilograms of cocaine were involved in the conspiracy. [—9—]

A. The Intent Instruction

To support a conviction for conspiracy, the evidence must show (1) the existence of a conspiracy, (2) the defendant's knowledge of the conspiracy, and (3) the defendant's knowing and voluntary participation in the conspiracy. *United States v. Dellosantos*, 649 F.3d 109, 116 (1st Cir. 2011). "Under the third element, the evidence must establish that the defendant both intended to join the conspiracy and intended to effectuate the objects of the conspiracy." *Id.*

The court instructed the jury on the third element of conspiracy as follows: "Here the allegation is that Mr. Paz and Mr. Marrero joined the conspiracy knowingly and willfully . . . . Acting knowingly and willfully, I already told you, means to do something that the law forbids. It means to act voluntarily and intelligently, and with a specific intent that the conspiracy be successful."[6] [—10—]

---

[4] Despite the two counts, we will follow the parties' lead and refer to "the conspiracy," singular.

[5] Delgado pleaded guilty to the importation count and, on the government's motion, the distribution count was dismissed. The district court sentenced Delgado to 135 months' imprisonment and we upheld the sentence. *See United States v. Delgado-Flores*, 777 F.3d 529 (1st Cir. 2015).

---

[6] In full, the relevant instructions were:

Here the allegation is that Mr. Paz and Mr. Marrero joined the conspiracy knowingly and willfully . . . . Acting knowingly and willfully, I already told you, means to do something that the law forbids. It means to

Paz and Marrero argue that the court did not adequately instruct the jury that the requisite intent for conspiracy is two-pronged, i.e., that a defendant must both intend to join the conspiracy and intend that the conspiracy achieve its aim. *United States v. Gonzalez*, 570 F.3d 16, 24 (1st Cir. 2009). Consequently, they argue, the court's instructions allowed the jury to convict them merely because they knew about the conspiracy.[7] They admit that they knew the conspiracy would use their clavos to smuggle drugs, but insist that they were indifferent to the conspiracy's success and, hence, did not join it. *See United States v. Burgos*, [—11—] 703 F.3d 1, 11 (1st Cir. 2012) ("[W]e have suggested that it is not reasonable to conclude that a defendant who is 'indifferent' to the conspiracy was a member of it."). Below, they sought to add language to the instructions that would have made the two-pronged nature of the requisite intent more

---

act voluntarily and intelligently, and with a specific intent that the conspiracy be successful. That is to say, with a bad purpose to disobey or disregard the law, and not because of mistake, accident, or other innocent reason. [—10—]

Proof that a defendant willfully joined in the agreement must be based upon the evidence of his own words and/or actions. . . .

Even if the defendant was not part of the agreement at the very start, the defendant can be found guilty of the conspiracy if the Government proves that the defendant willfully joined the agreement.

On the other hand, a person who has no knowledge of a conspiracy, but simply happens to act in a way that furthers some object of the conspiracy, does not thereby become a conspirator. The crime of conspiracy is complete upon the agreement to participate in such a way in which you take steps to make the criminal venture happen, succeed.

[7] Marrero suggests, though does not meaningfully argue, that the court's failure to properly charge the jury with the full intent requirement constituted structural error. However, "a jury instruction that omits an element of the offense" is not structural error. *Neder v. United States*, 527 U.S. 1, 8 (1999).

explicit, but the district court declined to add the language they proposed.[8]

Our review of a court's refusal to give a requested instruction is de novo. *United States v. Baird*, 712 F.3d 623, 628 (1st Cir. 2013). When, as here, the evidence is sufficient to support a requested instruction, our review proceeds in three steps: "We will reverse a district court's decision . . . only if the [requested] instruction was (1) substantively correct as a matter of law, (2) not substantially covered by the charge as rendered, and (3) integral to an important point in the case so that the omission of the instruction seriously impaired the defendant's ability to present his defense." *Id.* Paz and Marrero's challenge turns on the second step, whether the requested [—12—] instruction was substantially covered. The district court has broad discretion to determine "the precise manner that it explains legal concepts to the jury." *United States v. McFarlane*, 491 F.3d 53, 59 (1st Cir. 2007). The court need not accept verbatim the parties' preferred language. *Id.*

Here, the instruction explicitly stated the requirement that the defendants join the venture "knowingly and willfully," and that a finding of guilt depends on whether they acted "with a specific intent that the conspiracy be successful." The court further instructed, "Even if the defendant was not part of the agreement at the very start, the defendant can be found guilty of the conspiracy if the Government proves that the defendant willfully joined the agreement." The court's emphasis on willfully joining the conspiracy with the intent that it be successful was

[8] At trial, the defendants offered language from the Pattern Criminal Jury Instructions for the District Courts of the First Circuit § 4.18.371(1) (updated Apr. 21, 2015) and from *Burgos*, 703 F.3d at 11. In addition, during an in-chambers conference, Paz sought a "negative *Direct Sales* instruction," which would have explained that a defendant's knowledge that his goods or services will be used for an illegal purpose is not enough to prove that he intended to join the conspiracy. *See United States v. Brandon*, 17 F.3d 409, 449 (1st Cir. 1994); *Direct Sales Co. v. United States*, 319 U.S. 703, 712 (1943).

sufficient to convey the intent requirement to the jury. *See Gonzales*, 570 F.3d at 24 (equating the two-pronged intent requirement with an instruction that a defendant "willfully" join the conspiracy). Although the instructions might have been clearer if the court had adopted the language that the defendants proposed, we conclude that the instructions as rendered substantially covered the dual intents required for a conspiracy conviction and did not allow the jury to convict the defendants based solely on their knowledge that the secret compartments they built would be used for illegal purposes. [—13—]

B. The Drug Quantity Instruction

The district court based its sentences on the jury's finding that more than five kilograms of cocaine were involved in the conspiracy. Consequently, the court sentenced Paz and Marrero under 21 U.S.C. § 841(b)(1)(A), which mandates a sentence of ten years to life when five kilograms or more of cocaine are involved in the conspiracy. Other than the fact of a prior conviction, any fact that increases the mandatory minimum or maximum sentence must be submitted to a jury and proved beyond a reasonable doubt. *Alleyne v. United States*, 133. S. Ct. 2151, 2155 (2013) (minimum); *Apprendi v. New Jersey*, 530 U.S. 466, 490 (2000) (maximum). Paz and Marrero argue that the district court failed to instruct the jury that the drug amount had to be found "beyond a reasonable doubt." Therefore, they assert, there was no proper finding on drug quantity, and they should have been sentenced under 21 U.S.C. § 841(b)(1)(C), which provides a sentencing range of zero to twenty years when drug quantity is not determined. We conclude there was no error in the court's instructions as rendered.[9]

Here, the court began its instructions with a full explanation of the reasonable doubt

---

[9] Although Marrero concedes our review of this issue is for plain error, Paz contends the issue was preserved below because a relevant requested jury instruction was discussed and rejected in the trial judge's chambers. The defendants' claim fails under any standard of review.

standard, the government's [—14—] burden to prove guilt beyond a reasonable doubt, and a defendant's right to rely on the government's failure "to establish beyond a reasonable doubt any element of a crime charged against him." Later in its instructions, the court discussed the indictment, which charged the defendants with participating in a conspiracy involving more than five kilograms of cocaine. The court did not specifically refer to drug quantity at that point, but explained that the indictment "is simply an accusation" and that "the [g]overnment has to prove the defendants' guilt beyond a reasonable doubt." Then, explaining the elements of conspiracy, the court reiterated, "the [g]overnment must prove beyond a reasonable doubt that those involved shared a general understanding about the crime." Continuing to discuss the elements of conspiracy, the court stated: "You need not find that a defendant agreed specifically to or knew about all the details of the crime . . . . But the [g]overnment must prove beyond a reasonable doubt that the defendant knew the essential features and general aims of the criminal venture."

With the elements of conspiracy explained, the court then discussed jury deliberation procedures: selection of a foreperson, the requirement that the verdict be unanimous, each juror's duty to decide the matter for him- or herself, and the need to examine and reexamine one's position while maintaining [—15—] one's honest convictions. The court then discussed the verdict form:

The verdict form that you will use is this one that I have prepared. Very simple form. It talks about Count I and Count II, and simply asks you whether you find Mr. Paz and Mr. Marrero guilty or not guilty as charged.

I am also asking you another question. How much cocaine is involved in this conspiracy? That's the question, and the answer must be one of these two. More than five kilos of cocaine, or less than five kilos of cocaine. I don't want you to give me a specific. I just want you to tell me whether it's more than five or less than five. That's all.

According to Paz and Marrero, the district court's error was twofold: first, it did not include drug quantity in its discussion of the elements of conspiracy, and, second, it did not reiterate the reasonable doubt standard in its discussion of the verdict form, when the court asked the jury to determine drug quantity. This approach, they contend, permitted the jury to find drug quantity by a less stringent standard, thus violating their Fifth Amendment right to Due Process and their Sixth Amendment right to a jury verdict governed by the reasonable doubt standard.[10] [—16—]

We review the instructions as a whole, not piecemeal. *United States v. Melendez*, 775 F.3d 50, 55 (1st Cir. 2014); *Gonzalez*, 570 F.3d at 21. Assessing whether the jury was properly charged with the reasonable doubt standard, "the proper inquiry is not whether the instruction 'could have' been applied in an unconstitutional manner, but whether there is a reasonable likelihood that the jury *did* so apply it." *Victor v. Nebraska*, 511 U.S. 1, 6 (1994).

We acknowledge that the instructions might have been better if the court had discussed drug quantity alongside the other elements of the crime, or if the court had reiterated the reasonable doubt standard when it instructed the jury to make a finding on drug quantity. Nevertheless, the court repeatedly emphasized the reasonable doubt standard throughout the instructions. The drug quantity determination was then grouped together with the court's explanation that the jury would be asked to determine whether the defendants were guilty of conspiracy, a determination that the instructions made unequivocally subject to the reasonable doubt standard. Furthermore, the jury had a copy of the indictment during its deliberations, and the court emphasized that the accusations in the indictment, which included an accusation that the conspiracy involved more than five kilograms, had to be

---

[10] *See Sullivan v. Louisiana*, 508 U.S. 275, 278 (1993) ("It is self-evident, we think, that the Fifth Amendment requirement of proof beyond a reasonable doubt and the Sixth Amendment requirement of a jury verdict are interrelated.").

proved beyond a reasonable doubt. Hence, we do not think that there is "a reasonable likelihood that the jury [—17—] understood the instructions to allow conviction" without proof beyond a reasonable doubt of every element of the charged offense, including drug quantity.

Contrary to Paz and Marrero's assertion, this case is distinguishable from *United States v. Delgado-Marrero*, 744 F.3d 167 (1st Cir. 2014). In *Delgado*, the court instructed the jury on the elements of conspiracy, but did not ask the jury to make a finding as to the quantity of drugs involved. *Id.* at 183. After the jury deliberated and returned a guilty verdict, the court sent the jury back for a second deliberation to determine drug quantity, stating, "It's like another deliberation under the same terms and conditions." *Id.* On appeal, the government argued that the district court's "same terms and conditions" instruction was sufficient to convey to the jury that the reasonable doubt standard still applied. *Id.* at 187. However, in large measure because the jury had already returned a verdict before being asked to deliberate a second time, we held that instructional error had occurred. "[G]iven the timing and manner in which the question was presented, the jurors understandably may have failed to appreciate that the additional question represented something more than an inconsequential afterthought . . . ." *Id.*

The facts here differ significantly from those in *Delgado*. The finding on drug quantity was made as part of the original deliberations, not following an initial verdict during [—18—] resumed deliberations. Drug quantity was also included on the same verdict form as that used to determine the defendants' guilt or innocence on the substantive charges. We do not think "there is a reasonable likelihood," *Victor*, 511 U.S. at 6, that a juror in this case would have understood the instructions to permit the application of anything other than the reasonable doubt standard to the assessment of drug quantity. Therefore, the court did not fail to charge the jury with the reasonable doubt standard on an element that increased the mandatory minimum or maximum sentences.

III. Paz's Claims

Paz argues that the evidence was insufficient to support his conviction and that the district court erroneously increased his BOL by two levels for use of a "special skill."

A. Sufficiency of the Evidence

Our review of the sufficiency of the evidence is de novo. *United States v. Rodríguez-Martínez*, 778 F.3d 367, 371 (1st Cir. 2015). We view the evidence in the light most favorable to the verdict, giving "equal weight to direct and circumstantial evidence." *United States v. Appolon*, 715 F.3d 362, 367 (1st Cir. 2013). Importantly, the relevant inquiry is not whether a reasonable jury could have acquitted the defendant, but rather whether a reasonable jury "could have found that the government proved each element of the crime beyond a reasonable doubt." *Id.* (internal quotation marks omitted). [—19—]

As we explained above, to convict Paz of conspiracy, the jury had to find beyond a reasonable doubt that "(1) a conspiracy existed, (2) the defendant had knowledge of the conspiracy, and (3) the defendant knowingly and voluntarily participated in the conspiracy." *Dellosantos*, 649 F.3d at 116. Paz does not dispute that a conspiracy existed and that he had knowledge of it. His challenge to the sufficiency of the evidence is limited to the third element, under which the government had to prove that he intended to join the conspiracy and that he intended for its goals to be accomplished. *See id.* Paz advances the notion that he was indifferent to the conspiracy and lacked the requisite intent. He contends that he was simply "contracted" to perform "work orders" for clavo-related "services." He emphasizes that his services amounted to only seven to nine workdays scattered across several months, after which he was "never . . . seen or heard from again."

There are many ways to show that a defendant intended to join and advance a conspiracy, even where the defendant never actually handled the drugs. The defendant's intention to join "need not be express, but may be shown by circumstantial evidence." *United States v. Portalla*, 496 F.3d 23, 26 (1st Cir. 2007). Hence, "acts that furthered the conspiracy's purposes" may be evidence of the intent to join. *United States v. McDonough*, 727 F.3d 143, 156 (1st Cir. 2013). The requisite intent may also be shown through the knowing provision of peripheral services that aid in one of a [—20—] conspiracy's objectives, like the objective to avoid police detection. *Portalla*, 496 F.3d at 27. Ancillary functions like accounting, communications, and strong-arm enforcement are all examples of peripheral services that, when performed in the service of drug dealers, can support a conspiracy conviction. *United States v. García-Torres*, 280 F.3d 1, 4 (1st Cir. 2002).

Despite the arguably ancillary nature of the services Paz provided, a reasonable jury could have concluded that Paz's actions conveyed his intention to join and advance the conspiracy.[11] He participated in planning meetings where the intended use of his clavos—drug smuggling—was made explicit. He then constructed multiple clavos on two vessels designed for the specific purpose of storing and secreting cocaine. On these facts, a jury could reasonably conclude that Paz intended his ingenious compartments to achieve their aim, namely, that they conceal hundreds of kilograms of cocaine being smuggled into Puerto Rico for distribution. In addition, Paz guarded against sharing [—21—] secretive information with someone he thought untrustworthy: Moncho. That fact

---

[11] Paz's invocation of *United States v. Moreland*, 703 F.3d 976, 984 (7th Cir. 2012), is unpersuasive. In *Moreland*, the Seventh Circuit distinguished between co-conspirators and aiders and abettors, writing, "[K]nowledge of a buyer's intention to commit a crime with a supplier's goods doesn't imply an agreement between the buyer and the seller that the buyer do so. That knowledge, coupled with [supplying the goods,] could make him an aider and abettor of the buyer's crime but not, without more, a conspirator with the buyer." *Id.* Paz fails to acknowledge that the something "more" required for a conspiracy conviction—the intent to join the conspiracy—may be found circumstantially, "by words or action." *García-Torres*, 280 F.3d at 4.

would further support a reasonable jury's finding that Paz wanted his work to advance the conspiracy's objective of avoiding police detection. No more was required for a reasonable jury to find that Paz in fact intended to join the conspiracy and advance its goals.

Paz argues that it is unreasonable to conclude that he was a member of the conspiracy because members of the conspiracy did not consider him to be a member. He points, inter alia, to evidence in the record that Retamar instructed Moncho not to speak with Paz over the telephone. However, as the government notes, "the jury could have reasonably construed Retamar's testimony as showing his concern that police may have tapped Paz's telephone, unbeknownst to the latter." In addition, based on the fact that Retamar invited Paz to join him on the conspiracy's largest drug-smuggling excursion—the voyage to St. Croix to import 500 kilograms of cocaine—a reasonable jury could conclude that members of the conspiracy trusted Paz and considered him to be one of their own.

Finally, Paz emphasizes that he declined Retamar's invitation to participate in the voyage to pick up 500 kilograms of cocaine near St. Croix and was "never . . . seen or heard from [—22—] again" after declining that invitation.[12] A conspirator need not know "all of the details of the conspiracy or participate[ ] in every act in furtherance of the conspiracy." *United States* v. *Sanchez-Badillo*, 540 F.3d 24, 29 (1st Cir. 2008) (internal quotation marks omitted). Furthermore, an "inactive co-conspirator is presumed to be a continuing member of an ongoing conspiracy" unless he withdraws.[13] *United States v. Ngige*, 780 F.3d 497, 503 (1st Cir. 2015) (internal quotation marks omitted). Here, Paz essentially argues that, because his active participation came to an end, he never joined the conspiracy at all. But neither the fact that he declined to participate in one of the more dangerous aspects of the conspiracy (the drug run), nor the fact that his active involvement ended once he had completed the work he agreed to do, precludes a reasonable jury from finding that he joined the conspiracy when he built the clavos with the requisite knowledge and intent. [—23—]

Hence, the record contains ample evidence to support the jury's finding that Paz was a member of the conspiracy.

B. Sentence Enhancement

Paz appeals the two-level sentence enhancement he received for "us[ing] a special skill[ ] in a manner that significantly facilitated the commission or concealment of the offense." U.S.S.G. § 3B1.3. We review the district court's factual findings for clear error. *United States v. Prochner*, 417 F.3d 54, 60 (1st Cir. 2005).

The Guidelines define a "special skill" as "a skill not possessed by members of the general public and usually requiring substantial education, training or licensing. Examples would include pilots, lawyers, doctors, accountants, chemists, and demolition experts." U.S.S.G. § 3B1.3 cmt. n.4. Paz argues that he and his assistants were "hired to put covers on already existing cavities," and that the skills required to do that do not meet the meaning of a "special skill" as defined in the Guidelines. The record belies Paz's modest characterization of his work. His clavos were sophisticated compartments whose construction required more than a layperson's capabilities in carpentry, circuitry, and hydraulics. As Agent Reyes explained at trial,

---

[12] Relatedly, Paz insists it is unreasonable to find that he joined the conspiracy solely on the basis of his association with Delgado, the clavo-maker who joined Retamar on the drug-smuggling excursion. Of course, Paz is correct that mere association with a conspirator is not sufficient to prove beyond a reasonable doubt that a defendant is also a co-conspirator. *See Gonzalez*, 570 F.3d at 22. Here, however, Paz was not merely an associate of Delgado, but a knowing participant in construction activities that advanced the conspiracy.

[13] Withdrawing from a conspiracy requires that the conspirator "act affirmatively either to defeat or disavow the purposes of the conspiracy." *United States v. Pizarro-Berríos*, 448 F.3d 1, 10 (1st Cir. 2006).

Paz had replaced a wooden table (a piece of wood covering an open space) in the floor of the *Such Is Life* with a different, piston-operated table powered by a car battery. To access the compartment underneath, [—24—] a person had to complete an electrical circuit: "out of those screws [in the floor] . . . they selected two screws that went down and connected to [other] screws to make contact. So the person who was to open that needs to know which screws to touch with which cables to open or close it. There was no way for me from the outside to figure it out, because there's so many screws to try to make a combination. . . . I'd be playing the Lotto." The district court did not clearly err in determining that a member of the general public would lack the skills necessary to create such a mechanism.

Paz emphasizes that the offense here is conspiracy—an agreement—and contends that no special skill is required to make an agreement. The Guideline, however, applies either to facilitating the crime *or* concealing it. The purpose of Paz's work was to conceal the conspiracy by making drugs aboard the *Such Is Life* and the *Sheymarie* difficult to uncover. As indicated by the testimony of Agent Reyes, Paz achieved that purpose. In sum, there was no error in the district court's application of the two-level enhancement for use of a special skill.

IV. Marrero's Claims

Marrero makes three arguments particular to his appeal. First, he challenges the constitutionality of the conspiracy statutes as applied to him. Second, he contends that a *Petrozziello* error resulted in the improper admission of hearsay [—25—] evidence and gave rise to a prejudicial variance. Finally, he argues that the district court should have granted his Rule 29 motion for cumulative error. We address these arguments in turn.

A. As Applied Challenge to the Conspiracy Statutes

Marrero argues that the conspiracy statutes, 21 U.S.C. §§ 846 and 963, are unconstitutional as applied to him because those provisions did not give him fair notice of what constitutes participation in a conspiracy. In other words, he asserts that he did not have fair notice that, by knowingly building secret compartments to smuggle drugs for a drug conspiracy, he could be held accountable as a co-conspirator.[14]

Marrero is correct that the Fifth Amendment Due Process Clause gives him a "right to fair warning of that conduct which will give rise to criminal penalties." *Marks v. United States*, 430 U.S. 188, 191 (1977). In claiming a violation of that right, Marrero relies in particular on the vagueness doctrine, the aspect of the fair warning requirement that "bars enforcement of 'a statute which either forbids or requires the doing of an act in [—26—] terms so vague that men of common intelligence must necessarily guess at its meaning and differ as to its application.'" *United States v. Lanier*, 520 U.S. 259, 266 (1997) (Souter, J.) (quoting *Connally v. Gen. Constr. Co.*, 269 U.S. 385, 391 (1926)).[15]

Judicial interpretations may clarify an otherwise imprecise statute. *Id.* As Marrero concedes, the parameters of the conspiracy statutes are articulated in our case law. *See, e.g., Burgos*, 703 F.3d at 11 (explicating the third element of conspiracy, knowing and voluntary participation). Marrero nevertheless asserts that there is "no clear line" between lawful work on a vessel—such as

---

[14] Since Marrero raises his constitutional argument for the first time on appeal, our review is for plain error. *United States v. Diaz*, 519 F.3d 56, 65 (1st Cir. 2008). Marrero must show "(1) that an error occurred (2) which was clear or obvious and which not only (3) affected the defendant's substantial rights, but also (4) seriously impaired the fairness, integrity, or public reputation of the judicial proceeding." *United States v. Henderson*, 320 F.3d 92, 102 (1st Cir. 2003).

[15] "There are three related manifestations of the fair warning requirement," namely, the vagueness doctrine, the rule of lenity, and the principle that a court's "novel construction of a criminal statute" cannot be applied "to conduct that neither the statute nor any prior judicial decision has fairly disclosed to be within its scope." *Lanier*, 520 U.S. at 266 (discussing "fair warning" in the context of Fourteenth Amendment Due Process).

installing a GPS, fixing engines, or building cabinets—and conduct that "make[s] me a member of a conspiracy by mere knowledge of the improper intended use of the vessel and/or my services."

Marrero's argument, however, is flawed because he was not convicted for "mere knowledge" of the drug conspiracy and the conspirators' intent to use his services for unlawful ends. Rather, he was convicted because he was a knowing *participant* in the conspiracy. Marrero's attempt to characterize his conviction [—27—] as an arbitrary distinction between otherwise lawful activities therefore misses the mark. In the ancillary functions he identifies, it is not the nature of the defendant's services but the intent with which they are provided that distinguishes the innocent vendor from the co-conspirator.

Hence, Marrero's constitutional challenge fails. The statutes, in conjunction with our case law, gave him fair warning that knowingly participating in a drug conspiracy with the requisite intent could expose him to criminal penalties.[16]

B. Prejudicial Variance

Marrero contends that the district court erroneously admitted into evidence "hearsay about unrelated conspiracies and this amounts to prejudicial variance." We will untangle Marrero's argument and take the hearsay objection first. We will then address the multiple conspiracy and prejudicial variance arguments. [—28—]

1. Hearsay

Marrero challenges the district court's decision to admit the hearsay testimony of his co-conspirator, Paz. Although hearsay testimony generally is not admissible, an out-of-court statement made by a defendant's co-conspirator "during and in furtherance of the conspiracy" is not hearsay and may be introduced into evidence. Fed. R. Evid. 801(d)(2)(E), 802. To admit such evidence, the district court must determine by a preponderance of the evidence that the declarant and the defendant were members of the same conspiracy and that the statement was made in furtherance of the conspiracy. *See United States v. Ciresi*, 697 F.3d 19, 25 (1st Cir. 2012) (articulating the preponderance standard); *United States v. Goldberg*, 105 F.3d 770, 775-76 (1st Cir. 1997) (explaining that, following *United States v. Baines*, 812 F.2d 41, 42 (1st Cir. 1987), statements of a co-conspirator made before the defendant joined the conspiracy are also admissible). In this circuit, the district court's decision to allow testimony under the co-conspirator exception is called a *Petrozziello* ruling, after *United States v. Petrozziello*, 548 F.2d 20 (1st Cir. 1977).

A court may provisionally admit a statement under Rule 801(d)(2)(E) and defer its final *Petrozziello* ruling until the close of evidence. *Ciresi*, 697 F.3d at 25. "To preserve a challenge to a district court's *Petrozziello* ruling, a defendant must object on hearsay grounds when his or her co[-]conspirator's [—29—] statement is provisionally admitted and must renew the objection at the close of evidence." *Id.* at 25-26. Preserved challenges are reviewed for clear error; unpreserved challenges, for plain error. *Id.* at 26.

Marrero has specifically identified only one hearsay statement that he contends should not have been admitted: Retamar's testimony that, at their first meeting, Paz told him "it would be done," meaning, the clavo would be built. Marrero objected when that statement was admitted into evidence, citing

---

[16] To the extent his constitutional argument is really a mislabeled challenge to the sufficiency of the evidence, his challenge fails. A reasonable jury could have found that he was not "indifferent" to the conspiracy but was, rather, a member of it. *See Burgos*, 703 F.3d at 11. The jury could have determined that Marrero "ma[d]e it his own," *id.*, by building secret compartments that he knew would advance the conspiracy's objectives of smuggling cocaine for distribution while avoiding police detection. Marrero further demonstrated his intent to join the conspiracy by agreeing to join Retamar on the drug run. Although he later changed his mind and did not go on the drug run, his initial agreement would nevertheless support a reasonable jury's conclusion that he was a member of the conspiracy.

Petrozziello, and renewed his objection at the close of evidence. Hence, our review is for clear error.

The preponderance of the evidence easily supports the district court's assessment that Paz and Marrero were co-conspirators, just as it supports the court's conclusion that Paz's statement, "it would be done," was made in furtherance of the conspiracy. First, Retamar's testimony made clear that Paz and Marrero were co-conspirators. Retamar testified that Paz and Marrero attended multiple planning meetings with him to discuss building clavos, and that, working together, Paz and Marrero built clavos in both the *Sheymarie* and the *Such Is Life*. Second, it is more likely than not that Paz's statement, "it would be done," was made in furtherance of the conspiracy because it could easily be construed as a promise that he and his assistant, Marrero, would construct secret compartments to aid Retamar in smuggling hundreds [—30—] of kilograms of cocaine into Puerto Rico. Therefore, the court did not err, much less clearly err, in admitting Paz's statement into evidence.

2. Multiple Conspiracies and Prejudicial Variance

Marrero argues that the district court admitted evidence of multiple uncharged conspiracies, giving rise to a variance and prejudicial spillover. A variance occurs when the evidence at trial "proves different facts than those alleged in the indictment," such as when the indictment charges one conspiracy but the evidence supports multiple conspiracies. *Dellosantos*, 649 F.3d at 116 (internal quotation marks omitted). Three factors guide our assessment of whether the evidence was sufficient to prove that a set of criminal activities comprised a single conspiracy: "(1) the existence of a common goal, (2) overlap among the activities' participants, and (3) interdependence among the participants." *Ciresi*, 697 F.3d at 26. A single conspiracy may exist even if the participants or their respective roles change over time. *Id.*

Even if a defendant proves a variance, he must also prove that it was prejudicial. *Dellosantos*, 649 F.3d at 116. Prejudice may result from evidentiary spillover: "the transference of guilt to a defendant involved in one conspiracy from evidence incriminating defendants in another conspiracy in which the particular defendant was not involved." *United States v. Wihbey*, [—31—] 75 F.3d 761, 774 (1st Cir. 1996) (internal quotation marks omitted). To prevail on an evidentiary spillover claim, the defendant must prove "prejudice so pervasive that a miscarriage of justice looms." *United States v. Levy-Cordero*, 67 F.3d 1002, 1008 (1st Cir. 1995) (internal quotation marks omitted).

Marrero attempts to prove a variance by dividing the facts temporally into six sequential conspiracies corresponding to changes in personnel and discrete drug runs.[17] The evidence, however, points to a single conspiracy involving multiple transactions and players.[18] First, Marrero concedes that all six of the conspiracies he attempts to distill from the fact pattern share a common goal, namely, to sell drugs for profit. Second, there is a clear overlap among participants: either Retamar or Irizarry was involved in every aspect of the conspiracy, often [—32—] working in tandem. Finally, the participants worked interdependently. For example, Marrero provided the secret compartments that Retamar and Irizarry then used to smuggle drugs. Looking "to the totality of the evidence to see if it supports a finding of a

---

[17] The six conspiracies Marrero identifies are: (1) Retamar and Irizarry's drug smuggling work for their former employer; (2) Retamar's work (independent of Irizarry) for their former employer; (3) Retamar and Irizarry's importation of twenty kilograms of cocaine using one of their former employer's boats; (4) the conspiracy charged in the indictment, namely, to import and distribute more than five kilograms of cocaine using the *Sheymarie* and the *Such Is Life*; (5) the conspiracy Retamar ran in the time between his split with Irizarry and his arrest; and (6) the sting operation.

[18] The government contends that Marrero forfeited his multiple conspiracies argument for, among other reasons, failing to request a multiple conspiracy jury instruction. Since Marrero's argument cannot succeed on the merits, we need not decide whether he forfeited it.

single conspiracy," *Ciresi*, 697 F.3d at 26 (internal quotation marks omitted), we think the evidence at trial proved only one ongoing conspiracy that began when Retamar and Irizarry met and ran until the *Such Is Life* was confiscated. Hence, there was no variance.[19]

C. Cumulative Error

In his final argument, for cumulative error, Marrero identifies six motions he submitted to the district court and seeks to incorporate them by reference.[20] The substantive argument for [—33—] cumulative error is limited to the following in his opening brief: "We adopt said documents by reference and request this Honorable Court to evaluate the arguments presented therein, both de novo as well as non harmless cumulative error." As the government asserts, incorporation by reference is an ineffective method of preserving arguments for appeal. *See United States v. Orrego-Martinez*, 575 F.3d 1, 8 (1st Cir. 2009) (stating that incorporation of arguments by reference has been "consistently and roundly condemned" (internal quotation marks omitted)). Marrero attempts to elaborate in his reply brief, but he does not sufficiently develop an argument in support of any of the six motions.[21] Hence, his

cumulative error argument, like the arguments in the motions he seeks to incorporate by reference, is waived. *See United States v. Zannino*, 895 F.2d 1, 17 (1st Cir. 1990) ("[I]ssues adverted to in a perfunctory manner, unaccompanied by some effort at developed argumentation, are deemed waived."). [—34—]

V. Conclusion

We conclude that the district court properly instructed the jury on the elements of conspiracy and adequately charged the jury to apply the "beyond a reasonable doubt" standard to its finding on drug quantity. Both of Paz's individual challenges fail: the evidence was sufficient to support his conviction and the district court did not err in applying the two-level enhancement for a special skill. Marrero's challenges also fail: his argument that the conspiracy statutes are unconstitutional as applied to him is meritless, his hearsay and prejudicial variance arguments are unpersuasive, and his cumulative error arguments are waived. Thus, the defendants' convictions and sentences are *affirmed*.

So ordered.

---

[19] Marrero's best case for a variance is the evidence pertaining to Retamar and Irizarry's work for their former employer. However, the evidence presented on those facts—the so-called conspiracies #1 and #2—comprised no more than a handful of pages of the transcript at the very beginning of Retamar's two-day testimony. Furthermore, that portion of the testimony was aimed at establishing nothing more than how Retamar and Irizarry met and how each knew that the other was involved in drug trafficking. Marrero has not proved that the prejudice resulting from that testimony was "so pervasive that a miscarriage of justice looms." *Levy-Cordero*, 67 F.3d at 1008 (internal quotation marks omitted).

[20] The six motions are: a motion for judgment of acquittal and/or for new trial (DE 250); two motions to dismiss the indictment (DE 244, 246); two motions in limine regarding the alleged improper use of transcripts (DE 231, 247); and a motion for a sentence below the statutory minimum (DE 363).

[21] In support of one of the motions Marrero seeks to incorporate by reference—a motion to dismiss Count One of the indictment because it

allegedly used language permitting the jury to convict him for guilt by association—he does include a footnote quoting, but not discussing, *Joint Anti-Fascist Refugee Comm. v. McGrath*, 341 U.S. 123, 178-79 (1951), and *United States v. Allen*, 670 F.3d 12, 16 (1st Cir. 2012). He notes in his reply brief on appeal, "We understand that the nature of the defect in the Indictment is patent and requires no major argumentation." We reject this attempt to bypass our well-established waiver rules.

United States Court of Appeals
for the First Circuit

No. 15-1555

IN RE GRAND JURY PROCEEDINGS

Appeal from the United States District Court for the
District of Maine

Decided: September 4, 2015

Citation: 802 F.3d 57, 3 Adm. R. 73 (1st Cir. 2015).

Before **KAYATTA, SELYA,** and **DYK,** * Circuit Judges.

*Of the Federal Circuit, sitting by designation.

[—2—] **DYK,** Circuit Judge:

Appellant is the target of an ongoing grand jury investigation into an alleged scheme to defraud investors regarding the salvaging of a sunken vessel. The district court granted the government's motion to compel the production of documents from appellant's attorneys in connection with the grand jury investigation and granted the government's motion for a judicial determination that the crime-fraud exception applied to materials seized from appellant's home. The district court rejected appellant's claim of attorney-client privilege, holding that the crime-fraud exception applied. Although appellant requested *in camera* review of the documents that were the subject of the motion to compel, neither appellant nor appellant's attorneys ever produced the privilege log required under the Federal Rules. We affirm.

The P.N.[1] is a British cargo ship that was sunk by a German U-boat off the coast of Massachusetts on June 16, 1942.[2] [—3—]

---

[1] To preserve the confidentiality of grand jury proceedings, *see* Fed. R. Crim. P. 6(e), we use initials, as agreed by the parties, to refer to the relevant individuals and vessels.

[2] Much of the factual background for this case derives from an affidavit from Federal Bureau of Investigation Special Agent Mark Miller (the "Miller affidavit") that was attached to the government's February 19, 2015, motion to compel evidence from appellant's attorneys. Appellant's response to the motion to compel attached a November 25, 2014, affidavit that had previously

The government contends that appellant and appellant's company, S.H., raised $8 million from investors to salvage the P.N. by falsifying documents to make it appear as though the ship contained valuable cargo. Appellant currently contends that S.H. discovered the P.N. "[i]n approximately 2007."[3] E.M., who is now a witness for the government, is a shipwreck researcher hired by appellant to research the P.N. The government contends that appellant conspired with E.M. to falsify documents related to the P.N.'s cargo to defraud investors, whereas appellant contends that E.M. falsified the documents without appellant's knowledge. According to appellant, appellant first learned during a November 23, 2014, telephone conversation with E.M. that the documents had been altered.

The government asserts that the fraudulent activity dates back to August 29, 2006, the date that E.M. purchased Volume III of *Lloyd's War Losses*, a compendium of information about merchant ships owned by British, allied, and neutral countries that were [—4—] sunk or destroyed during World War II. According to E.M., appellant paid E.M. to purchase a copy of *Lloyd's War Losses*. The original entry for the P.N. from *Lloyd's War Losses* indicated that the ship sank on June 16, 1942, and listed her cargo as "1600 tons automobile parts & 4000 tons military stores." According to E.M., E.M. showed the entry to appellant who said that E.M. "needed

---

been filed in an associated admiralty action, but did not attach a counter affidavit to the Miller affidavit. Both parties incorporated the facts and arguments from the motion to compel into [—3—] their briefing on the motion for a judicial determination.

[3] Appellant has previously reported various dates for the discovery of the P.N. In a May 2008 confidential offering summary, appellant claimed that the P.N. was discovered on May 5, 2007. This May 5, 2007, date was repeated in a December 5, 2012, confidential offering summary. In a September 10, 2012, amended complaint in an admiralty action relating to the P.N., appellant claimed that S.H. "first located the wrecksite of the [P.N.]" in April of 2008. And at a January 7, 2014, deposition, appellant testified that S.H. discovered the wreck at "the end of 2007," and that appellant "think[s] it was in September."

to show more to get investors on board." E.M. "altered an image of the [P.N.] entry in *Lloyd's War Losses* to indicate that the ship was carrying 1,707,000 troy ounces of platinum." E.M. also admitted to heavily redacting the remainder of the document and adding a forged "declassification" stamp to conceal its origin. As discussed below, the altered document was later used to secure money from investors and was filed in the associated admiralty proceeding.

In May 2008, S.H. produced a confidential offering summary for potential investors. The summary claimed to have discovered the P.N. on May 5, 2007, and stated that "[i]ncluded in the bounty are seventy-one tons of platinum and a very real possibility of ten tons of gold bullion." It added that the ship's "manifest records" revealed that 1.5 tons of industrial diamonds were also aboard the ship with an "[u]nknown value at this time."[4] [—5—]

On August 19, 2008, S.H. filed an admiralty claim in federal district court seeking a warrant for the arrest of the P.N. and salvage or ownership rights to it. A claim for salvage requires three elements: "1. A marine peril. 2. Service voluntarily rendered when not required as an existing duty or from a special contract. 3. Success in whole or in part, or that the service rendered contributed to such success." *The "Sabine"*, 101 U.S. 384, 384 (1879); *see also Clifford v. M/V Islander*, 751 F.2d 1, 5 (1st Cir. 1984). "To obtain possession over the *res*, district courts sitting in admiralty may issue a warrant of arrest for a physical part of a shipwreck (an 'artifact') and, based on this arrest, exercise constructive jurisdiction over the entire shipwreck." *Great Lakes Exploration Grp., LLC v. Unidentified Wrecked & (For Salvage-Right Purposes), Abandoned Sailing Vessel*, 522 F.3d 682, 694 (6th Cir. 2008).

In its complaint in the admiralty action, S.H. claimed to be the salvor-in-possession of the P.N. and that it had effected the arrest by recovering six "metal pieces" from the vessel. The United Kingdom appeared in the action,

claiming ownership of the P.N. On August 26, 2008, the court issued the requested warrant naming S.H. salvor-in-possession of the ship based on the purported recovery of the six metal pieces on April 21, 2008.

Although the arrest warrant established the admiralty court's *in rem* jurisdiction over the P.N., it did not settle the [—6—] parties' ultimate rights, and the admiralty action continued with respect to that question. *See Fla. Dep't of State v. Treasure Salvors, Inc.*, 458 U.S. 670, 697 (1982) ("Of course, the warrant itself merely secures possession of the property; its execution does not finally adjudicate the State's right to the artifacts.").

The nature and value of the P.N.'s cargo was pertinent to the admiralty proceeding because "[t]he value of the property saved" is a factor in determining the amount of the salvage award. *The Blackwall*, 77 U.S. 1, 14 (1869); *see also R.M.S. Titanic, Inc. v. Wrecked & Abandoned Vessel*, 286 F.3d 194, 204 (4th Cir. 2002) ("Courts have held that [a salvage] award cannot exceed the value of the property itself."); *Allseas Maritime, S.A. v. M/V Mimosa*, 812 F.2d 243, 246 (5th Cir. 1987) ("The salvage award is . . . limited by the value of the property saved . . . ."); *Lambros Seaplane Base v. The Batory*, 215 F.2d 228, 234 (2d Cir. 1954) ("[A]mongst the factors which affect a salvage claim are the values . . . of the vessel or property saved . . . .").

On or about February 14, 2011, S.H. issued a second confidential offering summary for potential investors, repeating the prior claims about the P.N.'s cargo and adding that S.H. had a claim to the shipwreck because it had "filed an arrest warrant in the U.S. Federal Court." In response to the question of to whom "the material (cargo) belong[ed]," the same offering summary explained that "[i]f the original owner or owners are known or the [—7—] salvor desires not to dispute a third party's title claim to the wreck, then the salvor will seek a recovery award under the law of salvage, a well-established doctrine with significant international legal precedent, that has been in [the] past around 90% of the recovery."

---

[4] Appellant later testified that the information about diamonds aboard the ship "was just speculation."

In 2011, E.M.'s company, in a further effort to substantiate the claim that the P.N. contained valuable cargo when it sank, contracted with R.L., a private archival researcher, to review National Archives and Records Administration ("NARA") records regarding the P.N. and other vessels. On February 15, 2012, E.M. forwarded R.L.'s February 14, 2012, email to appellant, which indicated that R.L. had copied "cargo reports" "for earlier trips only."

On February 19, 2012, E.M. sent appellant a document that was purportedly "the last cargo of the [P.N.]" and was "on file at the National Archives." The document was titled "Cargo, Mail, and Passenger Report" (the "Cargo Report") and was date-stamped "FEB 6 1941" [not 1942, the date of the sinking]. Adjacent to a box labeled "GENERAL CARGO," the document contained a reference to "BULLION."

In a June 19, 2012, status report filing in the admiralty case, S.H. attached three altered documents: (1) the altered document derived from *Lloyd's War Losses* labeled as a "Copy of US Treasury Ledger–Listing Platinum as cargo" (the "Treasury Ledger"); [—8—] (2) a version of the Cargo Report purportedly from the P.N.'s final voyage that removed or completely obscured the "FEB 6 1941" date-stamp; and (3) a third document, a purported copy of a "US Treasury Department, Procurement Division" cargo listing (the "Treasury Procurement") altered to show that the P.N. contained 741 platinum bars and 4,889 gold bullion bars. A September 10, 2012, amended complaint in the admiralty case referred to the "[o]fficial documents of the United States Customs Service and the United States Treasury Department," which "contain a list of (at least part) of the commercial cargo being transported" and were "attached to the [June 19, 2012, status report]." According to E.M., appellant "pressured [E.M.] to alter the documents based on demands that [S.H.] was facing from potential investors who were interested in the [P.N.]."

S.H. issued a third confidential offering summary on December 5, 2012, attaching the same three documents (the Treasury Ledger, Cargo Report, and Treasury Procurement) that had been filed with the admiralty court, referring to them in the table of contents as "SMOKING GUN DOCUMENTS" and as evidence of valuable cargo aboard the P.N. This summary claimed that a remote-operated vehicle had entered the ship and the "bullion boxes [we]re then located." It also noted that "a federal admiralty claim has been issued" regarding the P.N. [—9—]

In a January 25, 2013, objection to the admiralty court's scheduling order, counsel for the United Kingdom questioned the authenticity of the documents. According to E.M., on or about June 24, 2013, E.M. traveled to NARA in Maryland at appellant's request to have copies of E.M.'s altered Treasury Procurement stamped with a NARA seal. Around the same time, NARA investigators reviewed the Treasury Procurement and Cargo Report from E.M. and concluded that they were fraudulent. NARA investigators located an original copy of the Cargo Report which, unlike the copy filed with the admiralty court, made no mention of bullion. An August 29, 2013, status report filed by S.H. in the admiralty action noted that E.M. attempted "to secure a certified copy of the [Treasury Procurement] document from the National Archives" but was "unsuccessful," such that "the validity of the document must remain in question."

On October 15, 2013, one of appellant's attorneys in the admiralty matter, Attorney D.H., moved to withdraw, citing a "fundamental disagreement" with "the client regarding how this action should be conducted," and that motion was granted. Attorney D.H. also sent an October 16, 2013, email to appellant and appellant's two remaining attorneys (Attorney G.B. and Attorney M.T.) entitled "False Smoking Gun Documents" and attached altered and unaltered versions of the Treasury Procurement document that had been filed in the admiralty matter. Attorney D.H. noted that "[t]hese issues were found by [Attorney D.H.'s associate] and [—10—] required [Attorney D.H.'s] withdrawal" because Attorney D.H. "d[id] not believe that the primary documents came from the archives." On the same day as Attorney D.H.'s email, Attorney G.B. moved to withdraw as counsel in the admiralty matter, and that motion was granted.

On October 22, 2013, appellant forwarded the February 19, 2012, email from E.M. that attached the Cargo Report to K.L., a former S.H. vessel crew member. Appellant asked K.L. to review the documents from E.M. to assess their legitimacy. At a meeting in or around November 2013, K.L. informed appellant and an investor that K.L. believed the documents were falsified, and, according to K.L., appellant "appeared upset but not surprised by [K.L.'s] findings."

On February 11, 2014, S.H. filed another status report in the admiralty action, which referred the court to the three documents filed on June 19, 2012, and explained that S.H. had been unable to verify the source of (or find an unredacted copy of) the Treasury Ledger or Treasury Procurement documents. In this status report, appellant also indicated that because the Cargo Report was dated in 1941, it did not relate to the P.N.'s final voyage in June 1942. Appellant filed a supplemental affidavit on June 12, 2014, claiming that appellant did not know in June 2012 that an unaltered version of the Cargo Report document existed.

On November 14, 2014, NARA agents interviewed E.M. On November 23, 2014, the government recorded a conversation between [—11—] appellant and E.M. During that conversation, appellant indicated that appellant was aware of the existence of a criminal investigation, an awareness which apparently colored the ensuing exchange. E.M. informed appellant that his earlier statements that a former federal agent (named J.M.) had led E.M. to the documents at issue was inaccurate. Later in the same conversation, the following exchange occurred:

E.M.: Mm-hmm. Yeah, but I mean, you knew—you knew those documents were fake a long time ago, you know?
APPELLANT: Not 100 percent, I didn't.
. . .

APPELLANT: No, we didn't [E.M.]. I'm telling you, we didn't. I've stuck up for them because I do not—that's why I stuck up for them because I had an idea, but I have no proof. The only proof I have is what you said this morning, right now.
E.M.: Well, we discussed it.
APPELLANT: What? Forging documents?
E.M.: No, we didn't say it in those words.
APPELLANT: Exactly. We didn't. You're right.

On December 4, 2014, the government executed a search warrant at appellant's home, seizing six metal pieces in addition to numerous computers and electronic media storage devices. And on December 22, 2014, a NARA agent interviewed the captain of the S.W. vessel (which was supposedly used by S.H. to recover the six metal pieces), who stated that no material was recovered from the P.N. while he was captain. Another crew member aboard the S.W. vessel at the time of discovery and for two subsequent trips stated that no material was recovered from the P.N. during those trips. [—12—]

In February 2015, the government served grand jury subpoenas on three of appellant's admiralty lawyers (Attorney M.T., Attorney D.H., and Attorney G.B.) and their law firms for materials "from 2006 until the present," including all documents provided by S.H. and communications with S.H. regarding the P.N.[5]

---

[5] The subpoena requested, *inter alia*, the following materials:

1. All documents, video, artifacts or other tangible material provided to you by [S.H.] relating to the [P.N.], the salvage thereof, or the solicitation of investments in [S.H.] relating to the salvage of the [P.N.], including historical documents, photographs, charts, maps, illustrations, ship artifacts, and any log books for the [S.W. vessel], [S.H. vessel], or any other vessel/ROV utilized by [S.H.].

2. All records of communications between [S.H.] and you, or between you and other attorneys representing [S.H.], regarding the [P.N.], the contents of the [P.N.]'s cargo, the salvage of the [P.N.], [the admiralty suit], or

Appellant's lawyers asserted the attorney-client privilege and work-product protection[6] in response, and on February 19, 2015, the government filed a motion to compel and a separate motion requesting a [—13—] determination that the materials seized from appellant's home fell under the crime-fraud exception.[7] The government attached the Miller affidavit, which summarizes the investigation of appellant and E.M.

On February 20, 2015, appellant filed a motion to intervene asserting the attorney-client privilege, which was granted.[8] On March 4, 2015, appellant filed an opposition to the government's motion to compel, joined by Attorney M.T. In that opposition, appellant argued for the first time that although the government had not requested *in camera* review, if the court was "inclined to grant the Motion [to compel], it is hard to imagine the

Court doing so before an *in camera* review has occurred."

Attorney D.H. and Attorney G.B. did not file a response in opposition to the government's motion to compel. At a March 26, 2015, hearing before the district court on the motion to compel, the government represented that Attorney D.H. and Attorney G.B. "are asserting the attorney-client privilege with respect to the [—14—] requested materials but are prepared to produce them upon a requisite court order, and they do not feel the need to be heard in opposition to the motion. They simply wanted the order in order to comply with their professional responsibility obligations." Neither appellant nor appellant's attorneys have filed a privilege log or otherwise identified any specific documents subject to the subpoena that they contended were not subject to the crime-fraud exception.

On March 11, 2015, S.H.'s remaining attorney in the admiralty action, Attorney M.T., moved to withdraw (like the other two attorneys who withdrew in 2013), and the motion was granted.

On April 17, 2015, the district court granted the government's motion to compel and the government's motion for a judicial finding that the crime-fraud exception applied to evidence seized from appellant's home,[9] finding that the government had proffered prima facie proof that (1) appellant "participated in a fraud," and (2) "that the admiralty action was connected to the fraud." The court relied on the Miller affidavit in finding sufficient evidence that appellant participated in a fraud by submitting falsified documents to the admiralty court showing that the P.N. was carrying valuable cargo and claiming that "war [—15—] records" showed that the P.N. was carrying valuable cargo. The district court also found evidence that the

---

the solicitation of investments relating to the salvage of the [P.N.], including but not limited to e-mail, letters, voicemails, and notes or memoranda relating to conversations.

3. All law firm records, including but not limited to memoranda, notes, e-mails, voicemails, billing records, and calendar entries relating to your firm's representation of [S.H.] with respect to the formation of or investments in any [S.H.] entity, the salvage of the [P.N.] or [the admiralty suit].

4. Drafts of pleadings and supporting exhibits, including affidavits, filed on behalf of [S.H.] in [the admiralty suit].

[6] Appellant has similarly asserted that the work-product protection applies here. For convenience, we have omitted discussion of the work-product protection, which the district court did not specifically address.

[7] Because the parties agreed that the motion for a judicial determination raised identical issues to the motion to compel, both parties adopted the facts and argument set forth in the briefing on the motion to compel in the motion for a judicial determination.

[8] Appellant asserts that appellant was the privilege-holder here, as opposed to S.H., a limited partnership "organized for the specific purpose of salvaging the cargo of the [P.N.]." The subpoena defined S.H. to include, *inter alia*, appellant and E.M. For privilege purposes, neither appellant nor the district court has distinguished appellant and S.H., the company owned by appellant.

---

[9] The district court limited the second subpoena category to omit the first reference to the P.N., because this category otherwise "may ensnare material unrelated to [appellant's] planning and engagement in the salvage of the [P.N.], including the investment scheme and admiralty lawsuit associated with it."

fraud began as early as 2006, based on the 2006 purchase of *Lloyd's War Losses*, which was the source of the fraudulent Treasury Ledger prepared in 2008. In addition, the court found that appellant had provided varying accounts of when the P.N. was discovered (*see supra* note 4), and that appellant's claim that S.H. recovered six pieces of metal from the P.N. was belied by statements by the S.W. vessel's captain that no objects were recovered during that time period.

Based on this evidence, the district court rejected appellant's claim that appellant had been duped by E.M., "conclud[ing] that [the] government's evidence supports its belief that [appellant] was [E.M.]'s co-conspirator, and not [appellant's] victim." Finally, the district court found sufficient evidence that the admiralty claim was part of the fraud because "[t]here could be no salvage operation for investors to invest in without a judicial determination that [appellant] had a lawful claim to the ship's cargo." The district court did not address appellant's request for *in camera* review. On May 15, 2015, the admiralty case was dismissed with prejudice.

Appellant appeals the grant of both the government's motions. We review the district court's rulings on questions of law de novo, findings of fact for clear error, and evidentiary determinations for an abuse of discretion. *In re Grand Jury* [—16—] *Subpoena (Mr. S.)*, 662 F.3d 65, 69 (1st Cir. 2011).

II.

Ordinarily, we would not have appellate jurisdiction over the district court's order granting the government's motion to compel prior to a citation for contempt. *See In re Grand Jury Subpoenas*, 123 F.3d 695, 696 (1st Cir. 1997). We have jurisdiction in the circumstances of this case, however, pursuant to *Perlman v. United States*, 247 U.S. 7 (1918). As this court has noted:

An exception to the rule requiring a contempt citation prior to appeal exists when subpoenaed documents are in the hands of a third party [the *"Perlman*

doctrine"]. In that case, the owner of the documents may seek immediate appeal of a district court's order requiring production of those documents.

Grand Jury, 123 F.3d at 696–97 (citing *Perlman*, 247 U.S. at 12–13). This court has applied the *Perlman* doctrine to circumstances where, as here, "a client seeks immediate appeal of an order compelling production of a client's records from his attorney." *Id.* at 699; *see also In re Grand Jury Subpoena (Custodian of Records, Newparent, Inc.)*, 274 F.3d 563, 570 (1st Cir. 2001).

With respect to the district court's declaratory order granting the government's motion for a judicial finding, we have jurisdiction because the declaratory order is a final judgment. *See* 28 U.S.C. § 2201 ("Any such declaration shall have the force and effect of a final judgment or decree and shall be reviewable as such."); *see also Langley v. Colonial Leasing Co. of New Eng.*, 707 [—17—] F.2d 1, 3 (1st Cir. 1983) (declaratory judgment order which "was in reality a full final judgment" was appealable).

III.

Appellant argues that the district court did not have a sufficient basis to find that appellant was engaged in a scheme to commit a crime or fraud.

The purpose of the attorney-client privilege is "to encourage full and frank communication between attorneys and their clients and thereby promote broader public interests in the observance of law and administration of justice." *Upjon Co. v. United States*, 449 U.S. 383, 389 (1981). In general, the burden is on appellant (as the party asserting the privilege here) to "establish the existence and applicability of the privilege . . . [using] sufficient information to allow the court to rule intelligently on the privilege claim." *Marx v. Kelly, Hart & Hallman, P.C.*, 929 F.2d 8, 12 (1st Cir. 1991); *see also Grand Jury*, 662 F.3d at 69 ("The burden of showing that documents are privileged rests with the party asserting the privilege.").

"The crime-fraud exception—one of several qualifications to the attorney-client privilege—withdraws protection where the client sought or employed legal representation in order to commit or facilitate a crime or fraud." *In re Grand Jury Proceedings*, 417 F.3d 18, 22 (1st Cir. 2005). The government has the burden of establishing the application of the crime-fraud exception by [—18—] establishing "a reasonable basis to believe that the lawyer's services were used by the client to foster a crime or fraud." *Grand Jury*, 417 F.3d at 23; *see also In re Grand Jury Proceedings (Gregory P. Violette)*, 183 F.3d 71, 75 (1st Cir. 1999). "To bring the crime-fraud exception to bear, the party invoking it must make a prima facie showing: (1) that the client was engaged in (or was planning) criminal or fraudulent activity when the attorney-client communications took place; *and* (2) that the communications were intended by the client to facilitate or conceal the criminal or fraudulent activity." *Violette*, 183 F.3d at 75. If the party asserting the crime-fraud exception makes this reasonable cause showing (also referred to as a prima facie case), the privilege is forfeited. *See Grand Jury*, 417 F.3d at 22–24.

Here, there was ample evidence for the district court to conclude under the applicable evidence standard that appellant was involved in a scheme to defraud investors as to the value of the cargo of the P.N. This included evidence that E.M. stated that the documents were falsified at appellant's direction, that the falsified documents were transmitted to potential investors and the admiralty court, that appellant's claim that the six metal pieces came from the P.N. was contradicted by the captain of the S.W. vessel that supposedly recovered them, and various other evidence from the Miller affidavit. [—19—]

Appellant contends that the subpoena is temporally overbroad because it reaches back to documents beginning in 2006, but 2006 is the year that appellant identified as the year during which appellant supposedly learned "something remarkable about" the P.N. after "scouring through" various records, and the year in which appellant caused E.M. to purchase the copy of *Lloyd's War Losses* eventually employed to perpetuate the fraud.

In light of what happened later, particularly appellant's direction to E.M. to utilize the *Lloyd's War Losses* book purchased in 2006 to perpetuate the fraud by altering its contents, it is reasonable to conclude that the fraud began in 2006.

And there was also sufficient evidence for the district court to conclude that at least some of the communications between appellant and appellant's attorneys with respect to the admiralty proceeding were intended by appellant to facilitate that fraudulent scheme. This included the fact that the fraudulently altered documents were filed with the court by counsel and that the admiralty action was referenced in various offering summaries. The admiralty proceeding itself would have been the source of any potential monetary recovery from the P.N., as S.H. represented to potential investors that it expected a salvage award amounting to approximately ninety percent of the value of the P.N.'s cargo.

Appellant argues that the district court failed adequately to consider contrary evidence that supported appellant's [—20—] contention that appellant was not involved in the crime or fraud. But this is clearly not so: the district court considered all evidence presented, and simply did not find appellant's evidence to be so compelling as to preclude a finding that there was a reasonable basis to conclude that appellant used appellant's lawyers to foster a fraud. As we have explained, ample evidence supported this finding.

IV.

Although we affirm the district court's conclusion that sufficient evidence exists to invoke the crime-fraud exception, that is not the end of the matter. Appellant alleges that the subpoena seeks documents that did not further the crime or fraud. In appellant's opposition to the government's motion to compel, appellant requested for the first time that the district court conduct an *in camera* review as an alternative to denying the motion. The district court did not address this request.

In camera review can perform two separate functions in the crime-fraud exception context. First, *in camera* review may be used to determine whether there is sufficient evidence to apply the crime-fraud exception to a claim of attorney-client privilege. In *United States v. Zolin*, 491 U.S. 554 (1989), the Supreme Court approved of the use of "*in camera* review to determine the applicability of the crime-fraud exception," upon "a showing of a factual basis adequate to support a good faith belief by a [—21—] reasonable person that *in camera* review of the materials may reveal evidence to establish the claim that the crime-fraud exception applies." *Id.* at 572 (internal quotation, citation omitted). As discussed above, there was ample evidence here for the district court to conclude that the crime-fraud exception applied without the need to resort to *in camera* review, nor did appellant seek *in camera* review for this purpose. *See Linder v. Nat'l Sec. Agency*, 94 F.3d 693, 696–97 (D.C. Cir. 1996) ("A court may rely on affidavits in lieu of an *in camera* review when they are sufficiently detailed . . . ."). Importantly, this is not a case in which *in camera* review of the subject documents would have helped the district court decide the issue that the parties put before it: whether the crime-fraud exception generally applied.

Second, *in camera* review may be sought for a different purpose—to determine whether specific documents evidence communications with attorneys in furtherance of the crime or fraud. This is because the crime-fraud exception requires "that the communications were intended by the client to facilitate or conceal the criminal or fraudulent activity." *Grand Jury*, 417 F.3d at 22 (quoting *Violette*, 183 F.3d at 75); *see id.* at 25 (suggesting the use of *in camera* review on remand to determine whether certain attorney-client communications were intended to perpetuate a crime or fraud). [—22—]

Appellant apparently seeks *in camera* review here to identify documents that remain privileged notwithstanding the existence of the crime-fraud exception because they were not in furtherance of the crime or fraud.[10]

The question is whether appellant has preserved appellant's claim for *in camera* review. Under Rule 45 of the Federal Rules of Civil Procedure, applicable to grand jury subpoenas, "[a] person withholding subpoenaed information under a claim that it is privileged or subject to protection as trial-preparation material must: . . . describe the nature of the withheld documents, communications, or tangible things in a manner that, without revealing information itself privileged or protected, will enable the parties to assess the claim." Fed. R. Civ. P. 45(e)(2)(A). "The operative language is mandatory and, although the rule does not spell out the sufficiency requirement in detail, [—23—] courts consistently have held that the rule requires a party resisting disclosure to produce a document index or privilege log." *Grand Jury*, 274 F.3d at 575.

Rule 45 does not specify when this description (normally in the form of a privilege log) must be provided. *See* 9A Charles Alan Wright & Arthur R. Miller, *Federal Practice and Procedure* § 2464 (3d ed. 2008) ("One problem presented by Rule 45[] is that it fails to provide any guidance as to when the claim of privilege or work product must be asserted by the person subpoenaed."). Addressing this gap, the District of Columbia and Second

---

[10] Appellant asserts that this includes certain documents (or portions of documents) relating to vessels other than the P.N. Documents relating solely to shipwrecks other than the P.N. are not within the scope of the subpoena, which is limited to materials "relating to" or "regarding the" P.N. and the associated admiralty suit. Appellant points to one aspect of the subpoena that might go beyond the P.N. and the associated admiralty suit: "[a]ll law firm records . . . relating to your firm's representation of [S.H.] with respect to the formation of or investments in any [S.H.] entity . . . ." As the government explains, however, appellant's affidavit represented that S.H. "was organized for the specific purpose of salvaging the cargo of the . . . [P.N.]," and "[a]ll of [S.H.'s] activities, and all documents generated or obtained by S.H., have related directly or indirectly to that [P.N.] salvage project." As such, this aspect of the subpoena is also limited to the P.N.

Circuits have imposed a requirement that "the information required under the Rule is provided to the requesting party within a *reasonable time*, such that the claiming party has adequate opportunity to evaluate fully the subpoenaed documents and the requesting party has ample opportunity to contest that claim." *Tuite v. Henry*, 98 F.3d 1411, 1416 (D.C. Cir. 1996); *see also In re DG Acquisition Corp.*, 151 F.3d 75, 81 (2d Cir. 1998) (citing and applying *Tuite*'s "reasonable time" requirement). We agree that this is the appropriate standard.

Here, in opposing the government's motion for a judicial determination that the crime-fraud exception applied to materials seized from appellant's home, Rule 45 was inapplicable and appellant was not required to provide a privilege log to argue against the government's crime-fraud theory. And even with respect [—24—] to the government's motion to compel (governed by Rule 45), neither party thought that a privilege log was necessary at that stage to address the applicability of the crime-fraud exception to the documents generally. For purposes of the crime-fraud exception, the government simply assumed that the subpoena sought documents that would otherwise have been privileged. Under those circumstances, there was no need for a privilege log to address that general question, and appellant's failure to provide a privilege log in opposition to the motion to compel did not deprive appellant of the right to contest the government's overall crime-fraud theory.

However, when appellant asserted the need for an *in camera* inspection in assessing the motion to compel, appellant essentially requested that the court make a document-by-document ruling as to whether any particular document might not be discoverable notwithstanding general application of the crime-fraud exception. The failure to produce a privilege log (or otherwise identify particular documents subject to the privilege) to support the need for *in camera* inspection waived appellant's right to seek *in camera* inspection.

Neither appellant nor appellant's attorneys ever produced a privilege log in response to the motion to compel nor otherwise complied with the requirements of Rule 45. Under this court's cases, that constitutes a waiver of the request for *in camera* [—25—] review. *See Grand Jury*, 274 F.3d at 576 ("A party that fails to submit a privilege log is deemed to waive the underlying privilege claim."); *Grand Jury*, 662 F.3d at 72; *see also Corvello v. New Eng. Gas Co.*, 243 F.R.D. 28, 34 (D. R.I. 2007) ("[I]n camera inspection is unnecessary where the party claiming privilege has failed to make a prima facie showing that the documents in question are privileged by submitting a privilege log that adequately described the documents and the basis for the claimed privilege.").

The requirement to comply with Rule 45 applies even where, as here, the allegedly privileged documents are in the possession of the client's attorneys, rather than the client, and the client has either knowledge of or access to them. As the attorneys' client (or former client), appellant had access to the attorneys' files. *See Me. Bar Rules* § 1.16(d); ABA Model Rules of Prof. Conduct 1.16(d); *see also* Maine Professional Ethics Opinion 120; Maine Professional Ethics Opinion 51. In *Grand Jury*, the allegedly privileged documents were in the possession of corporate counsel for the intervenor clients' parent company, but "the intervenors made no effort to prepare a privilege log" despite their "knowledge of the communications to which the subpoena pertained." 274 F.3d at 576. We held that because "[p]rivilege logs do not need to be precise to the point of pedantry[,] . . . a party who possesses *some knowledge* of the nature of the materials to which a claim of privilege is addressed cannot shirk his [—26—] obligation to file a privilege log merely because he lacks infinitely detailed information. To the contrary, we read Rule 45[] as requiring a party who asserts a claim of privilege to do the best that he reasonably can to describe the materials to which his claim adheres." *Id.* (emphasis added).

Here, appellant clearly "possesses some knowledge of the nature of the materials" sought by the subpoenas, *id.*, because at least two of the subpoenaed categories were necessarily in appellant's possession at one point: communications between appellant's company and appellant's attorneys, and materials provided by appellant's company to appellant's attorneys. Because appellant failed to produce a privilege log or any other "descri[ption] of the nature of the withheld documents," Fed. R. Civ. P. 45(e)(2), appellant's request for *in camera* review was not preserved.

AFFIRMED

Costs to the United States.

United States Court of Appeals
for the First Circuit

No. 14-1088

UNITED STATES

vs.

PEAKE

Appeal from the United States District Court for the District of Puerto Rico

Decided: October 14, 2015

Citation: 804 F.3d 81, 3 Adm. R. 83 (1st Cir. 2015).

Before **TORRUELLA, LYNCH,** and **THOMPSON,** Circuit Judges.

[—2—] **TORRUELLA,** Circuit Judge:

As a result of his conviction for participating in one of the largest antitrust conspiracies in the history of the United States, Defendant-Appellant Frank Peake ("Peake") raises a number of claimed errors with respect to his trial and sentencing for a serious price-fixing offense in violation of Section 1 of the Sherman Act, 15 U.S.C. § 1 ("Section 1"). Peake challenges: (1) the validity of his indictment; (2) the scope of the search warrant executed by the government; (3) the district court's denial of his pre-trial motion to change venue; (4) improper remarks made by the prosecutor during trial; (5) the district court's ruling permitting prejudicial testimony; (6) the district court's denial of his request for a theory-of-defense instruction; (7) the district court's denial of his request for a mistrial during jury deliberations, and (8) the length of his sentence, which was based on the amount of commerce affected by the charged conspiracy, and which Peake contends the court incorrectly computed. Finding no errors and concluding that the district court marshaled this trial in a commendable manner, we affirm. After a brief overview of the factual background, we will take each of the issues one by one.

I. Background

We recount the facts in the light most favorable to the jury verdict, as supported by the record. *See United States v. Andrade,* 94 F.3d 9, 10 (1st Cir. 1996). Since 2002, waterborne [—3—] cabotage between Puerto Rico and the mainland has been dominated by four freight carriers: Horizon Lines, Sea Star, Crowley, and Trailer Bridge. *See In re Puerto Rican Cabotage Antitrust Litig.,* 815 F.Supp.2d 448, 454 n.3 (D.P.R. 2011). And, because of Puerto Rico's geographical situation, Puerto Rico's consumers rely on these carriers to transport most goods imported to the island. *See* Merchant Marine Act of 1920, Pub. L. No. 66-261, 41 Stat. 988, 999 (1920) (codified as amended at 46 U.S.C. §§ 55101, *et seq.*). Seeking to maximize revenues, Horizon Lines and Sea Star agreed not to undercut each other in price and allocated precise market share quotas through an extensive conspiracy that included bid rigging and careful planning, coordination, and the kinds of day-to-day self-enforcement common of illegal agreements.

This behavior constituted an agreement in restraint of trade forbidden by Section 1. Peake, the former President and Chief Operating Officer ("COO") of Sea Star, played a managing role in the conspiracy, coordinating with competitors through meetings, phone calls, and emails, and attending to pricing or consumer-allocation disputes that his subordinates could not resolve on their own.

For example, during a meeting in Orlando in 2006, Peake coordinated with Horizon Lines executives to resolve existing disputes by agreeing to keep the market shares at their current levels, rather than reinstating the split in effect prior to his [—4—] joining the conspiracy in 2005. Later that year, the market allocation became imbalanced when Walgreens, a major importer of consumer goods to Puerto Rico, decided not to divide freight contracts between Horizon Lines and Sea Star, and instead allocated all of its freight to Horizon Lines. Peake quickly agreed with an executive from Horizon Lines that the company would compensate by shifting cargo to Sea Star vessels or using Transportation Service Agreements, whereby Horizon Lines would pay Sea Star to carry its cargo even though it had capacity to transport it in its own vessels.

While the conspiracy was in full swing, a Sea Star senior executive working with Peake became a government informant. Based on his description of the conspiracy, the government initiated an extensive investigation that included an FBI search of Sea Star's headquarters in 2008. Four of Peake's co-conspirators were charged with antitrust violations and pleaded guilty before the U.S. District Court for the Middle District of Florida, Jacksonville Division. Following these events, a grand jury in San Juan, Puerto Rico, returned an indictment against Peake in November 2011 on one charge of conspiracy to suppress and eliminate competition by agreeing to fix rates and surcharges for freight services in interstate commerce between the United States and Puerto Rico.

Peake's co-conspirators testified against him at trial, revealing his involvement in the conspiracy and their discussions [—5—] about setting surcharges, fees, and market share allocations. One such incident involved an email exchange between Peake and a competitor regarding prices offered to a client in an attempt to "avoid a price war."

After a nine-day trial, which took place over the course of three weeks, the jury found Peake guilty of participating in a conspiracy to fix the prices of Puerto Rico freight services, in violation of Section 1. The district court sentenced Peake to sixty months' imprisonment.

This appeal ensued.

II. The Indictment

Before addressing the main issues in this appeal, we briefly address an issue that, although Peake is raising on appeal for the first time, he claims would foreclose our jurisdiction on this matter.[1] Peake argues that

Puerto Rico is not a state, yet the indictment charges Peake under Section 1, which prohibits agreements in restraint of trade or commerce "among the several [—6—] States," and that his conviction must therefore be vacated.[2]   There are at least two insurmountable problems with this argument. First, it is well-settled that, for purposes of the Sherman Act, Puerto Rico is "to be treated like a state and not like a territory," therefore, Section 1 fully applies to Puerto Rico. *Córdova & Simonpietri Ins. Agency Inc. v. Chase Manhattan Bank N.A.*, 649 F.2d 36, 38, 44 (1st Cir. 1981). Second, the evidence in the record shows that part of the freight carried by the companies in the conspiracy originated in one state before being transported to a port in a second state to be shipped to Puerto Rico. Therefore, the commerce affected by the conspiracy was not only between a state and Puerto Rico, but also among the states. Thus, Peake was correctly charged, and the indictment is not defective.

We now move on to Peake's appeal of the district court's denial of his motion to suppress, and then address his other trial-related claims, before finally turning to the appeal of his sentence. [—7—]

III. Motion to Suppress

Peake appeals the district court's denial of his motion to suppress the government's search of his personal electronics. For the following reasons, we affirm the denial.

---

[1] "[J]urisdictional challenges to an indictment may be raised at any time," *United States v. Rosa-Ortiz*, 348 F.3d 33, 36 (1st Cir. 2003), but all other motions regarding a defective indictment, such as failure to state an offense, must be made *before*

trial, Fed. R. Crim. P. 12(b)(3)(B), and thus can only be reviewed for plain error if raised for the first time on appeal, *see United States v. Turner*, 684 F.3d 244, 255 (1st Cir. 2012). Here, it matters not whether we treat Peake's argument as a jurisdictional challenge, or as an untimely-made failure-to-state-a-claim argument to be reviewed for plain error, because, as we explain, Peake was correctly charged under Section 1, so there was no error at all.

[2] Peake argues that he should instead have been charged under Section 3 of the Sherman Act, which contains the same prohibitions, but applies to territories. 15 U.S.C. § 3(a) ("Every . . . conspiracy[] in restraint of trade or commerce . . . between any such Territory and another, or between any such Territory or Territories and any State or States . . . is declared illegal.").

A. Standard of Review

In reviewing a challenge to the district court's denial of a motion to suppress, "we view the facts in the light most favorable to the district court's ruling," and "review the district court's findings of fact and credibility determinations for clear error." *United States v. Camacho*, 661 F.3d 718, 723 (1st Cir. 2011) (citation and internal quotation marks omitted). However, we review the lower court's legal conclusions, including its determination of whether the government exceeded the scope of the warrant, *de novo*. *United States v. Fagan*, 577 F.3d 10, 12-13 (1st Cir. 2009).

A search warrant must "describ[e] the place to be searched" and the "things to be seized." U.S. Const. amend. IV. The authority conferred by the warrant "is circumscribed by the particular places delineated in the warrant and does not extend to other or different places." *Fagan*, 577 F.3d at 13. Search warrants also have a specificity requirement, meaning "that warrants shall particularly describe the things to be seized," which "prevents the seizure of one thing under a warrant describing another." *Marron v. United States*, 275 U.S. 192, 196 (1927). Even [—8—] though search warrants are limited to the particular places and things described in them, there is some breathing room in our analysis, since "search warrants and affidavits should be considered in a common sense manner, and hypertechnical readings should be avoided." *United States v. Bonner*, 808 F.2d 864, 868 (1st Cir. 1986) (citing *Spinelli v. United States*, 393 U.S. 410, 419 (1969)).

A draft warrant presented to a magistrate judge may be altered or modified by the judicial officer or at his direction. *See United States v. Hang Le-Thy Tran*, 433 F.3d 472, 481 (6th Cir. 2006); *United States v. Katoa*, 379 F.3d 1203, 1208 (10th Cir. 2004); *United States v. Arenal*, 768 F.2d 263, 267 (8th Cir. 1985). When part of a warrant is considered invalid, "evidence seized under the valid portion may be admitted." *United States v. George*, 975 F.2d 72, 79 (2d Cir. 1992). Furthermore, when a warrant is limited to authorize the seizure of only certain objects,

"container[s] situated within residential premises which are the subject of a validly-issued warrant may be searched if it is reasonable to believe that the container could conceal items of the kind portrayed in the warrant." *United States v. Rogers*, 521 F.3d 5, 9-10 (1st Cir. 2008).

B. The Search Warrants

In this case, a magistrate judge was presented with a draft warrant for his consideration. Upon reviewing it, he crossed [—9—] out a paragraph under Attachment A, which described the premises to be searched. The stricken paragraph allowed the search of "briefcases, laptop computers, hand-held computers, cell phones, Blackberries, and other movable document containers found on the premises described."[3] In Attachment B, the magistrate judge also struck the following text from the description of the property to be seized: "memory calculators, pagers, personal digital assistants such as Palm Pilot hand-held computers." The magistrate judge left standing, however, other references to electronically stored documents and records. As amended, Attachment B described the property to be seized as follows:

> As used above, the terms records, documents, programs, documentation, applications or materials include but are not limited to records, documents, programs, applications or materials

---

[3] The full text of the paragraph struck stated:

In order to minimize the prospect of the removal and subsequent destruction of any of the documents and records identified in Exhibit B to the Search Warrant, the search will include the briefcases, laptop computers, hand-held computers, cell phones, Blackberries, and other movable document containers found on the premises described above, and in the possession of, or readily identifiable as belonging to SEA STAR management, pricing, and sales personnel including, but not limited to, FRANK PEAKE, PETER A. BACI, CARL FOX, NED LAGOY, NEIL PERLMUTTER, ALEX CHISHOLM, MIKE NICHOLSON, EDWARD PRETRE, and WILLIAM BYRNES.

created, modified or stored in any form, including any optical, electrical, electronic, or magnetic form (such as any information on an optical, electrical, electronic or magnetic storage device), including floppy disks, hard disks, ZIP disks, CD-ROMs, [—10—] optical disks, backup tapes, printer buffers or other device memory buffers, smart cards . . . email servers, as well as opened and unopened e-mail messages and any printouts or readouts from any optical, electrical, electronic, or magnetic storage device . . . .

Additionally, the magistrate judge added two handwritten passages to the portion of the draft warrant governing the seizure of computers and other electronic devices, and ordered that any seized computers or electronic devices within the scope of the warrant be returned within thirty days of seizure. Specifically, the following language was inserted:

> In the event that computer equipment and other electrical storage devices must be transported to the appropriate laboratory, rather than searched on the premises, the search of computer equipment and other electronic storage devices must be completed within 30 days of seizure.

and

> If no evidence is found in the computer equipment and electronic storage devices by the end of the 30 day period, or if any electronically stored information is outside of the scope of the warrant, such shall be returned promptly.

Following the guidance provided in the warrant, the FBI raided Sea Star's headquarters on April 17, 2008, and seized Peake's personal laptop and Blackberry. The items were imaged (the data was copied) and returned to Peake on-site the same day. This evidence was not immediately reviewed, as the FBI was under the impression that Sea Star's servers stored copies of all seized

information relevant to the investigation. Images of Peake's computer and Blackberry were eventually sent to the Department of [—11—] Justice in Washington, D.C. More than four years passed before the government sought and obtained another search warrant from a magistrate judge in Washington, D.C., authorizing a search of these data copies. Their review revealed emails tying Peake to the conspiracy, which the government submitted as evidence at trial.

C. Appeal of the Suppression Ruling

Peake argues that the information collected from his personal computer and Blackberry should be suppressed because the two items were outside the scope of the initial warrant, and therefore illegally seized. He contends that when the magistrate judge struck the paragraph in Attachment A specifying computers and Blackberries as places that could be searched, doing so specifically disallowed any search and seizure of said items. A good faith exception to the purported violation of the initial warrant, Peake continues, cannot apply in the present case where the property seized was expressly disallowed by the issuing magistrate judge.

Peake also argues that the government did not have authority to image the seized electronics, and that the second warrant from the magistrate judge in Washington, D.C., did not cure the violation because it could not authorize a search of material outside the scope of the original warrant, especially after the thirty days permitted by the first warrant had passed. [—12—]

1. The First Warrant

Applying *de novo* review, we conclude that the information collected from the computer and Blackberry was within the scope of the original search warrant. We think Peake is mistaken in his reliance on the stricken paragraph; other, intact passages in the warrant expressly demonstrate that the magistrate judge approved searching for all documents and records that pertained to the conspiracy stored in "an electronic or digital format." That the warrant listed documents stored in electronic form on an electronic storage device, including email messages, and referred in Attachment B to Blackberry address books, confirms the legality of the FBI's search.

This case is analogous to *United States v. Rogers*, where we held that the government's seizure of a videotape was valid, even though videotapes were not listed in the warrant, because the warrant mentioned "photos," and a videotape was a plausible repository for a photo. 521 F.3d at 10. Or *United States v. Giannetta*, 909 F.2d 571, 577 (1st Cir. 1990), where we held that the officers could look in movable containers and wherever they had reasonable suspicion to think "documents could be hidden, which would include pockets in clothing, boxes, file cabinets and files," because "[a]s to document searches especially, the easily concealed nature of the evidence means that quite broad searches are permitted." [—13—]

Here, given that Peake's personal electronic devices were on the premises to be searched, and the warrant specifically mentioned electronically-stored documents, the FBI acted within the scope of the warrant when it searched Peake's devices. And the fact that the issuing magistrate judge had hand-written on the warrant that computers and electronic devices must be returned within thirty days is evidence enough that the scope of the warrant included these objected-to items. Futhermore, the government's imaging of the computer and Blackberry did not constitute a warrantless seizure because doing so was contemplated by the original warrant, which explicitly authorized the government to seize electronically-stored emails and documents.

Nor does the fact that the magistrate judge crossed out language in the warrant affect our conclusion. The warrant authorized a search of the "premises" of Sea Star's headquarters; thus, as the district court held in denying the motion to suppress, the magistrate judge could have reasonably crossed out the items mentioned in Attachment A, "briefcases, laptop computers, hand-held computers, cell phones, Blackberries and other movable

document containers," in order to indicate that the government should not be limited to searching solely in those places for records documenting the conspiracy, but should be permitted to search the entire premises. *See, e.g.*, *United States v. Bradley*, 644 F.3d 1213, 1266 [—14—] (11th Cir. 2011) (observing that warrant to search "premises" permitted search of the entire building).

As to the magistrate judge's crossing out of "personal digital assistant" in Attachment B, we conclude that the crossed-out text should simply be treated as nonexistent.[4] Peake does not point us to any case law establishing that eliminating a part of the text from a draft warrant necessarily means that the crossed-out statements have continued significance. *Cf. United States v. Thomas*, 489 F.2d 664, 672-73 (5th Cir. 1973) (stating that where a magistrate judge crossed out "in the daytime" while leaving the phrase "at any time in the day or night," the warrant "could be served at any time, day or night"). Thus, the agents would have been permitted to seize Peake's Blackberry, so long as the remaining text of the warrant was valid and authorized them to do so. As we explained above, the seizure and search of the Blackberry was authorized by the intact paragraphs of the warrant. We therefore conclude that the Blackberry was also lawfully seized and searched. [—15—]

2. The Second Warrant

Peake correctly argues that if his computer and Blackberry had been illegally seized, the government should not have been permitted to later obtain a more expansive warrant from an arguably friendlier forum in order to search previously-excluded items, as doing so

---

[4] Alternatively, the magistrate judge may have intended to eliminate *personal* items from the search, and limit the agents to seizing *company* property only. *See Bivens v. Six Unknown Named Agents of Fed. Bureau of Narcotics*, 403 U.S. 388, 395 n.7 (1971) ("[T]he Fourth Amendment confines an officer executing a search warrant strictly within the bounds set by the warrant." (quoting *Marron*, 275 U.S. at 196)). But Peake does not appear to argue that the information from his computer and Blackberry should have been suppressed because they were personal, and not company property, so we will not go down this road.

would weaken important Fourth Amendment protections. But here, we have concluded that the seized and imaged evidence Peake seeks suppressed was within the scope of the first warrant. We do not find that the government used the second warrant to unlawfully sidestep the first one, and we need not consider whether the second warrant was invalid. Nor do we need to reach the question whether the good faith exception applies. In sum, the suppression motion was properly denied. We turn now to Peake's pre-trial motion for change of venue.

IV. Motion for Change of Venue

Because Peake was indicted in Puerto Rico—while his co-conspirators' cases were brought in Jacksonville, Florida—Peake filed a pre-trial motion for change of venue under Federal Rule of Criminal Procedure 21(b) "for the convenience of the parties, any victim, and the witnesses, and in the interest of justice." Fed. R. Crim. P. 21(b). In his motion, Peake discussed the factors considered in *Platt v. Minnesota Mining & Manufacturing Co.*, 376 U.S. 240, 243-45 (1964), stressing that it was impracticable to hold a trial in Puerto Rico, since most persons [—16—] involved in the conspiracy and the investigation were in Jacksonville. *See also United States v. Quiles-Olivo*, 684 F.3d 177, 184 (1st Cir. 2012) (applying the *Platt* factors in a criminal case). Peake later filed supplemental briefing, arguing that change of venue was also proper under Federal Rule of Criminal Procedure 21(a) because it would be impossible to obtain a fair and impartial jury composed of Puerto Rican consumers.

The district court denied the motion, reasoning that any inconvenience suffered by Peake was outweighed by the interest of having the case heard in the jurisdiction most seriously affected by the conspiracy. It also explained that under Rule 21(a), transfer is a mandatory remedy if the court finds "an unacceptable level of prejudice," such as where "pervasive pretrial publicity has inflamed passions in the host community past the breaking point." *United States v. Walker*, 665 F.3d 212, 223 (1st Cir. 2011) (citing *United States v. Angiulo*, 497 F.2d 440, 440-42

(1st Cir. 1974) (per curiam)). The district court concluded that there was no pervasive pre-trial publicity inflaming the passions in the community to the point that Peake could not have a fair and impartial trial in Puerto Rico, and thus the court allowed the government to exercise its right to choose the venue at its prosecutorial discretion.

A district court's denial of the request for a change of venue is reviewed for abuse of discretion. *Quiles-Olivo*, 684 F.3d [—17—] at 181. We find no such abuse in the district court's denial. Peake did not allege any outside influence or publicity that could have affected, from the outset of trial, the jury's consideration of the evidence presented. Thus, we affirm the district court's ruling on the motion to change venue.

V. Trial

Peake's next set of issues on this appeal pertains to matters that arose at trial, and can be boiled down into four claims: the first is Peake's claim that he should have been granted a new trial on the basis of prosecutorial misconduct, the second is that the district court erred in permitting prejudicial testimony, the third is that the district court erred in denying his request for a jury instruction regarding his theory of defense, and the fourth is that the district court should have declared a mistrial when, during deliberations, the jury sent the judge a note stating that it could not come to a verdict. As we will explain, we find no error in the district court's handling of each of these matters, but first, we begin by providing some additional background on what happened during the trial.

Peake's trial was held in San Juan, Puerto Rico, in January 2013, and lasted nine days. In its opening argument on the second day of trial, the government made references to multiple national retail chains and franchises whose businesses purportedly experienced artificially higher shipping costs as a result of the [—18—] antitrust conspiracy, and stated that even the cost of school lunches had been affected by the conspiracy. Peake objected to these comments, which we will describe in more detail later, and filed a motion for mistrial. In his motion, he argued that the government had communicated to the jury that higher prices were being passed on to them as directly affected consumers, and reasoned that if jurors felt their personal financial interests were affected by the conspiracy, their judgment would be clouded. The district court took note of the motion on the morning of the third day of the trial, and granted the government three days to file its response.

As the trial continued, the government called Peake's coconspirators, Gabriel Serra, Gregory Glova, and Peter Baci, to the stand to provide testimony that established the existence of a conspiracy. On cross-examination, Peake also elicited testimony from the co-conspirators that he argues was exculpatory, but contends that, because the jurors at this point believed themselves to be "affected consumers," they were unable to fairly consider this purported exculpatory testimony that was critical to his defense.[5] [—19—]

On the fourth day of trial, the district judge had a discussion with the parties regarding the remarks made by the government during the opening statements when Peake raised an objection to the government calling witnesses whose retail and consumer business operations in Puerto Rico were affected by the

higher shipping rates generated by the conspiracy. Peake argued that the effect on market prices for consumers had nothing to do with whether there was an agreement amongst competitors to fix their prices. That is, Peake contended that the issue before the jury should be limited to the agreement, regardless of its effects, and argued that allowing the testimony of witnesses from affected businesses was in line with the government's inappropriate remarks during opening statements that the conspiracy affected Puerto Rican consumers. The government argued that the witnesses' testimony was necessary to demonstrate the antitrust harm to *direct* consumers of the shipping companies (and not to imply that members of the public who patronized those businesses, or *indirect* consumers, were affected),[6] because the government needed to establish that the [—20—] conspiracy affected interstate commerce, a required element of the charged offense.

The district judge agreed that testimony regarding the effect on the witnesses' companies showed that the conspiracy had impacted interstate commerce, which was an element of the offense, and thus ruled that testimony to that effect would be allowed. However, the district court warned the prosecutors against eliciting testimony beyond that scope, and noted that the implication in the government's opening that school lunch programs, and therefore children, had been affected by the conspiracy was "really way out of bounds." The district judge also offered, notwithstanding the yet-undetermined outcome of the motion for mistrial, to give a curative instruction to the jury that day that would address Peake's concerns about the

---

[5] For example, Baci testified that, during part of the conspiracy, Peake pushed for perfectly legal strategies that would negatively affect the stability of the "Florida 50/50" arrangement—the name given to the strategy of allocating equal market shares between Horizon Lines and Sea Star. One such pro-competition strategy that Peake had advocated for was for a third ship to serve the Puerto Rico-Jacksonville route; another was a "slap strategy" whereby Sea [—19—] Star would pursue the business of any company that tried to steal their clients. In his testimony, Serra confirmed Baci's statement that Peake wanted to add a third ship. He also testified that Peake authorized competitive shipping rates and that their meetings were strictly legal. In addition, on the stand, Glova could not identify any direct references to Peake in his records of communications made in furtherance of the conspiracy.

[6] Generally, there is a distinction between direct and indirect consumers in antitrust cases. *See Hanover Shoe, Inc. v. United Shoe Mach. Corp.*, 392 U.S. 481, 492-94 (1968). The harm to be [—20—] considered is only that to direct consumers. *See Ill. Brick Co. v. Illinois*, 431 U.S. 720, 752 (1977) ("Limiting defendants' liability to the loss of profits suffered by direct purchasers would thus allow the antitrust offender to avoid having to pay the full social cost of his illegal conduct in many cases in which indirect purchasers failed to bring suit.").

prosecutor's opening statement and clarify that jurors should not take into account the impact of the conspiracy on Puerto Rico's citizens. At the court's invitation, the parties submitted proposed curative instructions, and the district judge gave a version of the curative instruction to the jury that day.[7] [—21—]

Over Peake's objections, the government then called to the stand Gabriel Lafitte, who worked for the operator of Burger King restaurants in Puerto Rico, who testified that the conspiracy affected the costs paid by Burger King for products it sold on the island. Later in the trial, Ron Reynolds, a U.S. Department of Agriculture representative, testified to being offered "take-it-or-leave-it" rates for shipping services for food for school lunch programs in Puerto Rico.

After closing arguments, the jury began deliberations on the afternoon of Friday, January 25, 2013. While deliberating on the following Monday—January 28—the jury sent the district judge two notes, in which it stated that it could not reach a unanimous agreement. The second note, delivered on Monday evening after ten hours of deliberation, stated that each juror had reached a personal verdict, but that the jury as a whole was unable to reach unanimity. After the second note, Peake asked for a mistrial and the government asked for an *Allen* charge,[8] both of which the district court denied. Instead, the court asked the jury to "return [the next day] to continue deliberations." On Tuesday, the [—22—] jury

deliberated for another three hours and finally reached a unanimous guilty verdict.

After the verdict, Peake filed a Motion for New Trial and a Motion for Judgment of Acquittal under Federal Rules of Criminal Procedure 33 and 29 respectively, arguing, *inter alia*, that the district court erred in allowing the government to appeal to jury bias and prejudice, in refusing to give a theory-of-defense jury instruction, and in ordering the jury to continue deliberations.[9] The district court denied the motions. We turn now to Peake's appeal of the district court's various trial-related rulings.

A. Prosecutorial Misconduct

We address first Peake's argument that the district court should have granted him a new trial on grounds that the government's opening statement implied the conspiracy had impacted consumers, and therefore the jurors themselves, thus "poisoning the well."[10] [—23—]

---

[7] Near the end of trial, the court issued a memorandum opinion and order denying Peake's motion for a new trial, finding no misconduct [—21—] on the basis of the prosecutor's opening statement, but, even assuming misconduct, concluding that any prejudice was cured by the fact that the remarks were isolated, the jury was given a detailed curative instruction, and the objected-to statements did not bear on any elements of the charged offense.

[8] An *Allen* charge is "[a] supplemental jury instruction given by the court to encourage a deadlocked jury, after prolonged deliberations, to reach a verdict." Black's Law Dictionary (10th ed. 2014); *see Allen v. United States*, 164 U.S. 492 (1896).

[9] Peake does not appeal the district court's rulings on the other issues raised in the Rule 33 and 29 motions, which challenged the district court's denials of: (1) Peake's request to submit hearsay evidence from one of the co-conspirators; (2) Peake's objection to the admissibility of financial disclosures; and (3) Peake's request for a new trial on grounds that the government had failed to disclose exculpatory evidence in violation of *Brady v. Maryland*, 373 U.S. 83 (1963).

[10] Peake additionally claims that he was incorrectly prohibited from diminishing the negative effects of those statements because the government moved successfully to prohibit him from arguing that—despite the antitrust conspiracy—shipping costs remained reasonable and fair. But whether the agreed-upon prices charged by the conspirators were nonetheless fair or reasonable does not affect our conclusion. A *per se* Section 1 violation is not excused [—23—] by a showing that the supra-competitive prices were somehow still reasonable. *United States v. Socony-Vacuum Oil Co.*, 310 U.S. 150, 212-13 (1940); *see also United States v. Topco Assoc., Inc.*, 405 U.S. 596, 610 (1972) ("[N]aked restraints of trade are [not] to be tolerated because they are well intended or because they are allegedly developed to increase competition.").

In its opening statements, the government told the jury that "most consumer goods travel to Puerto Rico from the shipping lanes" affected by the conspiracy; that the conspiracy "was so significant that it affected billions of dollars of freight to and from Puerto Rico"; and that "[b]usinesses like Burger King, Office Max and Walgreens, businesses that have stores all over Puerto Rico, they were all paying more than they should have to ship freight to Puerto Rico because Sea Star and Horizon were conspiring, not competing." The government also told the jury that Burger King's shipping costs affected the price of hamburgers sold to customers, and that the federal government had incurred higher costs for the school lunch program, leaving it with "less money . . . to buy food for school children." The government added that the antitrust laws under which Peake was charged had been enacted out of the "concern[] that consumers need to buy things to feed and clothe their families."

Improper remarks by prosecutors are reviewed *de novo*. *United States v. Rodríguez*, 675 F.3d 48, 61 (1st Cir. 2012) (citing *United States v. Ayala-García*, 574 F.3d 5, 16 (1st Cir. 2009)). Even if misconduct occurred, we would still need to consider whether it was harmless. *United States v. González-Pérez*, 778 F.3d [—24—] 3, 19 (1st Cir. 2015), *cert. denied*, 135 S. Ct. 1911 (2015). In doing so, we determine whether the misconduct "so poisoned the well that the trial's outcome was likely affected, thus warranting a new trial." *Id.* (quoting *Rodríguez*, 675 F.3d at 62). "In making this determination, we focus on (1) the severity of the misconduct, including whether it was isolated and/or deliberate; (2) whether curative instructions were given; and (3) the strength of the evidence against the defendant." *Id.* at 19 (citing *Rodríguez*, 675 F.3d at 62).

Here, we agree that the prosecutor's remarks were improper. We therefore direct our inquiry at whether these statements were nonetheless harmless. As we explain, because of the extent and the level of detail the district court included in its curative instruction; the fact that the district judge intervened repeatedly in the examination of witnesses to

avoid any reference to end consumers; and the overwhelming amount of corroborating documentary evidence that tied Peake to the conspiracy, we conclude that the effects of the prosecutorial misconduct did not so poison the well that a new trial would be warranted.

First, the day after Peake filed his motion for a mistrial, the district court gave the jury the following comprehensive and detailed curative instruction:

> The fact that Puerto Rico may have potentially been affected or consumers and/or prices and/or business is not to be considered by [you] in your judgment as to the [—25—] innocence or guilt of the defendant. The effect on prices or consumers in Puerto Rico is not per se an element of the [offense].
>
> You are not to decide this case based on pity and sympathy to Puerto Rican businesses, to Puerto Rico, or to Puerto Rican consumers.
>
> The effect on Puerto Rico only is material as to potentially establishing an effect on interstate commerce. This case is about a potential conspiracy in violation of the antitrust law, and whether or not the defendant, Mr. Frank Peake, joined the conspiracy.
>
> Sympathy to Puerto Rico is, therefore, to play absolutely no role in your consideration of this case. Any statement that may have implied or that you may have understood that this is a case relating to the effect on Puerto Rico is an erroneous interpretation, and I don't want you to have that interpretation. So, therefore, any effect on Puerto Rico is not to be considered at all.

The court's instruction was arguably more detailed than the proposed instruction Peake submitted.[11] In addition, the district judge

---

[11] Peake's proposed curative instruction read as follows:

intervened in the questioning of the government's witnesses to prevent undue reference to the conspiracy's effect on Puerto [—26—] Rican consumers, and the instructions given to the jury after closing arguments again stressed these points. For example, they emphasized that the jury "must not be influenced by any personal likes or dislikes, prejudices or sympathy." The sixth instruction clarified that "[a]rguments and statements by lawyers are not evidence. The lawyers are not witnesses. What they say in their opening statements . . . and at other times . . . is not evidence." And the twenty-first instruction, labeled "What Not to Consider," contained the exact same curative instruction given to the jury on the fourth day of trial, with one important addition: instead of telling the jurors that the court did not want them to "have" an "erroneous interpretation" about statements implying that this case related to the effect on Puerto Rico, the court instructed, "I sternly order you not to take such statements into consideration."

We have stated that there is no miscarriage of justice requiring a new trial when there are curative instructions and the evidence does not "preponderate[] heavily against the verdict." *United States v. Mangual-García*, 505 F.3d 1, 14 (1st Cir. 2007) (quoting *United States v. Mooney*, 315 F.3d 54, 61 (1st Cir. 2002)). The degree of consideration and effort

---

I would like to instruct you that this case is not about pricing effects in Puerto Rico or whether prices in Puerto Rico have gone up or down. The only questions for you are whether there was a conspiracy as alleged in the indictment and whether Frank Peake knowingly and intentionally joined that conspiracy. I also instruct you that the prosecutor mentioned in opening statement that this case affected Puerto Rico and Puerto Ricans. This was improper. This case is not to be decided based on those factors. Therefore, I instruct you to disregard those comments. You should judge this case only on the evidence and not an appeal to sympathy or bias. Any such attempts by the prosecution in its opening statement or in the questioning of its witnesses should be disregarded.

on the part of the district court to respond to the defendant's valid concern over the prosecutors' appeal to the jury's personal interests allows us to conclude that it cured any prejudice. Indeed, curative instructions are "ordinarily an appropriate method of preempting a mistrial." *United States v. Trinidad-Acosta*, 773 F.3d 298, 308 [—27—] (1st Cir. 2014) (quoting *United States v. Sotomayor-Vázquez*, 249 F.3d 1, 18 (1st Cir. 2001)). We presume that juries follow instructions, *United States v. Gonzalez-Vázquez*, 219 F.3d 37, 48 (1st Cir. 2000), and there is nothing in the record to suggest that the instruction regarding the government's remarks was disregarded by the jury.

The strength of the government's corroborating evidence against Peake also supports our conclusion in this matter. *See Mangual-García*, 505 F.3d at 14 ("Nor can we say that the cumulative effect of the alleged errors, given the curative instructions that were given and the strength of the other evidence, constitutes a miscarriage of justice."); *Mooney*, 315 F.3d at 60 ("[W]e note that any lingering prejudicial effect from the remarks pales in comparison with the overwhelming strength of the government's evidence against the defendant."). Here, the government's case was robust. The testimony of co-conspirators and direct customers of the shipping companies established that there was a conspiracy to fix prices, that Peake knowingly participated, that the conspiracy had the effect of increasing shipping rates and surcharges, and that this affected interstate commerce. The government also introduced numerous exhibits, including emails sent by Peake himself from his company email, establishing the existence of a conspiracy. For example, in one email from July 11, 2005, Peake told Baci, his co-conspirator and subordinate, that he had learned that Horizon Lines had told Sea Star's clients that Horizon Lines [—28—] was willing to "work with them," and instructed Baci to come up with a "slap." Baci sent Horizon Lines an email the next day, expressing concern about the "level of distrust" building between Sea Star and Horizon Lines.

In another exchange between Peake and Serra from March 22, 2008, Peake complained to Serra that Horizon Lines had been "hurting" him by negotiating with Sea Star clients "Flexi, Goya, Atek and BK." Peake added a warning: "If you're swinging at Crowley[, one of the other freight carriers,] you are missing and hitting me." Serra responded with detailed information about Horizon Lines targeting certain clients and mentioned where he thought Sea Star would set prices. He concluded, "I'll have to go with the best info I have. Not sure communication and availability is working as well as it used to." Peake responded:

> BK I am not all that concerned about (we don't have much of that).
> I am the only one that will lose on ATEC, If I lose it (10 loads a week) I will have to fire back.
> Agree that things aren't working as well as they were. Pete [Baci] has similar complaints.
> Flexi is about fuel and you gave them a BSC discount. Tisk tisk.
> Goya is about you not charging for the overweight permits. Again tisk tisk. Same as cutting the rate in my book.

Serra wrote back, "I'll check them all . . . you are certainly not the target."

Given this fairly direct evidence of the conspiracy's existence, aims, and objectives, we find that the evidence presented at trial did not preponderate against the verdict. To [—29—] the contrary, the strength of the government's case weighs in favor of finding that the misconduct was harmless.[12] Thus, while we are concerned by the impropriety of the prosecutors' remarks, we are confident that the district court acted timely and decisively to instruct the jury in great detail to

---

[12] On this final point, we cannot ignore that a *per se* violation of Section 1 only requires that "an antitrust plaintiff [present] either direct or circumstantial evidence of defendants' 'conscious commitment to a common scheme designed to achieve an unlawful objective.'" *Evergreen Partnering Grp., Inc. v. Pactiv Corp.*, 720 F.3d 33, 43 (1st Cir. 2013) (quoting *Monsanto Co. v. Spray Rite Serv. Corp.*, 465 U.S. 752, 764 (1984)).

disregard the offending statements. And we are conscious that we should "not set guilty persons free simply to punish prosecutorial misconduct." *United States v. Vázquez-Botet*, 532 F.3d 37, 59 (1st Cir. 2008). The government's remarks did not so poison the well as to necessitate a new trial, and we affirm the district court's denial of a mistrial on grounds of prosecutorial misconduct.

B. Irrelevant and Unfairly Prejudicial Evidence

Peake argues that the district court also erred in permitting the testimony from witnesses involved in businesses harmed by the conspiracy because the testimony implied that the conspiracy impacted Puerto Rican consumers, therefore again causing the jurors to consider themselves victims of the charged conspiracy. Peake claims the testimony should have been excluded under Federal Rules of Evidence 402 and 403 either as irrelevant or because it caused "unfair prejudice" and had an "undue tendency to [—30—] suggest decision on an improper basis, commonly, though not necessarily, an emotional one." Fed. R. Evid. 403 advisory committee's note to 1972 proposed rules; *see also* Fed. R. Evid. 402 ("Irrelevant evidence is not admissible."); Fed. R. Evid. 403 ("The court may exclude relevant evidence if its probative value is substantially outweighed by a danger of . . . unfair prejudice . . . .").

We review a trial court's objected-to evidentiary rulings for abuse of discretion. *United States v. Romero-López*, 695 F.3d 17, 22 (1st Cir. 2012); *United States v. Rodríguez–Berríos*, 573 F.3d 55, 60 (1st Cir. 2009). That includes a trial court's determination under Rule 403 that evidence is more probative than prejudicial. *See United States v. Ramírez-Rivera*, Nos. 13-2285, 13-2289, 13-2291, 13-2320, 2015 WL 5025225, at *26 (1st Cir. Aug. 26, 2015) (citing *Walker*, 665 F.3d at 229).

Rule 403 "requires the trial court to exclude the evidence if its probative value is substantially outweighed by 'the danger of unfair prejudice.'" *United States v. Varoudakis*, 233 F.3d 113, 121 (1st Cir. 2000) (quoting Fed. R. Evid. 403). This analysis "'is a quintessentially fact-sensitive enterprise' which the district court is in the best position to make." *United States v. Soto*, Nos. 13-2343, 13-2344, 13-2350, 2015 WL 5011456, at *17 (1st Cir. Aug. 25, 2015) (quoting *United States v. Joubert*, 778 F.3d 247, 255 (1st Cir. 2015), *cert. denied*, 135 S. Ct. 2874 (2015)). All evidence is by design prejudicial, *Varoudakis*, 233 [—31—] F.3d at 122, but unfair prejudice refers "to the capacity of some concededly relevant evidence to lure the factfinder into declaring guilt on a ground different from proof specific to the offense charged." *United States v. DiRosa*, 761 F.3d 144, 153 (1st Cir. 2014) (quoting *Old Chief v. United States*, 519 U.S. 172, 180 (1997)). One such example is when "the evidence 'invites the jury to render a verdict on an improper emotional basis.'" *United States v. Landry*, 631 F.3d 597, 604 (1st Cir. 2011) (quoting *Varoudakis*, 233 F.3d at 122).

An abuse of discretion finding on a Rule 403 ruling "is not an easy one to make" and "only in 'extraordinarily compelling circumstances'" would we reverse the judgment of the district court. *DiRosa*, 761 F.3d at 154 (quoting *United States v. Doe*, 741 F.3d 217, 229 (1st Cir. 2013)); *see also Landry*, 631 F.3d at 604 ("Rule 403 judgments are typically battlefield determinations, and great deference is owed to the trial court's superior coign of vantage." (quoting *United States v. Shinderman*, 515 F.3d 5, 17 (1st Cir. 2008))).

Guided by the above framework, we do not find that the district court abused its discretion in permitting the testimony of representatives from businesses affected by the conspiracy. The witnesses never stated that the higher costs incurred by the direct customers of the shipping companies were indirectly transferred to their consumers, and the defense was also allowed to strike questions regarding the effect of the increased costs on the [—32—] businesses' bottom line. The testimony elicited by the government properly established the effects of fixing prices and rigging bids. After all, the conspiracy's effect on interstate commerce was an element of the offense the government was required to establish. *See Nat'l Collegiate Athletic Ass'n v. Bd. of Regents of Univ. of Okla.*, 468 U.S. 85, 104 (1984) ("Under the Sherman Act the criterion to be used in judging the validity of a restraint on trade is its impact on competition."). The government's examination of the witnesses was limited to establishing that element. Therefore, we find no abuse of discretion, and affirm the district court's ruling permitting the witnesses' testimony.

C. Theory of Defense Instruction

Peake next argues that he is entitled to a new trial because he was improperly denied his requested theory-of-defense jury instruction. Specifically, Peake requested the following instruction:

Mr. Peake does not contest that there was a conspiracy that existed between Gabriel Serra, Kevin Gill, Gregory Glova, and Peter Baci. Rather, he contends that he did not knowingly and intentionally participate in this conspiracy and did not knowingly and intentionally join the conspiracy as a member. Mr. Peake further contends that any discussions he had with Gabriel Serra were legitimate and competitive discussions and not anti-competitive conspiracy related. Mr. Peake also contends that he was competing with Horizon, including on market share and price.

Although this is Mr. Peake's defense, the burden always remains on the government to prove the elements of the offense beyond a reasonable doubt. If you do not believe the government has proven beyond a reasonable doubt that [—33—] Mr. Peake intentionally and knowingly joined the conspiracy, you must find him not guilty.

A defendant is "entitled to an instruction on his theory of defense so long as the theory is a valid one and there is evidence in the record to support it." *United States v. McGill*, 953 F.2d 10, 12 (1st Cir. 1992) (internal citation omitted). However, "the defendant has no right to put words in the judge's mouth. So long as the charge sufficiently conveys the defendant's theory, it need not parrot the exact language that the defendant prefers." *Id.* A district court's denial of a theory of defense instruction is reviewed *de novo. United States v. Baird*, 712 F.3d 623, 627-28 (1st Cir. 2013). But a trial court's refusal to give a particular instruction constitutes reversible error only if the requested instruction (1) was correct as a matter of law, (2) was not substantially incorporated into the charges as rendered, and (3) was integral to an important point in the case. *Id.* at 628.

Here, regardless of whether Peake should have been granted his instruction, there is no reversible error because the district court offered essentially the same instruction Peake requested, just in its own words. First, the instructions the district court gave stated that "the Government [must prove to the jury] that Mr. Peake is guilty of the crime with which he is charged beyond a reasonable doubt." Second, they mentioned that the government bears the burden of proving that Peake "knowingly and intentionally became a member of the conspiracy" and that the [—34—] "conspiracy . . . affected interstate commerce." Third, the instructions referenced the possibility that "competitors may have legitimate, lawful reasons to have contact with each other," and that "similarity of conduct . . . does not necessarily establish the existence of a conspiracy," because "there would be no conspiracy . . . [i]f actions were taken independently by them solely as a matter of individual business judgment." Comparing these passages with Peake's proposed instruction, we cannot conclude that anything Peake asked for was excluded. There is therefore no reversible error.

D. Jury Deliberations

The last trial-related argument Peake raises is that the district court erred in its response to the two notes from the jury, both received on the second day of deliberations, in which the jury stated it was not able to reach a unanimous verdict. Both times, the district judge sent a note back to the jury, asking the jurors to "continue deliberation." Peake argues that the district court should have declared a

mistrial after the second note because it was clear that the jury was at an impasse. Peake also argues that, if the court was going to respond to the note, it was at least required to include in its reply the three elements normally required in an *Allen* charge.

For some background, when a jury is deadlocked, the trial court may deliver an *Allen* charge, directing the jury to decide the [—35—] case if at all possible. Given the potential coerciveness of such an instruction, our case law holds that such a charge must be balanced by instructions that (1) communicate the possibility of the majority and minority of the jury reexamining their personal verdicts; (2) restate the government's maintenance of the burden of proof; and (3) inform the jury that they may fail to agree unanimously. *United States v. Angiulo*, 485 F.2d 37, 39 (1st Cir. 1973).

We review the district court's decision not to declare a mistrial or to provide additional guidance to a jury for abuse of discretion, *United States v. Vanvliet*, 542 F.3d 259, 266 (1st Cir. 2008), and we find there was no abuse of discretion here.

First, we note that the jury sent its notes on Monday afternoon and evening, during its first full day of deliberations, after having deliberated for only hours on Friday. It was thus not an abuse of discretion for the district court to conclude that, particularly after a nine-day trial, the jury needed more time to consider the evidence before a mistrial might be considered.

Second, the district judge's response to the jury, instructing it to "continue deliberations," was not an *Allen* charge, and therefore did not require the supplemental balancing instructions normally required in an *Allen* charge.[13] In a similar case, *United States v. Figueroa-Encarnación*, 343 F.3d 23, 31-32 [—36—] (1st Cir. 2003), we held that a district judge's instruction to the jury to go home, relax, and continue deliberations the following day contained no coercive elements and, as

---

[13] Indeed, we agree that it would have been premature to give one at this early point in the deliberations, after a nine-day trial.

such, was not an *Allen* charge requiring supplemental instructions. Likewise, here, the district court simply asked the jury to rest and come back in the morning to continue deliberations. This was no *Allen* charge. Accordingly, we find no abuse of discretion in the district court's response to the jury's notes during deliberation.

VI. Sentencing

As a final matter, Peake argues that, even if his conviction is not overturned, he should be resentenced. Peake raises only one argument regarding his sentence: that the district court incorrectly calculated the volume of commerce affected by the conspiracy, and therefore improperly applied, among other offense-level enhancements, a twelve-level enhancement under section 2R1.1 of the United States Sentencing Guidelines (U.S.S.G.). We deny the appeal of the sentence, finding that the district court correctly applied the sentencing guidelines.

We review a district court's interpretation and application of the sentencing guidelines *de novo. United States v. Stoupis*, 530 F.3d 82, 84 (1st Cir. 2008). However, "we will not upset the sentencing court's fact-based application of the guidelines unless it is clearly erroneous." *United States v. Santos-Batista*, 239 F.3d 16, 21 (1st Cir. 2001). [—37—]

For antitrust offenses affecting a volume of commerce of more than $1 million, the sentencing guidelines provide that the offense level should be adjusted by a certain number of levels according to the volume of commerce that was affected by the conspiracy, as indicated by a table provided therein. *See* U.S.S.G. § 2R1.1(b)(2). The district court found that more than $500 million in commerce was affected, and that a twelve-level enhancement applied under § 2R1.1(b)(2)(F). Peake argues the volume of commerce was, at most, approximately $386.2 million, and therefore only a ten-level enhancement should have been applied under § 2R1.1(b)(2)(E). He contends that, in calculating the volume of affected commerce, the district court erroneously included commercial activity that took place before

2005, which is when the indictment charged Peake with joining the conspiracy, and that the court also included commerce that was unaffected by the conspiracy.

After a thorough review of the sentencing record, we find that the district court did not err in determining that the affected volume of commerce was more than $500 million. First, the record shows that the district court would have reached its more-than-$500 million number for the volume of affected commerce even without including commerce that might have occurred before 2005, when Peake is charged with joining the conspiracy. So we will move on to Peake's second argument that the district court incorrectly [—38—] included in its calculation what he contends was "unaffected" commerce.

In calculating the "volume of commerce," the district court is to consider not just "the damage caused or profit made by the defendant," but the overall amount of sales during the conspiracy. *Id.* at § 2R1.1(b)(2) & cmt. 7 ("[T]he volume of commerce attributable to an individual participant in a conspiracy is the volume of commerce done by him or his principal in goods or services that were affected by the violation."); *see also United States v. Andreas*, 216 F.3d 645, 678 (7th Cir. 2000) ("[I]t is reasonable to conclude that *all sales* made by defendants during that period are 'affected.'" (quoting *United States v. SKW Metals & Alloys, Inc.*, 195 F.3d 83, 90 (2d Cir. 1999)) (emphasis added)). Although there is a presumption that all sales made during the conspiracy were affected, and should therefore be included in the volume of commerce calculation, this is a presumption that the defendant may rebut by offering evidence that some sales were not affected. *United States v. Giordano*, 261 F.3d 1134, 1146 (11th Cir. 2001).

In this case, the district court had before it data produced by Sea Star indicating that its total revenue between 2005 and 2008 amounted to over $565 million, and it used this number to conclude that the twelve-level enhancement applied. Peake argues that this was an error because the following revenue was "unaffected" commerce and should have been subtracted from the [—39—] total: (1) revenue from non-container freight that he contends was not a part of the antitrust conspiracy, (2) revenue from 2,634 customers that were never discussed in the conspiracy, (3) revenue from fuel surcharges, which Peake argues would have been charged even if there had been no conspiracy, and (4) revenue from Transportation Services Agreements, which Peake claims were routine and entirely lawful, and did not affect interstate commerce. However, in order to exclude this revenue from the volume of affected commerce calculations, Peake was required to show that these transactions were "completely unaffected" by the conspiracy. *Andreas*, 216 F.3d at 678-79. The district court found that Peake failed to do so.

This is essentially a factual question, and we find no clear error in the district court's findings that the objected-to revenue should have been included in the volume of commerce calculation. Testimony, particularly Baci's, and documentary evidence, including various emails, presented at trial showed that the conspirators had colluded to fix the fuel surcharges, and that revenue from the fuel surcharge was therefore a part of the conspiracy. The fixed surcharges affected all cargo transported, thus affecting all sales, including revenue from non-container freight and from all customers, even if that freight and those customers had never explicitly been made a part of the conspiracy. Finally, evidence at trial showed that Transportation Services Agreements were used in furtherance of the conspiracy. Thus, [—40—] finding no error in the district court's computation of a volume of affected commerce in excess of $500 million, we affirm the sentence.

VII. Conclusion

For the foregoing reasons, the conviction and sentence of Defendant-Appellant Frank Peake is

AFFIRMED.

United States Court of Appeals
for the First Circuit

No. 13-2155

UNITED STATES
vs.
PEÑA-SANTO

Appeal from the United States District Court for the
District of Puerto Rico

Decided: October 14, 2015

Citation: 809 F.3d 686, 3 Adm. R. 98 (1st Cir. 2015).

Before **TORRUELLA**, **SELYA**, and **DYK**,* Circuit
Judges.

*Of the Federal Circuit, sitting by designation.

[—3—] **TORRUELLA**, Circuit Judge:

Defendants-Appellants José Peña-Santo ("Peña-Santo"), José Ramón Vicente-Arias ("Vicente-Arias"), Jonathan Joel Gil-Martínez ("Gil-Martínez"), and Manuel Liriano de la Cruz ("Liriano") (collectively "Appellants") were jointly tried and convicted of conspiring to import cocaine and heroin into the United States, in violation of 21 U.S.C. §§ 952(a), 960, and 963, and conspiring to possess with intent to distribute cocaine and heroin on board a vessel subject to the jurisdiction of the United States, in violation of 46 U.S.C. §§ 70503(a)(1), 70504(b)(1), 70506(a). Peña-Santo and Liriano were additionally convicted of illegally reentering the United States, in violation of 8 U.S.C. § 1326(a)(2) and (b)(1). Appellants appeal their conspiracy convictions mainly on the grounds that improper expert testimony and the government's conduct warrant reversal of their convictions. They also assign error to the denial of their motions for judgments of acquittal. Finally, Gil-Martínez challenges the substantive reasonableness of his sentence. We have reviewed Appellants' claims carefully and do not find merit in any of them. Accordingly, we affirm.

I. *Facts*[1]

On the night of April 12, 2012, Ryan Perry, a Customs and Border Patrol ("CBP") agent working as a camera operator and [—4—] patrolling the waters from an aircraft, detected a target of interest with "lights out" seventeen nautical miles off the coast of Dorado, Puerto Rico, around 10:00 p.m. The target was a blue-colored wooden yola,[2] between twenty and twenty-five feet long, riding "very low" in the water, and carrying two motors and six fuel drums. A Maritime Patrol aircraft, along with the U.S. Coast Guard marine unit, the Puerto Rico Joint Forces of Rapid Action ("FURA," for its Spanish acronym), and a CBP helicopter, coordinated an intercept of the suspect vessel. When the Coast Guard marine unit approached the vessel, the individuals were moving "erratically" on the boat. Perry saw "objects being thrown from the yola." Another officer who joined the interception of the vessel, Luke Berguis from the Coast Guard, reported seeing "large, heavy bags being tossed over by the multiple crew members," as well as "small backpacks" and "smaller objects" that looked like cell phones and GPS units. Agent René Galarza, of U.S. Immigration and Customs Enforcement ("ICE"), after turning the helicopter's spotlight on the vessel also saw "individuals dumping what appeared to be bales."

At approximately 11:39 p.m., nearly four miles off the coast of Dorado, the Coast Guard marine unit intercepted the yola, which had six men on board, and ordered the men to raise their [—5—] hands, which they did after some initial hesitance. FURA, along with the Coast Guard marine unit, later retrieved the objects that had been thrown into the water, which turned out to be "six heavy dark colored [gym] bags wrapped in duct tape" that each had a "block shape." Inside the bags were eight kilograms of 50% pure heroin packaged

---

[1] We briefly summarize the relevant facts, reserving for our analysis a more detailed discussion of the facts relevant to each issue presented on appeal.

[2] A yola is a small fishing boat. For purposes of this opinion, "yola" and "vessel" will be used interchangeably.

in eight egg shapes and 146.5 kilograms of 74.8% pure cocaine packaged in 131 brick shapes. The six men, identified as Peña-Santo, Vicente-Arias, Gil-Martínez, Liriano, Bonifacio Toribio-Almonte, and Alejandro Difot-Santos, all citizens of the Dominican Republic, were arrested.

A grand jury returned a superseding indictment charging the six men with conspiracy to import cocaine and heroin into the United States, in violation of 21 U.S.C. §§ 952(a), 960, and 963 (Count 1), and conspiracy to possess with intent to distribute cocaine and heroin on board a vessel subject to the jurisdiction of the United States, in violation of 46 U.S.C. §§ 70503(a)(1), 70504(b)(1), 70506(a) (Count 2). Peña-Santo and Liriano were also charged with illegally reentering the United States, in violation of 8 U.S.C. § 1326(a)(2), (b)(1), respectively (Counts 3 and 4).[3] Difot-Santos and Toribio-Almonte pleaded guilty while Appellants were jointly tried. [—6—]

At trial the government presented the testimony of Perry, Berghuis, Galarza, Andrew Resk, and Joel Candelario, all of whom participated in the interception of the yola on April 12, 2012. Berghuis testified that wooden boats with low profiles and no navigation lights, such as the yola used by Appellants, are harder to see and to pick up on radar. He further testified that Appellants' yola was painted blue on both the outside and the inside, which made it "very hard to see at night" from an "aerial aspect"; that it had excessive horsepower and fuel for its size; and that it did not have any fishing or other recreational gear on board. Instead, it carried multiple open condoms, which, based on his experience, are often used to keep dry small objects such as wallets and cell phones. Berghuis also identified Appellants in court as four of the six men on board the yola when it was intercepted and testified that he observed

that more than one individual was needed to lift the bags which had been thrown overboard when the yola was approached by law enforcement.

The government also presented the testimony of Víctor Taboada, who was on patrol on the Coast Guard Cutter Cushing on the night of the interception; Abel Nasser, who works with ICE and the Department of Homeland Security; and Carmen Cacho ("Ms. Cacho"), a chemist employed by CBP. They testified about the type, purity, quantity, and weight of the narcotics recovered during the interception of the yola. [—7—]

In addition, the government presented the testimony of Drug Enforcement Administration agent Christopher Conchin ("Agent Conchin"), who had experience in narcotic cases and international maritime interdictions. The district court qualified Agent Conchin as an expert witness and allowed him to testify as to the value, packaging, and mode of transportation of narcotics. Agent Conchin testified regarding how narcotics' street price depends on the place of sale. He also testified that drugs are usually wrapped in plastic and packaged in same-size bricks. As to the mode of transportation, Agent Conchin testified that drugs are typically transported in go-fast boats or yolas, which are usually painted blue to blend in with the water, have more than one motor (usually two or three), are either open or have a compartment to "put stuff underneath," and carry numerous gasoline drums that are switched off during the voyage. In addition, he testified that vessels transporting narcotics generally have four to six people on board and that each has a specific duty. He further testified that, in his experience, "in the cases that [he has] worked, . . . individuals not connected with the trafficking of narcotics" have not been involved in the transportation.

After a four-day jury trial, Appellants were found guilty on all charges. Appellants moved for a judgment of acquittal [—8—] pursuant to Fed. R. Crim. P. 29, which the district court

---

[3] Peña-Santo and Liriano stipulated to the fact that they had been previously removed from the United States and that they had no petition pending with the U.S. Citizenship and Immigration Services to enter the United States lawfully. Peña-Santo further stipulated to the fact that he had a previous felony conviction.

denied.[4] The district court sentenced Peña-Santo to 120 months in prison, Vicente-Arias to 130 months, Gil-Martínez to 192 months, and Liriano to 240 months. In addition, they were each sentenced to five years of supervised release. These timely appeals followed.

II. *Discussion of Appellants' Claims*

A. Expert Testimony

1. Background

The government intended Agent Conchin to testify as to "the quantity of the narcotics, the value of the narcotics, and . . . to the fact that [Appellants] weren't just by happenstance" in the vessel. Appellants questioned the need for his testimony, arguing that the question before the jury of whether they were part of a conspiracy to distribute drugs did not require complex insight. The district court allowed the witness to testify only with respect to the value, packaging, and mode of transportation of drugs.

At trial, Agent Conchin testified that, in his experience, random people unconnected to drug trafficking would not be on board vessels with drugs. According to him,

> [t]he people that are on those boats are there for one purpose, and that's to get the drugs to where they're going, and they're there for protection. They're there to switch out the [—9—] hoses like I mentioned, because you can't do it with just [one] person. You have the captain who is the navigator to get you to where it's going, the exact point. You have a mechanic in case it breaks down and you have problems on the water. Everybody has a duty, a specific duty.

Appellants claim that the district court abused its discretion in allowing Agent Conchin to testify about the different roles of individuals on board vessels transporting drugs. They argue that this testimony should

have been stricken from the record because it exceeded the scope of the topics allowed by the district court. In addition, they claim that Agent Conchin improperly identified the roles of the Appellants in the charged conspiracy without having personal knowledge of it and that he addressed the ultimate issue for the jury—whether Appellants were members of the conspiracy and possessed the intent to import and distribute narcotics—which is prohibited by Rule 704(b) of the Federal Rules of Evidence and constitutes reversible error pursuant to this court's holdings in *United States v. Meises*, 645 F.3d 5 (1st Cir. 2011); *United States v. Flores-De-Jesús*, 569 F.3d 8 (1st Cir. 2009); and *United States v. Casas*, 356 F.3d 104 (1st Cir. 2004). We disagree.

2. Applicable Law and Analysis

It is well established that the district court "enjoys leeway in deciding to admit or exclude expert testimony." *United States v. Ladd*, 885 F.2d 954, 959 (1st Cir. 1989). Rulings on [—10—] preserved evidentiary objections are reviewed for abuse of discretion. *Casas*, 356 F.3d at 113. Review of unobjected-to evidentiary rulings is for plain error. *Id*. Under this exacting standard, an appellant must show that (1) there was an error, (2) which was clear or obvious, (3) that affected his substantial rights, and (4) also seriously impaired the fairness, integrity, or public reputation of judicial proceedings. *United States v. De Jesús-Viera*, 655 F.3d 52, 57 (1st Cir. 2011). Because Appellants did not meaningfully object to the testimony they now challenge, our review is for plain error.

Appellants' first argument—that Agent Conchin's testimony was inadmissible because it exceeded the scope of the topics allowed by the district court—falls flat at the outset. The district court allowed Agent Conchin to testify about the "mode of transportation" of drugs. Appellants cannot show that interpreting "mode of transportation" to include not only the physical description of vessels used to transport drugs, but also the process itself of transporting drugs in such vessels and the roles people perform while transporting the drugs amounts to error, much less clear or

---

[4] They also requested a new trial pursuant to Fed. R. Crim. P. 33, which was also denied.

obvious error. Thus, Appellants' claim cannot survive plain-error review.

Appellants' second argument suffers the same fate. "For expert testimony to be admissible under Fed. R. Evid. 702, it must 'be relevant to the task at hand' and helpful to the jury in its [—11—] deliberations." *United States v. García-Morales*, 382 F.3d 12, 18 (1st Cir. 2004) (quoting *United States v. López-López*, 282 F.3d 1, 14 (1st Cir. 2002)). This court has approved the admission of expert testimony regarding "the operation of criminal schemes and activities" in drug trafficking cases, finding such testimony relevant and "helpful to juries in understanding some obscure or complex aspect of the crime." *Id*. at 18-19 (quoting *United States v. Montas*, 41 F.3d 775, 783 (1st Cir. 1994) (noting that "expert testimony regarding the description of a typical drug network [is] relevant to provide context to the jury in evaluating the offenses charged" (alteration in original) (internal quotation marks and citation omitted) (quoting *United States v. Clarke*, 24 F.3d 257, 269 (D.C. Cir. 1994)); *see also, e.g.*, *Flores-de-Jesús*, 569 F.3d at 26 (holding that the expert witness "properly described the operation of drug points generally, including the various 'roles' typically involved in an intricate drug conspiracy and the practice of storing drugs intended for sale"); *Ladd*, 885 F.2d at 960 (holding that because "jurors are not expected to be familiar with the idiom and workings of the heroin community . . . [e]xpert interpretation of drug jargon and practices, supplied by one versed in the business, has often been admitted to assist the trier of fact in drug-trafficking cases").

The leeway enjoyed by the district court in determining the scope of expert witness testimony is limited by Rule 704(b) of [—12—] the Federal Rules of Evidence, which prohibits an expert witness from testifying that a "defendant did or did not have the mental state or condition that constitutes an element of the crime charged." Fed. R. Evid. 704(b). "This bar does not, however, apply to 'predicate facts from which a jury might infer such intent.'" *United States v. Schneiderhan*, 404 F.3d 73, 81 (1st Cir. 2005) (quoting *United States v. Valle*, 72 F.3d 210, 216 (1st Cir. 1995)).

Here, Agent Conchin provided proper expert testimony. Appellants do not contest that the challenged testimony was relevant. In addition, because the nature of narcotics trafficking by vessels is likely outside the knowledge of the average layman, we find that Agent Conchin's testimony was likely to assist the jury in understanding the evidence or determining a fact at issue. *See* Fed. R. Evid. 702; *Ladd*, 885 F.2d at 960.

Furthermore, contrary to Appellants' contentions, Agent Conchin's testimony was not disallowed by *Meises*, *Flores-de-Jesús*, or *Casas*. In those cases we "particularly condemned testimony from . . . agent[s], not based on personal knowledge, describing the roles played in the drug conspiracy by individual defendants" because "[s]uch descriptions amount to impermissible testimony from the agent[s] 'that each of the defendants was guilty of the conspiracy charged.'" *Meises*, 645 F.3d at 13 (quoting *Casas*, 356 F.3d at 119); *see also Flores-de-Jesús*, 569 F.3d at 24 (holding [—13—] that the court erred in allowing the expert witness to identify the appellants by name and role in the conspiracy, where this testimony was not based on his personal knowledge); *Casas*, 356 F.3d at 118, 120 (stating that the agent's testimony, which identified the roles of each defendant in the drug conspiracy despite lacking personal knowledge of it, was not an appropriate subject for expert testimony). Unlike in the cases cited by Appellants, Agent Conchin did not identify Appellants' roles in the charged conspiracy, nor did he even refer to Appellants in particular or to their yola. Rather, based on his experience in narcotics cases and international maritime interdictions, he referred to "the people that are on those boats" as he testified about the general roles involved in the transportation of drugs by vessels. Thus, he did not need to have personal knowledge of Appellants' specific roles in the charged conspiracy; his testimony was in line with our precedent. *See Flores-de-Jesús*, 569 F.3d at 26 (allowing an expert witness to describe "the operation of drug points generally, including the various 'roles' typically involved in an intricate drug conspiracy"); *García-Morales*, 382 F.3d at 18-19; *Ladd*, 885 F.2d at 960.

In addition, Agent Conchin's testimony did not encroach upon the jury's factfinding function regarding the ultimate issue of guilt. He merely provided facts from which the jury could infer culpable intent. *See Schneiderhan*, 404 F.3d at 81; *United States* [—14—] v. *DiMarzo*, 80 F.3d 656, 659-60 (1st Cir. 1996) (holding under similar circumstances that the agent's testimony that "in his experience, innocent observers are not invited to accompany criminals engaged in completing a drug deal" did not "encroach upon the jury's factfinding function regarding the ultimate issue of guilt"); *see also United States v. Valencia-Amezcua*, 278 F.3d 901, 909 (9th Cir. 2002) (allowing expert witness to testify about the "aversion of large-scale methamphetamine producers to allow unaffiliated individuals near clandestine operations"). Moreover, the district court clearly instructed the jury that "mere presence" on the yola was insufficient to establish guilt and that it was for the jury to decide whether the government had met its burden of proving the necessary mens rea. *See DiMarzo*, 80 F.3d at 660. Therefore, there was no error, plain or otherwise, in allowing Agent Conchin's testimony.

We note, however, one improper statement made by Agent Conchin during cross-examination. Because Agent Conchin's descriptions about drug trafficking referred to millions of dollars of profit, Liriano's defense counsel asked Agent Conchin in cross-examination whether he knew if Liriano had any possessions, such as a house or jewelry. Agent Conchin began to respond, "To answer your question, obviously people that transport drugs such as your client," but did not finish his response because he was immediately interrupted by defense counsel, who—although he did not object [—15—] to Agent Conchin's statement—said, "That's not my question." On appeal, Peña-Santo—but not Liriano—claims that this response constituted improper testimony on his guilt. Because Peña-Santo neither objected to nor moved to strike to the statement, we review only for plain error. *De Jesús-Viera*, 655 F.3d at 57.

Peña-Santos's claim fails under that stringent standard because he is unable to satisfy plain-error review's third and fourth prongs; that is, that it affected his substantial rights and that it seriously affected the fairness, integrity, or public reputation of the judicial proceedings. *Id.* Such an effect cannot be attributed to a "single, isolated [and fleeting] statement" like this one, which was made in response to a question by defense counsel regarding a matter outside the scope of Agent Conchin's testimony. *See United States v. Trinidad-Acosta*, 773 F.3d 298, 307 (1st Cir. 2014).

B. Sufficiency of the Evidence

Appellants claim reversible error by the district court in the denial of their respective motions for judgments of acquittal. *See* Fed. R. Crim. P. 29. They argue that the government demonstrated only that they were "merely present" on the vessel and that there was no evidence that they agreed to import or possess with intent to distribute the drugs. They also claim that the evidence presented at trial was consistent with their defense, [—16—] namely, that they were attempting to enter the United States illegally. We disagree.

1. Standard / Scope of Review

We review *de novo* the district court's denial of a Rule 29 motion for judgment of acquittal. *Trinidad-Acosta*, 773 F.3d at 310. In so doing, we view the evidence in the light most favorable to the jury's verdict, giving "equal weight to direct and circumstantial evidence." *United States v. Appolon*, 715 F.3d 362, 367 (1st Cir. 2013). We evaluate the sum of all the evidence and inferences drawn therefrom, and determine whether that sum is enough for any reasonable jury to find all the elements of the crime proven beyond a reasonable doubt. *United States v. Shaw*, 670 F.3d 360, 362 (1st Cir. 2012) ("Individual pieces of evidence viewed in isolation may be insufficient in themselves to prove a point, but in cumulation may indeed meet the mark."). Also, "[w]e do not assess the credibility of a witness, as that is a role reserved for the jury. Nor need we be convinced that the government succeeded in eliminating every possible theory consistent with the defendant's innocence." *Trinidad–Acosta*, 773 F.3d at 310–11 (quoting *United States v. Troy*, 583 F.3d 20, 24 (1st Cir. 2009)). We will uphold the verdict unless the evidence is so scant that a rational factfinder could not conclude that the government proved all the essential elements of the charged crime beyond a reasonable doubt. *United States v. Azubike*, 564 F.3d 59, [—17—] 64 (1st Cir. 2009). Accordingly, "defendants challenging convictions for insufficiency of evidence face an uphill battle on appeal." *United States v. Lipscomb*, 539 F.3d 32, 40 (1st Cir. 2008) (alterations omitted) (quoting *United States v. O'Shea*, 426 F.3d 475, 479 (1st Cir. 2005).

To sustain a drug-conspiracy conviction, the government must prove beyond a reasonable doubt that the defendant "knew about and voluntarily participated in the conspiracy, 'intending to commit the underlying substantive offense.'" *United States v. Acosta–Colón*, 741 F.3d 179, 190 (1st Cir. 2013) (quoting *United States v. Ortiz de Jesús*, 230 F.3d 1, 5 (1st Cir. 2000)). "An agreement to join a conspiracy may be express or tacit, and may be proved by direct or circumstantial evidence." *Trinidad–Acosta*, 773 F.3d at 311 (quoting *United States v. Liriano*, 761 F.3d 131, 135 (1st Cir. 2014)).

Appellants are right that their "'mere presence' at the scene of criminal activity is not enough" to convict them. *See United States v. Guerrero*, 114 F.3d 332, 342 (1st Cir. 1997). However, they grossly underestimate the strong circumstantial evidence supporting the jury's conclusion of guilt.

The evidence presented at trial, viewed in the light most favorable to the jury's verdict, showed that Appellants, along with two co-defendants, traveled from the Dominican Republic to the coast of Dorado, Puerto Rico, on a twenty-to-twenty-five-foot [—18—] wooden yola, which was painted blue both on the inside and outside to blend in with the water, had no navigation lights, and was riding "very low" in the water. Its lack of lights, low profile, color, and material made it very hard to be seen or be picked up on radar. It also had excessive horsepower and fuel for its size, and did not have any fishing or recreational gear on board. Instead, it carried six "block shape[d]" gym bags wrapped in duct tape, containing more than $3 million worth of heroin and cocaine. These bags were in plain view of everyone on board the yola.

Once the individuals on board the yola detected that they had been spotted by law enforcement, they started moving "erratically" on the boat, and "multiple crew members" started throwing the six bags, as well as small backpacks and objects that looked like cell phones and GPS units, into the water. The six bags were so large and heavy that more than one individual was needed to lift and throw each one overboard. Two different witnesses identified all four Appellants in open court as four of the six individuals on board the intercepted yola. There was also testimony that, when initially intercepted by law enforcement, Appellants first hesitated to comply with the officers' orders to stay put and raise their hands.

Furthermore, the jury also heard testimony from expert witness Agent Conchin about the way drugs are usually packaged (in "same size bricks"), the type of vessels used to transport drugs, [—19—] and the roles of people involved in the maritime transportation of narcotics.

This evidence, which included lay and expert witness testimony, a video,[5] and multiple photos,[6] coupled with the inferences that may be drawn therefrom, was enough for a reasonable jury to conclude beyond a reasonable doubt that Appellants were guilty of the conspiracy charges against them. Our conclusion is consistent with our precedent. For example, in *United States v. Cuevas-Esquivel*, 905 F.2d 510 (1st Cir. 1990), the defendants, who were apprehended on a thirty-to-forty-foot boat surrounded by

---

[5] On the video, the jury could see individuals on board the yola tossing bags overboard and law enforcement recovering them from the water, as well as the individuals' erratic movements when they were first detected by law enforcement and their hesitance to comply with the order to raise their hands.

[6] There were photos of the yola and the bags and drugs recovered from the water.

floating bales of marihuana, raised arguments similar to those pressed by Appellants here. In rejecting their argument of "mere presence," this court held that

> [r]ationality support[ed] the jury's finding. The jury could without undue strain conclude that it was simply incredible that with only four persons on board a relatively small vessel, on its way to "nowhere," with an open cargo hold, surrounded by a sea of floating marihuana bales which some of the crew had been seen dumping, that all four were not participants in this criminal venture. It is entirely reasonable for the jury to conclude that conspirators, engaged in conduct which by its nature is kept secret from outsiders, [—20—] would not allow the presence of innocent bystanders. Neither juries nor judges are required to divorce themselves of common sense, where, as here, the appellant's portrayal of himself as an innocent bystander is inherently unbelievable.

Id. at 515 (internal quotation marks and citation omitted) (quoting *United States v. Smith*, 680 F.2d 255, 260 (1st Cir. 1982)); *see also United States v. Rosa-Cariño*, 615 F.3d 75, 81 (1st Cir. 2010) (noting that "[d]rug smugglers handling . . . valuable drugs are unlikely to involve unknowledgeable outsiders"); *Guerrero*, 114 F.3d at 342 (noting that "where the circumstantial evidence permits a jury to conclude that activities aboard a vessel concern the obvious presence of contraband, the jury reasonably may infer the crew's knowing participation in the venture"); *United States v. Piedrahita-Santiago*, 931 F.2d 127, 130 (1st Cir. 1991) (holding where seven crewmembers were on board a "small" forty-foot vessel that "[a] larger crew than ordinarily needed for navigation purposes suggests that the crew was hired for the purpose of loading and unloading cargo rather than merely steering the vessel"); *United States v. Luciano-Pacheco*, 794 F.2d 7, 11 (1st Cir. 1986) (stating that "given the necessarily close relation of crewmembers cramped onto a vessel . . . with marijuana, it is entirely reasonable for the jury to conclude that conspirators . . . would reasonably not allow the presence of innocent bystanders in their midst while conducting a lengthy, illegal operation") (internal quotation marks and citation omitted) [—21—] (quoting *United States v. Beltrán*, 761 F.2d 1, 6 (1st Cir. 1985); *Smith*, 680 F.2d at 259-60 (1st Cir. 1982) (crewmember's presence on a vessel carrying large quantities of marihuana, together with reasonable inferences, supported the conviction notwithstanding defendant's contention that he was a mere passenger).

Although Appellants argue that the evidence was also consistent with their defense that they were on the vessel taking a ride to Puerto Rico with the sole intention of illegally entering the United States, it was up to the jury to believe or disbelieve their defense. The jury did not believe it and we cannot second-guess that determination. *See Trinidad-Acosta*, 773 F.3d at 310-11. "Nor need we be convinced that the government succeeded in eliminating every possible theory consistent with the defendant's innocence."[7] *Id.* at 311 (quoting *Troy*, 583 F.3d at 24). Thus, the district court properly denied Appellants' motions for judgment of acquittal.

C. Government's Statements

According to Appellants, the prosecutor made some improper remarks during trial that deprived them of a fair trial. [—22—] Some of these remarks were objected to by some appellants at trial, while others were not. We discuss each in turn.

This court reviews *de novo* whether objected-to remarks by the prosecution were improper and/or constituted misconduct. *See United States v. Sepúlveda-Hernández*, 752

---

[7] Although we have held that where the evidence is equally or nearly equally consistent with innocence as it is with guilt, "a reasonable jury must necessarily entertain a reasonable doubt," *O'Laughlin v. O'Brien*, 568 F.3d 287, 301 (1st Cir. 2009) (quoting *United States v. Flores-Rivera*, 56 F.3d 319, 323 (1st Cir. 1995)), that is not the case here, where the evidence establishing guilt was very strong.

F.3d 22, 31 (1st Cir. 2014); *United States v. Appolon*, 695 F.3d 44, 66 (1st Cir. 2012). If we conclude that statements were improper or constituted misconduct, we must then determine whether such statements resulted in prejudice to the Appellants. *United States v. Rodríguez*, 675 F.3d 48, 62 (1st Cir. 2012); *United States v. Azubike*, 504 F.3d 30, 38-39 (1st Cir. 2007); *United States v. Joyner*, 191 F.3d 47, 53 (1st Cir. 1999) ("[W]e review for harmless error, that is, whether the argument was 'sufficiently prejudicial to warrant a new trial under the circumstances'" (quoting *United States v. Rosales*, 19 F.3d 763, 767 (1st Cir. 1994))). In determining whether the prosecutor's remarks were harmless, "we evaluate the . . . comments as a whole, not in isolation," *Joyner*, 191 F.3d at 53 (quoting *Rosales*, 19 F.3d at 767), and "we focus on (1) the severity of the misconduct, including whether it was isolated and/or deliberate; (2) whether curative instructions were given; and (3) the strength of the evidence against the [Appellants]." *United States v. González-Pérez*, 778 F.3d 3, 19 (1st Cir. 2015) (citing *Rodríguez*, 675 F.3d at 62). The prosecutor's improper statements "are considered harmful if they 'so poisoned the well that the trial's [—23—] outcome was likely affected, thus warranting a new trial.'" *Id.* (quoting *Rodríguez*, 675 F.3d at 62).

Any unpreserved claims of prosecutorial misconduct are reviewed for plain error. *Id.*; *Rodríguez*, 675 F.3d at 64 (requiring defendant to prove there was an error, which was clear or obvious, that affected his substantial rights, and seriously impaired the fairness, integrity, or public reputation of the judicial proceedings).

1. Opening Statement

During her opening statement, the prosecutor stated:

You'll hear the Judge inform you that jurisdictional aspects is not an issue for you to determine. It's already been determined by this Court that the United States had jurisdiction over this vessel and that these individuals were on board this vessel which we had

jurisdiction over with the intent and knowledge to possess and distribute the narcotics.
Now, in this case there are no—

Peña-Santo's defense counsel immediately objected to the statement saying, "I object to that, Your Honor. That's not what the Court determined. That they knew that there were drugs on board is something for the jury. That's an issue of fact for the jury to decide." Gil-Martínez's counsel joined his objection and added that the district court's "ruling was regarding the jurisdiction, not that there were drugs inside the vessel." Faced with these objections, the prosecutor responded, "I don't believe I stated [—24—] that. You will have to determine whether those drugs were on board, and you'll see the video of them throwing them overboard."

Because only Peña-Santo and Gil-Martínez preserved this argument, our review of their claim is for harmlessness. While our review of Vicente-Arias and Liriano's claim would ordinarily be for plain error, because Appellants' claim fails under both standards of review, we limit our discussion to the more defendant-friendly standard.

The prosecutor's statement gave the impression that the court had already determined that Appellants had the "intent and knowledge to possess and distribute the narcotics," which was not correct and, thus, was improper. However, we still need to determine whether the statement was prejudicial.

A review of the record does not reveal that the prosecutor intended to mislead the jury. Rather, it suggests that she simply misspoke when trying to list a series of issues the government wanted to address as an introduction to the government's case. Furthermore, the prosecutor's improper statement was isolated and not deliberate. *See González-Pérez*, 778 F.3d at 19. Defense counsel for Gil-Martínez and Peña-Santo immediately objected to the statement and, although the district court made no comment or ruling after the objection, the prosecutor immediately retracted the statement by saying: "I don't believe I stated that. [—25—] You will have to determine whether those drugs were on board, and you'll see the video of them throwing them overboard."[8]

Also, while the district court did not give a curative instruction at the time, we note that one was not requested. Moreover, the district court repeatedly instructed the jury that attorneys' arguments were not evidence. During the preliminary instructions, the court stated, "[r]emember these are arguments. It's what the Government intends to prove in the case. It's not the actual evidence. The actual evidence will be coming in after the witnesses start coming in and presenting exhibits." Then, during the final jury instructions, the district court reiterated that it was the government who had to prove intent beyond a reasonable doubt. Specifically, it stated, "[f]or you to find a defendant guilty of this crime, you must be convinced that the Government has proven each of these things beyond a reasonable doubt . . . that the defendants agreed to import cocaine and heroin . . . [and] did so knowingly and intentionally." This militates against finding prejudice. *See United States v. Gentles*, 619 F.3d [—26—] 75, 82 (1st Cir. 2010) ("finding no error where defendant failed to request a curative instruction and court gave general instructions before deliberation as to what the jury could and could not consider as evidence" (citing *United States v. Robinson*, 473 F.3d 387, 398 (1st Cir. 2007))); *see also González-Pérez*, 778 F.3d at 21 ("[W]e ordinarily presume that juries follow instructions.").

Finally, we find it unlikely that any prejudice surviving the instructions could

---

[8] We note that the correction itself is problematic because it suggested that the video showed the defendants throwing packages overboard, whereas it was agreed that the defendants could not be identified as doing so from the video. No contemporaneous objection was made, so we review for plain error. As with the government's initial statement, the inaccurate reference in the correction does not amount to plain error, particularly given the admission in the testimony of the government's witness Agent Perry, that the defendants could not be identified in the video as throwing the packages overboard.

have affected the outcome of the case. The evidence of Appellants' guilt was strong enough to prevent any prejudice surviving the instructions from affecting the outcome of the case. In addition, the fact that this statement was made at the beginning of the trial also makes it less likely to have affected the outcome of the case. *See United States v. Mooney*, 315 F.3d 54, 60 (1st Cir. 2002) ("The context of the prosecutor's comments also weighs against finding that they likely affected the outcome of the trial. The comments occurred during opening arguments, not during summation where the last words the jury hears have significant potential to cause prejudice."). In sum, because we do not find that the prosecutor's statement "so poisoned the well that the trial's outcome was likely affected," *González-Pérez*, 778 F.3d at 19 (quoting *Rodríguez*, 675 F.3d at 62) (internal quotation marks omitted), Appellants' claim fails. [—27—]

2. Redirect Examination

On direct examination, Ms. Cacho, the chemist, testified about the tests she performed on some of the drugs in order to conclude that they were heroin and cocaine. During cross-examination, Gil-Martínez's defense counsel asked Ms. Cacho whether she knew if other tests—such as fingerprint analysis and DNA testing—had been performed on the packages containing the drugs. Defense counsel's point was that no tests linked the Appellants to the drugs. Ms. Cacho testified that she did not do anything other than analyze the chemical composition of the substances. On redirect examination, the prosecutor asked Ms. Cacho, "Did you watch the video of the defendants throwing the drugs into the water?" Gil-Martínez's defense counsel objected and stated that "[t]hat was not part of the cross-examination." The district court allowed the question, to which Ms. Cacho responded, "No."

Although they did not object at trial to the prosecutor's question to Ms. Cacho on redirect examination, Peña-Santo and Vicente-Arias now argue that it was a "loaded" and "speaking question" that aimed to confuse the jury by making them believe that there was direct evidence linking them to the crimes charged. They allege that, because there was no direct evidence or witness identifying them as throwing anything into the water and no one [—28—] could tell from the video whether they were the ones throwing the drugs overboard, they are entitled to a new trial.

Since Peña-Santo and Vicente-Arias failed to object to the question at the trial level, our review is only for plain error.[9] Their claim falls short because, at the very least, they failed to establish plain-error review's third and fourth prongs. Specifically, Peña-Santo and Vicente-Arias have not shown that their substantial rights were affected and that the fairness, integrity, or public reputation of their judicial proceedings were seriously impaired, especially because Ms. Cacho responded to the question in the negative. Although they argue that the question wrongly gave the impression that direct evidence (the video) showed them throwing the drugs overboard, the fact that Ms. Cacho responded that she had not seen the video—coupled with the fact that the jury examined the evidence (including the video) from which the government could lawfully suggest that the jury draw an inference that Appellants were the ones throwing the drugs overboard[10]—sufficiently attenuated any effect that the question [—29—] alone could have had. This is just not the kind of "blockbuster error" for which

"plain error review tends to afford relief." *Rodríguez*, 675 F.3d at 64.

3. Closing Argument

Peña-Soto and Vicente-Arias also challenge the following statement made by the government during its closing argument: "That's not someone's personal drug stash right there. $3.2 million is not something that the four of them are going to use casually at parties. Those are drugs that the four of them are going to sell at a profit, $3.2 million." Although they did not object to the statement at the trial level, Peña-Santo and Vicente-Arias assert that it satisfies the plain error standard of review since there was no evidence, either circumstantial or direct, that they intended to sell drugs for profit or that they stood to gain millions of dollars in profit. Relying on *Arrieta-Agressot v. United States*, 3 F.3d 525, 527 (1st Cir. 1993), they claim that the challenged statement was inflammatory by referring to money and wealth, and that the evidence showed, at most, that they acted as couriers (mules) or may have assisted on the boat. We disagree.

Although there was no direct evidence that Appellants intended to sell the drugs for profit, there is no error—plain [—30—] or otherwise—in referencing the amount or worth of the drugs and inviting the jury to draw the inference that the drugs were not for personal use. *See United States v. Bergodere*, 40 F.3d 512, 518 (1st Cir. 1994) (noting that "we have long recognized that factors such as the quantity and purity of the drugs confiscated by the authorities can support an inference of intent to distribute"); *see also United States v. Meadows*, 571 F.3d 131, 144-45 (1st Cir. 2009) (At closing argument, the prosecution may "ask jurors to draw reasonable inferences from the evidence."). And, even if the Appellants would not be the ones actually to sell the drugs and were instead couriers or mules, they were still part of the same conspiracy to import and distribute (and eventually sell for profit) controlled substances, which were the charged offenses. Furthermore, Peña-Santo's and Vicente's reliance on *Arrieta-Agressot* is misplaced. The improper comments in *Arrieta-*

---

[9] We note that only Gil-Martínez objected to the prosecutor's question at the trial level, but he did so on different grounds—that the question went beyond the scope of the cross-examination—and neither Peña-Santo nor Vicente-Arias joined his objection.

[10] The government may suggest to the jury which inferences should be drawn from the evidence as long as the government does not know that the suggested inferences are false or has very strong reasons to doubt those inferences. *See United States v. Kasenge*, 660 F.3d 537, 542 (1st Cir. 2011) (stating that "[a]lthough it is the jury's job to draw the inferences, there is nothing improper in the [—29—] Government's suggesting which inferences should be drawn," but noting that it is error for the government to propound inferences that it knows to be false, or has a very strong reason to doubt) (citations omitted).

Agressot had to do with the "evil" effect that the defendants' actions had on society. There, we established that a prosecutor's statement is improper if it serves no purpose besides inflaming the passions and prejudices of the jury. 3 F.3d at 527. Here, however, the prosecutor's reference to the worth of the drugs had the legitimate purpose of both refuting the Appellants' mere presence defense and suggesting that the jury draw an inference as to the required element of intent. *See Bergodere*, 40 F.3d at 518. Thus, their plain error claim fails. [—31—]

D. Peña-Santo's Cumulative Error Claim

Peña-Santo argues that if none of his previous claims of error is sufficient to vacate his conviction, their cumulative prejudicial effect requires that his conviction be vacated and his case remanded for a new trial.

We have acknowledged that "[i]ndividual errors, insufficient in themselves to necessitate a new trial, may in the aggregate have a more debilitating effect." *United States v. Sepúlveda*, 15 F.3d 1161, 1195-96 (1st Cir. 1993). "[C]laims under the cumulative error doctrine are sui generis." *Id.* at 1196. When reviewing such a claim a Court must consider:

> each such claim against the background of the case as a whole, paying particular weight to factors such as the nature and number of [] errors committed; their interrelationship, if any, and combined effect; how the district court dealt with the errors as they arose (including the efficacy—or lack of efficacy—of any remedial efforts); and the strength of the government's case.

Id. In addition, the length of the trial is another factor to be considered. *Id.*

Here, none of Peña-Santo's alleged errors—which are not many, considering the length of the trial—resulted in substantial prejudice and most of them are entirely without merit. Furthermore, as previously explained, the evidence against Peña-Santo was very strong, and the district court did not conduct the trial in a manner that undermined his right to a fair trial. Thus, [—32—] we reject his contention that his conviction was tainted by cumulative error. *See United States v. Flemmi*, 402 F.3d 79, 95 n.23 (1st Cir. 2005) ("[B]ecause we have found that none of [the defendant's] individual complaints resulted in substantial prejudice and that most are completely without merit, we reject the final contention that his conviction was tainted by cumulative error." (quoting *United States v. DeMasi*, 40 F.3d 1306, 1322 (1st Cir. 1994))). "The Constitution entitles a criminal defendant to a fair trial, not to a mistake-free trial." *Sepúlveda*, 15 F.3d at 1196 (citing *Delaware v. Van Arsdall*, 475 U.S. 673, 681 (1986)); *United States v. Polito*, 856 F.2d 414, 418 (1st Cir. 1988)).

E. Gil-Martínez's Sentencing Disparity Claim

Gil-Martínez claims that he received a disparately higher sentence than co-defendant Vicente-Arias, even though there was no evidence of dissimilar conduct among them and they both had the same Criminal History Category ("CHC").

1. Background

The Presentence Investigation Report ("PSR") recommended a Guidelines sentencing range ("GSR") for Gil-Martínez of 235 to 297 months of imprisonment.[11] The PSR did not identify any [—33—] information that would warrant a role adjustment or a departure. At the sentencing hearing, the district court considered the PSR's recommended GSR and took into account Gil-Martínez's "unfortunate rearing and upbringing." It considered that at times Gil-Martínez was unable to eat because his family could not afford food, he lived in a wooden house with a dirt floor, and he only had a fourth grade education because he left

---

[11] Pursuant to U.S. Sentencing Guidelines Manual § 3D1.2(d) (2004) ("U.S.S.G."), Counts One and Two were grouped together. These offenses resulted in a base offense level of thirty-eight, pursuant to U.S.S.G. § 2D1.1. Gil-Martínez had no previous criminal history and had a CHC of I. This yielded a GSR of 235 to 297 months of imprisonment.

school at a young age to help support his family. Gil-Martínez argued that a within-the-Guidelines sentence would be unreasonable when compared to Vicente-Arias's sentence of 130 months of imprisonment. He then requested to be sentenced to 120 months of imprisonment, the statutory minimum. He argued that sentencing him to a greater term of imprisonment would create a sentencing disparity.

The district court considered Gil-Martínez's request for a sentence similar to that of Vicente-Arias, who received a minor role reduction. The government opposed Gil-Martínez's request for a downwardly variant sentence of 120 months, arguing that, while Vicente-Arias had received a minor role reduction, Gil-Martínez had a number of roles onboard the yola, which distinguished him from Vicente-Arias. The government pointed out that Gil-Martínez had admitted to operating and fueling the yola. The district court concluded that it did not have any information that would support granting Gil-Martínez a minor role reduction like that Vicente-Arias received or otherwise sentencing him to a term of [—34—] imprisonment the same as or similar to that of Vicente-Arias. The court also considered the sentences imposed on other co-defendants. It noted that, although Peña-Santo received the statutory minimum sentence of 120 months of imprisonment, Peña-Santo's characteristics were different from those of Gil-Martínez because Peña-Santo was facing serious health conditions and his life expectancy was less than six months. The district court noted that although Gil-Martínez compared himself only to Vicente-Arias and Peña-Santo, the district court had also sentenced another co-defendant who had pleaded guilty pursuant to a straight plea to 188 months of imprisonment. The district court then stated that, in sentencing each defendant, it had taken into consideration "the particular situation of each and every one defendant" and had "individualized sentencing." After concluding that the court did not have any information to support a minor role reduction, and that Gil-Martínez was in good health, the district court imposed on Gil-Martínez a downwardly

variant sentence of 192 months of imprisonment.

2. Standard / Scope of Review

We review challenges to the reasonableness of a sentence "under a deferential abuse-of-discretion standard." *Gall v. United States*, 552 U.S. 38, 41 (2007). We first consider "whether the district court made any procedural errors, such as 'failing to calculate (or improperly calculating) the Guidelines range, [—35—] treating the Guidelines as mandatory, failing to consider the section 3553(a) factors, selecting a sentence based on clearly erroneous facts, or failing to adequately explain the chosen sentence—including an explanation for any deviation from the Guidelines range.'" *United States v. Maisonet-González*, 785 F.3d 757, 762 (1st Cir. 2015) (quoting *United States v. Rivera-Moreno*, 613 F.3d 1, 8 (1st Cir. 2010)). If the district court has committed no procedural error, we then review the substantive reasonableness of the sentence imposed for abuse of discretion. *United States v. Flores-Machicote*, 706 F.3d 16, 20 (1st Cir. 2013). "When conducting this review, we take into account the totality of the circumstances, including the extent of any variance from the Guidelines." *Maisonet-González*, 785 F.3d at 762 (quoting *Trinidad-Acosta*, 773 F.3d at 309). "A sentence will withstand a substantive reasonableness challenge so long as there is 'a plausible sentencing rationale and a defensible result.'" *Id.* (quoting *United States v. Martin*, 520 F.3d 87, 96 (1st Cir. 2008)).

In fashioning a sentence, judges must consider "the need to avoid unwarranted sentencing disparities among defendants with similar records who have been found guilty of similar conduct." 18 U.S.C. § 3553(a)(6). Although this provision is primarily aimed at national disparities, rather than those between co-defendants, *Martin*, 520 F.3d at 94, we have also held that if "'identically situated defendants' receive significantly disparate sentences, red [—36—] flags may indeed be raised." *United States v. Rivera-López*, 736 F.3d 633, 636 (1st Cir. 2013) (quoting *United States v. Mueffelman*, 470 F.3d 33, 41 (1st Cir. 2006)).

3. Analysis

We afford the district court wide discretion in sentencing because, after the court has calculated the GSR, "sentencing becomes a judgment call, and a variant sentence may be constructed based on a complex of factors whose interplay and precise weight cannot even be precisely described." *United States v. Politano*, 522 F.3d 69, 73 (1st Cir. 2008) (quoting *Martin*, 520 F.3d at 92). Gil-Martínez does not allege that the district court failed to consider the 18 U.S.C. § 3553(a) sentencing factors—including the need to avoid sentencing disparities—or commit any other procedural error. Rather, his challenge goes to the weighing of the section 3553(a) sentencing factors, specifically the factors establishing the need to avoid sentencing disparities and the history and characteristics of the defendant. As Gil-Martínez was sentenced below the applicable GSR, his challenge to the substantive reasonableness of his sentence faces an uphill battle. *See United States v. Joubert*, 778 F.3d 247, 256 (1st Cir. 2015) ("When, as in this case, a district court essays a substantial downward variance from a properly calculated guideline sentencing range, a defendant's claim of substantive unreasonableness will [—37—] generally fail." (quoting *United States v. Floyd*, 740 F.3d 22, 39-40 (1st Cir. 2014))).

As the Government correctly contends, a district court's consideration of sentencing disparity aims primarily at the minimization of disparities among defendants nationally and, while avoidance of disparities among co-defendants may be considered, "a defendant is not entitled to a lighter sentence merely because his co-defendants received lighter sentences." *United States v. Wallace*, 573 F.3d 82, 97 (1st Cir. 2009) (quoting *United States v. Marceau*, 554 F.3d 24, 33 (1st Cir. 2009)). Furthermore, contrary to Gil-Martínez's claim, he is not entitled to the same sentence as Vicente-Arias because they are not "identically situated," inasmuch as Vicente-Arias received a minor role reduction[12] and Gil-Martínez did not. *See Rivera-López*, 736

F.3d at 636; *United States v. Rivera-González*, 626 F.3d 639, 648 (1st Cir. 2010). At the sentencing hearing the district court stated that it would not grant Gil-Martínez a minor role reduction because it did not have any information supporting a minor role reduction, and, as the government argued, the information was to the contrary, with Gil-Martínez having admitted to operating and fueling the yola. The district court concluded that this information distinguished Gil-Martínez's role in the conspiracy from that of Vicente-Arias. Gil-Martínez has failed to show that these findings of fact [—38—] regarding his role in the conspiracy were clearly erroneous. *See United States v. Torres-Landrúa*, 783 F.3d 58, 66 n.10 (1st Cir. 2015). In addition, although Gil-Martínez selectively compares himself only to Vicente-Arias, the record shows that the district court did take into consideration the need to avoid sentencing disparities not only in relation to Vicente-Arias, but also in relation to his other co-defendants. It is clear from the record that the district court also took into consideration that another co-defendant, who had pleaded guilty pursuant to a straight plea, had received a sentence of 188 months of imprisonment, and that Peña-Santo, who was sentenced to the statutory minimum, received that sentence because he was sick and his life expectancy was less than six months. Because it is evident that the district court did consider the need to avoid sentencing disparities among defendants, as well as the other sentencing factors, sufficiently explained its chosen sentence, and arrived at a defensible result, *Maisonet-González*, 785 F.3d at 762, Gil-Martínez's challenge to the reasonableness of his downwardly variant sentence fails.

III. *Conclusion*

The record reflects that Appellants were afforded a fair trial, that the expert testimony of Agent Conchin was proper, and the evidence of their guilt was more than sufficient to support the jury's verdicts. In addition, the record shows that Gil-Martínez's [—39—] sentence was appropriate. Thus, Appellants' convictions and Gil-Martínez's sentence are affirmed.

---

[12] This resulted in Vicente-Arias having a lower GSR.

Affirmed.

United States Court of Appeals
for the First Circuit

No. 14-1194

UNITED STATES
vs.
CARELA

Appeal from the United States District Court for the
District of Puerto Rico

Decided: November 4, 2015

Citation: 805 F.3d 374, 3 Adm. R. 112 (1st Cir. 2015).

Before TORRUELLA, SELYA, and LYNCH, Circuit
Judges.

[—2—] TORRUELLA, Circuit Judge:

This appeal arises out of Defendant-Appellant Víctor Manuel Carela's ("Carela") involvement in a drug smuggling operation. Carela was convicted on two counts: (1) conspiracy to possess with intent to distribute five kilograms or more of cocaine; and (2) possession with intent to distribute five kilograms or more of cocaine. Finding no reversible error, we affirm his conviction and sentence.

I. *Background*

On September 16, 2012, a multi-agency[1] investigation was initiated in regard to suspected drug trafficking in the coastal area along Yabucoa and Maunabo, Puerto Rico. At 4:00 a.m. in the morning of September 17, 2012, Border Patrol agents observed an unlit vessel approaching Maunabo. The law enforcement officers participating in this investigation requested helicopter assistance from the Puerto Rico Police Department, which was shortly dispatched. The helicopter spotted a thirty-three foot vessel and communicated its location to law enforcement officers on the ground.

Around this same time, officers led a tactical land approach in the area and discovered a red Ford Excursion surrounded [—3—] by multiple gas tanks along with other supplies such as food and drink. Proceeding to the beach, officers uncovered 918.7 kilograms of cocaine hidden within the nearby bushes.

Later that day, officers for the Municipal Police of Yabucoa ("Yabucoa officers") were told that a shipment of drugs had been intercepted along the Maunabo coastline. The Yabucoa officers were instructed to patrol the area in order to locate individuals that may be linked to the intercepted shipment. The Yabucoa officers encountered Carela hitchhiking on a section of the PR-901 road that was two miles from the sea. When the Yabucoa officers approached Carela in a marked police vehicle, he jumped over the railing on the side of the road and down a precipice.

A few minutes later, the Yabucoa officers encountered Carela a second time. This time, the Yabucoa officers stopped their vehicle and approached Carela on foot. The Yabucoa officers asked Carela, who was dressed in jet skiing shoes and wet clothing, what he was doing in the area. Carela responded that he was collecting metal.[2] The Yabucoa officers continued to speak with Carela, who appeared agitated, tired and pale, and invited him to [—4—] drink some water in their car. While Carela was drinking water, the Yabucoa officers again asked him what he was doing in the area and Carela indicated that he had been on a boat. At this juncture, the Yabucoa officers arrested Carela and read him his rights. Carela had no identification or cell phone on his person and only a small amount of cash.

On the ride to the police station, Carela told the Yabucoa officers that he was supposed to be paid "$5,000 for the task, . . . but since it wasn't completed, he was not going to receive it." Later that day, Carela was interrogated by

---

[1] This investigation involved agents from the U.S. Customs and Border Patrol, U.S. Coast Guard, Puerto Rico Police Department, and Yabucoa Municipal Police Department.

[2] Carela did not have any metal on his person. Further, one of the Yabucoa Police officers that encountered Carela testified that she has never seen any individuals collecting metal in the area in which Carela was found.

Agent Carlos Martínez, a Homeland Security agent. Agent Martínez testified that Carela appeared "excited," "happy," "pumped up," and "very cooperative" during his interrogation. Carela admitted to the agent that he was hired for this "drug smuggling venture [and] that his job was to refuel the vessel that was coming in with the narcotics." Carela further admitted that he assisted in the offloading of narcotics from the vessel.

Carela was indicted on: (1) conspiracy to possess with intent to distribute five kilograms or more of cocaine; and (2) possession with intent to distribute five kilograms or more of cocaine. 21 U.S.C. §§ 841(a)(1), (b)(1)(A)(ii); 846. On April 22, 2013, Carela's first trial ended in a mistrial because the jury could not reach a unanimous verdict. Carela was tried a second [—5—] time and convicted on both counts. On January 22, 2014, Carela was sentenced to 196 months of incarceration. This timely appeal followed.

II. *Discussion*

Carela raises a number of issues on appeal. Specifically, Carela argues that: (1) the district court erred when it admitted an unexecuted draft contract into evidence in violation of the Federal Rules of Evidence; (2) the district judge made several improper remarks that violated Carela's constitutional rights; (3) the district court improperly admitted testimony in Spanish in violation of the Jones Act, 48 U.S.C. § 864; (4) the Government engaged in prosecutorial misconduct; and (5) Carela's sentence was both procedurally and substantively unreasonable. We consider Carela's contentions below.

A. The Unexecuted Draft Contract

1. Background

During the course of the second trial, the Government sought to introduce an unsigned copy of a draft sales contract (the "draft contract") via which Edwin Léon-Léon ("Léon") sold Carela the red Ford Excursion that law enforcement officers found on the beach on September 17, 2012. The Government also called Léon to testify that Léon and Carela had executed the draft contract. After hearing Léon's testimony, the district court [—6—] admitted the draft contract into evidence, over Carela's objections regarding the authenticity of the document, because Léon did not keep a copy of the original and Léon attested that he gave the original to Carela when the sale was executed.

Carela now argues that the draft contract was improperly admitted because it is proscribed hearsay and its admission requires a new trial.

Carela concedes that he did not object to the admission of the draft contract on hearsay grounds and that plain error review would normally apply. *See United States v. Avilés-Colón*, 536 F.3d 1, 22 (1st Cir. 2008). Nonetheless, Carela argues that because he objected to the admissibility of the draft contract on the ground that it could not be authenticated, we should apply closer scrutiny. *United States v. Jefferson*, 925 F.2d 1242, 1254 (10th Cir. 1991) (stating that closer scrutiny may be appropriate when the failure to preserve the precise grounds for error is mitigated by an objection on related grounds).

2. Applicable Law and Analysis

As noted above, we generally employ plain error review when a party has failed to preserve an objection in the lower court. *United States v. Acevedo-Maldonado*, 696 F.3d 150, 156 (1st Cir. 2012) (citing *United States v. Rodríguez*, 525 F.3d 85, 95 (1st Cir. 2008) (plain error review applies where defendant failed [—7—] to object on hearsay grounds)). Carela argues that we should apply closer scrutiny, but fails to cite to any case law affirming that we are bound to do so. Nonetheless, we note that his claims still fail under this rubric.

When reviewing for plain error, we ask whether "(1) an error occurred; (2) the error was clear and obvious; (3) the error affected the defendant's substantial rights; and (4) the error impaired the fairness, integrity, or public reputation of the judicial proceedings."

United States v. Ramos, 763 F.3d 45, 56 n.15 (1st Cir. 2014) (citation omitted).

Here, the prosecution sought to introduce the contract as additional evidence that linked Carela to the drug smuggling operation. The Government's case did not depend on the introduction of the draft contract into evidence because there was already ample evidence against Carela, which included: (1) Carela met law enforcement officers while hitchhiking in an area that is known to be a drug delivery point; (2) Carela was found within two miles of where the shipment of cocaine had been found several hours earlier while wearing jet skiing shoes in a disheveled and dehydrated state; (3) the Yabucoa officers who are from the area did not immediately recognize Carela; (4) Carela provided police with an unlikely story that he was in the area collecting metal even though the area is not known for metal collection; (5) Carela [—8—] admitted to the police that he had been on a boat and that he had accepted an offer of $5,000 to unload cocaine; and (6) Carela was wet when he was patted down. As a result, whether Carela did in fact purchase the Ford Excursion is not essential to link him to the drug conspiracy. Because there was an overwhelming amount of other evidence against Carela, we are unable to conclude that the admission of the draft contract somehow violated Carela's substantive rights.

In light of the ample evidence against Carela, the district court's admission of the draft contract did not impact Carela's substantial rights. Our conclusion would be the same under the closer scrutiny approach. Thus, we find that it was not plain error for the district court to admit the draft contract into evidence.

B. Whether the District Court Judge Erred by Commenting on the Evidence

1. Background

During the course of the second trial, the district court judge stated in open court that he would allow the draft contract to be presented as evidence because (1) the draft contract had been authenticated; (2) the draft contract was admissible because the original copy of the contract was lost or destroyed; and (3) the original contract could not be subpoenaed from the purchaser. [—9—]

In a subsequent sidebar conference, the district court judge again stated that he would admit the draft contract because Léon did not keep a copy of the original and the original copy of the draft was not available.

Carela argues that the district court's ruling violated his Fifth and Sixth Amendment rights because it improperly endorsed the Government's position. This ruling, Carela argues, deprived the jury of its corresponding factual determination because it prevented the jury from deciding whether the original sales contract ever existed, whether Léon kept a copy of the original contract, and whether Léon gave a credible explanation as to why the original contract was missing. Carela avers that the district court's ruling constituted error and requests a new trial.

2. Applicable Law and Analysis

Carela did not contemporaneously object to the comments at issue during the proceedings below. As a result, we review the district judge's comments under the plain error standard.

A trial judge "retains the common law power to question witnesses and to analyze, dissect, explain, summarize and comment on the facts and evidence." *Logue v. Dore*, 103 F.3d 1040, 1045 (1st Cir. 1997) (citations omitted). However, the judge may not overstep his bounds and give an impression of judicial bias. *United States v. Rivera-Rodríguez*, 761 F.3d 105, 111 (1st Cir. [—10—] 2014). Improper judicial intervention will seriously prejudice a defendant's case if there is a reasonable probability that, but for the error, the verdict would have been different. *Id.* at 112. In order to determine if there was judicial bias, we consider each intervention in the context of the trial as a whole, whether the comments were improper, and whether the complaining party can show serious prejudice. *Id.* at 111.

Federal Rule of Evidence 1008 establishes that the jury generally determines whether a writing produced at trial is the original writing. Fed. R. Evid. 1008. In the same vein, we have held that the Sixth Amendment guarantees a criminal defendant the opportunity for a jury to decide guilt or innocence. *United States v. Bello*, 194 F.3d 18, 25 (1st Cir. 1999).

Here, we do not find that the district court judge acted improperly or that he decided Carela's guilt or innocence. The statements that Carela objects to are part of the district court's ruling regarding the admissibility of the draft contract. In light of the trial as a whole, we cannot conclude that the district court's ruling to admit the draft agreement in open court somehow prejudiced Carela. As stated in the preceding section, there was significant evidence in this case against Carela. Thus, we cannot conclude that but for the district court's ruling the result of the proceeding would have been different. [—11—]

We further note that our review of the transcripts to which Carela refers yields no commentary or question by the trial judge that exceeds the bounds of acceptable judicial participation. *See Acevedo-García v. Monroig*, 351 F.3d 547, 561 (1st Cir. 2003).

As such, we find that the district court's comments were proper and did not endorse the Government's position.

C. Whether the Jones Act was violated

1. Background

Carela claims that the Jones Act[3] was violated because on the second day of trial, Agent Martínez testified to the Spanish version of Carela's statement. In simpler terms, Agent Martínez testified that Carela told him that he had been driving "*a red-type guagua, tipo guagua.*" Carela posits that there is no English meaning of the word "guagua" or "tipo" and that this statement violated the Jones Act and necessitates a new trial.

Carela further takes issue with what he characterizes as the prosecutor's attempt to get around the Jones Act by attempting to translate "guagua" as a red truck during the Government's [—12—] closing.[4] Carela vociferously argues that this is an inaccurate translation of the word "guagua," which according to Carela can only mean bus.

2. Applicable Law and Analysis

Carela readily concedes that no Jones Act objections were raised below. As a result, we review for plain error. *See United States v. Mescual-Cruz*, 387 F.3d 1, 12 (1st Cir. 2004).

In general terms, a prosecutor's comment does not violate the Jones Act so long as the proceedings were conducted in English. *United States v. Báez-Martínez*, 786 F.3d 121, 127 n.1 (1st Cir. 2015) (clarifying that an occasional reference to a foreign language word or phrase by a lawyer or witness does not offend the Jones Act).

Further, a violation of the English language requirement constitutes reversible error whenever the appellant can demonstrate that the untranslated evidence "has the potential to affect the disposition of an issue raised on appeal." *United States v. Rivera-Rosario*, 300 F.3d 1, 10 (1st Cir. 2002). However, there is no prejudice from a Jones Act violation if the untranslated evidence lacks such potential. *Id.* [—13—]

We cannot find that there was a Jones Act violation in this case. There is no dispute that testimony in question was delivered in English. It is true that the English testimony was peppered with Spanish colloquialisms. However, an occasional reference to a Spanish word or words does not offend the Jones Act.

---

[3] The Jones Act requires that all pleadings and proceedings in the United States District Court for the District of Puerto Rico be conducted in the English language. 48 U.S.C. § 864; *see also United States v. Millán-Isaac*, 749 F.3d 57, 63 (1st Cir. 2014).

[4] The prosecutor stated during his closing "[h]e tells us that he was in a red guagua, in a red truck, to go to the area to provide his services."

Carela did not suffer any prejudice here. The disputed statement lacks the potential to impact the disposition of the issue raised on appeal. As has already been discussed in this opinion, the record shows that there was ample evidence linking Carela to the charged conduct. The passing references to "guagua" and "tipo" lack any potential to change the outcome of this case. Although the prosecutor may have attempted to translate "guagua" during his closing remarks, the reference also lacked any potential to prejudice Carela or to affect the disposition of the case.

In light of the foregoing, we conclude that there was no violation of the Jones Act. We further conclude that Carela suffered no prejudice.

D. Alleged Prosecutorial Misconduct

1. Background

Carela maintains that the prosecutor's closing and rebuttal arguments constituted prosecutorial misconduct and merit [—14—] reversal.[5] Carela argues that the prosecutor improperly: (1) told the jury that the red Ford Excursion was registered in Carela's name when in fact it was not; (2) misrepresented the legal significance of the draft contract by calling it a contract instead of a draft contract and claiming that it certified the details of the sale; and (3) implied that Carela was charged with a conspiracy to possess with intent to distribute more than five kilograms of cocaine, and substantive possession in an uncharged conspiracy.

According to Carela, the context of the prosecutor's intentional misconduct must favor reversal because: (1) the allegedly improper statements were made during closing and rebuttal arguments after the court instructed the jury—a "delicate point in the trial process," *United States v. Taylor*, 54 F.3d 967, 977 (1st Cir. 1995); (2) the misconduct

---

[5] Carela argues that his Jones Act violations claims also qualify as forms of prosecutorial misconduct. However, as we have already stated in our preceding section, there was no Jones Act violation in this case.

occurred after the jury in the first trial had failed to convict him; and (3) the United States Attorney's Office in the District of Puerto Rico, where the case was tried, allegedly has a long-standing problem of prosecutorial misconduct during closing arguments. [—15—]

2. Applicable Law and Analysis

Because Carela did not raise these objections during trial, this Court reviews the prosecutor's comments under the plain error standard. *United States v. Glover*, 558 F.3d 71, 77 (1st Cir. 2009). In the context of prosecutorial misconduct, this Court reverses a district court "only if the prosecutor's remarks 'so poisoned the well that the trial's outcome was likely affected.'" *United States v. Vázquez-Larrauri*, 778 F.3d 276, 283 (1st Cir. 2015) (quoting *United States v. Kasenge*, 660 F.3d 537, 542 (1st Cir. 2011)). When determining whether there was prosecutorial misconduct, we consider the following factors: "(1) the severity of the prosecutor's misconduct, including whether it was deliberate or accidental; (2) the context in which the misconduct occurred; (3) whether the judge gave curative instructions and the likely effect of such instructions; and (4) the strength of the evidence against the defendant[]." *Id.* (citation and internal quotation marks omitted) (alteration in original). We further note that when assaying the prosecutor's remarks, context often determines meaning. *United States v. Sepúlveda*, 15 F.3d 1161, 1187 (1st Cir. 1993). In borderline cases, the standard of review can also figure importantly. *Id.* "[I]n the absence of a contemporaneous objection it seems fair to [—16—] give the arguer the benefit of every plausible interpretation of her words." *Id.* (citations omitted).

The Government concedes that the Ford Excursion was not registered to Carela. However, the Government argues that no error resulted from a twice made comment during a long closing. We note that an unintentional misrepresentation of the record may constitute misconduct under certain circumstances. *United States v. Azubike*, 504 F.3d 30, 38 (1st Cir. 2007).

Although the prosecutor's statements at issue were inaccurate, they did not so poison the well that "the trial's outcome was likely affected." *Vázquez-Larrauri*, 778 F.3d at 283 (citation omitted) (internal quotation marks omitted). In particular, two factors render the prosecutor's comments harmless: (1) "the district judge gave curative instructions" as to the jury's role in weighing the evidence and determining guilt, including effective direct reference to the evidentiary value to be given to lawyers' closing arguments; and, most importantly and as alluded to above, (2) "the strength of evidence against [Carela]" (i.e. his admissions and the circumstantial evidence) outweighs any risk of affecting Carela's substantial rights. *Id*.

Carela also takes issue with the prosecutor's statement that the draft contract certified that the Ford Excursion was being sold and that the draft agreement was "a very specific contract." [—17—] The Government again concedes that the prosecutor's word choice was far from ideal, but posits that these statements did not affect the outcome of trial. We also agree with the Government on this point. Although we encourage the Government to refrain from utilizing this type of language during trial and to ensure that its statements are factually accurate, we cannot conclude that Carela suffered prejudice here. As we have discussed throughout this opinion, there was an abundance of evidence against Carela in this case. In fact, Carela himself admitted to being part of the conspiracy. As such, we cannot conclude that the prosecutor's gaffes poisoned the well and impacted the outcome of trial.

Carela further claims that the prosecutor improperly implied that Carela was guilty of an uncharged conspiracy because he purchased the Ford Excursion.

[Carela] needed a van. He bought it before in July with other co-conspirators. As Mr. Edwin Léon Léon explained to you, the transaction was somebody came in and paid him cash for the vehicle. When he was selling it, two vehicles arrived, five or six individuals.

He thought he was selling to this individual, but then as they were ready to sign the documents, he said, "No, no, no. Please put it in the friend of my relative or friend, Mr. Víctor Manuel Carela." And he has the documents to purchase it.

That's a conspiracy. More than two individuals working together to accomplish what the object of the conspiracy is in this case. (Emphasis added) [—18—]

Although the use of the word "that" is somewhat ambiguous, we read the prosecutor's statement as referring to the charged conspiracy to smuggle cocaine and not a conspiracy to purchase the Ford Excursion. Moreover, we emphasize that in the absence of a contemporaneous objection, it seems fair to give the Government the benefit of every plausible interpretation of the words in dispute. *Sepúlveda*, 15 F.3d at 1187.

In light of the evidence against Carela, we conclude that Carela failed to show that the prosecutor's statements resulted in plain error.

E. Whether the Sentence was Unreasonable

1. Background

Lastly, Carela argues that his sentence was both procedurally and substantively unreasonable. Carela attacks his sentence on the ground that the court improperly considered evidence in Spanish in violation of the Jones Act. In simpler terms, the district court refused Carela's requested minor role adjustment because it relied on evidence that Carela admitted to driving a red "guagua." According to Carela, because there is no English language evidence that supports a finding that Carela drove the red Ford Excursion, his sentence is unreasonable.

Carela points out the following factors to support his contention that he only played a minor role (i.e. did not occupy [—19—] a position of trust): (1) "he was not trusted with the executed contract or any other documents related to ownership" of the red Ford Excursion; (2) he was not given the keys to the red Ford Excursion; (3) he did not pay for the red Ford Excursion; (4) he did not drive away in the red Ford Excursion at the time of sale; (5) he was not paid in advance, or for that matter was never paid, the $5,000 he was to receive for his services; and, finally, (6) his role is notably minor if the broad context of the drug smuggling conspiracy—an international operation requiring complex logistics management (i.e., coordination of travel from Venezuela to Puerto Rico) and substantial investment of funds in the product (i.e., cocaine), labor, and equipment (e.g., transport Vessel)—is taken into consideration. He thus avers that it was clear error to deny his requested minor role adjustment.

2. Applicable Law and Analysis

This Court reviews sentencing decisions for reasonableness based on a totality of the circumstances, and in a bifurcated manner: first, for procedural reasonableness, and second, for substantive reasonableness. *United States v. Ayala-Vázquez*, 751 F.3d 1, 29 (1st Cir. 2014). The district court's "legal determinations of the Sentencing Guidelines' meaning and scope" are reviewed *de novo*, and its factual determinations are reviewed for clear error. *United States v. Bryant*, 571 F.3d 147, [—20—] 153 (1st Cir. 2009). This Court will not "upset the sentencing court's fact-based application of the guidelines unless it is clearly erroneous." *United States v. Santos-Batista*, 239 F.3d 16, 21 (1st Cir. 2001) (citation omitted).

In order for a criminal defendant to qualify for a minor role reduction under United States Sentencing Guidelines § 3B1.2(b), he must satisfy a two-pronged test: (1) "he must demonstrate that he is less culpable than most of those involved in the offenses of conviction;" and, (2) "he must establish that he is less culpable than most of those who have perpetrated similar crimes." *United States v. Mateo-Espejo*, 426 F.3d 508, 512 (1st Cir. 2005) (citations omitted). Typically, "[r]ole-in-the-offense determinations [e.g., minor-role adjustments] are notoriously fact-sensitive." *United States v. Ortiz-Santiago*, 211 F.3d 146,

148 (1st Cir. 2000). We have held that in making these determinations a "defendant who participates in only one phase of a conspiracy may nonetheless be found to play a non-minor role in the conspiracy as a whole." *United States v. Vargas*, 560 F.3d 45, 51 (1st Cir. 2009). Finally, it must be noted that "[r]eliable hearsay is . . . admissible during sentencing proceedings." *United States v. Ramírez-Negrón*, 751 F.3d 42, 52 (1st Cir. 2014).

Here, we have already found that there is no Jones Act violation. Further, the district court did not commit a Jones Act [—21—] violation when it stated that Carela "drove the Ford Excursion." The district court's statement did not prejudice Carela such that reversal is required here. In fact, the district court refused Carela's proposed minor role adjustment on the grounds that Carela (1) used his name to purchase the red Ford Excursion that was used to bring 15 cans of gasoline to the landing site in order to refuel the transport vessel; (2) the red Ford Excursion was going to be used to transport 38 bales of cocaine found at the vessel landing site; (3) Carela was paid $5,000; and (4) when Carela used his name to purchase the red Ford Excursion there were other individuals with him and it was one of these other individuals who paid for the Ford Excursion.

Carela's involvement in the charged offenses was not dependent on his driving of the Ford Excursion. Thus, even if the brief reference to Carela driving the Ford Excursion could have constituted a Jones Act violation, it would not have prejudiced Carela.

Further, denying the minor role adjustment to Carela did not constitute clear error. Carela admitted to loading the cocaine onto a vehicle and transporting the cocaine. Carela also admitted that he had been hired to refuel the vessel that was transporting narcotics. [—22—]

Carela failed to establish that he was less culpable than the other participants in the offense, or indeed that he was less culpable than similarly situated offenders. A lack of profit or success in the criminal enterprise does not trigger a downward adjustment for a minor role. *Cf. United States v. García-Ortiz*, 657 F.3d 25, 29 (1st Cir. 2011) ("The essential predicate is a showing that the defendant is both less culpable than his confederates . . . and less culpable than the mine-run of those who have committed similar crimes." (citing *United States v. Ocasio*, 914 F.2d 330, 333 (1st Cir. 1990))). The record makes clear that the trial court fully considered the relevant factors in denying the minor role adjustment.

We further note that the district court varied downward when sentencing Carela from a suggested 235 to 293 months to a term of 196 months because the court felt that the guideline range was too harsh.

III. *Conclusion*

Having found no reversible error in the proceedings of the trial court, Carela's sentence and conviction are affirmed.

Affirmed.

This page intentionally left blank

United States Court of Appeals for the Second Circuit

United States Court of Appeals
for the Second Circuit

No. 13-3903

CONTINENTAL TERMINALS, INC.
vs.
WATERFRONT COMM'N OF N.Y. HARBOR

Appeal from the United States District Court for the
Southern District of New York

Decided: April 3, 2015

Citation: 782 F.3d 102, 3 Adm. R. 122 (2d Cir. 2015).

Before **RAGGI**, **CHIN**, and **CARNEY**, Circuit Judges.

[—2—] CHIN, Circuit Judge:

In this case, Continental Terminals, Inc. ("Continental") sued the Waterfront Commission of New York Harbor (the "Commission") for a declaratory judgment that its operations at a warehouse in Jersey City, New Jersey were outside the Commission's jurisdiction. Because we conclude that [—3—] Continental engages in stevedoring activities at the warehouse and that the warehouse is an "other waterfront terminal" within the meaning of the Waterfront Commission Act (the "Act"), we hold that its operations fall within the jurisdiction of the Commission.

STATEMENT OF THE CASE

A. *The Commission*

In August 1953, the States of New York and New Jersey entered into an interstate compact, the Act, to address pervasive corruption in New York Harbor. The Act created the Commission to govern operations at the Port of New York-New Jersey. *See Waterfront Comm'n of N.Y. Harbor v. Mercedes-Benz of N.A., Inc.*, 99 N.J. 402, 410 (1985).

When the Act was passed, most of the cargo coming through New York Harbor was handled in the "break-bulk" shipping method. *See id.* at 411-12. Individual pieces of cargo were loaded onto trucks, driven to the pier, and then unloaded. The cargo was then loaded piece-by-piece onto the vessel. Similarly, when cargo arrived in New York Harbor, it was unloaded from vessels piece-by-piece, placed on trucks, and then delivered to another destination. *Id.* at 412. [—4—]

Containerization transformed the shipping business. With containerization, a shipper loaded cargo into a box-shaped container, typically 20 feet long, 8 feet high, and 8 feet wide, *see In re M/V DG Harmony*, 394 F. Supp. 2d 649, 652 n.3 (S.D.N.Y. 2005), *aff'd in part, vacated in part, and rev'd in part*, 533 F.3d 83 (2d Cir. 2008), which was then loaded onto a truck, *see Waterfront Comm'n of N.Y. Harbor*, 99 N.J. at 411-12. The truck transported the container to the pier, where the container was lifted aboard a ship. *Waterfront Comm'n of N.Y. Harbor*, 99 N.J. at 412. Upon arrival at the final port, the container was removed from the vessel, eventually to be transported to a further destination. *Id.* Container ships are substantial in size and can hold thousands of containers. *See Harmony*, 394 F. Supp. 2d at 652 (describing container ship, which was 176.57 meters long and 27.5 meters wide, and could hold 1,799 containers). *See generally Ne. Marine Terminal Co. v. Caputo*, 432 U.S. 249, 269-79 (1977).

B. *Continental's Warehouse Operations in Jersey City*

Continental operates a number of warehouses in New Jersey, including a warehouse at 112 Port Jersey Boulevard, in Jersey City (the "112 Warehouse"). As part of its operations there, large cranes that sit on [—5—] "stringpieces"[1] lift containers of coffee from ships and move them to the Container Yard at the Global Marine Terminal. *See* Complaint, Ex. D. Continental then picks up the containers from the Container Yard and transports them to its facilities, including the 112 Warehouse.

---

[1] A "stringpiece" is "the heavy square timber laying along the top of the piles forming a dock front or timber pier." Special App. 4 n.2 (quoting United States Naval Supply Operational Training Center, Shiploading: A Picture-Dictionary of Shiploading Terms (1945)).

Once the containers arrive at the 112 Warehouse, Continental unloads them and removes their contents. Continental stores the freight for periods ranging from fewer than 30 days to up to 6 months. Continental provides a number of services for its customers, including unloading cargo; sampling and weighing cargo to facilitate sales between its customers (shippers and importers) and buyers; palletizing it; and strapping or wrapping it for future delivery. Continental draws samples from approximately 25% of its cargo and provides weighing services for approximately 10% of its cargo. As of October 2010, Continental transported between approximately 100 and 150 containers a week to its 112 Warehouse. [—6—]

C. *The Commission's Determination*

By letter dated April 12, 2011, the Commission advised Continental that it was required to obtain a stevedore license for its operations. Continental disputed that determination. By letter dated May 17, 2011, the Commission reiterated its decision that Continental was subject to the Commission's jurisdiction, and that it was required to be licensed as a stevedore. The letter advised that the Commission concluded that the "property line and building of [the 112 Warehouse]" were within 1,000 yards of a pier. The Commission advised Continental that its determination was "final" and therefore subject to judicial review.

The Commission identified three pinpoints for determining whether the 112 Warehouse was within 1,000 yards of a pier: (1) the corner of the Global Terminal fence line closest to Continental's facilities; (2) the corner of the Bayonne Tank Ro-Ro Pier closest to Continental's facilities; and (3) the corner of the Bayonne Pier located at the U.S. Coast Pier closest to Continental's facilities. A survey later revealed that at least two of these pinpoints were within 1,000 yards of the 112 Warehouse. Continental disputes that these are proper pinpoints. [—7—]

D. *Procedural History*

Continental commenced this action below on July 14, 2011, seeking (1) a declaratory judgment that its operations at the 112 Warehouse were outside the jurisdiction of the Commission and (2) a permanent injunction enjoining the Commission from requiring Continental to register and obtain a license for those operations. *Continental Terminals, Inc. v. Waterfront Comm'n of N.Y. Harbor*, No. 11 Civ. 4869, 2013 WL 5477487, at *1 (S.D.N.Y. Sept. 30, 2013).[2] The Commission filed a counterclaim seeking a declaratory judgment that Continental's warehouse operations fell within its jurisdiction. The parties cross-moved for summary judgment. On September 30, 2013, the district court issued a memorandum order denying Continental's motion for summary judgment and granting the Commission's motion. Judgment was entered accordingly on September 30, 2013. This appeal followed. [—8—]

DISCUSSION

A. *Applicable Law*

We review the granting of a motion for summary judgment *de novo. Scaria v. Rubin*, 117 F.3d 652, 653 (2d Cir. 1997) (per curiam).[3]

---

[2] The district court had subject matter jurisdiction over the case pursuant to 28 U.S.C. § 1331 because the case presents a federal question: the Commission is a bi-state agency formed pursuant to a compact between New York and New Jersey authorized by Congress, and interpretation of such a congressionally authorized compact presents a question of federal law. *See M.F. v. State of N.Y. Executive Dep't Div. of Parole*, 640 F.3d 491, 494 (2d Cir. 2011) (holding that interstate compact approved by Congress "has the force of federal law" and thus its interpretation "clearly presents a federal question"); *see also NYSA-ILA Vacation & Holiday Fund v. Waterfront Comm'n of N.Y Harbor*, 732 F.2d 292, 297 (2d Cir. 1984) ("[T]he Waterfront Commission Compact should be viewed as federal law.").

[3] The district court did not discuss the standard of review to be applied to the judicial review of a determination of the Commission, and it considered the question *de novo*. On appeal, the Commission suggests that its decision implementing the Act should be afforded "substantial deference." *See Waterfront Comm'n of N.Y. Harbor v. Constr. &*

Under the Act, a company engaging in "stevedoring" activities must be licensed by the Commission and its employees must be registered as longshoremen. N.Y. Unconsol. Laws § 9819. A "stevedore" is defined as:

a contractor (not including an employee) engaged for compensation pursuant to a contract or arrangement with a carrier of freight by water, in moving waterborne freight carried or consigned for carriage by such carrier on vessels of such carrier berthed at piers, on piers at [—9—] which such vessels are berthed or *at other waterfront terminals.*

Id. § 9806 (emphasis added). This includes contractors who "perform labor or services incidental to the movement of waterborne freight on vessels berthed at piers, on piers or at other waterfront terminals, including, but not limited to, cargo storage, cargo repairing, coopering, general maintenance, mechanical and miscellaneous work, horse and cattle fitting, grain ceiling, and marine carpentry." *Id.* § 9905(1)(b). The term also includes contractors who "perform labor or services involving, or incidental to, the movement of freight into or out of containers (which have been or which will be carried by a carrier of freight by water) on vessels berthed at piers,

Marine Equip. Co., 928 F. Supp. 1388, 1400 (D.N.J. 1996). In fact, the Commission's decision relies on two subsidiary findings: (1) under the Act, the 112 Warehouse was within 1,000 yards of a "pier"; and (2) under the Commission's own rulings interpreting the Act, Continental was engaged in stevedoring activity at the 112 Warehouse. The deference accorded to these determinations may vary as a result of their different contexts. *Compare Belmonte v. Snashall*, 2 N.Y.3d 560, 565-66 (2004) (observing that agency interpretation is entitled to deference if interpretation involves "some type of specialized knowledge," but that no deference is warranted where "the question is one of pure statutory reading and analysis"), *with Building Trades Emp'rs' Educ. Ass'n v. McGowan*, 311 F.3d 501, 507 (2d Cir. 2002) ("We defer to a state agency's interpretation of its own regulations, unless the interpretation is arbitrary or capricious."). We need not pursue the question further, however, because, even applying *de novo* review to the whole, we conclude that the Commission's determination that Continental is subject to its jurisdiction was correct.

on piers or at other waterfront terminals." *Id.* § 9905(1)(c).

Further guidance is provided by the Commission's Rulings, which define stevedoring activities to include "weighing and scaling," "strapping," and "sampling" at other waterfront terminals. Rulings of the Waterfront Commission of New York Harbor on the Applicability of the 1969 Legislative Amendments to [—10—] the Waterfront Commission Act to Certain Situations (the "Rulings") II.A.1,2.[4] The Rulings also define stevedoring activities to include "load[ing] or unload[ing] containers with freight which has been . . . carried by a carrier of freight by water . . . within 1,000 yards of a pier," as well

---

[4] The Rulings provide in pertinent part:

A. <u>Situations Requiring Licensing and/or Registration</u>

1. Companies engaged in weighing and scaling where the services are performed at piers, vessels or other waterfront terminals are required to be licensed as stevedores and their employees registered.

2. Companies which provide services such as . . . strapping, . . . crating, labeling, marking, . . . cargo inspection and sampling, etc. . . . [must] be licensed and its employees registered where the services are performed at a pier or marine terminal or other waterfront terminal . . . .

Rulings II.A.1, 2. Under the Rulings, a company engaging in "regular warehousing" is not required to obtain a stevedore license "even though it may on occasion load or unload containers incidental to its warehouse function, except for operations covered under Paragraph [1.A.3]." Rulings I.B.1. Paragraph 1.A.3 provides, in turn, that "[a] warehouse operation by a general stevedore (including loading and unloading of vessels) . . . or a consolidation or deconsolidation station (an operation which moves freight into or out of containers as a regular practice) which is a true extension of the stevedore's . . . or consolidation or deconsolidation station's regular operation and which is performed at a pier or other waterfront terminal requires that the company . . . be licensed as a stevedore and its employees performing the covered work be registered." Rulings I.A.3.

as services performed at deconsolidation stations, at which a business "receives containers from piers and [—11—] terminals and strips cargo from said containers for distribution to consignees." Rulings III.A.1.[5]

An "other waterfront terminal" is a "warehouse, depot or other terminal (other than a pier) which is located within one thousand yards of any [—12—] pier in the port of New York district and which is used for waterborne freight in whole or substantial part." N.Y. Unconsol. Laws § 9806.[6]

---

[5] The Rulings provide in pertinent part:

A. <u>Situations Requiring Licensing and/or Registration</u>

    1. Contractors who, for compensation pursuant to a contract or arrangement with any person, load or unload containers with freight which has been or will be carried by a carrier of freight by water at a pier or a marine terminal, or within 1,000 yards of a pier (other waterfront terminal), require licensing as stevedores and their employees require registration. . . . A deconsolidation station is a facility which in the regular course of business receives containers from piers and terminals and strips cargo from said containers for distribution to consignees. In determining whether . . . deconsolidation is conducted "in the regular course of business" the percentage of such . . . stripping as compared to the contractor's other work or services shall not be a factor.

B. <u>Situations Which Do Not Requiring Licensing and/or Registration</u>

    1. The occasional loading or unloading of containers as incidental to the function of a warehouse or other facility which is not primarily in the business of such loading or unloading of containers does not require the licensing of the company performing such work or the registration of its employees.

Rulings III.A., B.

[6] An "other waterfront terminals" is also defined as "any warehouse, depot or other terminal (other than a pier), whether enclosed or open, which is

B. *Application*

Continental argues that it was not required to be licensed as a stevedore under the Act for its activities at the 112 Warehouse because (1) its "primary function" is "regular warehousing (i.e., issu[ing] warehouse receipts)," and that any stevedoring activity was "incidental to its warehouse function," Appellant's Br. at 31 (quoting Rulings I.B.1), and (2) the 112 Warehouse is not an "other waterfront terminal" because it is not located within 1,000 yards of a "pier." We disagree, in both respects.

1. *Continental's Activities*

We conclude that the district court correctly held, as a matter of law, that Continental engages in "stevedoring activities." [—13—]

Continental provided quintessential stevedoring services under the Act, as it provided services "incidental to the movement of waterborne freight . . . at other waterfront terminals," N.Y. Unconsol. Laws § 9905(1)(b), and provided services "involving, or incidental to, the movement of freight into or out of containers . . . at other waterfront terminals," *id.* § 9905(1)(c). Continental also provided stevedoring services under the Commission's Rulings, which, as discussed above, require licensing and registration for companies and contractors who provide services including cargo storage; weighing, strapping, crating, labeling, marking, inspecting, and sampling cargo; and unloading containers with freight that has been carried by a carrier of freight by water. *See* Rulings II.A.1, 2 & III.A.1. As the undisputed facts show, Continental provided all of these services in connection with

---

located in a marine terminal in the port of New York district and any part of which is used by any person to perform labor or services involving, or incidental to, the movement of waterborne freight or freight." N.Y. Unconsol. Laws § 9905(10). A "marine terminal" is defined as "an area which includes piers, which is used primarily for the moving, warehousing, distributing or packing of waterborne freight or freight to or from such piers, and which, inclusive of such piers, is under common ownership or control." *Id.*

containerized cargo removed from ships—some 100 to 150 containers per week—at the 112 Warehouse. Continental picked up the cargo from various local steamship piers, took it back to its facilities, stored it, and provided the services identified above.

Continental argues, however, that its primary function is regular warehousing, and that the above-detailed activities were merely "incidental" to its regular warehousing activities. The district court correctly rejected this [—14—] argument. *Continental Terminals, Inc. v. Waterfront Comm'n of N.Y. Harbor*, No. 11 Civ. 4869, 2013 WL 5477487, at *4 (S.D.N.Y. Sept. 30, 2013). Even assuming that Continental's "primary function" is regular warehousing, the level of these other activities engaged in by Continental was more than "incidental." Indeed, Continental's business was to "go to the piers, marine terminals, pick up containerized freight," and then take the cargo back to its facility where it "unload[ed] the cargo, and then . . . palletize[d] . . . [it] and put it into the warehouse and h[e]ld it for the client," providing weighing, strapping, sorting, and other stevedoring services. Joint App. 42. Clearly, unloading containers was more than "incidental" to its warehouse function; indeed, Continental unloaded 100 to 150 containers per week.

2. *Other Waterfront Terminals*

The question remains whether Continental's stevedoring activities take place at an "other waterfront terminal." N.Y. Unconsol. Laws § 9806. The 112 Warehouse is an "other waterfront terminal" if it is a "warehouse, depot or other terminal" that "is located within [1,000] yards of any pier . . . and . . . is used for waterborne freight in whole or substantial part." *Id.* [—15—]

Continental argues that the 112 Warehouse is not within 1,000 yards of a "pier" because a "pier" is limited to structures located on the water that are used for loading and unloading waterborne freight from vessels. Under Continental's definition, a pier does *not* include the area where containers are stored after being removed from a vessel.

Thus, according to Continental, the correct measurement should be from the Global Marine Terminal stringpiece that directly abuts the water (the actual structure next to which boats dock) to the corner of the 112 Warehouse, which is 1,119.70 yards. Continental contends that the Container Yard that is part of the Global Marine Terminal should not be included.

The Commission argues that a "pier" is an area where waterborne freight is loaded, unloaded, and stored, including any area where containers are stored once removed from the vessel. The Commission contends that the correct measurement is from the Global Marine Terminal *fence line* (the border of the Container Yard where containers are stored) to the corner of the 112 Warehouse. It is undisputed that the distance from the Global Marine Terminal fence line to the corner of the 112 Warehouse is 521.99 yards. [—16—]

The district court held that the 112 Warehouse is an "other waterfront terminal" because it is located within 1,000 yards of a "pier." *Continental Terminals, Inc.*, 2013 WL 5477487, at *4. Specifically, the district court found that the "pier" included the Container Yard within the Global Marine Terminal, and that therefore the correct measurement was from the Global Marine Terminal fence line to the corner of the 112 Warehouse. *Id.* Using that pinpoint, the 112 Warehouse lies within 1,000 yards of a "pier."

We agree. As the district court noted, the definition of "pier" includes a "wharf." *Id.* at *3 (relying on N.Y. Unconsol. Laws § 9806). While a "wharf" is not defined in section 9806, it is defined in Black's Law Dictionary as a "structure on the margin of navigable waters, alongside of which vessels can be brought for the sake of being conveniently loaded or unloaded, or *a space of ground, artificially prepared, for the reception of merchandise from a ship or vessel*, so as to promote the discharge of such vessel." Black's Law Dictionary 1767 (4th ed. 1951) (emphasis added); *see Taniguchi v. Kan Pac. Saipan, Ltd.*, 132 S. Ct. 1997, 2002 (2012) (holding that "[w]hen a term goes undefined in a statute, we give the term its ordinary meaning," and then consulting "dictionaries in use when Congress enacted [statute in question]" for ordinary meaning); *see also* The Maritime and [—17—] Shipping Dictionary 654 (2006 ed.) (defining "wharf" as "[a] structure of open, rather than solid construction, along a shore or bank which provides berthing for ships and which generally provides cargo-handling facilities. A platform alongside navigable water where ships are loaded and unloaded."); Oxford-English Dictionary Vol. XX 185 (2d ed. 1989) (defining "wharf" as "[a] place raised or otherwise marked out on which stuff is deposited for subsequent removal to another place"). Because a "wharf" includes the area where containers are temporarily placed upon discharge while awaiting removal to another location, the Container Yard at the Global Marine Terminal is part of a "pier." Therefore, the Commission correctly used the fence line at the Container Yard as the point of measurement, which is 521.99 yards from the corner of the 112 Warehouse.

In urging otherwise, Continental argues that the Commission's interpretation equates a pier with a marine terminal, rendering the latter term superfluous under the Act. We disagree. A "marine terminal" is statutorily defined as "an area which includes piers, which is used primarily for the moving, warehousing, distributing or packaging of waterborne freight or freight from such piers, and which, inclusive of such piers, is under common ownership or control." N.Y. Unconsol. Laws § 9905(10). Thus, a marine terminal is distinct [—18—] from a pier because it consists of a larger area, including piers, which is under common ownership or control. Further, the movement of waterborne freight within a marine terminal is subject to more stringent licensing and registration requirements under the Act. *Compare id.* § 9806 (defining "other waterfront terminal" to include any warehouse located within 1,000 yards of a pier "and which is used for waterborne freight *in whole or substantial part*" (emphasis added)), *with id.* § 9905(10) (defining "other waterfront terminal" to include any warehouse located in a marine terminal and "*any part of which* is used by any

person to perform labor or services involving, or incidental to, the movement of waterborne freight" (emphasis added)). Accordingly, we identify no error in the Commission's interpretation.

Our conclusion is consistent with the modern-day realities of the handling of waterborne freight and port operations. Containerized freight is carried in large container ships, large cranes are used, and piers have expanded to accommodate the high volume of containers discharged from vessels. There must be room for "the reception of merchandise," Black's Law Dictionary 1767, and thus there must be storage areas adjacent to the stringpieces to which [—19—] containers can be moved and held temporarily until they can be carried away.[7] These storage areas—such as the Container Yard at the Global Marine Terminal—are an important part of the "pier" as they facilitate the high-volume discharge of merchandise from container ships. *See Continental Terminals, Inc. v. Waterfront Comm'n of N.Y. Harbor*, 486 F. Supp. 1110, 1115 (S.D.N.Y. 1980) (holding that Continental's definition of a "pier" as being limited to the stringpiece is "excessively restrictive"); *Mahoney v. City of Chelsea*, 478 N.E.2d 160, 163 (Mass. App. Ct. 1985) (experts agreeing that "commercial dock" includes "a storage area to which the cargo can be efficiently moved from the stringpiece and where it can be held until it is carried away"). Because the 112 Warehouse is within 1,000 yards of a "pier," it is an "other waterfront terminal," and Continental is within the jurisdiction of the Commission.[8] [—20—]

---

[7] As the Supreme Court has noted, "[c]ontainerization permits the time-consuming work of stowage and unstowage to be performed on land in the absence of the vessel. The use of containerized ships has reduced the costly time the vessel must be in port and the amount of manpower required to get the cargo onto the vessel. In effect, the operation of loading and unloading has been moved shoreward; the container is a modern substitute for the hold of the vessel." *Ne. Marine Terminal Co.*, 432 U.S. at 270.

[8] In light of our conclusion that the Commission's first pinpoint, the fence line at the Container Yard, is within 1,000 yards of the 112

CONCLUSION

For the foregoing reasons, the judgment of the district court is AFFIRMED.

Warehouse, we do not discuss the second and third pinpoints relied upon by the Commission.

United States Court of Appeals
for the Second Circuit

No. 13-2543

UNITED STATES

VS.

BENGIS

Appeal from the United States District Court for the
Southern District of New York

Decided: April 16, 2015

Citation: 783 F.3d 407, 3 Adm. R. 129 (2d Cir. 2015).

Before **WALKER, CABRANES,** and **CARNEY,** Circuit
Judges.

[—3—] **WALKER,** Circuit Judge:

Arnold Bengis and Jeffrey Noll pleaded guilty to conspiracy to commit smuggling and violate the Lacey Act, which prohibits trade in illegally taken fish and wildlife, and to substantive violations of the Lacey Act. David Bengis pleaded guilty to conspiracy to violate the Lacey Act. The district court (Lewis A. Kaplan, J.) entered a restitution order requiring Arnold Bengis, Noll, and David Bengis (jointly, "defendants") to pay $22,446,720 to South Africa. Defendants appeal the restitution order on a variety of grounds. In this opinion, we address only: (1) the government's contention that the appeal should be dismissed; (2) the defendants' contention that the restitution order violated their Sixth Amendment rights; and (3) David Bengis's contention that he should not be held liable for the entire restitution amount. We affirm the district court's judgment except as to the extent of David Bengis's liability and we remand the restitution order entered against David Bengis for further proceedings. Defendants' remaining arguments are resolved in a summary order filed simultaneously with this opinion. [—4—]

BACKGROUND

From 1987 to 2001, the defendants engaged in an elaborate scheme to harvest large quantities of South Coast and West Coast rock lobsters from South African waters for export to the United States in violation of both South African and U.S. law. At all relevant times, the South African Department of Marine and Coastal Management maintained fishing season quotas and issued harvesting and exporting permits for rock lobsters. Defendants, through their company, Hout Bay Fishing Industries Ltd. ("Hout Bay"), harvested rock lobsters in amounts that exceeded the authorized quotas and exported those lobsters to the United States.

In May 2001, South Africa seized a container of unlawfully harvested lobsters. South Africa declined to prosecute the individual defendants because it determined they were beyond the reach of South African authorities, but it charged Hout Bay with overfishing of South and West Coast Rock Lobsters in violation of South Africa's Marine Living Resources Act 18 of 1998. Arnold Bengis returned to South Africa and pleaded guilty on behalf of Hout Bay.

South Africa cooperated with a parallel investigation conducted by the United States. The individual defendants were eventually indicted in the United States District Court for the Southern District of New York, and, on March 2, 2004, Arnold Bengis and Jeffrey Noll pleaded guilty to: (i) violations of the Lacey [—5—] Act, 16 U.S.C. § 3372(a)(2)(A), which makes it a crime to, inter alia, import fish taken in violation of foreign law; and (ii) conspiracy to violate the Lacey Act and to commit smuggling, 18 U.S.C. § 545, in violation of 18 U.S.C. § 371. On April 2, 2004, David Bengis pleaded guilty to a misdemeanor count of conspiracy to violate the Lacey Act. The defendants were sentenced principally to terms of imprisonment of 46 months (Arnold Bengis), 30 months (Jeffrey Noll), and 12 months (David Bengis) and to a forfeiture order of $13,300,000 to the United States. Although the plea agreements acknowledged that restitution was a further possibility, the district court deferred addressing restitution.

The United States thereafter sought restitution on behalf of South Africa. In support of its application for restitution, the United States submitted a report prepared by the Ocean and Land Resource Assessment

Consultants ("OLRAC") that calculated restitution under two separate methods. The first method calculated the cost to South Africa of restoring the rock lobster fishery to the level that would have existed if the defendants had not engaged in overharvesting (the "catch forfeit" method); restitution under this method amounted to $46,775,150. The second method calculated the market value of the overharvested lobsters (the "market value" method); restitution under this method amounted to $61,932,630. [—6—]

The district court denied the government's request for restitution under both the Mandatory Victims Restitution Act of 1996 ("MVRA") and the Victim and Witness Protection Act of 1982 ("VWPA") because it concluded that South Africa was not a "victim" of the defendants' offenses. We vacated these orders on the basis that South Africa had a property interest in the illegally harvested lobsters and was therefore a "victim" under both the MVRA and VWPA. Because of South Africa's property interest in the lobsters, we held that the MVRA governed the restitution award to South Africa and remanded for calculation of the appropriate restitution amount. *United States v. Bengis*, 631 F.3d 33, 42 (2d Cir. 2011), *cert. denied*, 131 S. Ct. 2911 (2011).

On remand, the district court referred the government's request for restitution to Magistrate Judge Andrew J. Peck. Using the market value method, the magistrate judge recommended a restitution award of $54,883,550, which represented the market value of the illegally harvested lobster offset by the $7,049,080 the defendants had already paid to South Africa.

On March 11, 2013, the government moved to restrain the defendants from transferring their assets held in three trusts at the SG Hambros Bank located in the Channel Islands in the United Kingdom and to direct the defendants to deposit $54,883,550 with the Registry of the Court. On March 22, 2013, the Bengises made [—7—] substantial changes to the three trusts. Specifically, David Bengis was removed as a beneficiary of two of the trusts, Arnold Bengis resigned as protector,

and the Bengises appointed their family lawyer, Basil De Sousa, as the new protector.

On March 25, 2013, the district court entered an interim order restraining transfer or disposition of the assets held at SG Hambros except to the extent those assets exceeded $54,883,550. On June 14, 2013, the district court adopted the magistrate judge's recommended restitution order in part. The district court found that the government only had shown that the West Coast (and not the South Coast) rock lobsters were intended for the United States and that the restitution order should be limited to the market value of those lobsters. Therefore, the district court entered a restitution order of $22,446,720 and modified its restraining order to reflect the reduced amount of restitution.

Meanwhile, on June 10, 2013, before the restraining order was modified, the trustees of the SG Hambros trusts requested the bank to transfer the trusts' assets to a Swiss bank. Relying on the district court's restraining order, SG Hambros refused to comply with this request. The trustees then sued SG Hambros in the Channel Islands seeking to compel the transfer.

On October 17, 2013, the district court ordered the defendants and "all persons in active concert" with them to deposit funds up to [—8—] the restitution amount with the Clerk of Court (the "deposit order") and enjoined defendants and "all persons in active concert" with them from encumbering or transferring to any entity other than the Clerk of Court any property in which the defendants held an interest. Defendants' 2014 App'x 200. The defendants timely appealed both the underlying restitution award and the deposit order.

DISCUSSION

We review a district court's order of restitution and deposit order for abuse of discretion. *See United States v. Ojeikere*, 545 F.3d 220, 222 (2d Cir. 2008). The district court's legal conclusions are reviewed *de novo*, and its factual findings for clear error. *United*

States v. Amato, 540 F.3d 153, 158 (2d Cir. 2008).

I. Discretionary Dismissal of Appeal

Before turning to the merits of defendants' appeal, we address the government's contention that the appeal should be dismissed because the defendants tried to evade the court's power to execute its mandate. In support, the government points to the defendants' refusal to comply with the deposit order and the trustee's suit seeking to compel a transfer of the SG Hambros assets to a Swiss bank.

The government relies on *Stern v. United States*, 249 F.2d 720 (2d Cir. 1957). In *Stern*, we entered a provisional order dismissing an [—9—] appeal because the defendants showed "a determined effort to deprive the court of power to execute its mandate." *Id.* at 722. Specifically, the defendants had liquidated their assets, abandoned their U.S. citizenship, and fled to Czechoslovakia in a "successful attempt to render the court powerless to enforce its decree." *Id.*

In this case the actions of the defendants are more benign. The defendants, who have served their sentences, have continued to submit to the jurisdiction of the district court, have not renounced their U.S. citizenship, and are in no sense fugitives. As the government conceded at oral argument, the defendants have continued to appear at court proceedings when required. In addition, the defendants' efforts to transfer assets from SG Hambros to the Swiss bank were unsuccessful. Therefore, although we are troubled by the defendants' apparent efforts to place their assets beyond the court's reach rather than comply with the deposit order, the SG Hambros assets appear to remain available to satisfy the restitution award and the district court's contempt power reaches the defendants. Finally and significantly, the government has not sought to hold the defendants in contempt. In these circumstances, we decline to exercise our discretion to deny the defendants appellate review. *See In re Feit & Drexler, Inc.*, 760 F.2d 406, 414 (2d Cir. 1985) (declining to dismiss appeal where the defendant [—10—]

remained subject to the court's jurisdiction and the contempt process was available).

II. Defendants' *Apprendi* Challenge to the Amount of Restitution

Turning to the merits of the defendants' attack on the restitution order, we first address defendants' contention that the order violated their Sixth Amendment protections under *Apprendi v. New Jersey*, 530 U.S. 466 (2000). Under the sentencing scheme at issue in *Apprendi*, a defendant found guilty by a jury beyond a reasonable doubt for possession of a prohibited weapon was guilty of a second-degree offense. If in addition, however, a judge found by a preponderance of the evidence that the defendant's purpose for unlawfully possessing the weapon was to intimidate his victim on the basis of a particular characteristic the victim possessed, the judge could impose punishment identical to that which New Jersey provided for crimes of the first degree. *Id.* at 491. The effect of this enhancement was to increase the maximum penalty the defendant faced from 10 years to 20 years. *Id.* at 495. The Supreme Court held that this scheme violated the defendant's Sixth Amendment rights because "[o]ther than the fact of a prior conviction, any fact that increases the penalty for a crime beyond the prescribed statutory maximum must be submitted to a jury, and proved beyond a reasonable doubt." *Id.* at 490. [—11—]

In this case, the restitution amount reflects South Africa's loss, which was calculated based on the market value of the illegally harvested lobsters. The defendants' plea agreements did not specify the value of the rock lobsters they illegally imported. Defendants therefore argue that, under *Apprendi*, the restitution amount cannot be based on the value of the lobsters because that fact was neither admitted by the defendants nor found by a jury beyond a reasonable doubt.

This argument is unavailing because, unlike the terms of imprisonment at issue in *Apprendi*, the MVRA and VWPA specify no maximum restitution amount. Therefore, a judge cannot find facts that would cause the amount to exceed a prescribed statutory maximum. *See United States v. Reifler*, 446 F.3d 65, 118 (2d Cir. 2006) (holding that restitution is an indeterminate system that "fixes no range of permissible restitutionary amounts and sets no maximum amount . . . that the court may order").

Defendants also argue that the district court's calculation of South Africa's loss required it to engage in the same type of factfinding as the district court that imposed the fine held to violate *Apprendi* in *Southern Union Co. v. United States*, 132 S. Ct. 2344 (2012). In that case, the jury found that the defendant had violated an environmental statute, but it was not asked to determine the precise duration of the violation. The district court nevertheless determined [—12—] that the defendant had violated the statute for 762 days and assessed an $18 million fine based on a statutory maximum of $50,000 per day. *Id.* at 2349. The Court held that, under *Apprendi*, the district court's sentence could not exceed the $50,000 statutory maximum fine because it relied on facts that were not reflected in the jury verdict or admitted by the defendant. *Id.* at 2350.

Southern Union is inapposite. In *Southern Union*, but for the district court's finding that the defendant had violated the statute for 762 days, the maximum fine the defendant would have faced was $50,000. *Id.* at 2349. Thus, the district court imposed the fine above a statutory maximum. In this case there never was a determinate maximum restitution amount that defendants faced; under the MVRA, restitution is always determined with respect to the value of property that is lost. *See* 18 U.S.C. § 3663A(b). The district court could not, and did not, exceed a maximum that did not exist. *See Southern Union Co.*, 132 S. Ct. at 2353 ("Nor, *a fortiori*, could there be an *Apprendi* violation where no maximum is prescribed."). Therefore, any factfinding by the district court was not only permissible under *Apprendi* but was required to determine the appropriate amount of restitution under the MVRA.

Defendants' final argument is that restitution is similar to a fine whose maximum is determined with reference to the victim's loss. As defendants point out, the Court in *Southern Union* [—13—] referenced statutes in which the fine may be pegged to some factor of actual loss. 132 S. Ct. at 2351 n.4 (citing, inter alia, 18 U.S.C. § 3571(d), 18 U.S.C. § 645, and 18 U.S.C. § 201(b)). But each of those statutes posits two alternative fine amounts: a determinate statutory maximum and an amount based on the value of loss caused by the defendant. *See, e.g.*, 18 U.S.C. § 3571 (prescribing maximum fines based on the class of offense and "*alternative* fines" based on gain or loss) (emphasis added).

The Court determined that *Apprendi* was implicated when the district court chose to exercise its discretion to use an alternative valuation that exceeded the statutory maximum based on facts not found by the jury. *See Southern Union Co.*, 132 S. Ct. at 2351 ("[O]ur decisions broadly prohibit judicial factfinding that increases maximum criminal sentences, penalties, or punishments . . . ." (internal quotation marks and alterations omitted)). In contrast, restitution under the MVRA and VWPA has only one valuation—the amount of the victim's loss. There is no alternative maximum penalty. In sum, where, as here, there is no determinate statutory maximum that a district court can exceed, there is no range prescribed by statute and thus there can be no *Apprendi* violation.

For these reasons, we adhere to our decision in *United States v. Reifler* and join our sister circuits in concluding that judicial factfinding to determine the appropriate amount of restitution under [—14—] a statute that does not prescribe a maximum does not implicate a defendant's Sixth Amendment rights. *See United States v. Day*, 700 F.3d 713, 732 (4th Cir. 2012), *cert. denied*, 133 S. Ct. 2038 (2013); *United States v. Green*, 722 F.3d 1146, 1150 (9th Cir. 2013), *cert. denied*, 134 S. Ct. 658 (2013); *see also United States v. Wolfe*, 701 F.3d 1206, 1217 (7th Cir. 2012), *cert. denied*, 133 S. Ct. 2797 (2013) (finding that restitution is not a criminal penalty). Therefore the district court did not abuse its discretion by fixing the restitution amount at $22,446,720.

III. David Bengis's Liability for Restitution

The district court ordered Arnold Bengis, Jeffrey Noll, and David Bengis to "pay restitution to the Republic of South Africa, jointly and severally, in the amount of $22,446,720." Defendants' 2013 App'x 325. Separately from the other defendants, David Bengis argues that, because he allocuted to misdemeanor involvement in a conspiracy only from 1999 through August 1, 2001, the restitution ordered against him must exclude losses caused by the acts of the other defendants prior to 1999. The government responds that, because the primary purpose of the MVRA is to make victims of crime whole, the district court acted within its discretion by holding David Bengis jointly and severally liable for the entire restitution amount.

In general, "one who joins an existing conspiracy takes it as it is, and is therefore held accountable for the prior conduct of co-[—15—] conspirators." *United States v. Sansone*, 231 F.2d 887, 893 (2d Cir. 1956). In the context of sentencing for drug conspiracies, however, we have held that "[t]he late-entering coconspirator should be sentenced on the basis of the full quantity of narcotics distributed by other members of the conspiracy only if, when he joined the conspiracy, he could reasonably foresee the distributions of future amounts, or *knew or reasonably should have known what the past quantities were.*" *United States v. Miranda-Ortiz*, 926 F.2d 172, 178 (2d Cir. 1991) (emphasis added).

Restitution must be determined in a similar manner. *See United States v. Boyd*, 222 F.3d 47, 51 (2d Cir. 2000) (per curiam) (finding no plain error where the district court imposed a restitution order holding the defendant "liable for the reasonably foreseeable acts of all co-conspirators"). Thus, if David Bengis's understanding of the scope of the conspiracy he joined in 1999 was such that he knew or reasonably should have known about some or all of the conspiracy's past imports, his restitution order should encompass those amounts. However, if David Bengis joined the conspiracy without reasonable knowledge of his co-conspirators' past activities, then he should not be held liable for the loss caused by those activities. Of course, he would remain jointly and severally liable for the losses caused by the conspiracy after he joined it. [—16—]

On the record before us, we cannot determine whether David Bengis, when he joined the conspiracy in 1999, understood the scope of the conspiracy, such that he knew or should have known the extent of its adverse economic impact. Accordingly, we remand this matter to the district court in accordance with the procedures we set forth in *United States v. Jacobson*, 15 F.3d 19, 22 (2d Cir. 1994), to determine whether David Bengis knew or reasonably should have known the scope and impact of any or all of the past activities of the conspiracy he joined.

On remand, if the district court finds that a preponderance of the evidence shows that David Bengis knew or should have known of the scope and impact of the conspiracy prior to joining it, then the restitution order that has been entered against him may stand. *See United States v. Martinez*, 987 F.2d 920, 926 (2d Cir. 1993) (preponderance of the evidence standard applies to determination of whether defendant reasonably should have known the quantities of drugs sold by the conspiracy). If the district court determines, however, that the full scope and impact of the past activities of the conspiracy would not have been reasonably known to this defendant, then the district court should vacate the judgment and enter a new order reflecting the appropriate amount of restitution for which David Bengis is liable. This amount should include the amount of losses that occurred after David Bengis joined the [—17—] conspiracy and may include any amounts of prior losses of which he would have been reasonably aware. In the interest of judicial economy, this panel will retain jurisdiction over any subsequent appeal from the district court; either party may notify the Clerk of a renewed appeal within fourteen days of the district court's decision. *See Jacobson*, 15 F.3d at 22.

We have considered and find to be without merit the defendants' other arguments, including that (1) the district court abused its discretion by relying on the OLRAC Report and Ray Declaration in determining the appropriate amount of restitution; (2) South Africa was not a "victim" of David Bengis's offense; and (3) the district court abused its discretion by entering the deposit order against the defendants. The disposition of these arguments is set forth in a summary order filed simultaneously with this opinion.

CONCLUSION

For the foregoing reasons, the judgment is AFFIRMED in part, VACATED in part, and REMANDED for further proceedings consistent with this opinion.

United States Court of Appeals
for the Second Circuit

No. 13-1976

HICKS
vs.
VANE LINE BUNKERING, INC.

Appeal from the United States District Court for the
Southern District of New York

Decided: April 17, 2015

Citation: 783 F.3d 939, 3 Adm. R. 135 (2d Cir. 2015).

Before **WINTER, STRAUB,** and **HALL,** Circuit Judges.

[—2—] **WINTER,** Circuit Judge:

Vane Line Bunkering, Inc. appeals from a money judgment for Ciro Charles Hicks following a jury trial before Judge Forrest. The jury found that appellant breached its maritime law duty of providing maintenance and cure[1] following a shoulder injury Hicks sustained while working on board the Tug PATRIOT. It awarded Hicks the unpaid maintenance and cure and damages for pain and suffering caused by the breach. Further, the jury found that appellant's conduct was willful and awarded punitive damages. Finally, based on the jury's finding of willfulness, the district court granted Hicks's motion for reasonable attorney's fees.

Appellant argues that the evidence that appellant's acts and [—3—] omissions caused Hicks's pain and suffering was insufficient as a matter of law. Although it arguably waived the argument, appellant also objects to the award of punitive damages in addition to

---

[1] "Maintenance and cure" refers to the well-settled doctrine of maritime law that a seaman "injur[ed] in the performance of his duty is entitled to be treated and cured at the expense of the ship." *The Osceola,* 189 U.S. 158, 173 (1903), *superseded by statute on other grounds,* The Jones Act, 46 U.S.C. § 30104 (creating a statutory cause of action for negligence). Maintenance includes a seaman's living allowance and unearned wages. Gilmore & Black, The Law of Admiralty § 6–12, at 267–68 (2d ed. 1975).

and/or in excess of the amount of attorney's fees. We affirm.

BACKGROUND

In light of the jury verdict for appellee, we view the trial record in the light most favorable to him. *See Kosmynka v. Polaris Indus., Inc.,* 462 F.3d 74, 77 (2d Cir. 2006).

Hicks was employed by appellant as a deckhand on the Tug PATRIOT. On April 21, 2009, while on deck handling heavy towing gear, he injured his shoulder. Two days later, an orthopedist diagnosed a possible rotator cuff tear. The doctor injected Hicks with cortisone to relieve the pain and gave him a fit-for-duty slip. Prior to returning to work, Hicks was required to see a company doctor, who determined that Hicks was not fit for duty. Subsequently, appellant confirmed in writing its obligation under maritime law to pay sums for Hicks's maintenance and cure, reasonable medical expenses and maintenance costs until his full recovery, maximum improvement, or until his condition was declared permanent.

On July 1, 2009, Hicks underwent surgery on his shoulder. He experienced significant discomfort before and after the surgery. For several months following the procedure, he received [—4—] in-office and at-home physical therapy while continuing to experience significant pain. In December 2009, he informed his treating physician that he still had significant limitations of range of motion of his arm.

Appellant hired a private investigator to videotape Hicks surreptitiously. The video captured him on videotape planting a small tree and playing with his grandson. When Hicks's doctor requested funding for an additional MRI scan, he was shown this footage and a document detailing the physical requirements of Hicks's job. Based on this video and the suggestion—which appellant now admits was false—that Hicks's job required only light lifting, the doctor determined that Hicks was fit for duty. Appellant accordingly informed Hicks that it would terminate maintenance and cure payments effective May 9, 2010.

Beginning in August 2010, Hicks sought continuing care from a second doctor, who diagnosed a recurrent rotator cuff tear. In February 2011, this doctor recommended another surgery plus six months of rehabilitation to repair the additional damage. Under financial pressure caused by the meager maintenance and cure appellant had paid him—$15 per day compared to actual costs of $69.67 per day for food and lodging— and had now terminated, Hicks returned to work while still injured. Severe financial difficulties caused him to miss some of his physical therapy appointments. During this time, his house was put into [—5—] foreclosure, and he was unable to pay for health insurance.

In November 2011, Hicks brought the present action. His claims were based on negligence under the Jones Act and the maritime doctrines of unseaworthiness and maintenance and cure. The jury found that appellant had not been negligent and the PATRIOT was seaworthy, but that appellant had breached its obligation of maintenance and cure by paying Hicks an insufficient per diem and prematurely ceasing payments.

The jury awarded $77,000 in compensatory damages for past maintenance and cure from April 22, 2009 to the date of the verdict; $16,000 in future maintenance and $97,000 in future cure through April 2013; and $132,000 in compensation for past pain and suffering. The jury also found that appellant's failure to pay maintenance and cure was unreasonable and willful and awarded $123,000 in punitive damages. Based on the finding of willfulness, the district court, upon a motion under Fed. R. Civ. P. 54(d), granted Hicks an additional $112,083.77 in attorney's fees.

Appellant moved, unsuccessfully, for judgment as a matter of law or a new trial under Fed. R. Civ. P. Rules 50(b) and 59 respectively. This appeal followed.

DISCUSSION

We review a denial of a Rule 50(b) motion *de novo* and the denial of a Rule 59 motion for abuse of discretion. *See Fabri v.* [—6—] *United Techs. Int'l, Inc.*, 387 F.3d 109, 119 (2d Cir. 2004); *Devlin v. Transp. Commc'ns Int'l Union*, 175 F.3d 121, 131-32 (2d Cir. 1999). With respect to attorney's fees, because "resolution of the district court's grant of attorney's fees implicates a question of law, our review is *de novo.*" *Garcia v. Yonkers Sch. Dist.*, 561 F.3d 97, 102 (2d Cir. 2009).

We, therefore, consider: (i) the evidence underlying the award of pain and suffering damages, and (ii) the award of both punitive damages and attorney's fees.

a) *Pain and Suffering Damages*

An injured seaman may recover damages if the shipowner's failure to pay maintenance and cure caused pain and suffering by prolonging or aggravating the initial injury. *See Vaughan v. Atkinson*, 369 U.S. 527, 539 (1962) (Stewart, J., dissenting); *Cortes v. Baltimore Insular Line, Inc.*, 287 U.S. 367, 371 (1932); *Williams v. Kingston Shipping Co.*, 925 F.2d 721, 723 (4th Cir. 1991) (discussing availability of "money damages for any prolongation or aggravation of the physical injury"); *accord Hines v. J. A. LaPorte, Inc.*, 820 F.2d 1187, 1190 (11th Cir. 1987) (per curiam) (pain and suffering damages awarded where failure to pay maintenance "aggravated Hines' condition, prolonged his pain and suffering, and lengthened the time required for him to reach maximum cure").

In arguing that the evidence was insufficient as a matter of [—7—] law to support an award for pain and suffering, appellant relies heavily on statements by Hicks that his condition did not significantly improve after the initial injury. Appellant argues from these statements that Hicks's pain and suffering were entirely attributable to the original injury and not to appellant's failure to fulfill its maintenance and cure duties. However, under our caselaw, a plaintiff need not show an additional discrete injury or illness resulting from the failure to pay maintenance and cure. *See Rodriguez Alvarez v. Bahama Cruise Line, Inc.*, 898 F.2d 312, 314-15 (2d Cir. 1990) (duty to furnish maintenance and cure continues until seaman fully recovers). Rather, the prolonging or worsening of a condition as a result of the employer's breach will sustain a pain and suffering damages award. *See Messier v. Bouchard Transp.*, 688 F.3d 78, 84-85 (2d Cir. 2012) (duty to pay maintenance and cure extends to aggravation of preexisting illness). And, in maintenance and cure cases, "doubts regarding a shipowner's liability . . . should be resolved in favor of the seamen." *Padilla v. Maersk Line, Ltd.*, 721 F.3d 77, 81-82, 1 Adm. R. 34, 35 (2d Cir. 2013), *cert. denied*, 134 S. Ct. 1309 (2014) (citing *Atkinson*, 369 U.S. at 532).

In the present case, the jury could easily have found that appellant's discontinuation of maintenance and cure benefits caused injuries to Hicks, both physical and otherwise. It could [—8—] also have found that the insufficient payments forced Hicks back to work before physical therapy could render him fit. Indeed, Hicks's second doctor diagnosed a recurrent rotator cuff tear and determined the need for a second surgery, which would have required yet another long bout of physical therapy. Furthermore, Hicks suffered emotional distress stemming from the loss of his home and health insurance, both of which could have been found by the jury to have been caused, at least in part, by appellant's inadequate payments and discontinuation of benefits. *See, e.g., Sims v. U.S. of Am. War Shipping Admin.*, 186 F.2d 972 (3d Cir.), *cert. denied*, 342 U.S. 816 (1951).

Although appellant attempts to cast the causation issue as one of law, the causal link between the cessation of benefits and the harms to Hicks for which damages are sought was for determination by the jury. Based on the evidence, therefore, the district court did not abuse its discretion in holding that the jury acted reasonably in its award for pain and suffering.

b) *Attorney's Fees in Addition to Punitive Damages*

In the district court, the parties did not squarely address the issue of the amount of punitive damages recoverable in a maintenance and cure action. However, because this issue is a pure question of law, we may reach it regardless of waiver. *See Magi XXI, Inc. v. Stato della Città del Vaticano*, 714 F.3d 714, 724 (2d Cir. 2013) ("[W]e have exercised our discretion to hear [—9—] otherwise waived arguments . . . where the argument presents a question of law and there is no need for additional fact-finding.")(internal quotation marks and citations omitted).

We perceive a need to address the issue here. The judgment of the district court here is inconsistent with a decision of another district court in this circuit. *McMillan v. Tug Jane A. Bouchard*, 885 F. Supp. 452, 466 (E.D.N.Y. 1995) (holding that punitive damages in maintenance and cure cases are limited to reasonable attorneys' fees). The conflict is the result of our decision in *Kraljic v. Berman Enter., Inc.*, 575 F.2d 412, 415-16 (2d Cir. 1978). That decision held that, in maintenance and cure cases, the amount of punitive damages is limited to the amount of reasonable attorneys' fees.

As a result, we examine the decision in *Kraljic*, and the one by the Supreme Court, *Vaughan v. Atkinson*, 369 U.S. 527 (1962), that spurred it, in some detail. We also examine developments after *Kraljic*, including a Supreme Court decision, *Atlantic Sounding Co. v. Townsend*, 557 U.S. 404 (2009), that undermines *Kraljic*.

Kraljic, 575 F.2d at 416, reluctantly concluded that limiting punitive damages in maintenance and cure cases to reasonable attorney's fees was required by *Atkinson*. *Atkinson* was a cryptic decision embodied in an opinion written by Justice Douglas. It involved a shipowner's failure to pay maintenance [—10—] and cure, after which the ill seaman successfully sought damages for the unpaid amounts and counsel fees for being forced to go to court to remedy the owner's breach.

Atkinson's discussion of the attorney's fees issue was all of three paragraphs long and conflated the issues of compensatory and punitive damages. *Atkinson* noted that the seaman's claim for attorney's fees did not concern taxable costs; rather, it involved "necessary expenses" incurred as a result of the owner's breach of duty, 369 U.S. at 530, i.e. being "forced to hire a lawyer . . . to get what was plainly owed him," *id.* at 531. However, after this language, which clearly sounds in compensatory damages, *Kraljic*, 575 F.2d at 413 ("This might lead one to conclude that the award of attorney's fees was compensatory . . . ."), the *Atkinson* opinion then noted that the owner's conduct involved both the lack of any investigation into the seaman's claim and silence as to the claim's merits. 369 U.S. at 530-31. The *Atkinson* opinion described this conduct as a "recalcitrance" that was "callous," "willful," and "persistent." *Id.* This language was deemed by us to sound in punitive damages. *Kraljic*, 575 F.2d at 414 ("Recovery of [attorney's] fees is therefore based upon the traditional theory of punitive damages.")

The dissenters in *Atkinson* argued that there was no basis for an award of counsel fees as compensatory damages but that the [—11—] conduct of the owner might support an award of "exemplary damages in accord with traditional concepts of the law of damages." 369 U.S. at 540. The dissent noted, however, that punitive damages "would not necessarily be measured" by counsel fees but might provide "indirect compensation for such expenditures." *Id.*

Our decision in *Kraljic* read *Atkinson* to authorize punitive damages in maintenance and cure cases but to limit such damages to an award of reasonable attorney's fees. *Kraljic*, 575 F.2d at 416. We did so reluctantly, believing that we were "constrained" by *Atkinson*. *Id.* However, our rationale for reading *Atkinson* to impose such a limit, as best we can determine at this distance in time, was that *Atkinson* authorized an award of attorney's fees only where the owner's

conduct was sufficiently egregious to justify a punitive award. Based on the *Atkinson* dissent's view that a punitive award, but not one measured by fees, was available and our view in *Kraljic* that "[t]he seaman surely is not entitled to separate awards of both [punitive damages and fees]," *id.* at 414, we inferred that the *Atkinson* majority authorized an award of punitive damages but limited it to attorney's fees.

Lost in this chain of reasoning was the fact that the seaman in *Atkinson* sought only counsel fees and not punitive damages. The Supreme Court majority, therefore, had no reason to consider, much less discuss, the availability of punitive damages in excess [—12—] of, or in addition to, counsel fees. While the dissenters did mention punitive damages and the fact that they are not measured by attorney's fees, as described above, the majority ignored the dissent. The inference that we appeared to have drawn from the dissent, based in part on our view that separate awards of both punitive damages and counsel fees would be impermissible, *id.*, was certainly not an inescapable interpretation of the cryptic opinion in *Atkinson*. Indeed, *Kraljic*'s limitation of punitive damages to counsel fees is an outlier, expressly rejected by some courts, *e.g.*, *Hines*, 820 F.2d at 1189, simply ignored by others, *e.g.*, *Robinson v. Pocahontas, Inc.*, 477 F.2d 1048, 1051-52 (1st Cir. 1973), and adopted by no one outside this circuit. We conclude that it is no longer governing law in this circuit for two reasons.[2]

First, the landscape of Supreme Court caselaw has been substantially altered since *Atkinson* and *Kraljic*. In *Atlantic Sounding*, the Supreme Court held that punitive damages, as traditionally available under the common law, are available in claims arising under federal maritime law, including claims for maintenance and cure. *Atlantic Sounding*, 557 U.S. at 424. It is incontestable that traditional punitive damages are not limited

---

[2] We have circulated this opinion to all active members of this Court prior to filing. *See Shipping Corp. of India v. Jaldhi Overseas Pte Ltd.*, 585 F.3d 58, 67 & n.9 (2d Cir. 2009); *see also Kramer v. Time Warner Inc.*, 937 F.2d 767, 774 (2d Cir. 1991).

[—13—] to the amount of attorney's fees. Nowhere in the *Atlantic Sounding* opinion is there the slightest hint that such damages are limited to counsel fees. While *Atlantic Sounding* cited *Atkinson, id.* at 417—seemingly relying more on the dissenting than on the majority opinion—it never stated or implied that such a limit was contemplated, or was even an open issue left to the future. We believe, therefore, that *Kraljic*'s holding did not survive *Atlantic Sounding.*

The landscape has changed in another way that undermines *Kraljic.* While that opinion relied heavily upon the incompatibility of an award of punitive damages and a separate award of counsel fees, *see* 575 F.2d at 414, the availability of both punitive damages and attorney's fees awards in the same case, albeit for statutory violations but often on common law grounds with regard to punitive damages, is today not uncommon. *See, e.g., Stanczyk v. City of New York,* 752 F.3d 273, 275 (2d Cir. 2014) (in Section 1983 case, the jury awarded plaintiff compensatory damages and punitive damages, and the court subsequently awarded attorney's fees); *Kolstad v. Am. Dental Ass'n,* 527 U.S. 526, 529 (1999) ("[P]unitive damages are available in claims under Title VII of the Civil Rights Act of 1964."); *Farias v. Instructional Sys., Inc.,* 259 F.3d 91, 101-03 (2d Cir. 2001) (under Title VII, a plaintiff may be entitled to reasonable attorney's fees and punitive damages) (citing *Kolstad,* [—14—] 527 U.S. at 529); *Feltner v. Columbia Pictures Television, Inc.,* 523 U.S. 343, 346 (1998) and 17 U.S.C. §§ 504, 505 (under the Copyright Act, a court may "increase the award of statutory damages to a sum of not more than $150,000" and may "award a reasonable attorney's fee"); *Fort v. White,* 530 F.2d 1113, 1118 (2d Cir. 1976) (under the Fair Housing Act, a plaintiff may be awarded actual as well as punitive damages and attorney's fees); 35 U.S.C. §§ 284, 285 (under the Patent Act, the court "may increase the damages up to three times the amount found or assessed" and may award "reasonable attorney fees"); *accord Knorr-Bremse Systeme Fuer Nutzfahrzeuge GmbH v. Dana Corp.,* 383 F.3d 1337, 1347 (Fed. Cir. 2004) (in a patent infringement case, under 35 U.S.C. § 285, "[t]hat there were not actual damages does not render the award

of attorney fees punitive. Attorney fees are compensatory, and may provide a fair remedy in appropriate cases."); *cf. Jurgens v. CBK, Ltd.,* 80 F.3d 1566, 1573 n.4 (Fed. Cir. 1996) ("As a general rule, attorneys fees under [35 U.S.C. §] 285 may be justified by any valid basis for awarding increased damages under section 284. However, conduct which a court may deem 'exceptional' and a basis for awarding attorneys fees may not qualify for an award of increased damages. Even where damages are increased under section 284, a court may decline to award attorneys fees under section 285.") (internal citations omitted). [—15—]

Therefore, *Atkinson*'s holding that an award for attorney's fees may be made where the refusal to pay maintenance and cure was "callous," "willful," and "persistent" is not inconsistent with a punitive award. We also perceive no reason why *Atkinson*'s holding that counsel fees are available for a willful breach of an employer's maintenance and cure obligations is not settled law. Indeed, as noted, *Atlantic Sounding* cited *Atkinson* without any hint of reservation as to the award of fees. 557 U.S. at 417. Moreover, *Atlantic Sounding* also cited, seemingly with approval, a court of appeals decision affirming awards of both punitive damages and fees in maintenance and cure cases. *Id.* at 408 (citing *Hines,* 820 F.2d at 1188). Pending further developments in the Supreme Court, we follow those cases.[3]

CONCLUSION

We therefore affirm.

---

[3] We note one small departure from *Atkinson.* We believe that an award of punitive damages is for the jury while attorney's fees must be awarded under Fed. R. Civ. P. 54(d), which was promulgated in 1993. This departure aligns the award of fees in maintenance and cure cases with post-*Atkinson* practices regarding fees. *See Incandela v. Am. Dredging Co.,* 659 F.2d 11, 15 (2d Cir. 1981) (trial court assesses attorney's fees after a jury finding that defendant's behavior was "callous" or "recalcitrant").

𝖀𝖓𝖎𝖙𝖊𝖉 𝕾𝖙𝖆𝖙𝖊𝖘 𝕮𝖔𝖚𝖗𝖙 𝖔𝖋 𝕬𝖕𝖕𝖊𝖆𝖑𝖘
𝖋𝖔𝖗 𝖙𝖍𝖊 𝕾𝖊𝖈𝖔𝖓𝖉 𝕮𝖎𝖗𝖈𝖚𝖎𝖙

No. 13-1745

NATURAL RESOURCES DEFENSE COUNCIL
VS.
UNITED STATES ENVTL. PROTECTION AGENCY

On Petition for Review from the Environmental
Protection Agency

Decided: October 5, 2015
Amended: December 18, 2015

Citation: 808 F.3d 556, 3 Adm. R. 140 (2d Cir. 2015).

Before **SACK, CHIN,** and **CARNEY,** Circuit Judges.

[——4——] CHIN, Circuit Judge:

This case arises from the efforts of the Environmental Protection Agency ("EPA") pursuant to section 402(a) of the Clean Water Act (the "CWA"), 33 U.S.C. § 1342(a), to regulate the discharge of ballast water from ships.[1] A ship takes on and discharges ballast water to compensate for changes in its weight caused by activities such as loading and unloading cargo or consuming fuel or supplies. The amount of water can range from hundreds of gallons to as much as 25 million gallons—enough to fill thirty-eight Olympic-sized swimming pools. More than 21 billion gallons of ballast water are released in the United States annually. *See Nw. Envtl. Advocates v. EPA*, 537 F.3d 1006, 1013 (9th Cir. 2008).

When a ship takes on ballast water, it can inadvertently pick up organisms and their eggs and larvae, as well as sediment and pollutants. When the ship discharges ballast water, often in a new place, these organisms and pollutants are ejected into the surrounding waterbody, enabling these organisms to establish new, non-native populations. As a result, ships have become one of [——5——] the primary ways that invasive species are spread from one waterbody to another. *Id.* at 1012-13 ("All told, more than 10,000 marine species each day hitch rides around the globe in the ballast water of cargo ships." (quoting *Nw. Envtl. Advocates v. EPA*, No. C 03-05760 SI, 2006 WL 2669042, at *3 (N.D. Cal. Sept. 18, 2006)).

Invasive species cause severe economic and ecological harm, including by destroying native fish species and shellfish industries, creating algae blooms, and devastating tourism. Zebra mussels are a particularly destructive example. They were first introduced to Lake Erie in the 1980s by a freighter from Europe that discharged ballast water containing mussels.[2] These mussels have wreaked havoc in the Midwest and Northeast by blocking water intake and outtake at power plants and other industrial facilities, causing nearly $70 million in damage between 1989 and 1995. *Nw. Envtl. Advocates*, 537 F.3d at 1013. One study estimates the damage caused by invasive species collectively at "about $137 billion a year—more than double the annual economic damage [——6——] caused by all natural disasters in the United States." *Id.* (quoting *Nw. Envtl. Advocates*, 2006 WL 2669042, at *4).[3]

Ballast water discharge is particularly problematic in the Great Lakes. Vessels that sail exclusively in the Great Lakes, known as "Lakers," account for over ninety-five percent of ballast water volumes transferred in the Great Lakes. Unfortunately, Lakers are more likely than oceangoing vessels to spread invasive species because the short duration of their voyages allows organisms to survive in their ballast.

In April 2013, EPA issued a Vessel General Permit (the "2013 VGP"), pursuant to section 402 of the CWA, 33 U.S.C. § 1342, to regulate the discharge of ballast water from ships. In response, four environmental groups filed

---

[1] **Glossary of Acronyms**: As this opinion discusses the CWA and its intricacies, it contains a large number of acronyms. In addition to their definitions in the text, a separate glossary of acronyms is therefore set forth in the Appendix to this opinion.

[2] "From that humble start, the invaders colonized the Great Lakes and spread across the country on towed boats." Jim Robbins, *A Western Showdown*, N.Y. TIMES, Sept. 8, 2015, at D6.

[3] *See also* Robbins, *A Western Showdown*, at D6 (discussing damage caused by zebra and quagga mussels).

three Petitions for Review ("PFRs") alleging that EPA acted arbitrarily and capriciously in issuing the 2013 VGP: petitioner Natural Resources Defense Council ("NRDC") filed a PFR on May 3, 2013 in this Court; petitioners Northwest Environmental Advocates ("NWEA") and the Center for Biological Diversity jointly filed a PFR on May 3, 2013 in the United States Court of Appeals for the Ninth Circuit; and petitioner National Wildlife Federation ("NWF") filed a PFR on July 3, 2013 in the [—7—] United States Court of Appeals for the D.C. Circuit.[4] In an order dated May 24, 2013, the Judicial Panel on Multidistrict Litigation issued a Consolidation Order and assigned final venue for the first two petitions, and any subsequently filed petition, to this Court.

On May 31, 2013, the Lake Carriers' Association and the Canadian Shipowners Association (the "CSA") filed a motion to intervene, which was granted on October 7, 2013. On January 1, 2014, the CSA filed a PFR in this case. EPA and the CSA jointly moved to sever the CSA PFR from this case and hold it in abeyance; the motion was granted on May 23, 2014.

We find that EPA acted arbitrarily and capriciously in issuing parts of the 2013 VGP, and therefore remand this matter to the EPA for further proceedings.

BACKGROUND

A. *The CWA*

Congress created the CWA to limit pollution in the waters of the United States. *See* 33 U.S.C. § 1251(a) (objective of CWA is to "restore and [—8—] maintain the chemical, physical, and biological integrity of the Nation's waters"); *S. Fla. Water Mgmt. Dist. v. Miccosukee Tribe of Indians*, 541 U.S. 95, 102 (2004) (same); *Waterkeeper All., Inc. v. EPA*, 399 F.3d 486, 490-91 (2d Cir. 2005) (same). The CWA thus prohibits the "discharge of *any*

pollutant" from a "point source" to the "navigable waters" of the United States, except as permitted by the CWA. 33 U.S.C. §§ 1311(a), 1362 (emphasis added). The "discharge of a pollutant" includes "any addition of any pollutant to navigable waters from any point source." *Id.* § 1362(12)(A). A "pollutant" includes solid, industrial, agricultural, and biological waste. *Id.* § 1362(6). A "point source" is "any discernible, confined and discrete conveyance, including but not limited to any . . . vessel or other floating craft, from which pollutants are or may be discharged." *Id.* § 1362(14). "Navigable waters" is defined as "the waters of the United States, including the territorial seas." *Id.* § 1362(7). The discharge of polluted water from a vessel ballast tank is a point source discharge covered by the CWA. *See Nw. Envtl. Advocates*, 537 F.3d at 1021.

A key component of the statute is the establishment of water quality standards. Water quality standards are set by states for waters within their boundaries and are then reviewed for approval by EPA. *See* 33 U.S.C. § 1313; 40 [—9—] C.F.R. §§ 131.4, 131.10-.11; *see also NRDC v. EPA*, 279 F.3d 1180, 1183 (9th Cir. 2002) ("Under the CWA, each state sets its own water quality standards, subject to review and approval by the EPA."). EPA must ensure that the standard proposed by the state will comply with the requirements of the CWA before approving it. *See* 33 U.S.C. §§ 1311(b)(1)(C), 1313(a) 1342(a)(1); 40 C.F.R. § 122.4(d).

1. *National Pollutant Discharge Elimination System Permits*

An entity seeking to discharge a pollutant is required to obtain and comply with a permit that limits the amounts and kinds of pollutants being discharged. *See NRDC v. EPA*, 822 F.2d 104, 108 (D.C. Cir. 1987); *see also Waterkeeper All.*, 399 F.3d at 498 (discharge allowed "where . . . permits *ensure* that every discharge of pollutants will comply with all applicable effluent limitations and standards"). This permit, known as a National Pollutant Discharge Elimination System ("NPDES") permit, establishes enforceable

---

[4] All three petitions were timely filed within 120 days of the issuance of the VGP, as required under 33 U.S.C. § 1369(b)(1). Accordingly, this Court has jurisdiction over the petitions pursuant to section 509(b)(1)(F) of the CWA, 33 U.S.C. § 1369(b)(1)(F).

effluent limitations, as well as monitoring and reporting requirements.

NPDES permits, which are issued either by EPA or a state in a federally approved permitting system, see 33 U.S.C. § 1342, may be individual (issued to a specific entity to discharge pollutants at a specific place) or general [—10—] (issued to an entire class of dischargers in a geographic location), see 40 C.F.R. §§ 122.21, 122.28(a)(2), 124.1-.21, 124.51-.66. The permit here is a general permit.

Permits can impose two different types of standards on discharges: (1) technology-based standards and (2) water quality-based standards. See 33 U.S.C. §§ 1311(b)(1)(c) and (b)(2)(a), 1313, 1342(a). The 2013 VGP imposes both.

a. *Technology-Based Effluent Limits*

Technology-based effluent limits ("TBELs") set effluent limitations on a point source based on how effectively technology can reduce the pollutant being discharged. See 33 U.S.C. §§ 1311(b), (e), 1314(b); see also PUD No. 1 of Jefferson Cty. v. Wash. Dep't of Ecology, 511 U.S. 700, 704 (1994) (holding that, to achieve goals of CWA, EPA is required to "establish and enforce technology-based limitations on individual discharges into the country's navigable waters from point sources"). Congress designed this standard to be technology-forcing, meaning it should force agencies and permit applicants to adopt technologies that achieve the greatest reductions in pollution. See NRDC, 822 F.2d at 124 (holding that CWA seeks "not only to stimulate but to press development of new, [—11—] more efficient and effective technologies," which is "essential purpose of this series of progressively more demanding technology-based standards").[5]

In determining the standard for TBELs, EPA considers the source of the pollution (existing or new) and the type of pollutant. For nonconventional pollutants from existing sources, EPA is required to set effluent limits based on the "best available technology economically achievable" or "BAT." 33 U.S.C. § 1311(b)(2)(A).[6] BAT requires the "application of the best available technology economically achievable for such category or class, which will result in reasonable further progress toward the national goal of eliminating the discharge of all pollutants." Id.; see NRDC, 822 F.2d at 123 (CWA designed to progress "toward implementation of pollution controls to the full extent of the best technology which would become available"). Because invasive species are a [—12—] nonconventional pollutant from an existing source, ballast water discharges are subject to BAT.

EPA considers a number of factors in assessing whether a technology is BAT, including:

- the cost of achieving the effluent reductions,

- the age of equipment and facilities involved,

- the process employed,

- the engineering aspects of various control techniques,

- potential process changes,

- non-water-quality environmental impacts including energy requirements, and

---

[5] EPA issues national effluent limitation guidelines ("ELGs"), which establish limitations for all types of dischargers within a particular industry and for certain types of discharges. See 40 C.F.R. § 125.3(c)(1). ELGs are enforceable through their incorporation into a NPDES permit. In this case, no states have established numeric water quality

criteria for living organisms or aquatic nuisance species.

[6] For conventional pollutants from existing sources, the level of pollution control is based on best conventional pollutant control technology. Id. § 1311(b)(2)(E). New sources of pollution must meet new source performance standards, which are based on best available demonstrated control technology. Id. § 1316(a)(1). Neither standard is implicated here.

- other factors as EPA "deems appropriate."

See 33 U.S.C. § 1314(b)(2)(B).

EPA can mandate that BAT requires the use of a technology that is not currently available within a particular industry when (1) the technology is available in another industry, (2) EPA finds that the technology is transferrable from that other industry, and (3) EPA can reasonably predict that such technology will adequately treat the effluent. *See Kennecott v. EPA*, 780 F.2d 445, 453 (4th Cir. 1986) (citing *Tanners' Council of Am., Inc. v. Train*, 540 F.2d 1188, 1192 (4th Cir. 1976)). [—13—]

b. *Water Quality-Based Effluent Limits*

If the TBELs are insufficient to attain or maintain water quality standards, the CWA requires NPDES permits to include additional water quality-based effluent limits ("WQBELs"). *See* 33 U.S.C. §§ 1311(b)(1)(C), 1312(a); *NRDC*, 822 F.2d at 110 ("Whenever a technology-based effluent limitation is insufficient to make a particular body of water fit for the uses for which it is needed, the EPA is to devise a water-quality based limitation that will be sufficient to the task."). WQBELs are designed to ensure that the discharges authorized by the permit do not violate water quality standards. *See* 33 U.S.C. §§ 1313, 1342(a)(2).

The WQBELs, which supplement the TBELs, are based on the amount and kind of pollutants in the water. *See id.* § 1312(a). WQBELs are set without regard to cost or technology availability. *See NRDC v. EPA*, 859 F.2d 156, 208 (D.C. Cir. 1988) ("A technology-based standard discards its fundamental premise when it ignores the limits inherent in the technology. By contrast, a water quality-based permit limit begins with the premise that a certain level of water quality will be maintained, come what may, and places upon the permittee the responsibility for realizing that goal." (footnote omitted)). WQBELs may be [—14—] narrative where the calculation of numeric limits is "infeasible." *See* 40 C.F.R. § 122.44(k)(3).

No permit may be issued when "the imposition of conditions cannot ensure compliance with the applicable water quality requirements of all affected States." *Id.* § 122.4(d). Thus, permits must establish limits on discharges that will lead to compliance with water quality standards. *See Trs. for Alaska v. EPA*, 749 F.2d 549, 556-57 (9th Cir. 1984) (holding that permit must translate state water quality standards into end-of-pipe effluent limitations necessary to achieve those standards).

Because no states have established numeric water quality criteria for invasive species, EPA is required to establish WQBELs that ensure compliance with narrative criteria, designated uses, and antidegradation policies that comprise state water quality standards. The permit may then mandate "best management practices" ("BMPs") to control pollution. *See* 40 C.F.R. § 122.44(k)(3).

c. *Monitoring and Reporting Requirements*

NPDES permits also require both monitoring and reporting of monitoring results of TBELs and WQBELs to assure compliance with permit [—15—] limitations and facilitate enforcement. *See* 33 U.S.C. §§ 1314, 1318, 1342(a)(2); 40 C.F.R. § 122.44(i)(1)-(2).

B. *Regulatory History*

When the CWA was first being implemented in the 1970s, EPA regulations exempted discharges that were "incidental" to the "normal operation" of vessels from NPDES permitting requirements. *See National Pollutant Discharge Elimination System*, 38 Fed. Reg. 13,528, 13,530 (May 22, 1973) (codified at 40 C.F.R. § 125.4); *see also National Pollutant Discharge Elimination System; Revision of Regulations*, 44 Fed. Reg. 32,854, 32,902 (June 7, 1979) (codified at 40 C.F.R. § 122.3(a)). This exemption included ballast water discharges.

In 1999, the NWEA and other environmental organizations submitted a rulemaking petition to EPA seeking to repeal this exemption, then codified at 40 C.F.R. § 122.3(a). *See Final National Pollutant Discharge Elimination System (NPDES) General Permit for Discharges Incidental to the Normal Operation of a Vessel*, 73 Fed. Reg. 79,473, 79,475 (Dec. 29, 2008). EPA denied the petition. *See Nw. Envtl. Advocates*, 537 F.3d at 1013. The environmental groups challenged the denial in the United States District Court for the Northern District of California, while simultaneously filing a PFR in the United States Court of Appeals for the [—16—] Ninth Circuit, in case the district court lacked jurisdiction. The district court issued an order vacating the exemption, *see Nw. Envtl. Advocates*, 2006 WL 2669042, at *15, and the Ninth Circuit upheld the decision. *See Nw. Envtl. Advocates*, 537 F.3d at 1027. EPA finally repealed the exemption and issued a Vessel General Permit in 2008 (the "2008 VGP"). *Draft National Pollutant Discharge Elimination System (NPDES) General Permits for Discharges Incidental to the Normal Operation of a Vessel*, 73 Fed. Reg. 34,296 (June 17, 2008).

1. *The 2008 VGP*

Environmental groups, industry groups, and the State of Michigan challenged the 2008 VGP in a PFR filed in the United States Court of Appeals for the D.C. Circuit, arguing primarily that the 2008 VGP was inadequate because it contained only narrative provisions, not specific numeric limitations on discharges. In March 2011, EPA settled this matter, agreeing to: (1) set "numeric concentration-based effluent limits for discharges of ballast water expressed as organisms per unit of ballast water volume"; (2) set numeric effluent limits that "represent the applicable levels of technology-based control"; and (3) "include more stringent water quality-based effluent limitations" if needed to satisfy [—17—] applicable water quality standards. Settlement Agreement ¶¶ 9-13, *NRDC v. EPA*, No. 09-1089 (D.C. Cir. Mar. 8, 2011), ECF No. 1296922.

2. *The Creation of New Standards*

To create these new, more specific standards, EPA enlisted the help of its own

Science Advisory Board (the "SAB") and the National Research Council/National Academy of Sciences Committee on Assessing Numeric Limits for Living Organisms in Ballast Water (the "NAS Committee"). EPA posed a different question to each scientific body.

a. *The SAB*

In 2010, EPA asked the SAB to "provide advice on technologies and systems to minimize the impacts of invasive species in vessel ballast water discharge." App. at 599. Specifically, the SAB looked at four issues: (1) the performance of shipboard systems with available effluent testing data; (2) the potential performance of shipboard systems without reliable testing data; (3) system development for the shipboard systems identified in issues 1 and 2; and (4) the development of reliable information about the status of ballast water treatment technologies and system performance. In considering these questions, the SAB was to take into account *The International Convention for the Control and [—18—] Management of Ships' Ballast Water and Sediments* (the "IMO Standard"), adopted by the International Maritime Organization in 2004, which set certain concentration-based ballast water effluent limits. *Id.* at 610.[7]

In July 2011, the SAB issued its report *Efficacy of Ballast Water Treatment Systems: A Report by the EPA Science Advisory Board* (the "SAB Report"). The SAB identified fifty-one ballast-water treatment systems, with five categories of shipboard systems that could reliably achieve the IMO Standard. *Id.* at 601.[8] The SAB found that none of the systems could meet standards 100 or 1,000

---

[7] The Coast Guard proposed the same standard in a rulemaking in 2011 pursuant to its authority under the National Invasive Species Act. *See Standards for Living Organisms in Ships' Ballast Water Discharged in U.S. Waters*, 74 Fed. Reg. 44,632 (Aug. 28, 2009). In 2012, the Coast Guard finalized the rule, entitled *Standards for Living Organisms in Ships' Ballast Water Discharged in U.S. Waters*. 77 Fed. Reg. 17,254 (Mar. 23, 2012).

[8] The five categories were: (1) deoxygenation + cavitation; (2) filtration + chlorine dioxide; (3) filtration + UV; (4) filtration + UV + TiO2; and (5) filtration + electro-chlorination.

times greater than the IMO Standard. *Id.* at 602. The SAB also found that none of the fifty-one shipboard treatments identified could reliably achieve a "no living organism" standard. *Id.* [—19—]

b. *The NAS Committee*

EPA created the NAS Committee to examine "the relationship between the concentration of living organisms in ballast water discharges and the probability of nonindigenous organisms successfully establishing populations in U.S. waters." *Id.* at 235.

In its June 2011 report, *Assessing the Relationship Between Propagule Pressure and Invasion Risk in Ballast Water* (the "NAS Report"), the NAS Committee concluded (1) there was "no significant relationship between ballast volume and invasions," and (2) "[t]he current state of science does not allow a quantitative evaluation of the relative merits of various discharge standards in terms of invasion probability." *Id.* at 363. Essentially, the Committee said that it was unable to establish a reliable numeric limit on discharges that would guarantee protection against invasive species, other than zero.

3. *The 2013 VGP*

On March 28, 2013, EPA issued the 2013 VGP, the permit now before us, allowing vessels to discharge ballast water subject to certain limitations on the living organisms in the discharge. *Final National Pollutant Discharge Elimination System (NPDES) General Permit for Discharges Incidental to the Normal* [—20—] *Operation of a Vessel*, 78 Fed. Reg. 21,938 (Apr. 12, 2013).[9] This constituted final action on the permit pursuant to section 402(a) of the CWA, 33 U.S.C. § 1342(a). The 2013 VGP included TBELs, WQBELs, and monitoring and reporting requirements.

---

[9] EPA issued the draft NPDES VGP on November 30, 2011 with a 75-day notice-and-comment period. The public comment period ended on February 21, 2012. The 2013 VGP replaced the 2008 VGP, which expired on December 19, 2013.

a. *TBELs*

As discussed above, TBELs impose effluent limitations on a point source based on how much technology is able to reduce the amount of a pollutant at issue. *See* 33 U.S.C. §§ 1311(b), (e), 1314(b). In this instance, EPA chose to set the TBELs at the IMO Standard, which requires:

(1) Limiting discharges of organisms 50 micrometers or larger to a concentration of fewer than 10 living organisms per cubic meter of ballast water;

(2) Limiting discharges of organisms less than 50 micrometers and greater than or equal to 10 micrometers to concentrations of fewer than 10 living organisms per milliliter ("mL") of ballast water; and

(3) Limiting discharges of three types of pathogen and pathogen indicators: (1) *Vibrio cholerae*: fewer than 1 colony forming unit ("cfu") per 100 mL; (2) *Escherichia coli* ("E. coli"): fewer than 250 cfu per 100 mL; and (3) intestinal enterococci: fewer than 100 cfu per 100 mL. [—21—]

Vessel General Permit for Discharges Incidental to the Normal Operation of Vessels (VGP): Authorization to Discharge Under the National Pollutant Discharge Elimination System § 2.2.3.5, at 29 (Mar. 28, 2013), *available at* http://water.epa.gov/polwaste/npdes/vessels/upload/vgp_permit2013.pdf. The VGP did not set standards for other "small" organisms, such as bacteria or viruses.

b. *WQBELs*

The WQBELs in the 2013 VGP require: (1) oceangoing vessels entering the Great Lakes to continue to perform ballast water exchanges, and (2) all vessels to control discharges "as necessary to meet applicable water quality standards in the receiving water body or another water body impacted by [the] discharges." VGP § 2.2.3.7, at 43, § 2.3.1, at 59.

c. *Monitoring and Reporting Requirements for TBELs and WQBELs*

As noted above, NPDES permits must contain conditions that require both monitoring and reporting of monitoring results of TBELs and WQBELs to ensure compliance with water quality standards. *See* 33 U.S.C. § 1342(a)(2); 40 C.F.R. § 122.44(i)(1)-(2).

i) Monitoring and Reporting Requirements for TBELs

In the 2013 VGP, EPA established the following monitoring requirements for TBELs: [—22—]

(1) that vessels monitor the functionality of their ballast water treatment systems, if installed; and

(2) that vessels monitor the concentrations of the two "indicator" bacteria, *E. coli* and enterococci.[10]

VGP § 2.2.3.5.1.1.2, at 30, § 2.2.3.5.1.1.4, at 31-32.

The first requirement is known as functionality monitoring. Under this requirement, a ballast water treatment program is considered to be in compliance if it is "operating according to the manufacturers' requirements." App. at 96.

The second requirement is known as effluent biological organism monitoring. Under this requirement, vessels must collect

small-volume samples and analyze them for concentrations of two indicator pathogens. This is required between one and four times a year depending on the treatment system.

ii) Monitoring and Reporting Requirements for WQBELs

The only monitoring required for WQBELs is that ships report the *"expected* date, location, volume, and salinity of any ballast water to be [—23—] discharged." VGP § 4.3, at 72 (emphasis added). Permittees are not required to report actual locations, volumes, or composition of ballast water to be discharged.

d. *Lakers*

The 2013 VGP requires all Lakers to comply with non-numeric technology-based control measures, like ballast water exchange and other BMPs found in VGP § 2.2.3.3. App. at 85; *see* VGP § 2.2.3.3, at 27-28. Lakers are also subject to three ballast water management measures found in VGP § 2.2.3.4: (1) conducting an annual assessment of sediment accumulations; (2) minimizing the amount of water taken in nearshore environments; and (3) adequately maintaining sea chest screens, which keep larger organisms like fish out of ballast tanks. VGP § 2.2.3.4, at 28-29. In addition, all Lakers built on or after January 1, 2009, must comply with VGP § 2.2.3.5, which sets numeric ballast water discharge limits. VGP § 2.2.3.5.3.3, at 39.

DISCUSSION

A. *Standard of Review*

We review a NPDES permit under the Administrative Procedure Act to determine whether EPA's actions were "arbitrary, capricious, an abuse of [—24—] discretion, or otherwise not in accordance with law." 5 U.S.C. § 706(2)(A). To determine whether the agency's actions were "arbitrary and capricious," we consider whether the agency

'relied on factors which Congress has not intended it to consider, entirely

---

[10] EPA established effluent limits for *Vibrio cholerae*, but did not require monitoring in this respect because the "monitoring of this parameter would generally not result in the detection of the presence of this pathogen." App. at 99. The 2013 VGP also contains a third requirement that vessels with treatment systems that add or generate biocides, such as chlorine or ozone, to kill organisms must monitor ballast water discharges for residual biocides. *Id.* at 103. This requirement does not implicate TBELs.

failed to consider an important aspect of the problem, offered an explanation for its decision that runs counter to the evidence before the agency, or is so implausible that it could not be ascribed to a difference in view or the product of agency expertise.'

Islander E. Pipeline Co. v. McCarthy, 525 F.3d 141, 150-51 (2d Cir. 2008) (quoting *Motor Vehicle Mfrs. Ass'n. v. State Farm Mut. Ins. Co.*, 463 U.S. 29, 43 (1983)). We must be "satisfied from the record that 'the agency . . . examine[d] the relevant data and articulate[d] a satisfactory explanation for its action.'" *Id.* at 151 (quoting *State Farm*, 463 U.S. at 43). An agency's action is lawful "only if it rests 'on a consideration of the relevant factors.'" *Michigan v. EPA*, 135 S. Ct. 2699, 2706 (2015) (quoting *State Farm*, 463 U.S. at 43). We afford the agency's decision greater deference regarding factual questions involving scientific matters in its area of technical expertise. *See Balt. Gas & Elec. Co. v. NRDC*, 462 U.S. 87, 103 (1983); *Envtl. Def. v. EPA*, 369 F.3d 193, 204 (2d Cir. 2004).

In addition, judicial review of statutory interpretation by an agency is governed by *Chevron U.S.A. Inc. v. NRDC*, 467 U.S. 837, 842-45 (1984). Under [—25—] *Chevron*, we must first determine "whether Congress has directly spoken to the precise question at issue" in the CWA. *Id.* at 842. If so, we must give effect to the unambiguously expressed intent of Congress. *Id.* at 842-43. "[I]f the statute is silent or ambiguous with respect to the specific issue, the question for the court is whether the agency's answer is based on a permissible construction of the statute." *Id.* at 843. As the Supreme Court held in *Michigan v. EPA*, "[e]ven under this deferential standard, however, 'agencies must operate within the bounds of reasonable interpretation.'" 135 S. Ct. at 2707 (quoting *Util. Air Regulatory Grp. v. EPA*, 134 S. Ct. 2427, 2442 (2014)). We also grant deference to EPA's interpretation of its own regulations "unless that interpretation is 'plainly erroneous or inconsistent with the regulation." *Chase Bank USA, N.A. v. McCoy*, 131 S. Ct. 871, 880 (2011) (quoting *Auer v. Robbins*, 519 U.S. 452, 461 (1997)).

B. *Petitioners' Challenge*

Here, petitioners challenge EPA's issuance of the 2013 VGP as arbitrary and capricious, and not in accordance with law, on a number of grounds.

First, petitioners argue that the TBELs are arbitrary and capricious. Specifically, petitioners assert that EPA acted arbitrarily and capriciously and not [—26—] in accordance with the law when it: (1) selected the IMO standard as the standard for the TBELs; (2) failed to consider onshore treatment, limiting consideration to shipboard treatment; (3) failed to include numeric TBELs for viruses and protists; and (4) exempted Lakers built before 2009 ("pre-2009 Lakers") from the numeric TBELs of the 2013 VGP.

Second, petitioners argue that EPA acted arbitrarily and capriciously and not in accordance with the law in choosing narrative WQBELs, rather than numeric WQBELs, because, among other things, the narrative standard is too imprecise to guarantee compliance with water quality standards.

Finally, petitioners argue that EPA's monitoring and reporting requirements for TBELs and WQBELs are not in accordance with the law because they were inadequate to guarantee compliance.

1. *TBELs*

Under the CWA, EPA must apply BAT in establishing pollution controls for ballast water discharge. BAT requires the "application of the *best available technology economically achievable* for such category or class, which will result in reasonable further progress toward the national goal of eliminating the discharge of all pollutants." 33 U.S.C. § 1311(b)(2)(A)(emphasis added). BAT also requires "a commitment of the maximum resources economically possible to [—27—] the ultimate goal of eliminating all polluting discharges." *EPA v. Nat'l Crushed Stone Ass'n*, 449 U.S. 64, 74 (1980).

We hold that in failing to set TBELs that reflected BAT in the 2013 VGP, EPA acted arbitrarily and capriciously in a number of respects.

a. *The IMO Standard*

Petitioners argue that EPA failed to apply BAT when it chose the IMO Standard for TBELs in the 2013 VGP. They allege that EPA chose the IMO Standard first, and then worked "backwards" to determine which systems could achieve that standard. NWEA Br. at 36. In doing so, they contend, EPA improperly restricted the SAB's inquiry to whether certain technologies would meet what petitioners describe as "existing international consensus standards." *Id.* According to petitioners, EPA should have first considered what "available" technology was capable of achieving, and then created standards based on that capability. As a result, petitioners contend, EPA's standard did not achieve greater reductions in pollution discharges that were achievable with current technology.

We agree. EPA acted arbitrarily and capriciously when it chose the IMO Standard without adequately explaining why standards higher than the IMO Standard should not be used given available technology. [—28—]

In choosing the IMO Standard, EPA overlooked crucial portions of the SAB Report. The SAB identified a number of technologies that can achieve standards higher than IMO for one or more organism sizes, including all five of the technologies identified as also meeting the IMO Standard.[11] The SAB acknowledged that "these same five systems have the potential to meet a 10x IMO D-2/ Phase 1 standard [*i.e.*, the IMO Standard] in the near future." App. at 636. In describing the performance of those systems, the SAB

concluded that each would require only "reasonable/feasible modifications." *Id.* at 629-30,632. Indeed, according to the SAB Report, the Ecochlor, BalPure, and PeraClean systems can meet 100 times IMO for medium organisms, and Ecochlor can meet 10 times IMO for large organisms.

EPA should not have adhered to the IMO Standard without explanation when technologies could have exceeded IMO. Indeed, seeking to find systems that are capable of doing better than the current standard is in keeping with the technology-forcing aspect of the CWA. *See NRDC*, 822 F.2d at [—29—] 124. EPA should have first looked at the available ballast water technologies as identified by the SAB Report. Then, finding that those technologies could exceed the IMO Standard, EPA should have adjusted its standard accordingly, or explained why it would not. *See Islander E. Pipeline*, 525 F.3d at 151 (holding that agency must "examine[] the relevant data and articulate[] a satisfactory explanation for its action" (quoting *State Farm*, 463 U.S. at 43)(alterations omitted)).

EPA's counterargument that no more was necessary because it did not limit the SAB to considering the IMO Standard is unavailing. EPA insists that it gave the SAB a list of potential regulatory limits, and then asked the SAB to identify the systems that could reliably meet those limits. In support, EPA points to its Charge Question 1 to the SAB, which asked the SAB to identify "discharge standards that the available data [about existing systems] credibly demonstrate can be reliably achieved." App. at 607. EPA argues that in response to this charge, the SAB Report supports the conclusion that, "[b]ased upon the data available, no current ballast water treatment technologies were considered likely to meet standards more stringent than the IMO D-2/Phase I" standards. *Id.* at 91. [—30—]

While it is true that EPA did not strictly limit the SAB's consideration to the IMO Standard, EPA is incorrect in suggesting that the SAB Report supports the conclusion that no system could meet standards stricter than

---

[11] The record further demonstrates that existing shipboard technology can meet a standard between IMO and 10 times IMO. For instance, Hyde Marine Guardian has tested at 1.4 times IMO for large organisms; Optimarin has tested at 7.7 times IMO for large organisms; and Alfa Laval/AlfaWall PureBallast has tested at 4.5 times IMO for large organisms, and at 3.7 times IMO for medium organisms.

the IMO Standard. *Id.*[12] To the contrary, the record contradicts EPA's assertion that treatment systems that exceed the IMO Standard are not "available." In fact, as noted above, systems that exceed the IMO Standard are available.

Accordingly, by failing to consider adequately a standard more stringent than IMO, EPA failed to set permit limits that reflect BAT. *See* 33 U.S.C. § 1314(b)(2); *Nat'l Crushed Stone*, 449 U.S. at 74 (BAT requires "a commitment of the maximum resources economically possible to the ultimate goal of eliminating all pollution discharges"); *FMC Corp. v. Train*, 539 F.2d 973, 983-84 (4th Cir. 1976) [—31—] (upholding EPA's decision to set BAT based on data from a single pilot plant). In doing so, EPA acted arbitrarily and capriciously and not in accordance with law in choosing the IMO standard for the TBELs in the 2013 VGP.

b. *Onshore Ballast Water Treatment*

Petitioners also argue that EPA arbitrarily and capriciously limited its consideration to shipboard treatments, failing to consider onshore treatment. Petitioners argue that onshore facilities used in other industries, such as sewage treatment plants and drinking water treatment plants, were reasonable alternatives to shipboard treatment that

---

[12] The SAB actually stated that it could not *reliably test* for standards 100 or 1000 times more stringent than the IMO Standard:

The Panel also concludes that the [IMO Standard] . . . [is] currently measurable, based on data from land-based and shipboard testing. However, current methods (and associated detection limits) prevent testing of BWMS to any standard more stringent than [the IMO Standard] and make it impracticable for verifying a standard 100 or 1000 times more stringent.

Id. at 601. While we agree that we must defer to EPA's conclusions regarding the technical feasibility of testing for standards 100 or 1000 times more stringent than the IMO Standard, there is nothing in the record to suggest that it would not be possible to test for twice or even ten times the IMO Standard.

should have been considered. EPA concedes it directed the Board to "focus its limited time and resources on the status of shipboard treatment systems because such systems were either 'in existence or in the development process.'" EPA Br. at 56-57 (quoting SAB Report). It argues that onshore treatment was not "available," primarily because no onshore system was yet in existence.

While it is true that no onshore systems existed then—unsurprising considering ballast water treatment was not required at all until the effective date of the 2008 VGP— the record suggests that such onshore systems were technologically possible at that time. Yet, EPA chose to curtail discussion about onshore systems and failed to develop information necessary to evaluate their [—32—] availability. We conclude that by failing to consider onshore ballast water systems, EPA acted arbitrarily and capriciously.

What does "available" mean? As courts have interpreted the term in the CWA context, technologies that *could* be used for a particular discharge, even if they are not currently being used by that industry, are "available." As the Fourth Circuit noted,

The model technology [under consideration] may exist at a plant not within the . . . industry [at issue]. Congress contemplated that EPA might use technology *from other industries* to establish the Best Available Technology. Progress would be slowed if EPA were invariably limited to treatment schemes already in force at the plants which are the subject of the rulemaking. Congress envisioned the scanning of broader horizons and asked EPA to survey related industries and current research to find technologies which might be used to decrease the discharge of pollutants.

Kennecott, 780 F.2d at 453 (emphasis added) (citation omitted). This Court held similarly in *Hooker Chemicals & Plastics Corp. v. Train*,

That no plant in a given industry has adopted a pollution control device which could be installed does not mean that

that device is not "available." Congress did not intend to permit continuance of pollution by industries which have failed to cope with and attempt to solve the problem of polluted water. [—33—]

537 F.2d 620, 636 (2d Cir. 1976); *see also Cal. & Hawaiian Sugar Co. v. EPA*, 553 F.2d 280, 286 (2d Cir. 1977) (technology used "'in other industries with similar raw waste characteristics'" was "available" (quoting *Liquid and Crystalline Cane Sugar Refining Subcategory*, 39 Fed. Reg. 10,522, 10,522 (1974))); *Am. Petrol. Inst. v. EPA*, 858 F.2d 261, 264-65 (5th Cir. 1988) (holding that a process can be "deemed 'available' even if it is not in use at all" because "[s]uch an outcome is consistent with Congress' intent to 'push pollution control technology'" (quoting *Ass'n of Pac. Fisheries v. EPA*, 615 F.2d 794, 816 (9th Cir. 1980); *Weyerhaeuser Co. v. Costle*, 590 F.2d 1011, 1061 (D.C. Cir. 1978))).

For a technology in one industry to be "available" in a second industry: (1) the transfer technology must be available within the first industry; (2) the transfer technology must be transferable to the second industry; and (3) it must be reasonably predictable that the technology, if used in the second industry, will be capable of removing the increment required by the effluent standards. *See Kennecott*, 780 F.2d at 453 (citing *Tanners' Council*, 540 F.2d at 1192); *CPC Int'l Inc. v. Train*, 515 F.2d 1032, 1048 (8th Cir. 1975); *Hooker Chems.*, 537 F.2d at 636 ("But even if technology which is not presently in use can be treated as available and achievable, there must be some indication in the [—34—] administrative record of the reasons for concluding that such technology is feasible and may reasonably be expected to yield the effluent reduction mandated when applied to the particular industry."). For example, in *Kennecott*, the Fourth Circuit upheld EPA's use of manufacturing technology from one industry as part of a BAT determination for treating wastewater in a different industry. 780 F.2d at 453-54.

Here, we cannot evaluate whether onshore technology should be considered "available" because the record does not contain a full discussion of onshore treatment. This lack of information about onshore facilities, however, is a problem of EPA's own making because EPA went to great lengths to *foreclose* discussion of onshore treatment both by expressly limiting the SAB's mandate to studying shipboard treatment technology and consistently opposing any attempt by the SAB to consider onshore treatment.

EPA's effort to curtail discussion of onshore treatment is well documented in the record. In a letter dated February 10, 2012, thirteen scientists, eight of whom were members of the SAB and six of whom were members of the NAS Committee,[13] including the Chair of the NAS Committee, stated that the [—35—] SAB "never actually addressed the question of what is the best treatment that available technology can achieve" because EPA limited them to the narrower question of "whether *shipboard* treatment systems could meet *certain specific sets of standards.*" App. at 740. Furthermore, the scientists assert that their attempts to consider onshore treatments were actively thwarted by EPA:

During the SAB Panel meetings and discussions, some members of the Panel attempted to develop and include in the Panel report a more detailed assessment of onshore treatment, including its cost impacts, and an assessment of the full capability of shipboard treatment . . . . [T]hese assessments would have further demonstrated that available technology can achieve levels of treatment beyond what the EPA has proposed as controls. The EPA Office of Water, however, *consistently opposed including such information in the report.* As a result, some relevant information and analysis that could have been developed by the Panel was not, and some of what was developed by Panel members was *excluded* or *deleted* from the final report. *If there was less information developed on these issues and less provided in the report than the EPA considers sufficient, it is in large part because the EPA Office*

---

[13] One person was a member of both the SAB and the NAS Committee.

of Water opposed the development and inclusion of such information.

Id. at 744 (emphases added).

In light of these facts, we cannot well credit EPA's assertion that it lacked information to support a finding that onshore facilities were "available." While EPA states that it was "unaware of any onshore treatment facility currently [—36—] available in the U.S. that is capable of meeting the VGP's § 2.2.3.5 ballast water discharge standards," and that it did not "receive information indicating they are or would become available over the term of the VGP," *id.* at 544, in fact EPA turned a blind eye to significant information about onshore treatment.

Indeed, the lack of information about the "availability" of onshore treatment is due in large part to EPA's arbitrary and capricious decision to oppose developing such information. As a result, the TBELs were based on an incomplete record—one lacking meaningful discussion of an "available" treatment, namely onshore treatment. *See Humana of Aurora, Inc. v. Heckler*, 753 F.2d 1579, 1583 (10th Cir. 1985) (agency action is arbitrary and capricious when based on a flawed study); *Tex. Oil & Gas Ass'n v. EPA*, 161 F.3d 923, 935 (5th Cir. 1998) ("A regulation cannot stand if it is based on a flawed, inaccurate, or misapplied study."); *Almay, Inc. v. Califano*, 569 F.2d 674, 682 (D.C. Cir. 1977) (rejecting regulation produced "on the basis of the flawed survey"). Put another way, EPA's refusal to consider onshore treatment "entirely fail[s] to consider an important aspect of the problem" and "offer[s] an explanation for its decision that runs counter to the evidence before the agency." *Islander E. Pipeline*, 525 F.3d at 150-51; *see Tanners' Council*, 540 F.2d at 1191 ("[T]he agency must fully explicate [—37—] its course of inquiry, its analysis, and its reasoning."); *see also State Farm*, 463 U.S. at 43; *Hooker Chems.*, 537 F.2d at 636. Hence, it is arbitrary and capricious.

In fact, the SAB Report points out a number of reasonably predictable advantages to onshore treatment. The SAB Report states:

Use of reception facilities for the treatment of ballast water appears to be technically feasible (given generations of successful water treatment and sewage treatment technologies), and is likely to be more reliable and more readily adaptable than shipboard treatment.

App. at 605; *see also id.* at 694. The SAB Report also notes that onshore treatment has a number of advantages over shipboard treatment because onshore facilities are not subject to problems such as limited space, small and overburdened crews, vibrations, weight allowances, limited power, ship instability, and greater corrosion rates. *Id.* at 678-80. Regarding ship crews in particular, studies have shown that "many of these crews are already overburdened," "[o]peration by trained, dedicated personnel in reception facilities would likely result in more reliable performance," and "[m]aintenance and repair work are more likely to be done reliably" as well. *Id.* at 681. Onshore treatment can also be more effective by using superior technologies that are not available for shipboard treatment, such as settling tanks, granular filtration, and membrane filtration. *Id.* at 680-81. Indeed, EPA cites a number of studies that conclude that onshore treatment [—38—] facilities are a technically feasible option. *Id.* at 107. These studies date back to 1992, and proceed with some regularity thereafter—1996, 1999, 2000, 2002, 2007, 2008.

Moreover, onshore treatment would not necessarily be slower than shipboard treatment to implement. The SAB estimated that onshore implementation would take up to thirty months, while EPA allowed eight years to phase-in shipboard implementation. *See id.* at 684. Nor would onshore treatment necessarily be more expensive than shipboard treatment. Regional economic studies suggest that "treating ballast water in reception facilities would be at least as economically feasible as shipboard treatment." *Id.* at 694. In addition, the cost of monitoring and enforcement is likely to be lower with a smaller number of reception facilities compared with a larger number of shipboard systems. *Id.* at 605, 694. The Coast Guard also found that onshore treatment was generally less expensive per metric ton of ballast water than shipboard treatment. *Id.* at 679.

Of course, onshore treatment has many costs, including the cost of retrofitting vessels for onshore facilities, particularly ships from outside the United States, and the cost of shipping delays created by the time it takes to [—39—] discharge ballast onshore (though presumably shipboard treatment is not instantaneous). Costs alone, however, cannot determine BAT. *See* 33 U.S.C. § 1314(b)(2)(B). Furthermore, EPA failed to perform the economic analysis required to determine relative costs of the differing technologies in reaching its conclusion that onshore treatment was not economically achievable. *See Waterkeeper All.*, 399 F.3d at 516 ("[T]he Administrator is obligated to 'inquire into the initial and annual costs of applying the technology and make an affirmative determination that those costs can be reasonably borne by the industry.'" (quoting *Riverkeeper, Inc. v. EPA*, 358 F.3d 174, 195 (2d Cir. 2004))); *Nat'l Wildlife Fed'n v. EPA*, 286 F.3d 554, 563 (D.C. Cir. 2002) ("Although its analysis may be general, EPA 'has the heaviest of obligations to explain and expose every step of its [cost-benefit] reasoning.' . . . This duty to explain arises out of the need for reviewing courts to be able to discern the basis for EPA's decision." (internal citations omitted) (quoting *Am. Lung Ass'n v. EPA*, 134 F.3d 388, 392 (D.C. Cir. 1998))).

In light of these observations, the SAB and NAS Committee scientists concluded that "EPA should conduct a comprehensive analysis comparing biological effectiveness, cost, logistics, operations, and safety [—40—] associated with both shipboard [treatment] and reception facilities." App. at 606. If that analysis "indicate[d] that treatment at reception facilities is both economically and logistically feasible and is more effective than shipboard treatment systems, it should be used as the basis for assessing the ability of available technologies to . . . meet a given discharge standard." *Id.* EPA chose not to do so because the SAB "did not specify a timetable for that complex endeavor or suggest that is was possible to complete such

an analysis in time to inform the impending VGP." EPA Br. at 58-59. We do not find that answer compelling. There is no impediment to engaging in further study, and further study may advance the goals of the CWA.

Thus, EPA could have well found that onshore treatment was "available." Indeed, EPA's failure to consider onshore treatment is inconsistent with the CWA's mandate that TBELs be technology-forcing. Congress designed the CWA to force agencies and permittees to adopt technologies that achieve the greatest reductions in pollutants. *See NRDC*, 822 F.2d at 124 (holding that CWA seeks "not only to stimulate but to press development of new, more efficient and effective technologies," which is the "essential purpose of this series of progressively more demanding technology-based standards"). As Judge Starr [—41—] noted in *NRDC*, "the most salient characteristic of this statutory scheme, articulated time and again by its architects and embedded in the statutory language, is that it is technology-forcing." *Id.* at 123.

EPA's decision on this issue matters. As the SAB scientists pointed out, EPA's choice of system in this permit will have a long-term impact:

> [S]hipboard treatment and onshore treatment represent distinct approaches to ballast water management that would each require different large investments in infrastructure. . . . Thus *we are almost certain to be stuck for a very long time with whichever approach is used as the BAT* in setting discharge standards in 2013. It is thus of the utmost urgency that a fair and thorough comparison of the two approaches be made at this time.

App. at 744-45 (emphasis added). We conclude that EPA failed to give fair and thorough consideration to both onshore and shipboard treatment systems in setting the standard in the 2013 VGP, and we remand to EPA to give full consideration to the issue now.

c. *Viruses and Protists*

Petitioners also complain about the lack of numeric TBELs for viruses and protists (primarily single-celled organisms). EPA argues, however, that it could not set TBELs for viruses and protists in the 2013 VGP because EPA could not yet identify "suitable standardized test organisms and/or surrogate [—42—] parameters to determine treatment system performance at removing or eliminating viruses and protists and which also can be used in establishing technology-based discharge limitations." App. at 486; *see also* App. at 495 ("EPA does not believe that there are sufficient data available to establish numeric limits for protists or other bacteria.")

We agree that it was not arbitrary and capricious for EPA to decline to set TBELs for organisms for which it is unable to test and for which it has insufficient data to set numeric limits. *See Balt. Gas & Elec. Co. v. NRDC, Inc.*, 462 U.S. 87, 103 (1983) ("[A] reviewing court must remember that [where the agency] is making predictions, within its area of special expertise, at the frontiers of science . . . as opposed to simple findings of fact, a reviewing court must generally be at its most deferential."). Petitioners have not demonstrated that sufficient data are available. EPA has represented that it will consider including numeric TBELs for viruses and protists in the next version of the VGP. App. at 486. This is sufficient.

d. *Pre-2009 Lakers*

Petitioners allege that EPA's decision to exempt Lakers built before January 1, 2009 from numeric effluent limits of VGP § 2.2.3.5 was arbitrary and capricious. EPA based this decision on its finding that there was no treatment [—43—] technology "available" for these vessels either onboard or onshore. App. at 115-16. EPA expressed concern about the difficulty of finding effective onboard systems for pre-2009 Lakers due to their "unique operational and design constraints," such as the large volumes of fresh cold water they require, the short duration of their trips, their high pumping rates, and their uncoated

ballast tanks. *Id.* at 116.[14] In reaching that conclusion, EPA relied on the SAB Report, which advised that "specific constraints can greatly limit treatment options" for Lakers. *Id.* at 638. EPA also cited the costs of implementing these systems. *Id.* at 116.

We agree with petitioners that exempting the pre-2009 Lakers was arbitrary and capricious. First, the lack of supply of updated shipboard systems is not a legitimate reason to exempt pre-2009 Lakers from the 2013 VGP, as, again, the purpose of BAT is to force technology to keep pace with need. *See NRDC*, 822 F.2d at 124.

Second, EPA's decision was based on a flawed record that failed to consider an important aspect of the problem, namely the possibility of onshore [—44—] treatment. *See Islander E. Pipeline*, 525 F.3d at 150-51. EPA should have considered the comparable 'cost of achieving such effluent reductions' through onshore treatment versus shipboard treatment, rather than merely dismissing onshore treatment. EPA disregarded the SAB's recommendation that onshore treatment would benefit pre-2009 Lakers that are "engaged solely in regional trade." *Id.* at 684. The SAB points out that the space and power constraints posed by pre-2009 Lakers are "largely absent in reception facilities." *Id.* at 680. EPA's foreclosure of considering onshore treatments for pre-2009 Lakers—and indeed, all Lakers—seems shortsighted. *See supra* at 31-42.

Third, EPA imposed the 2013 VGP on Lakers built after 2009, even though post-2009 Lakers face many of the same challenges and constraints as pre-2009 Lakers, such as their short voyages, high pumping rates, and freshwater environment.[15]

---

[14] For example, certain treatment methods, such as electro-chlorination and ozonation, may only be effective in salt water, and others that use oxidizing chemicals may increase corrosion rates in uncoated tanks. *Id.* at 638.

[15] Intervenors argue that due to these constraints, ballast water treatment is infeasible for *all* Lakers, regardless of when they were built. EPA has concluded, however, that anyone building a ship designed to enter the market after 2009 was

While it is true that shipbuilders were on notice that post-2009 [—45—] Lakers would be subject to the 2013 VGP, in reality post-2009 boats appear to be similarly situated to pre-2009 Lakers. *See Islander E. Pipeline*, 525 F.3d at 150-51 (agency decision is arbitrary and capricious when agency offers explanation for decision that runs counter to evidence before agency). Thus, distinguishing pre-2009 and post-2009 Lakers was arbitrary and capricious.

The SAB Report supports our conclusion. Although the SAB Report acknowledged the limitations in treating ballast water from Lakers, it did not declare such treatment impossible. Instead, the SAB concluded that in light of these limitations, "[a] variety of environmental (e.g., temperature and salinity), operational (e.g., ballasting flow rates and holding times), and vessel design (e.g., ballast volume and unmanned barges) parameters" should be considered in determining the treatment standards. App. at 639.

EPA's exemption of the pre-2009 Lakers from the 2013 VGP was also arbitrary and capricious due to EPA's failure to conduct an appropriate and factually-supported cost analysis. Such an analysis might have shown that the cost of subjecting pre-2009 Lakers to the 2013 VGP was not unreasonably high, or, alternatively, that onshore treatment was economically feasible. For all these [—46—] reasons, EPA's decision to exempt pre-2009 Lakers from the 2013 VGP was arbitrary and capricious.

2. *WQBELs*

Under the CWA, NPDES permits must include WQBELs where the TBELs are

insufficient to maintain water quality standards. 33 U.S.C. § 1311(b)(1)(C); 40 C.F.R. § 122.44(d)(1)(vii)(A). Here, EPA concluded that "even at the IMO level of discharge, reasonable potential exists for such discharges to cause or contribute to violations of applicable water quality standards pursuant to 40 C.F.R. § 122.44(d)(1)(ii)." App. at 129. To address this concern, EPA established WQBELs to ensure compliance with water quality standards. EPA, however, chose to create narrative WQBELs because it believed numeric WQBELs were "infeasible" to calculate.[16] [—47—]

The WQBEL in the 2013 VGP states:

Your discharge must be controlled as necessary to meet applicable water quality standards in the receiving water body or another water body impacted by your discharges.

VGP § 2.3.1, at 59. In defending this standard, EPA relied in part on the NAS Report, which stated that "[t]he current state of science does not allow a quantitative evaluation of the relative merits of various discharge standards in terms of invasion probability." App. at 363.

Petitioners argue that this narrative WQBEL does not ensure compliance with water quality standards. We agree. This narrative standard is insufficient to give a shipowner guidance as to what is expected or to allow any permitting authority to determine whether a shipowner is violating water quality standards. By requiring shipowners to control discharges "as necessary to meet applicable water quality standards" without giving specific guidance on the discharge limits, EPA fails to fulfill its duty to "regulat[e] in fact, not only in principle." *Waterkeeper All.*, 399 F.3d at 498. As this Circuit held in *Waterkeeper Alliance*, NPDES permits "may issue only where such permits *ensure* that every discharge of pollutants will comply with all applicable effluent limitations and standards." *Id.* That is hardly the case

---

well aware of the impending VGP requirements, and could anticipate its impact on shipbuilding. App. at 117. Intervenors also contend that ships exclusively plying the Great Lakes do not pose a threat to water quality because they do not introduce any invasive species from outside the Great Lakes. EPA has properly rejected this argument, noting that Lakers can spread or more rapidly distribute invasive species already present in the Great Lakes. *Id.* at 501.

---

[16] Federal regulation permits such limits to be expressed narratively if the calculation of numeric limits is "infeasible." 40 C.F.R. § 122.44(k)(3).

here. EPA itself notes that it only [—48—] "generally expects that compliance with the [TBELs] . . . will control discharges as necessary to meet applicable water quality standards." VGP § 2.3.1, at 59. The WQBELs, although found by EPA to be required to *supplement* the TBELs, in fact add nothing. The WQBELs do not state how they will ensure compliance.

Even if determining the proper standard is difficult, EPA cannot simply give up and refuse to issue more specific guidelines. *See Am. Paper Inst., Inc. v. EPA*, 996 F.2d 346, 350 (D.C. Cir. 1993) (articulating that, even if creating permit limits is difficult, permit writers cannot just "thr[o]w up their hands and, contrary to the Act, simply ignore[] water quality standards including narrative criteria altogether when deciding upon permit limitations"). Scientific uncertainty does not allow EPA to avoid responsibility for regulating discharges. *See Massachusetts v. EPA*, 549 U.S. 497, 534 (2007) ("EPA [cannot] avoid its statutory obligation by noting the uncertainty surrounding various features of climate change and concluding that it would therefore be better not to regulate at this time.").

Moreover, EPA's reliance on the NAS Report is misplaced. EPA concedes that the NAS Committee "did not conclude that it is infeasible to calculate water quality-based effluent limits for ballast water discharges." App. [—49—] at 563. Rather, the NAS Committee found that it could not formulate a precise standard. In light of this uncertainty, it recommended further study of the issue. But EPA declined to engage in further study. *See* App. at 363-67. For all these reasons, EPA's WQBELs were arbitrary and capricious.

EPA's remaining counterarguments are unavailing. First, EPA asserts that petitioners fail to offer examples of "meaningful permit limits" for WQBELs. EPA Br. at 74. EPA, however, could articulate specific actions that vessels would be required to take to protect against site-specific threats. For example, if EPA or the shipowner became aware of an unusual risk posed by a specific port, EPA

could require vessels to take action to avoid such risk at that port, including not uptaking ballast water or not discharging into other ports the contaminated ballast water that was taken up. Toward that end, EPA has included a set of specific best management practices in the 2013 VGP § 2.2.3.3, further demonstrating the viability of this approach.

Second, EPA argues that under 40 C.F.R. § 122.44(k)(3) it may employ BMPs instead of "[n]umeric effluent limitations" for WQBELs when deriving numeric limitations is "infeasible." 40 C.F.R. §§ 122.44(k)(3). BMPs include "schedules of activities, prohibitions of practices, maintenance [—50—] procedures, and other management practices to prevent or reduce . . . pollution." *Id.* § 122.2. EPA argues that the narrative WQBEL is a BMP, and therefore it has discharged its duty under 40 C.F.R. § 122.2.[17]

But EPA's narrative WQBEL does not qualify as a BMP, as it is neither a practice nor a procedure. BMPs typically involve requirements like operating procedures, treatment requirements, practices to control runoff, spillage or leaks, sludge or waste disposal, or drainage from raw material storage; they can also be structural requirements including tarpaulins, retention ponds, or devices such as berms to channel water away from pollutant sources, and treatment facilities. *See NRDC v. Sw. Marine, Inc.*, 236 F.3d 985, 991 n.1 (9th Cir. 2000). Examples of BMPs that have been accepted as substitutes for effluent limits include: nutrient management plans for concentrated animal feeding operations, *see Waterkeeper All.*, 399 F.3d at 497, 502, filtration of stormwater runoff from ditches before it enters rivers and streams (by timber companies), and constructing roads with surfacing that minimizes sediment in runoff

---

[17] EPA also claims general prohibitions can be BMPs, citing 40 C.F.R. § 122.2, but does not offer an example of something as general as the WQBEL standard being found to be a BMP. As discussed herein, the EPA's characterization is inconsistent with regulations that require WQBELs to "ensure compliance." 40 C.F.R. § 122.4(d); *see Auer*, 519 U.S. at 461 (holding interpretation may not be inconsistent with regulation).

(by [—51—] timber companies), *see Decker v. Nw. Envtl. Def. Ctr.*, 133 S. Ct. 1326, 1338 (2013). The narrative standard here is nowhere as specific as any of these examples. Indeed, it requires nothing more of a shipowner than to meet the TBELs. This interpretation is hardly consistent with the regulations that require WQBELS to ensure compliance. *See Auer*, 519 U.S. at 461 (holding that courts should defer to agency's interpretation of its own regulations if not plainly erroneous or inconsistent with the regulation).

Third, EPA claims that WQBEL standards will be sufficiently maintained because EPA can take "corrective actions" *after* the permittee becomes aware of a violation. App. at 160. This is not reassuring. The point of a permit is to prevent discharges that violate water quality standards *before* they happen. *See* 33 U.S.C. §§ 1311(b)(1)(C), 1342(a)(2); 40 C.F.R. §§ 122.4(d), 122.44(d)(1). "Corrective action" is not an effective remedy in an invasive species context—it is difficult to eradicate a colony of zebra mussels after they are established. *See, e.g.*, Great Lakes Sci. Ctr., U.S. Geological Survey, *Zebra Mussels Cause Economic and Ecological Problems in the Great Lakes* 2 (rev. 2011) ("Once zebra mussels become established in a water body, they are impossible to eradicate with the technology available today. Many chemicals kill zebra mussels, but these exotics [—52—] are so tolerant and tough that everything in the water would have to be poisoned to destroy the mussel."); Robbins, *A Western Showdown*, at D6 (noting that officials in Western states have instituted elaborate and expensive inspection systems for boats because they "want desperately to keep the mussels out of blue-ribbon trout streams and pristine mountain lakes" as "once established [the mussels] are impossible to permanently eradicate"). This is all the more problematic because a vessel operator is not likely to know it has a discharge violation if, as discussed below, there are no monitoring require-ments.[18]

Accordingly, EPA acted arbitrarily and capriciously in issuing the WQBELs because they violate section 1342's requirement that NPDES permits ensure compliance with the CWA. *Cf. Waterkeeper All.*, 399 F.3d at 498.

Intervenors raise one additional argument. Under section 401 of the CWA, before EPA issues a permit, the state in which the discharge is to occur [—53—] must either certify, or waive its right to certify, that the discharge will comply with the state's water quality standards—commonly known as a "401 Certification." *NRDC*, 279 F.3d at 1183; *see also* 33 U.S.C. § 1341(a); 40 C.F.R. § 122.4(b). The intervenors argue that because "the 401 Certifications have been upheld, the matter is settled: the VGP will ensure compliance with the state water quality standards." Intervenors' Br. at 46. We disagree. EPA has an independent duty under the CWA to ensure compliance with state and federal water quality standards and may impose "additional permit conditions necessary to meet that end." *NRDC*, 279 F.3d at 1188. Such additional permit conditions may be necessary if state water quality standards are potentially less stringent than the CWA's," because "the CWA provides a federal floor, not a ceiling, on environmental protection." *Dubois v. U.S. Dep't of Agriculture*, 102 F.3d 1273, 1300 (1st Cir. 1996) (citations omitted).

3. *Monitoring and Reporting Requirements for TBELs and WQBELs*

Under the CWA, NPDES permits must contain conditions that require both *monitoring* and *reporting of monitoring results* of TBELs and WQBELs to ensure compliance.

---

[18] EPA's response is that petitioners' arguments regarding corrective action and BMPs are waived because they were not raised by petitioners in the comments to the permit. *See, e.g.*, *NRDC v. EPA*,

---

25 F.3d 1063, 1073-74 (D.C. Cir. 1994). Arguments can be considered, however, even if not raised during the notice and comment period. *See NRDC v. EPA*, 755 F.3d 1010, 1023 (D.C. Cir. 2014) ("EPA retains a duty to examine key assumptions as part of its affirmative burden of promulgating and explaining a nonarbitrary, non-capricious rule and therefore EPA must justify that assumption even if no one objects to it during the comment period." (internal quotation marks and alteration omitted) (quoting *Appalachian Power Co. v. EPA*, 135 F.3d 791, 818 (D.C. Cir. 1998)).

See 33 U.S.C. § 1342(a)(2); 40 C.F.R. § 122.44(i)(1)-(2). The regulations provide, in pertinent part: **[—54—]**

In addition to the conditions established under § 122.43(a), each NPDES permit shall include conditions meeting the following requirements when applicable.

. . .

(i) *Monitoring requirements.* In addition to § 122.48, the following monitoring requirements:

(1) To assure compliance with permit limitations, requirements to monitor:

(i) The mass (or other measurement specified in the permit) for each pollutant limited in the permit;

(ii) The volume of effluent discharged from each outfall;

(iii) Other measurements as appropriate including pollutants in internal waste streams under § 122.45(i); pollutants in intake water for net limitations under § 122.45(f); frequency, rate of discharge, etc., for noncontinuous discharges under § 122.45(e); pollutants subject to notification requirements under § 122.42(a); and pollutants in sewage sludge or other monitoring as specified in 40 CFR part 503; or as determined to be necessary on a case-by-case basis pursuant to section 405(d)(4) of the CWA.

(iv) According to sufficiently sensitive test procedures (i.e., methods) approved under 40 CFR part 136 for **[—55—]** the

analysis of pollutants or pollutant parameters or required under 40 CFR chapter 1, subchapter N or O.

. . .

(2) Except as provided in paragraphs (i)(4) and (i)(5) of this section, requirements to report monitoring results shall be established on a case-by-case basis with a frequency dependent on the nature and effect of the discharge, but in no case less than once a year. . . .

40 C.F.R. § 122.44(i)(1)-(2).

Enforcing compliance with a permit is the key to an effective NPDES program. *See NRDC v. Cty of L.A.*, 725 F.3d 1194, 1208 (9th Cir. 2013) ("[T]he NPDES program fundamentally relies on self-monitoring," and "Congress' purpose in adopting this self-monitoring mechanism was to promote straightforward enforcement of the Act." (internal quotations omitted)). We now turn to the monitoring and reporting requirements in the 2013 VGP.

a. *Monitoring Requirements for TBELs*

As previously discussed, the 2013 VGP requires vessels to monitor (1) the functionality of their ballast water treatment systems, if installed, and (2) the concentrations of the two "indicator" bacteria (*E. coli* and enterococci). · VGP § 2.2.3.5.1.1.2, at 30, § 2.2.3.5.1.1.4, at 31-32. **[—56—]**

The first requirement, known as "functionality monitoring," determines whether a ballast water treatment program is "operating according to the manufacturers' requirements." App. at 96. A shipowner is required to check a measurement that would "verify system functionality," such as how much chlorine the system is using each month. *Id.* at 1168. If the measurement is correct, it is assumed that the program is in compliance. If the equipment is not operating properly, the ship is not permitted to discharge ballast. The vessel owner is not required to take any measurement of pollutants or significant categories of living organisms in ballast water being discharged. Instead, the shipowner relies solely on the functioning of the treatment system to determine if the ship is complying with the permit. Treatment systems are inspected monthly. *See* VGP § 2.2.3.5.1.1.2, at 30 ("To assess the [system's] functionality, monitoring indicators of the [system's] functionality is required at least once per month for specific parameters that are applicable to your system.").

The second provision, effluent biological organism monitoring, requires vessels to collect small-volume samples from ballast discharge and analyze them for concentrations of two indicator pathogens, *E. coli* and enterococci. VGP § 2.2.3.5.1.1.4, at 31-32. The idea is that if there are significant [—57—] levels of these two pathogens in the sample, then treatment has not been effective. Vessels are not required to monitor *Vibrio cholera* or medium or large organisms regulated in the 2013 VGP. Sampling is required between one and four times a year, depending on the type of system.

Petitioners present two arguments about why these requirements do not accord with the law. First, petitioners argue that the 2013 VGP violates CWA regulations by not requiring vessels to monitor the *concentration* of living organisms. The regulations require monitoring of mass, volume, or "other measurement specified in the permit." 40 C.F.R. § 122.44(i)(1)(i)-(ii). Petitioners contend the unit of measurement for living organisms in the 2013 VGP should be concentration. Neither functionality monitoring nor testing for two indicator microorganisms measures concentration. Thus, according to petitioners, the monitoring and reporting requirements for TBELs violate 40 C.F.R. § 122.44(i)(1).

Second, petitioners argue that these monitoring requirements violate the requirement in 40 C.F.R. § 122.44(i)(1) that monitoring "assure[s] compliance with permit limitations." Relying on functionality monitoring instead of requiring an actual measurement of concentrations of organisms

means that neither EPA nor the public knows if the permittees are complying with the [—58—] TBELs. Similarly, petitioners argue that monitoring for the presence of the two "indicator bacteria," *E. coli* and enterococci, is not sufficient to monitor compliance with TBELs because it indicates only their presence in the water, not their quantity.

We disagree with petitioners and conclude that EPA's monitoring requirements were not arbitrary and capricious. The CWA regulations expressly allow for monitoring quantities other than mass or volume, namely some "other measurement specified in the permit[]" for each pollutant limited in the permit." 40 C.F.R. § 122.44(i)(1). Functionality monitoring and monitoring for the presence of indicator organisms qualify as such "other measurement."

And while there are potential alternatives, petitioners' urged alternative of direct monitoring is not required because "more sophisticated methods for enumerating living organisms in the larger size classes are not currently available for use by permittees." App. at 524. Current technology is not capable of adequately monitoring ballast water as it is being discharged because, EPA notes, such monitoring requires analyzing large volumes of water and is prohibitively expensive and impractical. According to EPA, testing medium and large organisms with shipboard systems can cost between $75,000 [—59—] and $125,000 per vessel per sampling event. Moreover, the process would be impractical, involving sampling and analyzing large volumes of water in labs and requiring "dozens of hours to collect and analyze those samples." EPA Br. at 89.

Given the difficult circumstances, EPA's monitoring requirements for TBELs were not arbitrary and capricious. *Cf. NRDC v. Costle*, 568 F.2d 1369, 1380 (D.C. Cir. 1977) ("[W]hen numerical effluent limitations are infeasible, EPA may issue permits with conditions designed to reduce the level of effluent discharges to acceptable levels."). In the face of the severe technological limitations on monitoring, it was reasonable for EPA to decline to require monitoring for parameters for which it is currently impractical to collect and analyze samples. Functionality monitoring and biological indirect monitoring are the only feasible options at present to assure compliance with the permit. We defer to EPA's decision that functionality monitoring and biological indicator monitoring, when used in combination, offer an acceptable "other measurement." *See Auer*, 519 U.S. at 461 (holding that courts should defer to agency's interpretation of its own regulations if not plainly erroneous or inconsistent with the regulation). [—60—]

b. *Monitoring Requirements for WQBELs*

Petitioners also argue that EPA acted arbitrarily and capriciously in failing to require that permittees monitor ballast water discharges to ensure compliance with WQBELs. The only monitoring requirement for WQBELs is that ships report the "*expected* date, location, volume, and salinity of any ballast water to be discharged" into U.S. waters or at a reception facility. VGP § 4.3, at 72 (emphasis added). There is no requirement to report actual volumes, locations, or composition of ballast water discharges.

We agree that failure to include monitoring requirements for WQBELs was arbitrary and capricious. The regulations require monitoring to "assure compliance with permit limitations." 40 C.F.R. § 122.44. Generally, "an NPDES permit is unlawful if a permittee is not required to effectively monitor its permit compliance." *NRDC*, 725 F.3d at 1207. Here, the reporting requirement provided little information on the quality of the ballast water, requiring only information on *expected* date, location, volume, and salinity. There is no way to derive from that information whether a vessel is actually in compliance with the WQBELs. Thus, because the 2013 VGP does not contain a mechanism to evaluate compliance with the WQBELs, the monitoring requirements are arbitrary and [—61—] capricious and not in accordance with the law. *See Waterkeeper All.*, 399 F.3d at 499 (failure of permit to include any mechanism for evaluating compliance with required technical standards rendered agency unable to

ensure compliance with water quality standards).

Our conclusion is further supported by the simple, but overlooked, options that EPA has in structuring WQBEL monitoring requirements. One possible condition EPA could consider including in the WQBELs would be to require shipowners to monitor the *actual* time, place, and volume of ballast water discharge, rather than the *expected* time, place, and volume. Another possible condition would be to require shipowners to monitor for a particular pathogen or pollutant if it became known that such a pathogen or pollutant is a problem in a particular port. Each of these options would provide more significant monitoring.

EPA's contentions on this point are unpersuasive. EPA argues that if a vessel is in compliance with the TBELs, it should be "generally expected to already be controlling [its] vessel discharges to a degree that is protective of water quality," rendering additional monitoring to demonstrate compliance with narrative WQBELs unnecessary. App. at 530. In defense of this position, EPA [—62—] also argues that 40 C.F.R. § 122.44(i) does not apply because of "practical constraints on the ability to collect and analyze the volumes of ballast water necessary to 'directly' detect and quantify such organisms at the levels of concern." EPA Br. at 98. According to EPA, it is simply "unrealistic" to have stricter monitoring.

This, however, is not a valid excuse in the WQBEL context. *See NRDC*, 859 F.2d at 208 (stating legislative history of CWA "strongly supports [the] position that Congress did not intend to tie compliance with water quality-based limitations to the capabilities of any given level of technology," and "a water quality-based permit limit begins with the premise that a certain level of water quality will be maintained, come what may, and places upon the permittee the responsibility for realizing that goal"). It is inconsistent to say that WQBELs are necessary to ensure that water quality standards are met, while specific enforcement of such WQBELs is unnecessary. More importantly, this lack of enforcement violates the CWA regulations, which mandate that no permit may be issued "[w]hen the imposition of conditions cannot ensure compliance with the applicable water quality requirements of all affected States." 40 C.F.R. § 122.4(d). [—63—]

Accordingly, EPA's failure to include monitoring for compliance with WQBELs was inconsistent with regulations and thus arbitrary and capricious.

C. *Remand*

Accordingly, we remand this matter to EPA for proceedings consistent with this opinion. The 2013 VGP is to remain in place until EPA issues a new VGP. *See Idaho Farm Bureau Fed'n v. Babbitt,* 58 F.3d 1392, 1405 (9th Cir. 1995) (holding that "[o]rdinarily when a regulation is not promulgated in compliance with the APA, the regulation is invalid. However, when equity demands, the regulation can be left in place while the agency follows the necessary procedures." (citation omitted)); *see also Allied-Signal, Inc. v. U.S. Nuclear Regulatory Comm.,* 988 F.2d 146, 150 (D.C. Cir. 1993) ("An inadequately supported rule, however, need not necessarily be vacated."); *Fertilizer Inst. v. EPA,* 935 F.2d 1303, 1312 (D.C. Cir. 1991) ("[W]hen equity demands, an unlawfully promulgated regulation can be left in place while the agency provides the proper procedural remedy."); *W. Oil & Gas Ass'n v. EPA,* 633 F.2d 803, 813 (9th Cir. 1980) ("[A] reviewing court has discretion to shape an equitable remedy, [and so] we leave the challenged designations in effect."). [—64—]

CONCLUSION

For the reasons set forth above, we **GRANT** the petition for review with respect to

(1) EPA's decision to set the TBELs at the IMO Standard,

(2) EPA's failure to consider onshore treatment for ballast water discharge,

(3) EPA's decision to exempt pre-2009 Lakers from the TBELS in the 2013 VGP permit,

(4) EPA's narrative standard for WQBELs, and

(5) the monitoring and reporting requirements established by EPA for WQBELs,

and **REMAND** for further proceedings in these respects.

We **DENY** the petition for review with respect to TBELs for viruses and protists and the monitoring and reporting requirements established by EPA for TBELs.

The 2013 VGP shall remain in place until EPA issues a new VGP. [—65—]

APPENDIX
Glossary of Acronyms

BACT — Best available demonstrated control technology

BAT — Best available technology economically achievable

BCT — Best conventional pollutant control technology

BMP — Best management practice

BWTS — Ballast water treatment systems

CSA — Canadian Shipowners Association

CWA — Clean Water Act

ELG — Effluent limitation guidelines

EPA — Environmental Protection Agency

IMO — International Maritime Organization

NAS — National Research Council/National Academy of Sciences

NPDES — National Pollutant Discharge Elimination System

NRDC Natural Resources Defense Council

NWEA Northwest Environmental Advocates

NWF National Wildlife Federation

PFR Petition for Review

SAB Science Advisory Board

TBEL Technology-based effluent limitation

VGP Vessel General Permit

WQBEL Water quality-based effluent limitation

This page intentionally left blank

This page intentionally left blank

United States Court of Appeals for the Third Circuit

United States Court of Appeals
for the Third Circuit

No. 14-3626

MAHER TERMINALS, LLC
vs.
PORT AUTH. OF N.Y. AND N.J.

Appeal from the United States District Court for the
District of New Jersey

Decided: October 1, 2015
Amended: November 12, 2015

Citation: 805 F.3d 98, 3 Adm. R. 164 (3d Cir. 2015).

Before **FISHER, JORDAN,** and **SHWARTZ,** Circuit
Judges.

[—3—] **FISHER,** Circuit Judge:

Although Maher Terminals, LLC ("Maher") challenges the rent it must pay under its lease agreement ("the Lease") with the Port Authority of New York and New Jersey ("the Port Authority"), this case is not a typical landlord-tenant dispute. Maher, a landside marine terminal operator, asserts that the rent due under the Lease violates the U.S. Constitution's Tonnage Clause, U.S. Const. art. I, § 10, cl. 3, as well as two related federal statutes, all of which historically have concerned taxes and fees imposed on vessels, their owners, and their passengers and crews. The District Court dismissed Maher's complaint in its entirety, reasoning that Maher's rent obligations did not violate the Tonnage Clause or its related statutes, and that Maher failed to establish admiralty jurisdiction for its remaining tort claim. We agree and hold that landside service providers like Maher are not within the class of plaintiffs that the Tonnage Clause or its related federal statutes were intended to protect, that is, they are outside each law's zone of interests. Accordingly, we will affirm.

I.

Maher is a marine terminal operator with its principal place of business in Elizabeth, New Jersey. Maher's primary business is to load and unload cargo on vessels—also known as stevedoring—and to berth vessels at its

terminal. The Port Authority is an entity created by a compact between New York and New Jersey with the consent of Congress. The Port Authority oversees various transportation systems and, of most relevance to this appeal, the Port of New York and New [—4—] Jersey, the third largest seaport in North America and the largest maritime cargo center on the eastern seaboard.[1]

The Port Authority leases many of its marine terminal facilities at the Port of New York and New Jersey to private companies like Maher, which in turn directly manage the terminals and provide stevedoring services to ships using those terminals. In October 2000, Maher signed a thirty-year lease with the Port Authority to rent the largest marine terminal at Port Elizabeth, consisting of 445 acres of improved land including structures and a berthing area.

The Lease divides Maher's rent into two categories. First, the "Basic Rental" charges Maher a fixed rate per acre of the terminal. When the complaint was filed in 2012, the Basic Rental was $50,413 per acre, totaling $22,433,612 for the year. The second form of rent—and this is the crux of the case—is the "Container Throughput Rental" ("Throughput Rental"), which is a variable charge based on the type and volume of cargo that is loaded and unloaded at Maher's terminal. For the first eight years of the Lease's term, Maher was exempted from paying any Throughput Rental. Since 2008, the Throughput Rental has been calculated based on the following formula: the first 356,000 containers loaded and unloaded by Maher are exempted from any fees; for containers 356,001 to 980,000, Maher pays a per-container fee set forth by a schedule in the Lease ($19.00 per container when the complaint was filed); and for each container over 980,000, Maher pays a lower fee ($14.25 per container when the complaint was filed).

In addition, Maher must load and unload a minimum amount of cargo annually as a condition of maintaining the [—5—] Lease

---

[1] Individual appellee Patrick Foye is the Port Authority's Executive Director.

(420,000 containers when the complaint was filed, which is subject to increase to 900,000 containers upon completion of certain harbor improvements), and Maher must pay an annual guaranteed minimum Throughput Rental equivalent to loading and unloading 775,000 containers (subject to the exemption for the first 356,000 containers), regardless of the number of containers Maher actually handles. All told, Maher paid roughly $12.5 million in Throughput Rental in 2010, and it expected the 2012 Throughput Rental to increase to $14 million.

According to Maher, the Port Authority profits from the Lease. The Port Authority also allegedly uses revenue from the Lease to fund harbor-improvement projects as well as projects wholly unrelated to the services that the Port Authority provides to Maher or vessels using the port.

In September 2012—nearly twelve years after the Lease's effective date—Maher sued the Port Authority in the U.S. District Court for the District of New Jersey. Maher's complaint alleged violations of the U.S. Constitution's Tonnage Clause, U.S. Const. art. I, § 10, cl. 3; the Rivers and Harbors Appropriation Act ("RHA"), 33 U.S.C. § 5(b); and the Water Resources Development Act ("WRDA"), 33 U.S.C. § 2236. Maher also asserted a negligence claim against the Port Authority for the way it established and collected fees.

The Port Authority moved to dismiss the complaint under Rules 12(b)(1) and 12(b)(6) of the Federal Rules of Civil Procedure, and in July 2014, the District Court granted the motion. The District Court reasoned that Maher lacked standing to bring its Tonnage Clause and RHA claims because it was not a protected vessel. Even if Maher had standing, the Tonnage Clause and RHA claims still failed, the District Court held, because Maher did not adequately plead that any fees imposed on vessels were not for services [—6—] rendered. The District Court also dismissed Maher's WRDA claim because Maher had not shown that the Port Authority imposed fees on vessels or cargo and because the WRDA did not prohibit the Port Authority

from using revenue from the Lease to finance harbor-improvement projects. Finally, the District Court decided that it lacked admiralty jurisdiction over Maher's negligence claim and declined to exercise supplemental jurisdiction over the claim. Maher filed this timely appeal.[2]

II.

The District Court exercised jurisdiction only under 28 U.S.C. § 1331, concluding that it lacked admiralty jurisdiction over Maher's negligence claim under 28 U.S.C. § 1333(1) and declining to exercise supplemental jurisdiction over that claim under 28 U.S.C. § 1367. We have jurisdiction under 28 U.S.C. § 1291.

Regardless of whether the District Court dismissed Maher's complaint for failure to state a claim or for lack of jurisdiction, our standard of review is the same: we exercise plenary review over the District Court's order. *Kaymark v. Bank of Am., N.A.*, 783 F.3d 168, 174 (3d Cir. 2015) (failure to state a claim); *Constitution Party of Pa. v. Aichele*, 757 [—7—] F.3d 347, 356 n.12 (3d Cir. 2014) (lack of jurisdiction, including lack of standing). And because any jurisdictional challenge here is facial, in either circumstance, we apply the same standard the District Court did, accepting as true the facts alleged in the complaint and drawing reasonable inferences in Maher's favor. *Kaymark*, 783 F.3d at 174; *Aichele*, 757 F.3d at 356 n.12, 358 (distinguishing facial attacks on jurisdiction from factual ones). We also may consider documents that are *"integral to or explicitly relied* upon in the complaint," *In re Burlington Coat Factory Sec. Litig.*, 114 F.3d 1410, 1426

---

[2] While Maher has been litigating this case, it has also been disputing the Lease's terms before the Federal Maritime Commission. *See Maher Terminals, LLC v. Port Auth. of N.Y. & N.J.*, No. 08-03, 2014 WL 7328474 (FMC Dec. 17, 2014). The FMC concluded that the Port Authority did not violate the Shipping Act, 46 U.S.C. § 40101, by giving an unreasonable preference to another terminal or imposing an unreasonable prejudice on Maher based on the terms of the Lease, including the minimum Throughput Rental. *Id.* at *1, *24.

(3d Cir. 1997) (internal quotation marks omitted), such as the Lease here.

With respect to Maher's negligence claim, we review the District Court's determination of its own admiralty jurisdiction de novo, *Sinclair v. Soniform, Inc.*, 935 F.2d 599, 601 (3d Cir. 1991), but we review the Court's refusal to exercise supplemental jurisdiction over state law claims for abuse of discretion, *Figueroa v. Buccaneer Hotel Inc.*, 188 F.3d 172, 175 (3d Cir. 1999).

III.

The central question on appeal is whether fees imposed on landside entities like Maher can support claims under the Tonnage Clause, the RHA, and the WRDA. A secondary question is whether the District Court correctly decided that it lacked admiralty jurisdiction, and declined to exercise supplemental jurisdiction over Maher's negligence claim. We address these issues in turn.

A.

The U.S. Constitution prohibits states from "lay[ing] any Duty of Tonnage" without the consent of Congress. U.S. Const. art. I, § 10, cl. 3. Maher alleges that several fees imposed by the Lease, but principally the Throughput Rental, [—8—] violate the Tonnage Clause.[3] Maher contends that the District Court

---

[3] On appeal, Maher also challenges the Cargo Facility Charge ("CFC"), which requires "a user of cargo handling services" to pay a fee "to the Port Authority, which will be collected by the terminal operator handling the user's cargo [i.e., Maher] for remittance to the Port Authority." J.A. 345. The Port Authority correctly points out that Maher's complaint only obliquely refers to the CFC, and that Maher did not raise the CFC before the District Court. At oral argument, counsel for Maher argued that the minimum volumetric guarantee, which we understand to be part of the Throughput Rental, also violates the Tonnage Clause. As explained below, however, the categories of fees challenged by Maher are ultimately unimportant because they do not change the fact that Maher is not a vessel or its representative and therefore cannot state a claim under the Tonnage Clause, the RHA, or the WRDA.

incorrectly concluded that Maher lacked standing to bring a Tonnage Clause claim and that Maher did not adequately plead a violation of the Tonnage Clause.

Standing involves "constitutional limitations on federal-court jurisdiction" on the one hand and "prudential limitations" on the other. *Warth v. Seldin*, 422 U.S. 490, 498 (1975). Here the District Court concluded that Maher's Tonnage Clause claim failed for lack of standing, but the Court did not explain whether its holding was based on constitutional or prudential limitations. We read the District Court's opinion as relying on prudential limitations, not [—9—] constitutional ones.[4] The District Court made no reference to the requirements of constitutional standing, instead explaining that Maher lacked standing because it was "not a vessel or other protected entity under the Tonnage Clause." *Maher Terminals, LLC v. Port Auth. of N.Y. & N.J.*, Civ. No. 2:12-6090 KM, 2014 WL 3590142, at *8 (D.N.J. July 21, 2014). In other words, the District Court concluded that Maher fell outside the class of plaintiffs who are protected by the Tonnage Clause. In so doing, the District Court effectively conducted a zone-of-interests

---

[4] In any event, we have no trouble concluding that Maher has constitutional standing to bring its claims. "Constitutional standing has three elements: injury in fact, causation, and redressability." *Shalom Pentecostal Church v. Acting Sec'y U.S. Dep't of Homeland Sec.*, 783 F.3d 156, 161 (3d Cir. 2015) (citing *Lujan v. Defenders of Wildlife*, 504 U.S. 555, 560–61 (1992)). Here the Port Authority argues that Maher suffers no injury in fact from fees that Maher passes on to vessels. This argument is unpersuasive. Maher is responsible for the fees regardless of whether it passes them on to vessels. *See Bacchus Imps., Ltd. v. Dias*, 468 U.S. 263, 267 (1984) (concluding that wholesalers had alleged an economic injury caused by a tax that they were liable to pay even if they could pass on the tax to customers). This conclusion applies to all of Maher's claims. To the extent the District Court's analysis was based on constitutional standing, *see Maher Terminals, LLC v. Port Auth. of N.Y. & N.J.*, Civ. No. 2:12-6090 KM, 2014 WL 3590142, at *8 & n.11 (D.N.J. July 21, 2014) (discussing Rule 12(b)(1) dismissal), the District Court was wrong. Still, we may affirm on any grounds supported by the record. *Tourscher v. McCullough*, 184 F.3d 236, 240 (3d Cir. 1999).

analysis. *See Lexmark Int'l, Inc.* [—**10**—] *v. Static Control Components, Inc.*, 134 S. Ct. 1377, 1387 (2014) (framing the zone-of-interests test as asking whether a particular plaintiff "falls within the class of plaintiffs" authorized to sue under a particular law).

We have previously categorized the zone-of-interests requirement as one of three components of prudential standing. *E.g., Freeman v. Corzine*, 629 F.3d 146, 154 (3d Cir. 2010).[5] But in *Lexmark International, Inc. v. Static Control Components, Inc.*, the Supreme Court criticized the placement of the zone-of-interests requirement within the rubric of prudential standing. 134 S. Ct. at 1387 ("[P]rudential standing is a misnomer as applied to the zone-of-interests analysis." (internal quotation marks omitted)); *see also Shalom Pentecostal Church*, 783 F.3d at 163 n.7. The Court clarified that the zone-of-interests requirement goes to whether a particular plaintiff has a cause of action under a given law, not a plaintiff's standing. *Lexmark*, 134 S. Ct. at 1387. Though *Lexmark* was decided only a few months before the District Court's decision in this case, we agree with Maher that *Lexmark* strongly suggests that courts shouldn't link the zone-of-interests test to the doctrine of standing and that the District Court erred by apparently doing so here. But putting aside the label that applies to the zone-of-interests test, we agree with the District Court that Maher still must satisfy this test to state a Tonnage Clause claim and, as explained below, that Maher fails the test. [—**11**—]

In applying the zone-of-interests test, we must discern the meaning and purpose of the Tonnage Clause using traditional methods of interpretation and ask whether it extends to Maher's claim. *Cf. id.* at 1388–89 (analyzing the meaning and purposes of the Lanham Act to determine the interests protected by the Act). We have applied the zone-of-interests

test "liberal[ly]" and have noted "that it is not meant to be especially demanding." *Oxford Assocs. v. Waste Sys. Auth. of E. Montgomery Cnty.*, 271 F.3d 140, 146 (3d Cir. 2001) (internal quotation marks omitted). The test is particularly generous in the context of challenges to agency actions under the Administrative Procedure Act, but it may be less so in other contexts. *Lexmark*, 134 S. Ct. at 1389.

Turning to the Tonnage Clause's meaning, "we are guided by the principle that the Constitution was written to be understood by the voters; its words and phrases were used in their normal and ordinary as distinguished from technical meaning." *District of Columbia v. Heller*, 554 U.S. 570, 576 (2008) (internal quotation marks and brackets omitted). Although the Constitution appears to speak broadly by prohibiting states from "lay[ing] any Duty of Tonnage," the term "Duty of Tonnage" had a well-known meaning to the founding generation. It referred to the common commercial practice of taxing "a ship . . . according to 'the internal cubic capacity of a vessel,' *i.e.*, its tons of carrying capacity." *Polar Tankers, Inc. v. City of Valdez*, 557 U.S. 1, 6 (2009) (quoting *Clyde Mallory Lines v. Alabama ex rel. State Docks Comm'n*, 296 U.S. 261, 265 (1935)). Further, tonnage duties referred to taxes "on the privilege of access by vessels to the ports of a state" and "were distinct from fees . . . for services facilitating commerce." *Clyde Mallory Lines*, 296 U.S. at 265.

To the Framers, the Tonnage Clause supported and shared a purpose with the Import-Export Clause, U.S. Const. [—**12**—] art. I, § 10, cl. 2, which generally prohibits states from taxing imports and exports. *See Clyde Mallory Lines*, 296 U.S. at 264–65. The purpose of the Import-Export Clause, in turn, was to prevent states with convenient ports from taxing goods travelling in commerce at the expense of consumers in less-fortunately located states. *See Polar Tankers*, 557 U.S. at 7. The Framers understood that the Import-Export Clause could be effectively "nullified" "[i]f the states had been left free to tax the privilege of access by vessels to their harbors." *Clyde Mallory Lines*, 296 U.S. at 265; *accord*

---

[5] The other two components of prudential standing are that a plaintiff first must "assert his or her own legal interests rather than those of third parties," and second must not assert "generalized grievances" that require courts to "adjudicat[e] abstract questions." *Freeman*, 629 F.3d at 154 (internal quotation marks and brackets omitted).

S.S. Co. v. Portwardens, 73 U.S. (6 Wall.) 31, 34–35 (1867). Although there was some disagreement about whether the Commerce Clause already prohibited tonnage duties, *Clyde Mallory Lines*, 296 U.S. at 265 n.1, the Tonnage Clause was adopted to "prevent that nullification" and to further restrain states from obtaining "geographical vessel-related tax advantages," *Polar Tankers*, 557 U.S. at 7.

To effectuate these purposes, the Supreme Court has interpreted the Tonnage Clause to prohibit more than only classic tonnage duties, i.e., taxes on a ship based on the ship's capacity; the Court has also said that a state cannot "'do that indirectly which she is forbidden . . . to do directly.'" *Id.* at 8 (alteration in original) (quoting *Passenger Cases*, 48 U.S. (7 How.) 283, 458 (1849)). Thus, the Tonnage Clause prohibits taxes that vary according to ratios other than a ship's capacity, such as the number of masts, mariners, or passengers. *Id.* It likewise prohibits taxes that are imposed not just on the vessel itself but also on the ship captain, owner, supercargo (the person in charge of the cargo on the ship), and passengers. *Id.*; *Passenger Cases*, 48 U.S. (7 How.) at 458–59. The Clause even prohibits flat taxes on a ship—those that do not vary according to tonnage—if they are for the privilege of entering a port. *Portwardens*, 73 U.S. (6 Wall.) at [—13—] 34–35. In sum, the Tonnage Clause's prohibition "embrace[s] all taxes and duties regardless of their name or form, and even though not measured by the tonnage of the vessel, which operate to impose a charge for the privilege of entering, trading in, or lying in a port." *Clyde Mallory Lines*, 296 U.S. at 265–66.

Consistent with the original understanding of tonnage duties, the Tonnage Clause does not prohibit states from charging vessels "for services rendered to and enjoyed by the vessel, such as pilotage, or wharfage, or charges for the use of locks on a navigable river, or fees for medical inspection." *Id.* at 266 (citations omitted). Charges for such services, even those that vary according to tonnage, are constitutional for at least two reasons. First, they are not taxes—which are assertions of sovereignty—but are instead demands for reasonable compensation—which are assertions of a right of property. *Packet Co. v. Keokuk*, 95 U.S. 80, 85 (1877). Second, charges for services are constitutional because they facilitate, rather than impede, commerce. *See Clyde Mallory Lines*, 296 U.S. at 265–66; *Keokuk*, 95 U.S. at 84 ("[A charge for services rendered] is not a hindrance or impediment to free navigation.").

Of course, a state may not escape the Tonnage Clause's reach merely by labelling a tax as a charge for services. *Keokuk*, 95 U.S. at 86; *Cannon v. City of New Orleans*, 87 U.S. (20 Wall.) 577, 580 (1874) ("A tax which is . . . due from all vessels arriving and stopping in a port, without regard to the place where they may stop, . . . cannot be treated as a compensation for the use of a wharf."). Vessels that pay a purported services charge must actually receive a proportionate benefit in return. *See State Tonnage Tax Cases*, 79 U.S. (12 Wall.) 204, 220 (1870) (striking down a tax because it was "an act to raise revenue without any [—14—] corresponding or equivalent benefit or advantage to the vessels taxed"). So it is constitutional for a state to demand "just" and "reasonable compensation" for services rendered, *Cannon*, 87 U.S. (20 Wall.) at 582, but the inverse must also be true: a state may not demand unjust and unreasonable compensation for services, even if services are actually rendered. Additionally, a reasonable charge for general services that benefit all ships that enter a port, such as policing services for a harbor, is constitutional, *see Clyde Mallory Lines*, 296 U.S. at 266–67, but a tax that has a "general, revenue-raising purpose" is probably not, *see Polar Tankers*, 557 U.S. at 10.

From this discussion, we conclude that the Tonnage Clause was meant to protect vessels as vehicles of commerce. *See Keokuk*, 95 U.S. at 84–85 ("[The Tonnage Clause] was designed to guard against local hindrances to trade and carriage *by vessels* . . . ." (emphasis added)). Tonnage duties were originally understood as taxes on vessels, and the modern formulation from *Clyde Mallory Lines* and *Polar Tankers* extending the Clause to all "charge[s] for the privilege of entering, trading in, or lying in a port" does nothing to change the fundamental object of the provision. The body of law surrounding the services exception to the Tonnage Clause drives home the point. Fees for services are allowed because they do not impede a vessel's free navigation in commerce and are only levied when a "passing vessel" elects to use those services, *see Keokuk*, 95 U.S. at 85, a concern that is plainly inapplicable to non-vessel plaintiffs. Therefore, to come within the Tonnage Clause's zone of interests, we hold that a plaintiff must allege an injury to a vessel as a vehicle of commerce.

Our conclusion does not conflict with the Supreme Court's admonition that the Tonnage Clause prohibits indirect [—15—] tonnage duties and, consequently, extends to taxes imposed not only on a vessel, but also on an owner, ship captain, supercargo, or the passengers; to the contrary, the two are very much consistent. Though these people are obviously not ships, the Tonnage Clause prohibits taxes imposed on them because they are representatives of ships. *See Passenger Cases*, 48 U.S. (7 How.) at 458 ("It is . . . a duty on the vessel . . . . It is a taxation of the master, as representative of the vessel and her cargo."). And unlike the landside provider of harbor services, these people travel with the ships moving as vehicles in commerce. As discussed above, the Tonnage Clause protects the rights of vessels to navigate free of local hindrances by prohibiting charges that the vessels do not choose to incur. Just as a tax on a vessel impedes the vessel's ability to freely move in commerce, taxes on the people on board the vessel have the same effect. Taxes on certain people (the owner, captain, supercargo, and crew) directly impact where a vessel decides to make port by taxing those responsible for the vessel's navigation, and taxes on passengers will likely indirectly impact a vessel's decisions by reducing demand for passage on the vessel. The interests of these people are the same as the interests of the vessels they occupy, so the Tonnage Clause prohibits taxes on them just as it prohibits taxes on the vessels themselves.

As a landside marine terminal operator challenging the rent it owes under the Lease, Maher is not a member of the class of plaintiffs that can state a claim under the Tonnage Clause. Maher's injury is not an injury to a vessel or its representative. Unlike a fee imposed on a vessel or the people on board, a fee imposed on Maher does not in and of itself impact a vessel's ability to freely navigate in commerce. Fees imposed on Maher affect vessels *only if* Maher passes on such fees to vessels that use its terminal for stevedoring services. [—16—] That it is not enough for Maher to satisfy the zone-of-interests test. A party may not contract its way into a law's zone of interests if that party does not itself have any protected interests under the law. *Cf. Freeman*, 629 F.3d at 157 ("[P]laintiffs who allege only that a party with whom they contract is subject to an undue burden on its ability to freely participate in interstate commerce are not within the zone of interests protected by the dormant Commerce Clause." (internal quotation marks omitted)). To hold otherwise would allow parties to evade the first prudential standing requirement: that parties must assert their own legal interests, not the interests of third parties. *See id.* at 154. Therefore, the Tonnage Clause is not concerned with taxes on any entity that has some relationship with vessels; rather, it prohibits taxes that are directed at vessels or their representatives. Vessels [—17—] may be able to challenge Maher's rent,[6] but Maher cannot assert the rights of third-party vessels.[7] [—18—]

---

[6] We do not hold that *vessels* or their representatives could never challenge tonnage duties that are passed through a private entity like Maher.

[7] Although third-party standing—standing to assert the legal interests of third parties—is allowed in "exceptional" circumstances, *Amato v. Wilentz*, 952 F.2d 742, 750 (3d Cir. 1991), Maher did not seek third-party standing here, mostly because it did not believe it needed to allege that the vessels paid the tonnage duties in this case. But even if Maher had made a third-party standing argument, it would have failed. In deciding whether Maher should have third-party standing, we consider, inter alia, (1) whether Maher had a close relationship with the third-party vessels and (2) whether the third-party vessels faced some obstacles to bringing their own lawsuits. *See Pa. Psychiatric Soc'y v. Green Spring Health Servs. Inc.*, 280 F.3d 278, 288–89 (3d Cir. 2002). Maher does not appear to have the requisite close

We are unpersuaded by Maher's argument that it satisfies the zone-of-interests test because it is "engaged in interstate commerce" and "seek[s] to vindicate interests related to the protection of interstate commerce." Maher Br. 32 (alteration in original) (internal quotation marks omitted). For support, Maher relies on cases applying the zone-of-interests test in the context of the dormant Commerce Clause. *See Freeman*, 629 F.3d at 156–57; *Oxford Assocs.*, 271 F.3d at 146. Though the Tonnage Clause supports the Commerce Clause (as well as the Import-Export Clause), the Tonnage Clause is not the Commerce Clause. The Tonnage Clause protects the free flow of commerce through a specific means— by protecting vessels operating as vehicles of commerce.

Nor is Maher within the Tonnage Clause's zone of interests because it pays fees that vary according to the volume of cargo moving through its port. In *Polar Tankers*, the Supreme Court said that the tax at issue there was "at the heart of what the Tonnage Clause forbids." 557 U.S. at 10. It did so in part because the tax "depend[ed] on a factor related to tonnage," i.e., a ship's cargo capacity, in that it applied to vessels only of a certain size. *Id*. But other cases teach us that whether a fee varies according to tonnage is not actually the touchstone of unconstitutional tonnage duties. *See Clyde Mallory Lines*, 296 U.S. at 265-66 (holding that the Tonnage Clause prohibits "all taxes and duties regardless of their name or form, *and even though not measured by the tonnage of the vessel*, which operate to impose a charge for

---

relationship with the allegedly-injured vessels. Fifteen years ago, Maher agreed to the Throughput Rental that it now claims violates the vessels' rights under the Tonnage Clause. Additionally, there are limited obstacles to vessels asserting their own claims under the Tonnage Clause if they believe they are paying unconstitutional tonnage duties. Finally, and perhaps most fundamentally, it is unclear from Maher's complaint whether any vessels are actually paying unconstitutional tonnage duties. Maher's allegations about passing on the fees to the vessels are quite vague, and Maher does not adequately allege that the vessels are paying unreasonable fees for the services they receive from Maher (the services provider) as a result of the rent due under the Lease.

the privilege of entering, trading in, or lying in a port" (emphasis added)); *Portwardens*, 73 U.S. (6 Wall.) at 35 (holding that the Tonnage Clause prohibits "*fixed*" fees as well as fees that vary with vessels' capacity (emphasis added)). We therefore do not read *Polar Tankers* or any of the Tonnage Clause [—19—] precedent as standing for the proposition that any fee on anyone or anything that varies according to cargo volume is an unconstitutional tonnage duty, as Maher does. What actually made the tax in *Polar Tankers* unconstitutional, and what Maher cannot show here, is that the tax was directed at *vessels* and was not in exchange for services. *See* 557 U.S. at 10 (noting that "the tax applie[d] only to large ships" and was "not for services provided to the vessel[s]"). The same is true of *Bridgeport & Port Jefferson Steamboat Co. v. Bridgeport Port Authority*, where the Second Circuit struck down a fee imposed on all passengers of a ferry under the Tonnage Clause. 567 F.3d 79, 88 (2d Cir. 2009). Although the tax in *Bridgeport* varied depending on whether the passenger was a person or vehicle, the tax was unconstitutional, in our view, because it was directed at a *vessel's passengers*.

If we unmoor the Tonnage Clause from taxes on vessels and allow landside entities to bring Tonnage Clause claims, we would transform the Tonnage Clause into a broad "Maritime Commerce Clause." Landside entities having some relationship to maritime commerce would be able to challenge not only volumetric charges like the one here, but any unreasonable state-imposed fees for the privilege of being in a port. *See Portwardens*, 73 U.S. (6 Wall.) at 35 ("It was not only a *pro rata* tax which was prohibited, but any duty . . . ."). So, for example, a restaurant renting state property in a port that serves food to mariners fresh off a vessel could state a claim under the Tonnage Clause by claiming that its rent is unreasonably high given the services provided by the state. We doubt the Framers intended the Tonnage Clause to sweep so broadly as to transform these and other landlord-tenant disputes into constitutional questions, especially given the conspicuous absence of vessels and cargo owners from this case complaining about the fees they are paying at the Port of [—20—] New York and New Jersey.[8] Although the Tonnage Clause should be interpreted in light of its general purposes of preventing nullification of the Import-Export Clause and stopping states from obtaining geographic advantages by taxing vessels, these purposes do not give us license to transform the Tonnage Clause into something it is not and was never intended to be.

In sum, while we hold that the District Court should not have couched its conclusion in terms of standing after *Lexmark*, we agree with the District Court's essential holding: Maher, as a landside entity, is outside the Tonnage Clause's zone of interests. This is not, as Maher contends, to elevate form over substance. Anchoring the Tonnage Clause to taxes on vessels and their representatives is the only way to preserve the Clause's meaning. Accordingly, Maher failed to state a Tonnage Clause claim.

B.

Maher next challenges the District Court's dismissal of its RHA claim. Under the RHA, taxes and fees from non-Federal interests (like the Port Authority) cannot be "levied upon or collected from any vessel or other water craft, or from its passengers or crew," except for, inter alia, "reasonable fees charged on a fair and equitable basis that – [—21—] (A) are used solely to pay the cost of a service to the vessel or water craft; (B) enhance the safety and efficiency of interstate and foreign commerce; and (C) do not impose more than a small burden on interstate or foreign commerce." 33 U.S.C. § 5(b).

---

[8] *State, Department of Natural Resources v. Alaska Riverways, Inc.*, 232 P.3d 1203 (Alaska 2010), is not to the contrary. There the Alaska Supreme Court struck down a per-passenger fee under the RHA that was assessed against a boat company ostensibly as rent for using unimproved shoreland. *Id.* at 1221. Unlike the plaintiff in that case, Maher is not a vessel operator so it does not have any independent interests protected by the Tonnage Clause or the RHA, its statutory equivalent.

By its terms, the RHA only applies to taxes and fees imposed on or collected from vessels, their passengers, or their crews. As a landside terminal, Maher is none of these and therefore cannot state a claim under the RHA. Maher itself recognizes that the RHA codifies the body of law surrounding the Tonnage Clause. Accordingly, we hold that Maher's RHA claim fails for the same reasons as its Tonnage Clause claim, and for the additional reason that the plain language of the RHA is explicitly limited to categories of entities that do not include Maher.

C.

We also reject Maher's argument that the District Court incorrectly dismissed its WRDA claim. The WRDA grants the consent of Congress to certain tonnage duties and cargo fees to finance harbor-improvement projects provided that such fees are imposed in accordance with the WRDA's requirements. 33 U.S.C. § 2236(a). Among other things, the WRDA permits the collection of fees only after the project has been completed. *Id.* § 2236(a)(1). Before fees may be imposed under the WRDA, there must be notice and a public hearing on the proposed fees, *id.* § 2236(a)(5), and the non-Federal interest must publicly file a schedule of harbor fees with the Federal Maritime Commission, *id.* § 2236(a)(6)(A). The WRDA allows "[a]ny person who . . . is . . . aggrieved by . . . a proposed scheme or schedule of port or harbor dues under this section . . . to seek judicial review of that proposed scheme or schedule," provided that the action is brought [—22—] within 180 days of the hearing required by § 2236(a)(5). *Id.* § 2236(b)(2).

Maher's WRDA claim fails for two reasons. First, the WRDA expressly applies only to fees imposed on vessels and on cargo. Here Maher is challenging neither. Granted, the Lease calculates Maher's rent based in part on the amount of cargo moving through Maher's terminal, but Maher's rent is not a fee on the cargo itself. Nor is it a tonnage duty, as explained above.

Second, we agree with the Port Authority that Maher has no WRDA claim because the

Port Authority never even purported to impose rent on Maher pursuant to the WRDA. The WRDA provides a limited private right of action to persons "aggrieved by . . . *a proposed scheme or schedule of port or harbor dues under this section*" and only allows for "judicial review of *that proposed scheme or schedule.*" *Id.* § 2236(b)(2) (emphasis added). Additionally, the 180-day time limit for bringing a WRDA claim is tied to the date of the public hearing required by the WRDA. *Id.* Because there is no WRDA schedule of fees for us to review, Maher has no WRDA claim.

Maher argues that such a reading of the WRDA is "preposterous," Maher Reply Br. 21, but we disagree. Nothing in the WRDA prohibits non-Federal interests from raising revenue in ways other than tonnage duties and cargo fees to finance harbor-improvement projects, as the Port Authority is allegedly doing in this case. Moreover, the WRDA merely provides congressional consent to tonnage duties and cargo fees that meet the WRDA's other requirements. In other words, it is a safe harbor for what would otherwise be unconstitutional duties. If a non-Federal interest imposes tonnage duties or cargo fees that do not comport with the WRDA's requirements, those duties and [—23—] fees would not have the consent of Congress, and the remedy would be a direct challenge under the Tonnage Clause or the Import-Export Clause.

Therefore, we hold that Maher cannot state a claim under the WRDA.

D.

Finally, we address Maher's negligence claim. The District Court concluded that it lacked federal admiralty jurisdiction over the claim, under 28 U.S.C. § 1333(1) and declined to exercise supplemental jurisdiction over the claim under 28 U.S.C. § 1367.

A proponent of admiralty jurisdiction for "a tort claim must satisfy conditions both of location and of connection with maritime activity." *Jerome B. Grubart, Inc. v. Great Lakes Dredge & Dock Co.*, 513 U.S. 527, 534 (1995). To satisfy the location test, "the tort [must have] occurred on navigable water or . . . [an] injury suffered on land [must have been] caused by a vessel on navigable water." *Id.* "[T]he tort occurs where the alleged negligence took effect." *Exec. Jet Aviation, Inc. v. City of Cleveland*, 409 U.S. 249, 266 (1972) (internal quotation marks omitted).

Maher's claim of negligence is that the Port Authority "negligently establish[ed] and collect[ed] charges and fees for the use of Maher's terminal . . . upon such bases and in such amounts as are unlawful." J.A. 49. Put simply, any negligence by the Port Authority occurred on land. Maher and the Port Authority are land-based entities. The Lease was negotiated on land, and payments were made on land. Accordingly, Maher cannot satisfy the location test for admiralty jurisdiction, so its claim arises not under federal law but state law. [—24—]

And because the District Court correctly dismissed all of Maher's federal claims over which it possessed original jurisdiction, the District Court did not abuse its discretion when it declined to exercise supplemental jurisdiction over Maher's state-law negligence claim. *See Hedges v. Musco*, 204 F.3d 109, 123 (3d Cir. 2000) (discussing 28 U.S.C. § 1367(c)(3)).

IV.

For the reasons set forth above, we will affirm the order of the District Court.[9]

(Reporter's Note: Concurring opinion in part and Dissenting opinion in part follows on p. 173).

---

[9] Based on our resolution of the case on the above-stated grounds, we do not reach the Port Authority's alternative arguments that Maher's claims are untimely.

[—1—] **JORDAN,** Circuit Judge, concurring in part and dissenting in part:

Although I concur in my colleagues' resolution of Maher's statutory and tort claims, I respectfully dissent from their conclusion that Maher has not stated a constitutional claim. The Majority Opinion runs contrary to a long line of Supreme Court precedent interpreting the Tonnage Clause. Most recently, in *Polar Tankers, Inc. v. City of Valdez, Alaska*, 557 U.S. 1 (2009), the Court reaffirmed its broad reading of that clause as prohibiting state and local governments from doing indirectly what they may not do directly, namely, lay a tax on shipping. *Id.* at 8. The Tonnage Clause forbids any attempt— "regardless of [its] name or form", *id.*—to raise revenue by charging duties on maritime commerce. That, however, is precisely what Maher alleges is the effect of the "Container Throughput Rental" assessments it must pay under the terms of its lease with the Port Authority. The assessments are a tax on the stevedores working with the vessels and will be passed on to the vessels, according to Maher. While those allegations may ultimately prove unfounded, I believe that Maher has pled sufficient facts to survive a motion to dismiss. I would therefore vacate the District Court's dismissal of the Tonnage Clause claim as to the Container Throughput Rental assessments.

The Constitution declares that "No State shall, without the Consent of Congress, lay any Duty of Tonnage ...." U.S. Const., art. I, § 10, cl. 3. My colleagues correctly note that the word "tonnage" literally refers to the "entire internal [—2—] cubical capacity, or contents of the ship or vessel expressed in tons of one hundred cubical feet ...." *In re State Tonnage Tax Cases*, 79 U.S. 204, 212 (1870). The term "'was used by the framers because at that day and time it was the customary mode of measuring the value of a ship.'" Erik M. Jensen, *Quirky Constitutional Provisions Matter: The Tonnage Clause, Polar Tankers, and State Taxation of Commerce*, 18 Geo. Mason L. Rev. 669, 683 (2011) (quoting Samuel Freeman Miller, Lectures on the Constitution of the United States 253 (photo reprint 1980) (New York & Albany, Banks & Bros. 1891)). But the Tonnage Clause has long since been extended to address taxation beyond the narrow reach inherent in that definition. It had to be, because, "taken in this restricted sense, the constitutional provision would not fully accomplish its intent." *So. Steamship Co. of New Orleans v. Portwardens*, 73 U.S. 31, 34 (1867). It was designed to support the Constitution's Import-Export Clause, which, as its name suggests, bars states from placing duties on imports or exports.[1] *In re State Tonnage Tax Cases*, 79 U.S. at 215 ("Tonnage duties are as much taxes as duties on imports or exports, and the prohibition of the Constitution extends as fully to such duties if levied by the States as to duties on imports or exports, and for reasons quite as strong [—3—] as those which induced the framers of the Constitution to withdraw imports and exports from State taxation."). By its very nature, the Tonnage Clause also serves the fundamental purpose of the Commerce Clause,[2] ensuring federal control over matters of interstate and foreign commerce. *See Dept. of Revenue of State of Wash. v. Ass'n of Wash. Stevedoring Cos.*, 435 U.S. 734, 754 (1978). In fact, James Madison "was of the opinion that the commerce clause independently restrained the states from imposing duties of tonnage." *Plaquemines Port, Harbor & Terminal Dist. v. Fed. Mar. Comm'n*, 838 F.2d 536, 546 (D.C. Cir. 1988). Nonetheless, the Tonnage Clause was added to the Constitution and so provided, along with the Import-Export Clause, a set of bars to complement the Commerce Clause barricade against state meddling in matters of national and foreign commerce.[3] These three

---

[1] The Import-Export Clause provides, "No State shall, without the Consent of the Congress, lay any Imposts or Duties on Imports or Exports, except what may be absolutely necessary for executing its inspection Laws: and the net Produce of all Duties and Imposts, laid by any State on Imports or Exports, shall be for the Use of the Treasury of the United States; and all such Laws shall be subject to the Revision and Controul of the Congress." U.S. Const. art. I, § 10, cl. 2.

[2] The Commerce Clause authorizes Congress to "regulate Commerce with foreign Nations, and among the several States, and with the Indian Tribes." U.S. Const. art. I, § 8, cl. 3.

[3] By including the Tonnage Clause, certain delegates to the Convention worried that it "would imply the opposite [– that states could otherwise

clauses in combination—the Commerce Clause, the Import-Export Clause, and the Tonnage Clause—are [—4—] meant to enhance the federal government's power to speak with one voice on matters of trade, to protect federal import revenues from state diversion, and to avoid discord among the states. *See Michelin Tire Corp. v. Wages*, 423 U.S. 276, 285-86 (1976).

The purposes meant to be accomplished by constitutional provisions, however, may not come easily or naturally. Self-interest is a powerful countervailing force. In the context of maritime commerce, that has manifested itself in repeated efforts by state and local authorities to circumvent the Tonnage Clause, often by merely calling a tax something else or moving the aim of it from a ship to a related target. The Supreme Court has been vigilant in recognizing and rejecting such creativity. "A State cannot take what would otherwise amount to a tax on the ship's capacity and evade the Clause by calling that tax 'a charge on the owner or supercargo,'[4] thereby 'justify[ing] this evasion of a great principle by producing a dictionary or a dictum to prove that a ship-captain is not a vessel, nor a supercargo an import.'" *Polar Tankers*, 557 U.S. at 8 (alteration in original) (quoting *Passenger Cases*, 48 U.S. (7 How.) 283, 459 (1849) (Grier, J., concurring)). Put differently, an indirect tax on shipping is just as offensive as a direct one. "The States cannot lay export duties, nor duties on imports, nor tonnage duties on vessels. If they tax the master and crew, *they indirectly lay a duty on the vessel*. If the passengers on board are taxed, *the* [—5—]

protected goods – the imports – are reached." *Passenger Cases*, 48 U.S. at 452 (Catron, J., concurring) (emphasis added). The allegations in this case present only the latest example of a self-interested local authority trying to tax commerce.

In levying its assessment upon the landside marine terminal operator rather than the vessel or its representatives, the Port Authority is playing the exact labeling game that the Framers of our Constitution intended to foreclose by adopting the Tonnage Clause. The Port Authority is indirectly taxing vessels, and thus the goods on those vessels, by moving the locus of its assessments somewhere else, in this instance, to the water's edge. We ought not permit this. My colleagues accept the argument that "the Tonnage Clause was meant to protect vessels" (Majority at 15), which is true, as far as it goes. But the Clause was never meant simply to protect vessels as such. The Framers were not worried about boats. They were worried about provincialism and protecting national control of commercial activity so that there would be a free flow of goods between the states and with other nations.[5] They

---

impose a tonnage duty –] and put the states in a worse position," *Plaquemines*, 838 F.2d at 546, but the Supreme Court has long rejected the notion that the absence of an express prohibition on states means that "any other commercial regulation, not expressly forbidden, to which the original power of the State was competent, may still be made," *Gibbons v. Ogden*, 22 U.S. (9 Wheat.) 1, 200 (1824) (Marshall, C.J.).

4 A "supercargo" is "[a] person specially employed and authorized by a cargo owner to sell cargo that has been shipped and to purchase returning cargo, at the best possible prices; the commercial or foreign agent of a merchant." Black's Law Dictionary 1575 (9th ed. 2009).

5 The Majority's reasoning gains no traction by invoking the "zone of interests" test. In Commerce Clause cases, as the Majority recognizes, "we have advocated a liberal employment of the zone of interests test, explaining that it is not meant to be especially demanding." *Oxford Assocs. v. Waste Sys. Auth. of E. Montgomery Cnty.*, 271 F.3d 140, 146 (3d Cir. 2001) (internal quotation marks omitted). The bar of the "zone of interests" test is so low that it is satisfied by plaintiffs who merely "seek to vindicate interests *related to* the protection of interstate commerce." *Freeman v.* [—6—] *Corzine*, 629 F.3d 146, 157 (3d Cir. 2010) (emphasis added). It would be odd, then, for the Tonnage Clause to have such a distinctly difficult "zone of interest" test, since the two clauses address the same concern.

In any event, the notion that Maher is not within the "zone of interests" of the Tonnage Clause is untenable. Maher's marine container terminal is the largest in the Port of New York and New Jersey, Maher unloads about one million ocean-shipping containers every year, and it paid $12.5 million in Container Throughput Rental assessments in 2010 alone. It is one of the world's largest multi-user marine container terminal operators, and has been operating at Port Elizabeth

understood basic economics, including the [—6—] way that indirect taxes on shipping would, if allowed, enrich coastal states at the expense of inland states. In the Federalist Papers, Alexander Hamilton noted that "[i]mposts, excises, and, in general, all duties upon articles of consumption, may be compared to a fluid, which will, in time, find its level with the means of paying them." The Federalist No. 21. The very fact that the Framers felt the Tonnage Clause was necessary as a backstop to the Import-Export Clause demonstrates their recognition of the illusory distinction between direct and indirect taxes on goods.

In the end, they knew, any charge on shipping—whether on the goods themselves, the vessels conveying the goods, or on some other surrogate for the vessels and goods— would be passed on to consumers. The citizens of one state [—7—] would benefit to the detriment of the citizens of another, and commerce would be impeded. According to Hamilton, "[t]he maxim that the consumer is the payer, is so much oftener true than the reverse of the proposition, that it is far more equitable that the duties on imports should go into a common stock, than that they should redound to the exclusive benefit of the importing States." The Federalist No. 35. Were such a tax on shipping permitted, whatever its guise, it would be "productive of inequality among the States; which inequality would be increased with the increased extent of the duties." *Id*. As a consequence, "the assumption of most founders was that ... an indirect tax is one which the ultimate consumer can generally decide whether to pay by deciding whether to acquire the taxed product"—in other words, the assumption was that indirect taxes will get passed on to consumers in the form of higher prices. Erik M. Jensen, *The Apportionment of "Direct Taxes": Are Consumption Taxes Constitutional*, 97 Colum. L. Rev. 2334, 2395 (1997).

---

for over 60 years. The Tonnage Clause seeks to protect against local assessments that impose a charge on maritime trade. *Polar Tankers*, 557 U.S. at 8. Maher's position as a major stevedoring business is thus more than enough to satisfy the "zone of interests" test.

For that reason, when an assessment is a revenue-raising tax on the privilege of "entering, trading in, or lying in port," *Clyde Mallory Lines v. Alabama ex rel. State Docks Comm'n*, 296 U.S. 261, 265-66 (1935), and not a reasonable reimbursement for services rendered, it constitutes an impermissible duty of tonnage because it undermines federal control over commerce, regardless of the target of the assessment.[6] Hence, "[t]he prohibition of a duty of tonnage [—8—] should ... be construed so as to carry out [its] intent. A mere adherence to the letter, without reference to the spirit and purpose, may in this case mislead as it has misled in other cases." *Keokuk N. Line Packet Co. v. City of Keokuk*, 95 U.S. (5 Otto) 80, 87 (1877). [—9—]

---

[6] It bears mention that the Tonnage Clause is one of the few limitations of the Constitution that is not absolute but instead only disallows states from enacting such duties "without the Consent of Congress." U.S. Const., art. I, § 10, cl. 3. The Port Authority is thus free to seek an Act of [—8—] Congress permitting the fees at issue here. Indeed, the Water Resources Development Act itself is specifically styled as congressional consent to impose an otherwise-impermissible duty of tonnage. *See* 33 U.S.C. § 2236(a). Rather than foreclose all such taxes, the Tonnage Clause operates to move decision-making over duties of tonnage to Congress, thereby ensuring its control over matters of national commerce. The potential permissibility of such taxes, with congressional assent, makes plain "the necessity of a rigid adherence to the demands of" the Tonnage Clause. *Cannon v. City of New Orleans*, 87 U.S. (20 Wall.) 577, 583 (1874).

> If hardships arise in the enforcement of this principle, and the just necessities of a local commerce require a tax which is otherwise forbidden, it is presumed that Congress would not withhold its assent if properly informed and its consent requested. This is a much wiser course, and Congress is a much safer depositary of the final exercise of this important power than the ill-regulated and overtaxed towns and cities, which are not likely to look much beyond their own needs and their own interests.

Id. By upholding the assessment levied here, the Majority forecloses the need for cooperative federalism and instead permits the Port Authority to make the decision alone, without proper input from Congress.

Unfortunately, the Majority has been misled. The test it offers for distinguishing this case from those in which a Tonnage Clause violation was found is that the non-vessel targets of taxation in those cases—the captain, crew, passengers, etc.—were unlike the stevedores here because those targets were "representatives of ships" who "travel with the ships moving as vehicles in commerce." (Majority at 16.) According to the Majority, taxes on such people might "indirectly impact a vessel's decisions" as to how and where to travel. (*Id.*) But how can it be thought that the Container Throughput Rental assessments at issue here will not—in theory anyway—do the very same thing? Maher alleges that, at public cargo facilities, the Port Authority collects all fees and assessments from the vessels. By contrast, at leased cargo facilities like Maher's, the "Port Authority collects fees and charges ... from the terminal operators, which in turn collect fees and charges from vessels and cargo using the terminals." (App. at 3.) In other words, vessels are charged directly at public facilities, and indirectly at leased facilities. According to the Majority, that amounts to a constitutional difference, with the Tonnage Clause acting as a restraint at the former set of facilities but not at the latter.[7] It is hard to [—10—] accept that conclusion, since national and international commerce is happening at both types of facilities, and thus the concerns motivating the Framers are fully in play at both.

Of course, the Majority's distinction places Maher at a disadvantage in comparison with public cargo facilities—why would a ship avail itself of a Maher terminal subject to indirect taxes, when it can have access to public terminals where fees can only be charged for services rendered? And the size of Maher's disadvantage is now at the whim of the Port Authority, itself the owner of the competing public cargo facilities. By my colleagues' reasoning, though, that is of no moment. All the Port Authority needs to do to avoid the Tonnage Clause is insert a middleman between itself and the vessels to be taxed. If the Port Authority charges Maher fees for the privilege of stevedoring in its port, and Maher passes those fees on to the vessels, the vessels themselves have no Tonnage Clause claim against the Port Authority because their payments, nominally paid to Maher, would not be considered taxes. And the vessels could not sue Maher for a Tonnage Clause violation, as it is not a sovereign entity. Only Maher can vindicate the Tonnage Clause interests at stake here. But, to the Majority, the Tonnage Clause becomes a dead letter once a landside middleman is inserted. If the Port Authority wants to raise some extra revenue, it can do exactly that—with this Court's blessing. That result effectively ignores the Supreme Court's injunction that "the prohibition against tonnage duties ... embrace[s] *all* taxes and duties *regardless of their name or form* ... which *operate to impose a charge for the privilege of entering, trading in, or* [—11—] *lying in a port.*" *Polar Tankers*, 557 U.S. at 8 (emphasis added) (internal quotation marks omitted).

The scope of constitutional protection should not be controlled by the fact that stevedoring services take place on land as well as on vessels. The Supreme Court has specifically commented on the necessity to maritime commerce of the work done by stevedores:

> Transportation of a cargo by water is impossible or futile unless the thing to be transported is put aboard the ship and taken off at destination. *A stevedore who in person or by servants does work so indispensable is as much an agency of commerce as shipowner or master.* Formerly the work was done by the ship's crew; but, owing to the exigencies of increasing commerce and the demand

---

[7] In the case of the Cargo Facility Charge, the Port Authority actually requires that the "user of cargo handling services" (i.e., the vessels) pay charges "to the Port Authority", but the charge "will be collected by the terminal operator", like Maher, "for remittance to the Port Authority." (App. at 345.) In other words, Maher is nothing more than the collector of such charges directly on behalf of the Port Authority, and keeps none of the assessment for itself. Presumably, the Majority would have no problem with such a levy, even if it otherwise violated the Tonnage Clause, [—10—] because the money first passed through the hands of the terminal operator.

for rapidity and special skill, it has become a specialized service devolving upon a class as clearly identified with maritime affairs as are the mariners.

Puget Sound Stevedoring Co. v. Tax Comm'n of Wash., 302 U.S. 90, 92 (1937) (emphasis added) (internal quotation marks omitted), *overruled by Dept. of Revenue of Wash. v. Ass'n of Wash. Stevedoring Cos.*, 435 U.S. 734 (1978).[8] The [—12—] Supreme Court has thus already disavowed the distinction that today's Majority draws. "What is decisive is the nature of the act, not the person of the actor." *Id.* at 94. *Cf. Complete Auto Transit, Inc. v. Brady*, 430 U.S. 274, 288 (1977) ("[A] focus on that formalism merely obscures the question whether the tax produces a forbidden effect.").

The *Passenger Cases* best bear out the point. One of the cases at issue there involved

---

[8] In *Puget Sound*, the Supreme Court struck down the State of Washington's effort to impose a business tax on a stevedoring company as a violation of the Commerce Clause. 302 U.S. 90 (1937). The Court reasoned that, because "[t]he business of loading and unloading" ships constitutes interstate commerce, Washington was *per se* not permitted to impose [—12—] its tax. *Id.* at 94. When Washington again tried to tax stevedores in 1974, the Supreme Court reconsidered and overruled its holding in *Puget Sound. See Dept. of Revenue of Wash. v. Ass'n of Wash. Stevedoring Cos.*, 435 U.S. 734 (1978). In changing the applicable law, the Supreme Court did nothing to alter its admonition in *Puget Sound* concerning the importance of stevedores in maritime commerce. In the later case, the Supreme Court reasoned that a tax on interstate commercial activity does not offend the Commerce Clause when the tax "applied to activity with a substantial nexus with the State, that are fairly apportioned, that do not discriminate against interstate commerce, and that are fairly related to the services provided by the State." *Id.* at 750. In light of this new, fact-intensive approach to challenges to state taxation under the Commerce Clause, the Court ultimately upheld the Washington tax at issue because "respondents relied below on the *per se* approach of *Puget Sound* and ... [therefore] they developed no factual basis on which to declare the Washington tax unconstitutional as applied to their members and their stevedoring activities." *Id.* at 751. In neither *Puget Sound* nor *Dept. of Revenue of Washington* did the Court consider the scope or applicability of the Tonnage Clause.

a two-dollar-per-passenger assessment, levied on the "master, owner, consignee, or [—13—] agent" of any vessel landing in the port of Boston, which had to be paid before any passengers could disembark. *Passenger Cases*, 48 U.S. (7 How.) at 456. The Supreme Court declared, by a five-to-four vote, that the tax was unconstitutional. *Id.* at 573. But with eight justices writing separately, the rationale of the Court was left unclear. Four justices relied on the Tonnage Clause, including Justice Grier, who concluded that it did not matter whether the tax was viewed as "a tax upon passengers or persons," or as a tax upon vessels. *Passenger Cases*, 48 U.S. (7 How.) at 460 (Grier, J., concurring). He persuasively discussed why such a distinction inevitably breaks down:

> It has been argued that this is not a tax on the master or the vessel, because in effect it is paid by the passenger having enhanced the price of his passage. Let us test the value of this argument by its application to other cases that naturally suggest themselves. If this act had, in direct terms, compelled the master to pay a tax or duty levied or graduated on the ratio of the tonnage of his vessel, whose freight was earned by the transportation of passengers, it might have been said, with equal truth, that the duty was paid by the passenger, and not by the vessel. And so, if it had laid an impost on the goods of the passenger imported by the vessel, it might have been said, with equal reason, it was only a tax on the passenger at last, as it comes out of his pocket, and, graduating it by the amount of his goods, affects only the modus or ratio by which its amount is calculated. In this way, the most stringent enactments may be [—14—] easily evaded. *It is a just and well-settled doctrine established by this court, that a State cannot do that indirectly which she is forbidden by the Constitution to do directly. ...* The Constitution of the United States, and the powers confided by it to the general government, to be exercised for the benefit of all the States, ought not to be nullified or evaded by astute verbal

criticism, without regard to the grand aim and object of the instrument, and the principles on which it is based.

Passenger Cases, 48 U.S. (7 How.) at 458-59 (Grier, J., concurring) (emphasis added).[9] Thus the necessary breadth of the Tonnage Clause. [—15—]

Justice Grier's expansive reading of the Tonnage Clause has since acquired dispositive weight with the endorsement of his position by the Court in *Polar Tankers. See Polar Tankers*, 557 U.S. at 8. Despite that, my colleagues apply an unduly restrictive reading to the *Polar Tankers* decision. According to them: "What actually made the tax in *Polar Tankers* unconstitutional, and what Maher cannot show here, is that the tax was directed at vessels and was not in exchange for services." (Majority at 20.) But that is not what the Supreme Court said. Far from limiting its reasoning to duties laid on vessels, the Supreme Court reiterated that the "prohibition against tonnage duties has been deemed to embrace all taxes and duties regardless of their name or form, and even though not measured by the tonnage of the vessel, which operate to impose a charge for the privilege of entering, trading in, or lying in a port." *Polar Tankers*, 557 U.S. at 8 (internal

---

[9] More recently, the Second Circuit adhered to this principle in *Bridgeport & Port Jefferson Steamboat Co. v. Bridgeport Port Auth.*, in holding that a passenger fee violated the Tonnage Clause. 567 F.3d 79, 88 (2d Cir. 2009). The amount of the passenger fee varied depending upon whether the passenger was a person, a car, a truck, or a bus. *Id.* at 83. Although the passenger fee was collected from passengers by the ferry company and thereafter remitted to the state, the state reimbursed the ferry company with an administrative fee for its trouble. *Id.* The *Bridgeport* Court correctly referred to the passengers as the fee payers, *id.* at 88, as the fee was ultimately passed on to passengers in the form an increase in ticket prices. Even though the fee represented a small percentage of overall ticket prices—in 2005 a one-way ferry ticket for a vehicle with unlimited passengers was $51.25, while the corresponding passenger [—15—] fee was $2.75, *id.* at 83—the Second Circuit recognized that such a fee charged to passengers, with no corresponding benefit to them, was impermissible under the Tonnage Clause.

quotation omitted). It would be hard to find more sweeping language than the words "regardless of their name or form" to describe the prohibited taxes, and likewise the words "entering, trading in, or lying in a port" seem intended to capture all trade-related activities in port.[10] *Id.* The Majority's restrictive reading of *Polar* [—16—] *Tankers* is at odds with the reasoning and language of the decision itself.

Although the present case involves a cargo throughput assessment levied on a stevedoring operation, conceptually, there is no difference between that and the fee levied in the *Passenger Cases*.[11] The Port Authority is "'do[ing] that indirectly which [it] is forbidden ... to do directly,'" evading [—17—] the Tonnage Clause "'by producing a dictionary or a dictum to prove that a [marine

---

[10] My colleagues warn that, if we unmoor the Tonnage Clause from taxes on vessels, then landside entities having some relationship to maritime commerce would be able to challenge any unreasonable state-imposed fees for the privilege of doing business at a port. For example, they say, a restaurant renting state property in a port could state a claim [—16—] under the Tonnage Clause by claiming that its rent is unreasonably high given the services provided by the state. That hypothetical misses the mark by a wide margin. To begin with, a rental fee is clearly reimbursement for a service rendered: providing the property on which the lessee can conduct its business. Further, unlike the restaurateur from the Majority's hypothetical, Maher does not have merely some tenuous relationship to maritime commerce. Maher is directly engaged in it. As the Supreme Court recognized in *Puget Sound*, such commerce could not occur without stevedores like Maher to load and unload seaborne cargo. The faithful construction of the Tonnage Clause that I propose will not, as the Majority fears, encompass disputes unrelated to volumetric charges. It will, instead, avoid arbitrary line-drawing that forecloses claims by entities that are clearly within the Tonnage Clause's zone of interest.

[11] The Majority implicitly recognizes as much. It announces that the Tonnage Clause applies to taxes on passengers because such duties "will likely *indirectly* impact a vessel's decisions by reducing demand," but then, inconsistently, says that the Clause does not apply to a fee on Maher because such a fee "does not *in and of itself* impact a vessel's ability to freely navigate in commerce." (Majority at 16.)

terminal operator] is not a vessel, nor a [stevedore] an import.'" *Polar Tankers*, 557 U.S. at 8 (quoting *Passenger Cases*, 48 U.S. (7 How.) at 458, 459 (Grier, J., concurring)).[12] [—18—]

In sum, the Majority errs in giving the Tonnage Clause a singularly narrow reading, and I would reverse the portion of the District Court's order that is based on that same errant view of the Constitution.

---

[12] While I dissent from my colleagues' narrow reading of the Tonnage Clause, I have no disagreement with their conclusion that the Basic Rental assessment does not violate that constitutional provision. The Basic Rental assessment, unlike the Container Throughput Rental, is more properly considered a fee for services rendered than a revenue-raising tax. The Port Authority owns the marine terminal and is entitled to "just compensation for the use of such property." *Cannon*, 87 U.S. (20 Wall.) at 582. Although the Basic Rental constitutes a fee for services, on the facts alleged by Maher, the Container Throughput Rental does not. According to Maher's complaint, the fees charged in the Container Throughput Rental "substantially exceed the costs of services provided by the Port Authority to the cargo or vessels" and "escalate at two to three year intervals without corresponding increases in the level of services provided by the Port Authority to the cargo or vessels." (App. at 42.) The fees are used to "subsidize other terminals" and "for other purposes not benefiting the vessels and cargo that use Maher's container terminal, including but not limited to, expenses to purchase and develop marine terminals for vessels that do not or cannot use Maher's container terminal." (App. at 44.) Also, the Container Throughput Rentals vary by the volume of cargo that is loaded and unloaded at Maher's terminal—thus striking at the very heart of the concerns motivating the Tonnage Clause—while any services provided do not. Maher pays a higher Container Throughput Rental [—18—] the more cargo it unloads, and, according to its Complaint, receives nothing from the Port Authority in return.

To the extent the District Court held that "most (if not all) of the rental charges and fees imposed by Port Authority against Maher would likely be the type of charges for services rendered that fall outside the Tonnage Clause's scope" (App. at 12-13 (internal quotations omitted)), it did not view the facts in the light most favorable to and draw all reasonable inferences in favor of Maher. In its Complaint, Maher repeatedly emphasized the disconnect between the amount paid and the services rendered, but the District Court did not adequately credit Maher's assertions.

This page intentionally left blank

United States Court of Appeals for the Fourth Circuit

United States Court of Appeals
for the Fourth Circuit

No. 14-1206

WU TIEN LI-SHOU
vs.
UNITED STATES

Appeal from the United States District Court for the
District of Maryland, at Baltimore

Decided: January 23, 2015

Citation: 777 F.3d 175, 3 Adm. R. 182 (4th Cir. 2015).

Before **WILKINSON, NIEMEYER,** and **KING,** Circuit
Judges.

[—2—] **WILKINSON,** Circuit Judge:

Wu Tien Li-Shou, a citizen of Taiwan,
seeks damages from the United States
for the accidental killing of her
husband and the intentional sinking of her
husband's fishing vessel during a NATO
counter-piracy mission. The district court
dismissed the action under the political
question and discretionary function doctrines.
For the reasons that follow, we affirm.

I.

Since the summer of 2009, the North
Atlantic Treaty Organization (NATO) has
conducted Operation Ocean Shield in the Gulf
of Aden and the Indian Ocean waters around
the Horn of Africa. NATO's offensive responds
to the recognition by the United States and its
allies that "Somali-based piracy against
chemical and oil tankers, freighters, cruise
ships, yachts, and fishing vessels poses a
threat to global shipping." J.A. 48 (Dec. 2008
U.S. National Security Council report).
"Piracy is a universal crime," President Bush
noted in June 2007. J.A. 59 (Memorandum
from the President). "The physical and
economic security of the United States . . .
relies heavily on the secure navigation of the
world's oceans for unhindered legitimate
commerce by its citizens and its partners." *Id.*

As part of Ocean Shield, the USS Stephen
W. Groves engaged the Jin Chun Tsai 68 (JCT
68), a Taiwanese fishing ship, in the early
morning of May 10, 2011. Pirates had hijacked
the JCT 68 [—3—] more than a year earlier,
transforming the commercial vessel into a
mothership from which the pirates launched
attacks using skiffs stored onboard. The ship
housed nearly two-dozen pirates in addition to
three hostages: the master and owner of the
ship, Wu Lai-Yu, and two Chinese
crewmembers.

The commander of NATO Task Force 508,
a commodore in the Royal Netherlands Navy,
directed the USS Groves "to shadow and then
disrupt the pirate mothership JCT 68." J.A. 64
(unclassified U.S. Navy investigation report).
In particular, the task force commander
ordered the USS Groves "to force JCT 68 to
stop and surrender, including the use of non-
disabling and disabling fire" starting with
verbal warnings, then warning shots, followed
by fire aimed at the skiffs. *Id.* 64-65. The USS
Groves commenced this sequence on the
morning of May 10. The shots ended almost
an hour later.

After the pirates had indicated their
surrender, a special team from the USS
Groves approached and boarded the JCT 68.
Weapons used by the pirates, including two
rocket-propelled grenade launchers, were
littered throughout the ship. The team found
Master Wu in his sleeping quarters "with the
crown of his head shot off." *Wu v. United
States,* 997 F. Supp. 2d 307, 309 (D. Md.
2014). Three pirates were also killed in the
engagement, and the two Chinese
crewmembers were rescued safely. The next
day, May 11, 2011, the USS Groves
intentionally sunk the JCT 68 [—4—] with
Wu's body on board pursuant to orders from
the NATO task force commander.

Two years later, Master Wu's widow
initiated this action against the United States,
seeking damages for her husband's death and
the loss of the JCT 68 under the Public
Vessels Act (PVA), 46 U.S.C. § 31101 *et seq.*,
the Suits in Admiralty Act (SIAA), 46 U.S.C.
§ 30901 *et seq.*, and the Death on the High
Seas Act (DOHSA), 46 U.S.C. § 30301 *et seq.*
The district court granted the government's
Rule 12(b)(1) motion to dismiss, reasoning
that the complaint presented a nonjusticiable

political question. *Wu*, 997 F. Supp. 2d at 309-10. The court also noted that even if subject matter jurisdiction were proper, Wu's claims would be "futile" in light of the discretionary function exception to any waiver of the government's sovereign immunity from suit. *Id.* at 309 n.2.

We review a dismissal under Rule 12(b)(1) *de novo. In re KBR, Inc., Burn Pit Litig.*, 744 F.3d 326, 333 (4th Cir. 2014). We apply the clear error standard to the "district court's jurisdictional findings of fact on any issues that are not intertwined with the facts central to the merits of the plaintiff's claims." *U.S. ex rel. Vuyyuru v. Jadhav*, 555 F.3d 337, 347 (4th Cir. 2009). [—5—]

II.

Wu challenges the district court's conclusion that her tort suit presents a nonjusticiable political question. Because allowing this action to proceed would thrust courts into the middle of a sensitive multinational counter-piracy operation and force courts to second-guess the conduct of a military engagement, we agree that the separation of powers prevents the judicial branch from hearing the case.

A.

The political question doctrine "is primarily a function of the separation of powers." *Baker v. Carr*, 369 U.S. 186, 210 (1962); *see also Taylor v. Kellogg Brown & Root Servs., Inc.*, 658 F.3d 402, 408 (4th Cir. 2011) (explaining the "genesis" of the doctrine in *Marbury v. Madison*, 5 U.S. (1 Cranch) 137 (1803)). It is not a matter of whether the dispute strictly falls within one of the categories over which the federal courts have subject matter jurisdiction. *Baker*, 369 U.S. at 198. Rather, a question is "political" and thus nonjusticiable when its adjudication would inject the courts into a controversy which is best suited for resolution by the political branches. *Id.* at 210-11. A case presents a nonjusticiable political question where there is

[1] a textually demonstrable constitutional commitment of the issue

to a coordinate political department; or [2] a lack of judicially discoverable and manageable [—6—] standards for resolving it; or [3] the impossibility of deciding without an initial policy determination of a kind clearly for nonjudicial discretion; or [4] the impossibility of a court's undertaking independent resolution without expressing lack of the respect due coordinate branches of government; or [5] an unusual need for unquestioning adherence to a political decision already made; or [6] the potentiality of embarrassment from multifarious pronouncements by various departments on one question.

Id. at 217. These formulations do not provide a clean, crisp test. *Id.* (noting "the impossibility of resolution by any semantic cataloguing"). Rather, we must undertake a "case-by-case inquiry." *Id.* at 211.

"Of the legion of governmental endeavors, perhaps the most clearly marked for judicial deference are provisions for national security and defense." *Tiffany v. United States*, 931 F.2d 271, 277 (4th Cir. 1991). Of course, "[t]he military does not enjoy a blanket exemption from the need to proceed in a non-negligent manner." *Id.* at 280. But it is not within the purview of "judicial competence" to review purely military decisions. *Lebron v. Rumsfeld*, 670 F.3d 540, 548 (4th Cir. 2012). We must be wary where plaintiff's "negligence claim would require the judiciary to question actual, sensitive judgments" made by the armed forces. *Taylor*, 658 F.3d at 411 (internal quotation marks omitted). Cases that require courts to second-guess these decisions run the risk not just of making bad law, but also of "imping[ing] on explicit constitutional assignments of [—7—] responsibility to the coordinate branches of our government." *Lebron*, 670 F.3d at 548.

B.

This case presents a textbook example of a situation in which courts should not interfere. Resolving this dispute would oblige the district court to wade into sensitive and particularized military matters. In order to reach a finding of negligence on the part of the United States, Wu would have the court consider the precise details of the military engagement: what kind of warnings were given, the type of ordnance used, the sort of weapons deployed, the range of fire selected, and the pattern, timing, and escalation of the firing. J.A. 8-9 (complaint); Appellant's Br. 5-7, 7 n.1. Wu is quite direct about this, criticizing the USS Groves for, among other things, "using exploding ordnance on the fishing boat rather than inert ordnance and firing into central compartments rather than at the skiffs on the bow or the boat's engines." Appellant's Br. 3. The case would not need to proceed to trial for the court to find itself enmeshed in this rigging. Discovery easily could draw the court and the parties into the technicalities of battle, with subpoenas issuing to NATO and American commanders on down to the Gunnery Direction Officer.

As judges, we are just not equipped to second-guess such small-bore tactical decisions. We also are ill-suited to [—8—] evaluate more strategic considerations. We do not know the waters. We do not know the respective capabilities of individual pirate ships or naval frigates. We do not know the functionality and limitations of the counter-piracy task force's assets. We do not know how a decision to tow and not to sink the JCT 68 would have affected the task force's mission by tying down valuable naval resources. We do not know the extent of the disruption to commercial shipping caused by any single ship or by Somali-based piracy generally. What we do know is that we are not naval commanders. These are questions not intended to be answered through the vehicle of a tort suit.

That is not all. This case threatens to involve the courts in the command structures of both the U.S. military and Operation Ocean Shield. Wu bases her claim of negligence on the USS Groves's failure to follow the proper rules of engagement. Appellant's Br. 8, 19-20; Reply Br. 4-5, 5 n.1. Specifically, she asserts that Navy vessels involved in what Wu terms as law enforcement "are governed by the law enforcement parameters set down by the U.S.

Coast Guard." Reply Br. 5 n.1. But selecting the proper rules of military engagement is decidedly not our job. This request that we do so encourages the courts to bull their way into the chain of command of a multinational operation. In fact, Wu would have us sit astride the top of the [—9—] command pyramid and decree the proper counter-piracy strategies and tactics to the NATO and American commanders below.

Moreover, Wu explicitly urges us to repudiate the NATO commander's direct order, see J.A. 67, to sink the JCT 68 under the rationale that "the U.S. Navy chain of command maintained control of the [USS Groves] at all times," Reply Br. 6. The disruption caused to our alliances by treating allied command decisions as advisory or second-rate is all too evident. One need only imagine the Dutch NATO commander fielding deposition questions in a federal lawsuit about decisions he made concerning naval vessels carrying military grade weapons in the context of a multinational counter-piracy mission in the Indian Ocean. Whatever protective orders courts might issue to avoid litigative tension within the NATO alliance would be under constant challenge, given the perceived relevance of the Dutch commodore's order to plaintiff's negligence claims.

Further, if we accepted Wu's invitation, we would open the door to allegations that soldiers and sailors should treat more skeptically the clear orders of their superiors. We would afford military personnel a reason and incentive to question orders—namely, to head off tort liability or at least the burdens of litigation that come with being sued. Allowing discovery here would permit inquiry into the wisdom of the order to sink the JCT 68. But the extent to which NATO counter-piracy operations [—10—] must accommodate "the property rights of shipowners" from various nations "dispossessed of their ships by pirates" is not justiciable without inquiry into every engagement with hijacked vessels, including vessels used by pirates as heavily armed bases for further disruptions of commercial shipping lanes. Appellant's Br. 21.

Wu next points to a provision in the Public Vessels Act, which allows litigating parties to subpoena crewmembers of a public vessel, as proof that there are procedures in place for deciding a case like this. *Id.* 38 n.12, 39. But crewmembers may only be subpoenaed if the Secretary who heads the department or the vessel's commander consents. 46 U.S.C. § 31110. More importantly, this procedure is beside the point. Subpoenaing members of the military is not necessarily itself an attack on the separation of powers. Asking probing questions about the strategy, tactics, and conduct of a military operation, however, is just such an affront.

It is, after all, the President who is commander-in-chief. U.S. Const. art. II, § 2, cl. 1; *see also Lebron*, 670 F.3d at 549. It is, after all, Congress which holds "plenary control over rights, duties, and responsibilities in the framework of the military establishment, including regulations, procedures, and remedies." *Chappell v. Wallace*, 462 U.S. 296, 301 (1983); *see also* U.S. Const., art. I, § 8, cl. 11 (power to declare [—11—] war); *id.* cl. 12-13 (power to establish an army and navy); *id.* cl. 14 (power "[t]o make Rules for the Government and Regulation of the land and naval Forces"). And, as our discussion has made abundantly clear, this controversy lacks discernible rules and standards for judicial resolution.

C.

Several of Wu's specific contentions merit mention. She objects to the district court's description of the altercation between the USS Groves and the JCT 68 as "a belligerent operation." *Wu*, 997 F. Supp. 2d at 309; Appellant's Br. 17-20, 29. In fact, Wu repeatedly characterizes Operation Ocean Shield as little more than an oceanic traffic stop or "a traditional police action on the high seas," and analogizes the incident with the JCT 68 to "a police officer stopping a vehicle on any highway." Appellant's Br. 10, 19, 20. She stresses that the government is attempting to escape responsibility by establishing a safe zone between belligerency and ordinary law enforcement actions. Thus the deference we offer is, under Wu's view, misplaced.

Wu misunderstands both the district court's use of the term "belligerent" and the law. Wu may be correct that the NATO's counter-piracy activities do not amount to "belligerency" in the law of war meaning. *See* Black's Law Dictionary 184 (10th ed. 2014) (defining "belligerency" as "the quality, state, or [—12—] condition of waging war"). But it is difficult for a court even to define what war *is*. *Campbell v. Clinton*, 203 F.3d 19, 26 (D.C. Cir. 2000) (Silberman, J., concurring) (questioning the existence of "a coherent test for judges to apply to the question what constitutes war"). Yet the district court did not say that the USS Groves's actions constituted "war," nor does the government assert that the frigate was engaged in "war." Gov't Br. 35 n.10. It is clear to us that the district court's use of the word "belligerent" was vernacular, not technical. That does not mean, however, that the USS Groves was engaged in a mere law enforcement action. Nothing about the events of May 10 and 11, 2011—from their far away location, to the international forces and threat involved, to the military command structure and equipment deployed—is "consistent with a traditional police action." *See* Appellant's Br. 19. American military forces typically do not take part in simple law enforcement, *see* 18 U.S.C. § 1385 (Posse Comitatus Act); 32 C.F.R. § 182.6(a)(3) (applying Posse Comitatus Act to the Navy), and there is nothing to suggest garden-variety police activity here.

Regardless, a state of war in the technical sense did not have to exist for the actions of the USS Groves to be unreviewable by the courts. As the Eleventh Circuit has noted, "judicial intrusion into military practices would impair the [—13—] discipline that the courts have recognized as indispensable to military effectiveness." *Aktepe v. United States*, 105 F.3d 1400, 1404 (11th Cir. 1997). That case involved negligence claims by Turkish sailors against the United States for injuries arising out of a NATO training exercise. *Id.* at 1401-02. War did not need to be declared for the political question doctrine to apply to this sort of tort suit against the United States. It is enough that plaintiff "ask[s] the courts to intrude in an area in which they have no rightful power and no compass." *Smith v. Reagan*, 844 F.2d 195, 202 (4th Cir. 1988) (refusing under the political question doctrine to entertain an action for a declaratory judgment under the Hostage Act). The cases Wu cites for the proposition that liability may attach to the United States for negligent acts of Navy vessels are not to the contrary, for none of them involved a military engagement. *See Ira S. Bushey & Sons, Inc. v. United States*, 398 F.2d 167 (2d Cir. 1968); *Pac.-Atl. S.S. Co. v. United States*, 175 F.2d 632 (4th Cir. 1949); *United States v. The Australia Star*, 172 F.2d 472 (2d Cir. 1949); *Bank Line v. United States*, 163 F.2d 133 (2d Cir. 1947); *Lind v. United States*, 156 F.2d 231 (2d Cir. 1946); *Ocean S.S. Co. of Savannah v. United States*, 38 F.2d 782 (2d Cir. 1930).

Wu also seems to suggest that because the USS Groves "recaptured" the JCT 68, the district court possessed admiralty [—14—] jurisdiction pursuant to the law of prize. *See* Appellant's Br. 33-35; Reply Br. 7. But the law of prize only applies where the captor demonstrates "an intention to seize and to retain as prize." *The Grotius*, 13 U.S. (9 Cranch) 368, 370 (1815); *see also* 28 U.S.C. § 1333 (granting federal district courts exclusive jurisdiction over claims "for the condemnation of property taken *as prize*" (emphasis added)). The law of prize in essence adjudicates claims to ownership. *See Jennings v. Carson*, 8 U.S. (4 Cranch) 2, 23 (1807) (The courts "decide who has the right, and they order its delivery to the party having the right."); 3 Op. Att'y Gen. 377 (1838); Thomas J. Schoenbaum, 1 Admiralty & Mar. Law § 3-2 (5th ed. 2011 & Supp. 2014). It is doubtful that the JCT 68 was ever a prize, because neither the USS Groves nor the NATO task force claimed or intended to claim ownership of the JCT 68. *See generally The Siren*, 80 U.S. (13 Wall.) 389, 391-93 (1871) (describing English origins of law of prize). As the district court recognized, "prize cases are *in rem* actions, not tort suits." *Wu*, 997 F. Supp. 2d at 309.

III.

Wu also challenges the district court's holding that the United States retains its sovereign immunity from suit because it was engaged in the exercise of a discretionary function. While this is framed as an alternative ground for decision, it decidedly is not because the political question doctrine and the [—15—] discretionary function exception to waivers of sovereign immunity overlap here in important respects. Wu contends that, although the exception applies to the Suits in Admiralty Act, it does not apply to suits brought under the Public Vessels Act and that, even if it did, the sinking of the JCT 68 was beyond the bounds of the USS Groves's discretion.

A.

The SIAA and the PVA both waive sovereign immunity for *in personam* admiralty suits. The SIAA does so where, "if a vessel were privately owned or operated, or if cargo were privately owned or possessed, or if a private person or property were involved, a civil action in admiralty could be maintained." 46 U.S.C. § 30903(a); *see also McMellon v. United States*, 387 F.3d 329, 334-37 (4th Cir. 2004) (en banc) (discussing history of government waiver as to admiralty suits). The PVA waives immunity for actions brought to recover "damages caused by a public vessel of the United States." 46 U.S.C. § 31102(a)(1). Neither statute contains an explicit exception to the scope of its waiver. In this respect, the statutes are unlike the Federal Tort Claims Act (FTCA), which expressly prohibits courts from hearing claims "based upon the exercise or performance or the failure to exercise or perform a discretionary function or duty on the part of a federal agency or an employee of the [—16—] Government, whether or not the discretion involved be abused." 28 U.S.C. § 2680(a).

Nevertheless, in *McMellon v. United States*, 387 F.3d at 349, this court sitting *en banc* held that "the SIAA must be read to include a discretionary function exception to its waiver of sovereign immunity." The discretionary function exception "is grounded in separation-of-powers concerns." *Id.* at 341 (citing *United States v. S.A. Empresa de Viacao Aerea Rio Grandense (Varig Airlines)*, 467 U.S. 797, 808, 814 (1984)); *see also Tiffany v. United States*, 931 F.2d 271, 276 (4th Cir. 1991). Because the separation of powers is a constitutional doctrine, "the courts must adhere [to it] even in the absence of an explicit statutory command." *Canadian Transp. Co. v. United States*, 663 F.2d 1081, 1086 (D.C. Cir. 1980). The SIAA must thus contain an implied discretionary function exception. Otherwise, the courts would become arbiters of "administrative and legislative . . . policy judgments." *Gercey v. United States*, 540 F.2d 536, 539 (1st Cir. 1976). That would be an "intolerable" result. *In re Joint E. & S. Dists. Asbestos Litig.*, 891 F.2d 31, 35 (2d Cir. 1989).

This logic applies with equal force to the PVA. The same separation-of-powers concerns that were present with the SIAA are present here. Without the discretionary function exception, "all administrative and legislative decisions concerning the [—17—] public interest in maritime matters would be subject to independent judicial review in the not unlikely event that the implementation of those policy judgments were to cause private injuries." *Gercey*, 540 F.2d at 539. That outcome is inconsistent with our Constitution. We are not alone in reaching this conclusion as to the PVA. In fact, every circuit to consider the issue has held that the PVA contains an implied discretionary function exception. *Thames Shipyard & Repair Co. v. United States*, 350 F.3d 247, 254 (1st Cir. 2003); *B & F Trawlers, Inc. v. United States*, 841 F.2d 626, 630 (5th Cir. 1988); *Tobar v. United States*, 731 F.3d 938, 945, 1 Adm. R. 420, 423-24 (9th Cir. 2013); *U.S. Fire Ins. Co. v. United States*, 806 F.2d 1529, 1534–35 (11th Cir. 1986), *abrogated on other grounds by United States v. Gaubert*, 499 U.S. 315 (1991).

B.

In applying the discretionary function exception, we look to FTCA cases for guidance. *McMellon*, 387 F.3d at 349. The discretionary function exception applies to "conduct" that "involves an element of judgment or choice." *Berkovitz v. United States*, 486 U.S. 531, 536

(1988). Where a case implicates such a choice, it does not matter "whether or not the discretion involved be abused." 28 U.S.C. § 2680(a). The conduct of a military engagement is the very essence of a discretionary function. Cases involving the use of military force lure courts [—18—] into considering "complex, subtle, and professional [military] decisions." *Gilligan v. Morgan*, 413 U.S. 1, 10 (1973). All military engagements involve discretionary decisions by military commanders of all ranks—choices that have to be made quickly during moments of pronounced pressure.

Wu's suit relies on questioning the wisdom of a series of discretionary decisions, some of which we noted in the preceding section. How should the warnings to the pirates have been framed? What type of ordnance should have been used? What weapons should have been used? At what range should the USS Groves have fired from? Where precisely should the fire have been directed? In light of the task force's resources and the goals of the counter-piracy mission, should the JCT 68 have been sunk? "The list of inquiries is virtually endless and the umbrella of negligence would encompass them all." *Tiffany*, 931 F.2d at 279. The Supreme Court has held "that the selection of the appropriate design for military equipment . . . is assuredly a discretionary function." *Boyle v. United Techs. Corp.*, 487 U.S. 500, 511 (1988). All the more so would operational decisions such as whether to sink a damaged pirate mothership in the waters off of the Horn of Africa count as discretionary functions too. Even if the NATO and American commanders abused their discretion "so as to frustrate the relevant policy," the fact that the function is discretionary *ab initio* exempts those [—19—] choices from judicial review. *Gaubert*, 499 U.S. at 338 (Scalia, J., concurring in part and concurring in the judgment). "The inquiry is thus whether the discretion exists, not whether in later litigation it is alleged to have been abused." *Holbrook v. United States*, 673 F.3d 341, 350 (4th Cir. 2012).

Wu insists that the USS Groves acted in contravention of law and thus that the government cannot claim the discretionary function exception as a safe harbor. Reply Br. 9-11. But Wu does not identify a law that would permissibly have circumscribed the USS Groves's course of action. Wu points to the *Annotated Supplement to the Commander's Handbook on the Law of Naval Operations* (Nov. 1997 ed.), Articles 18 and 19 of the 1958 Geneva Convention on the High Seas, and Articles 104 and 105 of the United Nations Convention on the Law of the Sea (UNCLOS). Appellant's Br. 32-33, 34 n.9; Reply 5 n.1, 7 n.3. The *Handbook*, however, notes that it provides only "general guidance" and "is not a comprehensive treatment of the law." *Handbook* 1 (Nov. 1997 ed.).[1] "International treaties," moreover, "are not presumed to create rights that are privately enforceable." *Goldstar (Panama) S.A. v. United States*, 967 F.2d 965, 968 (4th Cir. 1992). Non- [—20—] self-executing treaties "do not by themselves function as binding federal law." *Medellin v. Texas*, 552 U.S. 491, 504 (2008). The 1958 Geneva Convention on the High Seas contains no provision indicating that it is self-executing, and Wu offers no statutory provision implementing the Convention. Wu admits that the United States is not even a signatory to UNCLOS. Appellant's Br. 33.

In sum, nothing in this collection of documents deprives the United States and its NATO allies of the discretion inherent in sovereignty to conduct military operations free of judicial oversight or hindsight. Nothing in these documents purports to anticipate the myriad evolving circumstances that commanders encounter on the ground or on the seas, much less which of the many possible options those commanders should choose in responding to them. In short, the firing upon the JCT 68 and the subsequent sinking of that vessel were discretionary acts that the judiciary may not take it upon itself to review.

---

[1] Wu cites to the 1997 *Annotated Supplement*. The *Handbook* was reissued in 2007. That newer version also states that it provides only "general guidance" and "is not a comprehensive treatment of the law." *The Commander's Handbook on the Law of Naval Operations* 19 (July 2007 ed.).

IV.

Wu asserts that the district court should have allowed discovery or at least held an evidentiary hearing to establish that this case is justiciable. *See* Appellant's Br. 17-18, 29; Reply Br. 15-17. She points to our recent decision in *Al Shimari v. CACI Premier Tech., Inc.*, 758 F.3d 516, 534, 537 (4th Cir. 2014), as demonstration that discovery is needed to determine if [—21—] the claim may proceed. But that case is very different from the case at bar. *Al Shimari* involved a private contractor working for the federal government, a situation for which this Court has developed a specialized political question doctrine analysis. *See id.* at 533-34 (explaining test developed in *Taylor v. Kellogg Brown & Root Servs., Inc.*, 658 F.3d 402 (4th Cir. 2011)). More importantly, in *Al Shimari* we were "unable to assess whether a decision on the merits would require the judiciary 'to question actual, sensitive judgments made by the military.'" 758 F.3d at 536 (quoting *Taylor*, 658 F.3d at 411). The complaint and accompanying record in this case do not suffer from the same defects.

Whether or not every single fact in the Navy's unclassified investigative report is accurate, it quite clearly provided an overall picture of the military engagement. The district court was not required to litigate every fact in the report before making the political question or discretionary function determination, because litigating the facts would constitute just the sort of involvement that those doctrines are designed to avoid. We do not for a moment trivialize either Master Wu's death or the destruction of his ship, for which diplomatic [—22—] channels should in all kindness dictate recompense.[2] But whether or not the USS Groves properly approached and engaged the JCT 68 and whether or not the USS Groves should have sunk the vessel are matters of international import and military judgment in which we are loath to interfere. Under our constitutional system of separation-of-powers, these cases

---

[2] The government asserts that "[a]cting under its authority to conduct international relations," the United States has in fact made a payment to Master Wu's family. *See* Gov't Br. 4 n.1.

raise questions that the judiciary is not empowered to answer. The district court did not err in dismissing the suit. Its judgment is

AFFIRMED.

United States Court of Appeals
for the Fourth Circuit

No. 13-4895

UNITED STATES
VS.
BEYLE

Appeal from the United States District Court for the
Eastern District of Virginia, at Norfolk

Decided: April 3, 2015

Citation: 782 F.3d 159, 3 Adm. R. 190 (4th Cir. 2015).

Before **WILKINSON, GREGORY,** and **SHEDD,** Circuit
Judges.

[—3—] **WILKINSON,** Circuit Judge:

Appellants Abukar Osman Beyle and Shani Nurani Shiekh Abrar were each convicted on twenty-six criminal counts arising from the armed abduction and murder of four U.S. citizens off the coast of Somalia. Beyle and Abrar were part of a group of nineteen pirates who seized a yacht and captured the four Americans on board. The pirates headed for Somalia, but were intercepted by the United States Navy. During a final confrontation with the Navy, Beyle, Abrar, and another pirate shot and killed the four American hostages. The Navy secured the boat and apprehended the surviving pirates, who were transported to the United States to face criminal charges. After a weeks-long trial, a jury convicted Beyle and Abrar on all counts, and each defendant received multiple life sentences.

Beyle and Abrar now challenge their respective convictions on separate grounds. Beyle argues that the district court lacked jurisdiction over the murder and firearms charges against him because the Americans were not killed on the "high seas." Abrar, who maintains that he was kidnapped before the piracy operation, contends that he was unable to present certain witnesses who could have corroborated his duress defense. We conclude, however, that the site of the murders, thirty to forty nautical miles from the Somali coast, lay on the high seas and thus beyond the territorial sea of any nation. We further conclude [—4—] that Abrar was not denied his Fifth Amendment right to due process or his Sixth Amendment right to present witnesses material to his defense. The district court gave each of the defendants the fair trial that he deserved, and we affirm in all respects its judgment.

I.

In reviewing defendants' convictions by a jury, we consider the evidence in the light most favorable to the government. *Evans v. United States*, 504 U.S. 255, 257 (1992); *see United States v. Moye*, 454 F.3d 390, 394 (4th Cir. 2006) (en banc).

A.

The United States and its allies are engaged in a multinational battle against piracy in the waters off the Horn of Africa. Through the Gulf of Aden and much of the Indian Ocean, Somalia-based pirates have launched attacks against commercial and recreational vessels, from large freighters to personal yachts. *See* The White House, *United States Counter Piracy and Maritime Security Action Plan* annex A at 1 (June 2014); U.N. S.C. Rep. of the Sec'y-Gen. on the Situation with Respect to Piracy and Armed Robbery at Sea off the Coast of Somalia, U.N. Doc. S/2014/740 (Oct. 16, 2014). Piracy poses a threat not only to the free flow of global commerce, but also to [—5—] the individuals who navigate the seas. In 2011, armed Somali pirates attacked an estimated 3,863 seafarers and took some 555 individuals hostage. Oceans Beyond Piracy et al., *The Human Cost of Maritime Piracy, 2012*, at 3 (2013). Thirty-five of those hostages were killed. *Id.* at 7.

This case arises from one such attack. In early February 2011, a group of pirates, with the assistance of several investors and facilitators in Somalia, prepared to hijack a ship at sea. The investors provided a primary "mothership" for the voyage, as well as an attack skiff that the pirates would use to launch fast-moving assaults on their targets. The mothership, the *Alqasim*, was a captured Yemeni fishing boat, and four Yemeni fishermen on board were forced to operate the boat for the pirates. All of the pirates were Somali, except for one, another Yemeni fisherman who had been captured by Somali pirates but then decided to join their ranks. Among their supplies, the nineteen men brought various automatic firearms and a rocket-propelled grenade launcher.

Beyle and Abrar were part of this cohort. Beyle assisted with acquiring an outboard motor for the attack skiff. Abrar brought an AK-47 aboard the boat. One of the pirates drew up a list of the individuals who had participated in the mission, to allocate any eventual ransom shares. Both Beyle and Abrar were [—6—] on the list. The four captive Yemeni fishermen from the *Alqasim* were not.

The pirates set to sea on February 9, 2011. During their first nine days, they made a number of unsuccessful efforts, including chasing a large container ship. In at least one such attempt, Abrar carried the rocket-propelled grenade launcher.

On February 18, 2011, the pirates spotted a new target: a U.S.-flagged sailboat with four U.S. citizens aboard. The Americans had been sailing in the Arabian Sea as part of an international yacht rally, traveling a leg from India to Oman. Two of them, Scott Adam and Jean Adam, were husband and wife and owned this vessel, known as the *Quest*. The other two Americans were Phyllis Macay and Robert Riggle, who were friends of the couple.

Six of the pirates, including Beyle and Abrar, boarded the attack skiff. They moved swiftly to hijack the *Quest* and take the four Americans hostage. As the skiff approached, Beyle fired an AK-47 into the air. Once on board, Abrar first subdued the two women, and he then cut the boat's communication lines. At the time the pirates gained control, the nearest land was Oman or Yemen, approximately four hundred miles away. The pirates had traveled 940 to 960 miles from the Somali coast.

With the *Quest* secured, the remaining pirates took the supplies from the mothership and crowded onto the fifty-eight- [—7—] foot-

long *Quest*. They released the four Yemeni captives, who departed in the *Alqasim*. The nineteen pirates then set a course for Somalia. They intended to hold the Americans hostage on land and work through their coconspirators to secure a ransom.[1] The Americans were kept primarily in a horseshoe-shaped bench area around the helm. Beyle and Abrar were among the men assigned to guard the Americans, with guns ready. After hijacking the *Quest*, the pirates also used the Americans' cellular telephones to take photographs and record videos. Several pirates put on clothing belonging to their victims, and Abrar can be seen wearing a hostage's sunglasses and smiling.

The U.S. Navy was soon alerted to the attack, and a carrier strike group moved to intercept the *Quest*. After locating the boat, which was still hundreds of miles into the Indian Ocean, the Navy established radio communications with the pirates and began following the *Quest* as it proceeded to Somalia. The Navy's objective was to stop the *Quest* from entering Somali territorial waters and to secure the hostages' safe release. Claiming they lacked any negotiating authority, however, the pirates demanded that they be allowed to reach Somalia and engage in hostage negotiations through an interlocutor on land. The Navy made [—8—] clear to the pirates that they would not be permitted to take the hostages to Somalia. But time was running short: the pirates were on pace to reach Somalia within days. At one point during these exchanges, Abrar fired an AK-47 into the air above Scott Adam, as a warning to the Navy. The pirates variously threatened to kill the hostages and themselves.

On February 22, 2011, the Navy directed the pirates to stop proceeding toward Somalia. The Navy was determined to keep the *Quest* in international waters and prevent it from entering Somali territorial waters. But the pirates refused. The Navy began maneuvering to block the boat and informed the pirates

---

[1] The pirates' English-speaking negotiator in Somalia was later captured and convicted in a separate proceeding. We affirmed those convictions. *United States v. Shibin*, 722 F.3d 233, 1 Adm. R. 138 (4th Cir. 2013).

that these movements were peaceful. One pirate answered, "I will eat them like meat." J.A. 384.

Suddenly, another pirate fired a rocket-propelled grenade toward the USS *Sterett*, the Navy destroyer that had been following the *Quest* most closely. The rocket missed and splashed into the water, between the *Sterett* and a set of smaller boats carrying Navy SEALs. Bullets from the *Quest* began whizzing over the *Sterett*, but the Navy did not return fire. At that point, a group of three pirates—Beyle and Abrar, together with Ahmed Muse Salad, also known as "Afmagalo"—fired their automatic weapons and killed the four Americans. Scott Adam was shot seven times; Jean Adam was shot seven times; Phyllis Macay was shot eight times; Robert Riggle was shot nineteen times. At the time [—9—] of these events, it is undisputed the *Quest* was between thirty and forty nautical miles off the coast of Somalia.

Within a matter of minutes, a team of Navy SEALs headed for the *Quest*, boarded it, and secured it. By the time the SEALs arrived, all four Americans had been mortally wounded. Many pirates, including Beyle and Abrar, put their hands up and surrendered. The other shooter, Afmagalo, was the last to surrender. At the end of the encounter, four of the pirates were dead: two from the discharge of the pirates' own weapons, and two from the SEALs' raid.

The Navy took the remaining pirates into custody. While held aboard the USS *Enterprise*, an aircraft carrier, they were given *Miranda* warnings and questioned by the FBI. (One pirate, a juvenile, was released.) Abrar told the FBI that he had been forced to participate in the piracy mission. In Abrar's account, he was offered work as a mechanic in the coastal Somali town of Garacad, but was then kidnapped at gunpoint by two of the other pirates, Mohamud Salad Ali, also known as "Juguuf," and Mohamud Hirs Issa Ali, also known as "Sarindaaq." Abrar acknowledged that he had been the first pirate to board the *Quest*, and he contended that after the hijacking his role changed from mechanic to guard. According to Abrar, he did not leave

with the four Yemeni fishermen who were released on the *Alqasim* because he thought he would have been arrested in Yemen for piracy. [—10—]

Although Abrar admitted that he had been pointing a gun at Jean Adam before the concluding moments of carnage, he denied ever shooting any of the American hostages. Abrar, who is considered a member of the Bantu minority ethnic group in Somalia, claimed that he would not have received a share of any ransom. When confronted with the pirates' list of participants, Abrar suggested that his name may have been included simply to assuage his feelings.

B.

The fourteen remaining pirates, including Beyle and Abrar, were transported to the United States for criminal prosecution. A federal grand jury returned a three-count indictment against the pirates. Nine members of the group pleaded guilty to piracy under the law of nations, and two leaders, Sarindaaq and Juguuf, pleaded guilty both to piracy under the law of nations and to hostage-taking resulting in death. Each of the eleven pirates who entered guilty pleas was sentenced to at least one term of life imprisonment.

On July 8, 2011, the grand jury returned a superseding indictment containing twenty-six counts against each of the three pirates who had not pleaded guilty—Afmagalo, Beyle, and Abrar. The superseding indictment charged the codefendants with the following crimes: conspiracy to commit hostage-taking [—11—] resulting in death, in violation of 18 U.S.C. § 1203(a) (Count 1); hostage-taking resulting in death, in violation of 18 U.S.C. § 1203(a) and § 2 (Counts 2, 3, 4, and 5); conspiracy to commit kidnapping, in violation of 18 U.S.C. § 1201(c) (Count 6); kidnapping resulting in death, in violation of 18 U.S.C. § 1201(a)(2) and § 2 (Counts 7, 8, 9, and 10); conspiracy to commit violence against maritime navigation resulting in death, in violation of 18 U.S.C. § 2280(a)(1)(H) (Count 11); violence against maritime navigation resulting in death, in violation of 18 U.S.C. § 2280(a)(1)(G) and § 2

(Counts 12, 13, 14, and 15); murder within the special maritime and territorial jurisdiction of the United States, in violation of 18 U.S.C. § 1111 and § 2 (Counts 16, 17, 18, and 19); piracy under the law of nations, in violation of 18 U.S.C. § 1651 and § 2 (Count 20); the use, carry, brandish, and discharge of a firearm during a crime of violence, in violation of 18 U.S.C. § 924(c) and § 2 (Counts 21 and 26); the use, carry, brandish, and discharge of a firearm during a crime of violence resulting in death, in violation of 18 U.S.C. § 924(c) and (j) and § 2 (Counts 22, 23, 24, and 25). The superseding indictment also included the requisite notice of special findings for seeking capital punishment, and nine months later the government filed notices of its intent to seek the death penalty against Afmagalo, Beyle, and Abrar. [—12—]

Beyle and Abrar each filed pre-trial motions to dismiss. First, Beyle moved to dismiss Counts 16 through 19 and Counts 22 through 25 on the ground that the murders had taken place in Somali territorial waters, beyond U.S. jurisdiction. The district court denied the motion in a memorandum order. Second, Abrar moved to dismiss the indictment based on his inability to investigate or corroborate a duress defense. Abrar identified various witnesses located overseas—several individuals in Somalia, as well as the four Yemeni fishermen from the *Alqasim*—who he believed could provide meaningful character evidence to support his claim that he had been forced to join the piracy operation. The district court denied this motion as well.

The guilt phase of the codefendants' capital trial, which lasted from June 4 to July 8, 2013, featured extensive testimony from U.S. officials and from many of the pirates. The court issued a jury instruction on Abrar's duress defense for Counts 1 through 15 and Count 20—that is, for all the counts besides the murders and the various firearms offenses.

At the conclusion of the guilt phase of the trial, the jury convicted Afmagalo, Beyle, and Abrar on all twenty-six counts. The jury recommended sentences of life imprisonment.

The district court eventually sentenced each of the codefendants to three concurrent life sentences, plus eighteen consecutive life sentences and thirty consecutive years. [—13—]

Beyle and Abrar now appeal. Each argues his claim independently, and neither purports to join the other's grounds. The third convicted codefendant, Afmagalo, is not a party to this appeal.

II.

Beyle contends that the district court lacked jurisdiction over the charges of murder (Counts 16, 17, 18, and 19) and concomitant use of a firearm (Counts 22, 23, 24, and 25) because the underlying actions occurred within Somalia's territorial waters, not on the high seas. For many reasons, we find Beyle's claims unpersuasive.

A.

The Constitution grants Congress the power "[t]o define and punish Piracies and Felonies committed on the high Seas." U.S. Const. art. I, § 8, cl. 10. Congress has exercised this enumerated power to punish maritime crimes since the earliest days of the Republic. *United States v. Dire*, 680 F.3d 446, 455-56 (4th Cir. 2012) (discussing criminal piracy statutes from 1790 and 1819 and associated litigation).

The statutes under which Beyle was convicted fall well within Congress's constitutionally granted power to punish felonies on the high seas. The first statute proscribes murder [—14—] "[w]ithin the special maritime and territorial jurisdiction of the United States." 18 U.S.C. § 1111(b). The second statute defines the "special maritime and territorial jurisdiction of the United States" as including the "high seas, any other waters within the admiralty and maritime jurisdiction of the United States and out of the jurisdiction of any particular State," and "[a]ny place outside the jurisdiction of any nation with respect to an offense by or against a national of the United States." *Id.* § 7(1), (7). Finally, the statutory prohibition of the use of a firearm to cause the death of another tacks onto the underlying offense. *Id.* § 924(c), (j). Congress undoubtedly possesses the authority under the Define and Punish Clause to enact the criminal laws at issue in Beyle's appeal.

That said, the crux of Beyle's argument is not that the statutes under which he was convicted are facially unconstitutional, but rather that he was not on the high seas when he committed the actions for which he is to be punished. He asserts that the district court "mistakenly construed the law regarding the limits of the territorial seas" of Somalia. Appellants' Br. at 6. Beyle's appeal thus presents a single issue: is a person thirty to forty nautical miles off the Somali coast on the "high seas"? We review this question of law *de novo. United States v. Woolfolk*, 399 F.3d 590, 594 (4th Cir. 2005). [—15—]

B.

It is well-settled that the "high seas" encompass all those waters beyond the boundary of the various territorial waters. Simply put, "[o]utside the territorial sea are the high seas." *United States v. Louisiana*, 394 U.S. 11, 23 (1969); *see also Kiobel v. Royal Dutch Petroleum Co.*, 133 S. Ct. 1659, 1667 (2013) ("Piracy typically occurs on the high seas, beyond the territorial jurisdiction of the United States or any other country."); *United States v. Rodgers*, 150 U.S. 249, 259 (1893) ("[A] large body of navigable water[,] . . . open and unconfined, and not under the exclusive control of any one nation or people, . . . must fall under the definition of 'high seas'" . . . .). As we have noted, "beyond the territorial waters lie the high seas, over which no nation can exercise sovereignty." *R.M.S. Titanic, Inc. v. Haver*, 171 F.3d 943, 965 (4th Cir. 1999).

Customary international law supports this definition. Two international agreements are most relevant to the case at hand. First, the 1958 Geneva Convention on the High Seas, which the United States has ratified, defines "high seas" as "all parts of the sea that are not included in the territorial sea or in the internal waters of a State." Convention on the High Seas art. 1, *opened for signature* Apr. 29, 1958, 13 U.S.T. 2312, 450 U.N.T.S. 82

(entered into force Sept. 30, 1962). Second, the United [—16—] Nations Convention on the Law of the Sea ("UNCLOS") states that a nation's sovereignty covers only "the territorial sea." U.N. Convention on the Law of the Sea art. 2, *opened for signature* Dec. 10, 1982, 1833 U.N.T.S. 397 (entered into force Nov. 16, 1994). Although the United States has not signed or ratified UNCLOS, it "has recognized that [the treaty's] baseline provisions reflect customary international law." *United States v. Alaska*, 503 U.S. 569, 588 n.10 (1992) (internal quotation marks omitted); *Dire*, 680 F.3d at 459; Statement on United States Oceans Policy, 1983 Pub. Papers 378, 379 (Mar. 10, 1983) ("[T]he United States is prepared to accept and act in accordance with the balance of interests relating to traditional use of the oceans . . . .").

UNCLOS recognizes an exclusive economic zone ("EEZ") beyond a nation's territorial sea but within two hundred nautical miles of the coastal baseline. *See* UNCLOS, *supra*, arts. 55-59. Beyle insists that UNCLOS treats the EEZ as a distinct quasi-territorial entity and that the high seas do not begin until two hundred nautical miles from land. Because the *Quest* was within the EEZ when the murders occurred, he thus asserts that he was not on the "high seas" for the purposes of U.S. law.

While it is true that the part of UNCLOS that is titled "High Seas" concerns the waters extending beyond the borders of the EEZ, *see* UNCLOS, *supra*, art. 86, almost all of the treaty's [—17—] high-seas provisions apply with equal force inside the EEZ as they do outside it, *see id.* art. 58(1)-(2). The EEZ bordering a particular nation's territorial sea is merely a part of the high seas where that nation has special economic rights and jurisdiction. UNCLOS grants coastal nations certain rights to natural resources within the EEZ, as well as jurisdiction over marine scientific research and protection and preservation of the marine environment. *Id.* art. 56(1)(a), (b); *see also Titanic*, 171 F.3d at 965 n.3 (noting that the EEZ grants "exclusive control over [certain] economic matters . . . , but not over navigation").

Any allocation of economic rights, however, is a far cry from conferring on a nation the exclusive authority endemic to sovereignty to define and punish criminal violations. In effect, Beyle would have us use UNCLOS's grant of certain specific enumerated rights as a wedge to dramatically expand Somalia's plenary control past the twelve-nautical-mile maximum. But Beyle points to no court that has declared that a nation's full sovereign rights extend two hundred nautical miles from the coast. We decline to credit such a sweeping interpretation.

C.

If Beyle was beyond the bounds of Somalia's territorial sea, therefore, he was on the high seas and within the reach of [—18—] the U.S. criminal statutes under which he was convicted. The question then becomes where exactly Somalia's territorial sea ends and the high seas begin. The weight of authority points to an outer territorial limit of twelve nautical miles, which places the *Quest* on the high seas at the time of the murders.

UNCLOS explicitly restricts territorial seas from extending farther than twelve nautical miles from national coastlines. UNCLOS, *supra*, art. 3. At the time of the piracy at issue in this case, 161 nations had ratified UNCLOS, including Somalia. With nearly 170 signatory nations today, UNCLOS enjoys widespread acceptance in the international community. As noted above, although the United States is not a signatory to UNCLOS, this country recognizes the treaty's place as an accurate reflection of customary international law. It is, moreover, the policy of the United States not to respect claims that a territorial sea extends beyond twelve nautical miles. Office of Ocean Affairs, U.S. Dep't of State, Pub. No. 112, *Limits in the Seas: United States Responses to Excessive Maritime Claims* 7, 33 (1992); Fact Sheet, Office of the Press Sec'y, The White House, United States Oceans Policy (Mar. 10, 1983); *see* 33 C.F.R. § 2.22(b); *see also* The White House, *United States Counter Piracy and Maritime Security Action Plan* annex B at 2 (June 2014). Consistent with UNCLOS, the United States itself claims a territorial sea extending up to twelve nautical miles. 18 U.S.C. [—19—] § 2280(e); *Argentine Republic v. Amerada Hess Shipping Corp.*, 488 U.S. 428, 441 n.8 (1989); 33 C.F.R. § 2.22(a)(1)(ii), (iii), (iv) (applying a U.S. territorial sea of twelve nautical miles for determining U.S. criminal jurisdiction and the special maritime and territorial jurisdiction, and for interpreting international law); Proclamation No. 5928, 54 Fed. Reg. 777 (Dec. 27, 1988) (extending the U.S. territorial sea to twelve nautical miles "in accordance with international law").

We, too, have repeatedly stated that a nation's territorial waters generally extend to twelve nautical miles. *See United States v. Shibin*, 722 F.3d 233, 239, 1 Adm. R. 138, 141 (4th Cir. 2013); *Dire*, 680 F.3d at 460 n.11; *Titanic*, 171 F.3d at 965. The jury instructions given by the district court reflected this understanding, and earlier cases were predicated upon the same definition. J.A. 2704 ("The 'high seas' include areas of the seas that are outside the territorial seas of any nation. A nation's territorial seas are generally limited to an area within 12 nautical miles of the nation's coast."); *see, e.g.*, Excerpt of Proceedings (Jury Instructions) at 19-20, *United States v. Hasan*, No. 2:10-cr-56 (E.D. Va. Nov. 22, 2010) (same), ECF No. 356, *aff'd sub nom. Dire*, 680 F.3d 446.

Nevertheless, Beyle argues that customary international law does not apply to the determination of the extent of Somalia's territorial sea, because Somalia passed national legislation in [—20—] 1972 that extended its sea to two hundred nautical miles.[2] Even if we could or would credit any

---

[2] The validity of the 1972 Somali domestic legislation is itself doubtful and unclear. In June 2014, Somalia's president issued a proclamation stating that the country's exclusive economic zone stretched for two hundred nautical miles, but made no claim that full sovereignty extended so far. *See* Proclamation by the President of the Federal Republic of Somalia (June 30, 2014), *available at* http://www.un.org/depts/los/LEGISLATIONANDTREATIES/PDFFILES/SOM_2014_Proclamation.pdf. The following month, the country submitted an executive summary to the Commission on the Limits of the Continental Shelf, indicating in a table that a twelve-nautical-mile territorial claim existed, consistent with UNCLOS. *See Continental*

such territorial claim, it does not pass muster here. Somalia ratified UNCLOS in 1989, making a clear international commitment to a territorial sea of no more than twelve nautical miles.[3] Furthermore, Somalia also has never submitted a declaration indicating non-adherence to any UNCLOS provision, and in any event UNCLOS prohibits signatories from opting out selectively from its provisions. UNCLOS, *supra*, art. 310. The United States, moreover, explicitly does not recognize [—21—] any claim by Somalia to a two-hundred-nautical-mile territorial sea and has conducted operations well within the two-hundred-nautical-mile limit to make that policy known. Office of the Judge Advocate Gen., U.S. Navy, *Maritime Claims Reference Manual: Somalia* (2014). Indeed, the Navy maneuvered to block the *Quest* where it did precisely because it did not want the pirated vessel to sail into the twelve-nautical-mile territorial sea.

"The common and obvious meaning of the expression, 'high seas,' is also the true legal meaning," Daniel Webster once argued before the Supreme Court. *United States v. Bevans*, 16 U.S. (3 Wheat.) 336, 341 (1818). "The expression describes the open ocean, where the dominion of the winds and waves prevails without check or control." *Id.* Although Webster was not conversant with UNCLOS,

---

Shelf Submission of the Federal Republic of Somalia: Executive Summary 7 (July 21, 2014), *available* *at* http://www.un.org/depts/los/clcs_new/submissions_files/som74_14/Somalia_Executive_Summary_2014.pdf.

[3] We recognize that ratification of an international treaty that is not self-executing typically does not supersede inconsistent domestic law in a country that requires separate implementing legislation. *See Medellin v. Texas*, 552 U.S. 491, 504-05 (2008) (discussing treaties that are not self-executing in the context of U.S. law). Here, however, we need not decide whether the UNCLOS provision is self-executing. Even if it is not, the district court was justified in relying on Somalia's unequivocal international commitment, as embodied in its ratification of UNCLOS, and indeed in this case Somalia's own treaty implementation procedures are opaque and the status of its inconsistent domestic legislation is itself ambiguous.

he plainly grasped the point that expansive claims of territoriality would intrude upon the natural domain of the seas and the multinational interests therein. Nowhere is this truer than when litigants seek to extend customary international law as memorialized in treaties to claim territorial seas more than sixteen times the maximum breadth. The *Quest*, Beyle, and the victims were on the high seas when the murders occurred. [—22—]

D.

We are aware of no court that has held that Somalia's territorial sea extends past the twelve-nautical-mile boundary prescribed by UNCLOS, much less to two hundred nautical miles. We shall not be the first.

Piracy is an international problem. The primary anti-piracy statute in our criminal code, 18 U.S.C. § 1651, "incorporates" the "definition of piracy" under international law. *Dire*, 680 F.3d at 469. An essential element of the international crime of piracy is that the violence against persons, vessels, or property occurred "on the high seas" or "outside the jurisdiction of any" nation. UNCLOS, *supra*, art. 101(a)(i)-(ii); *see Shibin*, 722 F.3d at 240-44, 1 Adm. R. at 142-46; *Dire*, 680 F.3d at 465. In a reflection of that shared understanding, it has fallen to U.S. and North Atlantic Treaty Organization ("NATO") coalition forces to combat Somalia-based piracy. These naval forces conduct patrols in the Gulf of Aden, a vital shipping passageway between the Arabian Peninsula and the Horn of Africa. Parts of the Gulf of Aden off the Somali coast are under two hundred nautical miles wide. In essence, Beyle asks this court to treat the Gulf of Aden as a Somali territorial sea. As a practical matter, such a ruling would prove especially problematic for NATO maritime forces, which only operate in Somali territorial waters under [—23—] the consent of Somali authorities. Fact Sheet, Mar. Command, N. Atl. Treaty Org., Operation Ocean Shield, at 2 (Nov. 2014).

The risks of an extension of the Somali territorial sea include as well emboldened gangs of pirates, increased "investment" in piracy by Somalia-based financiers, and bridled NATO and multinational counter-piracy efforts. Such results would offend the United Nations Security Council's ongoing apprehension over the threat "to international navigation, the safety of commercial maritime routes and the safety of seafarers and other persons" posed by the violence of piracy and hostage-taking. S.C. Res. 1976, preambular ¶ 2, U.N. Doc. S/RES/1976 (Apr. 11, 2011). We decline to allow Beyle's challenge to his murder and firearm convictions to undermine this broader multinational effort.

In short, the structure of domestic and international law that Beyle seeks to topple protects commercial peace against piratical disruption, and we reject his challenge to his murder and firearms convictions.

III.

Abrar argues that he was denied his Fifth Amendment right to due process and his Sixth Amendment right to present witnesses material to his duress defense. In particular, he maintains that he was unable to access or subpoena certain [—24—] witnesses located abroad who could have corroborated his story that he had been kidnapped and forced to work as a pirate. Even though he concedes that duress is not a valid defense to the murder counts, he requests dismissal of the entire indictment as the "only remedy." Appellants' Br. at 30. We disagree with Abrar's contentions. The district court properly denied his motion to dismiss the indictment.

A.

The Fifth Amendment guarantees that "[n]o person shall . . . be deprived of life, liberty, or property, without due process of law." U.S. Const. amend. V. The right to due process "is, in essence, the right to a fair opportunity to defend against the [government's] accusations." *Chambers v. Mississippi*, 410 U.S. 284, 294 (1973). The Sixth Amendment provides that, "[i]n all criminal prosecutions, the accused shall enjoy the right . . . to have compulsory process for obtaining witnesses in his favor." U.S. Const. amend. VI. This right is violated when the

defendant is "arbitrarily deprived of 'testimony [that] would have been *relevant* and *material*, and . . . *vital* to the defense.'" *United States v. Valenzuela-Bernal*, 458 U.S. 858, 867 (1982) (alterations in original) (quoting *Washington v. Texas*, 388 U.S. 14, 16 (1967)). Fifth Amendment due process and Sixth Amendment compulsory process are [—25—] closely related, for the right "to call witnesses in one's own behalf ha[s] long been recognized as essential to due process." *Chambers*, 410 U.S. at 294; *see also Washington*, 388 U.S. at 19. At root, then, we are asked to determine whether one of the "elements of a fair trial" was absent in the proceedings below. *Chambers*, 410 U.S. at 295.

A criminal defendant's right to compulsory process is not unlimited. "Few rights," to be sure, "are more fundamental than that of an accused to present witnesses in his own defense," *Id.* at 302, and the right to compulsory process is "imperative to the function of courts" in our adversary system, *United States v. Nixon*, 418 U.S. 683, 709 (1974). But the right to compulsory process does not scorn practicality. Crucially, "the Sixth Amendment does not by its terms grant to a criminal defendant the right to secure the attendance and testimony of *any* and *all* witnesses." *Valenzuela-Bernal*, 458 U.S. at 867 (emphasis added). In concrete terms, the right to compulsory process is "circumscribed . . . by the ability of the district court to obtain the presence of a witness through service of process." *United States v. Moussaoui*, 382 F.3d 453, 463 (4th Cir. 2004).

Those practical limits are significant for the transnational context in which Abrar's claims arise. It is a "well[-]established and undisputed principle that the process power of the district court does not extend to foreign nationals [—26—] abroad." *Id.* at 463-64. A conviction does not become unconstitutional simply because the federal courts lack power to secure the appearance of a foreign national located outside the United States. *Id.*; *United States v. Theresius Filippi*, 918 F.2d 244, 246 n.2 (1st Cir. 1990); *United States v. Zabaneh*, 837 F.2d 1249, 1259-60 (5th Cir. 1988); *United States v. Greco*, 298 F.2d 247, 251 (2d Cir. 1962); *see also* 28 U.S.C. § 1783(a) (providing for subpoenas of "a national or resident of the United States who is in a foreign country," but not referencing foreign nationals abroad); Fed. R. Crim. P. 17(e)(2). After all, "the Sixth Amendment can give the right to compulsory process only where it is within the power of the federal government to provide it." *Greco*, 298 F.2d at 251.

All of the witnesses proffered by Abrar are foreign nationals located abroad. In his pretrial motion, Abrar named five individuals in Somalia, including a former landlord, his brother-in-law, and others who he believed could testify about his prior work as a driver or mechanic. He also wished to call the four Yemeni fishermen from the *Alqasim*, although he did not know their full names or their precise whereabouts. When Abrar renewed his motion at trial, his counsel identified two prospective witnesses for his duress defense, a shopkeeper and a garage manager in the Somali town of Garacad. All of those individuals are foreign nationals located outside the United [—27—] States, and as such they lay beyond the subpoena power of the district court.

Abrar's inability to access the proffered witnesses arose primarily from the security situation in Somalia—a matter beyond the control of the U.S. government. *See Security and Governance in Somalia: Consolidating Gains, Confronting Challenges, and Charting the Path Forward: Hearing Before the Subcomm. on Afr. Affairs of the S. Comm. on Foreign Relations*, 113th Cong. (2013); U.N. S.C. Rep. of the Sec'y-Gen. on Somalia, U.N. Doc. S/2014/699 (Sept. 25, 2014). The investigators who had traveled to Somalia on Abrar's behalf had been unable to leave the capital city of Mogadishu because of ongoing security threats. The domestic troubles within Somalia may complicate independent investigations or a potential service of process, but such exogenous difficulties need not halt the operations of the criminal justice system in the United States. This is especially the case where the immediate obstacles are not of the government's making.

Significantly, we do not even know whether the witnesses proffered by Abrar actually exist. During their visit to Mogadishu, Abrar's investigators apparently did contact some of Abrar's family members, but failed to obtain the cooperation of any witnesses. They did not even speak with the shopkeeper or the garage manager—the two witnesses identified at trial by [—28—] Abrar's counsel as "key" to his duress defense. J.A. 2364. Even if the district court were to direct individuals to travel through the dangerous conditions in Somalia to try to serve subpoenas on Abrar's proffered witnesses, it is uncertain how long such an effort would take or whether it would be fruitful. This is especially the case where the witnesses may be fictitious.

We owe substantial deference to the district court for these kinds of evidentiary determinations, and we review such decisions for abuse of discretion. *United States v. Medford*, 661 F.3d 746, 751 (4th Cir. 2011). After all, the district court has a bird's-eye view of the trial, knowledge of the intricacies of the case, and a sense of the context and background in which each evidentiary claim arises.

B.

Abrar cannot establish a constitutional violation from the "mere absence" of his proffered witnesses' testimony. *Valenzuela-Bernal*, 458 U.S. at 867. It is further doubtful that "their testimony would have been both *material* and *favorable* to his defense." *Id.* (emphasis added). The anticipated testimony of Abrar's proffered witnesses was relatively far afield: it would have consisted primarily of broad references to his activities before the events at issue in this case. According to Abrar's [—29—] own submission, the testimony would have pertained to his "trade as a mechanic and driver, his character for peacefulness, and the series of events leading up to his detainment by the other pirates." J.A. 121. Conceivably, the testimony may also have covered the discrimination Abrar confronted as a Bantu, although several of the pirates called by the government and other witnesses called by the defense did discuss that issue at trial. Critically, however, the proffered testimony would not directly substantiate Abrar's story that he was kidnapped at gunpoint by Juguuf and Sarindaaq, nor would it concern the events aboard the *Quest* or his relationship with the other pirates.

It is unclear—indeed doubtful—that such oblique testimony would be material to Abrar's duress defense. The testimony adduced at trial painted a deeply incriminating portrait of Abrar. Several of the other pirates testified that Abrar was a willing participant. Like all the other Somalia-based pirates who had boarded the *Alqasim*, including the one of Yemeni origin—and unlike the four captive Yemeni fishermen who were released after the hijacking of the *Quest*—Abrar would have received a share of any ransom. Abrar brought an AK-47 to the operation and, during at least one of the initial unsuccessful attacks, carried the rocket-propelled grenade launcher. He was the first pirate to board the *Quest*, and he promptly took control of the two American women and cut the **[—30—]** boat's communications lines. He stood guard over the hostages and had his gun trained on Jean Adam before the fatal shots were fired. From its viewing of the video evidence, the district court told Abrar at sentencing that, "if one were concluding, you were probably the shooter of Jean Adam." J.A. 3596. In that light, it is hard to imagine how testimony about Abrar's prior professional work could have been material to the determination of his guilt or punishment.

Despite the powerful evidence marshaled against him at trial, Abrar did not try to take advantage of the other sources available to him. The government represents that, in other piracy prosecutions in the Eastern District of Virginia, it has worked with defense counsel to develop various evidentiary accommodations for defendants, which might include testimony by telephone, depositions, and stipulations. Appellee's Br. at 52-53. Notably, Abrar also did not elicit testimony about his abduction from his two alleged kidnappers. Juguuf and Sarindaaq were in federal custody with the other pirates who had already pleaded guilty, and the government offered to make either of them available to testify on this point. But Abrar's counsel

declined the offer. He informed the court that he had spoken with Juguuf and Sarindaaq and knew that both would deny Abrar's story. While Abrar was certainly free to structure his defense as he thought best, his failure to adduce any direct evidence of **[—31—]** his story or to counter effectively the overwhelming case against him undermines whatever vague advantage he sought to gain from elusive overseas witnesses.

C.

In the proceedings below, the district court gave Abrar multiple opportunities to develop his duress argument. Of course, as a criminal defendant, Abrar was entitled not to take the stand. U.S. Const. amend. V. Had he chosen to testify, however, Abrar generally would have been subject to the same evidentiary rules as other witnesses. *Portuondo v. Agard*, 529 U.S. 61, 69 (2000). In particular, the government would have been allowed to attack his credibility on cross-examination. Fed. R. Evid. 608(a), 611(b). The district court, though, was prepared to make an exception: if Abrar took the stand and his counsel asked only about the facts surrounding his duress defense, the district court would limit the government's cross-examination of Abrar to that issue. But Abrar elected not to testify even in that controlled capacity. In addition, the court ultimately instructed the jury on Abrar's duress defense for most of the counts, despite the absence of significant evidentiary support. Although the government objected to this instruction below, it bears note that, even with a duress **[—32—]** instruction, the jury proceeded to convict Abrar on all twenty-six counts charged in the indictment.

Despite the opportunities afforded to Abrar, the weight of the evidence against him was simply overwhelming—and virtually uncontroverted. The district court ably presided over a twenty-eight-day jury trial spanning nearly two months and "watched every video and heard every piece of evidence." J.A. 3597. In the final analysis, the court's view of the matter was clear:

Four people were murdered, and they were murdered in a particularly heinous manner. The whole process of the conspiracy and the kidnapping was horrendous. . . . Frankly, you looked like you were having a good time at certain instances. I would challenge anyone to sit and look at all of these videos and any of these pictures and come to any conclusion other than you were a willing participant . . . . [N]one of the evidence, when you put it together, meets common sense of you being under duress. . . . You were a major player and you were a major shooter, and there is no question in my mind.

J.A. 3595-97. From all the evidence adduced at trial and the inferences that might have been drawn from it, the court concluded, Abrar's claim of duress "defie[d] . . . credibility." J.A. 3597. We see no reason to disturb the jury's and the court's assessments, much less to invoke the extraordinary remedy of dismissing the indictment. We thus affirm the district court's denial of Abrar's motion. [—33—]

IV.

For the foregoing reasons, the judgment is affirmed.

AFFIRMED

United States Court of Appeals
for the Fourth Circuit

No. 14-1434

WORLD FUEL SERVS. TRADING, DMCC
vs.
HEBEI PRINCE SHIPPING CO.

Appeal from the United States District Court for the
Eastern District of Virginia, at Norfolk

Decided: April 17, 2015

Citation: 783 F.3d 507, 3 Adm. R. 201 (4th Cir. 2015).

Before **WILKINSON, AGEE,** and **HARRIS,** Circuit Judges.

[—3—] **AGEE,** Circuit Judge:

World Fuel Services Trading, DMCC, ("DMCC") brought this in rem action against the M/V HEBEI SHIJIAZHUANG ("the Vessel") seeking to enforce a maritime lien for the supply of necessaries under the Federal Maritime Lien Act ("FMLA"), 46 U.S.C. § 31342(a). The district court held that DMCC was entitled to a maritime lien for the amount due for marine fuel (referred to as "bunkers") provided to the Vessel, and granted DMCC's motion for summary judgment. Hebei Prince Shipping Company, Limited, ("Hebei Prince"), the owner of the Vessel, appeals. For the reasons that follow, we affirm the judgment of the district court in favor of DMCC.

I.

A.

To provide context for the underlying dispute, we begin with a brief review of maritime lien law. A maritime lien is "[a] lien on a vessel, given to secure the claim of a creditor who provided maritime services to the vessel[.]" *Black's Law Dictionary* 1065 (10th ed. 2014). "It arises by operation of law and exist[s] as a claim upon the property." *Id.* (quoting Griffith Price, *The Law of Maritime Liens* 1 (1940)); *see also Triton Marine Fuels Ltd., S.A. v. M/V PAC. CHUKOTKA*, 575 F.3d 409, 416 (4th Cir. 2009) ("'[M]aritime liens are *stricti juris* [—4—] and cannot be created by

agreement between the parties; instead, they arise by operation of law, often depending on the nature and object of the contract.'" (quoting *Bominflot, Inc. v. M/V HENRICH S*, 465 F.3d 144, 146 (4th Cir. 2006)).

Congress enacted the FMLA in 1910, which altered several then-existing common law principles governing when a maritime lien would arise under United States law. *See id.* at 417. That initial legislation "provide[d] a single federal statute for the determination of maritime liens, and by providing this uniform scheme, the statute confer[red] domestic suppliers of necessaries with the same lien rights as previously enjoyed only by foreign suppliers under the common law." *Id.* at 418. The next major change to the FMLA occurred in "1971, when Congress enacted legislation essentially to void 'no lien' clauses in charters, as long as the supplier did not have actual knowledge of such clause." *Id.* at 418 n.5. Most recently, the FMLA was recodified as part of the Commercial Instruments and Maritime Liens Act, 46 U.S.C. §§ 31301-31343. For ease of reference, however, we will continue to refer to the relevant statutes as the "FMLA." "Despite [these] recodifications, the fundamental purposes underlying the FMLA have remained unchanged." *Triton Marine*, 575 F.3d at 417-18.

Generally speaking, a maritime lien arises more readily under the FMLA than under the laws of other maritime countries. [—5—] *E.g., Bominflot*, 465 F.3d at 147 ("The United States as well as a number of civil law nations . . . allow for broader use and enforcement of maritime liens[.]"). As a result, which nation's law governs a particular maritime contract may be significant in determining whether, or to what extent, a maritime lien exists.

B.

Hebei Prince, a corporation organized under the laws of China, owns the Vessel, which is registered in Hong Kong. The Vessel was leased to a Greek corporation, Tramp Maritime Enterprises Ltd. ("Tramp Maritime") under three consecutive time charters (maritime contracts of ship charter) covering the period from May 23, 2012 to

November 28, 2012. The terms of the time charters prohibited Tramp Maritime from incurring "any lien or encumbrance" against the Vessel. (J.A. 86.)

In October 2012, Tramp Maritime emailed Aristades P. Vogas of Bunkerfuels Hellas in Athens, Greece, to arrange for the purchase of bunkers to be delivered to the Vessel while it was docked at a port in the United Arab Emirates. The email reply from Vogas confirming the transaction ("the Bunker Confirmation") identifies the "seller" as "BUNKERFUELS A DBA/DIVISION OF WFS Trading DMCC" and the "buyer" as "MV HEBEI SHIJIAZHUANG AND HER OWNERS/OPERATORS AND TRAMP MARITIME ENTERPRISES LTD." (J.A. 21.) It also identifies APSCO JEDDAH [—6—] as the "physical supplier" of the bunkers. (J.A. 21.) The Bunker Confirmation further states:

ALL SALES ARE ON THE CREDIT OF THE VSL. BUYER IS PRESUMED TO HAVE AUTHORITY TO BIND THE VSL WITH A MARITIME LIEN. DISCLAIMER STAMPS PLACED BY VSL ON THE BUNKER RECEIPT WILL HAVE NO EFFECT AND DO NOT WAIVE THE SELLER'S LIEN. THIS CONFIRMATION IS GOVERNED BY AND INCORPORATES BY REFERENCE SELLER'S GENERAL TERMS AND CONDITIONS IN EFFECT AS OF THE DATE THAT THIS CONFIRMATION IS ISSUED. THESE INCORPORATED AND REFERENCED TERMS CAN BE FOUND AT WWW.WFSCORP.COM. ALTERNATIVELY, YOU MAY INFORM US IF YOU REQUIRE A COPY AND SAME WILL BE PROVIDED TO YOU.

(J.A. 21.)

APSCO JEDDAH delivered the bunkers to the Vessel according to the terms of the Bunker Confirmation. The Vessel's chief engineer signed the delivery notices and attached a "no lien" stamp, which stated "Bunkering Services and the bunkers are ordered solely for the account of Charterers and not for owners. Accordingly no lien or other claims whatsoever against the Vessel or her owners can arise." (J.A. 19, 20.)

Tramp Maritime subsequently received an invoice for the bunkers purporting to be from "BUNKERFUELS A Division of World Fuel Services Trading, DMCC" requesting payment. (J.A. 22.) The invoice stated that the amount due could be wire-transferred to a Bank of America account for "World Fuel Services Europe, Ltd." (J.A. 22.) Neither Tramp Maritime nor any other party paid the invoice. [—7—]

DMCC then filed this in rem action in the United States District Court for the Eastern District of Virginia asserting it was owed $809,420.50 for the unpaid bunkers,[1] and that it was entitled to enforce a maritime lien on the Vessel under the FMLA. It also moved for the court to issue a maritime warrant for the arrest of the Vessel, which was expected to port in Norfolk, Virginia, within fourteen days. The district court issued an order for the maritime arrest warrant, which was executed on the Vessel when it docked in Norfolk. Hebei Prince later posted a cash bond so that the Vessel could be released before resolution of the underlying complaint.

DMCC moved for summary judgment, which Hebei Prince opposed. Hebei Prince then filed a cross-motion for summary judgment, relying on the same grounds raised in its opposition to DMCC's motion. Challenging nearly every aspect of DMCC's claim, Hebei Prince argued: (1) DMCC was not a party in privity to the Bunker Confirmation and thus could not assert a maritime lien; (2) Greek law should apply to every aspect of the contractual dispute; (3) the Bunker Confirmation did not successfully incorporate the General Terms & Conditions on which DMCC relied; (4) the General Terms & Conditions could not apply to DMCC even if DMCC sought to incorporate them; (5) the General [—8—] Terms & Conditions' choice-of-law provision did not "choose" United States statutory maritime law such as the

---

[1] This amount reflected the amount due for the bunkers plus a contract-based administrative fee for past-due sums.

FMLA; (6) DMCC had actual knowledge of the prohibition of liens in Tramp Maritime's time charter and thus could not rely on the FMLA's presumption to bind the Vessel; and (7) principles of comity require rejecting the application of United States law to this transaction.

In a thorough opinion, the district court rejected all but one of Hebei Prince's arguments, and, in any event, that one area of agreement did not alter the court's ultimate holding. *See World Fuel Servs. Trading, DMCC v. M/V HEBEI SHIJIAZHUANG*, 12 F. Supp. 3d 792 (E.D. Va. 2014). In sum, the district court concluded that the Bunker Confirmation successfully incorporated the General Terms & Conditions DMCC relied upon to establish that United States law, including the FMLA, governed the existence and enforcement of a maritime lien. The district court also held that "no genuine issue of material fact regarding the existence of a maritime lien in this matter [exists and that], as a matter of law, [DMCC was] entitled to a maritime lien against the [V]essel." *Id.* at 810.

Following briefing and a hearing on the amount of damages to be awarded, the district court entered final judgment awarding DMCC $813,740.10. Hebei Prince noted a timely appeal. [—9—] Jurisdiction exists for the reasons discussed below in Section II.A.

II.

Hebei Prince raises the same arguments on appeal that it did in the district court. As for relief, it alternatively argues that we should dismiss the case for lack of admiralty jurisdiction, vacate the district court's award of summary judgment to DMCC and remand to resolve disputed issues of material fact, or vacate the district court's judgment and enter final judgment in its favor.

We review the district court's grant of summary judgment de novo, applying the same standard as the district court. *FDIC v. Cashion*, 720 F.3d 169, 173 (4th Cir. 2013). Summary judgment is appropriate if "there is no genuine dispute as to any material fact and the movant is entitled to judgment as a

matter of law." Fed. R. Civ. P. 56(a). In addition to construing the evidence in the light most favorable to Hebei Prince, the non-movant, we also draw all reasonable inferences in its favor. *Cashion*, 720 F.3d at 173.

To the extent Hebei Prince challenges not just the grant of summary judgment, but the district court's jurisdiction, we review legal conclusions regarding jurisdiction de novo and [—10—] factual findings for clear error. *Flame S.A. v. Freight Bulk Pte. Ltd.*, 762 F.3d 352, 356, 2 Adm. R. 117, 119 (4th Cir. 2014).

A.

Throughout its brief, Hebei Prince argues that the district court lacked admiralty jurisdiction and therefore the case should be dismissed. DMCC responds that Hebei Prince confuses the district court's admiralty jurisdiction with the merits of DMCC's claim of a maritime lien arising under the FMLA. We agree with DMCC.

The Supreme Court noted the distinction, specifically in the admiralty context, between establishing a court's jurisdiction and the determination of the merits of a cause of action over a century ago in *The Resolute*, 168 U.S. 437 (1897):

> Jurisdiction is the power to adjudicate a case upon the merits, and dispose of it as justice may require. As applied to a suit in rem for the breach of a maritime contract, it presupposes— First that the contract sued upon is a maritime contract; and second, that the property proceeded against is within the lawful custody of the court. These are the only requirements necessary to give jurisdiction. *Proper cognizance of the parties and subject-matter being conceded, all other matters belong to the merits.*
>
> . . . *[T]he question of lien or no lien is not one of jurisdiction, but of merits.*

It is true that there can be no decree in rem against the vessel except for the enforcement of a lien given by the maritime law . . .; but, if the existence of such a lien were a question of jurisdiction, then [—11—] nearly every question arising upon the merits could be made one of jurisdiction.

Id. at 439-40 (emphasis added). This admiralty-specific language is consistent with the Supreme Court's general statements in the non-admiralty context separating jurisdictional questions from those concerning the merits of an action. *E.g., Lexmark Int'l, Inc. v. Static Control Components, Inc.*, 134 S. Ct. 1377, 1387 n.4 (2014) ("'[T]he absence of a valid (as opposed to arguable) cause of action does not implicate subject-matter jurisdiction, *i.e.*, the court's statutory or constitutional *power* to adjudicate the case.'" (quoting *Verizon Md., Inc. v. Public Serv. Comm'n of Md.*, 535 U.S. 635, 642-43 (2002)).

Here, Hebei Prince acknowledges that the Bunker Confirmation was a maritime contract. *See Norfolk S. Ry. Co. v. Kirby*, 543 U.S. 14, 24 (2004) (stating that whether a contract is a "maritime contract," "depends upon the nature and character of the contract, and the true criterion is whether it has reference to maritime service or maritime transactions" (internal quotation marks and alteration omitted)). Similarly, Hebei Prince does not contest that the Vessel was physically within the "lawful custody of the court" at the time of its arrest. *See In re Millennium Seacarriers, Inc.*, 419 F.3d 83, 94 (2d Cir. 2005) ("[S]ubject matter jurisdiction lies in the [—12—] district court where the vessel or other *res* is located, but that jurisdiction does not attach until the vessel is arrested within the jurisdiction."). Thus, under the standard articulated in *The Resolute*, it is clear that the district court possessed admiralty jurisdiction.[2] *See*

Logistics Mgmt., Inc. v. One (1) Pyramid Tent Arena, 86 F.3d 908, 912-13 (9th Cir. 1996) (conducting this inquiry); *see also Wilkins v. Commercial Inv. Trust Corp.*, 153 F.3d 1273, 1276 (11th Cir. 1998) (same).

As a result, Hebei Prince's arguments that DMCC does not have an enforceable maritime lien under the FMLA do not implicate admiralty jurisdiction, but rather go to the merits of DMCC's action. The district court had admiralty jurisdiction to consider DMCC's claim, and we have jurisdiction over this appeal under 28 U.S.C. § 1291. [—13—]

B.

Before addressing Hebei Prince's substantive challenges to the district court's decision, we consider its threshhold arguments as to which country's law applies to the issues of contract formation.

In the district court, Hebei Prince argued that under *Lauritzen v. Larsen*, 345 U.S. 571 (1953), Greek law determined issues of contract between the parties, including whether DMCC was in privity of contract to the agreement and whether the Bunker Confirmation contained a binding choice-of-law provision. DMCC contended United States law applied, but that it made no real difference as the principles of contract law were the same under either country's law and would lead to the same result in its favor. After examining the terms of the Bunker Confirmation and the parties' arguments, the district court decided the most prudent course was to assume that Hebei Prince was correct and apply Greek law to any contract formation issues. As a corollary, the district court observed that it would reach the same

---

[2] The Ninth Circuit has held that admiralty jurisdiction can arise under the FMLA even where it would not also arise under common law admiralty jurisdiction. *See Ventura Packers, Inc. v. F/V JEANINE KATHLEEN*, 305 F.3d 913, 919 (9th Cir. 2002) ("Although a maritime contract may support admiralty jurisdiction, it is not an essential prerequisite to a civil action in admiralty to enforce a statutory necessaries lien."). *But see E.S.*

Binnings, Inc. v. M/V SAUDI RIYADH, 815 F.2d 660 (8th Cir. 1987) (concluding plaintiff could not proceed on a claim seeking enforcement of an FMLA maritime lien because the underlying contract was not a maritime contract and so the district court lacked admiralty jurisdiction), *overruled on other grounds by Exxon Corp. v. Cent. Gulf Lines, Inc.*, 500 U.S. 603, 612 (1991). We need not delve into that question here because jurisdiction exists in this case under traditional principles establishing admiralty jurisdiction.

conclusions on contract formation issues under United States law as it did applying Greek law.

On appeal, the parties do not make particularly robust arguments either as to the district court's choice of Greek law, its articulation of Greek contract law principles, or its conclusion that the same analysis would result under United [—14—] States law. Hebei Prince instead maintains that the court erred in its application of Greek law to the factual record. DMCC, in turn, maintains that while the district court should have applied United States law based strictly on the choice-of-law provision, it prevails under either country's law.

In *Lauritzen*, the Supreme Court set forth several factors for federal courts sitting in admiralty to consider in determining what country's law governs: "(1) the place of the wrongful act; (2) the law of the flag; (3) the allegiance of the injured party; (4) the allegiance of the defendant shipowner; (5) the place of contract; (6) the inaccessibility of a foreign forum; and (7) the law of the forum." *Trans-Tec Asia v. M/V HARMONY CONTAINER*, 518 F.3d 1120, 1124 (9th Cir. 2008) (citing *Lauritzen*, 345 U.S. at 583-92).

In *Triton Marine*, however, we found it unnecessary to conduct a *Lauritzen* choice-of-law analysis because the contract at issue contained a choice-of-law clause. *See Triton Marine*, 575 F.3d at 413; *see also Lauritzen*, 345 U.S. at 588-89 ("Except as forbidden by some public policy, the tendency of the law is to apply in contract matters the law which the parties intended to apply."). Relying on prior Supreme Court and Fourth Circuit case law, we concluded that "absent compelling reasons of public policy, a choice-of-law provision in a maritime contract should be enforced," and a *Lauritzen* choice-of-law analysis was [—15—] unnecessary. *Triton Marine*, 575 F.3d at 415; *see also Bominflot, Inc.*, 465 F.3d at 148 (holding that the choice of law question was "made easy" by the party's contractual provision agreeing that English law would

apply).[3] Thus, for the reasons set forth in *Triton Marine* and *Bominflot, Inc.*, a *Lauritzen* choice-of-law analysis is unnecessary in this case.

Moreover, we agree with the district court that the applicable law on the issues of contract formation would be the same whether Greek or United States law is applied. As we discuss in the context of the individual arguments below, Greek contract law does not differ in any material respect from the [—16—] corresponding principles of United States law. For this reason, too, we need not resolve the choice-of-law question, as it makes no discernible difference to the relevant analysis in the case at bar. *See Phillips Petroleum Co. v. Shutts*, 472 U.S. 797, 838 n.20 (1985) (Stevens, J., concurring in part and dissenting in part) ("If the laws of both states relevant to the set of facts are the same, or would produce the same decision in the lawsuit, there is no real conflict between them." (quotation marks and citation omitted)); *Hammersmith v. TIG Ins. Co.*, 480 F.3d 220, 230 (3d Cir. 2007) (stating that a conflict of law analysis is unnecessary if the

---

[3] The choice-of-law clause at issue in *Triton Marine* was located in the body of the contract. 575 F.3d at 413. In *Bominflot*, we avoided the *Lauritzen* choice-of-law analysis based on a choice-of-law provision that was incorporated by reference. 465 F.3d at 148; *see also Hawkespere Shipping Co., Ltd. v. Intamex, S.A.*, 330 F.3d 225, 233 (4th Cir. 2003) ("'Where the parties specify in their contractual agreement which law will apply, admiralty courts will generally give effect to that choice.'" (quoting *Chan v. Soc'y Expeditions, Inc.*, 123 F.3d 1287, 1297 (9th Cir. 1997))). These cases thus counsel that if we applied United States law to the question, we would enforce a contract's choice-of-law provision. Applied here, so long as the General Terms were successfully incorporated to the Bunker Confirmation, *see* analysis *infra* II.D at 28 n.6, it would govern the dispute.

Although Hebei Prince asserts various reasons why an otherwise incorporated choice-of-law provision should not be enforced against it, none demonstrates a compelling public policy. For example, we have previously rejected arguments that enforcing such provisions adversely affects the interests of—and works a fundamental unfairness against—a vessel owner who was not party to the contract containing the choice-of-law provision. *See Triton Marine*, 575 F.3d at 413-16.

laws of each jurisdiction are the same, or would lead to the same result, because there is no "conflict" in the law that needs to be resolved); *Okmyansky v. Herbalife Int'l of Am., Inc.*, 415 F.3d 154, 158 (1st Cir. 2005) ("[W]hen resolution of a choice-of-law determination would not alter the disposition of a legal question, a reviewing court need not decide which body of law controls."); *Fin. One Pub. Co. v. Lehman Bros. Special Fin., Inc.*, 414 F.3d 325, 331 (2d Cir. 2005) ("[W]e [do] not have occasion to embark on a choice-of-law analysis in the absence of an actual conflict between the applicable rules of two relevant jurisdictions."); *Cruz v. Am. Airlines, Inc.*, 356 F.3d 320, 331-32 (D.C. Cir. 2004) (same); *Modern Equip. Co. v. Cont'l W. Ins. Co.*, 355 F.3d 1125, 1128 n.7 (8th Cir. 2004) (same); *Schneider Nat'l Transp. v. Ford Motor [—17—] Co.*, 280 F.3d 532, 536 (5th Cir. 2002) (same). We will therefore follow the district court's approach in using principles of Greek law pertaining to contract formation, but noting the parallel analysis under United States law.

C.

Hebei Prince argues that the district court erred at the outset of the case as it contends that the record does not establish DMCC as a party in the underlying transaction and therefore without any right to bring the in rem action. Essentially, Hebei Prince contends DMCC was not in privity of contract with Tramp Maritime because it has not shown that it was an actual party to the Bunker Confirmation.[4] Consequently, Hebei Prince posits that DMCC cannot seek to enforce a maritime lien against the Vessel based on that agreement and that this problem requires

---

[4] Hebei Prince acknowledges that the Bunker Confirmation formed a contract between Tramp Maritime and another entity, but it disputes that DMCC is that other entity. In other words, Hebei Prince asserts that Tramp Maritime entered into an agreement with Bunkerfuels Hellas or even the entity identified on the Bunker Confirmation as "BUNKERFUELS A DBA/DIVISION OF WFS TRADING DMCC," but that no evidence in the record demonstrated that DMCC is either related by law to Bunkerfuels Hellas or is "BUNKERFUELS A DBA/DIVISION OR WFS TRADING DMCC." (*Cf.* J.A. 21.)

dismissal of the suit or, at the very least, remand to resolve a genuine issue of material fact as to DMCC's [—18—] standing to bring an action based on the Bunker Confirmation. We disagree.

Applying principles of Greek agency law, the district court concluded that Vogas had entered into the agreement with Tramp Maritime on behalf of his principal, DMCC. *See World Fuel Servs. Trading*, 12 F. Supp. 3d at 802 ("The Greek doctrine of 'ostensible authority' is much like the agency law recognized in the United States, where '[t]he essential underlying principle in the agency relationship is the power of an agent to commit his principal to business relations with third parties.'" (citation omitted)). The district court emphasized that in contrast to the record DMCC pointed to as evidence that it was the seller of bunkers to Tramp Maritime, Hebei Prince presented no "specific facts" supported in the record that created a "'genuine issue for trial,' as to whether [DMCC] was a party to the contract." *See id.* at 804 (quoting *Celotex Corp. v. Catrett*, 477 U.S. 317, 324 (1986)).

We agree with the district court that the record permits no conclusion but that DMCC sold Tramp Maritime the bunkers specified in the Bunker Confirmation through its agent, Vogas. Because DMCC filed a verified complaint, it contains a sworn statement indicating that its contents are "true and correct based upon [the] personal knowledge and documents available to" DMCC, and we can treat those components of it as "the equivalent [—19—] of an opposing affidavit for summary judgment purposes." *Williams v. Griffin*, 952 F.2d 820, 823 (4th Cir. 1991); *see also* Supp. Rules for Admiralty or Maritime Claims R. C(2) (requiring that the complaint in an in rem action be verified). (*See* J.A. 18, containing the verification of Richard D. McMichael, a "Director of WORLD FUEL SERVICES TRADING, DMCC.) The verified complaint states that "World Fuel Services Trading, DMCC, d/b/a Bunkerfuels" entered into the agreement memorialized in the Bunker Confirmation for its subcontractor APSCO to deliver bunkers to the Vessel. (J.A. 14.) Consistent with this assertion, the

Bunker Confirmation identifies the seller of the bunkers as "BUNKERFUELS A DBA/DIVISION OF WFS Trading DMCC." (J.A. 21.) Even more clearly, the invoice Tramp Maritime received after the bunkers had been delivered refers to "BUNKERFUELS A Division of World Fuel Services Trading, DMCC." (J.A. 22.)

While DMCC's name as specified in the verified complaint is "World Fuel Services Trading, DMCC," nothing in the record suggests that the "WFS Trading DMCC" identified on the Bunker Confirmation refers to an entity other than DMCC. All the record evidence points to the same conclusion: "WFS Trading DMCC" is "World Fuel Services Trading, DMCC," and "WFS" is simply an acronym for "World Fuel Services" rather than a formal designation of a separate entity. Examples of this practice [—20—] exist throughout this case: the website listed in the Bunker Confirmation (www.wfscorp.com) uses the elongated "World Fuel Services" throughout the website, the bunker invoice refers to both "World Fuel Services" and "WFS," as do other items in the record. (J.A. 21, 22.) Indeed, in other contexts, even Hebei Prince's filings use "WFS" and "World Fuel Services" interchangeably.

Furthermore, in his sworn declaration and deposition testimony, Jos Heijmen, the Senior Vice President of Credit & Risk Management of World Fuel Services Corporation, explained the relationship between the various entities. He stated that World Fuel Services Corporation is the parent corporation of "the World Fuel Services Group of Companies," which includes DMCC. (J.A. 252.) He observed that DMCC "is part of a network of affiliated and related companies that provide fuel to ocean-going vessels throughout the world, doing business under the trade name 'Bunkerfuels.'" (J.A. 252.) He noted that Bunkerfuels Hellas is the Athens, Greece branch of a World Fuel Services subsidiary, and that it "provide[s] marketing and promotion services to Greek ship operators/owners and local suppliers." (J.A. 252.) He stated that when a Bunkerfuels Hellas employee receives a bunker inquiry, the transaction is automatically routed

through "the World Fuel's affiliated company located in the geographic region of the world where the [—21—] bunkers will be delivered to the vessel." (J.A. 252.) And he identified DMCC as World Fuel Service's "provider of bunker fuel for ocean-going vessels in the [United Arab Emirates] and the Middle East," and that DMCC is organized under the laws of the United Arab Emirates with its principal place of business in Dubai. (J.A. 251.)

Heijmen also explained that Vogas is an employee of Bunkerfuels Hellas, and is authorized "to enter into contracts with [Greek vessel operators/owners like Tramp Maritime] on behalf of and for the World Fuel Services affiliate located where the ship required and was supplied bunkers," including transactions on behalf of DMCC. (J.A. 252-53.) He specifically stated that Vogas was authorized "by World Fuel Services Trading, DMCC, in October 2012 to act and enter on behalf of World Fuel Services Trading, DMCC into the contract with Tramp Maritime Enterprises, Ltd. that is at issue in this case." (J.A. 253.)

Hebei Prince's attempts to ignore or explain away this testimony amounts to no more than conjecture. Without record evidence to support its assertions, Hebei Prince speculates that DMCC may not be the entity it purports to be, that documents cannot mean what they say on their face, and that entities are not related in the only way they are described above. Hebei Prince's parsing of Heijmen's declaration and deposition [—22—] testimony goes beyond any common-sense reading of those documents. In sum, it attempts to manufacture doubt where none exists to obscure the relationship between DMCC and the transaction at issue. Based on the record in this case, the district court did not err in concluding that Hebei Prince failed to show a genuine issue of material fact as to whether Vogas entered into the Bunker Confirmation as the agent of the seller, DMCC.

Lastly, Hebei Prince asserts that even if Vogas was DMCC's agent, that fact "was not accurately disclosed and was misleading." (Opening Br. 19.) We readily reject that notion. The Bunker Confirmation hardly disguises the identity of the seller, "BUNKERFUELS A DBA/DIVISION OF WFS Trading DMCC." (J.A. 21.) Regardless of the effectiveness of the incorporation by reference, the Bunker Confirmation also refers to and directs readers to the "*SELLER'S* GENERAL TERMS AND CONDITIONS . . . FOUND AT WWW.*WFSCORP*.COM." (J.A. 21 (emphasis added).) In addition, the email addresses provided for both Vogas and Bunkerfuels Hellas contain the domain "*wfscorp*.com." (J.A. 21 (emphasis added).) The Bunker Confirmation plainly provides notice of Vogas' association with WFS subsidiary DMCC.

For these reasons, we conclude the district court did not err in concluding that DMCC was in privity of contract with Tramp Maritime. It follows that regardless of its eventual [—23—] success on the claim, DMCC could assert a cause of action based on an alleged breach of the Bunker Confirmation, including a claim that it had an enforceable maritime lien under the FMLA.

D.

Next, we address whether the district court erred in concluding Greek law would recognize the language contained in the Bunker Confirmation to validly incorporate World Fuel Service's General Terms & Conditions ("General Terms"). As noted, the Bunker Confirmation states it is

> GOVERNED BY AND INCORPORATES BY REFERENCE SELLER'S GENERAL TERMS AND CONDITIONS IN EFFECT AS OF THE DATE THAT THIS CONFIRMATION IS ISSUED. THESE INCORPORATED AND REFERENCED TERMS CAN BE FOUND AT WWW.WFSCORP.COM. ALTERNATIVELY, YOU MAY INFORM US IF YOU REQUIRE A COPY AND SAME WILL BE PROVIDED TO YOU.

(J.A. 21.)

The undisputed evidence in the record reflects that to reach the text of the General Terms on wfscorp.com, a user must click on two more links: either by clicking on a link labeled "Marine" and then on a second link labeled "Marine Terms and Conditions," which contains a .pdf version of the General Terms, or by hovering over a "By Sea" graphic, clicking on the link "learn more," and then clicking on a link labeled "Marine Terms and Conditions." (J.A. 316, 321-28.) [—24—]

The parties submitted declarations from Greek attorneys stating their respective opinions on whether and when terms are incorporated by reference, and whether and when a choice of law provision is enforceable under Greek law. Unsurprisingly, although the attorneys agreed about these broader points of Greek law, they disagreed about whether the Bunker Confirmation satisfied them.

The district court ruled that no genuine issue of material fact existed as to whether the Bunker Confirmation validly incorporated the General Terms. Based on the information provided by both parties, the district court noted that Greek law respected choice of law provisions, and also authorized contracts to incorporate other documents by reference. *See* Fed. R. Civ. P. 44.1 (stating, in relevant part, that "[i]n determining foreign law, the court may consider any relevant material or source, including testimony, whether or not submitted by a party or admissible under the Federal Rules of Evidence"). The district court observed that Hebei Prince's Greek attorney witness stated that such provisions must be drafted in "a clear, plain and explicit way" to be valid. *World Fuel Servs. Trading*, 12 F. Supp. 3d at 804. And it also observed that DMCC's Greek attorney witness stated that Greek law recognized that terms can be incorporated by reference so long as the contracting parties obtain knowledge of their [—25—] contents *or* be given the opportunity to obtain such knowledge. The court then held that the Bunker Confirmation's language satisfied both of these standards. That is, it was "sufficiently clear and explicit to direct Tramp [Maritime]—as well as anyone else who received the bunker confirmation—to the General Terms." *Id.*

The district court also rejected Hebei Prince's argument that the General Terms lacked the requisite clarity because the preamble did not identify DMCC by name. The court first observed that the preamble to the General Terms provided a non-exclusive list of corporations to which it applied, so DMCC's absence had no significance. Then, the court noted that the preamble stated that the General Terms applied to "'all subsidiaries of [WFS],'" and that the record evidence showed DMCC was a subsidiary of WFS. *Id.* at 796. Lastly, the court stated that since the Bunker Confirmation incorporated the General Terms, DMCC had adopted the document regardless of what the General Terms preamble purported its applicability to be.

Hebei Prince's arguments on appeal echo those it made to the district court, that the Bunker Confirmation did not validly incorporate the General Terms because it does not identify the specific internet site where those provisions could be located. In addition, it asserts that because the preamble to the General [—26—] Terms does not specifically refer to DMCC or Bunkerfuels, the document does not clearly apply to the transaction at issue.

The district court did not err in concluding that the Bunker Confirmation validly incorporated the General Terms into the agreement. The Bunker Confirmation plainly expresses that it incorporates the terms of another specific document, the General Terms. Consequently, Tramp Maritime, along with any other reader of the Bunker Confirmation, was immediately put on notice of the existence of a specific additional document that contained provisions that were also part of the Bunker Confirmation. In addition, the Bunker Confirmation provides two means of obtaining a copy of the General Terms: visiting the wfscorp.com website or asking for a copy. Although individuals in search of the General Terms need to click on two internal links to reach the text, the terms are readily found through wfscorp.com links identified by such relevant language as "By Sea," "Marine," and "Marine Terms and Conditions." *See One Beacon Ins. Co. v.*

Crowley Marine Servs., Inc., 648 F.3d 258, 266-70 (5th Cir. 2011) (using a similar standard (unambigious, clear, specific, conspicuous, and explicit) for valid incorporation by reference to conclude that terms and conditions available four clicks into the website contained in the contract were validly incorporated). Moreover, had any reader asked for a copy of the referenced document, the text would have been [—27—] readily reviewable in that form as well.[5] On its face, then, the Bunker Confirmation effectively incorporated the General Terms. As the district court concluded, the incorporation was "sufficiently clear and explicit to direct" readers to the General Terms and it "explicitly offered Tramp [Maritime] 'the opportunity to obtain knowledge' of the General Terms." *World Fuel Servs. Trading,* 12 F. Supp. 3d at 804.

The language in the preamble to the General Terms does not alter this conclusion. The preamble does not purport to identify an exhaustive list of entities to which it applies. Instead, it states that the group of companies to which it applies "includes, but is not limited to" certain delineated companies. (J.A. 23.) The preamble also states that it applies to "the World Fuel Services corporation Marine Group of companies . . . and their respective trade names, subsidiaries, affiliates and branch offices. This list includes all subsidiaries of [WFS] who have sold, are selling or will sell marine petroleum products and services, whether or not in existence on the effective date." (J.A. 23.) For the reasons already identified in part II.C, *supra,* DMCC and Bunkerfuels fall within the network of WFS marine companies. Accordingly, [—28—] the General Terms do not create doubt as to their applicability to DMCC or otherwise undermine the Bunker Confirmation's incorporation of the General Terms by reference.[6]

---

[5] Hebei Prince does not contend that it or Tramp Maritime ever requested a written copy of the General Terms. Nor does it contend that the website access procedure described above is inaccurate.

[6] Even if we had bypassed Greek law and instead applied United States law, we would reach the same result and conclude that the choice-of-law

E.

Having concluded that the Bunker Confirmation validly incorporated the General Terms as part of the formation of the governing contract between the parties, we turn to Hebei Prince's contention that the General Terms' choice-of-law provision does not encompass the FMLA. In that regard, the General Terms provide, in pertinent part:

> The General Terms and each Transaction shall be governed by the General Maritime Law of the United States and, in the event that the General Maritime Law of the United States is silent on the disputed issue, the law of the State of Florida, without reference to any conflict of laws rules which may result in the application of the laws of another jurisdiction. The General Maritime Law of the United States shall apply with respect to the existence of a maritime lien, [—29—] regardless of the country in which Seller takes legal action.

(J.A. 34.)

The district court rejected Hebei Prince's argument that the phrase "General Maritime Law of the United States" did not include the FMLA. Observing that United States maritime law has developed through both case law and statutes, the district court noted that "'when a statute resolves a particular issue, . . . the general maritime law must comply with that resolution.'" *World Fuel Servs.*, 12 F. Supp. 3d at 806 (quoting *Norfolk Shipbuilding*

& *Drydock Corp. v. Garris*, 532 U.S. 811, 817 (2001)). The court then traced the evolution of the FMLA from its original enactment in 1910 through its various amendments, which slowly altered principles previously established in the "general maritime law" concerning maritime liens under United States law. It concluded that since "general maritime" principles "must" give way to conflicting statutes where Congress has spoken on a particular issue, "the General Maritime Law of the United States" essentially changes to be consistent with the statutory principles. Accordingly, the district court ruled that the General Terms' choice of "General Maritime Law of the United States" included the FMLA. *Id.* at 807-08.

Citing to various cases and the legislative history of the FMLA, Hebei Prince contends this was error because the phrase [—30—] "General Maritime Law of the United States" is generally construed as a term of art to only encompass maritime case law rather than maritime statutory law.[7] Hebei Prince argues

---

clause was successfully incorporated. "Under general contract principles, where a contract expressly refers to and incorporates another instrument in specific terms which show a clear intent to incorporate that instrument into the contract, both instruments are to be construed together." *One Beacon Ins. Co.*, 648 F.3d at 267 (citing 11 Williston on Contracts § 30:25 (4th ed. 1999)). For the reasons articulated above, the parties' intent here is clearly expressed by the provisions in the Bunker Confirmation stating that it would be governed by the General Terms, as well as the language informing Tramp Maritime (or any reader) of two means of acquiring the text of the General Terms.

---

[7] For example, Hebei Prince observes that the Supreme Court has frequently distinguished between statutory and general maritime law. *See E. River S.S. Corp. v. Transamerica Delaval, Inc.*, 476 U.S. 858, 864 (1986) ("Absent a relevant statute, the general maritime law, as developed by the judiciary, applies."). In addition, it relies on the Fifth Circuit's discussion in *McBride v. Estis Well Serv., L.L.C.*, 731 F.3d 505, 1 Adm. R. 316 (5th Cir. 2013), in which the court stated:

> There are two primary sources of federal maritime law: common law developed by federal courts exercising the maritime authority conferred on them by the Admiralty Clause of the Constitution ("general maritime law"), and statutory law enacted by Congress exercising its authority under the Admiralty Clause and the Commerce Clause ("statutory maritime law").

Id. at 507-08, 1 Adm. R. at 316-17. Although it is unrelated to Hebei Prince's argument, we note that the panel decision in *McBride* has subsequently been vacated in light of the grant of rehearing en banc, 743 F.3d 458, 2 Adm. R. 170 (5th Cir. 2014), and en banc decision, 768 F.3d 382, 2 Adm. R. 320 (5th Cir. 2014). The en banc dissent still reiterates that under this construction of the term, DMCC faces a Catch-22 conundrum. On the one hand, the General Terms would not allow DMCC to rely on a maritime lien arising under the FMLA because "General Maritime Law of the United States" excludes statutory law. On the other hand, DMCC could not obtain a maritime lien under case law because the FMLA is now the sole means of obtaining a maritime lien for the provision of necessaries under [—31—] United States law. Consequently, Hebei Prince argues that the General Terms do not entitle DMCC to a maritime lien.

To be sure, the General Terms' choice-of-law provision could have been written in a way that would avoid this question entirely. In *Triton Marine*, for example, the relevant clause stated that the "agreement shall be governed by and construed in all particulars by the laws of the United States of America[.]" 575 F.3d at 412. So, too, the Ninth Circuit has reviewed a choice-of-law provision that selected "the general maritime laws of the United States and applicable United States Statutes." *Flores v. Am. Seafoods Co.*, 335 F.3d 904, 918 n.8 (9th Cir. 2003). Either of these constructions clearly incorporates federal statutory maritime laws such as the FMLA.

But even assuming, without deciding, that Hebei Prince's reading of the term "General Maritime Law of the United States" is correct and the FMLA is not part of the "General Maritime Law of the United States," Hebei Prince still cannot prevail. This is so because the General Terms alternatively provides if the "General Maritime Law of the United States is silent on the disputed issue, the law of the State of Florida [governs.]" (J.A. 34.)

Florida law resolves the issue in favor of DMCC because Florida law must be deemed to include United States law—by case law or by statute. The Supreme Court has long stated that "'a [—32—] fundamental principle in our system of complex national polity' mandates that 'the Constitution, laws, and treaties of

the United States are as much a part of the law of every state as its own local laws and Constitution.'" *Fidelity Fed. Sav. & Loan Ass'n v. de la Cuesta*, 458 U.S. 141, 157 (1982) (quoting *Hauenstein v. Lynham*, 100 U.S. 483, 490 (1879)). A choice-of-law provision directing us to the laws of Florida thus encompasses federal statutory law, including the FMLA. *See Atkinson v. General Elec. Credit Corp.*, 866 F.2d 396, 398-99 (11th Cir. 1989) (concluding, based in part on *Fidelity Fed. Sav. & Loan Ass'n*, that "Georgia law includes federal law" where a choice-of-law provision selected "the laws of the State of Georgia" but was silent as to federal statutory law's applicability). Accordingly, the General Terms' choice-of-law provision authorizes DMCC to pursue a maritime lien under the FMLA.

F.

Hebei Prince alternatively argues that even if the FMLA applies to the transaction, DMCC is still not entitled to a maritime lien because it has not satisfied all of the requirements under the FMLA. Once again, we disagree.

In relevant part, the FMLA provides that "a person providing necessaries to a vessel on the order of . . . a person [—33—] authorized by the owner" "has a maritime lien on the vessel" and "may bring a civil action in rem to enforce the lien." 46 U.S.C. § 31342(a). The FMLA creates a presumption that charterers (e.g., Tramp Maritime) have such "authority to procure necessaries for" the Vessel. *See* § 31341(a)(4)(B).

Hebei Prince contends that it produced proof rebutting this statutory presumption that Tramp Maritime had such authorization here. Alternatively, Hebei Prince maintains that the record demonstrates a genuine issue of material fact as to whether the presumption applies. It asserts DMCC had actual knowledge that Tramp Maritime was not authorized to enter into agreements that would give rise to a maritime lien against the Vessel and points to two prior contracts between Bunkerfuels Hellas and Tramp Maritime, where Tramp Maritime had placed no-lien stamps on the delivery receipts. Hebei

---

this same general principle. 768 F.3d at 405, 2 Adm. R. at 339 (Higginson, J., dissenting).

Prince contends these prior acts provided DMCC cognizable notice that Tramp Maritime could not procure necessaries in an agreement that would bind the Vessel. In addition, Hebei Prince maintains that upon seeing the no-lien stamp affixed to the delivery receipt for the bunkers at issue here, DMCC's sub-contractor APSCO could—and should—have engaged in self-help to immediately reclaim the bunkers. Hebei Prince asserts DMCC's failure to take such prompt action following actual notice of the no-lien provision caused it to waive the right to a maritime lien. [—34—]

We agree with the district court that no triable issue of fact exists on this issue. The statutory presumption discussed above can be rebutted only by proof that the seller had actual knowledge that the charterer lacked the ability to bind the vessel as part of the contract for necessaries. *See Triton Marine*, 575 F.3d at 418 n.5 (observing that in 1971 Congress recodified the FMLA "essentially to void 'no lien' clauses in charters, as long as the supplier did not have actual knowledge of such clause"); *Lake Charles Stevedores, Inc. v. PROFESSOR VLADIMIR POPOV MV*, 199 F.3d 220, 224-25 (5th Cir. 1999) (discussing cases in the Fifth and Eleventh Circuits holding the same, as well as recounting the changes in the statute leading to this conclusion). Put another way, "a supplier of necessaries ordered by a § 31341(a) entity subject to a no-lien clause not made known to the supplier has a maritime lien." *Lake Charles Stevedores*, 199 F.3d at 225.

None of the evidence Hebei Prince relies on demonstrates that DMCC had actual knowledge of the no-lien provision in Tramp Maritime's charter party. Hebei Prince does not contend that it or Tramp Maritime ever notified DMCC or Bunkerfuels Hellas of the terms of their charter party. This is so despite the Bunker Confirmation clearly stating that Tramp Maritime "is presumed to have authority to bind the [Vessel] with a maritime lien." (J.A. 21.) The Bunker Confirmation thus plainly contemplated [—35—] that a presumption of authority to obligate the Vessel existed, and there is no evidence that anyone attempted to notify DMCC to the contrary at any point between Tramp Maritime receiving the Bunker Confirmation and accepting delivery of the bunkers.

The no-lien stamps affixed to prior delivery notices when Tramp Maritime was operating under prior charter parties is insufficient to provide actual knowledge of the current charter party. Those prior stamps say nothing about the terms of Tramp Maritime's charter to operate the Vessel at the time it entered into the agreement set forth in the Bunker Confirmation.

The primary case Hebei Prince relies upon to satisfy its burden, *Belcher Oil Co. v. M/V GARDENIA*, 766 F.2d 1508 (11th Cir. 1985), materially differs from the facts here. In *Belcher Oil*, the supplier was notified *prior* to delivery of the bunkers that the charter party contained a no-lien clause prohibiting the charterer from obligating the vessel. *Id.* at 1510. Only as "corroborat[ion]" of this finding of actual knowledge did the Eleventh Circuit also note that the charterer had put disclaimer stamps on the bunkering certificates for prior deliveries from the same seller. However, the presumption against lien authority was only rebutted because the evidence showed the supplier actually knew the charterer was bound by a no-lien clause before delivery of the fuel. By contrast, there is no proof in this case that DMCC actually knew that the operative [—36—] charter party contained a no-lien clause. Accordingly, Hebei Prince cannot rebut the presumption based on prior contracts between Tramp Maritime and Bunkerfuels.

Hebei Prince's second argument fares no better, as the no-lien stamps affixed to the delivery notices did not provide timely actual notice of any no-lien clause in the charter party. This is so for at least two reasons. First, the Bunker Confirmation states that "[d]isclaimer stamps placed by [anyone] on the bunker receipt will have no effect and do not waive the seller's lien." (J.A. 21.) Despite this language, Tramp Maritime never contacted DMCC to convey the terms of the charter party or that it viewed the no-lien stamps as effective. Moreover, anyone reading the terms of the Bunker Confirmation would have reason to believe that even if a no-lien stamp was placed on the delivery receipt, it would be of no effect. Given the terms of the Bunker Confirmation, DMCC and its subcontractor APSCO both had reason to believe that any no-lien stamps were ineffective.

Second, delivery of the bunkers fulfilled DMCC's obligation under the Bunker Confirmation, and notice at that point of the no-lien provision would be too late to alter the terms of the existing agreement. Contrary to Hebei Prince's assertion, DMCC was not required to engage in self-help and demand immediate return of the bunkers upon learning that a no-lien stamp had [—37—] been affixed to the delivery notice. The out-of-circuit case it relies on for this assertion is not binding on us. *See Ferromet Res. v. Chemoil Corp.*, 5 F.3d 902, 903 (5th Cir. 1993). More importantly, the FMLA's provisions were not at issue before that court, and it did not discuss the presumption that arises under § 31341(a) or what evidence is sufficient to rebut it. *Id.*

Ferromet Resources involved a tort claim brought by the charterer against a supplier after the supplier of bunkers refused to unmoor from alongside the vessel until the delivery notice was signed without a no-lien stamp. The Eleventh Circuit held that a genuine issue of material fact existed as to when the supplier was notified that the charterer lacked authority to incur liens. If it was before delivery, then the charterer could likely recover damages incurred as a result of the delay caused by the supplier's refusal to unmoor. *Id.* at 905. If the supplier was not notified of the no-lien clause until delivery, then the supplier may have been entitled to engage in self-help. *Id.* Nothing in *Ferromet Resources* suggests that a supplier *must* engage in self-help or attempt to retrieve delivered bunkers simply because a no-lien stamp has been placed on the delivery receipt.

Accordingly, we conclude that § 31341(a)'s presumption of authority to procure necessaries applies to the Bunker Confirmation transaction. Hebei Prince failed to demonstrate or [—38—] even proffer evidence creating a genuine issue of material fact as to whether DMCC had actual knowledge of Tramp Maritime's lack of authority to bind the Vessel.

Given that the remaining § 31342(a) requirements are either uncontested or have already been resolved in DMCC's favor, we also conclude that DMCC was entitled to bring this action to enforce a maritime lien against the Vessel.

G.

Hebei Prince's final, comity-themed argument echoes throughout its brief. It contends that United States law with respect to maritime liens is so "out of step with existing international conventions and the law of other major maritime nations" that the Court should find a way to conclude no lien arose under the facts of this case. (Opening Br. 51.) As Hebei Prince acknowledges, its arguments align with those previously rejected in other cases, most directly *Triton Marine*. "'[A] panel of this court cannot overrule, explicitly or implicitly, the precedent set by a prior panel of this court. Only the Supreme Court or this court sitting en banc can do that.'" *Scotts Co. v. United Indus. Corp.*, 315 F.3d 264, 271 n.2 (4th Cir. 2002) (quoting *Mentavlos v. Anderson*, 249 F.3d 301, 312 n.4 (4th Cir. 2001)). Accordingly, we need not engage this argument further. [—39—]

III.

For the reasons explained above, we affirm the judgment of the district court granting summary judgment to DMCC.

AFFIRMED

United States Court of Appeals
for the Fourth Circuit

No. 14-1698

HUNTINGTON INGALLS INDUS., INC.
VS.
EASON

On Petition for Review of an Order of the Benefits
Review Board

Decided: June 2, 2015

Citation: 788 F.3d 118, 3 Adm. R. 214 (4th Cir. 2015).

Before **NIEMEYER** and **FLOYD**, Circuit Judges, and
HAMILTON, Senior Circuit Judge.

[—3—] HAMILTON, Senior Circuit Judge:

Huntington Ingalls Industries, Inc. (HI) petitions for review of the May 16, 2014 decision of the Benefits Review Board (BRB) upholding the August 16, 2013 decision of Administrative Law Judge (ALJ) Daniel Sarno, Jr. (Judge Sarno) granting the claim of Ricky Eason (Eason) for temporary partial disability under the Longshore and Harbor Workers' Compensation Act (LHWCA or the Act), 33 U.S.C. §§ 901-950.[1] For the reasons that follow, we grant the petition for review and remand the case to the BRB to enter an order dismissing Eason's claim for temporary partial disability under the LHWCA.

I

A

The LHWCA establishes a federal worker's compensation system for employees injured, disabled, or killed in the course of covered maritime employment. *See generally id.* § 907 (medical services and supplies to treat injury), *id.* § 908 (compensation for disability), *id.* § 909 (compensation for [—4—] death). Like

---

[1] Eason's filing of his disability claim brought the Director of the Office of Workers' Compensation Programs (OWCP), United States Department of Labor (the Director) into the case as an interested party. *Cf. Ingalls Shipbuilding, Inc. v. Dir., OWCP*, 519 U.S. 248, 262–70 (1997) (holding that the Director may appear as respondent in the courts of appeals when review is sought of a BRB decision).

other worker's "compensation regimes—limited liability for employers; certain, prompt recovery for employees—the LHWCA requires that employers pay [disability] benefits voluntarily, without formal administrative proceedings." *Roberts v. Sea-Land Servs., Inc.*, 132 S. Ct. 1350, 1354 (2012); *see also* 33 U.S.C. § 904 ("Every employer shall be liable for and shall secure the payment to his employees of the compensation payable under sections 907, 908, and 909 of this title.").

The LHWCA defines "[d]isability," in pertinent part, as "incapacity because of injury to earn the wages which the employee was receiving at the time of injury in the same or any other employment." 33 U.S.C. § 902(10). Four different categories of disabilities are set forth in the LHWCA: (1) permanent total disability; (2) temporary total disability; (3) permanent partial disability; and (4) temporary partial disability. *Id.* § 908(a)–(c), (e).

No standard is set forth in the LHWCA to determine the degree of a disability (total or partial) or the duration of a disability (permanent or temporary). Because disability under the LHWCA is an economic concept, *see Metro. Stevedore Co. v. Rambo*, 515 U.S. 291, 297 (1995) ("Disability under the LHWCA, defined in terms of wage-earning capacity . . . , is in essence an economic, not a medical, concept."), the degree of a [—5—] disability cannot be measured by medical condition alone, *Nardella v. Campbell Mach. Inc.*, 525 F.2d 46, 49 (9th Cir. 1975). Consideration must be given to the claimant's age, education, experience, mentality, ability to work as well as the extent of the physical injury, and the availability of suitable alternative employment. *Fleetwood v. Newport News Shipbuilding & Dry Dock Co.*, 776 F.2d 1225, 1227 n.2 (4th Cir. 1985). With regard to duration, a claimant remains temporarily disabled until he reaches "maximum medical improvement." *Stevens v. Dir., OWCP*, 909 F.2d 1256, 1259 (9th Cir. 1990). Maximum medical improvement marks the time where "normal and natural healing is no longer likely" to occur. *Pac. Ship Repair & Fabrication Inc. v. Dir., OWCP [Benge]*, 687 F.3d 1182, 1185 (9th Cir. 2012) (citation and internal quotation marks omitted). Thus, the "maximum medical improvement date 'triggers a change in the classification of a claimant's disability from temporary to permanent.'" *Id.* (quoting *Haw. Stevedores, Inc. v. Ogawa*, 608 F.3d 642, 653 (9th Cir. 2010)).

Which of the four categories of disability the claimant falls in dictates the amount of compensation paid to him by his employer. A permanently totally disabled employee is entitled to weekly compensation amounting to two-thirds of his pre-injury average weekly wage for as long as he remains permanently totally disabled. 33 U.S.C. § 908(a); *Roberts*, 132 S. Ct. at [—6—] 1354. The compensation payable for a temporary total disability remains fixed at that two-thirds figure, while weekly compensation for a permanent total disability is annually adjusted to reflect increases to the national average weekly wage. 33 U.S.C. § 910(f).

The LHWCA recognizes two types of permanent partial disability. One, commonly referred to as "unscheduled" or "non-scheduled" compensation, is based on the employee's actual loss of wage-earning capacity and, like total disability, is compensated at two-thirds of the difference between the employee's average weekly wage at the time of injury and his post-injury wage-earning capacity. *Id.* § 908(c)(21). The other, commonly referred to as "scheduled" compensation, covers specified body parts, and pays a fixed number of weeks of compensation at two-thirds of the employee's average weekly wage. *Id.* § 908(c)(1)-(17), (20). These scheduled amounts compensate for a presumed (not actual) loss of wage-earning capacity. *Korineck v. Gen. Dynamics Corp. Elec. Boat Div.*, 835 F.2d 42, 43-44 (2d Cir. 1987). For example, the loss of a leg under the schedule entitles a claimant to 288 weeks of compensation at two-thirds of his average weekly wage. 33 U.S.C. § 908(c)(2). For a partial loss of the use of a leg, which includes knee injuries, the number of weeks is multiplied by the percentage of loss. *Id.* § 908(c)(19). Thus, a claimant [—7—] with a 50% loss of the use of his leg would receive compensation for 144 weeks. Notably, a claimant who is permanently partially disabled due to a scheduled injury cannot choose to be compensated for his actual loss of wage-earning capacity under § 908(c)(21), even though the compensation under § 908(c)(21) potentially may be greater than the compensation paid under the schedule. *See Potomac Electric Power Co. [PEPCO] v. Dir., OWCP*, 449 U.S. 268, 270-71 (1980) (holding that a claimant who was permanently partially disabled due to a scheduled injury could not choose to be compensated for his actual loss of wage-earning capacity under § 908(c)(21) rather than being compensated for his loss as provided by the schedule).

Compensation for temporary partial disability is "two-thirds of the difference between the injured employee's average weekly wages before the injury and his wage-earning capacity after the injury in the same or another employment." 33 U.S.C. § 908(e). Under the LHWCA, temporary partial disability compensation cannot be paid for a period longer than five years. *Id.*

Once the claimant is classified in a particular disability category, he need not necessarily remain in such category. *Benge*, 687 F.3d at 1185. This is so because permanent/temporary and total/partial are fluid concepts and not "cast in stone." *Id.* at 1186. Reclassification of a disability requires a [—8—] showing of a "change[] [in] circumstances." *Id.* at 1185; *see also* 33 U.S.C. § 922 (providing that, with certain time limits, "on the ground of a change in conditions . . . , the deputy commissioner may . . . , whether or not a compensation order has been issued . . . , review a compensation case . . . [and] issue a new compensation order which may terminate, continue, reinstate, increase, or decrease such compensation, or award compensation"). For example, a claimant with a permanent partial disability may become permanently totally disabled or temporarily totally disabled if his injury worsens and renders him permanently or temporarily totally disabled. *See Benge*, 687 F.3d at 1185-87 (holding that permanent partial disability claimant became temporarily totally disabled following surgery to treat injury). Likewise, a claimant with a permanent total disability may be reclassified to having a permanent partial disability if suitable alternative employment becomes available. *See Stevens*, 909 F.2d at 1259-60 (holding that a permanent total disability changes to a permanent partial disability when suitable alternative employment becomes available to claimant). It is also possible that a disability deemed permanent and total or permanent and partial may improve "due to a remarkable recovery, advances in medical science, or other reasons" such that the claimant may be recharacterized as temporarily totally [—9—] disabled or temporarily partially disabled. *Benge*, 687 F.3d at 1185.

B

On September 28, 2008, Eason injured his right knee while employed as a pipe fitter at Newport News Shipbuilding and Dry Dock Company (NNS) in Newport News, Virginia.[2] He went to the medical clinic at NNS on October 1, 2008, complaining of pain in his right knee. The injury, which was diagnosed on October 14, 2008 as a torn meniscus requiring surgery, kept Eason completely out of work from October 2, 2008 through June 28, 2009. As a result, HI paid Eason temporary total disability benefits for this period.

On June 29, 2009, Eason returned to work at NNS full-time as a pipe fitter. On September 23, 2009, Eason was evaluated at Tidewater Physical Therapy and given a 14% lower extremity permanent impairment rating. Sometime in October 2009, Dr. David Hoang (Dr. Hoang), Eason's treating orthopedic surgeon, "signed off" on the 14% rating, and, thus, Eason reached maximum medical improvement for purposes of determining his eligibility for permanent partial disability compensation. (J.A. 180). Based on the 14% lower-extremity permanent impairment rating, HI [—10—] paid Eason from October 16, 2009 through May 17, 2010, and from May 19, 2010 through July 25, 2010,

40.28 weeks of scheduled compensation for permanent partial disability at $992.29 (two-thirds of his pre-injury average weekly wage of $1,488.43) per week. *See* 33 U.S.C. § 908(c)(2) (loss of leg provides 288 weeks of scheduled compensation); *id.* § (c)(19) (permanent partial loss "may be for proportionate loss or loss of use of the member").[3] Thus, for approximately seven months, Eason received scheduled permanent partial disability compensation in addition to his regular weekly salary for performing his duties as a pipefitter at NNS.

Eason continued to work full-time as a pipe fitter through May 17, 2010. On May 18, 2010, Eason met with Dr. Hoang and reported that "his left knee was acting up on him and his right knee was getting stiff intermittently, especially after sitting for awhile." (J.A. 180). Dr. Hoang noted "mild soreness" in the right knee and "tenderness" in the left knee, (J.A. 83), and he put Eason on light duty restrictions for both knees. These [—11—] light duty restrictions prevented Eason from performing his duties as a pipe fitter.

On his June 3, 2010 visit with Dr. Hoang, Eason reported that his left knee "still hurts" and that his right knee was "improving." (J.A. 83). Dr. Hoang advised Eason to "continue with the same work restrictions." (J.A. 84). On July, 16, 2010, Eason reported to Dr. Hoang that his right knee was "doing well" but the left knee was "grinding." (J.A. 84). Dr. Hoang directed Eason to "continue with the light duty [restrictions]." (J.A. 85). Over the next month, Eason's condition improved, and he returned to work full-time as a pipe fitter at NNS on August 10, 2010.

Between May 19, 2010 and August 9, 2010, NNS did not offer Eason light-duty employment within his restrictions. In

---

[2] At the time of Eason's injury, NNS was owned by Northrop Grumman Shipbuilding, Inc. (NGS). In 2011, HI purchased NNS from NGS. For ease of reference, we will refer to NGS as HI.

[3] HI paid 40.28 weeks of compensation for the scheduled injury, rather than 40.32 weeks (288 weeks x .14 = 40.32 weeks). Although the record under review is unclear as to why the difference exists, it may well be because HI paid an intervening day (May 18, 2010) of compensation for temporary total disability. In any event, the .04 difference is not at issue in this appeal.

addition, during this period, Eason did not seek suitable alternative employment within the relevant labor market.

C

Eason brought a claim against HI for temporary total disability or, alternatively, temporary partial disability for the May 19, 2010 through August 9, 2010 time period. In support of his claim, Eason argued that during this time period he "was not at maximum medical improvement." (J.A. 13). He posited that he was "undergoing ongoing medical treatment" and "under temporary [work] restrictions." (J.A. 13). Because no suitable [—12—] alternative employment was available, he argued he was entitled to temporary total disability compensation. Alternatively, Eason argued that, even if HI's alternative employment data were entitled to "any weight," he was entitled to temporary partial disability compensation because his pre-injury salary exceeded the salary of any alternative employment available. (J.A. 13). Eason posited that, even though he received scheduled permanent partial disability compensation for his knee injury, such compensation did not prevent the recovery of additional compensation for a temporary partial disability due to a flare up of that injury. In response, HI argued that Eason reached maximum medical improvement in October 2009. Because Eason reached maximum medical improvement at that time and received permanent partial disability compensation under the schedule, HI posited that he was not entitled to any additional temporary compensation—either total or partial—under the Supreme Court's decision in *PEPCO*. HI stressed that Eason's scheduled compensation for his knee injury presumed his actual loss of wage-earning capacity for that injury, such that any temporary compensation (total or partial) sought for a flare up of that injury already was covered by the payments made under the schedule.

A hearing was held before ALJ Richard Malamphy (Judge Malamphy). In his decision, Judge Malamphy found that Eason [—13—] reached maximum medical improvement in October 2009. He also found that the evidence did not support Eason's claim of temporary total disability. With regard to temporary partial disability, relying on the Supreme Court's decision in *PEPCO*, Judge Malamphy ruled that Eason's disability compensation for his knee injury was limited to the amount required by the schedule. He explained that "[t]he Act presumes that the scheduled award fully compensates claimant for any loss in wage-earning capacity" and, "[t]herefore, any temporary loss of wage earning capacity Claimant suffered is not compensable in addition to the scheduled award." (J.A. 184). In other words, Judge Malamphy held that the scheduled compensation award compensated Eason for his knee injury and that Eason was not entitled to additional compensation for any temporary partial loss of wage-earning capacity for that same injury.

On appeal, the BRB vacated Judge Malamphy's decision. The BRB affirmed Judge Malamphy's finding that Eason reached maximum medical improvement in October 2009. The BRB ruled, however, that this finding did not preclude the recovery of temporary partial disability compensation for Eason's knee injury. Referring to language in *PEPCO* that states "that a scheduled injury can give rise to an award for permanent total disability" and that "once it is determined that an employee is totally disabled the schedule becomes irrelevant," 449 U.S. at 277 n.17, [—14—] the BRB found that "the fact that permanent partial disability benefits were fully paid under the schedule is not determinative of a claimant's entitlement thereafter to permanent total, temporary total, or temporary partial disability benefits." (J.A. 188-89). Consequently, the BRB remanded the case to the ALJ to determine whether Eason's work restrictions from May 19, 2010 through August 19, 2010 prevented him from performing his usual work. If they did, the BRB stated, Eason would have established a *prima facie* case of temporary total disability. *See Newport News Shipbuilding & Dry Dock Co. v. Dir., OWCP*, 315 F.3d 286, 292 (4th Cir. 2002) (noting that an LHWCA "claimant must first establish a *prima facie* case by demonstrating an inability to return to prior employment due to a work-related injury"). The burden would then shift to HI to establish the availability of suitable alternative employment that Eason was capable of performing. *See id.* (outlining burden shift). According to the BRB, HI could meet its burden by showing that suitable alternative employment was available to Eason in the relevant labor market. *See id.* at 293 (noting that an employer meets its burden by demonstrating, *inter alia*, that suitable alternative employment was available in the relevant labor market). Thus, on remand, the BRB required the ALJ to determine if HI met its burden, such that its obligation to pay disability benefits would be reduced or eliminated. *See id.* ("Under our **[—15—]** precedent, if the employer meets its burden, its obligation to pay disability benefits is either reduced or eliminated, unless the disabled employee shows that he diligently but unsuccessfully sought appropriate employment." (citation and internal quotation marks omitted)).

On remand, the case was reassigned to Judge Sarno. Judge Sarno found that Eason was not able to return to his usual work from May 19, 2010 through August 9, 2010. However, Judge Sarno found that HI had established the availability of suitable alternative employment for 32 hours per week at $7.25 per hour. Judge Sarno concluded that Eason was temporarily partially disabled from May 19, 2010 through August 20, 2010 and entitled to compensation of $845.82 per week (two-thirds of the difference between $1,488.43 per week, Eason's average weekly wage at the time of the injury, and $219.70 per week, Eason's residual wage-earning capacity based on the national average weekly wage in 2008, the year of Eason's injury).[4] **[—16—]**

---

[4] Judge Sarno noted that HI had established that Eason had a wage-earning capacity under § 908(e) of $232.00 per week in 2010. This amount was adjusted downward to $219.70 per week in order to account for inflation between 2008 and 2010. *See Walker v. Wash. Metro. Area Transit Auth.,* 793 F.2d 319, 321 n.2 (D.C. Cir. 1986) ("In order to make a fair comparison between wages, the Board looks to the amount the post-injury job paid at the time of the claimant's injury. This allows the Board to compare the wages without worrying about the effect of inflation."); *Quan v. Marine Power & Equip. Co.,* 30 BRBS 124, 1996

HI appealed Judge Sarno's decision to the BRB, arguing once again that Eason was precluded from receiving any additional compensation in addition to that received under the schedule. The BRB found that it had already rejected that argument in its earlier decision. It also affirmed, as unchallenged on appeal, Judge Sarno's findings that Eason was unable to perform his usual work from May 19, 2010 through August 20, 2010 and that HI had established suitable available alternative employment. Consequently, it affirmed Judge Sarno's award of compensation for temporary partial disability from May 19 through August 20, 2010.[5] It is from this BRB decision that HI filed its timely petition for review.

II

We review the BRB's decision for errors of law and to ascertain whether the BRB adhered to its statutorily-mandated standard for reviewing the ALJ's factual findings. *Gilchrist v. Newport News Shipbuilding & Dry Dock Co.,* 135 F.3d 915, 918 (4th **[—17—]** Cir. 1998). As to the BRB's interpretation of the LHWCA, our review is *de novo* because the BRB is not a policy-making agency and, thus, its statutory interpretation is not entitled to any special deference from us. *Id.* However, the Director's reasonable interpretation of the LHWCA is entitled to some deference. *See Norfolk Shipbuilding & Drydock Corp. v. Hord,* 193 F.3d 797, 801 (4th Cir. 1999) ("We note that this is the result advocated by the Director of the Office of Workers' Compensation Programs, to whose reasonable interpretation of the LHWCA we accord some deference.").

WL 581786, at *4 (BRBS 1996) ("Sections 8(c)(21) and 8(h) (Continued) **[—16—]** require that a claimant's post-injury wage earning capacity be adjusted to account for inflation to represent the wages that the post-injury job paid at the time of claimant's injury.").

[5] Because he returned to work on August 10, 2010, Eason concedes that Judge Sarno (and the BRB) erroneously awarded temporary partial disability compensation from August 10, 2010 through August 20, 2010.

In its petition for review, HI challenges Judge Sarno's award of temporary partial disability benefits from May 19, 2010 through August 20, 2010. HI argues that a claimant, like Eason, who receives scheduled compensation for a permanent partial disability cannot subsequently receive additional temporary partial disability compensation because the receipt of scheduled permanent partial disability compensation for an injury includes any temporary partial disability compensation. Moreover, HI reads the LHWCA and *PEPCO* as precluding a claimant, like Eason, with a scheduled injury from receiving any additional temporary disability compensation—either total or partial—for the same injury.[6] Eason counters by arguing that receipt of scheduled [—18—] permanent partial disability compensation for an injury is not determinative of entitlement to temporary partial disability compensation for the same injury. According to Eason, *PEPCO* is not particularly helpful to HI because it only dealt with a permanent partial disability claim and not a claim, as here, for temporary partial disability. He suggests that his claim for temporary partial disability is viable because his knee injury flared up, preventing him from working as a pipe fitter from May 19, 2010 through August 9, 2010, though he apparently concedes that suitable alternative employment was available during that time. He also posits that his argument is supported by *PEPCO* because the Court there recognized the availability of total disability compensation for a scheduled injury.

The Director, while agreeing with the result urged by HI, takes a middle course. He agrees with HI that a scheduled permanent partial disability claimant cannot receive additional temporary partial disability compensation for the injury underlying the permanent partial disability compensation

---

[6] HI concedes that a claimant who receives scheduled (Continued) [—18—] permanent partial disability compensation is not precluded from subsequently receiving permanent total disability compensation. *See* Petitioner's Reply Br. at 2-3 (noting that scheduled compensation is "exclusive to all other forms of compensation, *except* for permanent total disability under 33 U.S.C. § 908(a) of the Act").

because such temporary compensation essentially is duplicative to the [—19—] scheduled compensation. He also agrees with HI that a claimant who receives scheduled permanent partial disability compensation is not precluded from subsequently receiving permanent total disability compensation. However, the Director disagrees with HI that a claimant who receives scheduled permanent partial disability compensation for an injury is precluded from receiving temporary total disability compensation for the same injury. According to the Director, the LHWCA's statutory framework supports his construction of the Act and nothing in *PEPCO* precludes reclassification of a scheduled permanent partial disability to a temporary total disability. However, because Eason's injury has remained permanent and partial, the Director posits that reclassification of his injury is not warranted, and, thus, Eason is precluded from recovering any additional disability compensation for his knee injury.

We agree with the position espoused by the Director, which we accord some deference. *Hord*, 193 F.3d at 801. Eason suffered a scheduled injury. Thus, his permanent partial disability compensation is set by the schedule. *PEPCO*, 449 U.S. at 270-71. Such scheduled compensation is presumed to cover Eason's actual *partial* loss of wage-earning capacity due to that *partial* disability. *See ITO Corp. of Balt. v. Green*, 185 F.3d 239, 242 n.3 (4th Cir. 1999) ("The presumed effect of scheduled disabilities on a claimant's wage-earning capacity has been set [—20—] by Congress within a fairly narrow range. Benefits are payable for a specific duration regardless of the actual impact of the disability on the claimant's prospects of returning to longshore (or any other) work."); *Bethlehem Steel Co. v. Cardillo*, 229 F.2d 735, 736 (2d Cir. 1956) (noting that, "as to any schedule loss, there is a conclusive presumption of loss or reduction of wage-earning capacity"). Once Eason's permanent partial disability compensation is set under the schedule, he is not entitled to receive *additional* disability compensation for the *same* scheduled injury unless the circumstances warrant a reclassification of that disability to permanent total or temporary total. *See, e.g., Benge*, 687 F.3d at

1185-87 (permitting claimant, who received unscheduled permanent partial disability compensation, to receive temporary total disability compensation because subsequent surgery rendered her temporarily totally disabled); *Hord*, 193 F.3d at 801-02 (allowing claimant, who was paid permanent partial disability compensation under the schedule to recover temporary total disability compensation); *DM & IR Ry. Co. v. Dir., OWCP*, 151 F.3d 1120, 1122-23 (8th Cir. 1998) (allowing a claimant who received permanent partial disability compensation to subsequently recover disability compensation for permanent total disability); *cf. PEPCO*, 449 U.S. at 277 n.17 ("Indeed, since the § 8(c) schedule applies only in cases of permanent partial disability, once it is [—21—] determined that an employee is totally disabled the schedule becomes irrelevant."). This is so because, once a disability becomes *total*, it makes no sense to apply a presumption designed to approximate a claimant's permanent *partial* disability compensation. A permanent or temporary total disability presumes the loss of *all* wage-earning capacity, while a permanent partial disability involves only a *partial* loss. *See Benge*, 687 F.3d at 1187 (noting that any total disability presupposes the loss of all wage-earning capacity). Thus, an increase in the disability compensation for the change from permanent partial to either permanent total or temporary total is warranted to account for the additional actual loss in wage-earning capacity. Such a conclusion comports with the basic purpose of the LHWCA, which is to provide compensation for the actual loss of wage-earning capacity. *See Korineck*, 835 F.2d at 44 (noting that the purpose of the LHWCA is "to provide work benefits for lost earning capacity.").

In contrast, in the case of a scheduled permanent partial disability that allegedly changes to a temporary partial disability because the claimant's injury flared up, there is no additional loss of wage-earning capacity. The claimant's loss of wage-earning capacity already is accounted for under the schedule. In other words, the scheduled compensation accounts for all the lost wages due the claimant under the LHWCA. To [—22—] hold otherwise would allow for an impermissible double recovery. *Cf. id.* ("Denying additional [scheduled] benefits to one already receiving benefits for total permanent disability serves to avoid double recoveries."). Like the claimant in *Korineck*, whose scheduled compensation claim was subsumed by the compensation he already was receiving for permanent total disability, Eason's temporary partial disability claim is subsumed by the compensation he received under the schedule. *Id.* at 43-44.

To be sure, in the case before us, there is no record evidence supporting a reclassification of Eason's disability to a permanent total or temporary total disability. His disability has remained permanent and partial since September 2008. His scheduled compensation is presumed to cover his actual loss of wage-earning capacity for any flare up of his knee injury that did not prevent him from working in some type of suitable alternative employment. *Green*, 185 F.3d at 242 n.3. Since Eason does not allege that the flare up rendered him permanently or temporarily totally disabled, he is not entitled to any additional disability compensation for his knee injury.

Eason's argument that the LHWCA permits the recovery of additional temporary partial disability compensation under the circumstances of this case is unpersuasive. First, his argument, if accepted, permits an impermissible double recovery. [—23—] He was compensated for his actual loss of wage-earning capacity due to his injury under the schedule and now he is seeking additional compensation for the same injury. We see nothing in LHWCA that permits such a double recovery. *See Port of Portland v. Dir., OWCP*, 932 F.2d 836, 839 n.1 (9th Cir. 1991) (noting that, under the LHWCA, "an employee may not obtain a double recovery for a disability for which compensation has already been paid"); *cf. Strachan Shipping Co. v. Nash*, 782 F.2d 513, 515 (5th Cir. 1986) (*en banc*) (noting that the "credit doctrine, created by the BRB for the singular purpose of avoiding double recoveries, provides that an employer is not liable for any portion of an employee's disability for which the employee has actually received compensation under the LHWCA"). Second, Eason's construction of the LHWCA defeats the intent of the schedule in the Act. The schedule is designed to provide quick compensation for certain permanent partial disabilities and, simultaneously, to fix the employer's liability exposure. *See PEPCO*, 449 U.S. at 282 ("The use of a schedule of fixed benefits as an exclusive remedy in certain cases is consistent with the employees' interest in receiving a prompt and certain recovery for their industrial injuries as well as with the employers' interest in having their contingent liabilities identified as precisely and as early as possible."); *see also Travelers Ins. Co. v. Cardillo*, 225 F.2d 137, 144 (2d Cir. 1955) (noting that [—24—] schedule "conclusively establishe[s]" the loss of wage-earning capacity and "its extent"). Yet, under Eason's construction of the LHWCA, the employer's liability exposure is anything but fixed. Rather, the liability exposure is subject to increase essentially any time a scheduled claimant is placed on temporary work restrictions. Such a construction of the LHWCA makes little sense.[7]

We also note that the Director understandably rejects HI's interpretation of the LHWCA because it forecloses the receipt of temporary total disability compensation following the receipt of scheduled disability compensation. HI's interpretation of the LHWCA has two flaws. First, it is inconsistent with *Benge* and *Hord*, where the permanent partial claimants were permitted to receive temporary total disability compensation after proper reclassification of their respective disabilities. *Benge*, 687 F.3d at 1185-87; *Hord*, 193 F.3d at 802. Second, HI's interpretation runs counter to the language of the LHWCA, which says that permanent partial disability compensation (scheduled or unscheduled)

shall be paid "in addition to" the compensation [—25—] paid for a "temporary total disability." 33 U.S.C. § 908(c). This language contains no temporal limitation. Thus, such additional temporary total disability compensation can be paid before the permanent partial disability compensation (for example, as in this case, Eason received temporary total disability compensation for his injury before receiving scheduled compensation for the same injury) or after (for example, as in *Benge*, where the claimant received temporary total disability compensation for her injury after receiving unscheduled compensation for the same injury). The receipt of such additional temporary total disability compensation ensures that the claimant is compensated for his actual loss in wage-earning capacity (including the loss *not* presumed by the schedule) and, thus, fulfills the basic purpose of the LHWCA. *See Korineck*, 835 F.2d at 44 (noting that the purpose of the LHWCA is "to provide work benefits for lost earning capacity"). Therefore, HI's construction of the LHWCA is inconsistent with the case law and thwarts the basic purpose of the LHWCA.

We realize that the schedule created by Congress allows for overcompensation in some instances and undercompensation in others. For example, a claimant with a scheduled injury may be compensated even though he never misses a day of work and, thus, incurs no actual wage loss whatsoever. At the same time, the schedule may undercompensate a claimant whose loss of wage [—26—] earning capacity may be greater than that compensated under the schedule. If a claimant who loses a hand only earns 50% of his pre-injury salary after reaching maximum medical improvement, the claimant would not, after 9.4 years, be compensated under the schedule as much as he would have been for an unscheduled injury. As recognized by the Supreme Court in *PEPCO*, such inequities simply are a manifestation of the system created by Congress which we are not at liberty to disturb. *See* 449 U.S. at 282-83 (noting that "requiring resort to the schedule may produce certain incongruous results" because, on the one hand, "even though a scheduled injury may have no actual effect on

---

[7] Of course, nothing prevents a claimant who is receiving scheduled permanent partial disability compensation from seeking additional compensation to reflect a higher percentage of *permanent* loss of the relevant body part due to the aggravation of the injury that gave rise to the scheduled compensation. *See New Haven Terminal Corp. v. Lake*, 337 F.3d 261, 268-69 (2d Cir. 2003) (discussing the interplay of the aggravation rule and the credit doctrine).

an employee's capacity to perform a particular job or to maintain a prior level of income, compensation in the schedule amount must be paid," while on the other hand, "the schedule may seriously undercompensate some employees"); *id.* at 284 (noting that the fact that the schedule "leads to seemingly unjust results in particular cases does not give judges a license to disregard it" where Congress employed "compelling statutory language"); *see also Green*, 185 F.3d at 242 n.3 ("Depending on one's point of view, this approach could reasonably be seen as either tending to overcompensate claimants with non-scheduled disabilities, or as under compensating those receiving payments pursuant to the schedule. Nonetheless, despite its inevitable inequities and the unwieldiness of its application, this aspect of the system [—27—] apparently functions in the manner intended by Congress, as evidenced by its being left essentially undisturbed since its enactment in 1927.").[8]

Finally, we reject both Eason's and HI's interpretation of *PEPCO*.[9] Eason interprets *PEPCO* as supporting his argument that a claimant who is receiving scheduled compensation for a permanent partial disability may receive additional compensation for temporary partial disability due to the same injury. HI's interpretation of *PEPCO* is quite different. It interprets the case as foreclosing a claimant who is receiving scheduled compensation for an injury from ever receiving temporary (total or partial) disability compensation for that injury.

---

[8] Of course, Eason is on the overcompensation end of the equation. He was awarded actual partial wage loss for the May 19 through August 20, 2010 time period at a compensation rate of $845.82 per week (two thirds of the difference between his average weekly wage of $1,488.43 and his residual wage-earning capacity of $219.70 per week). Thus, Eason would receive $11,237.22 in actual partial wage loss compensation. By contrast, Eason's scheduled award entitled him to $40,009.13 in compensation (40.32 weeks x $992.29 per week). Thus, his scheduled award paid him $28,771.91 more for a presumed loss of wage-earning capacity than he would have been entitled to for his actual loss.

[9] The BRB's interpretation of *PEPCO* is in line with Eason's interpretation of that case.

In *PEPCO*, the Supreme Court addressed whether a claimant who was permanently partially disabled due to a scheduled injury could choose to be compensated for his actual loss of wage- [—28—] earning capacity under § 908(c)(21), rather than being compensated for his presumed loss as provided by the schedule. 449 U.S. at 270.[10] The Court held that the LHWCA did not authorize such an election, and, therefore, a claimant's recovery for a scheduled injury "must be limited by the statutory schedule." *Id.* at 271. The Court focused on the language of § 908(c)(21), which calls for the payment of actual loss of wage-earning capacity "'[i]n all other cases'" of permanent partial disability. *Id.* at 274 (quoting 33 U.S.C. § 908(c)(21)). The Court interpreted this language to mean all permanent partial disability cases not specifically enumerated in the schedule, namely § 908(c)(1) to (20). *Id.* Thus, the Court held that injuries or disabilities covered by the schedule must be compensated according to the schedule, whereas permanent partial disabilities not covered by the schedule are subject to compensation based on the actual loss of wage-earning capacity. *Id.* at 278-82.

The Supreme Court in *PEPCO* rejected the argument that its construction of the LHWCA would not fulfill the remedial [—29—] purposes of the Act and that it would produce anomalous results that Congress probably did not intend. *Id.* at 280-84. The Supreme Court pointed out that the LHWCA represents a compromise between the interests of employers and employees. *Id.* at 282. The Court stated that the use of fixed scheduled benefits as an exclusive remedy "is consistent with the employees' interest in receiving a prompt and certain recovery for their industrial injuries as well as with the employers' interest in having their contingent liabilities identified as precisely and as early

---

[10] As noted earlier, unscheduled permanent partial disability awards are based on the actual loss of wage-earning capacity. 33 U.S.C. § 908(c)(21). The claimant in *PEPCO* sought wage-loss compensation under § 908(c)(21) because his loss of wage-earning capacity was over 40% and § 908(c)(21) would have provided far more compensation than the schedule otherwise allowed. 449 U.S. at 271.

as possible." *Id*. As noted above, the Court also recognized the incongruous results which the schedule could produce by over or undercompensating an employee for his actual loss in wage-earning capacity. *Id*. at 282-84. The Court stated, however, that this fact did not give it license to disregard the "compelling statutory language" and that it was up to Congress to reexamine the statute if anomalies were occurring frequently. *Id*. at 284.

Eason's interpretation of *PEPCO* is flawed. The Supreme Court in *PEPCO* did not imply, as he posits, that a claimant who is receiving scheduled compensation for a permanent partial disability can receive additional compensation for temporary partial disability due to the same injury. The Court merely said that a scheduled injury does not preclude an award of total disability. *Id*. at 277 n.17. This is not surprising since a [—30—] total disability increases the claimant's actual loss in wage-earning capacity. In any event, just because the Court cited with approval the receipt of total disability compensation following a scheduled injury, it does not follow that the Court would countenance the duplicative recovery that occurs when a claimant receives temporary partial disability compensation for an injury that the claimant already has received (or is receiving) scheduled compensation. As we noted above, the LHWCA does not permit such duplicative recoveries. *See Port of Portland*, 932 F.2d at 839 n.1 (noting that the LHWCA is designed to avoid double recoveries for the same injuries).

HI's interpretation of *PEPCO* also is flawed. The Court in *PEPCO* did not hold, as HI posits, that a claimant who is receiving scheduled compensation for an injury is foreclosed from receiving temporary (total or partial) disability compensation for that injury. Rather, as noted above, the Court simply held that a permanent partial disability claimant could not choose between the schedule and § 908(c)(21). 449 U.S. at 278-82. Thus, the Court did not address whether the receipt of scheduled compensation forecloses the receipt of additional temporary disability compensation, and we read nothing

in *PEPCO* lending support for HI's interpretation of the case.

In sum, the *PEPCO* decision is not outcome determinative for either Eason or HI. The case addressed a discrete issue, and [—31—] the reasons advanced by Eason and HI for an expansive reading of the decision are not compelling. *Cf. Korineck*, 835 F.2d at 44 (noting the "narrow issue" decided by the *PEPCO* Court).

III

For the reasons stated herein, we grant the petition for review and remand the case to the BRB to enter an order dismissing Eason's claim for temporary partial disability under the LHWCA.

PETITION GRANTED

United States Court of Appeals
for the Fourth Circuit

No. 14-1950

RECOVERY LTD. PARTNERSHIP

vs.

THE WRECKED AND ABANDONED VESSEL S.S.
CENTRAL AMERICA

Appeal from the United States District Court for the
Eastern District of Virginia, at Norfolk

Decided: June 22, 2015

Citation: 790 F.3d 522, 3 Adm. R. 224 (4th Cir. 2015).

Before **NIEMEYER, DUNCAN,** and **THACKER,** Circuit
Judges.

[—3—] **NIEMEYER,** Circuit Judge:

The S.S. *Central America*, loaded with tons of gold en route from San Francisco to New York, sank in a hurricane off the coast of South Carolina in 1857. Columbus-America Discovery Group ("Columbus-America"), acting as the agent for Recovery Limited Partnership ("Recovery Limited"), discovered the wreck in the 1980s, and the district court subsequently granted Columbus-America salvage rights.

For over two decades, Richard T. Robol and Robol Law Office, LLC (collectively, "Robol") represented Columbus-America in the proceedings to establish its salvage rights. During the same period, Robol also defended Columbus-America, Recovery Limited, and several other related business entities, including EZRA, Inc., against claims made by others for portions of the gold recovered from the sunken vessel. In addition, Robol leased commercial property in Columbus, Ohio, to EZRA, where documents relating to the salvage operation were stored.

In June 2013, an Ohio court placed several of the companies into receivership and ordered the Receiver to collect their property from all persons holding such property, including the companies' attorneys. The Receiver gave notice of the order to Robol, and thereafter— in July and August 2013—Robol turned over 36 file cabinets of materials that he had accumulated as counsel and landlord. Robol also encouraged Milton T. [—4—] Butterworth, Jr., an officer of Columbus-America, to turn over to the Receiver photographs, videos, and other materials related to the salvage of the S.S. *Central America*.

After Robol withdrew as counsel for the companies, he filed a claim in this *in rem* admiralty action to obtain a salvage award for himself, alleging that he had provided voluntary assistance to the Receiver in turning over files and documents related to the salvage operation, which proved useful in the continuing salvage of the sunken vessel.

The district court dismissed Robol's claim for failure to state a claim, concluding that Robol had been obligated to return the files and documents to his former clients under the applicable rules of professional responsibility and principles of agency law and therefore that his act of returning the materials to his former clients was not a voluntary act, as would be required for him to obtain a salvage award.

We agree with the district court and affirm.

I

In the mid-1980s, Thomas G. Thompson undertook to locate the wreck of the S.S. *Central America* and to recover its cargo of gold, valued at approximately $1.2 million in 1857. To that end, he set up a series of related business entities, including Recovery Limited, which he created to finance the project; [—5—] Columbus-America, which he formed to locate and salvage the ship on Recovery Limited's behalf; Columbus Exploration, LLC, which he set up to market the recovered gold; and EZRA, which he set up to pay labor costs associated with Recovery Limited's employees and consultants.

After several years of searching, Columbus-America located the wrecked ship 160 miles off the coast of South Carolina. In 1987, with Robol as counsel of record, it commenced this *in rem* action in admiralty, and the district court subsequently granted Columbus-

America salvage rights in the ship and its cargo. Continuously from 1988 until 1991, Columbus-America conducted salvage operations, recovering large amounts of gold and other artifacts. Following two trials and two appeals, we determined in 1995 that Columbus-America was entitled to a salvage award of 90% of the value of the gold and artifacts recovered and that various insurance companies that had paid claims for portions of the lost gold were entitled to the remainder. *See Columbus-Am. Discovery Grp. v. Atl. Mut. Ins. Co.*, 56 F.3d 556, 568-75 (4th Cir. 1995). Columbus-America and the insurance companies thereafter divided the treasure *in specie*, and, in July 2000, the district court closed the case.

Several years later, minority investors and former employees who had assisted in locating the *S.S. Central America* and recovering its cargo initiated legal actions in Ohio state [—6—] court against Thompson and the related business entities to obtain portions of the award. Robol represented all of the defendants, including Recovery Limited, in these actions until he withdrew as counsel in June 2011. During the course of the proceedings, which were consolidated and removed to the United States District Court for the Southern District of Ohio, it was discovered that 500 gold coins belonging to the related business entities had disappeared. *See Williamson v. Recovery Ltd. P'ship*, 731 F.3d 608, 617, 1 Adm. R. 348, 353 (6th Cir. 2013). The district court ordered Thompson to appear to explain the coins' whereabouts, but Thompson failed to do so, and, in August 2012, the court issued a bench warrant for his arrest. Thompson then fled and became a fugitive. In April 2015, after the U.S. Marshals Service finally located and arrested Thompson in a hotel room in Florida, he pleaded guilty to criminal contempt for failing to appear in federal court. His assistant later testified that Thompson had smuggled the missing gold coins to Belize.

Because of Thompson's disappearance, the Court of Common Pleas of Franklin County, Ohio, placed Recovery Limited and Columbus Exploration into receivership in June 2013, appointing Ira Kane as the Receiver. By order dated June 14, 2013, the court directed "[a]ny person who has (or, as of the time of the filing of this Entry, had) any fiduciary duty towards the Companies, by virtue of being either an officer, former officer, [—7—] or person holding any asset, object or thing that is, or at the time of the filing of this Entry was, the property of the companies, or either of them, . . . to surrender to and transfer to said Receiver any and all such property." The court also directed the Receiver to "conduct such maritime operations that are designed to make a positive financial return for the companies."

Pursuant to the court's order, "the Receiver served notice on all of the companies' attorneys," including Robol, "to turn over all company files and other property in their possession." *Williamson v. Recovery Ltd. P'ship*, No. 2:06-CV-00292, 2014 WL 1884401, at *3 (S.D. Ohio May 9, 2014), *appeal docketed*, No. 14-4231 (6th Cir. Dec. 12, 2014). Thereafter, during the period between July 25 and August 1, 2013, the Receiver retrieved 36 file cabinets of records from Robol that had been stored at Robol's property at 433 West Sixth Avenue in Columbus, Ohio (the "West Sixth Avenue property"), a portion of which Robol had leased to EZRA. *Id.*

Before Robol turned over the records to the Receiver, the Ohio district court had ordered Robol and his clients to provide the plaintiffs' accountant with various categories of documents, including inventories of the recovered gold and records of downstream sales of the gold, which the accountant needed in order to prepare a report on the financial condition of the [—8—] defendant-entities. *Williamson*, 2014 WL 1884401, at *1. Because the court found that Robol's clients had repeatedly failed in good faith to comply with its order, it twice held them in contempt. *Id.* Robol similarly failed to turn over inventories and records of downstream sales that he had possessed, repeatedly telling the court incorrectly that he had already provided all of the relevant documents in his possession, when, in fact, there were multiple unproduced documents among the files that the Receiver retrieved from Robol in July and

August 2013. *Id.* at *2–4. The Ohio district court consequently granted the plaintiffs' motion for sanctions, finding that Robol had acted in bad faith and additionally that his conduct rose "beyond mere bad faith to the level of 'fraud on the court.'" *Id.* at*13. The court ordered Robol to reimburse the parties for the costs incurred "in discovering [the] missing inventories, and the amount expended in prosecuting [the] Motion." *Id.* at*15.

Also in furtherance of the Ohio Court of Common Pleas' June 14, 2013 receivership order, Recovery Limited, through the Receiver, resumed salvage operations in the *S.S. Central America.* Between January and May 2014, Recovery Limited filed motions in this *in rem* action, which had been closed for nearly 14 years, seeking to reopen the case, to substitute it for Columbus-America as the real party in interest, and to declare [—9—] that it was the legal owner of salvage rights in the *S.S. Central America.* Recovery Limited also commenced a separate *in rem* action against the wreck and its cargo to declare itself the salvor for future salvage operations and to obtain a salvage award for all newly recovered gold and artifacts. The district court entered orders dated July 9, 2014, reopening this *in rem* action, granting Recovery Limited's motion to substitute itself as the salvor, and consolidating the two *in rem* actions under the original action's case number. At approximately the same time, on July 8, 2014, the court granted Robol's motion to withdraw as counsel of record for Columbus-America.

Robol now alleges that Recovery Limited and its related business entities owe him $2,092,882.17 plus interest in unpaid legal fees and that EZRA owes him $68,371.93 in rent that it failed to pay for the West Sixth Avenue property. To recover these amounts, Robol filed a "Verified Proof of Claim" in the Ohio receivership proceeding on January 7, 2014.

Additionally, Robol filed a "Verified Statement of Right, Interest, and Claim" in this proceeding on June 23, 2014, seeking a salvage award from the continuing salvage operations on the ground that he aided and assisted in these salvage operations by voluntarily releasing possession of documents over which he had a retaining lien for attorneys fees and a property [—10—] interest from EZRA's abandonment of them upon default of its lease. More specifically, he alleged that he assisted the salvage operation (1) by returning to the Receiver various "maritime and navigational charts, maritime maps, locational data, documents, drawings, historical data and accounts, shipwreck research and analysis, photographs, video," and other materials that he had acquired through his roles as counsel and as landlord and (2) by providing "assistance in obtaining site photography and video footage" held by Butterworth. Butterworth had served as Columbus-America's Director of Photography during the early stages of the salvage operation and thereafter as the company's Vice President, Acting President, and Chief Executive Officer. Robol alleged that this aid and assistance "was voluntary and involved items in which ... [he] had control, dominion, lien rights, ownership, and/other [sic] interests" and that Recovery Limited "utilized these materials in the salvage of the *S.S. Central America* to the benefit of the salvage," thus entitling him to a salvage award.

Recovery Limited, by its Receiver, filed a motion to dismiss Robol's claim under Federal Rule of Civil Procedure 12(b)(6), contending that the claim was not in the nature of a claim for a salvage award and that, in any event, Robol did not furnish his assistance voluntarily, as required to demonstrate a valid salvage claim. [—11—]

By order dated August 8, 2014, the district court granted Recovery Limited's motion and dismissed Robol's claim for a salvage award as a matter of law. The court concluded that Robol, who was licensed to practice law in both Virginia and Ohio, had a duty under Virginia Rule of Professional Conduct 1.16(e) "to supply the materials to [Recovery Limited] within a reasonable time of the termination of his representation of [Recovery Limited] or [Columbus-America]" and therefore that his action "was not 'voluntary.'" Although the court rejected Robol's argument that it should apply Ohio law, which, Robol claimed, would have permitted him to assert a retaining lien over some of the materials as a result of unpaid legal fees, it nonetheless recognized that such a lien would not have permitted Robol to use the materials for his own purposes, citing *Restatement (Third) of Agency* §§ 8.05, 8.09 cmt.b (2006). "*At best*," the court said, Robol might have "an *in personam* claim for attorney's fees or document storage fees." The court concluded further that the photographs and videos that Butterworth provided to the Receiver at Robol's urging had been prepared by Butterworth during salvage operations as an employee of Columbus-America, the agent of Recovery Limited, and therefore that they belonged to Recovery Limited.

From the district court's order dismissing Robol's claim, Robol filed this appeal. [—12—]

II

Robol contends first that, in turning over to the Receiver his former clients' documents relating to the salvage of the *S.S. Central America*, he provided *voluntary* assistance that proved useful in the renewed salvage operation, entitling him to a salvage award. A salvage award is, of course, compensation to persons "by whose *voluntary* assistance a ship at sea or her cargo or both have been saved in whole or in part from impending sea peril, or in recovering such property from actual peril or loss, as in cases of shipwreck, derelict, or recapture." *The Sabine*, 101 U.S. 384, 384 (1879) (emphasis added). Thus, a valid salvage claim requires a "[s]ervice *voluntarily rendered* when not required as an existing duty or from a special contract." *Id.* (emphasis added). As an initial matter, Robol argues that, in rejecting the allegations of his verified statement of claim that his actions in turning over documents to the Receiver were voluntary, the district court erred in failing to take his allegations as true, as required when ruling on a Rule 12(b)(6) motion. Specifically, he maintains that the district court should not have discredited his allegation that his "aid and assistance was voluntary" inasmuch as he returned documents over which he had "control, dominion, lien rights, [—13—]

ownership, and/other [sic] interests" because of his retaining lien for unpaid attorneys fees.

Robol's allegation of voluntariness, however, was no more than a legal argument that he was not required to return to his former clients' documents over which he had a retaining lien and that his doing so was therefore voluntary. And the district court appropriately treated his legal argument as one that it could—and indeed did—resolve as a matter of law. Relying on the existence of Robol's attorney-client relationship, the district court concluded that Robol had a preexisting duty to turn over the documents because the Virginia Rules of Professional Conduct preclude attorneys from exercising retaining liens. Regardless of whether the district court was correct on that point, it is clear that the court was not rejecting an allegation of fact, but rather Robol's legal conclusion. Of course, such legal conclusions are not entitled to the presumption of truth. *See Ashcroft v. Iqbal*, 556 U.S. 662, 678 (2009) ("[T]he tenet that a court must accept as true all of the allegations contained in a complaint is inapplicable to legal conclusions").

Robol also contends that, in reaching the conclusion that his action was not voluntary, the district court inappropriately went beyond the four corners of his verified statement of claim because its allegations did not include the facts necessary for [—14—] the court to reach that conclusion. The district court, however, did not go beyond the claim except to note that Robol had been counsel of record for Columbus-America and Recovery Limited and therefore that he owed a duty to return the materials relating to the salvage operation to his former clients. Robol can hardly dispute the court's reliance on the fact that he was counsel of record, as that is not only part of the record in this case, but also part of the record in virtually every case relating to the salvage operation. Courts are entitled to consider such matters of public record in relying on motions to dismiss. *See* 5B Charles Alan Wright et al., *Federal Practice and Procedure* § 1357 (3d ed. 2004); *see also, e.g., Walker v. Kelly*, 589 F.3d 127, 139 (4th Cir. 2009) (holding that a federal court may consider documents from a prior state court proceeding in conjunction with a motion to dismiss). Moreover, Robol stated in his sworn opposition to Recovery Limited's motion to dismiss that he "served as counsel for Columbus-America Discovery Group, Inc. ... and/or Recovery Limited Partnership ... at various times from 1987 until 2014 and with respect to various matters." In the same document, he also acknowledged that at least some of the documents that he turned over to the Receiver were the property of his clients in which he had asserted a retaining lien. The district court simply treated these matters as given and ruled as a matter of [—15—] law that Robol, as counsel for the entities, had an ethical duty to return the documents, notwithstanding any retaining lien that he claimed. Accordingly, we reject Robol's claim that the district court ailed to adhere to established principles for ruling on a Rule 12(b)(6) motion.

On the merits, Robol contends that because he relinquished possession of the documents despite his retaining lien, his acts were *voluntary*, entitling him to a salvage award commensurate with the value of the documents to the continuing salvage operation.

Modern standards of professional conduct, however, preclude Robol from exercising a retaining lien in such a manner. The Virginia Rules of Professional Conduct obligate an attorney to return to a former client documents furnished by the client and attorney work product, "whether or not the client has paid the fees and costs owed the lawyer." Va. Rules of Prof'l Conduct R. 1.16(e). Although Virginia at one time recognized the common-law right of an attorney to exercise a retaining lien, *see King v. Beale*, 96 S.E.2d 765, 768 n.2 (Va. 1957), the Virginia State Bar Standing Committee on Legal Ethics has since clarified that "the ethical mandate [to safeguard and return client property] virtually displaces the common law retaining lien," Va. Standing Comm. on Legal Ethics, Op. 1690 (1997) ("Holding a former client's files hostage does not comport with [—16—] a lawyer's post-representation duty to take reasonable steps for the continued protection of the client's interests").

Robol argues, however, that Ohio law, rather than Virginia law, governs his conduct because he turned the documents over to the Receiver in Ohio. *See* Va. Rules of Prof'l Conduct R. 8.5(b) (calling for application of the rules of the jurisdiction in which a lawyer's conduct occurred, for conduct not in connection with a court proceeding). He argues that Ohio law recognizes an attorney's retaining lien, citing *Foor v. Huntington National Bank*, 499 N.E.2d 1297, 1301 (Ohio Ct. App. 1986).

We need not decide, however, whether the ethics rules of Virginia or Ohio apply, because Robol's claim would fail under the rules of either jurisdiction. Although Ohio adopted the Model Rules of Professional Conduct, it modified them by deleting language recognizing a retaining lien—specifically, language authorizing a lawyer to "retain papers relating to the client to the extent permitted by other law," Model Rules of Prof'l Conduct R. 1.16(d)—and substituting for that language a provision that "[c]lient papers and property shall be promptly delivered to the client" upon termination of a representation, Ohio Rules of Prof'l Conduct R. 1.16(d); *see also Reid, Johnson, Downes, Andrachik & Webster v. Lansberry*, 629 N.E.2d 431, 435 (Ohio 1994) ("[A]n attorney who is discharged must yield the case file"); 6 Ohio Jur. 3d *Attorneys at Law* § 236 (cautioning [—17—] against the assertion of an attorney's retaining lien in light of the decision in *Lansberry*). Thus, despite the fact that an intermediate court in Ohio once recognized the common-law retaining lien, it appears that the Ohio Rules of Professional Conduct, which subsequently were adopted by the Ohio Supreme Court, have displaced the retaining lien by obligating an attorney to turn over files to the client upon the termination of a representation.

In any event, attorneys in Ohio and elsewhere are prohibited from asserting retaining liens when doing so would cause foreseeable prejudice to the client. *See* Ellen J. Bennett et al., Am. Bar Ass'n, Ctr. for Prof'l Responsibility, *Annotated Model Rules of Professional Conduct* R. 1.16 (7th ed. 2011) ("A lawyer asserting a retaining lien is subject to the requirements of Rule 1.16 and must take appropriate steps to protect the client's interests"); *see also* Ohio Bd. of Comm'rs on Grievances & Discipline, Op. 92-8 (1992) (stating, before the adoption of the Ohio Rules of Professional Conduct, that "[w]henever an attorney asserts a legal right to an attorney's retaining lien, the attorney must make sure that assertion of the right does not result in causing foreseeable prejudice to the rights of the client"). By Robol's own admission, the documents that he provided to the Receiver, including maps and navigational charts, saved Recovery Limited "in excess of $600,000" in its [—18—] efforts to relocate the wreck. Consequently, Robol would not have been permitted to retain possession of those documents to the exclusion of his former client and thereby force that former client, to its prejudice, to expend enormous time, effort, and expense to recreate the information contained therein.

Thus, the rules of professional conduct in both Virginia and Ohio have replaced the common-law retaining lien with an attorney's obligation to turn over all files to the client upon termination of the representation, especially when, as here, the failure to do so would cause foreseeable prejudice. Accordingly, we affirm the district court's conclusion that Robol had a preexisting duty to return files to his former clients, notwithstanding the fact that the clients had not paid him all of the legal fees to which he claimed entitlement, and therefore that his action was not voluntary.

III

Robol contends also that his return of the documents stored in the portion of the West Sixth Avenue property leased to EZRA was voluntary because, as he argues, he, not his clients, owned the documents. He reasons that EZRA's failure to pay rent for the property triggered default under the lease and that EZRA's failure thereafter to remove the documents effected an abandonment of them. He argues that he thereupon became the [—19—] owner of the documents and consequently that his turning over the

documents to the Receiver was a voluntary act. This argument fails for several reasons.

First, Robol has pointed to no Ohio law that would have entitled him to engage in self-help repossession of the West Sixth Avenue property upon the default of his tenant, and he has made no claim that he repossessed the property through judicial proceedings. Ohio courts have held that commercial lessors are entitled to self-help repossession of real property only where "a provision in the lease provides for self-help repossession." *Quigg v. Mullins*, No. L-89-314, 1991 WL 59886, at *5 (Ohio Ct. App. Apr. 19, 1991). Robol's lease with EZRA, however, did not contain such a provision. It provided that "if the Premises shall be abandoned . . . and the same continues for ten (10) days after written notice to Lessee by Lessor, then Lessor . . . may declare this Lease terminated and proceed *pursuant to the Ohio Revised Code* to repossess the Premises and remove Lessee." (Emphasis added). The Ohio Revised Code does not itself authorize self-help repossession, providing only a judicial remedy against defaulting tenants. *See* Ohio Rev. Code § 5321.03. Moreover, and more importantly, even if Robol had lawfully repossessed the West Sixth Avenue property, such repossession would not have entitled him to take ownership of the personal property on the [—20—] premises. *See Greer v. Bruce*, No. C-140121, 2014 WL 5817889, at *3 (Ohio Ct. App. Nov. 5, 2014) (holding a landlord liable for conversion of a defaulting tenant's property where there was "no evidence that [the tenant] had agreed to permit the [landlord] to summarily confiscate and sell the property stored on the [landlord's] land without compensating him for its value").

Second, in the accounting action in the Ohio district court, Robol conceded that the documents stored at the West Sixth Avenue property were not his, but rather his clients'. As he stated in an affidavit, "[t]he files provided to the Receiver were not 'Robol Law Office files' or 'Robol's files,'" but were rather "files owned and that had been controlled by the client." Such statements belie his claim that EZRA's conduct gave him ownership.

Third, when the Receiver, pursuant to the receivership order, contacted Robol seeking all company files in his possession, Robol not only failed to assert any ownership interest in the files—arguing to the contrary that they were client-owned files in which he had a possessory retaining lien—but also acquiesced in the Receiver's demand. In the face of this behavior, Robol can hardly now claim ownership in the files.

Fourth, any ownership of the files through EZRA's abandonment of them could not overcome Robol's overarching [—21—] ethical duty, discussed above, to return files to his former clients upon termination of the representation.

In sum, Robol's claim that he owned the files located at the West Sixth Avenue property and *voluntarily* turned them over to the Receiver is completely devoid of merit.

IV

Finally, Robol contends that he should receive a salvage award because he was able to convince Butterworth to return to the Receiver photographs and videos that proved useful in the renewed salvage operations. We reject this argument for the reasons given by the district court. Because Butterworth created the materials as an employee of Columbus-America during the initial salvage operations, the materials were not his to give, but rather belonged to his employer, and he was obligated by the receivership order to return them. Thus, Robol's encouragement was nothing more than a collateral push to have Butterworth comply with a preexisting legal obligation. Such effort by Robol cannot form the basis of a salvage award.

Moreover, when Robol contacted Butterworth about the materials, he was still counsel for Columbus-America. Consequently, he can hardly claim that providing such legal service to his clients entitles him personally to a salvage award. [—22—]

V

Finally, we note the questionable posture of Robol's claim in this case. For years, Robol represented Thompson, Columbus-America, Recovery Limited, and other related entities as legal counsel, assisting them in successfully obtaining a salvage award for their efforts in recovering gold and other artifacts from the wreck of the *S.S. Central America*. Now, after concluding his representation, he claims his own salvage award in competition with his former clients. And he does so largely on the basis that he "voluntarily" returned to his former clients their files related to the salvage effort. Whether this posture creates an impermissible conflict of interest or disloyalty is not something that we decide here, but it raises a disquieting question. *See* Ohio Rules of Prof'l Conduct R. 1.9(c)(1) (prohibiting an attorney from "us[ing] information relating to the [terminated] representation to the disadvantage of the former client"); Va. Rules of Prof'l Conduct R. 1.9(c)(1) (similar); *Restatement (Third) of Agency* § 8.05 & cmt. b (prohibiting an agent from using the property of his principal for his own purposes, even after the agency relationship has concluded). [—23—]

Nonetheless, we affirm the district court's dismissal of Robol's verified statement of claim for substantially the same reasons given by the district court.

AFFIRMED

United States Court of Appeals
for the Fourth Circuit

No. 14-4413

UNITED STATES
vs.
SAID

Appeal from the United States District Court for the
Eastern District of Virginia, at Norfolk

Decided: August 13, 2015

Citation: 798 F.3d 182, 3 Adm. R. 231 (4th Cir. 2015).

Before **KING** and **KEENAN**, Circuit Judges, and **DAVIS**, Senior Circuit Judge.

[—4—] **KING**, Circuit Judge:

In early 2010, a group of seven Somalis—including defendants Mohamed Ali Said, Mohamed Abdi Jama, and Abdicasiis Cabaase—boarded a small skiff and entered the Gulf of Aden (in the Indian Ocean between the Arabian Peninsula and the Horn of Africa), intending to seize a merchant ship at sea. Their objective was foiled by the British warship HMS Chatham, which was conducting a counter-piracy mission in the Gulf. Undeterred by their initial lack of success, Said, Jama, and Cabaase joined with defendants Abdi Razaq Abshir Osman and Mohamed Farah, plus two others, and returned from Somalia to the Gulf in the skiff in April 2010. During their April escapade, the defendants and their accomplices launched an attack on the USS Ashland, a United States Navy warship that they confused for a merchant vessel. The Ashland responded by destroying the skiff and killing one of the attackers.

After the defendants were apprehended and transported to the Eastern District of Virginia, they were tried and convicted of multiple offenses, including piracy as proscribed by 18 U.S.C. § 1651. At sentencing, the district court declined to impose statutorily mandated life sentences on the defendants, reasoning that such sentences would contravene the Eighth Amendment's prohibition against cruel and unusual punishment. [—5—] *See United States v.*

Said, No. 2:10-cr-00057 (E.D. Va. Feb. 28, 2014), ECF No. 260 (the "Eighth Amendment Order").[1]

The government, in pursuing its appeal in No. 14-4413, seeks relief from the district court's decision not to impose the life sentences required by § 1651. By their cross-appeals in Nos. 14-4420, 14-4421, 14-4423, 14-4424, and 14-4429, the defendants challenge the court's failure to dismiss the § 1651 charge, the jury instructions with respect to the piracy offense, and the sufficiency of the evidence supporting certain of their convictions. As explained below, we reject each of the defendants' contentions and affirm their convictions. We deem the government's appeal to be meritorious, however, and reverse the Eighth Amendment Order, vacate the defendants' sentences, and remand for resentencing.

I.

A.

1.

In approximately February 2010, defendants Said, Jama, and Cabaase—along with Jama Idle Ibrahim and three others—[—6—] acquired a small wooden skiff on the coast of Somalia and loaded it with a hooked ladder and weapons, including AK-47 assault rifles, a rocket-propelled grenade launcher (an "RPG"), a Singapore Assault Rifle 80 (an "SAR-80"), and a Tokarev 9-mm pistol.[2] They also equipped the skiff with two motors, enabling it to more swiftly traverse the sea. The group then left Somalia and travelled into the Gulf of Aden searching for a merchant ship to seize. The Gulf is one of the most heavily trafficked shipping corridors in the world, making it a prime location for piracy.

---

[1] The Eighth Amendment Order is published at 3 F. Supp. 3d 515 and also found at J.A. 886-902. (Citations herein to "J.A. __" refer to the contents of the Joint Appendix filed by the parties in these appeals.)

[2] We recite the facts in the light most favorable to the government, as the prevailing party at trial. *See United States v. Singh*, 518 F.3d 236, 241 n.2 (4th Cir. 2008).

On the afternoon of February 27, 2010, the skiff was intercepted in the Gulf of Aden by the HMS Chatham of the British Royal Navy. Upon encountering the skiff, the Chatham actioned a helicopter for a close investigation. The Somalis, recognizing the Chatham as a warship, attempted to flee in the skiff and threw weapons and their ladder overboard. Those actions were witnessed by the helicopter pilots, who conveyed information to a boarding team that had been dispatched in smaller boats from the warship.

The HMS Chatham's boarding team seized and searched the skiff, where team members discovered the pistol and ammunition [—7—] for that weapon and the AK-47s. The boarding team also apprehended and questioned the Somalis. Ibrahim, speaking as the group's leader, asserted that the Somalis were smugglers who had taken human cargo to Yemen and that one of their boats had broken down along the way.[3] Personnel of the Chatham photographed the Somalis, confiscated the pistol and ammunition, disabled one of the skiff's motors, spray-painted a red identification number on the skiff, and ordered the Somalis to return home.

2.

In April 2010, the five defendants in this case, along with Ibrahim and another man called the "Engineer," used the same skiff to enter the Gulf of Aden from Somalia. So that the skiff "would not be recognizable," the Somalis had obliterated the identification number spray-painted on it by Royal Navy personnel. See J.A. 415. To accomplish their goal of seizing a ship, the Somalis had obtained a replacement for the disabled motor and loaded the skiff with a hooked ladder, three AK-47s, and an RPG. Ibrahim and Jama led the new mission, and Said was [—8—] next in command. Farah drove the skiff, and

Cabaase and Osman supplied two of the weapons.

In the pre-dawn hours of April 10, 2010, the skiff swiftly approached a large ship believed by the Somalis to be a "cargo ship." See J.A. 444. Nearing the ship's aft on its port side, Said and Cabaase held loaded AK-47s, while Jama attempted to load the RPG with explosive rockets.[4] When the skiff was approximately twenty-five yards from the "cargo ship," Cabaase began shooting at it with his AK-47. The Somalis intended to "scare [the crew], and then after that[,] capture the ship." Id. The encounter took place about forty nautical miles off the coast of Yemen in international waters.

The targeted ship was actually the USS Ashland, a dock landing ship of the United States Navy, which was then transiting the Gulf of Aden transporting Marines and military equipment.[5] Several personnel aboard the Ashland—namely, Marine Lance Corporal John Curtis, Damage Control Fireman James [—9—] Hendershot, Seaman Donald Lane, Lieutenant Junior Grade Benjamin Towers, Lieutenant Brent Holloway, and Gunner's Mate Justin Myers— witnessed the Somalis' attack from several vantage points, including near the warship's aft, its mid-ship, and the bridge. Several of the witnesses saw Cabaase fire multiple rounds at the Ashland and heard bullets striking the ship. See, e.g., J.A. 153 (Curtis: "He was deliberately shooting . . . the weapon towards the front right over the bridge of the USS ASHLAND."); id. at 186 (Hendershot: "I saw a man stand up and bring a weapon up to his shoulder aiming at the ship . . . ."); id. at 282 (Myers: "You saw a muzzle flash followed by the sound of a weapon, and I also heard a

---

[3] Ibrahim later explained that the Somalis' cover story had to involve two boats to seem plausible, given that seven men claiming to be smugglers were aboard the skiff. Those who patrol the high seas and "see people smuggling people almost every day" would know that only two or three smugglers—and "not more than that"— generally carry out such missions. See J.A. 389.

[4] Unable to render the RPG operational, Jama sought the assistance of Ibrahim, who soon realized that the ammunition on board the skiff did not fit the RPG.

[5] As one of the Ashland's personnel later testified, the vessel "is one of the ships in the U.S. Navy inventory that actually looks like a merchant ship." See J.A. 203-04. With military equipment on board, the Ashland "could be misconstrued as . . . a merchant container vessel that isn't fully loaded." Id. at 204.

couple of clangs that sounded like ricochet on the side of the boat."). Indeed, Corporal Curtis witnessed Cabaase "load a magazine, rack it, fire like two to three times, bang, bang, bang. Bang, bang. He dropped the magazine, loads another one, racks it a couple of times, keeps shooting, bang, bang, bang." *Id.* at 153-54. The multiple shots fired at the Ashland were so startling that the warship's helmsman had difficulty with the steering.

Gunner's Mate Myers initially left his remote firing station inside the USS Ashland to observe the skiff's assault from the warship's deck. After watching Cabaase fire multiple times at the Ashland, Myers ran back to his duty station, where he controlled 25-mm machine guns loaded with armor-piercing [—10—] incendiary shells. The screen of the weapons system operated by Myers displayed images from an infrared camera mounted outside the ship. The camera zoomed in so closely on the skiff that it seemed "[a]lmost as if you [were] standing next to some of the people in the skiff." *See* J.A. 213. Myers's vantage point enabled him to see that Cabaase was aiming directly at the Ashland. After Cabaase began firing a second series of shots, the Ashland's Captain ordered Myers to return fire with a 25-mm machine gun, and Myers promptly fired two shots. As a result of those shots from the Ashland, a fire erupted on the skiff, the Engineer died, and Farah lost a leg.[6]

The defendants jumped off the burning skiff, and Ibrahim followed suit after throwing the RPG and two of the AK-47s overboard. While treading water, the Somalis agreed to tell the crew of the USS Ashland a story similar to the one that had been concocted for the personnel of the HMS Chatham—that the skiff was returning from smuggling refugees to Yemen. To explain why they were travelling on one small skiff, they would tell the Ashland's crew about transporting refugees on a second larger boat that had broken down before their return trip. The Somalis also agreed to explain that they were stranded without food or [—11—] fuel, and that the

---

[6] The defendants each suffered burns as a result of trying to put out the fire on the skiff, but Ibrahim was not injured.

Engineer (who was then deceased) had fired on the Ashland to alert the crew that they were in need of rescue.

The USS Ashland and its personnel apprehended the defendants and Ibrahim, took pictures of the skiff's remains, and seized its contents, including the weapons and the hooked ladder that were left aboard. The Somalis were subsequently transported to Virginia, where this prosecution was initiated.

B.

1.

On April 21, 2010, the grand jury in the Eastern District of Virginia at Norfolk returned an indictment against the defendants and Ibrahim. Nearly three months later, on July 7, 2010, the grand jury returned a superseding indictment. Those indictments—which dealt solely with the attack on the USS Ashland—charged the defendants and Ibrahim with, inter alia, piracy in contravention of 18 U.S.C. § 1651. That statute provides in full:

Whoever, on the high seas, commits the crime of piracy as defined by the law of nations, and is afterwards brought into or found in the United States, shall be imprisoned for life.

18 U.S.C. § 1651.

On June 9, 2010, the defendants and Ibrahim moved to dismiss the piracy charge of the initial indictment, contending that piracy under § 1651 requires a robbery at sea. Because [—12—] their effort to seize the Ashland was unsuccessful, the defendants and Ibrahim argued that the § 1651 piracy charge should be dismissed. The district court agreed with the defendants and granted their motion on August 17, 2010, dismissing the piracy charge from the superseding indictment.

On August 21, 2010, Ibrahim entered into a plea agreement with the United States Attorney, by which he agreed to assist the government in its prosecution of his cohorts. On August 27, 2010, Ibrahim pleaded guilty to three counts of the superseding indictment: attack to plunder a vessel, in contravention of 18 U.S.C. § 1659; performing an act of violence against an individual on a vessel, in contravention of 18 U.S.C. § 2291(a)(6); and using, carrying, and discharging a firearm during and in relation to a crime of violence, in violation of 18 U.S.C. § 924(c)(1)(A)(iii). On November 29, 2010, Ibrahim was sentenced to 360 months in prison.

2.

After Ibrahim was sentenced, the government filed an appeal contesting—as to the five defendants—the district court's dismissal of the § 1651 piracy charge. Following an oral argument conducted in this Court on March 25, 2011, we placed the government's appeal in abeyance pending argument and decision in *United States v. Dire*. The *Dire* appeals were brought by a separate group of Somalis who had been convicted of [—13—] piracy for their attack on the USS Nicholas, another Navy warship. The *Dire* defendants had intended to seize the Nicholas in the Indian Ocean, but their plan was foiled by the Nicholas's crew.

Like the defendants here, the *Dire* defendants argued that § 1651 requires a robbery—i.e., seizing or otherwise robbing a vessel. That contention is premised primarily on the Supreme Court's decision in *United States v. Smith*, 18 U.S. (5 Wheat.) 153, 162 (1820), where the Court indicated that it had "no hesitation in declaring, that piracy, by the law of nations, is robbery upon the sea." As the argument goes, because "a court must interpret a statute by its ordinary meaning at the time of its enactment," and because the language of § 1651 can be traced to an 1819 act of Congress, the *Smith* decision of 1820 constitutes "the definitive authority on the meaning of piracy." *See United States v. Dire*, 680 F.3d 446, 452 (4th Cir. 2012) (internal quotation marks omitted).

By our *Dire* decision, however, we rejected the theory that the meaning of piracy for purposes of § 1651 "was fixed in the early Nineteenth Century." *See* 680 F.3d at 467. That is, we excluded a static interpretation of

§ 1651 that would "render it incongruous with the modern law of nations and prevent us from exercising universal jurisdiction in piracy cases." *Id.* at 468-69. Rather, consistent with Congress's intent "to define piracy [—14—] as a universal jurisdiction crime," we concluded that "§ 1651 incorporates a definition of piracy that changes with advancements in the law of nations." *Id.* at 469. We recognized in *Dire* that, for decades, piracy has been defined by the law of nations to include:

(A) (1) any illegal act of violence or detention, or any act of depredation; (2) committed for private ends; (3) on the high seas or a place outside the jurisdiction of any state; (4) by the crew or the passengers of a private ship; (5) and directed against another ship, or against persons or property on board such ship; or

(B) (1) any act of voluntary participation in the operation of a ship; (2) with knowledge of the facts making it a pirate ship; or

(C) (1) any act of inciting or of intentionally facilitating (2) an act described in subparagraph (A) or (B).

Id. at 465 (alterations and internal quotation marks omitted) (drawing definition from the substantively identical Geneva Convention on the High Seas (the "High Seas Convention") and United Nations Convention on the Law of the Sea (the "UNCLOS")).

Because the foregoing definition of piracy encompassed the *Dire* defendants' conduct, we affirmed their convictions under § 1651. The very day we decided *Dire*—that is, May 23, 2012—we vacated the district court's dismissal of the § 1651 piracy charge in this case and "remand[ed] for such other and further proceedings as may be appropriate, consistent with our decision [—15—] in *Dire*."

See United States v. Said, 680 F.3d 374, 375 (4th Cir. 2012).[7]

3.

On August 8, 2012, after our remand to the district court, the grand jury returned a second superseding indictment against the defendants (the "operative indictment"), lodging additional charges stemming from the February 2010 encounter with the British warship HMS Chatham. As a result of Ibrahim's cooperation, the government investigators and the grand jury had obtained evidence supporting those additional counts. The operative indictment contained the following charges:

- Count One—Conspiracy to commit hostage taking (18 U.S.C. § 1203(a));

- Count Two—Conspiracy to commit kidnapping (18 U.S.C. § 1201(c));

- Count Three—Conspiracy to perform an act of violence against an individual on a vessel (18 U.S.C. § 2291(a)(9));

- Count Four—Conspiracy to use and carry a firearm and a destructive device during and in relation to, and possessing a firearm and a destructive device in furtherance of, a crime of violence, specifically the crimes charged in Counts One through Three and Five through Eight (18 U.S.C. § 924(o)); [—16—]

- Count Five—Piracy as defined by the law of nations (18 U.S.C. § 1651);

- Count Six—Attack to plunder a vessel (18 U.S.C. § 1659);

- Count Seven—Assault with a dangerous weapon on a federal officer

or employee (18 U.S.C. § 111(a)(1) and (b));

- Count Eight—Performing an act of violence against an individual on a vessel (18 U.S.C. § 2291(a)(6));

- Count Nine—Using and carrying a firearm during and in relation to, and possessing a firearm in furtherance of, a crime of violence, specifically the crimes charged in Counts One through Three (18 U.S.C. § 924(c)(1)(A)); and

- Count Ten—Using, carrying, and discharging a firearm during and in relation to a crime of violence, specifically the crimes charged in Counts One through Three and Five through Eight (18 U.S.C. § 924(c)(1)(A)(iii)).

Counts One through Four of the operative indictment encompass the time period in which the encounters with the HMS Chatham and the USS Ashland occurred. Counts Five through Eight, plus Ten, deal solely with the attack on the Ashland, and Count Nine relates only to the Chatham. Counts Five through Ten include allegations of aiding and abetting, pursuant to 18 U.S.C. § 2(a).

Defendants Said, Jama, and Cabaase were named in all ten counts of the operative indictment. Defendants Osman and Farah were named in all counts except Count Nine. Prior to trial, the [—17—] defendants again moved to dismiss the § 1651 piracy charge (Count Five of the operative indictment), which the district court denied on the basis of the *Dire* decision.

4.

The defendants' trial began in Norfolk on February 19, 2013, and concluded on February 27, 2013. The trial featured extensive testimony from personnel aboard the USS Ashland and the HMS Chatham during their encounters in 2010 with the defendants. Ibrahim was called to the stand by the government, and the prosecutors used

[7] The *Dire* defendants and the defendants in this case filed petitions for writs of certiorari in the Supreme Court, seeking to have the Court reverse our ruling in *Dire* concerning the ambit of § 1651. Those petitions were denied on January 22, 2013. *See* 133 S. Ct. 982 (2013).

his testimony to establish several details underlying their case.

Ibrahim began by explaining how he became involved in piracy activities. For example, after seeing "a lot of people in [his] neighborhood making a lot of money [and] buying houses and nice cars" from acts of piracy, he decided to "jump on that, too." J.A. 360. Thus, in November 2008, Ibrahim joined a group of Somali pirates—none of whom are involved in this case—on a mission to seize merchant ships near the coast of Yemen. That group forcibly seized a Danish ship called the CEC Future, using assault weapons and a ladder. The pirates removed the Future to Somalia and held it "until [they] got a ransom" in January 2009. *Id.* at 363. Ibrahim was paid $17,000 for that piracy mission.

In early 2010, Ibrahim sought out another piracy mission in order to "get more money." J.A. 365. In February 2010, he [—18—] joined Said, Jama, Cabaase, and three others on the mission to "seize a ship" that was thwarted by the HMS Chatham. *Id.* at 383. Thereafter, in April 2010, Ibrahim and the defendants set out with another plan to "seize a ship" and "make money." *Id.* at 403. Ibrahim described his and the defendants' subsequent attack on the USS Ashland and their apprehension by its personnel. After being indicted for the Ashland attack, Ibrahim explained, he decided to plead guilty and cooperate with the federal prosecutors, seeking a less severe sentence.[8]

At the close of the prosecution's case, on February 25, 2013, the defendants moved for judgments of acquittal. The trial court denied the motions. The defendants rested without calling witnesses. The defendants objected to the court's proposed instructions on piracy under § 1651, which adopted the legal principles recognized and applied in *Dire*. The court overruled the defendants' objections and instructed the jury in a manner consistent with *Dire*. At the conclusion of the six-day

trial, on February 27, 2013, the jury convicted the defendants on all counts. The defendants jointly filed a renewed motion [—19—] for judgments of acquittal on May 13, 2013, which the court denied on August 1, 2013.

5.

On October 4, 2013, prior to their sentencing hearings, the defendants filed a motion to invalidate § 1651's mandatory life sentence on Eighth Amendment grounds. By its Eighth Amendment Order of February 28, 2014, the district court granted the motion.

The Eighth Amendment Order concluded that life sentences in the circumstances of this prosecution would contravene the defendants' Eighth Amendment rights. The district court began its analysis by recognizing the Supreme Court's two-prong framework for assessing as-applied Eighth Amendment challenges to non-capital sentences, as spelled out in *Graham v. Florida*, 560 U.S. 48 (2010). The district court explained that, under prong one, a court must "compare the gravity of the offense and the severity of the sentence," and determine "if that comparison yields 'an inference of gross disproportionality,' which should be a 'rare' result." *See* Eighth Amendment Order 6 (quoting *Graham*, 560 U.S. at 60). Upon ascertaining an inference of gross disproportionality, the court moves to prong two, which requires it to "compare the sentence with sentences received with other offenders in the same jurisdiction and with sentences imposed for the same crime in other jurisdictions." *Id.* "If [—20—] that analysis confirms that the sentence is grossly disproportionate," the district court explained, "then to impose the sentence would violate the Eighth Amendment." *Id.*

At prong one of the Eighth Amendment analysis, the district court assessed whether an inference of gross disproportionality arose upon comparing the proposed life sentences with the gravity of the defendants' § 1651 piracy offenses. The court reasoned that, although piracy is generally a serious offense, "this was not a run-of-the-mill case of modern piracy." *See* Eighth Amendment Order 11. Indeed, the court explained that the

---

[8] After entering his guilty pleas in this case, Ibrahim pleaded guilty in the District of Columbia to charges relating to the 2008 seizure of the CEC Future. He was subsequently sentenced in that prosecution to twenty-five years in prison, to run concurrently with his sentence here.

defendants' offenses were more properly characterized as attempted piracy, in that "[n]o victims were caused any physical harm, and it is unclear whether there was even any property damage." *Id*. The court concluded that the defendants had satisfied prong one of the Eighth Amendment analysis by establishing the inference that life sentences would be grossly disproportionate to their piracy offenses. *Id*. at 12.

The district court then turned to prong two of the Eighth Amendment analysis, comparing the proposed life sentences with sentences imposed on other offenders in the same jurisdiction and with sentences imposed for piracy in other jurisdictions. The court observed that, with the exception of statutes punishing recidivist offenders, almost all of the "federal criminal statutes carrying a mandatory minimum life sentence [—21—] . . . involve the death of another person." *See* Eighth Amendment Order 13. The court also perceived that imposing "a life sentence for the conduct in this case [would be] unique internationally," on the premise that the "global average sentence for piracy is just over 14 years." *Id*. at 16. Accordingly, the court concluded that the "statutorily-mandated sentence violates the Eighth Amendment and cannot be imposed." *Id*.

By its Eighth Amendment Order, the district court directed the parties to submit supplemental briefing on the appropriate sentences for the defendants' piracy convictions, in view of the court's invalidation of the mandatory life sentence. In his supplemental brief, the United States Attorney urged the court to impose a life sentence on each of the defendants, asserting that such sentences were legally mandated. The defendants, by contrast, made recommendations of various non-life sentences.

The defendants' sentencing hearings were conducted on May 14 and 15, 2014. Said was sentenced to an aggregate of 500 months (140 months for his § 1651 piracy offense), Jama to 500 months (140 months for piracy), Cabaase to 510 months (150 months for piracy), Osman to 360 months (240 months for piracy), and Farah to 384 months (264 months for piracy). The government and the defendants timely noted their respective appeals, and we [—22—] possess jurisdiction pursuant to 28 U.S.C. § 1291 and 18 U.S.C. § 3742(b).

II.

Although the defendants are cross-appellants in these proceedings, we will review their contentions in the first instance, as our dispositions of their appeals could render moot the government's challenge to the defendants' non-life sentences for their 18 U.S.C. § 1651 piracy offenses. By their appeals, the defendants contend that the district court erred in denying their motion to dismiss the piracy charge and in instructing the jury on the elements of piracy under § 1651. The defendants also maintain that the court erroneously denied their motions for judgments of acquittal, arguing that the evidence was insufficient to prove piracy and certain other offenses.

A.

In contending that the district court erred with respect to the § 1651 piracy offense by declining to dismiss that charge and by erroneously instructing the jury, the defendants contest the court's reliance on *United States v. Dire*, 680 F.3d 446 (4th Cir. 2012). We review de novo a district court's denial of a motion to dismiss an indictment where the denial depends solely on questions of law. *See United States v. Hatcher*, 560 F.3d 222, 224 (4th Cir. 2009). We also review de novo the claim that [—23—] a jury instruction failed to correctly state the applicable law. *See United States v. Jefferson*, 674 F.3d 332, 351 (4th Cir. 2012).

The defendants again advance the contention—considered and rejected in *Dire*—that the definition of piracy under § 1651 is limited to robbery at sea. Nevertheless, the defendants concede that we are obliged to adhere to *Dire*, as one panel of this Court is not entitled to overrule another panel. *See McMellon v. United States*, 387 F.3d 329, 333-34 (4th Cir. 2004) (en banc). Furthermore, the defendants do not dispute that the district court faithfully applied the *Dire* principles. We thus have no trouble concluding that the court did not err in declining to dismiss the piracy charge or in instructing the jury on the elements of the § 1651 offense.[9]

B.

Turning to the evidentiary issues, each defendant challenges the sufficiency of the evidence as to the § 1651 piracy offense. Additionally, the defendants, except for Said, challenge the sufficiency of the evidence on the offenses [—24—] charged in Count One (conspiracy to commit hostage taking), Count Two (conspiracy to commit kidnapping), and Count Three (conspiracy to perform an act of violence against an individual on a vessel). Because Counts One through Three served as the predicate offenses for Count Nine (using and carrying a firearm during and in relation to, and possessing a firearm in furtherance of, a crime of violence), defendants Jama and Cabaase also seek vacatur of their Count Nine convictions.[10]

We review de novo a trial court's denial of a motion for judgment of acquittal. *See United States v. Reed*, 780 F.3d 260, 269 (4th Cir. 2015). In reviewing evidence sufficiency contentions, we are obliged to "view the evidence in the light most favorable to the government and sustain the jury's verdict if any rational trier of fact could have found the

essential elements of the crime charged beyond a reasonable doubt." *United States v. Barefoot*, 754 F.3d 226, 233 (4th Cir. 2014) (emphasis and internal quotation marks omitted). A defendant [—25—] challenging the sufficiency of the evidence faces a heavy burden, as "[r]eversal for insufficient evidence is reserved for the rare case where the prosecution's failure is clear." *United States v. Ashley*, 606 F.3d 135, 138 (4th Cir. 2010) (internal quotation marks omitted).

1.

The defendants first challenge the sufficiency of the evidence on the § 1651 offense, which relates solely to their attack on the USS Ashland. In support of their sufficiency contention, the defendants reiterate the argument that piracy requires a robbery at sea. As we have explained, however, their position is foreclosed by *Dire*.

Furthermore, the government presented sufficient evidence to prove that the defendants' conduct constituted piracy under the *Dire* principles. The evidence established, inter alia, the following:

- The defendants set out from Somalia in their skiff with the intent to seize a merchant ship and tools to do so, including a hooked ladder, three AK-47s, and an RPG;

- Seeking to capture the USS Ashland in international waters, Cabaase fired multiple AK-47 rounds at the Ashland from the skiff. *See Dire*, 680 F.3d at 465 (explaining that piracy includes "(A)(1) any illegal act of violence . . . ; (2) committed for private ends; (3) on the high seas . . . ; (4) by the crew or the passengers of a private ship; (5) and directed against another ship, or against persons or [—26—] property on board such ship" (alterations and internal quotation marks omitted));

- Farah drove the skiff as the defendants hunted a ship to seize and then targeted the Ashland. *See id.*

---

[9] Notably, we are not alone in our interpretation of § 1651. Other courts, including two courts of appeals, have adopted the definition of piracy announced in *Dire*. *See United States v. Ali*, 718 F.3d 929, 936-37 (D.C. Cir. 2013); *Inst. of Cetacean Research v. Sea Shepherd Conservation Soc'y*, 725 F.3d 940, 943, 1 Adm. R. 406, 406 (9th Cir. 2013).

[10] None of the defendants challenge their convictions of the offenses charged in Count Four (conspiracy to use and carry a firearm and a destructive device during and in relation to, and possessing a firearm and a destructive device in furtherance of, a crime of violence); Count Six (attack to plunder a vessel); Count Seven (assault with a dangerous weapon on a federal officer or employee); Count Eight (performing an act of violence against an individual on a vessel); and Count Ten (using, carrying, and discharging a firearm during and in relation to a crime of violence).

(further defining piracy as "(B)(1) any act of voluntary participation in the operation of a ship; (2) with knowledge of the facts making it a pirate ship" (alterations and internal quotation marks omitted); and

- Osman, along with Cabaase, had supplied two of the weapons, and Jama and Said, a leader and next in command for the mission, carried an RPG and an AK-47 during the Ashland attack. *See id.* (lastly defining piracy as "(C)(1) any act of inciting or of intentionally facilitating (2) an act described in subparagraph (A) or (B) (internal quotation marks omitted)); *see also United States v. Shibin*, 722 F.3d 233, 240, 1 Adm. R. 138, 143 (4th Cir. 2013) (recognizing "that the facilitating conduct of [subparagraph (C)] is 'functionally equivalent' to aiding and abetting criminal conduct, as proscribed by 18 U.S.C. § 2").

Accordingly, we are well satisfied that, on the evidence presented, a reasonable jury was entitled to conclude beyond a reasonable doubt that each of the defendants committed the § 1651 piracy offense.

2.

Next, defendants Jama, Cabaase, Osman, and Farah challenge the sufficiency of the evidence on the conspiracy offenses charged in Counts One through Three, encompassing the time period in which the encounters with the HMS Chatham and the USS Ashland occurred. As for Counts One and Two, the operative indictment alleged that the defendants conspired to commit [—27—] hostage taking and kidnapping, in that they went to sea with the intent to hijack a ship and hold the vessel and its crew for ransom. *See* 18 U.S.C. § 1203(a) (proscribing conspiracy to commit hostage taking); *id.* § 1201(c) (same for conspiracy to commit kidnapping). These four defendants contend that there was insufficient evidence to prove that they conspired to kidnap or hold any person hostage for ransom. They assert that

the evidence showed merely that they intended to seize a ship to make money.

Upon seizing a ship, however, the defendants would have had to either detain the crew members and personnel on board or throw them off the vessel. A reasonable jury could conclude that the defendants intended to pursue the former option—that is, detain the crew and other personnel—given that their shared goal was to "make money," and that they could do so by ransoming captives. *See, e.g.,* J.A. 403 (Ibrahim's testimony that the defendants' mutual objective at the time of the USS Ashland attack was "[t]o seize a ship so we can make money"). That evidence, illustrating the defendants' thirst for funds, was sufficient to prove that the defendants conspired to profit by kidnapping and holding crew members and personnel hostage in exchange for ransom. Tellingly, there was no commonsense alternative offered to the jury. Although these defendants now contend that they might have intended to make money by, for [—28—] example, selling the seized ship, they did not argue such a theory, or present any evidence supporting it, at trial. Indeed, the defense focused on convincing the jury that the defendants were smugglers rather than pirates.

Turning to Count Three, the operative indictment alleged that the defendants conspired to perform an act of violence against an individual on a vessel, and that such act of violence was likely to endanger the safety of those on board. *See* 18 U.S.C. § 2291(a)(9) (criminalizing conspiracy to "do anything prohibited under paragraphs (1) through (8)," including performing act of violence against individual on vessel, as proscribed by paragraph (6)). Jama, Cabaase, Osman, and Farah contend that their mere intent to seize a ship does not also prove an intention to perform an act of violence against the ship's crew or other personnel. Rather, according to these defendants, "[o]ne might seize a vessel by surprise or acquiescence." *See* Br. of Cross-Appellants 59.

The trial evidence, however, was more than sufficient to prove that, at the time of the encounters with the HMS Chatham and the

USS Ashland, the defendants were equipped and ready to commit violence against individuals on board in furtherance of their goal of seizing a ship. During the Ashland attack, they carried an RPG and three AK-47s—two provided by Cabaase and Osman—in their small, open skiff. While Farah drove the skiff [—29—] into position, Jama attempted to load the RPG, and Cabaase fired multiple rounds from his AK-47 at the Ashland in order "to capture the ship." *See* J.A. 444. From that evidence, a reasonable jury could conclude that these defendants conspired to perform an act of violence against an individual on a vessel, as part of their plan to forcibly seize a ship.

In these circumstances, the guilty verdicts on Count Three, as well as Counts One and Two, were adequately supported by the evidence. Because we therefore must affirm the convictions of Jama, Cabaase, Osman, and Farah on Counts One through Three, we also uphold Jama's and Cabaase's convictions on Count Nine.

III.

Having resolved each defendant's appeal against him, we turn to the government's appeal from the district court's Eighth Amendment Order. The government contends that the court erroneously determined that 18 U.S.C. § 1651's mandatory life sentence, as applied to the defendants, contravenes the Eighth Amendment's prohibition against cruel and unusual punishment. The defendants, by contrast, maintain that the court properly imposed non-life sentences for their piracy offenses. We review de novo the question of whether a sentence runs afoul of the Eighth Amendment. *See United States v. Cobler*, 748 F.3d 570, 574 (4th Cir. 2014). [—30—]

A.

We begin our consideration of the government's appeal by identifying the controlling legal framework. The Eighth Amendment provides that "[e]xcessive bail shall not be required, nor excessive fines imposed, nor cruel and unusual punishments inflicted." U.S. Const. amend. VIII. In deciding whether a punishment is cruel and unusual, we must examine the "evolving standards of decency that mark the progress of a maturing society." *Graham v. Florida*, 560 U.S. 48, 58 (2010) (internal quotation marks omitted). A punishment is cruel and unusual not only when it is "inherently barbaric," but also when it is "disproportionate to the crime." *Id.* at 59. Indeed, "[t]he concept of proportionality is central to the Eighth Amendment." *Id.*

Here, the defendants pursued as-applied challenges to § 1651's mandatory life sentence. *See Cobler*, 748 F.3d at 575 ("Under an as-applied challenge, a defendant contests the length of a certain [non-capital] sentence as being disproportionate given all the circumstances in a particular case." (internal quotation marks omitted)). As the district court recognized in its Eighth Amendment Order, the Supreme Court has adopted a two-prong test for assessing an as-applied challenge to the proportionality of a sentence. Under prong one, a court must determine whether a threshold comparison of "the gravity of the [—31—] offense and the severity of the sentence" produces "an inference of gross disproportionality." *See Graham*, 560 U.S. at 60 (internal quotation marks omitted) (relying on principles set forth in *Solem v. Helm*, 463 U.S. 277 (1983)). If prong one is satisfied, the court moves to an analysis of prong two. Under that prong, the court must "compare the defendant's sentence with the sentences received by other offenders in the same jurisdiction and with the sentences imposed for the same crime in other jurisdictions." *Id.* If that comparison "validates an initial judgment that the sentence is grossly disproportionate, the sentence is cruel and unusual." *Id.* (alterations and internal quotation marks omitted).

The Supreme Court has on one occasion—in its *Solem* decision of 1983—identified a non-capital sentence as being grossly disproportionate. There, the recidivist defendant (Helm) was sentenced to life without parole for uttering a $100 bad check. The Court observed that the matter involved "one of the most passive felonies a person could commit," in that the offense "involved neither violence nor threat of violence to any person"; Helm's prior offenses "were all relatively minor"; and life imprisonment was "the most severe punishment that the State could have imposed on any criminal for any crime." *See Solem*, 463 U.S. at 296-97 (internal quotation marks omitted). The Court further determined that "Helm has been treated in the same [—32—] manner as, or more severely than, criminals [in the same jurisdiction] who have committed far more serious crimes," and that "Helm was treated more severely than he would have been in any other State" except possibly one. *See id.* at 299-300. In those circumstances, the Court concluded that Helm's life sentence was "significantly disproportionate to his crime" and "therefore prohibited by the Eighth Amendment." *Id.* at 303. The *Solem* decision emphasized, however, that "outside the context of capital punishment, successful challenges to the proportionality of particular sentences will be exceedingly rare." *Id.* at 289-90 (alteration, emphasis, and internal quotation marks omitted).

Since *Solem* was decided, not a single "defendant before the Supreme Court has been successful in establishing even a threshold inference of gross disproportionality" in a non-capital case. *See Cobler*, 748 F.3d at 576. For example, in *Harmelin v. Michigan*, 501 U.S. 957 (1991), the Court rejected an as-applied Eighth Amendment challenge to a mandatory life sentence in a cocaine possession case. Justice Kennedy distinguished the "passive" check fraud crime in *Solem* from the "pernicious" drug offense at issue in *Harmelin*, observing that the latter crime "threatened to cause grave harm to society." *See Harmelin*, 501 U.S. at 1002 (Kennedy, J., concurring in part and concurring in the judgment) (internal quotation marks [—33—] omitted).[11]   In

rejecting Harmelin's Eighth Amendment challenge, Justice Kennedy also stressed the proposition that courts should give "substantial deference" to legislatures in determining the severity of punishments. *See id.* at 998-99 (internal quotation marks omitted).

The Supreme Court has more recently rejected an as-applied Eighth Amendment challenge for lack of an inference of gross disproportionality in *Ewing v. California*, 538 U.S. 11 (2003). Ewing received a sentence of twenty-five years to life under California's "three strikes" law for stealing $1,200 worth of golf clubs. Distinguishing his crime from that in *Solem*, the Court observed that the theft offense "was certainly not one of the most passive felonies a person could commit." *See Ewing*, 538 U.S. at 28 (internal quotation marks omitted). The Court then explained that, although Ewing's sentence was "a long one[,] . . . it reflect[ed] a rational legislative judgment, [—34—] entitled to deference, that offenders who have committed serious or violent felonies and who continue to commit felonies must be incapacitated." *Id.* at 30.

By our subsequent *Cobler* decision, we upheld a 120-year sentence imposed on a defendant who not only "possess[ed] large quantities of child pornography that he downloaded and shared on the Internet," but "also created depictions of his own sexual exploitation, molestation, and abuse of a four-year-old child." *See* 748 F.3d at 580. Applying the Supreme Court's two-prong test for an as-applied Eighth Amendment challenge, Cobler failed at prong one. We explained:

> Given the shocking and vile conduct underlying these criminal convictions, we hold that Cobler has failed to substantiate the required threshold inference of gross disproportionality. Even assuming, without deciding, that

---

[11] Although a majority failed to coalesce in *Harmelin* concerning the scope of the Eighth Amendment's proportionality guarantee, Justice Kennedy's opinion, which was joined by two of his colleagues, has been recognized by the Supreme Court as the controlling decision on that issue. *See Graham*, 560 U.S. at 59-60. It is thereby established that "the Eighth Amendment contains

---

> a 'narrow proportionality principle,' that 'does not require strict proportionality between crime and sentence' but rather 'forbids only extreme sentences that are "grossly disproportionate" to the crime.'" *Id.* (quoting *Harmelin*, 501 U.S. at 997, 1000-01 (Kennedy, J., concurring in part and concurring in the judgment)).

Cobler's 120-year term of imprisonment is functionally equivalent to a sentence of life imprisonment without the possibility of parole, we conclude that Cobler's multiple child pornography crimes are at least as grave as the drug offense in *Harmelin*, which the Supreme Court deemed sufficiently egregious to justify a similar sentence.

Id. (footnote omitted). Judge Keenan emphasized the rarity of cases in which an inference of gross disproportionality may be drawn, noting the singularity of the Supreme Court's *Solem* decision and distinguishing the check fraud offense there from the crimes perpetrated by Cobler. *See id*. ("Far from being 'one of the most passive felonies a person could commit,' Cobler's [—35—] heinous acts exploited, injured, and inflicted great harm on a most vulnerable victim." (quoting *Solem*, 463 U.S. at 296)).

On the issue of gross disproportionality, *Cobler* is typical of this Court's decisions.[12] Significantly, we have not identified a grossly disproportionate life sentence or putative life sentence in the wake of *Solem*. *See, e.g.*, *United States v. Dowell*, 771 F.3d 162, 167-69 (4th Cir. 2014) (eighty-year sentence for child pornography); *United States v. Myers*, 280 F.3d 407, 415-16 (4th Cir. 2002) (life sentence imposed under Armed Career Criminal Act for being felon in possession of firearm); *United States v. Kratsas*, 45 F.3d 63, 68-69 (4th Cir. 1995) (repeat drug offender's life sentence for conspiracy to distribute cocaine); *United States v. D'Anjou*, 16 F.3d 604, 612-14 (4th

---

[12] Our *Cobler* decision was rendered in April 2014—nearly two months after the district court had entered its Eighth Amendment Order in this case. The district court, upon being presented with *Cobler*, responded at defendant Said's sentencing hearing on May 14, 2014, that it

> read [*Cobler* and] understands that there has not been any precedent that would appear favorable to what the [Eighth Amendment Order] has ruled, but the precedent is usually the precedent until the precedent changes.

J.A. 1104.

Cir. 1994) (life sentence for conspiracy to distribute cocaine base). [—36—]

B.

With the foregoing legal framework in mind, we assess the government's challenge to the defendants' non-life sentences for their § 1651 piracy offenses. Prong one of the applicable analysis requires that we decide whether a threshold comparison of the gravity of the defendants' offenses and the severity of the proposed life sentences leads to an inference of gross disproportionality. *See Graham*, 560 U.S. at 60. The defendants contend that life sentences would be grossly disproportionate to their conduct, which, echoing the district court, they describe as mere "attempted robbery on the high seas" that "resulted in no property damage to the USS Ashland and no physical harm to any of its occupants." Br. of Cross-Appellants 39.

As discussed above, however, the defendants' § 1651 piracy offenses included committing illegal acts of violence for private ends (Cabaase), operating a pirate ship (Farah), and otherwise facilitating the violent acts (Said, Jama, and Osman). When the defendants engaged in that conduct, their piracy offenses were complete. Those offenses were hardly "passive"; rather, they involved "violence []or threat[s] of violence to [m]any person[s]." *See Solem*, 463 U.S. at 296. Indeed, the defendants' violent conduct was at least as severe as the cocaine possession in *Harmelin*. It is of no moment that no one aboard the USS Ashland was harmed before the defendants' attack [—37—] was thwarted. *Cf. Dowell*, 771 F.3d at 169 ("We reject out of hand the notion that the sexual abuse of a child can be considered nonviolent merely because it does not lead to physical or life-threatening injuries."). That is, "[t]he mere fact that [the defendants'] acts of [violence] did not inflict . . . physical injury [to the Ashland's personnel] does not render [life sentences] disproportionate." *See id*.[13]

---

[13] Of course, the defendants' attack on the USS Ashland was not casualty-free. The Engineer was killed and the defendants suffered burns when the Ashland returned fire.

Furthermore, § 1651's mandatory life sentence "reflects a rational legislative judgment, entitled to deference," that piracy in international waters is a crime deserving of one of the harshest of penalties. *See Ewing*, 538 U.S. at 30. The government has helpfully and cogently detailed why such an offense is sufficiently grave to merit life imprisonment. Above all, "for centuries, pirates have been universally condemned as *hostis humani generis*—enemies of all mankind—because they attack vessels on the high seas, and thus outside of any nation's territorial jurisdiction, with devastating effect to global commerce and navigation." *United States v. Dire*, 680 F.3d 446, 454 (4th Cir. 2012) (alterations and internal quotation marks omitted). Piracy was of such significance to the Framers that they expressly accorded Congress, in what is [—38—] known as the Define and Punish Clause, the power "[t]o define and punish Piracies and Felonies committed on the high Seas, and Offences against the Law of Nations." U.S. Const. art. I, § 8, cl. 10. In 1790, the First Congress created a series of crimes related to piracy, many of which were punishable by death. The piracy offense proscribed by § 1651 carried a mandatory death sentence from the offense's inception in 1819 until 1909, when Congress reduced the penalty to mandatory life.

The prevailing definition of piracy, "spelled out in the UNCLOS, as well as the High Seas Convention before it, has only been reaffirmed in recent years as nations around the world have banded together to combat the escalating scourge of piracy." *Dire*, 680 F.3d at 469. From 2005 to the fall of 2010, for example, Somali pirates hijacked approximately 170 vessels and fired upon some 280 more. *See* J.A. 952-53 (expert testimony at November 2010 trial of *Dire* defendants). Then, "[i]n 2011, armed Somali pirates attacked an estimated 3,863 seafarers and took some 555 individuals hostage." *See United States v. Beyle*, 782 F.3d 159, 162, 3 Adm. R. 190, 190 (4th Cir. 2015). As Judge Wilkinson aptly explained in the *Beyle* decision,

> [t]he United States and its allies are engaged in a multinational battle against piracy in the waters off the Horn

of Africa. Through the Gulf of Aden and much of the Indian Ocean, Somalia-based pirates have launched attacks against commercial and recreational vessels, from large freighters to personal yachts. Piracy poses a threat not only to the free flow of [—39—] global commerce, but also to the individuals who navigate the seas.

Id., 3 Adm. R. at 190 (citation omitted). Victims of piracy are robbed of their vessels, kidnapped, held hostage, and even tortured and murdered, while pirates are often able to find safe refuge in the territorial waters off Somalia and collect multi-million-dollar ransom payments. In these circumstances, we agree with the government "that Congress could with reason conclude [that piracy] calls for the strong medicine of a life sentence for those who are apprehended." *See* Br. of Appellant 39.[14]

We are satisfied that "the relationship between the gravity of [the defendants'] offenses and the severity of [their proposed] punishment fails to create the threshold inference of gross disproportionality that is required" to satisfy prong one of the Eighth Amendment analysis. *See Cobler*, 748 F.3d at 580. [—40—] Thus, without moving to prong two, we rule that the district court erred in invalidating § 1651's mandatory life sentence

---

[14] The defendants contend on appeal that we should not afford deference to Congress's judgment that piracy should be punished by life imprisonment, because when that penalty was fixed in 1909, the definition of piracy was limited to robbery at sea and did not include their violent conduct. For that same reason, the defendants also assert that imposing life sentences on them would violate the Define and Punish Clause. We must reject the defendants' theory, however, because Congress clearly meant to attach the mandatory life sentence to piracy, however defined by the law of nations at the relevant time. *See Dire*, 680 F.3d at 468-69 (recognizing that "§ 1651 incorporates a definition of piracy that changes with advancements in the law of nations," and that, in enacting § 1651, "Congress properly made an act a crime, affixed a punishment to it, and declared the court that shall have jurisdiction of the [offense]" (alterations and internal quotation marks omitted)).

as to these defendants and is obliged to impose such sentences on remand.

IV.

Pursuant to the foregoing, we affirm the various convictions of the defendants. We, however, reverse the Eighth Amendment Order, vacate the defendants' sentences, and remand for resentencing.

No. 14-4413 *REVERSED IN PART, VACATED IN PART, AND REMANDED*

Nos. 14-4420, 14-4421, 14-4423, 14-4424, and 14-4429 *AFFIRMED*

(Reporter's Note: Concurring opinion follows on p. 245).

[—41—] **DAVIS,** Senior Circuit Judge, concurring:

I join in full Judge King's excellent opinion. I write to express my agreement with one thoughtfully-expressed and eminently correct observation by the district court: Although modern piracy is a genuine, life-threatening scourge, not all piracy offenses are equal in severity, in heinousness, and in the dire consequences visited on innocent seafarers. Nor are all those who participate in such offenses deserving of life in prison as the sole conceivable "rational" punishment.[1] The civilized world knows this. The United States of America knows this too, but has not yet elected to act on that knowledge. Accordingly, because we are not legislators, and as Judge King demonstrates, because the Constitution has remarkably little to say about severe, but non-capital, criminal punishments, our hands are tied.

Perhaps, in the fullness of time, Congress will act on the certain knowledge we all share about criminal offenses and their punishments, and thereby empower federal district judges (and [—42—] not simply federal prosecutors) with discretion to fashion more individualized punishments in this small corner of federal criminal justice.

---

[1] Indeed, in this case, Mr. Ibrahim, who was "the group's leader" and who "led the new mission," *ante* at 7, would seem to have earned a life sentence. But he avoided that fate through the magic of "substantial assistance" and the fiction of "acceptance of responsibility," the coins of the federal prosecutorial realm. The inference is unavoidable that it is not really those who participate in piracy who receive a life sentence upon conviction (as we imagine Congress might believe), but rather those who are convicted after electing to go to trial.

United States Court of Appeals
for the Fourth Circuit

No. 14-2267

FLAME S.A.
vs.
FREIGHT BULK PTE. LTD.

Appeal from the United States District Court for the
Eastern District of Virginia, at Norfolk

Decided: November 24, 2015

Citation: 807 F.3d 572, 3 Adm. R. 246 (4th Cir. 2015).

Before **WILKINSON**, **AGEE**, and **HARRIS**, Circuit
Judges.

[—4—] **AGEE**, Circuit Judge:

Industrial Carriers, Inc., ("ICI"), a defunct maritime shipping company, breached numerous contracts in the final months of its operation. Among ICI's creditors were FLAME S.A. ("Flame"), who obtained a foreign judgment against ICI for breach of four Forward Freight Swap Agreements ("FFAs"), and Glory Wealth Shipping Pte. Ltd. ("Glory Wealth"), who obtained a foreign arbitration award against ICI based on the breach of a charter party.

Both Flame and Glory Wealth sought a writ of maritime attachment under Supplemental Rule B of the Federal Rules of Civil Procedure to attach the vessel M/V CAPE VIEWER when it docked in Norfolk, Virginia. Freight Bulk Pte. Ltd. ("Freight Bulk") is the registered owner of the vessel, but Flame and Glory Wealth asserted that Freight Bulk was the alter ego of ICI, and that ICI had fraudulently conveyed its assets to Freight Bulk in order to evade its creditors. For that reason, they argued that the U.S. District Court for the Eastern District of Virginia could enforce their claims against ICI through Freight Bulk. Following a bench trial, the district court awarded judgment to Flame and Glory Wealth, ordered the sale of the M/V CAPE VIEWER, and confirmed the distribution of the sale proceeds to Flame and Glory Wealth. [—5—]

Freight Bulk now appeals. Finding no merit to its claims, we affirm the judgment of the district court.

I.

A.

In 2008, Flame entered into four FFAs with ICI. After ICI defaulted on those contracts, Flame sued ICI in the High Court of Justice, Queen's Bench Division, Commercial Court, in London, England, alleging the breach and seeking monetary damages. The English court awarded judgment to Flame in the amount of $19,907,118.36 ("Flame's English judgment").

Flame had the English judgment recognized in the U.S. District Court for the Southern District of New York, and later registered the judgment in the U.S. District Court for the Eastern District of Virginia. It then sought and obtained the order of attachment against the M/V CAPE VIEWER.

Freight Bulk moved to vacate the order of attachment, contending the district court lacked subject matter jurisdiction because under either United States (federal) or English law, the FFAs were not maritime contracts. The district court denied Freight Bulk's motion and concluded it had admiralty jurisdiction, but certified the issue for interlocutory appeal. We granted Freight Bulk permission to file an interlocutory appeal. [—6—]

We then held that federal law governed our jurisdictional inquiry, and that the FFAs were maritime contracts under federal admiralty law. *Flame S.A. v. Freight Bulk Pte. Ltd.*, 762 F.3d 352, 2 Adm. R. 117 (4th Cir. 2014) (the "Interlocutory Appeal"). Because the FFAs were maritime contracts, we concluded that "the district court had subject matter jurisdiction to adjudicate the matter before it." *Id.* at 363, 2 Adm. R. at 125. We remanded the case to the district court for further proceedings.

B.

Separately, but also in 2008, Glory Wealth contracted for ICI to charter a vessel. After three installments, ICI stopped making payments under this agreement. Glory Wealth pursued arbitration against ICI in England and won an arbitration award (Glory Wealth's "English arbitration award"). Subsequently, Glory Wealth sought and obtained recognition of the arbitration award in the Southern District of New York. It did not register that judgment in the Eastern District of Virginia. Instead, Glory Wealth filed a complaint in the Eastern District of Virginia alleging that it was an ICI creditor who could maintain a maritime claim against ICI for breach of a charter party, as established by its English arbitration award.[1] It then sought [—7—] and obtained an attachment order for the M/V CAPE VIEWER pursuant to Supplemental Rule B.

C.

While the Interlocutory Appeal in Flame's case was pending, the district court consolidated the Flame and Glory Wealth cases based on the common questions of law and fact. Both complaints named other defendants in addition to Freight Bulk and ICI. One such co-defendant was the beneficial owner of Freight Bulk, Viktor Baranskiy, who is the son of ICI's final Chairman of the Board of Directors. Baranskiy is also the sole, beneficial owner of co-defendant Vista Shipping Ltd. ("Vista"). In fact, Baranskiy is the sole owner of numerous maritime companies—now, collectively known as the Palmira Group—of which Freight Bulk and Vista are just two.

The basic theory underlying both complaints was that Baranskiy aided ICI in evading its creditors by funneling money and other assets into multiple entities he controlled, including Vista and Freight Bulk. Vista was formed in late 2008, around the same time as ICI's failure. Freight Bulk, on

the other hand, was not formed until several years later. Consequently, the complaints relied on the interconnectedness of ICI with Vista and Vista with Freight Bulk to establish the requisite link showing Freight Bulk's responsibility as an alter ego for ICI's debts. The complaints alleged that Vista and Freight Bulk [—8—] were both formed with funds that originated from ICI and that ICI fraudulently transferred those funds and other assets in order to avoid its creditors.

The district court, with the assistance of a magistrate judge, oversaw "many, many" motions during discovery. *Flame S.A. v. Indus. Carriers, Inc.*, 39 F. Supp. 3d 769, 771 (E.D. Va. 2014). Freight Bulk repeatedly sought to delay the proceedings by obfuscation, often challenging the meaning and scope of discovery orders with meritless claims. As a result of Freight Bulk's noncompliance, Flame and Glory Wealth obtained sanctions in the form of certain presumptions to be applied at trial.

The evidence adduced at trial and the district court's factual findings are discussed below in the context of Freight Bulk's sufficiency challenge. But as background to our review, we note that things did not bode well for Freight Bulk when, by the end of the first day of his testimony, Baranskiy had provided inconsistent and evasive explanations for many of the key relationships and transactions at issue in the case. Even so, the district court expressed its surprise when Baranskiy and Freight Bulk's lead trial attorney "abandoned the case on the second morning of his testimony by not appearing" and instead left the country. *Id.* at 776. Local counsel notified the court of Baranskiy and lead counsel's decision and did not present any further evidence. [—9—]

Flame and Glory Wealth subsequently moved for judgment in their favor, which the district court granted. *Id.* at 790. In so doing, the court concluded that the evidence demonstrated that ICI, Vista, Freight Bulk, and Baranskiy were alter egos of one another. In addition, it found that ICI fraudulently transferred assets to Vista and related Palmira Group entities to avoid creditors, and

---

[1] Glory Wealth represented to the district court that it was in the process of having its English arbitration award reduced to a judgment in England.

that these latter entities had also fraudulently transferred funds to Freight Bulk. Accordingly, it held the defendants jointly and severally liable for ICI's debts, up to the value of the M/V CAPE VIEWER.[2] The court ordered the sale of the vessel, and later confirmed the sale and ordered distribution of the sale proceeds between Flame and Glory Wealth under a formula to which they had agreed.

Freight Bulk noted a timely appeal and we exercise jurisdiction pursuant to 28 U.S.C. § 1291. [—10—]

II.

On appeal, Freight Bulk raises six discrete issues and multiple sub-arguments. While we have reviewed its arguments in detail, we will only address its primary contentions of error. Those are: (1) that under Fourth Circuit precedent, United States substantive law does not apply to this dispute, which means the district court lacked subject matter jurisdiction; (2) that under Supreme Court precedent, actions to shift liability do not state an independent cause of action to establish subject matter jurisdiction, nor can a plaintiff rely on a prior lawsuit's basis for the court's jurisdiction in a subsequent suit to shift liability; (3) that the district court erred in distributing proceeds of the M/V CAPE VIEWER's sale to Glory Wealth because Glory Wealth failed to register its New York default judgment against ICI in the U.S. District Court for the Eastern District of Virginia; (4) that the district court abused its discretion by imposing certain discovery sanctions; (5) that the evidence was insufficient to support the

judgment as to both alter ego liability and fraudulent conveyance; and (6) that the district court judge exhibited personal bias against the defendants' Ukrainian nationality, which tainted the entire proceeding and requires a new trial. We address each issue in turn. [—11—]

A. Subject Matter Jurisdiction

Freight Bulk raises two new challenges to the district court's subject matter jurisdiction. Although the Court previously determined in the Interlocutory Appeal that the district court possessed admiralty jurisdiction over Flame's claims, the substantive questions we analyzed there are different from the arguments Freight Bulk now presents. Flame and Glory Wealth urge us to hold that the mandate rule precludes our reconsideration of the district court's subject matter jurisdiction.

We have reservations about whether a party can bring serial, piecemeal challenges to the district court's subject matter jurisdiction, and it is certainly a practice we do not encourage. However, we will address the merits of Freight Bulk's new arguments for two reasons. First, neither the Supreme Court nor we have directly opined on how to reconcile the mandate rule with subsequent distinct challenges to the Court's subject matter jurisdiction, a challenge that could ordinarily be raised at any time and even sua sponte. Second, Glory Wealth was not a party to the Interlocutory Appeal.

We review de novo whether the district court had subject matter jurisdiction. *See Vitol*, 708 F.3d at 533, 1 Adm. R. at 108. [—12—]

1.

Relying on *Dracos v. Hellenic Lines, Ltd.*, 762 F.2d 348 (4th Cir. 1985) (en banc), Freight Bulk contends that the district court lacked jurisdiction because the factors governing choice of law set out in *Lauritzen v. Larsen*, 345 U.S. 571 (1953), point against applying federal law to the parties' dispute. Because neither the parties nor the alleged wrongful conduct had any connection to the United

---

[2] The liability finding was limited in this manner because attachment proceedings under Supplemental Rule B confers only quasi in rem jurisdiction, which limits personal jurisdiction over the defendants in the case to the value of the attached vessel. *See* Supplemental Rule B(1)(a); *Vitol, S.A. v. Primerose Shipping Co. Ltd.*, 708 F.3d 527, 540, 1 Adm. R. 106, 114 (4th Cir. 2013). Flame and Glory Wealth had also sought to hold the defendants liable for the entire amount of their judgments against ICI, but the district court rejected that argument. Since they did not file a cross-appeal challenging that determination, it is not at issue in this appeal.

States, Freight Bulk asserts that *Dracos* requires us to conclude that the district court lacked subject matter jurisdiction.

Many of Freight Bulk's arguments conflate questions of choice of law with questions of subject matter jurisdiction, but our overriding impression is that Freight Bulk simply misunderstands our holding in *Dracos*. There, the plaintiff brought a negligence claim under the Jones Act and an unseaworthiness claim under general "American Maritime law." 762 F.2d at 350. The plaintiff asserted both tort claims against her deceased husband's employer, the owner of the ship upon which he had died. The plaintiff, her husband, and the defendant were all Greek individuals or corporations. The only connection to the United States was that the plaintiff's husband died while the ship was docked in Norfolk, Virginia. *Id.* at 350-51. [—13—]

Applying *Lauritzen*'s choice-of-law analysis, the district court found that federal tort law should not apply to the case, and without a federal claim to decide, the court dismissed the case for lack of jurisdiction. *Id.* at 351. We held that the district court's findings that the defendant's operations and connections to the United States were insufficient to require application of United States law to the plaintiff's claims were not clearly erroneous. *Id.* at 352. As a consequence, we agreed that federal tort law did not govern the plaintiff's claims and that the district court lacked jurisdiction to consider the case. *Id.* at 353.

Dracos thus held that when federal law does not provide the basis for a plaintiff's claims against the defendant, the district court is without subject matter jurisdiction. The court relied on the *Lauritzen* choice-of-law analysis to determine what law would govern the maritime tort action at issue, which in turn determined whether a federal tort claim existed.[3] Here, in contrast, Flame and Glory

Wealth do not need to look to *Lauritzen*'s choice-of-law analysis to pursue a claim under federal law. Instead, their claims rest on the long- [—14—] standing recognition that district courts have subject matter jurisdiction *in admiralty* both to enforce the judgments of foreign admiralty courts, *see Vitol*, 708 F.3d at 533, 538, 1 Adm. R. at 108, 112, and to consider the issues of alter ego and fraudulent transfer as part of an attachment proceeding pursuant to Supplemental Rule B, *see id.* at 537-38, 1 Adm. R. at 111-12.

In the Interlocutory Appeal, we held that the FFAs between Flame and ICI were maritime contracts, which meant that Flame's claim to enforce its English Judgment by means of a Supplemental Rule B attachment was cognizable under the district court's admiralty jurisdiction. *Flame*, 762 F.3d at 354-63, 2 Adm. R. at 117-25. None of Freight Bulk's arguments in this appeal challenge that holding, nor would it be able to do so as that holding is the law of the case. *Everett v. Pitt Cty. Bd. of Educ.*, 788 F.3d 132, 142 (4th Cir. 2015) (observing that with limited exceptions, once a court has established the law of the case, "it must be followed in all subsequent proceedings in the same case"[4]). Although Glory Wealth seeks to enforce its English arbitration award, its claim against ICI also arose from the breach of an indisputably maritime contract, namely, a charter party. *E.g., Kossick v. United Fruit Co.*, 365 U.S. 731, 735 (1961) ("Without doubt a [—15—] contract for hire either of a ship or of the sailors and officers to man her is within the admiralty jurisdiction."). Accordingly, Flame and Glory Wealth have claims arising squarely within federal admiralty jurisdiction. *See* 28 U.S.C. § 1333. At bottom, neither *Dracos* nor the *Lauritzen* choice-of-law analysis have any bearing on Flame and Glory Wealth's ability to bring the type of federal action they assert, nor in establishing the district court's admiralty jurisdiction over this case.

---

[3] Glory Wealth argues that *Dracos*'s reference to "jurisdiction" was imprecise and that recent Supreme Court precedent calls into question whether that analysis implicates the district court's subject matter jurisdiction. We need not address that argument because even a straightforward

reading of *Dracos* does not support Freight Bulk's position.

[4] Here and throughout the opinion, internal quotation marks, citations, alterations, or footnotes have been omitted in citations.

2.

Freight Bulk's second jurisdictional challenge is that *Peacock v. Thomas*, 516 U.S. 349 (1996), "precludes federal jurisdiction over alter ego and fraudulent conveyance claims that seek to shift liability for an existing judgment—including a maritime judgment—onto a non-party to that judgment." (Opening Br. 15.) Freight Bulk contends that Flame and Glory Wealth's allegations of alter ego and fraudulent concealment liability did not independently provide the district court subject matter jurisdiction. In addition, it asserts that the district court could not exercise ancillary, or supplemental, jurisdiction because *Peacock* prohibits a plaintiff relying on the court's jurisdiction in an earlier lawsuit to establish jurisdiction in a subsequent lawsuit to enforce a judgment. [—16—]

We disagree. Freight Bulk fails to grasp key substantive distinctions between federal question jurisdiction and admiralty jurisdiction when bringing suit to enforce a judgment. In *Peacock*, the Supreme Court held that the district court lacked jurisdiction to consider a "new action[] in which a federal judgment creditor [sought] to impose liability for a money judgment on a person not otherwise liable for the judgment." 516 U.S. at 351. Because the second action did not allege a new violation of any federal law, the district court did not have original jurisdiction in the second lawsuit pursuant to 28 U.S.C. § 1331 (federal question jurisdiction). *Id.* at 353-54. The Supreme Court also held that the district court did not have supplemental jurisdiction.[5] This was so, the Court concluded, because "[i]n a subsequent lawsuit involving claims with no independent basis for jurisdiction, a federal court lacks that threshold jurisdictional power that exists when ancillary claims are asserted in the same proceeding as

the claims conferring federal jurisdiction." *Id.* at 355.

While the plaintiff in *Peacock* sought to enforce a judgment arising from the court's federal question jurisdiction, Flame [—17—] and Glory Wealth sought to enforce a foreign judgment and arbitration award through the attachment of a vessel by invoking the district court's admiralty jurisdiction. This distinction matters because under long-standing Supreme Court jurisprudence, a district court's admiralty jurisdiction extends to claims to enforce foreign admiralty judgments. *See Pennhallow v. Doane Adm'rs*, 3 U.S. (3 Dall.) 54, 97 (1795) (opinion of Iredell, J.); *see also Vitol*, 708 F.3d at 538, 1 Adm. R. at 112 (stating "centuries of settled hornbook admiralty law establish that 'admiralty jurisdiction in the United States may be broadly stated as extending to . . . any claim to enforce a judgment of a foreign admiralty court'"); *Ost-West-Handel Bruno Bischoff GmbH v. Project Asia Line, Inc.*, 160 F.3d 170, 174 (4th Cir. 1998); 1-VII *Benedict on Admiralty* § 106.

This recognition of subject matter jurisdiction in the admiralty context "differs substantially from the law governing jurisdiction to enforce judgments rendered by federal courts exercising federal question jurisdiction under 28 U.S.C. § 1331." *D'Amico Dry Ltd. v. Primera Mar. (Hellas) Ltd.*, 756 F.3d 151, 155, 2 Adm. R. 69, 71 (2d Cir. 2014). While an enforcement action brought under § 1331 must demonstrate the existence of federal jurisdiction independent of the judgment to be enforced, a district court's ability to enforce foreign admiralty judgments has not been so limited. *Id.* at 155-56, 2 Adm. R. at 71 (collecting cases on [—18—] point). Similarly, as we reiterated in *Vitol*, the district court's admiralty jurisdiction includes the inherent authority to grant attachments, including an attachment of assets pursuant to Supplemental Rule B. *See* 708 F.3d at 537-38, 1 Adm. R. at 111-12.

Peacock only discussed the requirements of federal question jurisdiction under § 1331 and was unrelated to the scope of a district court's admiralty jurisdiction. As we have previously

---

[5] Supplemental jurisdiction, which is sometimes referred to as ancillary jurisdiction, "permit[s] disposition by a single court of claims that are, in varying respects and degrees, factually interdependent" and "enable[s] a court to function successfully, that is, to manage its proceedings, vindicate its authority, and effectuate its decrees." *Id.* at 354.

recognized in another context, "*Peacock* does not prohibit a federal court from taking jurisdiction over a postjudgment alter ego claim where an *independent* basis for jurisdiction exists." *C.F. Trust, Inc. v. First Flight Ltd. P'ship*, 306 F.3d 126, 133 (4th Cir. 2002). Here, that "independent basis" is the court's admiralty jurisdiction.

The Supreme Court's decision in *Swift & Co. Packers v. Compania Colombiana Del Caribe, S.A.*, 339 U.S. 684 (1950), confirms our conclusion that because the district court was properly exercising its admiralty jurisdiction, it could also consider the issues of alter ego and fraudulent conveyance. In *Swift*, the plaintiff filed suit against a defendant for nondelivery of cargo and attached the defendant's vessel. The plaintiff later sought to amend its allegations to include a second named defendant, which it argued was either the original defendant's alter ego or an entity to whom the original defendant had fraudulently transferred assets. *Id.* at 686. [—19—] Although the Supreme Court ultimately rejected plaintiff's alter ego claim, it first reiterated that "[t]he jurisdiction of a court of admiralty to determine the question of alter ego is undoubted." *Id.* at 689 n.4. Thus, under *Swift*, that "undoubted" authority exists in this case as well.

Swift reached the same conclusion on the issue of fraudulent conveyance. The district court had held (and the Fifth Circuit affirmed) that it could not consider the plaintiff's fraudulent conveyance claim because it ran too far afield from the admiralty claim that provided the basis for the court's jurisdiction. *Id.* at 689-90. The Supreme Court disagreed, observing that although there are restraints on the exercise of admiralty jurisdiction,

[The plaintiffs, as creditors of the defendant] went into admiralty on a claim arising upon . . . matters obviously within admiralty jurisdiction. As an incident to that claim, in order to secure respondents' appearance and to insure the fruits of a decree in [their] favor, they made an attachment . . . . The issue of fraud [arose] in connection with the attachment as a means of effectuating a

claim incontestably in admiralty. To deny an admiralty court jurisdiction over this subsidiary or derivative issue in a litigation clearly maritime would require an absolute rule that admiralty is rigorously excluded from all contact with nonmaritime transactions and from all equitable relief . . . . It would be strange indeed thus to hobble a legal system that has been so responsive to the practicalities of maritime commerce and so inventive in adapting its jurisdiction to the needs of that commerce.

Id. at 691. [—20—]

These principles govern this case as well: Flame and Glory Wealth filed enforcement claims that were "obviously within admiralty jurisdiction." Attendant to these claims was the Supplemental Rule B attachment. The issue of fraudulent conveyance arose in connection with those claims. And because the district court's admiralty jurisdiction had been invoked by the Supplemental Rule B attachment, it could also consider the latter.

Freight Bulk points to two cases where circuit courts have applied *Peacock* in a maritime context. *See Nat'l Mar. Servs., Inc. v. Straub*, 776 F.3d 783, 3 Adm. R. 638 (11th Cir. 2015); *Zamora v. Bodden*, 395 F. App'x 118 (5th Cir. 2010) (per curiam) (limiting its analysis to whether federal question jurisdiction exists). Neither is binding, of course, but we also find them unpersuasive to Freight Bulk's position.[6] Significantly,

---

[6] In fact, *Straub* cuts against Freight Bulk's argument with respect to the fraudulent transfer claim because the Eleventh Circuit distinguished *Peacock*, and concluded it *could* exercise ancillary jurisdiction in a supplementary proceeding to avoid a fraudulent transfer by a judgment debtor where jurisdiction in the original proceeding had been based in admiralty. *See Straub*, 776 F.3d at 786-88, 3 Adm. R. at 638-41. This was so because the suit "sought to disgorge [the defendant] of a fraudulently transferred asset, not to impose liability for a judgment on a third party," and liability would be limited to "the proceeds that [the judgment debtor] fraudulently transferred to [the defendant]." *Id.* at 787, 3 Adm. R. at 640. While we need not reach that analysis here since admiralty

neither [—21—] case considers whether *Peacock* applies to an action where an independent basis for establishing the district court's admiralty jurisdiction exists (apart from the fraud or alter ego theories). Nor does either case challenge that the district court's admiralty jurisdiction extends to enforcing foreign admiralty judgments in attachment proceedings.

To reiterate, then, unlike *Peacock* and the other cases Freight Bulk relies on, Flame and Glory Wealth brought proceedings in the district court to enforce an admiralty judgment and attach a vessel under Supplemental Rule B. The district court had admiralty jurisdiction under § 1333 to determine those claims, and as part of considering those claims, the court also had authority to consider the questions of alter ego and fraudulent conveyance. *See* 28 U.S.C. § 1367; *Vitol*, 708 F.3d at 537-39, 1 Adm. R. at 111-13.

Peacock's analysis thus has no bearing on the district court's subject matter jurisdiction over Flame and Glory Wealth's claims. For these reasons, the district court properly exercised jurisdiction over the parties' dispute.[7] [—22—]

B. Glory Wealth's Judgment Against ICI

Next, Freight Bulk contends the district court should not have permitted Glory Wealth to receive a share of the proceeds from the sale of the M/V CAPE VIEWER because Glory Wealth failed to register its New York judgment in the Eastern District of Virginia, "a perquisite to enforce[ment] . . . under 28 U.S.C. § 1963." (Opening Br. 38.) Freight Bulk

---

jurisdiction otherwise exists, Freight Bulk's attempt to distinguish *Straub* in its favor mischaracterizes that case's holding.

[7] Freight Bulk also contends that even if the district court possessed subject matter jurisdiction, the district court erred by adopting Virginia's fraudulent conveyance framework because it is an outlier among state-law provisions. Freight Bulk has not preserved this issue for appeal because it failed to raise it in the district court. As such, we will not consider it for (Continued) [—22—] the first time on appeal. *In re Under Seal*, 749 F.3d 276, 285-86 (4th Cir. 2014).

raises various arguments flowing from this main premise, all of which it asserts require "this Court [to] render judgment for Freight Bulk." (Opening Br. 40.) We need not consider the substance of Freight Bulk's arguments in light of two threshold considerations: waiver and harmlessness.

To start, Freight Bulk never argued to the district court that Glory Wealth's failure to formally submit the judgment it sought to be enforced precluded it from receiving a share of the proceeds from the sale of the M/V CAPE VIEWER. As such, Freight Bulk did not put the district court "on notice as to the substance of the issue" now raised on appeal, as required to preserve it for review. *Nelson v. Adams USA, Inc.*, 529 U.S. 460, 469 (2000). [—23—]

In addition, the record shows that between the district court's order holding Freight Bulk liable and the sale of the M/V CAPE VIEWER, Freight Bulk never argued that Glory Wealth's failure to formally introduce a judgment against ICI precluded it from recovering a portion of the proceeds. This was so even though the district court explicitly asked Freight Bulk if it had any objections to the distribution. At that time, Freight Bulk only expressed a somewhat indifferent concern that it did not know the basis for the agreed-upon allocation between Glory Wealth and Flame. We have refused to consider newly raised arguments absent "exceptional circumstances," that is to say, a "'fundamental error' or a denial of fundamental justice." *In re Under Seal*, 749 F.3d at 285-86. No exceptional circumstances exist in this case.

Another consideration demonstrates the absence of any such fundamental injustice and stands as an alternative basis to reject Freight Bulk's argument. Even assuming error, Freight Bulk would not be entitled to any relief as a consequence of Glory Wealth's failure to formally file its judgment. This is so because Flame registered an enforceable judgment in the district court against Freight Bulk in the amount of $19,907,118.36. That judgment far exceeds the approximately $8.3 million in proceeds arising from the sale of the M/V CAPE VIEWER. Flame's claim thus precluded Freight Bulk from any **[—24—]** portion of the proceeds from the sale. Prior to distribution of the proceeds, however, Flame and Glory Wealth mutually agreed how to divide the proceeds between themselves, and the district court entered judgment based on that agreement. Freight Bulk thus has no interest in how they resolved their competing claims. It has not been harmed by the alleged error, nor has it shown that it would be entitled to any relief as a result. *See* 28 U.S.C. § 2111 (stating the court will not consider harmless errors); Fed. R. Civ. P. 61 (same). Accordingly, we decline to consider the substance of Freight Bulk's argument.[8]

C. Discovery Sanctions

After finding that Freight Bulk had violated several of the court's discovery orders, the magistrate judge issued certain sanctions. Freight Bulk challenges only one of the findings and resulting sanctions: the failure to produce responsive ICI documents.[9] As a consequence of that violation, the magistrate **[—25—]** judge deemed "as established for purposes of" the proceedings, that "had any [ICI] documents been produced by [Freight Bulk] in compliance with the Court's discovery orders, those documents would have been favorable to [Flame and Glory Wealth] and harmful to [Freight Bulk]." (J.A. 1323.) The

district court overruled Freight Bulk's objections, agreeing that Freight Bulk controlled responsive ICI documents and yet had failed to produce them, and that the sanction was appropriate. (J.A. 1762-66, 1778-79.)

Freight Bulk contends this discovery sanction was improper because it did not possess, control, or have custody of responsive ICI documents and thus should not have been compelled to produce them. It also attacks the scope of the discovery order as being too broad. Freight Bulk further asserts that the sanctions "were overwhelmingly prejudicial" given that the district court repeatedly referred to the sanctions to "fill wide gaps" in the trial evidence. (Opening Br. 46.)[10] **[—26—]**

We typically review the substance of a district court's decision to impose discovery sanctions for abuse of discretion. *Hoyle v. Freightliner, LLC*, 650 F.3d 321, 329 (4th Cir. 2011). We are also obligated, however, to "disregard all errors and defects that do not affect any party's substantial rights." Fed. R. Civ. P. 61; *see also McNanama v. Lukhard*, 616 F.2d 727, 730 (4th Cir. 1980) (concluding error in compelling discovery was harmless); *Tagupa v. Bd. of Dirs.*, 633 F.2d 1309, 1312

---

[8] In light of our conclusion, we deny Glory Wealth's motion to supplement the record with the English judgment enforcing the arbitration award that it obtained after final judgment had been obtained in this proceeding.

[9] The district court also found that Freight Bulk had violated discovery orders by failing to produce (1) employee workbooks, (2) responsive emails from Baranskiy's account, (3) documents relating to a loan agreement between Sea Traffic and Freight Bulk, and (4) responsive email attachments. As a consequence, it authorized a sanction in the form of deeming the following facts established for purposes of the case: (1) Freight Bulk and Vista were alter egos of each other, and (2) the loan from Sea Traffic to Freight Bulk was a sham transaction (Continued) **[—25—]** and Freight Bulk was prohibited from offering evidence of repayment. In addition, the court held Freight Bulk and its counsel jointly and severally liable for attorneys' fees and expenses in pursuing the motions for sanctions.

[10] Freight Bulk's Opening Brief mentions one other discovery sanction in passing (deeming Freight Bulk and Vista to be alter egos). (Opening Br. 41.) Since the alter ego sanction was approved due to "the magnitude of [Freight Bulk's discovery] violations," (J.A. 1777), it was arguably based, at least in part, on Freight Bulk's failure to produce ICI documents. But (Continued) **[—26—]** since the failure to produce ICI documents was just one of five discrete categories of discovery violations leading to this sanction, it likely would have still been an appropriate exercise of the district court's discretion to have imposed it based on the other violations. In addition, Freight Bulk has failed to develop any argument in its opening brief discussing the propriety of this particular sanction. Its analysis solely involves the ICI documents. As such, Freight Bulk has not adequately developed any additional issues related to the propriety of the alter ego sanction for us to review on appeal. *See* Fed. R. App. P. 28(a)(8)(A); *see also Edwards v. City of Goldsboro*, 178 F.3d 231, 241 n.6 (4th Cir. 1999).

(9th Cir. 1980) ("The harmless error doctrine applies to discovery orders.").

We need not wade into the nuances of Freight Bulk's arguments because we readily conclude on this record that even if the district court abused its discretion on this issue, its error was harmless. Freight Bulk markedly overstates the impact that this discovery order and resulting sanction had on the district court's consideration of the case as a whole. Although [—27—] the negative inference from the ICI documents informed some of the factual findings underpinning the district court's analysis, each factual finding that noted the negative inference was supported by more than one piece of additional evidence that had been admitted at trial.[11] Moreover, by the time the court explained its legal conclusions as to each of the claims, it had so cabined the negative inference about the ICI documents that this evidence was only one of many facts supporting its analysis. *See Flame,* 39 F. Supp. 3d at 787-89.

More problematic, Freight Bulk's argument disregards the effect of the other negative inferences the district court relied on throughout its opinion and which arose from a key aspect of the trial: Baranskiy and his lead counsel's decision to abandon their case mid-trial. The district court identified that event as "[p]erhaps [the] most important in [the] case," observing that Baranskiy's testimony to that point had been "at times false, inaccurate, contradictory, and untruthful." *Id.* at 776. The district court concluded that Baranskiy's "desertion" prejudiced Flame and Glory Wealth, and found that had Baranskiy [—28—] continued to testify, "his testimony would have been substantially against his own interests in relation to" Vista, Freight Bulk, and ICI. *Id.* The district court then relied on *that* negative inference throughout its factual

findings and legal analysis. *E.g., id.* at 778, 779, 787-88, and 789. By the district court's own indication, these negative inferences were considerably more damaging to Freight Bulk than the negative inference created by the document discovery violation contested on appeal.

Based on the totality of the record, even if we assume that the district court erred in sanctioning Freight Bulk for failing to produce ICI documents, that error did not substantially affect the judgment. *See Taylor v. Va. Union Univ.,* 193 F.3d 219, 235 (4th Cir. 1999) (en banc) ("In order to conclude the district court's assumed evidentiary errors did not affect [the judgment], and therefore were harmless, 'we need only be able to say with fair assurance, after pondering all that happened without stripping the erroneous action from the whole, that the judgment was not substantially swayed by the error[s].'"), *abrogated on other grounds by, Desert Palace Inc. v. Costa,* 539 U.S. 90 (2003). Accordingly, we reject Freight Bulk's claim of error. [—29—]

D. Sufficiency of the Evidence

Freight Bulk next claims the evidence is insufficient to support the judgment in favor of Flame and Glory Wealth. It contends that the hallmarks for establishing alter ego liability are missing as between ICI, Vista, and Freight Bulk.[12] Freight Bulk further posits that the evidence did not establish the requisite fraud to support the fraudulent conveyance claim, but rather reflected legitimate business transactions. Neither argument has merit.

When evaluating the sufficiency of the evidence after a bench trial, we review the district court's factual findings for clear error and its legal conclusions de novo. *Universal Furniture Int'l, Inc. v. Collezione Europa USA, Inc.,* 618 F.3d 417, 427 (4th Cir. 2010).

---

[11] For example, although the district court noted the non-production of ICI documents showing when it became insolvent, testimony at trial supported an insolvency "as early as June 30, 2008" and "no later than mid-September," which also allowed the district court to make its ultimate finding "that ICI's insolvency began in July 2008 and continued through October 2008 and thereafter." *Flame,* 39 F. Supp. 3d at 777.

[12] As noted above, the alter ego analysis here is a two-step process showing Vista operated as an alter ego of ICI and that Freight Bulk is an alter ego of Vista.

1. Alter Ego

Although the corporate form ordinarily prohibits one entity from being liable for the acts of a separate, though related, entity, courts will pierce the corporate veil in "extraordinary circumstances," such as when the corporate form is being used for wrongful purposes. *Vitol*, 708 F.3d at 543-44, 1 Adm. R. at 117-18. The standard for piercing the corporate veil is high, but its purpose is to [—30—] "achieve an equitable result" by "focus[ing] on reality and not form, on how the corporation operated and the individual defendant's relationship to that operation." *Id.*, 1 Adm. R. at 117-18.[13]

Freight Bulk first contends that the district court erred in holding that ICI and Vista were alter egos. It points to the alter ego analysis in *Vitol*—wherein we concluded the evidence was insufficient to allege an alter ego claim—and maintains that certain allegations here were identical to, and in some cases less than, the allegations in *Vitol*. However, because numerous factors can support the conclusion that corporations are alter egos, the inquiry is fact-intensive and specific facts may be relevant in one case and irrelevant in another. *See Ost-West-Handel*, 160 F.3d at 174 ("Such a determination is to be made on a case-by-case basis."). To that end, Freight Bulk's focus on how the factors in this case align with those in *Vitol* is misplaced. The relevant inquiry is not whether any particular factor was present, but whether the totality of the evidence established during the trial demonstrated that ICI and Vista were alter egos of each other. [—31—]

On that point, the district court applied the proper legal standards, relied on factors we have previously identified as relevant, and concluded that the evidence supported an alter ego finding. The factors considered by the district court included ICI's insolvency; Baranskiy's siphoning of funds; the failure of ICI, Vista, and Palmira Group companies to observe corporate formalities and maintain corporate records; that Baranskiy controlled the acts of specific Vista officers as well as Vista and Palmira Group companies as a whole; and that ICI and Vista had some shared ownership and employees. *See Vitol*, 708 F.3d at 544, 1 Adm. R. at 117 (listing these factors as indicative of alter ego corporations).

Freight Bulk does not dispute most of these factual findings, and the few it does challenge were not clearly erroneous. For example, Freight Bulk points to Baranskiy's trial testimony to assert that ICI and Vista had only a negligible overlap in employees. But the district court did not find Baranskiy's testimony to be credible. *Flame*, 39 F. Supp. 3d at 776. Moreover, the district court's finding that ICI and Vista "shared the same employees performing substantially the same tasks" relied on four named management employees plus unnamed "others." *Id.* at 780. As the court's analysis reflects, the significant factor underpinning its finding on this point was not the percentage of overall shared employees, [—32—] but rather their roles and fluidity between ICI, Vista, and the other Palmira Group affiliates (including Freight Bulk). *Id.* This finding was an appropriate one to make under the record evidence and to be considered as part of the district court's alter ego analysis.

Similarly, Freight Bulk asserts the district court errantly found that Baranskiy's "working at [his] father's company [made him ICI's] alter ego." (Opening Br. 49.) Yet again, Freight Bulk mischaracterizes the basis for the district court's finding, which was not based on Baranskiy's status as an employee of both ICI and Vista. Instead, the court's conclusion followed a detailed explanation of Baranskiy's specific conduct as a conduit for cash between ICI and Vista. *See Flame*, 39 F. Supp. 3d at 776-83.

Freight Bulk also challenges the second step of the district court's analysis—*i.e.*, its conclusion that Freight Bulk and Vista were alter egos. Freight Bulk contends that "as a matter of law" they are not. (Opening Br. 50.)

---

[13] The parties do not dispute that federal common law applies to this analysis. *See Ost-West-Handel*, 160 F.3d at 174 ("[I]n an admiralty case, a court applies federal common law and can look to state law in situations where there is no admiralty rule on point.").

We reject this argument for two reasons, either of which would be sufficient on its own. First, one of the sanctions for Freight Bulk's cumulative discovery violations was the finding that Freight Bulk and Vista are "alter egos of one another." *Id.* at 773. For the reasons discussed in footnote 10, that sanction stands. As such, the district court could properly rely on it [—33—] at trial. *See* Fed. R. Civ. P. 37(b)(2)(A)(i) (stating that a proper sanction for discovery violations is "directing that . . . designated facts be taken as established for purposes of the action").

Second, and quite apart from the sanction-based finding, the evidence fully supports the district court's conclusion. The trial record established, among other things, Baranskiy's ownership and control of both entities; that officers do as Baranskiy directs rather than exercising independent decision making; that Freight Bulk is undercapitalized; that funds between Freight Bulk and Vista are intermingled amongst themselves and other Palmira Group entities; that Baranskiy's companies fail to observe corporate formalities and maintain proper records; that they share office space; and that dealings are not conducted at arm's length.

Freight Bulk's limited challenges to these findings again minimize Baranskiy's conduct and attack the court's findings as being based solely on his ownership of both Freight Bulk and Vista. Certainly not all corporations with a common owner are alter egos, but neither can a corporation escape alter ego liability solely on the basis of being a separate, formal entity sharing the same owner. Where, as here, the evidence shows a common owner who fails to observe corporate formalities and often comingles funds to avoid legal obligations, it is not [—34—] error to treat the entities as one. *E.g., De Witt Truck Brokers, Inc. v. W. Ray Flemming Fruit Co.,* 540 F.2d 681, 685 (4th Cir. 1976) ("[T]he mere fact that all or almost all of the corporate stock is owned by one individual . . . will not afford sufficient grounds for disregarding corporateness. But when substantial ownership of all the stock of a corporation in a single individual is combined with other factors clearly supporting disregard of the

corporate fiction on grounds of fundamental equity and fairness, courts have experienced 'little difficulty' and have shown no hesitancy in applying what is described as the 'alter ego' or 'instrumentality' theory in order to cast aside the corporate shield[.]").

Freight Bulk also mistakenly asserts that it cannot, as a matter of law, have been ICI's alter ego because it was established years after ICI's demise. This argument overlooks the requisite causal link between the entities through Vista. Freight Bulk does not deny that ICI and Vista were in existence at the same time. Since those two entities were alter egos, they are liable for each other's debts. *See Keffer v. H.K. Porter Co., Inc.,* 872 F.2d 60, 65 (4th Cir. 1989) (describing the effect of piercing the corporate veil). Similarly, because Vista and Freight Bulk are alter egos, they can be responsible [—35—] for each other's debts.[14] In short, Freight Bulk is liable for ICI's liabilities through Vista.

The district court properly applied our case law regarding alter ego liability to the facts presented. Our conclusion in a prior case applies equally here: "[T]his case patently presents a blending of the very factors which courts have regarded as justifying a disregard of the corporate entity in furtherance of basic and fundamental fairness." *Keffer,* 872 F.2d at 65.

2. Fraudulent Conveyance

Freight Bulk also raises multiple challenges to the district court's conclusion that ICI fraudulently conveyed assets to the defendants and related entities to avoid its

---

[14] As part of its argument, Freight Bulk selectively characterizes the Supreme Court's statement in *Swift* that the plaintiff could not pursue alter ego liability against a particular defendant since it came into existence after the underlying cause of action accrued. Significantly, however, the Supreme Court noted that "*apart from any transfer of assets by* [the originating defendant to an alleged alter ego company], the latter company could not be held personally liable on an alter ego theory." *Swift,* 339 U.S. at 689 n.4 (emphasis added). Here, Flame and Glory Wealth alleged a transfer of assets, so that principle does not apply.

creditors. Given no federal admiralty rules govern such a claim, the district court appropriately looked to Virginia law. *See Ost-West-Handel*, 160 F.3d at 174; *see also supra* n.7 (observing that Freight Bulk failed to preserve any argument that the district court should not have looked to Virginia [—36—] fraudulent transfer principles). The applicable Virginia statute treats as void any transfer of property "given with intent to delay, hinder or defraud creditors, purchasers or other persons of or from what they are or may be lawfully entitled to[.]" Va. Code § 55-80.

"In a suit to set aside a fraudulent conveyance, proof of the fraudulent intent must be 'clear, cogent and convincing.'" *Fox Rest Assocs., L.P. v. Little*, 717 S.E.2d 126, 132 (Va. 2011). However, because of the difficulty of establishing fraudulent intent, Virginia courts have traditionally relied on certain presumptions, known as "badges of fraud." *Id.* These "badges of fraud" include: the relationship of the parties, the grantor's insolvency, pursuit of the grantor by creditors at the time of the transfer, want of consideration, retention of the property by the grantor, fraudulent incurrence of indebtedness after the conveyance, gross inadequacy of price, and lack of security. *Id.* at 131-32; 9A Michie's Jurisprudence of Virginia & West Virginia §§ 12, 15 (2015). "Once a party has introduced evidence to establish a badge of fraud, a prima facie case of fraudulent conveyance is established[, and] the burden shifts [so that] the defendant must establish the bona fides of the transaction." *Fox Rest Assocs.*, 717 S.E.2d at 132.

At the outset, Freight Bulk asserts the district court inappropriately relied on adverse inferences in the absence of [—37—] evidence supporting Flame and Glory Wealth's claim. While Freight Bulk refers to "adverse inferences" in the plural, we note again that its prior challenge was only to the negative inference drawn from the failure to produce ICI documents, not from the district court's additional inferences arising from Baranskiy's trial conduct. Plus, we have already held that any error on this front was harmless. As to the inference arising from trial, the district court acted within its discretion in finding that any additional testimony from Baranskiy "would have been detrimental to [Freight Bulk's] positions." *Flame*, 39 F. Supp. 3d at 789; *see also Baxter v. Palmigiano*, 425 U.S. 308, 318 (1976) (noting, in the context of the Fifth Amendment's privilege against self-incrimination, that a court may draw "adverse inferences against parties to civil actions when they refuse to testify in response to probative evidence offered against them"); *Brice v. Nkaru*, 220 F.3d 233, 240 & n.9 (4th Cir. 2000) (discussing limitations on when an adverse inference can be made in a civil trial as a result of an opposing party's failure to testify or missing testimony, none of which are applicable here); *Streber v. Comm'r*, 138 F.3d 216, 221-22 (5th Cir. 1998) ("In general, a court may draw a negative inference from a party's failure to produce a witness 'whose testimony would elucidate the transaction.'" (quoting *Graves v. United States*, 150 U.S. 118, 121 (1893)). [—38—]

Next, Freight Bulk contends the evidence did not show that ICI transferred the charter for the M/V HARMONY FALCON to Vista, but rather that Vista simply entered into its own charter after ICI went bankrupt. The district court ably described the record evidence supporting its finding to the contrary. That evidence included proof that ICI and Vista both hid Vista's assumption of the charter; that Vista "paid [the] same charter rate for the same ship and route and cargo [as ICI had contracted for] despite the drop in shipping rates which [had] occurred"; that a subsidiary of ICI paid bunker rates for the charter Vista fulfilled; that Vista did not give ICI any consideration for the transaction; and that Vista "made about $1.7 million profit for the charter of the HARMONY FALCON, which sum ICI would have been entitled" to collect and apply to its debts. *Flame*, 39 F. Supp. 3d at 777-78. As the district court concluded, these facts are the very badges of fraud Virginia courts have indicated give rise to a prima facie case of fraudulent transfer. *Id.* at 785, 789. And Freight Bulk failed to rebut that presumption with evidence establishing the bona fides of the transaction.

Freight Bulk also contends Flame and Glory Wealth failed to establish fraud with respect to $1.58 million in payments ICI made to Baranskiy that it claims were commissions. The document Freight Bulk points to as proof for this position is an untitled, undated sheet of paper containing columns listing [—39—] clients and corresponding numbers without any context. We cannot say on the basis of this document that the district court clearly erred in rejecting Freight Bulk's assertion as to its meaning, particularly given the lack of credible corroborating testimony. Indeed, Baranskiy's testimony was contradictory throughout the duration of the case, including with respect to explaining money he received from ICI and money he used to capitalize Vista. As such, the district court did not clearly err in finding that these payments were actually payments ICI made to capitalize Vista.

As a final argument, Freight Bulk asserts that, at most, Flame and Glory Wealth established two discrete fraudulent transfers (the M/V HARMONY FALCON charter and $1.58 million cash) totaling only $3.28 million. As such, it contends the district court erred in holding that Freight Bulk was liable for the total amount of Flame and Glory Wealth's judgments against ICI, which were in the neighborhood of $60 million. Relatedly, Freight Bulk asserts that the district court should have capped Flame and Glory Wealth's recovery at $3.28 million rather than distributing the entire $8.3 million obtained from the sale of the M/V CAPE VIEWER.

This argument fails for two reasons. First, alter ego liability made Freight Bulk jointly and severally liable for the entirety of Flame and Glory Wealth's judgments against ICI. [—40—] Thus, even if Freight Bulk were correct as to the fraudulent conveyance claim, it would still not be entitled to a different result because of the district court's judgment on that issue. *Swift*, 339 U.S. at 689 n.4 (observing that if plaintiffs succeeded on a theory of alter ego, then the issue of fraudulent transfer would be irrelevant because they would be afforded relief under those standards). Second, the premise of Freight Bulk's argument—that the district

court only found two fraudulent conveyances—is incorrect. To the contrary, the district court found multiple fraudulent conveyances between ICI's alter egos, making Freight Bulk liable for the entire fraud perpetrated by ICI through Baranskiy and his compatriots. While its holding identified the charter of the M/V HARMONY FALCON in particular, it also identified the transfer of other "assets," "substantial funds," and "ostensible 'loans,'" which are in reality security—and interest-free transfers of funds[.]" *Flame*, 39 F. Supp. 3d at 789. In addition, the district court relied on the discovery sanction—unchallenged on appeal—that Vista provided funds to Sea Traffic, which were "then transferred to [Freight Bulk] for the purchase of the CAPE VIEWER," in a "sham transaction used to avoid creditors." *Id.* at 781. [—41—]

For these reasons, we conclude sufficient evidence supports the judgment against Freight Bulk on the fraudulent conveyance claim.

E. Judicial Bias

Lastly, Freight Bulk contends the district court demonstrated a personal bias against Ukrainians, which tainted the entire proceeding and requires reversal.[15] In support, Freight Bulk points to nine statements by the district court that purportedly show this prejudice.

To be sure, "[a] fair trial in a fair tribunal is a basic requirement of due process." *Caperton v. A.T. Massey Coal Co.*, 556 U.S. 868, 876 (2009). To protect the right to be heard by an impartial jurist, Congress has authorized parties to timely file an "affidavit that the judge before whom the matter is pending has a personal bias or prejudice either against him or in favor of any adverse party," and upon such a showing, "such judge shall proceed no further therein, but another

---

[15] Alternatively, Freight Bulk asserts the district court's bias requires reassignment to a different judge in the event of a remand. Because we have not found any other reversible error, we only consider the remaining portion of Freight Bulk's argument.

judge shall be assigned to hear such proceeding." 28 U.S.C. § 144. This is, of course, in addition to the judge's own duty to consider whether he must disqualify himself "in any proceeding in which [—42—] his impartiality might reasonably be questioned." 28 U.S.C. § 455(a).

At no time in the proceedings below did Freight Bulk challenge the district court judge's impartiality to hear the case. Accordingly, it has failed to preserve this claim for appellate review. *See In re Under Seal*, 749 F.3d at 285-86 (discussing the consequences of failing to preserve a claim for appeal); *see also Corti v. Storage Tech. Corp.*, 304 F.3d 336, 343 (4th Cir. 2002) (Niemeyer, J., concurring) ("[I]t remains the law of this circuit that when a party to a civil action fails to raise a point at trial, that party waives review of the issue unless there are exceptional or extraordinary circumstances justifying review."). Having reviewed Freight Bulk's arguments and paid particular attention to the exemplars it provided in the transcripts, we discern no exceptional or extraordinary circumstances in this case that would justify reviewing it on the merits.[16] [—43—]

III.

For the reasons detailed above, the judgment of the district court in favor of Flame and Glory Wealth is

AFFIRMED.

---

[16] Freight Bulk cites an out-of-circuit case to support its view that this Court should not deem its argument waived. *See United States v. Kaba*, 480 F.3d 152 (2d Cir. 2007). This criminal sentencing case did not involve an allegation of evidence of a judge's personal bias or prejudice, but rather a claim that the judge considered the defendant's nationality in deciding an appropriate sentence. *Id.* at 156-58. As such, it is inapposite.

Moreover, even assuming Freight Bulk preserved its argument, we find no error. We have reviewed the statements cited by Freight Bulk and conclude it has selectively quoted (Continued) [—43—] only parts of the record and taken the comments far out of context. Viewed in full, there is nothing in the district court's commentary to support such a claim.

This page intentionally left blank

United States Court of Appeals for the Fifth Circuit

United States Court of Appeals
for the Fifth Circuit

No. 12-30883

IN RE DEEPWATER HORIZON

UNITED STATES
VS.
BP EXPLORATION & PROD., INC.

Appeal from the United States District Court for the
Eastern District of Louisiana

Decided: January 9, 2015

Citation: 775 F.3d 741, 3 Adm. R. 262 (5th Cir. 2015).

ON PETITION FOR REHEARING EN BANC
(Opinion June 4, 2014, 753 F.3d 570, 2 Adm. R. 233)

Before **KING, BENAVIDES,** and **DENNIS,** Circuit
Judges.

[—1—] **BENAVIDES,** Circuit Judge:

The court having been polled at the request of one of its members, and a majority of the judges who are in regular active service and not disqualified not having voted in favor (Fed. R. App. P. 35 and 5th Cir. R. 35), the Petition for Rehearing En Banc is DENIED. Judge Clement, joined by Judges Jolly, [—2—] Jones, Owen, Elrod, and Southwick, dissents from the court's denial of rehearing en banc, and her dissent is attached.

In the en banc poll, 6 judges voted in favor of rehearing (Judges Jolly, Jones, Clement, Owen, Elrod and Southwick) and 7 judges voted against rehearing (Chief Judge Stewart and Judges Davis, Dennis, Prado, Haynes, Graves, and Costa).[1]

ENTERED FOR THE COURT:

Fortunato C. Benavides

UNITED STATES CIRCUIT JUDGE

---

[1] Judges Smith and Higginson are recused and did not participate in the consideration of the petition.

(Reporter's Note: Dissenting opinion follows on p. 263).

[—3—] CLEMENT, Circuit Judge, with whom JOLLY, JONES, OWEN, ELROD, and SOUTHWICK, join, dissenting from Denial of Rehearing En Banc:

The denial of the petition for rehearing en banc ensures that our precedent concerning liability for oil spills under the Clean Water Act remains unclear. The panel opinion's "controlled confinement" test does not follow from the text of the CWA. Compounding this, the panel's supplementary opinion conflicts with the panel opinion. These problems, coupled with the exceptional importance of the underlying issue, necessitated a rehearing. Hence, I respectfully dissent.

The CWA makes liable the "owner, operator, or person in charge of any vessel . . . or offshore facility from which oil . . . is discharged" into navigable waters. 33 U.S.C. §1321(b)(7)(A). Discharge is defined as "spilling, leaking, pumping, pouring, emitting, emptying or dumping." 33 U.S.C. § 1321(a)(2). The panel opinion, in turn, defines discharge as "the loss of controlled confinement." I believe that this "loss of controlled confinement" test is inconsistent with the text of the CWA. A rehearing en banc would have allowed us to consider more faithful interpretations of the Act.

Further, the panel's issuance of a supplemental opinion to clarify its first CWA interpretation suggests that the panel perceived an ambiguity in the CWA. This is concerning because a clear line of precedent exists holding that ambiguities in civil-penalty statues should be resolved in favor of the defendant. *See, e.g., Comm'r. v. Acker*, 361 U.S. 87, 91 (1959); *Diamond Roofing Co. v. Occupational Safety & Health Review Comm'n*, 528 F.2d 645, 649 (5th Cir. 1976).

Having created this "controlled confinement" test, the panel opinion misapplies it. The panel opinion holds that confinement was lost in the Well [—4—] when hydrocarbons moved from the formation into the Well. The panel reaches this conclusion despite the fact that the hydrocarbons then traveled through the blowout preventer and riser before entering the Gulf of Mexico. More significantly, the panel reaches its holding despite its contradictory finding that the Well—which was not designed to confine hydrocarbons—never confined the hydrocarbons at all. The panel opinion and supplementary opinion fail to reconcile the holding that controlled confinement was lost in the well with the finding that hydrocarbons were never confined in the well. This too should have been considered en banc.

Lastly, in its supplemental opinion, the panel changes the holding of the panel opinion. Thus, the law in our circuit is left unclear. The supplemental opinion attempts to overcome the fact that there was never confinement in the well. In the process, however, the supplementary opinion suggests that discharge is not defined as a loss of controlled confinement—as the panel opinion holds—but an absence of controlled confinement. This is no abstruse, metaphysical distinction. An absence of confinement test is not only further from the text of the CWA, it implicates a significantly broader swath of potentially liable actors. Further, the district courts are now left to harmonize this discord. I suspect that, as a consequence, we will be faced with addressing this issue again. We should have seized the opportunity now.

United States Court of Appeals
for the Fifth Circuit

No. 14-30032

MECHE
vs.
DOUCET

Appeals from the United States District Court for the
Western District of Louisiana

Decided: January 22, 2015

Citation: 777 F.3d 237, 3 Adm. R. 264 (5th Cir. 2015).

Before **DAVIS, WIENER,** and **HAYNES,** Circuit Judges.

[—1—] DAVIS, Circuit Judge:

Plaintiff-Appellant/Cross-Appellee Willie Meche ("Meche") filed this action seeking maintenance and cure and damages under the Jones Act and general maritime law against his former employer, Defendant-Appellee/Cross-Appellant Key Marine Services, L.L.C. ("Key"), and his former supervisor, Defendant-Appellee/Cross-Appellant Alex Doucet ("Doucet"). Following a bench trial, the district court ruled in Meche's favor and against Key and Doucet on his maintenance and cure claims, but against Meche on his unseaworthiness and Jones Act negligence claims. In addition to awarding maintenance and cure, the district court awarded Meche punitive damages, **[—2—]** attorney's fees, costs, and pre- and post-judgment interest against both Defendants.

Meche now appeals every adverse aspect of the district court's judgment. Key and Doucet cross-appeal and challenge the district court's judgment on several grounds. For the reasons described below, we vacate the entire judgment against both Doucet and Key. We affirm the district court's judgment in all other respects.

I.

Meche was the captain of the crew boat MISS CATHERINE, a vessel which served a drilling rig off the coast of Louisiana. On June 20, 2008, the vessel was tied to the rig, which was under tow to a new location near Cote Blanche, Louisiana. Meche claims that he injured his back on this date while lifting a hatch cover to check the oil on the vessel. Meche alleged that stormy conditions caused a five foot wave to hit the vessel and throw him over a railing.

Meche filed suit against Key (Meche's employer and the owner of the vessel) and Doucet (Meche's supervisor and the toolpusher on the rig under tow at the time of Meche's injury). Meche asserted claims under the Jones Act and general maritime law, including a claim for maintenance and cure, against both Defendants. Key and Doucet denied that the incident ever occurred and argued that Meche forfeited his right to maintenance and cure by lying about his preexisting spinal injuries on his pre-employment application and medical questionnaire.

The district court held a bench trial and issued findings of fact and conclusions of law. The court first found that Meche's testimony that he was thrown over the railing by a five foot wave was incredible because it conflicted with his contemporaneous descriptions of the incident, which all stated that he **[—3—]** had strained his back lifting a hatch cover to check the vessel's oil. The court also found that the weather and seas were calm at the time of Meche's injury, which further undermined Meche's testimony. Consistent with its finding that Meche merely strained his back while lifting the hatch cover, the district court concluded that Defendants were not negligent and that the vessel was not unseaworthy.

However, the court found that Meche aggravated his preexisting spinal injury when he lifted the hatch cover on the vessel. The court therefore ruled that Meche could recover maintenance and cure from both Key and Doucet.

The court rejected Defendants' argument that Meche forfeited his right to maintenance and cure by lying about his preexisting medical conditions on his pre-employment questionnaire. The court found that Key "did not require a pre-employment medical examination or interview." The court also found that "Meche did not consider his pre-existing condition to be a matter of importance." As a result, the district court concluded that "Meche did not intentionally conceal his medical history" and was therefore entitled to maintenance and cure.

The court further concluded that Key and Doucet had wrongfully refused to pay Meche maintenance and cure in bad faith. The court accordingly awarded Meche punitive damages and attorney's fees against both Defendants. Finally, the court awarded Meche pre-judgment interest, post-judgment interest, and costs.

Meche then appealed, and Key and Doucet cross-appealed. [—4—]

II.

"The standard of review for a bench trial is well established: Findings of fact are reviewed for clear error and legal issues are reviewed *de novo*."[1] A finding is clearly erroneous if it is without substantial evidence to support it, the court misinterpreted the effect of the evidence, or this court is convinced that the findings are against the preponderance of credible testimony."[2] "A district court finding may also be disregarded if it is infected by legal error."[3]

III.

Before turning to the merits of Meche's substantive claims, we must first consider Meche's argument that the district court impermissibly relied on evidence outside the record to evaluate his credibility. As noted above, the district court found that Meche provided multiple inconsistent accounts of the events surrounding his June 20, 2008 injury. In a recorded statement to a Key employee the

day after the injury, Meche stated that he had strained his back while lifting a hatch cover. Meche's incident report to Key from that date corroborates his initial statement that he merely strained his back, as does his statement to his physician on that date. By contrast, Meche recounted a very different story at trial: that the vessel turned against a five foot wave in severe weather, which threw him over a railing. Meche told his son, Bertrand, a third story: that the hatch fell on him and injured his back.

No one witnessed Meche's injury. Therefore, the district court's determination of what happened on June 20, 2008 depended entirely upon [—5—] Meche's credibility. Because of "Meche's conflicting accounts of the unwitnessed accident and the inconsistencies in his various statements and testimony," the district court had "serious doubts about whether or not an accident occurred and about his claims of negligence on the part of [Key]." The court accordingly found that "the only consistency in Meche's statements and testimony related to the incident is that . . . he felt a pain in his lower back while raising a hatch cover on the M/S MISS CATHERINE to perform routine maintenance."

Meche argues that the district court should not have relied on Bertrand's statement that the hatch fell on Meche when evaluating Meche's credibility because the parties did not introduce Bertrand's deposition testimony at trial. We conclude that the court's finding that Meche merely strained his back while lifting a hatch cover is not clearly erroneous because, as described above, the record evidence supporting this finding is overwhelming even without Bertrand's deposition testimony.

IV.

Meche also argues that the district court "erroneously relied on weather reports that calculated weather in the wrong area," rather than at the location where Meche sustained his injury. The district court, relying in part on the expert testimony of meteorologist Rob Perillo, made the following factual finding: "Based on the buoy reports and forecasts for June 20, 2008, winds were light and variable

---

[1] *Aransas Project v. Shaw*, 756 F.3d 801, 813 (5th Cir.), *reh'g denied*, --- F.3d ----, 2014 WL 7172014 (5th Cir. Dec. 15, 2014) (quoting *Kona Tech. Corp. v. S. Pac. Transp. Co.*, 225 F.3d 595, 601 (5th Cir. 2000)).

[2] *Id.* (quoting *Petrohawk Props., L.P. v. Chesapeake La., L.P.*, 689 F.3d 380, 388 (5th Cir. 2012)).

[3] *Id.* (citing *Elvis Presley Enters., Inc. v. Capece*, 141 F.3d 188, 196 (5th Cir. 1998)).

5-10 knots and seas 1-2 feet." This finding belied Meche's assertion that a five foot wave tossed him over a railing during a severe storm, and supported the court's finding that Meche merely strained his back while lifting a hatch cover on the vessel.

We reject Meche's challenge. Meche did not establish at trial that Perillo measured the weather at an incorrect location. To the contrary, Perillo testified [—6—] on redirect examination that his analysis would cover the area where Meche's injury occurred. The district court was consequently entitled to give Perillo's testimony whatever weight it deemed appropriate.

Moreover, the trial record contains other evidence that the weather was calm at the time and place Meche sustained his injury, namely the nearly contemporaneous incident report and another meteorologist's expert report tendered by Defendants. The district court's findings regarding the weather and condition of the seas at the time and location of the incident are therefore not clearly erroneous.

V.

Meche argues next that the vessel was unseaworthy in a number of respects, and that the district court's contrary finding is clearly erroneous. He first argues that the vessel was unseaworthy because it was inadequately lit. He contends that "[t]he lack of lights specifically prevented [him] from seeing the ocean and any wave action." He asserts that, if he had "been able to see the waves[,] he could have braced himself and not injured his back by holding the hatch." Given the district court's finding that Meche was not injured by the claimed wave action, Meche's purported inability to see the waves in the darkness is immaterial. The district court therefore did not err by rejecting this claim.

Meche next argues that the vessel was unseaworthy because Doucet ordered him to lift the hatch by himself. He asserts that lifting the hatch was a two-person job. The district court specifically found that "[l]ifting the hatch covers was a one man operation

which [Meche] performed daily as part of his job duties as the vessel captain," and that there was nothing unreasonably dangerous about lifting the hatch. The trial record supports the district court's finding. Thus, Doucet's alleged order that Meche lift the hatch by himself did [—7—] not render the vessel unseaworthy. The district court's reasonable finding that lifting the hatch covers was a routine, one-person job also resolves Meche's related claim that Doucet should have supervised Meche as he performed the task.

Finally, Meche contends that the vessel was unseaworthy because it was leaking oil. "Had the engine not excessively leaked oil," he argues, he "would not have been required to service it on every vessel use," and therefore would not have sustained an injury on June 20, 2008. However, Meche's injury was not "a direct result or a reasonably probable consequence" of the leaking oil.[4] Meche was injured not by the oil itself, but by straining his back lifting the hatch. As explained above, the district court reasonably found that there was nothing unreasonably dangerous about lifting the hatch. Thus, even if the leaking oil required Meche to lift the hatch more often, it did not render the vessel unseaworthy.

Thus, the district court properly ruled against Meche on all of his unseaworthiness claims.

VI.

Similarly, the district court's finding that Defendants were not negligent is fully supported by the record. Given the mechanism of the injury—lifting a hatch cover—the district court's conclusion that the routine task of lifting a hatch cover to check the oil did not raise an inference of negligence on the part of Defendants is fully supported.[5] [—8—]

---

[4] *See Phillips v. W. Co. of N. Am.*, 953 F.2d 923, 928 (5th Cir. 1992) (quoting *Johnson v. Offshore Express, Inc.*, 845 F.2d 1347, 1354 (5th Cir 1988)).

[5] Although the district court based its judgment on its finding that Meche "was not ordered to check the oil and . . . it was his decision to do so," we may affirm a judgment following a bench trial upon any basis supported by the record. *Mandel v. Thrasher*

VII.

We next consider whether the district court erred by awarding Meche maintenance and cure. "Maintenance and cure is a contractual form of compensation afforded by the general maritime law to seamen who fall ill or are injured while in the service of a vessel."[6] "Maintenance is a daily stipend for living expenses," whereas "cure is the payment of medical expenses."[7]

The vessel owner's obligation to provide this compensation does not depend on any determination of fault, but rather is treated as an implied term of any contract for maritime employment.[8] A seaman may recover maintenance and cure even for injuries or illnesses pre-existing the seaman's employment unless that seaman knowingly or fraudulently concealed his condition from the vessel owner at the time he was employed.[9]

A.

We must first vacate the maintenance and cure award against Doucet. To reiterate, Doucet was Meche's immediate supervisor and the toolpusher on duty on the rig under tow at the time of Meche's injury. It is hornbook law that the maintenance and cure duty extends only to the seaman's employer, or, in some cases, to the vessel *in rem*.[10] Because Doucet was not Meche's employer, he cannot be liable for maintenance and cure. It follows that we [—9—] must vacate the award of punitive damages, attorney's fees, pre- and post-judgment interest, and costs against him as well.

B.

We next consider whether the district court properly held Key liable to Meche for maintenance and cure. In *McCorpen v. Central Gulf Steamship Corp.*, we held that a seaman who "knowingly fail[s] to disclose a pre-existing physical disability during his [or her] pre-employment physical examination" may not recover maintenance and cure.[11] Key argues that the *McCorpen* rule precludes Meche from obtaining maintenance and cure in this case. For the following reasons, we agree.

1.

In order to establish a *McCorpen* defense, an employer must show that (1) the claimant intentionally mis-represented or concealed medical facts; (2) the non-disclosed facts were material to the employer's decision to hire the claimant; and (3) a connection exists between the withheld information and the injury complained of in the lawsuit.[12]

However,

[i]n cases involving a pre-existing illness or other disability, the courts have made a distinction between nondisclosure and concealment. Where the shipowner does not require a pre-employment medical examination or interview, the rule is that a seaman must disclose a past

---

(In re [—8—] *Mandel)*, 578 F. App'x 376, 382, 385 (5th Cir. 2014) (citing *United States v. Chacon*, 742 F.3d 219, 220 (5th Cir. 2014)).

[6] *Jauch v. Nautical Servs., Inc.*, 470 F.3d 207, 212 (5th Cir. 2006) (citing *McCorpen v. Cent. Gulf S.S. Corp.*, 396 F.2d 547, 548 (5th Cir. 1968)).

[7] *Lodrigue v. Delta Towing, L.L.C.*, No. Civ.A.03–0363, 2003 WL 22999425, at *6 n.51 (E.D. La. Dec. 19, 2003) (citing *Guevara v. Maint. Overseas Corp.*, 59 F.3d 1496, 1499 (5th Cir. 1995), *abrogated on other grounds by Atl. Sounding Co. v. Townsend*, 557 U.S. 404 (2009)).

[8] For that reason, we reject Defendants' argument that the district court's ruling on Meche's negligence claim requires us to vacate the maintenance and cure award.

[9] *Jauch*, 470 F.3d at 212 (citing *McCorpen*, 396 F.2d at 548).

[10] *See* GILMORE & BLACK, THE LAW OF ADMIRALTY 284-87 (2d ed. 1975); BENEDICT ON ADMIRALTY § 42, 4-5 (7th ed. 2013); FRANK L. MARAIST ET AL., ADMIRALTY 221 (6th ed. 2010).

[11] 396 F.2d at 548.

[12] *Brown v. Parker Drilling Offshore Corp.*, 410 F.3d 166, 171 (5th Cir. 2005) (citing *McCorpen*, 396 F.2d at 548-49).

illness or injury only when in his own opinion the shipowner would consider it a matter of importance. . . . On the other hand, where the shipowner requires a seaman to submit to a pre-hiring medical examination or interview and the seaman intentionally misrepresents or conceals material medical [—10—] facts, the disclosure of which is plainly desired, then he is not entitled to an award of maintenance and cure.[13]

Thus, in the nondisclosure context, the defendant must prove that the plaintiff subjectively believed that her employer would deem her medical condition a matter of importance.[14] The intentional misrepresentation/concealment standard, by contrast, is purely objective.[15] Our task is to decide which of the two standards applies in this case.

The district court found that Key "did not require a pre-employment medical examination or interview," and therefore applied the subjective nondisclosure standard. The court found that, "because [Key] never questioned Meche about any medical problems, but rather allowed him to continue working as a boat captain just as he had done for [his prior employer, Moncla Marine ("Moncla")] since 2006, Meche did not believe [Key] considered his existing medical problems a matter of importance." As a result, the court concluded that Meche could recover maintenance and cure.

Key argues that the district court should instead have applied the objective concealment standard. Although Key did not subject Meche to a pre-employment examination or interview, its predecessor, Moncla, did. Several months after Moncla hired Meche, Key purchased Moncla's marine division and thereby "acquired all of its assets and all of its liabilities." After reviewing Moncla's pre-employment medical

examination protocols and deeming them sufficient, Key hired Meche, along with Moncla's other former employees, without subjecting them to updated medical examinations.[16] Key therefore [—11—] argues that a misrepresentation to Moncla is tantamount to a misrepresentation to Key for the purposes of the *McCorpen* defense.

We agree.[17] As Key persuasively argues, it makes little economic or logical sense to require a successor company to reexamine its predecessor's employees solely for the purpose of avoiding maintenance and cure liability for their previously concealed medical conditions.[18] This is especially true when, as

---

[13] *McCorpen*, 396 F.2d at 548-49.

[14] *See Brown*, 410 F.3d at 174 (quoting *Vitcovich v. Ocean Rover O.N.*, No. 94-35047, 106 F.3d 411, 1997 WL 21205, at *3 (9th Cir. Jan. 14, 1997)).

[15] *See id.* (quoting *Vitcovich*, 1997 WL 21205, at *3).

---

[16] At trial, a Key employee described the acquisition process as follows: [—11—]

When we purchased the Moncla business, we brought all of our human resources personnel and our operations personnel into the—into what was the Moncla facility at that point in time . . . . We brought the personnel in, in shifts, and went through an on-boarding process where we completed the necessary documentation for our payroll processes, essentially.

During our due diligence prior to the purchase of Moncla's operations, we had assessed the training that Moncla was performing at the time, we had assessed their drug and alcohol testing protocols, and we had assessed their pre-employment physical capacity assessments, and we had determined that those were closely aligned with what Key was performing, so we had essentially accepted those such that we had them complete the necessary paperwork, put them in our payroll, and then brought them on essentially where is, as is, and made them Key employees.

[17] *See Lodrigue v. Delta Towing, L.L.C.*, No. Civ.A.03–0363, 2003 WL 22999425, at *1-2, *10 (E.D. La. Dec. 19, 2003) (applying objective concealment standard and holding that seaman intentionally concealed medical information from defendant where (1) prior employer conducted medical examination; (2) plaintiff failed to disclose medical facts to prior employer; and (3) defendant acquired prior employer's assets and employees without conducting new medical examinations).

[18] After all, a dishonest seaman who previously concealed his or her medical information on a pre-employment questionnaire is unlikely to volunteer

here, the predecessor has recently received an application for employment and conducted a thorough medical examination of the seaman, and the successor relied on the seaman's representations on the application and questionnaire when deciding to retain him.

More importantly, an intervening asset sale does not reduce the risk of injury to the seaman or to others resulting from the injured seaman's presence on the ship. "Employers need to be certain that each employee is physically [—12—] able to do the work, not only to protect the employer from liability, but also to protect the employees. This is the purpose of the preemployment health questionnaire, and of the *McCorpen* defense."[19]

Meche's arguments that an intervening asset sale should render the *McCorpen* defense inapplicable because the successor employer did not itself conduct a pre-employment medical examination are unpersuasive. He claims that "allow[ing] a current employer to rely on previous employer's [sic] medical examination or history or physical would effectively punish a seaman for his entire life for making a single mistake." That concern is unfounded. The rule we announce today only applies when a company purchases the division and keeps the predecessor's seamen in its employ. It would not, for example, punish a seaman who leaves his or her employer for an entirely unrelated company.

Therefore, an intervening asset sale does not automatically relieve a seaman from the consequences of his or her prior intentional concealment of material medical information. Because Moncla subjected Meche to a pre-employment medical examination, and because Key acquired Moncla shortly thereafter and relied on its prior medical examination when deciding to retain Meche, Key is entitled to the benefit of the *McCorpen* defense based on the representations Meche made in his employment application to

Moncla.[20] The district court should therefore have applied the objective intentional concealment standard, not the subjective nondisclosure standard.

2.

"[W]here findings are infirm because of an erroneous view of the law, a remand is the proper course unless the record permits only one resolution of [—13—] the factual issue."[21] For the following reasons, the trial record unequivocally establishes that Key satisfied all three elements of the *McCorpen* defense, so we need not remand for additional factual findings.

a.

It is clear that Meche "intentionally misrepresented or concealed medical facts."[22] The intentional concealment prong of the *McCorpen* defense does not require subjective intent to conceal.[23] The employer need only show that the seaman "[f]ail[ed] to disclose medical information in an interview or questionnaire that is obviously designed to elicit such information."[24]

Meche clearly concealed information about his prior spinal injuries from Moncla, and, by extension, from Key. The district court found that Meche sustained three prior work-related low back and neck injuries between 1984 and 1994, before he applied to work for Moncla. Meche received disability payments and sued his former employers for damages arising from these three injuries. Meche settled one of these lawsuits for $140,000.00 and another lawsuit for $30,000.00. Thus, Meche was clearly aware of his preexisting spinal

---

that information during a subsequent reexamination.

[19] *Brown*, 410 F.3d at 175.

[20] *See Lodrigue*, 2003 WL 22999425, at *1-2, *10.

[21] *See Pullman-Standard v. Swint*, 456 U.S. 273, 292 (1982) (citing *Kelley v. S. Pac. Co.*, 419 U.S. 318, 331-32 (1974)).

[22] *See Brown*, 410 F.3d at 171 (citing *McCorpen v. Cent. Gulf S.S. Corp.*, 396 F.2d 547, 548-49 (5th Cir. 1968)).

[23] *Id.* at 174 (quoting *Vitcovich v. Ocean Rover O.N.*, No. 94-35047, 106 F.3d 411, 1997 WL 21205, at *3 (9th Cir. Jan. 14, 1997)).

[24] *Id.* (quoting *Vitcovich*, 1997 WL 21205, at *3).

conditions at the time he applied to work for Moncla.

Meche's November 2006 pre-employment medical history questionnaire for Moncla nevertheless falsely states that he had not previously sustained "any low back injuries or trouble with [his] low back" or any "illness, injury, or claim arising out of [his] employment." Meche further swore on that [—14—] questionnaire that he did not "take any routine medication; prescribed or over the counter," even though he routinely used and filled prescriptions for hydrocodone. Meche signed his name on the questionnaire below a notice admonishing him that his "failure to answer truthfully any questions about previous injuries, disabilities, or other medical conditions may result in forfeiture of worker[']s compensation benefits."

Meche argues that he did not intentionally conceal his medical history from Moncla because he did not personally complete the written medical questionnaire. Rather, the district court found that Meche's daughter-in-law, Lesly,

> filled out the Moncla employment questionnaire because Meche doesn't read and write very well. Lesly Meche filled out the questionnaire for Meche and also filled out some of the paperwork at his physical examination. She began asking Meche the answers to the questions but before she finished, he was called to go for medical testing. She finished answering the questions herself and when Meche returned, he signed the questionnaire without reading it. She did not know whether or not Meche had neck or back problems.

Meche "signed the [questionnaire] under the statement declaring that all responses on the application were correct. Therefore, whether he personally checked 'No' to the questions about his prior injuries is inconsequential; by signing the final oath on the application, he averred that the information on the application was correct."[25] Because Meche in actuality "knew that the information on the application was not correct," Meche intentionally concealed his prior injuries as a matter of law.[26] [—15—]

We acknowledge that a seaman's failure to disclose his or her medical history on a pre-employment questionnaire does not necessarily amount to intentional concealment when the seaman lacks the requisite literacy skills to understand and complete the questionnaire.[27] Although the district court found that Meche "doesn't read and write very well," it did not find, and the record does not establish, that he lacked the literacy skills necessary to read and review Lesly's responses before swearing that her responses were correct. To the contrary, Meche admitted at trial that he personally filled out a different medical form for another employer detailing his prescription history several months before applying to work for Moncla. Meche's ability to understand what he was signing is clear from the record. Thus, his concealment of his medical history was intentional for the purposes of the *McCorpen* defense.

Meche also argues that he did not intentionally conceal his medical history because the district court found that he orally disclosed his past injuries and prior lawsuits to a Moncla representative before Moncla hired him. We hold that if a seaman intentionally provides false information on a pre-employment medical questionnaire and certifies that the information therein is true and correct, that seaman may not later argue that his concealment was not intentional based on his statement, which the employer disputes, that he verbally disclosed medical

---

[25] *Caulfield v. Kathryn Rae Towing*, CIV. A. No. 88-5329, 1989 WL 121586, at *2 (E.D. La. June 6, 1989).

[26] *Id.*

[27] *See McCorpen*, 396 F.2d at 549-50 (citations omitted); *Olympic Marine Co. v. Credeur*, Civ. A. No. 92-2062, 1992 WL 345322, at *2 (E.D. La. Nov. 10, 1992); *Bychurch v. Atl. Int'l Ltd.*, CIV. A. No. 89-0723, 1989 WL 113927, at *1 (E.D. La. Sept. 25, 1989); *Caulfield*, 1989 WL 121586, at *2.

information that contradicted the written questionnaire.[28] [—16—]

b.

Likewise, Key established at trial that the non-disclosed medical facts were material to its decision to retain Meche as an employee after it acquired Moncla's marine division.[29] Although the district court noted Meche's testimony that he told "everything" about his preexisting spinal condition to Michael Martens, the human resources representative at Moncla who hired Meche,[30] the record shows that Meche also testified that Martens said Meche needed to pass his physical to be hired. The record does not reflect that Meche disclosed his prior medical history to the doctor performing his physical. Therefore, we cannot conclude from this evidence that Meche's prior history was immaterial to the hiring decision.

Furthermore, the trial record contains no competent evidence that Key knew of Meche's medical condition but nevertheless opted to hire him.[31] Nor does the record suggest that Key knew of Moncla's agreement to hire Meche notwithstanding his prior spinal injuries. To the contrary, the record establishes that Key did not know of Meche's prior injuries, and would not have hired him if it did. Meche's "history of back injuries is the exact type of information sought by employers like [Key]" when deciding whether to hire a seaman.[32] "The fact that an employer asks a

specific medical question on an application, and that the inquiry is rationally related to the applicant's physical ability to perform his job duties, renders the information material [—17—] for the purpose of this analysis."[33] Key relied on Moncla's employment application, which specifically asked Meche about his preexisting condition and ultimately listed Meche as "Employable Without Accommodation," when deciding to hire him. Thus, Meche concealed material information from Key.

c.

Finally, "a connection exists between the withheld information and the injury complained of in the lawsuit,"[34] because the district court found that Meche "aggravated his pre-existing lumbar illness when he lifted the hatch cover on the M/V MISS CATHERINE on June 20, 2008." Therefore, Key unequivocally satisfied the causation element of the *McCorpen* defense at trial.[35]

Because Key established all three elements of its *McCorpen* defense, we vacate the maintenance and cure award against Key, as well as the award of pre- and post-judgment interest, costs, punitive damages, and attorney's fees.[36]

VIII.

In sum, we affirm the district court's judgment to the extent the court rejected Meche's Jones Act negligence and unseaworthiness claims against [—18—] Key

---

[28] *See Hughes v. Shaw Envtl., Inc.*, Civil Action No. 11-494, 2012 WL 729891, at *2-3 (E.D. La. Mar. 6, 2012); *Russell v. Seacor Marine, Inc.*, No. Civ.A. 00-339, 2000 WL 1514712, at *2 (E.D. La. Oct. 10, 2000).

[29] *Brown*, 410 F.3d at 171 (citing *McCorpen*, 396 F.2d at 548-49).

[30] *Cf. Jauch v. Nautical Servs., Inc.*, 470 F.3d 207, 212 (5th Cir. 2006) ("If the vessel owner would have employed the seaman even had the requested disclosure been made, concealment will not bar the seaman's recovery of maintenance and cure.").

[31] Meche insists that a human resources representative who worked for both Key and Moncla knew about Meche's condition, but that employee did not participate in either Key's or Moncla's decision to hire Meche.

[32] *Brown*, 410 F.3d at 175.

---

[33] *Id.*

[34] *Id.* at 171 (citing *McCorpen v. Cent. Gulf S.S. Corp.*, 396 F.2d 547, 548-49 (5th Cir. 1968)).

[35] *See id.* at 176.

[36] *See Boudreaux v. Transocean Deepwater, Inc.*, 721 F.3d 723, 728, 1 Adm. R. 275, 278 (5th Cir. 2013) (citing *Morales v. Garijak, Inc.*, 829 F.2d 1355, 1358 (5th Cir. 1987), *abrogated on other grounds by Guevara v. Maritime Overseas Corp.*, 59 F.3d 1496 (5th Cir. 1995)) (holding that "an employer is entitled to investigate a claim for maintenance and cure[,]" including the applicability of the *McCorpen* defense, "before tendering any payments to the seaman—without subjecting itself to liability for . . . punitive damages.").

and Doucet. We vacate the awards against Doucet and Key in their entirety and render judgment in favor of Key and Doucet.

AFFIRMED in part, VACATED in part, and JUDGMENT RENDERED for Key and Doucet.

United States Court of Appeals
for the Fifth Circuit

No. 14-20554

IN RE LLOYD'S REGISTER N. AM., INC.

Petition for a Writ of Mandamus to the United States
District Court for the Southern District of Texas

Decided: February 24, 2015

Citation: 780 F.3d 283, 3 Adm. R. 273 (5th Cir. 2015).

Before **SMITH**, **ELROD**, and **HIGGINSON**, Circuit Judges.

[—1—] **SMITH**, Circuit Judge:

Lloyd's Register North America, Inc. ("LRNA"), was the classification society responsible for certifying a ship that Irving Shipbuilding, Inc. ("Irving"), was building for Pearl Seas Cruises, LLC ("Pearl Seas"). Pearl Seas was dissatisfied with the ship and engaged in several years of arbitration and litigation with Irving. After those proceedings had concluded, Pearl Seas sued LRNA under various tort theories regarding LRNA's allegedly inadequate performance in certifying the ship and its alleged misdeeds during arbitration.

LRNA moved to dismiss on the ground of *forum non conveniens* ("FNC"), [—2—] claiming that a forum-selection clause in the Lloyd's Register Rules and Regulations for the Classification of Ships (the "LR Rules") and in the contract between LRNA and Irving required Pearl Seas to bring the claims in England. The district court denied the motion to dismiss without written or oral explanation. LRNA petitions for a writ of mandamus to direct the court to vacate its denial and dismiss for FNC. Because the district court clearly abused its discretion and reached a patently erroneous result, and because LRNA has no way effectively to vindicate its rights without a writ of mandamus, we grant the petition.

I.

The following facts are taken from Pearl Seas' First Amended Complaint. Pearl Seas

and LRNA communicated in 2006 about LRNA's potentially providing classification services for the vessels Pearl Seas would be operating. Those classification services would require LRNA to certify that the ship complied with certain standards, including the requirements of the ship's flag state (the Marshall Islands) and the classification society's own rules. Pearl Seas agreed that LRNA would be the classification society for its ships.

Later in 2006, Pearl Seas entered into a contract (the "Shipbuilding Contract") with Irving under which Irving would build a ship for Pearl Seas. LRNA then entered into a contract ("Classification Contract") with Irving under which LRNA would survey the ship during construction, ensuring that it complied with the rules and regulations specified in the Shipbuilding Contract, including the LR Rules. As construction continued, disputes arose between Irving and Pearl Seas. Irving invoked the arbitration clause in the Shipbuilding Contract in 2008, and contentious arbitration continued until Irving and Pearl Seas settled in 2013. [—3—]

II.

Pearl Seas sued LRNA in the court *a quo* in late 2013, alleging fraud, gross negligence, negligent misrepresentation, collusion, aiding and abetting, civil conspiracy, and promissory estoppel in tort. Each cause of action is essentially based on the theory that LRNA misrepresented the status of the vessel to Pearl Seas and to the arbitrators.

LRNA moved to dismiss for FNC, seeking enforcement of two forum-selection clauses that it said required the action to be brought in England. The first appears in the LR Rules and reads, "Any dispute about the Services or the Contract is subject to the exclusive jurisdiction of the English courts and will be governed by English law." The second appears in the Classification Contract between LRNA and Irving and reads, "Any dispute, claim, or litigation between any member of the LR Group and the Client arising from or in connection with the Services provided by LR shall be subject to the exclusive jurisdiction of the

English courts and will be governed by English law." Irving claimed that both of these clauses prevented Pearl Seas from bringing this suit in Texas.

Pearl Seas maintained that neither applied, because Pearl Seas was not a signatory to any agreement containing a forum-selection clause. The district court held a hearing in which it questioned the parties about numerous matters, including the motion to dismiss for FNC. A few weeks later, the court issued an order denying several of the motions to dismiss and the plaintiff's motion for *in camera* inspection. The court "explained" its decision in one sentence: "Having considered the motions, submissions, and applicable law, the Court determines that all motions should be denied."

III.

To be entitled to the extraordinary remedy of mandamus, LRNA has to [—4—] satisfy three requirements. First, it must have "no other adequate means to attain the relief [it] desires." *Cheney v. U.S. Dist. Court for Dist. of Columbia*, 542 U.S. 367, 380 (2004). Second, it has to show a "clear and indisputable" right to the writ. *Id.* at 381. And third, the court "must be satisfied that the writ is appropriate under the circumstances." *Id.*

A.

First, LRNA must show that it has no other "adequate means." The writ is not "a substitute for the regular appeals process," *id.* at 380–81, so LRNA must show that an ordinary appeal is inadequate. This requirement is satisfied: The usual appeals process does not provide an effective way to review a denial of a motion to dismiss for FNC. Immediate appellate review of the decision to deny is rarely available, and review after final judgment is ineffective to vindicate a wrongfully denied motion for FNC.

There is no adequate way immediately to review a denial of FNC. It is not reviewable under the collateral-order doctrine. *Van Cauwenberghe v. Biard*, 486 U.S. 517, 527 (1988). The defendant has the option of seeking leave for an interlocutory appeal under 28 U.S.C. § 1292(b), which is available only in limited circumstances. The question to be certified must be "a controlling question of law as to which there is substantial ground for difference of opinion," 28 U.S.C. § 1292(b), and even if it is, both the district court and the court of appeals must agree to permit the appeal. *See Gonzalez v. Naviera Neptuno A.A.*, 832 F.2d 876, 881 n.5 (5th Cir. 1987). Other courts of appeals that have considered the question have come to the same conclusion: Section 1292(b) is not an adequate substitute for mandamus.[1] [—5—]

LRNA is without adequate means to review the denial when the order is entered, but we must also evaluate whether the ordinary appeals process is otherwise adequate. That is a difficult requirement to satisfy. In most cases, relief from a potentially erroneous interlocutory order is available by appeal after final judgment. Even though the defendant may be required to engage in a costly and difficult trial and expend considerable resources before the court enters an appealable judgment, those unrecoverable litigation costs are not enough to make this means of attaining relief inadequate. *See Roche v. Evaporated Milk Ass'n*, 319 U.S. 21, 29–30 (1943). There has to be a greater burden, some obstacle to relief beyond litigation costs that renders obtaining relief not just expensive but effectively unobtainable. Under *Volkswagen*, a defendant's entitlement to FNC ordinarily cannot adequately be vindicated through the regular appeals process.

In *Volkswagen*, we were faced with a mandamus petition regarding a denial of a motion to transfer venue. We held that the

---

[1] *See In re Roman Catholic Diocese of Albany, N.Y., Inc.*, 745 F.3d 30, 36 (2d Cir. 2014); *In re Kellogg Brown & Root, Inc.*, 756 F.3d 754, 761 (D.C. Cir. 2014). In *In re Volkswagen of America, Inc.*, 545 F.3d 304, 319 (5th Cir. 2008) (en banc), the court did consider the *unavailability* of § 1292(b) certification to be relevant in concluding that a denial of a venue-transfer [—5—] motion qualified for mandamus relief. That does not mean, however, that § 1292(b) by itself provides sufficient review when it is available.

ordinary appeals process would not provide an adequate remedy for the erroneous decision not to order transfer. Two factors that we found convincing in the venue-transfer context are present here. First, a defendant is unlikely to be able to satisfy an appellate court, after final judgment, that a failure to transfer venue was sufficiently prejudicial as to be outcome-determinative. And second, the very harm sought to be avoided by transferring venue—"inconvenience to witnesses, parties and other"—will have worked irreversible damage and prejudice by the time of final judgment. *Volkswagen*, 454 F.3d at 319. Each of these reasons applies with equal force in the FNC context.

On appeal from a final judgment, the improper failure to transfer venue [—6—] is effectively unreviewable. The defendant would be in the unenviable position of having to show that "it would have won the case had it been tried in a convenient [venue]." *Id.* at 318–19 (citation omitted). The same ineffectiveness of review characterizes the denial of an FNC motion: If it is denied and the case proceeds through trial, the denial will not be considered reversible error "unless the moving party can demonstrate great prejudice arising from trial in the plaintiff's chosen forum." *McLennan v. Am. Eurocopter Corp.*, 245 F.3d 403, 423–24 (5th Cir. 2001). Such a standard does not provide adequate post-judgment review.[2] When one considers the instruction in *Atlantic Marine* that the private-interest factors of FNC analysis should automatically be weighed in favor of enforcing a forum-selection clause,[3] it is especially inapposite to force parties to rely on *post hoc* appellate evaluations of whether the clause was worth bargaining for.

---

[2] *See Volkswagen*, 545 F.3d at 318–19; *see also In re Ford Motor Co.*, 591 F.3d 406, 416 (5th Cir. 2009) (on petition for rehearing) ("[I]n these FNC cases, mandamus is appropriate on this prong because, if the issue is argued only on any eventual direct appeal, there is no way to show that the outcome of the case would have been different, and any inconvenience to the parties 'will already have been done by the time the case is tried and appealed.'" (quoting *Volkswagen*, 545 F.3d at 318–19)).

[3] *See Atl. Marine Constr. Co. v. U.S. Dist. Court for W. Dist. of Tex.*, 134 S. Ct. 568, 582 (2013).

Even if the standard of review were such that a defendant could convince an appeals court that the error justified reversal, we acknowledged in *Volkswagen* that the harm done by going through trial to final judgment would not be remediable on appeal. Unrecoverable litigation costs do not make review after final judgment inadequate, *see Roche*, 319 U.S. at 29–30, but the damage inflicted by the refusal to enforce a forum-selection clause is different from the costs that defendants face as a matter of course after denial of a motion that would otherwise terminate the litigation. The "inconvenience to witnesses, parties and other[s]," *Volkswagen*, 545 F.3d at 319, is one of the factors weighed [—7—] in determining whether an FNC motion should be granted. An FNC motion—like the venue-transfer motion at issue in *Volkswagen*—is a motion that asserts those damages are too high to justify trying the case where it was filed. If the matter must first proceed to final judgment before the denial of that assertion is evaluated, then the damage will always already be done. And "the prejudice suffered cannot be put back in the bottle." *Id.*

There is no reason to distinguish between the normal appeals process in the venue-transfer context, which we found lacking in *Volkswagen*, and that same process in the context of FNC. The first requirement for mandamus relief is therefore satisfied.

B.

The second requirement for mandamus relief is that the petitioner has a "clear and indisputable" right to it. *Cheney*, 542 U.S. at 381. In recognition of the extraordinary nature of the writ, we require more than showing that the court misinterpreted the law, misapplied it to the facts, or otherwise engaged in an abuse of discretion. And even reversible error by itself is not enough to obtain mandamus. *See Volkswagen*, 545 F.3d at 309–10. Rather, we limit mandamus to only "clear abuses of discretion that produce patently erroneous results." *Id.* at 310. We therefore must determine whether there was a clear abuse of discretion and whether the court reached a patently erroneous result.

Because we determine that both of these conditions are satisfied, this requirement for mandamus is met.

1.

In distinguishing between ordinary and "clear" abuses of discretion, we are guided by the principle reiterated in *Volkswagen* that mandamus must not become a means by which the court corrects all potentially erroneous orders. *See id.* at 309 (citing *Will v. United States*, 389 U.S. 90, 98 n.6 (1967)). A court [—8—] commits a clear abuse of discretion, however, when it "clearly exceeds the bounds of judicial discretion." *Id.* at 310. The district court's failure to provide an explanation of its denial of LRNA's motion clearly exceeded the bounds of judicial discretion given the facts and circumstances present here.

It is an abuse of discretion for a district court to grant or deny a motion to dismiss without written or oral explanation[4] or where, in ruling on a motion to dismiss for FNC, it "fails to address and balance the relevant principles and factors of the doctrine of [FNC]."[5] The district court provided no written or oral explanation for its decision.

In its response to the petition for mandamus, Pearl Seas claims that the court did not abuse its discretion because Pearl Seas provided an adequate legal and factual basis for denial in its brief, and the court indicated at a hearing that it "had reviewed the briefs and was well aware of the issues." That notion is unavailing. An explanation must be generated by the court, not inferred by the appellate court from the submissions of the

parties. A contrary rule would require us to guess the basis for the decision without guidance, essentially reducing us to the role of replacing the district court's discretion with our own in violation of *Volkswagen*, 545 F.3d at 312.

The transcript of the July 17 hearing is likewise insufficient to satisfy the requirement of a written or oral explanation. The court specifically said that it had not yet decided the question of the forum-selection clause and offered no conclusion as to its applicability or the propriety of granting or [—9—] denying the motion to dismiss. Whether the court's questions indicated that it understood the law and the briefings is immaterial.

Even though the court's failure to explain its decision is an abuse of discretion, that is not enough: It must be a "clear" abuse of discretion. That strict requirement is satisfied here. Denying dismissal without explanation and without any visible weighing of the factors of FNC takes the decision entirely outside the scope of judicial discretion, giving the parties and reviewing courts no way of understanding how the court reached its conclusion and providing no assurance that it was the result of conscientious legal analysis.

2.

We now turn to whether the district court reached a "patently erroneous result." Because the court failed to enforce a valid forum-selection clause, it did patently err.

a.

The first question is whether the forum-selection clause applies to this case. Pearl Seas is not a signatory to the contract between Irving and LRNA, but there are settled standards under which a non-signatory can be held to the terms of the contract. The doctrine on which the parties focus is the one that applies here: direct-benefits estoppel.

Direct-benefits estoppel holds a non-signatory to a clause in a contract if it "knowingly exploits the agreement" containing

---

[4] *See In re Air Crash Disaster Near New Orleans, La.*, 821 F.2d 1147, 1166 (5th Cir. 1987) (en banc), *vacated on other grounds sub nom. Pan Am. World Airways, Inc. v. Lopez*, 490 U.S. 1032 (1989), *reinstated in part by In re Air Crash Disaster Near New Orleans, La.*, 883 F.2d 17 (5th Cir. 1989) (en banc).

[5] *Id.* at 1166–67; *cf Rose v. Hartford Underwriters Ins. Co.*, 203 F.3d 417, 420 (6th Cir. 2000) ("Because the district court [decided a] motion without explanation, it has clearly abused its discretion in this case.").

the clause. *Bridas S.A.P.I.C. v. Gov't of Turkmenistan*, 345 F.3d 347, 361–62 (5th Cir. 2003). We have identified two specific ways in which a non-signatory can be bound under this theory. First, it may be bound "by knowingly seeking and obtaining 'direct benefits' from that contract." *Noble Drilling Servs., Inc. v. Certex USA, Inc.*, 620 F.3d 469, 473 (5th Cir. 2010). Second, it may be bound "by seeking to enforce the terms of that contract or asserting claims that must be determined [—10—] by reference to that contract." *Id.* Direct-benefits estoppel binds Pearl Seas to the forum-selection clause under the first method.[6]

To invoke direct-benefits estoppel under this theory, LRNA first must show that Pearl Seas knowingly exploited the contract during the contract's existence. *Id.* Pearl Seas must have known about the existence of the contract and its terms, *see id.* at 473–74, and acted to exploit that contract. Second, Pearl Seas must have obtained some benefit under the contract. *See id.* at 473. Because Pearl Seas knew about the contract between Irving and LRNA, acted to exploit it, and gained a benefit from it, Pearl Seas is bound by the forum-selection clause in the Classification Contract.

Pearl Seas' own complaint shows that it was aware of the existence of the Classification Society from the beginning of its relationship with LRNA. The Shipbuilding Contract required Irving to get a classification service that would provide the services at issue here, and Pearl Seas selected LRNA to provide the classification services for the ship. LRNA's performance was for the benefit of Pearl Seas, and the complaint describes LRNA as carrying out those duties and communicating with Pearl Seas. Pearl Seas' pleadings lead inexorably to the conclusion that it was aware of the Classification Contract and some of its basic terms, namely, ensuring compliance with particular

regulatory requirements in anticipation of a sale to Pearl Seas.

Additionally, Pearl Seas stated that it learned of the Classification Contract's content after arbitration had begun, which happened in early 2008. Pearl Seas contends that receipt of a contract during arbitration does not trigger direct-benefits estoppel. LRNA was not a party to the arbitration, however, [—11—] and much of the alleged wrongful conduct took place after the arbitration had begun.

If a nonsignatory receives a copy of a heretofore-unknown contract for the first time when it sues a signatory, that mid-litigation revelation likely is not enough for knowing exploitation of the contract under this version of direct-benefits estoppel. *See id.* at 473–74. But what matters is that Pearl Seas did in fact learn of the Classification Contract's content before much of the alleged wrongdoing and before this litigation between Pearl Seas and LRNA.[7] The knowledge test does not focus on the intent of the party providing information and would be equally met if Pearl Seas had received a copy of the contract after its agent had found a copy stuck to the bottom of his shoe.

LRNA must also show that Pearl Seas has received a direct benefit under the contract. *Id.* at 473. LRNA was performing its services for the benefit of Pearl Seas, examining the ship and communicating with Pearl Seas in the course of administering classification services. Indeed, Pearl Seas' own complaint repeats the *Otto Candies*[8] rule for negligent-misrepresentation claims against classification societies: LRNA provided its classification services knowing they were for the "guidance and benefit" of Pearl Seas.[9]

---

[6] Because the forum-selection clause from the Classification Contract binds Pearl Seas under this rule of direct-benefits estoppel, we need not determine whether the clause in the LR Rules also binds Pearl Seas, nor whether the second form of direct-benefits estoppel is satisfied here.

---

[7] Pearl Seas's brief and pleadings do not make clear exactly when it received a copy of the Classification Contract but show that it happened after arbitration had begun.

[8] *Otto Candies, L.L.C. v. Nippon Kaiji Kyokai Corp.*, 346 F.3d 530 (5th Cir. 2003).

[9] *Id.* at 535; *see Hellenic Inv. Fund, Inc. v. Det Norske Veritas,*, 464 F.3d 514, 519 (5th Cir. 2006) ("Any lingering doubt whether Hellenic garnered a benefit from [the classification society's]

And the complaint makes plain that LRNA did actually perform such services and provided reports directly to Pearl Seas as well. This likewise satisfies the requirement that Pearl Seas, in addition to knowing about the contract, has [—12—] exploited or embraced it during the life of the contract; Pearl Seas actively participated in ensuring that the parts of the contract benefiting it were performed.[10]

Pearl Seas contends that it did not receive a benefit because LRNA's performance was deficient. Unlike the situation in *Hellenic*, Pearl Seas did not receive the certification that was necessary to operate. Even if we assume that LRNA's performance was deficient, however, that partial performance was still a direct benefit to Pearl Seas. If LRNA had not performed under the contract at all, or had performed only those parts that did not benefit Pearl Seas, then this requirement of direct-benefits estoppel would not be met. But merely alleging that a benefit was deficient or outweighed by the negative aspects of the signatory's actions does not mean that no benefit was received.[11]

Pearl Seas also urges that direct-benefits estoppel cannot apply because the Classification Contract disclaims liability to, and enforceability by, third parties. But reciprocity and mutual enforceability are not requirements for direct-benefits estoppel, and Pearl Seas cites no authority that supports its position. Indeed, in its brief Pearl Seas at times discusses the doctrine of third-party beneficiary.

As this court has recognized, third-party beneficiary and direct-benefits estoppel are distinct doctrines. Third-party beneficiary doctrine looks at what the parties intended when they executed the contract, whereas direct-benefits estoppel looks at the actions of the parties after the contract was executed. *See Bridas*, 345 F.3d at 362 (quotation omitted). If we interpreted direct-benefits estoppel to require that the parties demonstrate an intention at the contracting [—13—] stage to create a third-party beneficiary, we would eliminate this distinction and collapse the doctrines.

Finally, Pearl Seas avers that LRNA cannot rely on direct-benefits estoppel because Pearl Seas alleged fraud, and this denies LRNA the benefit of equitable remedies. Pearl Seas provides no binding or persuasive authority for the proposition that a plaintiff can deny a defendant access to equitable remedies just by alleging fraud, especially where the fraud is unrelated to the applicability of the equitable doctrine. Pearl Seas does not assert that the claimed fraud played any role in bringing it within the scope of the forum-selection clause or allowed LRNA to hide any inequitable behavior behind a shield of equity. We decline to render direct-benefits estoppel inoperative by stating that an allegation of a defendant's wrongdoing is sufficient to deny the application of this clause.

b.

As the foregoing explanation shows, the forum-selection clause in the Classification Contract does apply to Pearl Seas' action against LRNA. That, however, is not the end of our analysis of whether LRNA has a "clear and indisputable" right to mandamus. Given that the forum-selection clause applies, we must determine whether the district court should have dismissed the complaint in accordance with that clause. In light of the Supreme Court's instructions in *Atlantic Marine*, the court erred when it denied the motion to dismiss.

Atlantic Marine laid out the process courts must follow in ruling on an FNC motion that seeks to enforce a valid forum-selection clause. Instead of independently weighing the private

---

performance of the [ ] contract is erased by Hellenic's own statements in its complaint: '[the classification society] knew, or should have known,' that its representations 'were intended for [Hellenic]'s *guidance and benefit* in a business transaction.'") (fourth modification in original).

[10] *See Noble Drilling*, 620 F.3d at 473; *E.I. duPont de Nemours & Co. v. Rhone Poulenc Fiber & Resin Intermediates, S.A.S.*, 269 F.3d 187, 200 (3d Cir. 2001).

[11] *See Hellenic*, 464 F.3d at 519; *Blaustein v. Huete*, 449 F. App'x 347, 350 (5th Cir. 2011) (per curiam).

interests of the parties, the court should "deem the private-interest factors to weigh entirely in favor of the preselected forum." *Atl. Marine*, 134 S. Ct. at 582. The court must then weigh the public- [—14—] interest factors, which include "the administrative difficulties flowing from court congestion; the local interest in having localized controversies decided at home; [and] the interest in having the trial of a diversity case in a forum that is at home with the law." *Id.* at 581 n.6 (quoting *Piper Aircraft Co. v. Reyno*, 454 U.S. 235, 241 n.6 (1981)). The plaintiff's choice of forum will not be given any weight, unlike in the ordinary FNC context. *Id.* at 581. The Supreme Court allows for the possibility that a court may properly refuse to grant the motion despite a valid forum-selection clause, but the forum-selection clause will prevail except in "unusual cases." *Id.* at 582.

Pearl Seas has not identified any factors that render this motion one of those unusual cases. In its response to LRNA's mandamus petition, Pearl Seas contends that Texas is the proper forum because the court needs to establish "uniform rules of conduct applicable to corporate entities in Texas," because some communications originated in Texas, and because LRNA is the defendant in a similar lawsuit in a Texas federal court. Those considerations are not enough to make enforcement of the forum-selection clause invalid.[12]

Pearl Seas raises additional concerns in its opposition to the mandamus petition. It theorizes that it would face "extreme juridical disadvantages in an English forum," but it does not identify what those disadvantages would be. Pearl Seas points out that the Fifth Circuit permits negligent misrepresentation claims against classification societies, but it

does not show that the remedies in English courts would be lacking. Pearl Seas claims that dismissing for FNC would deprive the plaintiff of available Texas and U.S. remedies and [—15—] would therefore violate public policy, but it does not point to a remedy that would be unavailable in England. Pearl Seas fails to show why this is the exceptional case in which a valid forum-selection clause should not be enforced.

In sum, the district court committed a clear abuse of discretion when it exceeded its judicial power and denied the FNC motion without explanation. The court, with the best of intentions, then reached a patently erroneous result when it declined to enforce a valid forum-selection clause. LRNA has a "clear and indisputable" right to issuance of the writ.

C.

The third requirement for mandamus is that we are satisfied that it "is appropriate under the circumstances." *Cheney*, 542 U.S. at 381. Because the writ is "supervisory in nature," we consider it especially appropriate where its issuance will have significance "beyond the immediate case." *Volkswagen*, 545 F.3d at 319. There is already an appeal pending from another case on this issue in the Fifth Circuit, and it is possible that more will be forthcoming now that the Supreme Court has strengthened the enforcement of forum-selection clauses in *Atlantic Marine*.

The petition for writ of mandamus is GRANTED.

(Reporter's Note: Dissenting opinion follows on p. 280).

---

[12] Additionally, the other LRNA case that was pending in Texas has since been dismissed for FNC. *See Vloeibare Pret Ltd. v. Lloyd's Register N. Am., Inc.*, No. 4-13-3653, 2014 WL 3908195 (S.D. Tex. Aug. 8, 2014). Even if the dismissal in that suit is reversed on appeal, we have limited *Atlantic Marine*'s applicability in multi-party litigation only where a single case involves parties both with and without valid forum-selection clauses. *See In re Rolls Royce Corp.*, 775 F.3d 671, 679, 2 Adm. R. 398, 402-03 (5th Cir. 2014).

[—15—] ELROD, Circuit Judge, dissenting:

Mandamus is an "extraordinary remedy" for correcting a "clear abuse of discretion" based on "extraordinary errors" leading to "a patently erroneous result." *In re Volkswagen of Am., Inc.*, 545 F.3d 304, 309, 318 (5th Cir. 2008) (en banc) (issuing the writ because the district court "disregard[ed] the specific [—16—] precedents of this Court in *In re Volkswagen I*"). Here, in its decision to mandamus the district court, the majority opinion creates two new legal rules about the doctrine of direct benefits estoppel, neither of which was compelled by our precedent. Because I do not believe the district court patently erred by not anticipating these two new rules, I respectfully dissent.

The majority opinion's first new rule concerns the extent of "direct benefit" a non-signatory must receive. In our most on-point precedent, *Hellenic Inv. Fund, Inc. v. Det Norske Veritas*, we applied direct benefits estoppel where the non-signatory shipowner received the benefit of a class certificate from the classification society. 464 F.3d 514, 516 (5th Cir. 2006). Our "direct benefit" analysis focused specifically on the shipowner's receipt of a class certificate; we did not hold that the classification society's preliminary inspections, standing alone, conferred a benefit on the shipowner. Rather, it was the issuance of the class certificate that conferred a benefit on the shipowner. Here, Pearl Seas never received a class certificate from LRNA. The majority opinion nonetheless holds that direct benefits estoppel applies because LRNA "examin[ed] the ship and communicat[ed] with Pearl Seas in the course of administering [incomplete] classification services." This is an extension of the holding in *Hellenic*. The majority opinion's new rule might be sensible, but an equally sensible rule is one requiring the issuance of a class certificate to trigger direct benefits estoppel, as occurred in *Hellenic*. The district court would not have patently erred by choosing the latter rule, even though the majority opinion prefers the former.

The majority opinion's second new rule concerns the knowledge requirement of the direct benefits estoppel doctrine. As the majority opinion recognizes, direct benefits estoppel only applies if the non-signatory knows about the existence and the terms of the contract containing the forum-selection clause. *See Noble Drilling Servs., Inc. v. Certex USA, Inc.*, 620 F.3d [—17—] 469, 473 (5th Cir. 2010). We have not previously addressed *when* the non-signatory must acquire this knowledge. Here, Pearl Seas acquired knowledge of the forum-selection clause after some of the alleged misrepresentations, but before other alleged misrepresentations. The majority opinion decides that direct benefits estoppel applies so long as the non-signatory gains knowledge "before much of the alleged wrongdoing and before [the non-signatory files its lawsuit]." The majority opinion's new rule seems sensible enough, but a different rule might be equally sensible—say, a rule that a non-signatory only can be bound if it learns about the forum-selection clause before its cause of action accrues (i.e. before the first misrepresentation). The district court would not have patently erred by choosing the latter rule, even though the majority opinion prefers the former.[1]

Finally, it is important to note that this is not merely a "time-and-place" dispute. If the forum-selection clause is enforced, Pearl Seas may only bring its claims in England. However, the parties acknowledged at oral argument that no cause of action exists in the English courts for a ship owner to allege negligent misrepresentation against a classification society. *Cf. Otto Candies, L.L.C. v. Nippon Kaiji Kyokai Corp.*, 346 F.3d 530 (5th Cir. 2003) (permitting negligent-

---

[1] Indeed, this likely is the ground on which the district court denied LRNA's motion to dismiss. In *Petrobras America, Inc. v. Vicinay Cadenas, S.A.*, 921 F. Supp. 2d 685, 694 (S.D. Tex. 2013), the same district court denied a motion to dismiss for *forum non conveniens* because "there [was] no evidence that [plaintiff] had actual knowledge of the *terms* of the Purchase Order." Pearl Seas, at a hearing in the district court, cited *Petrobras* and argued that it too lacked knowledge of the terms of the forum selection clause until after misrepresentations were made. LRNA did not offer any response to that argument.

misrepresentation claims against classification societies). Moreover, the Classification Contract expressly denies the right of any third party, such as Pearl Seas, to enforce the terms of the Classification Contract. Thus, the [—18—] majority opinion effectively deprives Pearl Seas of any forum for its grievances against LRNA to be heard.

Because I do not believe the district court patently erred, and because the majority opinion deprives Pearl Seas of any forum for its claim, I would deny the petition for writ of mandamus.

United States Court of Appeals
for the Fifth Circuit

No. 14-30059

OFFSHORE MARINE CONTRACTORS, INC.
vs.
PALM ENERGY OFFSHORE, L.L.C.

Appeal from the United States District Court for the
Eastern District of Louisiana

Decided: March 2, 2015

Citation: 779 F.3d 345, 3 Adm. R. 282 (5th Cir. 2015).

Before **HIGGINBOTHAM, CLEMENT,** and **HIGGINSON,**
Circuit Judges.

[—2—] **CLEMENT,** Circuit Judge:

Appellants Chet Morrison Well Services, L.L.C. and Chet Morrison Contractors, L.L.C. (collectively, "CM") appeal the order and reasons, judgment, and post-trial order entered by the district court on October 7, 2013, October 17, 2013, and December 30, 2013, respectively. For the reasons explained below, the district court's judgment and post-trial order are AFFIRMED.

FACTS AND PROCEEDINGS

Appellee Palm Energy Offshore, L.L.C. ("Palm") owned the mineral rights in an area of the Gulf of Mexico ("Gulf") called the West Delta 55 block ("WD55"). Palm also served as the court-appointed manager for appellee H.C. Resources, L.L.C. ("HCR") and its mineral holdings at another Gulf location, the Chandeleur 37 block ("C37"). Acting as HCR's manager, Palm asked CM to service one of HCR's wells at C37. CM agreed and chartered the L/B Nicole Eymard (the "Nicole Eymard") from appellee Offshore Marine Contractors, Inc. ("Offshore") beginning on July 15, 2008. The Nicole Eymard is a lift boat, a vessel with extendable legs that allow the ship to stabilize on the ocean floor to perform maintenance work at sea.

The ship departed Louisiana on July 18 and worked at C37 until July 27. On July 27, Palm, now acting on its own behalf, asked CM to send the Nicole Eymard to WD55. CM dispatched the ship to WD55. After completing the job at WD55, the crew of the Nicole Eymard attempted to retract the ship's legs from the ocean floor. The crew discovered that one of the legs was stuck. The crew worked to free the leg until August 18, when Offshore ordered the crew to sever the leg and return to port ahead of an approaching storm. In port, Offshore completed repairs on the ship on October 10. Offshore then sued CM and Palm for charter fees that accrued from July 15 to August 18, for "downtime charter" from August 19 to October 10, and for the cost of repairs. [—3—] CM and Palm then filed various counter- and cross-claims against each other and Offshore. CM and Offshore's claims against each other are governed in part by the terms of an oral charter agreement. CM and Palm's claims against each other are governed in part by the terms of a Master Service Agreement ("MSA"), and in part by a specific work order. The MSA contains an indemnity agreement ("Indemnity Agreement").

After a bench trial, the district court held that CM owed Offshore for charter fees that accrued from July 15 to July 27 while the Nicole Eymard was at C37, and for charter fees that accrued from July 28 to August 18 while the ship was at WD55. The court held that CM could recover the same fees from Palm. The court held that neither CM nor Palm owed Offshore for downtime charter fees from August 19 to October 10, or for repairs. The court held that CM and Palm owed prejudgment interest to Offshore and CM, respectively. The court further held that, under the Indemnity Agreement, CM owed Palm attorneys' fees and costs, which Palm incurred while defending against Offshore's claims.

CM, Offshore, and Palm filed motions to alter or amend the judgment under Fed. R. Civ. P. 59.[1] The court granted these motions to the extent they sought clarification regarding the court's order on prejudgment interest. The court explained that CM was liable to Offshore, and Palm to CM, for prejudgment interest at the rate of 1.5% per month. The court granted Palm's motion in

---

[1] CM also cited Rule 60 as a basis for its motion.

part, holding that Palm did not owe CM for on-site downtime charter fees that accrued from August 1 to August 18 while the Nicole Eymard was stuck at WD55. The court determined that the Indemnity Agreement barred CM from seeking repayment for those fees. The court denied the parties' motions in all other respects. [—4—]

CM appeals from the district court's judgment and its post-trial order.

STANDARD OF REVIEW

In admiralty cases tried without a jury, we review the district court's legal conclusions de novo and its factual findings under the clearly erroneous standard. *Stevens Shipping & Terminal Co. v. Japan Rainbow II MV*, 334 F.3d 439, 443 (5th Cir. 2003). "A finding is clearly erroneous when, although there is evidence to support it, the reviewing court, based on all of the evidence, is left with the definite and firm conviction that a mistake has been made." *Stolt Achievement, Ltd. v. Dredge B.E. LINDHOLM*, 447 F.3d 360, 363 (5th Cir. 2006). "If the district court's account of the evidence is plausible in light of the record, this Court may not reverse, even though convinced that had it been sitting as the trier of fact, it would have weighed the evidence differently." *Id.* at 363-64.

"If a finding is based on a mixed question of law and fact, this court should only reverse 'if the findings are based on a misunderstanding of the law or a clearly erroneous view of the facts.'" *Bertucci Contracting Corp. v. M/V ANTWERPEN*, 465 F.3d 254, 259 (5th Cir. 2006) (quoting *Tokio Marine & Fire Ins. Co. v. FLORA MV*, 235 F.3d 963, 966 (5th Cir. 2001)).

"Interpretation of the terms of a contract, including an indemnity clause, is a matter of law, reviewable *de novo* on appeal." *Duval v. N. Assur. Co. of Am.*, 722 F.3d 300, 303, 1 Adm. R. 270, 271 (5th Cir. 2013) (internal quotation marks omitted). Because the MSA and relevant work orders are "directly and proximately linked to a vessel involved in a maritime activity," general maritime law controls our interpretation of those agreements. *See Theriot v. Bay Drilling Corp.*, 783 F.2d 527, 539 (5th Cir. 1986); *cf. Reynaud v. Rowan Co.*, No. Civ. A. 98-1326, 1999 WL 65022, at *2 & n.3 (E.D. La. Feb. 5, 1999) (Clement, J.) (holding that contract to supply jackup rig was maritime in nature). Because the MSA contains a Louisiana choice of law provision, and the work in this case [—5—] was performed in Louisiana territorial waters, we apply Louisiana law when interpreting the MSA. *See Great Lakes Reinsurance (UK) PLC v. Durham Auctions, Inc.*, 585 F.3d 236, 243-44 (5th Cir. 2009) (holding that choice of law provision in maritime contract applies unless party opposing provision shows chosen state has "no substantial relationship to the parties or the transaction," or "state's law conflicts with the fundamental purposes of maritime law").[2]

DISCUSSION

I.

CM argues that the district court erred by finding that it was barred under the Indemnity Agreement from seeking repayment from Palm for charter fees that accrued from August 1 to August 18 while the Nicole Eymard was stuck at WD55.

As explained above, the Indemnity Agreement is part of the MSA. Thus our interpretation of the Indemnity Agreement is governed by Louisiana law. Under Louisiana law, "[t]he starting point for interpreting an indemnity provision is the language of the contractual provision." *Scarberry v. Entergy Corp.*, 136 So. 3d 194, 218 (La. Ct. App. 2014). "If the words of the contract are clear, unambiguous, and lead to no absurd consequences, the court need not look beyond the contract language to determine the true intent of the parties." *Boykin v. PPG Indus., Inc.*, 987 So. 2d 838, 842 (La. Ct. App. 2008) (citing and summarizing La. Civ. Code art. 2046). The Indemnity Agreement provides that CM "shall release, defend, protect, indemnify, and hold [Palm] harmless . . . from and against all suits, actions, claims,

---

[2] Neither party argues that these exceptions apply.

liabilities, damages, and demands based upon personal injury or death or property damage or loss . . . suffered by" CM or its subcontractors. [—6—]

In its October 7 order, the district court held that CM owed Offshore for charter fees that accrued from July 28 to August 18 while the Nicole Eymard was at WD55. *See Offshore Marine Contractors, Inc. v. Palm Energy Offshore, LLC* (*Offshore I*), No. 10-CV-4151, 2013 WL 5530273, at *7 (E.D. La. Oct. 7, 2013). The court further held that Palm had agreed to pay CM for those fees. *See id.* at *7-8. In its post-trial order, the district court affirmed its earlier holding to the extent that Palm still owes CM for charter fees that accrued while the Nicole Eymard was *working* at WD55. But the court held that the on-site downtime charter fees that accrued only because the Nicole Eymard was stuck on location were based on "property damage or loss," and thus "f[e]ll within the terms of the release" in the Indemnity Agreement. *Offshore Marine Contractors, Inc. v. Palm Energy Offshore, LLC* (*Offshore II*), No. 10-CV-4151, 2013 WL 6858911, at *6 (E.D. La. Dec. 30, 2013). Accordingly, the court held that Palm "[wa]s not liable to [CM] for charter fees during the period in which the Nicole Eymard was stuck [at WD55] (August 1, 2008 to August 18, 2008)." *Id.*

CM's argument turns on the meaning of the phrase "based upon . . . property damage or loss." In CM's view, the fact that its claim against Palm is for charter fees means that the claim cannot be based on property damage. But CM fails to recognize that the Indemnity Agreement covers not only claims based on "property damage" but also those based on "loss." Indemnification is required for claims "based upon personal injury or death or property damage or loss." Only damage is modified by "property." As used in the Indemnity Agreement, "loss" is general and not modified by "property."[3] The on-site

[—7—] downtime charter fees were a "loss," which is covered by the Indemnity Agreement.

We agree with the district court's interpretation of the Indemnity Agreement, and we discern no error in the district court's understanding of the relevant facts.

II.

CM argues that Palm breached its agreement to pay charter fees directly to Offshore, and that this breach precludes Palm from collecting attorneys' fees and costs from CM under the Indemnity Agreement.[4]

In *Offshore II*, the district court held that Palm never agreed to pay Offshore directly for the charter fees that accrued at WD55. *Id.*, 2013 WL 6858911, at *5. If Palm never agreed to pay Offshore directly, then no breach could have occurred. CM cites evidence that suggests that Palm agreed to pay Offshore directly. But the district court credited conflicting evidence that Palm never agreed to pay directly for the WD55 job. *See Offshore I*, 2013 WL 5530273, at *5 ("Williams [of CM] maintained that the [WD]55 project was supposed to be another direct billing arrangement, but Garrett [of Palm] testified that direct billing was never discussed." (footnote omitted)). CM fails to point to any evidence showing that the district court's balancing of the conflicting evidence was unreasonable.

Accordingly, CM fails to show that the district court clearly erred by crediting the evidence showing that there was no direct billing agreement.

---

[3] Where "property" is intended to modify both "damage" and "loss," the Indemnity Agreement makes the modification explicit. For example, the Indemnity Agreement provides that CM must provide comprehensive general liability insurance that covers "personal injury, sickness or death, and loss or damage to property." Elsewhere, it provides that Palm will pay CM for "damage to or loss of [CM's] downhole property or equipment."

[4] Palm moves the court to strike portions of CM's reply brief suggesting that Palm never paid for the charter hire of the Nicole Eymard. Because, even considering those portions of CM's brief, CM fails to show that the district court clearly erred, we dismiss Palm's motion as moot.

III. [—8—]

CM argues that the district court erred by failing to award it a 15% markup on all charter fees owed by Palm.

CM's strongest evidence is a corporate deposition of a Palm executive, Jonathan Garrett ("Garrett"). Opposing counsel asked Garrett:

> Well, let's just say the Court determines -- you've already told us that you committed to pay the charter hire, whatever was the reasonable charter hire.
>
> My question to you is: With your relationship with Chet Morrison, was your agreement to pay the charter hire plus 15 percent for this job on West Delta 55?

Garrett responded: "That's the -- yes, that's given --." This testimony suggests that CM and Palm had a blanket agreement that Palm would pay the markup whenever CM chartered vessels on its behalf. But at trial, Garrett testified that Palm never "issue[d] a blanket statement to [CM] that [it] would pay any and all invoices with a 15 percent markup" and that Palm "reserv[ed] the right to audit [CM's] invoice." A district court does not clearly err merely because it credits one of two conflicting testimonies. Cf. *United States v. Davis*, 76 F.3d 82, 85 (5th Cir. 1996) ("We see no error in the district court's determination that Wilson's cross-examination testimony was more worthy of credence than his direct testimony. . . ."). Moreover, we note that the district court's resolution of these conflicting testimonies was especially reasonable in this case, where the deposition question was convoluted and hypothetical, while the question at trial was clear and direct.

CM points to evidence that Palm paid a CM invoice that contained the markup. But CM concedes that the payment was later refunded, and other testimony suggests that Palm paid the invoice "accidentally." CM also points to testimony that Palm had paid CM the markup in the past. But the trial testimony cited above suggests that past markup payments were not promises to pay in the future. [—9—]

Finally, CM adduced evidence that it is customary for its customers to pay a markup. But "before a custom or usage will be considered binding by implication, the practice must appear to have been generally applicable as to the place in question or in reference to the particular trade with which it is connected." Richard A. Lord, 12 Williston on Contracts § 34.14 (4th ed. 2014). Such "binding effect . . . cannot be based on a few isolated instances, or the practice of a few persons in a business or trade in which numerous persons are engaged." *Id.*

Accordingly, CM fails to show that the district court clearly erred when it determined that Palm did not owe the markup payments.

IV.

CM argues that the district court clearly erred when it awarded prejudgment interest to Offshore at the rate of 1.5% per month because it never agreed to pay that rate. CM also contends that this case presents special circumstances that require an exception to the general rule that prejudgment interest applies.

"Under maritime law, the awarding of prejudgment interest is the rule rather than the exception, and, in practice, is well-nigh automatic." *Reeled Tubing, Inc. v. M/V Chad G*, 794 F.2d 1026, 1028 (5th Cir. 1986). "Admiralty courts enjoy broad discretion in setting prejudgment interest rates. They may look to the judgment creditor's actual cost of borrowing money, to state law, or to other reasonable guideposts indicating a fair level of compensation." *Gator Marine Serv. Towing, Inc. v. J. Ray McDermott & Co.*, 651 F.2d 1096, 1101 (5th Cir. Unit A July 1981) (internal citations omitted).

The district court set the interest rate based on Offshore's invoices. In doing so, the district court did not abuse its discretion. Courts often look to invoices when fixing prejudgment interest. *L&L Oil Co. v. M/V REBEL*, 96 F.3d 1445 (5th Cir. 1996) (unpublished table decision) (noting that district [—10—] court properly awarded interest based on rate called for in invoices); *Eagle Eye Distrib., Inc. v. Ben Parker, Inc.*, No. 3:09-CV-0095-L, 2009 WL 4251105, at *9 (N.D. Tex. Nov. 25, 2009) (looking to invoices to set 1.5% per month prejudgment interest rate). Courts award these amounts to "compensate[ ] for the use of funds to which the plaintiff was entitled, but which the defendant had use of prior to judgment," not on the grounds that the parties specifically agreed to the interest rate. *Reeled Tubing*, 794 F.2d at 1028. CM's argument that it never agreed to the invoice rate is irrelevant.

CM argues that special circumstances require an exception to the prejudgment interest rule. More specifically, CM contends that Offshore delayed litigation from 2008 to 2010. But the record shows that CM caused this delay, at least in part, by instructing Offshore to bill Palm directly. CM maintains that the district court should not have ordered payment of any interest rate higher than the federal interest rate, but it fails to cite any support for this assertion. CM argues that the prejudgment interest rate leads to an award that is far higher than Offshore could have earned on the withheld payments. Once again, CM fails to cite any support for this assertion. Finally, CM asserts that the district court's award ignores all of the *Reeled Tubing* factors. This general assertion is insufficient to show that the district court abused its discretion.

Accordingly, CM fails to show that the district court abused its discretion when it awarded Offshore prejudgment interest at the rate of 1.5% per month.

CONCLUSION

For the reasons explained, the district court's judgment and post-trial order are AFFIRMED.

United States Court of Appeals
for the Fifth Circuit

No. 14-30122

UNITED STATES

VS.

KALUZA

Appeal from the United States District Court for the
Eastern District of Louisiana

Decided: March 11, 2015

Citation: 780 F.3d 647, 3 Adm. R. 287 (5th Cir. 2015).

Before **HIGGINBOTHAM, JONES,** and **PRADO,** Circuit
Judges.

[—1—] **HIGGINBOTHAM,** Circuit Judge:

On April 20, 2010, a blowout of oil, natural gas, and mud occurred during deepwater drilling operations at the Macondo well, located on the Outer Continental Shelf ("OCS") in the waters of the Gulf of Mexico. At the time of the blowout, the *Deepwater Horizon*, a drilling rig chartered by BP plc ("BP") from Transocean Ltd. ("Transocean"), was attached to the Macondo well. Eleven men died from the resulting explosions and fires on the *Deepwater Horizon*. The blowout resulted in the discharge of millions of barrels of oil into the Gulf of Mexico.

Robert Kaluza and Donald Vidrine ("Defendants") were "well site leaders," the highest ranking BP employees working on the rig. Defendants were indicted by a federal grand jury in the Eastern District of Louisiana on [—2—] 23 counts, including 11 counts of seaman's manslaughter in violation of 18 U.S.C. § 1115. The district court granted Defendants' motion to dismiss for failure to charge an offense because neither defendant fell within the meaning of the criminal statute. The government appeals this determination. Because we agree that neither defendant falls within the meaning of the phrase "[e]very . . . other person employed on any . . . vessel," we AFFIRM.

I

A

In May 2008, BP, through one of its affiliated companies, obtained a lease from the United States to the oil and natural gas reservoirs at a site on the OCS in the Gulf of Mexico. The first well drilled by BP at this site was referred to as the Macondo well, approximately 48 miles from the Louisiana shoreline. The seabed was approximately 5,000 feet below sea level, and the potential reservoirs were located more than 13,000 feet below the seabed. BP and its affiliates entered into contracts with Transocean, whereby Transocean provided, *inter alia*, a drilling rig and crews to drill the Macondo well under BP's supervision. BP began drilling the Macondo well in October 2009 using Transocean's *Marianas* drilling rig and crew, but that work was halted in November 2009 due to a hurricane. In April 2010, BP resumed drilling the Macondo well using Transocean's *Deepwater Horizon* drilling vessel and crew.

The *Deepwater Horizon* was a mobile offshore drilling rig. It was "a dynamically-positioned semi-submersible deepwater drilling vessel."[1] The rig floated on two enormous pontoons extending 30 feet below the ocean's surface that acted as the vessel's hull, provided stability to the rig, kept the rig afloat, and allowed the drilling floor and other work areas to remain safely above the [—3—] water's surface. The *Deepwater Horizon* employed dynamic satellite positioning technology connected to directional thrusters that allowed the vessel to maintain its place over the wellhead. The rig had no legs or anchors connecting it to the seabed.

When the *Deepwater Horizon* arrived at the Macondo well, the crew assembled a drilling structure that attached the rig to the wellhead: the structure consisted of the Blow Out Preventer stack ("BOP") and the marine riser. The BOP, attached directly to the wellhead, was a five-story, 300-ton stack of

---

[1] *In re Oil Spill by the Oil Rig "Deepwater Horizon" in the Gulf of Mex., on April 20, 2010,* 808 F. Supp. 2d 943, 950 (E.D. La. 2011) (citations omitted).

components designed to close the well in case of an emergency. The BOP was attached to the marine riser, a pipe that was approximately 5,000 feet long and made primarily out of steel, twenty inches in diameter. The marine riser, in turn, was attached to the drill floor on the rig. In order to assemble this drilling structure, a section of the marine riser was joined to the BOP and then, as additional riser sections were added, the BOP was lowered to the seabed; remotely operated vehicles latched the BOP to the wellhead. All materials necessary to drill the well—the drilling tools, drilling mud, and other fluids—passed from the rig through the marine riser down to the wellhead.

The *Deepwater Horizon* maintained separate crews for different tasks, such as the "marine crew" and the "drill crew."[2] The marine crew was provided in its entirety by Transocean, and consisted of the master (i.e., the captain), the chief mate, the chief engineer, assistant engineers, dynamic positioning officers, able bodied seamen, the boatswain, and the offshore installation manager.[3] During the time that the vessel was attached to the well, certain [—4—] marine crew members were responsible for maintaining the location of the vessel over the wellhead. The drill crew was provided in part by BP, Transocean, and other companies, and consisted of the well site leaders, toolpushers

---

[2] There was also a "support crew" and other personnel not relevant to this appeal.

[3] 1 U.S. Coast Guard, *Report of Investigation into the Circumstances Surrounding the Explosion, Fire, Sinking and Loss of Eleven Crew Members Aboard the Mobile Offshore Drilling Unit Deepwater Horizon in the Gulf of Mexico, April 20– 22, 2010* app. D, D-4 (2011) [hereafter *Coast Guard Rep.*]. [—4—]

Although the offshore installation manager is listed as a member of the marine crew, his duties were more related to the drill crew. The master was in charge of the rig when it was moving from location to location. Once the rig arrived at a site and began drilling-related operations, the offshore installation manager took over, and the members of the drill crew provided by Transocean reported to him. Nat'l Comm'n on the BP Deepwater Horizon Oil Spill and Offshore Drilling, *Macondo: The Gulf Oil Disaster, Chief Counsel's Report* 33 (2011) [hereafter *Chief Counsel's Rep.*].

(i.e, drilling managers), the chief engineer, other engineers, drillers, assistant drillers, floorhands, roustabouts, mudloggers, and various other personnel.[4]

Although BP did not own the rig nor operate it in the normal sense of the word because daily production involved few BP employees, BP's engineering team designed the well and oversaw the implementation of the design. Most of BP's team for the *Deepwater Horizon* were based on shore. However, there were seven BP employees on the rig on the day of the explosion. Specifically, the two well site leaders were BP employees who were on the vessel at all times, splitting responsibility by 12-hour shifts, to direct the drill crew and contractors in their work while maintaining regular contact with the BP engineers on shore. The well site leaders were "the top BP employees" on the rig, and were known as "the company men." They were "the company's eyes and ears," making "important decisions regarding the course of drilling operations." According to BP's Drilling and Wells Operation Practice manual, the well site leaders were accountable for the execution of drilling and well operations in compliance with BP's health, safety, security, and environmental requirements. Under a different BP guide, in case of a well control incident, the well site leader was "responsible for ensuring all activities are carried out [—5—] in a safe and efficient manner at the location, and for proactively promoting the health, safety and welfare of all personnel on the Rig." Kaluza and Vidrine were the two well site leaders aboard the *Deepwater Horizon* on the day of the explosion.

Kaluza and Vidrine were industry veterans. Kaluza has a degree in petroleum engineering and 35 years' experience in the oil and gas industry, including more than eight years as a well site leader. He was ordinarily assigned to another rig, but was serving on the *Deepwater Horizon* on the day of the explosion. Vidrine had been a well site leader for more than 30 years. He had been working

---

[4] *Coast Guard Rep.* app. D, D-5 to D-8; *Chief Counsel's Rep.* at 30-34.

on the *Deepwater Horizon* since January 2010, and had previously worked on the Macondo well as a well site leader onboard another rig.

Well site leaders were responsible for conducting and assessing the validity of "negative pressure testing" or "negative testing," a process which assessed whether the cement pumped to the bottom of the well had hardened, thus forming an effective barrier between the well and the oil and gas reservoir. During the negative testing, the well was monitored for pressure increases and fluid flows. Either condition would indicate that the well was not secure and that oil and natural gas could be entering the well. An uncontrolled influx of fluids and gas from the surrounding rock into the well—known as a "kick"—could cause a catastrophic blowout up the well and onto the rig with the potential for ignition, explosions, casualties, death, and environmental damage. Competent negative testing was critical.

On April 20, 2010, the *Deepwater Horizon* crew was engaged in procedures to temporarily abandon the Macondo well, sealing it with cement so that a different vessel could later retrieve the oil and natural gas reserves. As part of this procedure, they attempted to perform negative tests multiple times to assess whether the well was properly sealed. Both defendants [—6—] participated in the negative testing. The indictment alleges that Defendants negligently or grossly negligently:

> failed to phone engineers onshore to advise them during the negative testing of the multiple indications that the well was not secure; failed to adequately account for the abnormal readings during the testing; accepted a nonsensical explanation for the abnormal readings, again without calling engineers onshore to consult; eventually decided to stop investigating the abnormal readings any further; and deemed the negative testing a success, which caused displacement of the well to proceed and blowout of the well to later occur.

After the failed negative testing, the well blew out within hours, the vessel exploded, eleven men died, and others were severely injured.

B

A federal grand jury in the Eastern District of Louisiana returned a 23-count superseding indictment charging Defendants with 11 counts of involuntary manslaughter in violation of 18 U.S.C. § 1112 (Counts 1-11); 11 counts of seaman's manslaughter in violation of 18 U.S.C. § 1115 (Counts 12-22); and 1 count of negligent discharge under the Clean Water Act in violation of 33 U.S.C. §§ 1319(c)(1)(A) and 1321(b)(3) (Count 23).

Defendants filed motions to dismiss based on several theories. With regard to Counts 12-22 (seaman's manslaughter), they first argued that the *Deepwater Horizon* was outside the territorial jurisdiction of the United States, and that § 1115 does not apply extraterritorially.[5] Second, Defendants argued that Counts 12-22 did not charge an offense—that they were not persons covered under 18 U.S.C. § 1115. Defendants also moved to dismiss all counts, [—7—] arguing that the underlying statutes were unconstitutionally vague as applied. The district court denied the motions to dismiss related to the *Deepwater Horizon*'s extraterritorial location, finding that the Outer Continental Shelf Lands Act (OCSLA) "extends federal law and political jurisdiction" to the rig, but dismissed Counts 12-22 for failure to charge an offense. The district court then denied the motion to dismiss for unconstitutional vagueness.

The government now appeals the dismissal of Counts 12-22, arguing that Defendants are persons covered under § 1115. Defendants urge alternatively that § 1115 did not apply on the *Deepwater Horizon* because it lacks extraterritorial reach, and the OCSLA did not apply federal law generally to the rig.

---

[5] Defendants also moved to dismiss Counts 1-11 (involuntary manslaughter), arguing that the *Deepwater Horizon* was outside the special maritime and territorial jurisdiction of the United States and thus that § 1112 did not apply on the rig by its terms. *See* § 1112(b).

II

We review the district court's legal determination regarding subject matter jurisdiction *de novo*.[6] We also review the district court's interpretation and application of a federal statute *de novo*.[7]

III

We begin by examining subject matter jurisdiction. "Federal subject matter jurisdiction is limited and must be conferred by Congress within the bounds of the Constitution."[8] Subject matter jurisdiction involves "the courts' statutory or constitutional *power* to adjudicate the case,"[9] and it can "never be forfeited or waived."[10] "The objection that a federal court lacks subject-matter [—8—] jurisdiction may be raised by a party, or by a court on its own initiative, at any stage in the litigation, even after trial and the entry of judgment."[11]

In the criminal context, subject matter jurisdiction is straightforward.[12] Here, the district court had subject matter jurisdiction under 18 U.S.C. § 3231, which provides that "[t]he district courts of the United States shall have original jurisdiction, exclusive of the courts of the States, of all offenses against the laws of the United States." As this is an appeal by the United States, we have jurisdiction pursuant to 18 U.S.C. § 3731.

IV

We find no occasion to address Defendants' argument that 18 U.S.C. § 1115 did not extend to the *Deepwater Horizon* because this issue does not concern subject matter jurisdiction and was not properly appealed.

Defendants argued below that the district court did not have "jurisdiction" because § 1115 did not extend to the *Deepwater Horizon*. The argument was that neither territorial nor extraterritorial jurisdiction existed. First, territorial jurisdiction did not obtain because the *Deepwater Horizon* was a foreign-flag vessel and operated in international waters 48 nautical miles from the coastline.[13] Second, extraterritorial jurisdiction did not obtain because the government had not overcome the presumption against extraterritorial application of federal law.[14] In response, the government relied [—9—] solely on the Outer Continental Shelf Lands Act ("OCSLA"), which explicitly extends federal law to the OCS and certain attachments to it. The district court agreed with the government, holding that the OCSLA extended federal law including § 1115 to the rig.

The provision of the OCSLA that the district court relied on was 43 U.S.C. § 1333(a)(1), which provides that:

---

[6] *United States v. Urrabazo*, 234 F.3d 904, 906 (5th Cir. 2000).

[7] *United States v. Gore*, 636 F.3d 728, 730 (5th Cir. 2011).

[8] *Elam v. Kan. City S. Ry. Co.*, 635 F.3d 796, 802 (5th Cir. 2011).

[9] *United States v. Cotton*, 535 U.S. 625, 630 (2002) (quoting *Steel Co. v. Citizens for Better Env't*, 523 U.S. 83, 89 (1998)).

[10] *Id.*

[11] *Arbaugh v. Y & H Corp.*, 546 U.S. 500, 506 (2006) (citation omitted); *see also* Fed. R. Crim. P. 12(b)(2) ("A motion that the court lacks jurisdiction may be made at any time while the case is pending.") (previously at 12(b)(3)(B)).

[12] *United States v. Scruggs*, 714 F.3d 258, 262 (5th Cir. 2013).

[13] *See United States v. Jho*, 534 F.3d 398, 405-06 (5th Cir. 2008) (noting that under international law a ship is subject to the territorial jurisdiction of its flag state); Antiterrorism & Effective Death Penalty Act of 1996, Pub. L. No. 104-132, § 901(a), 110 Stat. 1214, 1317 (extending territorial jurisdiction to the territorial sea of the United States, i.e, 12 nautical miles from the coastline).

[14] *See Morrison v. Nat'l Austl. Bank Ltd.*, 561 U.S. 247, 255 (2010) ("It is a longstanding principle of American law that legislation of Congress, unless a contrary intent appears, is meant to apply only within the territorial jurisdiction of the United States.") [—9—] (citations omitted) (internal quotation marks omitted); *see also Kiobel v. Royal Dutch Petrol. Co.*, 133 S. Ct. 1659, 1664 (2013) ("[The presumption against extraterritorial application] provides that [w]hen a statute gives no clear indication of an extraterritorial application, it has none.") (citations omitted) (internal quotation marks omitted).

The Constitution and laws and civil and political jurisdiction of the United States are extended to the subsoil and seabed of the outer Continental Shelf and to all artificial islands, and *all installations and other devices permanently or temporarily attached to the seabed, which may be erected thereon* for the purpose of exploring for, developing, or producing resources therefrom, or any such installation or other device (other than a ship or vessel) for the purpose of transporting such resources, to the same extent as if the outer Continental Shelf were an area of exclusive Federal jurisdiction located within a State.[15]

As we have explained, this provision imposes a situs test for the extension of federal law. "The OCSLA applies to all of the following locations":

(1) the subsoil and seabed of the OCS;
(2) any artificial island, installation, or other device if
    (a) it is permanently or temporarily attached to the seabed of the OCS, and
    (b) it has been erected on the seabed of the OCS, and
    (c) its presence on the OCS is to explore for, develop, or produce resources from the OCS;
(3) any artificial island, installation, or other device if
    (a) it is permanently or temporarily attached to the seabed of the OCS, and [—10—]
    (b) it is not a ship or vessel, and
    (c) its presence on the OCS is to transport resources from the OCS.[16]

There is no question that the *Deepwater Horizon* could not qualify as an OCSLA situs under either the first or third categories. The first category does not apply by its terms; the third category does not apply because the

Deepwater Horizon was a vessel.[17] For the *Deepwater Horizon* to be an OCSLA situs—so extending federal law, including § 1115, to the rig—it had to qualify within the second category. At the district court level, Defendants argued that the rig did not qualify as an OCSLA situs because it was not "erected on the seabed of the OCS." The government argued the square opposite, and the district court agreed with the government.

Defendants now try to renew this argument. However, we do not address it. To begin, the issue of whether the rig was an OCSLA situs does not implicate subject matter jurisdiction. We have previously explained that there are different provisions within the OCSLA for subject matter jurisdiction and choice of law. Through 43 U.S.C. § 1349(b)(1), the OCSLA grants subject matter jurisdiction to federal district courts.[18] By contrast, § 1333 is a choice-of-law provision that defines the applicable law on the OCS— whether federal, [—11—] maritime or state. We have held that this subject matter jurisdiction inquiry should not be conflated with the choice-of-law inquiry.[19] Although the district court was exercising subject matter jurisdiction on a different basis—namely § 3231, not § 1349(b)(1)—the principle is the

---

[15] 43 U.S.C. § 1333(a)(1) (emphasis added).

[16] *Demette v. Falcon Drilling Co.*, 280 F.3d 492, 497 (5th Cir. 2002), *overruled in part, on other grounds, by Grand Isle Shipyard, Inc. v. Seacor Marine, LLC*, 589 F.3d 778 (5th Cir. 2009) (en banc).

[17] Neither party contested the district court's assessment that the *Deepwater Horizon* was a vessel. In addition, we have previously treated the rig as a vessel. *In re Deepwater Horizon*, 745 F.3d 157, 164-66, 2 Adm. R. 171, 173-175 (5th Cir. 2014); *In re Deepwater Horizon*, 753 F.3d 570, 571-74, 2 Adm. R. 233, 233-236 (5th Cir. 2014); *see also* 33 C.F.R. § 140.10 ("Mobile offshore drilling unit or MODU means a vessel . . . capable of engaging in drilling operations for exploration or exploitation of subsea resources.").

[18] Section 1349(b)(1) grants district courts "jurisdiction of cases and controversies arising out of, or in connection with (A) any operation conducted on the outer Continental Shelf which involves exploration, development, or production of the minerals, of the subsoil and seabed of the outer Continental Shelf, or which involves rights to such minerals."

[19] *In re Deepwater Horizon*, 745 F.3d at 164, 2 Adm. R. at 173 ("[The] attempt to intertwine the Section 1349 jurisdictional inquiry with OCSLA's choice of law provision, 43 U.S.C. § 1333, fails because the provisions and the issues they raise are distinct.").

same; the inquiry regarding § 1333(a)(1)'s applicability does not raise subject matter jurisdiction issues. Defendants' argument instead goes to whether an offense is charged.[20] The question of whether the government has charged an offense goes to "the merits of the case,"[21] and the district court has the power to determine "whether the offense charged is a true offense."[22] Therefore, we are not obligated to examine this issue unless it has been properly appealed.

But this issue has not been properly appealed. While the United States appealed the district court's determination that Defendants did not fall within the meaning of § 1115, Defendants failed to cross-appeal the district court's determination that the *Deepwater Horizon* was erected on the seabed of the [—12—] OCS and OCSLA applied. "It is settled that an appellee may urge any ground available in support of a judgment even if that ground was earlier and erroneously rejected by the trial court."[23] But where the defendant fails to cross-appeal, his "failure to file a notice of appeal precludes him from receiving affirmative relief in this court."[24] In other words, if the government appeals and the defendant fails to cross-appeal, the defendant's rights under the judgment cannot be expanded.[25] Were we to reach the OCSLA situs issue and rule in Defendants' favor, that ruling would not only preserve the rights of Defendants, but would expand their rights. This because Defendants' liability under 18 U.S.C. § 1112—an issue not before us—also hinges on the OCSLA's extension of federal law to the *Deepwater Horizon*. Finally, Defendants themselves urge that we reach this issue only in the alternative, in case they do not prevail on the merits.

For all these reasons, we decline to decide whether the district court erred in deciding that the *Deepwater Horizon* qualified as an OCSLA situs because the issue is not properly before us.

V

We next turn to the merits of this appeal. Known as the "seaman's manslaughter" or "ship officer manslaughter" provision, § 1115 is currently titled "Misconduct or neglect of ship officers" and provides that:

> *Every captain, engineer, pilot, or other person employed on any steamboat or vessel*, by whose misconduct, negligence, or inattention to his duties on such vessel the life of any person is destroyed, and every owner, charterer, inspector, or other public officer, through whose fraud, neglect, connivance, [—13—] misconduct, or violation of law the life of any person is destroyed, shall be fined under this title or imprisoned not more than ten years, or both.

---

[20] *See Morrison*, 561 U.S. at 254 ("But to ask what conduct § 10(b) reaches is to ask what conduct § 10(b) prohibits, which is a merits question. Subject-matter jurisdiction, by contrast, refers to a tribunal's power to hear a case.") (internal quotation marks omitted); *United States v. Yousef*, 750 F.3d 254, 261-62 (2d Cir. 2014) ("In the criminal context, 18 U.S.C. § 3231 is all that is necessary to establish a court's power to hear a case involving a federal offense, whether or not the conduct charged proves beyond the scope of Congress' concern or authority in enacting the statute at issue."); *United States v. Delgado-Garcia*, 374 F.3d 1337, 1340-43 (D.C. Cir. 2004) (finding that defendants' argument that the statute of conviction did not apply extraterritorially, and thus that no offense had been stated against them, did not deprive the district court of subject matter jurisdiction); *see also United States v. Baker*, 609 F.2d 134, 135 (5th Cir. 1980) (in case hinging on whether possession with intent to distribute statute applied outside the territorial United States, framing the issue as whether or not the conduct "is a crime under 21 U.S.C.A. s 841(a)(1)").

[21] *Cotton*, 535 U.S. at 631; *see also Scruggs*, 714 F.3d at 262; *United States v. Longoria*, 298 F.3d 367, 372 (5th Cir. 2002) (en banc) (recognizing that the Supreme Court in *Cotton* overruled Fifth Circuit cases which had stated that failure to charge an offense was a "jurisdictional" error).

[22] *Delgado-Garcia*, 374 F.3d at 1342 (quoting *Lamar v. United States*, 240 U.S. 60, 65 (1916)).

[23] *Castellano v. Fragozo*, 352 F.3d 939, 960 (5th Cir. 2003) (en banc).

[24] *United States v. Coscarelli*, 149 F.3d 342, 343 (5th Cir. 1998) (en banc).

[25] *See id.* at 342-44; *Greenlaw v. United States*, 554 U.S. 237, 244 (2008) ("Under [the cross-appeal rule], an appellate court may not alter a judgment to benefit a nonappealing party.").

When the owner or charterer of any steamboat or vessel is a corporation, any executive officer of such corporation, for the time being actually charged with the control and management of the operation, equipment, or navigation of such steamboat or vessel, who has knowingly and willfully caused or allowed such fraud, neglect, connivance, misconduct, or violation of law, by which the life of any person is destroyed, shall be fined under this title or imprisoned not more than ten years, or both.[26]

Unlike the common law definition of manslaughter and the companion statutory definition for general manslaughter found in Section 1112, Section 1115 only requires the proof of any degree of negligence to meet the culpability threshold.[27] Moreover, the statute holds liable three groups of individuals:

(1) Every captain, engineer, pilot, or other person employed on any steamboat or vessel,

(2) Every owner, charterer, inspector, or other public officer, and

(3) When the owner or charterer of any steamboat or vessel is a corporation, any executive officer of such corporation, for the time being actually charged with the control and management of the operation, equipment, or navigation of such steamboat or vessel.[28]

Neither the second category (the owner provision) nor the third category (the corporate officer provision) is at issue; it is only the first category with which we are concerned. Specifically, the phrase "[e]very . . . other person employed on any . . . vessel" is the only relevant one because Defendants are not captains, engineers, or pilots and because the *Deepwater Horizon* was not a steamboat. [—14—]

The government argued below that the phrase was not ambiguous, and that the plain text included Defendants. The district court disagreed. It reasoned that the statute was ambiguous, and applied the principle of *ejusdem generis*[29] to define the phrase. The district court held that the phrase covered only persons with responsibility for the "marine operations, maintenance, and navigation of the vessel." Since Defendants were not such persons, they did not fall within the ambit of the statute.

A

On appeal, the government argues that the plain meaning of the statute is not ambiguous. The ordinary meaning of the phrase "[e]very . . . other person employed on any . . . vessel" easily encompasses Defendants. As confirmation of this plain text interpretation, the government points to the plain text of the other provisions in § 1115. It also points to others indicators—including statutory development, drafting history, statutory context, title, statutory purpose, and case law. The government argues that since the plain language is unambiguous, it was error to invoke *ejusdem generis*. Finally, the government points to the principle of *ex abundanti cautela*.[30]

In response, Defendants argue that *ejusdem generis* is not a canon of last resort, but rather a fundamental canon of statutory construction. There is no need to find ambiguity in the statute to apply the canon. Rather, Defendants argue that the government's position would lead to making

---

[26] 18 U.S.C. § 1115 (emphasis added).

[27] *United States v. O'Keefe (O'Keefe II)*, 426 F.3d 274, 278-79 (5th Cir. 2005). *Compare* 18 U.S.C. § 1112, *with id.* § 1115.

[28] *See* 18 U.S.C. § 1115.

[29] 2A Norman Singer & J.D. Shambie Singer, *Sutherland on Statutes and Statutory Construction* §47:17 (7th ed. 2014) ("*Ejusdem generis* means 'of the same kind,' and is a variation of the maxim *noscitur a sociis*. *Ejusdem generis* instructs that, where general words follow specific words in an enumeration describing a statute's legal subject, the general words are construed to embrace only objects similar in nature to those objects enumerated by the preceding specific words." (footnotes omitted)).

[30] *Circuit City Stores, Inc. v. Adams*, 532 U.S. 105, 140 (2001) (Souter, J., dissenting) (defining *ex abundanti cautela* as the abundance of caution principle).

the words "captain, engineer, [and] pilot" superfluous, and that *ejusdem generis* has to be applied [—15—] to give meaning to each word. Finally, Defendants argue that the principle of *noscitur a sociis*[31] also applies.

"The starting point in discerning congressional intent is the existing statutory text . . . ."[32] "When faced with questions of statutory construction, 'we must first determine whether the statutory text is plain and unambiguous' and, '[i]f it is, we must apply the statute according to its terms.'"[33] The parties disagree on whether the plain text of the statute needs to be found ambiguous before a canon of construction, such as *ejusdem generis*, can be applied.[34] However, as we explain below, the plain text of the statute is ambiguous, necessitating the use of canons of construction. In any case, there is no doubt that legislative history can only be a guide after the application of canons of construction. "Only after application of principles of statutory construction, including the canons of construction, and after a conclusion that the statute is ambiguous may the court turn to the legislative history. For the language to [—16—] be considered ambiguous, however, it must be susceptible to more than one reasonable interpretation or more than one accepted meaning."[35]

"When construing statutes and regulations, we begin with the assumption that the words were meant to express their ordinary meaning."[36] The government contends that the plain meaning of § 1115 is unambiguous as it contains no complicated or technical language. The definitions of each word in the phrase "[e]very . . . other person employed on any . . . vessel" are straightforward.

"Every" is defined as "[c]onstituting each and all members of a group without exception" or "[b]eing all possible."[37] "Other" is defined as "[b]eing the remaining ones of several."[38] "Person" is defined by the Dictionary Act to include individuals.[39] "Employed" is defined as "engaged in work or occupation; having employment; *esp.* [a person] that works for an employer under an employment contract."[40] "On" is "[u]sed to indicate position above and supported by or in contact with" an object.[41] "Any" "has an expansive meaning, that is, 'one or some indiscriminately of whatever kind.'"[42] "Vessel" is also defined by the Dictionary Act as "includ[ing] every description of watercraft or other artificial contrivance used, or capable

---

[31] 2A Singer & Singer, *supra* note 29, §47:16 ("*Noscitur a sociis* means literally 'it is known from its associates,' and means practically that a word may be defined by an accompanying word, and that, ordinarily, the coupling of words denotes an intention that they should be understood in the same general sense." (footnote omitted)).

[32] *Lamie v. U.S. Trustee*, 540 U.S. 526, 534 (2004).

[33] *Asadi v. G.E. Energy (USA), L.L.C.*, 720 F.3d 620, 622 (5th Cir. 2013) (quoting *Carcieri v. Salazar*, 555 U.S. 379, 387 (2009)).

[34] Precedent from the Supreme Court is not entirely clear on this point either. *Compare Garcia v. United States*, 469 U.S. 70, 74-75 (1984) (refusing to apply *ejusdem generis* because, among other things, the statute had a plain and unambiguous meaning), *with Circuit City Stores*, 532 U.S. at 114-20 (majority opinion) (applying *ejusdem generis* before concluding that the text was clear). Neither is precedent from our Court. *Compare United States v. Barlow*, 41 F.3d 935, 942 (5th Cir. 1994) (suggesting that a statute has to be opaque, translucent, or ambiguous before canons of statutory interpretation can be applied, including a resort to the rule of lenity and legislative history), *with Kornman & Assocs., Inc. v. United States*, 527 F.3d 443, 451 (5th Cir. 2008) (suggesting that statutory ambiguity can only be established after application of the principles of statutory construction, including the canons of construction).

[35] *Carrieri v. Jobs.com Inc.*, 393 F.3d 508, 518-19 (5th Cir. 2004) (internal citation quotation marks, and footnote omitted).

[36] *Bouchikhi v. Holder*, 676 F.3d 173, 177 (5th Cir. 2012).

[37] *The American Heritage Dictionary of the English Language* (5th ed. 2014), *available at* http://www.ahdictionary.com (accessed online).

[38] *Id.*

[39] 1 U.S.C. § 1.

[40] *Oxford English Dictionary* (3d ed. 2014), *available at* http://www.oed.com (accessed online); *see also* The American Heritage Dictionary of the English Language (defining "employ" as "[t]o provide work to (someone) for pay").

[41] *The American Heritage Dictionary of the English Language.*

[42] *United States v. Gonzalez*, 520 U.S. 1, 5 (1997) (quoting *Webster's Third New International Dictionary* 97 (1976)).

of being used, as a means of [—17—] transportation on water."[43] There is no question that the *Deepwater Horizon* was a vessel.[44]

Looking to these definitions, the government contends that the plain text of the phrase "[e]very . . . other person employed on any . . . vessel" is clear and unambiguous, bringing within its ambit every person employed on the *Deepwater Horizon*. Defendants, however, argue that the plain text is ambiguous because it is not clear whether the phrase does incorporate every person employed on the rig. Indeed, such an interpretation would render "captain," "engineer," and "pilot" superfluous. We agree. Both interpretations of the statute are reasonable. On the one hand, the phrase could be read to include everyone employed on the vessel. On the other hand, because such a reading would render certain terms superfluous, the phrase could be read to include a smaller group of those employed on the vessel. This ambiguity necessitates the use the canon of construction of *ejusdem generis*.

The government's argument that this Court has previously held § 1115 unambiguous fails. In *United States v. O'Keefe (O'Keefe II)*, we held that certain "terms [of § 1115] are unambiguous and therefore must be given their plain meaning."[45] In that case, this Court was dealing with Defendants' argument that the phrase "misconduct, negligence, or inattention" in § 1115 required the proof of either gross negligence or heat of passion.[46] Reading the plain text of the phrase "misconduct, negligence, or inattention," this Court found no ambiguity and affirmed that any degree of negligence was sufficient to obtain a conviction.[47] But that holding has no bearing on the meaning of "[e]very . . . other person employed on any . . . vessel." [—18—]

The government also argues that the invocation of *ejusdem generis* is improper for

other reasons. First, the government argues that the term "every other person" is already qualified by the requirement that they be "employed on any steamboat or vessel." Pointing to this limitation, the governments urges against further limitation. However, this argument does not answer the question of ambiguity inherent in the phrase "every other person." Second, the government argues there is no meaningful way to define the common attributes between "captain," "engineer," and "pilot," rendering the canon ineffectual.[48] To our eyes, however, the common attribute can be defined and applied to exclude Defendants. Third, the government argues that the "textbook" grammatical structure of the phrase is not enough to justify the use of *ejusdem generis*. The government points to cases where the Supreme Court and our Court have refused to read a statute using this canon of construction because the narrow reading was not "supported by evidence of congressional intent over and above the language of the statute."[49] We do not disagree with this accent, but emphasize below that the narrow reading using *ejusdem generis* comports with the statute's context, history, and purpose. Fourth, the government argues for the application of the principle of abundance of caution, which recognizes that Congress sometimes includes certain categories, though redundant, to ensure their inclusion in a list.[50] However, as explained below, *ejusdem generis* is the most appropriate canon of application in this case [—19—] because it comports with the statute's text wherein three specific terms are followed by a general term. By contrast, the abundance of

---

[43] 1 U.S.C. § 3.

[44] *See supra* note 17.

[45] *O'Keefe II*, 426 F.3d at 279.

[46] *Id.*

[47] *Id.* at 278-79.

[48] *See Ali v. Fed. Bureau of Prisons*, 552 U.S. 214, 225 (2008); *In re Dale*, 582 F.3d 568, 574-75 (5th Cir. 2009); *United States v. Amato*, 540 F.3d 153, 160-61 (2d Cir. 2008).

[49] *United States v. Powell*, 423 U.S. 87, 90 (1975); *see also United States v. Alpers*, 338 U.S. 680, 682-83 (1950); *United States v. Silva-Chavez*, 888 F.2d 1481, 1483-84 (5th Cir. 1989).

[50] *See Ali*, 552 U.S. at 226 ("Congress may have simply have intended to remove any doubt that officers of customs or excise were included in 'law enforcement officer[s].'"); *Alpers*, 338 U.S. at 684 (holding that Congress added a superfluous term because it "was preoccupied with making doubly sure" that the term was included within the coverage of the statute).

caution principle is more appropriate when the "[t]he phrase is disjunctive, with one specific and one general category, not . . . a list of specific items separated by commas and followed by a general or collective term."[51] Therefore, the district court's invocation of *ejusdem generis* was entirely proper.

B

Under the principle of *ejusdem generis*, "where general words follow an enumeration of specific terms, the general words are read to apply only to other items like those specifically enumerated."[52] "The rule of *ejusdem generis*, while firmly established, is only an instrumentality for ascertaining the correct meaning of words when there is uncertainty."[53] Importantly, the rule cannot be used to "obscure and defeat the intent and purpose of Congress" or "render general words meaningless."[54] "Canons of construction need not be conclusive and are often countered, of course, by some maxim pointing in a different direction."[55] "The limiting principle of *ejusdem generis* has particular force with respect to criminal statutes, which courts are compelled to construe rigorously in order to protect unsuspecting citizens from being ensnared by ambiguous statutory language."[56] [—20—]

The district court considered what "common attribute" or "class of persons" the statutory phrase implied. It concluded that in the context of the phrase, the terms "captain," "engineer," and "pilot" suggested a class of persons dealing with the operation and navigation of the vessel. Thus "every . . . other person" includes only those persons responsible for the "marine operations, maintenance, or navigation of the vessel." As a result, Defendants were excluded. The district court then consulted the legislative history and case law to confirm that Congress intended such a limitation. It noted that that the predecessor to § 1115 was enacted in 1838 to "provide for the better security of the lives of passengers on board of vessels propelled in whole or in part by steam,"[57] at a time when "steamboat collisions and boiler explosions were regular occurrences." The district court inferred that Congress intended "to hold those persons responsible for navigating the vessel accountable for their actions." Next, it noted that § 1115 had never been applied to employees on a drilling rig.

The government argues that even if the district court did not err in invoking *ejusdem generis*, it defined the common attribute incorrectly. According to the government, there are several other ways of defining the common attributes of "captain, engineer, [and] pilot." First, the government argues that "captain," "engineer," and "pilot" all denote individuals who work in service of the vessel. Second, that each is a person in a position of authority or with a substantial degree of responsibility for the safety of the vessel. Third, that each is responsible for the "operation, equipment, or navigation" of the vessel. By contrast, the government contends that the common attribute found by the district court has no purchase in the statutory text. Defendants argue that the district court correctly found that the common attribute involved [—21—] persons responsible for the "marine operations, maintenance, or navigation of the vessel."

We find that the district court's definition of the common attribute was correct. The three specific words define a general class of people, specifically those involved in the "marine operations, maintenance, or

---

[51] *Ali*, 552 U.S. at 225.

[52] *Garcia*, 469 U.S. at 74; *see also Hilton v. Sw. Bell Tel. Co.*, 936 F.2d 823, 828 (5th Cir. 1991) ("When general words follow an enumeration of persons or things, such general words are not to be construed in their widest extent, but are to be held as applying only to persons or things of the same general kind or class as those specifically mentioned. The rule is one of limitation, restricting general terms, such as 'any other' and 'and the like,' which follow specific terms, to matters similar to those specified.").

[53] *Powell*, 423 U.S. at 91 (quoting *Gooch v. United States*, 297 U.S. 124, 128 (1936)).

[54] *Christopher v. SmithKline Beecham Corp.*, 132 S. Ct. 2156, 2171 (2012) (quoting *Alpers*, 338 U.S. at 682).

[55] *Circuit City Stores*, 532 U.S. at 115.

[56] *United States v. Insco*, 496 F.2d 204, 206 (5th Cir. 1974).

[57] *See* Act of July 7, 1838, ch. 191, 5 Stat. 304.

navigation of the vessel." This conclusion is bolstered by examining the meaning of the terms "captain," "engineer," and "pilot." As relevant here, "Captain" is defined as "[t]he master or commander of a merchant ship or of any kind of vessel."[58] "Engineer" is defined as "[t]he operator of a steam engine, esp. on board a ship."[59] "Pilot" is defined as "[a] person who steers or directs the course of a ship; a helmsman or navigator, *spec.* a qualified coastal navigator taken on board temporarily to steer a ship into or out of a port, through a channel, etc."[60] All three terms refer to individuals involved in the "marine operations, maintenance, or navigation of the vessel."[61] In other words, all three are persons in positions of authority responsible for the success of a vessel *qua* vessel, i.e., in its function as something used or capable of being used as a means of transportation on water. Defendants do not fall within this definition.

The government's alternative common attributes do not persuade. As to the first one, defining the common attribute as someone "in service of the vessel" is too broad. For instance, a nanny employed by the vessel operator would fall under this definition. Congress did not intend to bring such a person within the scope of the statute. As to the second proffered definition, defining [—22—] the common attribute as someone in a position of authority or with a substantial degree of responsibility for the safety of the vessel sweeps too broadly. This because it fails to take into account that the "captain," "engineer," and "pilot" are all required for the *transportation* function of the vessel. Suppose a vessel had an armed guard officer to protect against pirates and other assailants. Under the government's definition, such a person

would be within the statutory meaning. But based on the statutory text and purpose, we are not persuaded that the statute was drafted to include such a person. As to the third proffered definition, characterizing the common attribute as responsibility for the "operation, equipment, or navigation" of the vessel has some appeal. This phrase is derived from the corporate officer provision of § 1115, and it does have purchase in the text. But this formulation likewise fails to account for the transportation-related duties conspicuously common to "captain," "engineer," and "pilot."

The government argues that even if the common attribute is persons in positions of responsibility who are involved in the "marine operations, maintenance, or navigation of the vessel," Defendants still fall within that definition. First, the government argues that the term "marine" cannot exclusively mean navigational activities or transporting passengers over water. Such a definition would be too restrictive. A captain has non-navigational duties because he is responsible for the entire vessel; an engineer's duties extend beyond propelling the vessel because the engineer also is responsible for the entire physical plant on the vessel, including air conditioning and refrigeration systems. To wit, the government argues that certain drilling engineers could also be held responsible under the statute. This argument echoes another argument of the government in support of the plain text interpretation: that the statute on its face does not limit the liability of "captain," "engineer," and "pilot" to only their failure in "marine" duties. There [—23—] is a certain tension here. If Defendants were "captains," "engineers," and "pilots," they could be responsible under § 1115 for failure in their *non*-marine duties. Nevertheless, *ejusdem generis* mandates that the general phrase ought to be limited to persons who are at least sometimes involved in the "marine operations, maintenance, or navigation of the vessel." Indeed, to say that engineers solely responsible for drilling were meant to be within the ambit of the statute takes the argument too far.

Second, the government argues that drilling could also be characterized as a

---

[58] *Oxford English Dictionary.*

[59] *Id.*

[60] *Id.*

[61] All three also refer to persons in positions of authority, i.e., ship officers. The district court decided that the "persons in positions of authority" qualifier did not constitute an additional limiting common attribute. We need not decide whether the district court erred in this conclusion because, in any case, Defendants do not fall within the meaning of persons responsible for "marine operations, maintenance, or navigation of the vessel."

"marine" function. In its eyes, a certain activity is "marine" simply because it is performed on water. Thus, Defendants were responsible for "marine operations" at the least. It is true that drilling might be characterized as a "marine" activity. But as we explained above, here, the "marine" limitation has to do with the vessel functioning as a vessel, i.e., in the transportation of people and things. This limitation is mandated by *ejusdem generis*, and the district court did not err in understanding "marine" this way.

Our reading of § 1115 is also supported by the other textual provisions within the statute. "In reading a statute, we must not look merely to a particular clause, but consider in connection with it the whole statute."[62] Although these provisions were added later by different sessions of Congress, they must be read consistently with earlier parts of the statute.[63] The owner provision—the second category of persons liable under § 1115—provides liability for "every owner, charterer, inspector, or other public official," and it is consistent with the exclusion of Defendants from the first category. While the owner provision does not have a similar limitation to "marine operations, [—24—] maintenance, or navigation of the vessel," it also lacks a general phrase. Next, the corporate officer provision—the third category—provides liability for "any executive officer" of the corporate owner or charterer of a vessel "for the time being actually charged with the control and management of the operation, equipment, or navigation" of such vessel "who has knowingly and willfully caused or allowed such fraud, neglect, connivance, misconduct, or violation of law, by which the life of any person is destroyed." Again, there is no limitation in this provision to "marine operations, maintenance, or navigation of the vessel." But this is consistent with the text because the corporate officer provision has a stricter *mens rea*

requirement: knowingly and willfully causing or allowing.

We find some guidance in the current title of § 1115: "Misconduct or neglect of ship officers." "[T]he title of a statute and the heading of a section are tools available for the resolution of a doubt about the meaning of a statute."[64] First, the reference to "ship officers" suggests that our focus on the "marine" nature of the common attribute is not misplaced. Second, the title suggests that only persons in positions of authority are liable.[65] As we explain below, however, the title was added long after the enactment of the manslaughter provision, and thus can offer only limited help.

Therefore, the text and context of § 1115 supports the conclusion that Defendants do not fall within the meaning of the statute.[66] [—25—]

C

As the conclusion that Defendants are outside the scope of coverage is reached by the text of § 1115, we need not reach the legislative history. We note quickly, however, that even the legislative history supports our conclusion.

1

Section 1115 was originally enacted as part of an 1838 act, whose title clarified that the act was intended "[t]o provide for the better security of the lives of passengers on board of vessels propelled in whole or in part by steam."[67] At the time, travel by steamboat was commonplace, but so were steamboat

---

[62] *Dada v. Mukasey*, 554 U.S. 1, 16 (2008) (internal quotation marks omitted).

[63] *Ali*, 552 U.S. at 222 ("Nonetheless, the [later] amendment is relevant because our construction of [the term] must, to the extent possible, ensure that the statutory scheme is coherent and consistent.").

[64] *Almendarez-Torres v. United States*, 523 U.S. 224, 234 (1998) (internal quotation marks omitted).

[65] *See supra* note 60.

[66] We agree with the district court that the application of *noscitur a sociis* is unnecessary here. Under that canon, "a term is interpreted by considering the meaning of the terms associated with it." *In re Katrina Canal Breaches Litig.*, 495 F.3d 191, 218 (5th Cir. 2007). Here, since the general term follows specific terms, *ejusdem generis* is the proper canon of construction.

[67] Act of July 7, 1838, ch. 191, 5 Stat. 304.

collisions and boiler explosions resulting in the deaths of hundreds of passengers and crewmembers.[68] The 1838 Act aimed to rectify these safety problems[69] by, *inter alia*, imposing steamboat licensing and inspection requirements and placing various obligations or liabilities upon vessel owners, masters, inspectors, captains, pilots, engineers, and others.[70] Section 12 of the 1838 Act was the first predecessor to today's § 1115, providing that

> every captain, engineer, pilot, or other person employed on board of any steamboat or vessel propelled in whole or in part by steam, by whose [—26—] misconduct, negligence, or inattention to his or their respective duties, the life or lives of any person or persons on board said vessel may be destroyed, shall be deemed guilty of manslaughter . . . .[71]

Section 12 had a lower degree of culpability than that required by other manslaughter statutes.[72] In 1864, Congress amended the seaman's manslaughter statute by adding the predecessor of the owner provision, the second category of persons liable under § 1115.[73]

Unfortunately, horrible steamboat accidents continued to occur.[74] "In 1871, Congress significantly overhauled the regulatory regime governing steam-powered vessels, adding provisions for watchmen, safety equipment, vessel design standards, inspection and testing of equipment, and licensing of captains, chief mates, engineers, and pilots."[75] The 1838 Act was repealed,[76] and the seaman's manslaughter provision was reenacted as § 57 of the 1871 Act.[77] Section 57 made minor changes to the seaman's manslaughter statute: it made the first category applicable to those "employed on any steamboat or vessel"[78] and it made the owner provision, the second category, applicable to "any owner or inspector, or other public officer."[79] [—27—]

By 1905, the statute was Section 5344 of the Revised Statutes of the United States. It was broadened again in response to another steamboat accident.[80] The owner provision, the second category, was broadened to apply to "every owner, charterer, inspector, or other public officer" and the word "neglect" was added to the list of acts or omissions which would lead to liability.[81] Additionally, the

---

[68] *United States v. O'Keefe* (*O'Keefe I*), No. 03-137, 2004 WL 224574, at *1 (E.D. La. Feb. 3, 2004); *United States v. Holmes*, 104 F. 884, 885 (N.D. Ohio 1900) ("[T]he purpose of the lawmakers was to prevent the constant recurrence of the serious accidents then prevailing in the navigation of the waters of the United States by vessels using steam."); *United States v. Warner*, 28 F. Cas. 404, 408 (C.C.D. Ohio 1848) ("It is a matter of public notoriety, and constitutes a part of the history of the times, that within a short period anterior to the date of this statute, numerous steamboat disasters had occurred in our country, attended with a melancholy loss of human life, under circumstances justifying the conclusion that there was gross negligence, yet without the possibility of proving, either positively or inferentially, a malicious intent."); *In re Charge to Grand Jury*, 30 F. Cas. 990, 990 (E.D. La. 1846) (noting "[t]he frequent loss of human life in consequence of explosions of the boilers of steamboats, of collisions and the burning of steamboats").

[69] *United States v. Ryan*, 365 F. Supp. 2d 338, 344 (E.D.N.Y. 2005).

[70] Act of July 7, 1838, §§ 1-13, 5 Stat. at 304-06.

[71] *Id.* § 12, 5 Stat. at 306.

[72] William Pitard Wynne & Brian Michael Ballay, *Seaman's Manslaughter: A Potential Sea of Troubles for the Maritime Defendant and a Clever Mechanism for Taking Arms Against the Slings and Arrows of Maritime Plaintiffs*, 50 Loy. L. Rev. 869, 895-96 (2004).

[73] Act of July 4, 1864, ch. 249, § 6, 13 Stat. 390, 391 (making "the owner or owners" liable). When Congress initially enacted the owner provision, it did not include ordinary negligence but only "fraud, connivance, misconduct, or violation of law" as the required conduct, unlike the current version of the statute. *Compare id.*, *with* 18 U.S.C. § 1115.

[74] *Ryan*, 365 F. Supp. 2d at 345.

[75] Wynne & Ballay, *supra* note 72, at 889; *see also* Act of Feb. 28, 1871, ch. 100, 16 Stat. 440.

[76] *Id.* § 71, 16 Stat. at 459.

[77] *Id.* § 57, 16 Stat. at 456.

[78] Thus removing the requirement that the vessel be steam-propelled.

[79] *Id.* § 57, 16 Stat. at 456.

[80] *Ryan*, 365 F. Supp. 2d at 346; *see also* Act of Mar. 3, 1905, ch. 1454. § 5, 33 Stat. 1023, 1025-26.

[81] *Ryan*, 365 F. Supp. 2d at 346.

corporate officer provision, the third category, was added.[82]

Congress then recodified the statute several times, first placing it at § 282 of the new Criminal Code,[83] then, in 1948, at its current location at 18 U.S.C. § 1115.[84] A title was also introduced to the section: "Misconduct or Neglect of Ship Officers."[85] The current version of § 1115 is substantively identical to the 1905 version.[86]

2

This legislative history shows a remarkable continuity for the phrase "[e]very . . . other person employed on any . . . vessel." While the other provisions—such as the owner provision and the corporate officer provision—have been amended several times, this general phrase has remained more or less the same.

The government points to several features of the legislative and drafting history in support of its plain text interpretation. We do not find any convincing. First, the government argues that the 1838 Act and the 1871 Act [—28—] demonstrate that Congress knows how to choose its words carefully and deliberately. The 1838 Act included different provisions imposing liability on different classes of people. Section 1 was applicable to "owners"; § 2 to "owner, master, or captain"; § 7 to "the master of any boat or vessel, or the person or persons charged with navigating said boat or vessel" propelled by steam.[87] The 1871 Act similarly included different provision imposing liability on different classes of people, such as owners, masters, captains, chief mates, mates, chief engineers, engineers, pilots, watchmen, "persons in command," and "the officer in charge of the vessel for the time

being."[88] We agree that Congress can choose its words carefully and deliberately. Indeed, it is for that very reason that the catchall phrase cannot mean everyone employed on the ship. Congress could have easily used the word "everyone" or "all persons" or "all." But it did not do so, and we must give meaning to its words.

Second, the government argues that Congress surely did not mean to include a "navigation" limitation on the general phrase. To begin, it points to § 7 of the 1838 Act which places a duty on a "master" of a vessel powered by steam "or the person or persons charged with navigating said boat or vessel." This express limitation, the government contends, shows that the "navigating" limit was not mean to apply to the first category in § 1115.[89] Next, the government points to the drafting history of § 12 of the 1838 Act. When first introduced in the Senate in December 1837, the provision was limited to "every captain, engineer, pilot, *or other person employed in navigating* any steamboat [—29—] or vessel propelled in whole or in part by steam."[90] The bill was referred to a select committee and reported out with amendment; the provision remained the same except for the addition of a comma between "person" and "employed."[91] The bill was then debated in the Senate and amended in various respects.[92] When the bill was engrossed for a third reading, the "navigating" limitation had been eliminated.[93] The provision now reached "every captain, engineer, pilot, *or other person, employed on board of any steamboat or vessel*

---

[82] *Id.*

[83] Act of Mar. 4, 1909, ch. 321, § 282, 35 Stat. 1088, 1144.

[84] Act of June 25, 1948, ch. 645, § 1115, 62 Stat. 683, 757.

[85] *Id.*

[86] The statute is now in two paragraphs and the explicit reference to "manslaughter" has been deleted.

[87] Act of July 7, 1838, §§ 1-13, 5 Stat. at 304-06.

[88] Act of Feb. 28, 1871, §§ 1-71, 16 Stat. at 440-59.

[89] *See Russello v. United States*, 464 U.S. 16, 23 (1983) ("[W]here Congress includes particular language in one section of a statute but omits it in another section of the same Act, it is generally presumed that Congress acts intentionally and purposely in the disparate inclusion or exclusion." (quoting *United States v. Wong Kim Bo*, 472 F.2d 720, 722 (5th Cir. 1972)).

[90] S. 1, 25th Cong., 2d Sess. § 13 (introduced by Sen. Grundy on Dec. 6, 1837) (emphasis added).

[91] S. 1, 25th Cong., 2d Sess. (as reported out of the Senate select committee on Jan. 9, 1838).

[92] Cong. Globe, 25th Cong., 2d Sess. 123-25 (Jan. 22, 1838); *id.* at 128-29 (Jan. 23, 1838).

[93] *Id.* at 129 (Jan. 23, 1838).

propelled in whole or in part by steam."[94] This was the state of the provision when it was enacted into law as § 12 of the 1838 Act, except that the comma between "person" and "employed" was again removed.[95] The removal of the "navigating" language, the government contends, shows that Congress intended no such limitation.[96] Finally, the government also points to some of the Senate debates, though it concedes that none of the debates explained why the "navigating" language had been removed.[97] To our eyes, however, the common attribute required by *ejusdem generis* is not the equivalent of importing the "navigating" term back into the statute. The common attribute is much broader: those individuals involved in the "marine operations, [—30—] maintenance, or navigation of the vessel." Therefore, we are satisfied that our reading of the statute is proper.

Third, the government points to other statutes passed around the same time to argue for its plain text interpretation. The government argues that Congress could have used the word "seamen," but did not do so. The logic of the argument is that "seamen" had a broad meaning, and Congress chose to use an even broader phrase than "seamen." However, this argument fails because "seamen" has nothing to do with the phrase, and the phrase must be read within the context of the statute. The government also points to the committee report of a failed 1840 bill that was meant to amend the 1838 Act.[98]

We do not find much meaning in this amendment precisely because Congress did not enact it. Similarly, the government points to two other statutes arguing that they have similar phraseology and their broad scope compels a broad reading of § 1115.[99] We disagree because the government fails to point to any case law holding as such, simply pointing to the plain statutory text.

The legislative history, then, supports a narrow reading of the statute that excludes Defendants from coverage. [—31—]

D

We turn to some remaining arguments the government proposes in favor of its plain text reading. First, the government points to the statutory purpose. But as discussed above, the statutory purpose indicates that reading § 1115 in light of *ejusdem generis* is appropriate. The statute was enacted to address the dangers of travel by steamboat, and it is persons responsible for that travel that should be held liable under the statute. Defendants were not responsible for the travel of the *Deepwater Horizon*.

Second, the government points to the case law in support of its reading. The government contends that no court has limited the general phrase to apply only to persons employed on a vessel in a "marine operations, maintenance, or navigation" capacity. The government points to cases and their broad language of

---

[94] *Id.* (emphasis added).

[95] Act of July 7, 1838, § 12, 5 Stat. at 306.

[96] *Russello*, 464 U.S. at 23-24 ("Where Congress includes limiting language in an earlier version of a bill but deletes it prior to enactment, it may be presumed that the limitation was not intended.").

[97] *See* Cong. Globe, 25th Cong., 2d Sess. 125 (Jan. 22, 1838) (Senator Sevier expressing concern of the broad sweep of the manslaughter provision); *id.* at 124 (Jan. 22, 1838) (Senator Smith speaking of provision as applying to "captain, pilot, engineer, or other person employed in navigating the boat").

[98] S. 247, 26th Cong., 1st Sess. (reported by the Senate Committee on Commerce on Mar. 2, 1840); S. Rep. No. 241, 26th Cong., 1st Sess., at 13 (Mar. 2, 1840) ("Any person employed on board of steamboats by whose negligence or misconduct the life of any passenger shall be destroyed, [is] to be

considered guilty of manslaughter, and punished by imprisonment.").

[99] Act of Mar. 24, 1860, ch. 8, § 1, 12 Stat. 3, 3 ("[E]very master or other officer, seaman or other person employed on board of any ship or vessel of the United States, who shall, during the voyage of such ship or vessel, under promise of marriage, or by threats, or by the exercise of his authority, or by solicitation, or the making of gifts or presents, seduce and have illicit connexion with any female passenger, shall be guilty of a misdemeanor . . . ."); *id.* at § 2, 12 Stat. at 3-4 ("[N]either the officers, seamen, or other persons employed on board of any ship or vessel bringing emigrant passengers to the United States, or any of them, shall visit or frequent any part of such ship or vessel assigned to emigrant passengers . . . .").

liability as proof.[100] Defeating this argument is the fact that no case before has dealt with the question before us today, i.e., whether someone on the drill crew of a drilling rig is liable under § 1115. The government argues there have been prosecutions under § 1115 for non-"marine" *activities*.[101] But these prosecutions have been of persons with primarily "marine" functions: the "captain," "engineer," and "pilot." When defining the general term, *ejusdem* [—32—] *generis* strongly suggests that the common attribute is a person responsible for the "marine operations, maintenance, or navigation of the vessel." Moreover, the case law actually seems to support Defendants; prosecutions under the first category of § 1115 have been limited to "captains," "engineers," "pilots," and others with responsibilities relating to vessel transport functions.[102] Thus, our focus on the

"marine" identities of these actors is not misplaced.

Finally, the government argues that the district court erred in invoking the rule of lenity. "The rule of lenity requires ambiguous criminal laws to be interpreted in favor of the defendants subjected to them."[103] The rule "vindicates the fundamental principle that no citizen should be held accountable for a violation of a statute whose commands are uncertain, or subjected to punishment that is not clearly prescribed."[104] According to the government, there is no ambiguity here in two ways. First, there is no ambiguity in the plain text. Second, even if there were ambiguity in the plain text, there is no ambiguity left after the application of *ejusdem generis*. [—33—] Therefore, the district court erred in applying the rule of lenity. The government misapprehends the district court's order. The district court clearly understood that the rule of lenity is only applied as a last resort. It only held that should there be any remaining ambiguity even after the application of *ejusdem generis*, the rule of lenity dictated that it be resolved in Defendants' favor.

---

[100] *See United States v. LaBrecque*, 419 F. Supp. 430, 435-36 (D.N.J. 1976) ("Section 1115 was, as noted, designed to punish persons employed on commercial vessels carrying persons for hire."); *see also United States v. Holtzhauer*, 40 F. 76, 78 (C.C.D.N.J. 1889); *United States v. Keller*, 19 F. 633, 637 (C.C.D.W. Va. 1884); *United States v. Collyer*, 25 F. Cas. 554, 576 (C.C.S.D.N.Y. 1855); *United States v. Taylor*, 28 F. Cas. 25, 26 (C.C.D. Ohio 1851); *Warner*, 28 F. Cas. at 407.

[101] *See Van Shaick v. United States*, 159 F. 847, 851 (2d Cir. 1908) (prosecution for failure to "maintain an efficient fire drill, to see that the proper apparatus for extinguishing fire was provided and maintained in efficient order and ready for immediate use and to exercise at least ordinary care in seeing that the life-preservers were in a fit condition for use"); *United States v. Beacham*, 29 F. 284, 284-85 (C.C.D. Md. 1886) (prosecution for absence of a rail on a saloon deck, which led to a passenger slipping overboard and drowning).

The government also points to cases involving prosecution under the owner provision which we do not find compelling. *See United States v. Fei*, 225 F.3d 167, 169-71 (2d Cir. 2000); *United States v. Allied Towing Corp.*, 602 F.2d 612, 613 (4th Cir. 1979).

[102] *See generally United States v. Oba*, 317 F. App'x. 698 (9th Cir. 2009) (captain); *O'Keefe II*, 426 F.3d 274 (captain); *United States v. Thurston*, 362 F.3d 1319 (11th Cir. 2004) (chief officer); *United States v. Hilger*, 867 F.2d 566 (9th Cir. 1989) (captain); *Hoopengarner v. United States*, 270 F.2d 465 (6th Cir. 1959) (speedboat owner and operator); *United States v. Abbott*, 89 F.2d 166 (2d Cir. 1937)

(master and chief engineer); *Van Schaick v. United States*, 159 F. 847 (2d. Cir. 1908) (captain); *Holtzhauer*, 40 F. 76 (captain and pilot); *Beacham*, 29 F. 284 (captain); *Keller*, 19 F. 633 (pilot); *In re Doig*, 4 F. 193 (C.C.D. Cal. 1880) (pilot); *Collyer*, 25 F. Cas. 554 (captain, pilot, engineer, captain's clerk, and owner); *United States v. Farnham*, 25 F. Cas. 1042 (C.C.S.D.N.Y. 1853) (captain); *Taylor*, 28 F. Cas. 25 (engineer); *Warner*, 28 F. Cas. 404 (captain, first mate, second mate, and wheelsman); *United States v. Schröder*, No. 06-0088, 2006 WL 1663663 (S.D. Ala. 2006) (captain); *United States v. Mitlof*, 165 F. Supp. 2d 558 (S.D.N.Y. 2001) (captain); *LaBrecque*, 419 F. Supp. 430 (captain of non-commercial vessel); *United States v. Vogt*, 230 F. Supp. 607 (E.D. La. 1964) (pilot); *United States v. Meckling*, 141 F. Supp. 608 (D. Md. 1956) (captain); *United States v. Harvey*, 54 F. Supp. 910 (D. Or. 1943) (pilot); *United States v. Knowles*, 26 F. Cas. 800 (N.D. Cal. 1864) (captain). Arguably, the prosecution of the captain's clerk in *Collyer* seems to buck this trend. But we do not put much stock in this one case as the clerk is also described as an "inferior officer." 25 F. Cas. at 564.

[103] *United States v. Santos*, 553 U.S. 507, 514 (2008) (plurality opinion).

[104] *Id.*

Counterarguments in favor of interpreting § 1115 to cover Defendants have purchase. Yet we are left with textual indeterminacy, as well as the incongruity of applying a statute originally developed to prevent steamboat explosions and collisions on inland waters to offshore oil and gas operations—all approaching a bridge too far. The primary thrust of legislative effect can bring light to the shadows of uncertainty.[105] At some point, and we think it here, the doctrine of lenity takes hold and dismissing this part of the indictment was not error.

VI

The judgment of the district court is AFFIRMED.

---

[105] *See generally Yates v. United States*, No. 13-7451, 3 Adm. R. 2 (U.S. Feb. 25, 2015).

United States Court of Appeals
for the Fifth Circuit

No. 14-30132

ASIGNACION
VS.
RICKMERS GENOA SCHIFFAHRTSGESELLSCHAFT
MBH & CIE KG

Appeal from the United States District Court for the
Eastern District of Louisiana

Decided: April 16, 2015

Citation: 783 F.3d 1010, 3 Adm. R. 304 (5th Cir. 2015).

Before STEWART, Chief Judge, and BENAVIDES, and
OWEN, Circuit Judges.

[—1—] OWEN, Circuit Judge: [—2—]

Rickmers Genoa Schiffahrtsgesellschaft mbH & Cie KG (Rickmers) sought to enforce a Philippine arbitral award given to Lito Martinez Asignacion for maritime injuries. The district court refused to enforce the award pursuant to the public-policy defense found in the Convention on the Recognition and Enforcement of Foreign Arbitral Awards (the Convention)[1] and the prospective-waiver doctrine. Rickmers appeals. We reverse and remand for the district court to enforce the award.

I

Asignacion, a citizen and resident of the Philippines, signed a contract to work aboard the vessel M/V RICKMERS DAILAN. Rickmers, a German corporation, owned the vessel, which sailed under the flag of the Marshall Islands.

Philippine law mandates that foreign employers hire Filipino workers through the Philippine Overseas Employment Administration (POEA), an arm of the Philippine government. POEA requires Filipino seamen's contracts to include the Standard Terms and Conditions Governing the Employment of Filipino Seafarers On Board Ocean Going Vessels (Standard Terms). Asignacion's contract incorporated the Standard Terms.

The Standard Terms include several provisions related to dispute resolution. Section 29, in part, provides:

In cases of claims and disputes arising from this employment, the parties covered by a collective bargaining agreement shall submit the claim or dispute to the original and exclusive jurisdiction of the voluntary arbitrator or panel of arbitrators. If the parties are not covered by a collective bargaining agreement, the parties may at their option submit the claim or dispute to either the original and exclusive jurisdiction of the National Labor Relations Commission (NLRC), pursuant to Republic Act of 1995 or to the original and [—3—] exclusive jurisdiction of the voluntary arbitrator or panel of arbitrators.

Section 31 provides:

Any unresolved dispute, claim or grievance arising out of or in connection with this Contract, including the annexes thereof, shall be governed by the laws of the Republic of the Philippines, international conventions, treaties and covenants where the Philippines is a signatory.

Section 20(B) provides that when a seaman suffers work-related injuries, the employer must provide the full cost of medical treatment until the seaman is declared fit to work or his level of disability is declared after repatriation to the Philippines. If the seaman is permanently disabled, he is entitled to scheduled disability benefits. Section 20(G) provides that the contract covers "all claims arising from or in the course of the seafarer's employment, including but not limited to damages arising from the contract, tort, fault or negligence under the laws of the Philippines or any other country."

---

[1] Convention on the Recognition and Enforcement of Foreign Arbitral Awards, June 10, 1958, 21 U.S.T. 2517, 330 U.N.T.S. 3.

While the M/V RICKMERS DAILAN was docked in the Port of New Orleans, Asignacion suffered burns when a cascade tank aboard the vessel overflowed. After receiving treatment at a burn unit in Baton Rouge for nearly a month, Asignacion was repatriated to the Philippines, where he continued to receive medical attention. The court below found that Asignacion sustained severe burns to 35% of his body, suffered problems with his body-heat control mechanism, and experienced skin ulcerations and sexual dysfunction. The record and the district court's opinion do not address Asignacion's current condition.

Asignacion sued Rickmers in Louisiana state court to recover for his injuries. Rickmers filed an exception seeking to enforce the arbitration clause of Asignacion's contract. The state court granted the exception, stayed litigation, and ordered arbitration in the Philippines. [—4—]

Arbitration commenced before a Philippine panel, which convened under the auspices of the Philippine Department of Labor and Employment. The panel refused to apply, or even consider applying, United States or Marshall Islands law, finding that Section 31 of the Standard Terms prevented the panel from applying any law besides Philippine law. The arbitrators accepted Rickmers's physician's finding that Asignacion had a Grade 14 disability—the lowest grade of compensable disability under the Standard Terms—which entitled Asignacion to a lump sum of $1,870.

Asignacion then filed a motion in the Louisiana state court asking that Rickmers show cause as to why the Philippine arbitral award should not be set aside for violating United States public policy. Rickmers removed the suit to federal court and brought a second action in the district court seeking to enforce the award.

The district court determined that the Convention provided the legal framework for analyzing the award and that the only defense Asignacion invoked was Article V(2)(b) of the Convention. Article V(2)(b) allows a signatory country to refuse enforcement if "recognition or enforcement of the award would be contrary to the public policy of that country."[2]

The district court proceeded to apply the traditional choice-of-law analysis for maritime injury cases, the *Lauritzen*[3]*–Rhoditis*[4] test, and concluded that the law of the vessel's flag—the Marshall Islands—should apply absent a valid choice-of-law clause. The court also found that the Marshall Islands adopts the general maritime law of the United States. The court then held that enforcing the arbitral award would violate the United States public [—5—] policy protecting seamen. The public-policy violation arose not from the arbitrator's failure to apply United States law but rather because applying Philippine law effectively denied Asignacion the "opportunity to pursue the remedies to which he was entitled as a seaman," i.e., maintenance and cure, negligence, and unseaworthiness. The court additionally held that the prospective-waiver doctrine, which invalidates certain combined choice-of-law and choice-of-forum provisions, applied to Asignacion's contract. Thus, the court entered an order refusing to enforce the Philippine arbitral award. Rickmers now appeals.

II

We review the district court's decision refusing to enforce the Philippine arbitral award under the same standard as any other district court decision.[5] We accept findings of fact that are not clearly erroneous and review questions of law *de novo*.[6]

III

The Convention applies when an arbitral award has been made in one signatory state and recognition or enforcement is sought in

---

[2] Convention art. V(2)(b).

[3] *Lauritzen v. Larsen*, 345 U.S. 571 (1953).

[4] *Hellenic Lines Ltd. v. Rhoditis*, 398 U.S. 306 (1970).

[5] *See Karaha Bodas Co. v. Perusahaan Pertambangan Minyak Dan Gas Bumi Negara*, 364 F.3d 274, 287 (5th Cir. 2004) (reviewing a district court judgment enforcing a foreign arbitral award).

[6] *Hughes Training Inc. v. Cook*, 254 F.3d 588, 592 (5th Cir. 2001).

another signatory state.[7] Both forums in this case, the United States and the Philippines, are signatories to the Convention.[8] An award's enforcement is governed by the Convention, as implemented at 9 U.S.C. § 201 *et seq.*, if the award arises out [—6—] of a commercial dispute and at least one party is not a United States citizen.[9] The award issued as a result of arbitration between Asignacion, a Filipino seaman, and Rickmers, a German corporation, is governed by the Convention.

A party to an award governed by the Convention may bring an action to enforce the award in a United States court that has jurisdiction.[10] The court "shall confirm" the award unless a ground to refuse enforcement or recognition specified in the Convention applies.[11] The Convention permits a signatory to refuse to recognize or enforce an award if "recognition or enforcement of the award would be contrary to the public policy of that country."[12]

Arbitral awards falling under the Convention are enforced under the Federal Arbitration Act (FAA).[13] An "emphatic federal policy" favors arbitral dispute resolution.[14] The Supreme Court has noted that this policy "applies with special force in the field of international commerce."[15] The FAA permits courts to "vacate an arbitrator's decision 'only

in very unusual circumstances.'"[16] A district court's review of an award is "extraordinarily narrow."[17] Similarly, a court reviewing an award under the Convention cannot [—7—] refuse to enforce the award solely on the ground that the arbitrator may have made a mistake of law or fact.[18] The party opposing enforcement of the award on one of the grounds specified in the Convention has the burden of proof.[19]

We have held that the Convention's "public policy defense is to be 'construed narrowly to be applied only where enforcement would violate the forum state's most basic notions of morality and justice.'"[20] In the context of domestic arbitral awards, the Supreme Court has recognized a public-policy defense only when an arbitrator's contract interpretation violates "'some explicit public policy' that is 'well defined and dominant, and is to be ascertained by reference to the laws and legal precedents and not from general considerations of supposed public interests.'"[21] The Eleventh Circuit has held that the "explicit public policy" requirement applies with the same force to international awards falling under the Convention.[22] We see no reason to depart from that standard here.[23]

---

[7] Convention, 21 U.S.T. at 2566 ("The United States of America will apply the Convention, on the basis of reciprocity, to the recognition and enforcement of only those awards made in the territory of another Contracting State."); *see also id.* art. I(3).

[8] *See, e.g., Lim v. Offshore Specialty Fabricators, Inc.,* 404 F.3d 898, 900-01 (5th Cir. 2005).

[9] *See* 9 U.S.C. § 202 (providing that commercial arbitral awards fall under the Convention except for certain awards entirely between United States citizens).

[10] 9 U.S.C. § 207.

[11] *Id.*

[12] Convention art. V(2)(b).

[13] *See Mitsubishi Motors Corp. v. Soler Chrysler–Plymouth, Inc.,* 473 U.S. 614, 631 (1985); *see also* 9 U.S.C. § 201 ("The [Convention] shall be enforced in United States courts in accordance with this chapter.").

[14] *Mitsubishi,* 473 U.S. at 631 (1985).

[15] *Id.*

[16] *Oxford Health Plans LLC v. Sutter,* 133 S. Ct. 2064, 2068 (2013) (quoting *First Options of Chi., Inc. v. Kaplan,* 514 U.S. 938, 942 (1995)).

[17] *Kergosien v. Ocean Energy, Inc.,* 390 F.3d 346, 352 (5th Cir. 2004), *abrogated on other grounds by Hall St. Assocs., L.L.C. v. Mattel, Inc.,* 552 U.S. 576 (2008).

[18] *Karaha Bodas Co. v. Perusahaan Pertambangan Minyak Dan Gas Bumi Negara,* 364 F.3d 274, 288 (5th Cir. 2004).

[19] *Id.* (citing *Imperial Ethiopian Gov't v. Baruch-Foster Corp.,* 535 F.2d 334, 336 (5th Cir. 1976)).

[20] *Id.* at 306 (quoting *M & C Corp. v. Erwin Behr GmbH & Co., KG,* 87 F.3d 844, 851 n.2 (6th Cir. 1996)).

[21] *United Paperworkers Int'l Union, AFL-CIO v. Misco, Inc.,* 484 U.S. 29, 43 (1987) (quoting *W.R. Grace & Co v. Local Union 759, Int'l Union of United Rubber, Cork, Linoleum and Plastic Workers of Am.,* 461 U.S. 757, 766 (1983)) (some internal quotation marks omitted).

[22] *Indus. Risk Insurers v. M.A.N. Gutehoffnungshütte GmbH,* 141 F.3d 1434, 1445 (11th Cir. 1998).

[23] *Cf. Mitsubishi Motors Corp. v. Soler Chrysler–Plymouth, Inc.,* 473 U.S. 614, 631 (1985) (noting

The parties do not dispute these standards. Rather, they disagree whether Asignacion's case provides the narrow circumstances that would [—8—] render the arbitral award unenforceable under the Convention because it violates United States public policy.

A

Asignacion's public-policy defense primarily turns on the adequacy of remedies under Philippine law. But at oral argument, Asignacion's counsel also urged that United States public policy requires that foreign arbitral panels give seamen an adequate choice-of-law determination; he argued that the arbitrators' exclusive reliance on the choice-of-law provision in Asignacion's contract did not constitute a choice-of-law determination, let alone a fair one.

To the extent that Asignacion's defense turns on the Philippine arbitrators' exclusive reliance on the contract's choice-of-law provision, courts are unable to correct this sort of unexceptional legal error (if one was in fact made) when reviewing an arbitral award.[24] Applying Philippine law to a Filipino seaman in Philippine arbitration, by itself, is not cause for setting aside the award, even if American choice-of-law principles would lead to the application of another nation's law.

B

Asignacion has the burden of proving that the Convention's public-policy defense applies.[25] The Philippine arbitrators awarded Asignacion $1,870. Were he to prevail in a suit under United States general maritime law, we

have little doubt his recovery would be greater.

As detailed above, the United States has a public policy strongly favoring arbitration, which "applies with special force in the field of international [—9—] commerce."[26] On the other hand, the United States has an "explicit public policy that is well defined and dominant"[27] with respect to seamen: maritime law provides "special solicitude to seamen."[28] Seamen have long been treated as "wards of admiralty,"[29] and the causes of action and the remedies available to seamen reflect this special status.[30] In addition to the foundational policies favoring arbitration and protecting seamen, other policies concerning international dispute resolution weigh in our decision.

The Supreme Court has rejected the "concept that all disputes must be resolved under our laws and in our courts,"[31] even when remedies under foreign law do not comport with American standards of justice. The Supreme Court has stated: "To determine that American standards of fairness . . . must [apply] demeans the standards of justice elsewhere in the world, and unnecessarily exalts the primacy of United States law over the laws of other countries."[32] Similarly, in

---

that the federal policy in favor of arbitral dispute resolution "applies with special force in the field of international commerce").

[24] *See Karaha Bodas*, 364 F.3d at 288 ("The court may not refuse to enforce an arbitral award solely on the ground that the arbitrator may have made a mistake of law or fact."); *id.* at 290 & n.27 ("Under the New York Convention, the rulings of the [arbitrators] interpreting the parties' contract are entitled to deference.").

[25] *See id.* at 288 (citing *Imperial Ethiopian Gov't v. Baruch-Foster Corp.*, 535 F.2d 334, 336 (5th Cir. 1976)).

[26] *Mitsubishi*, 473 U.S. at 631 (1985).

[27] *United Paperworkers Int'l Union, AFL-CIO v. Misco, Inc.*, 484 U.S. 29, 43 (1987) (internal quotation marks omitted).

[28] *Miles v. Melrose*, 882 F.2d 976, 987 (5th Cir. 1989).

[29] *U.S. Bulk Carriers, Inc. v. Arguelles*, 400 U.S. 351, 355 (1971).

[30] *See Mitchell v. Trawler Racer, Inc.*, 362 U.S. 539, 550 (1960) (noting that unseaworthiness liability is not tied to negligence); *Boudreaux v. Transocean Deepwater, Inc.*, 721 F.3d 723, 725-26, 1 Adm. R. 275, 276 (5th Cir. 2013) (noting that the right to maintenance and cure cannot be "contracted away by the seaman, does not depend on the fault of the employer, and is not reduced for the seaman's contributory negligence" (footnotes omitted)).

[31] *M/S Bremen v. Zapata Off-Shore Co.*, 407 U.S. 1, 9 (1972).

[32] *Scherk v. Alberto-Culver Co.*, 417 U.S. 506, 517 n.11 (1974) (citation and internal quotation marks omitted); *see also Haynsworth v. The Corporation*, 121 F.3d 956, 966 (5th Cir. 1997).

Romero v. International Terminal Operating Co., which addressed the application of choice-of-law principles to a seaman's claim, the Court stated:

> To impose on ships the duty of shifting from one standard of compensation to another as the vessel passes the boundaries of [—10—] territorial waters would be not only an onerous but also an unduly speculative burden, disruptive of international commerce and without basis in the expressed policies of this country. The *amount and type of recovery which a foreign seaman may receive* from his foreign employer while sailing on a foreign ship should not depend on the wholly fortuitous circumstance of the place of injury.[33]

Therefore, even with regard to foreign seamen, United States public policy does not necessarily disfavor lesser or different remedies under foreign law.

The importance of the POEA Standard Terms to the Philippine economy also weighs in favor of enforcement. As the Ninth Circuit has noted, "[a]rbitration of all claims by Filipino overseas seafarers is an integral part of the POEA's mandate to promote and monitor the overseas employment of Filipinos and safeguard their interests."[34] Asignacion points out, correctly, that the Convention directs a court to consider the public policy of the country in which it sits,[35] not the public policy of the arbitral forum. But, while Philippine public policy does not apply of its own force, our analysis of a foreign arbitral award is colored by "concerns of international comity, respect for the capacities of foreign

and transnational tribunals, and sensitivity to the need of the international commercial system for predictability in the resolution of disputes . . . even assuming that a contrary result would be forthcoming in a domestic context."[36] [—11—]

Asignacion maintains that in particularly egregious circumstances, a United States court may apply our choice-of-law and forum-selection laws as a means of implementing the Convention's public-policy defense and refusing to enforce an award.

The seminal maritime-injuries choice-of-law case is *Lauritzen v. Larsen*.[37] In *Lauritzen*, a Danish seaman injured in Cuba aboard a Danish-owned and flagged ship brought suit in the United States.[38] The seaman's contract provided that Danish law applied.[39] Unlike United States law, Danish law fixed maintenance and cure to a twelve-week period and provided a no-fault compensation scheme "similar to [American] workmen's compensation."[40] The Court enumerated a seven-factor test to determine choice of law[41] but also commented that "[e]xcept as forbidden by some public policy, the tendency of the law is to apply in contract matters the law which the parties intended to apply."[42] The Court then cautioned that "a different result would follow if the contract attempted to avoid applicable law," such as applying foreign law to a United States flagged ship.[43] The Court thus had little hesitation applying the contracted-for Danish law, as the law of the ship's flag.[44] [—12—]

---

[33] 358 U.S. 354, 384 (1989) (emphasis added).

[34] *Balen v. Holland America Line, Inc.*, 583 F.3d 647, 651 (9th Cir. 2009); *see also Marinechance Shipping, Ltd. v. Sebastian*, 143 F.3d 216, 221 n.25 (5th Cir. 1998) ("The effect of POEA intervention in employment contracts is to shift the balance of power slightly in favor of the employee in much the same way that a labor union or legislative enactment of minimum work standards increases the level of protection for employees in the United States.").

[35] Convention art. V(2)(b).

[36] *Mitsubishi Motors Corp. v. Soler Chrysler-Plymouth, Inc.*, 473 U.S. 614, 629 (1985).

[37] 345 U.S. 571 (1953).

[38] *Id.* at 573.

[39] *Id.*

[40] *Id.* at 575-76.

[41] *See id.* at 583-92 ((1) place of injury; (2) the vessel's flag; (3) plaintiff's domicile or allegiance; (4) shipowner's allegiance; (5) place of contract; (6) inaccessibility of a foreign forum; and (7) law of the forum); *see also Hellenic Lines Ltd. v. Rhoditis*, 398 U.S. 306, 309 (1970) (noting the *Lauritzen* factors are not exhaustive and considered the shipowner's base of operations).

[42] *Lauritzen*, 345 U.S. at 588-89.

[43] *Id.* at 589.

[44] *Id.* at 588-89.

Lauritzen's rule—that contractual choice-of-law provisions for foreign seamen are generally enforceable—favors Rickmers. However, the reach of the exception—which condemns a choice-of-law provision that attempts to "avoid applicable law"—is less clear. On one hand, Rickmers did little, if anything, to avoid applicable law through its contract with Asignacion. Rickmers had no say in the choice-of-law provision; POEA's Standard Terms mandated Philippine law. On the other hand, the Philippine government has arguably attempted to avoid the application of foreign law to its seamen. But it is far from certain that the *Lauritzen* Court condemned such choice-of-law clauses mandated by a foreign sovereign rather than a party to the contract.

Several cases from our court have ordered that a Filipino seamen's claims be resolved in Philippine arbitration or under Philippine law. Rickmers argues that these cases establish that applying Philippine law to Asignacion's claims does not violate public policy. Many of these cases simply weigh the *Lauritzen–Rhoditis* factors without addressing any public-policy concerns.[45] The decisions that reach public-policy considerations address policies irrelevant to the remedies at issue in the present case.[46]

---

[45] *See Quintero v. Klaveness Ship Lines*, 914 F.2d 717, 722-23 (5th Cir. 1990); *Cuevas v. Reading & Bates Corp.*, 770 F.2d 1371, 1378-79 (5th Cir. 1985), *abrogated on other grounds by In re Air Crash Disaster Near New Orleans, La.*, 821 F.2d 1147 (5th Cir. 1987) (en banc).

[46] *See Lim v. Offshore Specialty Fabricators, Inc.*, 404 F.3d 898, 900, 906 (5th Cir. 2005) (rejecting a public-policy challenge to Philippine arbitration based on Louisiana's policy disfavoring forum-selection clauses in employment litigation); *Marinechance Shipping Ltd. v. Sebastian*, 143 F.3d 216, 219-21 (5th Cir. 1998) (citing *Carnival Cruise Lines, Inc. v. Shute*, 499 U.S. 585 (1991)) (rejecting a challenge to contracts containing the POEA Standard Terms because individual Filipino seamen lacked bargaining power); *cf. Francisco v. STOLT ACHIEVEMENT MT*, 293 F.3d 270, 277-78 (5th Cir. 2002) (upholding an order to arbitrate in the Philippines and finding that the *suspension* of a Philippine law that would have otherwise limited remedies did not compel against arbitration).

Our decision in *Calix-Chacon v. Global International Marine, Inc.*[47] addressed the question of reduced remedies in foreign law. In *Calix-Chacon*, a [—13—] Honduran seaman signed a contract providing that Honduran law would apply and specifying a Honduran forum.[48] He brought a claim in an American court for maintenance and cure, and the district court held the forum-selection clause unenforceable on public-policy grounds because both general maritime law and the Shipowner's Liability Convention of 1936 (Shipowner's Convention) "express[ed] a strong public policy" against abridging maintenance and cure liability in contract.[49] On appeal, we concluded that under our precedents, the Shipowner's Convention did not require us to invalidate a foreign forum-selection clause when foreign law imposed a lower standard of care.[50] We vacated the district court's decision because it relied on the Shipowner's Convention and remanded for further analysis of the public-policy question under the general maritime law.[51]

In *Calix-Chacon*, we expressly refrained from addressing the general maritime law's weight in the public-policy analysis. Nonetheless, our conclusion that the Shipowner's Convention did not, as a matter of policy, prevail over a reduced standard of care in Honduran law, suggests we should be reluctant to conclude that lesser remedies make an award unenforceable on policy grounds.

In *Aggarao v. MOL Ship Management Co.*,[52] the District of Maryland, relying on the district court's decision in the present case, refused to enforce a Filipino seaman's arbitral award. The Philippine arbitrators determined that Aggarao had a Grade 1 disability—the highest grade under the POEA contract—and awarded him $89,100 in disability benefits,

---

[47] 493 F.3d 507 (5th Cir. 2007).

[48] *Id.* at 509.

[49] *Id.* at 510.

[50] *Id.* at 514 (citing *In re McClelland Eng'rs, Inc.* 742 F.2d 837, 839 (5th Cir. 1984)).

[51] *Id.*

[52] Civ. No. CCB–09–3106, 2014 WL 3894079 (D. Md. Aug. 7, 2014).

sick pay, and [—14—] attorney's fees.[53] The district court found that Aggarao had over $700,000 in unpaid medical debts, had to forgo necessary treatments, and would require lifetime care.[54] The Maryland district court found that Aggarao's limited remedies under the POEA contract violated public policy and refused to enforce the arbitral award.[55]

Asignacion contends that *Aggarao* is on all fours with his claims. We disagree. Unlike in *Aggarao*, the arbitrators found that Asignacion had a Grade 14 disability—the lowest compensable grade—and the district court made no findings related to the adequacy of the award vis-à-vis Asignacion's lasting injuries or unmet medical expenses. Rather, the district court only determined that the arbitration and award "effective[ly] deni[ed]" Asignacion the right to pursue his general maritime remedies. But that finding is insufficient to support the conclusion that the public policy of the United States requires refusing to enforce the award.

Asignacion's arbitral award does not represent the sum total of Rickmers's obligation to Asignacion under the POEA Standard Terms contract. Section 20(B) required Rickmers to pay Asignacion's medical costs until he was repatriated to the Philippines and his disability level was established. There is no dispute that Rickmers met its obligations under Section 20(B). At oral argument, Asignacion's counsel represents that he has incurred medical expenses after Rickmers's Section 20(B) obligation terminated. But our careful review of the record has found no evidence that the Philippine arbitral award was inadequate relative to Asignacion's unmet medical needs, let alone so inadequate as to violate this nation's "most basic notions of morality and [—15—] justice."[56] We conclude that the district court erred in determining that

Asignacion's award violated the public policy of the United States.

C

Finally, Rickmers contends that the district court erred by also relying on the prospective-waiver doctrine to refuse to recognize the Philippine arbitral award. We agree.

In *Mitsubishi Motors Corp. v. Soler Chrysler-Plymouth, Inc.*, the Supreme Court addressed a district court's enforcement of an agreement to arbitrate, which forced an auto dealer to arbitrate its antitrust claims under the Sherman Act, 15 U.S.C. § 1 *et seq.*, in Japan.[57] The Court commented, in dictum, that "in the event the choice-of-forum and choice-of-law clauses operated in tandem as a prospective waiver of a party's right to pursue statutory remedies for antitrust violations, we would have little hesitation in condemning the agreement as against public policy."[58] Similarly, in *Vimar Seguros y Reaseguros, S.A. v. M/V Sky Reefer*, the Court, again in dictum, suggested that *Mitsubishi*'s prospective-waiver doctrine might apply to contracts under the Carriage of Goods by Sea Act, 46 U.S.C. app. § 1300 *et seq.*[59] In both cases, the Court declined to apply the doctrine, in part, because it would be premature to do so; each case addressed the enforceability of an agreement to arbitrate, as opposed to awards in which the arbitrators actually failed to address causes of action under American statutes.[60] [—16—]

The present case is at the award-enforcement stage, unlike *Mitsubishi* and *Vimar*, and the district court applied the prospective-waiver doctrine. The district court noted that the antitrust laws in *Mitsubishi* and COGSA in *Vimar* applied to "business disputes between sophisticated parties." Because seamen are afforded special protections under United States law, unlike sophisticated parties, the district court concluded that the prospective-waiver

---

[53] *Id.* at *6-7.

[54] *Id.* at *5.

[55] *Id.* at *14.

[56] *Karaha Bodas Co. v. Perusahaan Pertambangan Minyak Dan Gas Bumi Negara*, 364 F.3d 274, 288 (5th Cir. 2004) (quoting *M & C Corp. v. Erwin Behr GmbH & Co., KG*, 87 F.3d 844, 851 n.2 (6th Cir. 1996)).

[57] 473 U.S. 614, 619-21 (1985).

[58] *Id.* at 637 n.19.

[59] 515 U.S. 528, 540-41 (1995).

[60] *See Mitsubishi*, 473 U.S. at 637 n.19; *Vimar*, 515 U.S. at 540.

doctrine prevented the enforcement of the Philippine arbitral award.

However, the prospective-waiver doctrine is limited to statutory rights and remedies. From *Mitsubishi* onwards, the Supreme Court has referred only to "statutory" rights and remedies when discussing the doctrine.[61] The Court recently continued that phrasing in *American Express Co. v. Italian Colors Restaurant*, where the Court refused to apply the doctrine to a waiver of class arbitration.[62] The Supreme Court has not extended the prospective-waiver doctrine beyond statutory rights and remedies. The district court therefore erred when it relied on the doctrine to afford Asignacion an opportunity to pursue his claims under the general maritime law. Additionally, to apply that doctrine in every case in which a seaman agreed to a choice-of-law provision that would result in lesser remedies than those available under laws of the United States would be at odds with the rationale of the Supreme Court's [—17—] reasoning in *Romero v. International Terminal Operating Co.*,[63] discussed above.

* * *

For the foregoing reasons, we REVERSE the order of the district court and REMAND for the district court to enforce the arbitral award.

---

[61] *See Mitsubishi*, 473 U.S. at 637 ("so long as the prospective litigant effectively may vindicate its statutory cause of action in the arbitral forum"); *id.* at 637 n.19 ("take cognizance of the statutory cause of action"); *id.* ("right to pursue statutory remedies"); *see also Vimar*, 515 U.S. at 540 ("right to pursue statutory remedies" (quoting *Mitsubishi*, 473 U.S. at 637 n.19)).

[62] *See* 133 S. Ct. at 2310 (2013) ("agreement forbidding the assertion of certain statutory rights"); *id.* at 2311 ("it is not worth the expense involved in *proving* a statutory remedy"); *id.* ("[i]t no more eliminates those parties' right to pursue their statutory remedy"); *see also id.* at 2319 (KAGAN, J., dissenting) (arguing that the doctrine should apply but noting that the doctrine "asks about the world today, not the world as it might have looked when Congress passed a given statute").

[63] 358 U.S. 354, 384 (1989).

United States Court of Appeals
for the Fifth Circuit

No. 13-31070

IN RE DEEPWATER HORIZON

STATE OF VERACRUZ
vs.
BP, P.L.C.

Appeal from the United States District Court for the
Eastern District of Louisiana

Decided: May 1, 2015

Citation: 784 F.3d 1019, 3 Adm. R. 312 (5th Cir. 2015).

Before **STEWART**, Chief Judge, and **JONES** and **HIGGINSON**, Circuit Judges.

[—2—] **STEWART**, Chief Judge: [—3—]

In April 2010, a blowout, explosion, and fire occurred aboard the mobile offshore drilling unit Deepwater Horizon as it was preparing to temporarily abandon a well 50 miles off the Louisiana coast. Millions of gallons of oil discharged into the Gulf of Mexico before the well was capped nearly three months later.

In September 2010, three Mexican states (Veracruz, Tamaulipas, and Quintana Roo (hereinafter, the "Mexican States" or "Plaintiffs")) filed substantially similar complaints in the Western District of Texas for damages incurred as a result of the oil spill. After the cases were consolidated in the Eastern District of Louisiana as part of the Deepwater Horizon multidistrict litigation, the district court in September 2013 granted summary judgment to the defendants—BP, Transocean, Halliburton, and Cameron[1]—because the Mexican states did not hold a sufficient "proprietary interest" in the allegedly damaged property. The Mexican States have appealed this judgment.

---

[1] The Mexican States sued many corporate entities, but for the sake of simplicity, and because the corporate niceties are not relevant to the dispute, we will refer to the companies by the names listed in the text above.

I. Factual and Procedural Background

The Mexican States each filed suit against BP (well owner, operator, and block lessee), Transocean (owner of the Deepwater Horizon), Halliburton (cement contractor), Anadarko (co-owner and co-lessee with BP), and Cameron (manufacturer of the blowout preventer)[2] for damages they allegedly incurred or would sustain as a result of the oil spill. These damages included "monitoring and preparing to respond to the oil spill; contamination and injury to the waters, estuaries, seabed, animals, plants, beaches, shorelines, etc., of [—4—] the Mexican States; lost taxes, fees, etc., due to reduced fishing activity and fishing-related industries; lost taxes, etc., due to diminished tourism; and the net costs of providing increased public services." *In re Oil Spill*, 970 F. Supp. 2d 524, 526 (E.D. La. 2013). The Mexican States brought claims alleging negligence, gross negligence, negligence per se, violations of the Oil Pollution Act ("OPA"), private nuisance, and public nuisance.

In December 2011, the district court dismissed the Mexican States' claim for negligence per se, the OPA claim,[3] and the two

---

[2] All claims against Anadarko were dismissed in December 2011 by the district court, and the Mexican States have not appealed the September 2013 judgment in favor of Cameron. Therefore, the only remaining defendants are BP, Transocean, and Halliburton (collectively, "Defendants").

[3] In an August 2011 order, the district court determined that the OPA did not displace substantive general maritime law. *See In re Oil Spill*, 808 F. Supp. 2d 943, 958–62 (E.D. La. 2011). The issue of whether the OPA displaces general maritime law is significant, and the subject of considerable debate both in and out of this circuit. *See e.g., South Port Marine, LLC v. Gulf Oil Ltd.*, 234 F.3d 58, 65 (1st Cir. 2000) ("Congress intended the OPA to be the sole federal law applicable in this area of maritime pollution"); *Gabarick v. Laurin Mar. (Am.) Inc.*, 623 F. Supp. 2d 741, 750 (E.D. La. 2009) ("OPA preempts general maritime law claims that are recoverable under OPA."); John J. Costonis, *The BP B1 Bundle Ruling: Federal Statutory Displacement of General Maritime Law (Part II)*, 44 Envtl. L. Rep. News & Analysis 10108 (2014) (critiquing the district court's decision in this case). However, the issue is insufficiently briefed. In light of our resolution, we need not

nuisance claims. The court preserved the negligence and gross negligence claims against the current Defendants "only to the extent there has been a physical injury to a proprietary interest." *In re Oil Spill*, 835 F. Supp. 2d 175, 182 (E.D. La. 2011). Discovery was eventually limited to the proprietary interest prong,[4] and the parties cross-moved for summary judgment.

In September 2013, the district court granted summary judgment to Defendants on the ground that the Mexican States lacked a proprietary interest sufficient to overcome application of the rule, announced in *Robins Dry* [—5—] *Dock & Repair Co. v. Flint*, precluding recovery for economic loss absent a proprietary interest in physically damaged property. *See* 275 U.S. 303, 307–09 (1927). After conducting an exhaustive inquiry into Mexican law, the court held that the Mexican federal government, rather than the states, is the true owner of the damaged property. In support of this determination, the district court pointed out that the Mexican federal government, in April 2013, brought a fundamentally similar lawsuit. That case is progressing, though no substantive orders have been issued. The court also stated that "it appears that the Mexican States lack legal standing." *In re Oil Spill*, 970 F. Supp. 2d at 541.

Plaintiffs timely appealed. The issues on appeal are: (1) whether the district court correctly determined that the *Robins Dry Dock* rule is applicable to the Mexican States' claims and (2) whether the district court correctly held that the Mexican States lack proprietary interests in the allegedly damaged property sufficient to maintain their claims.

---

reach and we express no opinion on Defendants' argument that the OPA displaces general maritime law in this or any other case.

[4] The parties continue to dispute whether oil actually entered or damaged Mexican waters, but the district court assumed actual damages for purposes of deciding the proprietary interest issue. We do the same.

II. Standard of Review

This court reviews a district court's grant of summary judgment de novo, applying the same standard as the district court and reviewing the facts in the light most favorable to the nonmovants. *See Tiblier v. Dlabal*, 743 F.3d 1004, 1007 (5th Cir. 2014). Summary judgment is proper "if the movant shows that there is no genuine dispute as to any material fact and the movant is entitled to judgment as a matter of law." Fed. R. Civ. P. ("FRCP") 56(a).

When inquiring into foreign law, courts may consider "any relevant material or source" whether or not presented by the parties. *See* FRCP 44.1 & advisory committee's note to 1966 adoption. The determination "must be treated as a ruling on a question of law." *Id.* "[D]ifferences of opinion among experts on the content, applicability, or interpretation of foreign law do not create a genuine issue as to any material fact." *Access Telecom Inc. v. MCI* [—6—] *Telecomms. Corp.*, 197 F.3d 694, 713 (5th Cir. 1999); *see also* 9A Charles Alan Wright & Arthur R. Miller, *Federal Practice & Procedure* § 2444 (3d ed. 1998).

III. Applicability of Robins Dry Dock

A threshold question is whether Plaintiffs' claims are even subject to the *Robins Dry Dock* rule precluding recovery "for economic loss if that loss resulted from physical damage to property in which [the plaintiff has] no proprietary interest." *In re Bertucci Contracting Co.*, 712 F.3d 245, 246, 1 Adm. R. 225, 225 (5th Cir. 2013) (internal quotation marks and citation omitted). This hard-edged, longstanding common law principle has been reaffirmed by an en banc panel of this court. *See State of La. ex rel. Guste v. M/V Testbank*, 752 F.2d 1019 (5th Cir. 1985) (en banc) (denying recovery to a wide variety of plaintiffs—including operators of marinas, cargo terminal operators, wholesale and retail seafood enterprises, among others—who sought damages from shipowners responsible for spilling chemicals into a Mississippi River gulf outlet). The rule's purpose is to limit the "consequences of negligence and exclude indirect economic repercussions, which can be widespread and open-ended." *Catalyst Old River Hydroelectric Ltd. v. Ingram Barge Co.*, 639 F.3d 207, 210 (5th Cir. 2011).

The Mexican States contend that the *Robins Dry Dock* rule is cabined to civil negligence and other unintentional conduct. They argue that *Robins Dry Dock* is inapplicable because both BP and Transocean pled guilty to criminal conduct arising from the Deepwater Horizon disaster. The only intentional conduct at issue here, however, is BP's guilty plea to intentionally obstructing a congressional investigation, which the Mexican States contend "exacerbated their damages by lulling regulatory authorities and others into deferring the taking of appropriate and mitigating action."[5] The balance of the guilty pleas involves only criminally negligent conduct. [—7—]

The Mexican States locate the purported exception in some of our case law. *See Amoco Transp. Co. v. S/S Mason Lykes*, 768 F.2d 659, 666 (5th Cir. 1985) ("This circuit and others have interpreted *Robins Dry Dock* to mean that there can be no recovery for economic losses caused by an *unintentional maritime tort* absent physical damage to property in which the victim has a proprietary interest." (emphasis added)); *Dick Meyers Towing Serv., Inc. v. United States*, 577 F.2d 1023, 1025 (5th Cir. 1978) (recognizing that a plaintiff may "not recover for interference with his contractual relations unless he shows that the interference was intentional or knowing"); *Kaiser Aluminum & Chem. Corp. v. Marshland Dredging Co.*, 455 F.2d 957, 958 (5th Cir. 1972) ("We agree that recovery by Kaiser is precluded as a matter of law because there is . . . no contention that the interference with Kaiser's contract rights was intentional."). These pronouncements are arguably dicta, as Defendants note.[6] But even

assuming the existence of a criminal or intentional conduct exception, the Fifth Circuit has not addressed the interplay between such conduct and *Robins Dry Dock*.

With one exception, the criminal conduct at issue here was exclusively negligent in nature, so we first address application of *Robins Dry Dock* in the context of criminal negligence. The First Circuit has confronted this issue. *See Ballard Shipping Co. v. Beach Shellfish*, 32 F.3d 623, 624 (1st Cir. 1994). In *Ballard Shipping*, an oil tanker ran aground in Rhode Island, spilling hundreds of thousands of gallons of oil into a bay. *Id.* The captain and the [—8—] shipping company pled guilty to criminally negligent violations of the Clean Water Act and paid out a total of over \$10 million in fines and cleanup costs. *Id.* Shellfish dealers alleging severe economic losses brought a lawsuit alleging violations of, *inter alia*, general maritime law. *Id.* The First Circuit affirmed the dismissal of the general maritime law claims based on *Robins Dry Dock*, holding that the claims did not fit into the "recognized exception[]" for claims based on "economic losses that are intentionally caused." *Id.* at 625 & n.1 (internal quotation marks and citation omitted). Effectively, the court held that criminal negligence did not bar application of *Robins Dry Dock*.[7]

---

[5] Transocean's guilty plea specifically admitted only "negligent conduct."

[6] At least one circuit has recognized a *Robins Dry Dock* exception for "economic losses that are intentionally caused." *See Ballard Shipping Co. v. Beach Shellfish*, 32 F.3d 623, 625 n.1 (1st Cir. 1994) (citing *Dick Myers*, 577 F.2d at 1025). *But see Nautilus Marine Inc. v. Niemela*, 170 F.3d 1195,

1196–1197 (9th Cir. 1999) (holding that "nothing in *Robins Dry Dock* or its progeny . . . support[s] [an] exception" for intentional or reckless tortious conduct, though suggesting that intentional interference with contractual relations may be such an exception).

[7] The lower court in *Ballard* provided a more focused discussion of the criminal negligence issue. *See In re Ballard Shipping Co.*, 810 F. Supp. 359, 364 (D.R.I. 1993). The court stated that the "*Robins Dry Dock* rule . . . should [not] be distorted or cease to operate because the criminal law imposes penalties on particular negligent behavior. As the federal law now deems criminal virtually all negligence resulting in an oil spill in navigable waters, . . . adopting the claimants' position would transform the *Robins Dry Dock* rule into a meaningless assertion. This Court does not believe that Congress intended that *Robins Dry Dock* be relegated to the scrap heap in this manner." *Id.* (citations omitted). Although the district court was ultimately reversed by the First Circuit on a different issue, its analysis on criminal negligence went unquestioned in that court.

We are persuaded by the First Circuit's analysis. To the extent that the *Robins Dry Dock* rule is concerned with the prospect of runaway recovery stemming from a negligent act, *see Amoco Transp.*, 768 F.2d at 668 ("The spectre of runaway recovery lies at the heart of the *Robins Dry Dock* rubric."), there is no principled reason to distinguish between civil and criminal negligence. This is especially so here because federal law has criminalized much negligence in the context of oil spills in navigable waters. *See In re Ballard Shipping Co.*, 810 F. Supp. 359, 364 (D.R.I. 1993); *cf.* David M. Uhlmann, *Environmental Crime Comes of Age: The Evolution of Criminal Enforcement in the Environmental Regulatory Scheme*, 2009 Utah L. Rev. 1223, 1246 (2009) ("As a matter of prosecutorial discretion, the government **[—9—]** considers criminal prosecution in most cases that involve significant harm or risk of harm to the environment.").

We next address the effect of BP's intentional criminal obstruction of a congressional investigation. The plea agreement states that BP did "corruptly, that is, with an improper purpose, endeavor to influence, obstruct, and impede" a congressional investigation. The Mexican States argue that the company's misrepresentations "lull[ed] regulatory authorities and others into deferring the taking of appropriate and mitigating action." The district court held that the misrepresentations were not "causally related to the blowout, the oil spill, or the alleged harm to the Mexican states." *In re Oil Spill*, 970 F. Supp. 2d at 528. We agree. The intent to obstruct a congressional investigation does not directly speak to the intent to cause damage to the Mexican States. *See* Dan B. Dobbs et al., *The Law of Torts* § 29 (2d ed. 2011) ("Intent is not a general state of mind. One has a purpose to accomplish, or a substantial certainty of accomplishing one or more specific objectives. The defendant might intend to touch and also intend his touching to have harmful effects. These are two different intents.").[8]

---

[8] The Mexican States argue that the "factual context" of the guilty pleas of Transocean and BP are sufficient to raise fact questions about

IV. Discussion

Robins Dry Dock bars recovery for economic damages absent physical injury to a plaintiff's proprietary interest. *See Catalyst Old River*, 639 F.3d at 210. To show a sufficient proprietary interest, the general rule is that a plaintiff must show he is an owner of the damaged property. When the plaintiff is clearly not the owner of the physically damaged property, therefore, *Robins Dry Dock* bars economic damage recovery. *See* 275 U.S. at 308–09 (barring a **[—10—]** time charterer of a steamship from recovery of lost profits where the defendant-dry dock negligently damaged the vessel). Thus, a production plant that suffered losses from interruption of gas services—because a barge negligently damaged another owner's pipeline—was denied recovery. *See Kaiser Aluminum*, 455 F.2d at 958. Likewise, a railroad that had to cease operation because of damage to another owner's bridge, despite the railroad's contractual right to use the bridge, could not recover. *See Louisville & N. R. Co. v. M/V Bayou Lacombe*, 597 F.2d 469, 470, 474 (5th Cir. 1979); *see also Dick Meyers*, 577 F.2d at 1025 (denying recovery for pecuniary losses suffered by a vessel operator when a river closed to traffic because of a negligently constructed and maintained lock).

By contrast, when the plaintiff is the owner of the physically damaged property, he can recover economic damages. In *Vicksburg Towing Co. v. Miss. Marine Transp. Co.*, for example, a dock owner who had leased the dock to another was still able to recover for economic damages sustained as a result of damage to the dock caused by the defendant's negligence. *See* 609 F.2d 176, 177 (5th Cir. 1980); *see also Catalyst Old River*, 639 F.3d at 209, 214 (permitting recovery by the owner of a hydroelectric station against a tow operator that negligently caused a barge to block intake channels that took in water to power the station's generators).

Halliburton's intentional conduct. Nowhere is there a direct allegation about Halliburton's intentional conduct, and the Mexican States provide no authority for such a sweeping reading of the purported exception to *Robins Dry Dock*.

The *Robins Dry Dock* Court itself, however, intimated that something perhaps just shy of outright ownership might suffice to show the requisite proprietary interest. The Court left open the possibility that a "demise" agreement might satisfy the proprietary interest requirement even if the "time charter" at issue in that case did not. *See* 275 U.S. at 308. This court in *Bayou Lacombe* provided a useful explanation of the distinction. With the time charter, the "owner's people continue to navigate and manage the vessel, but her carrying capacity is taken by the charterer for a fixed time." 597 F.2d at [—11—] 473 n.3 (quoting G. Gilmore & C. Black, *The Law of Admiralty* § 4–1, at 194 (2d ed. 1975)). The demise (or bareboat) charter, by contrast, allows the charterer to "take[] over the ship, lock, stock and barrel, and man[] her with his own people. He becomes, in effect, the owner pro hac vice." *Id.* This provides the charterer "complete control" of the vessel. *Id.*

The Mexican States point us to *Texas Eastern Transmission Corp. v. McMoRan Offshore Exploration Co.*, where this court "employed three criteria to evaluate proprietary interest: actual possession or control, responsibility for repair, and responsibility for maintenance." 877 F.2d 1214, 1225 (5th Cir. 1989) (citing *Bayou Lacombe*, 597 F.2d at 474). Characterization of these factors as sanctioning recovery for something less than ownership, however, misapprehends their origin and purpose. The *Bayou Lacombe* court, which originated the factors, explicitly noted that these were "incidents of ownership" rather than alternatives to it. *See* 597 F.2d at 474; *see also Texas E.*, 877 F.2d at 1225 ("Even were we to accept the proposition that repair of property endows one with a proprietary interest . . . ."); *Naviera Maersk Espana S.A. v. Cho-Me Towing Inc.*, 782 F. Supp. 317, 320 (E.D. La. 1992) ("[T]he Fifth Circuit clearly defines the term 'proprietary interest' to mean that a party must have control over the property tantamount to full ownership." (citing *Testbank*, 752 F.2d at 1024)). The reach of the definition of "proprietary interest" extends no further than the demise charter, which is "tantamount to, though just short of, an outright transfer of ownership." *Guzman v. Pichirilo*, 369 U.S. 698, 700 (1962).

With these principles in mind, we turn to the Mexican States' argument that they have carried their burden to show the necessary interest in the damaged property. They rely primarily on: (1) certain Mexican federal statutory provisions; (2) their own state constitutions; (3) two affidavits from state ministers from Quintana Roo and Tamaulipas; and (4) the affidavit of a real estate developer who affirms that he had substantial interaction with the [—12—] state of Tamaulipas about a development. Defendants contend that none of these affidavits or laws vests the requisite proprietary interest in the Mexican States. They chiefly rest on provisions in the Mexican Constitution, which they argue place ownership of all the property at issue in this litigation in the Mexican federal government.

We conclude that none of the Mexican States' cited sources show that they own the relevant property. Instead, as the district court held, both individually and collectively these sources suggest that the Mexican federal government is the true owner. We address these sources in turn.

A. *The Mexican Constitution*

Article 27 of the Mexican Constitution[9] contains the following broad statements about property ownership:

Ownership of lands and waters within the boundaries of national land territory[10] is vested originally in the

---

[9] Our translations of Mexico's Constitution derive entirely from an official version printed by the Mexican Supreme Court, and available on that court's official website at https://www.scjn.gob.mx/normativa/ConstEnglish/CONSTI%20INGLES%20SEPT%202010.pdf.

[10] "National land territory," as used in Article 27, is a term of art with an expansive definition. Defined in Article 42 of the Constitution, it includes: "I. The land territory of all the portions constituting the Federation; II. The territory of the islands, including the reefs and keys in adjacent seas; . . . IV. The continental shelf and the seabed and subsoil of the submarine areas of the islands,

Nation, which has had and has, the right to transmit title thereof to private persons, thereby constituting private property. . . .

The Nation has full ownership over all natural resources of the continental shelf and the seabed and subsoil of the marine areas of the islands . . . .

The Nation has full ownership over the waters of territorial sea in the extension and under the terms set forth by International Law . . . . [—13—]

In the cases established in [the preceding two paragraphs], the Nation's dominion is inalienable and not subject to the statute of limitation and the exploitation, use or enjoyment of the resources in question by private persons or by companies incorporated in accordance with Mexican laws, may not be undertaken save by means of concessions granted by the President of the Republic and in accordance with the rules and conditions set forth by the Laws.

Political Constitution of the United Mexican States ("Mexican Constitution"), Article 27, ¶¶ 1, 4–6.

This constitutional provision is essentially decisive of this case. Article 27 means that "Mexico's public domain over these assets is inalienable and cannot be taken away from the *federal government* by adverse possession, by either Mexican nationals or foreigners." Jorge A. Vargas, *Mexican Law: A Treatise for Legal Practitioners and International Investors* § 34.4 (2001) [hereinafter *Mexican Law: A Treatise*] (emphasis added); *see also* Jorge A. Vargas, *Mexican Law for the American Lawyer* 161 (2009).

The Mexican States propose a more holistic understanding of the critical word "Nation," a term not defined in the Mexican Constitution.

They argue that it embraces the entire Mexican people, and not only the federal government. However, that expansive reading is foreclosed by several interpretations of the term "Nation" in the context of the Mexican constitutional provisions outlined above. The Mexican Supreme Court has interpreted the term "Nation" narrowly, stating that "[t]he nation cannot be mistaken for a state, and consequently, State officials are not the ones who represent it because it is unique and represented by its federal agencies." *In re Oil Spill*, 970 F. Supp. 2d at 533 (citing *Nacion, Representacion de la*, [TA]; 5a. Epoca; 2a. Sala; S.J.F.; LII; Pag. 72 (Registro No. 332930)).[11] And one [—14—] commentator on Mexican law explicitly provides that "Nation," as used in Article 27, means the federal government. *See* Stephen Zamora et al., *Mexican Law* 495 (2004).[12] Professor Vargas proposes a more nuanced account of the distribution of sovereignty:

> Under Mexican law, all of the "elements" that compose the national territory of Mexico (including their corresponding natural resources) belong to the Mexican Nation (and not to the Federation or to each of the federal entities), with the legal and political understanding that the Nation is represented by the federal government.

---

[11] The Mexican States' arguments against our consideration of this case are unavailing. First, the States claim that the proper translation of the initial clause is "the nation cannot be mistaken for a *federal entity*," which would lead to a different conclusion. [—14—] We are unpersuaded that the translation the district court used is incorrect, however, because the official Mexican Supreme Court translation of the Mexican Constitution translates the same term—"entidad federativa"—as "state." *See* Mexican Constitution, Article 27, ¶ 5. Second, while the case appears not to be controlling precedent under Mexican law, we find persuasive the Mexican Supreme Court's interpretation of the Mexican Constitution. The Mexican States have not offered any subsequent Mexican Supreme Court decision that embraces their preferred interpretation of the term "Nation."

[12] Professor Zamora served as an expert for Halliburton in this case.

---

keys and reefs; [and] V. The waters of the territorial seas in the extension and under the terms established by International Law and domestic maritime laws."

Jorge A. Vargas, *Mexico and the Law of the Sea* 9 (2011) (footnotes omitted). Under either view, we conclude, the Mexican Constitution vests the federal government with the necessary proprietary interest for purposes of *Robins Dry Dock*.

This conclusion about federal supremacy is strengthened by the text in the sixth paragraph of Article 27, which clarifies that only the federal government, through Mexico's president, can allow "exploitation, use or enjoyment" of the long list of resources delineated in the preceding two paragraphs. *See* Mexican Constitution, Article 27, ¶¶ 4–6; *see also Corporacion Mexicana de Servicios Maritimos, S.A. de C.V. v. M/T Respect*, 89 F.3d 650, 653 (9th Cir. 1996), *as amended on denial of reh'g* (Aug. 28, 1996) ("Under Article 27 of the Constitution of the United Mexican States, the government of Mexico is the only entity that may own and exploit the country's natural [—15—] resources . . . . The Constitution permits the *federal government* to create organizations that manage and distribute these resources." (emphasis added) (citation omitted)).[13]

---

[13] The Mexican States claim that they own certain islands off their coasts. The root of this argument is a provision in Article 48 of the Mexican Constitution. That article states that "islands, keys and reefs of adjacent seas belonging to national land territory, the continental shelf, the sea beds of the islands, keys and reefs, the territorial seas, inland marine waters, and the space over national land territory, shall depend directly from the Government of the Federation, *with the exception of those islands over which the States have up to the present, exercised their jurisdiction*." Mexican Constitution Article 48 (emphasis added). Article 48 has resulted in great uncertainty in Mexico concerning ownership of these islands. *See generally* Vargas, *Mexico and the Law of the Sea* 405–484 (discussing history of relationship of states to Mexico's islands). However, the states have "abstained from enacting legislation to regulate islands offshore their coasts" in part because they have read Article 48 to provide that the "Federal Government . . . legally and politically exercise[s] control over Mexico's 'Insular territory.'" *Id*. at 455; *see also id*. at 439 (stressing that the islands have effectively been under federal control since passage of the 1917 constitution). We are not persuaded that the Mexican States have

B. *Mexican Federal Statutory Law*

An elaborate regime of Mexican federal statutory law—while certainly allotting some power to the states—further establishes federal supremacy with respect to the property at issue.

A few examples will suffice. The Mexican States have sought damages for harm to wildlife. But the General Law of Wildlife (GLW)[14] establishes, as relevant here, that the "Federal Attorney General's Office for Environmental Protection . . . shall exercise in an exclusive manner the action for liability for damage caused to wildlife and its habitat." GLW, Article 107. Additionally, while Mexico's General Law of Ecological Balance and Environmental Protection (GLEBEP) affords some power to Mexican states over environmental matters, *see* GLEBEP, Article 7, only the federal government is responsible for "[a]ttending to matters affecting the ecological balance . . . [—16—] originating in the territory or areas subject to other States' sovereignty and jurisdiction," *see* GLEBEP, Article 5. Given that the Deepwater Horizon incident "originated" outside Mexico's territorial boundaries, Article 5 signifies that the Mexican States have ceded the power to protect these resources to the Mexican federal government. *See Mexican Law: A Treatise* §12.61 (highlighting federal control over environmental enforcement); Zamora et al., *Mexican Law* 122 (observing that, in Mexico, "environmental protection remains almost exclusively a federal matter").

C. *State Constitutions*

The State Constitutions of Veracruz, Quintana Roo, and Tamaulipas provide that the individual states maintain a degree of autonomy and freedom. Article 1 of the Constitution of Veracruz, for example, states that it is "free and autonomous in its administration and internal governance." Article 1 of the Constitution of Quintana Roo

---

demonstrated the mandatory proprietary interest in these islands.

[14] We use the translations of Mexican federal statutory law and the Mexican States' constitutions provided to us by the parties.

explains that it is a "free state as its members determine the organization, function and objectives of its community." Article 1 of the Constitution of Tamaulipas states that it is "free, sovereign and independent in its government and internal administration," but also notes that it is "tied to the branches of government as part of the United Mexican States, in all that the Constitution expressly sets forth."

Although the language of the constitutions is expansive, there is substantial language in these documents recognizing the superior authority of the federal government. The Veracruz Constitution may, for example, note that the state is "free and autonomous," as Plaintiffs argue, but it also makes clear that this is the case only with respect to its "administration and internal governance." Tamaulipas may be "free" and "sovereign" but it is "tied to the branches of government as part of the United Mexican States." These state constitutions must yield to Article 27 of the federal constitution, which vests ownership of the relevant property "originally in the Nation." Mexican [—17—] Constitution, Article 27, ¶ 1; *see also* Mexican Constitution, Article 133 (containing a supremacy clause—similar to the American version embedded in Article VI of the U.S. Constitution—providing that the Mexican Constitution and federal law bind the states "notwithstanding any provision to the contrary in the local constitutions or local laws").

D. *Minister and Developer Affidavits*

The Mexican States rely greatly on three affidavits—two from state ministers, and one from a real estate developer—as further proof of their proprietary interests.[15] In the affidavits filed by the state ministers (the Tamaulipas Minister of Urban Development and the Environment and the Quintana Roo Minister of the Environment), they affirm that the states spent money out of their own treasuries to address oil that washed up on

---

[15] While the Mexican States complain that these affidavits were ignored by the district court, their own summary judgment briefs do not mention the state ministers and contain only one mention of the real estate developer in a reply brief.

beaches in their territory. Defendants do not appear to dispute this. However, some statements in these affidavits are flatly contradicted by the Mexican Constitution. For example, both ministers affirm that their respective states "own[], manage[], possess[] and maintain[] [their] beaches, waters, estuaries, rivers, waterways, lagoons and flora and fauna of the Gulf of Mexico." These claims conflict with the language of Article 27 of the Mexican Constitution, which again states that "[o]wnership of lands and waters within the boundaries of national land territory is vested originally in the Nation." Mexican Constitution, Article 27, ¶ 1. Even accepting the Mexican States' holistic interpretation of the term "Nation," it would still not be true that the Mexican States own this property. "Estuaries," "river waters," and "lagoons," furthermore, are explicitly committed to the Nation's ownership. Mexican Constitution, Article 27, ¶ 5. We do not find these affidavits persuasive. [—18—]

As to the real estate developer's declaration, while he avers that he spent much time in consultation with state authorities about the development of a "large scale tourism and beach resort," in that same declaration he provides a list of three pages of permits, agreements, and concessions he received from the federal government for that development.

E. *Application of Robins Dry Dock*

Ultimately, the question in this case is not whether the Mexican States have *some* authority to use or exploit *some* of the land and other resources at issue here. They likely do. The question is whether their property interests rise to the requisite level. They do not.

We recognize that the *Robins Dry Dock* analytical framework does not easily map on to an intragovernmental relationship. However, the Mexican Constitution is sufficiently clear about the distribution of property rights in the country for us to conclude that the Mexican States in no way resemble owners permitted to recover economic damages in our case law. *See e.g.*,

Vicksburg Towing, 609 F.2d at 177 (permitting the plaintiff to recover lost rental income after damage sustained to its dock because, although the dock was leased to another, the plaintiff remained the sole owner of the property).

Instead, the Mexican States far more closely resemble the railroad company disallowed economic damage recovery from a defendant who negligently damaged another owner's bridge, in spite of the company's right to use the bridge. *See Bayou Lacombe*, 597 F.2d at 474. They also resemble the oil company in *Texas Eastern* that could not recover for a defendant's negligent destruction of a pipeline it did not own, even though it maintained a laundry list of appurtenances to the pipeline. *See* 877 F.2d at 1225–26.

Seen through the prism of the perhaps less onerous demise charter analogy, the Mexican States' interests still do not stack up. Recall that the demise charterer "takes over the ship, lock, stock and barrel, and mans her [—19—] with his own people. He becomes, in effect, the owner pro hac vice." *Bayou Lacombe*, 597 F.2d at 473 n.3 (internal quotation marks and citation omitted). He maintains "complete control." *Id*. The time charterer, by contrast, can provide "orders as to ports touched, cargo loaded, and other business matters" and can have "tonnage under his control for a period of time, without undertaking the responsibilities of ship navigation and management of the long-term financial commitments of vessel ownership." *Id*.

According to the Mexican States, they "are in charge of the natural resources at issue" and have the right to "exploit" these assets. They also note through affidavits of state environmental ministers that they have—at their own expense—repaired, maintained, managed, developed and protected many of the relevant resources. But these interests do not even closely approximate the "complete control" maintained by the demise charterer. It could not be said that the states have taken over the property at issue "lock, stock and barrel." *Bayou Lacombe*, 597 F.2d at 473 n.3 (internal quotation marks and citation omitted). Rather, federal law places the bulk

of the power here in the hands of the federal government. The Mexican Constitution vests ownership of "lands and waters within the boundaries of national land territory" in the "Nation." Mexican Constitution, Article 27. The GLEBEP gives the federal government power over "matters affecting the ecological balance . . . originating . . . in areas beyond the jurisdiction of any State." *See* GLEBEP, Article 5. The GLW provides that only the federal government, as relevant here, can bring an action "for damage caused to wildlife and its habitat." *See* GLW, Article 107. The state constitutions, the above-listed laws, and Plaintiffs' cited affidavits bespeak a role for the states in managing some of the country's property. But [—20—] they do not provide the Mexican States with the crucial proprietary interest for purposes of *Robins Dry Dock*.[16]

V. Conclusion

We hold that the *Robins Dry Dock* doctrine bars recovery in this case for the Mexican States, and therefore AFFIRM the district court's decision.

---

[16] Federal primacy in the environmental arena is further highlighted by the parallel lawsuit brought by the Mexican federal government seeking damages that risk duplicating those potentially awarded in this litigation. *See Amoco Transp.*, 768 F.2d at 668–69 (recognizing that concerns about double recovery lie at the heart of *Robins Dry Dock*). Plaintiffs attempt to characterize that suit as evidence of the concurrent authority exercised by the states and the federal government. But it would be an exercise in futility to separate damages in the one case from those in the other when the complaints allege very similar harm. *Compare* Complaint at 37, *United Mexican States v. BP Exploration & Prod. Inc. et al.*, No. 2:13-cv-01441-CJB-SS (E.D. La. Apr. 19, 2013), ECF No. 1 (seeking relief for, *inter alia*, preventative and monitoring activities, economic damages, and damages to natural resources), *with*, *e.g.*, First Amended Complaint at 22, 28, *State of Quintana Roo v. BP, PLC et al.*, No. SA10CA0763 OG (W.D. Tex. Nov. 8, 2010), ECF No. 1 (praying for relief for, *inter alia*, response costs, economic damages, and damage to natural resources).

United States Court of Appeals
for the Fifth Circuit

No. 14-30488

ALEXANDER
vs.
EXPRESS ENERGY SERVS. OPERATING, L.P.

Appeal from the United States District Court for the
Eastern District of Louisiana

Decided: May 7, 2015

Citation: 784 F.3d 1032, 3 Adm. R. 321 (5th Cir. 2015).

Before **DAVIS, JONES,** and **CLEMENT,** Circuit Judges.

[—1—] **DAVIS,** Circuit Judge:

Plaintiff-Appellant Michael Alexander appeals from the district court's order granting Defendant-Appellee Express Energy Services Operating, L.P.'s ("Express") motion for summary judgment on seaman status, concluding that Alexander is not a seaman and dismissing Alexander's claims against Express with prejudice. We affirm.

I.

We begin with the controlling law. We review the district court's summary judgment ruling de novo, applying the same Fed. R. Civ. P. 56 [—2—] standards as the district court.[1] Summary judgment is appropriate "if the movant shows that there is no genuine dispute as to any material fact and the movant is entitled to judgment as a matter of law."[2] "The court is to consider evidence in the record in the light most favorable to the non-moving party and draw all reasonable inferences in favor of that party."[3]

A party asserting that a fact cannot be or is genuinely disputed must support the assertion by:

(A) citing to particular parts of materials in the record, including depositions, documents, electronically stored information, affidavits or declarations, stipulations (including those made for purposes of the motion only), admissions, interrogatory answers, or other materials; or

(B) showing that the materials cited do not establish the absence or presence of a genuine dispute, or that an adverse party cannot produce admissible evidence to support the fact.[4]

"Summary judgment is appropriate if the non-movant fails to make a showing sufficient to establish the existence of an element essential to that party's case," and we may affirm "on any ground supported by the record, even if it is different from that relied on by the district court."[5]

"To maintain a cause of action under the Jones Act, the plaintiff must be a seaman. Land-based workers are not seamen."[6] To qualify as a seaman, a plaintiff must prove that he meets both prongs of the test set out by the [—3—] Supreme Court in *Chandris, Inc. v. Latsis,* 515 U.S. 347 (1995). First, he must prove that his duties "contribut[e] to the function of the vessel or to the accomplishment of its mission," which does not necessarily require that the plaintiff "aid in navigation or contribute to the transportation of the vessel," but does require that he "be doing the ship's work."[7]

Second, and most important for our purposes here, a seaman must have a connection to a vessel in navigation (or to an identifiable group of such vessels) that is substantial in terms of both its

---

[1] *Bluebonnet Hotel Ventures, L.L.C. v. Wells Fargo Bank, N.A.,* 754 F.3d 272, 275 (5th Cir. 2014).

[2] Fed. R. Civ. P. 56(a).

[3] *Bluebonnet,* 754 F.3d at 276 (citation omitted).

[4] Fed. R. Civ. P. 56(c)(1).

[5] *Bluebonnet,* 754 F.3d at 276 (citations and internal quotation marks omitted).

[6] *Hufnagel v. Omega Serv. Indus., Inc.,* 182 F.3d 340, 346 (5th Cir. 1999) (citing *Harbor Tug and Barge Co. v. Papai,* 520 U.S. 548 (1997)).

[7] 515 U.S. at 357 (citations and internal quotation marks removed).

duration and its nature. The fundamental purpose of this substantial connection requirement is to give full effect to the remedial scheme created by Congress and to separate the sea-based maritime employees who are entitled to Jones Act protection from those land-based workers who have only a transitory or sporadic connection to a vessel in navigation, and therefore whose employment does not regularly expose them to the perils of the sea. *See* 1B A. Jenner, Benedict on Admiralty § 11a, pp. 2–10.1 to 2–11 (7th ed. 1994) ("If it can be shown that the employee performed a significant part of his work **on board the vessel** on which he was injured, with at least some degree of regularity and continuity, the test for seaman status will be satisfied" (footnote omitted)). This requirement therefore determines which maritime employees in *Wilander*'s broad category of persons eligible for seaman status because they are "doing the ship's work," [*McDermott Int'l, Inc. v. Wilander*, 498 U.S. 337, 355 (1991)], are in fact entitled to the benefits conferred upon seamen by the Jones Act because they have the requisite employment-related connection to a vessel in navigation.[8]

The Court emphasized that "[a] maritime worker who spends only a small fraction of his working time **on board a vessel** is fundamentally land [—4—] based and therefore not a member of the vessel's crew, regardless of what his duties are."[9] The Court adopted the Fifth Circuit's rule of thumb for ordinary cases that "[a] worker who spends less than about 30 percent of his time in the service of a vessel in navigation should not qualify as a seaman under the Jones Act," though courts may vary the rule depending on the facts of a particular case.[10] The Court explained that although the inquiry is fact-specific, "where undisputed facts reveal that a maritime worker has a clearly inadequate temporal connection to vessels in navigation, the court may take the question from the jury by granting summary judgment or a directed verdict."[11]

Even before *Chandris* was decided, the Fifth Circuit focused on the amount of the work the plaintiff actually performed *on a vessel*,[12] and following *Chandris*'s adoption of that rule, we must continue to apply it. We have referred to "the Supreme Court's teaching in *Chandris* that a seaman's connection with a vessel includes a temporal requirement, i.e. **that the worker spend a substantial part of his work time aboard the vessel**."[13]

Our pre-*Chandris* en banc decision in *Barrett* provides a useful example of how we have applied this rule. There, a worker who was a member of a contract maintenance crew working on production platforms in the Gulf of Mexico was injured. Because many of the platforms were too small to accommodate the maintenance crew and their equipment, a jack-up barge was positioned alongside the small platforms to provide additional work space and [—5—] hold some of the equipment. The plaintiff, Barrett, performed the vast majority of his work on the platform and only did incidental work on the adjacent vessel. Relying on the seminal *Robison* case, we held:

> *Robison* requires evidence that the worker was "assigned permanently to . . . *or* performed a substantial portion of his work on the vessel." This test is, of course, disjunctive, and permits a worker to be a crew member if he does substantial work on the vessel even

---

[8] *Id.* at 368-69 (emphasis added).
[9] *Id.* at 371 (emphasis added).
[10] *Id.*

[11] *Id.* (citations omitted).
[12] *See Barrett v. Chevron, U.S.A., Inc.*, 781 F.2d 1067, 1073-74 (5th Cir. 1986) (en banc) (noting that a plaintiff may be a seaman if he was either permanently assigned to a vessel or "performed a significant part of his work aboard the vessel with at least some degree of regularity and continuity" (discussing *Barrios v. Engine & Gas Compressor Servs., Inc.*, 669 F.2d 350, 353 (5th Cir. 1982); *Holland v. Allied Structural Steel Co.*, 539 F.2d 476, 484 (5th Cir. 1976))).
[13] *Nunez v. B&B Dredging, Inc.*, 288 F.3d 271, 276 (5th Cir. 2002) (emphasis added).

though his assignment to it is not "permanent."[14]

We made it clear that Barrett's work time on the vessel was inadequate to meet the seaman test: "Because he did not perform a substantial portion of his work aboard a vessel or fleet of vessels, he failed to establish that he was a member of the crew of a vessel."[15]

In short, to prove that he is a seaman, Alexander must prove both that (1) he contributed to the function of a vessel or to the accomplishment of its mission, and (2) he was assigned permanently to the vessel or spent a substantial part of his total work time—30% —aboard the vessel or an identifiable fleet of vessels. If he has failed to demonstrate at least a genuine dispute as to a material fact with respect to either prong, Express is entitled to summary judgment. With these standards in mind, we turn to the facts of the case.

II.

Alexander was employed as a lead hand/operator in Express's plug and abandonment ("P&A") department, which specializes in plugging decommissioned oil wells on various platforms off the coast of Louisiana for Express's customers. At his deposition, he described his duties as ensuring that [—6—] everything was set up and running properly on the deck of the platform and ensuring that the plugging operation was successful. He testified that the plugging operation essentially required the P&A team to check the pressure of the well with various gauges and valves to make sure it was ready to be killed. After that, the team would remove the bridge plug from the well, place a nipple in the well, and pump fluids down the well to kill it. Once the well was under control, the team would clean it and pump cement into it, then cut and remove the pipe.

On August 11, 2011, Alexander was injured while working on a P&A project on a platform owned by Apache Corporation which had four wells on it. At the time of the accident, a liftboat owned by Aries Marine Corporation ("Aries"), the L/B RAM X ("RAM X"), was positioned next to the Apache platform, with a catwalk connecting the vessel to the platform. The record shows that the permanent crane, which was operated by an Aries employee for the benefit of the P&A crew, was located on the liftboat, while other equipment, including wireline equipment, was located on the platform. Alexander testified that he and the P&A crew had set up the equipment on the platform before work began, and he was working on the platform. Alexander was injured when a wireline from the crane snapped, dropping a bridge plug/tool combination which had been suspended a foot above the deck, which then rolled onto his foot.

Alexander filed this action under the Jones Act, 46 U.S.C. § 30104 *et seq.*, against Express and other defendants. Express filed a motion for summary judgment on seaman status, arguing that Alexander was a platform-based worker who failed to satisfy either prong of the *Chandris* seaman status test. With respect to the first prong, Express argued that Alexander did not contribute to the function of a vessel or the accomplishment of its mission because he worked on the wells on non-vessel fixed platforms. With respect to [—7—] the second prong, Express argued that even though Alexander had shown that approximately 35% of his P&A *jobs* involved the use of an adjacent liftboat, he had failed to demonstrate that he spent at least 30% of his total work time on the adjacent liftboat.

In response, Alexander argued as to the first prong that he did in fact contribute to the function of the Aries liftboat. As to the second prong, Alexander erroneously stated that Express conceded that he spent 35% of his total job on Aries liftboats; Express only stated that 35% of his jobs involved an adjacent liftboat. Alexander then argued that, under *Roberts v. Cardinal Services, Inc.*, 266 F.3d 368 (5th Cir. 2001), and *Johnson v. TETRA Applied Technologies, L.L.C.*, No.

---

[14] 781 F.2d at 1073 (quoting *Offshore Co. v. Robison*, 266 F.2d 769, 779 (5th Cir. 1959); and *Davis v. Hill Eng'g, Inc.*, 549 F.2d 314, 326 (5th Cir. 1977)).

[15] *Id.* at 1076.

CIV.A. 11-1992, 2012 WL 3253184 (E.D. La. Aug. 7, 2012), which applied *Roberts*, he was allowed to count toward the *Chandris* temporal requirement *all* of his time on jobs that used an adjacent vessel (here, at least 35%), without regard to how much time he himself spent on the vessel. Significantly, Alexander never offered any evidence that he spent 30% or more of his work time on a vessel; rather, his argument on this prong depends entirely on his interpretation of *Roberts*.

The district court granted Express's motion for summary judgment on the first prong, concluding that Alexander's duties in this case were similar to those of the plaintiff in *Hufnagel*, which this court held did not contribute to the function of a vessel because those duties related to the fixed platform, not the vessel.[16] In a footnote at the end of the opinion, the district court opined that Alexander had also failed to meet the second prong.

As noted above, we may affirm the district court "on any ground supported by the record, even if it is different from that relied on by the district [—8—] court."[17] Pretermitting whether Alexander's duties contributed to the function of a vessel or the accomplishment of its mission, we conclude that Alexander has failed to demonstrate that he is a seaman under *Chandris*'s temporal connection prong. *Chandris* makes it clear that a seaman must spend a substantial amount of time, ordinarily 30%, actually working *on a vessel*. Alexander argues that *Roberts* means a plaintiff may count the amount of time he spent working on a platform toward that requirement if a vessel was merely adjacent to the platform and assisting with the platform work.[18] We cannot

accept Alexander's argument because we are bound to follow clear and controlling Supreme Court precedent.

The undisputed summary judgment evidence shows that approximately 65% of Alexander's jobs involved a fixed platform only, without the help of an adjacent vessel. Even on the other jobs involving a vessel adjacent to the platform, his work occurred mostly on the platform. It is not sufficient under *Chandris* (or indeed under *Barrett*) that Alexander was merely *near* a vessel on more than 30% of his jobs or that he performed some incidental work on a vessel on those jobs; to be a seaman, he must show that he actually *worked on a vessel* at least 30% of the time. Alexander has failed to produce sufficient evidence to prove that point, which is an essential element of seaman status.

We conclude that Alexander has failed to carry his burden of showing that he is a seaman. We therefore affirm the district court's order granting [—9—] Express's motion for summary judgment and dismissing Alexander's claims against Express with prejudice.

AFFIRMED.

---

[16] *See Hufnagel*, 182 F.3d at 347.

[17] *Bluebonnet*, 754 F.3d at 276 (citations and internal quotation marks omitted).

[18] The district court in *Johnson* also interpreted *Roberts* that way. *See* 2012 WL 3253184, at *4 ("However, the court counted the time plaintiff spent working alongside the employer's lift boats, which amounted to 24.88% of his time, separately from the time plaintiff spent working alongside lift boats owned by third parties, which amounted to 13.54%. Because plaintiff could not show that at least 30% of his time was spent in the service of a vessel or an identifiable fleet of vessels under common ownership or control, the court found that he could not prove seaman's status." (citations omitted)).

United States Court of Appeals
for the Fifth Circuit

No. 13-31296

IN RE DEEPWATER HORIZON

LAKE EUGENIE LAND & DEV., INC.
vs.
BP EXPLORATION & PROD., INC.

Appeal from the United States District Court for the
Eastern District of Louisiana

Decided: May 8, 2015

Citation: 785 F.3d 1003, 3 Adm. R. 325 (5th Cir. 2015).

Before **BENAVIDES, PRADO,** and **GRAVES,** Circuit Judges.

[—1—] **PRADO,** Circuit Judge: [—2—]

In these consolidated cases, BP Exploration & Production, Inc., BP America Production Company, and BP p.l.c. (collectively "BP") appeals three *Deepwater Horizon*-related settlement awards it paid to nonprofits through its Court-Supervised Settlement Program (CSSP). The district court denied discretionary review of these three awards even though BP argued that the Claims Administrator improperly interpreted the Settlement Agreement (the Agreement). The awards were based on the Claims Administrator's determination that nonprofits may count donations and grants as "revenue" under the terms of the Agreement (the Nonprofit-Revenue Interpretation). BP argues that 1) the Nonprofit-Revenue Interpretation violates the terms of the Agreement, 2) the Nonprofit-Revenue Interpretation puts the class settlement in violation of Rule 23 and Article III, and 3) even if the Nonprofit-Revenue Interpretation is upheld, each of these three awards is improper. We affirm the district court.

I. FACTUAL AND PROCEDURAL BACKGROUND

This case arises from the class action settlement of civil claims arising from the *Deepwater Horizon* oil spill. The Settlement Agreement negotiated by the parties and approved by the district court established the CSSP, through which class members can submit claims.

A. The Claims-Administration Process

The CSSP is managed by the Claims Administrator. After a claim determination has been made, BP or the claimant may appeal to an Appeal Panel.[1] A party may then appeal the Appeal Panel's determination to the district court of Judge Barbier in the Eastern District of Louisiana, which has [—3—] discretion to hear such appeals. Pursuant to a district court order of May 20, 2013, denials of discretionary review are not docketed.[2] Rather, the district court gives notice to the parties and posts decisions on the CSSP website.

The Settlement Agreement expressly includes nonprofits in the definition of entities who may recover pursuant to the settlement. The awards at issue were granted under the Business Economic Loss (BEL) framework. To recover under the BEL framework, a claimant must fall within one of twelve "Damage Categories" listed in § 1.3 of the Agreement. The Sealed Claimants recovered under the Economic Damage Category, which is summarized as encompassing "[l]oss of income, earnings or profits suffered by Natural Persons or Entities as a result of the DEEPWATER HORIZON INCIDENT." To recover in this category, a claimant must meet one of the "causation requirements" in Exhibit 4B of the Agreement. Claimants can establish causation by showing various "revenue patterns." If a claimant can show one of these revenue patterns, its compensation award is calculated under Exhibit 4C's "compensation framework"; compensation is based on a comparison of its pre- and post-spill revenue.

---

[1] Appeals of less than $1 million are heard by a single Appeal Panelist.

[2] BP appealed this order in a related case (the Final Rules appeal), also decided today, and we ordered the district court to begin docketing the denials of discretionary review. *See In re Deepwater Horizon*, No. 13-30843, 3 Adm. R. 341 (5th Cir. 2015).

B. The Claims Administrator's "Revenue" Interpretation

This appeal stems from the Claims Administrator's interpretation of "revenue" as it is used in Exhibits 4B and 4C of the Agreement. On November 30, 2012, the Claims Administrator determined that for nonprofit entities "grant monies or contributions shall typically be treated as revenue for the purposes of the . . . settlement agreement." BP challenged this interpretation [—4—] in the district court, and the court affirmed the Claims Administrator on December 12, 2012, via an email to the parties. BP never directly appealed this decision. After the Nonprofit-Revenue Interpretation went into effect, the Sealed Claimants, each a nonprofit organization, counted donations and grants as revenue in their calculations, and received awards through the CSSP.

- The Claimant in No.13-31296 (the *Cy Pres* Claimant) counted as revenue $331,395 in *cy pres* funds from a class action settlement.

- The Claimant in No.13-31299 (the Grant Claimant) counted as revenue its receipt of a large, one-time "Trust Grant."

- The Claimant in No. 13-31302 (the Legal-Services Claimant) included $157,500 in revenue that was based on "legal services performed by its legal fellows."

BP appealed the awards all the way to the district court, which denied its motion for discretionary review. BP now appeals these denials of discretionary review.[3]

---

[3] Also before the Court are BP's motion to supplement the record and file the supplemental record under seal, the Grant Claimant's motion to dismiss, and Class Counsel's motion to dismiss. The motion to supplement the record and file the supplemental record under seal is GRANTED, and both motions to dismiss are DENIED.

II. LEGAL BACKGROUND

This is the fifth appeal we have heard arising out of this class action settlement, and many of the issues presented relate to our earlier *Deepwater Horizon* decisions. Thus, we begin with a brief overview of the relevant portions of those cases.

A. *Deepwater Horizon I*

In *In re Deepwater Horizon* (*Deepwater Horizon I*), 732 F.3d 326, 1 Adm. R. 287 (5th Cir. 2013), BP appealed a district court order affirming the Claims Administrator's interpretation of the terms "revenue" and "expenses" in the Agreement. *Id.* at [—5—] 331, 1 Adm. R. at 288. This case centered on a dispute about accounting standards. In a Policy Announcement, the Claims Administrator stated that these terms encompassed only cash payments and disbursements, consistent with the cash-accounting method. *Id.* at 334, 1 Adm. R. at 291-92. BP disagreed and argued that the Agreement was to be governed instead by the accrual-accounting method, which requires matching of revenues and expenditures, and therefore the order allowed claimants to recover for inflated or nonexistent losses. *Id.* at 331–34, 1 Adm. R. at 288-92. We remanded to the district court for further proceedings on this contract-interpretation question. *Id.* at 339, 1 Adm. R. at 296.

B. *Deepwater Horizon II*

BP next challenged the class certification as violating Federal Rule of Civil Procedure 23 and Article III of the Constitution. *In re Deepwater Horizon* (*Deepwater Horizon II*), 739 F.3d 790, 795, 2 Adm. R. 140, 140 (5th Cir. 2014). At issue in *Deepwater Horizon II* was the district court's affirmance of two Claims Administrator Policy Announcements that interpreted Exhibits 4B and 4C of the Agreement. *Id.* at 795–96, 2 Adm. R. at 140-41. The Claims Administrator determined that Exhibit 4B, which sets forth various causation requirements for claimants, did not require any further proof of causation once a claimant had met one of the 4B criteria. *Id.* at 797, 2 Adm. R. at 142. The Claims Administrator also determined that Exhibit 4C, which provides the formula to calculate payments for BEL claimants, allowed the Claims Administrator to use the cash *or* accrual method of accounting in the calculation. *Id.*, 2 Adm. R. at 141-42.

BP argued that these interpretations broadened the class to include members whose injuries were not caused by the oil spill, in violation of Article III and Rule 23. *Id.* at 798–99, 2 Adm. R. at 142-43. We noted that the Fifth Circuit had not addressed the standard for Article III standing at the class-certification stage [—6—] and that other circuits are split between two tests. *Id.* at 800–02, 2 Adm. R. at 144-46. We held that the Agreement passed both tests and therefore declined to decide which approach was correct. *Id.* at 813, 2 Adm. R. at 155. We also rejected BP's numerous arguments that the Policy Announcements included class members with no injury and therefore violated Rule 23. *Id.* at 812–21, 2 Adm. R. at 154-162.

C. *Deepwater Horizon III*

The third appeal arose from our remand in *Deepwater Horizon I. In re Deepwater Horizon* (*Deepwater Horizon III*), 744 F.3d 370, 373–74, 2 Adm. R. 183, 183-84 (5th Cir. 2014), *cert. denied* 135 S. Ct. 754 (2014). On remand, "the district court held that the Settlement Agreement requires matching of revenues and expenses," as BP had originally argued. *Id.*, 2 Adm. R. at 183-84. However, the district court rejected BP's newly briefed argument—that the Claims Administrator's refusal to require specific evidence of causation violated Article III and Rule 23. *Id.* at 374, 2 Adm. R. at 184. Whereas *Deepwater Horizon II* addressed the certification of the class, *Deepwater Horizon III* "decide[d] . . . whether the implementation of the Settlement Agreement is defective." *Id.* at 375, 2 Adm. R. at 184. In spite of the decision in *Deepwater Horizon II*, BP again argued that any interpretation or implementation of the Agreement that does not require proof of causation "reanimates" the Article III and Rule 23 issues decided in that case. *Id.* at 376, 2 Adm. R. at 186. BP sought reversal of the district court's ruling and an injunction

preventing payment of claims to entities without evidence of causation. *Id.* at 373, 2 Adm. R. at 183. We affirmed the district [—7—] court's order, denied the injunction, and held that we were bound by our *Deepwater Horizon II* rulings on Rule 23 and Article III. *See id.* at 375–78, 2 Adm. R. at 184-88.

III. JURISDICTION

We have jurisdiction over this appeal under the collateral-order doctrine.[4] The three denials of discretionary review at issue "'(1) conclusively determine the disputed question, (2) resolve an important issue completely separate from the merits of the action, and (3) [are] effectively unreviewable on appeal from a final judgment,'" *Henry v. Lake Charles Am. Press, L.L.C.*, 566 F.3d 164, 171 (5th Cir. 2009) (quoting *Coopers & Lybrand v. Livesay*, 437 U.S. 463, 468 (1978)); *see also Montez v. Hickenlooper*, 640 F.3d 1126, 1129, 1132–33 (10th Cir. 2011) (finding appellate jurisdiction over a district court's collateral order affirming a special master's denial of an individual claim under a consent-decree dispute-resolution mechanism). The district court's refusal to review these three awards purported to conclusively determine the amount each nonprofit was to recover under the Agreement. The Nonprofit-Revenue Interpretation is "completely separate from the merits of BP's liability for the oil spill," *Deepwater Horizon I*, 732 F.3d at 332 n.3, 1 Adm. R. at 289 n.3. And the order would be effectively unreviewable if BP had to wait until the settlement of the entire class action, when awards "will have been distributed to potentially thousands of claimants and BP will have no practical way of recovering these funds should it prevail." *Id.*, 1 Adm. R. at 289 n.3. [—8—]

---

[4] Class Counsel and the Sealed Claimants argue that BP has waived its right to appeal individual awards under the terms of the Agreement. In the Final Rules appeal, we disagreed and held that BP had not waived its right to appeal individual awards. *See In re Deepwater Horizon*, No. 13-30843, 3 Adm. R. 341 (5th Cir. 2015).

A. Timeliness

We now turn to Appellees' arguments that these appeals are untimely under Federal Rule of Appellate Procedure 4. Rule 4(a)(1)(A) requires the notice of appeal to be filed "with the district clerk within 30 days after entry of the judgment or order appealed from." Timely notice of appeal is a mandatory prerequisite for this Court's appellate jurisdiction. *Resident Council of Allen Parkway Vill. v. U.S. HUD*, 980 F.3d 1043, 1048 (5th Cir. 1993).

Appellees present two timeliness arguments. First they argue that by failing timely to appeal the December 12, 2012 order affirming the Nonprofit-Revenue Interpretation, BP has effectively waived its general argument that the Interpretation violates the Agreement—as opposed to its specific challenges to the individual awards to the Sealed Claimants. In the alternative, they argue that the appeals of the district court's denials of discretionary review are untimely because Rule 4's thirty-day period should run from the time the order was sent to the parties, not from the time it was entered into the docket by BP.

1. The December 12 Order

Appellees argue that the Court lacks jurisdiction over this appeal because BP did not appeal the district court's December 12 order affirming the Nonprofit-Revenue Interpretation within thirty days of its docketing. They contend that BP is effectively appealing the December 12 order because it is challenging the Nonprofit-Revenue Interpretation. When the Interpretation was released, BP challenged it in the district court; the district court upheld the Interpretation in the December 12 order emailed to the parties. BP never filed a direct appeal of the order, instead waiting to appeal the specific awards to the three Sealed Claimants. By failing to appeal this determination, [—9—] Appellees contend, BP has waived any argument that the Nonprofit-Revenue Interpretation is incorrect.

In support of this argument, Appellees cite our decision in *Medical Center Pharmacy v.*

Holder, 634 F.3d 830 (5th Cir. 2011). In that case, a group of pharmacies sued for declaratory and injunctive relief from certain FDA regulations. *Id.* at 832. After the district court granted summary judgment to the plaintiffs, the FDA appealed, and we reversed. *Id.* at 832–33. On remand, the FDA presented an argument that it did not raise in its summary-judgment appeal and the district court entered judgment for the FDA. *Id.* at 834. On appeal, we held that the FDA had waived its argument by failing to raise it in the first appeal. *Id.* at 834–36.

Here, BP did not waive its challenge of the awards to the Sealed Claimants by failing to appeal the December 12 order. It is well established that parties are not required to appeal interlocutory orders. *See In re Chicken Antitrust Litig. Am. Poultry*, 669 F.2d 228, 236 (5th Cir. 1982) ("Making interlocutory appeals mandatory . . . would turn the policy against piecemeal appeals on its head."); *Caradelis v. Reinferia Panama, S.A.*, 384 F.2d 589, 591 n.1 (5th Cir. 1967) ("[Appellant] lost no rights by failing to take such an [interlocutory] appeal."). Appellees' reliance on *Medical Center Pharmacy* is misplaced; in that case, the party failed to raise an argument in its first appeal from a *final* judgment. 643 F.3d at 835–36. The December 12 order affirming the Nonprofit-Revenue Interpretation was not a final judgment. *See Deepwater Horizon I*, 732 F.3d at 332 n.3, 1 Adm. R. at 289 n.3. Thus, BP did not forfeit its right to appeal the nonprofit awards to the Sealed Claimants by failing to first appeal the December 12 order. *See Matherne v. Wilson*, 851 F.2d 752, 756 n.9 (5th Cir. 1988) ("[O]n principle, the interlocutory appeal is permissive, not mandatory, [—10—] and a party does not forfeit a right to appeal after judgment for failure to appeal interlocutorily." (citing 9 *Moore's Federal Practice* ¶ 110.8 (1986))).

2. The Denials of Review

Next we turn to Appellees' alternative argument that this appeal is untimely because BP did not appeal the awards to the Sealed Claimants within thirty days of the district court's denials of BP's motions for discretionary review. Pursuant to the district court's May 20 order, denials of discretionary review were not docketed. Rather, notice was given to the parties and decisions were posted on the CSSP website. The district court denied BP's motion for discretionary review in each case on September 4, 2013. On December 16, 2013, 100 days later, BP filed its notices of appeal with the denials of review attached.

Appellees assert that Rule 4's thirty-day limit should run from the day that the parties received notice of the denials of BP's motions for discretionary review via the CSSP website. Otherwise, Class Counsel argues, BP can "create federal appellate rights by docketing non-litigation material whenever it pleases." BP responds that these appeals are timely because they were filed the same day that the district court's orders were *entered* into the docket. *See* Fed. R. App. P. 4 ("[T]he notice of appeal must be 30 days after *entry* of the . . . order appealed from." (emphasis added)). BP challenges Appellees' equitable argument because the delay was caused by the May 20 order, which denied BP's request to have such decisions entered into the docket, rather than by any bad faith on BP's part.

We agree with BP. Rule 4's plain language makes clear that the thirty days run from the entry of the order. Rule 4(a)(7) explains that an order is "entered" when "the judgment or order is entered in the civil docket." Appellees' [—11—] equitable arguments are also unavailing; it was the district court's order, and not BP's conduct, that disadvantaged the parties, because undocketed orders are unappealable. *See In re Am. Precision Vibrator Co.*, 863 F.3d 428, 429 (5th Cir. 1989).[5] Thus, we hold that BP's appeals are timely, we have jurisdiction, and therefore proceed to the merits of the appeals.

---

[5] Pursuant to our opinion in the Final Rules appeal, the district court will now have to docket its decisions on individual awards. *See In re Deepwater Horizon*, No. 13-30843, 3 Adm. R. 341 (5th Cir. 2015). Therefore, BP will no longer be able to start the thirty-day clock whenever it chooses to file its notice of appeal. We reiterate here that we do not endorse BP's approach in future cases.

IV. DISCUSSION

The interpretation of a settlement agreement is a question of contract law that this Court reviews de novo. *Deepwater Horizon III*, 744 F.3d at 374, 2 Adm. R. at 184 (citing *Waterfowl L.L.C. v. United States*, 473 F.3d 135, 141 (5th Cir. 2006)). The Agreement gives the district court discretion to decide whether it will review an award at all. Thus, the district court's denials of review are reviewed for abuse of discretion. *See Wilton v. Seven Falls Co.*, 515 U.S. 277, 289–90 (1995) (applying an abuse-of-discretion standard to a district court's decision to entertain a declaratory-judgment action). However, the standard of review is effectively de novo because the district court was presented with purely legal questions of contract interpretation. *See United States v. Delgado–Nuñez*, 295 F.3d 494, 496 (5th Cir. 2002) ("[A]buse of discretion review of purely legal questions . . . is effectively *de novo* because '[a] district court by definition abuses its discretion when it makes an error of law.'" (second alteration in original) (quoting *Koon v. United States*, 518 U.S. 81, 100 (1996))). [—12—]

A. Plain-Language Challenges to the Nonprofit-Revenue Interpretation

This appeal concerns the Claims Administrator's interpretation of "revenue" as it is used in the BEL framework of the Agreement. BP first challenges the Nonprofit-Revenue Interpretation as inconsistent with the terms of the Agreement. Under general maritime law,[6] a court interprets, "to the extent possible, all the terms in a contract without rendering any of them meaningless or superfluous." *Chembulk Trading LLC v. Chemex Ltd.*, 393 F.3d 550, 555 (5th Cir. 2004).

1. The Language of Exhibits 4B and 4C

BP's contract-interpretation arguments scrutinize the language of Exhibit 4B, the

---

[6] The Agreement provides that it "shall be interpreted in accordance with General Maritime Law."

causation requirements, and Exhibit 4C, the compensation framework.

a. "Business revenue"

BP argues that "revenue" cannot mean donations and grants. To support its argument, BP first points toward Exhibit 4B, the causation requirements for claimants. A BEL claimant must meet one of the listed criteria to be eligible to recover under the Agreement.[7] The term "business revenue" appears four times in Exhibit 4B. In each instance, the clause "Total business revenue shows the following pattern" introduces a specific revenue pattern that claimants can use to establish causation.

BP argues that grants and donations are not "business revenue." This argument is based on two dictionaries that define "business" as "commercial" [—13—] activity carried on "for profit," *Black's Law Dictionary* 226 (9th ed. 2009), or "as a means of livelihood," *Webster's Third New International Dictionary* 302 (1976). By using the phrase "business revenue," BP contends, "the agreement plainly does not contemplate awards for lost grants and donations to non-profit entities."

This argument is unpersuasive. As the Amici point out, modern nonprofits are commercial entities that seek to generate cash surpluses. *See Girl Scouts of Manitou Council, Inc. v. Girl Scouts of U.S., Inc.*, 646 F.3d 983, 987–88 (7th Cir. 2011) ("The commercial activity of nonprofits has grown substantially in recent decades, fueled by an increasing focus on revenue maximizing . . . . The principal difference between [for-profit and nonprofit] firm[s] is . . . that a nonprofit enterprise is forbidden to distribute any surplus of revenues over expenses as dividends . . . ."). "Business," as it is used to modify "revenue" in the causation requirements, could just as easily include, "[b]y extension, transactions or matters of a noncommercial nature." *Black's Law Dictionary, supra; see also The American*

Heritage Dictionary 259 (3d ed. 1996) (defining business as, *inter alia*, "a specific occupation or pursuit").

As Appellees note, BP's interpretation conflicts with the Agreement's explicit inclusion of nonprofits as entities that may recover. For if they may recover, then they must be able to calculate their loss by taking into account their primary sources of income. In a footnote, BP argues those nonprofits that "engage in business activities involving commercial transactions," such as a museum operating a gift shop, could use those commercial revenues to meet the BEL causation criteria. But if a museum's gift-shop receipts are "business revenue" but its donations are not, as BP suggests, the museum must be categorized as an entity engaged in commercial activity "for profit" in its gift [—14—] shop operation, but not in its operation of the museum generally. This hair-splitting is not a sensible construction of the Agreement.

In light of the revenue-generating nature of modern nonprofits and the express inclusion of nonprofits as entities eligible for recovery under the BEL framework, we cannot extrapolate from the use of the word "business" an intent to limit "revenue" to funds obtained only through commercial, profit-seeking activity.

b. "Profit" and "Earn"

Next, BP argues that its interpretation of "revenue" is supported by language in Exhibit 4C, the compensation framework for BEL claimants. Exhibit 4C provides:

> Step 1 – The compensation framework for business claimants compares the actual *profit of the business* during a defined post-spill period in 2010 to the profit that the claimant might have expected *to earn* in the comparable post-spill period of 2010. . . . Step 1 compensation reflects the reduction in Variable Profit (which reflects the claimant's *revenue* less its variable costs) over this period.

---

[7] Not *all* claimants must meet one of the causation criteria; Exhibit 4B first lists groups of claimants that are exempt.

(emphasis added). BP argues that "revenue," used here to calculate the "Variable Profit," cannot include grants and donations because they do not relate to the "profit of a business." This is because profits are, according to *Black's*, "[t]he excess of revenues over expenditures in a *business transaction*," and, BP asserts, contributions are "plainly not the result of business transactions."

BP further challenges the Nonprofit-Revenue Interpretation because Exhibit 4C aims to allow recovery of "profit the claimant might have expected *to earn*." Again quoting *Black's*, BP argues that contributions and grants are [—15—] not earned because they are not "acquire[d] by labor, service, or performance," *Black's Law Dictionary* 584 (9th ed. 2009).

BP's profit argument relies on the assumption that nonprofits are not "businesses" in the "commercial, for-profit" sense. Yet BP offers no support for its assertion that gratuitous contributions and grants are not the result of business transactions. *Black's*, from which BP borrows its definition of "profit" and "earn," defines "business transaction" as "[a]n action that affects the actor's financial or economic interests, including the making of a contract." *Black's Law Dictionary* 241 (10th ed. 2014). When a nonprofit obtains a grant, fundraises, or accepts donations, its actions affect its financial and economic interests.

BP oversimplifies the work of nonprofits when it claims that they do not earn their revenue. Appellees and the Amici explain that nonprofits have to work to get contributions and improve their bottom line in order to keep their doors open.[8] Thus, the fact that Exhibit 4C seeks to compensate for "profit[s] the claimant[s] might have expected to earn," does not conflict with the Nonprofit-Revenue Interpretation.

---

[8] As one Amicus observes, "[w]ith more than $1 billion in revenue from grants and donations in the Louisiana health and human service not-for-profit sector alone, it comes as no surprise that not-for-profit corporations strive year after year to improve their services and programming to attract donors."

c. "Sales"

Next, BP contends that the Nonprofit-Revenue Interpretation renders Exhibit 4C's use of the word "sales" meaningless. Exhibit 4C provides:

Step 2 – Compensates claimants for incremental profits or losses the claimant might have been expected to generate in the absence of the spill *relative to sales* from the Benchmark Period. This calculation reflects a Claimant-Specific Factor that captures [—16—] growth or decline in the pre-spill months of 2010 compared to the comparable months of the Benchmark Period and General Adjustment Factor.

(emphasis added). The Claimant-Specific Factor (CSF) is calculated using the claimant's "total revenue" from certain pre- and post-spill time periods. Because revenue is a variable in the CSF calculation and the CSF is used to compensate for expected profits or losses "relative to *sales*," BP argues that donations and grants cannot be included as revenue.

But if the term "sales" were given the meaning that BP advocates, then for-profit service entities would be barred from claiming payments for services as revenue as well. For example, an attorney's fees are not "sales," yet an attorney could presumably include them as revenue in a BEL claim. Thus, BP's "sales" argument not only excludes grants and donations, it also excludes payments that are well within the meaning of the contract. *See Chembulk Trading LLC*, 393 F.3d at 555 ("A basic principle of contract interpretation . . . is to interpret, *to the extent possible*, all the terms in a contract without rendering any of them meaningless or superfluous." (emphasis added)).

BP's arguments regarding the use of the terms "business revenue," "profit of a business," and "earn" are unpersuasive. Although the use of the term "sales" is difficult to reconcile with the Nonprofit-Revenue Interpretation, the weight BP gives to the term also causes problems for revenue that all parties would agree should be included. Thus, considering the terms of the contract as a whole, notably the explicit inclusion of nonprofits in the list of entities that may recover under the BEL framework, we find that the [—17—] Nonprofit-Revenue Interpretation does not conflict with the language of Exhibits 4B and 4C.[9]

2. *The Language of Class Definition*

Finally, BP argues that the Nonprofit-Revenue Interpretation "produces awards to claimants that are not class members." BP highlights the summary description of the Economic Damage Category in § 1.3.1.2 of the Agreement: "Loss of income, earnings or profits suffered by Natural Persons or Entities as a result of the DEEPWATER HORIZON INCIDENT, subject to certain Exclusions."

BP argues that entities whose losses are based on "lost grants, donations, and similar receipts—as distinguished from lost profits from commercial transactions—are not encompassed" within this category. First, BP cites to the "Facts and Proceedings" section of *Deepwater Horizon I*, in which we explained that claimants in this category "must have conducted commercial activities in the Gulf Coast region during the relevant period." 732 F.3d at 329–30, 1 Adm. R. at 287. From this BP concludes that nonprofits whose damages are based "solely on gratuitous grants and other unearned awards" cannot join the class because they do not engage in commercial activities.

This argument is unavailing. BP attempts to use our mention of "commercial activities" in the facts section of a case that did not

address the nonprofit issue to contradict the Claims Administrator's determination. But [—18—] even if our language could be read as a binding summation of the Agreement's terms, BP has failed to show that nonprofits that operate on donation and grant funding are not engaged in commercial activity. *See supra* Part IV(A)(1)(a). Ultimately, BP fails to show that the Nonprofit-Revenue Interpretation violates the language of the Agreement.

B. Article III and Rule 23 Challenges to the Nonprofit-Revenue Interpretation

We now turn to BP's Rule 23 and Article III challenges. BP argues that many of the Article III and Rule 23 issues raised in *Deepwater Horizon II* are "reanimated" because the Nonprofit-Revenue Interpretation "'abandons' a fundamental premise of the agreement and class definition." BP does not seek decertification of the class on these grounds; rather BP argues that the Interpretation renders the Agreement illegal and, therefore, cannot be accepted. *See Walsh v. Schlecht*, 429 U.S. 401, 408 (1977) ("[A]mbiguously worded contracts should not be interpreted to render them illegal and unenforceable where the wording lends itself to a logically acceptable construction that renders them legal and enforceable."). We disagree and hold that the Nonprofit-Revenue Interpretation does not place the Agreement in violation of Rule 23 or Article III because the Interpretation does not alter our analysis in *Deepwater Horizon II*.

1. *Rule 23*

In *Deepwater Horizon II*, BP challenged class certification on numerous Rule 23 grounds following the district court's affirmance of a different Claims Administrator determination. 739 F.3d at 796, 2 Adm. R. at 141. The Claims Administrator determined the Agreement does not require claimants to provide proof of causation provided they meet one of the causation criteria enumerated in Exhibit 4B. *Id.* at 797–98, 2 Adm. R. at 141-43. There, BP argued that this determination put the [—19—] class certification in violation of numerous provisions of Rule 23. *Id.* at 799, 2 Adm. R. at

---

[9] BP also argues that a recent Claims Administrator interpretation barring most for-profit claimants from counting grants as revenue shows that the interpretation being appealed is incorrect. BP asserts that a Claims Administrator interpretation released on April 24, 2014, states that "'grants for 'for-profit' entities' 'shall not typically be treated as 'revenue' for purposes of the various calculations to be performed under the terms of the Agreement with regard to entities asserting [BEL] claims.'" However, this document is not contained in the record or in BP's supplemental record; thus we do not consider it.

143. All of these arguments rested on the "same central premise . . . that a class cannot be certified when it includes persons who have not actually been injured." *Id.* at 808, 2 Adm. R. at 151. Nevertheless, we held that certification was proper. *Id.* at 821, 2 Adm. R. at 162.

a. Adequacy

Rule 23(a)(4) requires that "the representative parties will fairly and adequately protect the interests of the class." "The adequacy inquiry . . . serves to uncover conflicts of interest between named parties and the class they seek to represent.'" *Amchem Prods., Inc. v. Windsor*, 521 U.S. 591, 625 (1997). Class representatives must "'be part of the class and possess the same interest and suffer the same injury as the class members.'" *Id.* (quoting *E. Tex. Motor Freight Sys., Inc. v. Rodriguez*, 431 U.S. 395, 403 (1977)).

BP argues that under the Nonprofit-Revenue Interpretation the class representatives are no longer "adequate." BP characterizes our opinion in *Deepwater Horizon II* as a "recogni[tion] that the district court's adequacy determination was based on its conclusion that the class representatives 'included individuals and businesses asserting each category of loss,'" and asserts "[t]hat is not so if the class includes non-profit entities that incurred no business loss." (quoting *Deepwater Horizon II*, 739 F.3d at 812–13, 2 Adm. R. at 155).

Even if we assume BP is correct that the Nonprofit-Revenue Interpretation allows entities without business loss to enter the class, our reasoning in *Deepwater Horizon II* still governs this appeal. We upheld the district court's adequacy determination, even accepting BP's argument that the class included individuals with no loss at all. 739 F.3d at 802, 2 Adm. R. at 146. We did so because, "in the context of Rule 23 requirements, '[c]lass certification is not precluded simply because a class may include persons who have not been [—20—] injured by the defendant's conduct.'" *Id.* at 813, 2 Adm. R. at 155 (alteration in original) (quoting

Mims v. Stewart Title Guar. Co., 590 F.3d 298, 308 (5th Cir. 2009)). BP has simply resurrected its failed adequacy argument from *Deepwater Horizon II*, and we remain bound by our previous determination that the class satisfies Rule 23(a)(4). *See Jacobs v. Nat'l Drug Intelligence Ctr.*, 548 F.3d 375, 378 (5th Cir. 2008).

b. Commonality and typicality

Next, BP argues that the Nonprofit-Revenue Interpretation violates Rule 23's requirement that there be "questions of law or fact common to the class." Fed. R. Civ. P. 23(a)(2). As was the case in *Deepwater Horizon II*, BP's commonality argument rests entirely on an out-of-context quotation from *Wal-Mart Stores, Inc. v. Dukes*, 131 S. Ct. 2541 (2011), that commonality requires that class members "have suffered the same injury."[10] *Id.* at 2551 (internal quotation marks omitted).

In *Wal-Mart*, the Court stated:

Commonality requires the plaintiff to demonstrate that the class members "have suffered the same injury[.]" This does not mean merely that they have all suffered a violation of the same provision of law. Title VII, for example, can be violated in many ways—by intentional discrimination, or by hiring and promotion criteria that result in disparate impact, and by the use of these practices on the part of many different superiors in a single company. Quite obviously, the mere claim by employees of the same company that they have suffered a Title VII injury, or even a disparate-impact Title VII injury, gives no cause to believe that all their claims can productively be litigated at

---

[10] In *Deepwater Horizon II* we observed: "Based on this single sentence, [BP suggests] that either the diversity of the class members' economic injuries or the inclusion of members who 'have suffered no injury at all' might preclude class certification. When quoted in its entirety, however, the relevant passage . . . demonstrates why both of these arguments are meritless." 739 F.3d at 810, 2 Adm. R. at 152-53.

once. *Their claims must depend upon a [—21—] common contention—for example, the assertion of discriminatory bias on the part of the same supervisor. That common contention, moreover, must be of such a nature that it is capable of classwide resolution—which means that determination of its truth or falsity will resolve an issue that is central to the validity of each one of the claims in one stroke.*

Id. (emphasis added) (citation omitted). In *Deepwater Horizon II*, we held that the "same injury" requirement could "be satisfied by an instance of the defendant's injurious conduct, even when the resulting injurious effects—the damages—are diverse." 739 F.3d at 810–11, 2 Adm. R. at 153. Thus, even assuming the Nonprofit-Revenue Interpretation allows recovery for class members with no business loss, it does not violate Rule 23(a)(2).[11]

c. Predominance

Next BP argues that the Nonprofit-Revenue Interpretation puts the class in violation of Rule 23(b)(3)[12] because the damages calculation now "results in significant awards based on extraordinary one-time grants" and fails to "connect a claimant's damages to the class theory of liability."

We have noted that "[c]lass treatment . . . may not be suitable [under Rule 23(b)(3)] where the calculation of damages is not susceptible to a mathematical or formulaic calculation, or where the formula by which the parties propose to calculate individual damages is clearly inadequate." *Bell Atl. Corp.*

v AT&T Corp., 339 F.3d 294, 307 (5th Cir. 2003); *see also Steering Comm.* [—22—] *v. Exxon Mobil Corp.*, 461 F.3d 598, 602 (5th Cir. 2006) ("[W]here individual damages cannot be determined by reference to a mathematical or formulaic calculation, the damages issue may predominate over any common issues shared by the class.").

Yet, "it is indeed 'possible to satisfy the predominance . . . requirements of Rule 23(b)(3) in a . . . mass accident class action' despite the particular need in such cases for individualized damages calculations." *Deepwater Horizon II*, 739 F.3d at 816, 2 Adm. R. at 157 (quoting *Exxon Mobil Corp.*, 461 F.3d at 603). This is the case "when a district court performs a sufficiently 'rigorous analysis' of the means by which common and individual issues will be divided and tried." *Id.*, 2 Adm. R. at 158 (quoting *Madison v. Chalmette Ref., L.L.C.*, 637 F.3d 551, 556 (5th Cir. 2011)).

BP argues that the Agreement's formula does not meet these standards, and therefore fails the predominance inquiry. First, BP argues that the Nonprofit-Revenue Interpretation results in large awards where "evidence of actual damages is lacking," which proves that the formula is "clearly inadequate," *Bell Atl. Corp*, 339 F.3d at 307. Next, BP argues that the formula fails to "connect a claimant's damages to the class theory of liability," as required by *Comcast Corp. v. Behrend*, 133 S. Ct. 1426, 1433 (2013) ("[A] model purporting to serve as evidence of damages in [a class action based on one theory of liability] must measure only those damages attributable to that theory.").

However, as we stated in response to BP's similar arguments in *Deepwater Horizon II*, these standards do not apply here, where the district court "did not list the calculation of the claimant's damages either in its list of common questions of fact or in its list of common questions of law." 739 F.3d at 816, 2 Adm. R. at 158 (footnotes and internal quotation marks omitted). *Comcast* "has no impact [—23—] on cases such as the present one, in which predominance was not based on common issues of damages but on numerous

---

[11] Based on its commonality argument, BP also contends that the class fails to meet Rule 23(a)(3)'s typicality requirement "since '[t]he commonality and typicality requirements of Rule 23(a) tend to merge.'" (quoting *Gen. Tel. Co. of Sw. v. Falcon*, 457 U.S. 14, 157 n.13 (1986)). This too is a failed argument resurrected from *Deepwater Horizon II*, and we again reject it. *See* 739 F.3d at 812 n.92, 2 Adm. R. at 154 n.92.

[12] This Rule requires that "the court find[] that the questions of law or fact common to class members predominate over any questions affecting only individual members." Fed R. Civ. P. 23(b)(3).

common issues of liability." *Id.* at 815, 2 Adm. R. at 157. We affirmed the district court's predominance determination because it was based on common issues apart from the calculation of damages. *See id.* at 816, 2 Adm. R. at 158 ("But even without a common means of measuring damages, in the district court's view, these common issues nonetheless predominated over the issues unique to individual claimants.").

Moreover, in *Deepwater Horizon II* we explicitly rejected the argument that the choice of "a formula for making voluntary payments under a settlement agreement could threaten the predominance of common questions over individual questions in litigation." *Id.* at 818, 2 Adm. R. at 160. Thus, even assuming BP's assertion that the Nonprofit-Revenue Interpretation "awards damages with no connection to many class members' causes of action," we remain bound by our earlier predominance determination under our rule of orderliness. *See Jacobs*, 548 F.3d at 378.

d. Fairness

Next, BP contends that the Nonprofit-Revenue Interpretation violates Rule 23(e)'s fairness requirement. This rule is meant to protect the nonparty class members. *Deepwater Horizon II*, 739 F.3d at 820, 2 Adm. R. at 161. BP argues that the Nonprofit-Revenue Interpretation permits entities with no colorable claim to recover, which results in claims that are not a "fair approximation" of their entitlement to relief, *Reed v. Gen. Motors Corp.*, 703 F.2d 170, 175 (5th Cir. 1983). However, we rejected a nearly identical argument in *Deepwater Horizon II*:

BP's argument ignores the six *Reed* factors altogether. Rather, BP relies on a short quotation from *Reed* to suggest that district courts should also ensure that settlement agreements are based on a "fair [—24—] approximation of [class members'] relative entitlement." . . . No other decision by our court or by any district court has every cited *Reed* for such a proposition. Nor can any of the six *Reed* factors be easily related to

the "fair approximation" analysis that BP proposes.

739 F.3d at 820, 2 Adm. R. at 161 (alteration in original). Nothing in the Nonprofit-Revenue Interpretation or BP's briefs changes our analysis now.

e. Ascertainability

Lastly, BP argues that the Nonprofit-Revenue Interpretation violates Rule 23's ascertainability requirement. To satisfy this requirement, "'the class sought to be represented must be adequately defined and clearly ascertainable.'" *Deepwater Horizon II*, 739 F.3d at 821, 2 Adm. R. at 162 (quoting *Union Asset Mgmt. Holding A.G. v. Dell, Inc.*, 669 F.3d 632, 639 (5th Cir. 2012)). BP contends that the Nonprofit-Revenue Interpretation "eliminates any rational demarcation between legitimate and illegitimate claimants" by permitting recovery to individuals without "*Business* Economic Loss."

In *Deepwater Horizon II*, we rejected BP's nearly identical argument that the Claims Administrator's "two Policy Announcements render[ed] the class definition irrational and therefore violate[d] the ascertainability requirement." 739 F.3d at 821, 2 Adm. R. at 162. This conclusion was based on our prior decision that "'the possibility that some [claimants] may fail to prevail on their individual claims will not defeat class membership' on the basis of the ascertainability requirement." *Id.*, 2 Adm. R. at 162 (alteration in original) (quoting *In re Rodriguez*, 695 F.3d 360, 370 (5th Cir. 2012)). Even assuming, as BP does, that the Interpretation permits recovery for individuals with no "business loss," we remain bound by our ascertainability determination from *Deepwater Horizon II*. *See Jacobs*, 548 F.3d at 378. [—25—]

2. Article III Standing

BP argues that the Claims Administrator, by interpreting "revenue" to include grants and contributions to nonprofit entities, has altered the class definition to include entities with "no colorable claim of injury." This violates Article III, BP argues, because the class now includes "a great many persons who have suffered no injury at the hands of [BP]," *Kohen v. Pac. Inv. Mgmt. Co.*, 571 F.3d 672, 677 (7th Cir. 2009).

Pursuant to Article III, a plaintiff must "allege (1) an injury that is (2) 'fairly traceable to the defendant's allegedly unlawful conduct' and that is (3) 'likely to be redressed by the requested relief.'" *Lujan v. Defenders of Wildlife*, 504 U.S. 555, 590 (1992) (Blackmun, J., dissenting) (quoting *Allen v. Wright*, 468 U.S. 737, 751 (1984)). "As *Lujan* emphasized, however the standard used to establish these three elements is not constant, but becomes gradually stricter as the parties proceed through 'the successive stages of the litigation.'" *Deepwater Horizon II*, 739 F.3d at 799, 2 Adm. R. at 144. We have not directly addressed how "to evaluate standing for the purposes of class certification and settlement approval under Rule 23," but other courts have taken two distinct approaches. *Id.* at 800, 2 Adm. R. at 144.[13]

Under the first approach, courts look at the *class definition* to "ensure that absent class members possess Article III standing." *Id.* at 801, 2 Adm. R. at 145. The Second Circuit has presented the most common formulation of this standard: "We do not require that each member of a class submit evidence of personal standing. [—26—] At the same time, no class may be certified that contains members lacking Article III standing. The class must therefore be defined in such a way that anyone within it would have standing." *Denney v. Deutsche Bank AG*, 443 F.3d 253, 263–64 (2d Cir. 2006) (citations omitted). This standard "does not require that each member of a class submit evidence of personal standing, so long as every class member

contemplated by the class definition can *allege* standing." *Deepwater Horizon II*, 739 F.3d at 804, 2 Adm. R. at 148 (internal quotation marks omitted).

Under the second, more permissive standard, courts look to whether the *named plaintiffs* or *class representatives* have standing, "ignor[ing] the absent class members entirely." *Id.* at 800, 2 Adm. R. at 144 (citing *Lewis v. Casey*, 518 U.S. 343, 395–96 (1996) (Souter, J., concurring in part, dissenting in part, and concurring in the judgment)). In *Kohen v. Pacific Investment Management Co.*, 571 F.3d 672 (7th Cir. 2009), the Seventh Circuit took this approach, reasoning that, although it "is true . . . that a class will often include persons who have not been injured by the defendant's conduct," such an "inevitability does not preclude class certification." *Id.* at 677. This is because at the class-certification stage, "many of the members of the class may be unknown, or if they are known still the facts bearing on their claims may be unknown." *Id.*

In *Deepwater Horizon II* we did not adopt either test because we found that the Agreement satisfied both. *See* 739 F.3d at 798–802, 2 Adm. R. at 142-46. Applying the *Denney* test, we noted that the class definition limited the Economic Damage Category to claims based on "'[l]oss of income, earnings or profits suffered . . . *as a result of* the DEEPWATER HORIZON INCIDENT.'" *Id.* at 803, 2 Adm. R. at 147 (alteration in original). Even looking beyond this definition paragraph to the entire Amended Complaint, we reasoned, "the result would be no different" because the complaint "include[d] numerous allegations of injuries to the absent class [—27—] members." *Id.*, 2 Adm. R. at 147. Thus "every class member contemplated by the class definition 'can *allege* standing.'" *Id.* at 804, 2 Adm. R. at 148 (quoting *Deepwater Horizon I*, 732 F.3d at 340–42, 1 Adm. R. at 296-98). Additionally, we found class standing under the more permissive *Kohen* test, which focuses on the standing of the named plaintiffs. *Id.* at 803, 2 Adm. R. at 146-47. This was because "each one of the[] named plaintiffs . . . identified an injury in fact that is

---

[13] Although BP is not seeking decertification of the class in this appeal, it argues that implementing the Nonprofit-Revenue Interpretation results in a class that could not have been certified. Thus, we analyze this issue pursuant to the Rule 23-stage Article III standards utilized in *Deepwater Horizon II*, where class certification was at issue. *See* 739 F.3d at 799–801, 2 Adm. R. at 143-45.

traceable to the oil spill." *Id.* at 803, 2 Adm. R. at 147.

BP argues that the class now fails both of these tests because "the class definition has been altered to include numerous entities that have no colorable claim of loss." Under the *Denney* test, BP contends, the class is no longer "defined in such a way that anyone within it would have standing," *Denney*, 443 F.3d at 264. Next BP argues that "even under the [*Kohen*] standard, 'a class should not be certified if it . . . contains a *great many persons* who have suffered no injury at the hands of the defendant," and the class now contains "an entire set of entities whose claims are based only on gratuitous contributions and that have no colorable claim of injury."

However, BP does not explain how the Nonprofit-Revenue Interpretation allows entities to recover for injuries that were not *caused* by BP's conduct. BP merely states that the Claims Administrator "has issued awards to nonprofit entities based on receipts that cannot qualify as 'revenue,' and thus awards are being issued to entities that have no colorable claim of injury." But whether contributions should qualify as "revenue" under the Agreement is irrelevant to the causal connection between BP's conduct and decreases in contributions to nonprofits. Moreover, Amici for Appellees cite to numerous sources showing how nonprofits are often harmed by calamities because "first, those affected by the calamity tend to slow their giving . . . and, second, donors shift their giving to those impacted directly by the disaster." [—28—]

We hold that the Nonprofit-Revenue Interpretation does not alter the class definition in violation of Article III. In *Deepwater Horizon II*, this Court found that the Agreement satisfied standing requirements for class certification. Here, BP has failed to show how treating contributions and donations as revenue results in a class of individuals with no colorable claim of injury.

C. Challenges to the Individual Awards

In each of the consolidated cases, BP argues that even if the Nonprofit-Revenue Interpretation is permissible, the individual award given to each Sealed Claimant violates the language of the Claims Administrator's own interpretation of the Agreement. We address each award in turn.

1. Cy Pres *Award, No. 13-31296*

The *Cy Pres* Claimant received $331,395 in *cy pres* funds from a class action settlement. This "extraordinary" award, according to the organization's director, was the largest single donation in the organization's history. BP argues that treating this windfall as "revenue" violates the Nonprofit-Revenue Interpretation, which states that "grant monies or contributions shall *typically* be treated as revenue," because this was a "one-time, extraordinary award." To hold otherwise, BP argues, would "read the word 'typically' out of the Non-Profit Policy."

The *Cy Pres* Claimant responds that it would characterize every donation it receives as a "'one-time, extraordinary payment' because there is no guaranty that any donation will be made or that any other donation will follow." BP's position, the Claimant argues, means that any unusually sized donation should be excluded from "revenue." This "makes little sense as a matter of practical reality. Non-profit entities receive many donations that are [—29—] one-time donor payments" resembling this *cy pres* donation. Finally, the Claimant notes the increasing frequency with which courts distribute *cy pres* awards in class action lawsuits to argue that this is not a "novel" source of revenue for nonprofit corporations. *See* Martin H. Redish et al., *Cy Pres Relief and the Pathologies of the Modern Class Action: A Normative and Empirical Analysis*, 62 Fla. L. Rev. 617, 653 (2010) ("[T]he use of class action cy pres awards by federal courts has increased since the 1980s and has accelerated sharply after 2000.").

We see no reason why "revenue" should be read to exclude donations simply because they were given by a court rather than a donor. The Nonprofit-Revenue Interpretation does not say that "typical donations" count as revenue; rather it says that "grant monies or contributions shall typically" count as revenue. "Typically" is not rendered meaningless by the inclusion of *cy pres* donations.

Moreover, denying this award because of its size would open the floodgates to a flurry of challenges to nonprofit awards, undermining the aims of the CSSP. As the Appeals Panel noted in reviewing this award, the CSSP calculations look at revenue on a business level, not on a customer or donor level. Reading limitations into the meaning of "revenue" based on the identity of the donor runs contrary to this agreed-upon framework. Thus, we find no abuse of discretion in the denial of review of the award to the *Cy Pres* Claimant.

2. Trust Grant, No. 13-31299

BP makes a similar argument regarding the Grant Claimant's award, which was based on its receipt of a "Trust Grant." BP argues that the inclusion of this "one-time, extraordinary receipt of grant money" distorted the Claimant's CSF and bestowed a windfall on this Claimant. [—30—]

The CSF is used in "Step 2" of the compensation framework to "compensate[] claimants for incremental profits or losses the claimant might have been expected to generate in the absence of the spill relative to sales from the Benchmark Period." The CSF aims to "capture the impact of pre-[spill] trends in the claimant's revenue performance that might have been expected in the post-[spill] Benchmark Period." Essentially, the CSF is a revenue growth rate metric used to ensure that a business that was growing leading up to the spill will be adequately compensated. It is calculated by "comparing revenue received in the four months leading up to the spill to revenue received in those same four months in the Benchmark Period." Thus, treating the Trust Grant as "revenue" increased the Grant Claimant's CSF, and therefore its award.

BP argues that this improperly inflated the CSF because grants normally did not make up a large portion of the Grant Claimant's revenue, yet this grant was "30% of Claimant's 2010 gross receipts *by itself.*" BP argues that because the grant was "atypical," it must be excluded to ensure that, in the language of Exhibit 4C, a claimant is compensated only "for incremental profits the claimant *might have been expected to generate*" in the post-spill period.[14]

In response, the Grant Claimant argues that BP is, "once again, trying to erect a causation test on appeal that does not exist in the Settlement Agreement and has already been resolved by this Court." The Claimant contends that BP seeks to require each claimant, nonprofit or otherwise, to show that revenues from certain sources would have continued to come in [—31—] absent the spill, thus "jettison[ing] the Settlement Agreements' Compensation Frameworks for an ad-hoc system."

We agree with the Claimant. By seeking to exclude revenue because it is "atypical," BP attempts to circumvent the causation requirements and compensation framework in the Agreement. BP now asks individual claimants to show that any revenue from the pre-spill period was of the type that they could have expected to continue earning after the spill. But that amounts to requiring that Claimants prove that their lost revenue was caused by the spill, which is precisely what we refused to require in *Deepwater Horizon II*. *See* 739 F.3d at 797, 821, 2 Adm. R. at 142, 162 (affirming the district court's approval of the Claims Administrator's statement that "the Settlement Agreement does not contemplate that the Claims Administrator will undertake additional analysis of causation issues beyond those criteria that are specifically set out in [Exhibit 4B]").

---

[14] BP also contends, as against the *cy pres* award, that this award should not be included as revenue because it is not "typical," per the language of the Nonprofit-Revenue Interpretation. This argument is practically identical to that raised against the *Cy Pres* Claimant, and for the reasons discussed in Part IV(C)(1), *supra*, it fails.

The parties agreed on Exhibit 4C's compensation framework to establish what claimants might have expected to earn after the spill. To accept challenges to the types of revenue included in those calculations because the claimants could not have expected to earn similar revenue after the spill defeats the purpose of the compensation framework itself. We therefore find no abuse of discretion in the district court's denial of review of the award to the Grant Claimant.

3. Legal Services, No. 13-31302

Finally, BP challenges the Legal-Services Claimant's award because it included $157,500 in revenue that was based on "legal services performed by [its] legal fellows." The Claimant valued its fellows' work at $150 per hour and multiplied that by the number of hours worked over the year. BP contends this [—32—] award is inconsistent with the plain language of the Agreement, namely the terms "profit," "earn," "financial performance," and "sales." Most of BP's textual arguments track BP's general attack on the Nonprofit-Revenue Interpretation; revenue is used to calculate a claimant's "actual *profit*" so that it can be compared to what the claimant "might have been expected to *earn*" during the post-spill period. *See supra* Part IV(A)(1). BP also points to Exhibit 4C's definition of the "Benchmark Period," which is chosen by a claimant "as the baseline for measuring its historical *financial* performance." Finally, BP argues that "if *voluntary* services are 'revenue,' it is difficult to discern why *compensated* services would also not be revenue."

We are not persuaded. BP argues that donated legal services are not "revenue" because they "do not enter into" the profit calculation. As the Legal-Services Claimant notes, certain donated services "requir[ing] specialized skills," including legal services, are included as revenue on financial statements prepared under Generally Accepted Accounting Principles (GAAP).[15] Moreover,

donated services affect the profit calculation because they free up organizations' cash donations, allowing nonprofits to manage and allocate a greater pool of money. Additionally, these are "earned" within the Agreement for the same reasons discussed in Part IV(A)(1)(b), *supra*; nonprofits have to work to attract skilled professionals to donate their time just as they have to work to obtain cash donations. [—33—]

BP's final argument—that if the donated legal services are revenue there is no reason why paid services would not also be revenue—obfuscates the crucial point that the legal services fall under the Non-Profit Interpretation precisely because they are *donated*. No party has suggested that non-profit organizations should be able to treat the services of paid employees as revenue; by contrast, the Non-Profit Interpretation, which we uphold here today, specifically instructs nonprofits to include donations in their revenue calculations.

Moreover, BP has not provided, and we do not see, any meaningful reason to distinguish this type of donation from other donations received by nonprofits.[16] Donated legal time is as valuable to the Legal-Services Claimant as a cash donation that would be used to pay for those services. And the loss of these in-kind donations would require the Claimant to divert cash from other operations to pay for the services instead. We therefore find no abuse of discretion in the district court's denial of review of the award to the Legal-Services Claimant.

---

[15] *See Stolt-Nielsen S.A. v. AnimalFeeds Int'l Corp.*, 559 U.S. 662, 674 n.6 (2010) ("Under . . . general maritime law, evidence of 'custom and usage' is relevant to determining the parties' intent when an express agreement is ambiguous."); Allan

B. Afterman, *WG&L GAAP Practice Manual* § 74.3.2 (2015) ("Contributions of services received . . . should be recognized *only* if they . . . [r]equire specialized skills, are provided by individuals having those skills, and would otherwise typically need to be purchased[.] Services requiring specialized skills would include those provided by . . . lawyers . . . .").

[16] BP asserts that in contrast to "[a]rms-length commercial sales," "voluntary donations of time have no readily discernible value, and are easily manipulated." Considering that these services are assessed when nonprofits prepare financial statements, we are unpersuaded that this award creates serious problems for the settlement process.

V. CONCLUSION

For the foregoing reasons, we AFFIRM the district court.

United States Court of Appeals
for the Fifth Circuit

No. 13-30843

IN RE DEEPWATER HORIZON

LAKE EUGENIE LAND DEV., INC.
vs.
BP EXPLORATION & PROD., INC.

Appeal from the United States District Court for the
Eastern District of Louisiana

Decided: May 8, 2015

Citation: 785 F.3d 986, 3 Adm. R. 341 (5th Cir. 2015).

Before **BENAVIDES, PRADO,** and **GRAVES,** Circuit
Judges.

[—1—] **BENAVIDES,** Circuit Judge:

This action involves the Economic and Property Damages Settlement Agreement ("Settlement Agreement") approved by the district court on December 21, 2012, between Appellants BP Exploration & Production, Inc., BP [—2—] America Production Company, and BP p.l.c. (collectively, "BP"), and Appellees, the certified Economic and Property Damages Class, in connection with the *Deepwater Horizon* oil spill of April 20, 2010. The Court Supervised Settlement Program ("Settlement Program" or "CSSP") was set up to compensate parties with economic losses caused by the oil spill. This specific dispute arises from the district court's order of May 20, 2013 ("May 20 Order"), approving the Final Rules Governing Discretionary Court Review of Appeal Determinations ("Final Rules") for claims processed through the Settlement Program, which has been challenged by BP.

I. INTRODUCTION

Under the Settlement Agreement, class members may submit claims to the Settlement Program, overseen and managed by a Claims Administrator whose decisions may be reviewed upon request by an Appeal Panel. The Appeal Panel reviews, *inter alia*, briefs from the parties, the Settlement Agreement,

relevant district court rulings, the claim file, the parties' submissions, and the Claims Administrator's decision. *See* Appeal Panel Rule 13 (Feb. 4, 2013) ("Appeal Panel Rules"), *available* *at* http://www.deepwaterhorizoneconomicsettlem ent.com/docs/Rules_Governing_the_Appeals_P rocess_-_Final.pdf. The materials presented to the Claims Administrator and Appeal Panel are not posted to the district court's civil docket but rather to a non-public Settlement Program website known as the DWH Portal. *See, e.g.,* Appeal Panel Rules 10(b), 11(b), 15, 17, 18, 23. Redacted versions of Appeal Panel decisions are made available to the public through the Settlement Program website. Appeal Panel Rule 24. Appeals in which the [—3—] compensation amount is at issue go through a baseball arbitration process,[1] and the Appeal Panel decision is considered "final." Agreement § 6.2.

The Settlement Agreement confers "continuing and exclusive jurisdiction over the Parties and their Counsel for the purpose of enforcing, implementing and interpreting" the Agreement on "the Court." Agreement § 18.1. The Agreement defines "Court" as "the United States District Court for the Eastern District of Louisiana, Judge Carl Barbier, presiding." Agreement § 38.40. The Settlement Agreement provides that "[t]he Court maintains the discretionary right to review any Appeal determination to consider whether the determination was in compliance with the Agreement. Upon reviewing such a determination, the Court shall treat the Appeal determination as if it were a recommendation by a Magistrate Judge." Agreement § 6.6.

Section 6 of the Settlement Agreement governs the claims appeal process. It leaves

---

[1] Under the baseball process, "the Claimant and the BP Parties exchange and submit in writing to the Appeal Panelist or Appeal Panel their respective proposals . . . for the base Compensation Amount they propose the Claimant should receive" and if the parties do not reach an agreement, "the Appeal Panelist or Appeal Panel must choose to award the Claimant either the Final Proposal by the Claimant or the Final Proposal by the BP Parties but no other amount." Agreement § 6.2.

room for the Settlement Program to "establish additional procedures for the Appeal Process not inconsistent with Exhibit 25." Agreement § 6.3. Exhibit 25, in turn, sets out procedures for filing and briefing appeals. Exhibit 25 allows the Appeals Coordinator, with the concurrence of the Claims Administrator, to "amend and/or adopt procedures as necessary to implement Section 6 of the Agreement after providing notice and a right to comment by the BP Parties and Lead Class Counsel." Agreement, Exhibit 25.

On April 29, 2013, the Claims Administrator released Draft Rules governing the district court's review of Appeal Panel decisions, and BP responded with comments objecting to the Draft Rules' limits on appellate [—4—] review by the Court of Appeals and the lack of provisions requiring documents and orders to be filed on the civil docket—similar arguments to the ones made in this appeal. Class Counsel also submitted comments.

The Final Rules that were adopted by the district court through its May 20 Order are at issue before us. BP challenges the Final Rules for not providing for the docketing of requests for district court review or district court orders regarding such requests, which, it argues, compromises a right to appeal from the district court to this court and violates Federal Rule of Civil Procedure ("FRCP") 79's provisions regarding the clerk's maintenance of the civil docket. Final Rule 12 states, "The Settlement Agreement provides no right of automatic appeal to the Court. Whether the determination of an Appeal Panel will be reviewed by the Court lies solely within the Court's discretion. Review of an Appeal Panel determination will be granted only in exceptional circumstances." Several provisions of the Final Rules implicate the question of whether there is a right to appeal claim determinations from the district court to this court under the Settlement Agreement. The Final Rules provide that requests for judicial review and related documents be posted to the DWH Portal rather than on the civil docket, and that the Appeals Coordinator be responsible for sending materials to and from the district court. *See* Final Rules 7, 8, 19, 21-

22. BP also challenges the Final Rules for preventing it from seeking judicial review of certain categories of awards. Final Rule 16, which was not in the Draft Rules, provides that for certain cases,[2] "no Request or Objection may be submitted and the processing of claims will not be suspended in such cases unless there is a further order of the Court." Under Final Rule 19, the Appeals Coordinator is not to submit any requests or objections for [—5—] these cases to the district court. District court decisions are posted to the DWH Portal and in redacted form on the Settlement Program's website. Final Rule 27.

To challenge the Final Rules, on June 17, 2013, BP filed a motion under FRCP 59(e) to amend the May 20 Order and the Final Rules. BP requested the court to amend the Rules to clarify (1) "that all requests for discretionary review, objections thereto, and Court orders regarding such requests will be entered into the appropriate Court docket"; (2)

> that a party may file a request for discretionary review on issues previously ruled on by the Court, that such requests must contain a clear notation that they are governed by [Final] Rule 16, that such requests will be filed in the appropriate Court docket, and that the clerk will promptly enter an order denying such requests[;]

and (3) "that a party filing a Request for Discretionary Review may append exhibits and attachments containing record evidence to requests for discretionary review."[3] The district court denied BP's motion on July 16, 2013, without elaboration, and BP then filed a Notice of Appeal on August 2, 2013, under Federal Rule of Appellate Procedure ("FRAP")

---

[2] These cases include those identified as "Contributions/Grant Revenue for Non-Profits issue" (a.k.a. "Non-Profit Policy"), "Alternative Causation issue" (a.k.a. "Alternative Causation Policy"), or "Matching of Revenue and Expenses issue" (a.k.a. "Matching Policy").

[3] According to BP, the Appeals Coordinator told BP via email that the district court would not accept requests that included any exhibits or documents attached.

4(a)(4)(A)(iv). Class Counsel moved to dismiss the appeal. This court carried the motion to dismiss the appeal with the case.

On September 4, 2013, the Appeals Coordinator notified BP that the district court had denied BP's requests for review of three awards to non-profit organizations. In accordance with Final Rules 16 and 19, the district court did not docket the requests for review, the underlying record, or the orders denying review. These denials are the subject of the appeals in Nos. 13-31296, 13- [—6—] 31299, and 13-31302 ("Non-Profit Appeals"). Class Counsel and the Non-Profit Appeals claimants moved to dismiss those appeals. Because jurisdiction over the Non-Profit Appeals hinges on our decision with respect to the Final Rules and the availability of further review by this court of individual claim determinations that have been reviewed or denied review by the district court, we consolidated the three Non-Profit Appeals and directed all four cases to be heard and decided by the same panel. In this specific appeal, we address (1) whether we have jurisdiction over the appeal of the May 20 Order that approved the Final Rules, (2) whether there is a right to appeal claim determinations from the district court to this court under the Settlement Agreement, (3) whether the Final Rules violate any right to appeal under the Settlement Agreement, and (4) whether the district court erred in categorically precluding certain categories of cases from its review through the Final Rules.

II. JURISDICTION OVER THIS APPEAL

As an initial matter, we must determine whether BP's notice of appeal was timely and whether we have jurisdiction over this appeal.

Under FRCP 59(e), a party may request "to alter or amend a judgment." FED. R. CIV. P. 59(e). "Such motions serve the narrow purpose of allowing a party to correct manifest errors of law or fact or to present newly discovered evidence." *Waltman v. Int'l Paper Co.*, 875 F.2d 468, 473 (5th Cir. 1989) (internal quotations omitted). Class Counsel argue that BP's appeal was untimely because it did not file its notice of appeal 30 days after the May

20 Order as required by FRAP 4(a)(1)(A), and because it did not make a proper FRCP 59(e) motion to fall under the exception of FRAP 4(a)(4)(A)(iv). They argue that BP's motion was not properly brought under FRCP 59(e) because it "focused on amending the [Final] Rules themselves, not the district court's order approving them," and because it raised arguments that had already been brought before the Appeals Coordinator. [—7—]

We find that these arguments lack merit. While it is true that BP sought to amend the Final Rules, the district court had incorporated and attached the Final Rules as part of its decision to adopt them in its May 20 Order. Thus, it was proper under FRCP 59(e) for BP to request the court to alter or amend the Final Rules, which BP believed offended its rights and violated the Settlement Agreement. While an FRCP 59(e) motion "is not the proper vehicle for rehashing evidence, legal theories, or arguments that could have been offered or raised before the entry of judgment," *Templet v. HydroChem Inc.*, 367 F.3d 473, 479 (5th Cir. 2004), and BP's motion did bring forth some of the arguments that had been presented to the Appeals Coordinator,[4] the motion was the first opportunity to present arguments regarding the Rules directly to the district court. It was also the first opportunity to address the alleged manifest error of law in Final Rule 16, which was not in the Draft Rules, and the new provision in Final Rule 19, which together preclude certain cases from any further review by the district court. Thus, we conclude that BP's motion to amend was proper.

As noted above, the district court adopted the Final Rules on May 20, 2013, and BP filed its motion to amend on June 17, 2013, which was timely. *See* FED. R. CIV. P. 59(e) ("A motion to alter or amend a judgment must be filed no later than 28 days after the entry of the judgment."). Under FRAP 4(a)(4)(A)(iv),

---

[4] *Compare* ROA.17974-ROA.17975 (comments to Appeals Coordinator about civil docket provisions), *with* ROA.17966 (seeking the district court "to clarify that all requests for discretionary review, objections thereto, and Court orders regarding such requests will be docketed in the appropriate docket of the Court").

the time to file a notice of appeal—within thirty days under FRAP 4(a)(1)(A)—started to run on July 16, 2013, when the district court issued its order denying the FRCP 59(e) motion. Thus, BP's notice of appeal filed on August 2, 2013, was timely. [—8—]

Having found that the appeal was timely, we next turn to whether we have jurisdiction over the appeal. BP invokes jurisdiction under the collateral order doctrine and 28 U.S.C. § 1292(a)(3). We find that jurisdiction is proper under the collateral order doctrine. To fall under the collateral order doctrine, "an 'order must (1) conclusively determine the disputed question, (2) resolve an important issue completely separate from the merits of the action, and (3) be effectively unreviewable on appeal from a final judgment.'" *Henry v. Lake Charles Am. Press, L.L.C.*, 566 F.3d 164, 171 (5th Cir. 2009) (quoting *Coopers & Lybrand v. Livesay*, 437 U.S. 463, 468 (1978) (numbering added)).

This court recently invoked the collateral order doctrine to hear an appeal involving an interpretation dispute over the same Settlement Agreement. In *In re Deepwater Horizon*, 732 F.3d 326, 1 Adm. R. 287 (5th Cir. 2013) ("*Deepwater Horizon I*"), the Claims Administrator had issued a Policy Announcement regarding the consideration of revenues and expenses in the calculation of reduction in variable profit and claimants' compensation (the Matching Policy noted in Final Rules 16 and 19 and further discussed in Part V.A, *infra*), 732 F.3d at 330-31, 1 Adm. R. at 287-89. BP alleged that the Claims Administrator misinterpreted the Settlement Agreement. *Id.* at 331, 1 Adm. R. at 288-89. The matter was brought before a Claims Administration Panel and eventually the district court, which affirmed the Policy Announcement. *Id.*, 1 Adm. R. at 289. BP filed a motion to reconsider, the district court upheld the Administrator's interpretation and denied BP's motion, and BP appealed. *Id.* at 331-32, 1 Adm. R. at 289.[5] This court stated

that it had [—9—] jurisdiction over BP's appeal of the district court's order under the collateral order doctrine with the following reasoning:

> The order conclusively determined the interpretation dispute, which is completely separate from the merits of BP's liability for the oil spill, and it will be effectively unreviewable on appeal from final judgment because, at that point, the improper awards will have been distributed to potentially thousands of claimants and BP will have no practical way of recovering these funds should it prevail.

Id. at 332 n.3, 1 Adm. R. at 289 n.3 (citing *Walker v. U.S. Dep't of Hous. & Urban Dev.*, 99 F.3d 761, 766-67 (5th Cir. 1996)). Like *Deepwater Horizon I*, the adoption of the Final Rules governing the district court's discretionary review of Appeal Panel decisions was a final decision by the district court with respect to the Rules, and is separate from the merits of BP's liability. The Final Rules affect the rest of the Settlement Program's administration, given that they will govern all future reviews by the district court. Because the Final Rules preclude appeals of certain cases to the district court, and because they are silent as to appeals to this court and lack requirements to file requests or docket orders on the civil docket, they would be unreviewable from a final judgment of claim determinations were we not to review them in this case. Thus, jurisdiction over this appeal exists under the collateral order doctrine. The motion to dismiss the appeal is DENIED.[6]

---

[5] BP also "filed a breach of contract claim against the Administrator and an emergency motion for a preliminary injunction to enjoin the Administrator from implementing the Settlement in accordance with the March 5 order and instead

to require the Administrator to implement BP's proposed interpretation." *Deepwater Horizon I*, 732 F.3d at 331, 1 Adm. R. at 289. The district court granted the Administrator's motion to dismiss BP's contract claim, and denied BP's request for injunctive relief. *Id.* at 331-32, 1 Adm. R. at 289.

[6] Because we conclude that jurisdiction is proper under the collateral order doctrine, we pretermit a determination as to whether there is also jurisdiction under § 1292(a)(3).

III. RIGHT TO APPEAL TO THIS COURT UNDER THE SETTLEMENT AGREEMENT

We now turn to the question of whether there is a right to appeal claim determinations from the district court to this court under the Settlement Agreement. While Class Counsel insist that the Final Rules are merely [—10—] operational rules for administering the Settlement Program that should be reviewed for abuse of discretion, *see Mullen v. Treasure Chest Casino, LLC*, 186 F.3d 620, 624 (5th Cir. 1999), the dispute before us results from a disagreement in how the Settlement Agreement should be interpreted as to appellate review. After all, BP claims that the Final Rules do not provide for appellate review by this court, which it argues it is entitled to under the Agreement absent an express waiver. It argues that this right to appeal has been violated by the Final Rules limiting the ability to file submissions regarding judicial review on the civil docket, as well as the Final Rules categorically precluding any judicial review for certain categories of cases. Class Counsel, on the other hand, argue that there is no right of appeal of individual claim determinations under the Agreement and that the Final Rules comply with the Agreement. The crux of the problem is that the Settlement Agreement is not clear one way or another, and our circuit has not yet specifically addressed the question of how to treat a settlement agreement's silence on whether there is a right to appeal from district court decisions on individual claims to this court.

We review issues related to interpreting settlement agreements *de novo. Waterfowl Ltd. Liab. Co. v. United States*, 473 F.3d 135, 141 (5th Cir. 2006). It is a "well-settled rule that the construction and enforcement of settlement agreements are governed by principles of local law applicable to contracts generally." *Fla. Educ. Ass'n, Inc. v. Atkinson*, 481 F.2d 662, 663 (5th Cir. 1973). The Settlement Agreement provides that it "shall be interpreted in accordance with General Maritime Law." Agreement § 36.1. "A basic principle of contract interpretation in admiralty law is to interpret, to the extent possible, all the terms in a contract without rendering any of them meaningless or superfluous." *Chembulk Trading LLC v. Chemex Ltd.*, 393 F.3d 550, 555 (5th Cir. 2004). [—11—]

In *Deepwater Horizon I*, this court interpreted the Settlement Agreement as preserving the parties' right to appeal to this court, but did so in dictum. After finding jurisdiction to hear the appeal under the collateral order doctrine, the court opined,

> Moreover, the procedures for resolving disputes concerning the Administrator's administration of the Settlement specify that a disagreement is "referred to the Court for resolution" if it is not resolved by the Claims Administration Panel. Based on its use throughout the Settlement, the term "the Court" appears to refer to the district court. Such an interpretation of the parties' agreement would render the district court's ruling final. However, the parties clearly intended a broader interpretation of the term—one that retained their right to appeal to this court—as shown by BP's appeal and Class Counsel's failure to object.

Deepwater Horizon I, 732 F.3d at 332 n.3, 1 Adm. R. at 289 n.3. BP relies on this heavily to argue that it has a right to appellate review of claim determinations. Class Counsel, on the other hand, claim that the conclusion was faulty, noting that

> [w]hile [they] are mindful of [the] observation that Class Counsel did not explicitly make this argument [that district court reviews are discretionary and not appealable] in response to the original appeal of [*Deepwater Horizon I*], Class Counsel did specifically raise this issue in the District Court[] [in its opposition to the motion for injunction and during the motion hearing], and strongly suggested that this Court had no jurisdiction to hear that appeal [in its brief].

After examining each of these references, we find that Class Counsel did argue that the court did not have jurisdiction over that appeal. BP asserted appellate jurisdiction under 28 U.S.C. §§ 1291, 1292, and the collateral order doctrine for the appeal of the district court's decision to uphold the Claims Administrator's interpretation. Class Counsel addressed each of these in turn to argue that there was no appealable order under these bases, and argued that jurisdiction was only proper over the dismissal of BP's separate suit [—12—] against the Claims Administrator pursuant to FRCP 12(b)(6). While Class Counsel did not make any arguments specific to whether there was appellate review by this court of claim determinations under the Settlement Agreement, it did not have to as the issue was not relevant in that case. We are not persuaded to follow the *Deepwater Horizon I* interpretation for the purpose of deciding the issue at hand because dictum by one panel does not bind future panels. *See Gochicoa v. Johnson*, 238 F.3d 278, 286 n.11 (5th Cir. 2000). In any event, the rationale for that dictum does not apply here given that Class Counsel have clearly objected to BP's appeal.

To support its position that there must be an express waiver of what is otherwise a right to appeal, BP relies on criminal and other unrelated cases for the proposition that waivers require proof of an "'intentional relinquishment or abandonment of' a 'known right,' and cannot be inferred from silence or by implication." Appellants' Br. 38 (quoting *United States v. Knowles*, 29 F.3d 947, 951 n.2 (5th Cir. 1994) (internal quotation omitted) (defining waiver in the context of conducting plain error review of the constitutionality of the Gun Free School Zones Act and noting that deviation from a legal rule is error unless there has been a waiver)) (citing *Harris v. Dallas Indep. Sch. Dist.*, 435 F. App'x 389, 396 (5th Cir. 2011) (finding that plaintiff waived discovery issue by withdrawing motion to compel discovery); *United States v. Dodson*, 288 F.3d 153, 160 (5th Cir. 2002) (considering waiver of rights under 21 U.S.C. § 851); *Wells Fargo Bus. Credit v. Ben Kozloff, Inc.*, 695 F.2d 940, 947 (5th Cir. 1983) (applying this concept of waiver to question of whether party

waived its rights to no-offset agreement)). None of these cases directly address the question of whether there is a known right to appeal from district court decisions [—13—] regarding claims from settlement agreements, and thus whether this concept of waiver would apply in that context.[7]

On the other hand, Class Counsel do not show convincing authority that parties may waive appellate rights without an express waiver in the context of settlement agreements. Instead, they summarize the appeals process to show that the rules regarding appeals are "exhaustive" and that the district court's review "serves as the last step in a multi-layered claims process." They then contrast this to the relative lack of guidelines regarding the district court's discretionary review to argue that this "clearly demonstrates that the Settlement Program, not the parties, were to enact the administrative rules" and that

> [t]his deference clearly evidences that the parties intended the Claims Administrator, through the Claims Coordinator, pursuant to Section 8 of Exhibit 25 of the Settlement Agreement, to amend and/or adopt procedures as necessary for administrative rules of timing, length of appeal documents, record evidence, and filing related to discretionary review.

They also argue that "parties to a settlement are free to contract away appellate review, especially when the parties privately contract for a separately detailed appellate review within the settlement program itself." However, they cite to no source for the

---

[7] BP also relies on *Federal Practice & Procedure*, which states, "The most likely occasion for waiver [of the right to Court of Appeals review] arises from a settlement agreement that calls for resolution of some disputed matter by the district court, coupled with an explicit agreement that the district court decision shall be final and that all rights of appeal are waived." 15A Charles Alan Wright et al., *Federal Practice and Procedure* § 3901 (2d ed. 2014). However, the idea that this is "the most likely occasion" is not an indication of an express waiver *requirement*.

proposition that parties may do so [—14—] without an express waiver.[8] In their motion to dismiss the appeal, Class Counsel argue,

> It is settled in this Court that a negotiated settlement that limits appellate review may be binding, and that by failing to negotiate for the inclusion of appellate review before the signing of the Settlement Agreement, BP has waived its right of appeal beyond that provided for in the Settlement Agreement; thus its appeal here is barred and should be dismissed.

For support, they cite to *Hill v. Schilling*, 495 F. App'x 480 (5th Cir. 2012) (per curiam), in which this court applied criminal cases dealing with appeal waivers in plea agreements to an interpretation of a settlement agreement, *id.* at 487 (citing *United States v. Palmer*, 456 F.3d 484, 488 (5th Cir. 2006); *United States v. Bond*, 414 F.3d 542, 546 (5th Cir. 2005); Charles Alan Wright et al., *Federal Practice and Procedure* § 3901 (2012)). The *Hill* panel dismissed the appeal as barred by the appeal waiver. *Id.* at 487-88. Yet *Hill* is not as helpful to Class Counsel as they wish because, unlike in *Hill*, *see id.* at 487, the instant case does not involve an express waiver. Favorably for the class, the court did not say that the waiver had to be an express one. Nevertheless, *Hill* was an

unpublished opinion and therefore not binding precedent with respect to whether this panel should also apply criminal cases dealing with appeal [—15—] waivers in plea agreements to the settlement agreement context. *See* 5th Cir. R. 47.5.4.

We find that similar cases from other circuits provide guidance in relation to this question. Class Counsel seek to emphasize the Settlement Agreement's use of the word "exclusive" in § 18.1 to refer to the district court's jurisdiction, but we find that a district court having such authority in the Settlement Program does not necessarily preclude further review by this court. In *United States v. International Brotherhood of Teamsters*, 905 F.2d 610 (2d Cir. 1990), a consent decree provided that the court-appointed administrator's decisions be "'final and binding, subject to the [district] Court's review as provided herein,' and . . . further provide[d] that the district court 'shall have exclusive jurisdiction to decide any and all issues relating to the Administrator's actions or authority' under the Consent Decree," *id.* at 615 (alteration in original). The Second Circuit found that it had jurisdiction to hear the appeal because "the phrase 'exclusive jurisdiction,' read in the context of the Consent Decree, [did] not unambiguously exclude appellate review" and was instead a venue requirement. *Id.*; *see also DeLoach v. Lorillard Tobacco Co.*, 391 F.3d 551, 558 (4th Cir. 2004) ("The district court's maintenance of 'continuing and exclusive jurisdiction' over an agreement is not inconsistent with this court's exercise of appellate jurisdiction to review the district court's orders."). We interpret the "exclusive" jurisdiction conferred on the district court by the Settlement Agreement to also leave open the possibility of further review by this court.

In *Montez v. Hickenlooper*, 640 F.3d 1126 (10th Cir. 2011), a class action alleging violations of disabled prisoners' rights resulted in a consent decree that set forth a plan for the defendants to bring the state prison system into compliance and established a claims procedure for injured inmates in which claims would be reviewed by a special master, subject to review by the district

---

[8] Citing to another class action settlement, Class Counsel assert that "the rule for settling parties is to exclude any right to court appellate review on claimant-specific issues. Typically, the claims administrator's determinations are final; there may be limited review by a special master." Appellees' Br. 36-37 (citing *In re Vioxx Prods. Liab. Litig.*, 760 F. Supp. 2d 640, 644-45 (E.D. La. 2010)). However, that settlement agreement expressly stated that certain determinations of the Claims Administrator, Gate Committee, Chief Administrator, and Special Master were "final, binding and Non-Appealable." *E.g.*, Vioxx Settlement Agreement §§ 2.6.1, 2.8, 3.2.3, 3.2.4, 4.2.7, 8.1.2, *available at* http://www.officialvioxxsettlement.com/documents/Master%20Settlement%20Agreement%20-%20new.pdf; *see id.* § 17.1.62 (defining "Non-Appealable" to include, *inter alia*, "any right of appeal to the MDL Court, any other Coordinated Proceedings court or any other court").

[—16—] court, *id.* at 1129. Like the instant case, the consent decree was silent about further review by the Court of Appeals after review by the district court. *Id.* Building off *International Brotherhood*, the Tenth Circuit stated,

> We simply hold that, when a consent decree does not resolve claims itself but instead simply establishes a mechanism under which the district court will resolve claims, the parties may appeal the district court's final resolution of such claims to this court unless the consent decree contains a clear and unequivocal waiver of the right to appellate review.

Id. at 1132.[9] Addressing whether there was appellate jurisdiction despite the fact that litigation was still ongoing and the district court's decision was not a final judgment as to all parties, the Tenth Circuit found that it had jurisdiction over the appeal of the district court's claim determination under the collateral order doctrine. *Id.* at 1132-33. We choose to follow these other circuits' decisions in similar cases involving consent decrees to hold that, where a settlement agreement does not resolve claims itself but instead establishes a mechanism pursuant to which the district court will resolve claims, parties must expressly waive what is otherwise a right to appeal from claim determination decisions by a district court. Given that there has been no such express waiver in the instant case, the parties have preserved their right to appeal from the district court to this court. Having found this, we next consider whether the Final Rules are in violation of this right to appeal by reviewing the Rules' lack of docketing provisions. [—17—]

---

[9] The *Montez* court also relied on "the somewhat analogous situation of appeals from district court orders reviewing arbitration decisions." 640 F.3d at 1132 (citing *MACTEC, Inc. v. Gorelick*, 427 F.3d 821, 830 (10th Cir. 2005) (holding that "contractual provisions limiting the right to appeal from a district court's judgment confirming or vacating an arbitration award are permissible, so long as the intent to do so is clear and unequivocal")).

IV. FEDERAL RULE OF CIVIL PROCEDURE 79

The record for the district court's review, as determined by the Final Rules, consists of:

(a) The Claims Administrator's Summary of Review, if one was prepared;
(b) The decision of the Appeal Panel and its written opinion, if one was prepared;
(c) The Initial and Final Proposals and supporting memoranda, as well as any *amicus* filings by Class Counsel submitted under the Rules Governing the Appeals Process; and
(d) Any additional portions of the claim file specifically requested by the Court for review.

Final Rule 23. Under the Rules, requests for review are to be submitted to the Appeals Coordinator rather than to the district court clerk. Final Rule 13. The Rules also provide that the district court's decisions to deny or grant a request for review, as well as final decisions upon review, are to be communicated to the parties by the Appeals Coordinator. Final Rules 21, 22, 27. As noted above, under the process set out in the Final Rules, the records for the district court's review are not placed on the civil docket but rather on the DWH Portal and in redacted form (without personally identifying information) on the Settlement Program website.

BP argues that the district court's failure to provide for the docketing of its orders regarding requests for review jeopardizes the right to appeal to this court and violates FRCP 79, which provides for the maintenance of a civil docket by the clerk. *See* FED. R. CIV. P. 79. Class Counsel argue, on the other hand, that FRCP 79 is merely ministerial in nature and not something that should interfere with the district court's administration of a private settlement agreement.

This court has recognized that undocketed orders cannot be appealed. *In re Am. Precision Vibrator Co.*, 863 F.2d 428, 429 (5th Cir. 1989). Entry of an [—18—] order on the civil docket is a prerequisite for the clock to start running for an appeal. *See* FED. R. APP. P. 4(a)(1)(A) ("In a civil case, . . . the notice of appeal required by Rule 3 must be filed with the district clerk within 30 days after entry of the judgment or order appealed from."); FED. R. CIV. P. 58(c)(2) (noting that judgment is entered "if a separate document is required, when the judgment is entered in the civil docket under Rule 79(a) and the earlier of these events occurs: (A) it is set out in a separate document; or (B) 150 days have run from the entry in the civil docket"). Class Counsel, after arguing that there is no right to appeal under the Settlement Agreement, argue in the alternative that the Final Rules have no bearing on BP's ability to appeal to this court given BP's ability to pursue the Non-Profit Appeals, in which BP docketed the district court's order denying review and then moved to supplement the record on appeal. However, leaving it to the appealing party to docket the district court's order grants that party the ability to determine the point at which the clock starts to run for the time to file a notice of appeal. We decline to endorse this approach. Instead, we conclude that the Final Rules violate the right for parties to appeal claim determinations to this court.

On this basis, we VACATE the district court's order adopting the Final Rules, and REMAND with instructions to adjust the Rules to comply with this opinion. The point at which a party seeks the district court's discretionary review is the point at which further review by this court becomes a possibility. Thus, it is at this point that requests should be docketed by the clerk so that a proper record is available in the event the case comes before this court.[10] [—19—]

V. DISTRICT COURT'S DECISION TO CATEGORICALLY PRECLUDE CERTAIN CASES FROM ITS REVIEW

We next consider the question of whether the district court erred in including provisions in the Final Rules that prevent judicial review of several categories of cases. As noted above,

Final Rules 16 and 19 preclude certain categories of cases from review by the district court. Specifically, requests for review and objections thereto for cases involving the Non-Profit Policy, Alternative Causation Issue, or Matching Policy are not submitted to the district court. Final Rules 16 and 19 provide that "the processing of claims will not be suspended in such cases unless there is a further order" by the district court. BP objects to Final Rules 16 and 19 on three grounds: (1) that these rules jeopardize BP's right to request judicial review of awards, (2) that the rules encumber the ability to appeal to this court, and (3) that the rules "wrongly insulate from review awards predicated on policy announcements that have been repudiated or not yet fully reviewed by this Court."

We review the district court's decision to preclude these cases from review—as part of its decision to adopt the Final Rules—for abuse of discretion since it was decided as part of its duties to manage the Settlement Program. *See Mullen*, 186 F.3d at 624. A decision premised on an error of law constitutes an abuse of discretion. *See Jethroe v. Omnova Solutions, Inc.*, 412 F.3d 598, 600 (5th Cir. 2005).

As to the first objection, we do not agree with BP's contention that the Final Rules improperly strip BP of its right to request judicial review of awards. Despite our holding above that there is a right to appellate review by this court of district court decisions regarding individual claims under the Settlement Agreement, this does not necessarily translate into the right of a party to obtain the *district court's* review of claim determinations. Under § 18.1 of the Settlement Agreement, parties may request review by the district court [—20—] to settle "[a]ny disputes or controversies arising out of or related to the interpretation, enforcement or implementation of the Agreement." However, it is clear from § 6.6 that "[t]he Court maintains the discretionary right to review any Appeal determination," which is not a right for the parties to be granted such review. We recognize that categorically precluding certain cases may frustrate the right to seek review in that an appealing

---

[10] We find no error in what comprises the record on district court review, as delineated by Final Rule 23.

party will know before filing a request for review that the district court will not grant review over the claim determination. However, we seek to preserve the district court's discretion under the Settlement Agreement—as agreed to by the parties—to decide which cases to review. We do not intend any part of this opinion to turn the district court's discretionary review into a mandatory review. To do so would frustrate the clear purpose of the Settlement Agreement to curtail litigation.

With respect to its second contention, BP argues that the Rules "preclude the parties from requesting relief from the district court, and thus from receiving *any* claim-specific order—docketed or not." Our holding above with respect to the docketing provisions addresses this objection. When the Rules are modified in accordance with this opinion so that requests for district court review are docketed, we expect the district court's decisions to grant or deny review to also be docketed. The parties will then receive a docketed claim-specific order and their ability to appeal to this court will be preserved.

To address BP's third contention, we consider developments to the three policies subsequent to the May 20 Order, which BP contends undermines the Rules' limitations on seeking review of awards involving the three policies.

A. Categorical Preclusion of Cases Involving the Matching Policy

BP's objection to the preclusion from judicial review of cases involving the Matching Policy is that the Final Rules have not been modified to reflect [—21—] the recent developments regarding the Matching Policy—namely, that the policy was set aside in *Deepwater Horizon I*, and has since been effectively superseded by a new policy approved by the district court. Recent developments regarding the Matching Policy muddy the waters for our review. We briefly summarize those recent developments.

In *Deepwater Horizon I*, this court set aside the Matching Policy[11] and remanded to the district court for further proceedings on the basis that the district court's interpretation of Exhibit 4C[12] of the Settlement Agreement was in need of further consideration. 732 F.3d at 339, 1 Adm. R. at 296. Shortly after that ruling, per the order to issue a "narrowly-tailored" preliminary injunction, *id.* at 346, 1 Adm. R. at 301, the district court ordered the Claims Administrator "to immediately suspend the issuance of any final determination notices or any payments with respect to those [business economic loss ("BEL")] claims in which the Claims Administrator determines that the matching of revenues and expenses is an [—22—] issue." *In re Deepwater Horizon*, MDL No. 2179, 2013

---

[11] In the Matching Policy, the Claims Admin

stated that, for both calculation of Variable Profit and purposes of causation, he would "typically consider both revenues and expenses in the periods in which those revenues and expenses were recorded at the time," and would "not typically re-allocate such revenues or expenses to different periods," but would "however, reserve the right to adjust the financial statements in certain circumstances, including but not limited to, inconsistent basis of accounting between benchmark and compensation periods, errors in previously recorded transactions and flawed or inconsistent treatment of accounting estimates."

Deepwater Horizon I, 732 F.3d at 330-31, 1 Adm. R. at 288.

[12] Exhibit 4C, which sets the compensation framework for business economic loss ("BEL") claims, lays out the calculation of variable profit for purposes of calculating compensation: (1) "Sum the monthly revenue over the period," then (2) "Subtract the corresponding variable expenses from revenue over the same time period." Agreement, Exhibit 4C. The interpretation issue arose from the difference in accounting methods used by claimants. Accrual-basis claimants recognize revenue "when the entity becomes entitled to receive payment, as opposed to when the payment is actually received," which "is sometimes referred to as 'matching' revenues and expenses." 732 F.3d at 333, 1 Adm. .R. at 291. Cash-basis claimants, on the other hand, "recognize revenue when cash from a given transaction is received and expenses when cash is paid." *Id.*, 1 Adm. R. at 290.

WL 5495266, at *1 (E.D. La. Oct. 3, 2013). Following further input from the parties, the district court ordered the Claims Administrator and Settlement Program to continue to process and pay BEL claims presented on the basis of matched, accrual-basis records. *See* Order 4, *In re Deepwater Horizon*, MDL 2179 (E.D. La. Oct. 18, 2013), ECF No. 11697. As for other BEL claims, the district court ordered the continued temporary suspension of final determination notices and payments "unless the Claims Administrator determines that the matching of revenues and expenses is not an issue with respect to any such claim." *Id.* at 5.[13]

After revisiting the issue of whether the Claims Administrator correctly interpreted the Settlement Agreement in the calculation of variable profit, the district court found that "the provision [in Exhibit 4C] for subtracting corresponding variable expenses requires that revenue must be matched with the variable expenses incurred by a claimant in conducting its business, and that does not necessarily coincide with when revenue and variable expenses are recorded." Order 5, *In re Deepwater Horizon*, MDL 2179 (E.D. La. Dec. 24, 2013), ECF No. 12055. On this basis, the court reversed its earlier ruling affirming the Matching Policy and remanded to the Claims Administrator "with instructions to adopt and implement an appropriate protocol or policy for handling BEL claims in which the claimant's financial records do not match

---

[13] The preliminary injunction was eventually extended to stay other BEL claims, including those involving the Alternative Causation and Non-Profit Policies. *See* Order 2, *In re Deepwater Horizon*, MDL 2179 (E.D. La. Dec. 5, 2013) ECF No. 11928 (amending the preliminary injunction and instructing the Claims Administrator to "continue to accept BEL claims and process said claims, but [to] temporarily suspend the issuance of final determination notices and payments of BEL claims, pending resolution of the BEL issues that are the subject of the pending remand [of *Deepwater Horizon I*]"). Class Counsel point out the extent of the stay, seemingly in response to BP's argument that Final Rules 16 and 19 wrongly enforce policies, but the stay has no bearing on whether it was an abuse of discretion for the district court to adopt Final Rules that allow for the categorical preclusion of cases involving the policies from its review.

[—23—] revenue with corresponding variable expenses." *Id.* No party appealed this instruction.

On May 28, 2014, the district court dissolved the injunction involving BEL claims and ordered that a new policy—the Claims Administrator's Policy 495 ("Business Economic Loss Claims: Matching of Revenue and Expenses")—"be applied to all BEL Claims currently in the claims process at any point short of final payment." Order 2, *In re Deepwater Horizon*, MDL 2179 (E.D. La. May 28, 2014), ECF No. 12948. On June 27, 2014, in an order clarifying the application of this new policy, the district court held, *inter alia*, that a determination by the Appeals Coordinator in "appeals when the issue of matching is contested" under Policy 495 would be "final and non-appealable." Order 2, *In re Deepwater Horizon*, MDL 2179 (E.D. La. June 27, 2014), ECF No. 13076. This seems to bring Policy 495 in line with Final Rules 16 and 19—by categorically precluding these cases from district court review.

In light of the recent developments highlighted above, we are unable to decide whether the district court's decision to categorically preclude review of cases involving the Matching Policy constituted an abuse of discretion. On remand, the district court should reconsider its decision to categorically preclude these cases from its review. In doing so, the district court should consider what effect, if any, the Final Rules have on cases involving Policy 495. In the event the court is of the view that these cases should be categorically precluded from review, the court should provide a rationale for such a finding.

B. Categorical Preclusion of Cases Involving the Alternative Causation Issue

With respect to the preclusion of cases involving the Alternative Causation Policy[14]

---

[14] The Alternative Causation Policy, released October 10, 2012, states as follows: [—24—]

The Settlement Agreement does not contemplate that the Claims Administrator

from judicial review, BP argues that the Final Rules should [—24—] be modified to account for this court's recent holding in *In re Deepwater Horizon*, 744 F.3d 370, 2 Adm. R. 183 (5th Cir. 2014), *cert. denied*, 135 S. Ct. 754 (2014) ("*Deepwater Horizon III*"). At issue in *Deepwater Horizon III* was whether the implementation of the Settlement Agreement was defective with respect to the Settlement Agreement's causation framework. *Id.* at 374-75, 2 Adm. R. at 184. *Deepwater Horizon III* arose from the remand of *Deepwater Horizon I*. On remand, after analyzing the Settlement Agreement and Alternative Causation Policy, the district court concluded that "the language of the Settlement Agreement did not require extrinsic inquiry into causation and that the Settlement Agreement had not violated Article III, Rule 23, or the Rules Enabling Act by eschewing the need for evidence of causation." *Id.* at 374, 2 Adm. R. at 184. After BP appealed this order, the *Deepwater Horizon III* majority found that "the parties explicitly contracted that traceability between the defendant's conduct and a claimant's injury would be satisfied at the proof stage, that is, in the submission of a claim, by a certification on the document that the claimant was injured by the *Deepwater Horizon* disaster." *Id.* at 376, 2 Adm. R. at 186. It thus concluded that "the Settlement Agreement does not require a claimant to submit *evidence* that the claim arose as a result of the oil spill," *id.* at 376-77, 2 Adm. R.

---

will undertake additional analysis of causation issues beyond those criteria that are specifically set out in the Settlement Agreement. Both Class Counsel and BP have in response to the Claims Administrator's inquiry confirmed that this is in fact a correct statement of their intent and of the terms of the Settlement Agreement. The Claims Administrator will thus compensate eligible Business Economic Loss and Individual Economic Loss claimants for all losses payable under the terms of the Economic Loss frameworks in the Settlement Agreement, without regard to whether such losses resulted or may have resulted from a cause other than the Deepwater Horizon oil spill provided such claimants have satisfied the specific causation requirements set out in the Settlement Agreement.

at 186, and affirmed the district court's order, *id.* at 378, 2 Adm. R. at 187-88. [—25—]

BP argues that the Final Rules should be modified to reflect the holding in *Deepwater Horizon III* that the Settlement Agreement contains a causal-nexus requirement—that a class member's injury be plausibly traceable to the oil spill—and that "implausible claims" that do not satisfy that requirement should be addressed as they arise. Rather than argue against the policy itself,[15] BP seems to argue that the Claims Administrator has refused to enforce the Settlement Agreement's causal-nexus requirement due to a *misapplication* of the Alternative Causation Policy. However, this argument does not show how the district court's decision to preclude from its review cases based on the Alternative Causation Policy is an abuse of discretion.

Though BP does not raise this as part of its argument, the Alternative Causation Policy was also at issue in *In re Deepwater Horizon*, 739 F.3d 790, 2 Adm. R. 140 (5th Cir. 2014), *cert. denied*, 135 S. Ct. 754 (2014) ("*Deepwater Horizon II*"). In *Deepwater Horizon II*, BP appealed from the district court's order certifying the class action and approving the settlement. *Id.* at 795, 2 Adm. R. at 140. In its appeal, BP argued, *inter alia*, that the Matching Policy and Alternative Causation Issue "permit[ted] claimants without any actual injuries caused by the oil spill to participate in the class settlement and receive payments," causing the Settlement Agreement to be in violation of Rule 23, the Rules Enabling Act, and Article III of the U.S. Constitution. *Id.* at 798, 2 Adm. R. at 142-43. This court rejected this argument and held that the district court did not abuse its discretion in certifying the class and affirmed the class certification order. *Id.* at 821, 2 Adm. R. at 162.

---

[15] Indeed, as this court has previously observed, no party ever formally objected to the Policy Announcement, and the district court order that adopted the Policy Announcement was never independently appealed. *In re Deepwater Horizon*, 739 F.3d 790, 797, 2 Adm. R. 140, 142 (5th Cir. 2014), *cert. denied*, 135 S. Ct. 754 (2014) ("*Deepwater Horizon II*").

Considering how *Deepwater Horizon II* and *Deepwater Horizon III* did nothing to nullify or call into question the Alternative Causation Policy, but [—26—] actually substantiated the policy, we find no error of law underlying the district court's decision to preclude cases involving the Alternative Causation Policy from its discretionary review. We thus find no abuse of discretion here.

C. Categorical Preclusion of Cases Involving the Non-Profit Policy

BP appears to argue that we should vacate the Final Rules with respect to the Non-Profit Policy[16] because the policy was not yet definitively reviewed by this court at the time of the May 20 Order. We find no merit to this argument. The district court may adopt rules regarding the administration of a settlement agreement before the basis has been definitively reviewed by this court. BP provides no authority for a rule to the contrary. In any event, we uphold the Non-Profit Policy in the Non-Profit Appeals,[17] also decided today.

VI. CONCLUSION

In sum, finding that we have jurisdiction over this appeal, we hold that the parties have a right under the Settlement Agreement to appeal claim determinations from the district court to this court. We also hold that the Final Rules violate this right with its lack of docketing provisions providing for a proper appeal to this court, and remand on that basis. On remand, we instruct the district court to reconsider its decision to categorically preclude cases involving the Matching Policy from its review in light of recent developments. We find no error in the decision to categorically preclude cases involving the Alternative Causation Issue from judicial review. We also find no error in the decision to categorically preclude cases involving the Non-Profit Policy. For the [—27—] foregoing reasons, we VACATE in part and AFFIRM in part the district court's May 20 Order adopting the Final Rules, and we REMAND for further proceedings consistent with this opinion.

---

[16] On November 30, 2012, the Claims Administrator announced the following policy: "Income received by not-for-profit entities in the form of grant monies or contributions shall typically be treated as revenue for that entity for purposes of the various required calculations under the terms of the Settlement Agreement."

[17] In the Non-Profit Appeals, the district court denied review of three claims in which awards were determined through the application of the Non-Profit Policy.

United States Court of Appeals
for the Fifth Circuit

No. 14-30269

IN RE DEEPWATER HORIZON

YOUNG
VS.
BP EXPLORATION & PROD., INC.

Appeals from the United States District Court for the
Eastern District of Louisiana

Decided: May 13, 2015
Revised: May 15, 2015

Citation: 786 F.3d 344, 3 Adm. R. 354 (5th Cir. 2015).

Before **KING**, **DAVIS**, and **OWEN**, Circuit Judges.

[—1—] **DAVIS**, Circuit Judge:

Defendants-Appellants BP Exploration & Production, Inc., BP Products North America, Inc., and BP Corporation North America, Inc. (collectively [—2—] "BP") appeal the district court's judgment in favor of Intervenor/Plaintiff-Appellee Elton Johnson ("Johnson"). The district court, over BP's objection, enforced a putative $2.7 million settlement agreement against BP in Johnson's favor. On appeal, BP asserts that the parties never formed a binding settlement agreement. In the alternative, BP argues that Johnson fraudulently induced BP into entering the settlement agreement, and that Johnson did not satisfy a condition precedent to recovery because he never signed a release. BP also claims that the district court awarded an unreasonable rate of prejudgment interest.

We hold that the parties formed a binding settlement agreement. We also hold that the district court correctly excused Johnson's failure to sign the release document. However, the district court should have held an evidentiary hearing to determine whether Johnson fraudulently induced BP into entering the settlement agreement. We therefore affirm the district court's order in part, but vacate the judgment and remand for further proceedings.

I.

In the wake of the April 2010 Deepwater Horizon explosion,[1] BP reached an agreement with the White House to establish the Gulf Coast Claims Facility ("GCCF"), an independent mechanism created to settle the numerous claims against BP. BP authorized the GCCF and its Claims Administrator, Kenneth R. Feinberg, to act on BP's behalf to fulfill its statutory obligations as a "responsible party" under the Oil Pollution Act of 1990 ("OPA"). BP also [—3—] authorized the GCCF to process certain non-OPA claims involving physical injury or death.

Although BP authorized the GCCF to settle claims on its behalf, BP does not control the GCCF and cannot prevent it from extending settlement offers. However, if the GCCF sends a claimant a determination letter offering the claimant more than $500,000 to settle his or her claims, BP may appeal that offer within fourteen days from the date of the determination letter.

A.

Intervenor/Plaintiff-Appellee Elton Johnson was a crew member aboard the M/V DAMON BANKSTON, a supply vessel operated by Tidewater Marine, LLC ("Tidewater"). The vessel was mud-roped to the Deepwater Horizon and was off-loading drilling mud on the night of the blowout. Johnson claims that he sustained physical injuries when the explosion rocked the vessel and threw him against a bulkhead. Johnson further claims that the stress from both the explosion and his attempts to save other seamen endangered by the casualty caused him emotional injury, including post-traumatic stress disorder.

---

[1] The facts of the Deepwater Horizon blowout are set forth in *United States v. BP Exploration & Prod., Inc. (In re Deepwater Horizon)*, 753 F.3d 570, 571, 2 Adm. R. 233, 233 (5th Cir. 2014) and *Lake Eugenie Land & Dev., Inc. v. BP Exploration & Prod., Inc. (In re Deepwater Horizon)*, 732 F.3d 326, 329, 1 Adm. R. 287, 287 (5th Cir. 2013).

Johnson sued BP for negligence in Louisiana state court in May 2010.[2] BP removed the case to the United States District Court for the Eastern District of Louisiana.

While Johnson's case remained pending before the district court, he submitted his claim to the GCCF. His submission included voluminous medical records from a number of healthcare providers. Those records suggested that, as a result of the explosion, Johnson suffered back and shoulder pain; reduced range of motion; popping or crunching in the shoulderblade; headaches; hearing problems; a cerebral concussion or other brain injury; anxiety; [—4—] irritability; depression; hallucinations; nightmares and sleeping problems; memory problems; temporary hearing loss; tinnitus; and post-traumatic stress disorder. Those medical records also indicated that Johnson was taking a number of prescription medications both for his physical pain and his psychological conditions. Johnson's submission to the GCCF also contained a report from a reha-bilitation/vocational specialist indicating that Johnson was vocationally disabled and therefore unable to work for the indefinite future. Johnson also submitted his past medical expense records, estimates of his future medical costs, and an economic appraisal quantifying how his injury affected his earning capacity.

The GCCF analyzed Johnson's submission and calculated his damages as follows:

The claimant's final payment offer is comprised of total economic loss, total medical expenses and non-economic loss. The claimant's economic loss of $758,452 is the projected loss of income through the claimant's remaining work life. The claimant's medical expenses are composed of $25,568 past medical expenses and $271,843 future medical expenses for a total of $297,411. The claimant's non-economic loss calculation is $750,000 plus 3 times the medical

expenses ($297,411 x 3 = $892,233) for a total non-economic loss of $1,642,233.

The GCCF therefore concluded that Johnson was entitled to receive a total of $2,698,095 as a result of his alleged injuries.

On September 23, 2011, the GCCF sent Johnson a Determination Letter containing the following language:

The amount of the Final Payment Offer ("Final Payment Offer")[] is **$2,698,095.00**, which is the amount that can be paid now if you decide to accept the Final Payment Offer and you sign a Release and Covenant Not to Sue (the "Release"). . . . If you want to be paid the Final Payment Offer and fully resolve the entire claim now, you can accept the Final Payment Offer. [—5—]

The Determination Letter instructed Johnson:

To accept the Final Payment Offer, check the box on the Election Form indicating that you accept the Final Payment Offer, sign it and return it to the GCCF no later than 90 days after the date of this Letter. We will then send you a Release to be signed and returned to be paid the Final Payment Amount. . . .

BP will have the right to appeal to [a] panel of three neutrals because the total monetary award is $500,000 or more. . . . [P]ayment of the Final Amount will not be made until the expiration of the 14-day period for the right of an appeal of this claim by BP. The expiration of the right of an appeal is 14 days from the date of this Letter.

Johnson signed the Final Payment Election Form the day after he received the Determination Letter. He checked the box on the Form indicating that he "elect[ed] to be paid the Final Payment Offer" and understood that "the GCCF w[ould] send [him] a Release and Covenant Not to Sue that [he] must sign and return to be paid." Johnson timely

---

[2] Johnson also sued Tidewater for maintenance and cure in the same case.

submitted the signed, completed Final Payment Election Form to the GCCF.

B.

On October 3, 2011, after Johnson submitted the Final Payment Election Form to the GCCF, but before BP's fourteen-day appeal period expired, BP sent Tidewater a letter explaining that the GCCF had offered to settle Johnson's claim, and that BP expected Tidewater to indemnify it for the entire settlement amount.

Tidewater strenuously objected. On October 5, 2011, Tidewater responded with a letter stating that, "[b]ased on the file materials we have, the settlement offered by the GCCF in the amount of nearly $2.7 million is excessive and unreasonable given the defenses to Johnson's claim that are available to Tidewater and BP, and the medical records Tidewater has been [—6—] provided." Notably, however, Tidewater's letter does not state that it had any reason to believe that Johnson fabricated his injury claims—the letter merely expressed Tidewater's belief that the Final Payment Amount was "excessive and unreasonable." Tidewater "request[ed] in the strongest terms that BP appeal the settlement."

BP responded that it "w[ould] not appeal the GCCF's settlement with Mr. Johnson." As a result, the fourteen-day appeal window closed without BP appealing the Final Payment Offer.

C.

On October 20, 2011, after BP's appeal period expired, Tidewater's counsel sent the GCCF a letter, complete with documentary exhibits, explaining that it had investigated Johnson's personal injury claims and had reason to believe they were fabricated.

Tidewater first pointed out that the sworn statements of other crew members on the vessel at the time of the explosion directly contradicted Johnson's version of events. One crewman maintained "that Johnson was not thrown, did not fall, did not lose consciousness or make any statement or complaint that he had been struck" at the time of the explosion. "Because of the drilling mud on the deck" of the vessel, Johnson "would have been covered in the mud" if he had fallen, yet two crewmen "reported that Johnson was not covered with any mud" after the explosion.

Another crewman stated that, on the morning after the explosion, he asked Johnson

> if [he was] OK after the previous night's events. Although Johnson stated that he did not sleep well, he specifically denied that he was injured. On several occasions during that day, Johnson (and the remainder of the Tidewater crew) were asked if they were injured and, each time, Johnson denied injury. Johnson performed his [—7—] assigned tasks that day without incident or issue, never complaining to anyone of any injury.

Tidewater further stated that, "[h]ad Johnson been injured or involved in any incident, it is standard Tidewater policy to prepare an accident report. No such report was prepared," and Johnson in fact "specifically denied that he had been injured."

Tidewater also opined that Johnson told several physicians inconsistent versions of the events leading to his alleged injuries. According to Tidewater, Johnson's various accounts differed with respect to (1) whether the explosion threw him against a door or merely caused him to fall down; (2) the distance he was thrown; (3) whether or not he lost consciousness; (4) whether he reported seeing hallucinations at the time of his alleged injury; and (5) the location on the vessel where the injury occurred.

D.

A week after the GCCF received Tidewater's letter, it retained Guidepost Solutions LLC ("Guidepost") to investigate Johnson's case. On January 24, 2012, Guidepost issued a report concluding that Johnson's claim was unsubstantiated. Guidepost concluded that there was "no credible evidence Johnson suffered injuries as a result of the incident, and multiple fellow crew members, one of whom was standing alongside Johnson at the time of the explosion, disputed the events and injuries Johnson later reported."

Guidepost's investigation corroborated the evidence that Tidewater set forth in its letter to the GCCF. Guidepost found that

[a]ll crew members were individually questioned shortly after the incident about any injuries they might have sustained, and Johnson never mentioned having been hurt. Additionally, Louis Longlois, who was with Johnson when the explosion occurred, disputed Johnson's claims of being thrown into a door and being [—8—] rendered dazed or unconscious. Johnson's behavior on the day of the explosion and immediately thereafter is inconsistent with statements attributed to him regarding his purported injuries.

Additionally, Guidepost's report recounts the following exchange Johnson allegedly had with Bill Wayne Marsh, a seaman on the vessel, shortly after the explosion:

Marsh said that once all of the survivors were pulled from the water and safely on deck, he saw Johnson again; during this meeting Johnson reportedly told Marsh he was going to "get some money out of Tidewater." Marsh recalled that he asked Johnson if he was hurt and that Johnson replied, "No, but everyone on the rig is going to get some money. Why not me?" Marsh said he then asked Johnson, "How do you expect to get money if you are not hurt?" According to Marsh, Johnson replied, "I'm all shook up." Marsh said Johnson never told him he was actually injured as a result of the explosion or the rescue operation.[3]

Guidepost also interviewed Johnson:

Johnson described his injuries at the time of the incident as a headache and stated that he did not realize he was injured until the following day when he was back at the Tidewater office in Amelia, Louisiana. Johnson stated that he never advised anyone he was injured until then. . . .

Johnson insisted that no one ever inquired as to his well-being or if he was injured at any time while on the vessel or on land . . . .

When asked about the conflicting statements he had provided to several of the different attending physicians regarding what happened to him during the explosion, Johnson explained that the doctors were all mistaken. Johnson could not explain the differences in his statements to physicians about the nature and extent of his injuries. Johnson refused to state that he was knocked "unconscious" as in being "knocked out." Instead he explained his condition as an "altered state," after his attorney, Cory Itkin, [—9—] suggested that was what had happened to him. Johnson continued to insist that the explosion knocked him back six feet.

Johnson denied speaking to the Associated Press, which had reported that he claimed to have been thrown seven feet into an engine room door and that he was knocked unconscious. Johnson's attorney, Itkin, suggested that Johnson's former attorneys, Steve Herman and Eddie Knoll[,] may have provided this information to the press.

As a result of its investigation, Guidepost concluded that "Johnson's claims of physical injury as a result of the Deepwater Horizon explosion appear to be fabricated." Nevertheless, Guidepost also concluded that "Johnson did not submit any overtly fraudulent document," so "a Finding of Potetnial [sic] Fraud is not supported by this investigation."

---

[3] The report noted, however, that Marsh exhibited poor recollection regarding many of the events surrounding the explosion.

E.

After reviewing Guidepost's investigative report, the GCCF issued a denial letter to Johnson (the "Denial Letter") on February 22, 2012. The Denial Letter informed Johnson that the GCCF "has terminated its process with respect to Mr. Johnson's claim, will not send Mr. Johnson a Release and Covenant Not to Sue for his signature, and, accordingly, will not issue to Mr. Johnson a Final Payment for his submitted claim."

BP never sent Johnson a Release to sign, and it has refused to pay Johnson the Final Payment Amount. Johnson insists he would have signed the Release if the GCCF had sent it to him.

F.

Displeased with BP's refusal to consummate the settlement, Johnson intervened in *Young et al. v. BP Exploration & Production Inc. et al.*, a Texas state court suit filed by another injured seaman represented by the same [—10—] plaintiff's attorney.[4] Johnson candidly admits that he took this unusual procedural step in an attempt to quickly get his claim heard by a court. Johnson's petition in intervention asserted claims of breach of contract, negligent misrepresentation, and tortious interference relating to BP's refusal to honor the putative settlement agreement.

BP removed *Young* to the United States District Court for the Southern District of Texas on March 30, 2012. Before the Judicial Panel on Multidistrict Litigation could decide whether to transfer *Young* to the Eastern District of Louisiana with the other Deepwater Horizon cases, the district court granted summary judgment in BP's favor. The court concluded that the parties never formed a valid settlement agreement because "the lack of a signed release prevented the formation of a contract." The court therefore ruled that "Johnson will take nothing from BP."

G.

Johnson appealed the district court's summary judgment order. A panel of this Court ruled

> that the practical and prudent course of action in this case is to vacate the judgment of the district court and have that court transfer this case to the Eastern District of Louisiana for disposition there . . . .

We are especially reluctant to decide the question of whether a binding settlement agreement arose here, given the complexities of the BP litigation and the administrative handling of related tort claims and settlement processes. We recognize that there should be some uniformity as to the manner in which such questions are answered—without consistency, we may be faced with serious and [—11—] disruptive unintended consequences. The proper way to insure this case is decided in a manner that does justice to all the parties involved—as well as those others affected by the *Deepwater Horizon* incident—is to refer the matter back to the court in which it arose. That court has detailed knowledge of all the aspects of the BP litigation and settlement programs, and is in the best position to decide this issue in a way that is consonant with the handling of this multitudinous litigation. Accordingly, we vacate the judgment of the district court and remand with instructions to the district court to transfer this case to the Eastern District of Louisiana.[5]

---

[4] On appeal, BP does not challenge the propriety of Johnson's intervention in *Young*. Mr. Young settled his claims against BP and his employers, leaving only Johnson in the case. As a result, the case has essentially become a simple two-party dispute with Johnson on one side and BP on the other.

---

[5] *BP Exploration & Prod., Inc. v. Johnson*, 538 F. App'x 438, 439-40 (5th Cir. 2013).

H.

With the case back before the Eastern District of Louisiana, Johnson moved the court to summarily enforce the putative settlement agreement with BP. BP opposed Johnson's motion and filed its own motion for summary judgment.

On March 10, 2014, the district court granted Johnson's motion and denied BP's motion.[6] The court reached its decision without holding an evidentiary hearing. Unlike the United States District Court for the Southern District of Texas, the court ruled that

> there is undisputed evidence that a binding settlement agreement was reached between Elton Johnson and the GCCF acting on behalf of BP. The agreement was to pay the total sum of $2,698,095 to Johnson in full settlement of all of his personal injury claims arising out of the DEEPWATER HORIZON casualty. In exchange, Johnson agreed to waive and release all potential claims against not only BP, but against any other party who might be liable in the casualty . . . The arguments made by BP in its attempt to avoid payment of the settlement are unavailing. [—12—]

The court therefore entered a judgment enforcing the settlement and awarding "costs and interest at a rate of 5% per annum from October 10, 2011 until paid."

BP now appeals that judgment. BP asks the Court to

> reverse the judgment below and direct the district court to grant BP's motion for summary judgment—either because

no contract was formed or because any contract included the execution of the GCCF release as a condition for payment.

Alternatively, BP requests that the Court vacate the grant of summary judgment to Johnson as improper and remand for a resolution of BP's fraud-in-the-inducement defense. Finally, whatever occurs on the merits, the interest rate should be remanded or reduced.

II.

The parties first dispute the applicable standard of review, as well as the proper way to characterize the procedural posture of the case. Johnson argues that the district court granted a motion to enforce a settlement agreement, which we must review under the deferential abuse of discretion standard. BP, by contrast, maintains that the district court actually granted summary judgment in Johnson's favor, so we should review that judgment *de novo*.

Neither party is fully correct. A district court may summarily enforce a settlement agreement if no material facts are in dispute,[7] and in such circumstances we review the district court's order for abuse of discretion only.[8] However, "when opposition to enforcement of the settlement is based not on the merits of the claim but on a challenge to the validity of the agreement itself, [—13—] the parties must be allowed an evidentiary hearing on disputed issues of the validity and scope of the agreement."[9]

This central issue—whether there was any disputed issue of material fact as to the validity of the settlement agreement[]—is similar to that which any court must address when ruling on

---

[6] Although Johnson also filed a motion to remand the case, neither the Eastern District of Louisiana nor the Southern District of Texas ruled on that motion before addressing the merits of the parties' arguments. After reviewing the record and the applicable law, however, we are satisfied that we may exercise subject matter jurisdiction over the case.

[7] *Mid-South Towing Co. v. Har-Win, Inc.*, 733 F.2d 386, 390 (5th Cir. 1984) (citing *Autera v. Robinson*, 419 F.2d 1197, 1200 (D.C. Cir. 1969)).

[8] *Harmon v. Journal Publ'g Co.*, 476 F. App'x 756, 757 (5th Cir. 2012).

[9] *Mid-South*, 733 F.2d at 390 (citing *Autera*, 419 F.2d at 1200).

a motion for summary judgment. This is not mere coincidence. The stakes in summary enforcement of a settlement agreement and summary judgment on the merits of a claim are roughly the same—both deprive a party of his right to be heard in the litigation.[10]

Because BP challenges the validity of its putative settlement agreement with Johnson, we will "treat [BP's] assertions as true, and will affirm the district court only if [Johnson] is entitled to enforcement of the agreement[] as a matter of law."[11] If not, we must remand for an evidentiary hearing[12] regarding the validity of the settlement agreement, because the district court did not hold one in this case.[13]

III.

Because Johnson alleged causes of action under general maritime law and the Jones Act against BP, federal contract law governs the validity and enforceability of Johnson's putative settlement agreement with BP.[14] However, [—14—] "the federal common law of release is largely undeveloped,"[15] and federal contract law is largely indistinguishable from general contract principles under state common law.[16] Thus, in reaching our decision,

we will rely not only on federal cases, but also on treatises and state contract law cases to the extent we find them persuasive.

IV.

BP argues that, for numerous reasons, the parties never formed a binding settlement agreement. As explained below, none of BP's arguments have merit.

A.

The parties first contest whether an offer and acceptance occurred in this case. Johnson argues that the Determination Letter constituted a valid offer to settle Johnson's claims, and he accepted that offer by submitting the Final Payment Election Form. Because BP did not appeal the GCCF's offer within the fourteen day window, Johnson insists that the parties formed an enforceable settlement agreement. BP responds that the Determination Letter was merely "a potential settlement *valuation*," not an offer. According to BP, since the release of Johnson's claims "represents the entire benefit of the bargain for BP, the release *is* the contract." Thus, BP argues, the GCCF cannot extend a valid offer until it mails a formal release to the claimant, and the claimant cannot accept the offer until he or she signs that release. Because [—15—] neither of those events occurred in this case, BP maintains that the parties never formed a contract.

We agree with Johnson. An offer is judged by the parties' overt acts and words, not by the subjective or secret intent of the offeror.[17] Here, a reasonable person would construe the Determination Letter as an offer because it repeatedly uses the language of offer and acceptance. The Determination Letter repeatedly states that the GCCF, on BP's behalf, is extending a "Final Payment *Offer*," and informs Johnson: "To *accept* the Final Payment Offer, check the box on the Election

---

[10] *Tiernan v. Devoe*, 923 F.2d 1024, 1031 (3d Cir. 1991) (internal citations omitted).

[11] *Id.* at 1032.

[12] In this respect, a contested motion to enforce a settlement agreement differs from a motion to summary judgment, which would instead result in remand for a trial on the merits if the non-movant identified a genuine issue of material fact.

[13] *See Mid-South*, 733 F.2d at 390 (citing *Autera*, 419 F.2d at 1200).

[14] *Borne v. A & P Boat Rentals No. 4, Inc.*, 780 F.2d 1254, 1256 (5th Cir. 1986) (citations omitted).

BP argues that Louisiana rather than federal law applies because the Release, which BP never mailed to Johnson and Johnson never signed, contains a choice of law clause. We need not decide whether that choice of law clause binds us here. BP does not argue that the result of the case would differ under Louisiana law, and in any event BP relies heavily on cases from outside Louisiana.

[15] *See Hisel v. Upchurch*, 797 F. Supp. 1509, 1518 (D. Ariz. 1992).

[16] *See, e.g., Flores v. Koster*, Civil No. 3:11-CV-0726-M-BH, 2013 WL 6153280, at *3 (N.D. Tex.

Nov. 22, 2013); *United States ex rel. Osheroff v. MCCI Group Holdings*, No. 10-24486-cv-SCOLA, 2013 WL 3991964, at *3-4 (S.D. Fla. Aug. 2, 2013); *Hisel*, 797 F. Supp. at 1518.

[17] 1 WILLSITON ON CONTRACTS § 4.1 (4th ed. 2014).

Form indicating that you accept the Final Payment Offer, sign it and return it to the GCCF no later than 90 days after the date of this Letter." Because Johnson did just that, and BP did not timely appeal, the parties formed a contract.

Furthermore, "[a] settlement is valid and enforceable even if it contemplates the parties signing a release at a later date"[18] unless the parties explicitly provide that a valid contract will not be formed until the parties execute a formal, finalized agreement.[19] Even if one party ultimately fails to execute or sign the final formal release documents, that does not void the original agreement or render it deficient from the outset.[20] Here, the Determination Letter states that the GCCF will send Johnson a Release only *after* he has accepted the offer: "To accept the Final Payment Offer, check the box on the Election Form indicating that you accept the Final Payment Offer, sign it and return it to the GCCF no later than 90 days after the date of this [—16—] Letter. *We will then send you a Release* to be signed and returned *to be paid the Final Payment Amount*." Because the Determination Letter does not state that a signed release is a prerequisite to *contract formation* (as opposed to a prerequisite to *payment*), the fact that Johnson ultimately did not sign the Release is immaterial to the question of whether the parties formed a binding contract.

BP insists that, even if the language in the Determination Letter would create an offer in the context of a typical settlement reached on the courthouse steps, it cannot create an offer in the context of proceedings before the GCCF. BP maintains that it, along with the White House, established the GCCF as a "sui generis" exception to the ordinary rules of contract formation. Thus, claims BP, only a signed release could constitute an offer and acceptance, notwithstanding the Determination Letter's repeated use of the words "offer" and "accept."

We disagree. Claims resolution facilities like the GCCF are far from "sui generis"— they are routinely established in large mass tort cases.[21] BP has not identified, and we have not found, any authority for the proposition that otherwise unambiguous offer language is less likely to create a binding contract in the mass tort claims resolution facility context than in a typical litigation environment, or that an objective person would not consider the Determination Letter an offer under these circumstances.

BP also argues that, if the GCCF offered to settle Johnson's claim without first sending him a release, it would be acting outside of its authorization. In support of its argument, it points to language in the GCCF's governing protocol and rules that, in its view, demonstrates that "the execution [—17—] of a release is not just a condition on payment but on acceptance itself." BP argues that, because that these protocols and rules were publicly available to claimants, and because Johnson agreed to be bound by those rules by voluntarily submitting his personal injury claim to the GCCF, an objective person in Johnson's position would not consider the Determination Letter an offer.

Again, we disagree. The language BP cites from the protocol and rules only confirms our interpretation that a signed release is a condition precedent to *payment*, not to contract formation.[22] Moreover, the Protocol and Rules state, on at least four separate occasions, that "[a] claimant has the right to

---

[18] *Davison v. Bay Area Credit Serv., LLC*, No. 12-03411-CV-S-DGK, 2013 WL 627003, at *1 (W.D. Mo. Feb. 20, 2013) (citations omitted). *Accord, e.g., Mastroni-Mucker v. Allstate Ins. Co.*, 976 A.2d 510, 522 (Pa. Super. Ct. 2009) (citations omitted).

[19] *See Gen. Metal Fabricating Corp. v. Stergiou*, 438 S.W.3d 737, 747-48 & n.8 (Tex. App. 2014) (citations omitted); 15A C.J.S. COMPROMISE & SETTLEMENT § 21 (2014).

[20] *May v. Anderson*, 119 P.3d 1254, 1256, 1259 (Nev. 2005); *Hagrish v. Olson*, 603 A.2d 108, 110 (N.J. Super. Ct. App. Div. 1992).

[21] *See* Deborah R. Hensler, *Alternative Courts? Litigation-Induced Claims Resolution Facilities*, 57 STAN. L. REV. 1429, 1430-31 (2005).

[22] *See* ROA 3972 ("*To receive a Final Payment*, a claimant will be required to sign a release . . ."); *id.* at 3964 ("Accepting *a final payment* requires the Claimant to sign a release of past and future claims.").

consult with an attorney of his or her choosing prior to accepting any settlement *or signing a release of legal rights.*" This language makes it clear that an acceptance of the settlement offer is independent of signing the Release.

Thus, because Johnson accepted the offer in the Determination Letter by its own terms by timely submitting the Final Payment Election Form and agreeing to subsequently sign the Release, and because BP declined to appeal that offer within the fourteen-day period, both an offer and acceptance occurred.

B.

BP next argues that the Determination Letter could not create a valid contract because it lacked material terms: namely, the exact terms of the Release. According to BP, the personal injury release terms were not publicly available, so Johnson could not have known what they were in advance. Thus, [—18—] argues BP, the parties could not have reached a meeting of the minds as to the essential terms of the contract.

A putative contract is unenforceable if it lacks material or essential[23] terms.[24] Release provisions are generally—though not always—material terms of settlement agreements.[25] However, even where the *existence* of a release is material, the *precise terms and specific language* of the release are not necessarily material.[26] Consequently,

"even where the scope of the release is disputed, . . . courts routinely enforce settlement agreements even where the precise wording of a release has not been finalized."[27] This remains true even when one of the parties ultimately fails to sign the finalized release.[28] [—19—]

Here, the Determination Letter contained the following description of the release that the GCCF promised to send Johnson if he accepted the offer:

> The Release waives and releases any claims for bodily injury that you have or

---

[23] The terms "essential" and "material" are effectively synonymous in this context. *See Gen. Metal*, 438 S.W.3d at 744 n.4.

[24] 17 C.J.S. CONTRACTS § 91 (2014).

[25] *See, e.g., Dillard v. Starcon Int'l, Inc.*, 483 F.3d 502, 508-09 (7th Cir. 2007).

[26] *See Blackstone v. Brink*, Civil Action No. 13-cv-0896 (KBJ), 2014 WL 3896018, at *9 (D.D.C. Aug. 11, 2014) (citations omitted) ("[W]hile the general agreement to release Plaintiffs' claims against Defendant Brink was a material element of the settlement agreement, the specific language of the release form was not."); *Schaffer v. Litton Loan Servicing, LP*, No. CV 05-07673 MMM (JCx), 2012 WL 10274678, at *15 (C.D. Cal. Nov. 13, 2012) ("[C]ourts generally find there is agreement on all of the material terms of settlement where the parties have agreed upon the monetary amount of the settlement payment and the fact that plaintiffs

---

will release specific claims. Agreement on the precise terms of a written settlement agreement [or] precise release language . . . is not required."); *Nicholas v. Wyndham Int'l, Inc.*, Civil No. 2001-147, 2007 WL 4811566, at *4 (D.V.I. Nov. 20, 2007) (citations omitted) ("[C]ourts routinely enforce settlement agreements even where the precise wording of a release has not been finalized."); *McDonnell v. Engine Distribs.*, Civil Action No. 03-1999, 2007 WL 2814628, at *8 (D.N.J. Sept. 24, 2007) ("The disputed terms[] concerning the scope of the release . . . all speak to the settlement's implementation. They are not, however, essentials of the settlement."); *Carlson v. State Farm Mut. Auto. Ins. Co.*, 76 F. Supp. 2d 1069, 1076 (D. Mont. 1999) ("Although the *release* was a material element, the *terms* of the release were not." (emphasis added)).

[27] *Mastroni-Mucker*, 976 A.2d at 521 n.5 (citations omitted).

[28] *See May*, 119 P.3d at 1256, 1259; *Hagrish*, 603 A.2d at 110.

Without contending that the Release included any material terms that Johnson could not have reasonably expected, the dissent suggests that the requirement that Johnson sign a release before BP and the GCCF disclosed the terms of that release prevented the formation of a contract. As the cases cited above demonstrate, however, even where the parties have not yet agreed to the precise terms and language of the release, they may nonetheless form a binding settlement agreement by agreeing to both the existence of a release and the amount of payment. Indeed, in the real world of tort litigation, it would be difficult to operate any [—19—] differently; when an attorney, with his or her client's consent, agrees to settle a case for a sum certain, the plaintiff inevitably realizes that the defendant has bought its peace, and will expect to sign a release that will discharge the defendant in the broadest terms.

may have in the future against BP and all other potentially responsible parties with regard to the Oil Spill, and prevents you from submitting any bodily injury claim seeking payment from a court.

This description fully apprises Johnson of both the existence of the Release and its breadth. The GCCF's decision to include these details of the scope of the Release further indicates that it sought to include all material terms of the settlement in its offer so that the settlement would be binding on Johnson once he signed and returned his acceptance. As a result, the Determination Letter contained all material terms. We cannot accept BP's argument that a binding settlement agreement was not perfected simply because the GCCF planned to send Johnson a formal release after Johnson accepted all the terms of the Final Payment Offer.

The cases BP cites in support of its argument are readily distinguishable. In *Nascimento v. Wells Fargo Bank, NA*,[29] for example, the court held that the parties never formed a valid settlement agreement because the parties never agreed to the essential terms of the contract's release provision.[30] In that case, however, the defendant mailed the plaintiff four separate acceptance letters, each containing radically different release provisions which in turn differed from the release terms contained in the plaintiff's offer letter.[31] The court therefore concluded that the parties never reached a meeting of the minds on [—20—] the release terms.[32] Here, by contrast, there exists a single release description in the Determination Letter, and it previewed the Release's essential terms to Johnson. The other case BP cites, *Corilant Financial*, involved a disputed earn-out payment provision in a proposed acquisition agreement, and therefore casts little light on

whether a description of a release in a settlement offer contains all material terms.[33]

BP nevertheless maintains that the parties could not have reached a meeting of the minds because the GCCF's formal release document contains terms that go far beyond those described in the thumbnail description in the Determination Letter. According to BP, the Determination Letter did not inform Johnson that (1) the Release applies to emotional injury as well as bodily injury claims; (2) the Release "extends to claims held by the releasing party's spouse, parents, heirs, estate, and other beneficiaries;" and (3) the Release contains a two-page list of released parties that are not explicitly mentioned in the Determination Letter, including Johnson's employer, Tidewater.[34] BP emphasizes that, whereas the description of the Release in the Determination Letter consists of a single sentence, the Release contains nine pages of detailed release terms. Thus, argues BP, Johnson could not have predicted these terms in advance, so he could not have agreed to all of the material terms of the settlement agreement at the time he submitted the Final Payment Election Form.

We disagree. The description of the Release in the Determination Letter is particularly broad; it informs Johnson that he will be releasing all claims [—21—] arising from the Deepwater Horizon explosion against all potentially responsible parties.[35] Johnson was represented by zealous and competent counsel at the time he accepted the Final Payment Offer. Johnson therefore would have anticipated that the Release would be lengthy

---

[29] No. 2:11–CV–1049 JCM (GWF), 2013 WL 6579575 (D. Nev. Dec. 13, 2013).

[30] *Id.* at *2-4.

[31] *Id.* at *3.

[32] *Id.*

[33] *See Fiduciary Fin. Servs. of S.W., Inc. v. Corilant Fin., L.P.*, 376 S.W.3d 253, 256-58 (Tex. App. 2012).

[34] BP also argues in passing that the Determination Letter is missing an additional essential term: a choice of law clause that is present in the Release. Because BP does not explain why this term is material, we conclude that BP has waived this argument on appeal.

[35] We reject BP's argument that an objective seaman would most naturally interpret the incredibly broad phrase "all other potentially responsible parties" to only include parties who would constitute "responsible parties" as that term is defined by OPA.

and exhaustive, and that it would encompass any and all legal claims arising from the incident that he or his successors might bring on his behalf against any defendant. Moreover, Johnson must have expected that the term "bodily injury" would include his emotional injury claims because he submitted copious psychological records to the GCCF. The Release therefore does not contain any terms that Johnson could not have anticipated. Thus, the parties reached a meeting of the minds as to all essential terms of the settlement agreement.

C.

BP also argues, and the dissent agrees, that the settlement agreement fails for lack of mutual consideration. BP claims that, if the parties' roles were reversed, and BP was trying to enforce the putative settlement agreement against Johnson, no court would force Johnson to sign a release he had never seen, given the law's solicitude for seamen as wards of admiralty. Thus, argues BP, if BP could not force Johnson to release his claims under the facts of this case, then Johnson should not be able to force BP to give him the Final Payment Amount.

In support of its argument, BP relies on the following language in the GCCF's internal protocols: "A claimant has a right to consult with an attorney of his or her choosing prior to . . . signing a release of legal rights." According to BP, this language necessarily means that a claimant could permissibly [—22—] decline to sign the release after accepting a final payment offer if he or she so chose. Thus, claims BP, an enforceable settlement agreement cannot arise under the GCCF's rules until the claimant actually signs a release.

Johnson has no quarrel with any of the Release's terms, and there is no question that he is willing and ready to sign the Release in its current form and settle all of his claims against all potentially responsible parties. But even if the roles were reversed, we reject BP's premise that it would be unable to require Johnson to sign the Release. A settlement will be enforced against a seaman if he

"relinquished his rights with an informed understanding of his rights and a full appreciation of the consequences when he executed a release."[36] "The adequacy of the consideration is just one factor, along with the adequacy of legal representation, and whether the parties negotiated in good faith, or if there is the appearance of fraud or coercion."[37]

We have no doubt that these factors would favor enforcement of the settlement agreement against Johnson if the parties' roles were reversed.[38] Johnson stands to receive generous consideration in exchange for the release of his claims.[39] Johnson is represented by competent and zealous counsel. There is no suggestion of bad faith, coercion, or fraud on the part of BP. Most importantly, as explained above, the description of the Release in the Determination Letter sufficiently apprised Johnson of the consequences of accepting the settlement agreement, as the Release does not contain any terms that Johnson could not reasonably have expected. Thus, Johnson relinquished [—23—] his rights with a full understanding of the consequences at the time he accepted the Final Payment Offer. Finally, the cases BP cites in support of its argument that it could not force Johnson to sign the Release if the roles were reversed all involve facts very different than those presented here.[40]

---

[36] *Stipelcovich v. Sand Dollar Marine, Inc.*, 805 F.2d 599, 606 (5th Cir. 1986) (citing *Bass v. Phoenix Seadrill/78, Ltd.*, 749 F.2d 1154, 1161 (5th Cir. 1985)).

[37] *Id.* (internal citations omitted).

[38] *See Strange v. Gulf & S. Am. S.S. Co.*, 495 F.2d 1235, 1236-37 (5th Cir. 1974) (enforcing settlement agreement against seaman even though seaman refused to execute release).

[39] *See Durden v. Exxon Corp.*, 803 F.2d 845, 848 (5th Cir. 1986).

[40] *See Castillo v. Spiliada Mar. Corp.*, 937 F.2d 240, 243 (5th Cir. 1991) (holding that district court erred in ruling that seamen's releases were valid as a matter of law where seamen presented evidence of language barriers, coercion, and inadequacy of the source and quality of legal counsel); *Halliburton v. Ocean Drilling & Exploration Co.*, 620 F.2d 444, 445 (5th Cir. 1980) (holding that seaman demonstrated genuine issue of material fact as to validity of release where seaman was not

BP claims, and the dissent agrees, that the language in the GCCF's protocols advising the claimant to seek legal counsel before signing the Release necessarily implies that a seaman could freely refuse to execute a release after submitting the Final Payment Election Form. We disagree. Even if a claimant could not refuse to sign the Release after accepting a settlement offer, that does not mean that an attorney's advice would necessarily be valueless. For instance, the attorney could review the Release to make sure it comports with the description in the Determination Letter upon which the parties agreed. In this case, the release language follows from the thumbnail description in the Determination Letter, so BP could require Johnson to sign it if the parties' roles were reversed.

In support of its argument that BP could not have forced Johnson to sign the Release if he declined to do so after submitting the Final Payment Election Form, the dissent cites the following language from the Release:

> You are under no obligation to accept the final payment offered to you by the Gulf Coast Claims Facility ("GCCF"). You are free to reject the final payment offered by the GCCF and to pursue other means of compensation. *If you want to file a lawsuit regarding the incident do not sign the Release.*[41] [—24—]

If that language was present in the offer letter, the dissent's argument would have significantly more force. But it is not; the language comes from the Release itself, which the GCCF never sent to Johnson, and Johnson never saw. Again, an offer is judged by the parties' overt acts and words, not by the subjective or secret intent of the offeror.[42] As explained above, all of the documents that Johnson and the GCCF actually exchanged manifest the parties' intent to form a contract to settle Johnson's claims and release BP from liability. Thus, BP could have held Johnson to the material terms of the Release, so the

settlement agreement does not fail for lack of mutuality.

In sum, each of the aforementioned challenges to contract formation fail.

V.

BP argues in the alternative that, even if a signed release was not a condition precedent to *formation* of a settlement agreement, it is at least a condition precedent to *payment* under the contract. Because Johnson never signed the Release, BP argues that Johnson may not recover the Final Payment Amount. Johnson responds that, because BP refused to mail the Release to Johnson, the doctrine of prevention excuses Johnson's failure to sign the Release.

"A condition precedent is either an act of a party that must be performed or a certain event that must happen before a contractual right accrues or a contractual duty arises."[43] "[T]he failure of a condition to occur excuses performance by the party whose performance is dependent on its occurrence."[44] [—25—]

However, "[f]ulfillment of a contract promise . . . is not excused by failure of a condition . . . which the promisor himself causes to happen."[45] "It is a principle of fundamental justice that if a promisor is himself the cause of the failure of performance, either of an obligation due him or of a condition upon which his own liability depends, he cannot take advantage of the failure."[46] This is known as the doctrine of prevention.[47]

The Determination Letter that BP sent to Johnson states: "The amount of the Final Payment Offer . . . is $2,698,095.00, which is the amount that can be paid now if you decide to accept the Final Payment Offer *and you*

---

represented by counsel and suffered diminished mental capacity).

[41] (Emphasis added).

[42] 1 WILLISTON ON CONTRACTS § 4.1 (4th ed. 2014).

[43] 13 WILLISTON ON CONTRACTS § 38:7 (4th ed. 2014).

[44] *Id.*

[45] *Ballard v. El Dorado Tire Co.*, 512 F.2d 901, 907 (5th Cir. 1975).

[46] *Id.*

[47] *E.g., W & G Seaford Assocs., L.P. v. E. Shore Mkts.*, 714 F. Supp. 1336, 1341 (D. Del. 1989).

sign a Release and Covenant Not to Sue (the "Release")." Thus, BP is correct that a signed release is a condition precedent to payment under the contract that has gone unfulfilled.

Nevertheless, BP's refusal to send Johnson the Release excuses his failure to sign it. The Determination Letter states that, if the claimant timely submits the Final Payment Election Form, and if BP opts not to appeal the settlement within fourteen days of the date of the Determination Letter, *"[w]e then will send you a Release* to be signed and returned to be paid the Final Payment Amount." Johnson submitted the Final Payment Election Form, BP did not exercise its appellate rights, and the GCCF never mailed the Release as promised. Johnson would have signed the release if the GCCF sent it to him. Thus, the GCCF—and, by extension, BP—prevented Johnson from signing the Release, which excuses his failure to do so.[48] Thus, the fact that Johnson never signed the Release does not categorically bar him from recovering under the agreement. [—26—]

BP responds that an exception to the doctrine of prevention exists when the party does not "improperly" prevent the condition precedent from occurring. According to BP, its refusal to send Johnson the Release was not "improper," so the doctrine of prevention does not excuse his failure to sign the Release. We need not decide whether this exception exists as a general matter. BP has not identified, and we have not found, any authority that would render the doctrine of prevention inapplicable under the facts of this case.[49] We therefore reject the argument.

---

[48] *See Ballard,* 512 F.2d at 907.

[49] *Mack Trucks, Inc. v. BorgWarner Turbo Systems, Inc.,* Civil Action No. 08-2681, 2011 WL 1045108, at *5-6 (E.D. Pa. Mar. 22, 2011), which BP cites in its brief, merely holds that a party may not raise the doctrine of prevention unless it produces evidence that "support[s] an inference that [the opposing party] frustrated [its] compliance with the condition precedent." The case is inapposite because there is no doubt that the GCCF and BP frustrated Johnson's compliance with the condition precedent by refusing to mail him the Release.

BP also argues that the GCCF's rules and protocols, to which Johnson agreed to be bound when he voluntarily submitted his personal injury claim to the GCCF, authorized the GCCF to withhold the Release from Johnson once it uncovered evidence that Johnson submitted a fraudulent claim. We have reviewed the GCCF's protocols and conclude that, although the GCCF is authorized to investigate fraud prior to extending a settlement offer, and the GCCF is empowered to "refer all evidence of false or fraudulent claims to appropriate law enforcement authorities," the GCCF rules contain no provision allowing the GCCF to repudiate an otherwise binding contract after BP's appeals period has expired merely because it later develops reason to believe that the claimant has submitted a false claim. Nor does the Determination Letter authorize the GCCF to refuse to mail the Release to the claimant after the claimant has accepted a Final Payment Offer.[50] [—27—]

BP insists that, if we rule in Johnson's favor on this issue, then BP has no remedy if a claimant submits a fraudulent claim that goes undiscovered until after the fourteen-day appeal window has expired. As BP persuasively argues, "[f]iling claims to a settlement facility . . . is not a game of beat-the-clock that allows unscrupulous claimants maintaining a deception until time runs out to keep their ill-gotten gains." This concern is well-taken, and we address it in the following section.

VI.

BP's final argument is that, even if BP and Johnson formed an otherwise valid contract, the settlement agreement is nonetheless unenforceable because Johnson fraudulently induced BP to enter the settlement. Specifically, BP claims that Tidewater's letter to the GCCF and Guidepost's investigation report demonstrate that Johnson fabricated

---

[50] *See Akanthos Capital Mgmt., LLC v. Compucredit Holdings Corp.,* 677 F.3d 1286, 1297 (11th Cir. 2012) (holding that a party may permissibly prevent a condition precedent from occurring if the "alleged 'prevention' is authorized by the contract").

his personal injury claims and thereby submitted a fraudulent claim to the GCCF.

A court may set aside a settlement agreement induced by fraud.[51] "The essential elements of fraudulent inducement into a settlement are no different from any action on fraud."[52] Thus, BP must prove:[53]

(1) a material representation was made; (2) the representation was false; (3) when the representation was made, the speaker knew it was false or made it recklessly without any knowledge of the truth and as a positive assertion; (4) the representation was made with the intention that it be acted upon by the other party; (5) the party [—28—] acted in reliance on upon the representation; and (6) the party suffered injury.[54]

As a general matter, a party may not challenge a settlement agreement on the basis of an alleged fraud that "relates to the underlying merits of the claim that was settled."[55] Were the rule otherwise,

It would allow a party to reopen any settled litigation if he later discovered evidence bolstering his prior litigation position. If a party was able to undo a binding settlement agreement by simply couching the prior litigation as "fraudulent," there would be no way to

assure the full and final resolution of any matter.[56]

Thus, "[a] settlement will not be set aside . . . merely because one party's case becomes stronger after the settlement is concluded."[57]

There is, however, a narrow exception to this general rule. Where the defendant subsequently uncovers previously unavailable evidence that the plaintiff was in fact *not injured at all*, or sustained only *de minimis* injuries, the defendant may argue that the plaintiff fraudulently induced it to enter into a settlement agreement.[58] In such circumstances, the district court must hold an evidentiary hearing to weigh the newly-discovered evidence of fraud.[59]

The Ninth Circuit's opinion in *Russell v. Puget Sound Tug & Barge Co.*[60] is particularly instructive in this regard.[61] In that case, a seaman swore at his deposition that he was permanently disabled as a result of an on-the-job [—29—] injury.[62] The seaman and the shipowner agreed to settle the seaman's personal injury claim.[63] After the parties settled the case, however, the shipowner obtained video evidence from its private investigators depicting the seaman performing rigorous physical activity without difficulty.[64] The Ninth Circuit reversed the district court's order enforcing the settlement agreement and remanded for an evidentiary hearing to determine whether the seaman submitted a fraudulent claim regarding his on-the-job injuries.[65] The Ninth Circuit

---

[51] *E.g.*, *Howard v. Chris-Craft Corp.*, 562 F. Supp. 932, 937 (E.D. Tex. 1982) (citations omitted).

[52] 15B AM. JUR. 2D COMPROMISE AND SETTLEMENT § 32 (2d ed. 2014) (citations omitted).

[53] BP argues that it need *not* make an *actual showing of fraud* to succeed on its defense, but rather need only show that the GCCF *possessed sufficient evidence to believe Johnson committed fraud* at the time it issued its Denial Letter. Because BP's argument is based on an inaccurate characterization of the GCCF's internal rules and is otherwise unsupported by legal authority, we reject it.

[54] *O'Hare v. Graham*, 455 F. App'x 377, 379-80 (5th Cir. 2011) (citations omitted).

[55] *Johnson v. King*, No. 10-CV-279-S, 2011 WL 4963902, at *14 (D. Wyo. Oct. 17, 2011) ("*King*").

[56] *King*, 2011 WL 4963902, at *14. *Accord Howard*, 562 F. Supp. at 933-38.

[57] *Howard*, 562 F. Supp. at 937.

[58] *See Russell v. Puget Sound Tug & Barge Co.*, 737 F.2d 1510, 1510-11 (9th Cir. 1984).

[59] *Id.* at 1510-11.

[60] *Id.*

[61] *See also City Equities Anaheim, Ltd. v. Lincoln Plaza Dev. Co. (In re City Equities Anaheim, Ltd.)*, 22 F.3d 954, 957 (9th Cir. 1994) ("[W]e have found enforcement upon motion inappropriate . . . where a settlement agreement was apparently procured by fraud.").

[62] *Russell*, 737 F.2d at 1510-11.

[63] *Id.* at 1511.

[64] *Id.*

[65] *Id.*

reached this conclusion even though the alleged fraud related directly to the merits of the seaman's claims—namely, the existence and extent of the seaman's injuries.[66]

Here, too, BP has produced evidence suggesting that Johnson did not sustain any injury on the date of the Deepwater Horizon blowout. As described in greater detail above, Johnson's co-workers stated that the force of the blast never caused him to fall, stumble, or lose consciousness. To the contrary, the seamen on duty maintained that Johnson performed his duties capably and did not exhibit any signs of injury whatsoever. BP also produced evidence that Johnson repeatedly denied being injured on the date of the incident. Because BP's evidence suggests that Johnson may have submitted a wholly fabricated claim to the GCCF, BP may raise fraudulent inducement as a defense to enforcement of the settlement.[67] [—30—]

The district court therefore erred by discounting BP's substantial evidence of fraud without holding an evidentiary hearing.[68] We must therefore vacate the judgment against BP and remand for further proceedings.[69]

---

[66] See id.

[67] See id. at 1510-11.

[68] We do not suggest that the evidence in the record is not conflicting. Johnson submitted his medical records into the record, which could demonstrate that he sustained some injury during the explosion. The strength of each side's evidence ultimately depends on a determination of each witness's credibility.

[69] In this connection, we advise the district court to reconsider the weight it gave to Guidepost's statement that "a Finding of Potetnial [sic] Fraud is not supported by this investigation." Although the Guidepost report does state that "Johnson did not submit any overtly fraudulent *document*" to the GCCF, the report nonetheless unequivocally concludes that "Johnson's *claims* of physical injury as a result of the Deepwater Horizon explosion appear to be fabricated."

We are also persuaded that the district court erred by concluding, at least on the record then before it, that BP could not prove justifiable reliance. The district court reasoned that Tidewater's October 20, 2011 letter to BP alerted BP to "Tidewater's suspicions about whether Johnson's accident had occurred as he alleged or whether he had exaggerated his injuries" before

VII.

BP argues that the district court erred by granting prejudgment interest at a rate of 5%. Because we have vacated the district court's judgment, we need not address this issue. If the district court again rules in Johnson's favor on remand, BP may address the issue with the district court at that time.

VIII.

In sum, we affirm the district court's order in part. We agree with the district court that Johnson and BP entered into a binding settlement [—31—] agreement. Although Johnson's failure to sign a release might ordinarily bar him from recovering under the settlement agreement, BP's refusal to send Johnson the release excuses that failure here.

However, the district court should have held an evidentiary hearing to evaluate whether Johnson fraudulently induced BP into entering the settlement agreement by submitting a fabricated claim to the GCCF. We therefore vacate the district court's judgment and remand for further proceedings.

AFFIRMED in part, VACATED, and REMANDED for further proceedings.

(Reporter's Note: Dissenting opinion follows on p. 369).

BP's appeal period expired. As BP correctly notes, however, Tidewater's letter merely advises BP of Tidewater's belief that the Final Payment Offer was "excessive and unreasonable;" it contains no indication that Tidewater had any reason at that time to believe that Johnson fabricated his claims entirely. Even if Tidewater did believe Johnson submitted a false claim to the GCCF, the letter does not express that belief to BP. Moreover, Tidewater and Guidepost did not complete their investigations of Johnson's claim until after BP's appeal period had already expired. Thus, as we read the record, BP, Guidepost, and Tidewater only became aware of the full extent of Johnson's alleged fraud after BP's opportunity to appeal had elapsed. In sum, what BP should have known—and when it should have known it—are genuine issues of material fact for the district court to resolve after an evidentiary hearing.

[—32—] OWEN, Circuit Judge, dissenting:

I disagree with the panel majority's conclusion that a contract was formed. Mutuality is lacking,[1] and I therefore respectfully dissent. The documents that the Gulf Coast Claims Facility (GCCF) prepared in connection with Elton Johnson's claims unequivocally permitted Johnson to change his mind before he actually signed a release, even after he had indicated that he was willing to accept the amount of $2,698,095.00 in settlement of his claims against the BP entities. Nothing that Johnson signed or to which he agreed *obligated* him to sign a release. To the contrary, the documents reflected that the formation of an enforceable agreement would not occur until Johnson actually assented to the Release. Johnson could have refused to sign a release, and BP could not have enforced a settlement agreement with Johnson. There was no settlement agreement that either BP or Johnson could have enforced when the GCCF sent the October 2011 letter denying Johnson's claims after further review.

The Determination Letter that the GCCF sent to Johnson provided that "[t]he amount of the Final Payment Offer . . . is $2,698,095.00, which is the amount that can be paid now if you decide to accept the Final Payment Offer and you sign a Release and Covenant Not to Sue (the "Release")." It is clear from these terms that accepting the Final Payment Offer *and* signing the Release are both necessary components of a settlement agreement. Importantly, the Determination Letter, in bold and italicized text, also informed Johnson that he had "the right to consult with an attorney of [his] [—33—] own choosing prior to accepting any settlement or signing a release of legal rights." This statement unquestionably permitted Johnson to consult with an attorney *"prior to accepting any settlement"* or *"signing a release of legal rights."* If checking the box on the Final Payment Form indicating an "elect[ion] to be paid the Final Payment Offer" constituted the formation of a settlement agreement, then the statement that Johnson had the right to consult with an attorney of his own choosing before accepting a settlement or signing a release would have conflicted with the Form, would have been virtually meaningless, and would have been misleading.

Consistent with the provisions in the Determination Letter regarding the right to consult counsel, the box Johnson checked on the Final Payment Election Form read: "I elect to be paid the Final Payment Offer described in my Determination Letter . . . . The GCCF will send you a Release and Covenant not to Sue that you must sign and return to be paid." This language informed Johnson that he could choose not to sign the Release, with the obvious consequence of not being paid. Johnson's ability to decline signing the Release demonstrates that BP could not enforce any agreement with Johnson until the Release was signed.

The language contained in the Release itself, although never read by Johnson, reflects that checking the box on the Final Payment Election Form did not give rise to an enforceable contract. The Release states that if a personal injury claimant decides not to accept a Final Payment from the GCCF, the claimant has the right to file suit.[2] The

---

[1] 1 WILLISTON ON CONTRACTS § 7:14 (4th ed. 2014) (explaining that mutuality of obligation can be viewed as simply another "way of stating that there must be valid consideration").

---

[2] The Release provides:

If you do not accept a Final Payment from the GCCF for your physical injury claim, you have the right to file a claim in court, including in the multidistrict litigation pending before the United States District Court for the [—34—] Eastern District of Louisiana, titled, *In re Oil Spill by the Oil Rig "Deepwater Horizon" in the Gulf of Mexico, on April 20, 2010* (MDL No. 2179). The multidistrict litigation is a consolidated grouping of federal lawsuits arising out of the Incident. Information regarding the multidistrict litigation may be obtained from the court's website at ww.laed.uscourts.gov.

. . .

You are under no obligation to accept the final payment offered to you by the Gulf Coast Claims Facility ("GCCF"). You are free to reject the final payment offered by the GCCF and to pursue other means of

Release emphasized: "You [—34—] are under no obligation to accept the final payment offered to you by the [GCCF]. You are free to reject the final payment offered by the GCCF and to pursue other means of compensation. If you want to file a lawsuit regarding the incident do not sign the Release." If the Form containing the Final Payment Offer constituted a binding settlement agreement, then the GCCF would not advise a claimant in the Release of his right to decline to sign the Release and to pursue a lawsuit. The Release is another clear indication that checking the box on the Form sent to Johnson did not constitute the formation of a binding contract.

The panel majority opinion asserts that "language in the GCCF's protocols advising the claimant to seek legal counsel before signing the Release" does not mean that Johnson could refuse to sign the Release.[3] The majority opinion reasons that an attorney's advice would not be "valueless," even if Johnson was obligated to sign the Release, since an "attorney could review the Release to make sure it comports with the description in the Determination Letter upon which the parties agreed."[4] But the structure of the sentence that appeared in bold type and was italicized in the [—35—] Determination Letter Johnson received advising him that he had "the right to consult with an attorney of [his] own choosing prior to accepting any settlement or signing a release of legal rights" does not make such a distinction clear. It did not clearly tell Johnson that once he checked the box on the Form, he was obligated to release his personal injury claims even if he thereafter consulted an attorney and was advised to pursue a different avenue to redress his claim.

The panel majority opinion concedes that the argument that there was no binding agreement "would have significantly more force"[5] if the statements in the Release advising the claimant that he is under no

obligation to accept the final payment offered by the GCCF and that he may file suit were also present in the Determination Letter. The majority opinion characterizes these Release provisions as "the subjective or secret intent of the offeror"[6] since Johnson did not see the Release prior to checking the box on the Form. However, the Release was not tailored for Johnson's individual claim. The Release is the standard release for personal injury claims used in the GCCF process, as Johnson recognized in the district court. It is an integral part of the GCCF claims process and reflects that unless and until a claimant signed the Release, the voluntary GCCF claims process did not result in any relinquishment of a claimant's rights against the BP entities. The Determination Letter that Johnson did receive reflected the GCCF's intent that there was no binding agreement until the Release was signed by stating that Johnson had the right to be paid only if he accepted the "Final Payment Offer *and* [he] sign[ed] a Release and Covenant Not to Sue." [—36—]

The documents are consistent throughout. Johnson had the right to walk away from the GCCF process even after he sent the Final Payment Election Form to the GCCF. Since Johnson had the right to walk away, the GCCF did as well. There was no binding settlement agreement at the time that the GCCF sent the letter denying Johnson's claims.

* * * * *

For the foregoing reasons, I dissent.

---

compensation. If you want to file a lawsuit regarding the incident do not sign the Release.

[3] *Ante* at 23.
[4] *Id.*
[5] *Ante* at 24.

[6] *Id.*

United States Court of Appeals
for the Fifth Circuit

No. 13-30156

COMAR MARINE, CORP.

vs.

RAIDER MARINE LOGISTICS, L.L.C.

Appeals from the United States District Court for the
Western District of Louisiana

Decided: July 6, 2015

Citation: 792 F.3d 564, 3 Adm. R. 371 (5th Cir. 2015).

Before **STEWART**, Chief Judge, **OWEN**, Circuit Judge,
and **MORGAN**, District Judge.*

* District Judge of the Eastern District of Louisiana,
sitting by designation.

[—3—] OWEN, Circuit Judge:

This case involves a contract dispute
between Comar Marine, LLC (Comar)
and four vessel-owning LLCs. Under the
contracts, Comar managed the vessels on
behalf of the vessel-owning LLCs. The vessel-
owning LLCs decided to terminate the
agreements prematurely, and Comar sued for
breach of contract. JPMorgan Chase Bank
(JPMorgan) and Allegiance Bank Texas
(Allegiance) provided the financing for the
vessel purchases and intervened to defend
their preferred ship mortgages. The district
court granted summary judgment in favor of
JPMorgan and Allegiance. After a bench trial,
the district court held, *inter alia*, that (1) the
vessel-owning LLCs materially breached the
agreements by terminating without cause, (2)
the termination fee in the agreements was
penal and thus unenforceable, (3) Comar did
not have valid maritime liens on the vessels,
and (4) Comar wrongfully arrested the
vessels. We affirm.

I

Chris St. Amand and Tracy Lirette agreed
to purchase three vessels from Comar: the
M/V Conqueror, the M/V Raider, and the M/V
Enforcer. Subsequently, St. Amand and
Lirette agreed to purchase another ship, the
M/V Marauder, from Comar. St. Amand and
Lirette purchased the vessels through a
network of limited liability companies
(collectively, with St. Amand and [—4—]
Lirette, the Owners). JPMorgan financed the
purchases of the Conqueror, Raider, and
Enforcer, while Allegiance provided financing
for the Marauder. Both banks secured their
loans with preferred ship mortgages. As a
condition precedent to the purchases, Comar
required the Owners to enter into identical
management agreements for each of the
vessels. Under the management agreements,
the Owners appointed Comar to market,
manage, and operate the vessels and to pay
Comar a monthly management fee equal to
the greater of $3,000 or 10% of the gross
income from each vessel that month. All
expenses Comar incurred in connection with
its provision of services were to be
"reimbursed . . . from funds held on account of
Owner[s]."

As the Gulf of Mexico charter market
deteriorated, Lirette notified Comar by e-mail
that the Owners were terminating their
agreements effective immediately and had
executed management agreements with
another company. Shortly thereafter, Comar
filed in personam actions against Lirette, St.
Amand, and the various LLCs and in rem
actions against the four vessels, asserting
breach of contract. Comar alleged that it was
owed both outstanding expenses as well as
termination fees, totaling approximately
$1,146,117.47. Comar sought and secured
arrests of the four vessels, on the ground that
its claims for necessaries and termination fees
under the agreements gave rise to maritime
liens. The Owners filed counterclaims against
Comar, asserting, *inter alia*, wrongful arrest
of the vessels. JPMorgan and Allegiance both
intervened in the litigation in order to defend
their rights as preferred mortgagees.

The district court set bonds on the four
vessels. With a loan from Allegiance, the
Owners were able to pay the bond to secure
the release of the Marauder. JPMorgan,
however, was unwilling to lend further funds
to the Owners; as a result, the Owners placed
the LLCs owning the Raider, Enforcer, and
Conqueror into bankruptcy. The Marauder
was under seizure for 35 days, [—5—] and the
three other vessels for 37 days, during which

they could not be chartered or otherwise profitably used.

As the litigation proceeded, Comar withdrew its claim for unpaid expenses and necessaries because the funds obtained from collecting outstanding accounts receivable were sufficient to satisfy those expenses. JPMorgan and Allegiance filed motions for summary judgment contending that Comar did not have maritime liens on the vessels. The district court granted the banks' motions. Comar appealed with respect to JPMorgan pursuant to 28 U.S.C. § 1292(a)(3).[1]

The remaining parties proceeded to a bench trial. The district court held that although the Owners breached the agreements by terminating without cause, the termination fee was penal and therefore unenforceable. In lieu of the termination fee, the district court awarded Comar damages of $3,000 per month from the date of termination until the date the agreements were scheduled to expire. The court also held that St. Amand and Lirette were personally liable for these damages as the guarantors of the agreements. Additionally, the court held that Comar had wrongfully arrested the vessels. Nonetheless, it declined to award the Owners damages because it found the Owners had failed to introduce evidence establishing the extent of their damages with reasonable certainty.

Comar and the Owners each submitted postjudgment motions requesting, among other things, that the court amend the judgment to award prejudgment interest. The court granted the Owners' request to offset the damages owed to Comar by the excess of the accounts receivable and denied [—6—] the remainder of the motions without discussion, citing "the Court's discretion and the 'peculiar circumstances' of this action." Both Comar and the Owners timely appealed the court's judgment; Comar also appealed the grant of summary judgment in favor of Allegiance.

This court consolidated the appeals with Comar's interlocutory appeal of the district court's grant of summary judgment in favor of JPMorgan.

II

We review the district court's grant of summary judgment in favor of Allegiance and JPMorgan de novo, "applying the same legal standard as the district court in the first instance."[2] Under that standard, "[t]he court shall grant summary judgment if the movant shows that there is no genuine dispute as to any material fact and the movant is entitled to judgment as a matter of law."[3]

The district court granted summary judgment in favor of both JPMorgan and Allegiance on two alternative grounds. First, it held that the breach of the management agreements did not give rise to liabilities that created maritime liens, and accordingly, that JPMorgan's and Allegiance's preferred ship mortgages had priority over other claims against the vessels. In the alternative, the district court held that even if the breach did give rise to maritime liens, Comar was precluded from asserting them as a joint venturer. Comar challenges both conclusions.

Assuming the agreements at issue are maritime contracts, as the parties have stipulated, the remaining inquiry is whether breach of these contracts gave rise to maritime liens.[4] Maritime liens are "*stricti juris* and will not be [—7—] extended by

---

[1] 28 U.S.C. § 1292(a)(3) ("[T]he courts of appeals shall have jurisdiction of appeals from . . . [i]nterlocutory decrees of such district courts or the judges thereof determining the rights and liabilities of the parties to admiralty cases in which appeals from final decrees are allowed.").

[2] *Turner v. Baylor Richardson Med. Ctr.*, 476 F.3d 337, 343 (5th Cir. 2007).

[3] FED. R. CIV. P. 56(a).

[4] *Effjohn Int'l Cruise Holdings, Inc. v. A&L Sales, Inc.*, 346 F.3d 552, 565 (5th Cir. 2003) ("[I]n determining whether a contract falls within admiralty, the true criterion is the [—7—] nature and subject-matter of the contract, as whether it was a maritime contract, having reference to maritime service or maritime transactions." (alteration in original) (quoting *Exxon Corp. v. Cent. Gulf Lines, Inc.*, 500 U.S. 603, 610 (1991))); *Wilkins v. Commercial Inv. Trust Corp.*, 153 F.3d 1273, 1276 (11th Cir. 1998) (stating the existence of a maritime contract is a prerequisite to a claim of a maritime lien rooted in contract).

construction, analogy or inference."[5] "Thus, to determine the validity of a maritime lien, we must normally refer to statutory law or those liens that have been historically recognized in maritime law."[6]

The Fifth Circuit has recognized that the breach of certain types of contracts gives rise to maritime liens.[7] Comar does not contend that the management agreements of the sort it entered into with the Owners are one such historically recognized type. Instead, it claims that the district court erred because the agreements are the functional equivalent, or at the very least analogous, to bareboat charters, contracts recognized as giving rise to maritime liens,[8] and such equivalency is sufficient to confer a maritime lien.

Our decision in *Walker v. Braus* provides a definition of a charter party:

> A "charter" is an arrangement whereby one person (the "charterer") becomes entitled to the use of the whole of a vessel belonging to another (the "owner"). . . . Under a bareboat or demise charter . . . the full possession and control of the vessel is transferred to the charterer. The stated consideration for a demise charter is payable periodically but without regard to whether the charterer uses the vessel gainfully or not. Under a bareboat or demise charter the vessel is transferred without crew, provisions, [—8—] fuel or supplies, i.e. "bareboat"; and when, and if, the charterer operates the vessel he must supply also such essential operating expenses. Because the charter's personnel operate and man the vessel during a demise charter, the charterer has liability for any and all casualties resulting from such operation and therefore provides insurance for such liability.[9]

Like a bareboat charter, Comar had full possession and control of the vessels, carried insurance for the vessels, and used its own crew, but unlike such a charter, Comar did not pay for the vessels' expenses, including insurance, and did not owe the Owners a periodic payment independent of whether the vessels were used. Rather, the Owners paid Comar a management fee and reimbursed Comar for expenses, such as equipment, supplies, and repairs. Comar sought charters on behalf of the Owners and then revenue, net of the agreed charges, was remitted to the Owners. Additionally, under a bareboat charter, "[s]ervices performed on board the ship are primarily for [the charterer's] benefit."[10] Here, the services performed by Comar were primarily for the Owners' benefit. The management agreements in the present case are not the functional equivalent of bareboat charters.

Even were the management agreements similar to bareboat charters, the decisions on which Comar relies do not hold that breach of a contract analogous to one historically recognized as giving rise to a maritime lien is sufficient to impose such a lien.[11] At most, the

---

[5] *Piedmont & George's Creek Coal Co. v. Seaboard Fisheries Co.*, 254 U.S. 1, 12 (1920); *Racal Survey U.S.A., Inc. v. M/V Count Fleet*, 231 F.3d 183, 192 (5th Cir. 2000) (citing *Piedmont*, 254 U.S. at 12).

[6] *Racal Survey*, 231 F.3d at 192 (citing *Lake Charles Stevedores, Inc. v. Professor Vladimir Popov MV*, 199 F.3d 220, 224 (5th Cir. 1999)).

[7] *See Int'l Marine Towing, Inc. v. S. Leasing Partners, Ltd.*, 722 F.2d 126, 130-31 (5th Cir. 1983) (holding that the breach of a charter party, including a bareboat charter party, gives rise to a maritime lien); *E.A.S.T., Inc. of Stamford, Conn. v. M/V Alaia*, 876 F.2d 1168, 1175 (5th Cir. 1989) (recognizing that there is a specific "universe of maritime contracts which may give rise to a maritime lien," and this "universe" includes a time charter).

[8] *Int'l Marine Towing*, 722 F.2d at 130-31.

[9] *Walker v. Braus*, 995 F.2d 77, 80-81 (5th Cir. 1993).

[10] *Reed v. S.S. Yaka*, 373 U.S. 410, 412 (1963).

[11] *See Krauss Bros. Lumber Co. v. Dimon S.S. Corp.*, 290 U.S. 117, 125 (1933) (determining a lien existed for overpayment of freight by mistake where such a lien had already been recognized for "overpayments similarly made but induced by other means"); *Logistics Mgmt., Inc. v. One (1) Pyramid Tent Arena*, 86 F.3d 908, 913-14 (9th Cir. 1996) (holding that a non-vessel-operating common carrier has the same right as a vessel owner or operator to assert a maritime lien for unpaid freight against the cargo it is responsible for

Ninth Circuit has held, and this [—9—] court has intimated, that a contract may give rise to a maritime lien if it imposes practically identical rights and responsibilities as historically recognized contracts, such as a subcharter.[12] As discussed above, the management agreements in the present case do not impose practically identical responsibilities as charters. Comar's reliance on our unpublished decision in *Action Marine* is misplaced.[13] While we did state that "breach of a maritime contract gives rise to a maritime lien despite the fact that no damage was sustained to the cargo," the citations supporting this statement were to our decisions in *International Marine Towing* and *Rainbow Line*, which stand for the uncontroversial proposition that breach of a charter gives rise to maritime lien.[14] Our decision in *Action Marine* dealt with a towing contract, not a management agreement.[15]

Finally, while the management agreements stated that Comar "is relying on the credit of the Vessel[s] to secure payment of [the management fees and advanced sums for

expenses] and shall have a maritime lien on the Vessel[s]," the Supreme Court has stated,

> [m]aritime liens are not established by the agreement of the parties, except in hypothecations of vessels, but they result from [—10—] the nature and object of the contract. They are consequences attached by law to certain contracts, and are independent of any agreement between the parties that such liens shall exist. They, too, are *stricti juris*.[16]

The district court correctly concluded that breach of the management agreements did not give rise to maritime liens.[17] We affirm the district court's grant of summary judgment in favor of Allegiance and JPMorgan. We do not reach whether the district court's alternate holding that Comar was a joint venturer and therefore foreclosed from asserting a maritime lien was erroneous.

III

Regarding the litigation between the Owners and Comar, Comar challenges the district court's holdings that (1) the termination fees were penal and therefore unenforceable and (2) Comar wrongfully arrested the vessels following the Owners' termination. The Owners contest the district court's (1) decision to not award the Owners damages arising from Comar's wrongful arrest, (2) conclusion that St. Amand and Lirette personally guaranteed the agreements, and (3) calculation of Comar's damages. Both parties contest the district court's decision to not award prejudgment interest.

---

transporting); *E.A.S.T. Inc.*, 876 F.2d at 1175 (agreeing with the district court that "breach of a time charter may create a maritime lien"); *Cardinal Shipping Corp. v. M/S Seisho Maru*, 744 F.2d 461, 466-67 (5th Cir. 1984) (acknowledging, without holding, that "[c]onceivably, [—9—] even the breach of a sub-subcharter . . . could give rise to liens, under the theory that the subcharterer . . . was entrusted with the use of the vessel"); *Int'l Marine Towing*, 722 F.2d at 130-32 (holding that a bareboat charterer is "entitled to a maritime lien against the vessel for the owner's breach of the charter party"); *Rainbow Line, Inc. v. M/V Tequila*, 480 F.2d 1024, 1027 (2d Cir. 1973) ("The American law is clear that there is a maritime lien for the breach of a charter party, and because the damages sought to be recovered by Rainbow are all of a maritime nature and flow directly from the breach of the charter, it has a maritime lien." (footnotes omitted)).

[12] *See Logistics Mgmt.*, 86 F.3d at 913; *Cardinal Shipping*, 744 F.2d at 466-67.

[13] *Action Marine, Inc. v. Norseman, M/V*, 189 F.3d 470 (5th Cir. 1999) (unpublished table decision) (per curiam).

[14] *Id.* at *1 (citing *Int'l Marine Towing*, 722 F.2d at 130 and *Rainbow Line*, 480 F.2d at 1027).

[15] *Id.*

[16] *Newell v. Norton*, 70 U.S. 257, 262 (1865).

[17] *See Racal Survey U.S.A., Inc. v. M/V Count Fleet*, 231 F.3d 183, 193 (5th Cir. 2000) ("The lack of precedential authority and the stricti juris nature of a maritime lien are damning to TMI's cause, and we conclude that TMI's attempt to extend the concept of a maritime lien is unavailing.").

A

"Whether a liquidated damage provision constitutes a penalty is a question of law,"[18] reviewable de novo.[19] "This court applies the two-part test [—11—] set forth in the *Restatement (Second) of Contracts* § 356, comment b."[20] The Restatement provides:

[T]wo factors combine in determining whether an amount of money fixed as damages is so unreasonably large as to be a penalty. The first factor is the anticipated or actual loss caused by the breach. The amount fixed is reasonable to the extent that it approximates the actual loss that has resulted from the particular breach, even though it may not approximate the loss that might have been anticipated under other possible breaches. Furthermore, the amount fixed is reasonable to the extent that it approximates the loss anticipated at the time of the making of the contract, even though it may not approximate the actual loss. The second factor is the difficulty of proof of loss. The greater the difficulty either of proving that loss has occurred or of establishing its amount with the requisite certainty (see § 351), the easier it is to show that the amount fixed is reasonable. To the extent that there is uncertainty as to the harm, the estimate of the court or jury may not accord with the principle of compensation any more than does the advance estimate of the parties. A determination whether the amount fixed is a penalty turns on a combination of these two factors. If the difficulty of proof of loss is great, considerable latitude is allowed in the

approximation of anticipated or actual harm. If, on the other hand, the difficulty of proof of loss is slight, less latitude is allowed in that approximation. If, to take an extreme case, it is clear that no loss at all has occurred, a provision fixing a substantial sum as damages is unenforceable.[21]

Under this court's precedent, the party seeking to invalidate the liquidated-damage provision has "the burden of proving that [it] is a penalty."[22] [—12—]

The termination-fee provision provides that if the Owners terminate the agreements, they are required to pay Comar "fifty (50%) percent of what COMAR would have earned as a Management Fee had [the] Agreement not been so terminated." "[W]hat COMAR would have earned" is

calculated by determining the average gross daily charter hire earned by the Vessel from inception of [the] Agreement up through the date of termination for all days the Vessel has actually worked. This average gross daily charter hire rate will then be multiplied by the number of days remaining under [the] Agreement but for [the] early termination.

The agreements provide the following example:

[I]f the Vessel's gross daily charter hire rate for days actually worked up through termination was $5,000 per day and there were 100 days left under [the] Agreement but for [the] early termination, Owner shall owe liquidated damages of $25,000 to COMAR [$5,000 average gross daily charter hire rate x 100 days x .05 (50% of 10%) = $25,000].

Under these provisions, the termination fee was $537,246.86. There is no evidence that the $537,246.86 amount calculated under the

---

[18] *Louis Dreyfus Corp. v. 27,946 Long Tons of Corn*, 830 F.2d 1321, 1331 (5th Cir. 1987).

[19] *McLane Foodservice, Inc. v. Table Rock Restaurants, L.L.C.*, 736 F.3d 375, 377 (5th Cir. 2013); *see also Theriot v. United States*, 245 F.3d 388, 394 (5th Cir. 1998) (per curiam) [—11—] ("In an admiralty action tried by the court without a jury, the factual findings of the district court are binding unless clearly erroneous. Questions of law are reviewed de novo." (citation omitted)).

[20] *Louis Dreyfus Corp.*, 830 F.2d at 1331.

[21] RESTATEMENT (SECOND) OF CONTRACTS § 356, comment b (citations omitted).

[22] *Farmers Exp. Co. v. M/V Georgis Prois*, 799 F.2d 159, 162 (5th Cir. 1986).

termination provisions approximated the actual loss that resulted from the Owners' early termination of the agreements.

With regard to whether the termination provisions approximated the loss anticipated at the time the contracts were executed, Comar argues that the formula was reasonable because the cyclical nature of the charter market makes it difficult to anticipate actual losses and the 50% discount figure is a reasonable approximation of the vessels' utilization rate. The district court found that the formula does not account for either previous or future nonworking days. The average gross daily charter-hire rate is calculated based only on the days the vessels worked, and that daily rate is multiplied by the number of days until the agreements' expiration. [—13—]

Comar contends, however, that the 50% discount serves to neutralize the inflation by anticipating that the vessels will only be used on 50% of the remaining days. This discount appears reasonable considering the vessels' yearly average utilization rates varied from 35% to 98% in the years preceding termination. Nonetheless, even assuming the 50% discount is a reasonable anticipation of what Comar's management fee would have been but for termination, we cannot conclude that the district court erred in holding that the termination fee is penal. As the district court noted, Charles Tizzard, Comar's president, and others testified that Comar incurs general and administrative expenses in its management of the vessels, and that most of the management fee it received paid those expenses and included only a small amount as profit. Tizzard testified that those expenses would decrease, but would not be eliminated, if the contracts were terminated. The termination fee formula, however, makes no deductions to account for the fact that Comar would have fewer expenses in the event of termination, and Comar has not quantified the expenses that would remain. We cannot say that the district court clearly erred in finding that the termination provisions do not provide a reasonable approximation of the loss anticipated at the time the contracts were formed.

Moreover, as the district court noted, the fact that breach of one agreement constitutes a breach of the other three agreements underscores the penal nature of the termination fee. Additionally, the termination fee is operative not only in the event the Owners terminate but also if the Owners sell the vessels and Comar "elects not to manage the Vessel[s] for a new owner." Comar does not, and reasonably could not, assert that the termination formula approximates the damages it would suffer in the event the Owners sell the vessels to a new owner willing to assume the Owners' obligations. Nor did the [—14—] agreements include a corresponding remedy for the Owners in the event of Comar's breach.

Accordingly, the district court did not commit reversible error in concluding that the termination-fee provision is unenforceable.

B

In lieu of the termination fees, the district court awarded Comar "$3,000 per calendar month, for each vessel, from the date of termination of the Agreements, August 14, 2009, through the end date of the Agreements, January 31, 2010," based on the agreements' default management fee and offset by what Comar owed the Owners after collecting the outstanding accounts receivable. The Owners challenge the award of $3,000 per month per vessel, contending it is clearly erroneous.

"A district court's damages award is a finding of fact, which this court reviews for clear error."[23] "If the award of damages is plausible in light of the record, a reviewing court should not reverse the award even if it might have come to a different conclusion."[24]

The district court found that the "[a]greements' default monthly management fee [of $3,000] . . . fixe[d] any uncertainty or difficulty otherwise involved in determining losses for non-working months . . . and provide[d] a ceiling for determining any

---

[23] *Jauch v. Nautical Servs., Inc.*, 470 F.3d 207, 213 (5th Cir. 2006) (per curiam).

[24] *St. Martin v. Mobil Exploration & Producing U.S. Inc.*, 224 F.3d 402, 410 (5th Cir. 2000).

alleged losses." The Owners argue that awarding the minimum payment specified in the agreements of $3,000 per month conflicts with the district court's finding that more than half of Comar's revenue from management fees went to general and administrative expenses and that the Owners' termination relieved Comar of paying at least some of [—15—] those expenses. But there is no indication that Comar would have only earned the $3,000 minimum under the agreements. Comar often earned management fees in excess of the minimum. The average monthly management fees in 2009 were $4,007 for the Conqueror, $5,789 for the Enforcer, $6,222 for the Marauder, and $5,615 for the Raider. In 2008, the average monthly management fees were even higher: $9,547 for the Conqueror, $10,532 for the Enforcer, $10,515 for the Marauder, and $9,481 for the Raider. The district court's award is "plausible in light of the record" and not clearly erroneous.[25]

C

Comar challenges the district court's holding that it wrongfully arrested the vessels after the Owners' termination. To recover for wrongful arrest of a vessel, there must be (1) no bona fide claim of a maritime lien on the vessel[26] and 2) a showing of "bad faith, malice,

or gross negligence [on the part] of the offending party."[27] [—16—]

Whether a maritime lien exists is a question of law,[28] reviewed de novo.[29] A finding of joint venture precluding such a lien is reviewed for clear error.[30] "The district court's determination . . . [of] bad faith . . . was a conclusion of fact, which we review under the deferential clear error standard."[31] The burden of proof lies with the party alleging wrongful arrest.[32] "[T]he advice of competent counsel, honestly sought and acted upon in

---

[25] *Id.*

[26] *See Arochem Corp. v. Wilomi, Inc.*, 962 F.2d 496, 500 (5th Cir. 1992) ("The district court correctly granted Wilomi's motion for summary judgment against Arochem's wrongful arrest claim because Wilomi acted neither in bad faith, nor with malice or gross negligence. A company does *not* wrongfully arrest cargo *by asserting a bona fide lien* to protect its interest." (emphases added)); *Cardinal Shipping Corp. v. M/S Seisho Maru*, 744 F.2d 461, 475 (5th Cir. 1984) (holding that because "there was a bona fide dispute over the validity of [the] lien" and "no evidence of . . . bad faith," this court would not award attorney's fees); *see also TTT Stevedores of Tex., Inc. v. M/V Jagat Vijeta*, 696 F.2d 1135, 1141 (5th Cir. 1983) ("Because we have held that TTT Stevedores had a good lien, we find Dempo entitled to no damages for wrongful seizure.").

[27] *Arochem Corp.*, 962 F.2d at 499 (quoting *Frontera Fruit Co. v. Dowling*, 91 F.2d 293, 297 (5th Cir. 1937)).

[28] *See E.A.S.T., Inc. of Stamford, Conn. v. M/V Alaia*, 876 F.2d 1168, 1171, 1173-74 (5th Cir. 1989) (stating that all issues presented in the case were questions of law, and existence of a maritime lien was one of the issues).

[29] *McLane Foodservice, Inc. v. Table Rock Restaurants, L.L.C.*, 736 F.3d 375, 377 (5th Cir. 2013); *Theriot v. United States*, 245 F.3d 388, 394 (5th Cir. 1998) (per curiam) ("In an admiralty action tried by the court without a jury, . . . [q]uestions of law are reviewed de novo.").

[30] *See Crustacean Transp. Corp. v. Atalanta Trading Corp.*, 369 F.2d 656, 660 (5th Cir. 1966) (holding that a finding of no waiver of the maritime lien—and thus a finding of no joint venture—"cannot be disturbed unless clearly erroneous"); *Fulcher's Point Pride Seafood, Inc. v. M/V Theodora Maria*, 935 F.2d 208, 211 (11th Cir. 1991) ("We review the district court's findings as to a joint venture's existence under the clearly erroneous standard.") (citing *Crustacean Transp. Corp.*, 369 F.2d at 660).

[31] *Dickerson v. Lexington Ins. Co.*, 556 F.3d 290, 300 (5th Cir. 2009).

[32] *See Cardinal Shipping Corp. v. M/S Seisho Maru*, 744 F.2d 461, 474 (5th Cir. 1984) ("In order to collect [attorney's] fees, the plaintiff must prove that the party seizing the vessel acted in bad faith, with malice, or with wanton disregard for the rights of his opponent."); *Furness Withy (Chartering), Inc., Panama v. World Energy Systems Assocs.*, 854 F.2d 410, 411 (11th Cir. 1988) ("It is an established principle of maritime law that one who suffers a wrongful attachment may recover damages from the party who obtained the attachment, provided he prove that such party acted in bad faith.").

good faith is alone a complete defense" to a claim of damages for wrongful arrest.[33]

Comar contends that it seized the vessels pursuant to valid maritime liens because, at the time of termination, the Owners owed it funds for necessaries. The district court found that the only amounts owed to Comar by the Owners as of the date of the arrest of the vessels was for the termination fees specified in the agreements, and that the termination fees were not for [—17—] any services that Comar actually rendered to the vessels. As of the date of the arrest, if Comar had collected and applied all outstanding accounts receivable from the operation of the vessels to the Owners' accounts payable, without considering the termination fees, Comar would have owed the Owners more than $21,000. The district court had previously held that the management agreements could not give rise to liabilities that would create maritime liens. We agree with the district court that Comar wrongly arrested the vessels.

We review the district court's finding of bad faith for clear error. Before the vessels were arrested, the Owners notified Glynn Haines, CEO of Comar, that they intended to terminate the agreements effective immediately because they had signed management agreements with another organization. Four days after the Owners terminated the agreements, Comar secured the arrest of the vessels. Comar argues that it was acting in good faith pursuant to legal advice that the outstanding expenses and accounts-receivable loans gave rise to maritime liens.

Due to conflicts in testimony, the district court found that neither Haines nor Tizzard were credible witnesses regarding Comar's arrest of the vessels. Haines provided inconsistent testimony regarding the extent to which Haines discussed the decision to arrest the vessels with counsel. Tizzard was

impeached on cross-examination and the district judge's questions regarding his role in the preparation of the damages claimed in Comar's original complaint and regarding the certainty of collecting the outstanding accounts receivable at the time of the arrests. Haines testified that the decision to arrest was made knowing that there were outstanding accounts receivable. Haines also stated that he had worked with the companies who owed these accounts and had had no difficulty collecting outstanding accounts receivable in the past. As noted above, other than the unenforceable termination fees, assuming Comar collected all accounts receivable, Comar owed the Owners over $21,000. [—18—] Haines testified that even if he had known that Comar owed the Owners, he still would have arrested the vessels because he did not know what legal options he had to freeze the vessels' accounts.

The district court found that, "at the time of arrest, because Comar knew (through Haines and Tizzard) . . . that Comar would ultimately owe the [Owners] money, Comar lacked probable cause to arrest the Vessels." The district court also found that although Comar had access to all relevant information, it acted before it made a complete assessment of who owed what and did not provide its legal counsel complete information. Furthermore, the district court noted that Comar amended the arrest complaint to include a claim for failure to repaint the vessels "even[] though the Vessels were at a shipyard being painted when [Haines] had them arrested." Under these circumstances, the district court did not clearly err in finding that Comar acted in bad faith when arresting the vessels and did not rely on legal advice in good faith.

D

The Owners assert that the court erred in declining to award them lost-profit and lost-equity damages arising from Comar's wrongful arrest of the vessels. "Determinations of the trial court concerning the amount of damages are factual findings,

---

[33] *Frontera Fruit Co. v. Dowling*, 91 F.2d 293, 297 (5th Cir. 1937); *accord Marastro Compania Naviera, S.A. v. Canadian Maritime Carriers, Ltd.*, 959 F.2d 49, 53 (5th Cir. 1992) (citing *Frontera Fruit Co.*, 91 F.2d at 297).

and we will set them aside only if clearly erroneous."[34]

As to lost profits, a court may only award damages for detention of a vessel "when profits have actually been, or may be reasonably supposed to have been, lost, and the amount of such profits is proven with reasonable [—19—] certainty."[35] In relation to detention damages following a "collision or other maritime tort," the Supreme Court has stated:

The best evidence of damage suffered by detention is the sum for which vessels of the same size and class can be chartered in the market. . . . In the absence of such market value, the value of her use to her owner in the business in which she was engaged at the time of the collision is a proper basis for estimating damages for detention, and the books of the owner, showing her earnings about the time of her collision, are competent evidence of her probable earnings during the time of her detention.[36]

Similarly, this court has stated detention damages "need not be proven with an exact degree of specificity"[37] nor with evidence of "a specific lost opportunity."[38] Rather, "the time honored rule in maritime cases . . . is to seek a fair average based on a number of voyages

before and after"[39] then deduct the costs avoided by the detention.[40]

The district court did not clearly err in concluding that the Owners had failed to introduce evidence to allow it to determine lost-profit damages with [—20—] reasonable certainty.[41] Lirette and St. Amand testified that Kilgore Marine contacted them regarding use of the vessels before and during the arrest of the vessels; however, there is no other evidence documenting this work. Lirette also testified that Kilgore Marine was "ready to put [one of the vessels] to work" after the wrongful arrest, at least one of the vessels was at work shortly after its release and repainting, and "Kilgore Marine ended up working the boats for most of what they've worked on since then until today." However, the Owners do not provide any indication of when all of the vessels were put back to work, the frequency of the work, or the profits from that work. Although the vessels operated at a profit in June 2009 (two months before the arrest of the vessels), the vessels, as a whole, operated at a loss the prior five months. Accordingly, the evidence does not leave us with a "definite and firm conviction that a mistake has been committed" by the district court.[42]

Regarding lost-equity damages, the Owners argue that when Comar seized the vessels, the Owners could not pay bond on three of them because they did not have sufficient funds and JPMorgan would not provide a loan. The Owners assert that Comar's wrongful arrest forced them to file for bankruptcy. The three

---

[34] *Marine Transp. Lines, Inc. v. M/V Tako Invader*, 37 F.3d 1138, 1140 (5th Cir. 1994); *accord In re M/V Nicole Trahan*, 10 F.3d 1190, 1193-94 (5th Cir. 1994).

[35] *The Conqueror*, 166 U.S. 110, 125, 127 (1897); *see also Marine Transp.*, 37 F.3d at 1140 ("A district court's lost profits methodology must permit it to arrive at a damages amount 'with reasonable certainty. No more is required.'" (quoting *Orduna S.A. v. Zen-Noh Grain Corp.*, 913 F.2d 1149, 1155 (5th Cir. 1990)) (some internal quotation marks omitted)); *M/V Nicole Trahan*, 10 F.3d at 1194.

[36] *The Conqueror*, 166 U.S. at 127; *see Cardinal Shipping*, 744 F.2d at 474 (referring to wrongful seizure of a vessel as a tort).

[37] *Marine Transp.*, 37 F.3d at 1140 (quoting *Mitsui O.S.K. Lines, K.K. v. Horton & Horton, Inc.*, 480 F.2d 1104, 1106 (5th Cir. 1973)).

[38] *Id.* at 1141 n.3; *accord M/V Nicole Trahan*, 10 F.3d at 1194-96.

[39] *Delta S.S. Lines, Inc. v. Avondale Shipyards, Inc.*, 747 F.2d 995, 1001 (5th Cir. 1984); *accord M/V Nicole Trahan*, 10 F.3d at 1194-96 (applying the *Avondale* rule to a 6.6-day detention for repairs following a collision).

[40] *Marine Transp.*, 37 F.3d at 1150 ("The damage that this loss represents is the ship's charter rate, less the variable or incremental expenses that would have been required of the owner to perform the charters, discounted by the probable utilization rate." (quoting *Kim Crest, S.A. v. M.V. Sverdlovsk*, 753 F.Supp. 642, 649 (S.D. Tex. 1990))).

[41] *Id.* at 1140.

[42] *Id.* (quoting *United States v. U.S. Gypsum Co.*, 333 U.S. 364, 395 (1948)).

entities that owned the vessels did file voluntary petitions for bankruptcy on September 21, 2009, approximately three days before the vessels were released from arrest. However, the vessels were not sold until nearly four years later, after the bankruptcies had been converted from Chapter 11 reorganizations to Chapter 7 liquidations because the Owners failed to make required payments to JPMorgan. Comar disputes that the arrests caused the Owners to lose equity in its vessels during liquidation, citing, among other reasons, JPMorgan's refusal to lend the Owners money to [—21—] pay the vessels' bonds, the Owners' business decisions, the poor market environment, and the Owners' failure to comply with the reorganization plans. The district court did not clearly err in denying such damages, even assuming lost-equity damages were available in the maritime context, which is a question we need not resolve.

E

The Owners contest the district court's holding that Lirette and St. Amand personally guaranteed the agreements. "The district court's interpretation of a contract is reviewed de novo, and [t]he contract and record are reviewed independently and under the same standards that guided the district court."[43] "[I]f the interpretation of the contract turns on the consideration of extrinsic evidence, such as evidence of the intent of the parties," we review for clear error.[44]

The parties agree that Louisiana law applies to the guaranty provision, and the district court applied Louisiana law to this issue. We assume that Louisiana law governs for purposes of this appeal.[45] Under Louisiana

law, a guaranty "must be expressed clearly and must be construed within the limits [—22—] intended by the parties to the agreement."[46] However, "[c]ontracts of guaranty . . . are subject to the same rules of interpretation as contracts in general."[47] Accordingly, "[c]ourts are bound to give legal effect to all such contracts according to the true intent of the parties, and this intent is to be determined by the words of the contract when these are clear and explicit and lead to no absurd consequences."[48]

The Owners acknowledge that the agreements contain a guaranty provision providing that "[t]he principal of the Owner, whose name is set forth below, hereby unconditionally guarantees the prompt and full payment of all obligations owed by Owner under this Agreement." They further concede that St. Amand and Lirette signed their names under the heading "GUARANTORS OF THIS AGREEMENT" and that, beneath their signatures appears the following language: "Tracy P. Lirette, Guarantor" and "Chris St. Amand, Guarantor." They assert, however, that the district court erred in concluding that they personally guaranteed the agreements

---

[43] *In re Liljeberg Enters., Inc.*, 304 F.3d 410, 439 (5th Cir. 2002) (alteration in original) (quoting *St. Martin v. Mobil Exploration & Producing U.S. Inc.*, 224 F.3d 402, 409 (5th Cir. 2000)) (internal quotation marks omitted).

[44] *Id.* (quoting *Nat'l Union Fire Ins. Co. v. Circle, Inc.*, 915 F.2d 986, 989 (5th Cir. 1990) (per curiam)).

[45] *See Kossick v. United Fruit Co.*, 365 U.S. 731, 735 (1961) (stating "an agreement to pay damages for another's breach of a maritime charter is not"

governed by admiralty law); *Angelina Cas. Co. v. Exxon Corp., U.S.A.*, 876 F.2d 40, 41 (5th Cir. 1989) ("Under the rule in *Thurmond v. Delta Well Surveyors*, 836 F.2d 952, 955 (5th Cir. 1988), state law governs disputes arising out of the performance of a separate non-maritime obligation of a mixed contract."); *cf. United States v. Little Joe Trawlers, Inc.*, 776 F.2d 1249, 1251 n.2 (5th Cir. 1985) ("[T]he parties have briefed and argued Texas law throughout this litigation, and the trial court applied Texas law. Therefore, we will refrain from changing the rules in the middle of the game, and in doing so, we apply Texas law.").

[46] *Regions Bank v. La. Pipe & Steel Fabricators, LLC*, 2011-0839, p. 4 (La. App. 1 Cir. 12/21/11); 80 So. 3d 1209, 1212; *see also* LA. CIV. CODE ANN. art. 3038 ("Suretyship must be express and in writing."); *Wooley v. Lucksinger*, 2006-1140, p. 7 (La. App. 1 Cir. 12/30/08); 7 So. 3d 660, 664 (citing LA. REV. STAT. ANN. § 10:1-201(b)(39)); LA. REV. STAT. ANN. § 10:1-201(b)(39) ("'Surety' includes a guarantor or other secondary obligor.").

[47] *Ferrell v. S. Cent. Bell Tel. Co.*, 403 So. 2d 698, 700 (La. 1981) (citing *Am. Bank & Trust Co. v. Blue Bird Rest. & Lounge, Inc.*, 279 So. 2d 720 (La. App. 1 Cir. 1973)).

[48] *Id.* (citing LA. CIV. CODE ANN. art. 1945).

because Lirette and St. Amand are not the "principal[s] of the [vessel] Owners." Rather, the principal of the vessel-owning LLCs is Gator Offshore, LLC (Gator). The guaranty provision and signature page appear as follows: [—23—]

ARTICLE 20. **PRINCIPAL OF OWNER GUARANTY.** The principal of the Owner, whose name is set forth below, hereby unconditionally guarantees the prompt and full payment of all obligations owed by Owner under this Agreement, including, without limitation, all Owner Expenses, the Management Fee and all other obligations owed by Owner (including the surviving indemnity obligations) owed under this Agreement.

[Signature page follows]

Executed in multiple originals, this 21 day of May 20 08

WITNESSES:

NAUTICAL OFFSHORE
CORPORATION, a/k/a COMAR

By:
Name: Charles B. Tizzard
Its: President

WITNESSES:

MARAUDER MARINE LOGISTICS, LLC,
OWNER

By: Gator Offshore, LLC, its Sole Member

By:
Name: Tracy P. Lirette
Its: Member

WITNESSES:

GUARANTORS OF THIS AGREEMENT:

By:
Tracy P. Lirette, Guarantor

By:
Chris St. Amand, Guarantor

The district court determined that the agreements clearly indicated that Lirette and St. Amand signed in their individual capacity as personal guarantors. If the guaranty provision refers to Gator ("[t]he principal of the Owner"), as the Owners argue, there would be no need for Lirette and St. Amand to sign again as "Guarantors of this Agreement." The contract is unambiguous that Gator's signature, through Lirette, indicates its consent to the terms of the contract, including the guaranty provision, while Lirette and St. Amand's signatures are separate, personal guarantees.

Even if the agreements were ambiguous, the district court found Lirette and St. Amand's testimony that they did not believe they were personally [—24—] guaranteeing the agreements to be incredible, and we see no clear error in the district court's findings as to their intent.[49]

---

[49] *See In re Liljeberg Enters., Inc.*, 304 F.3d 410, 439 (5th Cir. 2002).

F

"As a general rule, prejudgment interest should be awarded in admiralty cases—not as a penalty, but as compensation for the use of funds to which the claimant was rightfully entitled."[50] The district court has discretion to deny prejudgment interest "only when there are 'peculiar circumstances' that would make it inequitable for the losing party to be forced to pay prejudgment interest."[51] "Peculiar circumstances may be found where plaintiff improperly delayed resolution of the action, where a genuine dispute over a good faith claim exists in a mutual fault setting, where some equitable doctrine cautions against the award, or where the damages award was substantially less than the amount claimed by plaintiff."[52]

The district court denied Comar and the Owners prejudgment interest because of the "'peculiar circumstances' of this action." But it did not set forth what those peculiar circumstances were, contrary to what we have stated is the best practice for a district court denying prejudgment interest.[53] Nonetheless, we may still affirm the denial of prejudgment interest unless the record indicates the district court clearly erred when it found peculiar [—25—] circumstances existed.[54] For

---

[50] *Noritake Co. v. M/V Hellenic Champion*, 627 F.2d 724, 728 (5th Cir. Unit A 1980).

[51] *Id.*

[52] *Reeled Tubing, Inc. v. M/V Chad G*, 794 F.2d 1026, 1028 (5th Cir. 1986); *see also City of Milwaukee v. Cement Div., Nat'l Gypsum Co.*, 515 U.S. 189, 195-98 (1995).

[53] *Cantieri Navali Riuniti v. M/V Skyptron*, 802 F.2d 160, 165 n.9 (5th Cir. 1986) ("[T]he best practice for a trial court that refuses to award prejudgment interest would be for it to detail the peculiar circumstances it has found . . . ." (quoting *Noritake*, 627 F.2d at 729 n.4) (internal quotation marks omitted)).

[54] *Noritake*, 627 F.2d at 729 ("If the trial court explicitly denies prejudgment interest (rather than merely omitting any reference to it), then this is based on a factfinding that peculiar circumstances exist; the factfinding is sometimes explicitly set out, with the peculiar circumstances detailed in the court's findings of fact and conclusions of law, or it may be implicit in the denial of prejudgment interest without a listing of the circumstances. If the trial court was not clearly erroneous in finding

both Comar and the Owners, the awarded damages are substantially less than originally claimed.[55] Because the record reveals a peculiar circumstance on which the district court could have reasonably based its denial of prejudgment interest, the district court did not clearly err in denying prejudgment interest to Comar and the Owners.[56]

* * *

For the above reasons, we AFFIRM the district court's judgment.

---

that peculiar circumstances exist, then its denial of prejudgment interest was discretionary." (footnote omitted)); *see also In re Signal Int'l, LLC*, 579 F.3d 478, 501 (5th Cir. 2009) ("[T]he district court omitted any reference to prejudgment interest. Thus, under the framework established in *Noritake*, we analyze the record to determine if the existence of a peculiar circumstance was clear.").

[55] *See Reeled Tubing*, 794 F.2d at 1028 ("Peculiar circumstances may be found . . . where the damages award was substantially less than the amount claimed by plaintiff.").

[56] *See Noritake*, 627 F.2d at 729; *see also In re Signal Int'l*, 579 F.3d at 501.

United States Court of Appeals
for the Fifth Circuit

No. 14-30823

IN RE DEEPWATER HORIZON

LAKE EUGENIE LAND DEV., INC.
vs.
BP EXPLORATION & PROD., INC.

Appeal from the United States District Court for the
Eastern District of Louisiana

Decided: July 16, 2015

Citation: 793 F.3d 479, 3 Adm. R. 383 (5th Cir. 2015).

Before **STEWART**, Chief Judge, and **KING**, and **ELROD**, Circuit Judges.

[—1—] **STEWART**, Chief Judge:

In May 2012, BP Exploration & Production Inc. ("BP") and related entities reached a settlement with a class of individuals who suffered economic [—2—] and property damage after the Deepwater Horizon incident. That settlement agreement established a fund and an elaborate multi-tiered claims process. A provision in the agreement governs the scope and timing of the parties' access to information about these claims as they advance through that process. The district court determined that the provision did not entitle the parties to claim-specific information until an initial decision about a claim's eligibility had been made by the settlement program. BP appeals that decision. Counsel for the settlement class ("Class Counsel") argue chiefly that this court lacks jurisdiction to hear the appeal. We agree and DISMISS for lack of jurisdiction.

I. BACKGROUND

The district court approved the settlement and expressly adopted it in a December 2012 order. The agreement (the "Settlement Agreement" or the "Agreement") provides that the district court retains "continuing and exclusive jurisdiction over the Parties and their Counsel for the purpose of enforcing, implementing and interpreting th[e] Agree-

ment." At the time of briefing in this case, 288,000 claims had been filed, resulting in 75,000 awards totaling $5.2 billion.

The settlement regime ("Settlement Program") provides for the resolution of a variety of claims—e.g., business economic loss claims, vessel damage claims, coastal real property damage claims—through a wide array of procedures. Submitting a claim requires providing completed forms and documentation proof such as tax returns and profit/loss statements.

After the Settlement Program makes a determination about a particular claim's eligibility, a claimant or BP may, in certain circumstances, avail themselves of a multi-tiered internal review process crafted to "assure accuracy, transparency, independence, and adherence" to the terms of the Settlement Agreement. The deadline for internal appeal of an eligibility determination is a function of which party appeals and the amount of the [—3—] award, but all appeals must be filed within 30 days of notice of the award. Appeals are heard de novo by a panel, whose decision is intended to be "final." Discretionary review, however, is available in the district court, which treats the panel's decision like a magistrate judge's report and recommendation, reviewing de novo any dispositive issues. *See* Fed. R. Civ. P. 72(b)(3).

The disputed provision here, § 4.4.14 of the Settlement Agreement, governs access to information associated with individual claims and the precise timing of that access. The relevant excerpt reads:

> BP and Class Counsel shall have access to all Claim Files and Claims-related data transferred to or generated in the Settlement Program for any legitimate purpose including, without limitation, the operation of BP's separate [Oil Pollution Act] facility, prosecuting and defending appeals, reviewing and auditing the Settlement Program, reporting financial results, and pursuing indemnification, contribution, subrogation, insurance and other claims from third parties. However, BP and

Class Counsel shall not have access to any Claim Files for Claims that are being processed and have not yet been resolved in the Settlement Program except if the Claim File is needed by BP, a Claimant, or their counsel to prosecute or defend an Appeal.[1]

Class Counsel claim that BP violated § 4.4.14 by accessing claim-specific information on an internal site run by the Claims Administrator and used regularly by the parties in the normal operation of the Settlement Program. BP counters that it was permitted to do so under § 4.4.14. After this dispute arose, the Claims Administrator interpreted § 4.4.14 to permit both parties to access claim-specific information before issuance of an eligibility notice. After such notice, the Claims Administrator determined, BP and Class Counsel could view the internal work files of the program. [—4—]

In February 2014, Class Counsel brought a motion seeking to block BP's access to claim-specific information before the Settlement Program made an initial determination about a claim's eligibility. The district court determined in an order dated March 25, 2014 (the "March 25 Order") that neither BP nor Class Counsel should be permitted "access to any individual claim file before the Program issues a Denial Notice or an Eligibility Notice."

BP filed a motion for reconsideration and cited five examples of situations where access to pre-determination, claim-specific data on one claim helped the company detect an improper award on a post-determination claim. For example, in one case, BP's review of claim-specific data on a group of pre-determination individual claims for property damage to a single building revealed that a different claimant had already received a $1.8 million award for the same damage alleged by

the pre-determination claimants. BP appealed that award, and an appeals panel reversed it. BP's five examples show improper awards totaling about $4 million. The district court adhered to its prior holding in a June 6, 2014 order (the "June 6 Order") denying BP's motion for reconsideration.[2] The court noted that BP's request for "all pre-determination data is not justified either by the express terms of the Settlement Agreement or by the few examples it cites in its motion." While "no program handling hundreds of thousands of claims can be flawless," the court stated, the elaborate fraud-protection measures in place were sufficient to protect BP.

BP has appealed, citing two bases for jurisdiction. First, BP contends that this court has jurisdiction to review the district court's Orders under the collateral order doctrine. Alternatively, BP argues, this court can assert [—5—] jurisdiction under 28 U.S.C. § 1292(a)(1), which permits appellate jurisdiction in limited circumstances when, as relevant here, a court grants or modifies an injunction. Finally, on the merits, BP claims that the district court incorrectly interpreted the Settlement Agreement to prevent it from accessing claim-specific data on unresolved claims.

II. DISCUSSION

The Orders did not terminate all proceedings in this case, so the panel must first determine if jurisdiction exists. Because we conclude that we lack jurisdiction under either the collateral order doctrine or § 1292(a)(1), we do not reach the merits.

A. Collateral Order Doctrine

BP first invokes the collateral order doctrine as a basis for jurisdiction. As relevant here, 28 U.S.C. § 1291 provides that the courts of appeal have "jurisdiction of appeals from all final decisions of the district courts." Generally, a final decision is one "by which a district court disassociates itself from a case." *Swint v. Chambers Cnty. Comm'n*, 514 U.S.

---

[1] The Settlement Agreement defines "Claim" as "any demand or request for compensation . . . together with any properly completed form and accompanying required documentation, submitted by a Claimant to the Settlement Program." The terms "Claim File" and "Claims-related data" are not defined in the Settlement Agreement.

[2] For simplicity, we will refer to the March 25 and June 6 orders collectively as the "Orders."

35, 42 (1995). The collateral order doctrine—typically associated with *Cohen v. Beneficial Indus. Loan Corp.*, 337 U.S. 541, 545–46 (1949)—is "best understood not as an exception" to this finality rule, "but as a practical construction of it." *Will v. Hallock*, 546 U.S. 345, 349 (2006) (internal quotation marks and citations omitted).

The doctrine supplies jurisdiction for a "'small class' of pre-judgment orders that 'finally determine claims of right separable from, and collateral to, rights asserted in the action [and that are] too important to be denied review and too independent of the cause itself to require that appellate consideration be deferred until the whole case is adjudicated.'" *Lauro Lines s.r.l. v. Chasser*, 490 U.S. 495, 498 (1989) (quoting *Cohen*, 337 U.S. at 546). Put otherwise, we have jurisdiction under the collateral order doctrine when an order: (1) [—6—] conclusively determined the disputed question; (2) resolved an important issue separate from the merits of the case; and (3) is effectively unreviewable on appeal from a final judgment. *See Will*, 546 U.S. at 349; *Richardson-Merrell Inc. v. Koller*, 472 U.S. 424, 431 (1985) (citation omitted).[3]

"Importance" has sometimes been characterized as a discrete fourth requirement and other times been wrapped up in an analysis of both the second and third requirements. *See Mohawk Indus. Inc. v. Carpenter*, 558 U.S. 100, 107 (2009) (explaining that the question of whether a right is effectively unreviewable "cannot be answered without a judgment about the value of the interests that would be lost through rigorous application of a final judgment requirement" (internal quotation marks and citation omitted)); *Will*, 546 U.S. at 353 (recognizing that effective unreviewability requires that a "substantial public interest" be imperiled); *Lauro Lines*, 490 U.S. at 502 (Scalia, J., concurring) ("The importance of the right asserted has always been a significant part of our collateral order doctrine."); *Henry v. Lake Charles Am. Press LLC*, 566 F.3d 164, 178–181 (5th Cir. 2009) (analyzing

"importance" as a distinct fourth requirement); Eric J. Magnuson & David F. Herr, *Federal Appeals: Jurisdiction and Practice* § 2.4 (2015) (same).[4]

The Court has repeatedly stressed that the conditions for appeal under the collateral order doctrine are "stringent." *E.g.*, *Digital Equip. Corp. v. Desktop Direct Inc.*, 511 U.S. 863, 868 (1994). Expanding the doctrine to permit jurisdiction in too many cases risks allowing the exception to swallow the rule. [—7—] *See Will*, 546 U.S. at 349–50; *Digital Equip.*, 511 U.S. at 868; *Firestone Tire & Rubber Co. v. Risjord*, 449 U.S. 368, 374 (1981) (identifying the substantial finality interests in judicial efficiency and the "sensible policy of avoiding the obstruction to just claims that would come from permitting the harassment and cost of a succession of separate appeals from the various rulings to which a litigation may give rise" (internal quotation marks, alterations, and citation omitted)).

A brief comparison of the types of orders immediately appealable under the collateral order doctrine with those not immediately appealable is instructive. Immediately appealable orders include: those rejecting absolute immunity or qualified immunity; denying a state's claim to Eleventh Amendment immunity; and—in the criminal context—a defendant's adverse ruling on a double jeopardy defense. *See Will*, 546 U.S. at 350 (collecting cases). These types of orders, the Court explained, implicate weighty public interest concerns: in each one, "some particular value of a high order" was at issue. *Id.* at 352.

---

[3] It is undisputed here that the Orders were conclusive and separate from the merits.

[4] This court recently addressed the taxonomic uncertainty in this area in *NCDR, L.L.C. v. Mauze & Bagby, P.L.L.C.*, 745 F.3d 742, 748 n.5 (5th Cir. 2014) ("[I]t [is] not clear whether importance is a fourth requirement or is instead wrapped up in the second and third requirements."). This is an academic dispute. It is quite clear from both the Supreme Court's collateral order doctrine jurisprudence and our own that the importance of the asserted right is a significant component in the jurisdictional analysis under this doctrine.

By contrast, orders generally not immediately appealable under the collateral order doctrine include: denial of a motion to enforce a forum selection clause or to dismiss on forum non conveniens grounds, *see Lauro Lines*, 490 U.S. at 496; *Van Cauwenberghe v. Biard*, 486 U.S. 517, 527–530 (1988); discovery orders generally (including orders permitting discovery into otherwise-privileged, attorney–client communication because of waiver), *see* Richard L. Marcus et al., *Civil Procedure: A Modern Approach* 1149–51 (6th ed. 2013); *Mohawk*, 558 U.S. at 103, 108; attorney disqualification decisions, *see, e.g., Richardson–Merrell*, 472 U.S. at 426 (order disqualifying counsel in civil case not immediately appealable); *Flanagan v. United States*, 465 U.S. 259, 260 (1984) (same outcome in criminal case, despite Sixth Amendment rights at issue); and an order refusing to enforce a settlement agreement that [—8—] allegedly sheltered a party from suit, *see Digital Equip.*, 511 U.S. at 879, 884 ("Including [an immunity] provision in a private contract . . . is barely a prima facie indication that the right secured is 'important' to the benefited party.").[5]

The collateral order doctrine has been successfully invoked in favor of jurisdiction in three appeals in this court arising from this Settlement Program. In the first of these cases, this court heard an appeal arising from a dispute about an interpretation of the Settlement Agreement. *See In re Deepwater Horizon*, 732 F.3d 326, 329, 1 Adm. R. 287, 287 (5th Cir. 2013) ("*Deepwater Horizon I*"). The appeal involved an accounting methodology that potentially affected "thousands of claimants" and "hundreds of millions of dollars" in the business economic

loss recovery framework. *Id.* at 331, 332 n.3, 345, 1 Adm. R. at 288, 289 n.3, 301. We determined that the district court's order conclusively resolved the interpretive dispute, that the dispute was "separate from the merits of BP's liability for the oil spill," and that the order would "be effectively unreviewable on appeal from final judgment because, at that point, the improper awards will have been distributed to potentially thousands of claimants and BP will have no practical way of recovering these funds should it prevail." *Id.* at 332 n.3, 1 Adm. R. at 289 n.3 (citing *Walker v. U.S. Dep't of Hous. & Urban Dev.*, 99 F.3d 761, 766–67 (5th Cir. 1996)).

In two subsequent companion appeals, this court relied on *Deepwater Horizon I* to again find jurisdiction under the collateral order doctrine. One of these cases dealt with an order approving a set of final rules governing discretionary review in the district court of internal appeal determinations. *See* [—9—] *In re Deepwater Horizon*, 785 F.3d 986, 989, 3 Adm. R. 341, 341 (5th Cir. 2015) ("*Deepwater Horizon II*"). In that case, we asserted jurisdiction because the decision was conclusive and separate from the merits, and because:

> [t]he Final Rules affect the rest of the Settlement Program's administration, given that they will govern *all future reviews* by the district court. Because the Final Rules preclude appeals of certain cases to the district court, and because they are silent as to appeals to this court and lack requirements to file requests or docket orders on the civil docket, they would be unreviewable from a final judgment of claim determinations were we not to review them in this case.

Id. at 993, 3 Adm. R. at 344 (emphasis added). The underlying order therefore had substantial, settlement-wide ramifications.

The last relevant appeal (which in fact involved three consolidated appeals from individual awards) centered on another interpretive dispute about whether donations and grants could qualify as "revenue" for nonprofit organizations under the Settlement

---

[5] When assessing an order's appealability, courts should not engage in an "individualized jurisdictional inquiry." *Coopers & Lybrand v. Livesay*, 437 U.S. 463, 473 (1978). Instead, the focus should be on the "entire category to which a claim belongs." *Digital Equip.*, 511 U.S. at 868; *see also Mohawk*, 558 U.S. at 107. Thus, in *NCDR*, this court looked not to whether the order in that particular case was immediately appealable, but rather to whether orders in that context would generally "satisfy the conditions of the collateral order doctrine." 745 F.3d at 748 (citing *Henry*, 566 F.3d at 173).

Agreement for purposes of calculating loss. *See In re Deepwater Horizon*, 785 F.3d 1003, 1006, 3 Adm. R. 325, 325 (5th Cir. 2015) ("*Deepwater Horizon III*"). This court decided that the three awards had conclusively determined the recovery amount for the three claimants; that the dispute about the interpretation of the Settlement Agreement with respect to nonprofit revenue was completely separate from the merits; and that the order would be "effectively unreviewable if BP had to wait until the settlement of the entire class action, when awards 'will have been distributed to potentially thousands of claimants and BP will have no practical way of recovering these funds should it prevail.'" *Id.* at 1009, 3 Adm. R. at 327 (quoting *Deepwater Horizon I*, 732 F.3d at 332 n.3, 1 Adm. R. at 289 n.3).

BP rightly concedes that not every dispute over an interpretation of the Settlement Agreement resolved in the district court is immediately appealable to this court. But the two primary limiting principles it proposes are unsatisfying in this case. First, BP contends that this case, like the other BP [—10—] appeals in which this court permitted application of the doctrine, involves an important issue and effectively unrecoverable funds. Second, BP claims, this case arrives here in a post-judgment posture.[6] The thrust of this argument is that we need not fear opening up Pandora's Box by permitting wholesale abuse of the collateral order doctrine because appeals in the post-judgment context are rare. We take these arguments in turn.

BP's first contention is that its purported right to the information at issue in this case presents an important issue with effectively unrecoverable funds at stake. While these arguments might have justified immediate appealability in *Deepwater Horizon I, II,* and *III*, they fall short in this case. In each of the aforementioned cases, we determined that the

---

[6] The case is post-judgment in the sense that a final order approving the settlement has been entered. *See Bogard v. Wright*, 159 F.3d 1060, 1062 (7th Cir. 1998) (citing, *inter alia, Edwards v. City of Houston*, 78 F.3d 983, 993 (5th Cir. 1996) (en banc)).

orders at issue were effectively unreviewable at least in part based on their broad ramifications to the administration of the settlement. Appealability was endorsed in *Deepwater Horizon I* because the interpretation affected "potentially thousands of claimants." 732 F.3d at 332 n.3, 1 Adm. R. at 289 n.3. The same was true in *Deepwater Horizon III. See* 785 F.3d at 1009, 3 Adm. R. at 327. *Deepwater Horizon II* presented an even stronger case for appealability because the rules at issue might have prevented certain appeals to the district court and possibly all appeals to this court. *See* 785 F.3d at 992–93, 3 Adm. R. at 343-44. At issue in each of these cases was more than the right to an accurate interpretation of a Settlement Agreement provision. The right in these cases is better characterized as the right to an interpretation of the Settlement Agreement on an issue with a serious impact on the effective and fair administration of the settlement.

By that measure, the disputed issue in this case does not stack up. Here, BP claims, principally, that it needs specific information about pre- [—11—] determination "Claim A" in order to establish the legitimacy (or illegitimacy) of separate, but related, post-determination "Claim B." BP states that there have been about 288,000 claims filed and 75,000 awards totaling $5.2 billion at the time of briefing. But although by its own account it had "uninterrupted access to claimant-specific information" (except internal Settlement Program work files) for nearly 20 months, at the time of briefing BP had appealed 4,728 claim determinations, *see* Report by the Claims Administrator at 18, *In re Deepwater Horizon*, MDL No. 2179 (E.D. La. Nov. 26, 2014), ECF No. 13729, and directs the panel to only five fruitful appeals (from which it recouped about $4 million) where pre-determination information proved useful to its success. This does not constitute a showing of a disruption to the Settlement Program framework rising to the level of the disruptions in *Deepwater Horizon I, II,* and *III*, where either thousands of claims or all claims were unavoidably impacted by the interpretations at issue. *See Deepwater Horizon I*, 732 F.3d at 332 n.3, 1 Adm. R. at 289 n.3; *Deepwater Horizon II*, 785 F.3d at

992–93, 3 Adm. R. at 343-44; *Deepwater Horizon III*, 785 F.3d at 1009, 3 Adm. R. at 327. Here, by contrast, BP has shown a total of five claims in which this data appeared to have made any difference at all.[7]

We similarly see little merit in BP's argument that it needs this data for "reviewing and auditing the Settlement Program" and "pursuing indemnification, contribution, subrogation, insurance and other claims from [—12—] third parties." BP never justifies its need for pre-determination, claim-specific data to exercise these rights. If BP were seeking contribution or subrogation for a particular claimant's demonstrated loss, for example, it would presumably be because that claim's legitimacy had been conclusively determined. By that time, BP would have access to any data it needs related to that particular claim.

In addition, the Settlement Agreement has an entire preexisting framework in place to address fraud. Anyone—including members of the general public—can report fraud to the Claims Administrator, and a special master, former Federal Bureau of Investigation Director Louis Freeh, has been tasked with assisting the program with fraud prevention. The MDL docket reveals that Freeh has been actively bringing claims to recoup fraudulently obtained funds. Federal prosecutors, too, have brought criminal charges against individuals who have

allegedly committed fraud.[8] There was no comparable way to recoup improper awards in *Deepwater Horizon I, II,* or *III.*

Even were it otherwise, "[t]he mere identification of some interest that would be 'irretrievably lost' has never sufficed to meet the third *Cohen* requirement." *Digital Equip.*, 511 U.S. at 872. This is why immediate appealability is denied even when, as noted earlier, a criminal defendant seeks [—13—] reinstatement of his disqualified attorney, *see Flanagan*, 465 U.S. at 260, or, as in *Coopers & Lybrand v. Livesay*, an erroneous district court order would, as a practical matter, sound the death knell for plaintiffs' claims that might have been successful had the error been corrected on appeal. *See* 437 U.S. 463, 473–74 (1978) ("Perhaps the principal vice of the 'death knell' doctrine is that it authorizes *indiscriminate* interlocutory review of decisions made by the trial judge."). Orders like these result in harm far more irreparable than the injury at issue in this case. Here, BP will eventually come into possession of all the data it claims to need. At that time, it will be able to cross-check individual claims for fraud that has not already been detected and pursue any of a variety of available avenues to recoup improperly awarded funds.

---

[7] Still, BP argues, why is $4 million in proven fraud—detected at least in part with the assistance of pre-determination data—insufficient to confer a right to immediate appealability in this case? And BP correctly notes that both *Walker v. U.S. Department of Housing & Urban Development* and *Deepwater Horizon III*—both of which permitted appeal—involved amounts far below the $4 million at issue here. *See Walker*, 99 F.3d at 766–67 ($910,228.13); *Deepwater Horizon III*, 785 F.3d at 1007, 3 Adm. R. at 326 (involving awards totaling about $1.2 million). But this argument misses the mark. We reiterate that an individualized jurisdictional inquiry (one in which a court evaluates an order's appealability based on the particular facts presented, rather than looking to the category in which the asserted right falls) is improper. *See Mohawk*, 558 U.S. at 107; *NCDR*, 745 F.3d at 748; *Henry*, 566 F.3d at 173.

[8] When filling out paperwork to submit a claim, a claimant must declare under penalty of perjury that the information provided is true and accurate. One mandatory form for all claimants contains the following language: "I understand that false statements or claims . . . may result in fines, imprisonment, and/or any other remedy available by law to the Federal Government, and that suspicious claims will be forwarded to federal, state, and local law enforcement agencies for possible investigation and prosecution." The Department of Justice has placed a "high priority on promptly investigating and prosecuting all meritorious reports of fraud related to the oil spill and its aftermath." *See* U.S. Dep't of Justice, *Deepwater Horizon (BP) Oil-Spill Fraud, available at* http://www.justice.gov/criminal/oilspill/. A website owned and operated by BP that tracks legal developments related to the oil spill states that there have been 264 reported fraud cases leading to criminal charges, and 187 convictions stemming from reported fraud cases. *See The Whole Story*, State of the Gulf, https://www.thestateofthegulf.com/the-whole-story/fraud-tally/ (last updated June 24, 2015).

Walker v. U.S. Department of Housing and Urban Development, on which BP relies, is not to the contrary. *See* 99 F.3d at 766. In *Walker*, attorneys for plaintiffs in a housing discrimination class action won fees for work they undertook outside of the immediate scope of the litigation, including for monitoring a consent decree and pursuing environmental claims to address lead poisoning. *See id.* We held the fee order appealable under the collateral order doctrine in part because the victories did not result from litigation, so the orders were not "appealable or in any way subject to reversal." *Id.* By contrast, any fraudulently obtained award here— discoverable with the aid of the data BP seeks—will be uncovered sooner or later, since BP will eventually have access to this data. Even if this means BP will not be able to bring a timely appeal in the Settlement Program— which is far from certain—other avenues to challenge the award remain open. *See In re Deepwater Horizon*, 753 F.3d 516, 520 n.5, 2 Adm. R. 213, 215 n.5 (5th Cir. 2014) (Clement, J., dissenting from denial of rehearing en banc) ("BP may seek recovery for losses due to fraud in individual actions, [—14—] and government prosecutors may pursue those who submit fraudulent claims.").[9]

Interpreting effective unreviewability to permit appeal in this case would signify that each time BP could show a handful of claims arguably impacted by the district court's interpretation of the Settlement Agreement, it could immediately appeal to this court. The limited benefits of such unrestricted access to the appellate court are outweighed by the attendant systemic disruption and institutional cost. *See Mohawk*, 558 U.S. at 112; *Digital Equip.*, 511 U.S. at 884.

BP's second contention, that there is little prospect for abuse of the collateral order doctrine in the post-judgment context, is belied, first, by the sheer quantity of appeals that BP, Class Counsel, and individual plaintiffs have brought since reaching the Settlement Agreement. As noted above, BP has appealed: a determination about the accounting method in the business economic loss framework, *see Deepwater Horizon I*, 732 F.3d at 329–32, 1 Adm. R. at 287-90; an order approving the rules governing internal appeals procedures, *see Deepwater Horizon II*, 785 F.3d at 989, 3 Adm. R. at 341; and various claimant awards premised on an interpretation of the Settlement Agreement governing nonprofit awards, *see Deepwater Horizon III*, 785 F.3d at 1006, 3 Adm. R. at 325. BP has also challenged: the validity of the Settlement Agreement itself (No. 13-30095); the dismissal of a lawsuit to enjoin the Claims Administrator from distributing payment on business economic loss claims (No. 13-30329); the causation standards relevant to certain business losses (No. 13-31220); the denial of a motion to recoup business loss payments issued under a later-rejected accounting method (No. [—15—] 14-31165); and the denial of a motion to remove the Claims Administrator (No. 14-31299).

Class Counsel have filed their own various appeals, and dissatisfied individual claimants have done so as well. Although the collateral order doctrine has thus far supplied jurisdiction in Settlement Agreement disputes only in *Deepwater Horizon I, II,* and *III*—and some of the other decided appeals have asserted jurisdiction on other grounds—the potential for this "'narrow' exception . . . to swallow the general rule," *Digital Equip.*, 511 U.S. at 868 (citation omitted), is obvious enough.

The notion that we should loosen the strings in the context of post-judgment proceedings like this one is further undermined by the increasing frequency of court-supervised settlement agreements and consent decrees.[10] *See* Larry Kramer, *Consent*

---

[9] In *Deepwater Horizon I*, 732 F.3d at 332 n.3, 1 Adm. R. at 289 n.3, however, *Walker* was properly invoked because there is no indication that BP had recourse outside the immediate bounds of the settlement framework to address awards calculated under an improper accounting methodology. *See Walker*, 99 F.3d at 766.

[10] Although the Settlement Agreement at issue is not a consent decree, the judicial imprimatur associated with the incorporation of the Agreement in the approval order and the ongoing retention of jurisdiction renders the distinction thin. *See Kokkonen v. Guardian Life Ins. Co. of Am.*, 511 U.S. 375, 381 (1994); *Smyth ex rel. Smyth v. Rivero*,

Decrees and the Rights of Third Parties, 87 Mich. L. Rev. 321, 321 (1988) (recognizing that settlement by consent decree has become increasingly common in antitrust cases, "environmental cases, prison cases, school and housing desegregation cases, and especially employment discrimination cases"). Our circuit alone is home to a multitude of ongoing consent decrees related to, among other issues, desegregation of public workplaces, prisoner's rights, and health care mandates. [—16—]

In this case, as in the many others like it discussed above, an earlier decision of ours in a multidistrict litigation "of nearly unprecedented scope" illuminates the problem:

> Before the litigation is completed, the case will undoubtedly present numerous opportunities for parties dissatisfied with some aspect of a court ruling to claim entitlement to appellate review. In the context of such complex litigation it is important to remember that "we must be parsimonious in our analysis of appealability."

In re Corrugated Container Antitrust Litig., 611 F.2d 86, 89 (5th Cir. 1980) (citing *N. Am. Acceptance Corp. Sec. Cases v. Arnall, Golden & Gregory*, 593 F.2d 642, 645 (5th Cir. 1979)). The prospect for abuse of the collateral order doctrine in post-judgment proceedings is plainly evident. We therefore reject the notion that this would serve as an effective limiting principle were we to permit appeal here.

---

282 F.3d 268, 281 (4th Cir. 2002) ("Where a settlement agreement is embodied in a court order such that the obligation to comply with its terms is court-ordered, the court's approval and the attendant judicial over-sight (in the form of continuing jurisdiction to enforce the agreement) . . . may be functionally a consent decree . . . ."); *see also Buckhannon Bd. & Care Home, Inc. v. W. Va. Dep't of Health & Human Res.*, 532 U.S. 598, 618 (2001) (Scalia, J., concurring) ("[I]n the case of court-approved settlements and consent decrees, even if there has been no judicial determination of the merits, the outcome is at least the product of, and bears the sanction of, judicial action in the lawsuit." (emphasis omitted)).

We emphasize three additional reasons for our ruling today. First, we highlight the deference "owe[d] to the trial judge as the individual initially called upon to decide the many questions of law and fact that occur" over the course of a litigation. *Firestone Tire & Rubber Co.*, 449 U.S. at 374. "Permitting piecemeal appeals would undermine the independence of the district judge, as well as the special role that individual plays in our judicial system." *Id.*; *see also Mohawk*, 558 U.S. at 106–07; *Johnson v. Jones*, 515 U.S. 304, 315–17 (1995); *Richardson–Merrell*, 472 U.S. at 436. This is perhaps nowhere more true than in the management of the *Deepwater Horizon* class action litigation, the scope and size of which are nearly unprecedented. *See In re Corrugated Container Antitrust Litig.*, 611 F.2d at 89 (emphasizing special concerns about overuse of the collateral order doctrine in complex litigation).[11] [—17—]

Second, we call attention to the general rule that only serious and unsettled questions of law come within the collateral order doctrine. *See Nixon v. Fitzgerald*, 457 U.S. 731, 742 (1982) ("As an additional requirement, *Cohen* established that a collateral appeal of an interlocutory order must 'presen[t] a serious and unsettled question.'" (citing *Cohen*, 337 U.S. at 547)); *Baldridge v. SBC Commc'ns, Inc.*, 404 F.3d 930, 931 (5th Cir. 2005); *Davis v. E. Baton Rouge Parish Sch. Bd.*, 78 F.3d 920, 925–26 (5th Cir. 1996). *Deepwater Horizon I, II*, and *III* each involved issues that—regardless of how they were decided—would unquestionably and substantially impact the judicially-managed administrative framework. *See Deepwater Horizon I*, 732 F.3d at 332 n.3, 1 Adm. R. at 289 n.3 (large components of business economic loss framework affected);

---

[11] To the extent that interpretation of § 4.4.14 of the Settlement Agreement might rest on factual determinations about the parties' course of conduct, a point BP presses in its [—17—] briefing, deference to the district court is even more appropriate. *See* 15A Charles A. Wright & Arthur R. Miller, *Federal Practice and Procedure* § 3911.5 ("[T]he considerations that cause appellate courts to confide in trial court discretion should affect the timing of appeal as well as the scope of review.").

Deepwater Horizon III, 785 F.3d at 1009, 3 Adm. R. at 327 (same); *Deepwater Horizon II*, 785 F.3d at 992–93, 3 Adm. R. at 343-45 (all claims impacted). There is no comparable serious and unsettled question of law here.

Finally, effective appellate review of orders interpreting the settlement agreement can be had by other means. *See Mohawk*, 558 U.S. at 110–12; *Digital Equip.*, 511 U.S. at 883. First, aggrieved parties in this situation might employ 28 U.S.C. § 1292(b), which permits discretionary interlocutory appeal from a district court order "involv[ing] a controlling question of law as to which there is substantial ground for difference of opinion." The "discretionary appeal provision (allowing courts to consider the merits of individual claims) would seem a better vehicle for vindicating serious contractual interpretation claims than the blunt, categorical instrument of § 1291 collateral order appeal." *Digital Equip.*, 511 U.S. at 883 (citations omitted). Further, in extraordinary [—18—] cases, a writ of mandamus under the All Writs Act, 28 U.S.C. § 1651, is available to correct manifest injustices. *See Cheney v. United States Dist. Court for D.C.*, 542 U.S. 367, 380 (2004).[12] In light of the foregoing analysis, we are unpersuaded that the Orders here are appealable under § 1291.

B. § 1292(a)(1)

BP's second proffered basis for appellate jurisdiction is 28 U.S.C. § 1292(a)(1), which permits jurisdiction over appeals from "[i]nterlocutory orders . . . granting, continuing, modifying, refusing or dissolving injunctions." Just as it has done with the collateral order doctrine, the Court has "approach[ed] this statute somewhat gingerly

---

[12] BP mentioned mandamus relief in passing in its reply brief. Even if it has waived this argument, "[t]his court has the discretion to treat an appeal as a petition for a writ of mandamus." *In re Grand Jury Subpoena*, 190 F.3d 375, 389 n.16 (5th Cir. 1999). Failing to see an "exceptional circumstance[] amounting to a judicial usurpation of power or a clear abuse of discretion," *Cheney*, 542 U.S. at 380 (internal quotation marks and citations omitted), we do not believe mandamus relief is appropriate here.

lest a floodgate be opened" that permits immediate appeal over too many nonfinal orders. *Switz. Cheese Ass'n, Inc. v. E. Horne's Mkt., Inc.*, 385 U.S. 23, 24–25 (1966) (emphasizing a strong "congressional policy against piecemeal appeals").

A district court "grant[s]" an injunction when an action it takes is "directed to a party, enforceable by contempt, and designed to accord or protect some or all of the substantive relief sought in the complaint in more than a temporary fashion." *Police Ass'n of New Orleans Through Cannatella v. City of New Orleans*, 100 F.3d 1159, 1166 (5th Cir. 1996) (internal quotation marks and citation omitted); 16 Charles A. Wright & Arthur R. Miller, *Federal Practice and Procedure* § 3922 (3d ed. 2014); *see also* Black's Law Dictionary 855 (9th ed. 2009) (defining injunction as a "court order commanding or preventing an action"). A district court "modif[ies]" an injunction when it "changes the obligations imposed by the injunction." 16A Wright & Miller [—19—] § 3924.2. On the other hand, a court has not modified an injunction when it "simply implements an injunction according to its terms or [] designates procedures for enforcement without changing the command of the injunction." *Id.* Interpretation, then, is not modification. *See In re Seabulk Offshore Ltd.*, 158 F.3d 897, 899 (5th Cir. 1998). This court takes a practical view of modification, "look[ing] beyond the terms used by the parties and the district court to the substance of the action." *Id.*

In addition to showing that an order granted, modified, refused, or dissolved an injunction, a party challenging an interlocutory order must show "serious, perhaps irreparable, consequence[s]," because the § 1292(a)(1) "exception is a narrow one," *Gardner v. Westinghouse Broad. Co.*, 437 U.S. 478, 480 (1978) (internal quotation marks and citation omitted); *see also Carson v. Am. Brands, Inc.*, 450 U.S. 79, 84 (1981).

BP asserts that the March 25 Order interpreting § 4.4.14 of the Settlement Agreement constituted an injunction. Alternatively, BP proposes that the district court's approval of the settlement constituted an injunction, which was in turn modified by the March 25 Order and the subsequent denial of the motion for reconsideration. Class Counsel argue that neither the Orders nor the settlement approval provided injunctive relief, and alternatively that the Orders merely interpreted (rather than modified) any putative injunction.

Even assuming *arguendo* that the March 25 Order was an injunction or that the settlement approval order was an injunction modified by the Orders, BP has not shown "serious, perhaps irreparable, consequence[s]." *Gardner*, 437 U.S. at 480. As articulated in our discussion on the collateral order doctrine, any harm here is adequately reparable through the multiple avenues BP has to pursue awards obtained fraudulently. *See Sampson v. Murray*, 415 U.S. 61, 90 (1974) ("The possibility that adequate compensatory or other corrective relief will be available at a later date . . . weighs heavily against a claim of [—20—] irreparable harm." (internal quotation marks and citation omitted)); *Miss. Power & Light Co. v. United Gas Pipe Line Co.*, 760 F.2d 618, 629 (5th Cir. 1985) ("[I]t is nevertheless settled that an injury is 'irreparable' only if it cannot be undone through monetary remedies." (internal quotation marks, alterations, and citation omitted)). Further, there has been no showing, unlike in *Philip Morris USA Inc. v. Scott*, 131 S. Ct. 1, 4 (2010) (Scalia, J., in chambers), on which BP relies, that a "substantial portion" of the fraudulent awards "will be irrevocably expended."

III. CONCLUSION

We therefore DISMISS this appeal for lack of jurisdiction.

(Reporter's Note: Dissenting opinion follows on p. 393).

[—21—] **ELROD,** Circuit Judge, dissenting:

The majority opinion is well-reasoned, and were we writing on a clean slate, I might be inclined to join it.[1] Nevertheless, because I believe that *Deepwater Horizon I, II,* and *III* support a determination of jurisdiction under the collateral order doctrine, I respectfully dissent. The interlocutory order at issue here "conclusively determined the interpretation dispute, which is completely separate from the merits of BP's liability for the oil spill," *In re Deepwater Horizon,* 732 F.3d 326, 332 n.3, 1 Adm. R. 287, 289 n.3 (5th Cir. 2013) ("*Deepwater Horizon I*"), and it will be effectively unreviewable on appeal because BP will have no practical way to recover on appeal from final judgment. *See id.,* 1 Adm. R. at 289 n.3; *In re Deepwater Horizon,* 785 F.3d 986, 993, 3 Adm. R. 341, 344 (5th Cir. 2015) ("*Deepwater Horizon II*"); *In re Deepwater Horizon,* 785 F.3d 1003, 1009, 3 Adm. R. 325, 327 (5th Cir. 2015) ("*Deepwater Horizon III*"). In addition, the order at issue here will "affect the rest of the Settlement Program's administration," *Deepwater Horizon II,* 785 F.3d at 993, 3 Adm. R. at 344, and in particular, BP's ability to detect and appeal fraudulent awards.

---

[1] In creating the collateral order doctrine, the Supreme Court interpreted 28 U.S.C. § 1291—which confers appellate jurisdiction on the courts of appeals over only "final decisions" of federal district courts—to include a grant of authority to review certain orders traditionally considered non-final. *See Cohen v. Beneficial Indus. Loan Corp.,* 337 U.S. 541, 545–47 (1949). The Court recognized that this was a "practical rather than a technical construction" of § 1291. *Id.* at 546. Perhaps in part because of the doctrine's tension with the text of § 1291 and § 1292 (which expressly grants appellate jurisdiction over specified interlocutory orders), the Court cautioned that the doctrine should be limited to "that *small class*" of decisions that involve "serious and unsettled question[s]" and "which finally determine claims of right separable from, and collateral to, rights asserted in the action, too important to be denied review and too independent of the cause itself to require that appellate consideration be deferred until the whole case is adjudicated." *Id.* at 546, 547 (emphasis added).

BP has presented five examples of successful appeals in which access to pre-determination information was necessary, and these examples amount to $4 million in prevented fraud. In *Deepwater Horizon III,* we reviewed an [—22—] interlocutory order denying discretionary review of three individual awards to non-profits with disputed amounts totaling only about $1.2 million. 785 F.3d at 1007, 3 Adm. R. at 326; *see also ante,* at 11 n.7. Despite the relatively small number of awards and amount in controversy, we recognized that the order had implications for the calculation of awards made to other non-profits. *Id.* at 1009, 3 Adm. R. at 327. A similar inference is appropriate here. Because, as BP explains, the district court's order here impacts BP's ability to determine whether awards comply with the Settlement Agreement's award criteria, under our precedent, the order involves a question sufficiently important to trigger jurisdiction under the collateral order doctrine. *See id.,* 3 Adm. R. at 327 (determining jurisdiction under the collateral order doctrine and recognizing that the doctrine is limited to orders that "resolve an *important* issue completely separate from the merits" (emphasis added) (internal quotation marks omitted)). Moreover, the reasons for determining that we have jurisdiction are even stronger here than in *Deepwater Horizon III.* In this case, we deal not with potentially miscalculated awards, but rather with potentially fraudulent ones that should not have been awarded at all.

Therefore, I would determine that we have jurisdiction over this appeal under the collateral order doctrine and reach the merits. On the merits, I would reverse the judgment of the district court because it conflates the terms "Claims-related data" and "Claim Files" in § 4.4.14 of the Settlement Agreement. I respectfully dissent.

United States Court of Appeals
for the Fifth Circuit

No. 13-31281

WILCOX
vs.
WILD WELL CONTROL, INC.

Appeals from the United States District Court for the
Eastern District of Louisiana

Decided: July 24, 2015
Revised: August 11, 2015

Citation: 794 F.3d 531, 3 Adm. R. 394 (5th Cir. 2015).

Before **DENNIS, PRADO,** and **HIGGINSON,** Circuit Judges.

[—2—] PRADO, Circuit Judge:

This appeal arises from injuries sustained by Plaintiff–Appellant Joseph R. Wilcox while welding on an offshore platform. Wilcox, an employee of Defendant–Appellee Max Welders, L.L.C., was working as the borrowed employee of Defendant–Appellee–Appellant Wild Well Control, Incorporated, a subsidiary of Defendant–Appellee–Appellant Superior Energy Services, Incorporated. Wilcox sued the Defendants under, *inter alia*, the Jones Act. Superior and Wild Well filed a cross-claim for indemnity from Max Welders pursuant to a Master Service Agreement (MSA) or, in the alternative, Vessel Boarding, Utilization and Hold Harmless Agreement (VBA) between Superior and Max Welders. The district court granted summary judgment to all Defendants on the Jones Act claims because it found that Wilcox is not a Jones Act seaman and granted summary judgment to Max Welders on indemnity because 1) the MSA was void under Louisiana law and 2) the VBA did not apply to Wilcox's work. Wilcox, Superior, and Wild Well appeal these decisions. We affirm.

I. FACTUAL AND PROCEDURAL BACKGROUND

Max Welders is a contractor that provides various offshore construction, fabrication, and repair services. Max Welders employed Wilcox as a welder. During his employment with Max Welders, Wilcox worked in numerous locations, including a fabrication yard in Louisiana and on various rigs, barges, and vessels owned by Max Welders' customers. Wilcox concedes that during [—3—] his entire employment with Max Welders, he spent less than thirty percent of his time in service of any one vessel or group of vessels.

Energy Resource Technology GOM, Incorporated (ERT) hired Wild Well—a subsidiary of Superior—to decommission a well in the Gulf of Mexico ("the ERT job"). Wild Well contracted with Max Welders to provide welders to assist. Wilcox was one of the welders sent to work on the ERT job, which was expected to last for approximately two months. During this time, Wilcox was required to live on Wild Well's barge, the D/B SUPERIOR PERFORMANCE, which was on site at the well to provide support to the decommissioning work. Superior previously owned the D/B SUPERIOR PERFORMANCE. Wilcox allegedly sustained injuries on June 5, 2012, when gasses exploded while he was welding inside on the well platform. Wild Well concedes that, at the time of the accident, Wilcox was its borrowed employee.

Wilcox and his wife sued Max Welders, Superior, and Wild Well for negligence under the Jones Act, 46 U.S.C § 30104, and general maritime law (GML) unseaworthiness, or alternatively for vessel negligence against the D/B SUPERIOR PERFORMANCE under the Longshore and Harbor Workers' Compensation Act (LHWCA), 33 U.S.C. § 905(b). Superior and Wild Well jointly filed a cross-claim alleging that Max Welders had agreed to indemnify and hold harmless Superior and its subsidiaries against any personal-injury claims brought by Max Welders' employees pursuant to the 2004 MSA between Max Welders and Superior. They argued, in the alternative, that Max Welders owed them indemnity pursuant to a 2010 VBA between Superior and Wild Well.

Max Welders moved for summary judgment on Wilcox's Jones Act and GML claims, asserting that Wilcox was not a seaman. Max Welders also moved for summary judgment on Superior and Wild

Well's indemnity cross-claim, [—4—] contending that the MSA and VBA did not provide indemnity for Wild Well's demolition work for a third party. Superior and Wild Well then filed a cross-motion for summary judgment on their indemnity claims. The district court granted summary judgment to Max Welders on Wilcox's Jones Act and GML claims as well as on Superior and Wild Well's indemnity claims.

Superior and Wild Well later moved for summary judgment on Wilcox's Jones Act and GML claims, arguing that if Wilcox was not a seaman with respect to his employer, Max Welders, he was also not a seaman with respect to his borrowing employer, Wild Well. The district court granted this motion. The district court later granted summary judgment to Superior and Wild Well on Wilcox's remaining claims for vessel negligence under the LHWCA.

These consolidated cases encompass two appeals. First, Wilcox appeals the grant of summary judgment for Wild Well on Wilcox's Jones Act and GML claims based on his seaman status.[1] Second, Wild Well and Superior appeal the grant of summary judgment for Max Welders on indemnity.

II. DISCUSSION

This Court has jurisdiction to review a district court's final judgment pursuant to 28 U.S.C. § 1291. We review de novo a district court's grant of summary judgment, viewing "all facts and evidence in the light most favorable to the non-moving party." *Juino v. Livingston Par. Fire Dist. No. 5*, 717 F.3d 431, 433 (5th Cir. 2013). We apply the same standard as the district court in the first instance. *Turner v. Baylor Richardson Med. Ctr.*, 476 F.3d 337, 343 (5th Cir. 2007).

Summary judgment is appropriate "if the movant shows that there is no genuine dispute as to any material fact and the movant is entitled to judgment [—5—] as a matter of law." Fed. R. Civ. P. 56(a). A genuine dispute of material fact exists when the "evidence is such that a reasonable jury could return a verdict for the nonmoving party." *Royal v. CCC & R Tres Arboles, L.L.C.*, 736 F.3d 396, 400 (5th Cir. 2013) (quoting *Anderson v. Liberty Lobby, Inc.*, 477 U.S. 242, 248 (1986)).

A. Wilcox's Jones Act Claims

The district court granted summary judgment for Wild Well and Superior because it found that Wilcox was not a Jones Act seaman. The Supreme Court has articulated a two-prong test to determine seaman status under the Jones Act: 1) "an employee's duties must 'contribut[e] to the function of the vessel or to the accomplishment of its mission,'" and 2) "a seaman must have a connection to a vessel in navigation (or to an identifiable group of such vessels) that is substantial in terms of both its duration and its nature." *Chandris, Inc. v. Latsis*, 515 U.S. 347, 368 (1995) (quoting *McDermott Int'l, Inc. v. Wilander*, 498 U.S. 337, 355 (1991)).

At issue in this appeal is the substantial-connection prong.[2] The "fundamental purpose" of this inquiry "is to . . . separate the sea-based maritime employees who are entitled to Jones Act protection from those land-based workers who have only a transitory or sporadic connection to a vessel in navigation." *Id.* at 368. "Land-based maritime workers do not become seamen because they happen to be working on board a vessel when they are injured, and seamen do not lose Jones Act protection when the course of their service to a vessel takes them ashore." *Id.* at 361. Following *Barrett v. Chevron U.S.A., Inc.*, 781 F.2d 1067 (5th Cir. 1986) (en banc), we have generally "declined to find seaman status where the employee spent less than 30 percent of his time [—6—] aboard ship." *Chandris*, 515 U.S. at 367. The Supreme Court deemed this "an appropriate rule of thumb," but noted that "departure from it will certainly be justified in appropriate cases." *Id.* at 371.

---

[1] Wilcox does not appeal the grant of summary judgment on his LHWCA claims.

[2] The district court found a genuine issue of material fact regarding the contribution prong. Wild Well does not contest this finding.

Generally, the status of an employee who splits time between land and a vessel is "determined in the context of his *entire* employment with his current employer." *Barrett*, 781 F.2d at 1075 (internal quotation marks omitted); *see also Chandris*, 515 U.S. at 370–71. But if the employee "receives a new work assignment before his accident in which either his essential duties or his work location is *permanently changed*, he is entitled to have the assessment of the substantiality of his vessel-related work made on the basis of his activities in his new job." *Barrett*, 781 F.2d at 1075–76 (emphasis added); *see also Chandris*, 515 U.S. at 371–72 ("[W]e see no reason to limit the seaman status inquiry . . . exclusively to an examination of the overall course of a worker's service with a particular employer. When a maritime worker's basic assignment changes, his seaman status may change as well."). This reassignment exception applies only when an employee has "undergone a *substantial change* in status, not simply [by] serv[ing] on a boat sporadically." *Becker v. Tidewater, Inc.*, 335 F.3d 376, 389 (5th Cir. 2003) (emphasis added).

We addressed the *Barrett* reassignment exception in a borrowed-employee context similar to Wilcox's in *New v. Associated Painting Services, Inc.*, 863 F.2d 1205 (5th Cir. 1989).[3] The plaintiff worked for a painting company that sent employees to offshore drilling rigs and oil platforms. *Id.* at 1207. The employee was regularly assigned to different vessels owned by unrelated entities. *Id.* One week into an assignment to a drilling rig as a [—7—] borrowed employee, the plaintiff sustained injuries in an accident. *Id.* The employee argued that he was a seaman with regard to the painting company and the borrowing employer. *Id.* Although he did not satisfy the thirty-percent requirement based on his entire employment with the painting company, the employee asserted that the court

should look only to the time he worked for the borrowing employer because as a matter of law, he contended, the Barrett exception applied to his work as a borrowed employee. *Id.* at 1208–09. We held 1) that the plaintiff's status as a borrowed employee did not make him a Jones Act seaman; and 2) that because the summary-judgment evidence showed no permanent change to his essential work duties or work location, his status must be determined by looking to his entire employment with the painting company. *Id.*[4]

Wilcox argues that the district court erred in its substantial-connection analysis by refusing to determine Wilcox's status by reference to his period of employment with Wild Well, rather than his entire employment with Max Welders.[5] Wilcox disclaims reliance on the Barrett exception, and for good reason—there is no evidence in the record to support application of the [—8—] reassignment exception in this case. Wilcox's case presents facts that are strikingly similar to those in *New*. Like the borrowed employee

---

[3] Although *New* was decided before the Supreme Court's seminal decision in *Chandris*, we applied the *Robison* seaman-status test, which the Court "essentially accepted" in *Chandris*. *Nunez v. B&B Dredging, Inc.*, 288 F.3d 271, 274–75 (5th Cir. 2002). Thus, *New* remains binding. *See Jacobs v. Nat'l Drug Intelligence Ctr.*, 548 F.3d 375, 378 (5th Cir. 2008).

[4] We followed a similar analysis in a post-*Chandris* case. In *Becker v. Tidewater, Inc.*, 335 F.3d 376 (5th Cir. 2003), we refused to apply the reassignment exception to a land-based worker temporarily reassigned to a vessel. *Id.* at 390–91.

[5] Wilcox devotes a substantial portion of his brief to arguing that the district court granted summary judgment based on dictum from *New v. Associated Painting Services, Inc.*, 1987 WL 4944 (E.D. La. May 8, 1987). He suggests that the *New* district court created, and the district court in this case applied, a *per se* rule that a borrowed employee's seaman status must always be determined by looking at the time spent working for the original employer.

This argument mischaracterizes the district court's summary-judgment analysis in this case. The district court carefully analyzed and applied our *New* opinion, which affirmed the lower court. Wilcox also ignores the context of the summary-judgment order: in its prior order granting summary judgment to Max Welders, the district court had already addressed the argument that Wilcox's status should be determined based on the time spent as Wild Well's borrowed employee. When the district court disposed of Wild Well's summary judgment motion, the only remaining question was "whether the seaman status finding that was made with respect to Max Welders should also be applied to Wild Well."

in *New,* Wilcox was not permanently reassigned to work on Wild Well's vessel—the project was expected to last for approximately two months. Nor did his essential duties change—his primary duty continued to be welding. Wilcox does not point to any evidence suggesting a "fundamental change in status," *Becker,* 335 F.3d at 390, which would allow us to assess the substantial-relation prong with sole reference to Wilcox's time as a borrowed employee with Wild Well.

Conceding that the *Barrett* exception does not apply here, Wilcox instead asserts that he "started a new job with a new employer when he began work as Wild Well's borrowed employee," making Wild Well his "current employer," *Chandris,* 515 U.S. at 366, for the purposes of the seaman-status inquiry. Thus, Wilcox concludes, he has satisfied the substantial-connection prong because he spent more than thirty percent of his time with Wild Well aboard a vessel. He concedes that there is no direct support for this conclusion but argues that it is "suggested" by other pre-*Chandris* cases that recognize that a borrowed employee can become a seaman with regard to his borrowing employer. We decline to adopt such a rule.

The Supreme Court has recognized that in determining seaman status, "it [is] preferable to focus upon the essence of what it means to be a seaman and to eschew the temptation to create detailed tests to effectuate the congressional purposes, tests that tend to become ends in and of themselves." *Id.* at 369. Our thirty-percent rule and the *Barrett* reassignment exception "get[] at the . . . basic point [that] [t]he Jones Act remedy is reserved for sea-based maritime employees whose work regularly exposes them to the special hazards and disadvantages to which they who go down to sea in ships are subjected." *Chandris,* 515 U.S. at 370 (internal quotation marks omitted). We [—9—] do not here adopt a bright-line rule that courts performing the seaman-status inquiry must always look to an employee's entire employment with his nominal employer rather than his borrowing

employer.[6] Nevertheless, we also decline to adopt a rule that borrowed-employee status automatically requires courts look only to his period of employment with the borrowing employer.[7]

Wilcox supports his argument with *Roberts v. Williams–McWilliams Co.,* 648 F.2d 255 (5th Cir. 1981), in which this Court held that a borrowed employee was a seaman with regard to his borrowing employer. *See id.* at 262. In *Roberts,* we found "no reason to distinguish [the plaintiff] because he received his paycheck from the [nominal employer]." *Id.* at 262. There, the employee was under the complete control of the borrowing employer; he was sent to work on the vessel for an indefinite period of time and was expected to remain on the vessel until the completion of the project. *Id.* Importantly, the employee was assigned to work for the borrowed employer on his *second day* of work for the nominal employer. *Id.* at 257–58. Thus, the distinction at issue here—entire period of employment versus period of employment with the borrowing employer—was inconsequential in *Roberts.*

Here, there is good reason to distinguish Wilcox from Wild Well's permanent employees. While employed by Max Welders, Wilcox worked for 34 different customers on 191 different jobs, both offshore and onshore. He was [—10—] assigned to work for Wild Well on the D/B SUPERIOR PERFORMANCE for one specific project, which had a clear end

---

[6] Such a rule would enable employers to contract around Jones Act rights. *See Spinks v. Chevron Oil Co.,* 507 F.2d 216, 225 (5th Cir. 1975) (rejecting a rule that would "result in defeating Jones Act rights through contractual manipulations"), *overruled on other grounds by Gautreaux v. Scurlack Marine, Inc.,* 107 F.3d 331 (5th Cir. 1997) (en banc).

[7] Such a rule would be inconsistent with our reasoning in *New*—in which, after finding that the *Barrett* exception did not apply, we concluded that the district court "applied the proper legal standard" by reviewing the borrowed employee's entire employment with his nominal employer. 863 F.2d at 1208–09. Such a rule would also result in workers walking "into and out of [Jones Act] coverage in the course of his regular duties." *See Chandris,* 515 U.S. at 363.

date only two months after it began. Moreover, testimony indicates that, although crew would usually stay on a vessel for an entire job, they could request relief and leave the vessel before the job was complete.

Focusing on the "essence of what it means to be a seaman," *Chandris*, 515 U.S. at 369, we cannot say Wilcox demonstrated a genuine issue of material fact from which a reasonable jury could conclude that he qualifies for seaman status under the Jones Act. Therefore, we affirm the district court's grant of summary judgment to Wild Well on Wilcox's Jones Act claims.

B. The Indemnity Cross-Claims

We now turn to the district court's grant of summary judgment to Max Welders on Superior and Wild Well's indemnity claims. Because we affirm summary judgment on Wilcox's remaining claims against all Defendants, we need only address Max Welders' liability for defense costs. Superior and Wild Well filed a cross-claim for indemnity from Max Welders pursuant to the MSA or, in the alternative, the VBA between Superior and Max Welders.

1. The MSA

The MSA that Max Welders and Superior entered into in April 2004 contains an indemnity-and-defense provision. The district court assumed without deciding that the MSA applied to Wilcox's work and held the MSA's "obligations to defend [or] indemnify . . . are void and unenforceable" under the Louisiana Oilfield Anti-Indemnity Act (LOAIA).

Superior and Wild Well argue that this was error with reference to two key cases. In *Meloy v. Conoco, Inc.*, 504 So. 2d 833 (La. 1987), the Louisiana Supreme Court made clear that the LOAIA "does not apply where the indemnitee is not negligent or at fault," *id.* at 839. Thus, "the indemnitor's [—11—] obligation for cost of defense cannot be determined until there has been a judicial finding that the indemnitee is liable or that the charges against it were baseless." *Id.* In *Melancon v. Amoco Production Co.*, 834 F.2d 1238 (5th Cir.

1988), we affirmed summary judgment for a borrowing employer on an employee's LHWCA claim. *Id.* at 1247–48. Applying *Meloy*, we held that the district court erred in finding that the LOAIA voided the borrowing employer's indemnity agreement with the nominal employer and awarded the borrowing defense costs. *Id.* at 1248.

Max Welders argues that Wild Well and Superior have waived their argument that they are entitled to attorneys' fees under *Meloy* and *Melancon* because they did not present this argument to the district court. Superior and Wild Well counter that they could not raise their argument because they "were not conclusively determined to be 'not negligent'" until the district court dismissed Wilcox's final claim against them on February 14, 2014, "*after* the district court's Scheduling Order deadline" for pretrial motions.

"An argument not raised before the district court cannot be asserted for the first time on appeal." *XL Specialty Ins. Co. v. Kiewit Offshore Servs., Ltd.*, 513 F.3d 146, 153 (5th Cir. 2008) (citing *Stokes v. Emerson Elec. Co.*, 217 F.3d 353, 358 n.19 (5th Cir. 2000)). A party preserves an argument only if it is "raised to such a degree that the trial court may rule on it." *Id.* (quoting *Butler Aviation Int'l, Inc. v Whyte* (*In re Fairchild Aircraft Corp.*), 6 F.3d 1119, 1128 (5th Cir. 1993)), *abrogated on other grounds by Tex. Truck Ins. Agency, Inc. v. Cure* (*In re Dunham*), 110 F.3d 286 (5th Cir. 1997).

Superior and Wild Well did not have to wait for a conclusive determination of their liability to raise *Meloy* and *Melancon*. In its indemnity motion for summary judgment, Max Welders argued that the MSA's indemnity agreement was void under the LOAIA. Superior and Wild Well filed a cross- [—12—] motion for summary judgment, but only argued that the LOAIA did not govern the MSA because it did not "pertain to a well." They could have argued in their opposition that *Meloy* and *Melancon* precluded the district court from determining the validity of the indemnity provision before liability was determined, but they did not.[8] Because Wild Well and Superior failed to raise the *Meloy–Melancon* argument at the summary-judgment stage, we conclude that they have waived the argument on appeal. *See Provident Life & Accident Ins. Co. v. Goel*, 274 F.3d 984, 990 n.11 (5th Cir. 2001) ("As a general rule, arguments . . . not presented in the district court in connection with a summary judgment motion are waived on appeal and the appellate court will be unable to consider these materials in its review of the district court's decision." (quoting in a parenthetical 11 James Wm. Moore et al., *Moore's Federal Practice* ¶ 56.41[3][c] (3d ed. 1997))).

Because Superior and Wild Well have waived their argument for attorneys' fees based on *Melancon* and *Meloy*, we affirm the district court's summary-judgment holding that the MSA was void under the LOAIA.

2. *The VBA*

Superior and Wild Well also argue that they are entitled to defense costs and indemnity under the Vessel Boarding, Utilization and Hold Harmless Agreement (VBA) between Superior and Max Welders.[9] The district court [—13—] rejected this argument, but it did not distinguish between indemnity for Wild Well and indemnity for Superior in its analysis. After concluding that

the VBA did not apply to Wild Well, the district court granted summary judgment to Max Welders against *both* Wild Well and Superior. We address each indemnity issue in turn.

The VBA states it was "executed by Contractor [Max Welders] for the purpose of obtaining access from Owner [Superior] to vessels owned, chartered and/or operated by Owner . . . in order to allocate the risks and liabilities arising out of Owner granting to Contractor such access." It further provides:

> Contractor agrees to defend, indemnify and hold Owner harmless from and against any claims, losses, or demands of any kind arising as a result of personal injury, death or disease, that may be asserted by Contractor . . . or on behalf of any of its or their employees . . . no matter how occasioned . . . .

a. *Indemnity for Wild Well*

Before the district court, Superior and Wild Well argued that the VBA was intended as an addendum to the MSA that provided indemnity in connection with the D/B SUPERIOR PERFORMANCE, regardless of whether it was owned by Wild Well or Superior.[10] They conceded that the plain language of the agreement did not reflect this intent, but argued, based on parol evidence, that the VBA should be reformed to reflect that intent. They asserted that because this was a reformation issue, rather than an ambiguity issue, the parol evidence could be considered. The district court found the contract to be unambiguous and found the defendant's reformation argument [—14—] to be an "end-run" around the parol evidence rule. On appeal, Superior and Wild Well raise nearly identical arguments.

"Reformation is an equitable remedy used to correct errors or mistakes in contracts." *Am. Elec. Power Co. v. Affiliated FM Ins. Co.*, 556 F.3d 282, 287 (5th Cir. 2009) (internal

---

[8] Superior and Wild Well did cite to *Meloy* in the law section of their cross-motion for summary judgment on indemnity, noting that "[i]f the LOAIA applies to the Superior/Max MSA, then the defense, indemnity and insurance provisions will be void as a matter of public policy if there is any negligence on the part of Superior/Wild Well." (citing *Meloy*, 504 So. 2d 833). However, in the pertinent section of their brief, they only argue that the LOAIA does not apply because the agreement does not pertain to a well. This was most likely a strategic choice: because they also sought summary judgment on indemnity, the *Meloy–Melancon* issue could have precluded summary judgment in their favor.

[9] Max Welders points out that the VBA is not countersigned by Superior, and argues "[t]his alone renders the VBA inapplicable." However, it cites no authority for this [—13—] proposition. We find this argument to be inadequately briefed and abandoned. *See* Fed. R. App. P. 28(a)(8); *Yohey v. Collins*, 985 F.2d 222, 225 (5th Cir. 1993).

[10] Superior owned the D/B SUPERIOR PERFORMANCE when the VBA was signed in 2010 but transferred the vessel to Wild Well in 2011, prior to Wilcox's injury.

quotation marks omitted). The party seeking reformation bears the burden of establishing mutual error in the contract's creation. *Id.* Ordinarily the party must only show mistake by a preponderance of the evidence; but when a party seeks to reform a provision "to provide coverage for a 'substantially different and greater risk' than expressly covered, the party must demonstrate a mutual error by clear-and-convincing evidence." *Id.* at 287 n.4 (quoting *Samuels v. State Farm Mut. Auto. Ins. Co.*, 939 So. 2d 1235, 1240 (La. 2006)).

In *American Electric Power Co. v. Affiliated FM Insurance Co.*, we interpreted an insurance agreement that had been adopted by the defendant insurance company through a "prior loss" clause in its coverage agreement with the plaintiff. *Id.* at 284–85. The clause obligated the defendant to cover a loss if the prior insurance agreement did. *Id.* The prior agreement covered losses for the company and "any subsidiary *corporation* now existing or hereafter created or acquired." *Id.* at 285. The question was whether this provision covered subsidiary LLCs. *Id.* Before the district court, the plaintiff sought to introduce affidavits from the original parties to the agreement evincing that they intended to include LLCs in the coverage. *Id.* The district court, granting summary judgment for the defendant insurance company, found that "corporation" was unambiguous and, therefore, "struck the affidavits as impermissible parol evidence." *Id.* The plaintiff company filed a Rule 59(e) motion seeking reformation to match the original intent of the parties; the district court denied the motion. *Id.* [—15—]

This Court agreed that "corporation" was unambiguous and parol evidence was properly excluded. *Id.* at 286–87. We also affirmed the refusal to reform the agreement in part because "the use of the term 'corporation' is not the type of 'error' that reformation is intended to remedy." *Id.* at 288. We noted that the plaintiff "argue[d] that the original parties had a broader-than-usual meaning in mind when they purposefully included the word. In effect, [the plaintiff] attempt[ed] to make an end-run around the parol-evidence rule by framing its argument as a request for reformation." *Id.*

American Electric defeats Superior and Wild Well's reformation argument. The VBA defines "Owner" as "Superior Energy Services, L.L.C." There is nothing ambiguous about this term, which Superior and Wild Well now contend must be read to include all companies affiliated with Superior. The agreement clearly covers "vessels owned, chartered and/or operated by" Superior." As in *American Electric*, the parties seek to use parol evidence to show "the original parties had a broader-than-usual meaning in mind when they purposely included the word," *id.* Moreover, there is absolutely nothing in the agreement that even suggests it is meant as an addendum to the MSA, a document executed six years prior.

Superior and Wild Well argue that *American Electric* is distinguishable because "reformation of the contract at issue [in that case] would have been to the detriment of a third party." It is true that part of our reasoning in that case was that the requested reformation would hurt a third party. *See id.* at 287–88. But Superior and Wild Well do not explain how the alleged mistake—a failure to include language in the contract indicating that "Owner" referred not just to Superior, but also to any subsidiary it sold a vessel to—is "the type of 'error' that reformation is intended to remedy," *id.* at 288. To allow Superior and Wild Well, in spite of unambiguous contract language, to introduce [—16—] affidavits of its employees to show that the agreement was meant to include Wild Well and serve as an addendum to the MSA would most certainly be "an end-run around the parol-evidence rule . . . fram[ed] . . . as a request for reformation," *id.*

b. Indemnity for Superior

Superior also argues that even if the VBA does not provide for Wild Well's defense costs, "Superior had to defend itself in this case against allegations that it was negligent as the owner of the D/B SUPERIOR PERFORMANCE." Therefore, Superior argues, it is entitled to defense costs for defending against these allegations. We disagree.

The opening paragraph of the VBA states that it was "executed by Contractor [Max Welders] for the purpose of obtaining access from Owner [Superior] to vessels owned, chartered and/or operated by Owner, to provide employees of Contractor with working, living or operating support aboard the vessels of Owner, and in order to allocate the risks and liabilities arising out of Owner granting to Contractor such access." This statement makes clear that the risks and liabilities that are the subject of the VBA are those that arise out of Superior allowing Max Welders' employees to live, work, and operate aboard vessels that are owned and/or operated by Superior. Reading the indemnity provision's coverage for "claims . . . asserted . . . on behalf of [Max Welders'] employees" in the context of the VBA's opening language, it is clear that the parties only intended indemnity for claims of employees that had access to Superior's vessels. There was no Superior-owned vessel involved in Wilcox's injury, and therefore the VBA does not provide for defense costs. The unambiguous language of the VBA does not show that the parties intended it to cover any suit in which a Max Welders employee mistakenly or frivolously claims that a vessel was owned by Superior. [—17—]

III. CONCLUSION

For the foregoing reasons, we AFFIRM the district court's grant of summary judgment as to Wilcox's Jones Act claims and Superior and Wild Well's indemnity claims.

United States Court of Appeals
for the Fifth Circuit

No. 14-30422

JOHNSON
VS.
GLOBALSANTAFE OFFSHORE SERVS., INC.

Appeals from the United States District Court for the
Eastern District of Louisiana

Decided: August 13, 2015

Citation: 799 F.3d 317, 3 Adm. R. 402 (5th Cir. 2015).

Before **DENNIS, PRADO,** and **HIGGINSON,** Circuit Judges.

[—1—] **HIGGINSON,** Circuit Judge:

James Johnson, a superintendent aboard a drilling rig, was shot and seriously injured by a Nigerian gunman who invaded the rig. He claims that the negligence of other rig hands caused his injury, and he seeks to hold GlobalSantaFe Offshore Services, Inc. ("GSF") vicariously liable for the rig hands' negligence under the general maritime law. The district court granted GSF's motion for summary judgment, holding that no reasonable jury could find that GSF was the rig hands' employer. We AFFIRM.

FACTS AND PROCEEDINGS

On November 8, 2010, James Johnson was working as a drilling superintendent on the HIGH ISLAND VII, a drilling rig located near the [—2—] Nigerian coast. Prior to the evening of November 8, rig hands had moved a ball valve, attached to the blow-out preventer, in front of the stairs leading from the rig to a platform, in order to work on the blow-out preventer. When a boat was seen approaching the rig, the rig hands sought to raise the stairs, but the stairs were blocked by the ball valve. Nigerian gunmen used the stairs to board the rig, and one gunman shot Johnson in the leg. Johnson's leg was severely injured and required months of hospitalization, several surgeries, and a muscle transplant.

Johnson brought claims for negligence under the Jones Act and for unseaworthiness, maintenance and cure, and negligence under the general maritime law against PPI Technology Services, L.P. ("PPI"), PSL, Ltd. ("PSL"), Transocean Ltd., and Afren, PLC. Johnson later amended his complaint to add GSF as a defendant. These companies are related to one another in complex ways. Transocean Ltd., which has over 360 direct and indirect subsidiaries, owns and operates a large fleet that provides contract drilling services worldwide. In 2007, GlobalSantaFe Corporation, which GSF identifies as its corporate parent, merged with Transocean Inc., a subsidiary of Transocean Ltd. *See Bricklayers & Masons Local Union No. 5 Ohio Pension Fund v. Transocean Ltd.,* 866 F. Supp. 2d 223, 246 (S.D.N.Y. 2012). After the merger, GSF became an indirect subsidiary of Transocean Ltd. Under a contract signed March 11, 2010, Sedco Forex International, Inc. ("Sedco"), in association with Transocean Support Services Nigeria Limited, agreed to provide the HIGH ISLAND VII and drilling rig services to Afren Resources Limited. The HIGH ISLAND VII was owned by GlobalSantaFe International Drilling Inc., whose relationship to GSF is unclear. In March 2010, Johnson contracted with PSL to work for "Afren" on PSL's behalf.

The district court dismissed Afren, PLC following Johnson's motion for voluntary dismissal. The district court also dismissed Johnson's claims against [—3—] Transocean Ltd. because Johnson did not offer any information or argument opposing Transocean Ltd.'s motion to dismiss for lack of personal jurisdiction. The district court further dismissed Johnson's claims against PSL, finding that the court lacked personal jurisdiction over PSL. The district court ultimately granted PPI's motion for summary judgment, and that decision recently was affirmed on appeal. *Johnson v. PPI Tech. Servs., L.P.,* 605 F. App'x 366, 367 (5th Cir. 2015). The district court granted GSF's motion for summary judgment on Johnson's claims for negligence under the Jones Act and for negligence and unseaworthiness under the general maritime law. Johnson appeals only the district court's grant of summary judgment to GSF on his claim for negligence under the general maritime law.

STANDARD OF REVIEW

We review de novo a district court's grant of summary judgment, applying the same criteria used by the district court. *Gowesky v. Singing River Hosp. Sys.*, 321 F.3d 503, 507 (5th Cir. 2003). We may award summary judgment if, viewing all evidence in the light most favorable to the non-movant, the record demonstrates that there is no genuine issue of material fact and that the moving party is entitled to a judgment as a matter of law. *Estate of Sanders v. United States*, 736 F.3d 430, 435 (5th Cir. 2013); Fed. R. Civ. P. 56(a). A genuine issue of material fact exists "if the evidence is such that a reasonable jury could return a verdict for the nonmoving party." *Anderson v. Liberty Lobby, Inc.*, 477 U.S. 242, 248 (1986). "When the burden at trial rests on the nonmovant, the movant must merely demonstrate an absence of evidentiary support in the record for the nonmovant's case." *Int'l Ass'n of Machinists & Aerospace Workers, AFL-CIO v. Compania Mexicana de Aviacion, S.A. de C.V.*, 199 F.3d 796, 798 (5th Cir. 2000) (citing *Celotex Corp. v. Catrett*, 477 U.S. 317, 324 (1986)). We may affirm a grant of summary judgment "based on any rationale presented to the district court for [—4—] consideration and supported by facts uncontroverted in the summary judgment record." *Amazing Spaces, Inc. v. Metro Mini Storage*, 608 F.3d 225, 234 (5th Cir. 2010) (internal quotation marks and citations omitted).

DISCUSSION

In the absence of contrary regulation by Congress, federal courts have authority under the Admiralty Clause of the Constitution to develop federal common law governing maritime claims. *See* U.S. Const. art. III, § 2, cl. 1; *Exxon Shipping Co. v. Baker*, 554 U.S. 471, 489–90 (2008); *Romero v. Int'l Terminal Operating Co.*, 358 U.S. 354, 360–61, 382 (1959). "Drawn from state and federal sources, the general maritime law is an amalgam of traditional common-law rules, modifications of those rules, and newly created rules." *E. River*

S.S. Corp. v. Transamerica Delaval, Inc., 476 U.S. 858, 864–65 (1986) (footnote omitted).

Our court has noted that "[t]he recognized principle of agency law that imposes vicarious liability upon employers for the wrongful acts committed by employees while acting in the course of their employment is well ingrained in the general maritime law." *Stoot v. D & D Catering Serv., Inc.*, 807 F.2d 1197, 1199 (5th Cir. 1987). As stated in *Stoot*, the vicarious liability analysis requires two inquiries: (1) whether the defendant is the employer of the tortfeasor; and (2) whether the tortfeasor committed the tort while acting in the course of his employment. We focus on the first question and find that we need not reach the second question.[1]

As the district court observed, we have not expressly articulated a test for establishing an employment relationship in the context of a claim that the defendant is vicariously liable for negligence under the general maritime law. [—5—] However, given that our court has imported the general doctrine of vicarious liability from agency law into the general maritime law, *see id.* at 1199, we conclude that it is appropriate to rely on common law principles of agency to determine the employer's identity in the maritime analysis of vicarious liability. In addition, as explained below, some common law principles governing the employment relationship were developed in a maritime context, while others have been held to apply to maritime disputes.

I. Agency Law

Under the common law of agency, the existence of an employment relationship hinges on "'the hiring party's right to control the manner and means by which the product is accomplished.'" *Nationwide Mut. Ins. Co. v. Darden*, 503 U.S. 318, 323 (1992) (quoting *Cmty. For Creative Non-Violence v. Reid*, 490 U.S. 730, 751 (1989)). The Supreme Court has observed that "[c]ontrol is probably the most important factor under maritime law" to identify employment relationships, "just as it

---

[1] The district court held that a reasonable jury could find that the rig hands were negligent, and GSF does not appeal that determination.

is under the tests of land-based employment." *United States v. W. M. Webb, Inc.*, 397 U.S. 179, 192 (1970) (footnote omitted). Similarly, our court has held, in the maritime context, that "respondeat superior liability is predicated upon the control inherent in a master-servant relationship." *Barbetta v. S/S Bermuda Star*, 848 F.2d 1364, 1370 (5th Cir. 1988).

Agency law anticipates two common disputes relating to employment: disputes over whether an individual is the "borrowed employee" of another employer; and disputes over whether an individual is an independent contractor or an employee. Neither of these tests squarely fits the facts of Johnson's case: there is no indication that GSF was a borrowing or a lending employer, while at the same time, GSF does not allege that the rig hands were independent contractors. However, these two tests suggest factors relevant to [—6—] the analysis of whether GSF formed an employment relationship with the rig hands.

The borrowed servant doctrine, now familiar in agency and tort law, was developed in the admiralty context in *Standard Oil Company v. Anderson*, 212 U.S. 215 (1909). *See Drewery v. Daspit Bros. Marine Divers, Inc.*, 317 F.2d 425, 427 (5th Cir. 1963) (citing *Standard Oil* for the proposition that "[t]he doctrine of imputed negligence applies in admiralty"). "[U]nder the borrowed employee doctrine, an employer will be liable through respondeat superior for negligence of an employee he has 'borrowed,' that is, one who does his work *under his supervision and control*." *Gaudet v. Exxon Corp.*, 562 F.2d 351, 355 (5th Cir. 1977) (emphasis added); *see also Guidry v. S. La. Contractors, Inc.*, 614 F.2d 447, 455 (5th Cir. 1980) (holding that vicarious liability hinged on "whether, at the moment [the tortfeasor] was doing the work that led to [the] injury, he was acting in the business of and under the control of" the general or borrowing employer). To assess "control" under the borrowed servant doctrine, the Supreme Court has suggested consideration of "the power of substitution or discharge, the payment of wages, and other circumstances bearing upon the relation."

Standard Oil Co., 212 U.S. at 225. Relying on *Standard Oil*, we have articulated nine factors that courts should consider in determining whether an employee is a borrowed employee, including: "[w]ho has control over the employee and the work he is performing, beyond mere suggestion of details or cooperation;" "[w]hose work is being performed;" "[w]ho furnished tools and place for performance;" "[w]ho had the right to discharge the employee;" and "[w]ho had the obligation to pay the employee." *Gaudet*, 562 F.2d at 355 (citing *Ruiz v. Shell Oil Co.*, 413 F.2d 310, 312–13 (5th Cir. 1969)); *see also Jackson v. Total E & P USA, Inc.*, 341 F. App'x 85, 86–87 (5th Cir. 2009).

Other maritime disputes have focused on whether a party is an employee or an independent contractor. The Second Restatement of Agency lists factors [—7—] distinguishing employees from independent contractors, including "the extent of control which, by the agreement, the master may exercise over the details of the work;" "whether the employer or the workman supplies the instrumentalities, tools, and the place of work for the person doing the work;" and "whether or not the parties believe they are creating the relation of master and servant." Restatement (Second) of Agency § 220(2). The Court of Claims applied the Second Restatement's factors in the maritime context, in a case cited with approval by the Supreme Court. *See Cape Shore Fish Co. v. United States*, 330 F.2d 961, 964 n.5, 965 n.6 (Ct. Cl. 1964); *W. M. Webb, Inc.*, 397 U.S. at 182, 192 & n.17.

Indicia of the employer-employee relationship are also listed in an Internal Revenue Service regulation that the Supreme Court described as "a summary of the principles of the common law" and as sufficiently flexible to apply to the maritime context. *W. M. Webb, Inc.*, 397 U.S. at 193–94. Then and now, the regulation provides:

> Generally such [an employment] relationship exists when the person for whom services are performed has the right to control and direct the individual who performs the services, not only as to

the result to be accomplished by the work but also as to the details and means by which that result is accomplished. . . . The right to discharge is also an important factor indicating that the person possessing that right is an employer. Other factors characteristic of an employer, but not necessarily present in every case, are the furnishing of tools and the furnishing of a place to work, to the individual who performs the services.

26 C.F.R. § 31.3306(i)–1(b) (2015); 26 C.F.R. § 31.3121(d)–1(c)(2) (1970). Similarly, in analyzing employment relationships under anti-discrimination statutes, we have articulated the "common law control test" as hinging on "whether the alleged employer has the right to hire, fire, supervise, and set the work schedule of the employee." *Muhammad v. Dall. Cnty. Cmty. Supervision* [—8—] *& Corr. Dep't*, 479 F.3d 377, 380 (5th Cir. 2007) (internal quotation marks and citation omitted).

With these factors in mind, we examine the relationship between GSF and the rig hands whose negligence allegedly caused Johnson's injuries. Bradley A. McKenzie, global payroll manager for Transocean Offshore Deep Water Drilling, Inc. ("TODDI"), testified that GSF "is an entity that . . . the [TODDI] payroll department uses as a payroll company to distribute pay to . . . U.S. workers working internationally." McKenzie stated that, to his knowledge, GSF has no function other than "payroll." Similarly, Heather G. Callender, assistant secretary of GSF, stated in an affidavit: "[GSF] serves as a 'paymaster' for some expatriate employees. Its primary function is payroll. It does not perform services involving or related to security, protection, maintenance or safety on rigs." In its brief, GSF acknowledges that, in addition to providing payroll services, it "assists with immigration issues if they arise."

C. Stephen McFadin, GSF's president, stated in a declaration that GSF does not engage in any of the following: "operate rigs on a day to day basis;" "perform the day to day supervision and direction of the crew on a rig;"

"enter into drilling contracts;" or "charter rigs." A declaration by Emeka Ochonogor, principal rig manager for Transocean Support Services Nigeria Limited ("TSSNL"), stated that GSF "had nothing to do with the day-to-day operations of the HIGH ISLAND VII, and nothing to do with the day-to-day supervision or direction of the HIGH ISLAND VII's crew." Rather, Ochonogor said, "All the crew working on the HIGH ISLAND VII reported directly to one of the TSSNL rig managers working out of the Lagos office. TSSNL supervised the day-to-day operation of the HIGH ISLAND VII, including the crew on the rig."

The record reflects that in 2010, GSF issued W-2 forms to the following four individuals who worked on the HIGH ISLAND VII: Timothy Ashley, Danny Ball, James Robertson, and Jeffrey James. The W-2 forms of all four [—9—] workers listed GSF as their "employer," with an address of 4 Greenway Plaza in Houston, Texas. Ashley and Ball were responsible for security aboard the rig, and Ashley, the offshore installation manager, gave the rig hands day-to-day instructions. Johnson highlights testimony by James, the chief mechanic, that he received training at 4 Greenway Plaza, the address listed for GSF on several W-2 forms. Reading James's testimony in the light most favorable to Johnson, we infer that GSF trained James.

The record contains no evidence of most of the factors that would support a finding of an employment relationship. There is no evidence that GSF had the right to direct the rig hands or to control the details of their work. *See W. M. Webb, Inc.*, 397 U.S. at 189; *Gaudet*, 562 F.2d at 355; Restatement (Second) of Agency § 220(2)(a). There is no evidence that GSF hired or had the right to fire the rig hands. *See W. M. Webb, Inc.*, 397 U.S. at 193; *Standard Oil Co.*, 212 U.S. at 225; *Muhammad*, 479 F.3d at 380; *Gaudet*, 562 F.2d at 355. There is also no evidence that GSF furnished the rig or the equipment used on the rig. *See Gaudet*, 562 F.2d at 355; Restatement (Second) of Agency § 220(2)(e). Although it would be reasonable for the rig hands to assume that they were GSF employees based on their W-2 forms, none of the rigs hands so testified. Rather, James stated that he worked for "Transocean." Robertson said he believed his employer was based out of Houston, but did not identify his employer as GSF. James and Robertson testified that they did not believe GSF had "anything to do with the day-to-day operation" of the rig, and Ball testified that he believed Transocean controlled the day-to-day operation of the rig.

The only evidence favoring Johnson is that GSF paid the rig hands, that GSF is identified as the rig hands' "employer" on their W-2 forms, that GSF assisted with immigration matters, and that GSF trained the rig's chief mechanic. We must therefore decide whether a reasonable jury, based on these facts, could find that GSF and the rig hands created an employment [—10—] relationship that would support vicarious liability under the general maritime law.[2] Control is "the most important factor" in identifying an employment relationship under the general maritime law, *W. M. Webb, Inc.*, 397 U.S. at 192, especially where, as here, the plaintiff seeks to impose vicarious liability. *See Barbetta*, 848 F.2d at 1369–70. While payment of wages is relevant to control, it is not dispositive. *See Standard Oil Co.*, 212 U.S. at 225 ("[T]he payment of wages, and other circumstances bearing upon the relation . . . are not the ultimate facts, but only those more or less useful in determining whose is the work and whose is the power of control."). Absent from the record are other indicia of control, such as the right to supervise the rig hands or set their schedule, the right to hire or fire, and the provision of the place or instrumentalities of work. Given that there is little or no evidence of control, no reasonable jury could find that GSF employed the rig hands, applying common law principles of agency.

---

[2] The district court held that GSF was a mere "paymaster," and that a "paymaster" is not an employer under the general maritime law. On appeal, Johnson argues that the district court did not adequately define "paymaster," and GSF concedes that "the name [paymaster] is irrelevant." We do not explore whether GSF should be labelled a "paymaster," but rather focus on the facts of GSF's relationship with the rig hands.

II. The Jones Act

Johnson argues that we should consult caselaw applying the Jones Act to determine whether an employment relationship exists for purposes of assigning vicarious liability under the general maritime law. The Jones Act "create[s] a negligence cause of action for ship personnel against their employers." *Withhart v. Otto Candies, L.L.C.*, 431 F.3d 840, 843 (5th Cir. 2005); *see also* 46 U.S.C. § 30104. While vicarious liability hinges on an employment relationship between the defendant and tortfeasor, liability under the Jones Act depends on an employment relationship between the plaintiff-seaman and the defendant. *See Guidry*, 614 F.2d at 452. [—11—]

Jones Act cases may be useful to our analysis to the extent that these cases articulate common law principles. Our court has stated that "the common law's limits on employer liability are entitled to great weight in . . . Jones Act cases, subject to such qualifications as Congress has imported into those terms." *Beech v. Hercules Drilling Co.*, 691 F.3d 566, 571 (5th Cir. 2012) (internal quotation marks and citation omitted). Indeed, several of the factors that our court has cited in Jones Act cases to identify employment relationships are also relevant under the common law. *See Baker v. Raymond Int'l, Inc.*, 656 F.2d 173, 177–78 (5th Cir. Unit A Sept. 1981) (applying the borrowed servant doctrine under the Jones Act); *see also Volyrakis v. M/V Isabelle*, 668 F.2d 863, 866 (5th Cir. 1982) ("Control is the critical inquiry [under the Jones Act]. Factors indicating control over an employee include payment, direction, and supervision of the employee. Also relevant is the source of the power to hire and fire."), *overruled on other grounds by In re Air Crash Disaster Near New Orleans, La. on July 9, 1982*, 821 F.2d 1147 (5th Cir. 1987).

However, Jones Act caselaw should not control our analysis to the extent that it departs from common law principles of agency. The Supreme Court has held that the Jones Act "is entitled to a liberal construction to accomplish its beneficent purposes"—to "provide for the welfare of seamen." *Cox v.*

Roth, 348 U.S. 207, 210 (1955) (internal quotation marks and citation omitted). "Liberal construction is necessary because of the seaman's broad and perilous job duties." *Beech*, 691 F.3d at 570. We have cited the requirement of liberal construction in identifying employment relationships under the Jones Act. *See Guidry*, 614 F.2d at 455 ("The Jones Act is remedial legislation and as such should be liberally construed in favor of injured seamen." (citing *Spinks v. Chevron Oil Co.*, 507 F.2d 216, 224 (5th Cir. 1975), *overruled on other grounds by Gautreaux v. Scurlock Marine, Inc.*, 107 F.3d 331 (5th Cir. 1997)). "This [—12—] liberal construction has resulted in broader employer liability under the Jones Act . . . than would have been possible under the common law." *Beech*, 691 F.3d at 571; *see also Cosmopolitan Shipping Co. v. McAllister*, 337 U.S. 783, 790 (1949) ("assum[ing] without deciding that . . . the rules of private agency should not be rigorously applied" to identify employment relationships under the Jones Act). The requirement of liberal construction limits the usefulness of Jones Act cases in determining vicarious liability under the general maritime law, where our court has expressly adopted agency law. *See Stoot*, 807 F.2d at 1199 (noting that the vicarious liability doctrine from agency law is "well ingrained in the general maritime law"). Indeed, we have noted that "while the determination of vicarious liability is related to determining whether a defendant is an employer under the Jones Act, they are not assayed by identical standards." *Guidry*, 614 F.2d at 455.

The Jones Act case on which Johnson primarily relies is *Spinks v. Chevron Oil Company*. There, we held that an employee of Labor Services, Inc., who was injured while performing work for Chevron Oil Company, could sue Labor Services under the Jones Act for compensation for negligence. *Spinks*, 507 F.2d at 218. We held that although Spinks was a "borrowed employee" of Chevron, he also remained an employee of Labor Services, whose business included "the supplying of laborers to work on oil rigs and drilling barges." *Id.* at 220. As evidence that Spinks was an employee of Labor Services, we noted that Labor Services hired Spinks; Labor Services paid Spinks and withheld taxes and social security payments from his salary; a Labor Services employee could fire Spinks; and Labor Services made a profit from Spinks's work. *Id.* at 224–25. In *Guidry*, our circuit described the *Spinks* analysis:

> Spinks sued the company that had hired him and signed his checks, his payroll employer. This company in turn assigned him to do work with another firm . . . . In that context, we focus on whether the payroll employer has divested itself of all control over [—13—] the employee. Unless this has happened, the employee is entitled to look no further than the signature on his check.

Guidry, 614 F.2d at 454. Relying on *Spinks* and *Guidry*, Johnson argues that GSF is the rig hands' "payroll employer" and is therefore vicariously liable for their negligence even in the *absence* of evidence of control. Johnson suggests that the burden is on GSF to prove that it has "divested itself of all control" over Johnson.

As a threshold matter, we decline to shift the burden to GSF to demonstrate a lack of control. Such a rule would conflict with caselaw holding that vicarious liability hinges on control, and that payment of wages is relevant, but not dispositive, in determining control. *See Standard Oil Co.*, 212 U.S. at 225; *Barbetta*, 848 F.2d at 1370–71. In addition, we note that *Spinks* is distinguishable on its facts. First, the evidence of an employment relationship is stronger between Spinks and Labor Services than between the rig hands and GSF. In contrast to the relationship between Spinks and Labor Services, there is no evidence that GSF hired the rig hands or that a GSF employee could fire the rig hands. Second, the panel in *Spinks* appeared to assume that Labor Services was Spinks's original employer. The question was not whether Spinks and Labor Services had ever formed an employment relationship, but rather whether Labor Services ceased to be Spinks's employer, under the Jones Act, because it had assigned Spinks to work on Chevron's drilling barge. By contrast, there is no evidence that GSF ever formed an employment relationship with the rig hands. For both legal and factual reasons, Johnson's reliance on *Spinks* is inapposite.

III. Johnson's Additional Arguments

Johnson raises three additional arguments to support his position that GSF employed the rig hands. First, he notes that in two other lawsuits, GSF admitted to being an employer of other rig hands in 2008. Although Johnson [—14—] claims that one of these employees worked on the HIGH ISLAND VII, he points to no record evidence to support that claim. Evidence that GSF employed some rig hands in 2008 does not raise an inference that GSF employed the rig hands who were working on the HIGH ISLAND VII on the night of November 8, 2010.

Second, Johnson suggests that there is insufficient record support for GSF's claim that TSSNL was the rig hands' employer. However, because Johnson bears the burden at trial of demonstrating an employment relationship between GSF and the rig hands, GSF carries its burden at the summary judgment stage by pointing to an absence of evidence that it employed the rig hands. *See Int'l Ass'n of Machinists & Aerospace Workers, AFL-CIO*, 199 F.3d at 798. GSF need not prove that another entity employed the rig hands.

Finally, Johnson marshals policy arguments. He claims that a finding that TSSNL, and not GSF, employed the rig hands would lead to "a situation in which overseas rig hands will now fluctuate wildly in and out of employment relationships based merely upon where the rig is operating." However, on this record, the situation that Johnson fears might actually result from a finding that GSF employed the rig hands. McKenzie testified that while GSF distributes pay to Americans working on rigs in non-U.S. waters, Transocean Deep Water, Inc. distributes pay to Americans working on rigs in U.S. waters. Therefore, allowing the identity of the rig hands' employer to hinge on the W-2 form could cause employment relationships to change each time a rig moved between U.S. and non-U.S. waters.[3] [—15—]

CONCLUSION

GSF may not be held vicariously liable for the rig hands' alleged negligence because no reasonable jury could find an employment relationship between GSF and the rig hands. We therefore AFFIRM the district court's grant of summary judgment in favor of GSF.

---

[3] At the same time, we acknowledge concern that companies conceivably could delegate through contract each obligation reflecting an employment relationship, such that no one company exercises sufficient control over a tortfeasor to support vicarious liability.

United States Court of Appeals
for the Fifth Circuit

No. 14-31283

XL SPECIALTY INS. CO.
vs.
BOLLINGER SHIPYARDS, INC.

Appeals from the United States District Court for the
Eastern District of Louisiana

Decided: August 27, 2015

Citation: 800 F.3d 178, 3 Adm. R. 409 (5th Cir. 2015).

Before **STEWART**, Chief Judge, and **JONES**, and **GRAVES**, Circuit Judges.

[—2—] **JONES**, Circuit Judge:

Bollinger Shipyards won a multimillion dollar contract to upgrade eight United States Coast Guard 110-foot cutters to 123-foot craft. The vessels failed and the United States sued Bollinger. The defendant insurers refused to undertake Bollinger's defense. In Bollinger's suit to enforce the insurance contract, the district court in a comprehensive opinion, granted summary judgment for the insurers. We need not reach numerous issues raised concerning the insurance contracts' interpretation because we may affirm on a narrow basis.

BACKGROUND[1]

As part of the Coast Guard's "Deepwater" modernization program, Bollinger Shipyards converted eight 110-foot patrol boats (vessels it had built originally) to 123-foot patrol boats. The underlying lawsuit alleges that throughout the bidding and development stages of the project, the Coast Guard was concerned about the ability of the boats' hulls to accommodate the extensions. In response, Bollinger submitted a longitudinal strength analysis that compared the "required section modulus" for the redesign to the upgraded vessels' "actual" section modulus. This report showed that the redesigned boats would have well over twice the required strength.

[1] Nothing in this opinion should be taken as resolving any claim in the underlying lawsuit.

Bollinger later revised its reported figure down to a number still well above the "required" figure. This revised calculation allegedly produced three different results, two of which indicated the hull strength was *not* sufficient for the conversion. Bollinger allegedly did not disclose the problematic results but completed the work anyway and delivered the vessels. [—3—]

On September 10, 2004, one of the vessels Bollinger refitted "suffered a structural casualty that included buckling of the hull." The Coast Guard determined that all eight vessels were similarly and irreparably deficient; all of them are now "unusable" despite efforts to remedy the hull strength. The Department of Justice sent Bollinger a litigation hold letter in December 2006 and the Coast Guard revoked acceptance of the vessels on May 17, 2007. Bollinger cooperated with the Government investigation and entered into 21 successive agreements tolling the statute of limitations.

During the 21st tolling agreement, in July 2011, the United States sued Bollinger, alleging five causes of action: two under the False Claims Act and one each of common law fraud, negligent misrepresentation, and unjust enrichment. The district court dismissed the case for failure to state a claim, *United States v. Bollinger Shipyards, Inc.*, 979 F. Supp. 2d 721 (E.D. La. 2013), and this court reversed, 775 F.3d 255, 2 Adm. R. 390 (5th Cir. 2014). However, the Government had only appealed the dismissal of the FCA claims, and those are the only claims remaining in the underlying lawsuit. *See* Brief of United States at 13 n.5, *Bollinger Shipyards*, 775 F.3d 255, 2 Adm. R. 390 ("The United States also alleged liability under common law theories, but has not pursued those theories on appeal."). Trial is currently scheduled for April 11, 2016. Scheduling Order, *Bollinger Shipyards*, 979 F. Supp. 2d 721, No. 12-920-SSV-MBN (E.D. La. Apr. 14, 2015), ECF No. 193.

Just days before the Government filed suit, Bollinger advised its general maritime liability insurer XL Specialty[2] and excess insurer Continental of the impending civil claims. XL responded with a "reservation of rights" letter indicating that it was unsure whether the policy covered the Government's claims; meanwhile, Bollinger obviously continued to pay for its own defense. [—4—]

Before XL formally acted on Bollinger's claim, Bollinger sued XL and Continental in Louisiana state court to enforce its insurance policies, alleging common law breaches of contract and bad faith under Louisiana Revised Statutes §§ 22:1892 and 22:1973. Continental counterclaimed for a declaration that it owed Bollinger no duty to defend and no liability for bad faith. XL separately sued Bollinger in federal court for a declaratory judgment on coverage and removed the state case; the two were consolidated in the Eastern District of Louisiana. A few months later, Continental moved for and was granted summary judgment on the bad faith claims.

Bollinger and XL then filed competing summary judgment motions. The district court granted summary judgment for XL, holding "that the XL policy does not cover the United States' lawsuit and hence does not impose upon XL a duty to defend Bollinger[.]" *XL Specialty Ins. Co. v. Bollinger Shipyards, Inc.*, 57 F. Supp. 3d 728, 752 (E.D. La. 2014). The court granted summary judgment to Continental at the same time. Bollinger appealed and XL cross-appealed. We essentially agree with the district court on the points discussed below, and therefore affirm.

DISCUSSION

This court reviews appeals of summary judgment *de novo*, applying the same standard as the district court. *Roberts v. City of Shreveport*, 397 F.3d 287, 291 (5th Cir. 2005). Louisiana law applies in this diversity action. *See In re Katrina Canal Breaches Litig.*, 495 F.3d 191, 206 (5th Cir. 2007). "An insurance policy is a conventional obligation that constitutes the law between the insured and insurer, and the agreement governs the

nature of their relationship." *Peterson v. Schimek*, 729 So. 2d 1024, 1028 (La. 1999). "When the words of an insurance contract are clear and explicit and lead to no absurd consequences, courts must enforce the contract as written and may make no further interpretation in search of the parties' intent." *Id.* at 1028. [—5—]

"Whether an insurer has a duty to defend is determined solely by 'compar[ing] the allegations in the complaint against the insured with the terms of the policy' at issue— the so-called 'eight corners' rule." *Lamar Adver. Co. v. Cont'l Cas. Co.*, 396 F.3d 654, 660 (5th Cir. 2005) (quoting *Selective Ins. Co. of Se. v. J.B. Mouton & Sons, Inc.*, 954 F.2d 1075, 1077 (5th Cir. 1992)). This rule requires the court to compare the complaint for which coverage is sought with the terms of the insurance policy: "If 'there are any facts in the complaint which, if taken as true, support a claim for which coverage is not unambiguously excluded,' the insurer must defend the insured." *Lamar*, 396 F.3d at 660 (5th Cir. 2005) (quoting *In re Complaint of Stone Petroleum Corp.*, 961 F.2d 90, 91 (5th Cir. 1992)). The court considers the facts alleged in the underlying complaint rather than conclusory labels applied to claims. *Quick v. Ronald Adams Contractor, Inc.*, 861 So.2d 278, 282 (La.Ct.App.2003).

We discuss each policy in light of these general principles and find no ambiguities.

I. XL Specialty

The underlying complaint contained five causes of action: two FCA claims, common-law fraud, unjust enrichment, and negligent misrepresentation. Under the eight-corners rule XL is obliged to defend Bollinger unless all of the claims in the underlying suit are excluded from policy coverage. The district court concluded that all five claims in the underlying complaint fit into either Exclusion 28 or Exclusion 32, but it rejected XL's argument that other exclusions applied.[3] We

---

[2] Technically, some of XL's policies supplied excess as well as primary coverage.

[3] We do not reach other coverage issues raised in XL's brief and cross-appeal.

agree that Exclusions 28 and 32 exempt all claims.

A. Exclusion 28: Predetermined Level of Fitness

Exclusion 28 of Bollinger's insurance contract with XL provides that it

> shall not apply to . . . [t]he failure of your products to meet any predetermined level of fitness or performance and/or guarantee of [—6—] such fitness or level of performance and/or any consequential loss arising therefrom.

On appeal, Bollinger makes two arguments in support of its contention that this provision does not apply. First, Bollinger argues that Exclusion 28 does not preclude coverage for the claims in the underlying suit because the United States was seeking damages for the entire value of the vessels, not only the "work product" for which Bollinger was responsible. Second, Bollinger argues that the underlying suit did not allege a failure to meet a "predetermined level of fitness." We conclude, however, that Exclusion 28 applies to the government's unjust enrichment and negligent misrepresentation claims.

The precedent on which Bollinger relies for its first argument is inapposite. In *OSCA*, for example, the contractor "had only been hired to set a bridge plug inside of an already constructed well, and the allegedly faulty work damaged not only the plug but the entire well[.]" *Underwriters at Lloyd's London v. OSCA, Inc.*, No. 03-20398, 2006 WL 941794 (5th Cir. Apr. 12, 2006) (per curiam) (unpublished). The insurance policy at issue excluded coverage for claims

> arising out of the failure of any Insured's Products or of work . . . by or on behalf of any Insured to meet any warranty or representation by any Insured as to the level of performance, quality, fitness or durability or extent that such liability is for the diminished value or utility of Insured's Products or work by or on behalf of any Insured[.]

Id. at *20. Such "work product exclusions" typically restrict coverage on the basis of "the well-settled principle that liability policies are not intended to serve as performance bonds." *Rivnor Properties v. Herbert O'Donnell, Inc.*, 633 So. 2d 735, 751 (La. Ct. App. 1994); *see also Old River Terminal Co-op v. Davco Corp. of Tenn.*, 431 So. 2d 1068 (La. Ct. App. 1983). But work product exclusions do not apply in cases like *Hendrix Electric Co. v. Casualty Reciprocal Exchange*, 297 So. 2d 470 (La. Ct. App. 1974), in which [—7—]

> [t]he job involved running an underground electrical cable to an existing power distribution panel and installing a new circuit breaker in the panel. An employee accidentally dropped a metal strip and thereby caused a short which started a fire and destroyed the entire panel. The court held that the "damage was not to any 'work performed on or on behalf of the named insured.' The damage was to existing property of the Government, that is the panel and attached circuit breakers." Thus, the court found that the exclusion clearly did not apply.

OSCA, 2006 WL 941794, at *21 (citations omitted) (citing *Hendrix Elec.*, 297 So. 2d at 472); *see also Todd Shipyards Corp. v. Turbine Serv., Inc.*, 674 F.2d 401 (5th Cir. 1982) (distinguishing cases in which "[w]hat was lost to use in those cases was the insured's own product").

Bollinger argues that this is a case like *OSCA* and *Hendrix* because the United States is not seeking damages for Bollinger's work or product alone, but for the entirety of the eight vessels that all unexpectedly failed. Because the damage for which the United States seeks to recover is "the result of something" other than its work product, "Exclusion 28 was not triggered."

This argument cannot succeed. As the district court noted, the policy exclusions in those cases did not exempt the insurer from coverage for "consequential damages" arising from the failure of the insured's work. *See, e.g.,* OSCA, 2006 WL 941794, at *20.

Exclusion 28, by its own terms, exempts claims for damage not only to the insured's work product but also to things other than the insured's product.

Bollinger's second argument, that the underlying suit did not allege a failure to meet a "predetermined level of fitness," relies in part on the district court's previous dismissal of the underlying suit because the complaint did not, in the court's words, "allege what the program and contract requirements were for the converted vessels." *See United States v. Bollinger Shipyards, Inc.*, No. CIV. A. 12-920, 2013 WL 393037, at *1 (E.D. La. Jan. 30, 2013)). But just before that, the district court wrote, "The United States alleges that one of the [—8—] *requirements* was that Bollinger provide the Coast Guard with a Hull Load and Strength Analysis ('HLSA') in order to verify that the modified vessels met the program and contract *requirements*." *Id.* (emphases added).

Moreover, the district court was assessing whether the complaint met the FCA's materiality requirement as codified at 31 U.S.C. § 3729(a)(1)(B). In contrast, the issue in regard to this exclusion is not the FCA claims at all but the unjust enrichment and negligent misrepresentation claims. The United States pled that "Bollinger . . . was responsible for the . . . performance requirements" of the modified boats. Other "requirements" referenced in the complaint include "the *required* section modulus," a *requirement* to comply with American Bureau of Shipping standards, and a *requirement* to provide a hull strength analysis, which itself was used to determine conformity with "program and contract *requirements*." Even if the United States had not alleged sufficient facts to show materiality under the FCA—a determination this court reversed—that would not mean that the complaint did not allege liability because Bollinger's work failed to meet performance requirements.

Citing dictionaries, Bollinger also contends that its "representations" cannot amount to a "predetermination." The argument is that "representations" are unilateral and "predeterminations" imply bilateral agreement. But "predetermined" means only

"established, decided upon, or decreed beforehand." *OED Online*, http://www.oed.com/view/Entry/149830. It implies nothing about how a determination comes about, or who has the authority to determine. A single party can "determine" something, and can do so in advance: there is nothing inherently bilateral about predetermination. And even if there were, the complaint lays out straightforwardly that Bollinger failed to meet a requirement that the parties together determined in advance. The Deepwater contract required the vendor to submit a hull strength analysis, which stated the required longitudinal strength that Bollinger's work [—9—] failed to meet. As the district court noted, "the complaint makes plain that Bollinger, the party responsible for 'performance requirements,' recognized and communicated from the earliest stages of the project that the 'ABS required section modulus' was 3113 cubic inches." *Bollinger Shipyards*, 57 F. Supp. 3d at 755 (footnotes omitted). Thus, however many parties were involved in the predetermination, this was a predetermined level of fitness.[4]

B. Exclusion 32

With the factual basis for the unjust enrichment and fraudulent misrepresentation claims excluded under Exclusion 28, only the FCA and common law fraud claims remain. These fall out under Exclusion 32, which absolves XL from covering:

> e. Actual or alleged liability arising out of or incidental to any alleged violation(s) of any federal or state law regulating,

---

[4] Bollinger also suggests that the district court's reading of the work-products exclusion is overly broad, as it poses a hypothetical scenario in which "a Bollinger employee [] negligently left tools in a place that caused an innocent third party to trip and injure himself[.]" On this reading, XL could "deny coverage, even though the injury had nothing whatsoever to do with the predetermined level of fitness of Bollinger's work or product[.]" This hypothetical is nonsense: in such a situation, the complaint would not allege that the injury stemmed from Bollinger's work failing to meet a predetermined requirement, which is the first precondition of Exclusion 28.

controlling, and governing antitrust or the prohibition of monopolies, activities in restraint of trade, unfair methods of competition or deceptive acts and practices in trade and commerce, including, without limitation, the Sherman Act, the Clayton Act, the Robinson-Patman Act, the Federal Trade Commission Act and the Hart-Scott-Rodino Antitrust Improvements Act; or

f. Actual or alleged liability arising out of or contributed to by [Bollinger's] dishonesty or infidelity.

In the district court, Bollinger "rightfully concede[d] that these exclusions, by their plain terms, preclude coverage for the United States' common law fraud claims and its claims under the False Claims Act." *Bollinger Shipyards*, [—10—] 57 F. Supp. 3d at 757. Bollinger has changed its position following this court's reversal of the district court's FCA materiality decision, in which we focused on "reckless disregard" as the basis of an FCA claim. *See Bollinger Shipyards*, 775 F.3d at 260, 2 Adm. R. at 393. Bollinger continues to concede, however, that Exclusion 32.f "may" exempt the underlying fraud claim. Of course it does.

We need not decide whether "reckless disregard for the truth" qualifies as "dishonesty or infidelity" under 32.f, since the FCA claims clearly fall under Exclusion 32.e. It is irrelevant that the FCA is not listed among the statutes excluded, since the FCA is a "federal law . . . regulating . . . deceptive acts and practices in trade and commerce[.]" Bollinger itself cites authority holding that the FCA is the legal tool by which the Government seeks recompense for "deceptive practices directed at the public purse." *Cook Cnty., Ill. v. U.S. ex rel. Chandler*, 538 U.S. 119, 130-31, 123 S. Ct. 1239, 1247 (2003) (quoting *United States v. Halper*, 490 U.S. 435, 445, 109 S. Ct. 1892, 1900 (1989), *abrogated on other grounds by Hudson v. United States*, 522 U.S. 93, 118 S. Ct. 488

(1997)). Moreover, the alleged FCA violation need not itself be "deceptive." The plain language of Exclusion 32.e embraces laws that regulate deceptive acts, not allegations of deceptive acts.[5] [—11—]

II. Continental

Bollinger challenges the summary judgment awarded to Continental, its excess carrier, largely on the grounds of error in the district court's discussion of XL's policy coverage and prematurity. Both contentions fail.

Continental's excess coverage obligation is not implicated until Bollinger exhausts its lower-level coverages totaling $26 million, which it "has not yet come close to" doing. *Bollinger Shipyards*, 57 F. Supp. 3d at 764. Further, there are no claims remaining that could bring Bollinger's covered liability above this mark because the common law claims are no longer in the case. The remaining claims under the False Claims Act are not covered because Continental's policy insures Bollinger against liability for property damage and personal injury. FCA claims do not seek recovery for property damage or bodily injury, as such, but for "false" claims for payment to the government.[6] *See Bollinger Shipyards*, 57 F. Supp. 3d at 764; accord, *see Health Care Indus. Liability Ins. Prog. v. Momence Meadows Nursing Ctr., Inc.*, 566 F.3d 689 (7th Cir. 2009)(denying coverage on similar facts). As the district court held, "[b]ecause neither of the two claims remaining in the underlying

---

[5] Bollinger also argues that XL acted with bad faith in denying coverage, violating Louisiana Revised Statutes §§ 22:1892 & 22:1973. The fact that coverage was excluded pretermits this claim. *Cf. Cartwright v. Cuna Mut. Ins. Soc'y*, 476 So. 2d 915, 918 (La. App. 1985) ("an insurer's refusal to pay contested benefits is not without just and reasonable cause where that refusal is based on a reasonable interpretation of policy language which has not been construed to the contrary by the courts of this state").

[6] The district court's phrasing is felicitous: "though the underlying suit involves some *allegations* of physical damages, the United States' FCA claims cannot lead to *liability for damages* for physical damages." *Bollinger Shipyards*, 57 F. Supp. 3d at 765.

suit are covered by Continental's policies, Continental is entitled to summary and declaratory judgment that it has no duty to defend or indemnify Bollinger in the underlying suit." *Bollinger Shipyards*, 57 F.Supp.3d at 765. Bollinger's prematurity argument is no more than a Hail Mary under the circumstances of this case. **[—12—]**

CONCLUSION

The contract between the parties did not require XL to defend Bollinger from the claims the United States brought, and Continental's excess policy cannot give rise to coverage. The judgment of the district court is **AFFIRMED.**

United States Court of Appeals
for the Fifth Circuit

No. 14-31326

BARTO
vs.
SHORE CONSTR., L.L.C.

Appeal from the United States District Court for the
Eastern District of Louisiana

Decided: September 4, 2015
Revised: September 29, 2015

Citation: 801 F.3d 465, 3 Adm. R. 415 (5th Cir. 2015).

Before **BENAVIDES, CLEMENT,** and **HIGGINSON,**
Circuit Judges.

[—1—] **CLEMENT,** Circuit Judge:

Mark Barto, an employee of Shore Construction, L.L.C., ("Shore") was hurt when he fell while working on a derrick barge operated by McDermott, Inc. ("McDermott"). Barto sued McDermott under the Jones Act. He also sued Shore for cure under maritime law. After a bench trial, the district court entered a judgment against McDermott and Shore. McDermott appeals the district court's finding that it was completely at fault for the accident, as well as several components of the Jones Act damages award. Shore appeals a [—2—] portion of the cure award. We AFFIRM as to most issues but REVERSE and RENDER as to the award of future lost wages against McDermott.

FACTS AND PROCEEDINGS

Plaintiff-appellee Mark Barto was a Jones Act seaman employed by Shore. Shore assigned him to work as a rigger aboard Derrick Barge 50 ("DB 50"), a derrick barge operated by McDermott.

Barto had an accident while he was working on DB 50. Barto and several other crew members were performing an operation in which a cable was taken from a crane, inspected and subjected to maintenance, and spooled onto a large spooling machine. As the spooling machine slowly turned to reel in the cable, Barto was responsible for guiding the cable by tapping it to ensure that the cable lines did not overlap. He was offered no guidance on how to perform this task, which is not routine but instead is done approximately once every two years. Barto had been working on DB 50 for about 5 months and had never performed this task before. He was also "one of the lowest ranking riggers on the barge," as well as "the least experienced." The barge's crew included a superintendent, a foreman, several leadermen, and a number of more experienced riggers.

The spooling drum was elevated about eight to ten feet above the deck. To perform his task, Barto first tried to use a two-by-four wooden plank to tap the cable lines into place, which was the method used by the person he had seen performing the task previously. But Barto testified that he began having trouble reaching the spooling drum from the deck. So he decided to get a fir board and lay it across part of the spooling machine's frame so that he could stand on the board. He picked a board that "looked sturdy," although it already had a notch cut out of one end. The notch removed a little over half of the board's width from approximately the last foot of the board's length. After placing the board on the spooling frame, Barto stood on top of the board and [—3—] used a brass hammer to guide the cables. The district court credited Barto's testimony that he was standing approximately four feet from the deck and that the board's notched end extended over the frame so that it did not bear any weight.

The district court concluded that Barto's supervisors could easily see him on the board, and that they did not tell him to get down because they did not think it was unsafe. Barto also testified that a leaderman, Rene Vallecillo, came over and talked to Barto while he was standing on the board. Vallecillo told Barto to tap the cable lines if they overlapped on the spool, but he did not tell Barto to get off the board.

In the past, other McDermott employees, including leaderman Vallecillo, had used fir boards as makeshift scaffolding inside the spooling machine's frame. Some McDermott employees had instead performed the task by standing on the frame itself. Other McDermott employees, however, were able to perform the task by standing on the deck and tapping the cable using a two-by-four or even a four-by-four board.

The board on which Barto was standing ultimately broke at the notched end, and Barto fell. The district court found that, given that Barto had placed the board so that the notch overhung the frame, "somehow [the board] apparently moved on him as he was working and broke where the pictures depict that it broke, which is on the end where it was notched out."

After the accident, Barto began having pain in his left leg, lower back, and neck, and he could no longer work. Although Shore paid for most of the maintenance and cure requested by Barto, Shore refused to pay for the lumbar surgery recommended by Barto's neurosurgeon, Dr. Ilyas Munshi. Dr. Munshi recommended the surgery to reduce pain by removing pressure from the nerve sac. About one month before trial, Dr. Munshi performed a three-level laminectomy to remove bone at L2 to L5, which removed the pressure on the [—4—] nerve sac. He then performed a three-level fusion to strengthen the spine. Shore's expert witness, another neurosurgeon, admitted that Barto's nerve sac was compressed before the surgery but vigorously contested the surgery's necessity, maintaining that Barto's pain was on the wrong side to be caused by the nerve sac compression.

Dr. Munshi testified by deposition about two weeks after performing the surgery. He testified that it was too early to tell whether the surgery was successful, although Barto had reported improvement in his leg pain. Dr. Munshi testified that, even if the surgery was successful, "[t]here's a good chance, the most he may do is light duty work." Dr. Munshi also testified that, given his experience with other patients who had made a good recovery from the surgery he had performed, he "reasonably anticipate[s]" the following restrictions: "no frequent bending [or] stooping," weight lifting restrictions, and restrictions on "[a]nything that puts a lot of stress on his back." These restrictions would relate not only to work but

also to recreational activities, and they would be "long-lasting." At trial about one month later, Barto testified that he was not feeling any pain other than some neck pain "[o]ff and on" and some pain from the surgical incision. He testified that, because of the back and neck injuries, he could not do several things he enjoyed, such as "jogging, lifting weights, baseball, basketball, a lot of sports," "yard work," "fix[ing] on my car," and "[p]lay[ing] with my kids."

Barto sued McDermott for Jones Act negligence. He requested damages for, among other things, future lost wages and future "physical and mental pain and suffering and loss of enjoyment of lifestyle." He also sued Shore for cure, requesting that it pay for the surgery performed by Dr. Munshi.

The district court held a bench trial and then ruled from the bench. It held that McDermott was liable under the Jones Act, reasoning that McDermott failed to provide Barto with a safe place to work. The court also [—5—] held that Barto was not comparatively negligent. As to damages, the court held that McDermott owed Barto $400,000 in future general damages and $300,000 in future lost wages. Finally, the court held that Shore was liable for the surgery costs as cure.

STANDARD OF REVIEW

"The standard of review for a bench trial is well established: findings of fact are reviewed for clear error and legal issues are reviewed de novo." *Becker v. Tidewater, Inc.*, 586 F.3d 358, 365 (5th Cir. 2009) (quoting *In re Mid–South Towing Co.*, 418 F.3d 526, 531 (5th Cir. 2005)) (internal quotation marks omitted). Reversal is warranted under clear error review only if the court is "left with the definite and firm conviction that a mistake has been committed." *Jauch v. Nautical Servs., Inc.*, 470 F.3d 207, 213 (5th Cir. 2006) (per curiam) (quoting *Anderson v. City of Bessemer*, 470 U.S. 564, 573 (1985)) (internal quotation marks omitted).

Despite this court's typical deference to a district court's factual findings, "a judgment based on a factual finding derived from an incorrect understanding of substantive law must be reversed." *Mobil Exploration & Producing U.S., Inc. v. Cajun Const. Servs., Inc.*, 45 F.3d 96, 99 (5th Cir. 1995).

DISCUSSION

A. McDermott's Jones Act Liability

McDermott first argues that it is not liable under the Jones Act. We generally "review a district court's finding of negligence and apportionment of fault for clear error." *Jauch*, 470 F.3d at 213. But McDermott argues that we should automatically reverse here because the district court misunderstood the law. *See Mobil Exploration*, 45 F.3d at 99. Specifically, McDermott argues that the district court erroneously believed that a Jones Act employer has a duty to provide an absolutely safe place to work (rather than a reasonably safe [—6—] place to work, which is all that is required under *Gautreaux v. Scurlock Marine, Inc.*, 107 F.3d 331, 339 (5th Cir. 1997) (en banc)).

To demonstrate that the district court misunderstood the law, McDermott relies upon the district court's statement that "[u]nder the Jones Act, of course, the Jones Act employer has a duty, a nondelegable duty to provide a safe place to work." The court also found that "the safe method would have required—should have required proper scaffolding to be erected before employees were required to climb into or onto this spooling machine."

Upon a review of the entire record, we reject McDermott's contention that the experienced district judge misunderstood elementary principles of Jones Act liability. The district court never stated that a Jones Act employer has an absolute duty to provide a safe place to work. Further, the district court stated that "this is more of a negligence case to me than an unseaworthiness case," suggesting that the court recognized that a normal negligence standard of care applies under the Jones Act. Moreover, in their proposed findings of fact and conclusions of law, both parties provided the correct legal standard (ordinary negligence). It seems unlikely that the district court somehow *sua sponte* settled upon an incorrect legal standard. Also, some of the reasoning in the district court's ruling would made little sense if it thought that McDermott had an absolute duty to provide a safe place to work. For example, the court pointed out that "[t]here was scaffolding available on the DB 50. There was even an experienced scaffolding crew . . . ." If McDermott had an absolute duty to provide a safe place to work, it would not matter whether scaffolding was available. Instead, the district court seemed to weigh this fact as evidence that McDermott's failure to erect scaffolding was unreasonable. The court also held that Barto's supervisors "failed to properly supervise Mr. Barto . . . , particularly since this was not a routine job and something he had never done [—7—] before." This reasoning again suggests that the district court was trying to discern whether McDermott had exercised a reasonable amount of care.

Because we find that the district court did not misunderstand the law, we will reverse the negligence finding only if it was clearly erroneous. *Jauch*, 470 F.3d at 213. We hold that it was not. The record reveals ample evidence that the standard practice for performing Barto's assigned task on DB 50 involved seamen figuring out their own makeshift methods of reaching the spooling drum.[1] The district court did not clearly err in finding that McDermott failed to provide Barto with a reasonably safe place to work by failing to provide him with an appropriate way to reach the spooling drum.

---

[1] In particular, the DB 50 superintendent testified that using fir boards as scaffolding was acceptable and had been done in the past; a DB 50 leaderman testified that using a fir board was safe and that he had done so himself; and a more experienced DB 50 rigger testified that he had stood on top of the frame and used a brass hammer to perform Barto's task. Two of Barto's supervisors also testified that they saw him standing on either a board or the frame, and they apparently thought nothing of it. Admittedly, these supervisors testified that Barto was standing only two feet from the deck. But the district court found Barto's recollection that he was about four feet from the deck to be more credible.

B. Barto's Comparative Negligence

McDermott next challenges the district court's conclusion that Barto was not comparatively negligent for the accident. Again, this court "review[s] a district court's finding of negligence and apportionment of fault for clear error." *Jauch*, 470 F.3d at 213. We affirm based on this deferential standard of review.

We have held that:

A seaman . . . is obligated under the Jones Act to act with ordinary prudence under the circumstances. The circumstances of a seaman's employment include not only his reliance on his employer to provide a safe work environment but also his own experience, training, or education.

Gautreaux, 107 F.3d at 339. Comparative negligence "may reduce the amount of damages owed [to a seaman] proportionate to his share of fault." *Jauch*, 470 [—8—] F.3d at 213. The burden of proving comparative negligence is on the Jones Act employer. *Johnson v. Cenac Towing, Inc.*, 544 F.3d 296, 302 (5th Cir. 2008) ("[C]ontributory negligence is an affirmative defense [in a Jones Act case.]").

McDermott argues that Barto was comparatively negligent because he selected an improper board (i.e., a fir board with a notch in it) and failed to secure the board to the spooling machine's frame. The district court did not specifically explain why Barto was not negligent, even though he selected a notched board and failed to secure it. But the court generally explained its decision not to "impose any comparative fault," noting that Barto "was the low man on the totem pole. He was the least experienced. He had never performed this work before."

Moreover, the district court credited Barto's testimony that he had placed the notched end of the board over the frame such that the notched end was not supporting any part of his weight. The DB 50 superintendent testified that, if the notched portion had overhung the frame, "I think the board would have held [Barto's] weight." Also, the board apparently *did* hold Barto's weight for 25 to 30 minutes, further supporting an inference that Barto's selection of the board was not negligent. The district court therefore did not clearly err by finding that McDermott failed to prove that Barto was negligent in his selection of the board, given how he placed it on the frame.

McDermott also did not demonstrate that a reasonable seaman with Barto's "own experience, training, or education" would have realized that he had to secure the board. *See Gautreaux*, 107 F.3d at 339 ("The circumstances of a seaman's employment include . . . his own experience, training, or education."). Indeed, a DB 50 leaderman, Vallecillo, testified that, "[i]f I would have seen that the board wasn't banded [(i.e., wasn't secured to the frame)], I *probably* would have tell him something, but I didn't see that" (emphasis added). This testimony seems to indicate that even a leaderman would not [—9—] view the failure to secure the board as particularly unsafe, given that Vallecillo was unsure whether he would have told Barto to get off an unsecured board. To be sure, McDermott also presented evidence from a barge foreman that the board should have been secured to the frame. But again, McDermott bore the burden of proving that Barto was negligent, given his relative inexperience. Notably, the only other rigger who testified did not opine that the board should have been secured. And McDermott adduced no other testimony that a relatively inexperienced rigger like Barto should have known to secure the board. Further, there was no testimony that the people who had previously used fir boards to perform Barto's task had secured the boards. The district court therefore did not clearly err in finding that McDermott did not prove Barto's comparative negligence, given his relative inexperience.

C. Future General Damages

McDermott also challenges the district court's award of future general damages in the amount of $400,000. "A district court's damages award is a finding of fact, which this court reviews for excessiveness using the clear error standard." *Lebron v. United States*, 279 F.3d 321, 325 (5th Cir. 2002). "Put otherwise, '[w]e do not reverse a verdict for excessiveness except on the strongest of showings.'" *Id.* (quoting *Dixon v. Int'l Harvester Co.*, 754 F.2d 573, 590 (5th Cir. 1985)) (alteration in original).

Future general damages are available "for pain and suffering and impact on one's normal life routines." *Crador v. La. Dep't of Highways*, 625 F.2d 1227, 1230 (5th Cir. 1980). On appeal, McDermott focuses its argument on *only* pain and suffering, arguing that there is no evidence that Barto's pain will return now that he has had surgery. McDermott does *not* argue that Barto will be able to return to his normal life routines. This is particularly important because the district court noted that "[t]here is no question he's going to continue to need to be followed and will have some rather significant **[—10—]** permanent restrictions, as has been testified to by Dr. Munshi, with residual pain." Further, the district court's future general damages award specifically contemplated, in part, Barto's "permanent restriction of normal living— normal life activities and so forth." And Barto presented evidence that his life activities would be limited. He testified that he could no longer do things he enjoyed, such as "jogging, lifting weights, baseball, basketball, a lot of sports," "yard work," "fix[ing] on my car," and "[p]lay[ing] with my kids." And Dr. Munshi testified that, even if the surgery was completely successful, he expected that Barto would indefinitely need to avoid "[a]nything that puts a lot of stress on his back."

At oral argument, McDermott maintained that Barto produced insufficient evidence of the impact on his normal life routines. Specifically, McDermott argued that a seaman's own uncorroborated, self-serving testimony is not enough to prove this impact. This argument fails for three reasons. First, McDermott did not raise this argument in its appellate brief, so it is waived. *E.g., Am. Nat. Gen. Ins. Co. v. Ryan*, 274 F.3d 319, 325 n.3 (5th Cir. 2001). Second, Barto's testimony *was* corroborated: Dr. Munshi testified that, even after the surgery, Barto's recreational

activities would likely be restricted. Third, even if Barto's testimony were uncorroborated, the mere fact that testimony is uncorroborated and self-serving does not automatically mean that a factfinder is prohibited from crediting it. *See, e.g., Curry v. Fluor Drilling Servs., Inc.*, 715 F.2d 893, 895 (5th Cir. 1983) (rejecting defendant's complaint that district court credited plaintiff's self-serving and uncorroborated testimony).[2] **[—11—]**

McDermott next argues that the future general damages award violates our maximum recovery rule. "This judge-made rule essentially provides that we will decline to reduce damages where the amount awarded is not disproportionate to at least *one factually similar* case from the relevant jurisdiction." *Lebron*, 279 F.3d at 326 (quoting *Douglass v. Delta Air Lines, Inc.*, 897 F.2d 1336, 1344 (5th Cir. 1990)) (internal quotation mark omitted).

McDermott has not demonstrated that the rule is applicable here because it has not pointed to a damages award in a "*factually similar* case from the relevant jurisdiction." *Id.* In particular, in the case that McDermott offers as a comparator, the court awarded "$50,000 for future physical and mental pain and suffering." *Aycock v. Ensco Offshore Co.*, 833 So.2d 1246, 1248 (La. Ct. App. 2002). Nothing indicates that this award accounted for the "impact on [the plaintiff's] normal life routines." *Crador*, 625 F.2d at 1230. In contrast, the $400,000 award here explicitly accounted for the impact on Barto's everyday life. Thus, McDermott has failed to advance a suitable comparator for Barto's future general damages award, so the maximum recovery rule does not even come into play. *See Lebron*, 279 F.3d at 326 (noting that the maximum recovery rule "'does not become operative unless the award exceeds 133% of the highest previous recovery in the [relevant jurisdiction]' for a factually similar case"

---

[2] We note that McDermott has not raised an excessiveness challenge to the component of future general damages that compensates Barto for the impact on his normal life routines. We therefore express no opinion on whether the award was excessive.

(quoting *Douglass*, 897 F.2d at 1344 n.14) (alteration in original)).

D. Future Lost Wages

McDermott's final argument is that the district court erred by calculating Barto's lost wages according to an above-average work-life expectancy. A damages award for future lost wages should generally be based upon a seaman's work-life expectancy, meaning "the average number of years that a person of a certain age will both live *and* work." *Madore v. Ingram Tank Ships, Inc.*, 732 F.2d 475, 478 (5th Cir. 1984). "Such an average is not [—12—] conclusive. It may be shown by evidence that a particular person, by virtue of his health or occupation or other factors, is likely to live *and* work a longer, or shorter, period than the average." *Id.* "Absent such evidence, however, computations should be based on the statistical average." *Id.*

Here, the district court noted that expert economists provided wage loss estimates for work-life expectancies of age 55 to "age 67, which is the Social Security requirement age for Mr. Barto." The district court then said, "What I'm going to do is award something in the middle. I think that's a reasonable estimation of his loss of future earning capacity." Accordingly, the district court awarded Barto $300,000 for future lost wages. McDermott argues that the district court erred by relying upon an above-average work-life expectancy.

Barto's expert economist provided a range of estimates for Barto's future lost wages for two different retirement ages: 55.8 and 67. The age of 55.8 was selected based on a table of statistical work-life expectancies that had been prepared by other economists. In contrast, the age of 67 was selected because it is Barto's "full retirement age, as determined by the Social Security Administration." McDermott's expert economist provided a different range of estimates based on a retirement age of 58.2, which its expert selected based on a work-life expectancy table from the U.S. Department of Labor's Bureau of Labor Statistics.

Barto's economist did not provide any reason to believe that Barto would continue to work past his statistical work-life expectancy. The only relevant evidence Barto presented at trial was his testimony that he plans to work "[a]s long as I can retire. Whatever the retirement age is." This scant evidence was not enough to show that Barto "by virtue of his health or occupation or other factors, is likely to live *and* work a longer, or shorter, period than the average." *Madore*, 732 F.2d at 478. For one thing, Barto did not specifically testify that he planned to work until age 67. And nothing indicates that Barto knew that [—13—] this was the Social Security retirement age. Moreover, even if the district court believed that Barto wanted to work until age 67, *wanting* to work until age 67 is not the only or even the most significant factor in determining whether someone actually *will* work until age 67. As we have previously pointed out, an employee "might have become disabled before [the Social Security retirement age] as a result of illness or some other misadventure." *Id.* Or the employee "might have died before then." *Id.* Certainly Barto presented no evidence that such events were particularly unlikely given his health or other factors. Barto therefore did not successfully rebut the presumption that the average work-life expectancy should apply.

McDermott asks us to render judgment, reducing the future lost wages award from $300,000 to $209,533. The district court explicitly credited the vocational expert's opinion that Barto could still work as an unarmed security guard. Barto's own expert economist determined that his net future lost wages would be $209,533 if he worked as an unarmed security guard and retired at age 55.8. We therefore find it appropriate to render judgment in the amount of $209,533 for future lost wages.

Barto contended at oral argument that we should instead remand for the district court to determine future lost wages based on a retirement age of 58.2, the age selected by McDermott's expert economist. This age is about 2.5 years longer than the statistical work-life expectancy selected by Barto's expert economist. But at trial, Barto failed to provide an expert opinion on future lost wages assuming a retirement age of 58.2. "It is a basic concept of damages that they must be proved by the party seeking them." *Servicios-Expoarma, C.A. v Indus. Mar. Carriers, Inc.*, 135 F.3d 984, 995 (5th Cir. 1998). Barto should have presented a revised expert opinion at trial if he intended to argue that McDermott's slightly higher work-life expectancy should apply. We decline to remand to give Barto a second chance to prove future lost wages. [—14—]

E. Cure

Shore's sole argument on appeal is that Barto did not prove that the lumbar surgery was intended to improve his physical condition, so the surgery's cost was not available as cure. This question of fact is reviewed for clear error. *Becker*, 586 F.3d at 365. Moreover, "when there are ambiguities or doubts [as to a seaman's right to receive maintenance and cure], they are to be resolved in favor of the seaman." *Johnson v. Marlin Drilling Co.*, 893 F.2d 77, 79 (5th Cir. 1990) (quoting *Vaughan v. Atkinson*, 369 U.S. 527, 532 (1962)) (internal quotation marks omitted) (alteration in original).

"Cure involves the payment of therapeutic, medical, and hospital expenses not otherwise furnished to the seaman . . . until the point of 'maximum cure.'" *Pelotto v. L & N Towing Co.*, 604 F.2d 396, 400 (5th Cir. 1979). Maximum cure occurs "when it appears probable that further treatment will result in no *betterment* of the seaman's condition." *Id.* "Thus, where it appears that the seaman's condition is incurable, or that future treatment will merely relieve pain and suffering but not otherwise improve the seaman's physical condition, it is proper to declare that the point of maximum cure has been achieved." *Id.* It logically follows that, "when a particular medical procedure is merely palliative in nature or serves only to relieve pain and suffering, no duty to provide payments for cure exists." *Johnston v. Tidewater Marine Serv.*, No. 96-30595, 116 F.3d 478, 1997 WL 256881, at *2 (5th Cir. Apr. 23, 1997) (per curiam) (unpublished table opinion). For example, if a seaman's epilepsy is caused by

scarring in his brain, medicine for "[c]ontrol of seizures is not a cure, for the precipitative factor, the scarring, remains." *Stewart v. Waterman S.S. Corp.*, 288 F. Supp. 629, 633–35 (E.D. La. 1968), *aff'd*, 409 F.2d 1045 (5th Cir. 1969) (per curiam), *cited with approval in Pelotto*, 604 F.2d at 400. [—15—]

Here, Dr. Munshi testified that the purpose of the surgery was to remove pressure from the nerve sac, which caused at least some of Barto's pain. The removal of pressure from the nerve sac would thereby better Barto's physical condition by curing the root cause of his pain rather than merely correcting the symptom (pain). The surgery was therefore curative rather than merely palliative in nature. The surgery also corrected a physical abnormality that existed in Barto's body (pressure on the nerve sac) and thereby bettered his physical condition by restoring it to a normal, healthy condition. The district court therefore did not clearly err by requiring Shore to pay for the surgery as cure, particularly given that any doubts about cure "are to be resolved in favor of the seaman," *Johnson*, 893 F.2d at 79.

CONCLUSION

As to the award of future lost wages, we REVERSE and RENDER judgment that Barto is entitled to $209,533.00 for future lost wages against McDermott. In all other respects, we AFFIRM the district court's judgment.

United States Court of Appeals
for the Fifth Circuit

No. 15-30004

BARTEL
vs.
ALCOA S.S. CO.

Appeals from the United States District Court for the
Middle District of Louisiana

Decided: October 19, 2015

Citation: 805 F.3d 169, 3 Adm. R. 422 (5th Cir. 2015).

Before REAVLEY, ELROD, and HAYES, Circuit Judges.

[—3—] REAVLEY, Circuit Judge:

This consolidated action involves claims arising from the plaintiffs' alleged exposure to asbestos aboard vessels operated or owned by the various defendants. We must determine whether the cases, originally filed in state court, properly belong in federal court.

Plaintiffs Silas B. Bishop, Joseph L. Dennis, and Lawrence R. Craig worked for decades as merchant mariners aboard many different vessels and for many different employers. With their respective lawsuits, each alleges that he was exposed to asbestos over the course of his service and suffered serious disease or death as a result.[1] The plaintiffs sued their former employers in Louisiana state court under the Jones Act and general maritime law (unseaworthiness). They alleged that their injuries were attributable to the employers' failure to warn of the dangers of asbestos, to train their crews in using asbestos-containing products, and to adopt procedures for the safe installation and removal of asbestos. While all three plaintiffs served on various vessels during their careers, each of them served on at least one United States Naval Ship. United States Naval Ships are owned by the Navy but operated by civilian contractors. Here, Navy-owned vessels aboard which the plaintiffs worked were operated by defendants Mathiasen Tanker Industry, Incorporated, American President Lines Limited, and American Overseas Marine Corporation (the "Federal Officer Defendants").[2] [—4—]

The defendants argue that removal was warranted under the Federal Officer Removal Statute, 28 U.S.C. §1442(a)(1). Under this statute, an action "against or directed to . . . any officer (or any person acting under that officer) of the United States or of any agency thereof, in an official or individual capacity, for or relating to any act under color of such office" may be removed to federal court. 28 U.S.C. § 1442(a)(1). To qualify for removal, defendants must show that they are "persons" within the meaning of the statute, "that the defendants acted pursuant to a federal officer's directions and that a causal nexus exists between the defendants' actions under color of federal office and the plaintiff's claims." *Winters v. Diamond Shamrock Chem. Co.*, 149 F.3d 387, 398–400 (5th Cir. 1998). Additionally, they must assert a "'colorable federal defense.'" *Id.* at 400. The defendant bears the burden of making this showing, and we review the district court's determination *de novo*. *Id.* at 397.

It is undisputed that defendants, as corporate entities, qualify as "persons" within the meaning of the Federal Officer Removal Statute. *See Winters*, 149 F.3d at 398. For removal to be proper, it is necessary but not sufficient for a defendant to show it "acted pursuant to a federal officer's directions." *Winters*, 149 F.3d at 398. The defendant must

---

[1] Bishop and Dennis are deceased, and their estates are represented by William E. Bartel, the named party.

[2] These Federal Officer Defendants have since been dismissed from the action. While the claims against them gave rise to potential removability we now consider, our analysis is [—4—] unaffected by the dismissals. "To determine whether jurisdiction is present for removal, we consider the claims in the state court petition as they existed at the time of removal." *Manguno v. Prudential Prop. & Cas. Ins. Co.*, 276 F.3d 720, 723 (5th Cir. 2002). Moreover, "elimination of the federal officer from a removed case does not oust the district court of jurisdiction." *IMFC Prof'l Svcs. of Florida, Inc. v. Latin Am. Home Health, Inc.*, 676 F.2d 152, 159 (5th Cir. Unit B 1982). Our analysis proceeds as if the Federal Officer Defendants had not been dismissed.

also show "that a causal nexus exists between the defendants' actions under color of federal office and the plaintiff's claims." *Id.*

Here, defendants argue that the Federal Officer Defendants acted pursuant to a federal authority "when they contracted with the United States [—5—] Navy to operate and crew Navy ships with civilians." (Blue at 13.) And, they argue that this same fact also establishes a causal nexus exists between the plaintiff's injuries and the defendants' actions under color of office. To support these arguments, they provide a contract governing the relationship between the federal government and *one* Federal Officer Defendant, Mathiasen Tanker Industry, Incorporated. They also provide evidence that vessels operated by the remaining Federal Officer Defendants were Navy-owned.

The defendants' argument collapses the inquiry from two steps to one. That is, they believe the Navy's mere ownership and theoretical control of the vessels provides an adequate "causal nexus" between the Federal Officer Defendants' actions and the plaintiffs' claims. Inasmuch as the plaintiffs allege injuries arising from the intrinsic attributes of the ships, as delivered to the Federal Officer Defendants, defendants could have argued that mere operation of the ships supplies an adequate causal nexus. That is to say, if mere operation of intrinsically dangerous (unseaworthy) vessels caused injuries for which the Federal Officer Defendants may be liable, then that same mere operation may provide a causal nexus supporting removal. It is therefore important to understand the nature of the plaintiffs' allegations. As mentioned already, the plaintiffs' complaints are primarily concerned with failure to warn, failure to train, and failure to adopt procedures for the safe installation and removal of asbestos. These allegations are not concerned so much with vessel design as they are with vessel operation. At oral argument, however, the defendants argued the plaintiffs' allegations of unseaworthiness are broader and encompass the intrinsically unsafe nature of the vessels. We first address those claims concerned with the defendants' acts and omissions—the "failure to warn claims." We

then turn to the claims concerned with the intrinsic dangers posed by mere operation of the vessels—the "unseaworthiness claims." [—6—]

In adopting the magistrate judge's report and recommendation, the district court found that defendants failed to establish an adequate causal link because plaintiffs' claims were "analogous" to "failure to warn cases" where the government owns a work space infected with asbestos and the civilian contractor operating the facility fails to warn of the danger or otherwise mitigate the risk. *See Bartel v. Alcoa Steamship Co.*, 64 F.Supp.3d 843, 855 (M.D. La. 2014) (collecting cases). In their briefing, the defendants directly attacked this reasoning, relying extensively on an unpublished 1998 magistrate judge's ruling, *Lalonde v. Delta Field Erection. See* Case No. CIV.A.96-3244-B-M3, 1998 WL 34301466, at *1 (M.D. La. Aug. 6, 1998). That case, however, is distinguishable and cuts squarely against the defendants.

Like this case, *Lalonde* involved allegations of failure to warn, supervise, and make safe. *See id.* at *1. There, however:

> The federal government imposed numerous safety requirements at the facility, such as the wearing of protective equipment. *The United States required* that safety meetings be held in each department on a monthly basis, and, in addition, required plant-wide safety meetings be held on a monthly basis. *The government dictated* the topics of these meetings. In summary, [the defendant] operated a federal government-owned facility, exclusively for the government, *under the oversight and ultimate control of officers of the federal government.*

Id. at *3 (emphases added).

Thus, not only did the federal government own the facility, it exercised direct and continuing oversight of its operations, including safety briefings and practices. If there were any failure to warn in *Lalonde*, the failure was caused by the government's instructions.

This approach is proper. For example, in *Winters*, where the defoliator Agent Orange allegedly caused terminal cancer in the plaintiff, we asked "whether the government specified the composition of Agent Orange so as to supply the causal nexus between the federal officer's directions and the [—7—] plaintiff's claims." 149 F.3d at 398. After surveying a considerable evidentiary record, we concluded "that *the government's detailed specifications* concerning the make-up, packaging, and delivery of Agent Orange, *the compulsion to provide the product to the government's specifications*, and the *on-going supervision the government exercised* over the formulation, packaging, and delivery of Agent Orange" established that the defendants there "acted pursuant to federal direction and that a direct causal nexus exist[ed] between the defendants' actions taken under color of federal office and [the plaintiff's] claims." *Id.* at 400 (emphases added).

Here, the defendants can do no better than to show that the federal government owned the vessels in question. Even with respect to the Federal Officer Defendant that produced its contract with the government, Mathiasen Tanker Industry, Incorporated, there is no evidence showing that the government actually exercised continuing oversight over operations aboard ship. The contract provides that, in the absence of specific orders from the Navy, the vessel was to be operated "according to accepted commercial practices." There is no evidence that the government ever issued orders of any kind, let alone orders relating to safety procedures or asbestos. What little evidence there is suggests the Federal Officer Defendants operated the vessels in a largely independent fashion and, at a minimum, were free to adopt the safety measures the plaintiffs now allege would have prevented their injuries. Upon this ground the district court found remand proper. We agree.[3] [—8—]

At oral argument, the defendants introduced a new theory. Defendants faulted the district court and the magistrate judge for analyzing the plaintiffs' respective cases as failure-to-warn cases and overlooking the general unseaworthiness claims—*i.e.*, claims that the work environment was intrinsically unsafe. Counsel for defendants labelled this supposed error a "very important point" and "a major point of our complaints about what the magistrate judge did." When asked if this argument had been made in either the initial opposition to plaintiffs' motions to remand or in the subsequent objections to the magistrate judge's report and and recommendation, counsel for the defendants weakly offered that it "was mentioned in there." We have reviewed the oppositions and objections. The argument was never made. Moreover, the argument cannot be gleaned from the defendants' appellate briefs.

Absent "extraordinary circumstances," we will not consider an argument raised for the first time on appeal. *N. Alamo Water Supply Corp. v. City of San Juan, Tex.*, 90 F.3d 910, 916 (5th Cir. 1996). Further, "we do not generally consider points raised for the first time at oral argument." *Whitehead v. Food Max of Mississippi, Inc.*, 163 F.3d 265, 270 (5th Cir. 1998). There are no extraordinary circumstances here. *See N. Alamo Water Supply Corp.*, 90 F.3d at 916 ("Extraordinary circumstances exist when the issue involved is a pure question of law and a miscarriage of justice would result from our failure to consider it."). No miscarriage of justice will result if plaintiffs' claims are heard in state court rather than federal court. Without the benefit of adversarial briefing and trial court consideration, we decline the defendants' belated invitation to greatly expand the scope of federal officer removal jurisdiction in cases

---

[3] Defendants argue that requiring evidence like contracts or orders "places an unreasonable burden on the Federal Officer Defendants and ignores the fact that it ha[s] been more than twenty years since

Plaintiffs-Appellees' [*sic*] sailed on board these vessels and almost fifty years since some of the pertinent contracts were originally executed." While the defendants may find it inconvenient and difficult to locate evidence relating to events that occurred decades ago, that difficulty does not affect the burden of proof or permit us to guess that the evidence, if it were produced, would favor the defendants.

involving USNS vessels. We express no view on the merits of the argument. [—9—]

Because defendants did not establish the necessary causal nexus between their actions and the plaintiffs' claims, we need not decide whether the defendants have asserted a colorable federal defense. Likewise, we need not address plaintiffs' additional arguments in favor of remand.

AFFIRMED.

United States Court of Appeals
for the Fifth Circuit

No. 15-60112

RAMSAY SCARLETT & CO.

VS.

DIRECTOR, OFFICE OF WORKERS' COMPENSATION
PROGRAMS

Petition for Review of an Order of the Benefits
Review Board

Decided: November 12, 2015

Citation: 806 F.3d 327, 3 Adm. R. 426 (5th Cir. 2015).

Before **OWEN**, **GRAVES**, and **HIGGINSON**, Circuit Judges.

[—1—] **HIGGINSON**, Circuit Judge:

Ramsay Scarlett, the former employer of Ferdinand Fabre, age sixty-four, appeals the Benefits Review Board's affirmance of the Administrative Law Judge's order holding Ramsay Scarlett liable for medical expenses attributable to Fabre's asbestosis, under the Longshore Harbor Worker's Compensation Act, 33 U.S.C. §§ 901–950. We AFFIRM. [—2—]

Claimant Ferdinand Fabre was employed by Ramsay Scarlett from 1969 to 1991. During that time, Fabre primarily worked at the Port of Baton Rouge, though between approximately 1972 and 1976, he worked at a storage facility known as Sharp Station. *Id.* It is undisputed that Sharp Station is not a covered situs under the Longshore Harbor Workers' Compensation Act ("LHWCA"), 33 U.S.C. §§ 901–950; *see New Orleans Depot Servs., Inc. v. Dir., Office of Worker's Comp. Programs*, 718 F.3d 384, 393-94, 1 Adm. R. 228, 234-35 (5th Cir. 2013). Similarly, the parties do not dispute that the Port of Baton Rouge is a covered situs under the LHWCA. From 1991 to 2013, Fabre was employed by Westway, an employer also covered by the LHWCA and located at the Port of Baton Rouge.

The parties agree that Fabre was diagnosed with asbestosis in 2011. Fabre contends that he was exposed to asbestos while working for Ramsay Scarlett at both Sharp Station and the Port of Baton Rouge. The parties do not dispute that Fabre was exposed to asbestos while working at Sharp Station. Fabre alleges that, while working for Ramsay Scarlett at the Port of Baton Rouge, he was exposed to asbestos while changing the brakes and clutches of several types of equipment. Alleging that these conditions caused his asbestosis, Fabre filed a claim for medical benefits under the LHWCA on December 28, 2011. The Administrative Law Judge ("ALJ") issued a nineteen-page decision and order on September 10, 2013. After finding that Fabre established a prima facie case of coverage under the LHWCA, that Ramsay Scarlett did not rebut that case, and that Ramsay Scarlett was the last maritime employer, the ALJ ordered Ramsay Scarlett to pay for all "reasonable and necessary medical expenses arising out of [Fabre's] work-related occupational disease pursuant to 33 U.S.C § 907." Ramsay Scarlett appealed the ALJ's ruling, and on September 25, 2014, the Benefits Review Board [—3—] ("BRB") affirmed the ALJ's decision and order. Ramsay Scarlett timely appealed.

DISCUSSION

I.

We review decisions by the BRB only to determine whether it adhered to the proper scope of review—whether the ALJ's findings were supported by substantial evidence and were consistent with the law. *Ceres Gulf, Inc. v. Dir., Office of Worker's Comp. Programs*, 683 F.3d 225, 228 (5th Cir. 2012). Substantial evidence is "that relevant evidence—more than a scintilla but less than a preponderance—that would cause a reasonable person to accept the fact finding." *Id.* (citation omitted). Importantly, the ALJ remains the sole fact finder and must make all credibility determinations. *Id.* The BRB correctly cited this standard articulated in our case law.

II.

Under the LHWCA, the claimant establishes a prima facie case for coverage by showing that (1) a harm occurred and (2) the harm may have been caused or aggravated by a workplace condition. *Ceres Gulf, Inc.*, 683 F.3d at 229. If the claimant establishes these elements, a presumption arises that the claim falls under the LHWCA. *Id.*; 33 U.S.C. § 920(a). The burden then shifts to the employer to rebut the presumption "through facts—not mere speculation—that the harm was not work-related." *Ceres Gulf, Inc.*, 683 F.3d at 229 (citation omitted). This burden can be met by showing that working conditions did not cause the harm or that the employee was exposed to the same working conditions at a subsequent covered employer. *Avondale Indus., Inc. v. Dir., Office of Workers' Comp. Programs*, 977 F.2d 186, 190 (5th Cir. 1992). If the ALJ finds that the employer rebutted the presumption, then the ALJ must weigh all of the evidence to determine whether the harm was caused by the claimant's employment at the covered situs. *See Ceres Gulf, Inc.*, 683 [—4—] F.3d at 229. We hold that the BRB correctly held that the ALJ properly applied the LHWCA's burden-shifting framework and relied on substantial evidence when making his findings at each step.

Ramsay Scarlett first argues that Fabre's prima facie case is unsubstantiated because there was not substantial evidence to establish that Fabre was exposed to asbestos at the Port of Baton Rouge. When determining that Fabre established a prima facie case, the ALJ relied on Fabre's explicit deposition testimony and the report of Frank Parker, an industrial hygienist. Fabre testified that during his tenure at the Port of Baton Rouge, he changed brakes and clutches on a variety of equipment, including cranes, that he believed "definitely had asbestos on them" because "most of the things at that time probably had asbestos in them." Fabre stated that the components did not have warning labels on them, that he often had to blow out dust when installing the components, and that at an unknown time he read that these components contained asbestos. In his report, Parker reviewed Fabre's work history and concluded that Fabre was first exposed to asbestos at Sharp Station in the early 1970s. Parker also concluded that Fabre's exposure to asbestos,

while less, continued when he returned to the Port of Baton Rouge during the mid to late 1970s. Parker reported that during the time Fabre was employed by Ramsay Scarlett at the Port of Baton Rouge, he was exposed to asbestos because it was well documented that brakes and clutches, the components that Fabre handled, exposed workers to "significant concentrations of asbestos."

The ALJ credited the above-described evidence when finding that Fabre had met the low burden required to establish a prima facie case—that he suffered a harm that a workplace condition could have caused or aggravated. This evidence was more than a scintilla, and it might cause a reasonable [—5—] person to accept the ALJ's fact finding. *See Sonat Offshore Drilling v. Avondale Indus.*, 37 F. App'x 91, at *2 (5th Cir. 2002) (finding that the claimant's testimony and the testimony of one other employee was substantial evidence to justify a prima facie case); *see also Ingalls Shipbuilding, Inc. v. Dir., Office of Workers' Comp. Programs*, 991 F.2d 163, 165 (5th Cir. 1993) (defining substantial evidence as evidence that "a reasonable mind might accept as adequate to support a conclusion" (citation omitted)).

Ramsay Scarlett first attacks the credibility of Fabre's deposition testimony because his belief that he was exposed to asbestos arose only after he read a newspaper article describing the presence of asbestos in certain machinery. Ramsay Scarlett also contends that Fabre contradicted his assertions of exposure in two ways. Ramsay Scarlett points out that when Fabre was first diagnosed with asbestosis in 2011, he only mentioned his exposure at Sharp Station. Second, Ramsay Scarlett notes that Fabre did not feel the need to wear a protective mask at the Port of Baton Rouge, even though he wore one at Sharp Station. In addition to criticizing Fabre's statements, Ramsay Scarlett also criticizes Parker's report for failing to cite historical literature or other data and solely relying on the testimony of other longshoremen.

We have held that "under the [LHWCA], the ALJ, not the BRB, [is] entitled to assess the relevance and credibility of testimony, including expert testimony."[1] *Ceres Gulf, Inc.*, 683 F.3d at 229. The ALJ's reliance on Fabre's [—6—] deposition testimony and Parker's report that was elaborated in five paragraphs of record analysis under the caption "weighing the evidence" demonstrates that the ALJ found this evidence relevant and credible. The ALJ's statement that Parker relied on "scientific literature, his education and experience, and information generally relied upon my [sic] members of his profession" also demonstrates that the ALJ regarded the expert testimony as reliable. Ramsay Scarlett's credibility attack on Fabre's deposition testimony and Parker's report therefore fails. *See Ceres Gulf, Inc.*, 683 F.3d at 228.

Ramsay Scarlett also challenges Fabre's prima facie case on the ground that Fabre's exposure to asbestos at the Port of Baton Rouge would have been *de minimis* compared to his exposure at other non-maritime settings, such as Sharp Station. However, "[t]he Fifth Circuit has . . . held that, regardless of the brevity of the exposure, if it has the potential to cause disease, it is considered injurious." *Avondale Indus.*, 977 F.2d at 190. As a result, this argument also fails. The BRB did not err in finding that substantial evidence supported the ALJ's conclusion that Fabre established the presumption of a LHWCA claim.

Ramsay Scarlett next argues that even if Fabre did establish a prima facie case, Ramsay Scarlett rebutted the presumption. To rebut the claimant's established presumption, Ramsay Scarlett must provide "factual doubt" and "substantial evidence to the contrary." *See Ceres Gulf, Inc.*, 683 F.3d at 231; *Ortco Contractors, Inc. v. Charpentier*, 332 F.3d 283, 287 (5th Cir. 2003). The only evidence that Ramsay Scarlett itself submitted on the causation issue was evidence that, by 1976, the Occupational Health and Safety Administration [—7—] had adopted regulations regarding asbestos, which would have greatly limited any exposure to asbestos. But, Ramsay Scarlett did not present any evidence that these asbestos regulations or any additional safety measures were ever implemented at the Port of Baton Rouge. In addition, Ramsay Scarlett did not present any evidence contradicting Fabre's deposition testimony and Parker's report that there was asbestos in the brakes and clutches Fabre changed. Therefore, a reasonable mind could accept that Ramsay Scarlett did not provide factual doubt as to whether the working conditions of the Port of Baton Rouge caused Fabre's asbestosis.

Ramsay Scarlett also argues that it rebutted the presumption by proving that Ramsay Scarlett was not the last covered maritime employer. Ramsay Scarlett contends that Fabre was exposed to asbestos at Westway, another covered employer and his only subsequent employer. *Id.* Again, to rebut the presumption, Ramsay Scarlett must put forth "substantial evidence to the contrary" and provide "factual doubt." *See Ceres Gulf, Inc.*, 683 F.3d at 231; *Ortco Contractors, Inc.*, 332 F.3d at 287.

Because Fabre testified that he worked around cranes, trucks, and other equipment while employed at Westway, Ramsay Scarlett contends that Fabre could have been exposed to asbestos at Westway. Ramsay Scarlett contends that if such proximity evidence is enough to establish a prima facie case for Fabre, it is enough to establish that Westway was the last covered employer. When concluding otherwise, the ALJ relied on Fabre's deposition testimony that at Westway he was not exposed to asbestos and that he did not change brakes and clutches, the same components that exposed him to dust at the

---

[1] We have also held that "the formal rules of evidence do not apply in administrative proceedings but rather 'the admissibility of evidence depends on whether it is such evidence as a reasonable mind might accept as probative.'" *Atlantic Marine, Inc. v. Bruce*, 661 F.2d 898, 900 (5th Cir. Unit B 1981) (quoting *Young & Co. v. Shea*, 397 F.2d 185, 188 (5th Cir. 1968), *cert. denied*, 395 U.S. 920 (1969)). In addition, Ramsay Scarlett did not challenge the decision of the ALJ for relying on a fact unsupported by the record. 5 U.S.C. § 556 ("When [—6—] an agency decision rests on official notice of a material fact not appearing in the evidence in the record, a party is entitled, on timely request, to an opportunity to show the contrary.").

Port of Baton Rouge. Ramsay Scarlett did not put forth any factual evidence that contradicted Fabre's testimony that he was not exposed to asbestos and did not change brakes and clutches at Westway. As a result, there was substantial [—8—] evidence for the ALJ to conclude that Ramsay Scarlett did not rebut the presumption of a valid LHWCA claim because it did not provide factual doubt.

III.

Ramsay Scarlett also challenges the affirmance of the ALJ's order requiring Ramsay Scarlett to reimburse Fabre for annual flu and pneumonia vaccines and the treatment of conditions including pneumonia and bronchitis. The LHWCA requires an employer to reimburse a claimant for all medical expenses that arise from a work-related injury and defines "injury" as a disease or infection that arises "naturally" out of the employment. 33 U.S.C. §§ 902, 907. We have held that "[a] subsequent injury is compensable if it is the direct and natural result of a compensable primary injury, as long as the subsequent progression of the condition is not shown to have been worsened by an independent cause." *Miss. Coast Marine, Inc. v. Bosarge*, 637 F.2d 994, 1000 (5th Cir. 1981). We apply a liberal causation standard when determining the coverage of initial and subsequent injuries. *Bludworth Shipyard, Inc. v. Lira*, 700 F.2d 1046, 1051 (5th Cir. 1983).

When determining coverage of Fabre's medical treatment, the ALJ relied on the deposition of Dr. Gomes, the doctor who diagnosed Fabre with asbestosis at age sixty, and who Fabre now sees for a yearly x-ray and pulmonary function test. In his deposition, Dr. Gomes testified that patients with asbestosis require yearly flu and pneumonia vaccines to prevent chest infections and that asbestosis increases the likelihood that one will develop pneumonia and bronchitis. In response, Ramsay Scarlett contends that Fabre did not establish a causal link between asbestos exposure and these respiratory infections. Specifically, Ramsay Scarlett points out that Fabre had a history of pneumonia before his asbestosis diagnosis. Ramsay Scarlett also asserts [—9—] that pneumonia is not always

caused by asbestosis.[2] We defer to the ALJ's credibility determination and reliance on Dr. Gomes's testimony. *See Ceres Gulf, Inc.*, 683 F.3d at 228. Given the liberal causation standard, a reasonable mind could accept Dr. Gomes's testimony and "the common sense of the situation" as adequate to support the conclusion that these respiratory ailments are a natural result of asbestosis and that flu and pneumonia vaccines are necessary treatments for the disease. *See Atlantic Marine, Inc. v. Bruce*, 661 F.2d 898, 900 (5th Cir. Unit B 1981).

CONCLUSION

For the forgoing reasons, we AFFIRM the BRB's affirmance of the ALJ's order.

---

[2] Ramsay Scarlett also contends that the causation standard for subsequent injuries is a higher burden than the ALJ applied, citing, *Amerada Hess Corp., et al. v. Director, Office of Worker's Comp. Programs*, 543 F.3d 755 (5th Cir. 2008). In *Amerada Hess*, we remanded the case for the ALJ to determine whether there was substantial evidence to conclude that a heart condition was the "natural and unavoidable" result of a back injury. 543 F.3d. at 760–62. However, the court's decision rested on the fact that there was no expert testimony linking the two conditions. *Id.* at 762 (stating "no qualified physician testified to [the] effect" that "such treatment is necessary for a work-related condition" and "[i]t appears to us that such a finding would benefit from, if not require, support of medical experts"). Conversely, in his deposition, Dr. Gomes directly linked asbestosis to the relevant respiratory conditions.

United States Court of Appeals
for the Fifth Circuit

No. 15-30070

NGUYEN
VS.
AMERICAN COMMERCIAL LINES, L.L.C.

Appeal from the United States District Court for the
Eastern District of Louisiana

Decided: October 8, 2015
Revised: November 13, 2015

Citation: 805 F.3d 134, 3 Adm. R. 430 (5th Cir. 2015).

Before **KING, DENNIS,** and **OWEN,** Circuit Judges.

[—1—] PER CURIAM:

Following a collision, a barge owned by American Commercial Lines, L.L.C., discharged oil into the Mississippi River. A number of fishermen and others dependent on fishing filed claims under the Oil Pollution Act of 1990 against the owner of the barge for damages arising from the spill. The district court denied the motion of American Commercial Lines for summary judgment but certified to this court the two controlling issues of law concerning the requirements for proceeding under the Act. For the following reasons, we AFFIRM in part and REVERSE in part the order denying summary judgment. [—2—]

I. FACTUAL AND PROCEDURAL BACKGROUND

On July 23, 2008, a collision occurred on the Mississippi River in the Port of New Orleans between the M/V TINTOMARA and Barge DM-932, causing oil to discharge from the barge into the river. *See Gabarick v. Laurin Mar. (Am.) Inc.*, 753 F.3d 550, 551–52, 2 Adm. R. 228, 228 (5th Cir. 2014) (discussing the same oil spill at issue in this case). Following the discharge, the oil traveled downriver and entered various bodies of water, including estuaries within Plaquemines Parish, Louisiana. The United States Coast Guard designated Barge DM-932 as the source of the discharge and named American Commercial Lines, L.L.C., ("ACL"),

the owner of the barge, as the responsible party under the Oil Pollution Act of 1990 ("OPA"). ACL hired Worley Catastrophe Response, LLC, ("Worley") as its third-party claims administrator to handle any claims against ACL under the OPA for damages arising from the oil spill.

In June 2009, Michael A. Fenasci, an attorney representing commercial fishermen and others affected by the oil spill (the "claimants"), began submitting claims to Worley on form claim letters signed only by Fenasci—not the individual claimants. Attached to the form letters were copies of the individual fishermen's applicable licenses and selected copies of dock receipts for seafood sold to wholesalers. Each letter alleged that oil entered and contaminated the fishing grounds of the individual fisherman and that the oil disrupted fishing operations for approximately 25 days. The letters also stated that as a result of the pollution discharge, the fishermen suffered losses in earning capacity and in the subsistence use of harvested sea life. Each letter included a specific "evaluation of damages" that constituted the fisherman's demand under the OPA. Each evaluation included the claimant's gross loss of earning capacity, which was calculated by multiplying the gross loss of earnings per day by the total number of lost fishing days and then reduced by [—3—] 5% to account for overhead costs. All of the letters also alleged a loss of $60 per day in subsistence use of natural resources and $200 for hull cleaning.[1]

On July 23, 2009, Worley sent a letter to Fenasci stating that it had reviewed each of the 224 claims submitted thus far. Worley also requested additional documentation from each claimant. The documentation included the following: (1) a copy of the claimant's federal income tax return for 2007 and 2008; (2) a record of daily catch or sales data for the five months surrounding the spill; (3) an

---

[1] While the majority of claimants are fishermen, some are seafood wholesalers or others affected by the oil spill. The claim letters sent on behalf of these non-fishermen differed somewhat from the letters sent on behalf of the fishermen, but all of the letters included a demand for a specific amount of damages.

explanation, with support, for the number of lost fishing days; (4) a calculation demonstrating how the lost income per day was determined from the supporting materials provided by each claimant; (5) an explanation of how the $60 in subsistence loss was calculated; (6) the invoice for the hull cleaning; and (7) a map indicating where the claimant normally fished and normally stored his vessel. Fenasci responded to Worley's request by sending tax returns for the individual claimants, which had increased from 224 to 247. On December 2, 2009, Worley informed Fenasci that some of the submitted tax returns were missing information and reiterated its request for the other information it had previously demanded. On June 4, 2010, Wayne W. Yuspeh, the attorney currently representing the claimants, responded that both his office and Fenasci's office had previously forwarded a number of claims concerning the oil spill to Worley. He also stated that if no response with a good faith effort to settle the previously submitted claims was received within ten days, then a lawsuit would be filed. On July 22, 2011, Yuspeh sent notices of new and amended individual claims, and on July 25, 2011, the claimants filed this action. [—4—]

On November 9, 2012, the district court granted ACL's motion to dismiss under Federal Rule of Civil Procedure 12(c) and entered judgment accordingly on December 7, 2012. The court found that, by not providing Worley with the information it requested, the claimants had failed to comply with the OPA's requirement that claims first be properly presented to the responsible party. The court also explained that compliance with this presentment requirement was a mandatory condition precedent to commencing an action in court. However, the district court vacated its judgment on September 23, 2013, and directed ACL to file a motion for summary judgment. On July 18, 2014, the district court denied ACL's motion for summary judgment, stating that "[t]he Plaintiffs clearly satisfied the substantive presentment requirements imposed by the language of the OPA itself." On December 17, 2014, the district court denied ACL's motion for reconsideration but granted ACL's motion for certification of an interlocutory appeal under 28 U.S.C. § 1292(b).

The district court certified two issues of law for appeal: (1) "whether [the claimants] met proper presentment requirements when they failed to personally sign the claim forms . . . and did not provide certain specific requested items of evidence in support of their claims"; and (2) "whether the requirement of a 90-day waiting period after making proper presentment before starting litigation against the responsible party . . . coupled with the three-year limitation period for commencing an action against a responsible party . . . means that the [claimants] had to make a proper presentment at least 90 days before the expiration of the limitation period." The first issue is relevant to all claimants in this case, as none of them personally signed their claims or provided Worley with all of the documentation it requested. The second issue relates only to those claimants who first presented their claims to Worley on or after July 22, 2011, since these claimants failed to wait 90 days after first presenting their claims to file suit in order to avoid having their [—5—] claims time barred by the period of limitations. This court granted leave to appeal from the interlocutory order of the district court on January 27, 2015.

II. STANDARD OF REVIEW

A district court may certify an interlocutory appeal from an order if the court is "of the opinion that such order involves a controlling question of law as to which there is substantial ground for difference of opinion and that an immediate appeal from the order may materially advance the ultimate termination of the litigation." 28 U.S.C. § 1292(b). "Under 28 U.S.C. § 1292(b), a grant or denial of summary judgment is reviewed de novo, applying the same standard as the district court." *Castellanos-Contreras v. Decatur Hotels, LLC*, 622 F.3d 393, 397 (5th Cir. 2010) (en banc) (citing *First Am. Bank v. First Am. Transp. Title Ins. Co.*, 585 F.3d 833, 836–37 (5th Cir. 2009)). However, because review is only granted on "the issue[s] of law certified for appeal," *Tanks v. Lockheed Martin Corp.*, 417 F.3d 456, 461 (5th Cir.

2005), this court's "review only extends to controlling questions of law," *Castellanos-Contreras*, 622 F.3d at 397 (citing *Tanks*, 417 F.3d at 461). Summary judgment is proper "if the movant shows that there is no genuine dispute as to any material fact and the movant is entitled to judgment as a matter of law." Fed. R. Civ. P. 56(a). This court must construe "all facts and inferences in the light most favorable to the nonmoving party." *Dillon v. Rogers*, 596 F.3d 260, 266 (5th Cir. 2010) (quoting *Murray v. Earle*, 405 F.3d 278, 284 (5th Cir. 2005)).

III. PRESENTMENT UNDER THE OPA

Congress passed the OPA, 33 U.S.C. § 2701 *et seq.*, after the Exxon Valdez oil spill "to streamline federal law so as to provide quick and efficient cleanup of oil spills, compensate victims of such spills, and internalize the costs of spills within the petroleum industry." *Rice v. Harken Expl. Co.*, 250 F.3d 264, 266 (5th Cir. 2001) (citing S. Rep. No. 101-94 (1989), *as reprinted in* 1990 U.S.C.C.A.N. 722, 723). To facilitate prompt cleanup and compensation, the [—6—] OPA requires the "Coast Guard [to] identif[y] 'responsible part[ies]' who must pay for oil spill cleanup in the first instance." *United States v. Am. Commercial Lines, LLC*, 759 F.3d 420, 422, 2 Adm. R. 283, 283 (5th Cir. 2014) (quoting 33 U.S.C. § 2701(32)). "Responsible parties are strictly liable for cleanup costs and damages and [are] first in line to pay [for] . . . damages that may arise under OPA."[2] *Id.* at 422 n.2, 2 Adm. R. at 283 n.2 (citing 33 U.S.C. § 2702(a)). Individuals and entities harmed by an oil spill may file claims against the responsible party for damages. However, "to promote settlement and avoid litigation," *Johnson v. Colonial Pipeline Co.*, 830 F. Supp. 309, 310 (E.D. Va. 1993), the OPA establishes specific procedures which claimants must follow. Specifically, the statute provides:

(a) Presentment

---

[2] While responsible parties may be held strictly liable, these parties may later seek contribution and indemnification from other parties whose actions contributed to the oil spill. 33 U.S.C. §§ 2709–2710, 2713.

Except as provided in subsection (b) of this section, all claims for removal costs or damages shall be presented first to the responsible party or guarantor of the source designated under section 2714(a) of this title.

(b) Presentment to Fund

(1) In general

Claims for removal costs or damages may be presented first to the [Oil Liability Trust] Fund—

(A) if the President has advertised or otherwise notified claimants in accordance with section 2714(c) of this title;

. . .

(c) Election

If a claim is presented in accordance with subsection (a) of this section and—

(1) each person to whom the claim is presented denies all liability for the claim, or [—7—]

(2) the claim is not settled by any person by payment within 90 days after the date upon which (A) the claim was presented, or (B) advertising was begun pursuant to section 2714(b) of this title, whichever is later,

the claimant may elect to commence an action in court against the responsible party or guarantor or to present the claim to the [Oil Liability Trust] Fund.

33 U.S.C. § 2713.

Thus, under the OPA's presentment requirement, claimants must first present their claims to the responsible party and wait until that party denies all liability or until 90 days from the time of presentment have passed before "commenc[ing] an action in court against the responsible party."[3] 33 U.S.C. § 2713(c); *see also Am. Commercial Lines*, 759 F.3d at 425, 2 Adm. R. at 285 ("[I]f the responsible party has not paid the claim within 90 days, 'the claimant may elect to bring suit against the responsible party. . . .'" (quoting 33 U.S.C. § 2713(a))). In lieu of pursuing their claims in court, claimants may elect to file their claims against the Oil Liability Trust Fund (the "Fund"), which is a public trust fund established by the OPA to compensate those harmed by oil spills, if allowed by 33 U.S.C. § 2713(b).[4] In this case, no claimant has filed a claim against the Fund.

Neither party disputes that "the clear text of [33 U.S.C.] § 2713 creates a mandatory condition precedent barring all OPA claims unless and until a claimant has presented her claims in compliance with § 2713(a) . . . ." *Boca Ciega Hotel, Inc. v. Bouchard Transp. Co.*, 51 F.3d 235, 240 (11th Cir. 1995). However, the parties disagree over whether the claimants have properly [—8—] presented their claims to Worley, and the issues of law certified for appeal concern compliance with the presentment requirement. We first consider what supporting documentation claimants must include when they present their claims to a responsible party and conclude that the claimants have properly presented their claims to Worley. We then address whether claimants must present their claims to the responsible party at least 90 days before the end of the three-year period of limitations established by the OPA. *See* 33 U.S.C. § 2717(f)(1) (requiring that an action for damages be brought "within 3 years after . . . the date on which the loss and the connection of the loss with the discharge in

---

[3] Nothing in the record suggests that Worley or ACL ever "denie[d] all liability for [any] claim," 33 U.S.C. § 2713(c)(1), so our analysis of the presentment requirement focuses on the 90-day waiting period where relevant.

[4] If a claimant files a claim against the Fund, the government is subrogated to the claimant's rights under the OPA and may assert those rights in litigation to recoup any payments on claims. 33 U.S.C. § 2715.

question are reasonably discoverable with the exercise of due care.").

A. The Claimants Submitted Sufficient Information to Comply with the Presentment Requirement

Turning first to the issue of what information and supporting documentation claimants must submit to comply with the OPA's presentment requirement, there is no question that the claimants presented their claims and some supporting information to Worley. Neither ACL nor the claimants dispute that Worley received claim letters from all claimants or that each letter included a statement alleging losses from the oil spill and an evaluation of damages, which constituted the claimant's demand for damages under the OPA. Each letter also included applicable fishing licenses and selected dock receipts for seafood sold to wholesalers. Most claimants also submitted federal tax returns to support their claims. However, ACL contends that because the claimants failed to produce all of the information and supporting documentation Worley requested, the claimants have not properly complied with the OPA's presentment requirement.

"As in all statutory construction cases, [our analysis] begin[s] with the language of the statute," *Barnhart v. Sigmon Coal Co., Inc.*, 534 U.S. 438, 450 [—9—] (2002), so we turn to the language of the presentment requirement. In relevant part, the OPA requires that "all claims for removal costs or damages shall be presented first to the responsible party." 33 U.S.C. § 2713(a). The statute defines "claim" as "a request, made in writing for a sum certain, for compensation for damages or removal costs resulting from an incident." 33 U.S.C. § 2701(3). "Damages" are defined to include real property damage, loss of subsistence use of natural resources, loss of revenues, loss of profits, and loss of public services. 33 U.S.C. § 2701(5); *see also* 33 U.S.C. § 2702(b)(2). "Statutory definitions control the meaning of statutory words . . . in the usual case," *Burgess v. United States*, 553 U.S. 124, 129 (2008) (quoting *Lawson v. Suwannee Fruit & S.S. Co.*, 336 U.S. 198, 201

(1949)), and nothing in the plain language of any of these provisions or definitions suggests that claimants must submit anything more than what they have already submitted to Worley. We need not decide whether less documentation than what the claimants submitted here would satisfy the presentment requirement. Because the claimants have submitted sufficient supporting documentation, they have properly presented their claims to Worley under the OPA.

ACL's arguments, that more information and supporting documentation are required, are based on a misreading of the OPA. ACL urges this court to read 33 U.S.C. § 2713 together with § 2714 and argues that these two sections allow it, as the responsible party, to determine the required documentation for claims. ACL contends that because § 2713(a) refers to § 2714(a), which applies to the designation of the responsible party, this court must consider § 2714(b). Section 2714(b) requires a responsible party to "advertise the designation and the procedure by which claims may be presented, in accordance with regulations promulgated by the President." 33 U.S.C. § 2714(b)(1). ACL then points to 33 C.F.R. § 136.105—the OPA claims procedure regulation promulgated by the Coast Guard governing the supporting materials [—10—] claimants must include when filing claims against the Fund—as its justification for requiring claimants to submit additional information. This regulation requires claimants who file their claims against the Fund to provide, among other things, "[e]vidence to support the claim[s]." 33 C.F.R. § 136.105. Based on 33 U.S.C. §§ 2713 and 2714 and 33 C.F.R. § 136.105, ACL argues that it can require claimants to produce, as part of the presentment requirement, any documentation it desires as long as that documentation is consistent with 33 C.F.R. § 136.105.

We find, as the district court found, that ACL's reading of the statute is erroneous. First, ACL misreads the OPA by conflating the requirements for filing claims against the Fund with the requirements for presenting claims to a responsible party. The plain language of 33 U.S.C. § 2713(e) makes clear that 33 C.F.R. § 136.105 applies only to claims filed against the Fund and not to claims presented to responsible parties. Section 2713(e) empowers the "President [to] promulgate . . . regulations for the presentation, filing, processing, settlement, and adjudication of claims under this Act *against the Fund.*" 33 U.S.C. § 2713(e) (emphasis added). Based on this statutory language, 33 C.F.R. § 136.105 applies only to claims filed against the Fund and does not apply to claims presented to the responsible party.

Second, as an extension of its earlier argument, ACL contends that under the OPA, a claimant has only one claim. Therefore, ACL argues, the regulations governing that claim when it is filed against the Fund must also apply when it is presented to a responsible party. However, the fact that claimants possess only one claim does not imply that the requirements for submitting that claim cannot differ depending on whether the claim is being filed against the Fund or presented to the responsible party. The OPA defines a claim as "a request, made in writing, for a sum certain, for compensation for damages or removal costs resulting from an incident," and this definition [—11—] applies to all claims under the OPA. 33 U.S.C. § 2701(3). While § 2713(e) allows the President to promulgate regulations that expand what claimants must submit when filing their claims "against the Fund," it does not authorize the President to alter or expand the definition of a "claim" under the statute generally. Thus, the requirements for filing a claim against the Fund in 33 C.F.R. § 136.105 do not apply to claims presented to the responsible party. Because the plain text of 33 U.S.C. § 2713(e) establishes that 33 C.F.R. § 136.105 does not apply to claims presented to the responsible party, ACL cannot rely on this regulation to support its request for additional information.

Third, ACL correctly points out that other courts have held that the purpose of the presentment requirement "is to enable the parties to negotiate, if possible, a settlement of potential claims resulting from an oil spill without having to resort to litigation," and that "[i]n order to accomplish this purpose, the claim presented must inform the responsible party with some precision of the nature and extent of the damages alleged and of the amount of monetary damages claimed." *Johnson*, 830 F. Supp. at 311; *see also Turner v. Murphy Oil USA, Inc.*, No. 05-4206, 2007 WL 4208986, at *2 (E.D. La. Nov. 21, 2007). The purpose of the OPA can be achieved with the documentation the claimants submitted in this case, as that documentation provided sufficient information for ACL to decide if it wanted to settle a given claim. While ACL argues that it would be in a better negotiating position were it to obtain all of the information Worley requested, this is not a reason to expand the statute beyond its plain language. If ACL was not satisfied with the amount of information it received from the claimants, it remained free to determine it did not want to settle, deny the claims, and proceed to litigation where it would have access to the discovery process in the district court.

Finally, ACL argues that other environmental statutes which include citizen suits contain provisions requiring notice before a citizen can file suit. [—12—] ACL contends that, like the citizen suit notices in these statutes, the OPA requires that the presentment of a claim be adequate under some legal standard and offers 33 C.F.R. § 136.105 as that standard. *See, e.g.*, 33 U.S.C. § 1365(b). However, because this regulation does not apply when presenting claims to a responsible party under the OPA, it cannot serve as the legal standard for those claims. The OPA provides the legal standard against which a claim presented to a responsible party can be measured in 33 U.S.C. § 2701(3), which defines a claim generally. Using the statutory definition of claim as the standard of adequacy, the claim letters and supporting documentation submitted by the claimants are adequate.

In addition to requesting documentation and information beyond what the OPA requires the claimants to present to a responsible party, Worley also demanded that claimants individually sign their claim letters. ACL's arguments that claimants must sign their claim letters are based on its assertion

that 33 C.F.R. § 136.105 applies to claims presented to the responsible party. The regulation requires that "[e]ach claim must be signed in ink by the claimant certifying to the best of the claimant's knowledge and belief that the claim accurately reflects all material facts." 33 C.F.R. § 136.105(c). However, as discussed above, this regulation does not apply to claims presented to the responsible party, and the statute that does apply, 33 U.S.C. § 2701, nowhere requires that claimants individually sign their claims. Moreover, each claim letter at issue here was signed by the claimant's attorney, and ACL does not contend that the attorney lacked the authority to sign on the claimant's behalf. Therefore, the claims at issue here were not improperly presented simply because they lacked the signatures of individual claimants.

The district court correctly concluded that the claimants' claims were not barred for failing to sign their claims or to provide sufficient supporting [—13—] documentation. The plain language of the presentment requirement does not compel claimants to provide any explanation or documentation beyond what they have already submitted, and the purpose of the presentment requirement can be achieved with the information submitted. The district court also correctly determined that the claims were not improperly presented simply because the individual claimants did not sign their claim letters, as the signature requirement appears in a regulation not applicable to the presentment of claims to the responsible party.

B. The Claimants Must Comply With Both the Presentment Requirement and Three-Year Period of Limitations Under the OPA

We now address the second issue certified for appeal: whether claimants must present their claims to the responsible party at least 90 days before the end of the three-year period of limitations established by the OPA. The majority of claimants presented their claims to Worley in June and July of 2009 and did not file suit until July 2011, thus clearly presenting their claims at least 90 days prior to the expiration of the period of limitations. However, a number of claimants waited until July 22, 2011—nearly three years after the oil spill—to present their claims.[5] These claimants then commenced their actions along with all of the other claimants on July 25, 2011—only three days after first presenting their claims—because waiting the full 90 days would necessarily involve filing suit outside the three-year period of limitations. The district court held that "in this instance the failure to wait 90 days before submitting those claims should not be grounds for dismissal," and noted that "[m]ore than enough time has passed to cure this deficiency." We disagree. [—14—]

As before, our analysis begins with the language of the OPA. *Barnhart* 534 U.S. at 450; *see also Estate of Cowart v. Nicklos Drilling Co.*, 505 U.S. 469, 475 (1992). An action for damages is barred under the OPA unless it is brought:

within 3 years after—

> (A)   the date on which the loss and the connection of the loss with the discharge in question are reasonably discoverable with the exercise of due care, or

> (B)   in the case of natural resource damages under section 2702(b)(2)(A) of this title, the date of completion of the natural resources damage assessment under section 2706(c) of this title.

33 U.S.C. § 2717(f)(1). The provisions of the OPA establishing the presentment requirement and period of limitations do not refer to one another and therefore operate independently of each other. 33 U.S.C. § 2713, 2717; *see also Denehy v. Mass. Port Auth.*, 42 F. Supp. 3d 301, 308 (D. Mass. 2014) ("The

catch is that the OPA's presentment requirement operates independently of the law's other statutes of limitations."). Because these two provisions operate independently, the claimants cannot, as a general rule, rely on compliance with one to excuse non-compliance with the other. The claimants who failed to comply with the presentment requirement's 90-day waiting period in order to avoid filing suit outside the three-year period of limitations offer four reasons why their claims should nonetheless be allowed to go forward. None of these reasons is persuasive.

First, these claimants urge this court to apply the "Equity Doctrine under maritime law" to excuse their failure to wait 90 days after presenting their claims to Worley to file suit. The claimants point out that at least one court has allowed a claimant to commence an action against a responsible party without waiting 90 days from the time of presentment. In *Denehy*, the [—15—] Coast Guard did not designate a responsible party until "55 days before the end of the three-year window to file the instant lawsuit." *Id.* The court explained that "[a]t that point, [the claimant] simply could not have met both the presentment requirement and the statute of limitations." *Id.* The claimant in *Denehy* chose to comply with the period of limitations by filing a claim "a few days before the three-year deadline but scarcely a month after presenting claims to [the responsible parties]." *Id.* After noting that "[s]tatutes are to be interpreted in accordance with their 'plain and ordinary meaning,' in order to give practical effect to the beneficial goals that impelled Congress to enact the law," the court determined that "the two sections best may be harmonized equitably by staying [the] timely filed action until a 90-day period for presentment has passed." *Id.* at 309 (internal citations omitted).

The claimant in *Denehy* pointed to extenuating circumstances that made it impossible to wait 90 days prior to commencing an action against the responsible party—the Coast Guard did not identify the responsible party until less than 90 days before the expiration of the period of limitations. However, the claimants here point

---

[5] The district court referred to 48 claims filed within the 90-day presentment window, but the parties refer to 22 such claims. The number of claims filed in the 90-day window is not material to our analysis, and the district court can determine on remand the dates on which different claims were presented.

to no extenuating circumstances that precluded them from presenting their claims 90 days before they filed suit. Although the claimants advance a number of hypothetical scenarios that they argue warrant excusing non-compliance with the 90-day waiting period, we decline their invitation to speculate. Without some explanation for why the claimants did not comply with both the presentment requirement and three-year period of limitations, we need not decide whether extenuating circumstances could justify excusing their noncompliance with the 90-day waiting period as the court in *Denehy* did. *Cf. Eastman v. Coffeyville Res. Ref. & Mktg., LLC*, No. 10-1216-MLB-KGG, 2010 WL 4810236, at *4 (D. Kan. Nov. 19, 2010) (refusing to relate an OPA claim back to the date the original complaint was filed, in part, because "if the amended complaint were to relate back to the date of the [—16—] original complaint, the OPA claim would be treated as having commenced . . . before the 90 day[] [presentment period] had expired.").

Second, the claimants point to the purpose of the OPA, which is to compensate those affected by oil spills. They argue that this court must "do more . . . than simply read the letter of the OPA . . . in order to give practical effect to the beneficial goals that impelled Congress to enact the law." *Denehy*, 42 F. Supp. 3d at 309; *see also Rice*, 250 F.3d at 266. However, this court's "obligation is to give effect to congressional purpose so long as the congressional language does not itself bar that result." *Johnson v. United States*, 529 U.S. 694, 710 n.10 (2000). The statutory language of the OPA clearly requires that the claimants comply with both the 90-day waiting period and the three-year period of limitations. Therefore, claimants may not ignore the 90-day waiting period simply because the period of limitations is about to expire. We note that requiring the claimants to comply with the statutory language does not frustrate Congress's purpose. The claimants had ample time to pursue litigation against the responsible party given the Coast Guard's early identification of that party and the absence of any other factors delaying claimants' pursuit of their claims.

Third, the claimants argue that at least one district court has allowed unpresented claims to proceed. *See In re Oil Spill by the Oil Rig Deepwater Horizon in the Gulf of Mexico, on Apr. 20, 2010*, 808 F. Supp. 2d 943, 965 (E.D. La. 2011) *aff'd sub nom. In re DEEPWATER HORIZON*, 745 F.3d 157, 2 Adm. R. 171 (5th Cir. 2014). However, *Deepwater Horizon* involved over 100,000 individual claims in a multi-district litigation. While the court in that case declined to engage in the "impractical, time-consuming, and disruptive" task of reviewing so many claims to determine, *inter alia*, presentment prior to allowing them to proceed, the claimants here number less than 300, making the task of reviewing their claims much less arduous. *Id.* (noting that "[a] judge handling [a multi-district [—17—] litigation] often must employ special procedures and case management tools."). Moreover, the court in *Deepwater Horizon* held that "presentment is a mandatory condition-precedent with respect to Plaintiffs' OPA claims," despite its decision to not review individual claims because of the number of claims involved. *Id.*

Finally, the claimants argue that ACL tacitly denied their claims and that ACL was not prejudiced by the district court allowing the claims presented on July 22, 2011, to go forward. Based on this tacit denial and lack of prejudice, the claimants argue that their claims are not barred under the OPA. The claimants contend that, because ACL had not responded to any of the previous claims presented to it, they were justified in assuming it would not respond to the claims presented in July 2011. However, an assumption that claims would be denied is not sufficient to constitute compliance with the presentment requirement. The statute requires that claimants wait until "each person to whom the claim is presented denies all liability for the claim, or . . . the claim is not settled by any person by payment within 90 days after the date upon which . . . the claim was presented." 33 U.S.C. § 2713. Without an actual denial of all liability for a claim by the responsible party or compliance with the 90-day waiting period, the presentment requirement has not been satisfied.

Therefore, based on the plain language of the statute, the claimants in this case who failed to present their claims at least 90 days prior to commencing an action in court are barred from pursuing litigation against ACL.

IV. CONCLUSION

For the foregoing reasons, we AFFIRM in part and REVERSE in part the district court's order denying summary judgment. We REMAND for proceedings consistent with this opinion.

United States Court of Appeals
for the Fifth Circuit

No. 14-31321

IN RE DEEPWATER HORIZON

CAMERON INT'L CORP.
vs.
LIBERTY INS. UNDERWRITERS, INC.

Appeals from the United States District Court for the
Eastern District of Louisiana

Decided: November 19, 2015

Citation: 807 F.3d 689, 3 Adm. R. 439 (5th Cir. 2015).

Before **STEWART**, Chief Judge, and **CLEMENT**, and
ELROD, Circuit Judges.

[—1—] **CLEMENT**, Circuit Judge:

This is an insurance dispute arising out of
the *Deepwater Horizon* oil spill. Liberty
Insurance Underwriters, Inc. ("Liberty"),
appellee-cross-appellant here, insured
Cameron International Corporation
("Cameron"), appellant-cross-appellee here
and the manufacturer of the blowout
preventer used on *Deepwater Horizon*, for
potential losses associated with the blowout
preventer. After the spill, Cameron settled
with BP, the well owner, and sought the policy
benefits from Liberty to help cover the
settlement costs. For a [—2—] number of
reasons, Liberty refused to pay, so Cameron
sued. The district court granted summary
judgment for Cameron on its breach of
contract action, granted summary judgment
for Liberty on Cameron's claim under the
Texas Insurance Code, and denied Cameron's
motion for attorney's fees. Both parties
appealed.

CERTIFICATION FROM THE UNITED
STATES COURT OF APPEALS FOR THE
FIFTH CIRCUIT TO THE SUPREME
COURT OF TEXAS, PURSUANT TO ART. 5,
§ 3-C OF THE TEXAS CONSTITUTION AND
RULE 58.1 OF THE TEXAS RULES OF
APPELLATE PROCEDURE

TO THE SUPREME COURT OF TEXAS AND
THE HONORABLE JUSTICES THEREOF:

I.

This case turns, in part, on a complicated
arrangement of indemnification between some
of the parties involved in the spill. BP (a
nonparty here) owned the Macondo oil well
and the lease on the continental shelf. BP
contracted with Transocean (also a nonparty
here), which owned *Deepwater Horizon,* to
drill the well, and to indemnify[1] Transocean
for liability associated with drilling. Cameron
manufactured and sold Transocean the
blowout preventer connecting the rig to the
well, and Transocean indemnified Cameron
for liability associated with the blowout
preventer. In short, Cameron was indemnified
by Transocean, which was in turn indemnified
by BP.

Cameron did not rely solely on indemnification to protect itself. It created an
insurance "tower" of $500 million in coverage
by purchasing insurance from [—3—] various
insurers. Those insurance policies covered the
risk that Cameron would incur liability as the
blowout preventer's manufacturer. The first
$25 million in losses would be covered by one
insurer, the next $25 million in losses would
be covered by another, and so forth.[2] Liberty
sold Cameron a policy covering the $50 million
in losses between the first $100 million and
$150 million in losses. In other words,
Liberty's $50 million policy was excess of the
policies covering the first $100 million in
losses, and Cameron obtained other policies
that were excess of Liberty's policy.

---

[1] BP disputes that it owes Transocean
indemnification, and Transocean disputes that it
owes Cameron indemnification. Neither BP nor
Transocean has been found to owe indemnification.
Yet both BP's contract with Transocean and
Transocean's contract with Cameron contain
clauses that purport to indemnify under some
circumstances, and both Cameron and Transocean
sought indemnification under those clauses. This
opinion thus uses "indemnify" and "indemnification" as shorthand for "included a contractual
clause that one party interprets as indemnifying
it." But we express no opinion on whether BP or
Transocean owes indemnification under those
clauses.

[2] The precise details of the tower vary slightly
from this description, but those details are not
important here.

Like many insurance policies, Liberty's policy incorporated a subrogation clause. That clause provided that if Cameron could recover from a third party some or all of the losses paid under the policy, Cameron would transfer the rights to recover to Liberty, "do nothing after loss to impair these rights," and "help [Liberty] enforce them." For example, if Liberty paid Cameron $50 million for a covered loss, and a third party was potentially liable to Cameron for that same loss, Liberty would assert Cameron's rights against that third party and receive any recovery up to the amount Liberty paid Cameron.

After the spill, thousands of lawsuits were filed against BP, Transocean, Cameron, and others. Cameron sought indemnity (for its potential liability for pollution) from Transocean under the sales contract, and Transocean refused; Cameron thus sued Transocean, and Transocean counterclaimed. Transocean, in turn, sought indemnity from BP under its drilling contract, and BP refused; Transocean and BP thus also sued each other. And BP sued Cameron, claiming that, as the manufacturer of the blowout preventer, Cameron was responsible for the losses that BP incurred. [—4—]

As well as seeking indemnification from Transocean, Cameron notified Liberty after the spill of a potential loss covered by the policy. Initially, Liberty neither rejected nor paid Cameron's claim.

Following extensive litigation, BP and Cameron began to discuss settlement. The parties soon developed a framework for that settlement: BP would indemnify Cameron in exchange for $250 million,[3] but only if Cameron's insurers agreed to waive their subrogation rights and Cameron agreed to waive its indemnification rights against Transocean. Otherwise, BP feared, Cameron's insurers would cover Cameron's settlement costs, then step into Cameron's shoes and sue Transocean for indemnification, which would in turn sue BP for indemnification—for the very $250 million that BP just received. Why,

in other words, would BP settle for a payment from Cameron that Cameron would ultimately recoup—albeit in a circuitous fashion—from BP?

Alone among Cameron's insurers, Liberty objected to the settlement and declined to offer its policy limits of $50 million. Liberty did not agree to a settlement that waived its subrogation rights and Cameron's indemnification rights against Transocean, leaving Liberty on the hook for $50 million. Liberty also pointed out another clause in its policy that, in its view, meant that its obligation to pay had not yet been triggered: the Other Insurance Clause. That clause provided that "[i]f other insurance applies to a 'loss' that is also covered by this policy, this policy will apply excess of such other insurance." In turn, the policy defined "other insurance" as "any type of self-insurance, indemnification or other mechanism by which an Insured arranges for funding of legal liabilities." Liberty argued that because Cameron had not yet exhausted its legal remedies against Transocean, "other insurance"—namely, [—5—] Transocean's indemnification—"applie[d]" to the loss, so Liberty's policy was excess of that other insurance. Cameron disputed this interpretation.

Seeking to assuage Liberty's concerns about subrogation, Cameron and BP inserted additional language into the settlement purportedly preserving Liberty's subrogation rights. Then—despite Liberty's refusal to contribute its policy limits—Cameron went ahead with the settlement, putting up $50 million of its own money in addition to the $200 million its other insurers contributed.

Because Liberty continued to refuse to offer its policy limits, Cameron filed this suit, asserting claims for breach of contract and for violations of the Texas Insurance Code. Liberty moved under Rule 12(c) for judgment on the pleadings, but the district court denied most of that motion. On cross-motions for summary judgment, the district court granted Cameron a $50 million judgment on its breach of contract action. But the district court granted judgment in favor of Liberty on

---

[3] The parties did not immediately arrive at this number, but that is where they ended up.

Cameron's Texas Insurance Code claims and, in a later order, denied Cameron's request for attorney's fees incurred in this action.

Cameron appealed the district court's judgment against it on its claim under Chapter 541 of the Texas Insurance Code and on its claim for attorney's fees. Liberty cross-appealed the district court's judgment in favor of Cameron on its breach of contract claim.

II.

This court reviews de novo the district court's grants of summary judgment. *Morris v. Equifax Info. Servs., LLC*, 457 F.3d 460, 464 (5th Cir. 2006). Summary judgment is proper if "there is no genuine dispute as to any material fact and the movant is entitled to judgment as a matter of law." Fed. R. Civ. P. 56(a). The parties do not dispute that Texas law applies to this diversity case. *See Erie R.R. Co. v. Tompkins*, 304 U.S. 64, 78 (1938). [—6—]

III.

Liberty contends that the district court erred in granting Cameron's motion for partial summary judgment (and in denying Liberty's cross-motion for partial summary judgment) on its breach of contract claim. First, Liberty argues that Cameron is not entitled to recover under the policy because the Other Insurance Clause makes the policy apply only in excess of Cameron's (unexhausted) indemnity claim against Transocean. Second, Liberty argues that Cameron, not Liberty, breached the policy by impairing Liberty's subrogation rights in the BP settlement. We address each argument in turn.

a.

To begin with, it is undisputed that the policy covers the loss that Cameron suffered. But Liberty, pointing to the Other Insurance Clause, contends that because Cameron has an indemnification agreement with Transocean, "other insurance" "applies" to that loss. Thus, argues Liberty, Cameron is not yet entitled to coverage because Cameron has not exhausted that indemnification or

obtained a judicial determination that it is not entitled to indemnification. Cameron responds that its disputed indemnity claim against Transocean does not "appl[y]" to its loss because Transocean refused Cameron's demands for indemnification. Cameron also argues that its disputed indemnity claim against Transocean does not constitute "other insurance" at all.

To refresh, the Other Insurance Clause provides that "[i]f other insurance applies to a 'loss' that is also covered by this policy, this policy will apply excess of such other insurance." In turn, the policy defines "other insurance" as "any type of self-insurance, indemnification or other mechanism by which an Insured arranges for funding of legal liabilities." "'Other insurance' clauses are generally designed by insurers to 'avoid an insured's temptation or fraud of over-insuring . . . property or inflicting self-injury.'" *St.* [—7—] *Paul Mercury Ins. Co. v. Lexington Ins. Co.*, 78 F.3d 202, 206 (5th Cir. 1996) (quoting *Hardware Dealers Mut. Fire Ins. Co. v. Farmers Ins. Exch.*, 444 S.W.2d 583, 586 (Tex. 1969)).

Liberty argues that the district court should have interpreted the Other Insurance Clause to read, in effect, that if "other insurance" *potentially* applies to Cameron's loss, Liberty's policy is excess of that insurance. Until a final judicial determination that Transocean does not have to indemnify Cameron, then, Liberty's obligation to pay the policy benefits is not triggered, and thus it could not have breached the contract.

Cameron counters that the district court properly interpreted the Other Insurance Clause to mean that Liberty's policy is excess of other insurance if, but only if, that "other insurance" *actually and presently* applies. Thus, because Transocean refused to indemnify Cameron, Liberty was obligated to pay the policy benefits.

In our view, Cameron's interpretation is reasonable and Liberty's is not. The plain language of the clause supports Cameron's reading. Liberty's policy is excess only if other insurance "applies," present tense. *See Parrot*

Ice-Drink Prods. Of Am., Ltd. v. K & G Stores, Inc., No. 14-09-00008-CV, at *4, 2010 WL 1236322 (Tex. App.—Houston [14th Dist.] March 30, 2010, no pet.) (mem. op.) (use of present tense in contract establishes "relevant time period"). Liberty's interpretation requires the court to read the word "potentially" into the contract. *Tenneco Inc. v. Enter. Prods. Co.*, 925 S.W.2d 640, 646 (Tex. 1996) (noting that "courts will not rewrite agreements to insert provisions parties could have included"). Moreover, the clause provides that Liberty's policy being excess of other insurance is conditional on other insurance applying. Liberty reads this to mean that the policy is excess of other insurance until Cameron affirmatively shows that no other insurance exists. *But see Certain Underwriters at Lloyd's of London v. Cardtronics, Inc.*, 438 S.W.3d 779, 781 [—8—] (Tex. App.—Houston [1st Dist.] 2014, no pet.) (finding that to interpret clause to impose requirement of conclusive determination before recovery where "explicit statement of such a requirement is wholly absent" would be unreasonable). That reading would transform the Other Insurance Clause from a protection against double-insuring into a clause that makes Liberty's policy a policy of last resort.[4] Given the purpose for which Cameron obtained the policy—specifically, to be the primary insurance for the $100 million-$150 million layer of its insurance tower—the clause cannot bear that weight.

Context also indicates that Cameron's reading is correct. The policy states that it is "excess" to both other insurance and the underlying insurance (the first $100 million in the tower). As to the underlying insurance, however, the policy expressly provides that even if an underlying insurer is unable or refuses to pay, Liberty will not "drop down" in coverage. In other words, no matter what,

---

[4] As Cameron points out, this would place Liberty in quite a favorable position. Either Transocean indemnifies Cameron, letting Liberty off the hook, or Transocean refuses to indemnify Cameron and Cameron must pursue costly litigation against Transocean to obtain a final determination. Liberty could thus rightfully refuse to pay for years on end, something in tension—to say the least—with its policy term providing that it will "promptly pay" a covered loss.

Liberty's policy is excess to the underlying policies. The Other Insurance Clause contains no such provision; Liberty's policy is excess to other insurance only if other insurance "applies." Liberty thus asks us to read language into the Other Insurance Clause stating that the policy is excess even to "other insurance" that is uncollectible. But we refuse Liberty's invitation to read a provision into the policy, particularly because the policy includes that provision elsewhere in a similar context.

As the district court noted, moreover, under Liberty's reading, Cameron would be better off with no indemnification agreement at all—having both insurance and a disputed indemnity claim would leave Cameron less protected [—9—] than it would be with only insurance. Yet the policy does not specifically reference Cameron's indemnity agreement with Transocean, nor does it require Cameron to maintain any such agreement. *See AMHS Ins. Co. v. Mut. Ins. Co. of Az.*, 258 F.3d 1090, 1097 (9th Cir. 2001) (rejecting argument that "other insurance" clause required insured to exhaust other policy that insured was not required to maintain and that was not mentioned in policy). So because Cameron chose to maintain a potential alternative source of protection for its loss—something Liberty did not require it to do—Cameron would have to litigate with that alternative source before recovering anything from Liberty. *See* 2 Allan D. Windt, Insurance Claims & Disputes § 6:13, at 6-212 (6th ed. 2013) (noting that "[s]uch a result would be manifestly unfair and improper" and that "the insured should not be penalized because the additional insurance the insured happened to obtain proves to be uncollectible"); *cf. Hardware Dealers*, 444 S.W.2d at 586 (explaining that court must interpret competing "other insurance" clauses so that "the insured . . . [does not] have less coverage than if [it] had been protected by only one of the policies"). In short, we do not read the Other Insurance Clause to require that Cameron exhaustively litigate other potential sources of coverage before Liberty's payment obligation is triggered.

Liberty offers several counterarguments, but none convince. First, Liberty points to *Sherwin-Williams Co. v. Insurance Co. of Pennsylvania*, 105 F.3d 258 (6th Cir. 1997), and *Manpower Inc. v. Insurance Co. of Pennsylvania*, 807 F. Supp. 2d 806 (E.D. Wis. 2011), as supporting its argument. But those cases merely explain that an insured must exhaust its primary insurance before seeking coverage from its excess insurer; they do not involve an "other insurance" clause. *See Cardtronics*, 438 S.W.3d at 779-80 (distinguishing *Sherwin-Williams* and *Manpower* on that basis). Second, Liberty argues that the district court erred by finding that the Transocean indemnification [—10—] agreement is not "other insurance" at all. The district court found no such thing. The district court explained the principle that when an insured has two policies with competing "other insurance" clauses, those policies should not be construed to leave the insured with less coverage than if the insured had only one policy. Then, while acknowledging that the Other Insurance Clause covered indemnification, the district court simply pointed out that when the competing policy is not even an insurance policy—which it is not—that principle likely applies with even more force. Third, Liberty contends that Cameron's interpretation reads the word "excess" out of the Other Insurance Clause. It does not. Instead, it recognizes that Liberty's policy is excess of other insurance, but only if that other insurance actually applies; if other insurance does actually apply, the Other Insurance Clause preserves Liberty's right to sue that other insurer for contribution. Fourth, Liberty asserts that under Cameron's interpretation, Cameron would never need to attempt to enforce its indemnification agreement. That, however, ignores Liberty's subrogation rights: If Cameron refuses to seek indemnification, Liberty can pay the policy and then itself sue Transocean for indemnification.

For all these reasons, we hold that Cameron's interpretation of the Other Insurance Clause is reasonable and that Liberty's is unreasonable; thus, the Other Insurance Clause did not permit Liberty to withhold the policy benefits.[5]

b.

The above holding regarding the Other Insurance Clause does not end the matter. That is because Liberty argues that even if Cameron's interpretation of the Other Insurance Clause is correct, Cameron forfeited its right to coverage by breaching the policy's subrogation clause in settling with [—11—] BP. But because Liberty breached the contract by wrongfully denying coverage, thereby waiving its rights under the subrogation clause before Cameron settled, we do not reach whether Cameron's settlement violated the subrogation clause.

Our conclusion that Liberty breached the contract follows from our holding that Liberty's interpretation of the Other Insurance Clause was erroneous. The district court found that Liberty breached the policy before the settlement by wrongfully constructively denying Cameron's claim and by violating the policy's requirement that Liberty "promptly pay" Cameron's claim.[6] Before Cameron and BP settled, Liberty sent Cameron a series of letters in which it "decline[d] to offer its policy limits" and asserted that the "policy has not yet attached to this loss" because of Liberty's interpretation of the Other Insurance Clause. But as discussed, Liberty's interpretation of the Other Insurance Clause was erroneous, the loss was covered, and the policy had attached. Liberty was required to "promptly pay" Cameron the policy benefits—and it did not.[7] Instead, it wrongfully refused to pay Cameron unless and until Cameron obtained—after

---

[5] Because we conclude that Liberty's interpretation is unreasonable, we do not reach the question whether the doctrine of *contra proferentem* applies.

[6] The district court also found that Liberty breached the contract by refusing a reasonable settlement. Because we hold that Liberty breached the contract by constructively denying the claim, we do not address that issue.

[7] Liberty's argument that it did not "refus[e] to ever pay" is thus irrelevant. Liberty had to pay promptly.

what would have been extensive litigation—a final determination that Transocean did not owe it indemnification. Because Liberty breached the policy by wrongfully denying coverage under the Other Insurance Clause, it waived its subrogation rights. *See* 16 Lee R. Russ & Thomas F. Segalla, Couch on Insurance §§ 224:148, 224:152 (3d ed. 2005); *cf. Scottsdale Ins. Co. v. Knox Park Constr., Inc.*, 488 F.3d 680, 688 (5th Cir. 2007) (holding that insurer who refused coverage based on erroneous interpretation of policy waived consent-to-settle provision). [—12—]

We thus agree with the district court that Liberty breached the contract, before Cameron settled with BP, by constructively denying coverage and by violating the policy's "prompt payment" requirement. Because Liberty breached the contract, it waived its rights under the subrogation clause. Thus, even if Cameron violated that clause in its settlement with BP—a question that we do not reach— Liberty breached first.

IV.

Cameron argues that the district court erred in dismissing its claim under Texas Insurance Code Chapter 541. Chapter 541 authorizes policyholders to file private actions against insurers in order to recover "actual damages" caused by an insurer's "unfair method of competition or an unfair or deceptive act or practice in the business of insurance," and permits treble damages in certain circumstances. Tex. Ins. Code Ann. §§ 541.151, 541.003. Cameron alleged that Liberty violated Chapter 541 by wrongfully denying its claim under the policy. As actual damages, Cameron claimed only the policy benefits that Liberty denied and its attorney's fees related to this action.

Liberty argued below that under this court's decision in *Great American Insurance Co. v. AFS/IBEX Financial Services, Inc.*, to maintain a Chapter 541 claim, Cameron was required to assert some injury other than the policy benefits and attorney's fees. 612 F.3d 800, 808 & n.1 (5th Cir. 2010). Cameron countered that the district court should have instead applied the Supreme Court of Texas's

decision in *Vail v. Texas Farm Bureau Mutual Insurance Co.*, 754 S.W.2d 129 (Tex. 1988). There, the Supreme Court of Texas held that an insured who is wrongfully denied policy benefits *need not* show any injury independent from the denied policy benefits. 754 S.W.2d at 136. The district court agreed with Cameron that, under Texas law, Cameron need not assert any injury independent from the policy benefits as actual damages. Even so, the district court held that it was bound by this court's language to the contrary [—13—] in *Great American* and granted judgment for Liberty on Cameron's Chapter 541 claim.

Cameron argues on appeal that *Vail* is still good law in Texas—a proposition with which the district court agreed—and that *Great American* is an incorrect description of Texas law.[8] Liberty counters that the Supreme Court of Texas has sub silentio overruled *Vail*.

Because this issue turns on an important question of Texas state law, and because subsequent decisions from the Supreme Court of Texas and Texas's intermediate appellate courts arguably cast doubt on *Vail*'s continued vitality, we certify the question to the Supreme Court of Texas. *See* Tex. Const. art. V, § 3–c(a); Tex. R. App. P. 58.1. "The decision of whether to certify a question lies within our sound discretion." *Patterson v. Mobil Oil Corp.*, 335 F.3d 476, 487 (5th Cir. 2003) (citation omitted). We do not "lightly abdicate our mandate to decide issues of state law when sitting in diversity." *Jefferson v. Lead Indus. Ass'n, Inc.*, 106 F.3d 1245, 1248 (5th Cir. 1997). But certification "may be advisable where important state interests are at stake and the state courts have not provided clear guidance on how to proceed." *In re Katrina Canal Breaches Litig.*, 613 F.3d 504, 509 (5th Cir. 2010) (citation and internal quotation marks omitted).

The question here involves an important state interest—namely, the availability of a cause of action under the Texas Insurance Code where the insurer wrongfully denied the

---

[8] Cameron acknowledges that this panel is bound by prior panel decisions, but argues that the language in *Great American* on which the district court relied is non-binding dicta.

policy benefits but caused the insured no damages other than those denied benefits. Had this issue arisen immediately following *Vail*, there likely would have been "controlling [Texas] Supreme Court precedent" counseling against certification. Tex. R. App. P. 58.1; *see Vail*, [—14—] 754 S.W.2d at 136. But in *Great American*, this court interpreted a more recent case from the Supreme Court of Texas, *Provident American Insurance Co. v. Castañeda*, 988 S.W.2d 189, 198-99 (Tex. 1998), as setting out the opposite rule from that in *Vail*.[9] 612 F.3d at 808 & n.1. And since we decided *Great American*, the Supreme Court of Texas has not addressed the issue—although some recent decisions from Texas intermediate appellate courts indicate that (contrary to the view we expressed in *Great American*) *Vail*, not *Castañeda*, governs the issue. *See United Nat'l Ins. Co. v. AMJ Invs., LLC*, 447 S.W.3d 1, 11 (Tex. App.—Houston [14th Dist.] 2014, pet. dism'd) *reh'g overruled* (Oct. 7, 2014), *rev. dismissed* (Mar. 27, 2015) (explicitly rejecting insurer's independent-injury argument, citing *Vail* and distinguishing *Castañeda*); *USAA Tex. Lloyd's Co. v. Menchaca*, No. 13-13-00046-CV, 2014 WL 3804602, at *9 (Tex. App.—Corpus Christi, July 31, 2014, pet. filed) (mem. op.) (approvingly quoting *Vail*'s holding that independent injury is not required). Rather than second-guess our reading of current Texas law, we find it prudent to obtain clarity from Texas itself. The parties' arguments regarding whether *Vail* remains good law "illuminate the magnitude and wide ramifications . . . for insurance law" that this issue presents. *In re Deepwater Horizon*, 728 F.3d 491, 500, 1 Adm. R. 280, 286 (5th Cir. 2013), *certified question answered*, No. 13-0670, 2015 WL 674744 (Tex. Feb. 13, 2015),

reh'g withdrawn (May 29, 2015). We thus conclude that certification is appropriate here. [—15—]

V.

Cameron argues that the district court abused its discretion in denying its motion for attorney's fees. After the district court granted Cameron's motion for summary judgment and awarded Cameron $50 million plus interest, Cameron moved for attorney's fees under Federal Rule of Civil Procedure 54(d)(2). The district court denied that motion, holding that Cameron "impliedly waived" its claim for attorney's fees.[10]

In the district court's view, by the time Cameron moved for attorney's fees, the district court "twice ha[d] considered and dismissed Cameron's theories regarding attorney's fees." Thus, because the district court had "already expended considerable time and effort to resolve [the parties'] dispute, which has included two claims for attorneys' fees," and because the dispute "represents only a fraction of a percent of this massive and very active multidistrict litigation" (MDL 2179, *In re Deepwater Horizon*), the district court was "simply not inclined to hear a third theory concerning [Liberty's] purported liability for attorneys's [sic] fees when that theory could have been presented before the Court issued the" judgment for Cameron. Put another way, the district court found that Cameron should have included its request for attorney's fees in its summary judgment briefing.

Cameron, however, did not waive its claim for attorney's fees, impliedly or otherwise. To impliedly waive its claim, Cameron must have, through some "act from which an

---

[9] Even before we decided *Great American*, some Texas intermediate appellate courts similarly had interpreted *Castañeda* as requiring an independent injury. *See, e.g.*, *Laird v. CMI Lloyds*, 261 S.W.3d 322, 328 (Tex. App.—Texarkana, 2008, no pet.) ("An insured is not entitled to recover extra-contractual damages unless the complained-of actions or omissions cause injury independent of the injury resulting from a wrongful denial of policy benefits."); *United Servs. Auto. Ass'n v. Gordon*, 103 S.W.3d 436, 442 (Tex. App.—San Antonio, 2002, no pet.) *reh'g overruled* (March 12, 2003) (same).

[10] The district court acknowledged in its summary judgment order that, under Texas law, Cameron would be entitled to recover reasonable attorney's fees absent waiver, a point which Liberty does not dispute. Indeed, because Cameron prevailed on its breach of contract claim, the "award of reasonable fees is mandatory." *Mathis v. Exxon Corp.*, 302 F.3d 448, 462 (5th Cir. 2002); *see Grapevine Excavation, Inc. v. Md. Lloyds*, 35 S.W.3d 1, 5 (Tex. 2000) (same).

intention to waive may be inferred or from which waiver follows as a legal result," misled Liberty to its prejudice "into the honest belief [—16—] that such waiver was intended or consented to." *Wells Fargo Bus. Credit v. Ben Kozloff, Inc.*, 695 F.2d 940, 947 (5th Cir. 1983). Cameron requested fees in its amended complaint and moved for fees within fourteen days after the district court entered judgment as required by Rule 54(d)(2). Liberty responds that, having raised claims for attorney's fees during summary judgment, Cameron was required to present all such claims at that time. Despite Liberty's argument, though, Cameron did not present a *substantive claim for attorney's fees incurred in this litigation* during summary judgment. That much is revealed by examining the context in which Cameron discussed its "two claims for attorneys' fees."

First, as discussed above, Liberty moved for summary judgment on Cameron's claim for recovery under Chapter 541 of the Texas Insurance Code, arguing that Cameron had not suffered any "actual damages." Cameron responded that its actual damages were the withheld policy benefits and its attorney's fees in litigating this action. After rejecting Cameron's argument that the withheld policy benefits constituted actual damages, the district court also rejected Cameron's argument that its attorney's fees—standing alone—could constitute actual damages, and granted judgment for Liberty on Cameron's Chapter 541 claim. The district court did not, however, address Cameron's entitlement to attorney's fees incurred in this litigation other than to note that Texas law provides that a prevailing party in a breach of contract action may recover reasonable attorney's fees.

Second, both parties moved for summary judgment on Cameron's claim that, under the policy, Liberty had to reimburse Cameron for its attorney's fees related to the underlying MDL proceedings—proceedings distinct from this litigation. The district court granted summary judgment for Liberty, finding that it did not have to reimburse Cameron for those fees. Put differently, the district court denied one of Cameron's *substantive claims for relief* in this [—17—] litigation; again, it did not

address Cameron's entitlement to attorney's fees incurred in *this* litigation.

To sum up, Cameron did not present a claim for attorney's fees incurred in this litigation on either purported "claim"—and the issue was certainly not "squarely presented," as Liberty contends. None of Cameron's arguments during summary judgment regarded its entitlement to attorney's fees incurred in this litigation. Nor did the district court reject any claim for attorney's fees incurred in this litigation— indeed, the district court acknowledged that Texas law provides for recovery of attorney's fees in cases like this. Because Cameron did not present any claim for attorney's fees incurred in this litigation until it filed its motion for attorney's fees, Cameron did not waive that claim.

Liberty counters that whether Cameron waived its right to attorney's fees is a procedural issue governed by federal law.[11] But this argument is both meritless and irrelevant.[12] Liberty contends that, under federal law, because Cameron discussed attorney's fees during summary judgment, but did not raise the present argument regarding attorney's fees, that argument is waived. *See Brady Nat'l Bank v. Gulf Ins. Co.*, 94 F. App'x 197, 205 (5th Cir. 2004) (holding that federal law applies to bar party from presenting argument on appeal where party did not present argument below); *see also Kiewit E. Co. v. L & R Constr. Co.*, 44 F.3d 1194, 1203-04 (3d Cir. 1995) (holding that where plaintiff raised argument for recovery of attorney's fees from one defendant during summary judgment, alternative argument for recovery of attorney's fees from another defendant raised for first time after trial was waived). But as discussed, Cameron did not present a claim for attorney's fees incurred [—18—] during this litigation during summary judgment and then present a new argument

---

[11] Liberty also argues that Cameron waived its claim for attorney's fees because it did not include a request for attorney's fees in its complaint or amended complaint. But Cameron *did* request attorney's fees in its amended complaint.

[12] The district court did not mention which standard of waiver it was applying.

regarding that claim in its later motion for attorney's fees, as in *Brady* and *Kiewit*. Instead, Cameron merely discussed attorney's fees in the context of arguments regarding other issues unrelated to its entitlement to attorney's fees incurred in this litigation. So the federal waiver rule that Liberty cites both does not apply (because the question is whether Cameron waived a claim, not an argument) and is irrelevant (because Cameron never presented any claim for attorney's fees incurred in this litigation during summary judgment).

In sum, Cameron did not waive, impliedly or otherwise, its claim for attorney's fees incurred in this litigation. And as Cameron points out, moving for attorney's fees during summary judgment would have been premature: Cameron did not know whether it would prevail, let alone on which claims it would prevail. *See, e.g., Amerisure Ins. Co. v. Navigators Ins. Co.*, 611 F.3d 299, 313 n.5 (5th Cir. 2010) (attorney's fees request premature where entitlement to recovery was unresolved); *see also* Fed. R. Civ. P. 54(d)(2)(B)(i) (requiring fee motions to be filed "no later than 14 days after the entry of judgment"). Under Texas law, prevailing on the merits is an essential element for recovering attorney's fees, so a motion for attorney's fees before the merits had been resolved would necessarily have failed. *See State Farm Life Ins. Co. v. Beaston*, 907 S.W.2d 430, 437 (Tex. 1995). Because Cameron did not impliedly waive its claim for attorney's fees, the district court abused its discretion in denying Cameron's motion.

VI.

For the reasons described above, we AFFIRM the district court's grant of summary judgment for Cameron on its breach of contract claim. We REVERSE the district court's denial of Cameron's motion for attorney's fees [—19—] and REMAND for a determination of the proper amount of those fees. And we certify the following question to the Supreme Court of Texas:

Whether, to maintain a cause of action under Chapter 541 of the Texas Insurance Code against an insurer that wrongfully withheld policy benefits, an insured must allege and prove an injury independent from the denied policy benefits?

We disclaim any intention or desire that the Supreme Court of Texas confine its reply to the precise form or scope of the question certified.

United States Court of Appeals
for the Fifth Circuit

No. 14-20619

LICEA
VS.
CURACAO DRYDOCK CO.

Appeals from the United States District Court for the
Southern District of Texas

Decided: November 23, 2015

Citation: 627 Fed. Appx. 343, 3 Adm. R. 448 (5th Cir. 2015).

Before JONES, SMITH, and SOUTHWICK, Circuit Judges.

[—2—] JONES, Circuit Judge:

These are appeals from a garnishment action. Appellees—Alberto Justo Rodriguez Licea, Fernando Alonso Hernandez, and Luis Alberto Casanova (together "Plaintiffs")—were successful plaintiffs in an underlying action against the Curacao Drydock Company ("Curacao"). The garnishees' appeals raise numerous questions. We hold that the court lacked personal jurisdiction over two garnishees, improperly exercised *quasi in rem* jurisdiction over a debt owed by one of them, and erroneously failed to follow Texas procedure as to the third garnishee.

BACKGROUND

The underlying action was filed in 2006 under the Alien Tort Statute and RICO in the Southern District of Florida. *Licea v. Curacao Drydock Co.*, 584 F. Supp. 2d 1355 (S.D. Fla. 2008). It alleged that Plaintiff-Appellees endured human trafficking, false imprisonment, and forced labor in a modern-day slavery conspiracy between Curacao and the Cuban government. *Id.* at 1356-63. After initially appearing and filing several motions, Curacao "repeatedly flouted [the] Court's authority and refused to defend the matter." *Id.* at 1357. The court entered default judgment against Curacao on the issue [—3—] of liability and held a separate trial to set damages, at which Curacao did not appear. *Id.* at 1357-58. The plaintiffs won an $80 million

judgment: $50 million in compensatory damages and $30 million in punitive damages. *Id.* at 1366. There was no appeal from that action. The plaintiffs registered their judgment in the Southern District of Texas pursuant to 28 U.S.C. § 1963 on May 7, 2013.

Three garnishees are Appellants in these cases: Formosa Brick Marine Corporation ("FBMC"), Formosa Plastics Marine Corporation ("FPMC"), and Formosa Plastics Corporation, America ("FPCA") (together "Garnishees"). Though it is not entirely clear from the record, FPCA may be the parent company of both FBMC and FPMC, FBMC and FPMC might be brother-sister corporations, and/or FPMC might own FBMC. In any case, the entities are related in a corporate family. FBMC and FPMC are Liberian corporations with their principal place of business in Taiwan but no apparent contacts with Texas. FPCA, however, is registered to do business in Texas, has a registered agent, and operates a large processing plant in the state.

Pursuant to FED. R. CIV. P. 64, TEX. R. CIV. P. 657-79, and the TEX. CIV. PRAC. & REM. CODE Ch. 63, the plaintiffs sought writs of garnishment against FBMC, FPMC, and FPCA in partial satisfaction of their judgment against Curacao. FPCA was served with process through its statutory agent for service.

FPMC and FBMC were both "served" by United States Marshals through the masters of vessels. Putative service upon FPMC was made on the master of *M/V FPMC 30* while it was docked in Corpus Christi, Texas and, again on the master of *M/V FPMC 19* when that vessel was conducting cargo operations in Texas City, Texas. FBMC was also putatively served through the master of *M/V FPMC 19* when it was conducting cargo operations in Texas [—4—] City. At the time of service, each vessel was owned by other entities, and FPMC operated the vessels under contract with the owners. Consequently, neither FBMC nor FPMC was directly served with process. The record indicates no other connection between Texas and either FBMC or FPMC.

FPMC and FBMC nevertheless answered the writs of garnishment and moved to dismiss. Both garnishees objected that the court lacked personal jurisdiction and that service was improper. FPMC denied that it was indebted to Curacao, while FBMC admitted it owed $2,639,000 to Curacao. The district court initially denied these motions without prejudice, and both parties later filed amended motions to dismiss raising the same issues.

FPCA filed a verified answer that denied any indebtedness to Curacao or that it knew any person who was so indebted. After receiving no controverting response or affidavit, FPCA moved for discharge from the proceedings, which was denied.

Responding to plaintiffs' motion to interplead funds, FBMC deposited $2,639,000 with the clerk for the Southern District of Texas, subject to its amended motion to dismiss. FBMC and FPMC again objected to personal jurisdiction and service of process in their objection to the district court's proposed final judgment.

The district court issued a final judgment on September 19, 2014, awarding the $2,639,000 to Plaintiffs and discharging Garnishees' liability to Curacao for that amount.

In its opinion, the district court found that "Plaintiffs provided the court with uncontroverted evidence showing that FPMC Brick Marine Corporation [the owner of the *M/V FPMC 19*] and FBMC are alter egos of FPMC and thereby each other." The district court also found that FPCA, FBMC, and [—5—] FPMC were all alter egos of each other. Serving the masters therefore effectuated service on all Garnishees.[1]

The district court noted that because Garnishees were served with writs while in Texas, the funds they owe Curacao are subject

---

[1] The district court cited *Witham v. The James E. McAlpine*, 96 F.Supp. 723 (E.D. Mich. 1951) for the proposition that "[s]ervice on a captain of a ship . . . has long been the equivalent of service on the corporation."

to garnishment under the court's *quasi in rem* jurisdiction. It cited *United States Rubber v. Poage*, 297 F.2d 670 (5th Cir. 1962)). The court rejected Garnishees' argument that *Poage* was overruled by subsequent Supreme Court decisions.

The district court also found that it would be fair to exercise jurisdiction over the Garnishees because this proceeding imposes a slight burden on them compared to normal litigation and because of the alter egos' extensive activities in Texas. Further, because FPCA did not object to personal jurisdiction and is the alter ego of FPMC and FBMC, its amenability can be imputed to the two other corporations.

Following this judgment, this court granted FPMC's and FBMC's motion to stay enforcement of the judgment pending appeal and to accept the previously deposited amount as security in lieu of a supersedeas bond.

STANDARDS OF REVIEW

Questions of jurisdiction, service of process, and the denial of the motion to discharge are issues of law reviewed de novo. *Herman v. Cataphora, Inc.*, 730 F.3d 460, 465 (5th Cir. 2013); *Af-Cap, Inc. v. Republic of Congo*, 462 F.3d 417, 423 (5th Cir. 2006); *Bullion v. Gillespie*, 895 F2d 213, 216 (5th Cir. 1990). The district court's finding of alter ego is a fact that is reviewed for clear error. *United States v. Jon-T Chems., Inc.*, 768 F.2d 686, 694 (5th Cir. 1985). [—6—]

DISCUSSION

As a preliminary matter, FED. R. CIV. P. 64 and 69 provide that the law, both substantive and procedural, of the state where the federal court sits governs writs of garnishment unless a federal statute provides otherwise. The parties have briefed Texas law and have not called attention to any applicable federal statute. Texas law also governs the alter ego determinations, which bear on the exercise of jurisdiction over and proper service on FPMC and FBMC. *See Jackson v. Tanfoglio Giuseppe, S.R.L.*, 615 F.3d 579, 586-88 (5th Cir. 2010) (applying state alter ego law to find lack of personal jurisdiction over a non-resident); *Hargrave v. Fibreboard Corp.*, 710 F.2d 1154, 1159 (5th Cir. 1983) (noting that state law of the forum controls whether a defendant is amendable to service through its alter egos under a long-arm statute). The principal error by the district court in addressing the issues was its failure to apply Texas law.

Separate appeals were filed by FPCA, on one hand, and FBMC and FPMC on the other. The common issue raised by the Garnishees is whether the district court erred in finding that they are all alter egos of each other. Jurisdiction and service of process on FPMC and FBMC depend on the alter ego findings. Other issues concern the district court's failure to apply substantive Texas law to the garnishment and its failure to dismiss FPCA as required by Texas law when a garnishee files an uncontroverted affidavit denying possession of any account subject to garnishment. We address these points in turn.

I. Corporate Alter Ego

The district court found that "FPMC Brick Marine Corporation [the owner of the *M/V FPMC 19*] and FBMC are alter egos of FPMC and thereby of each other." It also found that FPMC, FBMC, and FPCA are all alter egos [—7—] of each other. As a result, the court held that service on the vessel masters was sufficient to serve all of the entities, and that FPCA's failure to challenge personal jurisdiction could be imputed to FPMC and FBMC. These findings of alter ego, which did not cite a single supporting case, were erroneous.

Texas law recognizes that the corporate form can be disregarded in certain circumstances. *See Castleberry v. Branscum*, 721 S.W.2d 270, 272-73 (Tex. 1986). One of the bases for doing so is the alter ego doctrine, whereby "a corporation is organized and operated as a mere tool or business conduit of another corporation." *Id.* at 272. Proof of imputed contacts or an alter ego relationship may be the basis for exercising jurisdiction over a non-resident defendant. *See BMC Software Belg., N.V. v. Marchand*, 83 S.W. 3d

789, 798 (Tex. 2002); *see also Hargrave v. Fibreboard Corp.*, 710 F.2d 1154, 1160 (5th Cir. 1983).

The Texas Supreme Court has "acknowledged that jurisdictional veil-piercing and substantive veil-piercing involve different elements of proof" given that jurisdiction implicates due process considerations that cannot be overridden by statutes or common law. *PHC-Minden, L.P. v. Kimberly-Clark Corp.*, 235 S.W.3d 163, 174-75 (Tex. 2007).[2] The court outlined the following factors relevant for jurisdictional veil-piercing:[3] [—8—]

> To "fuse" the parent company and its subsidiary for jurisdictional purposes, the plaintiffs must prove the parent controls the internal business operations and affairs of the subsidiary. But the degree of control the parent exercises must be greater than that normally associated with common ownership and directorship; the evidence must show that the two entities cease to be separate so that the corporate fiction should be disregarded to prevent fraud or injustice.

PHC-Minden, 235 S.W.3d at 175 (quoting *BMC Software*, 83 S.W.3d at 799). Other factors to consider are "the amount of the subsidiary's stock owned by the parent corporation, the existence of separate headquarters, the observance of corporate formalities, and the degree of the parent's control over the general policy and administration of the subsidiary." *Id.* (citing

---

[2] For this reason, some alter ego cases cited by the parties are inapposite because they recite factors to consider in substantive veil piercing rather than jurisdictional veil piercing. *E.g. United States v. Jon-T Chems., Inc.*, 768 F.2d 686, 691-92 (5th Cir. 1985) (the "laundry list" factors).

[3] The law in this area addresses parent-subsidiary corporations, but it is applicable to other intracorporate relationships as well. The parties discuss the relationships among the entities in this case as if FPCA is the parent of both FBMC and FPMC, and the district court found that FPMC is the parent of FBMC and FPMC Brick Marine Corporation. It is unclear from the record what the actual relationships are.

4A WRIGHT & MILLER, FEDERAL PRACTICE & PROCEDURE § 1069.4). However, "[a] subsidiary corporation will not be regarded as the alter ego of its parent merely because of stock ownership, a duplication of some or all of the directors or officers, or an exercise of the control that stock ownership gives to stockholders." *Id.* (quoting *Gentry v. Credit Plan Corp. of Houston*, 528 S.W.2d 571, 573 (Tex. 1975)). There must be a "plus factor, something beyond the subsidiary's mere presence within the bosom of the corporate family." *Id.* at 176 (quoting *Dickson Marine, Inc. v. Panalpina, Inc.*, 179 F.3d 331, 338 (5th Cir. 1999)). Not pertinent to *jurisdictional* veil piercing analysis, however, are allegations of fraud[4] and a common name among the entities. *Id.* at 175. [—9—]

In this case, the district court found an alter ego[5] relationship among FPMC Brick Marine Corporation (the owner of the *M/V FPMC 19*), FBMC, and FPMC because: (1) FPMC operated the *MV FPMC 19*; (2) FPMC Brick Marine Corporation and FBMC are both owned by FPMC;[6] (3) ship operations are performed out of FPMC's office; (4) FPMC lists the vessels on its website even though "nominally owned" by other entities; and (5)

FPMC's organizational chart indicates that the master of each vessel reports to FPMC. It also found that FPCA, FBMC, and FPMC (all of the Garnishees) are alter egos of each other because: (1) all of the entities report to and are run by the same founder; (2) they share a group administrative office that combines several functions together; and (3) management of the entities is controlled at the "Formosa Plastics Group level."[7] Plaintiffs repeat these conclusions on appeal and cite portions of the record that consist of their own statements as to these "facts."

The court relied almost exclusively on two "organizational charts" submitted by Plaintiffs (taken from Garnishees' website) in finding alter ego. [—10—] The first chart apparently shows the internal reporting structure of FPMC and the second purports to show the various levels of ownership of the entities. The charts are not probative.

First, the charts do not actually depict corporate structure. There is no indication of ownership; they do not indicate which entity owns what, which entities are parents, or subsidiaries, or brother/sister. Nor is it even clear that the "entities" on the chart are formal entities, because they have no corporate form designations. Normal organizational charts make distinctions for, *e.g.*, corporations, LLC's, disregarded entities, or foreign entities. Further, Garnishees FPCA and FBMC are not even represented on the charts.

Second, the charts do not show the functional relationship among the entities. "In determining whether an alter ego relationship exists, the court should focus on the relationship between the corporation and the entity or individual that allegedly abused corporate formalities." *Zahra Spiritual Trust v. United States*, 910 F.2d 240, 245 (5th Cir. 1990) (citing *Castleberry*, 721 S.W.2d at 272). As Garnishees correctly put it, the organizational charts are "irrelevant because they are not probative of the issue of alter ego. They show only the structure, but not the

---

[4] Garnishees are thus incorrect to stress that fraud is necessary in order to find alter ego for jurisdictional purposes.

[5] The district court actually seemed to apply the single business entity theory for piercing the jurisdictional veil, not the alter ego theory. *See Castleberry*, 721 S.W.2d at 272 ("Many Texas cases have blurred the distinction between alter ego and the other bases for disregarding the corporate fiction and treated alter ego as a synonym for the entire doctrine of disregarding the corporate fiction."); *see also Goodyear Dunlop Tires Ops., S.A. v. Brown*, 131 S. Ct. 2846, 2857 (2011) (declining to address single business entity argument). The single business entity theory would pierce the veil "when two or more corporations associate together and, rather than operate as separate entities, integrate their resources to achieve a common business purpose." *S. Union Co. v. City of Edinburg*, 129 S.W.3d 74, 86 (Tex. 2003) (internal quotation and citation omitted). The Texas Supreme Court has never endorsed this theory in any context. *PHC-Minden*, 235 S.W.3d at 173.

[6] It is unclear how the district court found this, as the page in the record it cites to for this proposition does not so indicate.

[7] It is unclear what this level is as there is no entity called "Formosa Plastics Group."

relationships between the Formosa entities." They do not indicate any "plus factor" that entails "something beyond the subsidiary's mere presence within the bosom of the corporate family." *PHC-Minden*, 235 S.W.3d at 176. At best, they demonstrate mere affiliation, which is insufficient to pierce the veil, or common names, which are irrelevant to jurisdictional veil piercing. They do not even appear to show that the entities share common functions; the "Group Administration" boxes report to the Execupive [sic] Board, but there is no indication that these functions are performed for the entities listed on the chart. In no way do these descriptions suggest control "greater than that normally associated with common [—11—] ownership and directorship" or that the "entities cease to be separate so that the corporate fiction should be disregarded to prevent fraud or injustice." *PHC-Minden*, 235 S.W.3d at 175.

In sum, the charts are not evidence that satisfies the tests endorsed by the Texas Supreme Court for jurisdictional veil piercing. The district court's findings of alter ego were clearly erroneous. Because this means that neither FBMC nor FPMC was effectually served with process, nor can personal jurisdiction be asserted over these entities based on an alter ego relationship with FPCA, we must remand with instructions to dismiss the garnishment proceeding against FBMC and FPMC.

II. District Court's Exercise of *Quasi in Rem* Jurisdiction

"Quasi in rem actions are based on a claim for money begun by attachment or other seizure of property when the district court has no jurisdiction over the person of the [judgment] defendant, but has jurisdiction over either property that the court can apply to the satisfaction of the defendant's debt or persons who themselves owe an obligation to the defendant that the court can apply to the satisfaction of the debt." *Stena Rederei AB v. Comision de Contratos del Comite Ejecutivo General del Sindicato Revolucionario de Trabajadores Petroleros de la Republica Mexicana, S.C.*, 923 F.2d 380, 391 (5th Cir.

1991) (citation omitted). The district court here relied several times on its finding that "[t]he Formosa Entities were served with writs of garnishment while in the state" to support its exercise of *quasi in rem* jurisdiction over the debt owed to Curacao. It is unclear on which basis the court predicated *quasi in rem* jurisdiction: whether it emanated from service of process or personal jurisdiction based on alleged alter ego status of FBMC or FPMC, or on the debt itself being "found" in Texas. For good reason, the Garnishees challenge any *quasi in rem* jurisdiction. [—12—]

To the extent that the court believed it could exercise jurisdiction over the debt via the persons of the Garnishees, it was misguided. Our previous discussion eliminates *quasi in rem* jurisdiction on this basis.

Alternatively, the "presence" of the debt in Texas might provide a basis for the exercise of jurisdiction over it for the Plaintiffs' benefit. *See Shaffer v. Heitner*, 433 U.S. 186, 207, 97 S. Ct. 2569, 2581 (1977) ("[P]resence of property in a State may bear on the existence of jurisdiction by providing contacts among the forum State, the defendant, and the litigation."). Setting aside due process minimum contacts concerns, the prerequisite to this theory is a determination under state law that the debt (or other property) is actually found in the state. *Rush v. Savchuk*, 444 U.S. 320, 328 n.14, 100 S. Ct. 571, 577 n.14 (1980); *see also United States Rubber v. Poage*, 297 F.2d 670, 674 (5th Cir. 1962). Texas allows attachment or garnishment only of a debt whose situs is within the jurisdiction of the court. *T.&H. Smith & Co. v. Taber*, 40 S.W. 156, 157 (Tex. Civ. App. 1897); *see also Wirt Franklin Petrol. Co. v. Gruen*, 139 F.2d 659, 660 (5th Cir. 1944) ("Garnishment is in the nature of a proceeding in rem, as to which the situs of the res is generally determinative for purposes of jurisdiction."). The situs of the debt under Texas law is either the domicile of the creditor, *Gerlach Merc. Co. v. Hughes-Bozarth-Anderson Co.*, 189 S.W. 784, 788 (Tex. Civ. App. Amarillo 1916), or wherever the debtor may be found. *T&H.Smith*, 40 S.W. at 157. The first condition is inapplicable here, and the second is a reprise of the failed attempts to serve or find personal jurisdiction over FBMC or FPMC in Texas. Consequently, the debt to Curacao was not "found" in Texas.

III. Discharge of FPCA as Garnishee

At the outset, we noted that federal courts must follow state procedural and substantive law relating to garnishments. In Texas, a putative garnishee [—13—] may file an answer to the writ of garnishment served on him. *See* Tex. R. Civ. P. 665. The garnishee's answer "shall be under oath, in writing and signed by him, and shall make true answers to the several matters inquired of in the writ of garnishment." *Id.* If either the plaintiff or the defendant is not satisfied with the garnishee's answer, "he may controvert the same by his affidavit stating that he has good reason to believe, and does believe, that the answer of the garnishee is incorrect." Tex R. Civ. P. 673. In the absence of a controverting affidavit, it is presumed that the garnishee's answer is true. *Snyder Nat. Bank v. Pinkston*, 219 S.W.2d 606, 607 (Tex. Civ. App. Dallas 1949).

If the garnishee's answer goes uncontroverted, the court must enter judgment discharging the garnishee when it appears from the answer that: (1) the garnishee is not indebted to the defendant and was not so indebted when served with the writ of garnishment; (2) the garnishee does not possess any effects of the defendant and had not possessed any when the writ was served; and (3) the garnishee has either denied knowledge of any other persons indebted to the defendant or possessing effects belonging to the defendant or else has named such persons. Tex R. Civ. P. 666. This rule is jurisdictional; the trial court has no authority to proceed against the garnishee other than to discharge him on his answer. *Goodson v. Carr*, 428 S.W.2d 875, 879 (Tex. Civ. App. Houston 1968). Thus, if the garnishee's answer denies indebtedness and is uncontroverted, the garnishee must be dismissed from the action. *Gray v. Armour & Co.*, 104 S.W.2d 486, 487 (Tex. Comm'n App. 1937, opinion adopted); [—14—] *J.C. Hadsell & Co., Inc. v. Allstate Ins. Co.*, 516 S.W.2d 211, 213-14 (Tex. Civ.

App. Texarkana 1974); *Snyder*, 219 S.W.2d at 607.[8]

In this case, FPCA filed a verified answer to the writ of garnishment that was under oath, in writing, and (1) denied indebtedness to Curacao, (2) denied possession of Curacao's effects, and (3) denied knowledge of other persons so indebted. FPCA subsequently moved for discharge after its answer went uncontroverted. Plaintiffs' unsworn response to this motion cannot be construed as controverting the answer as required by Texas law; the response merely restated plaintiffs' contentions that the Garnishees are alter egos of each other without controverting that FPCA was not indebted to Curacao. FPCA should have been discharged.

CONCLUSION

For the foregoing reasons, the final judgment of garnishment against FBMC, FPMC, and FPCA is **REVERSED** and the case is **REMANDED** with instructions to **DISMISS**. The funds in the registry of court, together with interest thereon, must be **DISBURSED** to FBMC.

---

[8] Further, "[w]here the garnishee is discharged upon his answer, the costs of the proceeding, including a reasonable compensation to the garnishee, shall be taxed against the plaintiff." Tex. R. Civ. P. 677. Costs include attorney fees, *J.C. Hadsell*, 104 S.W.2d at 213-14, but FPCA waived any such claim by failing to assert it.

This page intentionally left blank

United States Court of Appeals for the Sixth Circuit

United States Court of Appeals
for the Sixth Circuit

No. 14-2135

ST. CLAIR MARINE SALVAGE, INC.
vs.
BULGARELLI

Appeal from the United States District Court for the
Eastern District of Michigan at Detroit

Decided: July 22, 2015

Citation: 796 F.3d 569, 3 Adm. R. 456 (6th Cir. 2015).

Before **COLE**, Chief Judge, and **MERRITT** and
BATCHELDER, Circuit Judges.

[—1—] BATHELDER, Circuit Judge:

Defendant Michael Bulgarelli owns a boat that ran aground in Lake St. Clair, necessitating the services of a salvage ship to tug it free by towing it several feet. Plaintiff St. Clair Marine Salvage, Inc., alleges that the agreed-upon price was approximately $9,000, while Bulgarelli insists he was quoted a price range of $1,000–$1,200. The district court denied St. Clair Marine's motion for summary [—2—] judgment in this maritime case, citing the obvious dispute on a question of material fact. Following a bench trial in admiralty, the magistrate judge entered judgment in favor of Bulgarelli, finding that St. Clair Marine had engaged in fraud when the captain of its salvage vessel induced Bulgarelli to sign the salvage contract at issue. We AFFIRM.

I.

On August 18, 2012, Michael Bulgarelli's 36-foot Sea Ray boat ran aground on Michigan's Lake St. Clair. Groundings fall into two categories: "soft" groundings where the boat can be freed by a tug from a tow boat, and "hard" groundings where the vessel's weight is bearing upon the bottom of the vessel, endangering the craft and those aboard. Bulgarelli contacted Tow Boat US, which dispatched a salvage vessel from St. Clair Marine commanded by Captain William Leslie to assist Bulgarelli. Leslie claims that when he arrived, he conferred with Bulgarelli, and quoted Bulgarelli the price of $250 per foot of the Sea Ray's 36-foot length. Bulgarelli, however, insists that the quoted price was $1,000–$1,200, and that Leslie assured him that insurance would pay the bill. Bulgarelli signed the contract, which did not include a printed price, but has "$250.00 FT" (i.e., "per foot") scrawled in its bottom margin. Bulgarelli claims that handwriting was not present on the paper when he signed it, and since St. Clair did not use copies at the time, Leslie had exclusive possession and personal control of the sole copy of the contract once he and his vessel departed the area upon completing the operation. Calling this a "hard" grounding in high winds and very rough waters, Leslie claims that he used his vessel to "churn up" the waterbed in front of Bulgarelli's vessel to "dig out" the Sea Ray, "tucked" his boat under the Sea Ray's bow, and pulled it into the channel, in a process that took 29 minutes. Bulgarelli and a corroborating witness provided a very different account, saying that the wind and water were both calm, and that Leslie merely secured a tow line, tugged the Sea Ray first from one angle, then from a second, and pulled the vessel free in a process that took less than ten minutes. In either event, once the Sea Ray was free, Leslie departed that area of the lake, and promptly drafted a narrative report of the incident, in which he claimed, *inter alia*, that he knew from the initial phone call that this would be a "hard" grounding, and provided details of his account. [—3—]

St. Clair Marine filed a three-count complaint in U.S. District Court for the Eastern District of Michigan, invoking the district court's admiralty jurisdiction under 28 U.S.C. § 1333, seeking enforcement of a maritime lien, alleging breach of a maritime salvage contract, and claiming quantum meruit/unjust enrichment. Bulgarelli counter-claimed for fraud, innocent misrepresentation, and reformation. Bulgarelli also filed an affidavit accusing Leslie of physically altering the contract at some point after Bulgarelli signed it, adding the handwritten notation "$250.00 FT." The district court denied St. Clair Marine's motion for summary judgment, given the factual dispute about the agreed-upon price and the allegation that one party had deceived the other in forming the contract.

The parties consented to have the case tried by a magistrate judge, who conducted a bench trial and found Bulgarelli and his corroborating witness credible and persuasive, while finding Leslie not credible. The court also found that Leslie could not have known from the brief initial phone call that this was a "hard" grounding, and inferred from the tone and structure of Leslie's written account that it was intended to persuade its reader rather than objectively convey the facts of the situation, and thus was designed to deceive Bulgarelli's insurance provider as to the nature of the salvage job. The court further found that Leslie was not credible when, on cross-examination, he professed not to recall the salient facts regarding previous lawsuits involving unpaid towing/salvage fees for towing jobs which he had performed. Consequently, the court made a finding of fact that Leslie had quoted the price of $1,000–$1,200 to Bulgarelli while assuring him that his insurance would cover the entire cost, intending all along to bill Bulgarelli's insurance company for $9,000. The court further found that Leslie had added the handwritten margin note of $250 per foot to the sole copy of the contract after Bulgarelli had signed it, and thus that it was not part of the agreement to which Bulgarelli assented. The court accordingly found that Leslie had engaged in fraud in the procurement of the towing contract, and voided the contract.

II.

We begin, as the district court did, by confirming our jurisdiction. Because the requisite elements of diversity jurisdiction under 28 U.S.C. § 1332 are not present here, in order for us to have appellate jurisdiction under 28 U.S.C. § 1291, the district court must have had admiralty [—4—] jurisdiction under 28 U.S.C. § 1333. In the absence of admiralty jurisdiction, we would dismiss this matter, leaving the parties the option of pursuing it in Michigan's courts.

The Supreme Court long ago held that for disputes arising from contracts for salvage carried out between vessels upon the water, "there can be no doubt of the jurisdiction of a Court of Admiralty. . . [it] is the only Court where such a question can be tried." *Houseman v. Cargo of The Schooner North Carolina*, 40 U.S. (15 Pet.) 40, 48 (1841). Much more recently, the Court noted that "The Rules of Construction Act defines a 'vessel' as including 'every description of watercraft or other artificial contrivance used, or capable of being used, as a means of transportation on water.'" *Lozman v. City of Riviera Beach*, 133 S. Ct. 735, 739, 1 Adm. R. 2, 2 (2013) (quoting 1 U.S.C. § 3). No one disputes that Bulgarelli's boat and Leslie's salvage boat are both vessels that are "capable of being used" for water transportation, or that this lawsuit arises from a dispute over the contract price charged for salvage services. Although *Houseman* is almost two centuries old, as a Supreme Court precedent that is directly on point and has never been overruled, it fully controls our analysis here. *Agostini v. Felton*, 521 U.S. 203, 237 (1997).[1] The district court therefore had jurisdiction to hear this case, and we have appellate jurisdiction to review the district court's judgments.

III.

St. Clair Marine appeals the district court's denial of its motion for summary judgment, arguing in essence that the material facts surrounding the salvage contract were not genuinely in dispute, and that St. Clair Marine was entitled to summary judgment on both its claim for breach of that contract and on Bulgarelli's counterclaim for fraud. Although neither party addresses the threshold question of whether the order denying summary judgment is appealable

---

[1] We note that the Supreme Court's recent restatement of the test for determining admiralty jurisdiction, *see Norfolk S. Ry. v. James N. Kirby, Pty. Ltd.*, 543 U.S. 14, 24, 27–28 (2004), as well as the Court's reasoning that the "fundamental interest giving rise to maritime jurisdiction is the protection of maritime commerce," *Exxon Corp. v. Cent. Gulf Lines, Inc.*, 500 U.S. 603, 608 (1991) (internal quotation marks omitted), are consistent with its 1841 decision in *Houseman*.

following a full trial on the merits, we must.
[—5—]

Confronted with a circuit split on the issue, the Supreme Court, in *Ortiz v. Jordan*, 562 U.S. 180 (2011), said:

> May a party, as the Sixth Circuit believed, appeal an order denying summary judgment after a full trial on the merits? Our answer is no. . . Once the case proceeds to trial, the full record developed in court supersedes the record existing at the time of the summary-judgment motion.

Id. at 183–84. Although *Ortiz* was a case in which summary judgment had been sought and denied on qualified immunity grounds, the Court's holding is not limited to such cases. This circuit has interpreted *Ortiz* as "leav[ing] open the possibility that [in] cases 'involv[ing] . . . [only] disputes about the substance and clarity of pre-existing law'" the denial of summary judgment may still be considered on appeal following a full trial on the merits. *See Nolfi v. Ohio Ky. Oil Corp.*, 675 F.3d 538, 545 (6th Cir. 2012).

Here, the district court denied summary judgment because it concluded that material facts regarding the contract remained in dispute, and hence, this is not a case involving only legal issues. But even if the district court's order denying summary judgment in this case is appealable, the appeal is meritless. St. Clair Marine argues that the contract Bulgarelli signed contained a merger clause specifying that the written contract represents the entirety of the agreement between the parties, and thus federal courts may not look beyond the written instrument to decide this case. Because the document contained the notation "$250.00 FT" along its bottom margin, St. Clair Marine argues, it was entitled to summary judgment in its favor. Citing the rule against using verbal statements as parol evidence to defeat the plain language of a written contract, St. Clair Marine contends that Bulgarelli's claim that St. Clair Marine quoted him a significantly lower price may not be considered by the court. That rule generally prohibits the use of

verbal evidence in contract interpretation when that extrinsic oral evidence contradicts the clear and unambiguous written terms found within the four corners of the contractual instrument. *See Rufflin v. Mercury Record Prods., Inc.*, 513 F.2d 222, 223–24 (6th Cir. 1975).

"When a contract is a maritime one, and the dispute is not inherently local, federal law controls the contract interpretation." *Norfolk S. Ry. v. James N. Kirby, Pty. Ltd.*, 543 U.S. 14, 22–23 (2004). Both parties argue that this case is controlled by Michigan law; both parties argue [—6—] that Michigan law militates in their respective favor. Both parties are wrong. Federal law controls in this case.

The general rule in contract law is:

> When two parties have made a contract and have expressed it in a writing to which they have both assented as the complete and accurate integration of that contract, evidence, whether parol or otherwise, of antecedent understandings and negotiations will not be admitted for the purpose of varying or contradicting the writing.

6 Peter Linzer, *Corbin on Contracts* § 25.2 (Joseph M. Perillo ed., 2010).

First, we have permitted the use of extrinsic parol evidence in maritime cases in appropriate circumstances. *See Royal Ins. Co. of Am. v. Orient Overseas Container Line Ltd.*, 525 F.3d 409, 422 (6th Cir. 2008). And second, we hold that the rule limiting court review to the four corners of the contractual document does not apply in a case such as this, where one party alleges that something within those four corners was surreptitiously added by the other party after the fact, with the deceptive purpose of altering the agreement, and the first party would have had no way of knowing about the alteration. In such a situation, one party has *not* assented to the entire agreement. Contractual duties are discharged for such alterations. *Restatement (Second) of Contracts* § 286 (1981).

The printed contract contains no mention of price at all. Leslie claims they agreed in writing to a price of $9,000; Bulgarelli says the agreement as to price was a verbal agreement of $1,200 or less. Bulgarelli's affidavit alleging that Leslie altered the agreement by writing in the margin that the rate would be $250 per foot of the Sea Ray's length is more than a scintilla of evidence in opposition to St. Clair Marine's motion, and is enough to create a genuine issue of material fact.[2] The district court correctly denied St. Clair Marine's motion for summary judgment. [—7—]

IV.

A.

We turn now to the district court's final judgment. Following a bench trial, we review de novo the district court's conclusions of law, and its findings of fact for clear error. *Russell v. Lundergan-Grimes*, 784 F.3d 1037, 1045 (6th Cir. 2015).

Federal law governs here as well. When Congress has not enacted law on a particular admiralty question, "in the absence of some controlling statute, the general maritime law, as accepted by the Federal courts, constitutes part of our national law." *S. Pac. R.R. Co. v. Jensen*, 244 U.S. 205, 215 (1917), *superseded in part on other grounds by statute*, Longshoremen's and Harbor Workers' Compensation Act, codified at 33 U.S.C. § 901 *et seq.* Since there is no federal statute governing this case, we recur to federal common law, and are empowered to make decisional law for the interpretation of maritime contracts in admiralty cases. *Kirby*, 543 U.S. at 23. For admiralty cases alleging breach of contract, "we look both to the federal maritime law of contracts as well as to general principles of contract interpretation." *Royal Ins. Co.*, 525 F.3d at 421.

"Admiralty courts have traditionally been vigilant in protecting mariners from unscrupulous and dishonest salvors." *Jackson Marine Corp. v. Blue Fox*, 845 F.2d 1307, 1309 (5th Cir. 1988); *see also, e.g., The Elfrida*, 172 U.S. 186, 194 (1891); *The Bello Corrunes*, 19 U.S. (6 Wheat.) 152, 173 (1821); *The Albany*, 44 F. 431, 434 (E.D. Mich. 1890). Given the "heightened vulnerability" of a vessel's master when his ship and crew are in distress, the law takes a dim view of salvors who engage in "dishonesty, corruption, fraud, [or] falsehood" during towing or salvage operations. *Jackson*, 845 F.2d at 1310 (quoting *Church v. Seventeen Hundred and Twelve Dollars*, 5 F. Cas. 669 (S.D. Fla. 1853) (No. 2713)) (internal quotation marks omitted). A court sitting in admiralty will not enforce a contract "where the salvor has [] taken advantage of his power to make an unreasonable bargain." *Post v. Jones*, 60 U.S. (19 How.) 150, 160 (1857). So even if the agreed upon price were $9,000, the salvage contract might be void if the non-salvor was in a state of distress at the time he signed the contract, especially in a situation where the non-salvor is an unsophisticated novice as the pilot of a vessel. Admiralty courts are empowered to void contracts that were entered into under such circumstances, or—as [—8—] is the case here—where the master of the distressed vessel "has been corruptly or recklessly induced to sign." *The Elfrida*, 172 U.S. at 194. Salvage contracts can be set aside when they are, *inter alia*, "corruptly entered into, or made under fraudulent representations, [or] a clear mistake or suppression of important facts." *Id.* at 192.

B.

We have not had occasion to articulate a rule that would control cases in admiralty in which the non-salvor party claims that the salvage contract was procured by fraud. The Fifth Circuit has held that for maritime contracts:

> To prevail on a claim that a contract was fraudulently procured, the party that was deceived must show that (1) the deceiving party made a material misrepresentation or nondisclosure, (2)

---

[2] A mere scintilla of evidence by the nonmoving party is insufficient to defeat summary judgment; "there must be evidence on which the jury could reasonably find for the [nonmoving party]." *Anderson v. Liberty Lobby, Inc.*, 477 U.S. 242, 252 (1986).

the representation was false or the nondisclosure implied that the facts were different from what the deceived party understood them to be, (3) the deceiving party knew that the representation was false or that the nondisclosure implied the existence of false facts, (4) the deceiving party intended the deceived party to rely on the misrepresentation or nondisclosure, and (5) the deceived party detrimentally relied upon the misrepresentation or nondisclosure.

Black Gold Marine, Inc. v. Jackson Marine Co., 759 F.2d 466, 470 (5th Cir. 1985). The district court here applied the *Black Gold Marine* rule, and we agree that it is properly applied to cases such as this one.

The district court was not clearly erroneous in its factual findings. The court found Bulgarelli and corroborating witness credible and persuasive, while finding Leslie not credible, and also found that Leslie's written account was designed to deceive. These findings led the district court to find that the agreed-upon price was $1,000–$1,200, that Leslie verbally conveyed that price to Bulgarelli, and that the contradictory written notation was fraudulently added after the fact as an alteration to the document that Bulgarelli had signed. St. Clair Marine points to nothing in the record that demonstrates that those findings are clearly erroneous.

Applying the *Black Gold Marine* rule to these facts, we conclude that all of its factors are satisfied: Leslie made a material misrepresentation; it was false; Leslie knew it was false; Leslie intended for Bulgarelli to rely upon it; and Bulgarelli did so to his financial detriment. The district court did not err in holding that the contract is void. [—9—]

C.

It is a general principle of maritime law "that the master of a vessel is the agent and representative of the owner and as such can bind the owner by acts performed within the scope of the agency," including torts and contract issues. *Jackson*, 845 F.2d at 1309–

10. Here, Leslie's actions were entirely within the scope of his employment duties as he was acting as an agent of St. Clair Marine. Accordingly, the captain's improper actions are imputed to his employer. Because this contract was procured by fraud, St. Clair Marine cannot enforce the salvage contract against Bulgarelli.

V.

For the foregoing reasons, we AFFIRM the judgment of the district court.

United States Court of Appeals
for the Sixth Circuit

No. 14-2381

HERR
vs.
UNITED STATES FOREST SERV.

Appeal from the United States District Court for the
Western District of Michigan at Marquette

Decided: October 9, 2015

Citation: 803 F.3d 809, 3 Adm. R. 461 (6th Cir. 2015).

Before **SUTTON** and **DONALD**, Circuit Judges, and
ZOUHARY, District Judge.*

* The Honorable Jack Zouhary, United States District
Judge for the Northern District of Ohio, sitting by
designation.

[—2—] SUTTON, Circuit Judge:

David and Pamela Herr bought waterfront property on Crooked Lake in the Upper Peninsula of Michigan and planned to use their gas-powered motorboat on it. That plan was dashed when the U.S. Forest Service threatened to enforce a regulation that bans non-electric motorboats from the ninety-five percent of the lake that falls within a National Wilderness Area. The Herrs responded with this lawsuit, seeking to enjoin enforcement of the regulation on the ground that the relevant federal statute preserves their state-law property right to use all of the lake. The district court held that a six-year time bar on the action was jurisdictional and that the Herrs had waited too long to file this lawsuit. We reverse based in large part on a Supreme Court decision handed down after the district court's decision. *See United States v. Kwai Fun Wong*, 135 S. Ct. 1625 (2015).

I.

Nestled in old-growth forest 120 miles from Marquette, Crooked Lake is three miles long and is one of thirty-six interconnected glacial lakes that offer all manner of activities for those who appreciate the outdoors. Most of Crooked Lake rests in the federally protected Sylvania Wilderness Area, which the U.S. Forest Service oversees under the Michigan Wilderness Act of 1987, 101 Stat. 1274. A National Wilderness Area like Sylvania "preserv[es] the wilderness character of [an] area" by minimizing human impact. 16 U.S.C. § 1133(b). One way the Act advances this goal is by prohibiting motorized vehicles in the area except those permitted by the Forest Service. *Id.* § 1133(c), (d)(1).

That rule would seem to bar gas-powered motorboats from Crooked Lake, and for the most part that is true. *See* 36 C.F.R. § 293.6. But a sliver of the lake—the northern part of the northernmost bay—falls outside the Sylvania Wilderness and thus beyond the Forest Service's reach. On the northern shore of that bay sits the only private property on Crooked Lake: approximately ten privately owned lots. For some time, the owners have used gas-powered motorboats on the lake's waters. [—3—]

No one protests the use of these motorboats on the part of the lake outside the wilderness. But inside the protected zone, the Forest Service says, the landowners, like the general public, must abide by all restrictions on motorized boats. One restriction, found in the Forest Service's 2006 forest-management plan for the Sylvania Wilderness, bans motorboats from the wilderness portion of Crooked Lake except for those powered by electric motors with less than four horsepower. U.S. Forest Serv., *Final Environmental Impact Statement for 2006 Ottawa National Forest Plan* 3-48 (2006). The agency may punish violations of the requirement with a fine of up to $5,000 or a prison sentence of up to six months (or both). *See* 16 U.S.C. § 551; 18 U.S.C. §§ 3559(a)(7), 3571(b)(6).

When this restriction went into effect, David and Pamela Herr, a married couple, were occasional visitors to Crooked Lake, having vacationed there at various times since 1979. In September 2010, they became landowners, buying two of Crooked Lake's waterfront lots. One reason the couple bought the property was to "use gas-powered motorboats" on the lake. R. 4 at 11. That would not pose a problem, the seller said, because he had boated "on the entire surface of Crooked Lake without hindrance by the Forest Service." *Id.*

At first no problems arose after the Herrs bought the property. "Each summer from 2010–2012," the couple bought "a pass from the Forest Service . . . to use the Forest Service boat landing on Crooked Lake" as lake access for "their gas-powered motorboat." *Id.* They used "the entire surface of Crooked Lake" during that time, and the Forest Service never stopped them. *Id.*

Things changed in 2013. The Forest Service informed the Herrs by letter that local "Forest Service personnel [would start] fully enforc[ing]" the motorboat restrictions against them (and others) "within the wilderness portion of Crooked Lake." R. 4-5 at 2. Until this letter, so far as the pleadings show, the Forest Service had not enforced the 2007 forest order against private landowners.

In May 2014, the Herrs filed this lawsuit under the Administrative Procedure Act to enjoin the Forest Service from enforcing the motorboat restriction against them. *See* 5 U.S.C. § 702. Their lawsuit turned on two legal premises—one state, one federal. Under state law, lakefront real estate owners have a property right to use the *entire* surface of the lake for boating and sailing. *People v. Hulbert*, 91 N.W. 211, 211–12, 218 (Mich. 1902). Under federal law, the [—4—] Forest Service's authority over Crooked Lake is "[s]ubject to valid existing rights." Michigan Wilderness Act, § 5, 101 Stat. 1274, 1275; *see* 36 C.F.R. § 293.3. Two environmental organizations and two other Crooked Lake property owners intervened to support the Forest Service. The private-party intervenors hope to preserve the peace and quiet of the area's "[p]ristine glacial lakes"—with their accompanying "world-class smallmouth bass fisheries," R. 15-1 at 1, often accessed by canoes, kayaks, or boats that run on small electric-powered motors. The district court dismissed the Herrs' 2014 complaint for lack of jurisdiction, reasoning that the limitations period governing this action was jurisdictional, that the six-year limitations clock started when the Forest Service issued the relevant order in 2007, and that the

limitations period ended in 2013—one year before they filed the lawsuit.

II.

The Herrs' appeal raises two questions: (1) Does the statute of limitations (28 U.S.C. § 2401(a)) impose a jurisdictional barrier on the power of the federal courts to hear this case? And (2) did the six-year limitations period run before they filed this lawsuit?

A.

Jurisdiction. For the last decade, the Supreme Court has been on a mission to rein in profligate uses of "jurisdiction," a word with "many, too many, meanings." *Arbaugh v. Y&H Corp.*, 546 U.S. 500, 510 (2006). The meaning that counts here, and the one the Court has become disciplined about distinguishing from others, is subject-matter jurisdiction. Properly understood, subject-matter jurisdiction turns on whether a federal court has "statutory or constitutional *power* to adjudicate the case" before it. *Steel Co. v. Citizens for a Better Env't*, 523 U.S. 83, 89 (1998). The stakes of the inquiry are high. In the absence of subject-matter jurisdiction, a federal court must dismiss the lawsuit—no matter how far along the litigation has progressed (including to the last-available appeal), no matter whether the parties forfeited the issue, no matter indeed whether the parties have waived it. *Henderson ex rel. Henderson v. Shinseki*, 562 U.S. 428, 434–35 (2011); *see* Fed. R. Civ. P. 12(h)(3). That is strong medicine for litigants, attorneys, and judges alike. Before the courts will assume that Congress has imposed such a limit on its power, they require the legislature to "clearly state[]" that a given statute implicates the judiciary's subject-matter jurisdiction. *Sebelius v. Auburn Reg'l Med. Ctr.*, 133 S. [—5—] Ct. 817, 824 (2013); *see also, e.g.*, *Henderson*, 562 U.S. at 435–36; *Reed Elsevier, Inc. v. Muchnick*, 559 U.S. 154, 161–62 (2010); *Union Pac. R.R. Co. v. Bhd. of Locomotive Eng'rs, Cent. Region*, 558 U.S. 67, 81 (2009). Our court has picked up on the message. *See Brentwood at Hobart v. NLRB*, 675 F.3d 999, 1002–04 (6th Cir. 2012); *Hoogerheide v. IRS*, 637 F.3d 634, 636 (6th Cir. 2011).

Kwai Fun Wong, decided *after* the district court's decision in this case, applied this clear-statement rule to a neighboring statute of limitations that, like § 2401(a), governs lawsuits against the federal government. *See* 28 U.S.C. § 2401(b). Here is what that statute says: "A tort claim against the United States shall be forever barred unless it is presented in writing to the appropriate Federal agency within two years after such claim accrues or unless action is begun within six months after the date of mailing, by certified or registered mail, of notice of final denial of the claim by the agency to which it was presented." *Id.* Deploying "traditional tools of statutory construction," the Court concluded that § 2401(b) was not jurisdictional. *Kwai Fun Wong*, 135 S. Ct. at 1632. The statute's text "does not speak in jurisdictional terms," the Court noted, "or refer in any way to the jurisdiction of the district courts." *Id.* at 1633. It merely "say[s] only what every time bar, by definition, must: that after a certain time a claim is barred." *Id.* at 1632. The Court also observed that, when Congress enacted § 2401(b) as part of the Federal Tort Claims Act, it placed the Act's jurisdictional provisions apart from the statute of limitations. *Id.* at 1633. "Congress's separation of a filing deadline from a jurisdictional grant indicates that the time bar is not jurisdictional." *Id.* *Kwai Fun Wong* acknowledged that § 2401(b)'s "language is mandatory" but found that of "no consequence," as statutes of limitations frequently speak in mandatory terms. *Id.* at 1632.

In ruling that the statute of limitations in § 2401(b) does not erect a non-forfeitable (and non-waivable) jurisdictional bar, *Kwai Fun Wong* removes some of the suspense from this appeal. Section 2401(a), the subsection at issue today, says that "every civil action commenced against the United States shall be barred unless the complaint is filed within six years after the right of action first accrues." That language, like the language in § 2401(b), most naturally relates to how and when to process a claim, not the power of the court. The statute does not "speak in jurisdictional terms." *Zipes v. Trans World Airlines, Inc.*, 455 U.S. 385, 394 (1982). [—6—] It "reads like an ordinary, run-of-the-mill statute of limitations, spelling out a litigant's filing obligations without restricting a court's authority." *Kwai Fun Wong*, 135 S. Ct. at 1633 (quotations omitted). For these reasons, the Court concluded, § 2401(b) does not contain a clear statement limiting subject-matter jurisdiction.

It is tempting to leave it at that. If *Kwai Fun Wong* establishes that § 2401(b) does not establish a jurisdictional bar on our power, then it would seem that the similarly worded § 2401(a) does not do so either. Although *Kwai Fun Wong* removes some of the suspense from this appeal, however, it does not remove all of it.

The apparent contextual clue suggested by the sibling pairing of these statutes of limitations is misleading. The codification of two provisions next to each other does not necessarily mean that they were enacted together or for that matter that they share common roots. In this instance, subsection (b) comes from the Federal Tort Claims Act, § 420, 60 Stat. 812, 845 (1946), while subsection (a) comes from the Tucker Act, § 1, 24 Stat. 505, 505 (1887). The potential inference created by the codified pairing thus is not a real inference. We do not "infer[] that Congress, in revising and consolidating the laws, intended to change their effect, unless such intention is clearly expressed." *Fourco Glass Co. v. Transmirra Prods. Corp.*, 353 U.S. 222, 227 & n.8 (1957); *cf. Wachovia Bank v. Schmidt*, 546 U.S. 303, 314–15 (2006). Section 2401 contains no such indication. Even so, that does not alter our ultimate conclusion. It means only that a potential *additional* reason for treating subsection (b) as non-jurisdictional does not exist. That does not undermine the many other ways in which the Court's cases, including *Kwai Fun Wong*, indicate that this statute of limitations does not limit our jurisdiction over this case.

One other complication requires a longer (a few pages longer) digression, covering the history of the Big and Little Tucker Acts, two other Supreme Court decisions, and the role of stare decisis. First the history. In 1887, Congress passed the Tucker Act, which waived some of the federal government's sovereign immunity, authorizing a range of private-party lawsuits against the government for money damages and other relief. Tucker Act, §§ 1–2, 24 Stat. at 505; *see Dep't of Army v. Blue Fox, Inc.*, 525 U.S. 255, 260 (1999). Before then, Congress had permitted only a few money-damages lawsuits against the federal government, all in the Court of Claims. *See* Act of Mar. 3, 1863, § 2, 12 Stat. 765, 765; *Langford v. United States*, 101 U.S. [—7—] 341, 343–44 (1879). And those lawsuits had been governed by an 1863 statute of limitations, which provided that "every claim against the United States . . . shall be forever barred unless" filed "within six years after the claim first accrues." Act of Mar. 3, 1863, § 10, 12 Stat. at 767.

The Tucker Act expanded the federal courts' jurisdiction over money-damages lawsuits against the federal government in two ways. A provision now known as the Big Tucker Act enlarged the Court of Claims' jurisdiction. *See* Tucker Act, § 1, 24 Stat. at 505; *Fisher v. United States*, 402 F.3d 1167, 1172 (Fed. Cir. 2005) (en banc in relevant part). And a provision now called the Little Tucker Act authorized the district and circuit courts to hear any lawsuit that could be brought in the Court of Claims as long as the amount in controversy did not exceed $10,000. *See* Tucker Act, § 2, 24 Stat. at 505; *United States v. Bormes*, 133 S. Ct. 12, 15 (2012). Governing both provisions, Big and Little, was a new six-year statute of limitations, which provided that "no suit against the Government of the United States, shall be allowed under this act unless the same shall have been brought within six years after the right accrued for which the claim is made." Tucker Act, § 1, 24 Stat. at 505. This 1887 provision did not repeal the 1863 statute of limitations, meaning that both laws governed lawsuits in the Court of Claims unless they were "absolutely irreconcilable." *United States v. Greathouse*, 166 U.S. 601, 605 (1897).

In 1911, Congress reorganized several statutes regulating federal-court procedure. Act of Mar. 3, 1911, 36 Stat. 1087. In the process, it created new, separate statutes of limitations for the Big and Little Tucker Acts.

For the Big Tucker Act, Congress used the language from the 1863 Court of Claims statute of limitations. *See id.* § 156, 36 Stat. at 1139. For the Little Tucker Act, Congress used the language from the 1887 statute of limitations. *See id.* § 24(20), 36 Stat. at 1093. Congress moved the Big Tucker Act's limitations provision to its current home (28 U.S.C. § 2501) in 1948. It moved the Little Tucker Act's limitations provision, the one at issue today, to its current home (28 U.S.C. § 2401(a)) at the same time.

To the Forest Service, this history shows that § 2401(a) limits subject-matter jurisdiction. The thinking goes like this. In *United States v. Sherwood*, 312 U.S. 584, 591 (1941), the Court noted in dicta that the "jurisdiction of district courts" under the Little Tucker Act is "as restricted as is that of the Court of Claims" under the Big Tucker Act. And in *John R. Sand & Gravel Co.* [—8—] *v. United States*, 552 U.S. 130, 134 (2008), the Court held that the Big Tucker Act's statute of limitations (§ 2501) is jurisdictional because a prior decision (*Kendall v. United States*, 107 U.S. 123 (1883)) had held that § 2501's predecessor, the 1863 statute of limitations for the Court of Claims, limits the Court of Claims' subject-matter jurisdiction. The force of stare decisis, *John R. Sand* held, allowed § 2501 to remain jurisdictional despite the prevailing current in the caselaw that time bars do not create jurisdictional bars. 522 U.S. at 138–39. All of this, says the Forest Service, means that the Little Tucker Act's limitations period (§ 2401(a)) also deprives the federal district courts of subject-matter jurisdiction over claims more than six years old.

The key link is *John R. Sand*, and it does not provide the necessary foundation for this argument. The decision does not establish that other statutes of limitations sharing language and features of the *John R. Sand* statute of limitations must be treated as jurisdictional on stare decisis grounds. Otherwise, several cases resolved during the Court's ten-year push to straighten this area out would have come out differently. To use the most salient example, *John R. Sand* held that a limitations statute saying that late claims against the United States "shall be barred" created a jurisdictional limitation. 28 U.S.C. § 2501. But *Kwai Fun Wong* held that a statute saying late claims against the United States "shall be forever barred" did not create a jurisdictional limitation. 28 U.S.C. § 2401(b). *John R. Sand* thus must mean something else.

The decision stands only for the modest proposition that, if the Court has already definitively interpreted a statute (there § 2501 or its predecessor) to erect a jurisdictional bar, it would respect that holding in future cases on stare decisis grounds. That indeed is how the Court distinguished *Irwin v. Department of Veterans Affairs*, 498 U.S. 89 (1990), which considered a similarly worded statute. "*Irwin*," the Court remarked, "dealt with a different limitations statute. That statute, while similar to the present statute in language, is unlike [§ 2501] in the key respect that the Court had not previously provided a definitive interpretation." 552 U.S. at 137. *John R. Sand*'s own accounting of itself makes it a ticket good for one destination and one destination alone: § 2501. And that explanation does not help the Forest Service because today's statute, like the one at issue in *Irwin*, is not § 2501. We know of no Supreme Court cases holding that § 2401(a) (or its predecessor) is jurisdictional or that § 2401(a) must be interpreted like § 2501. Respect for precedent justifies *John R. Sand*, but that is all. **[—9—]**

A critical feature of stare decisis—perhaps the salient feature of it—is that it requires courts to preserve error. All three explanations for the doctrine—stability, predictability, and ease of judicial administration—have work to do in preserving mistakes. Only the last one— allowing judges to work less hard— plays a role when it comes to correctly decided prior decisions. Much as these explanations may justify the doctrine in both settings, they disappear when parties seek to *extend* precedent—especially flawed precedent. Stare decisis may require courts to give respect to prior mistaken decisions. It may even require courts to cover prior mistakes with bubble wrap and lock them in safe places. But it does not require courts to extend them.

What of the fact that § 2401(a) has roots in the Little Tucker Act, § 2501 has roots in the Big Tucker Act, and the statutes of limitations for both were once coextensive? This historical excursion does not present the full picture. Congress altered the Little Tucker Act's statute of limitations—the one at issue here— in 1948. It separated the Little Tucker Act's limitations period and jurisdictional grant into sections. *Compare* 28 U.S.C § 41(20) (1940), *with* Act of June 25, 1948, §§ 1346, 2401(a), 62 Stat. 869, 933, 971. And it broadened the Little Tucker Act's statute of limitations. It now governs "*every* civil action commenced against the United States," 28 U.S.C. § 2401(a) (emphasis added), while the prior version governed only actions seeking money damages "not exceeding $10,000," 28 U.S.C. § 41(20) (1940). Congress thus extended the Little Tucker Act's statute of limitations beyond small money-damages actions. *See, e.g., Walters v. Sec'y of Def.*, 725 F.2d 107, 113–14 (D.C. Cir. 1983); *Werner v. United States*, 188 F.2d 266, 268 (9th Cir. 1951). This change, when combined with Congress's decision to separate the Little Tucker Act's statute of limitations from the jurisdictional grant, demonstrates that § 2401(a) was designed to serve as a standard, mine-run statute of limitations without jurisdictional qualities. That leaves us with a statute (§ 2401(a)) that does not clearly impose a jurisdictional limit.

What of the canon that directs courts to construe waivers of sovereign immunity narrowly? Does that trump the canon that insists on a clear statement before courts will treat limitations on causes of action as jurisdictional? *Kwai Fun Wong* (and *Irwin* before it) rejected the same argument. The Court in both cases "declined to count time bars as jurisdictional merely **[—10—]** because they condition waivers of immunity." *Kwai Fun Wong*, 135 S. Ct. at 1637. It instead treated them as it would any other statute of limitations. So do we.

Regardless, the Forest Service responds, *McDonald v. Resor*, 34 F.3d 1068, at *2 (6th Cir. 1994) (unpublished order), indicates that § 2401(a) "is a condition of federal court jurisdiction." That is a stretch. *Resor* is a nonprecedential case. It made the point only in dicta. It provided no analysis to support the point. It predates *Arbaugh* and the other cases designed to clean up this area. And it relied on a case discussing § 2501, not § 2401(a), for this proposition. To the extent we wish to consider dicta from pre-*Arbaugh* cases, we would pick a published case going the other way. *See United States v. Knott*, 69 F.2d 907, 910–11 (6th Cir. 1934).

After today's decision, it is true, there is a 4–3 circuit split on the point, with four of the circuits favoring the government's position that § 2401(a) creates a jurisdictional bar. *Compare Konecny v. United States*, 388 F.2d 59, 61–62 (8th Cir. 1967); *Ctr. for Biological Diversity v. Hamilton*, 453 F.3d 1331, 1334 (11th Cir. 2006) (per curiam); *Mendoza v. Perez*, 754 F.3d 1002, 1018 (D.C. Cir. 2014); *and Hopland Band of Pomo Indians v. United States*, 855 F.2d 1573, 1576–77 (Fed. Cir. 1988), *with Clymore v. United States*, 217 F.3d 370, 374 (5th Cir. 2000); *Herr v. U.S. Forest Serv.*, No. 14-2381 (6th Cir. Oct. 9, 2015); *and Cedars-Sinai Med. Ctr. v. Shalala*, 125 F.3d 765, 770 (9th Cir. 1997). Many of these cases, however, have not grappled with the Supreme Court's recent cases limiting the concept of jurisdiction. None has considered the impact of *Kwai Fun Wong*, decided just this year. When the D.C. Circuit has noted the apparent conflict between its decision and the *Arbaugh* line of cases, it has acknowledged the point each time yet steered the basis for decision to other grounds. *See Mendoza*, 754 F.3d at 1018 n.11; *P & V Enters. v. U.S. Army Corps of Eng'rs*, 516 F.3d 1021, 1026–27 & n.2 (D.C. Cir. 2008); *Felter v. Kempthorne*, 473 F.3d 1255, 1260 (D.C. Cir. 2007); *Harris v. FAA*, 353 F.3d 1006, 1013 n.7 (D.C. Cir. 2004). The *Arbaugh* rule together with its application in *Kwai Fun Wong* gives us comfort in siding with the non-jurisdictional side of this split. Section 2401(a) does not limit a federal court's subject-matter jurisdiction. [—11—]

B.

Statute of limitations. That a limitations period is not jurisdictional does not mean it is not mandatory. We must determine (1) whether the Herrs filed this claim within the limitations period and if not (2) whether they are entitled to equitable tolling.

Here is the timeline: The Herrs rented property on the lake at various times since 1979; the agency rule at issue went into effect in 2007; the Herrs bought their lakefront property in 2010; and they filed this lawsuit in 2014. The statute creates a six-year limitations period, making the start of the six-year clock the dispositive issue. If the time period began running in 2007 when the Forest Service promulgated this regulation, the statute required the Herrs to file the lawsuit within the next six years—by 2013. If the time period began running when they purchased their property, this 2014 lawsuit comes well within the six-year limitations period.

The limitations period in § 2401(a) begins to run when a party's "right of action first accrues"—"as soon as (but not before) the person challenging the agency action can institute and maintain a suit in court," *Spannaus v. DOJ*, 824 F.2d 52, 56 (D.C. Cir. 1987). This comports with the general rule that "a statute of limitations begins to run . . . when the plaintiff can file suit and obtain relief," *Heimeshoff v. Hartford Life & Accident Ins. Co.*, 134 S. Ct. 604, 610 (2013) (quotations omitted), for "the injury upon which [his] action is based," *Kach v. Hose*, 589 F.3d 626, 634 (3d Cir. 2009).

To file a lawsuit under the Administrative Procedure Act, parties must satisfy two requirements. They must know or have reason to know that the challenged agency action caused them to suffer a "legal wrong" or "adversely affected or aggrieved" them "within the meaning of a relevant statute." 5 U.S.C. § 702; *see Stupak-Thrall v. Glickman*, 346 F.3d 579, 584 (6th Cir. 2003). And the challenged agency action must be "final," 5 U.S.C. § 704, "determin[ing] rights or obligations" and "mark[ing] the consummation of the agency's decisionmaking process," *Sackett v. EPA*, 132 S. Ct. 1367, 1371–72 (2012). Once the challenged agency action becomes final and invades a party's legally protected interest, the party's right to redress that injury under the APA accrues, *see Lujan v. Nat'l Wildlife Fed'n*, 497 U.S.

871, 882–83 (1990), and § 2401(a)'s six-year clock starts ticking. [—12—]

In their complaint, the Herrs allege that the Forest Service's 2007 forest order invaded their state-law property right to use their gas-powered motorboat on all of Crooked Lake, a right that section 5 of the Michigan Wilderness Act protects. Both parties agree that the 2007 forest order constitutes final agency action. And both appear to agree that the deprivation of a property right would "aggrieve[]" the Herrs "within the meaning of" section 5, a provision that protects private property rights from abrogation by the Forest Service. *See* 5 U.S.C. § 702. When, then, did the forest order abridge the Herrs' alleged property right?

September 2010. That is when the Herrs purchased their waterfront property on Crooked Lake. The Herrs allege that their property right "to use the entire surface" of Crooked Lake "ar[ose], by operation of [Michigan] law, as an incident to [their] ownership of property adjoining the banks" of the lake. R. 4 at 5. If that is correct, they had no property right to use all of Crooked Lake until they owned lots abutting the lake. The Herrs thus could not have become "aggrieved" by the Forest Service's invasion of that property right until they became property owners on the lake—until they purchased their waterfront real estate in September 2010. Only at that point could the Herrs meet both requirements to bring this lawsuit under the APA by pleading final agency action *and* an injury to their rights under the Michigan Wilderness Act. Only at that point did their "right of action" under the APA "accrue[]." 28 U.S.C. § 2401(a). And only at that point did the six-year limitations period begin to run. The Herrs thus had until September 2016 to challenge the Forest Service's gas-powered boat restriction, a deadline they met by more than two years.

The Forest Service tries to counter this conclusion in several ways. It argues that a right of action under the APA accrues upon final agency action regardless of whether that action aggrieved the plaintiff. But that contradicts the text of the statute and

Supreme Court precedent to boot. Only "[a] person suffering legal wrong because of agency action, or adversely affected or aggrieved by agency action within the meaning of a relevant statute," 5 U.S.C. § 702 says, "is entitled to judicial review thereof." If a party cannot plead a "legal wrong" or an "adverse[] [e]ffect[]," *id.*, it has no right of action. *See, e.g., Match-E-Be-Nash-She-Wish Band of Pottawatomi Indians v. Patchak*, 132 S. Ct. 2199, 2210 (2012); *Ass'n of Data Processing Serv. Orgs. v. Camp*, 397 U.S. 150, 153 (1970); *see also Lexmark Int'l, Inc. v. Static Control* [—13—] *Components, Inc.*, 134 S. Ct. 1377, 1387 nn.3–4 (2014). No doubt, the party must *also* plead final agency action, *see* 5 U.S.C. § 704, but that is another necessary, but not by itself a sufficient, ground for stating a claim under the APA.

Some courts, it is true, have suggested that an APA claim "first accrues on the date of the final agency action." *Hardin v. Jackson*, 625 F.3d 739, 743 (D.C. Cir. 2010); *see, e.g., Latin Ams. for Soc. & Econ. Dev. v. Adm'r of the Fed. Highway Admin.*, 756 F.3d 447, 464 (6th Cir. 2014). But these cases show why we don't read precedents like statutes. These cases all involved settings in which the right of action happened to accrue at the same time that final agency action occurred, because the plaintiff either became aggrieved at that time or had already been injured. A classic example would be an agency that issues a rule without following all requirements of notice-and-comment rulemaking. *See* 5 U.S.C. § 553(c). This denial of process to the public at large violates the statute, and any party concretely injured by the action (say, a party who has to pay a fee because of the rule) may sue to correct that wrong. The clock for the injured party begins to tick the moment the agency took its final action because the agency's lack of notice-and-comment rulemaking already legally injured the party. But that is not the case when, as here, the party does not suffer any injury until *after* the agency's final action. *See Wind River Mining Corp. v. United States*, 946 F.2d 710, 714–16 (9th Cir. 1991).

Southwest Williamson County Community Ass'n v. Slater, 173 F.3d 1033 (6th Cir. 1999), is not to the contrary. It held that the limitations period for challenging an agency's environmental assessments started to run when final agency action occurred even though the plaintiff-association did not come into existence until later. *Id.* at 1036. The reason, however, is that the association did not allege harms to *itself* as an organization, *cf. Havens Realty Corp. v. Coleman*, 455 U.S. 363, 379 (1982); it sought relief on behalf of its members, *see Sierra Club v. Morton*, 405 U.S. 727, 739 (1972); *Nat'l Wildlife Fed'n v. Hodel*, 839 F.2d 694, 704 n.7 (D.C. Cir. 1988). Nothing in the case suggests that any member first became aggrieved after, rather than when, final agency action occurred.

Even if a claimant needs to suffer an injury to bring an APA challenge, the Forest Service maintains that the Herrs sustained an injury when it issued the order in 2007. Because the Herrs have boated on Crooked Lake since the late 1970s through vacation rentals, the Service argues, **[—14—]** they had a recreational interest that the 2007 forest order infringed. Yes and no. Yes, the boating restriction harmed the couple's recreational interests in 2007 and perhaps might have given them *a* right of action under the APA at that time. But no, *this* right of action did not accrue at that time. A "right of action," as understood when Congress enacted 28 U.S.C. § 2401(a), is "a legal right to maintain an action, growing out of a *given transaction or state of facts and based thereon.*" *Black's Law Dictionary* 1560 (3d ed. 1933) (emphasis added); *see* Act of June 25, 1948, § 2401(a), Pub. L. No. 80-773, 62 Stat. 869, 971. Such a right arises from a fact pattern that demonstrates a specific "legal wrong"—"an act authoritatively prohibited by a rule of law." *Black's Law Dictionary* 1849 (10th ed. 2014); *see* 1A C.J.S. *Actions* §§ 54, 55; 1 Am. Jur. 2d *Actions* §§ 1, 2; *see also McMahon v. United States*, 186 F.2d 227, 230 (3d Cir. 1950), *aff'd*, 342 U.S. 25 (1951).

Different legal wrongs give rise to different rights of action. *See Am. Fire & Cas. Co. v. Finn*, 341 U.S. 6, 13 (1951); *Baltimore S.S. Co. v. Phillips*, 274 U.S. 316, 321 (1927); *Union Pac. Ry. Co. v. Wyler*, 158 U.S. 285, 291–92 (1895). That is so even if the different *legal* wrongs stem from the same order. *See* 1A

C.J.S. *Actions* § 189; 1 Am. Jur. 2d *Actions* § 76. The upshot is this: Even if the Herrs had *some* right of action to remedy *some* legal wrong related to their recreational interests in 2007, they could not have had *this* right of action to remedy *this* legal wrong—the infringement of a property right in violation of the Michigan Wilderness Act—until they obtained that property right in 2010.

The Forest Service also looks to the Herrs' predecessor in interest, the prior owner of the lakefront lots, to defeat this lawsuit. The prior owner held title to the property in 2007, which means that his right of action to challenge the boating restriction as infringing his property rights arose in 2007. The Herrs, the theory goes, do not have their own independent right of action; their right stems from the one that accrued to the lots' prior owner in 2007, which "ran with the land" after the 2010 sale. That right of action expired in 2013, the theory continues, making this action late all the same.

Property law says otherwise. Once a right of action accrues, it becomes a "piece" of intangible personal property called a "chose in action." *Sprint Commc'ns Co. v. APCC Servs., Inc.*, 554 U.S. 269, 275 (2008). Choses of action to enforce property rights do not, as a general **[—15—]** matter, automatically transfer when the underlying property changes hands. *See, e.g., Peters v. Bowman*, 98 U.S. 56, 58–59 (1878) (right to enforce covenant does not run with land); *Ginsberg v. Austin*, 968 F.2d 1198, 1201 (Fed. Cir. 1992) (right to recover outstanding rent payments does not run with land); *In re Nucorp Energy Sec. Litig.*, 772 F.2d 1486, 1490 (9th Cir. 1985) (right of action under Rule 10b-5 does not automatically transfer when security is sold); *see also Restatement (Second) of Contracts* § 317 (1981); *Restatement (First) of Property* § 552 (1944). No doubt, one may *assign* a chose in action to another party, *see Sprint*, 554 U.S. at 275–77, but that requires the assignor to "manifest an intention to transfer the right" to the assignee, *Restatement (Second) of Contracts, supra*, § 324; *see Restatement (First) of Property, supra*, § 552 cmt. c. No such intention appears in this record. The Herrs' deed says only that they acquired the "premises" of their lots from the prior owner. R. 4-1 at 2.

Nor does § 2401(a) alter this conclusion. The statute contains no language suggesting that the limitations period starts when a plaintiff's predecessor in interest could first file a lawsuit. Congress knew how to impose such a limitation. It has done so before. In the Quiet Title Act, it barred any civil action unless "commenced within twelve years of the date . . . the plaintiff *or his predecessor in interest* knew or should have known of the claim of the United States." 28 U.S.C. § 2409a(g) (emphasis added). Section 2401(a) contains no such statement, and "[w]e do not lightly assume that Congress has omitted from its adopted text requirements that it nonetheless intends to apply." *Jama v. Immigration & Customs Enforcement*, 543 U.S. 335, 341 (2005).

If the transfer of property alone permits new APA challenges arising from ownership of that property, the Service warns, agency regulations will never be safe from attack. That is not true in one sense. As just shown, Congress knows how to make statutes of limitations run against current owners and "predecessors in interest." It simply chose not to do so here.

That argues much too much in another sense. A federal regulation that makes it six years without being contested does not enter a promised land free from legal challenge. Regulated parties may always assail a regulation as exceeding the agency's statutory authority in enforcement proceedings against them. *See NLRB Union v. Fed. Labor Relations Auth.*, 834 F.2d 191, 195 (D.C. Cir. 1987); *Functional Music, Inc. v. FCC*, 274 F.2d 543, 546 (D.C. Cir. [—16—] 1958); *see also Wind River*, 946 F.2d at 714 (collecting cases). That is true of old and new regulations. *See Horne v. Dep't of Agric.*, 135 S. Ct. 2419, 2424–25 (2015) (regulatory regime dating back to 1937); *Long Island Care at Home, Ltd. v. Coke*, 551 U.S. 158, 163 (2007) (regulation promulgated in 1975). Recall that the Forest Service has threatened criminal action against the Herrs. Does anyone really think that the Herrs would not be allowed to challenge the

Forest Service's administrative authority to put them in jail for six months or fine them $5,000 based on its interpretation of this statute? *See Chevron, U.S.A., Inc. v. Nat. Res. Def. Council, Inc.*, 467 U.S. 837 (1984); *cf. Carter v. Welles-Bowen Realty, Inc.*, 736 F.3d 722, 729–36 (6th Cir. 2013) (Sutton, J., concurring). That is a steep climb. Any such theory of repose is a mirage in still another sense. Regulated parties may always petition an agency to reconsider a longstanding rule and then appeal the denial of that petition (as the denial counts as final agency action). 5 U.S.C. § 553(e); *see NLRB Union*, 834 F.2d at 195.

Our decision adds only a modest wrinkle to this regime. When a party *first* becomes aggrieved by a regulation that exceeds an agency's statutory authority more than six years after the regulation was promulgated, that party may challenge the regulation without waiting for enforcement proceedings. That makes sense, as courts "normally do not require plaintiffs to bet the farm . . . by taking the violative action before testing the validity of the law." *Free Enter. Fund v. Pub. Co. Accounting Oversight Bd.*, 561 U.S. 477, 490–91 (2010) (quotations omitted).

Even if the Herrs filed their complaint within § 2401(a)'s time limits, the Forest Service contends that they failed to exhaust their administrative remedies, 7 U.S.C. § 6912(e), and contends that this requirement (too) is jurisdictional. Not so on both fronts. The exhaustion requirement in § 6912(e) does not affect our power to hear the case. Unless Congress "clearly state[s]" its intention to deprive courts of subject-matter jurisdiction, as explained, "courts should treat the [procedural] restriction as nonjurisdictional." *Kwai Fun Wong*, 135 S. Ct. at 1632 (quotations omitted). That rule applies to exhaustion requirements no less than it does to time bars. *See id.* And § 6912(e)'s exhaustion requirement does not speak in jurisdictional terms. It includes none of the "sweeping and direct" language needed to remove our power to hear unexhausted claims. *Weinberger v. Salfi*, 422 U.S. 749, 757 (1975). It instead speaks in the nomenclature of claim-processing requirements. So far, all circuits to address this question [—17—] agree. *Munsell v. Dep't of Agric.*, 509 F.3d 572, 580–81 (D.C. Cir. 2007) (collecting cases from the Fifth, Eighth, and Ninth Circuits).

Any effort to exhaust in this case, moreover, would be futile. Courts may excuse exhaustion provisions when the agency "predetermined the issue before" the plaintiff filed the lawsuit. *McCarthy v. Madigan*, 503 U.S. 140, 148 (1992). Courts have discussed the applicability of that principle under § 6912(e). *E.g., Ace Prop. & Cas. Ins. Co. v. Fed. Crop Ins. Corp.*, 440 F.3d 992, 1000 (8th Cir. 2006). If administrative review would "come to naught," if any efforts before the agency would be "pointless," the courts do not insist that litigants go through the motions of exhausting the claim anyway. *Dozier v. Sun Life Assurance Co. of Can.*, 466 F.3d 532, 535 (6th Cir. 2006). "Pointless" aptly describes the Herrs' would-be administrative review. Other similarly situated Crooked Lake property owners previously challenged the lawfulness of the motorboat restrictions in 2007. But the Forest Service rejected their challenges and stood by its restrictions. And the Forest Service's defense in this lawsuit offers no reason to think it would treat the Herrs any differently, especially after it threatened criminal enforcement of the order against them. The Herrs could thus "fairly assume that the *same* [agency] would apply" the *same* standard to the *same* facts to reach the *same* result. *Cf. Dozier*, 466 F.3d at 535 (emphasis added). The law does not force them to take on hopeless causes.

For these reasons, we reverse and remand for further proceedings consistent with this opinion.

United States Court of Appeals for the Seventh Circuit

United States Court of Appeals
for the Seventh Circuit

No. 14-2155

AWOK ANI-DENG

VS.

JEFFBOAT, LLC

Appeal from the United States District Court for the Southern District of Indiana, New Albany Division

Decided: January 27, 2015

Citation: 777 F.3d 452, 3 Adm. R. 472 (7th Cir. 2015).

Before **WOOD**, Chief Judge, and **POSNER**, and **EASTERBROOK**, Circuit Judges.

[—1—] POSNER, Circuit Judge:

The plaintiff filed a scattershot of discrimination and related claims against her former employer, Jeffboat (a division of American Commercial Lines), the nation's largest inland shipbuilder and second-largest manufacturer of barges. The district judge dismissed all the claims, some on the pleadings and the rest on summary judgment. [—2—]

A woman of Sudanese extraction, the plaintiff worked in Jeffboat's shipyard in Jeffersonville, Indiana as a welder from January 2006 until she was laid off in October 2011. She had been until late in her employment by Jeffboat a welder first class. Welders first class do the most difficult—and dangerous—welding jobs, such as overhead welding and welding in confined spaces. Welders second class do less demanding and safer welding jobs, and there are also welders third class, who do even less demanding jobs. In a two-week period in June 2011, the plaintiff, who had on 12 previous occasions sought first aid for work-related injuries, experienced two more such incidents, becoming dizzy and nauseous while welding in confined spaces. At the end of the month Jeffboat demoted her to welder third class. (According to the collective bargaining agreement between Jeffboat and the union that represented the plaintiff, at the time the plaintiff was demoted a welder first class received $21.10 per hour while a welder third class received $15.69 per hour.) The plaintiff claims that the company demoted her in retaliation for her having complained to the EEOC the previous February that the company was discriminating against her because of her sex and national origin.

She was laid off in October 2011, but the layoff was part of a general reduction in force based on seniority and in January 2012 the company notified her by certified mail that she was being recalled—she hadn't enough seniority to avoid the reduction but she had enough to be among the laid-off workers who were recalled. The letter stated that if she wanted to return to work she had to notify the company by 3:30 p.m. on a date in January that was five working days after the letter was mailed. She failed to reply within the deadline. However, on 6:00 p.m. on that fifth day her hus- [—3—] band called the company to report that his wife did want to return to work. But the company had closed for business at 3:30, so he was able only to leave a voicemail.

Jeffboat is unionized and its collective bargaining agreement requires an employee, in order to secure his or her seniority, to "report for work within five (5) working days after being notified by certified letter to report." The plaintiff's husband phoned the company on the fifth day, but because the call was made after the close of business that day no one in the company received timely notice. The company informed the plaintiff that she'd missed the deadline and therefore would not be recalled; her employment with Jeffboat was over.

The plaintiff never received the certified recall letter that noted the deadline, but only because, as she admitted, she had failed to apprise the company that she had moved and that therefore her address was no longer the address in the company's records. The union's chief steward and an employee of Jeffboat's human resources department twice phoned her to remind her of the deadline (though no such attempt to remind is required by the collective bargaining agreement), but they were unable to reach her either time. The chief steward called a third time, now using his personal cell phone, but still failed to reach her. The chief steward then tracked down the plaintiff's husband, another Jeffboat employee, on the shipyard premises, and told him of the deadline, but as we said he failed to comply.

So far as appears, then, the plaintiff was demoted because of the company's safety concerns, which seem entirely legitimate given the dangerousness of the work and the incidence of safety violations, which have included deaths, see [—4—] OSHA Regulation News Release, Feb. 16, 2012, www.osha.gov/pls/oshaweb/owadisp.show_document?p_table=NEWS_RELEASES&p_id=21831 (visited Jan. 26, 2015); she was laid off as part of a general reduction in force; and she would have been recalled if only she'd responded in time to the recall notice—and there is no valid reason she couldn't have responded in time. She seems to think that notice would have been timely had she or her husband left a voicemail message with Jeffboat at one second before midnight on the fifth day. But that's wrong because the company would not have received *meaningful* timely notice. Neither did it receive such notice when the plaintiff's husband left a voicemail message two and a half hours after the office that received the message had closed.

The only evidence of discrimination or retaliation against the plaintiff is an affidavit by Evelyn Miller, a former employee of Jeffboat who was still employed by the company when the plaintiff missed the recall deadline. In fact Miller was the other party to the abortive phone calls placed by the chief union steward. Miller's affidavit states that the company's labor relations manager "would regularly manipulate the workforce," "would review the seniority list for the different classes of jobs in order to find ways in which to terminate the employment of workers," and had "searched for a way to terminate the employment of" the plaintiff in stages, first by demoting her from welder first class to welder third class "for too many First Aid Visits," which Miller calls "unusual and not a real reason to demote a worker at Jeffboat," the "real reason" being the plaintiff's complaints "about how she was treated as a woman, as an

African and as a non-English speaker by those who had supervision over her work." The affidavit goes on to state that many white and [—5—] male welders first class also went to First Aid because of overheating "yet, they experienced no demotion or reclassification," and that anyway the overheating was Jeffboat's fault for failing to provide enough fans. And finally the affidavit asserts that the plaintiff was "laid-off in violation of the CBA … in retaliation to her complaint to the EEOC and other complaints."

The affidavit was entitled to no weight, as it had no foundation. "A [lay] witness may testify to a matter only if evidence is introduced sufficient to support a finding that the witness has personal knowledge of the matter," Fed. R. Evid. 602; *United States v. Joy*, 192 F.3d 761, 767 (7th Cir. 1999); *Visser v. Packer Engineering Associates, Inc.*, 924 F.2d 655, 659–60 (7th Cir. 1991) (en banc), though personal knowledge can include inferences, *id.*; *Gustovich v. AT&T Communications, Inc.*, 972 F.2d 845, 849–50 (7th Cir. 1992) (per curiam)—most of our personal knowledge is inferential. The affidavit itself could have contained the requisite evidence, since it is under oath. Had Miller's affidavit stated for example that she had overheard a company official say that he'd get the plaintiff fired because she was foreign, the affidavit, or at least that part of it, would have been admissible. But without such first-hand evidence in the affidavit itself—and there wasn't any—Miller needed discovery to establish the admissibility of the assertions in the affidavit. The plaintiff's lawyer inexcusably failed to conduct the necessary discovery. His discovery requests for pertinent company records missed the district court's discovery deadline. If it's true as Miller's affidavit states that the plaintiff's numerous "First Aid Visits" were attributable to the company's failure to provide enough fans, one would expect complaints to have [—6—] been made by the welders to the union and by the union to OSHA. Discovery would have revealed such complaints.

The statement in the affidavit that "too many First Aid Visits" are not a "real reason" why a welder is demoted is hardly credible, since a high accident rate would get Jeffboat into trouble with OSHA; but in any event the affidavit does not indicate how a human resources officer would know the "real reason" for demotion of a welder with injury problems. The affidavit fails also to indicate what basis the affiant had for thinking that white welders and male welders (white or black?) who made many First Aid Visits because of overheating were not punished by being demoted, or how the affiant learned that the company's labor relations manager was trying to fire the plaintiff in stages—did he tell the affiant that? Did she overhear him tell someone else? There is no evidence to suggest that Miller had personal knowledge of the manager's supposed scheming.

As for the charge that the plaintiff's supervisors mistreated her because of her sex, African origin, and language difficulties, Miller's affidavit should have named the alleged miscreants or at least provided some basis for identifying them. And contrary to another assertion in Miller's affidavit, it is apparent that the plaintiff does speak English, albeit not as well as a native English speaker. The chief union steward and Miller would have spoken to her in English had they reached her on the phone, and even her lawyer at oral argument acknowledged that she speaks "limited" English. Although her first deposition was conducted through an interpreter, confirming that she has difficulty with English, at her second deposition she appears to have understood most [—7—] of the questions, which were in English, though at times she relied on an interpreter.

Without the affidavit, the plaintiff had nothing. The district judge was therefore on sound ground in dismissing her suit.

AFFIRMED.

United States Court of Appeals
for the Seventh Circuit

No. 14-1171

KAWASAKI KISEN KAISHA, LTD.
vs.
PLANO MOLDING CO.

Appeals from the United States District Court for the
Northern District of Illinois, Eastern Division

Decided: March 31, 2015

Citation: 782 F.3d 353, 3 Adm. R. 475 (7th Cir. 2015).

Before **FLAUM**, **WILLIAMS**, and **TINDER**, Circuit Judges.

[—1—] FLAUM, Circuit Judge:

On April 21, 2005, a Union Pacific freight train derailed in Oklahoma. The train was carrying two steel injection molds being delivered to Plano Molding Company in Illinois. The derailment occurred after the molds broke through the floor of their shipping container, causing that train car and many behind it to derail and resulting in approximately $4 million in total damage. The [—2—] molds had been manufactured in China and shipped to the United States before being transferred to the Union Pacific train for the final leg of their journey.

At issue in this case is the reason that the molds broke through the floor. The appellants are three companies that were involved in the shipment of the molds and sustained losses from the accident: Kawasaki Kisen Kaisha, Ltd., "K" Line America, Inc. (collectively, "K-Line"), and Union Pacific Railroad Co. ("Union Pacific"). They sued Plano, claiming that Plano was at fault because a company it hired packed the molds into the shipping container improperly, causing the floor of the container to break and ultimately causing the derailment. If true, Plano would be liable to appellants for breach of a warranty found in a document known as the "World Bill of Lading," which provided contractual terms for the shipment of the molds. Plano, in defense, argued that the molds were properly packed and that they fell through the floor of the container because the container was defective.

In a bench trial, the district court found in favor of Plano, concluding that appellants had not proved that the molds were improperly packed. The court also held that the derailment was in fact caused by deficiencies in the container. On appeal, the plaintiffs contest these factual conclusions, as well as a number of other aspects of the district court's opinion. For the reasons set forth below, we affirm.

I. Background

Plano is an Illinois corporation that designs, manufactures, and sells plastic storage boxes. In 2004, Plano identified a need to purchase two new steel injection molds, which [—3—] it uses to manufacture its plastic boxes, and so it contacted CMT International, Inc. ("CMT"), a company that assists customers in the United States who wish to purchase products from Asia. CMT provided Plano with bids, and Plano selected Kunshan Yuanjin Plastic & Electronic Co., Ltd. ("Kunshan"), a Chinese company, to make the molds. Kunshan manufactured the molds and loaded them into wooden crates.

Plano hired World Commerce Services ("World"),[1] a non-vessel operating common carrier,[2] to arrange for the shipment of the molds from China to Plano's factory in Illinois. World then contracted with the THI Group LTD ("THI") and K-Line for the physical shipment of the molds. THI, in turn, hired Shanghai Haixing Yuancang Container Transportation Co. ("Haixing") to load the molds into an intermodal shipping container

---

[1] Plano contends that it was actually CMT that retained World's services. For the purposes of this appeal, however, this dispute is irrelevant.

[2] As their name suggests, non-vessel operating common carriers do not own or operate ships or other means of freight transportation. Rather, they act primarily as coordinators of shipping logistics, and contract with carriers to actually move goods. They do, however, assume common carrier responsibility, 46 U.S.C. § 40102(6), (16), and often issue their own bills of lading. See, e.g., Sompo Japan Ins. Co. of Am. v. Norfolk S. Ry. Co., 762 F.3d 165, 168–69, 2 Adm. R. 78, 78-79 (2d Cir. 2014).

and hired Shanghai Ocean Tally Company as a "checker," which ensured that the molds were properly loaded. That shipping container carried Plano's molds (inside of their wooden crates) from the moment they were packed in China until the Union Pacific train derailed in Oklahoma. Both World and K-Line issued bills of lading covering the shipment of the molds. K-Line handled the ocean [—4—] part of the voyage, but subcontracted the overland movement of the molds within the United States to Union Pacific. Once the shipping container carrying Plano's molds arrived in the U.S., it was transferred from K-Line to Union Pacific, which began transporting the container by train from California to Illinois. During the voyage, the molds somehow broke through the floor of the shipping container, causing the train to derail in Oklahoma. The accident caused approximately $2 million in damage to the cargo of K-Line's customers and $2 million in costs to Union Pacific.

Appellants sued in federal court, attempting to hold Plano liable for certain damages caused by the derailment and seeking indemnification for claims made against appellants by third parties who suffered damages in the accident. The district court initially granted summary judgment in Plano's favor on all of appellants' claims, but this court reversed on one claim—a breach of contract claim based on a warranty in the bill of lading issued by World. *Kawasaki Kisen Kaisha, Ltd. v. Plano Molding Co.*, 696 F.3d 647, 657–58 (7th Cir. 2012). We remanded to the district court to determine whether Plano was subject to the terms of the World Bill of Lading. After a one-day trial, the district court held that Plano was bound by the World Bill of Lading and could be held liable to appellants if it violated the terms of that agreement. *Kawasaki Kisen Kaisha, Ltd. v. Plano Molding Co.*, No. 07 C 5675, 2013 WL 3791609, at *8 (N.D. Ill. July 19, 2013) ("*Kawasaki I*"). Plano does not appeal that ruling.

The district court then held a three-day trial to determine whether Plano breached Clause 10(2) of the World Bill of Lading, which states: [—5—]

If Carrier receives the goods already packed into containers:

...

(2) Merchant warrants that the stowage and seals of the containers are safe and proper and suitable for handling and carriage and indemnifies Carrier for any injury, loss, or damage caused by the breach of this warranty

Plano, the parties agree, was a "Merchant" as defined in Clause 2(3) of the World Bill of Lading. The World Bill of Lading defined World as the "Carrier," but Clause 3 provides that World's contractors and subcontractors—including all of the appellants—are entitled to all of the Carrier's rights under the Bill of Lading.

The trial consisted largely of expert testimony. Appellants sought to prove that Plano breached Clause 10(2) by improperly stowing and securing the molds in the shipping container.[3] There was no direct evidence of how the molds were packed into the container, and neither party presented witnesses who were involved in the loading of the container. That is in part because the container was packed in China, making it difficult to obtain this information. [—6—]

The derailment itself also made it very difficult to determine after the fact how the container had been loaded. Much of what was inside of the container before the crash ended up outside of it, spread over the miles-long crash site. About 60% of the floor of the container was missing after the accident, allowing much to fall out during the derailment. There was, however, some physical evidence about the stowage of the

---

[3] As stated above, Plano itself did not actually pack its molds into the shipping containers; rather, Haixing did, and its work was checked by Shanghai Ocean Tally. However, assuming, as the district court did, that these companies were hired by Plano to pack the molds, Plano would be liable for those companies' breach of Clause 10(2) just as if Plano itself had packed the container. Therefore, to avoid unnecessary complexity, we will conduct our analysis as if Plano itself packed the molds.

molds. Together, the two molds weighed 25,000 pounds, and each was packed into its own wooden crate. One mold was much larger than the other—it weighed 18,900 pounds, while other weighed 6,100 pounds. When packing shipping containers, packers use wooden pallets, wooden beams, and other types of dunnage (all types of inexpensive waste materials) to support and distribute the weight of cargo. After the derailment, all that was found in the shipping container was one 43-inch long wooden pallet, which presumably supported, at least in part, the weight of one of the crates. There were remnants of wooden pallets found at the accident site, as well as a wide variety of other debris that could have served as dunnage. Exhibit 281, a photograph taken at the derailment scene, appears to show two pallets that survived the accident, as well as several long wooden boards. It is not clear, however, which shipping container the pallets and wood came from, as the derailment caused multiple containers to break open and spill their contents.

Appellants' theory of the case was that the molds were packed in a way that did not sufficiently distribute their weight in the container. They based this contention on the guidelines set forth in Circular 43-D, a publication of the Association of American Railroads, an industry trade group. Appellants argued that the guidelines in Circular 43-D, which was entered into evidence, should serve as the stand- [—7—] ard of care in this case. Appellants did not claim that the total weight of the molds violated the Circular 43-D guidelines, but rather that the weight was too concentrated. Regarding the concentration of weight in a shipping container, Circular 43-D states that "not more than 25,000 lbs. uniformly distributed in any 10 linear feet can be loaded."

Appellants' argument was presented largely through its expert witness, Dr. Robert Vecchio. Vecchio theorized that the pallet found in the shipping container following the accident was one of two identical 43-inch pallets that were originally used to support the molds, with each pallet supporting one crate. The larger of the two crates weighed 18,900 pounds; spread out over 43 inches, that translates to over 5,000 pounds per linear foot, which is double the amount allowed for in Circular 43-D. Vecchio admitted, however, that a 43-inch pallet would have been sufficient to disburse the weight of the smaller crate.

Vecchio also argued that the crates were not properly secured ("lashed") within the shipping container, which allowed the crates to exert "dynamic amplification"—in other words, bouncing—on the floor of the container. His theory was that the combination of a failure to secure the crates and a failure to distribute the crates' weight properly led to overstressing of the container floor, eventually causing the floor to break. To support his theory, Vecchio noted that no lashing material was found inside of the container or around the train following the derailment. Additionally, he referred to a number of "significant dents" in the wood floor of the container that were found after the derailment. According to Vecchio, these dents were caused by dynamic amplification [—8—] of the crates, which only could have occurred if the crates were not properly lashed.

The parties' experts referred to numerous investigative reports about the derailment at trial. The most important report, on which both appellants and Plano relied heavily and which was introduced into evidence, was produced by a company called Intertek Caleb Brett. Appellants focused on the Intertek report's statement that the crates were placed in the center of the container, arguing that this implied that the weight of the crates was not properly distributed. On the other hand, the Intertek report stated that the crates were secured and lashed, contrary to Vecchio's theory. Another important piece of evidence was a "Testification" produced by the Shanghai Ocean Shipping Tally Company, the company that supervised the loading of Plano's molds into the shipping container. The Testification, like the Intertek report, stated that the cargo was loaded in the middle of the container. However, it also stated that the crates were "packed sound," which could imply that the crates' weight was properly distributed and that the cargo was properly lashed. Finally, a post-derailment email from Joana Feng of the THI Group to World's John Wember stated that "wooden brackets" had been used "to fix the case[s] in order not to move when transmitting." On cross-examination, Vecchio stated that he had not previously seen the Testification or Feng's email, and therefore did not take either into account when formulating his report.

The district court found that appellants had not provided sufficient evidence to prove that the weight of Plano's crates was not distributed properly. Without any direct evidence as to how the container was packed, the court said that it was [—9—] pure speculation for Vecchio to assume that the crates were supported by two 43-inch pallets. Although only one pallet was found in the container after the derailment, the district court noted that a second pallet—which even Vecchio assumed had been present—could have been large enough to support the larger crate. Moreover, the crates may have been supported by other pieces of dunnage. According to the district court, any of these scenarios was equally plausible given that more than enough wood to adequately support the crates was found at the site of the accident.

The district court also found that there was not enough evidence to support appellants' claim that the crates had not been properly lashed. The court criticized Vecchio for disregarding the Intertek report's finding that the crates had been properly secured and lashed, when Vecchio otherwise relied heavily on the report and had said that it "provided the best available information" and that he "had no reason not to believe it." The district court also stated that Vecchio's conclusion was belied by the email from Feng to Wember stating that the crates had been fixed to prevent movement. The district court downplayed the fact that no lashing material had been found at the accident site, stating that it could have been lost or destroyed during the accident, or that investigators may have not even searched for it. The court also rejected Vecchio's theory that the dents in the container's floor were caused by dynamic amplification of the crates. The dents, the court noted, could have preexisted the loading of the crates into the container or could have been created when the crates were loaded or during the violent derailment. [—10—]

Both appellants and Plano also presented a great deal of evidence regarding the cause of the derailment, most of which focused on the condition of the shipping container. Because we ultimately agree with the district court's conclusion that appellants failed to prove that Plano breached Clause 10(2), and therefore do not reach the issue of causation, we provide only a brief summary of this evidence here. In essence, Plano and its experts argued that the container was defective, mostly due to the condition of its welds. Plano's position was that the molds fell through the floor of the shipping container not because they were packed improperly, but rather because the floor of the container was defective and gave way. Appellants, conversely, argued that the welds, and the container as a whole, were sound. The district court agreed with Plano, finding that the shipping container was defective and that "defective welds in the shipping container caused the molds to fall through the bottom of the container and cause the derailment." *Kawasaki Kisen Kaisha, Ltd. v. Plano Molding Co.*, No. 07 C 5675, slip op. at 23 (N.D. Ill. Mar. 6, 2014) ("*Kawasaki II*").

II. Discussion

Appellants' central argument is that the district court clearly erred by finding that appellants failed to meet their burden of proving that Plano breached Clause 10(2), and that this breach caused the Union Pacific derailment. Before turning to this general issue, we address appellants' arguments regarding more specific aspects of the district court's opinion. We apply federal maritime law because jurisdiction exists under 28 U.S.C. § 1333. *See Norfolk S. Ry. Co. v. Kirby*, 543 U.S. 14, 24–25 (2004) (finding bills of lading involving [—11—] overseas shipment of goods to be maritime contracts even where the last leg of the journey was by rail).

First, appellants argue that the district court ignored the guidance of *Daubert v. Merrell Dow Pharmaceuticals*, 509 U.S. 579

(1993), when it assessed the testimony of their expert, Vecchio. Specifically, they claim that it was improper for the district court to find Vecchio's theory less "credible" than the theories presented by Plano's experts. *Daubert*, they argue, precludes a judge acting as a trier of fact from questioning an expert witness's conclusions. Appellants misunderstand a court's role in assessing expert testimony. It is true, as appellants point out, that the *Daubert* Court said a judge's focus when assessing expert testimony "must be solely on principles and methodology, not on the conclusions that they generate." *Id.* at 595. The Court, though, was referring to a judge's analysis, under Federal Rule of Evidence 702, of whether to admit expert testimony[4] at all. *Id.* at 594–95. In making this determination, a judge acts as a "gatekeeper" to ensure that expert testimony is not admitted into evidence unless it is sufficiently reliable. *Dhillon v. Crown Controls Corp.*, 269 F.3d 865, 869 (7th Cir. 2001). The district court here performed this gatekeeping analysis for each expert. In fact, the court did so both before the trial and in its final opinion, after both appellants and Plano once again asked the court to exclude the other side's expert testimony under *Daubert*. Neither party contends that the judge performed these analyses incorrectly. [—12—]

Once an expert's testimony is admitted, it is treated no differently than lay testimony. *See United States v. Christian*, 673 F.3d 702, 712 (7th Cir. 2012) (citing Federal Criminal Pattern Jury Instructions of the Seventh Circuit 3.07); *United States v. Mansoori*, 304 F.3d 635, 654 (7th Cir. 2002) (endorsing a jury instruction stating that "the fact that an expert has given an opinion does not mean that it is binding upon you or that you are obligated to accept the expert's opinion as to the facts."). When expert testimony has been admitted under *Daubert*, the "soundness of the factual underpinnings of the expert's analysis and the correctness of the expert's

conclusions based on that analysis are factual matters to be determined by the trier of fact." *Stollings v. Ryobi Tech., Inc.*, 725 F.3d 753, 765 (7th Cir. 2013) (quoting *Smith v. Ford Motor Co.*, 215 F.3d 713, 718 (7th Cir. 2000)). In a bench trial, once the court has fulfilled its gatekeeping function, it becomes a trier of fact that needs to assess the evidence itself—not just the methodology underlying that evidence. The judge, as trier of fact, was required to play his "essential role as the arbiter of the weight and credibility of expert testimony." *Id.* In concluding that Plano's experts were more credible than Vecchio, the judge properly scrutinized each expert's assumptions, reasoning, and conclusions, as is the duty of the trier of fact.

Next, appellants argue that the district court was wrong to believe that they had made an argument regarding the proper securing and lashing of the molds within the shipping container. Appellants claim that they never made such an argument; rather, they only argued that the weight of the molds was not sufficiently dispersed. Appellants also claim that the district court was incorrect when it stated that "Dr. Vecchio's theory of the accident hinges on the idea that the [—13—] Molds were not lashed down properly in the Container." *Kawasaki II*, No. 07 C 5675, slip op. at 17. If appellants are correct, it is possible that the district court's mistake caused it to wrongly discredit Vecchio's testimony.

But appellants are wrong about their own argument. In their Post-Trial Closing Statement, appellants devoted more than a page to this argument, stating that "the post-derailment investigation did not unearth any evidence" that the molds were secured and that the "'dents' Vecchio found in the plywood floor, however, show the steel molds were not properly secured against vertical movement." To support their lashing argument, they then quoted from Vecchio's testimony, demonstrating that Vecchio's theory indeed assumed that the crates were not lashed. Appellants' complaints about the district court, therefore, are not credible. Even more disturbing is appellants' criticism of the district court for using the word "bouncing" to refer to Vecchio's

---

[4] More precisely, *Daubert* dealt with the standard for admitting expert *scientific* testimony. *Daubert*, 509 U.S. at 582. The *Daubert* standard was later extended to apply to all expert testimony in *Kumho Tire Co., Ltd. v. Carmichael*, 526 U.S. 137, 141 (1999).

testimony about "dynamic amplification." In their closing argument, appellants thrice referred to dynamic amplification as bouncing; in fact, they did not use the correct term, "dynamic amplification," at all.[5] [—14—]

We now turn to the heart of this appeal: whether the district court clearly erred by finding that appellants failed to prove that Plano breached Clause 10(2) of the World Bill of Lading. Appellants challenge both the district court's allocation of the burden of proof and its determination that appellants did not meet their burden. We review de novo a district court's allocation of the burden of proof. *Chi. Prime Packers, Inc. v. Northam Food Trading Co.*, 408 F.3d 894, 898 (7th Cir. 2005). We review a district court's findings of fact under the clearly erroneous standard. Fed. R. Civ. P. 52(a)(6); *United States v. U.S. Gypsum Co.*, 333 U.S. 364, 395 (1948) ("A finding is 'clearly erroneous' when although

---

[5] Appellants also take issue with the district court's statement that it was "assum[ing], without finding, that Plano is subject to Clause 10.2." *Kawasaki II*, No. 07 C 5675, slip op. at 28. Appellants argue that this was a settled issue, and therefore that no assumption was necessary. Though this assumption was in the appellants' favor, and therefore did not impact the outcome below, we think it is worthwhile to provide some clarification on this matter. The appellants contend that, by questioning whether Plano was "subject to" Clause 10(2), the district court contradicted its July 19, 2013 ruling that Plano was bound to the World Bill of Lading. We appreciate the appellants' point, as we think that the district court's discussion here was imprecise. Clause 10(2) has a condition precedent; it [—14—] only applies if the "Carrier receives the goods already packed into containers." At trial, the parties disputed whether this condition had been satisfied. The district court, though, did not decide the issue because it concluded that, even if Clause 10(2) was triggered, Plano had not breached the warranty found in that Clause. As we explain below, this conclusion was sound. At that point in the litigation, it was settled that Plano was *subject* to Clause 10(2) because it was bound as a party to the terms of the World Bill of Lading. Rather, the question was whether the Clause was *applicable* in this case—that is, whether Plano's duty to safely and properly stow the molds was triggered. This is clearly what the district court meant to say. Regardless, neither the misstatement nor the district court's decision not to definitively rule on the matter caused appellants any prejudice.

there is evidence to support it, the reviewing court on the entire evidence is left with the definite and firm conviction that a mistake has been committed.").

Normally, the party claiming breach of a warranty under a maritime contract—here, appellants—bears the burden of proof. *See, e.g., Cent. Oil Co. v. M/V Lamma-Forest*, 821 F.2d 48, 49 (1st Cir. 1987). Appellants argue, however, that in this [—15—] case the burden should fall on Plano to prove that the molds were packed properly because Plano has readier access to knowledge about the facts in question—how the shipping container was actually packed in China. Specifically, appellants point to Plano's contractual relationships with World and THI, either of which could have inquired with its agents—Haixing and Shanghai Ocean Tally—about how the containers were loaded. They also argue that Plano's engineering vice-president has a home in China, and that he should have investigated how the container was actually loaded.

Appellants' argument is based on John Henry Wigmore's rule that "the burden of proving a fact is said to be put on the party who presumably has peculiar means of knowledge enabling him to prove its falsity if it is false." 9 Wigmore, Evidence § 2486, at 275 (3d ed. 1940). The Supreme Court has also endorsed this rule: "the ordinary rule, based on considerations of fairness, does not place the burden upon a litigant of establishing facts peculiarly within the knowledge of his adversary." *Campbell v. United States*, 365 U.S. 85, 96 (1961). Wigmore's "rule" is not mandatory; rather, it is a "policy consideration" to be "applied in certain cases" as "a rule of fairness." *Erving Paper Mills v. Hudson-Sharp Machine Co.*, 332 F.2d 674, 678 (7th Cir. 1964); *see also* Wigmore, *supra*, at 275 ("The truth is that there is not and cannot be any one general solvent for all cases. It is merely a question of policy and fairness based on experience in the different situations.").

Appellants point to two cases in which this maxim was employed. In *Erving Paper Mills*, a products liability case, we said that the manufacturer of a product should bear the bur- [—16—] den of proving that the product was suitable for sale to others in the ordinary course of its business. 332 F.2d at 678. And in *Shanghai Automation Instrument Co., Ltd. v. Kuei*, 194 F. Supp. 2d 995, 1004 (N.D. Cal. 2001), a district court in California held that the burden of proof should shift to the defendants where the plaintiff alleged that certain funds received by the defendants were improperly converted for personal use. The defendants, the court noted, had sole possession of information regarding how the funds were spent. We found a number of other cases in which this rule was employed. For example, in *Shatterproof Glass Corp. v. Libbey-Owens-Ford Co.*, the Sixth Circuit shifted the burden of proof to the defendant, which had peculiar knowledge of the royalty rates it had paid to various patent holders. 482 F.2d 317, 324 (6th Cir. 1973). And in *PepsiCo, Inc. v. Redmond*, a trade secrets case brought by Pepsi against a former employee who had joined a rival corporation, the district court granted Pepsi's requested injunction barring Redmond from divulging trade secrets. 1996 WL 3965, at *1 (N.D. Ill. Jan. 2, 1996). The court forgave Pepsi's inability to prove what job duties Redmond would have at his new job, shifting the burden to Redmond on this issue because the details of his job duties were peculiarly within his and his new employer's knowledge. *Id.* at *21. These cases are representative of the others that we examined.

For a number of reasons, we decline to apply this type of burden shifting in this case. First, the information at issue is not "peculiarly within the knowledge" of Plano. *Campbell*, 365 U.S. at 96. In each of the above-cited cases where the burden of proof was shifted, the adversary itself had peculiar knowledge of the information at issue. Here, in contrast, not only does Plano lack "peculiar" (i.e., "exclusive") [—17—] knowledge of the information at issue, it lacks any knowledge whatsoever—Plano simply has no information about how the shipping container was actually loaded. Appellants argue that Plano has a closer relationship with the foreign companies that possess this knowledge, and therefore that Plano has easier access to that information. Even if that is true, those companies are separate entities from Plano, and the mere fact that Plano may have a closer relationship with them does not bring this information peculiarly within *Plano's* knowledge. Moreover, appellants have not demonstrated that Plano would actually be able to acquire the information at issue. The mere fact that Plano has, in the past, had contractual relationships with the foreign companies that possess the relevant information does not mean that Plano currently has unfettered access to that information. It is similarly irrelevant that a Plano vice-president has a personal home in the country where those companies are based. China is vast (over 9.5 million square kilometers) and has the largest population on earth; appellants fails to explain how Plano's vice-president would have easy access to the information at issue. *See* Central Intelligence Agency, The World Factbook: China (2014), *available at* https://www.cia.gov/library/publications/the-world-factbook/geos/ch.html (last visited Mar. 3, 2015). In sum, fairness does not dictate that the burden of proof on this issue be shifted to a party with no actual knowledge of the relevant information and, it seems, no ready way to acquire it.

The district court, therefore, properly held appellants to the burden of proving by a preponderance of the evidence that Plano breached the warranty in Clause 10(2). That burden required appellants to prove it was more likely than not [—18—] that Plano breached the warranty. *See Bunge Corp. v. Carlisle*, 227 F.3d 934, 937 (7th Cir. 2000). The district court did not clearly err by finding that appellants failed to meet this burden.[6]

Appellants presented no evidence of how the molds were *actually* packed into the shipping container. The fact that only one relatively small pallet was found in the container after the crash means little—most of the container's contents likely fell out during

---

[6] Appellants do not appeal the district court's finding regarding how the molds were lashed and secured within the container; rather, they claim that they never made an argument about lashing in the first place. Therefore, we not need review that aspect of the district court's opinion.

the derailment. As the district court noted, large amounts of wood—and even some complete pallets—were found near the derailment site, any of which could have come from the container in question. Appellants argue that it was "wild speculation" for the district court to suggest that the wood found at the crash site may have supported Plano's molds. But appellants overlook the fact that *they* had the burden of proving that the crates were improperly supported. Because they had no direct evidence of how the container was loaded, appellants had to resort to circumstantial evidence—the fact that only one small pallet was found in the container post-derailment. Appellants argued that an inference should be made from this discovery that the pallet in the container was the only one used to support the molds, or that there were at most two pallets of identical size. That inference was weakened by the fact that there was ample wood found at the crash site that could have served as support for the molds. The district court did not find that these scraps had supported the molds. Rather, it found that the [—19—] existence of the wood undermined appellants' argument that the molds had been improperly supported. Moreover, Vecchio's assumption that the molds were supported by two identical and insufficiently supportive pallets was based on pure speculation. The missing pallet (or pallets) could just as easily have been much larger, or, conversely, nonexistent; there was simply no way to know based on what was found in the container post-derailment. Appellants repeatedly complain that Plano presented no evidence to suggest that the molds were properly packed. As the defendant, though, Plano did not have to prove anything.

Appellants have not produced enough evidence to prove that Plano breached the warranty found in Clause 10(2). Their final argument, however, is that they should not have to affirmatively prove breach, but rather that breach should be presumed based on the circumstances of this case. They argue, "[c]arriers receiving a sealed container cannot possibly [prove how the container was loaded]—it is a ridiculous burden to carry, hence the warranty. When 'K' Line proved

there was no evidence anywhere of proper weight dispersing material for the larger crate, and without proper dispersal the stress was excessive, its *prima facie* case was made." Reply Br. 17. Appellants are wrong about the purpose of the warranty—it exists to create a contractual duty, not to shift the burden of proof. Their general contention, though, is that the nature of an accident should provide a presumption of breach because, absent the presumption, carriers will rarely be able to provide direct evidence of breach, rendering the warranty a nullity. This argument is underdeveloped, and appellants provide no case law to support this approach, but we interpret it to be an attempt to import the doctrine of res ipsa loquitur into the realm of contract law. [—20—]

Aside from whether the res ipsa loquitur doctrine can ever apply in a breach of contract case, it is clear that the doctrine should not apply in this case. We are sympathetic to appellants' argument that it will often be exceedingly difficult for a carrier to affirmatively prove that a shipping container was improperly packed when a derailment—precisely the type of injury a warranty of proper stowage is intended to prevent—has led to the destruction of the most probative evidence. This problem, however, was known to the parties when they agreed to be bound by the World Bill of Lading. With that problem in mind, appellants could have insisted upon a provision in the Bill of Lading stating that, in a case such as this, where a derailment is caused by a merchant's goods breaking through the floor of a shipping container, there would be a presumption that the container was mispacked.[7] As the Bill of

---

[7] Clause 10(5) of the World Bill states: "Merchant shall inspect containers before stuffing them and the use of the containers shall be *prima facie* evidence of their being sound and suitable for use." Therefore, it is evident that the parties knew how to incorporate evidentiary presumptions into the Bill of Lading. The failure to do so explicitly in Clause 10(2) demonstrates that the parties did not wish to create such a presumption.

The presumption included in Clause 10(5), we note, does not impact our analysis of whether Plano breached its duty under Clause 10(2). As the district court correctly stated, "[t]he question of

Lading was actually written, however, there is no such presumption, and a carrier must affirmatively prove breach and causation. We decline to effectively rewrite the terms of the Bill of Lading by presuming breach. [—21—]

Because we agree with the district court's conclusion that appellants did not meet their burden of proving that Plano breached Clause 10(2), we do not need to review its findings that the shipping container was defective and that those defects caused the molds to fall through the container floor, ultimately causing the derailment. Plano had no obligation to explain why the accident occurred. Once the district court found that appellants had not met their burden of proving that Plano had breached Clause 10(2), the actual cause of the accident became legally irrelevant.[8] Therefore, we agree with the district court that Plano is not liable to appellants for damages stemming from the derailment.

III. Conclusion

We AFFIRM the judgment of the district court.

---

whether the stowage and seals were safe and proper is a different question than whether the container was sound and suitable." *Kawasaki II*, No. 07 C 5675, slip op. at 27–28.

[8] The district court's finding regarding the cause of the accident, we note, was not in itself sufficient to relieve Plano of liability. To prevail, appellants had to prove, in addition to breach, that Plano's breach caused the derailment. The district court found that the defective state of the shipping container was a but-for cause of the accident. However, the fact that a container's defective state was a but-for cause of a derailment does not mean that a merchant's improper stowage of goods was not *also* a but-for cause. Under those circumstances, the merchant could conceivably be liable because its breach was a cause (though not the only cause) of damage.

United States Court of Appeals
for the Seventh Circuit

No. 14-1825

LU JUNHONG
VS.
BOEING CO.

Appeals from the United States District Court for the
Northern District of Illinois, Eastern Division

Decided: July 8, 2015

Citation: 792 F.3d 805, 3 Adm. R. 484 (7th Cir. 2015).

Before **WOOD**, Chief Judge, and **CUDAHY**, and
EASTERBROOK, Circuit Judges.

[—1—] EASTERBROOK, Circuit Judge:

On July 6, 2013, a Boeing 777 hit the seawall that separates the ocean from the end of a runway at San Francisco International Airport. The plane's tail broke off, 49 persons sustained serious injuries, and three of the passengers died, though the other 255 passengers and crew aboard suffered only minor or no injuries. The [—2—] flight, operated by Asiana Airlines, had crossed the Pacific Ocean from Seoul, Korea. The National Transportation Safety Board concluded that the principal cause of the accident was pilot error: the pilots approached too low and too slow, and by the time they attempted to add power and execute a missed approach, it was too late. Only three seconds remained until the impact, the plane was about 90 feet above the ground, and the "airplane did not have the performance capability to accomplish a go-around." *Aircraft Accident Report: Descent Below Visual Glidepath and Impact with Seawall, Asiana Airlines Flight 214* (NTSB June 24, 2014) at 126. The Board believed that the pilots would have had to act eight or nine seconds earlier (a total of 11 or 12 seconds before reaching the seawall) to avoid hitting it. *Id.* at 84–85.

Suits brought in federal courts in California, and some other district courts, were consolidated by the Panel on Multidistrict Litigation in the Northern District of California under 28 U.S.C. §1407(a). Some passengers filed suit against Boeing in state courts of Illinois, contending that the plane's autothrottle, autopilot, and low-airspeed-warning systems contributed to the pilots' errors. Boeing removed these suits to federal court, asserting two sources of jurisdiction: admiralty, plus federal officials' right to have claims against them resolved by federal courts. 28 U.S.C. §§ 1333, 1442. The Panel on Multidistrict Litigation then decided that these suits, too, should be transferred to California to participate in the consolidated pretrial proceedings. But before receiving the Panel's formal directions to transfer the suits to California, the district court remanded them for lack of subject-matter jurisdiction. 2013 U.S. Dist. LEXIS 175699 (N.D. Ill. Dec. 16, 2013), reconsideration denied, 2014 U.S. Dist. LEXIS 50210 (N.D. Ill. Apr. 11, 2014). The court concluded that Boeing did [—3—] not act as a federal officer for the purpose of §1442 and that the tort occurred on land, when the plane hit the seawall, rather than over navigable water. Boeing appealed, as it is entitled to do: removal under §1442 is an exception to 28 U.S.C. §1447(d), which makes most remands non-reviewable. We stayed the remand orders.

I

First in line is the question whether Boeing was entitled to remove under §1442(a)(1), which offers a federal forum to "[t]he United States or any agency thereof or any officer (or any person acting under that officer) of the United States or of any agency thereof, in an official or individual capacity, for or relating to any act under color of such office". Boeing obviously is not the United States, a federal agency, or a federal officer, but it maintains that it is a "person acting under [a federal] officer" because federal regulations require it to assess and certify the airworthiness of its planes.

Boeing contends that it is "acting under" the Federal Aviation Administration because "the FAA has granted Boeing authority to use FAA-approved procedures to conduct analysis and testing required for the issuance of type, production, and airworthiness certifications for aircraft under Federal Aviation Regulations. In carrying out those functions,

Boeing is subject to FAA control, and it acts as a representative of the FAA Administrator." Instead of sending a cadre of inspectors to check whether every aircraft design meets every particular of every federal rule and policy, the FAA allows Boeing (and other firms) to do some of the checking itself. In particular, Boeing maintains, FAA Order 8100.9A authorizes and requires it to analyze the adequacy [—4—] of its autopilot and autothrottle systems and certify that they meet the regulatory requirements of 14 C.F.R. §25.1309.

It would be linguistically possible to call self-certification a form of "acting under" the FAA. Yet all businesses must ensure that they comply with statutes and regulations. Sometimes they use the information internally, to decide whether they must make changes. Sometimes they must certify compliance. For example, Boeing's brief on this appeal closes with three certifications: (1) that the brief was properly filed with the court and served on opposing counsel; (2) that the portions subject to a length limit contain 11,882 words and that it meets the typeface requirements of Fed. R. App. P. 32; and (3) that all of the materials required by Seventh Circuit Rule 30 have been included in the appendix. Would Boeing's lawyers say that these certifications make Boeing (or its law firm) persons "acting under" the judiciary? Yet certifications just demonstrate a person's awareness of the governing requirements and evince a belief in compliance. Judges often call lawyers "officers of the court," but no one should think that this means that a lawyer can use §1442 to remove a state-law malpractice suit to federal court. A figure of speech does not make someone a federal officer or a person "acting under" one. *See Howard v. St. Germain*, 599 F.3d 455 (5th Cir. 2010) (treating a lawyer's invocation of §1442 as sanctionably frivolous).

This analysis implies that the right question is whether being subject to governmental requirements is enough to make a person one "acting under" the author of those regulations, for the purpose of §1442. And we know from *Watson v. Philip Morris Cos.*, 551 U.S. 142 (2007), that being

regulated, even when a federal agency "directs, supervises, and moni- [—5—] tors a company's activities in considerable detail" (*id.* at 145), is not enough to make a private firm a person "acting under" a federal agency.

Watson sued a cigarette manufacturer, contending that it had cleverly manipulated the testing of its products to show low levels of tar and nicotine. The manufacturer contended that, to the contrary, it had tested exactly as federal officials required and that any deviation from those protocols was forbidden. As an entity merely following orders, the manufacturer asserted, it should be treated the same as the agency that issued the orders. The Court observed that regulation is ubiquitous, and much regulation can be called complex; if following federal rules allowed litigation in federal court, then all food and drug suits, and many others too, would be removable. The Court thought that neither the language nor the history of §1442 justified reading it to cover the activities of regulated businesses. Instead, the Court concluded, persons "acting under" federal officials are those who provide aid in law enforcement, such as a local police officer who accompanies a federal agent on a drug raid and acts under the federal agent's direction.

This is where Boeing sees its opening. It does not *just* follow regulations; it also certifies compliance with them and in the process reduces the size of the federal bureaucracy. An employee of the FAA who certified the airworthiness of Boeing's autopilot and autothrottle systems would be covered by §1442. Since the FAA has conscripted the regulated company's staff to perform those functions, Boeing maintains, it too comes within §1442.

The problem with this argument is the one we stated at the outset. *Every* regulated firm must use its own staff to [—6—] learn whether it has satisfied federal regulations. The staff of an electric utility running a coal-fired generation station must ensure that the equipment (much of it covered by detailed regulations) meets the EPA's specifications (and those of the host state) and is in working order. The staff also must monitor the stack gasses to ensure that the plant does not emit too much sulfur dioxide or particulate matter. It is a detail whether the firm sends the EPA a report (a "self-certification") of compliance, or instead sends reports only when it finds non-compliance, or sends no reports at all and waits for inspectors to appear. Likewise with safety apparatus (and safety inspections) under the Occupational Safety and Health Act and hundreds of other federal statutes. We do not see any correlation between the required certifications and acting-under status. The Supreme Court in *Watson* gave, as one example of someone obviously *not* "acting under" a federal agency, a person filing a tax return. 551 U.S. at 152. Yet the taxpayer must interpret and apply a complex statute and voluminous regulations, and the end of every return is a certification that this has been done and all income (and deductions) reported honestly. That process of self-reporting enables the IRS to have a smaller workforce, just as Boeing's procedures cut the FAA's payroll, but if taxpayers (and lawyers who certify that their briefs comply with rules) are not covered by §1442, neither is Boeing.

The list of people who have to certify things is exceedingly long. For example, every employer with a federal contract must certify that it has paid workers the prevailing wage. *See* 29 C.F.R. §§ 3.3, 3.4; *United States v. Clark*, No. 14-1251 (7th Cir. May 28, 2015). We doubt that the Justices would see a dispositive difference between certified compliance and ordinary compliance. Indeed, *Watson* rejected an argument [—7—] by the cigarette maker that a federal agency hadn't "just" required compliance with regulations but also had "delegated authority" to the manufacturer to determine compliance with those regulations. The Court thought that inadequate to make the manufacturer a person "acting under" the agency. 551 U.S. at 154–57.

Boeing replies that the relation between cigarette manufacturers and the Federal Trade Commission (the agency that regulated testing) was *faux* delegation, while its relation with the FAA is *real* delegation. Boeing points to 49 U.S.C. §44702(d)(1), which permits the FAA to conserve its resources by transferring some checking and certification functions to manufacturers, and the FAA used that power in Order 8100.9A. Note, however, that this is still a power to certify *compliance*, not a power to design the rules for airworthiness. The FAA permits Boeing to make changes to its gear after finding that the equipment as modified meets the FAA's standards; it does not permit Boeing to use gear that meets Boeing's self-adopted criteria.

When discussing the possibility that delegation might create "acting under" status, the Court mentioned rule making rather than rule compliance as the key ingredient, 551 U.S. at 157, and the FAA's order does not allow Boeing to change substantive rules. That some of the FAA's own rules are general—for example, §25.1309(b) says that "airplane systems and associated components, considered separately and in relation to other systems, must be designed so that ... [t]he occurrence of any failure condition which would prevent the continued safe flight and landing of the airplane is extremely improbable"—does not confer on Boeing or other [—8—] manufacturers a power to make rules, as opposed to interpret and apply them as best it can.

If the FAA gave Boeing a power to issue a *conclusive* certification of compliance, even though not to establish substantive standards, the situation would come closer to what *Watson* suggested might suffice. As far as we can see, however, nothing that Boeing says is conclusive in the sense that a court must treat its self-certification as establishing that its flight-control systems *do* meet all federal rules. If the FAA itself were to reach that conclusion, a court could not gainsay the decision in a tort suit or under the Administrative Procedure Act (unless, perhaps, the FAA's decision were arbitrary and capricious). Boeing's self-certification does not have that effect, however; it does not prevent either a court or the FAA itself from taking a fresh look and reaching a contrary conclusion.

Magnin v. Teledyne Continental Motors, 91 F.3d 1424, 1428 (11th Cir. 1996), supports Boeing's position. Boeing does not identify, however, any post-*Watson* decision reaching a similar conclusion, for the FAA or any other agency that has delegated, not the power to make rules, but the power to certify compliance with them. We think that *Magnin* is inconsistent with *Watson* and cannot be considered authoritative. So we agree with the district court that §1442 does not support removal.

II

Plaintiffs maintain that, once we reach this conclusion, the appeal is done. That's because 28 U.S.C. §1447(d) reads: "An order remanding a case to the State court from which it was removed is not reviewable on appeal or otherwise, ex- [—9—] cept that an order remanding a case to the State court from which it was removed pursuant to section 1442 or 1443 of this title shall be reviewable by appeal or otherwise." Boeing's argument that §1442 supplies jurisdiction having been rejected, plaintiffs contend, there is nothing more for a court of appeals to do, for a district court's conclusion that federal jurisdiction does not exist is unreviewable. *See, e.g., Kircher v. Putnam Funds Trust*, 547 U.S. 633 (2006); *Gravitt v. Southwestern Bell Telephone Co.*, 430 U.S. 723 (1977).

Boeing offers a different take on the scope of federal jurisdiction. It observes that when a suit is "removed pursuant to section 1442" (as this was) the district court's "order" of remand is reviewable on appeal. To say that a district court's "order" is reviewable is to allow appellate review of the *whole* order, not just of particular issues or reasons. So *Yamaha Motor Corp., U.S.A. v. Calhoun*, 516 U.S. 199, 205 (1996), holds with respect to 28 U.S.C. §1292(b), which permits a court of appeals to review an interlocutory order if the district court certifies that particular issues meet the statutory requirements. The Court held that although the district judge must find that important issues are presented and that their resolution could advance the case's disposition, once the appeal has been accepted the court of appeals reviews the "order" rather than just the issues. *See also Edwardsville National Bank & Trust Co. v. Marion Laboratories, Inc.*, 808 F.2d 648, 650 (7th Cir.

1987) (when a statute provides appellate jurisdiction over an order, "the thing under review is the order", and the court of appeals is not limited to reviewing particular "questions" underlying the "order"). Boeing maintains that §1447(d) should be understood the same way. [—10—]

And so we *have* understood the relation between §1447(d) and an appeal that is an exception to its limit on review of remands. In *Brill v. Countrywide Home Loans, Inc.*, 427 F.3d 446 (7th Cir. 2005), a district court remanded a class action that had been removed by a defendant that invoked the Class Action Fairness Act. The judge held that that Act did not authorize the removal and that the case was otherwise not within the scope of federal jurisdiction, and remanded. The Class Action Fairness Act authorizes appellate review of remands of cases that had been removed under its auspices. A court of appeals may accept an appeal of "an order of a district court" that has remanded after finding that the Act does not permit removal. 28 U.S.C. §1453(c)(1). After discussing the propriety of removal under the Act, we went on to decide that the suit *also* came within federal-question jurisdiction. That conclusion was consistent with §1447(d), *Brill* held, because, once the district court's "order" was before the court of appeals, all of the reasons the district court gave in support of that order were reviewable. 427 F.3d at 451–52. *Brill* relied on *Yamaha Motor* for this conclusion.

Section 1447(d) itself authorizes review of the remand order, because the case was removed (in part) pursuant to §1442. *Brill* establishes that once an appeal of a remand "order" has been authorized by statute, the court of appeals may consider all of the legal issues entailed in the decision to remand.

Once again another court of appeals has come to a contrary conclusion. *Jacks v. Meridian Resource Co.*, 701 F.3d 1224, 1229 (8th Cir. 2012), holds that, even when a statute authorizes review of a remand order, only the issue behind the exception to §1447(d) is reviewable; consideration of other is- [—11—] sues is blocked by §1447(d), the court stated. For this proposition, it cited—

nothing. *Jacks* did not discuss the significance of the statutory reference to review of an "order." It did not mention *Yamaha Motor.* It did not mention *Brill.* And the omissions are understandable. The court pointed out, 701 F.3d at 1228, that neither side had cited authority or made a coherent argument. *Jacks* unknowingly created a conflict with *Brill.* The leading treatise supports *Brill's* approach:

> Review should ... be extended to all possible grounds for removal underlying the order. Once an appeal is taken there is very little to be gained by limiting review; the only plausible concern is that an expanded scope of review will encourage defendants to rely on strained arguments under [§1442 or] §1443 in an effort to support appeal on other grounds. Sufficient sanctions are available to deter frivolous removal arguments that this fear should be put aside against the sorry possibility that experience will give it color.

Edward H. Cooper, 15A *Wright & Miller Federal Practice & Procedure* §3914.11 (2014 rev.) (citations omitted).

We recognize that *Thermtron Products, Inc. v. Hermansdorfer*, 423 U.S. 336 (1976), and a few other decisions that went out of their way to find exceptions to §1447(d), are not admired these days at the Supreme Court. The holding of *Thermtron*—that a case remanded for reasons outside the scope of §1447(c) can be reviewed on appeal despite §1447(d)—is not supported by the text of §1447(d) and does not fit comfortably with the current Justices' approach to statutory interpretation. Decisions such as *Kircher*, which direct courts of appeals not to go behind a judge's stated reason for a remand, even if it seems clear that some other reason is responsible (or that the judge used words imprecise- [—12—] ly), show the Court's restiveness with the latitude *Thermtron* took with the statutory language. *See also Powerex Corp. v. Reliant Energy Services, Inc.*, 551 U.S. 224, 229–30 (2007) (strongly suggesting that *Thermtron* was wrongly decided); *Carlsbad Technology, Inc. v. HIF Bio, Inc.*, 556 U.S. 635, 641–42, 642–43 (2009) (concurring opinions disparaging *Thermtron*).

Our application of *Yamaha Motor* and *Brill* to the word "order" in §1447(d) does not rely on *Thermtron's* approach but is entirely textual. The Court remarked in *Kircher*, 547 U.S. at 641 n.8, that Congress has on occasion made the rule of §1447(d) inapplicable to particular "orders"—and for this the Court cited, among other statutes, §1447(d) itself. We take both Congress and *Kircher* at their word in saying that, if appellate review of an "order" has been authorized, that means review of the "order." Not particular reasons *for* an order, but the order itself.

This is not a matter of pendent appellate jurisdiction here any more than in *Yamaha Motor.* There is only one order and only one appellant, while pendent appellate jurisdiction involves an extra order, an extra appellant, or both. *See Swint v. Chambers County Commission*, 514 U.S. 35 (1995); *Clinton v. Jones*, 520 U.S. 681, 707 n.41 (1997); *Allman v. Smith*, No. 14-1792 (7th Cir. June 24, 2015), slip op. 3–4. If one "order" is the thing appealed, as *Yamaha Motor* and *Brill* concluded, nothing is "pendent" when considering all of the issues that led to the order. This is the same as the proposition that an appeal from a district court's order denying a Rule 59 motion brings up the whole judgment, without the need for a separate appeal of the original judgment. *See, e.g., Foman v. Davis*, 371 U.S. 178, 181 (1962). To appeal an "order" is to pre- [—13—] sent all issues that led to that order, without entailing any element of "pendent" jurisdiction.

If we go beyond the text of §1447(d) to the reasons that led to its enactment, we reach the same conclusion. The Supreme Court has said that §1447(d) was enacted to prevent appellate delay in determining where litigation will occur. *See, e.g., Kircher*, 547 U.S. at 640; *United States v. Rice*, 327 U.S. 742, 751 (1946). Since the suit must be litigated somewhere, it is usually best to get on with the main event. *See also, e.g., Van Cauwenberghe v. Biard*, 486 U.S. 517 (1988). But once Congress has authorized appellate review of a remand order—as it has authorized review of suits removed on the authority of §1442—a court of appeals has been authorized to take the time necessary to determine the right forum. The marginal delay from adding an extra issue to a case where the time for briefing, argument, and decision has already been accepted is likely to be small.

Some litigants may cite §1442 or §1443 in a notice of removal when all they really want is a hook to allow appeal of some different subject. But a frivolous removal leads to sanctions, potentially including fee-shifting, *see* 28 U.S.C. §1447(c), and after today it would be frivolous for Boeing or a similarly-situated defendant to invoke §1442 as a basis of removal. *See Martin v. Franklin Capital Corp.*, 546 U.S. 132 (2005); Fed. R. App. P. 38. What's more, a court may resolve frivolous interlocutory appeals summarily. *See Abney v. United States*, 431 U.S. 651, 662 n.8 (1977). A district judge may, after certifying that an interlocutory appeal is frivolous, proceed with the litigation (including a remand), *see Apostol v. Gallion*, 870 F.2d 1335 (7th Cir. 1989), and if the appeal is [—14—] frivolous the court of appeals will deny a motion for a stay, so the case can continue without delay.

III

The relation between aviation accidents and the admiralty jurisdiction has been fraught ever since *Executive Jet Aviation, Inc. v. Cleveland*, 409 U.S. 249 (1972), modified the former situs requirement and asked, not where a wreck ended up (land or water), but whether the events leading to the accident have enough connection to maritime activity. A plane had taken off from an airport adjoining Lake Erie, collided with a flock of gulls that gathered at the garbage dump off the end of the runway, settled back to earth in the heap of garbage, and was carried by its inertia into the lake, where it sank. The Justices thought that this had nothing to do with maritime affairs, even though the gulls may have made their living eating fish (in addition to refuse), and held the admiralty jurisdiction unavailable.

But the approach articulated in *Executive Jet* has caused problems. The price of throwing out one case that did not seem connected to maritime commerce was to unsettle the rules for many other cases with stronger connections. *Sisson v. Ruby*, 497 U.S. 358 (1990), suggested that the Justices had begun to rue the *Executive Jet* decision, and though it was not overruled the Court did hold that damage caused by a fire in the washer/dryer of a yacht tied up at a dock was within the admiralty jurisdiction. A few years later, the Court responded to the Great Chicago Flood—a hole in the bottom of the Chicago River introduced water to tunnels that carried it to basements throughout the Loop, causing injury inland—by holding that this event, too, was within the admiralty jurisdiction because the cause was maritime. *Jerome B. Grubart,* [—15—] *Inc. v. Great Lakes Dredge & Dock Co.*, 513 U.S. 527 (1995). Again the result of *Executive Jet* survived, though the applicable legal standard changed.

The parties and the district court read the interaction of these decisions (and there are others that need not be mentioned) in three ways. Plaintiffs maintain that aviation accidents are outside the admiralty jurisdiction (unless perhaps a flying boat or float plane is involved); as fallbacks they contend that when the injury occurs on land there cannot be admiralty jurisdiction and that in any event a defendant cannot remove under the admiralty jurisdiction. Boeing contends that admiralty jurisdiction is available when an accident has a maritime cause, which Boeing understands to mean a cause that occurred while the plane was over navigable waters. The district court did not accept any of these approaches. Instead it held that admiralty jurisdiction is available only when an accident becomes inevitable while the plane is over water.

We start with the inevitability standard, which as far as we can tell lacks a provenance in the Supreme Court's decisions or in any appellate opinion. And it has the further problem of not supporting the judgment, because the choice between "cause" (Boeing's argument) and "inevitable cause" (the district court's holding) cannot affect the outcome.

As the district judge saw things, until the crash the pilots had only to rev the engines, pull up on the yoke, and execute a missed approach. Their failure to do this caused the accident, but hitting the seawall never became inevitable over water. When Boeing asked the district judge to reconsider, contending that the record did not support the judge's understanding of the facts, the judge replied that the record did [—16—] not show beyond all doubt that the plane was doomed at any moment while it was over navigable water.

Both the district judge's opinion and his order denying reconsideration were issued before the NTSB released its report, which concluded that by 10 seconds before impact a collision *was* certain; a 777 aircraft lacks the ability to accelerate and climb fast enough, no matter what the pilots did in the final 10 seconds. This means that, while the plane was over San Francisco Bay (part of the Pacific Ocean), an accident became inevitable. And the plaintiffs' own theory of liability pins a portion of the blame on Boeing because, about 4.5 nautical miles from the seawall, the autothrottle system disengaged—apparently without the pilots recognizing what had happened—and caused the plane to descend faster than the pilots appreciated. *NTSB Report* at 79–84.

The autothrottle system did exactly what it had been programmed to do. We have nothing to say about whether it should have been programmed differently, whether its design played a role in the accident, or whether Boeing should have done more to educate airlines (and their pilots) about how it would react when pilots issued the commands that Asiana's pilots did on the descent into San Francisco. But, if Boeing is liable at all, it must be because something about how this system was designed or explained created an unacceptable risk of an accident—and the system's performance (including the interaction between pilots and the automation design) occurred before the plane hit the seawall.

The district judge may have thought that federal jurisdiction depends on a high degree of certainty that jurisdictional facts exist.

That seems to be the point of an "inevitability" approach, coupled with insistence on proof that relevant [—17—] facts and inferences be established beyond dispute. Yet the rules are otherwise. Jurisdictional allegations control unless it is legally impossible for them to be true (or to have the asserted consequences). *See St. Paul Mercury Indemnity Co. v. Red Cab Co.*, 303 U.S. 283, 289 (1938) (asking whether it "appears to a legal certainty" that the plaintiff cannot satisfy a jurisdictional requirement). That's equally true of a defendant's allegations in support of removal. *See Dart Cherokee Basin Operating Co. v. Owens*, 135 S. Ct. 547, 553–54 (2014). Given the NTSB's findings, it is possible for Boeing to show that this accident was caused by, or became inevitable because of, events that occurred over navigable water.

Is that sufficient? *Grubart* says that admiralty jurisdiction is available when an "injury suffered on land was caused by a vessel on navigable water", if the cause bears a "substantial relationship to traditional maritime activity." 513 U.S. at 534 (internal quotation marks omitted). This plane crossed the Pacific Ocean, a traditional maritime activity, and the cause of the accident likely occurred over the water. But an airplane is not a "vessel" and it was "over" rather than "on" the water. Does that make a difference?

Not functionally. An airplane, just like an ocean-going vessel, moves passengers and freight from one continent to another. It crosses swaths of the high seas that are outside of any nation's territory, and parts of the seas adjacent to the United States but outside any state's territory. It is a traditional, and important, function of admiralty law to supply a forum and a set of rules for accidents in international commerce. And *Executive Jet* itself said as much, though with a hedge, in remarking that a trans-ocean flight "might be thought to bear a significant relationship to traditional mari- [—18—] time activity because it would be performing a function traditionally performed by water-borne vessels". 409 U.S. at 271.

Before the Wright Brothers, admiralty jurisdiction necessarily was limited to vessels on navigable waters. Perhaps the invention of the submarine (under rather than on the water) was its first logical extension. When aircraft came along, courts had a lot of difficulty classifying them for many purposes. See Arthur R. Miller, 14AA *Wright & Miller Federal Practice & Procedure* §3679 (2014 rev.). But just as judges have not doubted that Congress can establish an air force even though the Constitution mentions only an army and a navy, so judges have concluded that airplanes over navigable waters should be treated the same as vessels—when a connection to maritime activity exists, as it didn't in *Executive Jet*.

Executive Jet treated it as settled that airplanes are within the scope of the Death on the High Seas Act, 46 U.S.C. §30302, which brings within the admiralty jurisdiction any death that is "caused by wrongful act, neglect, or default occurring on the high seas" more than three nautical miles from shore. 409 U.S. at 263–64. *Offshore Logistics, Inc. v. Tallentire*, 477 U.S. 207 (1986), later applied that statute when a helicopter went down in the ocean. If accidents that occur because of a cause *over* the water are treated as *on* the water for the purpose of this statute, it is hard to see any stopping point—provided that the accident meets the functional requirements articulated in *Grubart*. For 28 U.S.C. §1333(1), which creates admiralty jurisdiction, does not mention vessels or demand that the cause or injury be "on" the water. It says only that district courts have jurisdiction of: "Any civil case of admiralty or maritime jurisdiction, saving to suitors in all cases all other remedies to which they are otherwise [—19—] entitled." This is close to circular. District courts have admiralty jurisdiction in "[a]ny civil case of admiralty or maritime jurisdiction". That leaves only the *Grubart* standard, which as we have said is satisfied functionally.

True, we have in this litigation an accident apparently caused by events over water, but producing injury on land, and there's no tort without injury. Yet neither §1333(1) nor §30302 requires the whole tort to occur on the water. Section 30302 speaks of a *cause* on the water (or, after *Offshore Logistics*, over the

water), and so does *Grubart*—for even if admiralty did not initially cover water-based causes of injury on land, it has done so ever since the Extension of Admiralty Jurisdiction Act, 46 U.S.C. §30101, on which *Grubart* relied to bring harm from the flooding of Chicago's basements within admiralty jurisdiction.

We are not saying that the Death on the High Seas Act applies to these cases. The plaintiffs do not rely on it. Section 30307(c) creates an exception to the Act for deaths that occur within 12 nautical miles of shore. Nor are we saying that a flight scheduled to take off and land within the United States drifts in and out of admiralty as it crosses lakes and rivers along the way. The Justices remarked in *Executive Jet* that for "flights within the continental United States, which are principally over land, the fact that an aircraft happens to fall in navigable waters, rather than on land, is wholly fortuitous." 409 U.S. at 266. That opinion wrapped up this way: "we hold that, in the absence of legislation to the contrary, there is no federal admiralty jurisdiction over aviation tort claims arising from flights by land-based aircraft between points within the continental United States." *Id.* at 274. [—20—]

But Asiana 214 was a trans-ocean flight, a substitute for an ocean-going vessel—as flights from the contiguous United States to and from Alaska, Hawaii, and overseas territories also would be—and thus within the scope of *Executive Jet*'s observation that this situation "might be thought to bear a significant relationship to a traditional maritime activity". *Id.* at 271. The Supreme Court's holding in *Offshore Logistics* that an accident caused by problems in airplanes *above* water should be treated, for the purpose of §30302, the same as an accident caused *on* the water carries the implication that the general admiralty jurisdiction of 28 U.S.C. §1333(1) also includes accidents caused by problems that occur in trans-ocean commerce. Admiralty then supplies a uniform law for a case that otherwise might cause choice-of-law headaches.

Most appellate decisions on this subject since *Executive Jet* agree. *See Miller v. United States*, 725 F.2d 1311, 1315 (11th Cir. 1984) (flight from Bahamas to Florida is within admiralty jurisdiction); *Williams v. United States*, 711 F.2d 893, 896 (9th Cir. 1983) (flight from California to Hawaii is within admiralty jurisdiction); *Roberts v. United States*, 498 F.2d 520, 524 (9th Cir. 1974) (flight from California to Vietnam is within admiralty jurisdiction). The one exception, *United States Aviation Underwriters, Inc. v. Pilatus Business Aircraft, Ltd.*, 582 F.3d 1131 (10th Cir. 2009) (flight between Japan and Russia), stressed that the flight was not commercial; maybe the Tenth Circuit would find admiralty jurisdiction for commercial aviation such as Asiana 214. It is enough for us to say that we accept the majority position.

Plaintiffs tell us that, even if the events come within §1333(1), Boeing still was not allowed to remove the suits under 28 U.S.C. §1441(a). Yet that section permits removal of [—21—] any suit over which a district court would have original jurisdiction—and, if these suits are within the admiralty jurisdiction, that condition is satisfied. Plaintiffs' brief asserts: "admiralty jurisdiction does not provide a basis for removal absent an independent basis for federal jurisdiction. *Oklahoma ex rel. Edmondson v. Magnolia Marine Transp. Co.*, 359 F. 3d 1237, 1241 (10th Cir. 2004) (no removal of admiralty actions in the absence of independent basis for removal); *Morris v. TE Marine Corp.*, 344 F. 3d 439, 444 (5th Cir. 2003) (same); *In re Chimenti*, 79 F. 3d 534, 537 (6th Cir. 1996) (same); *Servis v. Hiller Sys. Inc.*, 54 F.3d 203, 207 (4th Cir. 1995) (same)." There plaintiffs stop; they don't explain why.

The appellate cases cited in this passage rely on *Romero v. International Terminal Operating Co.*, 358 U.S. 354 (1959), which took the saving-to-suitors clause at the end of §1333(1) to mean that plaintiffs who elect to litigate a common-law maritime claim in state court are entitled to keep their preferred forum, when the defendant is a citizen of the forum state, unless some other jurisdictional grant also applies and permits removal. To put this otherwise, *Romero* held that an admiralty claim under §1333 is not a federal-question claim under §1331, for federal questions always have been removable without regard to the defendant's citizenship or residence.

Oddly, however, plaintiffs do not mention the saving-to-suitors clause and do not cite *Romero* or any similar decision by the Supreme Court. Perhaps they have left them out because they no longer provide assistance. When the Supreme Court decided *Romero*, and when the courts of appeals decided the four cases on which plaintiffs rely, 28 U.S.C. §1441(b) said this: [—22—]

Any civil action of which the district courts have original jurisdiction founded on a claim or right arising under the Constitution, treaties or laws of the United States shall be removable without regard to the citizenship or residence of the parties. Any other such action shall be removable only if none of the parties in interest properly joined and served as defendants is a citizen of the State in which such action is brought.

That's why it mattered in *Romero* whether a maritime case under §1333(1) counted as one arising under federal law (sentence one) or as an "other" action within federal jurisdiction (sentence two). The Court held in *Romero* that it was an "other" action. If the language had remained unchanged, it would matter to our case as well, for Boeing's headquarters are in Illinois. But in 2011 Congress amended §1441(b) to read:

(b) REMOVAL BASED ON DIVERSITY OF CITIZENSHIP.—(1) In determining whether a civil action is removable on the basis of the jurisdiction under section 1332(a) of this title, the citizenship of defendants sued under fictitious names shall be disregarded. (2) A civil action otherwise removable solely on the basis of the jurisdiction under section 1332(a) of this title may not be removed if any of the parties in interest properly joined and served as defendants is a citizen of the State in which such action is brought.

Federal Courts Jurisdiction and Venue Clarification Act of 2011, §103, Pub. L. No. 112-63, 125 Stat. 759. This amendment limits the ban on removal by a home-state defendant to suits under the diversity jurisdiction.

Perhaps it would be possible to argue that the saving-to-suitors clause itself forbids removal, without regard to any language in §1441. But plaintiffs, who have not mentioned the saving-to-suitors clause, do not make such an argument. We do not think that it is the sort of contention about sub- [—23—] ject-matter jurisdiction that a federal court must resolve even if the parties disregard it. Our conclusion that §1333(1) supplies admiralty jurisdiction shows that subject-matter jurisdiction exists. Plaintiffs thus could have filed these suits directly in federal court (as many victims of this crash did). If the saving-to-suitors clause allows them to stay in state court even after the 2011 amendment, they are free to waive or forfeit that right—which given the scope of §1333(1) concerns venue rather than subject-matter jurisdiction. Boeing therefore was entitled to remove these suits to federal court.

IV

One observation in closing. Our conclusions about admiralty jurisdiction, and the appellate-jurisdiction ruling that allowed us to consider the admiralty question, are compatible with the Multiparty, Multiforum Trial Jurisdiction Act of 2002, codified in 28 U.S.C. §1369 and §1441(e). This statute supplies federal jurisdiction when an accident with multistate features entails the deaths of 75 or more persons. Like most other grants of federal jurisdiction, it does not say that it is an exclusive means to federal court. A law granting one sort of jurisdiction does not implicitly negate others. *See, e.g., Breuer v. Jim's Concrete of Brevard, Inc.*, 538 U.S. 691 (2003). No one doubts, for example, that if an air crash has only one victim, that person's estate could sue the plane's manufacturer under the diversity jurisdiction, 28 U.S.C. §1332, if they were citizens of different states.

Likewise with the admiralty jurisdiction. Federal litigation in most air crashes will continue to rely on the diversity jurisdiction (potentially including the Class Action Fairness Act, §1332(d), if more than 100 injured persons pursue a class action or a mass action) or the Multiparty, Multiforum Trial Jurisdiction [—24—] Act; adding the possibility of admiralty jurisdiction when the cause of an accident occurs during a trans-ocean flight does not change the forum in which most aircraft suits are litigated.

The district court's decision is reversed, and the case is remanded with instructions to rescind the remand orders and transfer these cases to the Northern District of California for consolidated pretrial proceedings under 28 U.S.C. §1407, consistent with the decision of the Panel on Multidistrict Litigation.

United States Court of Appeals
for the Seventh Circuit

No. 14-2009

WESTFIELD INS. CO.
vs.
VANDENBERG

Appeal from the United States District Court for the
Northern District of Illinois, Eastern Division

Decided: August 6, 2015

Citation: 796 F.3d 773, 3 Adm. R. 494 (7th Cir. 2015).

Before **POSNER, RIPPLE,** and **KANNE,** Circuit Judges.

[—1—] RIPPLE, Circuit Judge:

Scot Vandenberg was injured when he fell from the upper deck of a yacht anchored in Lake Michigan. He filed suit in Illinois state court, alleging that the owners and operators of the yacht were negligent. He eventually settled with the defendants. Under the settlement agreement, the defendants agreed to pay Mr. Vandenberg $25 million through the assignment of their claims against [—2—] their insurers. Westfield Insurance Company ("Westfield") was the insurance provider for Rose Paving Company ("Rose Paving"), one of the defendants. Westfield disputed that its insurance policies with Rose Paving covered the yacht accident and brought a declaratory judgment action in the district court. Mr. Vandenberg, as the assignee of Rose Paving, opposed the action. The district court granted Westfield's motion for judgment on the pleadings; it decided that the Westfield policies did not provide coverage for Mr. Vandenberg's injury. Mr. Vandenberg asks that we review that determination. We now hold that the accident occurring on the yacht is not covered by the insurance policies and accordingly affirm the district court's judgment.

I

BACKGROUND

A.

In September 2009, Mr. Vandenberg was attending a five-hour cruise on a chartered yacht when he fell from the upper deck. The accident occurred when he turned to respond to someone calling his name and, as he shifted his weight, the bench upon which he was sitting tipped over. The bench was not secured to the deck, nor did the upper deck have a railing. The fall left Mr. Vandenberg paralyzed from the chest down. The yacht was owned by RQM, Inc. ("RQM"), a closely held corporation owned by Michael Rose, Carl Quanstrom, and Alan Rose. Mr. Vandenberg alleged that Rose Paving, a company run by Alan Rose, was a booking agent that maintained a marketing relationship for the chartering of the yacht. [—3—]

At the time of the accident, Rose Paving was insured by Westfield under a commercial general liability ("CGL") policy and by an umbrella policy (collectively "the policies"). The application for the CGL policy listed as insureds Rose Paving Co., Rose Paving & Seal Coating Inc., and Bridgeview Investments.[1] This application included a "schedule of hazards," which listed "concrete construction," "Contractors Executive Supervisors," and "subcontractors."[2] The application also asked whether the applicant owned, hired, or leased any watercraft. Rose Paving marked the "no" box.[3] The umbrella section of the application similarly asked whether the applicant owned or leased a watercraft. Rose Paving did not answer that question.

The insurance contract included "common policy declarations" applicable to both the CGL and umbrella policies, which listed Rose Paving's business as "concrete construction."[4] The CGL policy declarations also contained a

---

[1] Bridgeview Investments was listed as an additional insured in its capacity as the manager or lessor of Rose Paving's business premises.

[2] R.56-2 at 49.

[3] *Id.* at 50.

[4] R.56-1 at 54.

"general liability schedule," which listed the premises and operations covered by the contract and included "contractors" and "subcontracted work—in connection with construction, reconstruction, repair or erection of buildings."[5] The CGL and [—4—] umbrella policies further provided that Westfield would be legally obligated to pay for damages "to which this insurance applies."[6] They then listed certain exclusions, including liability that "aris[es] out of the ownership, maintenance, use or entrustment to others of any ... watercraft owned or operated by or rented or loaned to any insured."[7] Finally, the policies provided that, by accepting coverage, Rose Paving agreed that "[t]he statements in the Declarations are accurate and complete," that "[t]hose statements are based upon representations" Rose Paving made to Westfield, and that Westfield "issued th[e] policy in reliance upon [those] representations."[8]

B.

Before Westfield filed this declaratory action, the parties had commenced several actions, the particulars of which are not pertinent to our decision today.[9] Mr.

---

[5] *Id.* at 60. The CGL policy declarations determine the scope of both policies. Although the umbrella policy did not contain a similar liability

(continued...) [—4—]

(...continued)
schedule, it applied only if Westfield had been "obligated to pay the 'retained limit'" under the CGL policy. R.56-2 at 25; *see also id.* at 29 ("'Retained limit' means the available limits of 'underlying insurance' scheduled in the Declarations ....").

[6] R.56-1 at 68 (CGL policy); R.56-2 at 13 (umbrella policy).

[7] R.56-1 at 78; R.56-2 at 15.

[8] R.56-1 at 86; R.56-2 at 25.

[9] To summarize briefly, in March 2010, Mr. Vandenberg filed an action against RQM in the Circuit Court of Cook County, Illinois, seeking to recover money damages for his injuries. In August 2010, RQM filed a maritime action in federal court seeking exoneration from liability for the

(continued...) [—5—]

(...continued)
accident or a limitation of liability to the value of the yacht. The district court enjoined Mr. Vandenberg from pursuing his claims against RQM and ordered the parties to refrain from filing

Vandenberg [—5—] ultimately entered into a settlement agreement with the defendants, disposing of the then-pending state court and maritime actions. Under this agreement, Rose Paving, along with Carl Quanstrom, Michael Rose, Alan Rose, Dough Management, and Location Finders International, agreed to pay $25 million, to be satisfied solely through an assignment of their rights of recovery under their insurance policies. Rose Paving, Michael Rose, and Alan Rose agreed to pay an additional $300,000 directly, and RQM's insurer agreed to pay $2 million. The settlement agreement was accepted by the Circuit Court of Cook County, Illinois, on October 10, 2012. [—6—]

In January 2012, Westfield filed this declaratory action. It sought a determination that it owed no duty under Rose Paving's insurance policies to defend or to indemnify any of the defendants in the state court action. Westfield alleged that the policies did not cover the underlying accident because the operation of a seventy-five-foot yacht fell outside the scope of the risks and liabilities for which the policies provided coverage. Alternatively, Westfield maintained that the "watercraft exclusion" barred coverage and that Rose Paving's conduct released Westfield from contractual liability under the policies.

---

additional lawsuits. Mr. Vandenberg then dismissed his first state court action. In August 2011, Mr. Vandenberg filed a second suit in the Circuit Court of Cook County, Illinois. He alleged that the defendants were negligent because they failed to provide railing or other protection on the top deck, allowed Mr. Vandenberg to access the top deck of the yacht, failed to warn about the lack of railings, and "[a]llowed a bench to be placed inches from the rear of the unrailed top deck." R.56-1 at 41. The district court overseeing RQM's maritime action ordered Mr. Vandenberg to stay his state court action.

Mr. Vandenberg also provided Westfield with an unfiled amended complaint five months before settlement. The amended complaint included allegations that Rose Paving negligently owned, maintained, or used an unstable bench. The stay imposed by the district court in RQM's maritime action prevented Mr. Vandenberg from filing the amended complaint.

Westfield filed a motion for judgment on the pleadings. Mr. Vandenberg, as the assignee of Rose Paving, responded with a combined response and cross-motion for summary judgment. The district court granted Westfield's motion for judgment on the pleadings and denied Mr. Vandenberg's motion for summary judgment. The court concluded that the insurance policies covered only Rose Paving's construction business. The court relied on the business description provided in the common policy declarations, the "schedule of hazards" listed in the application, and Rose Paving's representation that it did not own, hire, or lease any watercraft.

The district court later denied Mr. Vandenberg's motion to alter the judgment under Federal Rule of Civil Procedure 59(a). Mr. Vandenberg now appeals the court's [—7—] decision granting Westfield's motion for judgment on the pleadings.[10]

II

DISCUSSION

Mr. Vandenberg asks us to review the district court's decision on the scope of the Westfield insurance policies. He maintains that the policies provide coverage for his injuries because of the broad terms employed in the text. More precisely, he takes the view that, because the Westfield policies do not exclude expressly accidents such as the one on the yacht, the accident and his injuries are covered. Westfield responds that the policies apply only to Rose Paving's construction business and, in the alternative, that the accident falls under the watercraft exclusion contained in the policies.[11]

The interpretation of an insurance policy is a matter of state law. *See Koransky, Bouwer & Poracky, P.C. v. Bar Plan Mut. Ins. Co.*, 712 F.3d 336, 341 (7th Cir. 2013). Because the parties agree that Illinois law applies, we look to the [—8—] decisions of the Supreme Court of Illinois for guidance. *See id.* We review de novo the district court's decision granting a Rule 12(c) motion for judgment on the pleadings. *See Matrix IV, Inc. v. Am. Nat'l Bank & Tr. Co.*, 649 F.3d 539, 547 (7th Cir. 2011). For the reasons set out more fully below, we agree with the district court that the policies do not provide coverage for Mr. Vandenberg's accident. We also conclude that Rose Paving's use of the yacht was excluded from coverage by the policies' watercraft exclusion.

A.

We first address the scope of the Westfield insurance policies. Mr. Vandenberg makes two major arguments to support his interpretation of the policies. First, he submits that the business designation, on its own, is insufficient to limit the scope of the policies. Second, he contends that, under Illinois law, an insurer must "expressly exclude" a risk from the insurance policy if the insurer does not intend to insure against that particular risk.[12] He therefore maintains that because the Westfield policies do not expressly exclude non-construction-related injuries, the policies provide coverage.

Under Illinois law, "[a]n insurance policy is a contract, and the general rules governing the interpretation of other types of contracts also govern the interpretation of insurance policies." *Hobbs v. Hartford Ins. Co. of the Midwest*, 823 N.E.2d 561, 564 (Ill. 2005). When interpreting an insurance policy, [—9—] "our primary objective is to ascertain and give effect to the intention of the parties, as expressed in the policy language." *Id.*; *accord Crum & Forster Managers Corp. v. Resolution Tr. Corp.*, 620 N.E.2d 1073, 1078 (Ill. 1993) ("[T]he primary function of the court is to ascertain and enforce the

---

[10] The district court had jurisdiction pursuant to 28 U.S.C. § 1332. We have jurisdiction under 28 U.S.C. § 1291.

[11] Westfield also maintains that it never breached its duty to defend Rose Paving because it filed a declaratory action and that it is not bound by the settlement because the settlement was overtly collusive, breached multiple policy conditions, and forfeited coverage. Because we decide that Westfield prevails under its first two

theories, we do not address its remaining contentions.

[12] Appellant's Br. 26.

intentions of the parties as expressed in the agreement."). To achieve that goal, we "must construe the policy as a whole, taking into account the type of insurance for which the parties have contracted, the risks undertaken and purchased, the subject matter that is insured and the purposes of the entire contract." *Crum & Forster Managers Corp.*, 620 N.E.2d at 1078; *accord Oakley Transp., Inc. v. Zurich Ins. Co.*, 648 N.E.2d 1099, 1106 (Ill. App. Ct. 1995) (noting that "an insurance policy is not to be interpreted in a factual vacuum and without regard to the purpose for which the insurance was written").

After reviewing the insurance application and the terms of the policies, we conclude that the district court correctly determined that Westfield and Rose Paving intended to enter into an insurance agreement under which Westfield provided coverage only for Rose Paving's construction-related business. We begin with the actual text of the policies. In that respect, we first note that the policies' "common policy declarations" list Rose Paving's business as "concrete construction."[13] The "general liability schedule" also explains that Westfield is providing coverage for work done "in connection with construction, reconstruction, repair [—10—] or erection of buildings."[14] The policies thus reflect, explicitly, the parties' intent to insure only Rose Paving's construction business.

The situation before us today is closely akin to the one before the Appellate Court of Illinois in *Heritage Insurance Co. v. Bucaro*, 428 N.E.2d 979 (Ill. App. Ct. 1981). There, the court determined that similar representations were sufficient to limit the scope of an insurance policy. The court determined that the underlying insurance policy did not cover automobile acquisitions because "[t]he activities enumerated in the policy concern[ed] operations relating to automobile *dismantling*." *Id.* at 982 (emphasis in original). The court relied on the description of hazards, which "include[d] salvage or junking of parts, and store operations," and that the policy listed the insured's business as "Automobile Dismantling." *Id.* at 981. "Due to the limited nature of the policy purchased," the court concluded that it was "implausible to assume that protection was expected for liability of the type that has been created here." *Id.* at 982. The Illinois court's methodology and conclusion reinforces our view of the proper interpretation of the Westfield policies.

The insurance application also supports our interpretation. *See Dash Messenger Serv., Inc. v. Hartford Ins. Co. of Ill.*, 582 N.E.2d 1257, 1263 (Ill. App. Ct. 1991) (relying on the insurance application to determine the risks for which the parties contracted); *see also A.D. Desmond Co. v. Jackson Nat'l Life Ins. Co.*, 585 N.E.2d 1120, 1122 (Ill. App. Ct. 1992) [—11—] ("When, as in this case, an insurance policy is issued which makes the application for insurance part of the policy, the application becomes and is construed as part of the entire insurance contract."). The policies at issue here provide that Rose Paving agreed that "[t]he statements in the Declarations are accurate and complete," that "[t]hose statements are based upon representations" Rose Paving made to Westfield, and that Westfield "issued th[e] policy in reliance upon [those] representations."[15] Rose Paving stated in its application that it was engaged in the construction business. Consistent with that representation, the parties listed in the schedule of hazards the risks that they intended to cover, including "concrete construction," "Contractors Executive Supervisors," and "subcontractors."[16] Rose Paving's representations in the insurance application therefore reinforce our construction of the text of the insurance policies and our conclusion that the parties did not intend to cover an accident occurring on the yacht.

Mr. Vandenberg submits that it is inappropriate to rely on the business designation in the insurance contract. We need not determine whether, in all cases, Illinois courts would consider a business designation contained in an insurance policy,

---

[13] R.56-1 at 54.
[14] *Id.* at 60.

[15] R.56-1 at 86; R.56-2 at 25.
[16] R.56-2 at 49.

standing alone, to be a sufficient indication of party intent to circumscribe the scope of an insurance agreement. Here, our decision need not rely solely on the business designation. As we have noted earlier, the business designation *and* the general liability schedule contained in [—12—] the contract, as well as the incorporated representations in the insurance application, express, *uniformly*, the parties' intent to limit the scope of the insurance policies to Rose Paving's known business, construction. *See Heritage Ins. Co.*, 428 N.E.2d at 981–82 (holding that, because the description of hazards included only "Automobile Dismantling" and the business of the insured was listed as "Automobile Dismantling," "it is evident that the policy provides coverage only for occurrences arising out of specified activities [automobile dismantling] taking place on the insured premises"). The district court correctly recognized that Rose Paving "operated multiple independent businesses (paving and yacht charters), purchased insurance for only one of those businesses (paving), and later sought coverage for a different business (yacht charters)."[17] In this case, therefore, the business designation contained in the insurance contract, when read with the other evidence of the parties' intent, substantiates forcefully that the parties entered into an agreement to insure only Rose Paving's construction business.

Nor can we accept Mr. Vandenberg's contention that the policies provide coverage for any and all liabilities unless they are explicitly excluded. In assessing this submission, our task is, of course, to determine the intent of the parties, as expressed by the insurance policy. *See Hobbs*, 823 N.E.2d at 564; *Crum & Forster Managers Corp.*, 620 N.E.2d at 1078. Here, we believe that the text and structure of the policies makes clear that the parties intended to insure against the [—13—] risks of operating a construction company. If the parties intended to exclude a risk associated with running such a business, we would expect them to have recited that exclusion in the contract. A policy does not need to exclude

from coverage liability that was not contemplated by the parties and not intended to be covered under their agreement. *See Dash Messenger Serv., Inc.*, 582 N.E.2d at 1263 (noting that an insurer should expressly exclude a risk from coverage "if an insurer does not intend to insure against a risk *likely to be inherent in the insured's business*" (emphasis added)). Because Rose Paving's policies were manifestly designed to cover only its construction business, however, we would not expect those policies to address risks not inherent in that business.[18] To hold otherwise would require [—14—] the parties to conjure up and exclude explicitly any and all activities in which Rose Paving might engage. Such a speculative exercise in hypotheticals would be nonsensical.

---

[18] Other courts, when faced with analogous circumstances, have adopted similar interpretations. *See Steadfast Ins. Co. v. Dobbas*, No. CIV. S-05-0632 FCD JFM, 2008 WL 324023, at *6 (E.D. Cal. Feb. 5, 2008) (holding that, because the policy describes the business of the insured as "Railroad Contractor" and "[t]he Declarations page tailored for this particular policy limited the coverage of the policy based upon the business description," the "policy unambiguously provide[d] coverage … *only* for injuries relating to the business of 'Railroad Contractor'" (emphasis in original)); *Gemini Ins. Co v. S & J Diving, Inc.*, 464 F. Supp. 2d 641, 650 (S.D. Tex. 2006) (holding that the insurance policy applied "only to marine survey operations" and not to the company's involvement with an outdoor rock concert because it would be unreasonable "to conclude that the policy covers any and all activity, not specifically excluded, when the insured negotiated as, and described itself to be, a marine operation"); *Cooper v. RLI Ins. Co.*, No. CV 9403617128, 1996 WL 367721, at *8 (Conn. Super. Ct. June 3, 1996) (holding that the CGL policy "does not provide coverage for accidents associated with business activity different from the business activity for which coverage was initially sought"); *cf. Phila. Indem. Ins. Co. v. 1801 W. Irving Park, LLC*, No. 11 C

(continued...) [—14—]

(...continued)
1710, 2012 WL 3482260, at *5 (N.D. Ill. Aug. 13, 2012) (holding that the insurance policy provided coverage because the insured "was a single entity that performed multiple services as a part of its condominium development business—which was a named insured on the Policies").

---

[17] R.89 at 10.

In sum, Mr. Vandenberg has not provided a cogent rationale to support his conclusion that Westfield and Rose Paving intended to enter into an insurance contract of endless scope, covering any and all businesses operated by Rose Paving. Construing the policies as a whole, we conclude that both Westfield and Rose Paving intended that the insurance policies provide coverage only for Rose Paving's construction-related business. Accordingly, the policies do not provide coverage for Mr. Vandenberg's injury on the yacht.[19] [—15—]

B.

The policies' watercraft exclusion provides an independent basis for affirming the district court's judgment. The Westfield policies exclude from coverage "'[b]odily injury' ... arising out of the ownership, maintenance, use or entrustment to others of any ... watercraft owned or operated by or rented or loaned to any insured."[20] In his state court complaint, Mr. Vandenberg alleged that Rose Paving negligently had "[f]ailed to provide railing or equivalent protection of the top deck peripheral areas which were accessible to passengers," "[f]ailed to prevent SCOT VANDENBERG ... from accessing the top deck of the yacht," "[a]llowed ... SCOT VANDENBERG[] to access areas of the top deck which did not have railings or equivalent protection," "[f]ailed to warn ... SCOT VANDENBERG[] of the lack of railings or

equivalent protection on the top peripheral areas of the top deck," and "[a]llowed a bench to be placed inches from the rear of the unrailed top deck."[21] [—16—]

Mr. Vandenberg submits that, under Illinois law, the negligent maintenance, ownership, and use of the bench was a concurrent cause of his injuries and, therefore, the watercraft exclusion does not preclude coverage. Westfield maintains that the watercraft exclusion bars coverage under the policies because the use of the yacht was intertwined inextricably with all theories of recovery.

We have recognized previously that, under Illinois law, an insurance policy does not provide coverage for claims that are "intertwined" with an excluded liability. *See Nautilus Ins. Co. v. 1452-4 N. Milwaukee Ave., LLC*, 562 F.3d 818, 822 (7th Cir. 2009). In *Nautilus*, we addressed whether a claim seeking compensation for property damage

---

[19] Mr. Vandenberg also submits that, because the umbrella policy does not have the same limitations as the CGL policy, it was intended to apply beyond Rose Paving's construction business. He relies on the absence of a business description in the separate umbrella policy document. But, as Westfield points out, the identification of Rose Paving's business is contained in a document labeled "common policy declarations" that summarizes the entire agreement. R.56-1 at 54. Specifically, the document states that "this policy consists of the following coverage parts" and lists the "commercial umbrella coverage part." *Id.* Mr. Vandenberg fails to invite our attention to any documentation that would support a determination that Westfield, through the umbrella policy, intended to insure activities beyond Rose Paving's construction business.

[20] *Id.* at 78; R.56-2 at 15.

[21] R.45-1 at 8–9. In his unfiled amended complaint, Mr. Vandenberg alleged that Rose Paving negligently "[p]rovided a wobbly bench to be used by SCOT VANDENBERG from which he fell." R.13-1 at 4. However, an insurer's duty to defend is limited to those allegations contained in the operative complaint. *See Mass. Bay Ins. Co. v. Unique Presort Servs., Inc.*, 679 N.E.2d 476, 478 (Ill. App. Ct. 1997) ("It is well settled that the allegations of the complaint are dispositive of the insurer's duty to defend and not the findings of the underlying

(continued...) [—16—]

(...continued)
litigation."); *Oakley Transp., Inc. v. Zurich Ins. Co.*, 648 N.E.2d 1099, 1102 (Ill. App. Ct. 1995) (noting that a "court must ordinarily confine its inquiry to a comparison of the allegations of the underlying complaint and the relevant provisions of the insurance policy in determining a duty to defend"). Indeed, the Appellate Court of Illinois recently decided that Mr. Vandenberg's unfiled complaint should not be considered under the doctrine of "true but unpleaded facts." *See Md. Cas. Co. v. Dough Mgmt. Co.*, No. 1-14-1520, 2015 WL 4002569, at *9 (Ill. App. Ct. June 30, 2015). The court held "that the self-serving allegations in an unfiled amended complaint cannot be presumed true and are not the type of facts intended to be covered by the true but unpleaded facts doctrine." *Id.*

was barred by the insurance policy's contractor-subcontractor exclusion. *See id.* at 821–23. We concluded that "the presence of an alternative theory of relief … is insufficient to trigger coverage" when the plaintiff does not allege an "injury independent of the" injury sustained as a result of the excluded liability. *Id.* at 823. Thus, we found it determinative [—17—] that "the statutory claims in the underlying complaints [sought] recovery for the same loss as all the other claims—the property damage arising out of the faulty excavation performed by [the defendant's] contractors and subcontractor—and coverage for *that* property damage is excluded by the contractor-subcontractor exclusion." *Id.* at 822 (emphasis in original).

In reaching our conclusion in *Nautilus*, we relied, in part, on the decision of the Supreme Court of Illinois in *Northbrook Property & Casualty Co. v. Transportation Joint Agreement*, 741 N.E.2d 253 (Ill. 2000). In *Northbrook*, the court held that a policy exclusion bars coverage for injuries associated with excluded conduct, even if a plaintiff proceeds under an alternative theory of recovery that implicates the excluded conduct only indirectly. The Illinois court explained:

> The policy excludes injuries arising from the school districts' use or operation of a motor vehicle. Allegations that the school districts inadequately planned and inspected bus routes or failed to warn bus drivers of potential hazards along the routes are nothing more than rephrasings of the fact that the students' injuries arose from the school districts' use or operation of a motor vehicle. Contrary to the appellate court's holding, the students' complaints failed to allege that the injuries arose from events wholly independent of any negligent operation of the bus. Northbrook therefore has no duty to defend the school districts in the underlying lawsuits. [—18—]

Id. at 254–55 (citation omitted) (internal quotation marks omitted). Thus, in order to succeed, the allegations in Mr. Vandenberg's complaint must be "wholly

independent of any negligent operation of the [watercraft]."[22] *Id.* at 254 (internal quotation marks omitted). [—19—]

---

[22] The decisions of the Appellate Court of Illinois reflect the distinction between dependent and independent claims. *Compare Mass. Bay Ins. Co.*, 679 N.E.2d at 479 ("In this case, the underlying plaintiffs' count XXVII is specifically dependent upon the fact that their injuries occurred in a vehicle accident. This drug-testing regulation would not apply to the underlying plaintiffs' negligence action if their injuries had been caused by some instrumentality other than a vehicle. Thus, the negligence alleged in count XXVII is inextricably intertwined with the policy's excluded instrumentality, namely, the vehicle."), *with Mount Vernon Fire Ins. Co. v. Heaven's Little Hands Day Care*, 795 N.E.2d 1034, 1043 (Ill. App. Ct. 2003) ("[W]e find after reviewing the allegations in the underlying complaint that the victim's death resulted from nonvehicular conduct on the part of Heaven's Little Hands and its employees. The allegations in the complaint assert multiple theories of negligence including a failure to maintain a proper census of the children attending the day-care facility. Had Leon kept an accurate head count of the children inside the van or if someone inside Heaven's Little Hands had noticed Tyrelle's absence soon after the van in question had arrived at the day care facility, Tyrelle would not have died. In short, the van is the situs, rather than the cause, of Tyrelle's death."), *and Louis Marsch, Inc. v. Pekin Ins. Co.*, 491 N.E.2d 432, 437 (Ill. App. Ct. 1985) ("Thus if a trier of fact concluded that Marsch had failed in its duty to Chizmar under the Road Construction Injuries Act, the fact that the dump truck was the instrumentality which ultimately injured Chizmar would be but one of two concurrent causes of the injury, one excluded under the Aetna policy, the other not so excluded. If the liability of an insured arises from negligent acts which constitute non-auto-related conduct, the policy should be applicable regardless of the automobile exclusion or the fact that an automobile was involved in the occurrence."), *and U.S. Fid. & Guar. Co. v. State Farm Mut. Auto. Ins. Co.*, 437 N.E.2d 663, 666 (Ill. App. Ct. 1982) ("In the present

(continued...) [—19—]

(...continued)

case, the complaint alleges negligent acts which are potentially within the coverage of the policy, such as the failure to adequately supervise the children and the negligent operation of the day care center. These alleged acts are separate and distinct from any allegations relating to the negligent operation of the automobile.").

The Appellate Court of Illinois recently reaffirmed these principles and applied them to the same state court complaint at issue here. In *Maryland Casualty Co. v. Dough Management Co.*, No. 1-14-1520, 2015 WL 4002569 (Ill. App. Ct. June 30, 2015), the court addressed whether an identically worded watercraft exclusion in an insurance contract barred coverage for the injuries that Mr. Vandenberg sustained on the yacht. *See id.* at *7. In that action, Maryland Casualty Co., the insurer that had provided coverage to Dough Management, maintained that it had no duty to defend or indemnify Dough Management under its insurance policy. *See id.* at *2–3. The court noted that the "policy specifically exclude[d] coverage for any bodily injury 'arising out of the ownership, maintenance, use, or entrustment to others of any ... watercraft owned or operated by or rented or loaned to any insured.'" *Id.* at *7 (second alteration in original). The court concluded that "the Vandenbergs only alleged [in their state court complaint] that the insureds failed to properly maintain the yacht by failing to provide a railing on the top deck, allegations that fall squarely under the watercraft exclusion." *Id.* "Therefore, based on the personal injury complaint," the court continued, "the Vandenbergs' claims are excluded under the CGL policy." *Id.* [—20—]

With the guidance of the Appellate Court of Illinois, we reach the same conclusion. Mr. Vandenberg fell from the top deck of the yacht after the bench on which he was sitting tipped over. Because the top deck of the yacht did not have a railing, he fell a substantial distance, resulting in his injuries and paralysis. In his state court complaint, Mr. Vandenberg recognized that his injury would not have occurred if Rose Paving had provided a railing or prevented him from accessing the top deck of the yacht. Thus, the accident and Mr. Vandenberg's resulting injuries were not "wholly independent of" the negligent operation, maintenance, or use of the yacht. *Northbrook Prop. & Cas. Co.*, 741 N.E.2d at 254 (internal quotation marks omitted). Mr. Vandenberg's injuries therefore come under the policies' watercraft exclusion, and the policies do not provide coverage.

Conclusion

The judgment of the district court is affirmed.

AFFIRMED

United States Court of Appeals
for the Seventh Circuit

No. 14-2451

SWEATT

vs.

UNION PAC. R.R. CO.

Appeal from the United States District Court for the Northern District of Illinois, Eastern Division

Decided: August 6, 2015

Citation: 796 F.3d 701, 3 Adm. R. 502 (7th Cir. 2015).

Before **RIPPLE**, **KANNE**, and **TINDER**, Circuit Judges.

[—1—] KANNE, Circuit Judge:

Appellant Ronald Sweatt is an African-American male who worked for Union Pacific Railroad Company ("Union Pacific"). Union Pacific hired him in 2006 to perform manual labor jobs, and during his time there, he did just that. He served as a Laborer, Assistant Foreman, Trackwalker, Trackman, and Tie Inserter. After a few years on the job, Sweatt manifested pain in his shoulder and hands. The pain progressed to the point that Sweatt could no [—2—] longer do his job. So he sought a less strenuous position—Security Officer—through Union Pacific's Vocational Rehabilitation Program. Sweatt did not get the job.

Sweatt subsequently filed suit against Union Pacific. For his physical injuries, he alleged violations of the Federal Employers' Liability Act ("FELA"). For the denial of the Security Officer position, he alleged violations of the Civil Rights Act of 1991 and the Age Discrimination in Employment Act ("ADEA"), among other statutes.[1] He bundled these claims into one action (with five counts) in the Northern District of Illinois. Discovery ensued, and Union Pacific eventually filed a motion for summary judgment on each of Sweatt's claims. The district court granted Union Pacific's motion in its entirety. For the reasons below, we affirm.

I. Background

Sweatt's job as a railroad worker was hard work. No one disputes that. During his time at Union Pacific, he operated spike mauls, hydraulic tampers, and spiker guns. He swung sledgehammers, pulled spikes with claw bars, and assisted with welding. He also inserted—and removed—railroad ties. Unsurprisingly, this strenuous work caused Sweatt to develop pain in his shoulder and hands. Sweatt addressed his shoulder pain in his deposition.

A. I started having a lot of pain during 2009, the year 2009, that year when I was up at Lake Street when we started doing a lot of tampering [sic]. [—3—]

Q. What time of year was it?

A. What time of year?

Q. Uh-huh—yes.

A. Oh, like in the summer.

Q. Somewhere in June or July or August?

A. It might have been—I know it was—it was warm. It might have been before then.

Q. So it could have been before June?

A. Yeah.

Q. And when you would use the claw bars back probably before June of 2009, you would notice the pain in your shoulder?

A. Yes. Because when I would—when I would use the—use the claw bar, it was just—it was unbearable, you know, I would, you know, try to—I called one of the guys, come over, you know, and give me a hand.

---

[1] Sweatt also brought claims under the Americans with Disabilities Act, 42 U.S.C. § 12101 et seq., and the Illinois Human Rights Act, 775 ILCS 5/2-103, but those claims are not before us on appeal.

Q. Did you seek medical attention at that time?

A. See I—over the counter I was taking pain medication because I didn't want—I didn't really want no time off work.

During that same timeframe, Sweatt began experiencing pain in his hands. He attributed the cause of the hand pain to repetitive use of hydraulic tools and other hand tools. On November 19, 2009, Sweatt saw a medical professional to address the hand pain. His provider for that healthcare visit, Nurse Practitioner Valentin, entered the following note into Sweatt's medical record: "complaining of bilateral hand pain. The patient has had pain in his hands for quite a while [—4—] now. He might have carpal tunnel syndrome. He does repetitive motion at his job."

Eleven days later, on November 30, 2009, Sweatt met with Dr. Coates. According to Dr. Coates, Sweatt first complained of hand pain, which he attributed to his work at Union Pacific, in May of 2009. Sweatt was a Trackman at the time. Upon examination, Dr. Coates believed that Sweatt was unable to perform the job of Trackman.

We pay particular attention to these dates. They are significant because Union Pacific contends that Sweatt's FELA claims[2] are barred by the statute of limitations. To recap:

---

[2] Sweatt alleged nine theories of negligence against Union Pacific under the FELA. According to Sweatt, Union Pacific: (1) neglected to provide him with a reasonably safe place to work; (2) neglected to provide him with safe and proper tools; (3) neglected to provide him with the proper safety equipment; (4) neglected to inspect and maintain its equipment; (5) neglected to warn him about defective tools and equipment; (6) negligently created and permitted a dangerous and hazardous workplace condition; (7) neglected to adopt safe customs and practices; (8) neglected to adopt safe methods and procedures; and (9) committed other acts of negligence. These separate

- May / June 2009–Sweatt notices hand pain. He also describes experiencing "unbearable" shoulder pain. Sweatt requests coworkers to help him use claw bars.

- Nov. 19, 2009–Sweatt sees Nurse Practitioner Valentin for bilateral hand pain.

- Nov. 30, 2009–Sweatt sees Dr. Coates. Dr. Coates says Sweatt is unfit to perform the duties of Trackman. [—5—]

- Nov. 30, 2012–Sweatt files suit.

Given this series of events, the district court agreed with Union Pacific. It ruled the claims time-barred by the applicable three-year statute of limitations, 45 U.S.C. § 56, and granted summary judgment in favor of Union Pacific.

That brings us to Sweatt's age- and race-based discrimination claims. These claims flow from Sweatt's rejection for the Security Officer position, a position he sought once he could no longer perform his manual-labor jobs. In January 2011, Union Pacific gave Sweatt an opportunity to participate in the Vocational Rehabilitation Program ("VRP"). This program facilitates job placement for railroad workers who are no longer able to perform their existing jobs to due injury or illness. VRP Counselors try to place workers in their previous jobs, in different jobs within Union Pacific, or in positions outside Union Pacific. During their placement efforts, VRP Counselors help workers develop skills in interviewing and résumé drafting.

Sweatt seized the opportunity. When he learned of an open Security Officer position in the greater Chicago area, he expressed interest and applied. Union Pacific scheduled him for an interview in Omaha, Nebraska, where its corporate headquarters are located.

---

harms resulted, he alleged, in "permanent injuries to his shoulders, arms, hands and wrists and the bones, muscles, tissues, ligaments and internal parts thereof."

Before Sweatt left, VRP Counselor Elizabeth Watson gave him a document that alerted him to areas of interest that could be discussed during the interview. The document, "Information requested on Personal History form for background check," requested information pertaining to arrests, traffic citations, military service, family, education, and references. Watson discussed the form with Sweatt and generally helped him to prepare for the interview. [—6—]

Sweatt arrived in Omaha on March 16, 2011. Before he began his interviews, he completed a "Personal History Statement." This document was different from the form Watson had given him. Under a heading entitled "ARRESTS," the form asked if he had ever been convicted of a misdemeanor or a felony offense. It also asked if he had ever been on probation or parole, and if he had ever been under indictment or charges for a criminal offense. The form then provided an admonishment: "A conviction may not disqualify you, but a false statement will." Sweatt answered "no" to each of the questions.

Then he met with Candace Girard, Director of Disability Management. She informed him that Union Pacific favors a candidate with integrity and honesty because a Security Officer is charged with guarding multi-million dollar vehicles. After his meeting with Girard, Sweatt met with Bruce Finger, Director of Internal Placement, and Ken Eultgen, Director of Homeland Security. Finger used an "Interview Questioner's Form," the same form he always used when interviewing candidates for the Security Officer position. In accordance with that form, Finger asked Sweatt if he had ever been arrested or convicted of a misdemeanor or felony. Sweatt answered in the negative, and Finger recommended Sweatt for the position.

Then Union Pacific ran a background check. Union Pacific first conducted an "eVerifile" criminal report, which it runs on all prospective employees. That report returned a clean record. The background check did not stop there, however. When someone applies for a position in the police de- [—7—]

partment,[3] Union Pacific conducts a more thorough investigation. So Special Agent James Weller, Union Pacific (Northern Region), ran a "LEADS/NCIC" criminal check on Sweatt. LEADS/NCIC (Law Enforcement Agencies Data System / National Crime Information Center) is a computerized database that is maintained by the government. It facilitates background checks on all prospective employees in the Northern Region. Here, it indicated that Sweatt had been arrested in the Homewood-Flossmoor area of Illinois. The report disclosed a case number from the Flossmoor Police Department and a State ID number for the arrest. Agent Weller confirmed the arrest.

He then contacted Sweatt's former supervisor, Richard Johnson, who gave Sweatt a positive referral. Johnson stated that Sweatt earned an award for his hard work, never abused sick time, and never gave anyone a hard time. He recommended Sweatt for the job. After receiving a similar, positive referral from Sweatt's former employer of fifteen years, Agent Weller conducted an in-person interview of Sweatt.

During that interview, Agent Weller asked Sweatt if he had ever been arrested. Sweatt again said "no." Agent Weller asked him that question at least three times, and each time Sweatt gave him the same answer—"no." Armed with the background report, Agent Weller decided to confront Sweatt [—8—] with the details of the arrest. He asked Sweatt if he had been arrested in Flossmoor, Illinois. Sweatt finally acknowledged that he had. He quickly called the incident a misunderstanding, noting that the judge tossed the case out of court. He also added that it was a domestic dispute, and that he remained friends with everyone involved.

---

[3] According to Union Pacific's website, the railroad police force dates to the mid-nineteenth century, "when the number of U.S. Marshals was insufficient to police America's growing rail network." *See* https://www.up.com/aboutup/community/safety/special_agents/index.htm (last visited on July 24, 2015).

Agent Weller summarized the results of his background investigation and sent his final report to Jack Harris, Northern Division Captain. Upon review, Harris emailed Finger to memorialize his concerns about the inconsistencies in Sweatt's responses to the arrest questions. Finger, who had previously recommended Sweatt, e-mailed Mark Kalinowski, Regional Director, asking for his opinion on the matter. Kalinowski responded with a negative endorsement on Sweatt's candidacy. In his view, Sweatt did not deserve the Security Officer position due to his untruthfulness related to the prior arrest. Recall Girard's notice: Union Pacific was looking for a person with integrity and honesty.

Finger subsequently notified Sweatt in writing that he was disqualified for the Security Officer position. The form letter, dated March 31, 2011, stated that Sweatt's "background investigation has disclosed information and circumstances that disqualify you as a candidate for Security Officer."

Sweat subsequently filed suit against Union Pacific, alleging, in part, age- and race-based discrimination. In support of his case, Sweatt offers nineteen comparators who have been offered the position of Security Officer since 2009. He argues that these comparators reveal a less-than-level playing field when it comes to competition for the Security Officer position. In his view, the case boils down to questions of [—9—] credibility, so his claims should have survived summary judgment.

There is more. Sweatt links the district court's judgment against him to its case management procedure ("CMP") regarding summary judgment. He argues that Judge Sara L. Ellis exceeded her authority by promulgating a CMP that prevents parties from filing separate statements of fact.[4] In Sweatt's view, this rule is inconsistent with Local Rule 56.1 and Federal Rule of Civil Procedure 83. We unfurl this novel argument below.

---

[4] Under the CMP, the parties must file a "joint" statement of undisputed facts.

II. ANALYSIS

We review a district court's grant of summary judgment *de novo. Hanover Ins. Co. v. N. Bldg. Co.*, 751 F.3d 788, 791 (7th Cir. 2014). Summary judgment is appropriate where the admissible evidence reveals no genuine issue of any material fact. FED. R. CIV. P. 56(c); *Lawson v. CSX Transp., Inc.*, 245 F.3d 916, 922 (7th Cir. 2001). A fact is "material" if it is one identified by the law as affecting the outcome of the case. *Anderson v. Liberty Lobby, Inc.*, 477 U.S. 242, 248 (1986). An issue of material fact is "genuine" if "the evidence is such that a reasonable jury could return a verdict for the nonmoving party." *Anderson*, 477 U.S. at 248. We "construe all facts and reasonable inferences in the light most favorable to the non-moving party." *Apex Digital, Inc. v. Sears, Roebuck, & Co.*, 735 F.3d 962, 965 (7th Cir. 2013). Here, Sweatt is the non-moving party. So we construe all facts and reasonable inferences in his favor. [—10—]

A. FELA Claims

Our discussion begins with Sweatt's FELA claims. The FELA affords redress to injured employees of railroad companies that are engaged in interstate commerce. 45 U.S.C. § 51 *et seq.; see also Conrail v. Gottshall*, 512 U.S. 532, 542 (1994) ("Cognizant of the physical dangers of railroading that resulted in the death or maiming of thousands of workers every year, Congress crafted a federal remedy that shifted part of the human overhead of doing business from employees to their employers.") (internal quotation marks and citations omitted). In crafting this remedy, Congress imposed a three-year statute of limitations. 45 U.S.C. § 56 ("No action shall be maintained under this chapter unless commenced within three years from the day the cause of action accrued.").

In cases like this one, where the statute of limitations is at issue, the date of accrual is key. Accrual is defined in two parts: notice of injury and notice of cause. *See Fries v. Chicago & Nw. Transp. Co.*, 909 F.2d 1092, 1095 (7th Cir. 1990) ("[O]nce a plaintiff is in possession of the critical facts of both injury and governing cause of that injury the action accrues even though he may be unaware that a legal wrong has occurred.") (citation omitted). Actual notice is not required for accrual. *Tolston v. Nat'l R.R. Passenger Corp.*, 102 F.3d 863, 866 (7th Cir. 1996). After a condition manifests itself, the question becomes whether the plaintiff knew or, through the exercise of reasonable diligence, *should have known* of the cause of his injury. *Id.*

Here, Sweatt was on notice of his injuries and the cause of his injuries as early as May or June 2009. Sweatt testified that he first observed his hand and shoulder pain in the summer months of 2009: "I started having [shoulder] pain [—11—] during 2009 ... like in the summer." When asked if it was "in June or July or August," he answered, "I know it was ... warm. It might have been before then." Dr. Coates corroborated that testimony. He testified that Sweatt first noticed his hand pain in May of 2009. And Nurse Practitioner Valentin's notes from Sweatt's November 19, 2009, appointment states that he experienced "pain in his hands for quite a while now." Clearly then, Sweatt's injury manifested itself well before November 30, 2009—the critical three-year mark from his filing in district court. *See Green v. CSX Transp., Inc.*, 414 F.3d 758, 763 (7th Cir. 2005) ("When the specific date of injury cannot be determined because an injury results from continual exposure to a harmful condition over a period of time, a plaintiff's cause of action accrues when the injury manifests itself.").

Sweatt's arguments to the contrary are unavailing. He first argues that "intermittent pain associated with a minor injury" is insufficient to trigger accrual of a claim under the FELA. We do not disagree with that proposition of law, *see Green*, 414 F.3d at 764; we disagree with its applicability to this case. Sweatt's own testimony belies the notion that he experienced "intermittent pain associated with a minor injury." Indeed, he described his shoulder pain as "unbearable," particularly when using the claw bar.[5] He testified that he

needed help from his coworkers to use that tool. And by November 30, 2009 (exactly three years before he filed this action), Dr. Coates opined that Sweatt could no longer per-[—12—] form the work as a Trackman.[6] To be sure, Sweatt testified that he did not miss work as a result of these injuries. But his effort in working in the face of injury does not forestall the date of accrual.

Sweatt next argues that he was unaware that his malady was anything more than muscle soreness. This plea of ignorance is similar to the argument the appellant advanced in *Fries*. In that case, the appellant argued that the statute of limitations for his FELA claim was tolled until a doctor diagnosed him with the relevant injury. 909 F.2d at 1095. We rejected that argument, and held that a plaintiff cannot wait until he receives a medical diagnosis to begin pursuit of his claim. *Id.* We are not alone in this approach. In the cause-of-injury context, the Fifth Circuit also rejects the use of a medical diagnosis as a starting point for the statute of limitations. *See Emmons v. S. Pac. Transp. Co.*, 701 F.2d 1112, 1122 (5th Cir. 1983) ("[W]e think it sufficient for purposes of commencement of the limitations period that the plaintiff knew his complained of condition was work related, and that it is not additionally necessary that he have been formally so advised by a physician.").

Regarding cause of injury, Sweatt immediately linked his pain to his employment with Union Pacific. He testified that he first noticed the pain when he started doing a lot of tamping on the railroad tracks. He called his shoulder pain "unbearable," particularly when he would use the claw bar—a tool specific to his job at Union Pacific. Nurse Practitioner [—13—] Valentin's November 19, 2009, note corroborates the work-related nature of the injury. She wrote that Sweatt *"does repetitive motion at his job"* (emphasis added). And Dr. Coates also testified that Sweatt associated the pain with his work.

---

[5] We are unsure why Sweatt questions the district court's reliance on this fact. It is beyond

dispute that he testified to enduring "unbearable" pain.

[6] Dr. Coates performed corrective surgery on Sweatt's shoulder in March 2010.

This connection is no leap of logic. After all, Sweatt had performed heavy-duty jobs at Union Pacific for a period of nearly three years. Like a machinist who, after years working in a loud, industrial room, develops hearing loss, *Fries*, 909 F.2d at 1093–94, Sweatt knew or through the exercise of reasonable diligence should have known that his injuries were caused by his work for Union Pacific.

Based on our *de novo* review of the record, Sweatt's FELA claims for the injuries to his shoulder and hands began to accrue well before November 30, 2009. That puts them outside the relevant three-year period, rendering them time-barred by the statute of limitations.

B. Race and Age Discrimination Claims

Sweatt's next issue concerns his *prima facie* cases of age and race discrimination. He brings these claims in light of Union Pacific's failure to hire him as a Security Officer.[7] Because Sweatt did not present direct evidence that he was discriminated against, the district court resorted to the burden-shifting method of *McDonnell Douglas Corp. v. Green*, 411 U.S. [—14—] 792, 802–05 (1973).[8] Under this method, a plaintiff must show that: (1) he is a member of a protected class; (2) he applied for and was qualified for an open position; (3) despite his qualifications, he was rejected for the position; and (4) a similarly situated person outside his protected class was hired for the position instead, or the position remained open. *Gore v. Ind. Univ.*, 416 F.3d 590, 592 (7th Cir. 2005). We note that this familiar burden-shifting framework also applies to age discrimination claims under the

ADEA. *Krchnavy v. Limagrain Genetics Corp.*, 294 F.3d 871, 875 (7th Cir. 2002).

In any event, if a plaintiff can establish this *prima facie* case, then the defendant must present evidence demonstrating a legitimate, nondiscriminatory reason for not hiring the plaintiff for the position. *Norman-Nunnery v. Madison Area Tech. Coll.*, 625 F.3d 422, 432 (7th Cir. 2010). The plaintiff must then present evidence that the stated reason for not hiring was merely pretextual. *Zaccagnini v. Chas. Levy Circulating Co.*, 338 F.3d 672, 675 (7th Cir. 2003). Pretext is defined as "a dishonest explanation, a lie rather than an oddity or an error." *Peele v. Country Mut. Ins. Co.*, 288 F.3d 319, 326 (7th Cir. 2002).

Here, Sweatt cannot make out a *prima facie* case for either age- or race-based discrimination. Specifically, he fails to establish the final prong dealing with similarly situated indi- [—15—] viduals.[9] Although similarly situated individuals "need not be identical in every conceivable way," they "must be 'directly comparable' to the plaintiff 'in all material respects[.]'" *Coleman v. Donahoe*, 667 F.3d 835, 846 (7th Cir. 2012). This record reveals no candidates for the Security Officer position—past or present—who were comparable to Sweatt in all material respects, and yet were treated more favorably than he was (i.e. hired).

We begin our analysis with Sweatt's race discrimination claim under § 1981. Union Pacific offered nineteen people jobs as Security Officers in the past five years. Sweatt uses these individuals as his comparators. Discovery revealed their racial makeup: fifteen were Caucasian, three were Hispanic, and one was African-American. Nine of these individuals hailed from the Northern Region where Sweatt sought his Chicago position. Of those individuals, one was outside Sweatt's

---

[7] Given the briefing in this case, it is unclear whether Sweatt's race discrimination claim is brought under the Civil Rights Act of 1964, 42 U.S.C. § 2000e-2, or the Civil Rights Acts of 1991, 42 U.S.C. § 1981. (Appellant's Br. 36.) Sweatt's complaint alleges a violation under § 1981, so our analysis proceeds under that statute.

[8] Although the district court laid out the *McDonell Douglas* framework, it proceeded directly to analysis of pretext. *Sweatt v. Union Pac. R.R. Co.*, No. 12 C 9579, 2015 U.S. Dist. LEXIS 76156, at *22-23 (N.D. Ill. June 3, 2014).

[9] Union Pacific appears to concede that Sweatt was qualified for the position of Security Officer, which satisfies prong 2 of Sweatt's *prima facie* case. Although we doubt that an applicant who is not forthright in an interview is qualified for a position that depends on honesty and integrity, we accept Union Pacific's concession for purposes of our analysis.

protected class and was untruthful on the topic of traffic citations in his paper application. He was hired. But importantly, that candidate immediately rectified the discrepancy in his paper application during his interview. Sweatt, by contrast, did not. During Sweatt's interview, he denied being arrested, and he corrected himself only when confronted by Agent Weller with the specific details of the arrest. That makes Sweatt and this particular comparator qualitatively different. [—16—]

The same story plays out when we consider individuals hired by Union Pacific for Security Officer *outside* the Northern Region. Three individuals from this pool also had prior arrests and/or charges brought against them. Unlike Sweatt, however, each of these individuals forthrightly admitted to their prior misdeeds during the interviews. Collectively, then, these comparators are not comparable to Sweatt in all material aspects. It's not the initial lie; it's the cover-up, the persistence in the lie. Sweatt, unlike each of his purported comparators, engaged in the latter activity. The comparators, therefore, are not directly comparable in all material respects, *Coleman*, 667 F.3d at 846, and Sweatt cannot establish his *prima facie* case for race discrimination.

Sweatt's alternative argument, that members outside his protected racial class were treated more favorably than he was because *some* of their summary reports do not state that they had background checks performed, is also unavailing. The fact that a summary report does not contain language indicating that a background check was performed does not mean that it was not performed. It simply means that the check, if one occurred, was not included in the report. And even if this argument somehow satisfied Sweatt's *prima facie* case, which it does not, Sweatt presents no evidence suggesting that Union Pacific's reason for not hiring him—his dishonesty during the interview—is pretextual. *EEOC v. Target Corp.*, 460 F.3d 946, 960 (7th Cir. 2006) ("To satisfy [pretext], a plaintiff must show that (a) the employer's nondiscriminatory reason was dishonest; and

(b) the employer's true reason was based on discriminatory intent.").

Our § 1981 analysis applies with equal force to Sweatt's ADEA claim. Sweatt was born on August 6, 1956, so on the [—17—] date of his interview, March 16, 2011, he was fifty-four. Under the ADEA, that means he was a member of a protected class, 29 U.S.C. § 631 ("The prohibitions in this chapter shall be limited to individuals who are at least 40 years of age."), which covers prong 1 of his *prima facie* case. Union Pacific does not contest prongs 2 or 3. It does not have to. Because once again, the insurmountable hurdle for Sweatt is prong 4. None of Sweatt's purported comparators made the same fatal mistake that Sweatt made during his interview—persisting in a lie about criminal history. As a result, his comparators are not similar in all material respects, and Sweatt cannot make out his *prima facie* case for age discrimination.

Before we address Sweatt's argument regarding the district court's CMP, we pause to make some final observations on the discrimination claims. We do not doubt Sweatt's explanation that the Flossmoor arrest was a misunderstanding, that the judge tossed the case, and that Sweatt remained friends with all relevant parties. But these facts, which we accept as true, do not change the fact that Sweatt was not forthcoming about the incident during his interview. In the context of an interview for a position where honesty and integrity are paramount (Girard told him so), Sweatt's lack of candor understandably served as the death knell for his candidacy. Sweatt offers no evidence sufficient to create a genuine issue of material fact that the true reason behind the failure to hire was age or race discrimination.

C. The District Court's Summary Judgment Procedure

Sweatt argues that the district court's CMP denies a non-movant the ability to respond to the movant's statement of facts. He further argues that the CMP prohibits a non- [—18—] movant from submitting additional facts that he believes would defeat the motion.

This, he contends, contravenes Local Rule 56.1. And in this case, he claims, it prejudiced him below. We disagree.

Our analysis begins with the relevant portion of Judge Ellis's CMP:

Motions for summary judgment and responses must comply with Local Rules 56.1(a)(1)–(2) and 56.1(b)(1)–(2), as well as the procedures outlined herein. Parties are directed to file **a joint statement of undisputed material facts** that the parties agree are not in dispute. The joint statement must include—for each undisputed fact—citations to admissible evidence. The joint statement of undisputed material facts shall be filed separately from the memoranda of law and shall include the line, paragraph, or page number where the supporting material may be found in the record. **The parties may not file—and the court will not consider—separate documents of undisputed facts.** If the nonmoving party refuses to join in the statement, the moving party will nevertheless be permitted to file the motion, accompanied by a separate declaration of counsel explaining why a joint statement was not filed. Failure to stipulate to an undisputed fact without a reasonable basis for doing so may result in sanctions.

Judge Sara L. Ellis, Case Management Procedures, *available at* http://c.ymcdn.com/sites/www.7thcircuitbar.org/resource/resmgr/2014_materials/Ellis.pdf (last visited July 24, 2015) (emphasis in original). [—19—]

This CMP is concerned solely with a statement of *undisputed material facts* to which *both parties agree*. Nothing in this CMP prohibits *one* party from responding to *another* party's version of the *disputed* facts. And nothing in this CMP prohibits a party from submitting additional facts, as the need may arise. The laudable goal of this CMP is to remove the chaff from the grain in a given case, thereby allowing the parties—and the court—to focus on the facts that are actually in dispute.

Judge Ellis's CMP does not disadvantage a party. If a party refuses to agree to a joint statement, that party can still proceed with its motion for summary judgment. It simply must include a statement explaining why the joint statement was not filed. We note that in this case, the district court allowed Sweatt to amend the joint statement by including five additional facts. That procedure inured to Sweatt's benefit here.

Further, by its own terms, the CMP conforms to the Local Rules of the Northern District of Illinois. The relevant Local Rule, 56.1, directs each party to file "a statement of material facts as to which the moving party *contends* there is no genuine issue … ." N.D. Ill. L.R. 56.1 (emphasis added). That rule aspires to the goal achieved by Judge Ellis's CMP—agreeing that certain material facts are beyond dispute. In practice, however, there is a difference between *contending* that a fact is beyond dispute and *agreeing* that a fact is beyond disputed. Local Rule 56.1(3) focuses on the former. The Committee Comment acknowledges this fact. N.D. Ill. L.R. 56.1 cmt. ("The judges of this Court have observed that parties frequently include in their LR56.1 statements facts that are unnecessary to the motion and/or *are disputed*.") (emphasis [—20—] added). Judge Ellis's CMP, on the other hand, encourages the parties to work together to focus on the latter. We find no fault in that. And we certainly find no inconsistency between the CMP and Local Rule 56.1.

Because we find Local Rule 56.1 wholly consistent with Judge Ellis's CMP, we need not discuss Sweatt's remaining argument concerning Federal Rule of Civil Procedure 83. *See* Fed. R. Civ. P. 83 (allowing a judge to "regulate practice in any manner consistent with federal law, rules adopted under 28 U.S.C. §§ 2072 and 2075, and the district court's local rules"). It is without merit.

III. Conclusion

For the foregoing reasons, the judgment of the district court is AFFIRMED.

United States Court of Appeals for the Eighth Circuit

United States Court of Appeals
for the Eighth Circuit

No. 13-3023

IN RE GENMAR HOLDINGS, INC.

Appeal from the United States Bankruptcy Appellate Panel for the Eighth Circuit

Decided: January 28, 2015

Citation: 776 F.3d 961, 3 Adm. R. 512 (8th Cir. 2015).

Before **LOKEN**, **BEAM**, and **COLLOTON**, Circuit Judges.

[—1—] **LOKEN**, Circuit Judge: [—2—]

The bankruptcy trustee for Chapter 7 debtor Genmar Holdings, Inc. commenced this adversary proceeding seeking to avoid as preferential a $65,000 payment made to Michael Calandrillo within ninety days of bankruptcy. *See* 11 U.S.C. § 547(b). The bankruptcy court[1] granted the trustee summary judgment. The Bankruptcy Appellate Panel (BAP) affirmed. Calandrillo appeals, arguing the payment was a "contemporaneous exchange for new value" that may not be avoided under § 547(c)(1).[2] Reviewing the grant of summary judgment *de novo*, we agree with the BAP that Calandrillo failed to prove the parties to the transaction intended a contemporaneous exchange and

---

[1] The Honorable Dennis D. O'Brien, United States Bankruptcy Judge for the District of Minnesota.

[2] At oral argument, Calandrillo raised two other issues. First, he contends that the $65,000 payment should be deemed to have been made outside the § 547(b)(4)(A) ninety-day preference period. We decline to consider this fact-intensive issue because it was not raised either to the bankruptcy court or to the BAP. *See Singleton v. Wulff*, 428 U.S. 106, 120-21 (1976). Second, he argues the bankruptcy court erred in ruling that the trustee's amended complaint adding Calandrillo as a defendant related back to the date of the original complaint because the applicable statute of limitations does not expressly allow relation back. *See* Fed. R. Civ. P. 15(c)(1)(A); 11 U.S.C. § 546(a). We decline to consider this issue because it was not argued in Calandrillo's brief on appeal, and the contention appears to be contrary to the alternative provisions in Rule 15(c)(1)(A)-(C), as the BAP discussed.

therefore affirm. *See Contemporary Indus. Corp. v. Frost*, 564 F.3d 981, 984 (8th Cir. 2009) (standard of review).

The relevant facts are undisputed. In April 2007, Calandrillo purchased a boat manufactured by Hydra-Sports, a subsidiary of Genmar Tennessee, a subsidiary of Genmar Holdings. Calandrillo claimed the boat was defective and commenced an arbitration proceeding. On February 19, 2009, Calandrillo entered into a settlement agreement with "Genmar Tennessee, Inc. . . . together with its . . . parents [and] subsidiaries." Calandrillo agreed to convey title to the boat to Genmar Tennessee, [—3—] free of liens and encumbrances; Hydra-Sports agreed to pay Calandrillo $205,000 in the following manner:

A. Hydra-Sports shall pay to the Bank (which currently holds a lien on the Boat) such amounts as necessary to obtain a discharge of the Bank's lien on the Boat, and it is an express condition of this agreement that Hydra-Sports is to receive a lien waiver from the Bank immediately upon payment to the Bank . . .

B. The remainder of the Settlement Payment shall be paid to the trust account of [Calandrillo's attorneys], in trust for and on behalf of [Calandrillo], no sooner tha[n] 15 days after Genmar Tennessee receives the lien waiver confirming the Bank's discharge of the lien and all title assignment documents . . . for the Boat.

The next day, the bank received $140,000 from a Genmar entity and issued a lien waiver. On February 25, Calandrillo executed a bill of sale conveying the boat to Genmar Tennessee. On March 4, he sent documents assigning title to Genmar Tennessee. On March 23, Genmar Holdings sent Calandrillo a check for the $65,000 settlement balance. On June 1, 2009, Genmar Holdings and twenty-one subsidiaries, including Genmar Tennessee, filed for bankruptcy. The trustee brought this suit seeking recovery of the $65,000 payment from Calandrillo as a preferential transfer. The $140,000 payment to the bank a month earlier was outside the ninety-day preference period in § 547(b).

The avoidance of preferential transfers under § 547 "is intended to discourage creditors from racing to dismember a debtor sliding into bankruptcy and to promote equality of distribution to creditors in bankruptcy." *In re Jones Truck Lines, Inc.*, 130 F.3d 323, 326 (8th Cir. 1997). Contemporaneous new value exchanges are excepted from avoidance because they "encourage creditors to continue doing business with troubled debtors who may then be able to avoid bankruptcy altogether," and "because other creditors are not adversely affected if the debtor's estate receives new value." [—4—] *Id.* To qualify for this exception, the creditor transferee must prove that an otherwise preferential transfer was "(A) intended by the debtor and the creditor . . . to be a contemporaneous exchange for new value given to the debtor; and (B) in fact a substantially contemporaneous exchange." § 547(c)(1).

Calandrillo claims that the § 547(c)(1) exception applies to the $65,000 payment because he provided new value to the debtor when he conveyed the boat in a contemporaneous exchange. "The critical inquiry in determining whether there has been a contemporaneous exchange for new value is whether the parties intended such an exchange." *In re Gateway Pac. Corp.*, 153 F.3d 915, 918 (8th Cir. 1998). Calandrillo bears the burden of proving this fact. § 547(g); *Jones Truck Lines*, 130 F.3d at 328. Here, the BAP affirmed the bankruptcy court's conclusion that Calandrillo presented no evidence permitting a reasonable fact-finder to find that the parties to the settlement agreement intended a contemporaneous exchange for new value. We agree.

Calandrillo's conveyance of the boat was completed on March 4, when he sent executed title documents to Genmar Tennessee. He received payment of the $65,000 settlement balance on March 23. This time lag, by itself, does not resolve whether the transaction was intended to be a "contemporaneous exchange." *See* 5 Resnick & Sommer, *Collier on*

Bankruptcy ¶ 547.04[1][a] at 547-44 (16th ed. 2014) ("the passage of time does not necessarily negate that intent"). Many exchanges the parties intend to be contemporaneous cannot be completed instantly, or even within a few days. For example, in *In re Lewellyn & Co., Inc.*, 929 F.2d 424, 428 (8th Cir. 1991), we upheld the bankruptcy court's finding that the parties intended stock purchases settled seven business days later to be contemporaneous exchanges. In cases where contemporaneous intent was found after trial, or conceded by the trustee, even a substantial delay in one part of the exchange has not defeated the § 547(c)(1) exception if the creditor explained why a reasonable delay was consistent with the requisite intent. *See In re Dorholt*, 239 B.R. 521, 525 (B.A.P. 8th Cir. 1999) (sixteen [—5—] days to perfect a security interest; summary judgment for trustee reversed), *aff'd* 224 F.3d 871 (8th Cir. 2000); *In re Kerst*, 347 B.R. 418, 424 (Bankr. D. Colo. 2006) (delayed car refinancing); 4 William L. Norton Jr., *Norton Bankruptcy Law & Practice* § 66:35 (3d ed. 2014). "[C]ontemporaneity is a flexible concept which requires a case-by-case inquiry into all relevant circumstances." *Dorholt*, 224 F.3d at 874 (quotation omitted).

In this case, the essential question of the parties' intent is not conceded or obvious. Calandrillo argues the requisite intent can be found in the settlement agreement. The settlement agreement provided that Genmar Tennessee would make two payments to re-acquire clear title to the allegedly defective boat. First, the bank holding a substantial lien would be paid and provide a lien waiver. Initially satisfying an existing lien creditor is not inconsistent with the parties intending a contemporaneous exchange. Second, after Calandrillo transferred the necessary title documents to Genmar Tennessee, he would be paid the $65,000 balance of the "purchase" price. Again, providing a reasonable time for the buyer to review title documents is a type of delay that, if reasonable, would not be inconsistent with the parties intending a contemporaneous exchange. But here, the settlement agreement provided that the final $65,000 payment would be made to Calandrillo *no sooner than* fifteen days after

Genmar Tennessee received the lien waiver and title documents. Thus, on its face, the settlement agreement reflected that what might have been a contemporaneous exchange of a boat for $205,000 was instead a short-term loan of $65,000 to the debtor. A debtor's repayment of a loan within ninety days of bankruptcy is an avoidable preference.

Calandrillo produced no evidence explaining the reason for this open-ended payment delay in the settlement agreement. The absence of an explanation why a *mandatory* delay of at least fifteen days was reasonably necessary brings this case squarely within the purview of our decision in *In re Armstrong*, 291 F.3d 517, 525 (8th Cir. 2002). In *Armstrong*, a casino provided chips to a gambler in exchange for [—6—] "markers" that would be paid out of the gambler's bank account when deposited by the casino. But while the casino would deposit a customer's personal check when received, it agreed to hold the gambler's markers for fourteen days before making the deposits, later extended to thirty days. We upheld the bankruptcy court's conclusion there was no evidence of an intended contemporaneous exchange. Instead, the gambler incurred debts when the markers were signed that did not become due for thirty days. Agreeing not to deposit the markers until a certain date "convert[ed] a negotiable instrument into a loan." *Id.* at 524. Likewise here, a reasonable fact-finder could only conclude that the settlement agreement's unexplained fifteen-day holding period evidenced the intent to provide the debtor a short-term loan.

For this reason, we conclude the bankruptcy court and the BAP properly granted summary judgment to the trustee because there was no evidence the parties intended a contemporaneous exchange, a critical issue on which Calandrillo had the burden of proof. Given our resolution of this issue, we need not—and do not—address other issues disputed by the parties, including whether there was new value within the meaning of § 547(c)(1)(A), whether the discrepancy between $65,000 and the total amount paid for the boat would affect the § 547(c)(1) analysis, whether there was "in fact a substantially contemporaneous exchange" for purposes of § 547(c)(1)(B), and whether debtor Genmar Holdings could have the requisite intent in a transaction between Calandrillo and Genmar Tennessee.

The judgment of the BAP is affirmed.

United States Court of Appeals
for the Eighth Circuit

No. 13-3800

UNITED STATES
vs.
BROWN

Appeals from the United States District Court for the District of Minnesota - St. Paul

Decided: February 10, 2015

Citation: 777 F.3d 1025, 3 Adm. R. 515 (8th Cir. 2015).

Before **MURPHY, SMITH,** and **GRUENDER,** Circuit Judges.

[—2—] **MURPHY,** Circuit Judge: [—3—]

Appellees Michael Brown, Jerry Reyes, Marc Lyons, and Frederick Tibbetts were indicted under the Lacey Act which makes it unlawful to "sell . . . any fish . . . taken, possessed, transported, or sold in violation of . . . any Indian tribal law." 16 U.S.C. § 3372(a)(1). The indictments alleged that appellees had netted fish for commercial purposes within the boundaries of the Leech Lake Reservation in violation of the Leech Lake Conservation Code, then sold the fish. Appellees are Chippewa Indians, and they moved to dismiss the indictments on the ground that their prosecution violates fishing rights reserved under the 1837 Treaty between the United States and the Chippewa. The district court[1] granted the motions to dismiss. The United States appeals, arguing that its application of the Lacey Act did not infringe on appellees' fishing rights. We affirm.

I.

A.

During the early 1800s Chippewa Indians occupied much of present day Minnesota and Wisconsin. Ronald N. Satz, *Chippewa Treaty Rights: The Reserved Rights of Wisconsin's Chippewa Indians in Historical Perspective* 1

---

[1] The Honorable John R. Tunheim, United States District Judge for the District of Minnesota.

(Carl N. Haywood, ed., 1996). At least three thousand Chippewa resided in seven village centers at locations including Leech Lake. *Id.* In Minnesota they controlled the land east of the Mississippi River and north of the Crow Wing River. William Watts Folwell, *A History of Minnesota* 80-81, 88 (Solon J. Buck, ed., 1921).

Hunting, fishing, gathering, and trapping were essential to the survival and ways of life of Indian tribes throughout North America. *Cohen's Handbook of Federal Indian Law* § 18.01 at 1154 (Nell Jessup Newton ed., 2012). Such activities [—4—] "were not much less necessary to the existence of the Indians than the atmosphere they breathed." *United States v. Winans*, 198 U.S. 371, 381 (1905). Throughout their territory the Chippewa fished, hunted, trapped, gathered wild rice, and tapped maple trees for sugar. Satz, *Chippewa Treaty Rights* at 1-2. Fishing and hunting were of such importance that a boy's first success was publicly celebrated. *Id.* at 2. In addition to fishing for subsistence purposes, Chippewa Indians sold their catch to traders, from whom they also bought fishing nets. *Id.* at 29.

The United States made several treaties with Chippewa Indians during the nineteenth century, including two relevant to this case. In July 1837, over one thousand Chippewa Indians gathered at Fort Snelling while their chiefs negotiated with Wisconsin Territorial Governor Henry Dodge who represented the United States. Documents Related to the Negotiation of the Treaty of July 29, 1837, reprinted in Satz, *Chippewa Treaty Rights* 131-153, at 131 ("1837 Treaty Journal"). The United States sought to purchase land east of the Mississippi River in present day central Minnesota and Wisconsin because of its desirable pine timber. *Id.* at 131-32, 140.

During these negotiations, the Chippewa chiefs emphasized the importance of reserving their rights to fish, hunt, and gather on the land, also called usufructuary rights. According to the treaty journal, Ma-ghe-ga-bo stated, "Of all the country that we grant to you we wish to hold on to a tree where we get our living, & to reserve the streams where we drink the waters that give us life." 1837 Treaty Journal at 142. The secretary who recorded the proceedings noted that he transcribed the statement as provided by the underqualified interpreters, but he "presume[d] it to mean that the Indians wish to reserve the privilege of hunting & fishing on the lands and making sugar from the Maple." *Id.* Flatmouth, chief of the Pillager band which resided at Leech Lake, reiterated the importance of reserving usufructuary rights on the ceded lands: [—5—]

> My Father. Your children are willing to let you have their lands, but they wish to reserve the privilege of making sugar from the trees, and getting their living from the Lakes and Rivers, as they have done heretofore, and of remaining in this Country. . . . You know we can not live, deprived of our Lakes and Rivers; . . . we wish to remain upon them, to get a living.

Id. at 145.

Governor Dodge agreed to reserve these rights for the Chippewa Indians. 1837 Treaty Journal at 146. Article 5 of the 1837 treaty provides, "The privilege of hunting, fishing, and gathering the wild rice, upon the lands, the rivers, and the lakes included in the territory ceded, is guarantied to the Indians, during the pleasure of the President of the United States." Treaty with the Chippewa, July 29, 1837, art. 5, 7 Stat. 536 ("1837 Treaty").

The area surrounding the Leech Lake Reservation was not part of the territory ceded in 1837. *See* 1837 Treaty, art. 1. That reservation was established, and additional territory in northern Minnesota was ceded, in an 1855 treaty. Treaty with the Chippewa, February 22, 1855, art. 1-2, 10 Stat. 1165 ("1855 Treaty"). Several Chippewa chiefs again gathered at Fort Snelling for the negotiations. Documents Related to the Negotiation of the Treaty of February 22, 1855 at 1 ("1855 Treaty Journal), available at http://digital.library.wisc.edu/1711.dl/History.I T1855no287 (last visited Jan. 27, 2015). Colonel George Manypenny, Commissioner of

Indian Affairs, represented the United States. *Id.* According to the treaty journal, the Chippewa chiefs understood the United States to have a straightforward goal. In the words of Flatmouth, chief of the Pillager band residing near Leech Lake, "It appears to me that I understand what you want, and know your views from the few words I have heard you speak. You want land." *Id.* at 18. [—6—]

In contrast to the 1837 negotiations, there is no record of a discussion of usufructuary rights, and the treaty is silent on that subject. *See* 1855 Treaty Journal; 1855 Treaty. Reservations within the ceded territory were negotiated. Flatmouth requested a reservation "at Lake Winn[ibigoshish], Cass Lake, and Leech Lake" and the treaty thus established the Leech Lake Reservation. 1855 Treaty Journal at 29; 1855 Treaty, art. 2.

B.

In more recent years, courts have determined that treaty reservations of usufructuary rights to the Chippewa Indians remain in effect. In *Leech Lake Band of Chippewa Indians v. Herbst*, 334 F. Supp. 1001 (D. Minn. 1971), the Leech Lake Band sought a declaratory judgment that the state of Minnesota could not regulate fishing, hunting, and gathering wild rice within its reservation. The United States, also a plaintiff, contended "that the treaty protected rights to hunt, fish, trap and gather wild rice are property rights to be used in whatever fashion the Indians, as owners, desire, whether to eat, clothe, or sell." The district court determined that the Chippewa Indians' usufructuary rights had not been terminated by the 1889 Nelson Act, and it enjoined enforcement of state fish and game laws against Indians on the reservation. *Herbst*, 334 F. Supp. at 1006. The case ended in a settlement in which the Leech Lake Band created its own conservation code and agreed to enforce the code in tribal courts.

A subsequent case involving another band of Minnesota Chippewa Indians made its way to the Supreme Court. *Minnesota v. Mille Lacs Band of Chippewa Indians*, 526 U.S. 172 (1999). The state of Minnesota argued that the

Mille Lacs Band had lost the hunting, fishing, and gathering rights guaranteed by the 1837 treaty through an executive order in 1850, the 1855 treaty, and Minnesota's admission into the Union in 1858. *Id.* at 175-76. Analyzing the historical context of the 1855 treaty, the Court concluded that the lack of discussion of usufructuary rights in the [—7—] negotiations "suggest[ed] that the Chippewa did not understand the proposed Treaty to abrogate their usufructuary rights as guaranteed by other treaties." *Id.* at 198. The Court determined that the rights reserved under the 1837 treaty had not been extinguished by the subsequent executive order, 1855 treaty, or admission of Minnesota into the Union. *Id.* at 195, 202, 208.

C.

In 2010, the Minnesota Department of Natural Resources began "Operation Squarehook," an investigation into illegal sales of game fish, mostly walleye, in northern Minnesota. Minn. Dept. of Natural Res., "Operation Squarehook: Frequently Asked Questions," available at http://www.dnr.state.mn.us/enforcement/op_squarehook_faq.html (last visited January 27, 2015). State law enforcement worked with the U.S. Fish and Wildlife Service and authorities from the Red Lake and Leech Lake Indian Reservations. *Id.* The investigation focused on allegations that tribal members caught walleye on lakes within the reservations and illegally sold the fish to non Indians at below market rates. *Id.* Defendants were among over thirty people charged with criminal offenses as a result of the investigation, ten of whom were named in federal court indictments. *Id.*

The factual allegations against defendants relate to fishing within the Leech Lake Reservation. This reservation includes a number of lakes, such as Leech Lake, Cass Lake, Lake Winnibigoshish, and Six Mile Lake. Brown, Reyes, and Lyons are enrolled members of the Leech Lake Band, and Tibbetts is an enrolled member of the White Earth Band.[2] Both bands are part of the Minnesota Chippewa Tribe, a federally recognized Indian tribe. Indian Entities Recognized and Eligible To [—8—] Receive Services From the United States Bureau of Indian Affairs, 79 Fed. Reg. 4748-52 (January 29, 2014).

The indictments allege that defendants have taken fish by gill net for commercial purposes within the Leech Lake Reservation, violating the band's conservation code. Defendants had then sold the fish to non Indians, some of whom were also indicted. Section 22.01(2) of the conservation code prohibits taking game fish by gill net other than for personal use, and § 23.01 prohibits taking fish for commercial purposes within the reservation, except for non game fish when authorized by a permit from the band's conservation committee. Conservation Code of the Leech Lake Band of Chippewa Indians, §§ 22.01(2), 23.01. Walleye are included in the definition of "game fish." *Id.* § 11.01(10). Violations of sections 22.01 and 23.01 are punishable in tribal court by a fine of up to five hundred dollars, imprisonment for up to 180 days, both, "or any other penalty as deemed appropriate by the Judge." *Id.* at § 51.03(1).

Defendants were indicted in the District of Minnesota for violations of the federal Lacey Act, which makes it unlawful to sell fish taken "in violation of any Indian tribal law." 16 U.S.C. § 3372(a)(1). The indictments alleged that defendants had sold fish worth more than $350 knowing the fish were taken in violation of the Leech Lake conservation code. Such a violation is punishable by a fine of up to $20,000, imprisonment for up to five years, or both. 16 U.S.C. § 3373(d)(1).

Defendants moved to dismiss the indictments, arguing that the government could not prosecute them for exercising their right to fish on tribal waters. They claimed that the 1837 treaty reserved this right and that because Congress had not abrogated their

---

[2] The government has not suggested that Tibbetts's membership in the White Earth Band provides him different fishing rights from those of the other defendants.

treaty right, the indictment must be dismissed. At a hearing on defendants' motions, the United States "agree[d] that there's no issue as to whether the 1837 Chippewa Treaty applies in the Leech Lake region." The government argued [—9—] however that the prosecution did not implicate the defendants' treaty rights because the Lacey Act was a law of general applicability.

While considering these arguments, the district court examined the 1837 treaty and its historical context, including the negotiations between the Chippewa chiefs and Governor Dodge. The court concluded that the statements made in those negotiations demonstrated that all parties understood the 1837 treaty to reserve "a broad right to fish as they had been accustomed—without restriction." This right included selling the fish to make a living and did not limit the method used for catching them. The defendants' alleged actions therefore fell within the protections of the treaty. The district court concluded that the Lacey Act did not abrogate the usufructuary rights reserved under the 1837 treaty. The indictments were dismissed, and the United States appeals.

II.

A.

The United States argues that prosecuting defendants under the Lacey Act does not implicate usufructuary rights. In considering that argument we must examine the scope of the rights protected by the 1837 treaty, a treaty the United States admits is applicable. When seeking to determine the meaning of Indian treaties, "we look beyond the written words to the larger context that frames the Treaty, including the history of the treaty, the negotiations, and the practical construction adopted by the parties." *Mille Lacs Band*, 526 U.S. at 196 (quotation omitted). We interpret such treaties liberally, resolving uncertainties in favor of the Indians, and we "give effect to the terms as the Indians themselves would have understood them." *Id.* at 196, 200.

The wording of the 1837 treaty is broad, guaranteeing a "privilege of hunting, fishing,

and gathering the wild rice, upon the lands, the rivers, and the lakes included [—10—] in the territory ceded." 1837 Treaty, art. 5. The historical importance of these activities in Chippewa life and the emphasis of the Chippewa chiefs on usufructuary rights during their negotiations with the United States indicate that the Indians believed they were reserving unrestricted rights to hunt, fish, and gather throughout a large territory. This case presents no issue of whether the treaty protection includes the use of new technologies since the Chippewa used nets to catch fish at the time the treaty was made.

The history suggests that the Chippewa Indians' exercise of their usufructuary rights included selling what they hunted, fished, or gathered in order to make a modest living. Other cases considering the 1837 treaty have reached the same conclusion. *Mille Lacs Band of Chippewa Indians v. Minnesota*, 861 F. Supp. 784, 838 (D. Minn. 1994); *Lac Courte Oreilles Band of Lake Superior Chippewa Indians v. Wisconsin*, 653 F. Supp. 1420, 1435 (W.D. Wis. 1987). Where "Indians engaged in commercial fishing prior to and at the time of their treaties, as was the case in . . . the Great Lakes area, the treaties will be read to entitle them to fish commercially today." *United States v. Dion*, 752 F.2d 1261, 1265 n.11 (8th Cir. 1985) (en banc) (quotation omitted), *rev'd in part on other grounds*, 476 U.S. 734 (1986). Moreover, as recently as the 1970s the United States argued in the *Herbst* case that usufructuary rights on the Leech Lake Reservation included the right to sell fish. This history, the text of the 1837 treaty, and evidence of the parties' understanding of it show that the treaty guaranteed a broad right to fish that includes right to sell them.

On appeal, the United States attempts to retreat from its earlier admission that the rights reserved under the 1837 treaty apply on the Leech Lake Reservation. It acknowledges that the the Chippewa Indians have on reservation rights "inherent in [the band's] sovereignty" and cites *Cohen's Handbook of Federal Indian Law* § 18.03[1] at 1158-59. As this treatise notes, "[e]xclusive on-reservation hunting, fishing, and gathering rights are implied from the establishment of a reservation for the exclusive use of a tribe." *Id*. The Supreme Court has explained that "[a]s a [—11—] general rule, Indians enjoy exclusive treaty rights to hunt and fish on lands reserved to them . . . [and] [t]hese rights need not be expressly mentioned in the treaty." *United States v. Dion*, 476 U.S. 734, 738 (1986). Individuals may assert these rights "unless [they] were clearly relinquished by treaty or have been modified by Congress." *Id*.

The United States suggests no reason why the right to net and sell fish would not be part of the usufructuary rights reserved by the establishment of the Leech Lake Reservation in the 1855 treaty. The context of the 1855 treaty establishing the Leech Lake Reservation indicates that this "general rule" applies. As the Supreme Court noted in *Minnesota v. Mille Lacs Band*, the silence regarding usufructuary rights in the 1855 treaty and the negotiations leading up to it suggest that the Chippewa Indians did not believe they were relinquishing such rights. 526 U.S. at 198. Historical sources indicate that the Chippewa practiced such activities during the time period when the reservation was established. Even if the 1837 treaty does not apply, the rights it protects are relevant because in this particular case the Chippewa would have understood similar broad rights to apply on the Leech Lake Reservation. We therefore conclude that the exclusive on reservation fishing rights of the Chippewa Indians protect the rights to fish and to sell fish.

B.

The United States raises several arguments why the prosecution does not conflict with Chippewa fishing rights reserved under the 1837 treaty or implied by the establishment of the Leech Lake Reservation in the 1855 treaty. First, the government contends that such right is one that may be asserted by a band or tribe, but not by an individual. In support of this argument, the government cites a Tenth Circuit case for the proposition that the right asserted in court proceedings is "the right of an individual of the community," part of the "tribal right to hunt or fish." [—12—] *United States v. Fox*, 573 F.3d 1050, 1053-54 (10th Cir. 2009).

It is well settled, however, that an individual Indian may assert usufructuary rights in a criminal prosecution. For example, the Supreme Court stated in *United States v. Dion* that hunting and fishing "treaty rights can be asserted by Dion as an individual member of the Tribe." 476 U.S. at 738 n.4. Evaluating usufructuary rights in *United States v. Winans*, the Court explained that while "the negotiations were with the tribe," treaties "reserved rights, however, to every individual Indian, as though named therein." 198 U.S. at 381.

Fox does not help the government's argument in this case. The defendant in *Fox*, a Navajo Indian and a convicted felon, was prosecuted under 18 U.S.C. § 922(g) for possessing a shotgun and rifle on the Navajo Reservation, even though he claimed to possess the guns solely for hunting. 573 F.3d at 1051. Although the Tenth Circuit was "skeptical of the [government's] position that hunting rights guaranteed by treaty only benefit the tribe collectively, as opposed to its individual members," *id*. at 1053, it decided that Fox was ineligible to assert a treaty hunting right because the treaty provided that Navajo Indians who commit crimes may be "tried [by the United States] and punished according to its laws." *Id*. at 1054-55. Part of Fox's punishment was the loss of the privilege to possess firearms. *Id*. The present case is easily distinguishable, for defendants here are not subject to any prior federal criminal punishment prohibiting the use of gill nets for commercial fishing.

The United States also argues that this Lacey Act prosecution supports rather than undermines tribal sovereignty because it is predicated on a violation of the Leech Lake Band's conservation code. Since defendants allegedly fished in ways prohibited by the band, usufructuary rights do not protect them, the government contends. The government does not, and cannot, cite any authority for the proposition that the Leech Lake Band's fishing regulations have altered the scope of rights protected in the 1837 treaty or by the establishment of the reservation in the 1855 treaty. Whether or not [—13—] a Lacey Act prosecution in this case could promote tribal sovereignty, a tribe does not abrogate its own rights by electing to regulate those rights. Tribal fishing laws enforceable in tribal court do not change the scope of treaty protections which tribal members may assert as a defense to prosecution by the United States.

Finally, the United States also relies on a Ninth Circuit case holding that Indians could be prosecuted for taking fish within Indian Country in violation of tribal regulations. *United States v. Sohappy*, 770 F.2d 816 (9th Cir. 1985). The Ninth Circuit described the "crucial issue" there as "whether the treaties reserved to the tribes *exclusive* jurisdiction over enforcement of tribal fishing law against Indians." *Id.* at 818 (emphasis in original). The court decided that a treaty which reserved the "right to take fish at all 'usual and accustomed places'" was not exclusive but was to be shared 'in common with citizens of the Territory.'" *Id.* at 819. There was no language in the treaty "purporting to exempt Indians from the laws of general applicability throughout the United States." *Id.* at 820 (quotation omitted). In such circumstances, the Ninth Circuit concluded, concurrent federal jurisdiction over fishing did not violate treaty rights. *Id.* at 819-20.

An affirmance of the district court in this case does not conflict with *Sohappy* because that case evaluated rights under a particular treaty with materially different language and parties. The Supreme Court has instructed courts to analyze the history, purpose, and negotiations of the treaty at issue in a particular case. *See Mille Lacs Band*, 526 U.S. at 202. The Ninth Circuit determined in *Sohappy* that a right to take fish "in common with citizens of the Territory" was not an exclusive right. 770 F.2d at 819. In contrast, the 1837 treaty applicable here reserves broad usufructuary rights with no such limiting language, and the on reservation rights implied in the 1855 treaty are exclusive. These are critical differences which distinguish the case before our court. [—14—]

The United States nonetheless urges that its Lacey Act prosecutions are valid because the treaty does not "exempt Indians from the laws of general applicability throughout the United States." *Sohappy*, 770 F.2d at 820. Because the activity for which defendants were prosecuted (selling fish they caught on the Leech Lake Reservation) falls within the scope of the Chippewa Indians' exclusive usufructuary rights, we need not now consider whether the 1837 treaty exempted the Chippewa from other laws of general applicability. This conclusion is consistent with our decision in *United States v. White*, 508 F.2d 453 (8th Cir. 1974).

In *White*, we affirmed the dismissal of an indictment against a member of the Red Lake Band for violating the Eagle Protection Act, 16 U.S.C. § 668(a), by shooting at a bald eagle on the reservation. *Id.* at 454. We stated there that "areas traditionally left to tribal self-government, those most often the subject of treaties, have enjoyed an exception from the general rule that congressional enactments, in terms applying to all persons, includes Indians and their property interests." *Id.* at 455. After determining that the Red Lake Band had reserved hunting rights, the court continued, "To affect those rights, then, by 16 U.S.C. § 668, it was incumbent upon Congress to expressly abrogate or modify the spirit of the relationship between the United States and Red Lake Chippewa Indians on their native reservation." *Id.* at 457-58. As Congress had not so acted, the court concluded, the district court had properly dismissed the indictment. *Id.* at 458-59.

Other treaty rights decisions show that *White* furnishes the correct analysis for the issues presented here. In *United States v. Dion* which was decided after *Sohappy*, the Supreme Court also employed an abrogation analysis when determining whether treaty rights precluded prosecution of a Yankton Sioux Indian under the Eagle Protection Act. 476 U.S. at 737-39. Later in *United States v. Gotchnik*, we again evaluated the scope of treaty protections and whether Congress abrogated those protections when determining that treaty fishing rights did not preclude federal [—15—] prosecution for using motor vehicles in the Boundary Waters Canoe Area Wilderness. 222 F.3d 506, 508-11 (8th Cir. 2000).

The United States points out that two of our cases have cited *Sohappy*. *United States v. Stone*, 112 F.3d 971, 973-74 (8th Cir. 1997); *United States v. Big Eagle*, 881 F.2d 539, 540 n.1 (8th Cir. 1989). In neither of these cases is it clear that the Indian defendants were prosecuted for actions that fell within their treaty hunting and fishing rights. Stone was charged with violating the Airborne Hunting Act within Indian country by using a plane to drive a moose toward hunters on the ground. *Stone*, 112 F.3d at 972. The hunters were not prosecuted. *See id.* Big Eagle was charged with taking fish on the reservation of a tribe to which he did not belong in violation of that tribe's rules. *Big Eagle*, 881 F.2d at 539-40. Neither decision considered the history, purpose, and negotiations of a treaty claimed to protect the defendant's actions. *See Stone*, 112 F.3d at 973-74; *Big Eagle*, 881 F.2d at 540. Moreover, even if these cases were to conflict with *White*, we would be obligated to follow *White* as the earliest case on point. *Mader v. United States*, 654 F.3d 794, 800 (8th Cir. 2011) (en banc).

After giving full consideration to the arguments by the United States, we conclude that appellees are entitled to assert the Chippewa Indians' fishing rights and that this prosecution under the Lacey Act conflicts with those rights.

III.

Although Congress may abrogate Indian treaty rights, it must make its intention to do so "clear and plain." *Dion*, 476 U.S. at 738. There must be "clear evidence that Congress actually considered a conflict between its intended action on the one hand and Indian treaty rights on the other, and chose to resolve that conflict by abrogating the treaty." *Id.* at 740. The United States does not argue that Congress abrogated Chippewa fishing rights through the Lacey Act. That Act itself makes clear that Congress did *not* intend to abrogate Indian rights: it provides that [—16—]

[n]othing in this chapter shall be construed as . . . repealing, superseding, or modifying any right, privilege, or immunity granted, reserved, or established pursuant to treaty, statute, or executive order pertaining to any Indian tribe, band, or community.

16 U.S.C. § 3378(c)(2). Congress has thus not abrogated the rights asserted by defendants.

IV.

We conclude that the historic fishing rights of the Chippewa Indians bar this prosecution of defendants for taking fish within the Leech Lake Reservation and selling them. The judgment of the district court is affirmed.

United States Court of Appeals
for the Eighth Circuit

No. 14-2234

ST. PAUL FIRE & MARINE INS. CO.
VS.
ABHE & SVOBODA, INC.

Appeal from the United States District Court for the
District of Minnesota - Minneapolis

Decided: August 20, 2015 (Amended October 6, 2015)

Citation: 798 F.3d 715, 3 Adm. R. 522 (8th Cir. 2015).

Before **WOLLMAN**, **BEAM**, and **COLLOTON**, Circuit
Judges.

[—1—] **COLLOTON**, Circuit Judge:

Following the sinking of a leased barge during a storm, industrial painting contractor, Abhe & Svoboda, Inc. ("Abhe"), filed a claim for insurance coverage. Abhe invoked a Protection and Indemnity insurance policy issued by maritime underwriters, St. Paul Fire and Marine Insurance Company ("St. Paul Fire"), as part of a package marine insurance policy. St. Paul Fire denied Abhe's claims and then [—2—] filed suit in the district court seeking a declaration that the policy was void under the doctrine of *uberrimae fidei*. That doctrine requires that parties to an insurance contract must accord each other the highest degree of good faith. Abhe filed several counterclaims, including a claim for negligence, and both parties moved for summary judgment.

The district court granted St. Paul Fire's motion for summary judgment, declaring the package policy void under the principle of *uberrimae fidei* because Abhe failed to disclose material facts in its application for insurance coverage. The court also dismissed Abhe's counterclaims with prejudice. Abhe appeals, arguing principally that the district court failed to consider the element of reliance in assessing St. Paul Fire's *uberrimae fidei* defense. We conclude that reliance is an element of the defense, and that there are disputed issues of fact as to whether it is satisfied, so we reverse and remand for further proceedings.

I.

Abhe is a Minnesota company that repairs and paints dams, bridges, and other infrastructure. In 2010, Abhe contracted with the Rhode Island Bridge and Turnpike Authority to paint and repair the Pell Bridge, a bridge that hangs over Narragansett Bay in Rhode Island. To assist in painting the bridge, Abhe leased two barges from Sterling Equipment, Inc. These barges were "dumb" barges, meaning that they had no motor or means of propulsion and were intended to serve solely as stationary equipment platforms. The parties refer to these barges as SEI-34 and SEI-120.

The leasing agreement with Sterling required Abhe to have a professional surveyor assess the barges "[t]o establish the condition of the Vessel[s] at the time of delivery and re-delivery." The survey report for SEI-34 noted that there were pinholes in the deck, the under-deck tanks were not watertight from one another, and there was mud, sand, and water in some tanks. The report did not note any holes in [—3—] SEI-34's hull and did not recommend any repairs. The survey also valued SEI-34 at $90,000, which reflected the value of the scrap metal, "plus a little bit more because the barge was still useful."

In March 2011, Abhe anchored the barges under the Pell Bridge and began painting. Over the next seven months, Abhe used SEI-34 as a stationary equipment platform. During this time, Abhe employees regularly inspected the barge, looked for holes, and fixed pinholes found in the deck. Abhe also installed a utility pump to remove any water that accumulated in SEI-34's bilge.

During the first three months of its work on the Pell Bridge project, Abhe was covered under its existing Marine Hull and Protection and Indemnity insurance policy. But instead of renewing its policy with its existing insurer, Abhe purchased a package marine insurance policy from St. Paul Fire. St. Paul Fire did not request that Abhe complete an application for insurance, but instead accepted the application that Abhe provided to its previous insurer in May 2010. The schedule of vessels attached to that application was outdated and did not include SEI-34 or the other vessels that Abhe leased for the Pell Bridge project. The 2010 application also indicated that none of the scheduled vessels was surveyed within the last two years because the survey of SEI-34 had yet to be performed at the time of the application.

On May 3, 2011, Abhe sent St. Paul Fire an updated schedule of vessels, which included SEI-34 as a leased barge with a value of $225,000, reflecting its agreed value on its charter application with Sterling. Abhe did not provide St. Paul Fire with the November 2010 survey of SEI-34, and St. Paul Fire did not attempt to survey any of Abhe's marine equipment, as it was entitled to do under the policy. St. Paul Fire issued Abhe a Marine Hull and Protection and Indemnity Policy effective July 1, 2011, through July 1, 2012. [—4—]

On October 29, 2011, a severe nor'easter struck the Newport area. During that storm, SEI-34 sank to the bottom of Narragansett Bay and landed upside down, crushing most of the equipment that was welded to its deck. The Coast Guard intervened shortly thereafter and ordered Abhe to remove the wreck from the bay. If Abhe failed to do so within a specified period of time, the Coast Guard would federalize the wreck, which would empower the government to clear the wreck and hold Abhe liable for all associated costs.

Abhe contacted a marine salvage company, Donjon Marine Co., Inc., to negotiate the wreck removal. At St. Paul Fire's request, Abhe provided St. Paul Fire with SEI-34's survey and lease agreement, salvage plans, and a proposed wreck-removal contract from Donjon. Abhe then turned over negotiation of the Donjon contract to St. Paul Fire, and St. Paul Fire retained an attorney to negotiate the contract on Abhe's behalf.

After the wreck had been submerged for over five weeks, Donjon raised SEI-34's hull and all equipment that was still attached to the deck. Donjon then refused to recover the remaining barge equipment based on a

provision in the wreck-removal contract that it negotiated with St. Paul Fire. Because the Coast Guard's deadline for federalizing the wreck was approaching, Abhe retained new companies to remove the remaining barge equipment for an additional cost.

During negotiations of the wreck-removal contract, St. Paul Fire agreed to guarantee fifty percent of the payments due Donjon and prepaid that amount. Donjon then pursued Abhe for the other half of the money. Abhe and Donjon proceeded to arbitration regarding Donjon's obligations to Abhe under the wreck-removal contract. Abhe sought defense and indemnification from St. Paul Fire for the arbitration, but St. Paul Fire refused, citing Abhe's non-disclosure of SEI-34's 2010 survey as a reason for the coverage denial. [—5—]

The arbitrators concluded that Donjon breached its contract with Abhe by failing to raise all of the equipment, and the panel awarded Abhe $665,351.15 in compensatory damages, interest, and attorney's fees. The panel disallowed Abhe's claim for loss of the barge and other "overhead" items, including employee salaries, overtime, and damages not specifically tied to the recovery of the remaining equipment.

While the arbitration was pending, St. Paul Fire filed this action in the district court, seeking a declaratory judgment that it had no duty to defend or indemnify Abhe for several reasons. Abhe filed three counterclaims, including one alleging negligence by St. Paul Fire.

The district court granted St. Paul Fire's motion for summary judgment, concluding that the insurance policy was void *ab initio* because Abhe breached its duty of good faith under the doctrine of *uberrimae fidei* by failing to disclose the 2010 survey of SEI-34 on its application for insurance. The court thus denied Abhe's cross-motion for partial summary judgment as moot and dismissed Abhe's counterclaims with prejudice.

Abhe appeals, arguing that the district court applied the wrong legal standard in determining that it breached its duty of good faith. We review the district court's grant of summary judgment *de novo*, viewing the evidence in the light most favorable to Abhe and giving Abhe "the benefit of all reasonable inferences to be drawn from the evidence." *Country Life Ins. Co. v. Marks*, 592 F.3d 896, 898 (8th Cir. 2010). [—6—]

II.

A.

This dispute concerns a marine insurance contract and therefore is governed by the principle of *uberrimae fidei*, or utmost good faith. *See N.Y. Marine & Gen. Ins. Co. v. Cont'l Cement Co.*, 761 F.3d 830, 839, 2 Adm. R. 468, 473 (8th Cir. 2014). Under the doctrine of *uberrimae fidei*, "the parties to a marine insurance policy must accord each other the highest degree of good faith." *Knight v. U.S. Fire Ins. Co.*, 804 F.2d 9, 13 (2d Cir. 1986). This duty of good faith requires the insured to "disclose to the insurer all known circumstances that materially affect the risk being insured." *Id.*; *see also Kilpatrick Marine Piling v. Fireman's Fund Ins. Co.*, 795 F.2d 940, 942 (11th Cir. 1986). Because the insured is in the best position to know of any facts that may be material to the risk, the insured is obligated to disclose those facts to the insurer, regardless of whether the insurer makes a specific inquiry. *See Knight*, 804 F.2d at 13.

The parties agree that Abhe was required to disclose all material facts to St. Paul Fire, but they dispute whether there is another element to an insurer's claim that a policy is void for non-disclosure. Abhe argues that an insurer cannot void a policy under the doctrine of *uberrimae fidei* without showing both that the insured failed to disclose a material fact *and* that the non-disclosure induced the insurer to issue the policy. The district court reasoned that St. Paul Fire was entitled to void the policy solely because a survey of a vessel's condition could "possibly influence the mind of a prudent and intelligent insurer"—*i.e.*, that the non-disclosure was material. Abhe asserts that the district court applied the wrong standard and that it failed to examine whether St. Paul Fire actually relied on the non-existence of SEI-

34's survey when deciding whether to issue the policy to Abhe. [—7—]

There is surprisingly little authority on whether a showing of reliance is required to void an insurance policy under the doctrine of *uberrimae fidei*. The principal case to address the question directly is *Puritan Insurance Co. v. Eagle Steamship Co. S.A.*, 779 F.2d 866 (2d Cir. 1985), which held that reliance is a necessary element of the *uberrimae fidei* defense:

> The principle of *uberrimae fidei* does not require the voiding of the contract unless the undisclosed facts were material *and relied upon*. A fact is not material unless it is something which would have controlled the underwriter's decision, and a marine insurance policy cannot be voided for misrepresentation where the alleged misrepresentation was not relied upon and did not in any way mislead the insurer.

Id. at 871 (emphasis added) (internal citation and quotation marks omitted).

St. Paul Fire argues that *Puritan* does not stand for the proposition that an insurer must *always* show reliance before invoking the *uberrimae fidei* defense. Instead, St. Paul Fire suggests that an insurer is required to show actual reliance only where the insurer had actual knowledge of the claimed non-disclosure and bound the risk anyway. According to St. Paul Fire, reliance should factor into a court's decision only where the underwriter bound the insurance with knowledge of the material information but did not rely upon it.

St. Paul Fire's contention is inconsistent with *Puritan*. The insured in that case failed to disclose two losses suffered by two of its vessels on its application for insurance. *Id.* at 868. The insurer was made aware of the first loss, but the second loss was not disclosed to the insurer until the next insurance renewal period. *Id.* at 869. Even though the insurer had no knowledge of the second loss, the Second Circuit upheld the district court's finding that while the insured should have disclosed the second loss to the insurers, the insurers "failed to prove that they would not have undertaken the risk had they been fully informed of this loss." *Id.* at 870. *Puritan* [—8—] thus requires that an insurer seeking to void a policy show reliance on an insured's non-disclosure, regardless of whether the insurer had knowledge of the undisclosed material fact at the time that it decided to issue the policy.

We find the Second Circuit's reasoning persuasive. In general contract law, a misrepresentation by omission has no legal effect "unless it induces action by the recipient, that is, unless [the recipient] manifests his assent to the contract in reliance on it." Restatement (Second) of Contracts § 164 cmt. c (1981). Before a party can rescind a contract due to the other party's non-disclosure or misrepresentation, he must show that the misrepresentation induced him to enter the contract. *Id.* In other words, a party is required to show a causal connection between the other party's omission and the issuing of the contract. *See* R. Lord, 27 Williston on Contracts § 69:32 (4th ed. 2014). We discern no reason why the requirement of causation should be removed in the context of marine insurance contracts.

St. Paul Fire's proposed rule also would create a moral hazard on the part of marine insurers. It would have the perverse effect of encouraging insurers to assume unreasonable risks and to issue insurance polices that they otherwise would not have issued. Under the rule proposed by St. Paul Fire, if an insurer knows that an applicant for insurance failed to disclose or misrepresented a fact that other prudent insurers may deem to be material, that insurer would have an incentive to issue the policy anyway, collect premiums from the insured, and then use the doctrine of *uberrimae fidei* to void the policy if an accident occurs and the insured seeks to invoke the policy's protection. Allowing an insurer to void a policy based on the *uberrimae fidei* defense in that situation would not further the purpose of the doctrine to protect the insurer against liability caused by an insured's failure to act in good faith.

We have required that insurers demonstrate actual reliance before voiding a policy based on the principle of *uberrimae fidei* in other circumstances. In *Shipley v. Arkansas Blue Cross & Blue Shield*, 333 F.3d 898 (8th Cir. 2003), we addressed [—9—] an insurer's effort to void an insurance policy, governed by ERISA, because of alleged material omissions in the insurance application. The court recognized that "[i]nsurance polices are traditionally contracts *uberrimae fidei*," and "[i]f a party's manifestation of assent is induced by either a fraudulent or a material misrepresentation by the other party *upon which the recipient is justified in relying*, the contract is voidable by the recipient." *Id.* at 903 (emphasis added) (internal quotation marks omitted). We upheld the district court's grant of summary judgment in favor of the insurer, but only after determining that the insurer showed actual reliance on the insured's mis-representations. *Id.* at 905-06.

Similarly, in *Countryside Casualty Co. v. Orr*, 523 F.2d 870 (8th Cir. 1975), we addressed an insurer's claim to have an automobile insurance policy declared void *ab initio* on the ground that the insured misrepresented his history of traffic violations, arrests, and convictions for public drunkenness on his application for insurance. *Id.* at 871-72. The district court granted summary judgment in favor of the insurer, reasoning that "the insurance company relied upon the misrepresentations and would not have issued the policy had it known the true facts that existed at the time." *Id.* at 875 (internal quotation marks omitted). In affirming the district court, we applied the common law rule that "a material misrepresentation made on an application for an insurance policy *and relied upon by the insurance company* will void the policy." *Id.* at 872 (emphasis added).

While most circuits have not explicitly recognized reliance as a distinct element of the *uberrimae fidei* defense, some courts have applied a subjective test for materiality that asks whether the insurer in fact would have found the omitted information to be material. The standard applied by these circuits effectively requires a showing of actual reliance by the insurer, because it defines a material fact as one that the insurer relied upon. *See, e.g., I.T.N. Consolidators, Inc. v. N. Marine Underwriters Ltd.*, 464 F. App'x 788, 794 (11th Cir. 2012) ("Because all parties knew of the loss here, a misrepresentation that no known loss had occurred could not have [—10—] led [the insurer] to rely on that statement, and would in no way constitute a material misrepresentation in breach of *uberrimae fidei*."); *Certain Underwriters at Lloyd's, London v. Inlet Fisheries, Inc.*, 518 F.3d 645, 655 (9th Cir. 2008) ("[The insurer] produced overwhelming and unrefuted evidence that any of these undisclosed facts would have affected its decision to offer the policy were it known."). To satisfy the materiality element of the *uberrimae fidei* defense in these jurisdictions, insurers must show that they would not have issued the policy, or would have issued it at a different premium, if they had known about the omitted fact. Other decisions applying *uberrimae fidei* rely on evidence of actual reliance or inducement on the part of the insurer, even where they have not articulated reliance as a requirement distinct from materiality. *See, e.g., Certain Underwriters at Lloyd's v. Montford*, 52 F.3d 219, 222 (9th Cir. 1995); *Gulfstream Cargo, Ltd. v. Reliance Ins. Co.*, 409 F.2d 974, 980 (5th Cir. 1969).

These decisions are consistent in substance with our conclusion, but we think clarity is enhanced by preserving actual reliance and objective materiality as distinct elements. In one of its earliest cases concerning a marine insurer's *uberrimae fidei* defense, the Supreme Court applied an objective test for materiality, concluding that "[h]ad [the undisclosed fact] been known, it is reasonable to believe that a prudent underwriter would not have accepted the proposal as made." *Sun Mut. Ins. Co. v. Ocean Ins. Co.*, 107 U.S. 485, 509-10 (1883); *see also AGF Marine Aviation & Transp. v. Cassin*, 544 F.3d 255, 264-65 (3d Cir. 2008); *Grande v. St. Paul Fire & Marine Ins. Co.*, 436 F.3d 277, 282-83 (1st Cir. 2006); *Kilpatrick*, 795 F.2d at 942-43. While materiality examines whether a fact would have influenced the judgment of a *reasonable and prudent* underwriter, *e.g., Cont'l Cement Co.*, 761 F.3d at 841, 2 Adm. R. at 474-75, reliance examines whether there was a causal connection between the misrepresentation or concealment of that material fact and the *actual* underwriter's decision to issue the policy. *See* 2 Thomas J. Schoenbaum, *Admiralty and Maritime Law* § 19-14 (5th ed. 2011). [—11—]

B.

St. Paul Fire argues that even if reliance is an element of the defense, there is no genuine issue of fact for trial on whether it relied on Abhe's failure to disclose the 2010 survey. The insurer argues that its underwriter, Ed King, received, reviewed, and relied upon Abhe's insurance application before deciding to insure SEI-34. King also testified that the 2010 survey of SEI-34, which indicated a lack of watertight bulkheads and pinholes in the hull, would have been "very important in underwriting [the] risk." Abhe countered, however, with evidence that in June 2012, King renewed coverage for SEI-120, despite receiving an on-hire survey for that vessel that showed the vessel lacked watertight bulkheads. We conclude that this evidentiary dispute is sufficient to create a genuine issue of material fact as to whether St. Paul Fire relied on Abhe's failure to disclose SEI-34's lack of watertight bulkheads in issuing the insurance policy for that barge.

Alternatively, St. Paul Fire asserts that Abhe's over-valuation of SEI-34 in its insurance application was an additional breach of *uberrimae fidei* that independently entitles it to summary judgment. King testified that if Abhe had disclosed the fact that SEI-34 had a scrap value of $90,000, he would have questioned whether the barge "might be an unacceptable risk." Abhe, however, produced evidence that SEI-34's stated value of $225,000 accurately reflected the barge's value as expressed in Abhe's charter agreement with Sterling. Abhe's marine insurance expert also testified that, for insurance purposes, the appropriate value of a leased vessel is the value specified in the charter agreement. We therefore conclude that a genuine issue of material fact exists as to whether undisclosed information regarding

SEI-34's value was material and actually induced St. Paul Fire to issue coverage to Abhe.

If the case proceeds to trial on the defense of *uberrimae fidei*, we also believe that the question of materiality should be considered by the trier of fact to resolve disputed issues of fact. The district court concluded succinctly that Abhe's non- [—12—] disclosure of the 2010 survey was material because "a prudent insurer would want to know that bulkheads designed to protect a vessel from sinking would not operate as intended." Abhe presented evidence, however, that other recent surveys of SEI-34 stated that the barge was suitable for use as an equipment barge despite having non-watertight bulkheads. Abhe also presented testimony from its expert surveyor that a lack of watertight bulkheads and a need to pump water from the bilge is common and is not a concern on barges that are used as construction platforms. As we do not think it can be "universally affirmed" on this record that the existence of non-watertight bulkheads "must always be material to the risk," *McLanahan v. Universal Ins. Co.*, 26 U.S. 170, 189 (1828), there is a genuine dispute for trial on materiality as well.

*   *   *

For the foregoing reasons, we reverse the judgment of the district court and remand the case for further proceedings consistent with this opinion.

**United States Court of Appeals
for the Eighth Circuit**

No. 14-1867

IN RE AMERICAN RIVER TRANSP. CO.

Appeal from the United States District Court for the
Eastern District of Missouri – St. Louis

Decided: August 25, 2015

Citation: 800 F.3d 428, 3 Adm. R. 528 (8th Cir. 2015).

Before **RILEY,** Chief Judge, **WOLLMAN** and **MELLOY,**
Circuit Judges.

[—1—] WOLLMAN, Circuit Judge: [—2—]

This case comes to us on appeal a second time after the district court *sua sponte* dismissed the limitation action brought by the American River Transportation Company (Artco), concluding that the limitation proceeding could not go forward because the United States' potential claims were not subject to the Limitation of Shipowners' Liability Act, 46 U.S.C. §§ 30501-30512 (the Limitation Act). The district court declined to hold the United States in contempt for violating the court's order enjoining suits outside the limitation proceeding. We reverse the court's dismissal of Artco's limitation action, affirm its denial of Artco's motion to hold the government in contempt and for sanctions, vacate the district court's order as to the remaining motions, and remand for further proceedings.

I.

This dispute arises from damage done to the government's lock and dam after barges separated from the M/V Julie White, a towboat owned by Artco, and allided with the lock and dam and appurtenant structures. The government informed Artco of the damage, and, in accordance with Federal Rule of Civil Procedure F (Rule F), Artco commenced this action under the Limitation Act in the Eastern District of Missouri, seeking limitation of its liability to the government or exoneration for the government's damages.

The district court issued an order enjoining the prosecution of any separate suits "whatsoever" against Artco or the vessel at issue "in respect of any claim arising out of or connected to" the allision and directing potential claimants to file claims by June 15, 2011. Before the time for filing claims had expired, the government filed a motion to dismiss Artco's complaint, arguing that the government's claim alleging a violation of the Rivers and Harbors Act (RHA), 33 U.S.C. § 408, was not subject to limited liability and therefore need not be litigated in the Rule F proceeding. The government never filed a timely claim in the limitation proceeding. The district court granted the motion to dismiss, holding that the government's potential § 408 claim [—3—] was not subject to the Limitation Act and that the government could pursue it in a separate proceeding *in personam*. The district court then dismissed Artco's limitation action in its entirety.

Artco appealed, and we held in *In re American River Transportation Co.* (*Artco I*), 728 F.3d 839, 1 Adm. R. 378 (8th Cir. 2013), that because the government never filed a claim in the Rule F proceeding, it lacked statutory standing to move to dismiss Artco's limitation action. We reversed the district court's dismissal of Artco's limitation action on that basis and remanded the case. We did not address whether the government's claim was subject to limited liability under the Limitation Act or whether the government could pursue an *in personam* remedy.

On remand, the parties filed four new motions. Artco filed a motion for a final decree of exoneration based on the government's failure to file a claim and the lack of any other claims in the limitation action. The government moved for permission to file a late claim in the limitation proceeding. The government also initiated a new and separate proceeding based on the same incident, filing a complaint against Artco in the Eastern District of Missouri that alleged claims under the RHA, 33 U.S.C. §§ 408-409. *See United States v. Am. River Transp. Co.*, No. 4:14-cv-00050-AGF (E.D. Mo. filed Jan. 13, 2014). In response, Artco filed in the limitation proceeding a motion to impose sanctions and to hold the government in contempt for violating the district court's injunction against the prosecution of separate suits. The government then filed a motion to consolidate the actions.

The district court disposed of all four motions in a single order. It denied Artco's motion for a decree of exoneration, stating that we had left intact its prior holding that the government's claims were not subject to limited liability under the Limitation Act and that the government could pursue an *in personam* remedy for its § 408 claim. The court concluded that its prior injunction had been overbroad and therefore denied Artco's motion to hold the government in contempt, to impose [—4—] sanctions, and to direct dismissal of the government's separate suit. As there were no claims filed against Artco in the limitation action, the court denied the government's motion for leave to file a late claim, denied as moot the government's motion to consolidate, and directed dismissal of the limitation action.

Artco appeals, arguing that the government's claim under § 408 of the RHA is subject to the Limitation Act, that the district court's dismissal of its limitation action is contrary to our holding in *Artco I*, that an absence of claims in a limitation action does not justify dismissal of the action but rather should result in exoneration or default judgment, and that the district court erred in refusing to hold the government in contempt and to impose sanctions for violating the injunction.

II.

"Congress passed the Limitation Act in 1851 'to encourage ship-building and to induce capitalists to invest money in this branch of the industry.'" *Lewis v. Lewis & Clark Marine, Inc.*, 531 U.S. 438, 446 (2001) (quoting *Norwich & N.Y. Transp. Co. v. Wright*, 80 U.S. (13 Wall.) 104, 121 (1871)). The Limitation Act limits vessel owners' liability for damage or injury to the value of the vessel and its freight, as long as the damage or injury occurs without the owner's privity or

knowledge. 46 U.S.C. § 30505. The Limitation Act provides:

(a) . . . . [T]he Liability of the owner of a vessel for any claim, debt, or liability described in subsection (b) shall not exceed the value of the vessel and pending freight.

(b) . . . . Unless otherwise excluded by law, claims, debts, and liabilities subject to limitation under subsection (a) are those arising from any embezzlement, loss, or destruction of any property, goods, or merchandise shipped or put on board the vessel, any loss, damage, or injury by collision, or any act, matter, or thing, loss, damage, or [—5—] forfeiture, done, occasioned, or incurred, without the privity or knowledge of the owner.

Id.

The Limitation Act, in conjunction with Rule F, also allows vessel owners, within six months of receiving written notice of a claim, to commence a limitation action to have multiple related claims against them disposed of in a concursus, through a single proceeding. 46 U.S.C. § 30511; Fed. R. Civ. P. Supp. R. F. The court presiding over the limitation proceeding fixes a date for filing claims and issues a concursus injunction to enjoin the prosecution of "any action or proceeding against the plaintiff or the plaintiff's property with respect to any claim subject to limitation in the action." *See* Fed. R. Civ. P. Supp. R. F(3)-(4). The concursus procedure helps "to ensure the prompt and economical disposition of controversies in which there are often a multitude of claimants." *Md. Cas. Co. v. Cushing*, 347 U.S. 409, 415 (1954) (plurality opinion).

The government argues that its RHA claim under § 408 is not subject to the Limitation Act. Section 408 states, in pertinent part, "It shall not be lawful for any person or persons to . . . injure . . . or in any manner whatever impair the usefulness of any . . . work built by the United States . . . for the preservation and improvement of any of its navigable waters . . . ." 33 U.S.C. § 408. It thus imposes strict liability on vessel owners whose vessels impair or injure public works on navigable waters. *United States v. Fed. Barge Lines, Inc.*, 573 F.2d 993, 997 (8th Cir. 1978); *United States v. Ohio Valley Co.*, 510 F.2d 1184, 1186 (7th Cir. 1975).

We review *de novo* the question at the center of this appeal: whether § 408 implicitly repealed the Limitation Act, such that a claim under § 408 is not subject to the limitations of liability set forth above. *See Highmark Inc. v. Allcare Health* [—6—] *Mgmt. Sys., Inc.*, 134 S. Ct. 1744, 1748 (2014) ("[Q]uestions of law are reviewable *de novo* . . . ." (internal quotations omitted)).

The repeal of statutes by implication is not favored. *Morton v. Mancari*, 417 U.S. 535, 549 (1974). "A new statute will not be read as wholly or even partially amending a prior one unless there exists a 'positive repugnancy' between the provisions of the new and those of the old that cannot be reconciled." *Blanchette v. Conn. Gen. Ins. Corps.*, 419 U.S. 102, 134 (1974) (quoting *In re Penn Cent. Transp. Co.*, 384 F. Supp. 895, 943 (Reg'l Rail Reorg. Ct. 1974)). "[W]here provisions in the two acts are in irreconcilable conflict, the later act to the extent of the conflict constitutes an implied repeal of the earlier one . . . ." *Radzanower v. Touche Ross & Co.*, 426 U.S. 148, 154 (1976) (quoting *Posadas v. Nat'l City Bank of N.Y.*, 296 U.S. 497, 503 (1936)). "[W]hen two statutes are capable of co-existence," however, "it is the duty of the courts, absent a clearly expressed congressional intention to the contrary, to regard each as effective." *Morton*, 417 U.S. at 551. "[T]he rule is to give effect to both if possible." *Id.* (quoting *United States v. Borden Co.*, 308 U.S. 188, 198 (1939)).

The parties dispute whether there is an irreconcilable conflict between the Limitation Act and § 408. Artco contends that there is nothing inherently conflicting between a statute that provides a cause of action and another that limits it. Artco argues that only an *in rem* remedy is available for violations of § 408 and that therefore the limitations on liability built into the RHA and Limitation Act are consistent. The government argues that it may pursue an *in personam* remedy for violations of § 408 and that § 408 is therefore in irreconcilable conflict with the Limitation Act, which limits damages to the value of the vessel and its freight. The government notes that a vessel owner has six months to initiate a limitation action after receiving a claim in writing, whereas the government has three years to bring suit under the RHA. Finally, the government points to the conflicting nature of the competing objectives of the two acts and their differing standards of liability. [—7—]

A.

The RHA does not explicitly provide for an *in personam* cause of action for violations of § 408. Instead, it specifically provides for fines of up to $25,000 per day against the vessel's owner under § 411, and an *in rem* remedy against the vessel to recover damages under § 412, which states that

> any [vessel] used or employed in violating any of the provisions of sections 407, 408, 409, 414, and 415 of this title shall be liable for the pecuniary penalties . . . and in addition thereto for the amount of the damages done by said [vessel] . . . and said [vessel] may be proceeded against . . . by way of libel in any district court of the United States having jurisdiction thereof.

33 U.S.C. § 412. The government contends that, in addition to the express *in rem* cause of action against the offending vessel for violations of § 408, it has an implicit *in personam* cause of action against the vessel owner.

In support of its argument, the government relies primarily on *Wyandotte Transportation Co. v. United States*, 389 U.S. 191 (1967), in which the Supreme Court held that an implicit *in personam* remedy was available for violations of another provision of the RHA, § 409. At that time, § 409 made it unlawful to "voluntarily or carelessly sink, or permit or cause to be sunk, vessels . . . in navigable channels" and made it the duty of the vessel owner to "commence the immediate removal" of a sunken vessel. 33 U.S.C. § 409 (1964) (amended 1986). In *Wyandotte*, the United States brought an action for a declaratory judgment that certain vessel owners must remove their sunken vessels, as well as a claim *in personam* to recover the significant costs it incurred in removing a sunken barge loaded with 2.2 million pounds of chlorine. 389 U.S. at 194-96. The Court cited *Texas & Pacific Railway Co. v. Rigsby*, 241 U.S. 33 (1916), and *J. I. Case Co. v. Borak*, 377 U.S. 426 (1964), for the proposition that it is proper for courts to fashion [—8—] an appropriate remedy if criminal liability is inadequate to ensure full effectiveness of a statute, the interest of the plaintiff falls within the class the statute was intended to protect, and the plaintiff's harm is of the type the statute was intended to remedy. *Wyandotte*, 389 U.S. at 202-03. Applying this same reasoning to the facts of *Wyandotte*, the Court held that because § 409 placed the duty to remove negligently sunken vessels on the vessel owner principally for the benefit the government, because the penalties were insufficient to effectuate the purposes of § 409, and because the express *in rem* remedy was insufficient to fully compensate the government for performing the vessel owner's duty, the Court would infer the existence of an *in personam* remedy and declaratory relief. *See id.* at 201-05.[1] The Court noted that "[i]t would be surprising if Congress intended that, in such a situation, the Government's commendable performance of [the vessel owner's] duty must be at Government expense." *Id.* at 204-05.

We have heretofore not decided whether *Wyandotte* should be extended to allow the government to maintain an *in personam* cause of action for a violation of § 408. Post-*Wyandotte*, the Supreme Court has altered its statutory-interpretation analysis and its approach to implying the existence of remedies that Congress has not expressly created. The Court's retreat from implying remedies in accordance with the principles laid out in *Rigsby*, *Borak*, and *Wyandotte* cautions against simply extending *Wyandotte* by analogy and reading an *in personam* cause of action into § 408. *See Corr. Servs. Corp. v. Malesko*, 534 U.S. 61, 67 n.3 (2001) ("Since our decision in *Borak*, we have retreated from our previous willingness to imply a cause of action where Congress has not provided one."); *Merrill Lynch, Pierce, Fenner & [—9—] Smith, Inc. v. Curran*, 456 U.S. 353, 377 (1982) (chronicling the Court's departure from the principles laid out in *Rigsby*); *Touche Ross & Co. v. Redington*, 442 U.S. 560, 578 (1979) ("[I]n a series of cases since *Borak* we have adhered to a stricter standard for the implication of private causes of action . . . .").

A search for congressional intent has become the primary focus in determining whether a statute includes an implied remedy, with the statute's text and structure being the starting point of the court's inquiry. *Alexander v. Sandoval*, 532 U.S. 275, 286-88 (2001). "[W]here a statute expressly provides a remedy, courts must be especially reluctant to provide additional remedies. In such cases, '[i]n the absence of strong indicia of contrary congressional intent, we are compelled to conclude that Congress provided precisely the remedies it considered appropriate.'" *Karahalios v. Nat'l Fed'n of Fed. Emps., Local 1263*, 489 U.S. 527, 532-33 (1989) (second alteration in original) (internal citation omitted) (quoting *Middlesex Cnty. Sewerage Auth. v. Sea Clammers*, 453 U.S. 1, 15 (1981)).

There is disagreement among the circuits regarding whether there is an implied *in personam* remedy for violations of § 408. The Sixth Circuit held in *Hines, Inc. v. United States*, 551 F.2d 717 (1977), that the government could pursue an *in personam* remedy for violations of § 408. The outcome in *Hines* depended on the court's conclusion that the "legal logic" the Supreme Court used to interpret § 409 in *Wyandotte* was equally applicable to § 408. *Id.* at 724. Yet, as explained above, the Court has abandoned the interpretive logic that it employed in

---

[1] The Court also noted that allowing a *negligent* vessel owner to limit its liability to be exclusively *in rem* would be inconsistent with the Limitation Act, whose "privity or knowledge" standard prevents vessel owners from limiting their liability when they are at fault because of their own negligence. *Wyandotte*, 389 U.S. at 205-06. But the Court expressly declined to determine whether the Limitation Act's limitation of liability would apply to a § 409 claim. *Id.* at 205 n.17.

Wyandotte, and we see no reason why we should apply it to our analysis of § 408 merely because § 408 and § 409 are part of the same act. *See Sandoval*, 532 U.S. at 287 ("Not even when interpreting the same [act] that was at issue in *Borak* have we applied *Borak's* method for discerning and defining causes of action.").

Furthermore, the Sixth Circuit in *Hines* suggested that § 408, which imposes strict liability, was even more likely to include an implied *in personam* remedy than [—10—] § 409, then a negligence-based liability provision.[2] *See* 551 F.2d at 724. Yet *Wyandotte* relied on § 409's then-negligence standard as support for inferring an implied *in personam* cause of action. *See* 389 U.S. at 204-05; *supra* note 1. We do not agree that § 408's strict liability standard makes it any more likely, under the *Wyandotte* Court's now-disfavored reasoning, that Congress intended to provide an *in personam* remedy. To the contrary, § 408's strict liability standard renders much of *Wyandotte's* reasoning inapplicable.

We find more persuasive the opinions of the Fifth and Tenth Circuits, which have held that only an *in rem* remedy is available for violations of § 408. *See United States v. Jantran, Inc.*, 782 F.3d 1177, 3 Adm. R. 630 (10th Cir. 2015); *In re Barnacle Marine Mgmt. Inc.*, 233 F.3d 865 (5th Cir. 2000). As both circuits note, the *Wyandotte* Court emphasized the duty-creating language of § 409 in inferring the existence of an *in personam* remedy. *Jantran*, 782 F.3d at 1182, 3 Adm. R. at 633; *Barnacle*, 233 F.3d at 870. Such language is absent from § 408. Without the duty-creating language, there is no "textual hook" that could serve as a strong indicia of congressional intent to imply an *in personam* cause of action. *Jantran*, 782 F.3d at 1182, 3 Adm. R. at 633.

Furthermore, like the Tenth Circuit in *Jantran*, we decline to adopt the government's position that we should be particularly willing to infer the existence of a remedy that benefits the government rather than private parties. *See id.* at 1183, 3 Adm. R. at 634. The argument that the costs of repairing public works damaged by vessels should fall on the vessels' owners rather than taxpayers is one better addressed to Congress, and the government has pointed to no persuasive indication of any implied congressional intent that an *in personam* remedy exist for violations of § 408. We also reject the government's contention that it follows from the identical introductory language of § 408 and § 409—"It shall not be lawful"—that § 408 contains the same implied [—11—] remedies that the *Wyandotte* Court read into § 409. "Such a reading would require us to . . . base our analysis on what is, essentially, a boilerplate introduction." *Jantran*, 782 F.3d at 1183, 3 Adm. R. at 634.

The government argues that denying it an *in personam* remedy for its § 408 claim will frustrate Congress's goal of "provid[ing] funds for the replacement and maintenance of improvements made by the United States." *United States v. Fed. Barge Lines, Inc.*, 573 F.2d 993, 997 (8th Cir. 1978). But the overall purpose of the RHA is not, in itself, a strong indicia of Congress's intent to provide an *in personam* remedy. It is not for us to re-craft the RHA to better effectuate Congress's goals while ignoring its express choice of remedies. *Cf. In re Cavanaugh*, 306 F.3d 726, 731-32 (9th Cir. 2002) ("Congress enacts statutes, not purposes, and courts may not depart from the statutory text because they believe some other arrangement would better serve the legislative goals."). The RHA expressly provides for an *in rem* remedy in § 412 and penalties in § 411. In the absence of strong indicia that Congress intended to provide an *in personam* remedy, we decline to impose one by judicial fiat.

We thus turn to the interaction between the Limitation Act and the RHA and the question whether the *in rem* remedy Congress provided for violations of § 408 conflicts with the Limitation Act. As a threshold issue, it has been suggested that a claim *in rem* by its very nature simply falls outside the coverage of the Limitation Act because it is a claim against the vessel itself and therefore does not

---

[2] Congress later amended the statute's language and removed the negligence standard from § 409. *See* Pub. L. 99-662, § 939(a), 100 Stat. 4082, 4199 (1986).

concern "liability of the owner of a vessel" within the plain meaning of 46 U.S.C. § 30505. *See Artco I*, 728 F.3d at 845 n.2, 1 Adm. R. at 382 n.2 (Riley, C.J., dissenting) (noting that the Limitation Act limits only the *in personam* liability of the owner of a vessel); *Ohio Valley*, 510 F.2d at 1188-89 (same); *see also Tug Allie-B, Inc. v. United States*, 273 F.3d 936, 955 n.6 (11th Cir. 2001) (Black, J., concurring) ("I have difficulty understanding how the [—12—] Limitation Act could apply to a proceeding *in rem*, as the statute explicitly applies solely to "the *owner* of any vessel.").[3]

We disagree. Although the Limitation Act speaks in terms of the "liability of the owner of a vessel for any claim, debt, or liability," in all practical senses a successful suit *in rem* results in the vessel owner's liability via the deprivation of the owner's property. *See Place v. Norwich & N.Y. Transp. Co.*, 118 U.S. 468, 503 (1886) ("A man's liability for a demand against him is measured by the amount of property that may be taken from him to satisfy that demand. In the matter of liability, a man and his property cannot be separated."). The Supreme Court has repeatedly stated that the Limitation Act applies to proceedings *in rem* against ships as well as to proceedings *in personam* against vessel owners and that the limitation extends to vessel owners' property as well as to their persons. *See Just v. Chambers*, 312 U.S. 383, 386 (1941); *Hartford Accident & Indem. Co. v. S. Pac. Co.*, 273 U.S. 207, 215-16 (1927); *Place*, 118 U.S. at 502-04. Although the limitations of liability available under the Limitation Act may rarely have practical effect when there is only a single claimant asserting a claim *in rem*, the vessel owner may still benefit from

the protections of the Limitation Act and the concursus procedure when there are multiple claimants. The text of Rule F, which states that the concursus injunction shall cover "any action or proceeding against the plaintiff *or the plaintiff's property* with respect to any claim subject to limitation in the action," confirms our [—13—] interpretation. Fed. R. Civ. P. Supp. R. F(3). In sum, then, claims *in rem* can be subject to the Limitation Act.

Having determined that claims *in rem* can be subject to the Limitation Act, there is no remaining source of conflict between the Limitation Act and Congress's choice of remedy for § 408 claims under the RHA. The *in rem* remedy inherently limits recovery for violations of § 408 to the value of the property, which is consistent with the Limitation Act's standard limiting a vessel owner's liability to the value of the ship and its freight.

B.

A vessel owner may obtain limitation of liability under the Limitation Act only if the injury or loss occurs without the owner's "privity or knowledge." 46 U.S.C. § 30505. The government argues that the privity-or-knowledge element is in irreconcilable conflict with the strict liability standard imposed by § 408 because negligence, unseaworthiness, and culpability are concepts foreign to the imposition of strict liability. Artco counters that the differing standards of culpability are reconcilable; the test for determining whether a claimant can establish liability will simply be different from the test for determining whether the vessel owner is entitled to limitation of liability. We agree with Artco that there is no inherent repugnancy between § 408's strict liability standard and the Limitation Act.

Generally, determining whether there is privity or knowledge requires a two-step inquiry: first, whether negligence or unseaworthiness caused the accident; and second, if so, whether the vessel owner was privy to, or had knowledge of, that causative agent. *In re MO Barge Lines, Inc.*, 360 F.3d 885, 890 (8th Cir. 2004). "Privity generally means some personal participation of the

---

[3] The government has not emphasized this point. Indeed, it would be inconsistent to argue both that a provision is in conflict with the Limitation Act's limits on liability because it gives rise to a claim *in personam* and that a claim *in rem* is never subject to the Limitation Act. The circuits' views on this matter reflect this contradiction. *Compare Tug Allie-B*, 273 F.3d at 944, 946 n.12 (concluding that the availability of an *in personam* remedy under a later-enacted statute places it in conflict with the Limitation Act), *with Ohio Valley*, 510 F.2d at 1188-89 (stating that the Limitation Act applies only to claims *in personam*).

owner in the fault or negligence that caused or contributed to the loss or injury." *Id.* at 890-91 (citing *Coryell v. Phipps*, 317 U.S. 406, 411 (1943)). The modern trend is to interpret [—14—] "privity or knowledge" for purposes of the Limitation Act as including constructive knowledge—*i.e.*, knowledge exists if the vessel owner could have discovered the causative agent through reasonable inquiry. *See Suzuki of Orange Park, Inc. v. Shubert*, 86 F.3d 1060, 1064 (11th Cir. 1996) (listing cases).

It is true that the Limitation Act typically applies to claims founded on a negligence theory. *Tug Allie-B*, 273 F.3d at 943. But the government points to nothing in the language or history of the Limitation Act that limits its application to claims involving a standard of reasonable care. Nor does the case law support the government's view. For example, courts apply the Limitation Act to claims of unseaworthiness, which are essentially strict liability claims. *See Yamaha Motor Corp., U.S.A. v. Calhoun*, 516 U.S. 199, 207-08 (1996) ("[A] series of th[e] Court's decisions transformed the maritime doctrine of unseaworthiness into a strict-liability rule."). Nevertheless, in evaluating whether a vessel owner's privity or knowledge precludes limitation in a claim of unseaworthiness, courts generally look to whether the owner exercised reasonable diligence with respect to the unseaworthy condition. *E.g.*, *Brister v. A.W.I., Inc.*, 946 F.2d 350, 356 (5th Cir. 1991). Thus, there is no requirement that the culpability standard in the privity-or-knowledge element be congruent with the culpability standard for liability. The fact that assessing privity or knowledge will require factfinders to identify the causative agent and then determine the vessel owner's culpability as to that causative agent—extra steps that may otherwise be unnecessary in a § 408 claim—does not place the Limitation Act and § 408 in irreconcilable conflict.

C.

The government argues that the Limitation Act and § 408 are irreconcilable because a vessel owner has six months to initiate a limitation proceeding under the Limitation Act, *see* 46 U.S.C. § 30511(a), while the statute of limitations for a § 408 [—15—] claim is three years, *see* 28 U.S.C. § 2415(b).[4] We do not agree. The six-month window for a vessel owner to initiate a limitation action commences after the owner receives written notice of a claim, not six months after the occurrence of the accident. *See* 46 U.S.C. § 30511(a). It is thus possible for the filing period in a limitation action to be even longer than the three-year limitations period under § 408, depending on when the allegedly injured party gives notice of its claim. Moreover, many maritime claims, such as personal injury claims under the Jones Act, are subject to the Limitation Act, *e.g.*, *In re E. River Towing Co.*, 266 U.S. 355, 366-68 (1924) (holding that Jones Act claims are subject to the Limitation Act), despite having a three-year statute of limitations, *see* 46 U.S.C. §§ 30104, 30106; 45 U.S.C. § 56. Thus, subjecting the government's § 408 claim to the Limitation Act's six-month filing period simply puts the government in the same position as others whose claims courts have already held are subject to the Limitation Act.

Because the available remedies, liability standard, and statute of limitations for § 408 claims can be reconciled with the Limitation Act, we conclude that the Limitation Act has not been implicitly repealed with respect to § 408. The government's § 408 claim is thus subject to limitation of liability and the limitation proceeding prescribed by the Limitation Act and Rule F.

III.

The government argues that regardless of whether its § 408 claim is subject to the Limitation Act, it is the only potential claimant in the limitation action and therefore the district court properly dismissed the action. [—16—]

The doctrine invoked by the government, first set forth by the Supreme Court in *Langnes v. Green*, 282 U.S. 531, 539-44 (1931), allows the district court to dissolve or relax a concursus injunction in a limitation

---

[4] Artco does not dispute that the three-year statute of limitations in 28 U.S.C. § 2415(b) applies to the government's § 408 claim.

proceeding in certain situations. The central aim of the Limitation Act and limitation proceedings is to provide a right to limitation of a vessel owner's liability and to apportion the limitation fund among multiple claimants. *See Lake Tankers Corp. v. Henn*, 354 U.S. 147, 152 (1957). Yet in the saving-to-suitors clause, Congress reserved claimants' choice of remedies—such as common-law remedies— and their right to pursue them in state court where they may, for example, obtain a jury trial. *Id.* at 153 (citing 28 U.S.C. § 1333). To ensure harmony between the Limitation Act and the saving-to-suitors clause, courts permit claimants to pursue their claims outside of the limitation proceeding in two situations: where there is a single claimant, or where the total claims do not exceed the value of the limitation fund. *Lewis*, 531 U.S. at 451. To satisfy themselves that a vessel owner's right to limitation will be protected, district courts may obtain from claimants stipulations that their damages will not exceed the limitation fund and waivers of claims of *res judicata* concerning issues bearing on limitation of liability. *Id.* at 453-54. As long as the vessel owner's right to limited liability will not be jeopardized, the court has discretion to dissolve or modify a concursus injunction to give claimants the right to pursue their claims in state court.[5] *See id.* at 454; *Lake Tankers*, 354 U.S. at 153-54. On the other hand, "[i]f the district court concludes that the vessel owner's right to limitation will not be adequately protected—where for example a group of claimants cannot agree on appropriate stipulations or there is uncertainty concerning the adequacy of the fund or the number of claims—the court may proceed to adjudicate the merits, deciding the issues of liability and limitation." *Lewis*, 531 U.S. at 454. [—17—]

The concerns that led to the development of the foregoing doctrine—the right of claimants to pursue their choice of remedies in their chosen forum and the right to a jury trial, if desired—do not appear to be at issue here.

The government urges us to hold that it is entitled to pursue its admiralty claim in a separate proceeding in the same federal district in which Artco filed the limitation proceeding. Some courts have given the Supreme Court's cases on the doctrine a broad reading and have held that it is not founded solely in the saving-to-suitors clause and that it protects claimants' rights not only to assert common-law rights in state courts, but also to assert other rights elsewhere, including in other federal courts. *See Inland Dredging v. Sanchez*, 468 F.3d 864, 864-68 (5th Cir. 2006); *Kreta Shipping, S.A. v. Preussage Int'l Steel Corp.*, 192 F.3d 41, 48-50 (2d Cir. 1999). But even under such an interpretation, it is not clear that the doctrine should apply here, where the government asserts claims in admiralty, without a jury demand, in the same federal district in which the limitation proceeding is ongoing.

Even assuming that the doctrine applies to the facts at hand, however, the district court did not follow the procedures ordinarily employed to protect a vessel owner's right to limitation of liability. The court made no effort to ensure that Artco's right to limitation would be protected and in fact concluded that Artco had no such right.[6] Most importantly, the district court explicitly said that it was dismissing Artco's action because the government's claim was not subject to the Limitation Act, not because there was a single potential claimant or because the claims would not exceed the limitation fund. The government did not ask to have the injunction dissolved or relaxed in order to pursue its separate claims; to the contrary, it moved to consolidate this action with the other. The district court therefore did not exercise its discretion under the doctrine, but rather dismissed the action for an entirely different reason. We decline to affirm the dismissal on an alternative ground [—18—] that is questionable, was raised for the first time on appeal, and would require us to substitute our discretion for that of the district court.

---

[5] Although the decision has been described as one of discretion, in certain circumstances a district court's failure to dissolve the injunction constitutes an abuse of discretion. *See Valley Line Co. v. Ryan*, 771 F.2d 366, 372-73 (8th Cir. 1985).

[6] We acknowledge, however, that Artco's right to limited liability for the § 408 claim may be inherently protected because of the *in rem* nature of the cause of action.

IV.

Artco argues that the district court erred in denying Artco's motion to hold the government in contempt for noncompliance with the district court's concursus injunction. We disagree. In *Artco I*, the district court had held that the government's § 408 claim was not subject to the Limitation Act. On appeal, we did not decide whether the government's § 408 claim was subject to limitation, and we suggested the possibility that if the government had a claim that was not subject to the Limitation Act, it could assert that claim independently from the limitation proceeding. *See Artco I*, 728 F.3d at 844, 1 Adm. R. at 381 ("*CF Industries* and similar cases demonstrate only that the government need not appear in the limitation proceeding at all to assert its claims when those claims are not subject to the Limitation Act."). Although the government's filing of a separate suit violated the plain terms of the district court's injunction, our opinion and the district court's prior holding suggested that the injunction may have been overbroad to the extent it enjoined separate proceedings for claims not subject to the Limitation Act. The district court thus did not abuse its discretion in denying the motion to hold the government in contempt and to impose sanctions. *See Wycoff v. Hedgepeth*, 34 F.3d 614, 616 (8th Cir. 1994) (standard of review).

V.

We reverse the district court's *sua sponte* dismissal of Artco's limitation action. We affirm the district court's denial of Artco's motion to hold the government in contempt and to impose sanctions. We vacate the district court's denial of Artco's motion for a decree of exoneration, the denial of the government's motion to file a late claim, and the denial as moot of the government's motion to consolidate, and we [—19—] remand the case for consideration of those motions and for further proceedings consistent with this opinion.

(Reporter's Note: Concurring opinion follows on p. 537).

[—19—] RILEY, Chief Judge, concurring in the judgment:

Faced with "the unenviable task of deciding whether an impossibly obscure law (the [RHA]) prevails over a hopelessly anachronistic one (the Limitation Act)," we are—as the Fifth Circuit once described it—"adrift on muddied waters that lie at the convergence of two desultory streams of nineteenth century thought." *Univ. of Tex. Med. Branch at Galveston v. United States*, 557 F.2d 438, 441 (5th Cir. 1977) (agreeing with commentary from 1957 that the Limitation Act "has been due for a general overhaul for the past seventy-five years; seventy-five years from now that statement will be still true, except that the overhaul will then be one hundred and fifty years overdue" (quotation omitted)). Piloting between these two antediluvian acts, the majority makes a sound argument why the government's RHA claim is subject to the Limitation Act. Though I disagree with the majority's reconciliation of these two Acts, *see In re Am. River Transp. Co.*, 728 F.3d 839, 848, 1 Adm. R. at 384-85 (8th Cir. 2013) (Riley, C.J., dissenting), I believe we need not confront this statutory Scylla and Charybdis[7] and that the dismissal should be reversed for another reason.

By "marshalling" all assets and claims subject to the Limitation Act into a single concursus proceeding, *Valley Line Co. v. Ryan*, 771 F.2d 366, 372 (8th Cir. 1985), Artco's limitation proceeding is meant to provide the exclusive forum[8] in [—20—] which claimants could pursue these claims. *See* Fed. R. Civ. P. Supp. Rule F(3) ("[T]he [district] court shall enjoin the further prosecution of any action or proceeding against the plaintiff or the plaintiff's property with respect to any claim subject to limitation in the action."). Injured parties with such claims must, upon receiving notice of a limitation action, pursue them "in the limitation action under pain of default." 2 Thomas J. Schoenbaum, *Admiralty and Maritime Law* § 15-5, at 184-86 (5th ed. 2011). Indeed, the clerk of court in this case notified potential claimants that claims against Artco must be raised in a timely fashion in the limitation proceeding "or be defaulted."

Upon denying the government's motion to file a late claim and concluding there was no claim against Artco, the proper course was not to dismiss the limitation proceeding but to enter a default judgment in Artco's favor as against all properly noticed potential claimants with claims subject to the Limitation Act. *See, e.g., Langnes*, 282 U.S. at 540-41 (noting that no further claims appeared imminent because the time for filing "had expired and default had been noted"); *In re Fun Time Boat Rental & Storage, LLC*, 431 F. Supp. 2d 993, 1002 (D. Ariz. 2006) ("Since the Court concludes that [potential claimants] failed to properly file any claim in this action . . . [, the vessel owner] is entitled to exoneration from liability regarding the injuries suffered by [potential claimants] and that this action should be terminated."). On this ground, I concur in the majority's judgment that the district court's dismissal be reversed and remanded.

On remand, the district court should consider the remaining motions and should enter a default in Artco's favor only if it again denies the government's request to file a late claim.

---

[7] The Odyssey of Homer, Book XII, 194-95 (S.H. Butcher & A. Lang transls., The Macmillan Co. 1906) (1879).

[8] A line of cases following *Langnes v. Green*, 282 U.S. 531, 539-44 (1931), commands district courts in specific situations to relax their injunctions on collateral proceedings. *See, e.g., Lake Tankers Corp. v. Henn*, 354 U.S. 147, 153 (1957); *Valley Line*, 771 F.2d at 372-73. I agree with the majority that this doctrine does not provide an alternative basis for affirming the dismissal. *See ante* at 17. Under this [—20—] doctrine, the point is to simply "*dissolve* or *relax* a concursus *injunction* . . . in certain situations," *ante* at 16 (emphasis added), so as to preserve the injured parties' rights by permitting a parallel action *alongside* the limitation proceeding. *See Valley Line*, 771 F.2d at 372-73. It is not a basis for *dismissing* the limitation proceeding. *See id.*

This page intentionally left blank

United States Court of Appeals for the Ninth Circuit

United States Court of Appeals
for the Ninth Circuit

No. 13-15145

ALI
vs.
ROGERS

Appeal from the United States District Court for the
Northern District of California

Decided: March 19, 2015

Citation: 780 F.3d 1229, 3 Adm. R. 540 (9th Cir. 2015).

Before **SCHROEDER,** Senior Circuit Judge, **SILVERMAN,** Circuit Judge, and **GARBIS,** Senior District Judge.*

* The Honorable Marvin J. Garbis, Senior District Judge for the U.S. District Court for the District of Maryland, sitting by designation.

[—3—] SILVERMAN, Circuit Judge:

Abdulhalim Ali was a seaman aboard a tanker ship owned by the United States Maritime Administration, an agency of the federal government, but operated by a private company under a contract. At all material times, the ship was in navigable water. Ali alleges that the human resources director of the company operating the ship ordered the ship's captain to fire him because he is of Yemeni origin. Ali brought a civil rights lawsuit naming as defendants the H.R. director and the captain of the ship, but not the United States. We hold today, as the district court did, that the conduct complained of had such a sufficient maritime connection that the plaintiff's complaint includes at least one claim that could have been brought as a "civil action in admiralty" against the private wrongdoers, and therefore, pursuant to the Suits in Admiralty Act and the Public Vessels Act, should have been brought against the United States. These statutes, which are [—4—] analogous to the Federal Torts Claim Act, waive the government's sovereign immunity in admiralty actions involving U.S. government-owned vessels, and in doing so provide the exclusive remedy for such actions. Because Abdulhalim Ali sued the H.R. director, rather than the United States, his complaint was properly dismissed for lack of jurisdiction. (The captain was never served.)

Mohamed Ali alleges that the day after Abdulhalim Ali was fired, he (Mohamed) was present in the hiring hall of the Seafarers International Union and saw a listing for a job aboard the same government-owned ship from which Abdulhalim Ali was fired. Mohamed Ali alleges that he was not hired on the orders of the H.R. director because of his religion and national origin, violating both his constitutional rights and his union's collective bargaining agreement with the company. He named only the H.R. director as a defendant. We also hold today that because Mohamed Ali could have brought suit in admiralty for breach of the collective bargaining agreement relating to the crewing of this U.S.-owned vessel, his exclusive remedy—including for his civil rights claims, which he could have alleged as being closely linked to the putative breach of contract claim—was against the United States. Therefore, his complaint, too, was properly dismissed for lack of jurisdiction.

I. Background

In reviewing an order dismissing a case for failure to state a claim, we "take as true all factual allegations in the complaint and draw all reasonable inferences in the plaintiff's favor." *Silva v. Di Vittorio*, 658 F.3d 1090, 1101 (9th Cir. 2011). [—5—]

Plaintiffs Abdulhalim Ali and Mohamed Faisal Ali alleged the following: They are both Yemen-born Muslims who are now United States citizens. Both belong to the Seafarers International Union. In January 2010, Abdulhalim Ali was on the crew of the SS PETERSBURG, a vessel owned by the United States Maritime Administration, an agency of the United States Department of Transportation. Interocean American Shipping Corporation had contracted with the United States to provide civilian personnel to operate the PETERSBURG. Interocean also has a collective bargaining agreement with the union, under which Abdulhalim Ali was employed on the PETERSBURG.

Robert Rogers is a Vice President of Interocean and Director of its human resources department. On January 23, 2010, Rogers, "acting under color of law," ordered the captain of the PETERSBURG, William Bartlett, to terminate the employment of anyone on the ship "who appeared to be of Yemanese [sic] origin and/or of Arabic descent and/or a follower of Islam." In compliance with that order, Captain Bartlett fired Abdulhalim Ali and ordered him to leave the ship, which was in navigable waters, and Ali left. The following day, Mohamed Ali, who was in the union hiring hall in Oakland, California, saw a listing for a position on the PETERSBURG. His seniority in the union ranks meant that he had first choice of jobs, and he applied for the position. However, Rogers directed that Ali should not be hired, and that the job should instead be given "to another union member who was apparently not of Yemanese [sic] origin, Arabic descent and/or a follower of Islam."

Abdulhalim Ali and Mohamed Ali sued Rogers exactly two years after the date on which Abdulhalim Ali's employment was terminated, each bringing claims under [—6—] 42 U.S.C. §§ 1981 and 1983. Abdulhalim Ali described his claims as being for "Wrongful Termination - Discrimination," while Mohamed Ali's claims were for "Discrimination in Contracting" and "Discrimination in Hiring." The district court dismissed the complaint for lack of subject matter jurisdiction. Noting that there was no dispute that the PETERSBURG is a "public vessel owned by the United States . . . [and] operated by Interocean" as the United States' agent, the district court concluded that the plaintiffs were required, by the terms of both the Clarification Act, 50 App. U.S.C. § 1291, and the Suits in Admiralty Act ("SIAA"), 46 U.S.C. §§ 30901 et seq., to sue only the United States for admiralty claims. The district court concluded that both plaintiffs' claims satisfied the location and nexus tests for admiralty jurisdiction, so since the claims were filed against Rogers, rather than the United States, the district court dismissed the complaint with prejudice.

Abdulhalim Ali and Mohamed Ali now appeal. We have jurisdiction under 28 U.S.C. § 1291 to review the district court's final decision.

II. Discussion

A. Standard of Review

We review *de novo* a district court's order dismissing a case for lack of subject matter jurisdiction. *Gruver v. Lesman Fisheries Inc.*, 489 F.3d 978, 982 (9th Cir. 2007).

B. Statutory Framework

The SIAA waives sovereign immunity for the United States in cases where "a civil action in admiralty could be [—7—] maintained" against a private person in the same situation. 46 U.S.C. § 30903(a).[1] That is, if a vessel is owned by the United States, and someone is harmed by the vessel or one of its employees, and the harm is one for which, if the vessel were privately owned, the harmed individual could have sued its owner in admiralty, then the person can bring—indeed, must bring—that admiralty claim against the United States. *Id.*; *see Dearborn v. Mar Ship Operations, Inc.*, 113 F.3d 995, 996 (9th Cir. 1997) (through the SIAA, government is subject to "the same liability . . . as is imposed by the admiralty law on the private shipowner"). This makes the SIAA "the maritime analog to the FTCA." *Huber v. United States*, 838 F.2d 398, 400 (9th Cir. 1988). In plain terms, the SIAA applies when (1) a vessel is owned by the United States or operated on its behalf, and (2) there is a

---

[1] 46 U.S.C. § 30903(a) provides in full:

(a) In general.—In a case in which, if a vessel were privately owned or operated, or if cargo were privately owned or possessed, or if a private person or property were involved, a civil action in admiralty could be maintained, a civil action in admiralty in personam may be brought against the United States or a federally-owned corporation. In a civil action in admiralty brought by the United States or a federally-owned corporation, an admiralty claim in personam may be filed or a setoff claimed against the United States or corporation.

remedy cognizable in admiralty for the injury. *See Williams v. Central Gulf Lines*, 874 F.2d 1058, 1061–62 (5th Cir. 1989) (framing SIAA inquiry in two parts: first, whether the vessel is owned by United States or an agent, and second, whether the claim stated is a "traditional admiralty claim"). The SIAA provides no cause of action; it just waives sovereign immunity where [—8—] an admiralty remedy is available. *Dearborn*, 113 F.3d at 996 n.1.

The SIAA has a two-year statute of limitations. 46 U.S.C. § 30905. Further, any remedy available under the SIAA is exclusive of any other remedy "arising out of the same subject matter" that the plaintiff might bring against the individual who actually caused the harm at issue. 46 U.S.C. § 30904.[2] That is, "where a remedy lies against the United States, a suit against an agent of the United States 'by reason of the same subject matter' is precluded." *Dearborn*, 113 F.3d at 997. As the Fifth Circuit has explained, "a remedy is provided" within the meaning of the SIAA when, "one, the underlying maritime law would permit the seaman to state the same claim against a private party, and two, the United States has waived its sovereign immunity with respect to that claim." *Martin v. Miller*, 65 F.3d 434, 442 (5th Cir. 1995). Moreover, the remedy available against the United States need not be the same as that available against a private party for this provision to apply. *See id.* at n.4. After an extensive review of the legislative history and case law surrounding the SIAA, the Fourth Circuit explained that the exclusivity provision's language was intended to enshrine a Supreme Court case holding that the SIAA "furnish[es] the exclusive remedy in admiralty against the United States . . . on all maritime causes of action arising out of the possession or operation" of vessels. *Manuel v. United States*, 50 F.3d 1253, [—9—] 1257 (4th Cir.

1995) (quoting *Johnson v. U.S. Shipping Bd. Emergency Fleet Corp.*, 280 U.S. 320, 327 (1930), *overruled in part on other grounds by Brady v. Roosevelt Steamship Co.*, 317 U.S. 575, 578 (1943)). The Fourth Circuit acknowledged that this may lead to a "harsh result" in some cases, because of the resulting lack of certain remedies for seamen, but explained that the exclusivity language "clearly dictates this result." *Id.* at 1260.

Also relevant to this case is another statutory waiver of federal sovereign immunity in the admiralty context, the Public Vessels Act ("PVA"). 46 U.S.C. §§ 31101 *et seq.* The PVA applies to "civil action[s] in personam in admiralty . . . for damages caused by a public vessel of the United States." 46 U.S.C. § 31102(a)(1). Claims under the PVA have certain limitations that SIAA claims do not, but none that are relevant here. More importantly, the PVA makes all claims subject to the SIAA, including its statute of limitations and its exclusivity provision, except to the extent to which the two are inconsistent. 46 U.S.C. § 31103; *see also Dearborn*, 113 F.3d at 996–97 (noting that the SIAA's exclusivity rule is incorporated by reference into the PVA). Though some circuits interpret the term "damages" caused by a public vessel narrowly (i.e., as encompassing only physical injuries), we recently reaffirmed that the PVA includes claims arising out of the conduct of employees on a public vessel, not merely direct physical damages. *See Tobar v. United States*, 639 F.3d 1191, 1198 (9th Cir. 2011). And despite expansive revisions to the SIAA, the Supreme Court continues to rule that any suit for damages caused by a public vessel falls under the PVA; under *Tobar* and predecessor cases, those damages will include contract damages. *Id.* Any other admiralty claim against a federally-owned vessel will fall [—10—] under the SIAA. *United States v. United Cont'l Tuna Corp.*, 425 U.S. 164, 181 (1976).[3]

---

[2] 46 U.S.C. § 30904 provides in full:

If a remedy is provided by this chapter, it shall be exclusive of any other action arising out of the same subject matter against the officer, employee, or agent of the United States or the federally-owned corporation whose act or omission gave rise to the claim.

---

[3] Rogers argues that a third admiralty statute, the Clarification Act, applies to Abdulhalim's claims because he was employed on a vessel owned by the federal Maritime Administration. 50 App. U.S.C. § 1291(a). But this statute only covers claims for "death, injuries, illness, maintenance

C. Admiralty Jurisdiction

The Constitution's grant of federal jurisdiction for admiralty, "codified at 28 U.S.C. § 1333(1), allows the filing of claims related to maritime contracts and maritime torts." *In re Mission Bay Jet Sports, LLC*, 570 F.3d 1124, 1126 (9th Cir. 2009). Over time, courts have developed tests for both types of claim that determine whether a claim has sufficient "maritime flavor" that a litigant may properly invoke federal admiralty jurisdiction. *See Owens-Illinois, Inc. v. U.S. Dist. Court for W. Dist. of Washington, at Tacoma*, 698 F.2d 967, 969–70 (9th Cir. 1983); David J. Bederman, *Admiralty Jurisdiction*, 31 J. Mar. L. & Com. 189, 206 (2000) (tracing development and contours of admiralty jurisdiction).

1. Tort

Tort claims may sound in admiralty jurisdiction if they satisfy a test with three components showing that the claim has the requisite maritime flavor. *Christensen v. Georgia-* [—11—] *Pac. Corp.*, 279 F.3d 807, 814 (9th Cir. 2002). The relevant tort or harm must have (1) taken place on navigable water (or a vessel on navigable water having caused an injury on land), (2) "a potentially disruptive impact on maritime commerce," and (3) a "substantial relationship to traditional maritime activity." *Jerome B. Grubart, Inc. v. Great Lakes Dredge & Dock Co.*, 513 U.S. 527, 534 (1995). We look at a tort claim's general features, rather than at its minute particulars, to assess whether there is the requisite connection; thus, for instance, when a crane on a river barge flooded a tunnel, the Supreme Court spoke of "damage by a vessel in navigable water to an underwater structure," and when two girls were thrown off a Sea-Doo into San Diego's Mission Bay,

the Ninth Circuit described the incident as "harm by a vessel in navigable waters to a passenger." *Id.* at 539; *Mission Bay Jet Sports*, 570 F.3d at 1129.

2. Contract

As with torts, in determining whether there is admiralty jurisdiction over a given contract, the court's task is to determine whether it is adequately maritime in nature. Federal courts have admiralty jurisdiction over a contract "if its subject matter is maritime." *La Reunion Francaise SA v. Barnes*, 247 F.3d 1022, 1024 (9th Cir. 2001) (quoting *Royal Ins. Co. of America v. Pier 39 Ltd.*, 738 F.2d 1035, 1036 (9th Cir. 1984)). The answer to the question of whether a given contract is a "maritime" contract " 'depends upon . . . the nature and character of the contract,' and the true criterion is whether it has 'reference to maritime service or maritime transactions.'" *Norfolk S. Ry. Co. v. Kirby*, 543 U.S. 14, 24 (2004) (quoting *N. Pac. S.S. Co. v. Hall Bros. Marine Ry. & Shipbuilding Co.*, 249 U.S. 119, 125 (1919)). Of particular relevance to this case, it is well settled that "a contract for [—12—] hire either of a ship or of the sailors and officers to man her is within the admiralty jurisdiction." *Kossick v. United Fruit Co.*, 365 U.S. 731, 735 (1961).

D. Plaintiffs' Claims Are Subject to the Public Vessels Act and Suits in Admiralty Act

Having outlined the general landscape (or should we say seascape?) of admiralty jurisdiction and waivers of sovereign immunity, we consider whether plaintiffs' claims are sufficiently maritime in nature that they should have been brought under the PVA and SIAA rather than against Rogers.

As noted, it is undisputed that the PETERSBURG is a "public vessel of the United States." Therefore, assuming some form of damages is involved, both Abdulhalim Ali and Mohamed Ali's claims are subject to the PVA, and through it the SIAA, if they have claims that can be properly characterized as "civil action[s] in personam in admiralty." 46 U.S.C. § 31102.

---

and cure, loss of effects, detention, or repatriation, or claims arising therefrom," as well as claims for "collection of wages and bonuses and making of allotments," requiring such claims to first go through an administrative exhaustion process and then, if they are administratively disallowed, be brought under the SIAA. *Id*. We cannot agree that Abdulhalim's claims are for the type of harms specifically covered by the Clarification Act.

We hold that Abdulhalim Ali's allegations against Rogers establish that his claims have the requisite maritime flavor to constitute a "civil action in personam in admiralty" and be subject to the PVA and SIAA. 46 U.S.C. §§ 31102–31103. Ali alleged that the PETERSBURG's captain fired him from the ship's crew, in violation of the collective bargaining agreement, while he was aboard the ship, and while the ship was docked in navigable waters. The district court treated Ali's claims as tort claims, noting that Ali's termination from the ship's crew could potentially have disrupted the ship's activities because it was then missing a crew member; furthermore, the activity in which he was engaged, crewing a ship, is one of the most basic "traditional maritime [—13—] activities" that exists. We need express no opinion as to whether Ali's discrimination claims could be considered admiralty torts. His claims under §§ 1981 and 1983 also include allegations raising a breach of contract claim. Such a claim would be indisputably maritime in nature, since Ali's contract was for employment to operate the PETERSBURG on navigable waters. *See Kossick*, 365 U.S. at 735.

Given that the PETERSBURG is a public vessel, and Ali's claims are based on conduct resulting from its operation, the PVA's waiver of sovereign immunity is applicable, and Ali is thus able to sue the United States. But PVA claims are also generally subject to the SIAA, and the SIAA's exclusivity provision precludes any claims arising from the same facts from being brought against any parties but the United States. *See* 46 U.S.C. § 30904. Consequently, Ali not only *could* sue the United States, if he wanted any relief, he was *required* to do so. *See id.*; *see also Manuel*, 50 F.3d at 1259–60. Since Ali's discrimination claim against Rogers is "a suit against an agent of the United States 'by reason of the same subject matter' [it] is precluded." *Dearborn v. Mar Ship Operations, Inc.*, 113 F.3d 995, 997 (9th Cir. 1997) (quoting 46 U.S.C. § 30904).

Mohamed Ali also pleaded his claims under §§ 1981 and 1983. However, he was neither aboard the PETERSBURG nor yet hired to work on its crew when Rogers directed that he not be hired, for allegedly discriminatory reasons. Therefore, the harm did not take place on navigable waters as required for admiralty tort jurisdiction. However, Ali alleged that he was entitled to the benefit of his union's collective bargaining agreement and that Rogers breached this contract by a discriminatory refusal to hire him as a crew member of the PETERSBURG. Such an agreement plainly will have [—14—] "reference to maritime service or maritime transactions," thereby satisfying the "true criterion" for what makes a maritime contract, and qualifying for admiralty contract jurisdiction. *Norfolk S. Ry. Co.*, 543 U.S. at 24 (citation omitted). Although Ali's portion of the complaint pleaded claims under §§ 1981 and 1983, he *could* have brought a breach of contract claim in admiralty jurisdiction. Such an action would be "a civil action in admiralty [that] could be maintained," so *both* that claim *and* his discrimination claims, which "aris[e] out of the same subject matter" and are closely linked to the contract claim, are subject to the SIAA's exclusivity provision. 46 U.S.C. §§ 30903, 30904.[4] Therefore, Ali was required to bring his claims against the United States, not against Rogers. Since he did not, the district court rightly concluded that it lacked subject matter jurisdiction over the claims. In holding that these plaintiffs' claims are barred by the SIAA, we express no view on the merits of these claims in admiralty. Our inquiry is a jurisdictional one only.

III. Conclusion

Neither party has argued that plaintiffs' discrimination claims could be brought as admiralty claims; therefore, we reiterate that we express no opinion on that issue. Rather, we conclude that because Abdulhalim Ali and Mohamed Ali's claims both involved a contract for employment or potential employment aboard a public vessel of the United States and have sufficient maritime connection, they were required to [—15—] bring those claims

---

[4] Like Abdulhalim's claim, Mohamed's claims are subject to the SIAA by way of the PVA, since contract damages caused by a public vessel are subject to the PVA. *Tobar v. United States*, 639 F.3d 1191, 1198 (9th Cir. 2011).

against the United States. Since they sued Rogers instead, the district court correctly determined that it lacked subject matter jurisdiction over their claims.[5]

AFFIRMED.

---

[5] We do not remand with instructions that the district court give leave for plaintiffs to amend their complaint, because the SIAA's two-year statute of limitations has run, 46 U.S.C. § 30905, and the plaintiffs make no argument that any sort of tolling or relation back applies.

United States Court of Appeals
for the Ninth Circuit

No. 13-17005

GUAM INDUS. SERVS., INC.
VS.
ZURICH AM. INS. CO.

Appeal from the United States District Court for the
District of Guam

Decided: June 1, 2015

Citation: 787 F.3d 1001, 3 Adm. R. 546 (9th Cir. 2015).

Before **SCHROEDER, KOZINSKI,** and **SMITH,** Circuit Judges.

[—4—] PER CURIAM:

This insurance coverage case arises out of the sinking of a dry dock, loaded with barrels of oil, during a typhoon on Guam. The issues pertain to whether either of two insurance policies covered costs of damage to the dock and the clean up which was accomplished before any of the oil leaked out of the containers into the Pacific Ocean.

Guam Industrial Services, Inc. ("Guam Industrial") owned the dry dock. At the time of the sinking, one of its insurance policies covered damage to the dock, and one covered liability for property damage caused by pollutants. After the dock sank, Guam Industrial filed a claim under each policy. The insurers denied the claims, and Guam Industrial brought suit. The district court granted summary judgment for the insurers, finding that the first policy was voidable because Guam Industrial had failed to maintain the warranty on the dock, and that the coverage under the second policy was never triggered because no pollutants were released. Guam Industrial and its CEO, Mathews Pothen, appeal. We affirm.

BACKGROUND

Guam Industrial owned and operated a dry dock called the Machinist, located in Apra Harbor, Guam. The dry dock sank on January 2, 2011. Guam Industrial had insured the dry dock under two policies: a Hull and Machinery

Policy, which was underwritten collectively by Zurich American Insurance Company ("Zurich") and Starr Indemnity and [—5—] Liability Company ("Starr"), and an Ocean Marine Policy, which was underwritten by Zurich alone.

The Hull and Machinery Policy covered damage to the dry dock resulting from certain specified "perils" that included lightning, earthquake, pirates, assailing thieves, and various types of accidents and malfunctions. As a condition of coverage, the policy required Guam Industrial to obtain and maintain Navy Certification for the dry dock ("the Navy Certification warranty"). Such certification ensures that the dock has satisfied a certain level of structural integrity. It is the highest standard in the industry.

It appears, however, that Guam Industrial never obtained Navy Certification. Instead, Guam Industrial obtained "commercial" certification from a company called Heger Dry Dock, Inc. In October 2010, that commercial certification expired. Heger Dry Dock informed Guam Industrial that it would not renew the certification unless Guam Industrial undertook significant repairs. Guam Industrial then took the dry dock out of commission to conduct these repairs. The dock sank while it was undergoing the repairs.

When the dry dock sank, it took with it various containers in which were stored approximately 113,000 gallons of oil. None of the containers were breached, however. Following the incident, the Coast Guard issued a letter informing Guam Industrial that it had to remove the sunken containers holding the oil or face the possibility of fines and strict liability for any contamination to the surrounding waters. Guam Industrial recovered the containers, expending approximately $647,000; no oil ever leaked out of the containers and into the water. [—6—]

Guam Industrial then filed a claim under the Hull and Machinery Policy with Zurich and Starr. The insurers denied the claim on the basis of the breach of the requirement to obtain Navy Certification.

Guam Industrial also filed a claim with Zurich under the Ocean Marine Policy. That policy generally covered "all sums which the insured shall become legally obligated to pay and shall have damages because of . . . [p]roperty damage." The policy also contained a "Pollution Exclusion Clause," which generally excluded coverage for any damages caused by the "actual or potential discharge" of pollutants. The scope of this exclusion was narrowed by an endorsement that was attached to the policy ("Endorsement No. 10"). Together, the exclusion and the endorsement specified that the policy would cover the costs of any damage caused by "the discharge, dispersal, release, or escape" of any pollutants into the environment, provided the discharge was accidental rather than intentional. Zurich denied the claim because no actual discharge of pollutants had occurred.

After the denial of both claims, Guam Industrial brought this suit in the District of Guam, invoking diversity jurisdiction, against Zurich and Starr, seeking to recover on both policies. The district court granted summary judgment in favor of Zurich and Starr. It concluded that the Hull and Machinery Policy did not provide coverage because Guam Industrial had breached the Navy Certification warranty. The court rejected Guam Industrial's position that Zurich and Starr had to demonstrate that the breach caused the sinking of the dry dock, because applicable law required strict compliance with certification requirements. [—7—]

The district court further concluded that the Ocean Marine Policy coverage for property damage caused by pollution was never triggered because the oil never left the containers. There was no "discharge, dispersal, release, or escape" of any pollutant into the waters of Apra Harbor, and hence no property damage within the terms of the policy.

Guam Industrial now appeals.

HULL AND MACHINERY POLICY AND THE LACK OF CERTIFICATION

The Hull and Machinery Policy covering damage to the dry dock was underwritten by both Zurich and Starr, and required, as a condition of coverage, that Guam Industrial obtain and maintain Navy Certification for the dry dock. Guam Industrial breached the warranty because the dry dock was never Navy Certified. Deciding whether the insurance policy mandates strict compliance with its requirement of Navy Certification requires interpretation of the policy.

To interpret a marine insurance policy, we usually must first determine whether to apply state or federal law. *See Wilburn Boat Co. v. Fireman's Fund Ins. Co.*, 348 U.S. 310, 313–14 (1955). Generally, courts are to "apply state law unless an established federal rule addresse[s] the issues raised, or there [is] a need for uniformity in admiralty practice." *Yu v. Albany Ins. Co.*, 281 F.3d 803, 808 (9th Cir. 2002). That being said, we do not need to determine whether to apply federal or state law in this instance because both sources of law lead to the same rule: that marine insurance policy warranties are to be strictly construed. The federal [—8—] rule, if one in fact exists,[1] is that "admiralty law requires the strict construction of express warranties in marine insurance contracts; breach of the express warranty by the insured releases the insurance company from liability even if compliance with the warranty would not have avoided the loss." *See Lexington Ins. Co. v. Cooke's Seafood*, 835 F.2d 1364, 1366 (11th Cir. 1988). The state majority rule also provides that express warranties in marine

---

[1] In *Wilburn Boat Co. v. Fireman's Fund Ins. Co.*, the Supreme Court declared that no established federal rule addressed marine insurance policy warranty clauses, and that the clauses should be interpreted using state law. 348 U.S. at 314-16. Since *Wilburn Boat*, however, a few circuits have announced the "federal rule" identified above. *See Lexington Ins. Co. v. Cooke's Seafood*, 835 F.2d 1364, 1366 (11th Cir. 1988); *see also Lloyd's of London v. Pagan-Sanchez*, 539 F.3d 19, 24 (1st Cir. 2008). This circuit has neither announced a federal rule nor disclaimed such a rule.

insurance policies should be strictly construed. *See Yu*, 281 F.3d at 808–09.

Guam's courts have not yet spoken on this specific issue, and where state courts are silent, "federal court[s] must make a reasonable determination of the result the highest state court would reach if it were deciding the case." *Med. Lab. Mgmt. Consultants v. Am. Broad. Cos.*, 306 F.3d 806, 812 (9th Cir. 2002) (internal quotation marks omitted). We think that it is reasonable to conclude that the Supreme Court of Guam would likely follow the majority rule. Guam's insurance statutes are derived from California law, which requires strict compliance with warranties when they are material. Cal. Ins. Code § 447. Ultimately, whether derived from federal admiralty law or state law, we conclude that the law requires strict compliance with marine insurance policy warranties, even when the breach of the warranty did not cause the loss. Applying that law to these facts, there is no question that [—9—] Guam Industrial failed to comply with the Navy Certification warranty.

Guam Industrial contends that the insurers waived their right to demand strict compliance with the Navy Certification warranty because they had accepted commercial certification. Under Guam law, conduct that is inconsistent with an intent to demand strict compliance may constitute waiver. *See Guam Hous. & Urban Renewal Auth. v. Dongbu Ins. Co., Ltd.*, 2001 Guam 24, ¶ 18. The district court nevertheless correctly granted summary judgment in favor of the insurers, because even if they had waived the insistence on Navy Certification, the dry dock lacked even commercial certification when it sank. Though the insurers may have waived their right to insist on the Navy Certification warranty, they did not waive their right to insist on at least commercial certification. *See id.* at ¶ 16 (waiver must be intentional).

OCEAN MARINE POLICY

Zurich was also the insurer on an Ocean Marine Policy, covering liability for property damage caused by pollutants. The Ocean Marine Policy, in material part, limits coverage to claims "arising out of the discharge, dispersal, release, or escape of . . . oil . . . or pollutants into or upon . . . any watercourse or body of water." It is undisputed that no oil leaked out of the containers and into the water in the harbor. Thus, the policy's coverage could be triggered only if the sinking of the containers constituted a "discharge, dispersal, release, or escape" of oil or pollutants into the waters of the Bay. It did not. [—10—]

Cases in this Circuit that deal with similar property damage insurance clauses involving pollution have arisen in situations where pollutants had unquestionably leaked into the environment. *See, e.g., Aeroquip Corp. v. Aetna Cas. & Sur. Co.*, 26 F.3d 893, 893 (9th Cir. 1994) (dealing with the leakage of 7,500 gallons of diesel fuel into the soil, but coverage denied because leakage not "sudden and accidental" as required under the policy); *Intel Corp. v. Hartford Acc. & Indem. Co.*, 952 F.2d 1551, 1559 (9th Cir. 1991) (insurer's reliance on pollution exclusion not waived in connection with hazardous waste solvents that had slowly leaked out of storage tanks and into the groundwater and soil). Thus, we have had no occasion to consider whether the disposal into the environment of containers holding contaminants can constitute a discharge of pollutants, even if no contaminants leaked into the environment.

Contract law requires that we give unambiguous[2] insurance policy terms "their ordinary meaning." *Klamath Water Users Protective Ass'n v. Patterson*, 204 F.3d 1206, 1210 (9th Cir. 1999) ("Whenever possible, the plain language of the contract should be considered first."). Under the ordinary meaning of Endorsement No. 10, Zurich would provide coverage of Guam Industrial's damages only if either (1) oil or (2) pollutants escaped or were discharged, dispersed, or released into the water. We agree with Guam Industrial's Opening Brief, where it outlined the "ordinary meaning" for the insurance policy terms:

---

[2] No party argues (unlike the dissent) that the language of Endorsement No. 10 is ambiguous.

The plain ordinary meaning of discharge is the release of something from "confinement, [—11—] custody, or care". [sic] *Webster's Ninth New Collegiate Dictionary* (1989). A dispersal is the "act or result of dispersing", [sic] and disperse includes the meaning "to spread or distribute from a fixed or constant source". [sic] *Id.* An escape is the "act of escaping or the fact of having escaped: as . . . leakage or outflow esp. of steam or a liquid" and release includes "to set free from restraint". [sic] *Id.*

Bl. Br. 39. Applying these definitions to the facts of this case, it is clear that *barrels or containers* were discharged, dispersed, and released, but that oil was not. In fact, all parties agree that the oil remained sealed inside its containers at all relevant times. Thus, under the ordinary meaning of Endorsement No. 10, Zurich's coverage cannot be said to have been triggered by a "discharge, dispersal, release, or escape" of oil.

Further, sealed barrels, regardless of their contents, do not qualify as "pollutants" under the plain meaning of Endorsement No. 10. Endorsement No. 10 provides a list of specific substances whose "discharge, dispersal, release or escape" triggers the clause. The substances listed are "smoke, vapors, soot, fumes, alkalis, toxic chemicals, liquids or gases, waste materials, oil or other petroleum substance or derivative (including any oil refuse or oil mixed wastes)." These specific substances are then followed by the catchall terms "or other irritants, contaminants or pollutants." The sealed barrels discharged in this case clearly do not qualify as any of the specified substances. Thus, the only question is whether sealed barrels fall within the catchall terms. "It is . . . a familiar canon of statutory construction that [catchall] clauses are to be read as bringing within a statute categories [—12—] similar in type to those specifically enumerated." *Paroline v. United States*, 134 S. Ct. 1710, 1721 (2014) (alteration in original) (quoting *Federal Maritime Comm'n v. Seatrain Lines, Inc.*, 411 U.S. 726, 734 (1973)). When applying this canon of construction to the Endorsement, it is clear that barrels and other containers are not

similar to the listed substances. Instead, the Endorsement limits the term "pollutants" to chemicals and other hazardous substances. Solid, non-hazardous items, such as barrels, are not similar in type to the specifically enumerated hazardous substances. Thus, under the ordinary meaning of the policy terms, a sealed barrel cannot be an "irritant[], contaminant[] or pollutant." Neither oil nor pollutants were discharged, dispersed, or released, nor did they escape, into the waters of Apra Harbor in this case.

The dissent argues that we err by not construing the Ocean Marine Policy in favor of the insured (Guam Industrial). As the authority cited by the dissent recognizes, *"should ambiguities exist in the language of the policy provisions*, they are to be liberally construed in favor of the insured" to "protect[] . . . the objectively reasonable expectations of the insured." *Yasuda Fire & Marine Ins. Co. v. Heights Enterprises*, 1998 Guam 5 ¶ 12–13 (emphasis added) (internal quotation marks omitted). However, we find no ambiguity in the terms of the Ocean Marine Policy. Without an ambiguous term or provision, we have nothing to "construe" in favor of the insured. Surely, the dissent cannot intend to suggest that any time an insurer and an insured have a genuine disagreement concerning an insurance contract provision, a reviewing court must accept the insured's interpretation. That contention has absolutely no support in our precedent. *See Klamath Water Users Protective Ass'n*, 204 F.3d at 1210 ("The fact that the parties dispute a [—13—] contract's meaning does not establish that the contract is ambiguous . . . .").

Instead, our precedent clearly requires that we apply the ordinary meaning of the contract terms. *See, e.g., id.* at 1210. Utilizing Guam Industrial's own "ordinary meanings" of the terms in Endorsement No. 10, we conclude that Guam Industrial's damages were not covered by the Ocean Marine Policy.

At least one other Circuit has expressly held that the relevant act of pollution for purposes of similar insurance coverage occurs when the contaminant leaks out of a container, not when the container is disposed of. In *Patz v. St. Paul Fire & Marine Ins. Co.*, 15 F.3d 699, 702 (7th Cir. 1994), the Seventh Circuit addressed a similar insurance clause that provided coverage for accidental "discharge, dispersal, release, or escape" of contaminants or pollutants. The insured had put sludge into barrels and then buried the barrels. *Id.* at 703. The insurer had contended the burial constituted the pollution and was not accidental. The court held that the relevant act of pollution occurred not when the barrels were buried but when the sludge leaked out of the barrels. *Id.* ("As the barrels themselves were not contaminants, no discharge of contaminants into the soil occurred until the barrels leaked or broke.").

We agree with the Seventh Circuit that the containers themselves are not pollutants. Just as there was no pollution in *Patz* when the barrels were buried in the ground, there was no pollution in this case when the dry dock sank and the containers fell into the water. Under the pollution clause in the insurance policy, pollution would have occurred only [—14—] when and if the oil leaked out of the containers, which it did not.

The district court correctly ruled that since there was no actual discharge of pollutants, even though the containers of oil were submerged after the sinking, Guam Industrial's costs of retrieving the containers from the sea were not covered by the policy's allowance of coverage for cleanup after the "discharge, dispersal, release, or escape" of pollutants.

CONCLUSION

The district court correctly granted summary judgment in favor of the defendant insurance companies on both the Hull and Machinery Policy, and on the Ocean Marine Policy.

AFFIRMED.

(Reporter's Note: Dissenting opinion follows on p. 551).

[—14—] **KOZINSKI,** Circuit Judge, dissenting in part:

If you slap a silk suit on a monkey, you still won't want to take it to the prom. And if you pour crude oil into a barrel, you still won't want it in your hot tub.

Zurich's Ocean Marine Policy covers claims "arising out of the discharge, dispersal, release, or escape of . . . oil . . . or pollutants into . . . any watercourse or body of water." Guam Industrial paid for this coverage and Zurich happily accepted the premiums. (Insurance companies seldom have trouble with this part of the bargain.) What risk was Zurich paid to assume? The risk that something nasty would get into the water and Guam Industrial would be under a legal obligation [—15—] to clean it up. That's just what happened here: Some very nasty stuff—barrels containing over 100,000 gallons of industrial oil—plunged into the harbor when the dry dock sank. To no one's surprise, the Coast Guard immediately issued Guam Industrial a clean-up notice. This wasn't an invitation to the prom; it was a clean-up-or-else-we'll-do-it-ourselves-and-make-you-pay-through-the-nose notice. Guam Industrial did what the law required of it and, thanks to its careful efforts, none of the oil mixed with the water. Why should Zurich's obligation to pay for the clean-up turn on the largely fortuitous circumstance that none of the barrels leaked right away? Sooner or later the monkey will rip off the silk suit and the barrels at the bottom of the ocean will release gunk where the fishes live. Which is no doubt why the Coast Guard gave Guam Industrial a notice to clean up the barrels of oil but not the other debris from the sinking.

Like the majority, I start with the dictionary definitions of "discharge," "dispersal," "release" and "escape" to ascertain their ordinary meaning. A "discharge" is a "release from confinement, custody, or care." *Merriam-Webster's Collegiate Dictionary* 356 (11th ed. 2003). A "dispersal" is the act of "spread[ing] or distribut[ing] from a fixed or constant source." *Id.* at 361. A "release" is the act of "set[ting] free from restraint [or] confinement," *id.* at 1051, and an "escape" is "flight from confinement," *id.* at 425. The

majority concludes that "*barrels or containers were discharged, dispersed, and released*" from the dry dock. Op. at 11. It then follows that the contents of those barrels were likewise "discharged, dispersed, and released" from the dry dock.

Let's say you place your cell phone in your backpack while hiking, and the backpack falls into a crevice and can't [—16—] be recovered. You'd certainly be right in claiming that you lost your cell phone, even though the phone is still inside your backpack. What matters is that the backpack and its contents are no longer in your control. If the phone was insured against loss, no insurance company (except maybe Zurich) would claim that the phone isn't lost because it's still inside your backpack.

Endorsement No. 10 lists the "discharge, dispersal, release, or escape" of "smoke, vapors, soot, fumes, alkalis, toxic chemicals, liquids or gases, waste materials, oil or other petroleum substance or derivative . . . or other irritants, contaminants or pollutants" as hazards covered by the policy. The majority claims that "[s]olid, non-hazardous items, such as barrels, are not similar in type to the specifically enumerated hazardous substances" in the Endorsement. Op. at 12. But we're not talking here about empty barrels; we're talking about barrels filled with a known pollutant. Nor are we talking about indestructible barrels—something that exists only in graphic novels. In the real world, barrels are merely temporary containment devices that will corrode or break over time. At that point, whatever lurks inside—oil, acid, arsenic, radioactive waste, you name it—will spill out.

Of course, we must read the catchall clause, "or other irritants, contaminants or pollutants," as "bringing within a [contract] categories similar in type to those specifically enumerated." *Paroline* v. *United States*, 134 S. Ct. 1710, 1721 (2014) (internal quotation marks omitted). But are oil barrels all that different from "waste materials" or the very substance contained within the barrels—industrial oil? Once underwater, barrels filled with oil pose a threat to the environment and will eventually cause the same kind of harm. Would you let your kids swim in waters where there are [—17—] submerged barrels filled with toxic waste? Would you drink from a well in which such barrels were dropped? Most people wouldn't. The Coast Guard certainly considered the barrels sufficiently polluting to order that Guam Industrial remove them.

The majority misplaces its reliance on a Seventh Circuit case that held for the insureds. *See Patz* v. *St. Paul Fire & Marine Ins. Co.*, 15 F.3d 699 (7th Cir. 1994). The insureds in *Patz* buried sealed barrels of paint sludge on their property. A few years later, the sludge leaked from the barrels and the Patzes were ordered to clean up the mess. *Id.* at 702. They sought reimbursement for their clean-up costs under a policy that covered the *accidental* "discharge, dispersal, release or escape" of contaminants or pollutants. The insurance company denied coverage, arguing that the discharge was not accidental because the Patzes had buried the barrels of sludge intentionally. *Id.* The Seventh Circuit did say that "the barrels themselves were not contaminants" at the time they were buried, and that "no discharge of contaminants into the soil occurred until the barrels leaked or broke," *id.* at 703, but it did so while construing the insurance contract—as it was required to do—in favor of the insureds. It acknowledged that "[a]t first and even second glance, [the insurance company's] interpretation . . . has a great deal to recommend it. Excluded from coverage, on the most natural reading of the clause, are all discharges (etc.) of waste materials, except those that are sudden and accidental." *Id.* Construing the Patzes' burial of the barrels as an act of pollution may have been the more plausible interpretation, but the Seventh Circuit adopted the less plausible interpretation which favored the insureds. [—18—]

The real lesson of *Patz*, which my colleagues overlook, is that when it comes to construing insurance contracts, the insured need not have the best interpretation or even one just as good as the insurer's. The insured's interpretation need only be plausible. "A well settled general principle of insurance law is that . . . ambiguities . . . are to be liberally construed in favor of the insured." *Yasuda Fire & Marine Ins. Co.* v. *Heights Enters.*, 1998 Guam 5 ¶ 12. An ambiguous term must be interpreted "in the manner in which the promisor believed the promisee understood it at the time of its making" so as to "protect[] . . . the objectively reasonable expectations of the insured." *Id.* at ¶ 13 (internal quotation marks omitted). The majority has hung this venerable maxim of insurance law by its tail.

Guam Industrial argues that the language of Endorsement No. 10 unambiguously covers the sinking of the oil barrels, while Zurich argues that the language unambiguously excludes such coverage. Where "both parties claim a contract is unambiguous but advance different rational arguments as to its meaning, a court is not limited by the parties' failure to specifically assert ambiguity." *Minex Res., Inc.* v. *Morland*, 467 N.W.2d 691, 696 (N.D. 1991); *see also Comm'r of the Gen. Land Office of Tex.* v. *SandRidge Energy, Inc.*, 454 S.W.3d 603, 612 (Tex. App. 2014) ("We may conclude that a contract is ambiguous even when, as is the case here, the parties do not assert ambiguity.").

The cost of fishing out submerged oil barrels at the command of the Coast Guard is the kind of risk for which dry dock owners would seek coverage when buying insurance. It doesn't matter whether oil mixes with water immediately or sometime later; the risk is the same. After all, dry dock owners have every reason to expect that the Coast Guard will [—19—] order the immediate removal of barrels filled with pollutant, whether or not they ruptured when the dry dock sank. *See* 33 U.S.C. § 1321(c)(1)(A) (requiring the President, acting through the Coast Guard, to ensure "mitigation or prevention of a substantial threat" of an oil spill).

The policy's pollution exclusion clause is designed to exclude coverage for pollution occurring during the normal course of an insured's business. *See Minerva Enters., Inc.* v. *Bituminous Cas. Corp.*, 851 S.W.2d 403, 404 (Ark. 1993) ("the [pollution] exclusion is intended to prevent persistent polluters from getting insurance coverage for general polluting activities"); *Thompson* v. *Temple*, 580 So. 2d 1133, 1134–35 (La. Ct. App. 1991) ("Pollution exclusion clauses are intended to exclude coverage for active industrial polluters, when businesses knowingly emitted pollutants over extended periods of time.") (citing cases); *Molton, Allen & Williams, Inc.* v. *St. Paul Fire & Marine Ins. Co.*, 347 So. 2d 95, 99 (Ala. 1977) ("It is believed that the intent of the 'pollution exclusion' clause was to eliminate coverage for damages arising out of pollution or contamination by industry-related activities. . . . The pollution exclusion was no doubt designed to decrease the risk where an insured was putting smoke, vapors, soot, fumes, acids, alkalis, toxic chemicals, liquids or gases, waste materials or other irritants, contaminants or pollutants into the environment."). Losing control of pollutants as a result of an unexpected and unintended event—here, the sinking of the dry dock during high surf conditions—is nothing like the types of events contemplated by the pollution exclusion clause. Endorsement No. 10 clears up any doubt by specifying that "[t]his [pollution] exclusion shall not apply" where "the occurrence [that] arose from Maritime Operations" was "caused by some [—20—] intervening event neither foreseeable nor intended by the insured." This is just what happened here.

No rational dry dock owner would buy a policy that covers government-ordered pollution clean-up if containment vessels filled with toxic waste break apart upon sinking but not if they remain intact. It's absurd. Zurich's denial of coverage is the type of slimy conduct that gives insurance companies a bad name. This opinion should serve as fair warning to those who would throw away good money doing business with Zurich.

United States Court of Appeals
for the Ninth Circuit

No. 13-35866

ALASKA WILDERNESS LEAGUE
vs.
JEWELL

Appeal from the United States District Court for the
District of Alaska

Decided: June 11, 2015

Citation: 788 F.3d 1212, 3 Adm. R. 554 (9th Cir. 2015).

Before **FARRIS**, **NELSON**, and **NGUYEN**, Circuit Judges.

[—5—] **NGUYEN**, Circuit Judge:

Shell Gulf of Mexico Inc. and Shell Offshore Inc. (collectively "Shell") for many years have sought to develop offshore oil and gas resources in the remote Beaufort and Chukchi seas on Alaska's Arctic coast. Shell secured leases for the Beaufort Sea in 2005 and 2007, and the Chukchi Sea in 2008, but its exploration efforts have been waylaid by a variety of legal, logistical, and environmental problems, including multiple lawsuits,[1] the wreck of one of its drill rigs,[2]

---

[1] *See, e.g., Resisting Envtl. Destruction on Indigenous Lands, REDOIL, v. EPA*, 716 F.3d 1155 (9th Cir. 2013) (challenging permitting of exploratory drilling in the Beaufort and Chukchi Seas); *Native Vill. of Point Hope v. Salazar*, 680 F.3d 1123, 1128 (9th Cir. 2012) (challenging the approval of exploration plans in the Beaufort Sea); *Inupiat Comm. of the Arctic Slope v. Salazar*, 486 F. App'x 625 (9th Cir. 2012) (mem.) (challenging the approval of exploratory drilling plans in the Chukchi Sea); *Native Vill. of Point Hope v. Salazar*, 378 F. App'x 747 (9th Cir. 2010) (mem.) (challenging the approval of exploration plans in the Beaufort and Chukchi Seas); *Alaska Wilderness League v. Kempthorne*, 548 F.3d 815 (9th Cir. 2008), *vacated*, 559 F.3d 916 (9th Cir. 2009) (challenging the approval of exploration plans in the Beaufort Sea), *dismissed as moot sub nom.*, *Alaska Wilderness League v. Salazar*, 571 F.3d 859 (9th Cir. 2009); *see also Ctr. for Biological Diversity v. Salazar*, 695 F.3d 893 (9th Cir. 2012) (challenging the authorization of incidental take of polar bears and Pacific walruses related to exploration activity in the Chukchi Sea); *Ctr. for*

and the temporary suspension of drilling activities in the [—6—] Arctic after the Deepwater Horizon Spill.[3] We review here another challenge, a claim by a coalition of environmental groups that the Bureau of Safety and Environmental Enforcement ("BSEE") acted unlawfully in approving two of Shell's oil spill response plans ("OSRPs"). The district court granted summary judgment in favor of the federal defendants and intervenor-defendant Shell. We affirm.

BACKGROUND

I.

The Statutory Schemes

We begin with an overview of the complex statutory backdrop to BSEE's approval of the OSRPs in this case.

The Outer Continental Shelf Lands Act ("OCSLA"), 43 U.S.C. § 1331 *et seq.*, establishes a four-stage process for the exploration and development of offshore oil and gas resources. First, the Secretary of the Interior prepares and maintains a five-year oil and gas leasing program. 43 U.S.C. § 1344(a). Second, the Secretary may grant oil and gas leases for submerged lands in the outer continental shelf at a lease sale, subject to certain terms and provisions. *See id.* § 1337(a)–(b). Third, a lessee must "submit an exploration plan to the Secretary for approval," *id.* § 1340(c)(1), accompanied by an Oil Spill Response Plan required under [—7—] the Clean Water Act, *see* 30 C.F.R. § 550.219 (the approval of which is at issue in this case). In the fourth and final phase, if exploration reveals oil or gas, a lessee must then submit "a development and production

---

Biological Diversity v. Kempthorne, 588 F.3d 701 (9th Cir. 2009) (same, as to the Beaufort Sea).

[2] *See* Gary Braasch, *The Wreck of the Kulluk*, N.Y. TIMES, Dec. 30, 2014, at MM24.

[3] U.S. Dep't of the Interior, Decision Memorandum Regarding the Suspension of Certain Offshore Permitting and Drilling Activities in the Outer Continental Shelf, July 12, 2010, at 1 *available at* http://www.doi.gov/deepwaterhorizon/loader.cfm?csModule=security/getfile&PageID=38390.

plan" for the Secretary's approval. 43 U.S.C. § 1351(a)(1). Each stage triggers certain environmental analysis, and the Bureau of Ocean Energy Management ("BOEM") is responsible for managing the process, including the necessary environmental reviews. *See Native Vill. of Point Hope v. Salazar*, 680 F.3d 1123, 1128 (9th Cir. 2012).

While OCSLA governs the development of oil and gas resources, the Clean Water Act provides a framework for preventing and responding to potential oil spills. *See* 33 U.S.C. § 1321(b). The Clean Water Act mandates oil spill contingency planning at four levels: the national, regional, and area levels, and, lastly, at the level of individual owners and operators of offshore oil facilities. First, at the national level, the President prepares a National Contingency Plan that sets forth "efficient, coordinated, and effective action to minimize damage from oil and hazardous substance discharges." *Id.* § 1321(d)(2). Second, Regional Response Teams, co-chaired by the Environmental Protection Agency and the Coast Guard, prepare Regional Contingency Plans that coordinate "planning, preparedness, and response activities" across federal agencies, "states, local governments, and private entities." 40 C.F.R. § 300.105(a); *see also id.* at 300.115. Third, Area Committees prepare Area Contingency Plans that, "when implemented in conjunction with the National Contingency Plan, [are] adequate to remove a worst case discharge, and to mitigate or prevent a substantial threat of such a discharge." 33 U.S.C. § 1321(j)(4)(C)(i). [—8—]

Fourth and finally, and most relevant to this litigation, the President must promulgate regulations that require owners and operators of offshore oil facilities[4] to submit an OSRP "for responding, to the maximum extent practicable, to a worst case discharge . . . of oil or a hazardous substance." *Id.* § 1321(j)(5)(A)(i). The Secretary of the Interior

delegated this responsibility to BSEE.[5] 56 Fed. Reg. 54,757, 54,761-62 (Oct. 18, 1991); 76 Fed. Reg. 64,432-01, 64,448 (Oct. 18, 2011). OSRPs must comply with the Clean Water Act's six requirements, listed at 33 U.S.C. § 1321(j)(5)(D), one of which is compliance with the governing Area Contingency Plan. *Id.* § 1321(j)(5)(D)(i); 30 C.F.R. § 550.219. BSEE must "promptly review" submitted plans, "require amendments to any plan that does not meet the requirements of this paragraph," and "*shall . . .* approve any plan that meets" the statutory requirements. *Id.* § 1321(j)(5)(E)(i)–(iii) (emphasis added). [—9—]

Environmental consultation occurs at several points throughout both OCSLA and the Clean Water Act's four-tiered processes. National Environmental Policy Act ("NEPA") and Endangered Species Act ("ESA") consultations occur when oil and gas exploration leases are first issued (at OCSLA's second stage), 43 U.S.C. § 1344(a)(1) & (b)(3); *see also Sec'y of the Interior v. California*, 464 U.S. 312, 338 (1984), and again when lessee exploration plans are submitted (at OCSLA's third stage), 43 U.S.C. § 1340(c). Additional environmental review takes place upon submission of lessee development and production plans (OCSLA's fourth stage), including another round of NEPA review, *see id.* § 1351(c), and the submission of environmental impact statements ("EIS") to the governors of any affected states, *id.* § 1351(f)–(g). The Secretary may "approve, disapprove, or require

---

[4] While OCSLA refers to "lessees," the Clean Water Act refers to "owners and operators." *Compare* 43 U.S.C. § 1331 et. seq. *with* 33 U.S.C. § 1321. Because this case concerns the approval of OSRPs under the Clean Water Act, we primarily employ the term "operators."

[5] Initially, a single agency, the Minerals Management Service ("MMS"), managed compliance with both OCSLA and the Clean Water Act. *See* 76 Fed.Reg. 64,432, DOI Secretarial Order No. 3229. After the Deepwater Horizon oil spill in 2010, however, the Secretary divided MMS into three new entities. *Native Vill.*, 680 F.3d at 1127 (quoting Press Release, U.S. Dep't of Interior, Salazar Divides MMS's Three Conflicting Missions (May 19, 2010), *available at* http://www.doi.gov/news/pressreleases/Salazar-Divides-MMSs-Three-Conflicting-Missions.cfm). BOEM now manages the development of offshore resources under OCSLA, and BSEE is responsible for the "enforcement of safety and environmental functions" under the Clean Water Act, including approval of the OSRPs at issue here. *Id.* at 1128.

modifications" of development plans, and must reject any plan that would "probably cause serious harm or damage to . . . the marine, coastal, or human environments," when weighed against the extent of the threat and the potential advantages of allowing production. *Id.* § 1351(h)(1).

Likewise, the Clean Water Act has several types of environmental review built in throughout its various stages. At the Area Contingency Plan level, Area Committees must consult with both the U.S. Fish and Wildlife Service and the National Oceanic and Atmospheric Administration to prepare "a detailed annex containing a Fish and Wildlife and Sensitive Environments Plan" that "provide[s] the necessary information and procedures to immediately and effectively respond to discharges that may adversely affect" the environment. 40 C.F.R. § 300.210(c)(4)(I). An operator's OSRP must be consistent with the protocols established at this stage. *See* 33 U.S.C. § 1321(j)(5)(D)(i). The National [—10—] Contingency Plan also lays out procedures for emergency consultation in the case of an actual oil spill. *See* 40 C.F.R. § 300.305(e).

II.

The Current Dispute

The case before us arises in the context of these overlapping statutory schemes, and represents "the latest chapter in a long-running saga beginning back in April 2002, when the Minerals Management Service ("MMS") established a five-year lease sale schedule for the outer continental shelf of Alaska." *Native Vill.*, 680 F.3d at 1126. After Shell acquired offshore oil leases in the Beaufort Sea in 2005 and 2007, and in the Chukchi Sea in 2008, it submitted exploration plans, and the required OSRPs, for activities that were scheduled to commence in the summer of 2010. MMS, which was then in charge of approving exploration plans and OSRPs, *id.* at 1127, approved Shell's Beaufort Sea OSRP in March of that year and approved Shell's Chukchi Sea OSRP the following month.

The April 2010 Deepwater Horizon oil spill in the Gulf of Mexico shifted the landscape in a number of ways. BOEM assumed control over the approval of exploration plans, and BSEE assumed responsibility for approving OSRPs. *Id.* at 1128. Also, following a moratorium on all oil and gas drilling, the Department of the Interior issued new guidance regarding the content and analysis that should be provided in OSRPs. *See, e.g.,* U.S. Department of the Interior, Bureau of Ocean Energy Management, Regulation, and Enforcement, *Information Requirements for Exploration Plans, Development and Production Plans, and Development* [—11—] *Operations Coordination Documents on the OCS* 3 (2010), *available at* http://www.boem.gov/Regulations/Notices-To-Lessees/2010/10-n06.aspx.[6] In response, Shell updated its OSRPs for the Chukchi and Beaufort Seas in May 2011, and again in early 2012. BSEE approved the two OSRPs in February and March of 2012, respectively.

Following these approvals, Plaintiffs sued the Secretary of the Interior and the Department of the Interior under the Administrative Procedure Act, challenging BSEE's approval of the OSRPs. Shell successfully intervened. The parties filed cross-motions for summary judgment. The district court, following extensive briefing and argument, granted summary judgment in favor of the federal defendants and Shell. *Shell Gulf of Mex. v. Ctr. for Bio. Diversity, Inc.*, No. 3:12-CV-00048-RRB (D. Alaska Aug. 5, 2013). This appeal followed.

STANDARDS OF REVIEW

"We review the grant of summary judgment de novo, thus reviewing directly the agency's action under the Administrative Procedure Act's ("APA") arbitrary and capricious standard." *Gila River Indian Cmty.*

---

[6] These revised guidelines were then superceded in January 2015. U.S. Department of the Interior, Bureau of Ocean Energy Management, *Information Requirements for Exploration Plans, Development and Production Plans, and Development Operations Coordination Documents on the OCS for Worst Case Discharge and Blowout Scenarios* (2015), *available at* http://www.boem.gov/NTL-2015-N01/.

v. United States, 729 F.3d 1139, 1144 (9th Cir. 2013), *as amended* (July 9, 2013) (quoting *Gifford Pinchot Task Force v. U.S. Fish & Wildlife Serv.*, 378 F.3d 1059, 1065 (9th Cir. 2004)) (internal [—12—] quotation marks omitted). Review under this standard "is narrow, and [we do] not substitute [our] judgment for that of the agency." *Ecology Ctr. v. Castaneda*, 574 F.3d 652, 656 (9th Cir. 2009) (quoting *Lands Council v. McNair*, 537 F.3d 981, 987 (9th Cir. 2008) (en banc)) (alterations in original) (internal quotation marks omitted). Rather, reversal is only proper

> if the agency relied on factors Congress did not intend it to consider, entirely failed to consider an important aspect of the problem, or offered an explanation that runs counter to the evidence before the agency or is so implausible that it could not be ascribed to a difference in view or the product of agency expertise.

Id. (quoting *Lands Council*, 537 F.3d at 987) (internal quotation marks omitted).

Additionally, under *Chevron, U.S.A., Inc. v. Natural Res. Def. Council, Inc.*, 467 U.S. 837 (1984), we engage in a three-step inquiry when reviewing an agency's interpretation of a statute that it is entrusted to administer. First, we must decide whether Congress intended "the agency to be able to speak with the force of law when it addresses ambiguity in the statute or fills a space in the enacted law." *United States v. Mead Corp.*, 533 U.S. 218, 229 (2001). Next, we ask "whether Congress has directly spoken to the precise question at issue. If the intent of Congress is clear, that is the end of the matter; for the court, as well as the agency, must give effect to the unambiguously expressed intent of Congress." *Chevron*, 467 U.S. at 842–43. Finally, if the statute is silent or ambiguous as to the issue at hand, we then defer to the [—13—] agency's reading so long as its interpretation is a reasonable one. *Id.* at 843.

DISCUSSION

I.

The Administrative Procedures Act

Plaintiffs argue that BSEE's approval of the OSRPs was arbitrary and capricious in violation of the Administrative Procedures Act. *See* 5 U.S.C. § 706(2)(A). According to Plaintiffs, Shell assumed that, in the event of a worst case discharge, Shell would achieve a mechanical recovery of 90 to 95 percent of any oil spilled in the Arctic Ocean—an assumption that Plaintiffs characterize as unrealistic and unsupported. Plaintiffs, however, have misread the record, which shows that Shell never assumed a 90 to 95 percent mechanical recovery rate. And even assuming that it did, BSEE did not rely on any such assumption in approving Shell's OSRPs.

The pertinent portion of Shell's OSRPs reads as follows:

> To scale the potential shoreline response assets needed, and for planning purposes, Shell based these assets upon the assumption that 10 percent of the 25,000-[barrels of oil per day ("bopd")] discharge escapes the primary offshore recovery efforts at the blowout. This unrecovered 2,500 bopd is assumed to drift toward the mainland . . . . It is assumed that half of the oil reaching the nearshore environment is recovered by the [—14—] skimming systems dispatched from [a large, mobile oil spill response barge and tug]. The remaining 1,250 bopd are assumed to migrate toward the shoreline where [Shell's spill response contractor] would mobilize personnel and equipment to intercept the oil and deploy boom for shoreline protection.[7]

Thus, on a straightforward reading of the OSRPs, Shell made two assumptions—that 10

---

[7] This quote is taken from Shell's Chukchi Sea OSRP. Pls.' Excerpts of R. at 959, ECF No. 24-10. An analogous claim was made in Shell's Beaufort Sea OSRP. *See* Pls.' Excerpts of R. at 907, ECF No. 24-10.

percent of spilled oil would "drive toward the mainland," half of which would be recovered by skimming systems and half of which would "migrate toward the shoreline"—for purposes of "scal[ing] the potential shoreline response assets needed." Nothing in the OSRPs' text suggests that Shell was predicting a 90 to 95 percent mechanical recovery rate. Indeed, Shell's OSRPs make clear that it was estimating the potential shoreline response assets needed in order to comply with an Alaska state law requiring certain calculations regarding the magnitude of a worst case scenario oil spill. BSEE's regulations identify the specific information an operator must provide when discussing its worst case discharge scenario, and these regulations do not require an estimated recovery rate for spilled oil. *See* 30 C.F.R. § 254.26(a)–(d). In short, the record simply does not support Plaintiffs' claim that Shell assumed an impossibly high recovery rate of almost 100 percent.

Moreover, it is equally clear from the administrative record that BSEE did not rely on a purported 90 to 95 percent [—15—] mechanical recovery rate in approving Shell's OSRPs. While Shell's OSRPs were under consideration, the National Oceanic Atmospheric Administration expressed concern that "Shell was claiming it would mechanically recovery 95 percent of oil spilled in any incident, which is many times more than the best performance currently achievable." Pls.' Excerpts of R. at 286, ECF No. 24-3. BSEE responded that "this was a misreading of the plan, which is not a performance standard. Shell is claiming to have the capacity to store up to 95 percent of the [worst case discharge] volume, not that it would be able to actually collect that much." *Id.* This record shows that BSEE internally acknowledged some "confusion" over the "planning v. performance issue" in the OSRPs, but nonetheless reaffirmed its view that Shell was "in no way claiming an ability to recover 90 percent of the oil." *Id.* at 288. Thus, Plaintiffs' claim that BSEE's approval of the OSRPs was arbitrary and capricious on the ground that Shell assumed an impossibly high recovery rate fails.

II.

The Endangered Species Act

Next, Plaintiffs argue that BSEE should have engaged in ESA consultation before approving the OSRPs. Section 7 of ESA requires federal agencies to consult with the appropriate environmental agencies before taking an action that may affect endangered species or habitats. 16 U.S.C. § 1536(a)(4); *see also Nat'l Res. Def. Council v. Jewell*, 749 F.3d 776, 779 (9th Cir. 2014). Even if there is agency "action," however, ESA consultation is triggered only if "there is *discretionary* Federal involvement or control," 50 C.F.R. § 402.03 (emphasis added), because consultation [—16—] would be merely a "meaningless exercise" if the agency lacks the power to implement changes that would benefit endangered species, *Sierra Club v. Babbitt*, 65 F.3d 1502, 1509 (9th Cir. 1995).[8]

Here, we need not decide whether BSEE's approval of the OSRPs constitutes agency action. Even assuming, without deciding, that the approval of the OSRPs was agency action, we conclude that it was a nondiscretionary action and thus ESA's consultation requirement was not triggered. Because Congress has "delegat[ed] administrative authority" to the agency to interpret this statute, *Chevron's* framework applies. *See Adams Fruit Co., Inc. v. Barrett*, 494 U.S. 638, 649 (1990) ("A precondition to deference under *Chevron* is a congressional delegation of administrative authority."). As discussed below, at *Chevron* Step One, we find the relevant provisions of the Clean Water Act ambiguous, and therefore "Congress has [not] directly spoken to the precise question at issue." *Chevron*, 467 U.S. at 842. At *Chevron* Step Two, we find the agency interpretation reasonable, and therefore we must accord its interpretation deference. *See id.* at 843.

---

[8] Because we determine that discretionary agency action did not occur, we need not decide whether the action "may affect a listed species or designated critical habitat." *Karuk Tribe of Cal. v. U.S. Forest Serv.*, 681 F.3d 1006, 1027 (quoting *Turtle Island Restoration Network v. Nat'l Marine Fisheries Serv.*, 340 F.3d 969, 974 (9th Cir. 2003) (internal quotation marks omitted)).

A. *Chevron* Step 1: The Statute's Ambiguity

The Clean Water Act, as amended by the Oil Pollution Act of 1990, offers three pertinent instructions regarding the content and approval of operators' OSRPs. First, at [—17—] 33 U.S.C. § 1321(j)(5)(A)(i), the statute states that "[t]he President shall issue regulations which require an . . . operator . . . to prepare and submit to the President a plan for responding, to the maximum extent practicable, to a worst case discharge, and to a substantial threat of such a discharge, of oil or a hazardous substance." Second, at § 1321(j)(5)(D), the statute lists six requirements that OSRPs "shall" meet. Specifically, OSRPs must

(i) be consistent with the requirements of the National Contingency Plan and Area Contingency Plans;

(ii) identify the qualified individual having full authority to implement removal actions, and require immediate communications between that individual and the appropriate Federal official and the persons providing personnel and equipment pursuant to clause (iii);

(iii) identify, and ensure by contract or other means approved by the President the availability of, private personnel and equipment necessary to remove to the maximum extent practicable a worst case discharge (including a discharge resulting from fire or explosion), and to mitigate or prevent a substantial threat of such a discharge;

(iv) describe the training, equipment testing, periodic unannounced drills, and response actions of persons on the vessel or at [—18—] the facility, to be carried out under the plan to ensure the safety of the vessel or facility and to mitigate or prevent the discharge, or the substantial threat of a discharge;

(v) be updated periodically; and

(vi) be resubmitted for approval of each significant change.

Id. The statute then *mandates* approval if the above requirements are met, stating that "the President shall . . . approve any plan that meets the requirements of this paragraph." *Id.* § 1321(j)(5)(E)(iii). All three instructions—the "maximum extent practicable" language, the six enumerated statutory criteria, and the President's "shall approve" requirement—fall within the same statutory section (specifically, paragraph (5)). Pursuant to the Clean Water Act's directive, the agency has issued regulations that set forth what an operator must do to meet the criteria set out in this section. 30 C.F.R. pt. 254.

We find the statute ambiguous in two ways—in the statutory language itself, and in the statute's structure. The text does not explicitly grant or deny BSEE discretion to consider additional environmental factors in the OSRP approval process. Section 1321(j)(5)(A)(i), which directs the agency to issue regulations requiring operators "to prepare and submit . . . a plan for responding, to the maximum extent practicable, to a worst case discharge," suggests agency discretion because of the open-ended nature of the phrase "maximum extent practicable." On the other hand, § 1321(j)(5)(D) reads like a checklist statute, and BSEE *must* approve "any plan that meets the requirements of this [—19—] paragraph," 33 U.S.C. § 1321(j)(5)(E)(iii). Thus, these sections suggest no agency discretion.

The statute's structure adds to the ambiguity. These two directives are listed in two separate portions of the paragraph that delineates an OSRP's requirements. It is unclear how the broad language of section 1321(j)(5)(A)(i), with its reference to the "maximum extent practicable," interacts with the finite statutory criteria of section 1321(j)(5)(D). "And that means we . . . face a statute whose halves do not correspond to each other–giving rise to an ambiguity that calls for *Chevron* deference." *Scialabba v. Cuellar de Osorio*, 134 S. Ct. 2191, 2210 (2014) (plurality opinion). We must defer to the agency's interpretation of the statute unless it is unreasonable. *Chevron*, 467 U.S. at 843.

B. *Chevron* Step 2: The Reasonableness of the Agency's Interpretation

Reaching *Chevron*'s second step, we must determine if the agency's interpretation of the ambiguous governing statute is a reasonable one. When "the agency's answer is based on a permissible construction of the statute," we must defer to the agency's view and not "impose [our] own construction on the statute." *Chevron*, 467 U.S. at 843; *see also Young v. Cmty. Nutrition Inst.*, 476 U.S. 974, 981 (1986) (noting that the court is "preclude[d] . . . from substituting its judgment for that of the [agency]" when the agency's interpretation of a statute it administers is "sufficiently rational").

BSEE argues that the purpose of an OSRP is to ensure that private operators have response capacity consistent with federal contingency plans in the event of a worst case [—20—] discharge. Thus, Congress has limited its discretion to reviewing an OSRP to determine if it meets the six enumerated requirements of section 1321(j)(5)(D) and the agency's coterminous implementing regulations. BSEE reads its regulations as providing further refinement of the statutory criteria and the framework under which compliance with the criteria will be assessed. Since the statute mandates that the President (and now, BSEE by delegation) "shall . . . approve any plan that meets the requirements of this paragraph," 33 U.S.C. § 1321(j)(5)(E), BSEE contends that it lacks discretion to consider factors apart from these delineated statutory criteria.

We conclude that BSEE's interpretation of the statute is reasonable, and thus we must defer to the agency. Significantly, the sections on which the agency relies, § 1321(j)(5)(D)–(E), speak directly to what a plan *shall* contain and what the agency *shall* approve. Section 1321(j)(5)(A)(i), in contrast, is more circuitous, discussing what the President's *implementing regulations* should require. *See id.* ("The President shall issue regulations which require an owner or operator . . . to prepare and submit to the President a plan for responding, to the maximum extent practicable, to a worst case discharge . . . ."). In other words, the agency reads § 1321(j)(5)(A)(i) as an instruction to issue regulations that delineate how operators can comply with the statutory checklist enumerated at § 1321(j)(5)(D). Thus, the agency reasonably understands its discretion to be constrained by § 1321(j)(5)(D)'s list of requirements which, upon their satisfaction, trigger mandatory agency approval of the OSRP.

Our deference to the agency's reading is similar to that provided by the Supreme Court in *Young v. Community* [—21—] *Nutrition Institute*, 467 U.S. 974 (1986). In *Young*, the Supreme Court considered a statute which required the Food and Drug Administration ("FDA") to "promulgate regulations limiting the quantity [of poisonous or deleterious substances that cannot be avoided within foods] therein or thereon to such an extent as [the agency] finds necessary." 476 U.S. at 977 (quoting 21 U.S.C. § 346). The FDA interpreted this provision to "give it the discretion to decide *whether* to promulgate" a quantity limit, while the plaintiffs interpreted the statute to require the agency to set a limit whenever a poisonous substance was present. *Id.* at 977 (emphasis added), 980. Applying the *Chevron* framework, the Court first found the statutory language to be ambiguous as to the question of the agency's discretion and then deferred to the FDA's interpretation, finding it "to be sufficiently rational to preclude a court from substituting its judgment for that of the [agency]." *Id.* at 980–81. No regulation explicitly reflected the agency's view of its discretion, but its position was consistent with the statutory scheme and longstanding agency policy. *Id.* at 977, 981–84.

Just like in *Young*, BSEE's position is consistent with the statute's scheme and the agency's longstanding policy. The applicable regulations "provide specific instructions to operators as to what they must do to meet [the] Clean Water Act requirements," which then trigger the agency's mandatory approval under § 1321(j)(5)(E)(iii). *E.g., compare* 30

C.F.R. § 254.5(b) (requiring the OSRP to "be consistent with the National Contingency Plan and the appropriate Area Contingency Plan(s)") *with* 33 U.S.C. § 1321(j)(5)(D)(i) (imposing the same requirement); *compare* 30 C.F.R. § 254.23(g) (requiring information about procedures the operator "will follow in the event of a spill") *with* 33 U.S.C. § 1321(j)(5)(D)(iii) (requiring the OSRP to "identify, and [—22—] ensure by contract or other means . . . the availability of, private personnel and equipment necessary to remove to the maximum extent practicable a worst case discharge"). Further, BSEE's interpretation is consistent with the Department's longstanding position on the interaction of its regulations with the statute. When promulgating its 1997 final rule, MMS understood its regulatory requirements to be coextensive with the statutory requirements, stating in the rule's preamble that "[t]he rule will bring MMS regulations into conformance with the Oil Pollution Act of 1990." Response Plans for Facilities Located Seaward of the Coast Line, 62 Fed. Reg. 13991, 13991 (Mar. 25, 1997). Moreover, the Department has expressly confirmed this understanding in its briefing on appeal. The fact that "the Secretary's interpretation comes to us in the form of a legal brief . . . does not, in the circumstances of this case, make it unworthy of deference," so long as it "reflect[s] the agency's fair and considered judgment on the matter in question." *Auer v. Robbins*, 519 U.S. 452, 462 (1997).

The legislative history of the Oil Pollution Act's passage lends further support to BSEE's interpretation. *See Natural Res. Def. Council v. Envtl. Prot. Agency*, 526 F.3d 591, 603 (9th Cir. 2008) (providing that we may look to legislative history to assist our interpretation of an ambiguous statute under *Chevron*). In its comments on the Senate version of the Oil Pollution Act of 1990, much of whose language was incorporated into the House Bill that ultimately passed and amended the Clean Water Act, the Committee on Commerce, Science, and Transportation noted that the bill imposed "[s]pecific requirements for the [oil spill contingency] plans." S. Rep. 101-99, at 4 (1989), *reprinted in* 1990 U.S.C.C.A.N. 749, 752. This suggests that Congress likely

meant to impose specific obligations upon operators in their oil spill response [—23—] preparations, and not create an amorphous standard for the Executive Branch to interpret and enforce. *See also* 136 Cong. Rec. S11931-01 (Aug. 2, 1990) (statement of Sen. Warner) (noting that "[t]he bill imposes rigorous new contingency planning requirements on areas and vessels," while obliging "the President to take charge of all major oilspills and to determine when cleanup is complete").

The dissent focuses on the breadth of § 1321(j)(5)(A)(i)'s "maximum extent practicable" language and emphasizes that because this language reads like a broad mandate, the evaluation of which would require significant agency discretion, BSEE must engage in ESA consultation before approving an OSRP. Under the dissent's view, §1321(j)(5)(A)(i)'s "maximum extent practicable" language serves as an independent "standard" that must be met in addition to the list of enumerated requirements at § 1321(j)(5)(D). The dissent's reading of the statute, however, gives short shrift to the ambiguity in the statute's text and structure.

Of course, we agree that § 1321(j)(5)(A)(i)'s "maximum extent practicable" language is broad, and the statute arguably could be read to support the dissent's interpretation. But we must accord *Chevron* deference to the agency's alternative understanding. While focusing on § 1321(j)(5)(A)(i), the dissent largely overlooks the presence of § 1321(j)(5)(D), which lays out a list of specific requirements that OSRPs must meet. BSEE reads this subsection, and the mandatory agency approval required once the specific requirements are met, *see* § 1321(j)(5)(E), to eliminate its discretion. This interpretation is assuredly a "permissible construction" of the ambiguous statutory language and structure. *Chevron*, 467 U.S. at 843. And it is not our role to displace the [—24—] agency's reasonable construction of a statute that it is responsible for administering. *See Mead*, 533 U.S. at 229 ("[A] reviewing court has no business rejecting an agency's exercise of its generally conferred authority to resolve a particular statutory ambiguity simply because the agency's chosen resolution seems unwise.").

The dissent resists the *Chevron* deference that we must give to the agency's interpretation by finding the implementing regulations to be an unreasonable interpretation of the statute. The regulations define "maximum extent practicable" to mean "within the limitations of available technology, as well as the physical limitations of personnel." 30 C.F.R. § 254.6. The dissent argues that this definition is incomplete because it fails to account for the superlative nature of the word "maximum" and instead provides a definition only of what is "practicable." Since the definition is incomplete, the dissent reasons, it is therefore unreasonable, obviating the need for this court to apply *Chevron*'s framework.

Tellingly, even Plaintiffs do not rely on the purported vagueness of the agency's implementing regulations. To the contrary, Plaintiffs' counsel *conceded* the adequacy of the regulatory definition at oral argument, stating that "[t]he regulations clearly define maximum extent practicable" and that "the regulations are fully consistent with" the maximum extent practicable standard. Oral Argument at 7:55, 8:44, *available at* http://www.ca9.uscourts.gov/media/view_video.php?pk_vid=0000006548. We also do not find the regulatory definition to be problematic. "In the absence of . . . a definition, we construe a statutory term in accordance with its ordinary or natural meaning." *F.D.I.C. v. Meyer*, 510 U.S. 471, 476 (1994). A natural reading of the regulation [—25—] indicates that operators must be prepared to respond to an oil spill to the highest degree possible (to the "maximum"), not exceeding "the limitations of available technology . . . [and] the physical limitations of personnel." 30 C.F.R. § 254.6. While the agency could have been more explicit by specifying that "maximum extent practicable" means the *highest degree* of response possible "within the limitations of available technology," *id.*, such a clarification would be superfluous since the plain meaning of "maximum" leads to the same reading. Therefore, we cannot say that the agency

regulation constitutes an "[im]permissible construction of the statute." *Chevron*, 467 U.S. at 843.

More importantly, this regulatory definition is largely peripheral to our analysis. We defer to the agency's interpretation here not because of its regulatory promulgation, but because we face a "statutory inconsistency . . . giving rise to an ambiguity that calls for *Chevron* deference." *Cuellar de Osorio*, 134 S. Ct. at 2210 (plurality opinion). The text and structure of the statute are unclear as to whether the statute grants the agency discretion to use a broad, indeterminate standard to review OSRPs, or whether it mandates approval of plans that meet the requirements of § 1321(j)(5)(D). "Confronted with a self-contradictory, ambiguous provision in a complex statutory scheme, the [agency] chose a textually reasonable construction consonant with its view of the purpose and policies underlying . . . [the] law." *Id.* at 2213. We do not "assume as our own the responsible and expert agency's role," and instead defer to BSEE's reasonable interpretation of the gap in a statute it has been tasked with interpreting. *Id.*

We address a number of additional arguments raised by Plaintiffs. They note that the statutory sections governing the [—26—] federal government's spill plans, at §§ 1321(d)(1)–(2), (j)(4)(B)–(D), contain the same "shall approve" formulations, and yet are admittedly subject to ESA's consultation requirements. These provisions, however, are different. Section 1321(d)(1) states that the President "shall prepare and publish a National Contingency Plan for removal of oil and hazardous substances pursuant to this section." Nothing in the text prohibits such a plan from being prepared in light of concerns that an ESA consultation might raise. Similarly, § 1321(d)(2) specifies that the National Contingency Plan "shall provide for efficient, coordinated, and effective action to minimize damage from oil and hazardous substance discharges," and "shall include, but not be limited to" a list of enumerated factors. This suggests that a National Contingency Plan could (and should) contain *additional* factors that might be deemed necessary after an ESA consultation occurs. Likewise, while the President shall "review and approve Area Contingency Plans," this language does not suggest that *any* plan meeting a list of set requirements must be approved. *Compare id.* § 1321(j)(4)(B)–(D) *with id.* § 1321(j)(5)(D)–(E).

Section 1321(j)(5)(E)'s language, in contrast, requires that the President "shall . . . approve any plan that meets the requirements of this paragraph." This language leaves no room for the inclusion of additional factors. The absence of agency discretion is apparent not from the words "shall approve" alone, but from the phrase "shall . . . approve *any plan that meets the requirements of this paragraph.*" *Id.* § 1321(j)(5)(E) (emphasis added).

Plaintiffs next argue that "[t]he regulations never say that so long as a plan addresses in some fashion various questions, the agency must conclude the plan meets the statutory [—27—] mandates." Pls.' Opening Br. at 46. Yet, 30 C.F.R. § 254.9(b) explicitly states that the information in the OSRP is collected to "ensure that the owner or operator . . . is prepared to respond to an oil spill" and to "verify compliance with the mandates" of the Oil Pollution Act's amendments to the Clean Water Act. In any event, such an explicit pronouncement is not a prerequisite for *Chevron* deference to apply. *See, e.g., Young,* 476 U.S. at 981–82 (deferring to the FDA's interpretation of an ambiguous statutory provision even in the absence of a regulation explicitly stating the agency's position); *Fernandez v. Brock,* 840 F.2d 622, 633 (9th Cir. 1988) (deferring to the Secretary of Labor's interpretation of statute that was ambiguous as to the presence of agency discretion).

Finally, plaintiffs argue that ESA's consultation requirement is triggered because BSEE exercises discretion in deciding *whether* the six statutory criteria are met. This position, however, is irreconcilable with the Supreme Court's decision in *National Association of Home Builders v. Defenders of Wildlife,* 551 U.S. 644, 671 (2007), which held that ESA cannot defeat an agency's

nondiscretionary statutory directive. The statute at issue there listed nine statutory criteria; if those criteria were satisfied, the agency bore a nondiscretionary duty to perform a specific action (namely, transfer certain permitting powers to state authorities). *Id.* at 661. *Home Builders*'s analysis is directly applicable here.[9] BSEE may only determine whether the [—28—] statutory criteria in 33 U.S.C. § 1321(j)(5)(D) have been met, and if they have been met, BSEE must approve the plan. Since determining *whether* the statutory criteria have been achieved does not trigger ESA's consultation requirement, Plaintiffs' argument must again fail.

In sum, deferring to the agency's interpretation of the statute that it has been entrusted to administer, and its own regulations, we hold that BSEE's approval of the OSRPs was a nondiscretionary act that did not trigger a requirement for inter-agency consultation under the ESA.

III.

The National Environmental Policy Act

Finally, Plaintiffs argue, and the dissent agrees, that BSEE violated NEPA by failing to prepare an Environmental Impact Statement ("EIS") before approving the OSRPs. NEPA requires federal agencies to provide an EIS for all "major Federal actions significantly affecting the quality of the human environment." 42 U.S.C. § 4332(C); *see also Dep't of Transp. v. Pub. Citizen,* 541 U.S. 752, 757 (2004). NEPA's implementing regulations define "[m]ajor Federal action" to include

---

[9] The dissent points out that *Home Builders* relied in part on the fact that ESA was passed after the statute requiring the transfer of permitting power, while the provisions of the Clean Water Act at issue here were enacted in 1990, post-dating ESA's 1972 passage. *See Home Builders,* 551 U.S. at 662–64. This factual distinction in timing does not change the [—28—] outcome of our analysis. *See, e.g., Grand Canyon Trust v. United States Bureau of Reclamation,* 691 F.3d 1008, 1020 (9th Cir. 2012) (relying on *Home Builders* to hold that agency action required in part by a 1992 statute did not require ESA consultation).

"actions with effects that may be major and which are potentially subject to Federal control and responsibility." 40 C.F.R. § 1508.18. Even when a major federal action occurs, however, NEPA remains subject to a "rule of reason" that frees agencies from preparing a full EIS [—29—] on "the environmental impact of an action it could not refuse to perform." *Pub. Citizen*, 541 U.S. at 769. Thus, "where an agency has no ability to prevent a certain effect due to its limited statutory authority over the relevant actions," the agency "[does] not need to consider the environmental effects arising from" those actions. *Id.* at 770; *see also Sierra Club*, 65 F.3d at 1513 ("The [Bureau of Land Management's] inability meaningfully to influence Seneca's right-of-way construction leads us to conclude that the procedural requirements of NEPA do not apply to this case.").

Here, as our ESA analysis suggests, BSEE reasonably concluded that it must approve any OSRP that meets the statutory requirements. *See* 33 U.S.C. § 1321(j)(5)(D)–(E). Thus, even assuming, without deciding, that BSEE's approval of Shell's OSRPs constitutes a "major Federal action," its approval is not subject to NEPA's requirements.

The dissent accepts Plaintiffs' argument that no authority prevents BSEE from requiring Shell to make changes to the OSRPs in order to minimize adverse environmental effects. On the contrary, BSEE's authority is just so constrained. The governing statute mandates that the agency "shall . . . approve any plan that meets the requirements" of the statutory section. *Id.* § 1321(j)(5)(E). This language is similar to the statutory mandate at issue in *Public Citizen*, where the governing statute required that the Federal Motor Carrier Safety Administration ("FMCSA") "*shall* register a person to provide transportation . . . as a motor carrier if [it] finds that the person is willing and able to comply with" that statute's requirements. *Pub. Citizen*, 541 U.S. at 766 (alterations in original) (quoting 49 U.S.C. § 13902(a)(1)). Examining this statutory mandate, the Supreme Court found that FMCSA

registration of cross-border motor carriers did not trigger [—30—] NEPA review because "FMCSA [had] no ability categorically to prevent the cross-border operations of . . . motor carriers, [and thus] the environmental impact of the cross-border operations would have no effect on FMCSA's decisionmaking." *Id.* at 768. NEPA review was not required because the FMCSA lacked the power to consider environmental consequences outside of its statutory obligation. *See id.* at 768–70.

The statute here similarly restricts BSEE's discretion. BSEE is required to approve an OSRP that meets the statute's requirements, which the agency reasonably interprets to be the checklist of six requirements set forth in § 1321(j)(5)(D). Applying NEPA to this process, then, would merely "require an agency to prepare a full EIS due to the environmental impact of an action it could not refuse to perform," which would clearly violate NEPA's "rule of reason." *Pub. Citizen*, 541 U.S. at 769.

This does not mean that NEPA review is entirely absent. Indeed, the NEPA environmental assessment that is required to be conducted as to Shell's exploration plan expressly considered the environmental effects of Shell's OSRPs. As mentioned *supra*, an operator's OSRP, which is the fourth step of the Clean Water Act's oil spill response framework, must be submitted in conjunction with a lessee's exploration plan, which is OCSLA's third step. 30 C.F.R. § 550.219. In a memorandum dated February 17, 2012, BSEE clarified that the Chukchi OSRP was considered in the development of an environmental assessment of Shell's Revised Exploration Plan for the Chukchi Sea. Similarly, Shell's Beaufort Sea OSRP was considered in the exploration plan Shell submitted regarding its Flaxman Island Leases. Thus, both of the OSRPs at issue here underwent NEPA review at OCSLA's [—31—] third step—which is consistent with the requirement that OSRPs be submitted at this stage. *See id.* In sum, we conclude BSEE is not required to prepare an EIS prior to approving the OSRPs.

CONCLUSION

BSEE's approval of Shell's OSRPs was not "arbitrary, capricious, . . . or otherwise not in accordance with law." 5 U.S.C. § 706(2)(A). In its OSRPs, Shell never asserted, nor did BSEE ever rely on, a 90 to 95 percent mechanical recovery rate for spilled oil. According deference, as we must, to BSEE's interpretation of the statute and its own regulations, BSEE lacked discretion to deny approval once it determined that the OSRPs satisfied the statutory requirements. Therefore, ESA consultation and NEPA review were not required.

AFFIRMED.

(Reporter's Note: Dissenting opinion follows on p. 566).

[—31—] NELSON, Senior Circuit Judge, dissenting:

I agree with the majority that the Bureau of Safety and Environmental Enforcement (the Bureau) did not act in an arbitrary or capricious manner in approving the oil response plans, and I concur in the majority opinion as to that issue. I respectfully dissent, however, from the remainder of the majority opinion.

In my view, the Bureau was required to engage in consultation pursuant to the Endangered Species Act (ESA) before approving Shell's oil response plans. Moreover, the [—32—] Bureau should have conducted analysis pursuant to the National Environmental Policy Act (NEPA) before approving the oil response plans. Thus, I would reverse the grant of summary judgment as to ESA consultation and compliance with NEPA.

1. ESA Consultation

The majority holds that the Bureau's approval of an oil response plan is a nondiscretionary action, and, thus, the Bureau had no obligation to consult pursuant to the ESA. I disagree.

a. Agency Action

The first question is whether the Bureau engaged in agency action. It did. The duty to consult exists only where "agency action" is present. *Natural Res. Def. Council v. Houston*, 146 F.3d 1118, 1125 (9th Cir. 1998). Agency action includes "federal agencies' authorization of private activities," such as the Bureau's approval of the oil response plans here. *Karuk Tribe of Cal. v. U.S. Forest Serv.*, 681 F.3d 1006, 1021 (9th Cir. 2012); 33 U.S.C. § 1321(j)(5)(F).

Of course, not all agency actions necessitate consultation. Indeed, only those actions that "may affect" a protected species trigger the requirement, 50 C.F.R. § 402.14(a), though the "may affect" requirement is an admittedly low threshold, *Karuk Tribe*, 681 F.3d at 1027. Here, the approval of the oil response plans satisfies the "may affect"

standard. In the event of an oil spill, Shell would have to carry out its oil response plan, which governs the protection of wildlife. 30 C.F.R. § 254.5(a). Thus, the Bureau's decision to approve the [—33—] oil response plans, or to require amendments to those plans, "may affect" a protected species.

b. Agency Discretion

Next, we must consider whether the Bureau had discretion to approve the oil response plans. It did. "The ESA's consultation duty is triggered . . . only when the agency has authority to take action and discretion to decide what action to take. There is no point in consulting if the agency has no choices." *Ctr. for Food Safety v. Vilsack*, 718 F.3d 829, 842 (9th Cir. 2013). What is more, "the discretionary control retained by the federal agency also must have the capacity to inure to the benefit of a protected species." *Karuk Tribe*, 681 F.3d at 1024.

"Whether an agency must consult does not turn on the *degree* of discretion that the agency exercises regarding the action in question, but on whether the agency has any discretion to act in a manner beneficial to a protected species or its habitat." *Natural Res. Defense Council v. Jewell*, 749 F.3d 776, 784 (9th Cir. 2014) (en banc). In other words, if the agency could take action that benefits protected species, the agency must conduct ESA consultation. *See id.; see also Karuk Tribe*, 681 F.3d at 1024 ("[T]o avoid the consultation obligation, an agency's competing statutory mandate must require that it perform specific nondiscretionary acts rather than achieve broad goals."). Ultimately, "[t]he relevant question is whether the agency *could* influence a private activity to benefit a listed species, not whether it *must* do so." *Karuk Tribe*, 681 F.3d at 1025.

In my view, the Bureau's decision to approve or reject an oil spill response plan is precisely the kind of discretionary [—34—] act that triggers ESA consultation. The Oil Pollution Act requires private owners or operators of vessels and facilities, such as Shell, to prepare an oil spill response plan. 33 U.S.C. § 1321(j). This response plan must explain how an operator like Shell will respond "to the maximum extent practicable, to a worst case discharge, and to a substantial threat of such a discharge, of oil or a hazardous substance." 33 U.S.C. § 1321(j)(5)(A)(i). The phrase "maximum extent practicable" suggests that Congress intended entities like Shell to create plans that have the capacity to respond to an oil spill to the greatest possible degree, given logistical constraints. *See* 30 C.F.R. § 254.6 (defining "maximum extent practicable" as "within the limitations of available technology, as well as the physical limitations of personnel"). At the same time, this broad, subjective standard does not direct the Bureau to act in a specific or clearly defined way, but, rather, contemplates that the Bureau will exercise its judgment when determining whether an oil response plan satisfies the "maximum extent practicable" requirement. *See Karuk Tribe*, 681 F.3d at 1024–25.

The implementing regulations bolster my view, as they make clear that the Bureau can exercise its discretion to benefit a protected species. For instance, the regulations require both an owner or operator to identify resources of "environmental importance" that could be harmed by a "worst case discharge scenario" and to provide strategies that will be used to protect those resources. 30 C.F.R. §§ 254.26(a), (c). In addition, the regulations also call for an owner or operator to explain how, in the event of an oil spill, it will "protect beaches, waterfowl, other marine and shoreline resources, and areas of special . . . environmental importance." 30 C.F.R. § 254.23(g)(4). Furthermore, Shell's response plans themselves underscore the importance of [—35—] protecting wildlife. Each plan devotes an entire appendix to discussing wildlife protection tactics and includes measures to protect wildlife.

Shell and the government would have us hold that the Bureau lacked discretion here because the Oil Pollution Act states that the Bureau "shall approve" any oil response plan that meets the statutory criteria. 33 U.S.C. § 1321. This compulsory language, the argument goes, reflects the absence of Bureau discretion. I disagree. The Bureau cannot avoid consultation here because it is not obligated to "perform specific nondiscretionary acts." *Karuk Tribe*, 681 F.3d at 1024. Neither the Oil Pollution Act nor its implementing regulations sets forth a rigid, mechanical set of requirements that specify when the Bureau must approve an oil response plan. There is no checklist to be ticked off; approval is not rote. Rather, the Bureau must consider a wide range of environmental, ecological and other factors in deciding whether an oil response plan meets the "maximum extent practicable" standard.

Shell and the government note that the Bureau interprets the implementing regulations as coextensive with the "maximum extent practicable" standard. Thus, they contend, and the majority agrees, both that the regulations do not give the Bureau any discretion and that we should accord *Chevron* deference to the Bureau's interpretation of the Oil Pollution Act. Yet again, I disagree.

Our analysis pursuant to *Chevron, U.S.A., Inc. v. Natural Res. Def. Council, Inc.*, 467 U.S. 837 (1984), involves two questions. First, we ask "whether Congress has directly spoken to the precise question at issue." *Id.* at 842. If so, the court "must give effect to the unambiguously expressed intent [—36—] of Congress." *Id.* at 842–43. But "if the statute is silent or ambiguous with respect to the specific issue, the question for the court is whether the agency's answer is based on a permissible construction of the statute." *Id.*

Here, I do not believe the implementing regulations contain a reasonable definition of "maximum extent practicable." The regulations reference the phrase only once. They provide: "Maximum extent practicable means within the limitations of available technology, as well as the physical limitations of personnel, when responding to a worst case discharge in adverse weather conditions." 30 C.F.R. § 254.6. If this occupies the full and complete definition of "maximum extent practicable," it is unreasonable and not entitled to deference. The word "maximum," a superlative, means "the highest possible magnitude or quantity of something," or "highest, greatest." *Maximum*, Oxford English Dictionary, http://www/oed.com/view/Entry/115275?redire ctedFrom=maximum#eid (last visited April 27, 2015). Thus, the phrase "maximum extent practicable" also has a superlative quality and therefore must refer to the greatest option in a range of possibilities. But the Bureau's definition is not a superlative, as it refers to a range of possibilities, taking into account practical limits. Thus, it gives effect only to the term "practicable" while ignoring the term "maximum." We should not defer to this nonsensical and incomplete definition. *Coronado-Durazo v. I.N.S.*, 123 F.3d 1322, 1324 (9th Cir. 1997) ("We are not obligated to accept an interpretation that is demonstrably irrational or clearly contrary to the plain and sensible meaning of the statute." (internal quotation marks and citation omitted)). The regulations merely clarify that owners and operators, such as Shell, will not be held to an impossibly high standard that [—37—] exceeds current technological capabilities and other logistical constraints.

The majority relies on the *Nat'l Ass'n of Home Builders v. Defenders of Wildlife*, 551 U.S. 644 (2007), to hold that the Bureau has no discretion to determine whether Shell complied with the six statutory factors enumerated in the Oil Pollution Act. I find this argument unpersuasive. In *Home Builders*, the Supreme Court noted that the Clean Water Act required the Environmental Protection Agency to approve an application to transfer permitting authority to a state, unless that state lacked the authority to perform the nine functions spelled out in the statute. *Id.* at 661. The Court described the statutory language as "mandatory" and the list of nine functions as "exclusive," holding that "if the nine specified criteria are satisfied, the EPA does not have the discretion to deny a transfer application." *Id.* At the same time, however, the ESA required consultation, in addition to the nine enumerated factors. *Id.* at 662. Faced with these irreconcilable statutory directives, the Court held that the later-enacted ESA did not amend the Clean Water Act in part because requiring ESA consultation would "engraft[] a tenth criterion onto the [Clean Water Act]." *Id.* at 663.

This case, however, differs in significant respects from *Home Builders*. First, the Supreme Court's analysis in *Home Builders* hinged in part on the fact that the ESA came after the Clean Water Act. *See id.* at 662–64. Here, however, the Oil Pollution Act of 1990 postdated the ESA. 33 U.S.C. § 2701 et seq. (Oil Pollution Act); 16 U.S.C. § 1531 et seq. (ESA, passed in 1972). In fact, Congress passed the Oil Pollution Act after ESA consultation already had been required for seventeen years. Thus, the concern that ESA consultation implicitly amended an exclusive set of statutory [—38—] requirements of the Oil Pollution Act by adding a new requirement beyond the original enactment is absent here. Moreover, both parties in *Home Builders* appeared to agree that the state possessed the authority to perform each of the nine enumerated functions but disagreed about whether ESA consultation added an extra step to the process. *See* 551 U.S. at 662. The question here is of a different sort. It is not whether the "maximum extent practicable" standard adds an additional step to the approval process for oil spill response plans but about how to interpret "maximum extent practicable," which is one of many subjective items the Bureau must consider in whether to approve an oil spill response plan.

2. NEPA Consultation

The majority holds that because the Bureau had no choice but to approve any oil response plan that met the enumerated requirements in the Oil Pollution Act, the Bureau was exempt from NEPA review. I disagree.

NEPA "declare[s] a national commitment to protecting and promoting environmental quality." *Ashley Creek Phosphate Co. v. Norton*, 420 F.3d 934, 945 (9th Cir. 2005). NEPA achieves these broad goals by "merely prohibit[ing] uninformed—rather than unwise—agency action." *Robertson v. Methow Valley Citizens Council*, 490 U.S. 332, 351 (1989). Specifically, NEPA requires agencies to prepare a detailed environmental impact statement (EIS) for "major Federal actions significantly affecting the quality of the human environment." 42 U.S.C. § 4332(2)(C).

An EIS "must inform decisionmakers and the public of the reasonable alternatives which would avoid or minimize adverse impacts or enhance the quality of the human environment." *League* [—**39**—] *of Wilderness Defenders-Blue Mountains Biodiversity Project v. U.S. Forest Serv.*, 689 F.3d 1060, 1068–69 (9th Cir. 2012) (internal quotation marks and citation omitted).

Here, the Bureau did not conduct any NEPA analysis, which the majority forgives, reasoning that approval of the oil response plan fell within the "rule of reason." *Dep't of Transp. v. Pub. Citizen*, 541 U.S. 752, 769 (2004). In other words, where an agency is obligated to take specific action, an analysis of the environmental impact of that action serves no purpose. *Id.* But this exception does not apply where an agency has "statutory authority to regulate the environmental consequences" of a major federal action. *League of Wilderness Defenders-Blue Mountains Biodiversity Project v. U.S. Forest Serv.*, 549 F.3d 1211, 1217 (9th Cir. 2008). That is the circumstance here.

The Bureau did in fact possess the kind of discretion that necessitated NEPA review. The Oil Pollution Act and its implementing regulations grant the Bureau significant authority to regulate the activities of owners and operators of offshore facilities. The regulations demand that the plan include provisions for protecting wildlife and areas of special environmental importance. 30 C.F.R. §§ 254.23(g)(3)–(4), (7). In addition, the Bureau must apply the broad and amorphous "maximum extent practicable" standard in considering the validity of an oil response plan. 33 U.S.C. §§ 1321(j)(5)(A)(i) & (D)(iii). This subjective process gives the Bureau the authority to require amendments to the plan. *Id.* at § 1321(j)(5)(E)(ii). Thus, I would hold that because the Bureau regulates the response activities and prevention efforts of entities like Shell, and because it retains authority to ensure that those entities' response efforts will protect the [—**40**—] environment effectively in the event of an oil spoil, it is not exempt from its duty to conduct NEPA review.

Morever, the Oil Pollution Act specifically directs the Bureau to consider environmental factors in its decisionmaking process. Thus, requiring NEPA analysis is squarely in line with "NEPA's core focus on improving agency decisionmaking." *Pub. Citizen*, 541 U.S. at 769 n.2; 40 C.F.R. § 1500.1(c). Because environmental protection lies at the core of the Bureau's duties pursuant to the Oil Pollution Act, NEPA review would not offend the rule of reason.

I also do not think that the Bureau discharged its duty to conduct NEPA review by relying on previous analyses that considered the environmental impact of oil and natural gas exploration in the Arctic. Certainly, an agency may rely on prior analysis to discharge its duties pursuant to NEPA. *See Pub. Citizen*, 541 U.S. at 767; 40 C.F.R. § 1500.1(c) ("NEPA's purpose is not to generate paperwork—even excellent paperwork—but to foster excellent action."); 43 C.F.R. § 46.120(b) ("If existing NEPA analyses include data and assumptions appropriate for the analysis at hand, the [agency] should use these existing NEPA analyses and/or their underlying data and assumptions where feasible.").

But an agency cannot discharge its duties pursuant to NEPA solely by relying on prior analyses if those analyses do not fulfill NEPA's purpose of ensuring "that the agency has taken a hard look at the environmental effects of the proposed action." *Ctr. for Biological Diversity v. U.S. Forest Serv.*, 349 F.3d 1157, 1166 (9th Cir. 2003) (internal quotation marks and citation omitted). Here, the documents on which the Bureau relied did not discuss alternatives to approving Shell's response plans. *N. Idaho Cmty. Action Newtork v. U.S. Dep't* [—**41**—] *of Transp.*, 545 F.3d 1147, 1153 (9th Cir. 2008) (noting an EIS requires "rigorous" evaluation of alternatives); 43 C.F.R. § 46.120(c). The prior analyses do provide some consideration of oil spill response techniques, but they have nothing to say about alternatives to Shell's proposed plans. The Bureau did not discharge its duty pursuant to NEPA.

Because I would reverse the grant of summary judgment to Shell as to the duty to conduct ESA consultation and NEPA analysis, I respectfully dissent.

United States Court of Appeals
for the Ninth Circuit

No. 13-35163

CHMM, LLC
vs.
FREEMAN MARINE EQUIP., INC.

Appeal from the United States District Court for the
District of Oregon

Decided: June 29, 2015

Citation: 791 F.3d 1059, 3 Adm. R. 571 (9th Cir. 2015).

Before **KOZINSKI**, **FISHER**, and **DAVIS**,* Circuit
Judges.

* The Honorable Andre M. Davis, Senior Circuit
Judge for the U.S. Court of Appeals for the Fourth
Circuit, sitting by designation.

[—3—] **KOZINSKI**, Circuit Judge:

The economic loss doctrine precludes recovery against a manufacturer for physical damage that the manufacturer's defective product causes to the "product itself." *E. River S.S. Corp.* v. *Transamerica Delaval Inc.*, 476 U.S. 858, 866–71 (1986). But the manufacturer can be sued for physical damage the product causes to "other property." *Id.* at 867–68. We consider whether a vessel owner may sue for the physical damage a defective vessel component causes to property that the owner adds to the vessel before the vessel is delivered. Put another way, is property added by the owner to a vessel prior to the delivery of the vessel considered "other property"?

I. Background

CHMM, LLC is the owner of M/Y JAMAICA BAY, a 59.5-meter luxury yacht. In 2006, CHMM contracted with Nobiskrug GmbH to "construct, equip, launch and complete [the yacht] at [Nobiskrug's] shipyard and to sell and deliver [the yacht] to [CHMM]" for approximately €34.2 million. Nobiskrug subcontracted with Freeman Marine Equipment for the manufacture of a "weathertight" door for installation in the yacht. This door provided access from the foredeck to the interior of the yacht.

The shipbuilding contract between Nobiskrug and CHMM states that "the Interior Outfit of the Yacht is to be provided by [CHMM]" and that "delivery and installation of the Interior Outfit has to be executed within the time frame laid down in [Nobiskrug's] Construction Schedule." CHMM [—4—] contracted with third parties for the purchase and installation of the items in the yacht's interior. The yacht that Nobiskrug ultimately delivered to CHMM contained a finished interior outfit.

In 2011, while the yacht was at sea en route to the Bahamas, the Freeman door allegedly malfunctioned, letting in a substantial amount of water. The subsequent flooding severely damaged the yacht and its interior, including woodwork, furniture, carpeting, electrical wiring, and electronics. CHMM estimates it would cost over $18 million to repair the damage.

CHMM sued Freeman, alleging five tort claims— negligence, defect in design, defect in manufacture, failure to properly instruct in the installation and use of the door and negligent misrepresentation. Freeman moved to dismiss on the ground that recovery for physical damage to the yacht's interior was barred by the economic loss doctrine announced in *East River Steamship*. While this motion was pending, CHMM amended its complaint to add a sixth claim for breach of "contract, quasi-contract and/or warranty."

The magistrate judge construed the motion as against the amended complaint and determined that the economic loss doctrine barred CHMM's five tort claims because the interior of the vessel was "integrated into" the completed vessel and was therefore part of the product itself. The magistrate judge held that the portion of the sixth count that alleged breach of contract should be dismissed because CHMM had no contractual relationship with Freeman. But the magistrate judge concluded that it would be premature to dismiss the breach of quasi-contract or express warranty claims without giving CHMM an opportunity for discovery. The district [—5—] court adopted the magistrate judge's Findings and Recommendation in full and granted CHMM leave to file a second amended complaint "to the extent that [CHMM] seeks tort remedies for damage to 'other property' added after delivery of the Vessel by Nobiskrug to [CHMM]."

CHMM now appeals the district court's interlocutory order dismissing the five tort claims as barred by the economic loss doctrine. We have jurisdiction under 28 U.S.C. § 1292(a)(3), which allows us to hear appeals from "[i]nterlocutory decrees of . . . district courts . . . determining the rights and liabilities of the parties to admiralty cases." 28 U.S.C. § 1292(a)(3); *see All Alaskan Seafoods, Inc.* v. *M/V Sea Producer*, 882 F.2d 425, 427 (9th Cir. 1989) ("To fall within the ambit of section 1292(a)(3), it is sufficient if a[] [district court] order conclusively determines the merits of a particular claim as between the parties."); *see also Sea Lane Bahamas Ltd.* v. *Europa Cruises Corp.*, 188 F.3d 1317, 1321 (11th Cir. 1999) ("As a general rule, a district court's order resolving one or more claims on the merits is appealable under § 1292(a)(3), irrespective of any claims that remain pending."). We review de novo, accepting all facts alleged in the amended complaint as true and construing them in the light most favorable to CHMM. *Barker* v. *Riverside Cnty. Office of Educ.*, 584 F.3d 821, 824 (9th Cir. 2009).

II. Discussion

We have described the economic loss doctrine, as applied in products liability cases, as follows:

> If a plaintiff is in a contractual relationship with the manufacturer of a product, the plaintiff can sue in contract for the normal [—6—] panoply of contract damages, including foreseeable lost profits and other economic losses. Whether or not the plaintiff is in a contractual relationship with the manufacturer, the plaintiff can sue the manufacturer in tort only for damages resulting from physical injury to persons or to property *other than the product itself*.

Giles v. *Gen. Motors Acceptance Corp.*, 494 F.3d 865, 874 (9th Cir. 2007) (emphasis added). This doctrine is rooted in "[t]he distinction that the law has drawn between tort recovery for physical injuries and warranty recovery for economic loss." *Seely* v. *White Motor Co.*, 403 P.2d 145, 151 (Cal. 1965) (en banc). As Chief Justice Traynor explained in *Seely*, this distinction rests on the understanding that a manufacturer "can appropriately be held liable for physical injuries caused by defects by requiring his goods to match a standard of safety defined in terms of conditions that create unreasonable risks of harm," but he "cannot be held [liable] for the level of performance of his products in the consumer's business unless he agrees that the product was designed to meet the consumer's demands." *Id.*

The Supreme Court relied on *Seely* in applying the economic loss doctrine to products liability cases in *East River*. 476 U.S. at 871. There, supertanker charterers sought recovery in tort for damage caused by defective turbine parts. The Court held that the charterers were precluded from tort recovery because "there was no damage to 'other' property," as "each supertanker's defectively designed turbine components damaged only the turbine itself." *Id.* at 867. The Court reasoned: [—7—]

> Damage to a product itself is most naturally understood as a warranty claim. Such damage means simply that the product has not met the customer's expectations, or, in other words, that the customer has received "insufficient product value." The maintenance of product value and quality is precisely the purpose of express and implied warranties. Therefore, a claim of a nonworking product can be brought as a breach-of-warranty action. Or, if the customer prefers, it can reject the product or revoke its acceptance and sue for breach of contract.

Id. at 872 (citations and footnote omitted).

The Court added that a contract or warranty action has a "built-in limitation on liability" in the form of the "agreement of the parties and the requirement that consequential damages, such as lost profits, be a foreseeable result of the breach." *Id.* at 874. By contrast, permitting tort recovery for "all foreseeable claims for purely economic loss could make a manufacturer liable for vast sums," as products liability law imposes "a duty to the public generally." *Id.* Indeed, it's "difficult for a manufacturer to take into account the expectations of persons downstream who may encounter its product." *Id.* Thus, the Court observed, the economic loss doctrine "account[s] for the need to keep products liability and contract law in separate spheres and to maintain a realistic limitation on damages." *Id.* at 870–71.

A decade later, the Court revisited this "corner of tort law" in *Saratoga Fishing Co.* v. *J.M. Martinac & Co.*, 520 U.S. 875, 877 (1997). Martinac built a fishing vessel in [—8—] which it installed a hydraulic system designed by Marco Seattle Inc. Joseph Madruga purchased the vessel and added equipment—a skiff, fishing net and spare parts. Madruga then sold the vessel, which contained the additional equipment, to Saratoga Fishing Company. The vessel later caught fire and sank as a result of a defective hydraulic system, after which Saratoga Fishing filed a tort suit against Martinac and Marco Seattle.

There was no dispute that the "product itself" consisted "*at least* of a ship as built and outfitted by its original manufacturer and sold to an initial user." *Id.* at 877. The question was whether Saratoga Fishing, the subsequent user, could recover in tort for "the physical destruction of *extra equipment . . . added* by the initial user after the first sale and then resold as part of the ship when the ship itself is later resold to a subsequent user." *Id.* The Court held that the equipment added by Madruga was "other property" and, as such, Saratoga Fishing was eligible to recover in tort for damage to that equipment.

When a manufacturer places an item in the stream of commerce by selling it to an Initial User, that item is the "product itself" under *East River*. Items added to

the product by the Initial User are therefore "other property," and the Initial User's sale of the product to a Subsequent User does not change these characterizations.

Id. at 879.

Freeman argues that *Saratoga Fishing* established a "bright-line rule stating that the product is defined at the time [—9—] it enters the stream of commerce, and that any items added after that time constitute 'other property' for purposes of the economic loss doctrine." Freeman views as dispositive that the yacht wasn't "placed into the stream of commerce, *i.e.*, was not delivered to CHMM, until the [yacht] was fully complete." Its position is that the damaged property in the interior of the yacht consists of the "product itself," for which tort recovery is unavailable, because CHMM added that property *before* Nobiskrug delivered the completed yacht from the shipyard.

A closer look at *Saratoga Fishing* reveals that it draws no bright-line rule based on the time of delivery. Rather, in determining whether items added to a product can be considered "other property," the Court focused on who added those items to the product—the user or the manufacturer of the product.

Saratoga Fishing observed that "[s]tate law often distinguishes between items added [by a user] to or used in conjunction with a defective item purchased from a Manufacturer (or its distributors) and (following *East River*) permits recovery for the former when physically harmed by a dangerously defective product." 520 U.S. at 880 (citing, for example, *A.J. Decoster Co.* v. *Westinghouse Electric Corp.*, 634 A.2d 1330 (Md. 1994) (chicken farm owner could recover in tort for the death of his chickens caused by a defective chicken house ventilation system)). The Court also cited another admiralty case, *Nicor Supply Ships Associates* v. *General Motors Corp.*, 876 F.2d 501 (5th Cir. 1989), which held that a ship charterer who added seismic equipment to the ship may recover in tort for damage to that equipment caused by a defective engine. The Court concluded that it would maintain the distinction the case law [—10—] suggests "between the components added to a product by a manufacturer before the product's sale to a user" and "those items added by a user to the manufactured product." *Saratoga Fishing*, 520 U.S. at 884.

Saratoga Fishing does not turn on the *timing* of the addition to the product. What matters for purposes of tort recovery is that the items were added by the user. This is because there is a fundamental difference between the situation where "a defective manufactured product causes [damage] to property added by the Initial User" and the situation in *East River*, where "a defective component causes [damage to] the manufactured product, other than the component itself." *Id.* at 883. As the Court explained in *Saratoga Fishing*, the latter situation is well-suited for a warranty action, while the former is not:

> Initial users, when they buy, typically depend upon, and likely seek warranties that depend upon, a manufacturer's primary business skill, namely, the assembly of workable product components into a marketable whole. Moreover, manufacturers and component suppliers can allocate through contract potential liability for a manufactured product that does not work, thereby ensuring that component suppliers have appropriate incentives to prevent component defects that might destroy the product. There is no reason to think that initial users systematically control the manufactured product's quality or . . . systematically allocate responsibility for user-added equipment [] in similar ways. [—11—]

Id. at 883–84 (citations omitted). This reasoning holds true regardless of whether the user added items "after the initial sale," as in *Saratoga Fishing*, *id.* at 884, or, as here, prior to it. In both instances, the manufacturer of the product to which the user added items had no responsibility for manufacturing or assembling the user-added items.

"Manufacturers of integrated products can avail themselves of warranty provisions and can spread the risk of product defect over their entire market." *All Alaskan Seafoods, Inc.* v. *Raychem Corp.*, 197 F.3d 992, 995 (9th Cir. 1999). For example, "[w]hen purchasing component parts, [they] can exercise market power to negotiate price and allocation of downstream risks of defective components." *Id.* They can also "impose specifications on component suppliers." *Id.* And they can "use the same components in multiple iterations of the same product" in order to achieve economies of scale. *Id.* But a manufacturer who lacks responsibility for the manufacture or assembly of user-added items isn't in a position to work with component suppliers of user-added items in such ways. Warranty law is thus ill-suited to protect against a malfunctioning product that causes physical damage to user-added items.

Freeman argues that "[t]he initial purchaser of a vessel has the opportunity to negotiate warranties with the various vessel builders with which it contracts—before vessel delivery into the stream of commerce—whereas such warranties typically are unavailable from those builders for equipment added after delivery." But the Supreme Court rejected this very argument in *Saratoga Fishing*. In discussing whether the initial user should have been expected to offer a warranty to the subsequent purchaser for the items the initial user added to the vessel, the Court stated: [—12—]

> Of course, nothing prevents a user/reseller from offering a warranty. But neither does anything prevent a Manufacturer and an Initial User from apportioning through their contract potential loss of any other items—say, added equipment or totally separate physical property—that a defective manufactured product, say, an exploding engine, might cause. *No court has thought that the mere possibility of such a contract term precluded tort recovery for damage to an Initial User's other property.*

520 U.S. at 882 (emphasis added).

None of the cases Freeman cites in support of its proposed bright-line rule are on point. *See, e.g., All Alaskan Seafoods, Inc.,* 197 F.3d at 993–95 (the act of resale does not preclude the subsequent user from tort recovery); *Sea-Land Serv., Inc.* v. *Gen. Elec. Co.,* 134 F.3d 149, 154–55 (3d Cir. 1998) (a defective replacement component by the same manufacturer is part of the product itself); *Petroleum Helicopters, Inc.* v. *Avco Corp.,* 930 F.2d 389, 393 (5th Cir. 1991) (a defective interchangeable component by the same manufacturer is part of the product itself); *Shipco 2295, Inc.* v. *Avondale Shipyards, Inc.,* 825 F.2d 925, 929 (5th Cir. 1987) (manufacturer assembled the entire vessel, and thus the product was the completed vessel); *Exxon Shipping Co.* v. *Pac. Res., Inc.,* 835 F. Supp. 1195, 1201 (D. Haw. 1993) (a defective interchangeable component purchased directly from the manufacturer is part of the product itself). Freeman claims that these cases show that courts "evaluated the object of the parties' bargain, which was the acquisition of a fully-functioning product." However, in *All Alaskan Seafoods,* we [—13—] interpreted *Saratoga Fishing* as having "rejected the view . . . that would define the 'product' . . . as the object of the purchaser's bargain." 197 F.3d at 994. In so doing, we emphasized "the distinction between components incorporated by a manufacturer before sale to an initial user and those items added by a user of the manufactured product." *Id.*

The rule of *Saratoga Fishing* can thus be distilled as follows: Where the manufacturer of a product had no responsibility for manufacturing or assembling items that the user adds to the product, the user-added items are considered "other property" for purposes of the economic loss doctrine.

In applying this rule to our case, we begin by examining Section 2.10 of the Shipbuilding Contract, entitled "Interior Outfit," which sets forth the respective responsibilities of CHMM ("the Purchaser" and user) and Nobiskrug ("the Builder" and manufacturer):

(a) The Interior Outfit of the Yacht is to be provided by the Purchaser. The Builder does not assume any responsibility or liability with regard to the Interior Outfit, except as provided herein. The interface between the scope of work of the Builder and the Interior Outfit is described in the Interior Outfitting Demarcation List.

(b) The Purchaser will supply and install the Interior Outfit by using materials and methods which are consistent with the requirements and Specifications related to specified noise and vibration standards as pre-approved by [—14—] the Builder, the Classification Society and the Flag State and in compliance with the weight limits for the Interior Outfit as stipulated in the Weight Limits List attached as Schedule 11. The delivery and installation of the Interior Outfit has to be executed within the time frame laid down in the Builders' Construction Schedule and in the Action List by the contractor(s) chosen and employed by the Purchaser who will not interfere with the Builders' scope of work. Any delay in delivering and installing of the Interior Outfit shall be a Permissible Delay.

(c) The Purchaser shall furnish the Builder with all documentation related to the Interior Outfit which is needed for Classification of the Yacht.

The "Interior Outfitting Demarcation List" specifies that Nobiskrug's scope of work is the "bare ship," while CHMM's is the Interior Outfit. To further clarify matters, the Contract defines "Interior Outfit" as "the Interior Outfit of the Yacht for which [CHMM] is responsible."

In Section 2.10, Nobiskrug disclaims "any responsibility or liability with regard to the Interior Outfit," with the exception of pre-approving the noise and vibration standards that CHMM used for the Interior Outfit and obtaining Classification certificates for the yacht once it received the relevant documentation from CHMM. CHMM, on the other hand, is responsible for "supply[ing] and install[ing] the Interior Outfit by using materials and methods which are consistent" with certain industry specifications; completing [—15—] delivery and installation of the Interior Outfit "within the time frame laid down in [Nobiskrug's] Construction Schedule"; ensuring that the contractors CHMM hired to work on the Interior Outfit don't "interfere with [Nobiskrug's] scope of work"; and providing Nobiskrug with "all documentation related to the Interior Outfit which is needed for Classification of the Yacht."

The relevant facts can be boiled down to the following: (1) Nobiskrug was responsible for manufacturing the bare ship; (2) CHMM, the user, added items to the bare ship; and (3) Nobiskrug wasn't responsible for manufacturing or assembling these user-added items. Under *Saratoga Fishing*, the items in the Interior Outfit consist of "other property," while the bare ship consists of the "product itself."

As discussed above, this is not a case within the wheelhouse of warranty law. CHMM and Nobiskrug didn't work together to manufacture or assemble the Interior Outfit *and* the bare ship. Rather, CHMM assumed sole responsibility for providing and installing items in the Interior Outfit, and Nobiskrug assumed sole responsibility for manufacturing the bare ship. It's unreasonable to expect CHMM to depend upon a warranty from Nobiskrug that the bare ship would not damage any items in the Interior Outfit. And it should come as no surprise that Nobiskrug did not offer such a warranty; the shipbuilding contract states that the warranties provided therein "apply only to the work of [Nobiskrug], [Nobiskrug's] employees, and of its subcontractors and suppliers."

It makes no difference that CHMM added the items comprising the Interior Outfit prior to the delivery of the yacht from Nobiskrug's shipyard. CHMM agreed in the [—16—] Shipbuilding Contract to complete the Interior Outfit by the time Nobiskrug finished construction of the bare ship. Perhaps this arrangement was made to speed up the process so CHMM didn't have to wait until the bare ship was ready to then outfit the interior

and receive the necessary registration and Classification certificates. Whatever the parties' motivations, CHMM shouldn't be penalized for not waiting until after the delivery of the bare ship to outfit the interior.

Nobiskrug subcontracted with Freeman to provide the door connecting the foredeck to the interior of the yacht, and there is no dispute that this door is part of the product. CHMM's claim is that the product (the bare yacht, which included the Freeman door) caused physical damage to other property (the Interior Outfit). The economic loss doctrine does not bar CHMM from suing in tort for damage to the Interior Outfit caused by the allegedly defective Freeman door.

REVERSED and REMANDED.

United States Court of Appeals
for the Ninth Circuit

No. 13-35773

TULALIP TRIBES
VS.
SUQUAMISH INDIAN TRIBE

Appeal from the United States District Court for the Western District of Washington

Decided: July 27, 2015

Citation: 794 F.3d 1129, 3 Adm. R. 577 (9th Cir. 2015).

Before **PAEZ, BYBEE,** and **CALLAHAN,** Circuit Judges.

[—3—] **PAEZ**, Circuit Judge:

In this treaty fishing rights case, the Tulalip Tribes ("the Tulalip") invoked the district court's continuing jurisdiction as provided by the permanent injunction in *United States v. Washington*, 384 F. Supp. 312, 419 (W.D. Wash. 1974) (*Decision I*), aff'd, 520 F.2d 676 (9th Cir. 1975), by filing a request for determination of the scope of the Suquamish Indian Tribe's ("the Suquamish") usual and accustomed fishing grounds and stations ("U&A"). The Tulalip sought a determination that the Suquamish's U&A, as determined by Judge Boldt in 1975, does not include Possession Sound, Port Gardner Bay, the mouth of the Snohomish River, and the bays on the west side of Whidbey Island (Admiralty Bay, Mutiny Bay, Useless Bay, and Cultus Bay). Ruling on cross-motions for summary judgment, the district court concluded that Judge Boldt did not intend to exclude the contested areas from the Suquamish's U&A and entered judgment accordingly. Reviewing de novo, we affirm. [—4—]

I. Background

There is a lengthy background to the complex litigation over the treaty fishing rights of the Indian tribes in Western Washington. The historical background of the treaty negotiations is detailed in Judge Boldt's *Decision I*. We will not repeat that background, although we do note several key facts to give context to the issues we address here. Although Judge Boldt's rulings resolved many key issues over the extent of the Indian tribes' treaty fishing rights, there have been a number of post-judgment subproceedings seeking clarification of Judge Boldt's rulings. This case is one such subproceeding.

In 1854 and 1855, several Indian tribes entered into treaties with Isaac Stevens, Washington Territorial Governor, on behalf of the United States. *Decision I*, 384 F. Supp. at 330. One of these treaties was the Treaty of Point Elliott, 12 Stat. 927 (signed January 22, 1855; ratified March 8, 1859; proclaimed April 11, 1859) ("the Treaty"), which is the treaty at issue here. *Decision I*, 384 F. Supp. at 355. Through these treaties, the United States "acquire[d] vast Indian lands." *Id.* at 330. As part of the negotiations, the tribes reserved the right to fish at "all usual and accustomed grounds and stations," including those off reservation. *Id.* at 332.

In 1970, the United States filed a lawsuit against the State of Washington, among others, on behalf of several Western Washington Indian tribes, later joined by other tribes as intervenor plaintiffs. *Id.* at 327. The plaintiffs sought a declaratory judgment regarding the tribes' reserved treaty fishing rights and an injunction to enforce those rights. *Id.* at 327–28. In *Decision I*, Judge Boldt held that tribes that were [—5—] parties to the Treaty, or "Treaty Tribes," had a "right to take anadromous fish outside of reservation boundaries . . . limited . . . by geographical extent of the usual and accustomed places." *Id.* at 407. Judge Boldt also defined the Treaty Tribes' U&As throughout his ruling, and in later decisions.[1]

Judge Boldt took great care to define Treaty Tribes' U&As. According to Judge

---

[1] In *Decision I*, the court "retain[ed] jurisdiction . . . for the life of this decree to take evidence, to make rulings and to issue such orders as may be just and proper upon the facts and law and in implementation of this decree." 384 F. Supp. at 408. To invoke the court's continuing jurisdiction, a party must satisfy various procedural prerequisites and then file and serve a "Request for Determination." *Id.* at 419.

Boldt, the words "[u]sual and accustomed . . . indicate the exclusion of unfamiliar locations and those used infrequently or at long intervals and extraordinary occasions." *Id.* at 332. He defined a U&A as "every fishing location where members of a tribe customarily fished from time to time at and before treaty times, however distant from the then usual habitat of the tribe, and whether or not other tribes then also fished in the same waters." *Id.* Conversely, "occasional and incidental trolling" while traveling through thoroughfares does not constitute a U&A. *Id.* at 353. Judge Boldt's findings "set forth . . . some, but by no means all, of [the plaintiff tribes'] principal usual and accustomed fishing places." *Id.* at 333. After all, "[a]lthough there are extensive records and oral history from which many specific fishing locations can be pinpointed, it would be impossible to compile a complete inventory of any tribe's" U&As. *Id.* at 353.

In determining the tribes' U&As, Judge Boldt found anthropological reports prepared by Dr. Barbara Lane, an [—6—] expert witness, to be "highly credible" and "very helpful in determining by direct evidence or reasonable inferences the probable location and extent of" U&As. *United States v. Washington*, 459 F. Supp. 1020, 1059 (W.D. Wash. 1978) (*Decision II*); *see also Decision I*, 384 F. Supp. at 350 (finding that Dr. Lane's reports "have been exceptionally well researched and reported and are established by a preponderance of the evidence").

Neither party to this subproceeding was a party to this litigation when Judge Boldt issued *Decision I*; both intervened afterwards. *Decision II*, 459 F. Supp. at 1028. Appellant, the Tulalip, is a political successor in interest to various groups of Indians that were parties to the Treaty. *Id.* at 1039. Appellee, the Suquamish, was an original party to the Treaty. *Id.* at 1040. Because neither tribe was a party to the *Decision I* proceedings, Judge Boldt determined their respective U&As in orders issued after his original order recognizing off-reservation fishing rights. The court held that the Suquamish had a right to fish at U&As outside of reservation boundaries. *Id.* at 1041. Later, the court

declared that the Suquamish's U&A includes "the marine waters of Puget Sound from the northern tip of Vashon Island to the Fraser River including Haro and Rosario Straits, the streams draining into the western side of this portion of Puget Sound and also Hood Canal." *Id.* at 1049.

In June 2005, in a separate subproceeding, the Upper Skagit Tribe filed a Request for Determination that Saratoga Passage and Skagit Bay are not within the Suquamish's U&A. We affirmed the district court's judgment that neither Saratoga Passage nor Skagit Bay lie within the Suquamish's U&A. *Upper Skagit Indian Tribe v. Washington*, 590 F.3d 1020, 1026 (9th Cir. 2010). [—7—]

Here, the Tulalip requested a determination that the inland marine waters east of Admiralty Inlet but west of Whidbey Island (Admiralty Bay, Mutiny Bay, Useless Bay, and Cultus Bay), as well as Saratoga Passage, Penn Cove, Holmes Harbor, Possession Sound, Port Susan, Tulalip Bay, and Port Gardner, do not lie within the Suquamish's U&A.

The Tulalip filed a motion for summary judgment asking the court to declare that the Suquamish's U&A is "limited to the west side of Puget Sound," and that "the Suquamish tribe does not have adjudicated usual and accustomed fishing grounds and stations in the marine waters of Saratoga Pass[age], Holmes Harbor, Port Susan, Possession Sound, or Port Gardner, and on the west side of Whidbey Island, including Useless Bay, Mutiny Bay, and Admiralty Bay."[2] The district court granted the motion as to Skagit Bay, Saratoga Passage, Penn Cove, Holmes Harbor, and Port Susan, following our opinion in the Upper Skagit subproceeding. The court, however, denied the motion as to Possession Sound, Port Gardner Bay, and the bays on the west side of Whidbey Island, specifically Admiralty Bay, Mutiny Bay, Useless Bay, and Cultus Bay, and declared that the Suquamish

---

[2] The Tulalip's motion in the district court was styled as a "Motion for Declaratory Judgment." The parties, however, do not dispute that the district court treated the motion as a summary judgment motion.

U&A included these waters. Upon making these determinations, which resolved all disputed issues, the court entered a final judgment.

The Tulalip timely appealed. The Tulalip's challenge before us, however, is limited to the district court's ruling that, in determining the Suquamish's U&A, Judge Boldt did not intend to exclude the mouth of the Snohomish River, [—8—] Possession Sound, Port Gardner Bay, and the bays on the west side of Whidbey Island (Admiralty Bay, Mutiny Bay, Useless Bay, and Cultus Bay).

II. Jurisdiction and Standard of Review

We have jurisdiction under 28 U.S.C. § 1291. *See United States v. Muckleshoot Indian Tribe*, 235 F.3d 429, 432 n.1 (9th Cir. 2000) (*Muckleshoot III*)[3] (citing *Van Cauwenberghe v. Biard*, 486 U.S. 517, 521–22 (1988) for the proposition that jurisdiction under § 1291 is proper when the district court's judgment in a subproceeding is final as to all disputed issues).

Our review is de novo, as the Tulalip appeal the district court's entry of summary judgment. *Muckleshoot v. Lummi*, 141 F.3d 1355, 1357 (9th Cir. 1998) (*Muckleshoot I*); *Muckleshoot III*, 235 F.3d at 432 (reviewing de novo a determination on summary judgment regarding Judge Boldt's finding of the Muckleshoot Tribe's U&A).

III. The Suquamish's U&A

In *Upper Skagit*, we drew on our prior decisions interpreting Judge Boldt's U&A findings for various tribes to develop a two-step mode of analysis. First, the moving party bears the burden of offering evidence that a U&A finding was "ambiguous, or that Judge Boldt intended something other than [the text's] apparent meaning." *Upper Skagit*, 590 F.3d at 1023 (citing *Muckleshoot I, Muckleshoot Indian Tribe v.* [—9—] *Lummi Indian Nation*, 234 F.3d 1099 (9th Cir. 2000)

(*Muckleshoot II*), and *Muckleshoot III*). Second, the moving party bears the burden of showing that "there was no evidence before Judge Boldt" that would indicate that the contested area was included or excluded in the U&A of the nonmoving tribe. *Id.*

We have determined previously that, for the finding describing the Suquamish's U&A, Judge Boldt intended something different than the language's apparent meaning, which neither the Suquamish nor the Tulalip contest. *Upper Skagit*, 590 F.3d at 1025 (affirming the district court's determination that the Upper Skagit Tribe met its burden on the first prong). In *Upper Skagit*, the district court's reasoning, which we affirmed, began with a finding that the apparent meaning of the term "Puget Sound" from the Suquamish's U&A included the waters at issue in that case—Saratoga Passage and Skagit Bay. *Id.* at 1023. But, the district court determined that nothing before Judge Boldt demonstrated that the Suquamish fished in those contested waters, or traveled through those areas on their way to the Fraser River area. *Id.* at 1023–24. Therefore, the district court reasoned, Judge Boldt must have intended something other than the language's apparent meaning in defining the Suquamish's U&A. *Id.* It does not matter that the contested areas at issue here are slightly different; the finding that Judge Boldt intended something different than the plain text of the Suquamish U&A finding remains intact. We adhere to that determination and do not analyze further prong one of the *Muckleshoot* analytical framework.

Under prong two, the Tulalip have "the burden to show that there was no evidence before Judge Boldt that the Suquamish fished . . . or traveled" through the contested [—10—] areas. *See Upper Skagit*, 590 F.3d at 1023. All the contested waters here surround Whidbey Island, which is on the east side of Puget Sound. In *United States v. Suquamish Indian Tribe*, 901 F.2d 772, 778 (9th Cir. 1990), we stated that the "Suquamish . . . were not entitled to exercise fishing rights on the east side of Puget Sound." However, this statement is from the concluding paragraph of an opinion where we did not address the

---

[3] As in the prior cases where we have discussed all three *Muckleshoot* cases, we name them chronologically, rather than based on the order in which they appear in this opinion.

boundaries of the Suquamish's U&A. Rather, in that case, we affirmed the district court's finding that the Suquamish did not merge or consolidate with the Duwamish,[4] and therefore was not the successor in interest to the Duwamish's fishing rights. *Id.* at 777–78. Thus, *Suquamish* does not control the status of the contested waters in this subproceeding.

For analysis, we divide the contested areas into two categories: those east of Whidbey Island (Possession Sound, Port Gardner Bay, and the mouth of the Snohomish River) and those west of Whidbey Island (Cultus Bay, Useless Bay, Mutiny Bay, and Admiralty Bay).

A. Eastern Contested Waters

We have made determinations previously about waters north of the eastern contested waters, east of Whidbey Island. In *Upper Skagit*, we affirmed the district court's determination that the Suquamish's U&A does not include Skagit Bay and Saratoga Passage. 590 F.3d at 1026. We stated that "[t]here is no evidence in the record before Judge [—11—] Boldt that the Suquamish fished or traveled in the waters on the eastern side of Whidbey Island." *Id.* at 1025.

Evidence that was before Judge Boldt indicates that the eastern contested waters are distinguishable from those at issue in *Upper Skagit*. In particular, the evidence before Judge Boldt demonstrates that the Suquamish traveled to the mouth of the Snohomish River and the waters immediately surrounding it to fish.

Materials from Dr. Lane, namely her reports and trial testimony, constitute evidence before Judge Boldt that the Suquamish traveled to the eastern contested waters to fish. The Suquamish, Dr. Lane explained, "had very limited kinds of resources within their home territory because almost uniquely of [the other tribes in this case] they had no large streams in their territory." The Suquamish "did in fact go to the larger rivers on the mainland in order to harvest salmon because they had no rivers in their own country." They "were accustomed to harvest their fall and winter salmon supplies at the rivers on the east side of Puget Sound. Modern Suquamish, as well as neighbouring Indians, have attested that the Suquamish traditionally fished at the mouths of the Duwamish and Snohomish Rivers as well as in the adjacent marine areas." Dr. Lane's testimony and reports constitute evidence that the Suquamish traveled to the mouth of the Snohomish river and the areas immediately surrounding it to fish. In light of this evidence, the Tulalip failed to meet their burden to show that there was "no evidence" before Judge Boldt that the Suquamish fished in or traveled through the eastern contested areas. *See id.* at 1023.

The Tulalip argue that we already determined this issue in *Upper Skagit*. We disagree. The evidence here relates to [—12—] the mouth of the Snohomish River and its immediate surroundings, rather than the waters further north or the waters east of Whidbey Island more generally. Indeed, Dr. Lane stated several times that the mouths of rivers and the surrounding areas were unique. First, she testified, as noted above, that the Suquamish "did in fact go to the larger rivers on the mainland in order to harvest salmon because they had no rivers in their own country." Despite its proximity to Whidbey Island, the Snohomish River is a large river on the mainland. Second, Dr. Lane explained that people "would gather to troll for the salmon as they gathered in the bays just prior to their entry into the rivers." This evidence supports the district court's determination that Judge Boldt intended to include Possession Sound and Port Gardner Bay in Suquamish's U&A because salmon would swim through the marine waters just before entering the Snohomish River. By contrast, Skagit Bay and Saratoga Passage, discussed in *Skagit Bay*, were larger bodies of water separate from a river. Third, Dr. Lane's opinion about the Suquamish's harvest "on the east side of Puget Sound" including "at the

---

[4] The Duwamish's U&A on the eastern side of Puget Sound included Lake Washington, Lake Union, Lake Sammamish, the Black and Cedar Rivers, and the lower White or Duwamish River below its junction with the Green River. *Id.* at 774 n.2.

mouths of the Duwamish and Snohomish rivers as well as in the adjacent marine areas" is distinct from Skagit Bay and Saratoga Passage because the river mouths are not near those areas.

As the district court concluded, in light of this evidence, the Tulalip cannot demonstrate that there was "no evidence" before Judge Boldt that the Suquamish fished or traveled in the eastern contested waters. *See Upper Skagit*, 590 F.3d at 1023. We hold that the Tulalip did not satisfy its burden to show that Judge Boldt intended to exclude the eastern contested waters from the Suquamish's U&A. [—13—]

B. Western Contested Waters

As with the eastern contested waters, the Tulalip must "show that there was no evidence before Judge Boldt that the Suquamish fished . . . or traveled through" the western contested waters. *See id.*

The Tulalip failed to meet that burden here because the record contains evidence that the Suquamish fished in these waters. Dr. Lane explained in a Suquamish-specific report that the Suquamish territory included "possibly. . . the west side of Whidbey Island. It is difficult at this time to establish the precise nature of Suquamish use of the west coast of Whidbey Island."[5] While Dr. Lane added that "there appears to be no clear evidence of Suquamish winter villages on the west side of Whidbey Island," she reported elsewhere that the "Suquamish travelled [*sic*] to Whidbey Island to fish." Moreover, there is other evidence supporting the Suquamish's use of the western contested waters. Dr. Lane explained generally that "[t]he deeper saltwater areas, the Sound, the straits, and the open sea, served as public thoroughfares, and as such, were used as fishing areas by anyone travelling [*sic*] through such waters." As

indicated by the plain text of the Suquamish's U&A, the Suquamish traveled from "the marine waters of Puget Sound from the northern tip of Vashon Island to the Fraser River." *Decision II*, 459 F. Supp. at 1049. When traveling from Vashon Island to the Fraser River, the Suquamish would have passed through the waters west of [—14—] Whidbey Island, and likely would have fished there while traveling. This general evidence, too, constitutes some evidence before Judge Boldt and supports the district court's determination that Judge Boldt did not intend to exclude these contested bay areas from Suquamish's U&A.

Therefore, we hold that the Tulalip did not meet its burden to demonstrate that there was no evidence before Judge Boldt supporting Suquamish fishing or traveling through the western contested waters. *See Upper Skagit*, 590 F.3d at 1023.

IV. Conclusion

The Tulalip did not meet its burden to show that the contested areas in this subproceeding should be excluded from Suquamish's U&A. Therefore, we affirm the district court's judgment.

AFFIRMED.

---

[5] Dr. Lane cited two treaty-time accounts: one from Achilles de Harley, who mentioned that the "Soquamish" occupied the west side of Whidbey Island in 1849, and one from George Gibbs, who wrote in 1854 that the Snohomish and Skagit tribes occupied Whidbey Island, but omitted the Suquamish.

United States Court of Appeals
for the Ninth Circuit

No. 14-15781

CHINATOWN NEIGHBORHOOD ASS'N
VS.
HARRIS

Appeal from the United States District Court for the
Northern District of California

Decided: July 27, 2015

Citation: 794 F.3d 1136, 3 Adm. R. 582 (9th Cir. 2015).

Before **REINHARDT, NOONAN,** and **HURWITZ,** Circuit Judges.

[—4—] **HURWITZ,** Circuit Judge:

California's "Shark Fin Law" makes it "unlawful for any person to possess, sell, offer for sale, trade, or distribute a shark fin" in the state. Cal. Fish & Game Code § 2021(b). The plaintiffs in this action claim that the Shark Fin Law violates the Supremacy Clause by interfering with the national government's authority to manage fishing in the ocean off the California coast, and the dormant Commerce Clause by interfering with interstate commerce in shark fins. The district court dismissed the plaintiffs' amended complaint with prejudice, and we affirm.

I.

A.

The Magnuson-Stevens Fishery Conservation and Management Act ("MSA"), 16 U.S.C. §§ 1801-1884, "was enacted to establish a federal-regional partnership to [—5—] manage fishery resources." *Nat'l Res. Def. Council, Inc. v. Daley*, 209 F.3d 747, 749 (D.C. Cir. 2000). Under the MSA, the federal government exercises "sovereign rights and exclusive fishery management authority over all fish, and all Continental Shelf fishery resources, within the exclusive economic zone" ("EEZ"), 16 U.S.C. § 1811(a), which extends from the seaward boundary of each coastal

state to 200 miles offshore,[1] *id.* § 1802(11); *City of Charleston v. A Fisherman's Best, Inc.*, 310 F.3d 155, 160 (4th Cir. 2002). The MSA expressly preserves the jurisdiction of the states over fishery management within their boundaries. *See* 16 U.S.C. § 1856(a)(1).

To manage fishing in the EEZ, the MSA calls for the creation of regional Fishery Management Councils ("FMCs"), composed of state and federal officials and experts appointed by the Secretary of the National Marine Fisheries Service ("NMFS"). 16 U.S.C. § 1852(b)(1)-(2). With the cooperation of "the States, the fishing industry, consumer and environmental organizations, and other interested persons," *id.* § 1801(b)(5), the NMFS and FMCs develop and promulgate Fishery Management Plans ("FMPs") to "achieve and maintain, on a continuing basis, the optimum yield from each fishery," *id.* § 1801(b)(4).[2] In [—6—] the MSA, "optimum yield" means the amount of fish that "will provide the greatest overall benefit to the Nation, particularly with respect to food production and recreational opportunities, and taking into account the protection of marine ecosystems." *Id.* § 1802(33); *see also* 50 C.F.R. § 600.310(e)(3).

B.

Shark finning is the practice of removing the fins from a living shark. The primary market for shark fins is to make shark fin soup, a traditional Chinese dish.

Even before the Shark Fin Law was passed, federal and state law prohibited finning in the waters off the California coast. In 1995, the California legislature made it "unlawful to sell, purchase, deliver for commercial purposes, or possess on any commercial fishing vessel . . . any shark fin or

---

[1] In California, the seaward boundary is three miles offshore. *Vietnamese Fishermen Ass'n of Am. v. Cal. Dep't of Fish & Game*, 816 F. Supp. 1468, 1470 (N.D. Cal. 1993).

[2] *See, e.g.*, Fishery Management Plan for U.S. West Coast Fisheries for Highly Migratory Species, Pacific Fishery Management Council [—6—] (July 2011), *available at* http://www.pcouncil.org/wp-content/uploads/HMS-FMP-Jul11.pdf.

shark tail or portion thereof that has been removed from the carcass." Cal. Fish & Game Code § 7704(c); see 1995 Cal. Legis. Serv. ch. 371, § 1 (S.B. 458). In 2000, Congress added finning prohibitions to the MSA, which, as amended in 2011, make it unlawful to remove the fins from a shark at sea, possess detached fins aboard fishing vessels, transfer them from one vessel to another, and land them onshore. See 16 USC § 1857(1)(P); Conservation of Sharks, Pub. L. No. 111-348, § 103(a)(1), 124 Stat. 3668, 3670 (2011); Shark Finning Prohibition Act, Pub. L. No. 106-557, § 3, 114 Stat. 2772 (2000). [—7—]

In 2011, after finding that shark finning nonetheless continued to "cause[] tens of millions of sharks to die each year," thereby threatening a critical element of the ocean ecosystem, and that "California is a market for shark fin" that "helps drive the practice of shark finning," 2011 Cal. Legis. Serv. ch. 524, § 1(d), (f) (A.B. 376), the California legislature passed the Shark Fin Law, which makes it a misdemeanor to possess, sell, trade, or distribute detached shark fins in California, see Cal. Fish & Game Code §§ 2021(b), 12000.

C.

The plaintiffs are associations whose members previously engaged in cultural practices and commerce involving shark fins. They claim that the Shark Fin Law is preempted by the MSA because it interferes with federal management of shark fishing in the EEZ, and with the federal government's prerogative to balance the various statutory objectives of the MSA. They also claim the law runs afoul of the dormant Commerce Clause by interfering with commerce in shark fins between California and other states, and by stemming the flow of shark fins through California into the rest of the country.[3]

In August 2012, the plaintiffs moved the district court to preliminarily enjoin the enforcement of the Shark Fin Law. The district court denied the motion, and we

[—8—] affirmed, agreeing that the plaintiffs had failed to show a likelihood of success on the merits of their preemption and dormant Commerce Clause claims.[4] See Chinatown Neighborhood Ass'n v. Brown, 539 F. App'x 761, 762-63 (9th Cir. 2013) (mem.). On December 9, 2013, the plaintiffs filed an amended complaint. The district court granted the defendants' motion to dismiss with prejudice on March 24, 2014. [—9—]

II.

We have jurisdiction over this appeal under 28 U.S.C. § 1291. We review a district court's grant of a motion to dismiss de novo, Cousins v. Lockyer, 568 F.3d 1063, 1067 (9th Cir. 2009), and the denial of leave to amend for abuse of discretion, Toth v. Trans World Airlines, Inc., 862 F.2d 1381, 1385 (9th Cir. 1988).

---

[3] The plaintiffs also claimed below that the Shark Fin Law violates the Equal Protection Clause, but they abandoned this claim at oral argument.

[4] The federal government raised tentative preemption concerns in an untimely amicus brief filed with this Court while the appeal from the denial of the preliminary injunction was before us. See Chinatown Neighborhood Ass'n v. Brown, 539 F. App'x 761, 763 (9th Cir. 2013) (mem.). That brief relied in part on an NMFS notice of proposed rulemaking—which proposed regulations that have not been adopted—suggesting that under certain circumstances, the MSA would preempt state laws that have the effect of regulating fishing within the EEZ. See Magnuson-Stevens Act Provisions; Implementation of the Shark Conservation Act of 2010, 78 Fed. Reg. 25,685, 25,687 (May 2, 2013). We declined to consider the federal government's position on preemption in determining whether the district court had abused its discretion in denying preliminary injunctive relief because that position was first presented in an untimely amicus brief on appeal, but said that the federal government could "rais[e] these arguments in the permanent injunction proceedings." Chinatown Neighborhood Ass'n, 539 F. App'x at 763. The federal government did not file an amicus brief in connection with the motion to dismiss or the present appeal, but the defendants have submitted correspondence from the NMFS stating that the Shark Fin Law "is not preempted by the Magnuson-Stevens Act, as amended." In light of our conclusions below, we need not rely on this position.

III.

The MSA does not have an express preemption provision. Even absent such a provision, however, a federal statute has preemptive effect if it conflicts with state law. This can occur when "compliance with both federal and state regulations is a physical impossibility," *Fla. Lime & Avocado Growers, Inc. v. Paul*, 373 U.S. 132, 142-43 (1963), or when a state law "stands as an obstacle to the accomplishment and execution of the full purposes and objectives of Congress," *Arizona v. United States*, 132 S. Ct. 2492, 2501 (2012).[5] In assessing the preemptive force of a federal statute, the purpose of Congress, as "discerned from the language of the pre-emption statute and the statutory framework surrounding it," is the "ultimate touchstone." *Medtronic, Inc. v. Lohr*, 518 U.S. 470, 485-86 (1996) (quotation marks omitted). [—10—]

A presumption against preemption applies generally, but is especially strong when, as here, "Congress has legislated in a field which the states have traditionally occupied." *McDaniel v. Wells Fargo Invs., LLC*, 717 F.3d 668, 674 (9th Cir. 2013); *see also Bayside Fish Flour Co. v. Gentry*, 297 U.S. 422, 426 (1936) (explaining the historic control of states over fish in state waters); *N.Y. State Trawlers Ass'n v. Jorling*, 16 F.3d 1303, 1309-10 (2d Cir. 1994) ("The interest of a state in regulating the taking of its fish and wildlife resources has been long established."). Thus, the California statute cannot be set aside absent "clear evidence" of a conflict. *Geier v. Am. Honda Motor Co.*, 529 U.S. 861, 885 (2000); *see also McClellan v. I-Flow Corp.*, 776 F.3d 1035, 1039 (9th Cir. 2015) ("[T]he historic police powers of the States were not to be superseded unless that was the clear and manifest purpose of Congress." (alteration omitted)).

A.

Although the plaintiffs argue the Shark Fin Law interferes with the federal government's authority under the MSA to manage shark fishing in the EEZ, they do not identify any "actual conflict between the two schemes of regulation." *Fla. Lime*, 373 U.S. at 141. To be sure, the California statute restricts certain economically viable uses for sharks that are lawfully harvested from the EEZ and landed in California. But the MSA does not mandate that a given quantity of sharks be harvested from the EEZ—and even if it did, detached fins are not the only viable use for harvested sharks. As the plaintiffs recognize, "[t]he use of approximately 95% of any legally fished shark for shark oil, shark meat, shark skin, etc. is still permitted" under the California regime. The plaintiffs point to no "clear and manifest" intent of Congress to preempt regulation such as [—11—] the Shark Fin Law, *McClellan*, 776 F.3d at 1039; rather, they have alleged nothing more than the prospect of a "modest impediment" to general federal purposes, *Pharm. Research & Mfrs. of Am. v. Walsh*, 538 U.S. 644, 667 (2003). This does not suffice to overcome the presumption against preemption. *See Sprietsma v. Mercury Marine*, 537 U.S. 51, 67 (2002) (finding no preemption in the absence of conflict with an "authoritative message" from Congress); *P.R. Dep't of Consumer Affairs v. Isla Petrol. Corp.*, 485 U.S. 495, 501 (1988) (same); *Fla. Lime*, 373 U.S. at 146-52 (same).[6] [—12—]

---

[5] Under the doctrine of "field preemption," state law is preempted if it regulates "conduct in a field that Congress, acting within its proper authority, has determined must be regulated by its exclusive governance." *Arizona*, 132 S. Ct. at 2501. The plaintiffs have abandoned any claim of field preemption.

---

[6] The cases relied upon by the plaintiffs that invalidate state regulations with effects on fishing in the EEZ are unpersuasive because in each case, the invalidated regulations either directly proscribed what federal law affirmatively allowed, *see A Fisherman's Best*, 310 F.3d at 173-76 (Fourth Circuit case finding preempted a city resolution forbidding access to ports for vessels using longline tackle, which was the only fishing method authorized by the applicable FMP), or directly banned activity within the EEZ that was legal under federal law, *see Vietnamese Fishermen Ass'n*, 816 F. Supp. at 1475 (concluding an FMP permitted the use of gill nets in certain places within the EEZ, and invalidating a California proposition banning the use of gill nets in the EEZ); *Bateman v. Gardner*, 716 F. Supp. 595, 597-98 (S.D. Fla. 1989) (finding preempted a Florida statute that banned fishing in portions of the EEZ where federal law

B.

The plaintiffs emphasize that even when state and federal purposes overlap, a conflict in the method of achieving those purposes can be grounds for setting aside a state law. *See Arizona*, 132 S. Ct. at 2505 ("[C]onflict in technique can be fully as disruptive to the system Congress enacted as conflict in overt policy."). They discern in the MSA a balancing of competing objectives in fishery management and a corresponding congressional intent to preclude state legislation that promotes one of these objectives—conservation—over others. *See, e.g., id.* (finding state law preempted from interfering "with the careful balance struck by Congress with respect to unauthorized employment" of undocumented workers).

The MSA indeed recognizes various competing values. *See* 16 U.S.C. § 1801(b) (listing "conserv[ing] and manag[ing] the fishery resources found off the coasts of the United States," "promot[ing] domestic commercial and recreational fishing under sound conservation and management principles," and "encourag[ing] the development by the United States fishing industry of fisheries which are currently underutilized or not utilized . . . in a non-wasteful manner" as objectives of the MSA). Among them, however, conservation is paramount. *See Nat. Res. Def. Council, Inc. v. Nat'l Marine Fisheries Serv.*, 421 F.3d 872, 879 (9th Cir. 2005) ("The purpose of the Act is clearly to give conservation of fisheries priority over short-term economic interests."); *Daley*, 209 F.3d at 753 ("[U]nder the . . . [MSA], the Service must give priority to conservation measures."). Indeed, in the particular context of shark fishing, the amendments to the MSA addressing finning make the primacy of conservation un-

---

allowed it), *aff'd*, 922 F.2d 847 (11th Cir. 1990) (mem.). In *Southeast Fisheries Association v. Chiles*, a case cited in the dissent, the Eleventh Circuit suggested in dicta that state-law daily quotas on landing Spanish Mackerel would interfere with a federal annual quota on catch of that fish in the EEZ. 979 F.2d 1504, 1509-10 (11th Cir. 1992). There too, state law directly conflicted with what federal law allowed.

ambiguous. *See* 16 U.S.C. § 1857(1)(P). This is, [—13—] accordingly, not the rare circumstance in which a state law interferes with a "deliberate effort to steer a middle path," *Crosby v. Nat'l Foreign Trade Council*, 530 U.S. 363, 378 (2000) (quotation marks omitted), or to strike a "careful balance," *Arizona*, 132 S. Ct. at 2505.

The MSA's provision for broad state-level participation in the implementation of the statutory objectives further undermines any inference of interference with Congress's method. *See, e.g.*, 16 U.S.C. § 1852(a)(2) ("Each [FMC] shall reflect the expertise and interest of the several constituent States in the ocean area over which such Council is granted authority."); *see also id.* § 1853(b)(3)(B) (permitting FMPs to limit commerce in fish caught within the EEZ "consistent with any applicable . . . State safety and quality requirements"); *id.* § 1856(a)(1) ("[N]othing in this chapter shall be construed as extending or diminishing the jurisdiction or authority of any State within its boundaries."); *Daley*, 209 F.3d at 749 ("The Fishery Act was enacted to establish a federal-regional partnership to manage fishery resources."). Courts have found conflicts between state and federal schemes with overlapping purposes when the federal scheme is comprehensive and exclusive, *see, e.g., Arizona*, 132 S. Ct. at 2504-05 (immigration); *Crosby*, 530 U.S. at 380-88 (international sanctions), but not when, as here, the federal scheme is cooperative, *see Wyeth v. Levine*, 555 U.S. 555, 575 (2009) ("The case for federal pre-emption is particularly weak where Congress has indicated its awareness of the operation of state law in a field of federal interest, and has nonetheless decided to stand by both concepts and to tolerate whatever tension there is between them." (alteration omitted)); *DeHart v. Town of Austin, Ind.*, 39 F.3d 718, 722 (7th Cir. 1994) ("[G]iven the clear [—14—] expressions of Congressional intent to foster cooperation with state and local governments and the different, albeit overlapping, purposes behind the [federal] Act and the . . . Ordinance, we discern no Congressional intent to ban state or local legislation . . . .").

C.

The plaintiffs' attempt to draw a negative inference from Congress's failure in the MSA to address on-land activities related to finning, *see* 18 U.S.C. § 1857(1)(P) (referring to activities at sea, aboard fishing vessels, and during landing), is similarly meritless. Silence, without more, does not preempt—"a clear and manifest purpose of pre-emption is always required." *Isla Petrol.*, 485 U.S. at 503 (quotation marks omitted). There is no "authoritative federal determination" that on-land activities are "best left *unregulated.*" *Id.*[7] To the contrary, the federal scheme [—15—] expressly preserves the ability of states to regulate fishing-related activities within their boundaries. *See* 16 U.S.C. § 1856(a)(1).

D.

The plaintiffs amended their original complaint after we remanded the case upon affirming the denial of a preliminary injunction. At the hearing on the motion to dismiss the amended complaint, the district court asked plaintiffs' counsel during the discussion of the preemption claim whether "you've got the complaint where you want it," and counsel responded affirmatively. Based on this representation, the court found that a second round of amendments would be futile

and granted the motion to dismiss with prejudice.

The plaintiffs assert for the first time on appeal that they could plead additional facts to support the preemption claim, and ask us to find that the district court abused its discretion in failing to grant leave sua sponte. Even making the charitable assumption that this argument was preserved for appeal, *see Alaska v. United States*, 201 F.3d 1154, 1163-64 (9th Cir. 2000) ("Where a party does not ask the district court for leave to amend, the request on appeal to remand with instructions to permit amendment comes too late." (alterations and quotation marks omitted)); *Reyn's Pasta Bella, LLC v. Visa USA, Inc.*, 442 F.3d 741, 749 (9th Cir. 2006) (relying on *Alaska* for the proposition that "we generally will not remand with instructions to grant leave to amend unless the plaintiff sought leave to [—16—] amend below"), we cannot conclude on this record that the district court abused its discretion in dismissing with prejudice.[8]

"Although leave to amend 'shall be freely given when justice so requires,' it may be denied if the proposed amendment either lacks merit or would not serve any purpose because to grant it would be futile in saving the plaintiff's suit." *Universal Mortg. Co. v. Prudential Ins. Co.*, 799 F.2d 458, 459 (9th Cir. 1986) (quoting Fed. R. Civ. P. 15(a)). The first amended complaint makes no allegations of a direct conflict between the California statute and any unambiguous federal mandate. At oral argument on this appeal, plaintiffs' counsel asserted that the plaintiffs could remedy this defect by alleging that state bans on commerce in shark fins affect the ability of commercial fishers to reap the optimum yields prescribed in FMPs for shark harvests. But the MSA does not preempt a state law simply because it may affect the

---

[7] The plaintiffs rely on regulations that limit the circumstances under which sharks may be sold on land. *See* 50 C.F.R. § 635.31(c)(1), (5). But these regulations *limit*, rather than encourage, commerce in sharks. *Cf.* 16 U.S.C. § 1853(b)(3) (permitting FMPs to "establish specified *limitations* which are necessary and appropriate for the conservation and management of the fishery on the . . . sale of fish caught during commercial, recreational, or charter fishing" (emphasis added)). The plaintiffs also rely on a statement by Representative George Miller during floor debates on the federal finning prohibition act that the "Act will not prevent United States fishermen from harvesting sharks, bringing them to shore, and then using the fins or any other part of the shark." 146 Cong. Rec. H11571 (Oct. 30, 2000). But a lone statement in the legislative history is not a "clear and manifest" expression of Congress's intent to preempt, and in any event, this statement merely describes the limits of federal law.

---

[8] The dissent correctly notes the "strong showing" required in the district court to justify dismissal with prejudice, but ignores the deferential abuse-of-discretion standard governing our review of the district court's failure to grant leave to amend. At the very least, it is even more difficult to perceive an abuse of discretion when the plaintiffs never sought leave to amend below.

realization of optimum yields—if that were so, a wide array of state regulations affecting commercial fishing, such as taxes or labor laws, would be potentially suspect. Indeed, Congress expressly foreclosed any interpretation of optimum yield that would have such a broad preemptive effect by [—17—] preserving state jurisdiction over commerce in fish products within state borders. *See* 16 U.S.C. § 1856(a)(1).

The plaintiffs concede that no provision of federal law affirmatively guarantees the right to use or sell shark fins onshore, and they do not dispute that there are commercially viable uses for sharks besides their detached fins. That resolves the preemption issue. *See Fla. Lime*, 373 U.S. at 146-47 ("[W]e are not to conclude that Congress legislated the ouster of this California statute . . . in the absence of an unambiguous congressional mandate to that effect."). Leave to amend would therefore be futile. *Cf. ReadyLink Healthcare, Inc. v. State Comp. Ins. Fund*, 754 F.3d 754, 761-62 (9th Cir. 2014) ("Preemption is almost always a legal question, the resolution of which is rarely aided by development of a more complete factual record." (quotation marks omitted)).[9]

IV.

"The Supreme Court has adopted a two-tiered approach to analyzing state economic regulation under the [—18—] Commerce Clause." *Ass'n des Eleveurs de Canards et d'Oies du Quebec v. Harris*, 729 F.3d 937, 948 (9th Cir. 2013) (quotation marks omitted), *cert. denied*, 135 S. Ct. 398 (2014). If a state statute "directly regulates or discriminates

---

[9] Our conclusion is bolstered by the posture in which the request to amend was made. The original complaint was filed three years ago, since then, there has been ample opportunity to explore the scope of the preemption claim, including in litigating the preliminary injunction and the appeal from the denial of the preliminary injunction. The plaintiffs had the benefit of this litigation, and its resolution, before filing the first amended complaint. *Cf. AmerisourceBergen Corp. v. Dialysist W., Inc.*, 465 F.3d 946, 953-54 (9th Cir. 2006) (affirming denial of leave to amend based on delay between learning of basis for amendment and seeking leave).

against interstate commerce, or . . . its effect is to favor in-state economic interests over out-of-state interests," it is "struck down . . . without further inquiry." *Brown-Forman Distillers Corp. v. N.Y. State Liquor Auth.*, 476 U.S. 573, 579 (1986). When, however, a state statute has only indirect effects on interstate commerce and regulates evenhandedly, it violates the Commerce Clause only if "the burdens of the statute so outweigh the putative benefits as to make the statute unreasonable or irrational." *UFO Chuting of Haw., Inc. v. Smith*, 508 F.3d 1189, 1196 (9th Cir. 2007) (alteration omitted).

A.

The plaintiffs claim the Shark Fin Law is per se invalid under the Commerce Clause because it regulates extraterritorially by curbing commerce in shark fins between California and out-of-state destinations, and by preventing the flow of shark fins through California from one out-of-state destination to another. But a state may regulate commercial relationships "in which at least one party is located in California." *Gravquick A/S v. Trimble Navigation Int'l, Ltd.*, 323 F.3d 1219, 1224 (9th Cir. 2003). And even when state law has significant extraterritorial effects, it passes Commerce Clause muster when, as here, those effects result from the regulation of in-state conduct. *See Rocky Mtn. Farmers Union v. Corey*, 730 F.3d 1070, 1101-04 (9th Cir. 2013) (upholding California statute imposing fuel standards that affect out-of-state fuel producers because the standard applies only to fuels consumed in California), *cert. denied*, 134 S. Ct. 2875 [—19—] (2014); *Ass'n des Eleveurs*, 729 F.3d at 948-51 (upholding California statute banning sale of products from force-fed birds, even though it affected out-of-state producers and exports from California); *cf. Sam Francis Found. v. Christies*, 784 F.3d 1320, 1323-24 (9th Cir. 2015) (en banc) (invalidating a California statute that "facially regulates a commercial transaction that takes place wholly outside of the State's borders" (quotation marks omitted)). Thus, nothing about the extraterritorial reach of the Shark Fin Law renders it per se invalid.

The plaintiffs' reliance on *Healy v. Beer Institute*, *Brown-Forman Distillers Corp. v. New York State Liquor Authority*, and *Baldwin v. G.A.F. Seelig, Inc.* is misplaced. In each of those cases, the Supreme Court struck down price-control or price-affirmation statutes that had the effect of preventing producers from pricing products independently in neighboring states. *See Healy*, 491 U.S. 324, 326, 334 (1989) (Connecticut statute requiring beer distributors to affirm that Connecticut prices were at least as low as prices in other states); *Brown-Forman*, 476 U.S. at 575, 582-83 (New York statutes barring distillers from selling liquor at prices higher than prices in other states); *Baldwin*, 294 U.S. 519, 521-22 (1935) (New York statute prohibiting sale of milk in New York if acquired from Vermont farmers at price lower than price available to New York farmers). We have recognized the sui generis effect on interstate commerce of such price-control regimes and the correspondingly limited scope of these cases. *See Ass'n des Eleveurs*, 729 F.3d at 951 ("*Healy* and *Baldwin* are not applicable to a statute that does not dictate the price of a product and does not tie the price of its in-state products to out-of-state prices." (alteration and quotation marks omitted) (quoting *Walsh*, 538 U.S. at 669)). The Shark Fin [—20—] Law does not fix prices in other states, require those states to adopt California standards, or attempt to regulate transactions conducted wholly out of state, and the price-control cases are therefore inapposite. *See Rocky Mtn.*, 730 F.3d at 1102-03.

B.

The plaintiffs claim that even if the Shark Fin Law is not an impermissible direct regulation of extraterritorial conduct, it should be struck down under *Pike v. Bruce Church, Inc.*, because "the burden [it] impose[s] on [interstate] commerce is clearly excessive in relation to the putative local benefits." 397 U.S. 137, 142 (1970). Our precedents, however, preclude any judicial "assessment of the benefits of [a state] law[] and the . . . wisdom in adopting" it unless the state statute either discriminates in favor of in-state commerce or imposes a "significant burden on interstate commerce." *Nat'l Ass'n of Optometrists & Opticians v. Harris*, 682 F.3d 1144, 1156 (9th Cir. 2012); *see also Ass'n des Eleveurs*, 729 F.3d at 951-52. Here, the plaintiffs do not allege the Shark Fin Law has any discriminatory effect, and they cannot establish a significant burden on interstate commerce.

"[O]nly a small number of . . . cases invalidating laws under the dormant Commerce Clause have involved laws that were genuinely nondiscriminatory . . . ." *Nat'l Ass'n of Optometrists*, 682 F.3d at 1150 (quotation marks omitted). These cases address state "regulation of activities that are inherently national or require a uniform system of regulation," *id.* at 1148—most typically, interstate transportation, *see, e.g., Raymond Motor Transp., Inc. v. Rice*, 434 U.S. 429, 447-48 (1978) (state regulation of truck length); *see also Ass'n des Eleveurs*, 729 F.3d at 952 [—21—] ("[E]xamples of courts finding uniformity necessary fall into the categories of transportation or professional sports leagues." (alteration and quotation marks omitted)).

The Shark Fin Law does not interfere with activity that is inherently national or that requires a uniform system of regulation. The purpose of the Shark Fin Law is to conserve state resources, prevent animal cruelty, and protect wildlife and public health. *See* 2011 Cal. Legis. Serv. ch. 524, § 1 (A.B. 376) (listing purposes). These are legitimate matters of local concern. *See, e.g., Merrifield v. Lockyer*, 547 F.3d 978, 986 (9th Cir. 2008); *UFO Chuting*, 508 F.3d at 1196. And to the extent the Shark Fin Law is effectively a means of ocean fishery management, fishery management is an inherently cooperative endeavor—with state and federal jurisdiction over the oceans divided according to distance from shore, *see* 16 U.S.C. §§ 1802(11), 1811(a), 1856(a)(1), and with state and federal cooperation contemplated even in the management of federal waters, *see, e.g., id.* § 1852(a)(2). There is, accordingly, no significant interference with interstate commerce. *See Ass'n des Eleveurs*, 729 F.3d at 952; *Nat'l Ass'n of Optometrists*, 682 F.3d at 1156.

"Because the [Shark Fin Law does] not impose a significant burden on interstate commerce, it would be inappropriate for us to determine [its] constitutionality . . . based on our assessment of the benefits of th[e] law[] and the State's wisdom in adopting [it]," or the availability of less-burdensome alternatives. *Nat'l Ass'n of Optometrists*, 682 F.3d at 1156-57; *see also Ass'n des Eleveurs*, 729 F.3d [—22—] at 952 (finding an inquiry into "whether the benefits of the challenged laws are illusory" unwarranted because the regulation of the foie gras market is not inherently national).[10]

V.

We **AFFIRM** the judgment of the district court.

(Reporter's Note: Dissenting opinion, in part, follows on p. 590).

---

[10] Because none of the plaintiffs' constitutional claims survive the motion to dismiss, the district court properly dismissed the claim under 42 U.S.C. § 1983. *See West v. Atkins*, 487 U.S. 42, 48 (1988).

[—23—] REINHARDT, Circuit Judge, dissenting in part:

I dissent in part because the plaintiffs must be granted leave to amend the complaint with respect to their preemption claim.[1] "[I]n a line of cases stretching back nearly 50 [now 65] years, we have held that in dismissing for failure to state a claim under Rule 12(b)(6), 'a district court should grant leave to amend *even if no request to amend the pleading was made,* unless it determines that the pleading *could not possibly be cured* by the allegation of other facts.'" *Lopez v. Smith*, 203 F.3d 1122, 1127 (9th Cir. 2000) (emphasis added) (citations omitted); *see also Sharkey v. O'Neal*, 778 F.3d 767, 774 (9th Cir. 2015). In my view, the defects in plaintiffs' preemption claim *could* be cured by amendment, and the majority's other suggested reasons for affirming the denial of leave to amend are also without merit.

The majority first states in dictum that the issue of the denial of leave to amend the complaint may have been waived. As the foregoing statement of the law regarding dismissals with prejudice makes clear, however, whether the plaintiffs asked the district court for leave to amend is irrelevant. The majority incorrectly suggests that *Alaska v. United States*, 201 F.3d 1154, 1163–64 (9th Cir. 2000), broadly held that a party cannot raise the issue for the first time on appeal, Maj. Op. at 15-16, but that case neither considered nor abrogated our longstanding rule regarding dismissals under Rule 12(b)(6). Rather, it merely held that **[—24—]** the government could not seek to amend its *answer* to the complaint on appeal from judgment on the pleadings where it had intentionally adopted its *answer* as a strategic litigating position. *See Alaska*, 201 F.3d at 1163. In so doing, *Alaska* relied on cases holding that a party cannot wait until an appeal of *summary judgment* to seek leave to amend a pleading, *id.* at 1163–64—a rule that makes sense in light of the time and expense that a disposition at that stage entails. By contrast, there is a strong presumption that a

plaintiff with a plausible legal claim who simply fails to master the art of the well-pleaded complaint must be allowed to cure pleading defects—whether or not it makes a request to do so before the district court.

The majority also alludes in dictum to the fact that the plaintiffs voluntarily amended their complaint on one prior occasion and that it has been three years since the original complaint was filed. True, the presumption that a dismissal should be without prejudice may be rebutted by a finding of "undue delay, bad faith or dilatory motive . . . , repeated failure to cure deficiencies by amendments previously allowed, [or] undue prejudice to the opposing party by virtue of allowance of the amendment . . . ." *Sharkey*, 778 F.3d at 774 (internal citation and quotations marks omitted). However, absent prejudice to the opposing party—which the district court did not find and the defendants do not assert—there must be a "*strong* showing" of one of the other factors to justify a dismissal with prejudice. *Id.* (emphasis added and citation omitted). A single, good-faith prior amendment of the complaint cannot satisfy this high bar. Nor can the mere passage of **[—25—]** time.[2] More important, the district court relied solely on the purported futility of an amendment. We cannot affirm based on a finding of repeated failure to cure or undue delay that the district court did not make. *See id.* (holding that the district court must provide an explanation for dismissal with prejudice).

Nor are the majority and the district court correct that the plaintiffs' pleading defects could not possibly be cured by amendment. I agree that the plaintiffs' complaint as

---

[1] The plaintiffs do not contest the denial of leave to amend with respect to their Commerce Clause claim on this appeal.

[2] This case is not akin to *AmerisourceBergen Corp. v. Dialysist W., Inc.*, cited by the majority, in which the district court found that the defendant would be prejudiced by the plaintiff's attempt "twelve months into the litigation, . . . [to] drastically change[ ] its litigation theory" without explanation. 465 F.3d 946, 953 (9th Cir. 2006). As explained below, the problem with the operative complaint in this case could be cured by the pleading of additional facts; unlike in *AmerisourceBergen*, the plaintiffs do not seek to change their strategy altogether.

currently drafted fails to "identify any actual conflict between" the Shark Fin Law and "the federal government's authority under the [Magnuson-Stevens Act] to manage shark fishing in the [exclusive economic zone]." Maj. Op. at 10 (quotation marks omitted). It includes nothing beyond "mere conclusory statements," *Ashcroft v. Iqbal*, 556 U.S. 662, 678 (2009), that the Shark Fin Law conflicts with "the [Magnuson-Stevens Act], federal implementing regulations and federal [Fisheries Management Plans]." First Amended Complaint for Declaratory and Injunctive Relief at 12 ¶ 57, *Chinatown Neighborhood Ass'n v. Harris*, No. CV 12-03759 WHO (N.D. Cal. Dec. 9, 2013). However, the [—26—] plaintiffs assert that, if permitted to amend the complaint, they could plead additional facts demonstrating that (1) the federal government has adopted specific quotas for shark fishing pursuant to the optimum yield provisions of the Magnuson-Stevens Act and that (2) the Shark Fin Law poses an obstacle to achievement of those quotas because it significantly reduces otherwise legal shark fishing.[3] As outlined below, if such facts were properly pleaded, this would constitute a plausible claim for relief.

As relevant here, conflict preemption occurs where "the challenged state law 'stands as an obstacle to the accomplishment and execution of the full purposes and objectives of Congress,'" *Arizona v. United States*, 132 S. Ct. 2492, 2501 (2012), including where it "would interfere with the careful balance struck by Congress," *id.* at 2505. A central purpose and objective of the Magnuson-Stevens Act is to "achieve and maintain, on a continuing basis, the optimum yield from each fishery," 16 U.S.C. § 1801(b)(4), which is the "amount of fish which — (A) will provide the greatest overall benefit to the Nation, particularly with respect to food production and recreational opportunities, and taking into account the protection of marine ecosystems; [and] (B) is prescribed on the basis of the maximum sustainable yield from

the fishery . . . ." *Id.* § 1802(33). As the majority explains, the Magnuson-Stevens Act creates a framework under which regional [—27—] Fishery Management Councils comprised of federal and state stakeholders collaborate to adopt Fishery Management Plans designed to achieve optimum yield. *Id.* § 1851(a). In short, Fishery Management Plans seek to maximize the commercial and recreational benefits of fisheries in the exclusive economic zone without compromising the long-term sustainability of them. *See id.*; *Natural Res. Def. Council, Inc. v. Daley*, 209 F.3d 747, 753 (D.C. Cir. 2000).

One of the things a Fishery Management Plan may do to achieve optimum yield is establish a quota for the amount of a particular species of fish that should be caught. A plaintiff states a cognizable preemption claim where a Fishery Management Plan has established such a quota and a state law interferes with the achievement of that quota. *Se. Fisheries Ass'n v. Chiles*, 979 F.2d 1504, 1510 (11th Cir. 1992) (holding that the plaintiffs stated a cognizable preemption claim where a Fishery Management Plan established an annual quota for the total catch of Spanish Mackerel while state law established a daily limit on the number of Spanish Mackerel that a commercial vessel could bring into a state port). Notwithstanding the majority's statement to the contrary, the Magnuson-Stevens Act provision that preserves a state's "jurisdiction or authority . . . *within its boundaries*," 16 U.S.C. § 1856(a)(1) (emphasis added), does not authorize a state to adopt laws that pose an obstacle to the federal government's authority to manage and maximize the productivity of fisheries within *its own respective territory*, *see id.* § 1811(a) ("the United States claims, and will exercise . . . sovereign rights and exclusive fishery management authority over all fish . . . within the exclusive economic zone."). *See also City of Charleston v. A Fisherman's Best*, 310 F.3d 155, 174–76, 179 (4th Cir. 2002) (holding that city resolution banning [—28—] vessels that use longline tackle from docking at city marina was preempted by Fishery Management Plan designating "longline" as the authorized gear for catching swordfish).

---

[3] Federal law bans the inhumane *practice* of shark finning—of removing the fin from a shark on a boat—but it does not prohibit the landing of an intact shark carcass or the subsequent detachment and sale of a fin. *See* 16 U.S.C. § 1857(1)(P).

Although the plaintiffs' pleadings as presently drafted fail to point to a Fishery Management Plan regulating sharks or setting a shark quota, at oral argument defendants and their amicus curiae admitted that there are a number of Fishery Management Plans in place around the country that do so. Even if those Fishery Management Plans are silent with regard to the sale of shark *fins* (as the defendants and their amici represented at oral argument), the plaintiffs could establish that the Shark Fin Law is preempted by adducing clear evidence that it poses an obstacle to the achievement of an optimum yield of sharks specified in an Fishery Management Plan because it results in a significant decrease in otherwise legal shark fishing. The plaintiffs asserted at oral argument that if permitted to amend their complaint, they would provide additional facts demonstrating that the number of sharks caught in the exclusive economic zone has dropped significantly and that they have lost millions in revenue due to the Shark Fin Law.[4] If the fin is the main part of a shark

---

[4] The plaintiffs did not, as the majority contends, concede that "there are commercially viable uses for sharks besides their detached fins." Maj. Op. at 17. The majority improperly relies on two statements in the record to hold that the plaintiffs conceded the matter. First, it cites plaintiffs' counsel's statement at oral argument that a letter from the Director of the California Department of Fish and Wildlife was not a "big deal." That letter states that "revenue from the sale of sharks harvested in federal waters off California derives mostly from the sale [—29—] of the meat of the shark, not from the sale of fins after the shark is legally harvested and landed with fins naturally attached." Although that assertion may indeed prove true, our job at the motion to dismiss stage is to test the sufficiency of the *plaintiffs'* allegations. We cannot simply accept as true a state government official's position regarding a factual matter.

Second, the majority relies on a footnote in the operative complaint stating that "[t]he use of approximately 95% of any legally fished shark . . . is still permitted." This statement, however, says nothing about the relative commercial value of the parts of a shark or whether the ban on the sale of sharks is an obstacle to the achievement of optimum yield—matters that involve factual

that has [—29—] commercial value and thus California fishermen largely cease catching sharks in exclusive economic zone fisheries, the federal objective of achieving optimum yield might be unconstitutionally impaired by the state's ban on the sale of fins—i.e., the balance between conservation and economic interests struck by the Fishery Management Council in adopting a quota could be upset. While I express no opinion on the likelihood that such a claim would ultimately succeed on the merits, the command that "leave to amend shall be freely given" requires that the plaintiffs at least be given a chance to adequately plead their claim. *Sharkey*, 778 F.3d at 774 (citation omitted).

Finally, the majority's assertion that in dismissing the complaint with prejudice the district court properly relied on a representation by the plaintiffs that amendment would be futile is erroneous. The comment on which the majority and the district court rely is ambiguous at best. In response to the district court's inquiry, "you've got the complaint [—30—] where you want it . . . ?", plaintiffs' counsel responded "you are correct." Counsel likely meant only that he believed that he had made sufficient averments to support the claims at the motion to dismiss stage, as the district court's inquiry followed counsel's lengthy argument to that effect. This is different from a representation that should the district court conclude that the allegations in the complaint were insufficient, the plaintiffs could not provide further allegations. The district court and the majority err by treating counsel's ambiguous representation as sufficient to dislodge "the presumption in favor of granting leave to amend." *Id*. It would have taken little effort by the district court to clarify the matter before permanently depriving the plaintiffs of an opportunity to pursue their case.

I respectfully dissent.

---

questions that cannot be decided against the plaintiffs at the motion to dismiss stage.

United States Court of Appeals
for the Ninth Circuit

No. 13-16383

NOVAK
vs.
UNITED STATES

Appeal from the United States District Court for the District of Hawaii

Decided: July 30, 2015

Citation: 795 F.3d 1012, 3 Adm. R. 593 (9th Cir. 2015).

Before **CLIFTON**, **SMITH**, and **FRIEDLAND**, Circuit Judges.

[—4—] **CLIFTON**, Circuit Judge:

This action challenges the constitutionality of the Jones Act's cabotage provisions, which prohibit foreign competition in the domestic shipping market. Plaintiffs allege that these provisions impair interstate trade between Hawaii and the rest of the United States to such an extent that they violate the Constitution. The district court dismissed the action with prejudice, concluding that Plaintiffs failed to satisfy what it framed as prudential standing requirements because they alleged only generalized grievances shared with all residents and businesses in Hawaii.

We affirm the dismissal of this action. Plaintiffs have alleged more than generalized grievances and have demonstrated an "injury in fact," but have not met their burden to show causation or redressability, the other two elements of Article III standing. Although it is possible that Plaintiffs could establish standing if they amended their complaint, any amendment would be futile because Plaintiffs' challenge to the Jones Act would fail on the merits. An amended complaint would, we conclude, be subject to dismissal for failure to state a claim because the enactment of the Jones Act was not beyond the authority assigned to Congress under the Commerce Clause. To the contrary, that statute is precisely the kind of legislation, a regulation of interstate commerce, that the Commerce Clause empowers Congress to enact. [—5—]

I. Background

Plaintiffs are six individuals and one corporation.[1] All reside in Hawaii and claim to have suffered pecuniary injury when they purchased "domestic ocean cargo shipping services on west coast Hawaii routes." They sued the United States, claiming that the root of their problem is found in the cabotage provisions of the Jones Act, formally known as the Merchant Marine Act of 1920. Cabotage is the transport of goods or passengers between two points in the same country. Black's Law Dictionary 243 (10th ed. 2014).

The purpose of the Jones Act is to support this country's merchant marine and its shipbuilding and repair facilities, at least in part so they may be available in times of war or national emergency. 46 U.S.C. § 50101. One way the statute aims to accomplish this objective is by limiting the domestic shipping market to American companies, excluding foreign competitors. Under the cabotage provisions, any ship carrying cargo between two points in the United States must have been "built in the United States," 46 U.S.C. § 12112(a)(2)(A), and be "wholly owned by citizens of the United States," id. § 55102(b)(1). [—6—]

According to Plaintiffs, these provisions violate the basic tenets of the Commerce Clause because they have effectively "impaired, hindered, and substantially affected and completely cut off Hawaii from interstate commerce." "In the absence of highways and railways," the complaint alleges, "the Jones Act promises to nullify interstate commerce to the State of Hawaii."

---

[1] The individual plaintiffs and appellants are Patrick Novak, Daniel Rocha, Ken Schoolland, Bjorn Arntzen, Philip Wilkerson, and William Akina; the corporate plaintiff and appellant is Kenner Inc. The action was filed as a putative class action on behalf of all persons and entities who purchased shipping services between the continental United States and Hawaii in compliance with the Jones Act from at least September 1, 1959 to the present. Plaintiffs did not seek class certification prior to dismissal of the action by the district court. Although they initially sought damages and injunctive relief, Plaintiffs have abandoned their claim for damages.

Plaintiffs' theory is that, by excluding foreign competition, the cabotage provisions have created "an essentially monopolistic Hawaiian ocean shipping market" that has resulted in "high prices" and "a de facto duopoly" of two established firms in the Hawaii-mainland shipping market. Plaintiffs contend that all Hawaii residents and businesses, including themselves, have been harmed not only by the increased shipping costs, but also by the resultant inflated cost of doing business in Hawaii because higher shipping costs lead to higher prices for imported goods. Plaintiffs assert that interstate trade between Hawaii and the rest of the United States has been significantly stifled to such an extent that the effect of the Jones Act's restrictions amounts to "an unlawful restraint of trade and interstate commerce, thereby violating the Commerce Clause of the United States Constitution." Plaintiffs filed this action against the United States, asserting a single cause of action under the Commerce Clause.

The district court granted the government's motion to dismiss the action with prejudice, holding that Plaintiffs failed to establish standing on prudential grounds because they alleged only generalized grievances. Specifically, the court concluded that "Plaintiffs assert only generalized claims on behalf of an extremely broad class of persons or entities that pay for interstate shipping or are consumers of goods that [—7—] have been shipped in interstate commerce. . . . This type of broad, generalized allegation is simply insufficient to meet standing requirements." The court's order cited *Arizonans for Official English v. Arizona*, 520 U.S. 43, 64 (1997), and *United States v. Hays*, 515 U.S. 737, 743 (1995), among other authorities.

Plaintiffs appealed.

II. Discussion

We review de novo a district court's determination on the issue of standing. *Levine v. Vilsack*, 587 F.3d 986, 991 (9th Cir. 2009). "Where standing is raised in connection with a motion to dismiss," we "accept as true all material allegations of the complaint, and construe the complaint in favor of the complaining party." *Id.* (alteration, citation, and quotation marks omitted). We also "presume that general allegations embrace those specific facts that are necessary to support the claim." *Jewel v. Nat'l Sec. Agency*, 673 F.3d 902, 907 (9th Cir. 2011) (citation and quotation marks omitted). We may affirm on any proper ground supported by the record. *Hartmann v. Cal. Dep't of Corr. & Rehab.*, 707 F.3d 1114, 1121 (9th Cir. 2013).

A. Standing

The "irreducible constitutional minimum" of Article III standing consists of (1) "injury in fact," (2) "a causal connection between the injury and the conduct complained of," and (3) a likelihood "that the injury will be redressed by a favorable decision." *Lujan v. Defenders of Wildlife*, 504 U.S. 555, 560–61 (1992) (quotation marks omitted). [—8—] "The party invoking federal jurisdiction bears the burden of establishing these elements." *Id.* at 561.

1. Injury in Fact

"[A]n injury in fact" is "an invasion of a legally protected interest" that is "concrete and particularized" and "actual or imminent, not conjectural or hypothetical." *Id.* at 560 (quotation marks omitted). Because a generalized grievance is not a particularized injury, a suit alleging only generalized grievances fails for lack of standing. *Lexmark Int'l, Inc. v. Static Control Components, Inc.*, 134 S. Ct. 1377, 1387 n.3 (2014); *Lance v. Coffman*, 549 U.S. 437, 439–40 (2007) (per curiam); *Newdow v. Rio Linda Union Sch. Dist.*, 597 F.3d 1007, 1016 (9th Cir. 2010).

The district court determined that Plaintiffs alleged only generalized grievances and consequently dismissed their action for lack of standing.[2] In so doing, the district court mistakenly focused only on the size of

---

[2] Although the district court framed its analysis under the prudential standing rubric, the Supreme Court subsequently clarified that the rule barring adjudication of generalized grievances is really a matter of constitutional standing under Article III. *Lexmark*, 134 S. Ct. at 1387 n.3.

the population allegedly harmed. "[T]he fact that a harm is widely shared does not necessarily render it a generalized grievance." *Jewel*, 673 F.3d at 909; *see also Federal Election Comm'n v. Akins*, 524 U.S. 11, 24 (1998) (recognizing that "where a harm is concrete, though widely shared, the Court has found 'injury in fact.'"). Indeed, the instances in which the Supreme Court has labeled a plaintiff's claim a "generalized grievance" "invariably appear[ ] in cases where the harm at issue is not only widely shared, but is also of an abstract and [—9—] indefinite nature— for example, harm to the common concern for obedience to law." *Id. at* 23 (citation and internal quotation marks omitted).

Plaintiffs' claim is not a generalized grievance because the harm they allege is not entirely "of an abstract and indefinite nature." *Id.* Plaintiffs allege in their complaint that each of them individually suffered "pecuniary injury and damages as a result of the Jones Act" when they "purchased domestic ocean cargo shipping services." This alleged injury is not the kind of abstract or indefinite harm that the Supreme Court has held to be insufficient to confer standing. *See, e.g., Lance*, 549 U.S. at 441–42 (holding that plaintiffs lacked standing because "[t]he only injury [they] allege is that the law . . . has not been followed"); *Allen v. Wright*, 468 U.S. 737, 754 (1984) ("This Court has repeatedly held that an asserted right to have the Government act in accordance with law is not sufficient, standing alone, to confer jurisdiction on a federal court."), *abrogated on other grounds by Lexmark Int'l*, 134 S. Ct. 1377; *Schlesinger v. Reservists Comm. to Stop the War*, 418 U.S. 208, 217, 219–20 (1974) (holding that the "generalized interest of all citizens in constitutional governance . . . is an abstract injury" that is an insufficient basis for standing).

2. Causation

The second required element for Article III standing is causation. This means that "there must be a causal connection between the injury and the conduct complained of." *Lujan*, 504 U.S. at 560. "When . . . as in this case, a plaintiff's asserted injury arises from the government's allegedly unlawful regulation (or lack of regulation) of *someone else*, . . . causation and redressability ordinarily [—10—] hinge on the response of the regulated (or regulable) third party to the government action or inaction—and perhaps on the response of others as well." *Id.* at 562. "'[M]ore particular facts are needed to show standing'" in such cases. *Mendia v. Garcia*, 768 F.3d 1009, 1013 (9th Cir. 2014) (citing *Nat'l Audubon Soc'y, Inc. v. Davis*, 307 F.3d 835, 849 (9th Cir. 2002)). "That's so because the third parties may well have engaged in their injury-inflicting actions even in the absence of the government's challenged conduct." *Id.* "To plausibly allege that the injury was not the result of the *independent* action of some third party, the plaintiff must offer facts showing that the government's unlawful conduct is at least a substantial factor motivating the third parties' actions." *Id.* (citation and quotation marks omitted).

We dealt with a somewhat analogous issue in *San Diego County Gun Rights Committee v. Reno*, 98 F.3d 1121 (9th Cir. 1996). In that case, members of various gun rights groups sued the Attorney General of the United States, as well as other government officials, challenging the Violent Crime Control and Law Enforcement Act of 1994 ("VCCA"). *Id.* at 1124. The plaintiffs argued, among other things, that they had standing because they had suffered an economic injury. *Id.* at 1130. They asserted that the VCCA had caused the price of the affected firearms to increase from 40% to 100%. *Id.* We reasoned that "[a]lthough the [VCCA] may tend to restrict supply, nothing in the Act directs manufacturers or dealers to raise the price of regulated weapons," and that "[u]nder *Lujan*, plaintiffs' injury [did] not satisfy the requirements of Article III because it [was] the result of the independent action of some third party not before the court." *Id.* [—11—]

Here, Plaintiffs suggest that the cabotage provisions of the Jones Act allowed two companies (not parties to this suit) to establish a duopoly whereby they are able to dominate the Hawaii shipping market and charge exorbitant rates. Plaintiffs' own complaint, however, also alleges that the

Hawaii shipping market "has several characteristics that made it easy" for the two shipping companies in that market to keep prices high, independent of the Jones Act: "market concentration, significant barriers to entry, ease of information sharing, lack of viable alternatives to ocean shipping, and the commodity nature of ocean shipping services." In this light, Plaintiffs themselves have alleged facts showing that the two companies "may well have engaged in their injury-inflicting actions even in the absence of the government's challenged conduct." *Mendia*, 768 F.3d at 1013. This is fatal to Plaintiffs' effort to allege causation.

3. Redressability

The third element of Article III standing, redressability, requires that it "be likely, as opposed to merely speculative, that the injury will be redressed by a favorable decision." *Lujan*, 504 U.S. at 561 (citation and internal quotation marks omitted). Although "[p]laintiffs need not demonstrate that there is a 'guarantee' that their injuries will be redressed by a favorable decision," *Graham v. Fed. Emergency Mgmt. Agency*, 149 F.3d 997, 1003 (9th Cir. 1998), *abrogated on other grounds by Levin v. Commerce Energy, Inc.*, 560 U.S. 413 (2010), they do need to "show that there would be a 'change in a legal status'" as a consequence of a favorable decision "and that a 'practical consequence of that change would amount to a significant increase in the likelihood that the plaintiff would obtain relief that directly redresses the injury suffered.'" *Renee v. Duncan*, 686 F.3d 1002, 1013 (9th [—12—] Cir. 2012) (citing *Utah v. Evans*, 536 U.S. 452, 464 (2002)). There is no standing if, following a favorable decision, whether the injury would be redressed would still depend on "the unfettered choices made by independent actors not before the courts." *ASARCO Inc. v. Kadish*, 490 U.S. 605, 615 (1989).

Here, Plaintiffs have not shown a likelihood that the shipping companies would lower their prices if the challenged provisions of the Jones Act were invalidated. On the contrary, as we have noted, Plaintiffs themselves have alleged several reasons—

"market concentration, significant barriers to entry, ease of information sharing, lack of viable alternatives to ocean shipping, and the commodity nature of ocean shipping services,"—that suggest prices might remain high even if the Jones Act were invalidated. Indeed, Plaintiffs allege that the two shipping companies serving the Hawaii market have engaged in a "conspiracy" to keep prices high. But, as Plaintiffs acknowledge in their complaint, the Jones Act "does not permit collusion, market sharing, market allocation, market manipulation or price fixing." This suggests that enjoining enforcement of the Jones Act would not redress the alleged conspiracy between the shipping companies. According to Plaintiffs' own complaint, any such conspiracy would be the result of "the unfettered choices made by independent actors not before the courts." *ASARCO*, 490 U.S. at 615.

B. Leave to Amend

We must next decide whether Plaintiffs should be granted leave to amend in order to correct the deficiencies we have identified. Under Rule 15(a) of the Federal Rules of Civil Procedure, leave to amend a party's pleading "should [be] [—13—] freely give[n] . . . when justice so requires," because the purpose of the rule is "to facilitate decision on the merits, rather than on the pleadings or tech-nicalities." *Chudacoff v. Univ. Med. Ctr. of S. Nev.*, 649 F.3d 1143, 1152 (9th Cir. 2011) (alterations in original) (citation and quotation marks omitted). Nevertheless, the "general rule that parties are allowed to amend their pleadings . . . does not extend to cases in which any amendment would be an exercise in futility or where the amended complaint would also be subject to dismissal." *Steckman v. Hart Brewing, Inc.*, 143 F.3d 1293, 1298 (9th Cir. 1998) (citations omitted). Futility alone can justify a court's refusal to grant leave to amend. *See Bonin v. Calderon*, 59 F.3d 815, 845 (9th Cir. 1995).

We decline to order that leave be granted to amend the complaint. We conclude that amendment would be an exercise in futility because even if Plaintiffs established standing, they would still fail to state a claim.[3] Plaintiffs' claim under the Commerce Clause would not survive a motion to dismiss because the Commerce Clause does not limit the authority of Congress to regulate interstate commerce. By its terms, the Commerce Clause empowers Congress to "regulate Commerce with foreign Nations, and among the several States." U.S. Const. art. I, § 8, cl. 3. As [—14—] Plaintiffs themselves acknowledge, the broad power of Congress has been well established for nearly 200 years, at least since *Gibbons v. Ogden*, 22 U.S. 1 (1824). There may sometimes be debates as to whether a given enactment by Congress falls within its authority under the Commerce Clause— debates that might turn on whether the regulated activity has a sufficient effect on interstate commerce. *See, e.g., Nat'l Fed'n of Indep. Bus. v. Sebelius*, 132 S. Ct. 2566, 2587 (2012). But "[t]he commerce clause is in no sense a limitation upon the power of Congress over interstate and foreign commerce." *Prudential Ins. Co. v. Benjamin*, 328 U.S. 408, 423 (1946).

Plaintiffs' complaint is aimed squarely at a regulation of commerce among the several states, specifically shipping between Hawaii and the other states. Indeed, Plaintiffs allege that the Jones Act violates the Commerce Clause because its cabotage provisions constitute "an unlawful restraint of trade and interstate commerce." Thus, they acknowledge that the regulation at issue here concerns interstate commerce.

That the regulation may be a "restraint of trade" does not matter. As noted above, the Commerce Clause does not limit the power of Congress to regulate interstate commerce. *Id.* Quite the opposite, it is well established that, by virtue of the Commerce Clause, Congress has broad authority to regulate the channels and instrumentalities of interstate commerce, as well as any activity substantially relating to interstate commerce. *See, e.g., United States v. Lopez*, 514 U.S. 549, 558 (1995); *Prudential Ins.*, 328 U.S. at 423.

It is true that the purpose of the Commerce Clause is to encourage and promote interstate commerce. *Bos. Stock Exch. v. State Tax Comm'n*, 429 U.S. 318, 328 (1977). But [—15—] the Supreme Court has made clear that this means the Clause prevents *states* from burdening interstate commerce. *See General Motors Corp. v. Tracy*, 519 U.S. 278, 287 (1997) ("The negative or dormant implication of the Commerce Clause prohibits state taxation or regulation that discriminates against or unduly burdens interstate commerce and thereby impedes free private trade in the national marketplace.") (citations, alteration, and quotation marks omitted). As to Congress, however, it is solely a grant of power to regulate the realm of interstate commerce, not a restriction.[4] In particular, contrary to Plaintiffs' implied assertion, the antitrust laws are not written into the Commerce Clause as a limit on Congress' power. The Commerce Clause does not provide a legal basis for Plaintiffs' claim.

---

[3] Strictly from a standing perspective, it would not necessarily be futile for Plaintiffs to amend their complaint. Materials outside the record support the notion that the Jones Act causes economic injury to residents of Hawaii. *See, e.g.,* U.S. Int'l Trade Comm'n, The Economic Effects of Significant U.S. Import Restraints xviii (2002) (estimating that the economic welfare gain from the "complete liberalization of maritime cabotage services under the Jones Act . . . would be slightly more than $656 million"). If Plaintiffs cured the deficiencies we have identified in their complaint, they might well be able to establish Article III standing to challenge the Jones Act.

---

[4] The federal government only has the powers granted to it by the Constitution. The definition of interstate commerce under the Commerce Clause thus affects the scope of the authority given Congress by that clause, and court decisions emphasizing limits on the definition of interstate commerce are sometimes described as limiting the authority of Congress. *See, e.g., Lopez*, 514 U.S. at 566 ("Congress' authority is limited to those powers enumerated in the Constitution, and . . . those enumerated powers are interpreted as having judicially enforceable outer limits . . . ."). Here, however, there is no dispute that the Jones Act regulates interstate commerce under any definition, and the Commerce Clause places no limits on the power of Congress to regulate within that interstate commerce realm. "[T]he sovereignty of Congress, though limited to specified objects, is plenary as to those objects." *Gibbons*, 22 U.S. at 197.

On appeal, perhaps in tacit recognition that the legal theory espoused in their complaint was not viable, Plaintiffs have argued that, even if the Jones Act is a valid exercise of congressional power derived from the Commerce Clause, it violates protections guaranteed under the Due Process Clause of the Fifth Amendment. In the context of the Commerce [—16—] Clause, we have held that "the requirements of due process are satisfied if the law passed . . . has a reasonable relation to a legitimate legislative purpose and is not arbitrary, capricious or discriminatory." *Boylan v. United States*, 310 F.2d 493, 498 (9th Cir. 1962). Plaintiffs do not argue that the Jones Act's cabotage provisions are not reasonably related to a legitimate legislative purpose, nor do they assert that the provisions are arbitrary or capricious.

Plaintiffs do contend that the Jones Act is discriminatory because its effects on Hawaii commerce are disproportionate as compared to the rest of the United States. But that alleged discrimination does not support a viable cause of action, whether framed as a matter of due process or as an attempt to enforce a supposed structural limitation on federal power under the Commerce Clause. "There is no requirement of uniformity in connection with the commerce power." *Currin v. Wallace*, 306 U.S. 1, 14 (1939); *see also Am. Trucking Ass'ns v. United States*, 344 U.S. 298, 322 & n.20 (1953) (explaining that the Due Process Clause is not violated even where a regulatory scheme causes some businesses to fail); *Sec'y of Agric. v. Cent. Roig Ref. Co.*, 338 U.S. 604, 616–19 (1950) (explaining that legislation did not offend the Due Process Clause even where it set different quotas for sugar from refiners in island territories than from refiners on the mainland, thereby creating inequalities); *see generally* Thomas B. Colby, *Revitalizing the Forgotten Uniformity Constraint on the Commerce Power*, 91 Va. L. Rev. 249 (2005) (considering historical arguments in favor of an inherent uniformity constraint on the commerce power, but recognizing that the Supreme Court has for decades consistently stated that no such constraint exists). [—17—]

The closest that Plaintiffs come to identifying legal support for their due process theory is to quote, in both their opening brief and their reply brief, from the Supreme Court's 1939 decision in *Currin*, specifically the first sentence of the following paragraph:

If it be assumed that there might be discrimination of such an injurious character as to bring into operation the due process clause of the Fifth Amendment, that is a different matter from a contention that mere lack of uniformity in the exercise of the commerce power renders the action of Congress invalid. For that contention we find no warrant. It is of the essence of the plenary power conferred that Congress may exercise its discretion in the use of the power. Congress may choose the commodities and places to which its regulation shall apply. Congress may consider and weigh relative situations and needs. Congress is not restricted by any technical requirement but may make limited applications and resort to tests so that it may have the benefit of experience in deciding upon the continuance or extension of a policy which under the Constitution it is free to adopt. As to such choices, the question is one of wisdom and not of power.

Currin, 306 U.S. at 14. The first sentence might acknowledge that there could be a due process limitation on some exercises of power, but it does not support Plaintiffs' claim that the Jones Act crosses the line. The rest of the [—18—] paragraph provides the most telling response, especially the final sentence. It is not for us to evaluate the wisdom of the Jones Act. That task is for Congress. Congress has the power to regulate interstate commerce, and it is up to Congress to decide how to exercise it. As Chief Justice Marshall stated nearly 200 years ago, "[t]he wisdom and the discretion of Congress, their identity with the people, and the influence which their constituents possess at elections, are, in this, as in many other instances . . . the sole restraints . . . to secure them from its abuse." *Gibbons*, 22 U.S. at 197.

Likewise, although it is true that "[t]he liberty protected by the Fifth Amendment's Due Process Clause contains within it the prohibition against denying to any person the equal protection of the laws," *United States v. Windsor*, 133 S. Ct. 2675, 2695 (2013), "equal protection is not a license for courts to judge the wisdom, fairness, or logic of legislative choices," *FCC v. Beach Commc'ns, Inc.*, 508 U.S. 307, 313 (1993). Where, as here, rational basis review applies and "there are plausible reasons for Congress' action, our inquiry is at an end." *Id.* at 313–14 (quotation marks omitted). This is not, for instance, a case involving invidious racial discrimination, *e.g.*, *Bolling v. Sharpe*, 347 U.S. 497, 500 (1954), or indeed a case of intentional, invidious discrimination of any kind, *see generally Vill. of Arlington Heights v. Metro. Hous. Dev. Corp.*, 429 U.S. 252, 265 (1977) (holding that a "discriminatory intent or purpose is required to show a violation of the Equal Protection Clause").

Thus, we decline to order that leave be granted for Plaintiffs to amend their complaint because, for the reasons discussed above, it would be futile to do so. [—**19**—]

C. Procedural Due Process

Plaintiffs also assert that the district court violated their right to procedural due process by ruling on the government's motion to dismiss without an oral hearing. We reject this argument. Plaintiffs admit they "had [an] opportunity to present arguments counter to Defendant's motion," but they do not explain why that opportunity to present arguments in writing was inaedquate for purposes of due process. It was sufficient. *See Cleveland Bd. of Educ. v. Loudermill*, 470 U.S. 532, 546 (1985) ("The essential requirements of due process . . . are notice and an opportunity to respond. The opportunity to present reasons, either in person *or in writing*, why [a] proposed action should not be taken is a fundamental due process requirement." (emphasis added)). The district court did not err in ruling on the government's motion without an oral hearing.

III. Conclusion

Plaintiffs' complaint fails to make the showing necessary to establish Article III standing. We affirm the dismissal of the action and we decline to grant leave to amend the complaint.

AFFIRMED.

(Reporter's Note: Concurring opinion follows on p. 600).

[—19—] FRIEDLAND, Circuit Judge, concurring:

I concur in Judge Clifton's thoughtful opinion, which faithfully applies our circuit precedent. I write separately to express my view that *San Diego County Gun Rights* [—20—] *Committee v. Reno*, 98 F.3d 1121 (9th Cir. 1996), which drives the opinion's conclusion that Plaintiffs lack Article III standing, should be reconsidered in an appropriate case.

Gun Rights ignores one of the most basic rules of microeconomics. According to *Gun Rights*, the fact that a law "restrict[s] supply" of a good is insufficient to support the inference that the law causes an increase in the price of that good. 98 F.3d at 1130. But the law of supply and demand tells us that, when demand for a good remains constant, a decrease in the supply of that good will cause an increase in price. *See* DAVID BESANKOW & RONALD R. BRAEUTIGAM, MICROECONOMICS 37 (4th ed. 2010); *see also* CHARLES ALAN WRIGHT, ARTHUR R. MILLER & EDWARD H. COOPER, 13A FEDERAL PRACTICE & PROCEDURE § 3531.5 n.35 (3d ed. 2008) (criticizing the causation analysis in *Gun Rights* for failing to recognize that "[r]estriction of lawful supply inevitably increases the price absent a change in the demand schedule").

In accordance with basic economics, plaintiffs should be able to show that a challenged statute has caused an increase in price by showing that it has decreased supply. But *Gun Rights* prevents plaintiffs from establishing causation in this manner unless they can show that the statute actually "directs manufacturers or dealers to raise the price of regulated" goods. 98 F.3d at 1130. This contravenes the rule that causation may be indirect: "causation may be found even if there are multiple links in the chain connecting the defendant's unlawful conduct to the plaintiff's injury." *Mendia v. Garcia*, 768 F.3d 1009, 1012 (9th Cir. 2014). As long as plaintiffs can show, "without relying on speculation or guesswork," that challenged governmental conduct is "at least a substantial factor" behind an injury, they can establish [—21—] causation. *Id.* at 1013. The

law of supply and demand requires no speculation or guesswork, so there should be little doubt that a statute reducing supply is at least a substantial factor behind a rise in price.

Were it not for *Gun Rights*, I would conclude that Plaintiffs have standing to challenge the Jones Act. At a minimum, Plaintiffs allege that the Jones Act limits the supply of vessels available to serve the Hawaii shipping market. This alone should be sufficient to establish that the Jones Act causes prices in that market to be higher than they otherwise would be. But, regrettably, *Gun Rights* requires more.

That said, this case is a poor vehicle for revisiting *Gun Rights* because, as Judge Clifton's opinion explains, Plaintiffs have failed to state a claim whether or not they have established standing. I expect the day will come, however, when it will be necessary to reconsider how plaintiffs injured by high prices can show that a defendant's challenged conduct caused those prices to increase. When it does, we should overrule *Gun Rights* and bring the law of our circuit into conformity with fundamental principles of economics.

United States Court of Appeals
for the Ninth Circuit

No. 13-17358

MARILLEY
VS.
BONHAM***

Appeal from the United States District Court for the
Northern District of California

Decided: September 18, 2015

***Petition for rehearing en banc granted on Feb. 26, 2016.

Citation: 802 F.3d 958, 3 Adm. R. 601 (9th Cir. 2015).

Before **GRABER** and **WATFORD**, Circuit Judges, and
FRIEDMAN,* District Judge.

* The Honorable Paul L. Friedman, United States
District Judge for the District of Columbia, sitting by
designation.

[—3—] **FRIEDMAN**, District Judge:

Commercial fishers in California are subject to a bevy of fees. For certain fees, however, non-residents are charged two to three times more than residents. Plaintiffs represent a class of non-resident commercial fishers who contend that California's discriminatory fees violate the Privileges and Immunities Clause of the United States Constitution. Because California has failed to offer a closely related justification for its discrimination against non-residents, we agree with plaintiffs and therefore affirm the district court's grant of summary judgment to the plaintiff class.

BACKGROUND

The named plaintiffs are commercial fishers residing outside California. They represent a class of non-residents [—4—] who, since 2009, have purchased commercial fishing licenses, registrations, or permits from California and paid higher fees than residents. Plaintiffs sued Charlton Bonham, in his official capacity as the Director of the California Department of Fish and Game, alleging that the differential fees violate the Privileges and Immunities and Equal Protection Clauses of the United States Constitution.

Plaintiffs challenge four specific fees: general commercial fishing license fees, commercial fishing vessel registration fees, Herring Gill net permit fees, and Dungeness Crab vessel permit fees. *See* Cal. Fish & Game Code §§ 7852, 7881, 8550.5, 8280.6. While the parties dispute the prevalence of Herring Gill and Dungeness Crab permits, it is undisputed that, at a minimum, non-resident commercial fishers must purchase the general license to fish in California waters and a vessel registration to do so from a boat they own or operate. *See id.* §§ 7852, 7881. In 2012–13, the relevant fees were as follows:

- Commercial fishing license: $130.03 for residents; $385.75 for non-residents;

- Commercial fishing vessel registration: $338.75 for residents; $1,002.25 for nonresidents;

- Herring Gill net permit: $359.00 for residents; $1,334.25 for non-residents;

- Dungeness Crab vessel permit: $273.00 for residents; $538.00 for non-residents. [—5—]

All four licenses would set a resident back $1,100.78, but a non-resident $3,260.25.

Following discovery, the parties filed cross-motions for summary judgment. The district court concluded that California had failed to demonstrate a genuine issue of material fact and granted summary judgment to the plaintiff class on its Privileges and Immunities Clause claim. The district court then entered final judgment as to plaintiffs' Privileges and Immunities Clause claim pursuant to Rule 54(b) of the Federal Rules of Civil Procedure.[1]

---

[1] The district court expressly did not reach or enter final judgment on plaintiffs' Equal Protection Clause claim. We therefore lack jurisdiction over that claim. *See* 28 U.S.C. § 1291.

STANDARD OF REVIEW

We have jurisdiction under 28 U.S.C. § 1291. We review a grant of summary judgment de novo. *See Pac. Shore Props., LLC v. City of Newport Beach*, 730 F.3d 1142, 1156 (9th Cir. 2013). Viewing the evidence in the light most favorable to the State, we must decide whether there are any genuine disputes of material fact and whether the district court correctly applied the substantive law. *See Olsen v. Idaho St. Bd. Of Med.*, 363 F.3d 916, 922 (9th Cir. 2004).

DISCUSSION

The Privileges and Immunities Clause provides that "[t]he Citizens of each State shall be entitled to all Privileges and Immunities of Citizens in the several States." U.S. Consti. art. IV, § 2, cl. 1. This clause "was designed 'to place the citizens of each State upon the same footing with citizens of [—6—] other States, so far as the advantages resulting from citizenship in those States are concerned.'" *Sup. Ct. of Va. v. Friedman*, 487 U.S. 59, 64 (1988) (quoting *Paul v. Virginia*, 75 U.S. (8 Wall.) 168, 180 (1869)); *see also Toomer v. Witsell*, 334 U.S. 385, 395 (1948) (The Clause "was designed to insure to a citizen of State A who ventures into State B the same privileges which the citizens of State B enjoy."). The Clause thus "establishes a norm of comity" between residents and non-residents of a State, *Austin v. New Hampshire*, 420 U.S. 656, 660 (1975), to create "a national economic union," *Council of Ins. Agents & Brokers v. Molasky-Arman*, 522 F.3d 925, 934 (9th Cir. 2008) (quoting *Sup. Ct. of N.H. v. Piper*, 470 U.S. 274, 280 (1985)).[2]

The Clause, however, "is not an absolute." *Molasky-Arman*, 522 F.3d at 934 (quoting *Toomer*, 334 U.S. at 396). "While it bars 'discrimination against citizens of other States where there is no substantial reason for the discrimination beyond the mere fact that they are citizens of other States . . . it does not

---

[2] "While the Privileges and Immunities Clause cites the term 'Citizens,' for analytic purposes citizenship and residency are essentially interchangeable." *Friedman*, 487 U.S. at 64.

preclude disparity of treatment in the many situations where there are perfectlyvalid independent reasons for it." *Id.* (quoting *Toomer*, 334 U.S. at 396). We therefore employ a two-part test to determine whether disparate treatment violates the Clause. "First, the activity in question must be 'sufficiently basic to the livelihood of the Nation' . . . as to fall within the purview of the Privileges and Immunities Clause." *Friedman*, 487 U.S. at 64 (quoting *United Bldg. & Constr. Trades Council v. Mayor and Council of Camden*, 465 U.S. 208, 221–22 (1984)). "Second, if the challenged restriction deprives nonresidents of a protected privilege, we [—7—] will invalidate it only if we conclude that the restriction is not closely related to the advancement of a substantial state interest." *Id.* at 65 (citing *Piper*, 470 U.S. at 284). California contends that the differential license fees pass muster under both parts of this test. We disagree.

A

California does not dispute that plaintiffs' right to pursue "a common calling is one of the most fundamental of those privileges protected by the Clause." *Camden*, 465 U.S. at 219; *see also Toomer*, 334 U.S. at 403 ("Thus we hold that commercial shrimping in the marginal sea, like other common callings, is within the purview of the privileges and immunities clause."). It instead argues that, in addition to demonstrating that the affected activity is protected, plaintiffs must make two additional showings.

First, California argues that our decision in *International Organization of Masters, Mates, & Pilots v. Andrews*, 831 F.2d 843 (9th Cir. 1987), requires plaintiffs to show that the differential fees exclude them, in whole or in part, from commercial fishing. This showing cannot be made, California claims, because the percentage of non-resident commercial fishers in California has increased, not decreased. In *Andrews*, we held that the Clause was not violated by a statute regarding cost of living wage adjustments because the statute was "designed to provide equity between the wages of [citizen] and non-[citizen] workers." *Andrews*, 831 F.3d at 846.

The statute in *Andrews* thus created equality, not inequality, and therefore did not run afoul of the Privileges and Immunities Clause because, we said, "the appellants ha[d] not shown that they are prevented or discouraged by the State from pursuing employment." *Id.* [—8—]

California contends that our choice of the words "prevented or discouraged" upset decades of precedent and added an exclusion requirement to the first part of the test. We disagree. As we recited in *Andrews* just two paragraphs before, the first step requires only that "we determine first whether [the statute] burdens" rights protected under the Clause. *Id.* at 845. An exclusion requirement would undermine the purpose of the Clause because permitting a State to freely discriminate against non-residents up to the point they are driven out would not "place the citizens of each State upon the same footing with citizens of other States." *Lunding v. N.Y. Tax Appeals Tribunal*, 522 U.S. 287, 296 (1998) (quoting *Paul*, 75 U.S. (8 Wall.) at 180). And, to any extent that *Andrews* may have implied that a plaintiff must demonstrate exclusion from pursuing their common calling, the Supreme Court's subsequent statement in *Friedman* makes clear that "[n]othing in [its] precedents . . . supports the contention that the Privileges and Immunities Clause does not reach a State's discrimination against nonresidents when such discrimination does not result in their total exclusion from the State." 487 U.S. at 66.[3]

Second, California argues that *McBurney v. Young*, 133 S. Ct. 1709 (2013), the Supreme Court's most recent Privileges and Immunities Clause decision, requires that plaintiffs show that the differential fees were enacted for a "protectionist purpose." The Supreme Court in *McBurney* did note that prior cases "struck laws down as violating the [—9—] privilege of pursuing a common calling only when those laws were enacted for the protectionist purpose of burdening out-of-state citizens." *Id.* at 1715. California urges us to read that statement to mean that proof of a protectionist purpose always is required to meet step one of our privileges and immunities inquiry. We cannot accept that interpretation of *McBurney*.

When the Court determines that the Privileges and Immunities Clause does not apply at all, it says so. For example, in *Baldwin v. Fish & Game Commission*, 436 U.S. 371, 388 (1978), the Court held that, because elk hunting was "not basic to the maintenance or well-being of the Union," the state's decision to charge non-residents more than residents for elk-hunting licenses "simply [did] not fall within the purview of the Privileges and Immunities Clause." In *McBurney*, the Court rejected one of McBurney's arguments—that Virginia's law denied them "the right to access public information on equal terms with citizens" of Virginia—for similar reasons, holding that the Privileges and Immunities Clause did not "cover[] this broad right." 133 S. Ct. at 1718.

By contrast, with respect to McBurney's common calling argument, the Court held that the Virginia law at issue did not "abridge [non-residents'] ability to engage in a common calling *in the sense prohibited by the Privileges and Immunities Clause*." *Id.* at 1715 (emphasis added). The Court reached that conclusion because the statute had only an "incidental effect" on the pursuit of a common calling, and because the distinction it made between citizens and non-citizens had a "distinctly nonprotectionist aim." *Id.* at 1716. This reasoning, along with the Court's discussion of earlier cases involving statutes with protectionist purposes, is a part of step *two* of the inquiry, which requires the state to [—10—] point to a "substantial reason[]" for the discrimination. *Friedman*, 487 U.S. at 67. "Part and parcel to this analysis is determining whether [the state has] demonstrated a substantial factor unrelated to economic protectionism to justify the discrimination." *Connecticut ex rel. Blumenthal v. Crotty*, 346 F.3d 84, 97 (2d Cir. 2003).

---

[3] Our conclusion is supported by the fact that, as the district court noted, our "most recent Privileges and Immunities Clause decision, *Molasky-Arman*, contains no discussion at all—at either step of the inquiry—of the extent to which the challenged law's increased burden on nonresidents led to any deterrence or exclusion."

Requiring proof of a legislature's protectionist purpose at the *first* step of the inquiry, as California urges, would negate the *second* step's burden on the state to provide a valid justification for the discrimination against non-residents. Moreover, an intent requirement would undermine the Clause's purpose to "plac[e] the citizens of each State upon the same footing with citizens of other States," *Lunding*, 522 U.S. at 296 (quoting *Paul*, 75 U.S. (8 Wall.) at 180), by mandating different outcomes depending upon a State's motive. We therefore reject California's invitation to read *McBurney* as a dramatic overhaul of the first step of the settled two-step inquiry.

To reiterate, contrary to California's arguments, the first step of the Privileges and Immunities Clause inquiry asks only whether the challenged statute directly burdens a protected activity. It is undisputed that California's commercial fishing license fees are significantly higher for non-resident fishers than for residents. And it is common sense that commercial fishing license fees directly affect commercial fishing. Those facts alone satisfy plaintiffs' burden at the first step of the inquiry. *See Toomer*, 334 U.S. at 396 (a statute that charged $25 to residents for commercial shrimping licenses, but charged $2,500 to non-residents "plainly and frankly discriminate[d] against non-residents" and thus satisfied the first step); *Mullaney v. Anderson*, 342 U.S. 415, 417–18 (1952) (holding that the Privileges and [—11—] Immunities Clause "would bar any State from imposing" a $5 license fee on resident fishers and a $50 fee on non-residents unless a State offered a substantial, closely related justification at the second step of the inquiry).

B

At the second step, the burden shifts to the State to demonstrate that "substantial reasons exist for the discrimination and [that] the degree of discrimination bears a close relation to such reasons." *Friedman*, 487 U.S. at 67.[4] To determine whether the State's

proffered justifications bear a close relation to the discrimination, we must "consider[] whether, within the full panoply of legislative choices otherwise available to the State, there exist alternative means of furthering the State's purpose without implicating constitutional concerns." *Id.*

The Supreme Court has noted that "[t]he State is not without power . . . to charge non-residents a differential which would merely compensate the State . . . for any conservation expenditures from taxes which only residents pay." *Toomer*, 334 U.S. at 398–99. California argues that it is doing just that—merely compensating itself for [—12—] expenditures on conservation and enforcement efforts from which non-residents benefit. But California claims that *Toomer* allows for inequality at step two and therefore *any* fee differential is permissible so long as the State does not "overcompensate" itself *in the aggregate*, which, according to California, means only that the amount collected from non-residents cannot exceed their collective "fair share" of the State's expenditures. These differential fees thus are permissible, according to California, because the total additional amount collected from non-residents (approximately $400,000) constitutes a mere 3% of the budget shortfall between costs and revenues (approximately $14.6 million) but non-residents comprise approximately 11% of the commercial fishers in California.

We are unpersuaded. Although we agree that obtaining compensation for expenditures the State makes for conservation or enforcement is a permissible state objective, the additional fees charged to non-residents must bear a close relation to the "taxes which only residents pay." *Toomer*, 334 U.S. at 399;

---

[4] California argues that the district court applied a purportedly different rule taken from the Supreme Court's "tax" cases, as opposed to its "common calling" cases, and failed to consider California's justifications for the discrimination. The Supreme Court, however, has employed the same two-step inquiry for both "tax" and "common calling" cases. *Compare Friedman*, 487 U.S. at 64–65 (challenge to a residency requirement for admission to the State bar), *with Lunding*, 522 U.S. at 296–98 (challenge to a differential income tax deduction). The district court applied the correct test and properly considered California's asserted State objectives.

see also Molasky-Arman, 522 F.3d at 934 (noting that "a 'substantial reason' for discrimination does not exist 'unless there is something to indicate that non-citizens constitute a peculiar source of the evil at which the statute is aimed'") (quoting *Toomer*, 334 U.S. at 398). In other words, a State may justify a differential fee by showing either that it is closely related to the costs of addressing a burden non-residents uniquely impose or that it approximates the amount in "taxes which only residents pay" towards the relevant State expenditures from which non-residents also benefit. *Toomer*, 334 U.S. at 399; *see also Tangier Sound Waterman's Ass'n v. Pruitt*, 4 F.3d 264, 267 (4th Cir. 1993) (*Toomer* permits state to discriminate against non-residents where state "establishes an 'advancement of a substantial [—13—] state interest' as a reason for the disparate treatment, and, in the facts of this case, evenly or approximately evenly distributes the costs imposed on residents and nonresidents to support those programs benefiting both groups."). Such a differential would "bear[] a close relation to the achievement of [a] substantial state objective[]," *Friedman*, 487 U.S. at 70, because it would address the particular evil non-residents present, unfairly benefiting from residents' tax expenditures. It also would place non-residents "upon the same footing with," *id.* at 64, or at least in "substantial equality" with California residents, *Toomer*, 334 U.S. at 396, by forcing an individual non-resident who benefits from the State's expenditures to contribute an amount substantially equal to that which an individual resident contributes across all fees and related taxes.

California does not claim, however—nor has it presented any evidence that shows—that the fee differential approximates the amount in taxes a resident contributes to the State's expenditures related to commercial fishing. *Mullaney*, 342 U.S. at 418; *see also Hicklin v. Orbeck*, 437 U.S. 518, 527 (1978) ("[T]he discrimination the [statute] works against nonresidents does not bear a substantial relationship to the particular 'evil' they are said to present."). California alone bore the step two "burden of showing that the discrimination is warranted by a substantial state objective and closely drawn to its achievement." *Friedman*, 487 U.S. at 68. It failed to carry that burden, despite ample opportunity to develop and support its offered justification and "all the facts. . . in [its] possession." *Mullaney*, 342 U.S. at 418–19. [—14—]

CONCLUSION

For the above reasons, we hold that California's differential commercial fishing license fees, Cal. Fish & Game Code §§ 7852, 7881, 8550.5, and 8280.6, violate the Privileges and Immunities Clause. Charging non-residents two to three times the amount charged to residents plainly burdens non-residents' right to pursue a common calling, in this case commercial fishing. Such discrimination violates the Privileges and Immunities Clause unless the State carries its burden to show "that such discrimination bears a close relation to the achievement of substantial state objectives." *Friedman*, 487 U.S. at 70. Although its stated objective, compensation for State expenditures for conservation or enforcement, is valid, California has failed to show that the differential fee charged to a non-resident is closely related to a resident's share of the State's expenditures.

AFFIRMED.***

(Reporter's Note: Dissenting opinion follows on p. 606).

*****(Reporter's Note: On February 26, 2016, the U.S. Ninth Circuit ordered that this case be reheard en banc.)*****

[—14—] **GRABER**, Circuit Judge, dissenting:

I respectfully dissent. Although I agree fully with the majority's analysis at step one of the inquiry, I would hold, at step two, that the differential fees survive summary judgment. Further evidentiary development is necessary to determine whether the nonresident fees "merely compensate the State for any added enforcement burden [nonresidents] may impose or for any conservation expenditures from taxes which only residents pay." *Toomer v. Witsell*, 334 U.S. 385, 399 (1948). [—15—]

We have little guidance to assist us in determining what the United States Supreme Court meant in the foregoing passage from *Toomer*. Only twice since *Toomer* has the Court quoted the phrase "taxes which only residents pay" in a privileges and immunities context, and in neither case did it explain the meaning of those words. *Baldwin v. Fish & Game Comm'n*, 436 U.S. 371, 401 (1978); *Mullaney v. Anderson*, 342 U.S. 415, 417 (1952). As I explain in more detail below, two state supreme courts have reached different conclusions about the proper interpretation of that phrase. But we do not know which (if either) of those courts got it right, because the Supreme Court denied certiorari in *both* cases. *Carlson v. Alaska Commercial Fisheries Entry Comm'n*, 519 U.S. 1101 (1997); *Glaser v. Salorio*, 449 U.S. 874 (1980). Further complicating our interpretive task, the Privileges and Immunities Clause of Article IV "is not one the contours of which have been precisely shaped by the process and wear of constant litigation and judicial interpretation over the years since 1789." *Baldwin*, 436 U.S. at 379.

Acknowledging those limitations, we must decide how to interpret the phrase "taxes which only residents pay." *Toomer*, 334 U.S. at 399. On the one hand, as the State urges, the phrase could be read to refer to residents' aggregate tax contribution to commercial fishing. Under that reading, California permissibly could charge differential fees to nonresidents so long as those fees do not exceed the nonresidents' fair share of the portion of commercial fisheries management

costs that California residents' tax dollars fund.

The New Jersey Supreme Court has interpreted *Toomer* in this way. In *Salorio v. Glaser*, 414 A.2d 943 (N.J. 1980), the plaintiffs challenged New Jersey's imposition of an [—16—] Emergency Transportation Tax, which applied only to nonresident users of the state highway system. Although it found the record insufficiently developed to render a final decision, the New Jersey Supreme Court held that a tax that applied only to nonresidents could, in theory, pass constitutional muster, because "[t]he Constitution does not entitle nonresident commuters to a 'free ride.' The State may exact from them a fair share of the cost of adequate transportation facilities without violating the Privileges and Immunities Clause." *Id.* at 954. The court read *Toomer* and other Supreme Court cases to authorize a state to "impose upon nonresidents the additional expenses occasioned by their activities within the state, or the reasonable costs of benefits which they receive from the state." *Id.* at 953.

Applying the *Salorio* court's reasoning here, nonresidents are on "equal footing" with residents so long as they are not charged more than their "fair share" of commercial fisheries management expenses that residents' tax dollars fund. California introduced evidence that nonresidents purchased 11% of commercial fishing licenses, while the differential fees for out-of-state licenses equaled only 3% of the net general fund contributions to the Department of Fish and Wildlife ("DFW") budget. The State asserts that it constitutionally could charge differential fees that total up to 11% of the DFW's general fund-supported commercial fishing expenditures, so the smaller fee that California actually charges is—*a fortiori*—permissible.

On the other hand, Plaintiffs read "taxes which only residents pay," *Toomer*, 334 U.S. at 399, very differently. They contend that the phrase requires a per capita calculation of a California resident's tax burden related to DFW's commercial fishing budget. The

Alaska Supreme Court [—17—] adopted this alternative interpretation in *Carlson v. State*, 798 P.2d 1269 (Alaska 1990). There, the plaintiffs challenged Alaska's commercial fishing fees, which were three times higher for nonresidents than for residents. The state urged the court to follow *Salorio*. But the Alaska Supreme Court rejected the New Jersey Supreme Court's interpretation of *Toomer*:

> Implicit in *Salorio* is the notion that it is permissible to require nonresidents to pay up to 100% of their *pro rata* share of expenditures regardless of what percentage of their *pro rata* share residents are in fact paying. In other words, *Salorio*, as applied to this case, seems to add up to a general proposition that the state may subsidize its own residents in the pursuit of their business activities and not similarly situated nonresidents, even though this results in substantial inequality of treatment.

Carlson, 798 P.2d at 1278. The court held that the proper inquiry was "whether all fees and taxes which must be paid to the state by a nonresident to enjoy the state-provided benefit are substantially equal to those which must be paid by similarly situated residents when the residents' *pro rata* shares of state revenues to which nonresidents make no contributions are taken into account." *Id.*

Under the *Carlson* court's approach, the state would have to divide general fund expenditures for commercial fishing management by the total number of California taxpayers; the quotient would represent the maximum permissible differential fee. The State introduced evidence that net [—18—] annual general fund outlays for commercial fisheries management total at least $12 million. Thus, for instance, if there were 12 million taxpayers in California, the per capita formula would limit the permissible differential fee to $1 per nonresident fisher.[1]

According to Plaintiffs, this formula puts residents and nonresidents on "equal footing" because their out-of-pocket costs to support commercial fisheries are the same.

I would reject the per capita formula. The purpose of the Privileges and Immunities Clause is to "place the citizens of each State upon the same footing with citizens of other States, so far as the advantages resulting from citizenship in those States are concerned." *Paul v. Virginia*, 75 U.S. (8 Wall.) 168, 180 (1868). In my view, the per capita approach does not advance that goal. The per capita formula attributes to each resident a pro rata contribution to every program and activity supported by a state's general fund expenditures. But that sort of rigid across-the-board calculation does not accurately reflect the real benefit that a taxpayer obtains through his or her tax dollars. Taxpayer dollars support a large number of state-funded programs. Education, natural resources management, healthcare services, corrections and rehabilitation, infrastructure, and transportation all are at least partially funded with state tax revenues in California. In a given year, an individual taxpayer likely receives no direct benefit from some of those programs, but a benefit that far [—19—] exceeds his or her pro rata contribution from others. This is the deal that we make when we pay taxes: We all put a portion of our income into a big pot and it is spent in a variety of ways, some of which benefit us directly and some of which do not.

California residents subsidize each other with their taxes. For example, suppose that each taxpayer's share of state support for secondary schools is $1 per year. A certain California taxpayer has a teenager who attends public high school. That taxpayer's per capita "payment" for the educational benefit is $1, but the benefit to the taxpaying parent is worth much more than that. The parent agrees to subsidize a number of other activities in the state, including commercial

---

[1] This illustrative example likely is a generous estimate, as the population of California was nearly 39 million in 2014. U.S. Census Bureau, State & County Quick Facts, http://quickfacts.census.gov/qfd/states/06000.html.

Thus, the permissible differential likely would be less than $1 under the per capita formula, even though a substantial number of California residents—for example, minor children—are not taxpayers.

fishing. In exchange, taxpayers without school-age children subsidize public education.[2] The per capita formula permits a nonresident fisher to obtain the same benefit as a resident fisher, but the nonresident does not have to subsidize *any* other programs or activities in California in exchange. The per capita formula thus *systematically disadvantages the resident* vis-à-vis the nonresident.

Instead of using a per capita formula, I would adopt the *Salorio* court's "fair share" approach. At step two of the privileges and immunities inquiry, the state must show that the discrimination against nonresidents is "closely related to [—20—] the advancement of a substantial state interest." *Supreme Court of Va. v. Friedman*, 487 U.S. 59, 65 (1988). We recently reiterated that "[a] 'substantial reason' for discrimination does not exist 'unless there is something to indicate that non-citizens constitute a peculiar source of the evil at which the statute is aimed.'" *Council of Ins. Agents & Brokers v. Molasky-Arman*, 522 F.3d 925, 934 (9th Cir. 2008) (quoting *Toomer*, 334 U.S. at 398)). Nonresidents increase the amount of commercial fishing activity in California's coastal waters. That increased activity, in turn, requires the state to spend more money than it otherwise would spend on commercial fisheries management, including enforcement and conservation. Because nonresidents are a "peculiar source" of those additional costs, I would hold that not subsidizing nonresident participation in an activity funded with residents' tax dollars is a substantial reason for discrimination. *See Tangier Sound Waterman's Ass'n v. Pruitt*, 4 F.3d 264, 268 (4th Cir. 1993) (assuming, without deciding, that such an interest is

permissible under the Privileges and Immunities Clause).

Turning to the "close relationship" requirement, I would hold that the State has the burden to show three things. First, it must isolate the state expenditures that benefit only the licensees.[3] *See id.* (rejecting Virginia's differential license fee in part because it unfairly charged nonresident [—21—] commercial fishers "for programs funded by all taxpayers to benefit all fishermen, whether commercial or sport fishermen"). Second, it must determine what portion of those expenditures fairly may be characterized as deriving "from taxes which only residents pay." *Toomer*, 334 U.S. at 399; *see Tangier*, 4 F.3d at 267 (striking down Virginia's differential commercial fishing license fees in part because the state calculated the fee without considering nonresident fishers' payment of state sales and use taxes); *Salorio*, 414 A.2d at 955 (discussing whether property and sales taxes are "taxes imposed upon residents alone" in light of the fact that some nonresidents pay them). And third, it must assess what portion of qualifying expenditures is fairly allocable to the nonresidents as "the additional expenses occasioned by their activities within the state."[4] *Salorio*, 414 A.2d at 953; *see also*

---

[2] Of course, some commercial fishers are parents whose children attend public school. But that fact just demonstrates that each taxpayer benefits directly from a different set of state programs supported by his or her tax dollars. The value of the taxpayer-funded investment in a given program to each individual taxpayer who benefits from that program varies. The value is less than the taxpayer's total tax bill, but more—generally, significantly more—than the taxpayer's strict pro rata contribution to the program.

[3] These expenditures would include any costs associated with programs or activities in which only licensees participate—for example, the cost of enforcing rules such as size of fish or season limits. They also would include conservation expenditures made necessary by licensees' activities. If the state engages in conservation activities designed to keep fish stocks at a certain level, some of those activities benefit only licensees. To count those costs, the state must separate general conservation activities from conservation activities directed to the effect of commercial fishing.

[4] It may be, as the State asserts, that multiplying the qualifying expenditures by the percentage of commercial fishers who are nonresidents is the appropriate way to calculate those nonresidents' fair share, but that is not necessarily the case. *See Salorio v. Glaser*, 461 A.2d 1100, 1106 (N.J. 1983) ("Although the State has not shown that New York commuters cause higher average costs per commuter than New Jersey commuters, the New York commuter does exacerbate the peak load. Accordingly, both incremental and average costs are pertinent factors

Tangier, 4 F.3d at 267 (holding that "the record does not disclose that the Commonwealth of Virginia has shown that it created any credible method of allocating costs as between residents and nonresidents").

I would hold that the "close relationship" requirement of step two is satisfied so long as the state charges a differential [—22—] fee that, in the aggregate, does not exceed[5] the amount that the state spends that (1) benefits only licensees, (2) derives from taxes that only residents pay, and (3) is fairly allocable to nonresidents.[6] This test puts residents and nonresidents on "substantially equal footing" with respect to commercial fishing: Residents reap the benefit of the tax dollars that they alone pay, and nonresidents cannot be required to pay more than their "fair share" of the benefits they enjoy that are subsidized by those resident-paid tax dollars.

This fair share approach accurately reflects the relative benefit that residents and nonresidents obtain from a state's general fund expenditures. Suppose that a state charges a $50 license fee to resident commercial fishers. Over and above the revenue collected from those fees, the state spends $1 million in tax-supported funds on

commercial fisheries management. If 10,000 people per year obtain licenses, the benefit of the $1 million subsidy to each fisher is $100. Thus, a nonresident may be charged the $50 fee that residents pay, plus a $100 differential. If only 5,000 people obtain licenses, [—23—] each nonresident may be charged a $200 differential. This variance makes sense, because the benefit to each fisher of the tax-supported outlay decreases as more people use the resource. The per capita approach makes less sense because it is unresponsive to such changes; so long as a state's tax rate and general fund outlay on the commercial fisheries program remain unchanged, the permissible differential is fixed. It is the same whether 10 or 10,000 people obtain licenses and use the resource.

Plaintiffs raise the specter of a year in which only one nonresident purchases a commercial fishing license. They argue that the state's approach would permit California to collect hundreds of thousands of dollars from that single licensee. Not so. The fair share formula accounts for this possibility. Assuming the scenario described above, in a year in which a single nonresident and 4,999 residents obtain licenses the permissible differential for that nonresident would remain $200.[7]

Finally, Plaintiffs challenge the "fair share" approach because, using it, the state could set nonresident license fees ten, twenty, or even a hundred times higher than resident license fees. They point out that the Supreme Court has rejected nonresident fees at such ratios before. *See Mullaney*, 342 U.S. at 418 (invalidating nonresident fees ten times [—24—] higher than resident fees); *Toomer*,

---

in determining the costs attributable to the New York commuter."); *Salorio*, 414 A.2d at 955 (questioning a "strict percentage computation" that assumed equal transportation costs for nonresident and resident commuters).

[5] Because the Privileges and Immunities Clause neither bars the residents of a state from deciding to use their tax dollars to subsidize the activities of nonresidents nor precludes a state from providing a greater benefit to nonresidents than it provides to residents, it is permissible for a state to charge *less* than the maximum allowable differential.

[6] The test here is one of "substantial equality of treatment," not absolute equality. *Austin v. New Hampshire*, 420 U.S. 656, 665 (1975). So long as the state "fairly attempts to distribute the burdens and costs of government to those receiving its benefits" pursuant to a reasonable methodology, I would hold that the requirements of the Privileges and Immunities Clause are met. *Salorio*, 414 A.2d at 952; *see also Travelers' Ins. Co. v. Connecticut*, 185 U.S. 364, 371 (1902) ("It is enough that the state has secured a reasonably fair distribution of burdens, and that no intentional discrimination has been made against nonresidents.").

---

[7] The only way the permissible differential charged to a nonresident would skyrocket is if the overall number of fishers obtaining licenses plunged to single digits. But if that happened, the state likely would slash its commercial fisheries management spending. And if it did not cut spending, it is hard to see how the State could prove that the full $1 million in my example benefitted just a handful of fishers, because it is not reasonable to attribute hundreds of thousands of dollars in enforcement and conservation costs to a single fisher.

334 U.S. at 389 (striking down nonresident fees one hundred times higher than resident fees). And they urge us to rely on the ratio of nonresident to resident fees here (roughly three to one)[8] to reject the "fair share" analysis. Plaintiffs' argument is flawed for two reasons.

First, the Supreme Court did not reject the differential fees because of the *size* of the ratio. Rather, it rejected the nonresident fees because Alaska and South Carolina had failed to show any *connection* between the differential and state spending on services to the nonresidents. *See Mullaney*, 342 U.S. at 418 & n.1 (rejecting the state's argument that the differential fees merely compensated the state for enforcement against nonresidents because the state had not calculated the cost of that enforcement and the total amount of differential fees collected "may easily have exceeded the entire amount available for administration" of the office in charge of enforcement); *Toomer*, 334 U.S. at 398 (noting that "[n]othing in the record indicate[d] . . . that any substantial amount of the State's general funds [was] devoted to shrimp conservation" and that, even if there had been such evidence, it "would not necessarily support a remedy so drastic as to be a near equivalent of total exclusion").

Second, focusing on the size of the ratio requires consideration of fees in a vacuum. That isolation makes little sense in light of the Supreme Court's statement that a state may charge a fee designed to "compensate [it] for any added [—25—] enforcement burden [nonresidents] may impose or for any conservation expenditures from taxes which only residents pay." *Toomer*, 334 U.S. at 399. In *Salorio*, the tax at issue applied *only* to nonresidents. On appeal after remand, the New Jersey Supreme Court ultimately invalidated the tax—but not because the nonresident-to-resident ratio was too high. The problem was that, during a period of two

decades, the revenues collected by the state through the tax had exceeded the costs attributable to nonresidents by a factor of more than two. *Salorio v. Glaser*, 461 A.2d 1100, 1107 (N.J. 1983). Focus on the size of the ratio per se is misplaced; the privileges and immunities inquiry requires consideration of all taxes and fees paid by residents and nonresidents in support of commercial fishing.

Because it applied a different test, the district court did not address whether the net general fund outlay benefits only licensees, whether that outlay derives solely from taxes that only residents pay, or what portion of qualifying costs is properly allocable to nonresident fishers. Thus, on the current record, I would hold that we cannot determine whether the differential fees are permissible under the Privileges and Immunities Clause. Accordingly, I would reverse the summary judgment of the district court and remand for further proceedings.*****

(Reporter's Note: On February 26, 2016, the U.S. Ninth Circuit ordered that this case be reheard en banc.)

---

[8] The ratio of nonresident fees to resident fees for commercial fishing licenses and commercial boat registrations is three to one. For dungeness crab vessel permits, the ratio is lower (two to one); and for herring gill net permits, the ratio is higher (nearly four to one).

United States Court of Appeals
for the Ninth Circuit

No. 13-35866

ALASKA WILDERNESS LEAGUE
vs.
JEWELL

On Petition for Panel Rehearing and Petition for
Rehearing En Banc

Decided: December 29, 2015

Citation: 811 F.3d 1111, 3 Adm. R. 611 (9th Cir. 2015).

Before **FARRIS, NELSON,** and **NGUYEN,** Circuit
Judges.

[—3—] ORDER

Judges Farris and Nguyen voted to deny
the petition for rehearing. Judge Nelson
voted to grant the petition for rehearing.
Judge Nguyen voted to deny the petition for
rehearing en banc, and Judge Farris so
recommended. Judge Nelson recommended
granting the petition for rehearing en banc.

The full court was advised of the petition
for rehearing en banc. A judge requested a
vote on whether to rehear the matter en banc,
and the matter failed to receive a majority of
the votes of the nonrecused active judges in
favor of en banc consideration. Fed. R. App. P.
35.

The petition for panel rehearing and the
petition for rehearing en banc are **DENIED**.
No future petitions for rehearing or petitions
for rehearing en banc will be entertained.

*(Reporter's Note: Dissenting opinion follows
on p. 612).*

[—4—] **GOULD,** Circuit Judge, with whom **FLETCHER** and **CALLAHAN,** Circuit Judges, join, dissenting from the denial of rehearing en banc:

I respectfully dissent from denial of rehearing en banc in this case, which concerns decisions by the Bureau of Safety and Environmental Enforcement (BSEE) not to engage in consultation pursuant to the Endangered Species Act (ESA), and not to prepare an environmental impact statement (EIS) pursuant to the National Environmental Policy Act (NEPA), before approving Shell's oil spill response plans for offshore drilling in the Beaufort and Chukchi Seas. The majority's ESA analysis rests first on an erroneous decision to grant BSEE *Chevron* deference, based on the majority's finding an ambiguity in the statute where none exists, and second on an incorrect analogy to *National Association of Home Builders v. Defenders of Wildlife*, 551 U.S. 644 (2007). The majority incorrectly interpreted the statute that governs oil spill response plans, the 1990 amendments to the Clean Water Act (CWA), as imposing non-discretionary duties; it granted *Chevron* deference to BSEE on this issue based on a perceived statutory ambiguity. But the statute's clear language demonstrates without ambiguity that BSEE exercises discretion in reviewing and approving oil spill response plans. Both parts of the majority opinion lead to an unprecedented and unwise constraining of the powers of the ESA and NEPA.

The majority's decision in this case encourages federal agencies to abrogate their oversight by deciding that a statute's requirements limit their discretion to the point of taking the ESA and NEPA off the table. The majority invites federal agencies to ignore their ESA and NEPA obligations, await a challenge, and then defend their inaction under the [—5—] guise of *Chevron* deference. However, the federal courts should not be so eager to accept, under the guise of *Chevron,* an agency decision that violates existing case law interpreting the ESA and NEPA, as well as the very logic of those statutes. *Chevron* was meant to prevent courts from imposing their own construction of a statute where Congress has not "directly addressed the precise question at issue." *Chevron, U.S.A.,*

Inc. v. Nat. Res. Def. Council, Inc., 467 U.S. 837, 843 (1984). Instead, courts should defer to an agency's "permissible interpretation of a statute." *Id. Chevron* was not meant to force courts into deferring to an agency's contention that it lacks discretion over statutorily mandated requirements. Such a ruling invites abrogation of statutory responsibilities.

I.

A central flaw in the majority's decision is that it finds an ambiguity in 33 U.S.C. § 1321(j)(5) where none exists. According to this statute, part of the 1990 amendments to the CWA passed after the Exxon *Valdez* disaster, an oil company's oil spill response plan must show that the company is capable of "responding, to the maximum extent practicable, to a worst case discharge, and to a substantial threat of such a discharge, of oil or a hazardous substance." 33 U.S.C. § 1321(j)(5)(A)(i). To comply, the proposed plans must meet six specific requirements. 33 U.S.C. § 1321(j)(5)(D). The statute then directs that the President "shall" take several actions after an oil company submits its plan: "promptly review" it, "require amendments" to a plan that does not meet the statutory requirements, and "approve any plan" that does meet the requirements. 33 U.S.C. § 1321(j)(5)(E). According to the majority, the "shall" language suggests that BSEE "*must* approve" any conforming [—6—] plan, and thus has no discretion over the adequacy of the plans. *Alaska Wilderness League v. Jewell,* 788 F.3d 1212, 1220, 3 Adm. R. 554, 559 (9th Cir. 2015) (emphasis in original). This led the majority to find an ambiguity in the statute: "It is unclear how the broad language of section 1321(j)(5)(A)(i), with its reference to the 'maximum extent practicable,' interacts with the finite statutory criteria of section 1321(j)(5)(D)." *Id.,* 3 Adm. R. at 559. "And that means we . . . face a statute whose halves do not correspond to each other—giving rise to an ambiguity that calls for *Chevron* deference." *Id.,* 3 Adm. R. at 559 (quoting *Scialabba v. Cuellar de Osorio,* 134 S. Ct. 2191, 2210 (2014)).

However, there is no ambiguity in the statute that warrants *Chevron* deference. The

CWA amendments unambiguously give BSEE discretion over oil spill response plan approval. Section 1321(j)(5)(A)(i) requires an oil spill response plan to respond "to the maximum extent practicable to a worst case discharge, and to a substantial threat of such a discharge, of oil or a hazardous substance." According to the majority, "the open-ended nature of [this] phrase . . . suggests agency discretion." *Alaska Wilderness*, 788 F.3d at 1220, 3 Adm. R. at 559. The majority agreed with Judge Nelson, who dissented, that this portion of the statute could be read to "serve[] as an independent 'standard' that must be met in addition to the list of enumerated requirements at § 1321(j)(5)(D)." *Id.* at 1222, 1229, 3 Adm. R. at 561, 568 (Nelson, J., dissenting) ("[T]he phrase 'maximum extent practicable' . . . has a superlative quality and therefore must refer to the greatest option in a range of possibilities.").

The majority is wrong that the statute's "halves do not correspond to each other." *Id.* at 1220, 3 Adm. R. at 559. Like the broad language in § 1321(j)(5)(A)(i), one of the six explicit criteria requires removal of a worst case discharge "to the maximum [—7—] extent practicable." 33 U.S.C. § 1321(j)(5)(D)(iii). Accepting the majority's conclusion that this phrase "suggests agency discretion," there is no ambiguity entitling BSEE to *Chevron* deference on the issue of its discretion, because the phrase appears in both parts of the statute. *See Chevron*, 467 U.S. at 842 ("If the intent of Congress is clear, that is the end of the matter . . . ."). The majority ignored that the statute's specific requirements include the same phrase as the statute's introduction, which the majority and dissent agreed suggests agency discretion over response plan approval.

As explained more fully below, this case is unlike *Home Builders* because the statutory duty at issue does not restrict BSEE's discretion over approval of oil spill response plans. The majority makes much of the statute's requirement that BSEE "shall" approve any plan that "meets the requirements of this paragraph," but it ignores the substance of those requirements. 33 U.S.C. §§ 1321(j)(5)(E)(i) & (iii). The

requirements do not constitute mere "triggering events," as in *Home Builders*; they require a thorough evaluation of a response plan. *Home Builders*, 551 U.S. at 669.

First, one of statute's explicit requirements is that response plans must "be consistent with the requirements of the National Contingency Plan [NCP] and Area Contingency Plans." 33 U.S.C. § 1321(j)(5)(D)(i). The NCP contains numerous phases of operational responses to a spill, including a special response to worst case discharges, *see* 40 C.F.R. §§ 300.300–300.335, and includes several protections for endangered species. *See, e.g.*, 40 C.F.R. § 300.135(k). The NCP also requires that environmental evaluations "be performed to assess threats to the environment, especially sensitive habitats and critical habitats of species protected [—8—] under the [ESA]." 40 C.F.R. § 300.430(e)(2)(i)(G). However, the majority does not explain how BSEE could determine whether a response plan meets the NCP's numerous independent requirements if BSEE's oversight role is truly just to check the boxes in a "checklist." *Alaska Wilderness*, 788 F.3d at 1220, 3 Adm. R. at 559. Whether an oil company's oil spill response plan is "consistent with the requirements of the [NCP] and Area Contingency Plans" is far from a mechanical determination or "triggering event[]." *Home Builders*, 551 U.S. at 669.

Second, the CWA amendments require that a company's response plan "remove . . . a worst case discharge," specifically defining the term "remove" to mean "containment and removal of the oil . . . from the water and shorelines or . . . such other actions as may be necessary to prevent, minimize, or mitigate damage to the public health or welfare, including . . . fish, shellfish, wildlife, and public and private property, shorelines, and beaches." 33 U.S.C. § 1321(a)(8). Whether an oil spill response plan provides the means to "remove" a worst case discharge is also a question that requires evaluation of the plan—it is not simply a "triggering event[]." *Home Builders*, 551 U.S. at 669.

Third, other sections of the CWA governing the federal government's spill plans, 33 U.S.C.

§§ 1321(d)(1)–(2) & (j)(4)(B)–(D), contain the same "shall" language as the sections governing oil spill response plans, yet are undisputedly subject to ESA consultation. The majority asserts that "[t]hese provisions . . . are different," but does not say why. *Alaska Wilderness*, 788 F.3d at 1224, 3 Adm. R. at 562. The majority tries to distinguish § 1321(d)(1), which requires the President to prepare and publish an NCP, by claiming that "[n]othing in the text prohibits such a plan from being prepared in light [—9—] of concerns that an ESA consultation might raise." *Id.*, 3 Adm. R. at 562. But the majority does not explain why its analysis of the statute at issue here looks for explicit *mention* of ESA consultation whereas its analysis of a parallel provision looks for an explicit *prohibition* on ESA consultation. It is the majority's inconsistent textual analysis, not any meaningful distinction in CWA provisions, that produces these contrary results.

Fourth, the majority attempts to distinguish response plan approval from the NCP, which according to the statute should "include, but not be limited to" a number of factors "that might be deemed necessary after an ESA consultation occurs," including "water pollution control and conservation and trusteeship of natural resources (including conservation of fish and wildlife)." 33 U.S.C. § 1321(d)(2); *Alaska Wilderness*, 788 F.3d at 1224, 3 Adm. R. at 562-63. This argument by the majority apparently is intended to bolster its conclusion that unlike the NCP, 33 U.S.C. § 1321(j)(5)(E) "leaves no room for the inclusion of additional factors." *Alaska Wilderness*, 788 F.3d at 1224, 3 Adm. R. at 563. But the majority does not mention that, as explained above, one of the very requirements BSEE must consider before approving an oil spill response plan is its "consisten[cy] with the requirements of the [NCP]." 33 U.S.C. § 1321(j)(5)(D)(i); *Alaska Wilderness*, 788 F.3d at 1224, 3 Adm. R. at 562-63. It is unavailing to distinguish response plan approval from the supposedly more broad-based NCP, when consistency with the NCP is one of the factors to be considered in approving an oil spill response plan.

Fifth, as the dissent explained, BSEE's implementing regulations make clear that the agency can exercise its discretion to benefit protected species. *Alaska Wilderness*, 788 F.3d at 1228, 3 Adm. R. at 567 (Nelson, J., dissenting). For example, the regulations require operators to identify resources of [—10—] "environmental importance" that could be harmed by a "worst case discharge scenario," and to provide strategies to protect them. 30 C.F.R. §§ 254.26(a), (c). The regulations also require operators to identify procedures to "protect beaches, waterfowl, other marine and shoreline resources, and areas of special . . . environmental importance." 30 C.F.R. § 254.23(g)(4). The majority does not explain how BSEE's cursory review of an oil spill response plan could be consistent with the agency's own regulations. These regulations underscore that § 1321(j)(5)(D) is not just a "checklist statute." *Alaska Wilderness*, 788 F.3d at 1220, 3 Adm. R. at 559.

BSEE reasoned that its implementing regulations define "maximum extent practicable" as "within the limitations of available technology, as well as the physical limitations of personnel, when responding to a worst case discharge in adverse weather conditions." 30 C.F.R. § 254.6; Federal Defendants' Opposition to Rehearing En Banc at 12–13. According to BSEE, nothing in this language gives it the discretion to consider a wide range of factors consistent with the general meaning of the word "maximum." *Id.* at 12. That argument persuaded the majority. But Judge Nelson's dissent persuasively explains the unreasonableness of this reasoning. *See Alaska Wilderness*, 788 F.3d at 1229, 3 Adm. R. at 567-68 (Nelson, J., dissenting). Even under BSEE's definition of "maximum extent practicable," BSEE must determine whether Shell's response plans met the standard. And, as even the majority reasoned, the term "maximum extent practicable" "suggests agency discretion because of [its] open-ended nature . . . ." *Id.* at 1220, 3 Adm. R. at 559.

Finally, further evidence that the CWA amendments contemplated active review comes from 33 U.S.C. §§ 1321(j)(5)(E)(ii) &

(iii), which direct BSEE to "require [—11—] amendments to any plan that does not meet the requirements of this paragraph," or to approve a plan that does meet them. That Congress has given BSEE the responsibility to decide whether an oil spill response plan meets the statutory criteria, and has directed the agency to require amendments to nonconforming plans, is further evidence that the statute imparts discretion. Nowhere does the majority explain why Congress would task BSEE with requiring amendments to a nonconforming plan if it truly sought to cabin the agency's discretion or to make the requirements of the CWA amendments mere "triggering events." *Home Builders*, 551 U.S. at 669.

The approval process for oil spill response plans requires agency discretion. It was wrong to grant BSEE *Chevron* deference on this issue.

II.

Two flawed holdings flow from the majority's erroneous *Chevron* determination. Specifically, the majority narrowed the application of both the ESA and NEPA. First, the majority's approach sets a dangerous precedent for ignoring ESA § 7. Undisputedly, ESA consultation is only required when an agency takes a "discretionary" action. 50 C.F.R. § 402.03. As explained above, however, response plan approval pursuant to the requirements of 33 U.S.C. § 1321(j)(5)(D) is discretionary because it requires BSEE to analyze *whether* the requirements have been met. BSEE should therefore be required to consult under the ESA. The majority concluded otherwise based on its incorrect analogy to *Home Builders*. At issue in *Home Builders* was a requirement in CWA § 402(b) that the Environmental Protection Agency (EPA) "shall approve" a transfer of CWA [—12—] permitting authority from the federal government to a state upon a showing that the state had met nine specified criteria.[1] *Home*

---

[1] To become the permitting authority, the state must demonstrate that it has the ability: (1) to issue fixed-term permits that apply and ensure compliance with the CWA's substantive requirements and which are revocable for cause; (2)

Builders, 551 U.S. at 650–51. The Supreme Court described the "shall approve" language in CWA § 402(b) as "mandatory" and held that EPA did not have discretion to deny a transfer application. *Id.* at 661. Because the ESA required consultation for all discretionary agency actions, the Court's majority concluded that application of the ESA would impermissibly "engraft[] a tenth criterion onto the CWA." *Id.* at 663. Here, the majority claims that, like CWA § 402(b), the six requirements for response plan approval in 33 U.S.C. § 1321(j)(5)(D) are mandatory, and the ESA is not applicable.

However, this case differs from *Home Builders* for at least three reasons. First, *Home Builders* hinged partially on the fact that the ESA was passed after the CWA, and did not explicitly overrule CWA § 402(b). *Home Builders*, 551 U.S. [—13—] at 662. But here, 33 U.S.C. § 1321(j)(5) postdates the ESA by seventeen years. There is no concern here, as there was in *Home Builders*, that ESA consultation would implicitly amend a prior statute.

The second distinction is that in *Home Builders*, the parties appeared to agree that the state had authority to perform each of the nine enumerated functions in CWA § 402(b). *Home Builders*, 551 U.S. at 672 ("[T]here is no

---

to inspect, monitor, and enter facilities and to require reports to the extent required by the CWA; (3) to provide for public notice and public hearings; (4) to ensure that the EPA receives notice of each permit application; (5) to ensure that any other State whose waters may be affected by the issuance of a permit may submit written recommendations and that written reasons be provided if such recommendations are not accepted; (6) to ensure that no permit is issued if the Army Corps of Engineers concludes that it would substantially impair the anchoring and navigation of navigable waters; (7) to abate violations of permits or the permit program, including through civil and criminal penalties; (8) to ensure that any permit for a discharge from a publicly owned treatment works includes conditions requiring the identification of the type and volume of certain pollutants; and (9) to ensure that any industrial user of any publicly owned treatment works will comply with certain of the CWA's substantive provisions. 33 U.S.C. §§ 1342(b)(1)–(9).

dispute that Arizona has satisfied each of those statutory criteria"); *see also Alaska Wilderness*, 788 F.3d at 1229, 3 Adm. R. at 568 (Nelson, J., dissenting). The parties' disagreement was instead about whether ESA consultation added an extra step to transfer of permitting authority. Here, the question is not whether the ESA adds an *extra* step to the approval process, but how much discretion there is in the *existing* steps of 33 U.S.C. § 1321(j)(5)(D). On this the parties do not agree. This distinction means that although *Home Builders* is controlling precedent, its particular outcome does not bind this case.

Third, the conditions in § 1321(j)(5)(D) that must be met for response plan approval are substantively different than the conditions for state permitting authority in *Home Builders*. There, the Supreme Court characterized the conditions as "triggering events" with a mechanical cause and effect. *Home Builders*, 551 U.S. at 669. Arizona had to show that it had the ability to perform nine specific tasks. Once it had done so, the agency had no choice but to transfer CWA permitting authority. *Id.* at 669. This reading is consistent with the Supreme Court's conclusion that CWA § 402(b) imposed nondiscretionary requirements on EPA. *Id.* at 661. Here, as explained above, the requirements are not simple enough to be considered mere "triggering events." *Id.* at 669. [—14—] They require evaluation of whether an oil spill response plan actually meets, for example, the requirement that it be consistent with the NCP, or the requirement that it ensure the availability of personnel and equipment necessary to remove a worst case discharge to the "maximum extent practicable." 33 U.S.C. §§ 1321(j)(5)(D)(i), (iii).

By not correcting the majority's holding through en banc rehearing, we have permitted a gross alteration of Supreme Court precedent and given federal agencies unwarranted and unprecedented authority over whether their statutory duties are discretionary or not, which directly impacts whether ESA consultation is required. ESA consultation is required for "any action authorized, funded, or carried out by" a federal agency—with the rare exception for cases such as *Home Builders*, where a statute's requirements are clearly "triggering events" rather than independent requirements, and where there is no dispute that the requirements have been met. Neither is true of the statute at issue here, 33 U.S.C. § 1321(j)(5). This is clear from the statute itself, and the majority was wrong to adopt the agency's contrary interpretation under the guise of *Chevron*.

The majority's decision also misapplies NEPA precedent. NEPA requires federal agencies to prepare an EIS for all "major Federal actions significantly affecting the quality of the human environment." 42 U.S.C. § 4332(2)(C). In a narrow exception, NEPA does not apply where an agency lacks the discretion to consider environmental values in its decision making process. *See Dep't of Transp. v. Public Citizen*, 541 U.S. 752, 767–69 (2004). Here, the majority held that BSEE reasonably concluded that it "must approve any [response plan] that meets the statutory requirements." *Alaska Wilderness*, 788 F.3d at 1225, 3 Adm. R. at 564. "Thus, even assuming, [—15—] without deciding, that BSEE's approval of Shell's [response plans] constitutes a 'major Federal action,' its approval is not subject to NEPA's requirements." *Id.*, 3 Adm. R. at 564. The majority analogized this case to *Public Citizen*, where the governing statute required the Federal Motor Carrier Safety Administration (FMCSA) to register a person to provide transportation as a motor carrier if it found the person willing and able to comply with the statute's requirements. *Public Citizen*, 541 U.S. at 766. NEPA review was not required in *Public Citizen* because the agency lacked the power to consider environmental consequences outside its statutory obligation. *Id.* at 768–70.

The majority's analogy to *Public Citizen* is unsupported. As explained above, § 1321(j)(5)(D) imposes a discretionary duty on BSEE. In *Public Citizen*, the Supreme Court held that FMCSA did not have to account for certain environmental effects in its environmental assessment because it had "no ability to countermand" executive action by the President, so its action did not have a "reasonably close causal relationship" to any negative environmental impacts. *Public Citizen*, 541 U.S. at 766–67. That is not the case here, because BSEE does have the authority to consider environmental values in its decision-making process. BSEE's approval of response plans is discretionary, and it would provide a "reasonably close causal relationship" between the agency action and environmental effects, including a "worst case discharge," stemming from a potential spill. *See Public Citizen*, 541 U.S. at 767; 33 U.S.C. § 1321(j)(5)(A)(i).[2] [—16—]

In sum, the impact of the majority's decision is to take the ESA and NEPA off the table when considering oil spill response plans, which are a required component of offshore drilling proposals. This violates the language of 33 U.S.C. § 1321(j)(5), which by its terms requires discretionary evaluation of oil spill response plans. The statute calls on BSEE to assess whether response plans give protection to the "maximum extent practicable." 33 U.S.C. § 1321(j)(5)(A)(i). A federal agency cannot determine if protection is to the "maximum extent practicable" without exercising some discretion in judgment. If discretion is needed, then claimants with standing, and the federal courts, must be part of the approval process until decisions are made in litigation.

---

[2] Deference to BSEE's views may also be tempered here because we are assessing whether BSEE's review and approval of an oil spill response plan under the CWA is non-discretionary *within the meaning of NEPA*. As the D.C. Circuit has explained, "the court owes no deference to the [—16—] [agency's] interpretation of NEPA . . . because NEPA is addressed to all federal agencies and Congress did not entrust administration of NEPA to [BSEE] alone." *Grand Canyon Trust v. Fed. Aviation Admin.*, 290 F.3d 339, 342 (D.C. Cir. 2002). Moreover, Congress demonstrated in the CWA that it knows how to exempt agency approvals from environmental review. *See* 33 U.S.C. § 1371(c) (exempting certain actions by EPA from NEPA review). That Congress did not similarly exempt BSEE's oil spill response plan approval, pursuant to the CWA, from NEPA or ESA review strongly suggests that Congress intended the statutes to apply.

III.

I agree with the majority that the ESA and NEPA do not require an agency to provide redundant analysis. NEPA and its implementing regulations accommodate this concern by allowing agencies to take a "tiered" approach to environmental review. *See* 40 C.F.R. § 1502.20 (encouraging tiering of NEPA review). We have also allowed for tiering of ESA review. *See Gifford Pinchot Task Force v. U.S. Fish & Wildlife Serv.*, 378 F.3d 1059, 1067–68 (9th Cir. 2004). Thus, BSEE's NEPA and ESA review of the proposed [—17—] approval of Shell's oil spill response plans need not be burdensome or redundant if the foreseeable impacts of approving the plans, and reasonable alternatives, were already addressed in an EIS and biological opinion completed at an earlier stage of development. If this were the case, BSEE could, for example, prepare a shorter environmental assessment tiered to the earlier EIS to satisfy NEPA. *See* 40 C.F.R. § 1508.9 (describing an environmental assessment). Here, the majority does not address whether BSEE satisfied NEPA and the ESA through tiered environmental review. Rather, the majority rules that oil spill response plan approval is exempt from the ESA and NEPA altogether.

It is true that BSEE reviewed Shell's oil spill response plans only after other higher-level planning activities, including preparing an EIS for each of its five-year leasing programs and preparing a biological opinion evaluating the likelihood that drilling will jeopardize species protected by the ESA. *See, e.g.*, NMFS, Beaufort and Chukchi Seas Biological Opinion, http://goo.gl/YECHFu. But an oil spill response plan may raise significant environmental risks beyond those analyzed at a granular level at a previous stage of development. For example, alternative means of containing an oil spill, such as the controversial use of dispersants, may themselves significantly impact listed species, other environmental resources, and the safety of first responders and the public to varying degrees. Review of these risks and of alternative response actions would not be redundant or duplicative if they were not considered in a previous EIS and biological opinion. Indeed, the higher planning levels govern the whole gamut of offshore drilling operations. Oil spill response plans—while nominally a "lower," implementation-level action—are the first component to be deployed when a spill actually happens. It [—18—] is ill-advised for the court to accept, under the guise of *Chevron*, BSEE's refusal to complete NEPA and ESA review of these plans, especially since these plans may not be as effective in redressing spills and preserving the environment as they could be with environmental review of alternatives and input from federal wildlife agencies.

I also emphasize this case's importance notwithstanding Shell's recent suspension of its Arctic drilling program. Although the program is on hold, and the administration has recently canceled existing Arctic lease sales, oil markets are cyclical and it is all but certain that higher future oil prices, a warming Arctic, or both will once again make drilling in the Arctic cost-effective. The Department of the Interior's latest five-year drilling plan still includes offshore lease sales in Alaska. Whenever Shell begins its Arctic drilling permitting process again, BSEE will give Shell's oil spill response plans the same cursory review it did here. If this case is not corrected by Supreme Court review, it will have two severe consequences. First, it will preclude judicial review of oil spill response plans when Shell's Arctic drilling plans resume. In light of BSEE's obvious reluctance to give the term "maximum extent practicable" its natural meaning in 33 U.S.C. §§ 1321(j)(5)(A)(i) & (j)(5)(D)(iii), it is undeniable that Shell's oil spill response plans will not be as responsive to the needs of endangered and threatened species as they would be with ESA consultation. And it is all but certain that BSEE's review of the response plans—the first line of defense in the event of a major oil spill—will be far more cursory than it would be if the public process, review of foreseeable impacts, and consideration of alternatives necessary under NEPA were provided. [—19—]

Second, and equally important, our court now has chosen to accept an agency's own opinion about the scope of its discretion in order to make this case fit into the narrow exceptions of *Home Builders* and *Public Citizen*. By ignoring our proper role in this litigation, we have enabled BSEE's abrogation of its oversight role over response plan approval, and we have invited other federal agencies to do the same any time a statutory duty could arguably be cast as "mandatory" or "nondiscretionary." The message we send to agencies, and to oil companies, is "we trust you and will rely on your judgment without review by federal agency experts and public input." This is not the role envisioned by Congress when it passed the 1990 CWA amendments, which require an oil spill response plan to demonstrate its ability to respond, "to the maximum extent practicable, to a worst case discharge," or when it passed the ESA, which requires "[e]ach Federal agency" to consult with federal wildlife agencies to "insure that any action authorized, funded, or carried out by such agency" is not likely to jeopardize protected species or adversely modify their critical habitat. 33 U.S.C. § 1321(j)(5)(A)(i); 16 U.S.C. § 1536(a)(2). It is not the role envisioned by NEPA, which mandated that "all agencies" shall utilize a "systematic, interdisciplinary approach" in planning and decision making, and shall prepare an EIS for all major federal actions significantly affecting the human environment, which include "any irreversible and irretrievable commitments of resources which would be involved in the proposed action should it be implemented." 42 U.S.C. § 4332. It is not the role for the courts *Chevron* envisioned by approving deference to an agency's "permissible construction of the statute" only in response to statutory ambiguity. *Chevron*, 467 U.S. at 843. [—20—]

Although this case deals with a complicated regulatory framework, at bottom it turns on simple answers to simple questions: If an oil company submits an oil spill response plan to BSEE, does the federal government have discretion to consider alternative response actions in order to ensure that any approved plan responds to a worst case spill to the maximum extent practicable? Could alternative methods of responding to a spill themselves have varying impacts on listed species that now thrive in the Beaufort and Chukchi Seas, such as the bowhead whale, the humpback whale, the bearded seal, and the Steller sea lion, as well as other aspects of the human environment? *See* BOEM Biological Opinion, Lease Sale 193, http://goo.gl/YECHFu. If such dangers and alternative courses of action are present, is it the aim of Congress to have the agency that oversees drilling perform public environmental review of the proposed plan and consult with federal agencies that oversee listed species? If Congress has required that an oil spill response plan must respond to the spill to the maximum extent practicable, will that not require a discretionary judgment of the regulating agency, here the Bureau of Safety and Environmental Enforcement? The answers to these questions are "yes." Only if BSEE scrutinizes whether an oil spill response plan gives protection to the maximum extent practicable will our treasured public trust resources be protected to the maximum extent practicable.

By not correcting the majority's holding through en banc review, we have let stand a decision that misapplies core principles of administrative and environmental law, and have set a dangerous precedent of deferring to a federal agency's view of its own discretion, even when a statute is not ambiguous. I respectfully dissent.

United States Court of Appeals
for the Ninth Circuit

No. 13-70613

SHIRROD
vs.
DIRECTOR, OFFICE OF WORKERS' COMPENSATION
PROGRAMS

On Petition for Review of a Decision and Order of the
Benefits Review Board

Decided: December 31, 2015

Citation: 809 F.3d 1082, 3 Adm. R. 620 (9th Cir. 2015).

Before **TASHIMA** and **BEA**, Circuit Judges, and
BURNS, * District Judge.

* The Honorable Larry A. Burns, District Judge for the U.S. District Court for the Southern District of California, sitting by designation.

[—3—] BEA, Circuit Judge:

ichard Shirrod was awarded benefits under the Longshore and Harbor Workers' Compensation Act ("Longshore Act") for injuries he sustained while working on a barge-refitting project for Respondent Pacific Rim Environmental Resources, LLC ("Pacific Rim").[1] During the workers'-compensation proceedings, an administrative law judge ("ALJ") awarded Shirrod $33,581.17 in attorney's fees for work Shirrod's attorney, Charles Robinowitz, performed before the ALJ, as is authorized under a fee-shifting provision of the Longshore Act. *See* 33 U.S.C. § 928(a). The Benefits Review Board ("BRB") affirmed the ALJ's fee award. The [—4—] fee award is based on an hourly rate for Robinowitz's services of $340 per hour. Shirrod contends the formula on which this $340-per-hour rate is based is flawed. We agree. We grant Shirrod's petition for review, vacate the BRB's decision and order, and remand this case for further proceedings.

I

Shirrod sustained permanent injuries to his knee and ankle during the course of his employment with Pacific Rim. Shirrod was working in Oregon on a project to refit two rail cars and a barge to carry solid waste from ocean-going barges to waste dumps. Shirrod filed a claim for workers'-compensation benefits under the Longshore Act, and it is undisputed that he is entitled to such benefits. Shirrod's case was overseen by ALJ Steven Berlin.

The Longshore Act permits a claimant to recover attorney's fees in some circumstances and, in this case, Shirrod requested attorney's fees for work Robinowitz performed before Judge Berlin, mostly during 2010. The fee request totaled $38,786.17, including 86.75 hours for Robinowitz's services at $400 per hour, 8.25 hours of legal-assistant services at $150 per hour, and $2,848.67 in costs. Shirrod submitted several affidavits and legal-industry fee surveys to support the proposed $400-per-hour rate for Robinowitz's services, including the Oregon State Bar's 2007 Economic Survey ("Bar Survey"), which provides billing rates for legal services in several Oregon markets. Robinowitz has been a lawyer in private practice in Portland, Oregon, since 1969. [—5—]

Judge Berlin approved an attorney's-fee award of $33,581.17; he reduced the rate for Robinowitz's services to $340 per hour but approved Shirrod's fee request in all other respects. In determining the proper rate for Robinowitz's services, Judge Berlin primarily relied on the analysis developed by ALJs in two earlier Longshore Act cases in which Robinowitz served as counsel: *DiBartolomeo v. Fred Wahl Marine Constr.*, ALJ No. 2008-LHC-01249 (Dep't of Labor Oct. 26, 2009) (ALJ Gerald Etchingham), and *Castillo v. Sundial Marine Tug & Barge Works, Inc.*, ALJ No. 2010-LHC-00341 (Dep't of Labor Apr. 22, 2011) (ALJ Jennifer Gee).[2]

---

[1] We affirmed the amount of Shirrod's benefits under the Longshore Act in a separate appeal. *See Shirrod v. Pac. Rim Envt'l Res., LLC*, No. 14-73291, __ F. App'x __, 2015 WL 6468110 (9th Cir. Oct. 27, 2015).

[2] *DiBartolomeo* was affirmed by the BRB, *DiBartolomeo v. Fred Wahl Marine Constr.*, No. 10-0257, 2010 WL 3514186, at *6 (Ben. Rev. Bd. Aug. 30, 2010), and *Castillo* was vacated by the BRB on grounds not relevant to this appeal, *Castillo v.*

The claimants in this case, *DiBartolomeo*, and *Castillo* submitted similar affidavits and legal-industry fee surveys to support the hourly rate requested for Robinowitz's services. In each case, the presiding ALJ rejected that evidence as not probative of the market rates for Longshore Act litigation and instead found it necessary to develop a proxy market rate. Both Judge Gee in *Castillo* and Judge Berlin in this case relied on the $316.42-per-hour rate Judge Etchingham calculated in *DiBartolomeo* as a proxy market rate.

In *DiBartolomeo*, Judge Etchingham "estimat[ed] the value of Mr. Robinowitz's services in the Portland market" using data from the 2007 Survey of Law Firm Economics by Altman Weil Publications ("Altman Weil Survey"). He [—6—] determined that Robinowitz's credentials and performance merited a rate in the 75th percentile. As a result, Judge Etchingham averaged the 75th-percentile hourly billing rates for lawyers practicing in areas he found relevant to Longshore Act litigation—employment law ($365), maritime law ($320), personal-injury law ($335), and workers'-compensation law ($200)—and Oregon lawyers with over 30 years of experience ($325). He thus calculated a proxy market rate of $309 per hour for Robinowitz's services, which he increased to $316.42 to account for inflation.

Judge Etchingham disavowed any reliance on the Bar Survey, even though the Bar Survey includes more detail about billing rates in various Oregon markets, including Portland. Judge Etchingham determined that the Altman Weil Survey was a better source of data because it is published every year and provides billing rates for lawyers practicing employment law and maritime law, whereas the Bar Survey is published every four to five years and does not include separate rates for those practice areas.

Judge Berlin agreed with Judge Etchingham's approach in *DiBartolomeo* and adopted the $316.42-per-hour proxy market

---

Sundial Marine Tug & Barge Works, Inc., No. 11-0400, 2012 WL 894005, at *3–*4 (Ben. Rev. Bd. Feb. 23, 2012).

rate Judge Etchingham calculated for Robinowitz's services. Judge Berlin then increased this rate to $320 to account for inflation and to $340 to acknowledge Robinowitz's recent accomplishments. He thus approved a fee award totaling $33,581.17. The BRB affirmed this fee award.

II

We have jurisdiction to review final orders of the BRB. 33 U.S.C. § 921(c). The BRB's decisions are subject to the [—7—] provisions of the Administrative Procedure Act. *See Haw. Stevedores, Inc. v. Ogawa*, 608 F.3d 642, 648 (9th Cir. 2010). Thus, we must set aside decisions of the BRB that are "arbitrary, capricious, an abuse of discretion, or otherwise not in accordance with law." 5 U.S.C. § 706(2)(A). The BRB must accept an ALJ's factual findings unless they are contrary to law, irrational, or not supported by substantial evidence. *Van Skike v. Dir., OWCP*, 557 F.3d 1041, 1045–46 (9th Cir. 2009). We independently evaluate the evidence in the administrative record to ensure the BRB adhered to the correct standard of review. *See id.*; *Bumble Bee Seafoods v. Dir., OWCP*, 629 F.2d 1327, 1329 (9th Cir. 1980).

III

If an employer or insurance carrier denies liability for a Longshore Act claim, it must pay a "reasonable attorney's fee" to the claimant if the claimant successfully prosecutes his claim with the aid of an attorney. 33 U.S.C. § 928(a). A successful claimant may collect attorney's fees for work his attorney performed before ALJs, the BRB, and District Directors in the Office of Workers' Compensation Programs. *Id.*; 20 C.F.R. §§ 702.132, 802.203.

The term "reasonable attorney's fee" has evolved toward a uniform definition in all federal fee-shifting statutes, including the Longshore Act. *See Christensen v. Stevedoring Servs. of Am.*, 557 F.3d 1049, 1052 (9th Cir. 2009). The lodestar method, which requires multiplying a reasonable hourly rate by the number of hours reasonably expended on the case, is the starting point for the calculation of attorney's fees. *Id.* at 1053 & n.4. The goal of the lodestar method is to "produce[] an award that roughly approximates the fee that the prevailing attorney would have received if he or she had [—8—] been representing a paying client who was billed by the hour in a comparable case." *Perdue v. Kenny A. ex rel. Winn*, 559 U.S. 542, 550–51 (2010) (emphasis omitted). As such, an attorney's hourly rate is to be calculated "according to the prevailing market rates in the relevant community" and should be "in line with [the rates] prevailing in the community for similar services by lawyers of reasonably comparable skill, experience and reputation." *Christensen*, 557 F.3d at 1053 (quoting *Blum v. Stenson*, 465 U.S. 886, 895–96 (1984)).

Determining the prevailing market rate for claimants' attorneys in Longshore Act cases has proven difficult, as the Longshore Act prohibits claimants from negotiating fees with their attorneys. *See* 33 U.S.C. § 928(e); *Christensen*, 557 F.3d at 1053; 20 C.F.R. §§ 702.132(a), 802.203(f). We have held that fees in Longshore Act cases should be "commensurate with those which [claimants' attorneys] could obtain by taking other types of cases." *Christensen*, 557 F.3d at 1053 (quoting *Camacho v. Bridgeport Fin., Inc.*, 523 F.3d 973, 981 (9th Cir. 2008)). Prior to our decisions in *Christensen* and *Van Skike*, Longshore Act fee awards were typically based on fee awards from earlier Longshore Act cases. *Id.* at 1054; *accord Van Skike*, 557 F.3d at 1046–47. In *Christensen*, we found that self-referential approach improper, because it did not look to rates in an independently operating market and, hence, did not produce "market" rates, as is required by the Supreme Court's decision in *Blum v. Stenson*. *See* 557 F.3d at 1054–55. As such, we held that, in Longshore Act cases, the "relevant community" must be defined "more broadly than simply fee awards under the [Longshore Act]." *Id.*; *accord Van Skike*, 557 F.3d at 1046–47. Recognizing that the relevant decisionmaker has wide—but not unlimited—discretion when making attorney's-fee awards, *see Kenny A.*, [—9—] 559 U.S. at 558, we ultimately left it to the BRB, ALJs, and District Directors to determine the "relevant community" and the

prevailing market rates in that community, as long as the decisionmaker provides adequate justification. *Christensen*, 557 F.3d at 1055.

A. The "relevant community"

Our review of the fee award must begin by investigating just what was the "relevant community" that Judge Berlin used when he awarded fees for Robinowitz's services. Judge Berlin left the "relevant community" undefined but used language suggesting that the "relevant community" was either the state of Oregon or the city of Portland.[3] The BRB, in its review of the fee award, also made no express mention of the "relevant community." However, which is the "relevant community" need not necessarily be decided anew in each decision awarding fees. *See Christensen*, 557 F.3d at 1055. We take the "relevant community" here to be Portland, Oregon, the "relevant community" determined by the ALJs in the two prior cases on which Judge Berlin relied. *See DiBartolomeo*, ALJ No. 2008-LHC-01249, slip op. at 7 ("[T]his Court is left with the task of estimating the value of Mr. Robinowitz's services in the Portland market."); *Castillo*, ALJ No. 2010-LHC-00341, slip op. at 3 ("I find that the [—10—] 'relevant community' for Mr. Rabinowitz [sic] is the city of Portland.").[4]

---

[3] For instance, Judge Berlin stated that "the present record contains no evidence that attorneys in Oregon are increasing billing rates" and compared Robinowitz to "Oregon trial lawyers," but also applied a Portland-specific inflation adjustment to the proxy market rate he adopted.

[4] Echoing the BRB's decision affirming the ALJ's fee award in *DiBartolomeo*, Pacific Rim contends that Judge Berlin had the discretion to treat the state of Oregon or the city of Portland as the "relevant community." *See DiBartolomeo*, 2010 WL 3514186, at *4 ("[T]he appropriate community in this case could reasonably be found to be the state of Oregon, the greater Portland metropolitan area, or the city of Portland."). Even if this is so, we review only what Judge Berlin and the BRB did, not what they could have done. *See SEC v. Chenery Corp.*, 318 U.S. 80, 93–94 (1943). Because Judge Berlin adopted the analyses in *DiBartolomeo* and *Castillo*, we assume he also adopted the "relevant community" from those cases. If Judge Berlin sought to deviate from those decisions on that point, he should have done so expressly and provided justification sufficient to enable

We also agree with Shirrod that Portland is the right "relevant community" in this case. In civil litigation, we typically recognize the forum where the district court sits as the "relevant community" for purposes of fee-shifting statutes. *Christensen*, 557 F.3d at 1053; *Barjon v. Dalton*, 132 F.3d 496, 500 (9th Cir. 1997). By analogy, a determination of the "relevant community" in Longshore Act cases should focus on the location where the litigation took place. But, because district courts are not involved in cases under the Longshore Act, we must look to other indicia to determine where the litigation took place and, thus, which is the "relevant community." Here, all factors point to Portland as the location of the litigation: Counsel to Shirrod and Pacific Rim maintain their offices in Portland; hearings before Judge Berlin occurred in Portland. *Cf. Newport News Shipbuilding & Dry Dock Co. v. Holiday*, 591 F.3d 219, 229 [—11—] (4th Cir. 2009) (noting that the "relevant community" should "turn[] on inquiries about the lawyer and client"); 20 C.F.R. § 802.203(d)(4) ("The rate awarded by the [BRB] shall be based on what is reasonable and customary in the area where the services were rendered for a person of that particular professional status.").[5]

B. Applicability of the proxy market rate to the Portland market

We next examine whether the proxy market rate developed by Judge Etchingham in *DiBartolomeo* and relied upon by Judge Berlin in this case adequately reflects market rates for Portland, Oregon, the "relevant community." We conclude that it does not because it is based entirely on data not tailored to Portland, even though reliable information about attorney billing rates in Portland was readily available.

The proxy market rate adopted by Judge Berlin is based on five constituent rates from the Altman Weil Survey: the 75th-percentile rates for lawyers practicing employment, maritime, personal-injury, and workers'-compensation law, and the 75th-percentile rate for Oregon lawyers with over 30 years of experience. *See DiBartolomeo*, ALJ No. 2008-LHC-01249, slip op. at 7–8. The constituent rates do not relate specifically to Portland, Oregon, the "relevant community"; [—12—] one of the rates is expressly geographically limited—but encompasses the entire state of Oregon—and, although it is not entirely clear from the record, the practice-area rates appear to be national in scope. *See id*. We hold that it was error for Judge Berlin to apply a rate bearing no direct nexus to the "relevant community." *See Camacho*, 523 F.3d at 979 (vacating an attorney's-fee award because the market rate was based "almost exclusively" on data for judicial districts other than the Northern District of California, the "relevant community").

To be sure, if the "relevant community" were defined differently,[6] or if reliable data on attorney's fees in the "relevant community" did not exist, using the proxy market rate—or the constituent rates on which it depends—

---

meaningful review by the BRB and by us. *See Christensen*, 557 F.3d at 1055; *Finnegan v. Dir., OWCP*, 69 F.3d 1039, 1041 (9th Cir. 1995); *cf. FCC v. Fox Television Stations, Inc.*, 556 U.S. 502, 514–15 (2009).

[5] We acknowledge that the "relevant community" may depend on the facts of specific cases, and we decline to construct a bright-line rule. Instead, we leave it to the BRB, ALJs, and District Directors to determine the "relevant community" in individual cases, as long as the decision is adequately justified and supported by substantial evidence. *See Christensen*, 557 F.3d at 1055. To facilitate meaningful review, we urge these decisionmakers to make their findings regarding the "relevant community" explicit. *Cf. Camacho*, 523 F.3d at 979.

[6] The Seventh Circuit has suggested that the "relevant community" could be national in scope. *See Jeffboat, LLC v. Dir., OWCP*, 553 F.3d 487, 490 (7th Cir. 2009) ("Jeffboat takes the word 'community' to mean 'local market area.' It would be just as consistent, however, to read the word as referring to a community of practitioners; particularly when, as is arguably the case here, the subject matter of the litigation is one where the attorneys practicing it are highly specialized and the market for legal services in that area is a national market."). As stated previously, we leave it to the BRB, ALJs, and District Directors to determine the "relevant community" in the first instance but note that we have not adopted this position and *Jeffboat* has not been widely followed with respect to this point.

could be permissible. *Cf. id.* (suggesting the market rate may be based on rates for communities "comparable to" the "relevant community"). Here, however, the Bar Survey does provide attorney's-fee information specific to the "relevant [—13—] community" of Portland, Oregon.[7] Although Judge Etchingham in *DiBartolomeo* gave two reasons for favoring the Altman Weil Survey over the Bar Survey—which Judge Berlin implicitly adopted in this case—we find those reasons unconvincing.

First, Judge Etchingham stated that the Altman Weil Survey is a better source of information because it is published every year, whereas the Bar Survey is published only every four to five years. *DiBartolomeo*, ALJ No. 2008-LHC-01249, slip op. at 7 n.2. But if Judge Etchingham—and other ALJs relying on his analysis and methodology—preferred the Altman Weil Survey because it is published annually, we would expect them to calculate proxy market rates for each year using the data published for that year. However, to determine proxy market rates for years after 2007, Judge Etchingham in *DiBartolomeo*, Judge Gee in *Castillo*, and Judge Berlin in this case merely adjusted the proxy market rate calculated from the 2007 Altman Weil Survey using inflation data. *See id.* at 8; *Castillo*, ALJ No. 2010-LHC-00341, slip op. at 11–12 & n.10. We see no reason why the ALJs could not have made the same inflation adjustments to the figures in the Bar Survey.

Second, Judge Etchingham stated that he relied on the Altman Weil Survey because it includes billing rates for attorneys practicing employment law and maritime law, [—14—] which the Bar Survey lacks. *DiBartolomeo*, ALJ No. 2008-LHC-01249, slip op. at 7 n.2. Judge Etchingham did not explain why he disregarded the data for the practice areas—

personal-injury law and workers'-compensation law—that the surveys have in common and for which the Bar Survey contains data specific to the Portland market. Relatedly, Judge Etchingham did not explain why the Altman Weil Survey's billing rate for Oregon attorneys with over 30 years of experience was superior to the Bar Survey's billing rate for Portland attorneys with the same amount of experience. *See id.* Nor did Judge Etchingham attempt to harmonize the data in the two surveys in any other way. *Cf., e.g.*, *Ramsey v. Cascade Gen., Inc.*, No. 11-0875, 2012 WL 3903607, at *2–*4 (Ben. Rev. Bd. Aug. 29, 2012) (affirming an attorney's-fee award that was "based on averages of the rates in the Altman Weil Survey, the Oregon Bar Survey and the average hourly rate for all Portland attorneys with 21–30 years of experience, regardless of practice area").

Because the lodestar method requires a "reasonable attorney's fee" to be based on market rates in the "relevant community," we hold that the BRB erred in affirming an attorney's-fee award based on a proxy market rate not tailored to the "relevant community," which, in this case, Judge Berlin found to be Portland.

C. Use of billing rates for workers'-compensation practice

The proxy market rate applied by Judge Berlin depends in part on the 75th-percentile rate, from the Altman Weil Survey, for attorneys practicing workers'-compensation law. *See DiBartolomeo*, ALJ No. 2008-LHC-01249, slip op. at 7–8. Shirrod contends that it was error to include that rate, [—15—] because it is artificially low and does not represent a market rate. We agree.

The proxy market rate includes, among its constituent rates, a $200-per-hour rate reported by attorneys practicing workers'-compensation law, which is significantly lower than the other rates on which the proxy market rate depends.[8] *See id.* Judge

---

[7] We have no reason to doubt the reliability of the data in the Bar Survey, as it supplies the benchmark for attorney's-fee awards in the District of Oregon, *see* D. Or. Civ. R. 54-3(a), and the BRB and ALJs have relied on it in the past, *see, e.g.*, *Christensen v. Stevedoring Servs. of Am.*, 43 Ben. Rev. Bd. Serv. (MB) 145, 146 (2009); *see also Castillo*, 2012 WL 894005, at *3–*4.

[8] By our calculation, the proxy market rate would have been higher by nearly $30 per hour if the rate for workers'-compensation lawyers had been excluded.

Etchingham included that rate as part of the proxy market rate he calculated in *DiBartolomeo* because he found that workers'-compensation law "employ[s] legal skills similar to those required by Longshore practice," *id.* at 7, and the BRB affirmed, *see DiBartolomeo v. Fred Wahl Marine Constr.*, No. 10-0257, 2010 WL 3514186, at *5 (Ben. Rev. Bd. Aug. 30, 2010). Judge Berlin in this case agreed with Judge Etchingham that "Oregon state workers' compensation fees are analogous and relevant to a determination of the billing rate applicable to trial-level work" in Longshore Act cases, and the BRB affirmed this decision, giving scant discussion to the use of rates reported by workers'-compensation lawyers.

Yet, the BRB previously recognized that billing rates reported by workers'-compensation lawyers do not necessarily represent market rates that are usable in a lodestar calculation. In *Christensen*, we vacated the BRB's decision awarding fees for work Robinowitz performed before it because the fee award was not based on market rates. *See* 557 F.3d at 1052–55. On remand from us, the BRB initially calculated a proxy market rate "by reference to an average of the rates for workers' compensation, plaintiff personal injury [—16—] civil litigation, and plaintiff general civil litigation cases." *Christensen v. Stevedoring Servs. of Am.*, 43 Ben. Rev. Bd. Serv. (MB) 145, 146–47 (2009). However, the BRB reconsidered this decision, excluded the workers'-compensation rate, and recalculated the fee award based only on the average of the other two rates. *Christensen v. Stevedoring Servs. of Am.*, 44 Ben. Rev. Bd. Serv. (MB) 39, 40 (2010). It did so because it found the reported workers'-compensation rate to be artificially low and thus not reflective of market rates: Fees paid to claimants' attorneys are typically capped by state law and often paid out of the compensation award, whereas insurers and employers are able to negotiate discounts with attorneys who defend against workers'-compensation claims because they supply a steady stream of work. *Id.* In response to the employer's request for reconsideration of this decision, the BRB added that "[f]ees awarded by state administrative law judges are not necessarily

based on market considerations, just as rates set by administrative law judges in longshore cases have been held to be non-market-based rates." *See Christensen v. Stevedoring Servs. of Am.*, 44 Ben. Rev. Bd. Serv. (MB) 75, 75 (2010) (citing *Christensen*, 557 F.3d 1049; *Van Skike*, 557 F.3d 1041), *aff'd sub nom. Stevedoring Servs. of Am. v. Dir., OWCP*, 445 F. App'x 912 (9th Cir. 2011).

Although Judge Berlin did not mention the BRB's decision on reconsideration in *Christensen* by name, he gave two reasons why it would not apply to this case. *First*, Judge Berlin noted that BRB decisions regarding attorney's fees for appellate work performed before the BRB—such as *Christensen*—are "less instructive" than BRB decisions reviewing attorney's-fee orders for trial-level work performed before ALJs—such as the BRB's decision affirming Judge Etchingham's attorney's-fee award in *DiBartolomeo*. We see [—17—] nothing in the BRB's *Christensen* decision that would detract from its applicability to attorney's-fee orders for trial-level work. We do not dispute that the skills involved in resolving state workers'-compensation claims are similar to those involved in litigating Longshore Act cases and may be more relevant to trial-level work than appellate work. *See, e.g., DiBartolomeo*, 2010 WL 3514186, at *5. But, in *Christensen*, the BRB excluded rates reported by workers'-compensation lawyers not because workers'-compensation practice was irrelevant, but because structural factors caused workers'-compensation lawyers to report unusually low—and non-market—hourly rates. *See* 44 Ben. Rev. Bd. Serv. (MB) at 40. If reported rates for workers'-compensation practice do not reflect *market* rates in the "relevant community," they cannot be used in a lodestar calculation, no matter how similar the skills involved are. *See Christensen*, 557 F.3d at 1054–55 (rejecting reliance on the hourly rates awarded to attorneys in previous Longshore Act cases); *accord Van Skike*, 557 F.3d at 1046–47.

Second, and relatedly, Judge Berlin called the cap on fees for claimants' attorneys in Oregon workers'-compensation cases an "open market factor" and suggested that rates reported by workers'-compensation lawyers are market rates because workers'-compensation attorneys "freely choose to represent injured workers in cases very similar to [Longshore Act cases], and they do so knowing of the cap." But this reasoning contradicts the BRB's decision in *Christensen*; there, the BRB found rates reported by Oregon workers'-compensation attorneys not representative of market rates in part because the total fee paid to claimants' attorneys is capped by statute. *See* 44 Ben. Rev. Bd. Serv. (MB) at 40; *see* [—18—] *also, e.g.,* Or. Rev. Stat. § 656.308(2)(d).[9] We share the BRB's skepticism that billing rates reported under such a regime reflect rates that are "sufficient to induce a capable attorney to undertake the representation," *Kenny A.,* 559 U.S. at 552, because the fee cap may reduce *reported* hourly rates below *expected* hourly rates.

For example, suppose that an Oregon workers'-compensation attorney reasonably expects to earn $400 per hour and spend 10 hours on a case. He then spends 15 hours on the case—for a total expected fee of $6,000—but his fee is capped by statute at $4,500. Because of the fee cap, the attorney's average hourly rate for the case is $300, or $100 lower than the hourly rate he expected when he accepted the client. Notwithstanding the operation of the fee cap in that case, the attorney would still expect to receive $400 per hour in his *next* case. If, in the next case, the attorney spends only 10 hours, basing his fee on the $300-per-hour rate earned in the first case would undercompensate him, as that rate represents a blend of full compensation for some time and no compensation for other time. The lodestar method already requires the relevant decisionmaker to award

attorney's fees only for the number of hours reasonably expended on the litigation—and to award no compensation for any unreasonably spent time. *See, e.g., Blum,* 465 U.S. at 888. Using a billing rate that is depressed because it assumes that [—19—] counsel will not be fully compensated would doubly reduce the attorney's-fee award. *See Kenny A.,* 559 U.S. at 546 (noting that the lodestar method includes the factors relevant to determining a "reasonable attorney's fee" and adjustments to the lodestar calculation may not be made "based on a factor that is subsumed in the lodestar calculation"); *see also City of Burlington v. Dague,* 505 U.S. 557, 560–67 (1992) (rejecting as impermissible double-counting a lodestar enhancement that accounts for the risk the attorney will not collect a contingent fee).

We recognize that we are not in a position to evaluate whether the billing rate for workers'-compensation practice included in the proxy market rate in fact suffers from the flaw we described or the other defects adverted to by the BRB in *Christensen*. To the extent that it does not, and if it otherwise reflects market rates in the "relevant community," the BRB, ALJs, and District Directors may be able to use it. But the BRB's published *Christensen* decision has precedential value, *see Price v. Stevedoring Servs. of Am.,* 697 F.3d 820, 827 (9th Cir. 2012) ("In practice as well as theory, it is the BRB's published decisions . . . that are precedential and determine the rights of future parties."), and it provides good reasons to doubt that the rate for workers'-compensation practice is a market rate for Longshore Act claimants' work. As far as we can tell, the BRB has not repudiated its *Christensen* decision, and it did not distinguish *Christensen* or justify a departure from *Christensen* in this case. We thus find that the BRB acted arbitrarily in allowing partial reliance on a rate reported by workers'-compensation lawyers that, according to the BRB's own decisions, is not a market rate for claimant Longshore Act representation. *See Christensen,* 557 F.3d at 1054–55; *Camacho,* 523 F.3d at 979; *see also Andia v. Ashcroft,* 359 F.3d 1181, 1184 (9th Cir. 2004) ("The [Board [—20—] of

---

[9] As mentioned previously, the practice-area rates identified by Judge Etchingham in *DiBartolomeo* and adopted by Judge Berlin in this case, which come from the Altman Weil Survey, appear to be national in scope, not Oregon-specific. Nonetheless, we offer our view on Judge Berlin's reasoning because he assumed the workers'-compensation rate from *DiBartolomeo* reflected the rate paid to claimants' attorneys in Oregon, and caps on fees for claimants' attorneys seem to be commonplace nationwide. *Cf., e.g., Ramsey,* 2012 WL 3903607, at *3 & n.3.

Immigration Appeals] acts 'arbitrarily' and 'contrary to law' if it fails to apply and follow its own prior decisions.").

IV

For the reasons discussed, we hold that the BRB erred in affirming Judge Berlin's award of attorney's fees for work performed by Robinowitz because the proxy market rate on which the award depends does not adequately represent market rates in the "relevant community," here, Portland, Oregon. We grant Shirrod's petition for review, vacate the BRB's decision and order, and remand this case for further proceedings.

PETITION FOR REVIEW GRANTED; VACATED and REMANDED.

This page intentionally left blank

United States Court of Appeals for the Tenth Circuit

United States Court of Appeals
for the Tenth Circuit

No. 13-7060

UNITED STATES
vs.
JANTRAN, INC.

Appeal from the United States District Court for the
Eastern District of Oklahoma

Decided: April 9, 2015

Citation: 782 F.3d 1177, 3 Adm. R. 630 (10th Cir. 2015).

Before TYMKOVICH, EBEL, and PHILLIPS, Circuit Judges.

[—1—] TYMKOVICH, Circuit Judge:

The Miss Dixie is a cargo line boat operated by Jantran, a company involved in maritime transportation on the Verdigris River in Oklahoma. While [—2—] operating on the river, the Miss Dixie struck and extensively damaged a lock maintained by the Army Corps of Engineers. After repairing the lock, the Corps sued Jantran for the costs of repair.

One would think such a suit would be a routine matter, but because of the federal maritime legal regime at play, we are required to revisit basic principles of civil procedure involving *in personam* and *in rem* jurisdiction. For purposes of this case, if federal law allows an *in personam* action against Jantran as ship owner and operator, the company will be personally liable for all of the Corps's damages in repairing the lock. But if federal law only allows an *in rem* action against the damage-causing vessel, the Corps would be limited to seeking damages capped at the value of the Miss Dixie.

The district court dismissed the Corps's suit, concluding that federal law does not allow the Corps to seek *in personam* damages directly from the owners of a vessel that damages a structure on navigable waters. As the court found, the applicable statute, the Rivers and Harbors Act, 33 U.S.C. §§ 401–27, only allows *in rem* claims against the vessel that caused the damage—here the Miss Dixie.

We agree with the district court that the Act does not authorize *in personam* actions against the owners of the vessel. The Act only allows the Corps to proceed *in rem* against the vessel itself. We therefore AFFIRM. [—3—]

I. Analysis

While carrying cargo, the Miss Dixie lost power, struck, and damaged a lock operated by the Army Corps of Engineers. The United States then commenced in district court an *in personam* civil action against Jantran under § 408 of the Rivers and Harbors Act.

The Rivers and Harbors Act was enacted in 1899, and in large part is designed to establish a national legal framework that would help regulate harm to the nation's waterways. *Wyandotte Transportation Co. v. United States*, 389 U.S. 191, 201 (1967). To this end, the Act prohibits conduct that might damage or obstruct river structures like dams, locks, or levees. In particular, § 408 makes it unlawful for any person to damage a federal water-control structure, stating that:

> It shall not be lawful for any person or persons to . . . alter, deface, destroy, move, injure, obstruct by fastening vessels thereto or otherwise, or in any manner whatever impair the usefulness of any seawall, bulkhead, jetty, dike, levy, wharf, pier or other work built by the United States, in whole or in part, for the preservation and improvement of any of its navigable waters or to prevent floods . . . .

33 U.S.C. § 408. A related provision, § 409, establishes that it "shall not be lawful . . . to sink, or permit or cause to be sunk, vessels or other craft in navigable channels." *Id.* § 409. Section 409 further provides that, in the event of a violation, "it *shall be the duty* of the owner, lessee, or operator of such sunken craft to commence the immediate removal of the same, and prosecute such removal diligently." *Id.* (emphasis added). [—4—]

Nothing in the Rivers and Harbors Act, however, expressly authorizes the government to bring an action against a ship owner or operator to enforce these provisions. Rather, the Act provides two kinds of remedies for violations of § 408. First, § 411 authorizes criminal fines and penalties for "[e]very person and every corporation that shall violate, or that shall knowingly aid, abet, authorize, or instigate a violation of the provisions of sections 407, 408, 409, 414, and 415."[1] *Id.* § 411.

Second, § 412 provides that the government may proceed *in rem* against any vessel used to violate the Rivers and Harbors Act:

[A]ny boat, vessel, scow, raft, or other craft used or employed in violating any of the provisions of sections 407, 408, 409, 414, and 415 of this title shall be liable for the pecuniary penalties specified in section 411 of this title, and in addition thereto for the amount of the damages done by said boat, vessel, scow, raft, or other craft, which latter sum shall be placed to the credit of the appropriation for the improvement of the harbor or waterway in which the damage occurred, and said boat, vessel, scow, raft, or other craft may be proceeded against summarily by way of libel in any district court of the United States having jurisdiction thereof. [—5—]

Id. § 412. In sum, § 408 prohibits damaging or obstructing a federal water-control structure, while sections 411 and 412 provide criminal and civil *in rem* actions, respectively.

Nonetheless, the Corps argues that § 408 should be read to also authorize *in personam* actions. Although it concedes that the text of § 408 does not expressly establish an *in*

personam remedy, the Corps contends the Supreme Court has already construed the similarly worded § 409 as allowing precisely that type of relief. Section 409 of the Act states that, "It shall not be lawful to . . . sink or permit or cause to be sunk, vessels or other craft in navigable waters." *Id.* § 409. Despite the lack of any reference in the statute to *in personam* relief, the Supreme Court held in *Wyandotte* that § 409 impliedly authorizes a personal right of action against ship owners to further a purpose of full compensation for maritime damages. *See* 389 U.S. 191. The Corps argues that without an implied personal right of action, § 408, like § 409, is inadequate to fully compensate the United States for its losses. As a matter of consistency, the Corps contends § 408 must therefore contain an implied right to *in personam* relief for the same reasons.

We disagree, but our analysis first requires a brief detour through basic civil procedure. The differences between *in rem* and *in personam* actions have a number of practical consequences. First, in contrast to a traditional *in personam* [—6—] action where the defendant is typically a person or business,[2] the defendant in an *in rem* action under the Act is the vessel itself.[3] This follows from traditional maritime law, where a party injured by a maritime vessel automatically obtains a lien on that vessel at the time of the accident. 2 *Benedict on Admiralty* § 21 (7th ed. 1987) ("The principle is that one . . . who, through the instrumentality of the ship, has suffered a wrong that is within the maritime jurisdiction, shall have by way of security or redress, an enforceable interest in the ship."). Under maritime law, after the creation of the lien the injured party can then bring an *in rem* action against the vessel itself and foreclose its lien if successful in the action. *Id.* This process highlights the second unique feature of *in rem* actions: *in rem* recoveries are

---

[1] In larger part, "Every person and every corporation that shall violate, or that shall knowingly aid, abet, authorize, or instigate a violation of the provisions of sections 407, 408, 409, 414, and 415 of this title shall be guilty of a misdemeanor, and on conviction thereof shall be punished by a fine of up to $25,000 per day, or by imprisonment (in the case of a natural person) for not less than thirty days nor more than one year, or by both such fine and imprisonment . . . ." 33 U.S.C. § 411.

[2] "(Of a legal action) brought against a person rather than property." *Black's Law Dictionary* 862 (9th ed. 2009).

[3] "Involving or determining the status of a thing, and therefore the rights of persons generally with respect to that thing." *Black's Law Dictionary* 862 (9th ed. 2009).

necessarily limited to the value of the vessel itself.

Why would the statute express a preference for *in rem* actions? Although perhaps unusual for inland torts, the Act's apparent preference for *in rem* over *in personam* proceedings is in line with the principles and practices of maritime law. Maritime law has long recognized that "a ship is, of necessity, a wanderer," which "visits shores where her owners are neither known nor accessible." 2 *Benedict on Admiralty* § 21. Accidents happen, and with maritime vessels [—7—] accidents often happen far from home. Frequently the negligent party will be a ship captain of insufficient means to satisfy a judgment, and the responsible ship owner may be a foreign entity difficult to sue and unlikely to satisfy a judgment. Thus, maritime law historically recognized an aggrieved party might find his "best and surest pledge for . . . compensation and indemnity" in the ship itself and, as a result, traditional maritime law grants an injured party a lien in the vessel that caused his injury. *Id.* §§ 21–22. The injured party can then foreclose his lien and receive compensation by filing an *in rem* action against the ship itself. *Id.* § 21.[4]

In another case, our finding that § 408 expressly provides an *in rem* action might be the end of the story. But the Supreme Court complicated the analysis in *Wyandotte*.

Despite a lack of an express *in personam* remedy in the Rivers and Harbors Act, the Supreme Court found in *Wyandotte* that the Act impliedly authorizes injunctive relief and *in personam* damages actions for violations of §409. 389 U.S. at 200. There, the petitioners abandoned three vessels that had sunk on the Mississippi. Because two of those vessels were obstructing the waterway, while the third was at risk of leaking highly toxic chemicals into the [—8—] river, the United States sought an injunction requiring the owners of the first

two vessels to remove them and initiated the emergency removal of the third. *Id.* at 194–195. As part of its suit, the United States also sought reimbursement for the costs it incurred in removing the third vessel. *Id.* at 196.

Construing language in § 409 that imposed "a duty o[n] the owner, lessee, or operator of such sunken craft to commence the immediate removal of the same," 33 U.S.C. § 409, the Court found the statute created an implied right to injunctive relief, *Wyandotte*, 389 U.S. at 203–04. The Court observed that the purpose of the Act was to "prevent obstructions in the Nation's waterways" and the criminal and *in rem* remedies given in the Act were inadequate to effectuate this purpose. *Id.* at 201. Without an injunctive remedy the United States could not enforce the ship owners' "duty" to remove obstructions, and the costs of removal to the United States would have been significantly greater than the value of the offending ships. To deny injunctive relief would have allowed the ship owner to avoid his duty and thus "shift[] responsibility for the consequences of his negligence onto his victim" by forcing the United States itself to remove the ships. *Id.* at 204.

Finding the availability of injunctive relief to enforce a ship owner's duty to remove his wrecked vessel, the Court went on to hold that it was "but a small step from declaratory relief to a civil action for the Government's expenses incurred in removing a negligently sunk vessel." *Id.* at 204. The Court thus [—9—] found that § 409 also must impliedly authorize *in personam* actions because "[i]t would be surprising if Congress intended that . . . the Government's commendable performance of Wyandotte's duty must be at Government expense." *Id.* at 204–05.

Although sections 408 and 409 are different, the government nonetheless argues that because the language and purposes of the two provisions are similar, they should be interpreted to authorize similar remedies. The government points out that § 408, which, like § 409, begins by declaring that "It shall not be lawful" to engage in certain prohibited conduct (namely, damaging a federal water-

---

[4] This case presents a slight wrinkle since Jantran sold the Miss Dixie after the accident. But that fact is of no importance. Maritime liens "follow the ship into the hands of anyone in whose possession she may come, including an innocent purchaser." *Id.* § 22.

control structure). *See* 33 U.S.C. § 408. From this broad language, the government argues *Wyandotte*'s policy of full compensation controls and we should conclude that the criminal and *in rem* penalties provided for in the Rivers and Harbors Act are inadequate to compensate the United States for its losses.

The parties observe that *Wyandotte* has led to a split in the circuits over the proper interpretation of § 408. In a 1977 case, *Hines, Inc. v. United States*, 551 F.2d 717 (6th Cir. 1977), the Sixth Circuit allowed an *in personam* recovery against a ship owner under § 408. In that case, the government sought to recover for damage that occurred when two barges struck a federal dam, caught fire, and sank. At issue was whether the Limitation of Liability Act of 1851, which limits damages in maritime accidents to the value of the offending vessel, *see* 46 U.S.C. § 183, restricts the damages available under § 408. **[—10—]**

We do not find *Hines* persuasive. First, it is far from clear that the Sixth Circuit even addressed the question of whether § 408 authorizes *in personam* relief. Rather, the court seems to have assumed that such relief was available and instead focused on the conflict between the two statutes at issue. Second, even assuming that the Sixth Circuit did decide the question, its opinion contains limited textual analysis and thus is of limited persuasive value.

More recently, in *Barnacle Marine Management Inc. v. United States*, 233 F.3d 865, 870 (5th Cir. 2000), the Fifth Circuit addressed the very issue we face in this appeal. Relying on the plain language of the Act, the court found that §408 did not authorize *in personam* actions. *Id.* Specifically, the court found that the Supreme Court's decision in *Wyandotte* was not controlling, because "the *Wyandotte* Court expressly relied on language peculiar to § 409" that "create[s] a *duty* on the owner of the sunken vessel to remove it." *Id.* (emphasis added). The court explained that it was the unique, duty-creating language of § 409 that caused the Supreme Court to find that the section contained an implied right to injunctive relief, and that it was the right to

injunctive relief that justified finding an implied *in personam* action in § 409. *See id.* ("The Court stated that '[i]t is but a small step from declaratory relief to a civil action . . . .'" (quoting *Wyandotte*, 389 U.S. at 204)). Because § 408 does not, by its terms, create any duties, the Fifth Circuit found that *Wyandotte* was not applicable. *Id.* The Fifth Circuit also correctly observed that the Supreme Court has in recent years **[—11—]** avoided creating implied rights of action, concluding lower courts "should be reluctant to imply a remedy broader than Congress expressly provided." *Id.* (citing *Karahalios v. Nat'l Fed'n of Fed. Emps., Local 1263*, 489 U.S. 527, 532–33 (1989); *California v. Sierra Club*, 451 U.S. 287 (1981); *Touche Ross & Co. v. Redington*, 442 U.S. 560 (1979)).

We find this analysis persuasive. In our view, *Wyandotte* is best read as relying on the unique, duty-creating language of § 409. Section 409's creation of a duty to remove sunken vessels was of obvious relevance to the Court's finding that the government could obtain an order directing ship owners to remove those same sunken vessels and, as the Court stated, "[i]t is but a small step from declaratory relief to a civil action." *Wyandotte*, 389 U.S. at 204. The Court further highlighted the importance of § 409's duty-creating language to its *in personam* holding by noting that "[i]t would be surprising if Congress intended that . . . the Government's commendable performance of Wyandotte's *duty* must be at Government expense." *Id.* at 204–05 (emphasis added).

In response, the government argues that Congress did not intend for the lack of a statutory duty under § 408 to imply that it authorizes fewer remedies than does § 409. Rather, the absence of duty language in § 408 merely reflects the undesirability of having private parties repair government locks and dams. Although this may explain why § 408 does not contain an independent duty, this observation does not affect our analysis. The simple fact is that § 409 *does* **[—12—]** contain an explicit duty, and that duty was key to finding an implied right to injunctive relief in *Wyandotte*. Because § 408 contains no such duty, there is no textual hook from which to infer that Congress intended for § 408 to authorize *in personam* relief.

We also reject the government's contention that sections 408 and 409 should be read to authorize the same remedies simply because they both begin, "It shall be unlawful to . . . ." *See* 33 U.S.C. §§ 408, 409. Such a reading would require us to ignore the subsequent, relevant differences in the statutes and base our analysis on what is, essentially, a boilerplate introduction. As a result, we find that our analysis is not bound by the Supreme Court's decision in *Wyandotte* and rely on the text of the Rivers and Harbors Act.

The structure and text of the Act provide additional clues. The Act contains two remedy sections—sections 411 and 412—and one would not ordinarily expect a non-remedial section, such as § 408, to authorize broader remedies by implication than those already expressly provided. In fact, the Supreme Court has repeatedly observed that, "It is . . . an 'elemental canon' of statutory construction that where a statute expressly provides a remedy, courts must be especially reluctant to provide additional remedies. In such cases, in the absence of strong indicia of contrary congressional intent, we are compelled to conclude that Congress provided precisely the remedies it considered [—13—] appropriate." *Karahalios*, 489 U.S. at 532–33; *see also, e.g., Sierra Club*, 451 U.S. 287.

Despite this guidance, the government contends we should decline to apply the presumption against implied remedies in interpreting the Rivers and Harbors Act because the implied remedies would be in favor of the United States and not private parties.

We are not persuaded. First, the government has not advanced any argument explaining why we should favor inferring public remedies over private ones. Nonetheless, our analysis likely would not change even if the government had presented a clear policy argument for preferring public remedies. The proposition that courts ought to be reluctant to find implied remedies where an act expressly provides other remedies is, in

essence, a variation of the negative implication, or *expressio unius*, canon, which holds that "the expression of one thing implies the exclusion of others." Antonin Scalia & Bryan A. Garner, *Reading Law: The Interpretation of Legal Texts* 107 (2012). This canon is based on "how people express themselves and understand verbal expression." *Id.* It guides us to the most principled interpretation of the text itself—it is not merely a policy-based rule of thumb that can be set aside because of countervailing policy concerns. Given this, we reject the argument that the negative implication canon only applies when private remedies are at issue. *See also United States v. City of Philadelphia*, 644 F.2d 187, 191–92 (3d Cir. 1980) ("We reject the [—14—] argument that *Wyandotte* established a different standard for inferring rights of action in favor of the government than the standard applicable to private litigants.").

This conclusion, however, does not end our analysis. As noted above, the Supreme Court has held a court still may infer an omitted remedy when there are "strong indicia of contrary congressional intent." *See Karahalios*, 489 U.S. at 532–33. To this end, the government asserts that Congress could not have intended that the only civil recoveries under § 408 be *in rem* against the offending ship as it is possible to violate § 408 without using a ship at all. As the government correctly asserts, § 408 begins by stating that "[i]t shall not be lawful for *any person* or persons to . . . *in any manner whatever* impair the usefulness" of any federal water control structure. 33 U.S.C. § 408 (emphasis added). It is thus possible to violate § 408 without using a ship by, for instance, standing on top of a protected structure and striking it with a sledgehammer.

Although this argument might have merit, the government fails to demonstrate that it would, in fact, be limited to *in rem* relief in such cases. If someone did decide to take a sledgehammer to a federal dam, we can find no reason why the United States could not sue outside of the Rivers and Harbors Act and recover on a negligence or trespass theory. The government has not pointed to any other language in the Act that demonstrates a congressional intent to [—15—] provide for an *in personam* remedy in lieu of other civil remedies available to the Corps.

Because nothing in the text of the Rivers and Harbors Act indicates a congressional intent to allow for an implied cause of action against Jantran, we are compelled to find no other remedies are available. We thus hold that the government may not bring *in personam* actions against vessel owners for violations of § 408 of the Act.

II. Conclusion

The District Court's Order dismissing the action is AFFIRMED.

This page intentionally left blank

United States Court of Appeals for the Eleventh Circuit

United States Court of Appeals
for the Eleventh Circuit

No. 13-15349

NATIONAL MARITIME SERVS., INC.
vs.
STRAUB

Appeal from the United States District Court for the
Southern District of Florida

Decided: January 13, 2015

Citation: 776 F.3d 783, 3 Adm. R. 638 (11th Cir. 2015).

Before **PRYOR** and **JORDAN**, Circuit Judges, and
WALTER, * District Judge.

*Honorable Donald E. Walter, United States District
Judge for the Western District of Louisiana, sitting by
designation.

[—1—] PRYOR, Circuit Judge: [—2—]

This appeal requires us to decide whether the district court had ancillary jurisdiction over a supplementary proceeding to avoid a fraudulent transfer by a judgment debtor. National Maritime Services, Inc., sued Burrell Shipping Company, LLC, for amounts owed for management and custodial services provided for a vessel. After National Maritime obtained a judgment in its favor, it discovered that Burrell Shipping had transferred all of its assets to its owner, Glenn F. Straub. National Maritime then initiated a supplementary proceeding, Fed. R. Civ. P. 69; Fla. Stat. § 56.29(6), to void the transfer, and the district court later entered a judgment against Straub. Because the district court had ancillary jurisdiction over this supplementary proceeding and the record supports the finding of a fraudulent transfer, we affirm.

I. BACKGROUND

National Maritime filed a complaint in the district court against Burrell Shipping and Straub for breach of contract and unjust enrichment. The claims arose from management and custodial services that National Maritime had provided for the M/V Island Adventure, a vessel owned by Burrell Shipping. The district court had subject matter jurisdiction based on the maritime nature of the controversy, 28 U.S.C. § 1333. While that action was pending, Burrell Shipping sold the vessel, its only asset, to a boat scrapper for $2,249,000. Burrell Shipping then transferred the proceeds of the sale to Straub. [—3—]

Straub is the sole owner of Burrell Shipping and its president, chief operating officer, and managing member. Straub is also the director and president of Burrell Industries, Inc. To facilitate the purchase of the vessel, Straub loaned Burrell Industries $3.2 million in exchange for a promissory note. Burrell Industries in turn loaned Burrell Shipping $3.2 million by a promissory note. Burrell Shipping then granted Burrell Industrials a mortgage for the vessel to secure the promissory note and purchased the vessel from the United States Marshals Service.

After a bench trial in June 2011, the district court entered a final judgment in favor of National Maritime and against Burrell Shipping in the amount of $99,660.05, plus interest. But the district court ruled that Straub was not individually liable to National Maritime. National Maritime attempted to execute on its judgment, but was unsuccessful because Burrell Shipping had no assets.

National Maritime then initiated a supplementary proceeding against Straub in "accord[ance] with the procedure of the state where the court is located." Fed. R. Civ. P. 69(a). Based on a Florida law that permits a trial court to void a transfer of property that "has been made . . . by the judgment debtor to delay, hinder, or defraud creditors," Fla. Stat. § 56.29(6)(b), National Maritime asked the district court to void the transfer of proceeds from Burrell Shipping to Straub. [—4—]

After our decision in *Jackson-Platts v. General Electrical Capital Corporation*, 727 F.3d 1127 (11th Cir. 2013), the district court raised *sua sponte* the question whether it had subject-matter jurisdiction to entertain the supplementary proceeding against Straub. After the parties submitted memoranda of law, the district court ruled that it had subject-matter jurisdiction. The district court explained that it had "ancillary jurisdiction [because] . . . National Maritime is seeking assets of the Judgment Debtor, Burrell [Shipping], that are found in the hands of a third party, Straub." *Nat'l Maritime Servs., Inc. v. Straub*, 979 F. Supp. 2d 1322, 1326 (S.D. Fla. 2013).

The district court found that before the sale of the vessel Burrell Shipping had never generated its own revenues and had operated on loans or funds provided by Burrell Industries. When Burrell Shipping sold the vessel, its liabilities "exceeded its assets by at least $4 million." *Id.* To close the sale, Burrell Shipping had to deliver the vessel to the buyer free of all encumbrances. Burrell Industries agreed to release the mortgage in exchange for the proceeds of the sale, but the proceeds were transferred directly to Straub, not Burrell Industries.

The district court found that Straub is an insider of Burrell Shipping and of Burrell Industries. The district court also found that Straub "controlled and received the transfer" and failed to provide consideration for the transfer. *Id.* The district court determined that, "[a]t the time of the transfer, Straub was aware or [—5—] should have been aware that Burrell [Shipping]'s liabilities exceeded its assets, he was aware or should have been aware of the pending lawsuit against Burrell [Shipping] and himself, and he was aware or should have been aware that Burrell [Shipping] owed National Maritime in excess of $90,000.00." *Id.*

The district court ruled that the transfer of proceeds was fraudulent on two grounds. First, the district court found that the transfer was made with "actual intent to hinder, delay, or defraud," Fla. Stat. § 726.105(1)(a). *Straub*, 979 F. Supp. 2d at 1327–29. Second, the district court found that the transfer was made to an insider for an antecedent debt when the insider should have known that the debtor was insolvent, Fla. Stat. § 726.106(2). *Straub*, 979 F. Supp. 2d at 1329–30. The district court ruled that the transfer was void and entered judgment against Straub in the amount of the final judgment against Burrell Shipping.

II. STANDARDS OF REVIEW

Two standards of review govern this appeal. First, we review *de novo* issues of subject-matter jurisdiction. *Jackson-Platts*, 727 F.3d at 1133. Second, "[a]fter a bench trial, we review the district court's conclusions of law *de novo* and the district court's factual findings for clear error." *Crystal Entm't & Filmworks, Inc. v. Jurado*, 643 F.3d 1313, 1319 (11th Cir. 2011) (internal quotation marks and citation omitted). [—6—]

III. DISCUSSION

This appeal presents two issues. First, we must decide whether the ancillary jurisdiction of the district court extended to the supplementary proceeding initiated by National Maritime. Second, we must decide whether the district court erred when it determined that Burrell Shipping fraudulently transferred the proceeds to Straub. We address each issue in turn.

A. The District Court Had Subject-Matter Jurisdiction to Hear the Supplementary Proceeding Initiated by National Maritime.

The parties agree that ancillary jurisdiction is the only possible basis for subject-matter jurisdiction over the supplementary proceeding. This Court has not addressed when a supplementary proceeding falls within the ancillary jurisdiction of a district court. We conclude that the district court had ancillary jurisdiction over this supplementary proceeding.

Ancillary jurisdiction exists in two circumstances: "(1) to permit disposition by a single court of claims that are, in varying respects and degrees, factually inter-dependent; and (2) to enable a court to function successfully, that is, to manage its proceedings, vindicate its authority, and effectuate its decrees." *Peacock v. Thomas*, 516 U.S. 349, 354, 116 S. Ct. 862, 867 (1996) (quoting *Kokkonen v. Guardian Life Ins. Co.*, 511 U.S. 375, 379–80, 114 S. Ct. 1673, 1676 (1994)). The latter category encompasses "a broad range of supplementary proceedings involving third parties to assist in the protection and enforcement of [—7—] federal judgments—including attachment, mandamus, garnishment, and the prejudgment avoidance of fraudulent conveyances." *Id.* at 356, 116 S. Ct. at 868 (citations omitted). But ancillary jurisdiction does not extend to "a new lawsuit to impose liability for a judgment on a third party." *Id.* at 359, 116 S. Ct. at 869.

The decision of the Supreme Court in *Peacock* is instructive. After the plaintiff in *Peacock* won a judgment against his employer, the plaintiff initiated a supplementary proceeding to pierce the corporate veil of his employer to reach assets of a third party. *Id.* at 351–52, 116 S. Ct. at 865–66. The Supreme Court held that ancillary jurisdiction did not extend to the supplementary proceeding because the effect of the plaintiff's claim would be "to impose liability for a money judgment on a person not otherwise liable for the judgment." *Id.* at 351, 116 S. Ct. at 865. As the Court explained, the claim was more than an attempt "to force payment . . . or to void postjudgment transfers." *Id.* at 357 n.6, 116 S. Ct. at 868 n.6.

In contrast with *Peacock*, the district court had ancillary jurisdiction over this supplementary proceeding because National Maritime sought to disgorge Straub of a fraudulently transferred asset, not to impose liability for a judgment on a third party. Unlike the defendant in *Peacock*, Straub is not personally liable for the judgment against Burrell Shipping. *Id.* at 351, 116 S. Ct. at 865. Straub's liability is limited instead to the proceeds that Burrell Shipping fraudulently [—8—] transferred to him. If the value of the transferred proceeds was less than the value of the judgment against Burrell Shipping, National Maritime would have no recourse against Straub for the excess amount. The claim asserted by National Maritime is not "a new lawsuit [that] impose[s] liability for a judgment on a third party." *Id.* at 359, 116 S. Ct. at 869.

Our decision follows the approaches of other authorities. Both the Second and Ninth Circuits have upheld the exercise of ancillary jurisdiction in this circumstance, *Epperson v. Entm't Express, Inc.*, 242 F.3d 100, 103–07 (2d Cir. 2001); *Thomas, Head & Griesen Emps. Trust v. Buster*, 95 F.3d 1449, 1453–55 (9th Cir. 1996), and the First and Tenth Circuits have suggested in dicta that they would reach the same conclusion, *Ellis v. All Steel Const., Inc.*, 389 F.3d 1031, 1034 (10th Cir. 2004); *U.S.I. Props. Corp. v. M.D. Const. Co.*, 230 F.3d 489, 498 (1st Cir. 2000). Our decision also comports with the ruling in *Dewey v. West Fairmont Gas Coal Company*, where the Supreme Court approved of the exercise of ancillary jurisdiction over a claim to avoid a fraudulent transfer of assets to a third party. 123 U.S. 329, 332–33, 8 S. Ct. 148, 150 (1887). Although the claim to avoid the fraudulent transfer in *Dewey* was asserted before the entry of a judgment against the transferor, *id.* at 332, 8 S. Ct. 149–50, we see no reason why the result should be different when the claim is asserted after the entry of a judgment. *See Buster*, 95 F.3d at 1455. "[T]he fact that the joinder . . . took place after judgment [—9—] is not dispositive of whether the court has jurisdiction to effectuate its judgment by recapturing the judgment debtor's fraudulent conveyances." *Id.*; *see also Swift & Co. Packers v. Compania Colombiana Del Caribe, S.A.*, 339 U.S. 684, 694–95, 70 S. Ct. 861, 867–68 (1950) ("The basis of admiralty's power is to protect its jurisdiction from being thwarted by a fraudulent transfer, and that applies equally whether it is concerned with executing its judgment or authorizing an attachment to secure an independent maritime claim.").

Straub argues that our holding in *Jackson-Platts* establishes that any supplementary proceeding brought under section 56.29(6) is a new action that seeks to impose new liability on a third party, but we disagree. *Jackson-Platts* did not foreclose the exercise of ancillary jurisdiction in this circumstance. Although we described the supplementary proceeding in *Jackson-Platts* as a "'suit[] involving a new party litigating the existence of a new liability,'" 727 F.3d at 1135 (quoting *Butler v. Polk*, 592 F.2d 1293, 1296 (5th Cir. 1979)) (alteration in original), that description does not apply to this supplementary proceeding. In *Jackson-Platts*, the plaintiff brought the supplementary proceeding to impose liability for the entire judgment on new defendants who had conspired to strip the original defendants of all of their assets. *Id.* at 1132. In contrast, National Maritime sought to recover only a fraudulently transferred asset from a third party. [—10—]

B. The District Court Did Not Err When It Concluded that Burrell Shipping Fraudulently Transferred the Proceeds of the Sale to Straub.

Straub argues that the district court erred when it ruled that the transfer of the proceeds was fraudulent. To determine whether a transfer is fraudulent within the meaning of section 56.29(6)(b), Florida courts look to the Uniform Fraudulent Transfer Act, *id.* §§ 726.101–.112. *Morton v. Cord Realty, Inc.,* 677 So. 2d 1322, 1324 (Fla. Dist. Ct. App. 1996). The Act provides that a preferential transfer to an insider is void if the "claim arose before the transfer was made, . . . the transfer was made to an insider for an antecedent debt, the debtor was insolvent at that time, and the insider had reasonable cause to believe that the debtor was insolvent." Fla. Stat. § 726.106(2). The district court found that all of these conditions were met, *Straub,* 929 F. Supp. 2d at 1330, and Straub does not contest these findings.

Straub argues that National Maritime failed to establish that the transfer was made "without reasonably equivalent value," but this argument misses the boat. Reasonably equivalent value is not an element of proof under section 726.106(2) or any associated defenses, *see* Fla. Stat. § 726.109. Although subsection (1) of section 726.106 provides that a transfer is fraudulent if it occurred "without receiving a reasonably equivalent value," subsection (1) is unrelated to whether a transfer to an insider is fraudulent under subsection (2). *Id.* § 726.106.

Straub also argues that the transfer is not voidable because he gave "new value" for the transfer, *id.* § 726.109(6), but this argument too fails. Section [—11—] 726.109(6) provides that a transfer to an insider is not voidable "[t]o the extent the insider gave new value to . . . the debtor after the transfer was made." *Id.* § 726.109(6). Straub presented no evidence that he gave any value after the transfer was made; he instead proved only that he released

the antecedent debt. But section 726.109(6) applies when an insider gives new value after a transfer. *See Unif. Fraudulent Transfer Act* § 8 cmt. 6 (2006) (explaining that section 726.109(6) "is adapted from § 547(c)(4) of the Bankruptcy Code, which permits a preferred creditor to set off the amount of new value subsequently advanced against the recovery of a voidable preference").

The district court did not err. The record supports its decision that the transfer to Straub was a fraudulent transfer to an insider, Fla. Stat. § 726.106(2). And we need not address whether the transfer alternatively was fraudulent because Burrell Shipping "inten[ded] to hinder, delay, or defraud," *id.* § 726.105(1)(a).

IV. CONCLUSION

We **AFFIRM** the judgment in favor of National Maritime and against Straub.

(Reporter's Note: Concurring opinion follows on p. 642).

[—12—] JORDAN, Circuit Judge, concurring:

I join the Court's opinion in full. Although there is language in *Jackson-Platts v. General Electric Capital Corp.*, 727 F.3d 1127, 1134-39 (11th Cir. 2013), which can be read as cutting against a finding of ancillary jurisdiction here, the case is distinguishable because the plaintiff there, though seeking to void a fraudulent transfer, wanted to hold the new parties liable for the entire underlying judgment. Here, as the Court points out, National Maritime's claim against Mr. Straub in the supplementary proceeding was limited to the value of the fraudulently transferred assets. We should not read *Jackson-Platts* more broadly given that the Supreme Court has twice held that district courts have jurisdiction to entertain ancillary proceedings challenging fraudulent transfers by defendants. *See Swift & Co. Packers v. Compania Colombiana Del Caribe, S.A.*, 339 U.S. 684, 690-95 (1950) (fraudulent transfer of vessel which had been attached pre-judgment in initial admiralty action); *Dewey v. West Fairmont Gas Coal Co.*, 123 U.S. 329, 332-33 (1887) (pre-judgment fraudulent transfer of assets to non-diverse defendant).

United States Court of Appeals
for the Eleventh Circuit

No. 13-13243

AIG CENTENNIAL INS. CO.
vs.
O'NEILL

Appeals from the United States District Court for the
Southern District of Florida

Decided: April 10, 2015

Citation: 782 F.3d 1296, 3 Adm. R. 643 (11th Cir. 2015).

Before TJOFLAT and CARNES, Circuit Judges, and
DuBOSE,* District Judge.

*Honorable Kristi DuBose, U.S. District Judge for the
Southern District of Alabama, sitting by designation.

[—2—] TJOFLAT, Circuit Judge:

This case involves a disputed marine insurance policy covering a sixty-six foot sport-fishing vessel, the *Bryemere*. It comes to us on appeal from an eight-day bench trial conducted in the United States District Court for the Southern District of Florida. Finding no reversible error, we affirm.

I.

A.

Brian O'Neill first set his sights on the *Bryemere* in 2006. He signed a purchase-and-sale agreement for the vessel in March 2007, which fixed its price at $1.575 million plus the trade of another vessel valued at $700,000. O'Neill's acceptance was contingent on a successful marine survey and sea trial to examine the *Bryemere* before purchase. O'Neill hired Thomas Price, a marine surveyor, to [—3—] conduct the pre-purchase investigation. Price documented his findings and issued an initial report estimating the *Bryemere*'s market value at approximately $1.875 million. O'Neill's project manager for the transaction, L.J. Gallagher, later contacted Price to request an increase in the vessel's valuation. Price acquiesced, reissuing the initial pre-purchase investigation but upping the *Bryemere*'s market value to $2.35 million. The survey also revealed that the

vessel was in working condition but in need of repairs. O'Neill knew he would be on the hook for procuring these improvements, so he sought a reduction in the purchase price. The seller agreed, lowering the cost of the vessel by $150,000 for an adjusted sale price of $2.125 million.

As he negotiated the *Bryemere*'s price, O'Neill began laying the ground work for its eventual purchase. He incorporated a limited-liability company in the state of Rhode Island, Carolina Acquisition, LLC ("Carolina") to take ownership of the vessel. O'Neill is Carolina's only shareholder, and Carolina is the *Bryemere*'s registered title owner. With Carolina at his side, O'Neill turned his focus toward two remaining tasks: financing and insuring the *Bryemere*. [—4—]

O'Neill applied for a preferred ship mortgage—a specific type of mortgage governed by federal law[1]—with Bank of America, N.A. ("BOA") to fund the *Bryemere*'s cost. Acting through a mortgage broker, Beacon Marine Credit ("Beacon"), O'Neill submitted to BOA an initial loan request for $1.83 million. BOA granted the loan. Although it was O'Neill who filed the original

---

[1] The terms of a preferred ship mortgage are governed by 46 U.S.C. §§ 31301–31343. A preferred mortgage "is a lien on the mortgaged vessel in the amount of the outstanding mortgage indebtedness secured by the vessel." *Id.* § 31325(a). Prior to 1920, courts sitting in admiralty lacked jurisdiction to hear cases regarding ship mortgages. *See, e.g., Bogart v. The Steamboat John Jay*, 58 U.S. 399, 401–02, 15 L. Ed. 95 (1854) ("[Admiralty courts] have no jurisdiction in questions of property between a mortgagee and the owner. . . . [M]ere mortgage of a ship . . . is a contract without any of the characteristics or attendants of a maritime loan . . . ."). Congress changed this state of affairs by passing the Ship Mortgage Act of 1920, which was later recodified as the Maritime Commercial Instruments and Liens Act of 1988, Pub. L. No. 100-710, 102 Stat. 4735 (codified as amended at 46 U.S.C. §§ 31301–31343). In so doing, Congress enabled "a mortgagee to bring a cause of action *in rem* for the foreclosure of a preferred ship's mortgage" and endowed "federal district courts exclusive original jurisdiction to hear that cause of action." *Beluga Holding, Ltd. v. Commerce Capital Corp.*, 212 F.3d 1199, 1202 (11th Cir. 2000) (footnote omitted).

application, O'Neill signed the mortgage in his capacity as managing member of Carolina.[2] With Carolina as the mortgagor, O'Neill assumed the role of guarantor in his personal capacity. The *Bryemere*, meanwhile, served as collateral: the loan agreement gave BOA a security interest in the vessel such that, in the event of default, BOA could repossess the *Bryemere*, sell it, and use the proceeds to pay [—5—] down any outstanding debt. 46 U.S.C. § 31325(b)(1) ("On default of any term of the preferred mortgage, the mortgagee may enforce the preferred mortgage lien in a civil action in rem . . . .").

After submitting the initial application, O'Neill, acting through Beacon, asked for an increase in the loan amount from $1.83 million to $1.976 million; BOA granted that request. The loan amount was set, and the preferred ship mortgage was signed and dated on April 18, 2007.

C.

As a condition of the loan, BOA required proof of insurance for the *Bryemere*. In addition, BOA requested that the insurance policy contain a mortgage clause that would protect BOA's interests as a mortgagee in the event the underlying insurance policy was found void.[3] Unfortunately for all parties involved, this straightforward request quickly turned Sisyphean.

1.

It all started when O'Neill's insurance broker, Willis of Pennsylvania, Inc. ("Willis"), sought an insurance quote for the *Bryemere* from AIG Centennial Insurance Company

---

[2] The mortgage lists Carolina as the "mortgagor" and "100% sole owner" of the *Bryemere*. Accompanying the mortgage is a certificate of documentation, issued by the U.S. Coast Guard, as further proof that Carolina owned the *Bryemere*. A certificate of documentation is one of the prerequisites for establishing a preferred ship mortgage. 46 C.F.R. § 67.1.

[3] Also known as a "standard mortgage clause," or a "standard mortgagee clause," it "protects the mortgagee's interest even if the insured mortgagor does something to invalidate the policy." Black's Law Dictionary 1104 (9th ed. 2009).

("AIG"). Susan Bonner, an underwriter, handled the [—6—] application process on behalf of AIG. Sharon King, a broker, was assigned to O'Neill's case on behalf of Willis. The first problem arose when, instead of working directly with King, O'Neill delegated the task of obtaining insurance for the *Bryemere* to his executive secretary, Desiree Foulds. And the problem was compounded when, instead of explaining the insurance-application process to Foulds, King forwarded the application to Foulds without comment and returned the application Foulds had completed to Bonner without reviewing it for accuracy or completeness. Needless to say, this was a recipe for error.

As she filled out the insurance application, Foulds made three mistakes that are relevant to this appeal. First, she listed O'Neill as the owner of the vessel. Carolina, in fact, held legal title to the *Bryemere*. *See supra* part I.A. Second, in response to a question about whether the owner or captain had ever suffered any "losses," she disclosed one prior loss in 2003, when O'Neill lost a boat due to a fire. But in the marine-insurance context, the term "loss" encompasses not only the total physical loss of a vessel but also any damage causing injury to the property insured. Under this rubric—and by his own admission at trial—O'Neill had suffered two additional losses that went undisclosed: propeller damage to his Ocean yacht and a blown engine on his sailing vessel. Third, Foulds listed the *Bryemere*'s purchase price as $2.35 million. The closing statement, however, reflects a purchase price of $2.125 million. [—7—]

2.

Foulds sent the completed application to King; King then forwarded it to Bonner at AIG. Bonner received the application and, in reliance thereon, sent King an insurance quote over email on April 17, 2007. The quote listed O'Neill as the named insured. Bonner's email, to which the insurance quote was attached, contained a request that O'Neill submit a signed letter of compliance, indicating that he would complete the repairs to the *Bryemere* recommended by Price's initial marine survey. Two days later, on April 19, 2007, at 5:07 p.m., King sent an insurance binder to Foulds. An insurance binder is "[a]n insurer's memorandum giving the insured temporary coverage while the application for an insurance policy is being processed or while the formal policy is being prepared." Black's Law Dictionary 190 (9th ed. 2009). The binder listed O'Neill as the named insured. Four minutes later, King sent a revised binder to Foulds listing Carolina as the named insured. King testified, and the District Court found, that she changed the named insured on the binder in response to a request made by BOA.[4] [—8—] But King never informed Bonner that Carolina—not O'Neill—should have been the named insured on the policy.

The next day, April 20, AIG issued the final policy. The declarations page of that policy listed O'Neill as the named insured and the policy's effective date as April 19, 2007. As BOA requested, the policy also contained a standard mortgage clause. In contrast with the preferred ship mortgage, there is no indication that O'Neill took out the insurance policy in his capacity as managing member of Carolina LLC. The insurance application names only "J. Brian O'Neill" as the insured under the policy.

---

[4] Based on this testimony, the District Court found that BOA, having reviewed the initial insurance binder and having spotted the error in the named insured, "request[ed] the binder be revised to reflect 'Carolina Acquisition, LLC' as the named insured on the Policy." "We review factual findings made by a district court after a bench trial for clear error, which is a highly deferential standard of review." *Renteria-Marin v. Ag-Mart Produce, Inc.*, 537 F.3d 1321, 1324 (11th Cir. 2008). BOA believes that this factual finding was clearly erroneous. We disagree.

King testified point-blank that BOA asked her to issue a revised binder with Carolina as the named insured. King's testimony to this effect was unambiguous. And although King later [—8—] clarified that BOA's request was communicated to her through Foulds, "[t]he credibility of a witness is in the province of the factfinder and this court will not ordinarily review the factfinder's determination of credibility." *Crystal Entm't & Filmworks, Inc. v. Jurado*, 643 F.3d 1313, 1320 (11th Cir. 2011) (quotation marks omitted).

II.

Following the *Bryemere*'s purchase, O'Neill invested $225,000 to pay for the repairs recommended by Price's marine survey. On June 29, 2007, the *Bryemere* departed Palm Beach, Florida, for Newport, Rhode Island. During the voyage, the crew "noticed considerable flexing in the vessel's hull." Upon arrival in Rhode Island, several marine experts inspected the *Bryemere* and concluded that it suffered from a number of structural defects rendering the vessel, in the words of [—9—] one marine surveyor, "un-seaworthy, dangerous and unsafe for any use."[5] O'Neill then submitted a claim to AIG for coverage under his insurance policy.

In response, AIG filed in the United States District Court for the Southern District of Florida a declaratory judgment action seeking affirmation that the insurance policy was void ab initio as to both O'Neill and BOA. After an eight-day bench trial, the District Court issued an order finding that neither O'Neill nor BOA could recover under the policy. As for O'Neill, the District Court held that the misrepresentations regarding O'Neill's prior loss history and the *Bryemere*'s purchase price—contained in the application for insurance completed by Foulds on O'Neill's behalf—rendered the policy void ab initio under the maritime doctrine of *uberrimae fidei*, or utmost good faith. As for BOA, the District Court held, among other things, that the named insured on the policy, O'Neill, was not the mortgagor on the loan and that BOA had no rights under the standard mortgage clause as a result. O'Neill and BOA timely appealed.

III.

On appeal, O'Neill and BOA advance two lines of argument. O'Neill contends that the District Court erred in holding that his misrepresentations on the [—10—] insurance

---

[5] Unsurprisingly, these defects inspired litigation. Carolina brought suit against the *Bryemere*'s seller and Price, the marine surveyor, among others. At trial, O'Neill testified that the case settled for $1.95 million.

application violated the duty of utmost good faith—and thus voided the insurance policy—because the terms "purchase price" and "loss history" were ambiguous and because, in any event, the misrepresentations were not material. As a corollary to this argument, O'Neill says that the District Court improperly addressed the misrepresentation of his loss history, an issue he claims rested outside the scope of the pleadings and the pretrial stipulation.

BOA, meanwhile, maintains that the standard mortgage clause is a valid contract binding on both BOA and AIG. And like O'Neill, BOA also identifies a procedural misstep: the District Court, BOA argues, should not have ruled on the validity of the standard mortgage clause in the first place because it, too, was outside the scope of the pleadings and the pretrial stipulation. We address these arguments in turn.

A.

Marine insurance is a curious legal creature, bearing the markings of both the state common law of contracts and the federal common law of admiralty. Although the Admiralty Clause of the United States Constitution vests the federal courts with jurisdiction to hear maritime-contract cases,[6]

"it does not follow . . . [—11—] that every term in every maritime contract can only be controlled by some federally defined admiralty rule." *Wilburn Boat Co. v. Fireman's Fund Ins. Co.*, 348 U.S. 310, 313, 75 S. Ct. 368, 370, 99 L. Ed. 337 (1955). In the absence of a "judicially established federal admiralty rule," we rely on state law when addressing questions of marine insurance. *Id.* at 314, 320–21, 75 S. Ct. at 370, 373–74.

1.

The age-old federal marine-insurance doctrine of *uberrimae fidei* governs O'Neill's argument and provides "the controlling federal rule even in the face of contrary state authority." *Steelmet, Inc. v. Caribe Towing Corp.*, 747 F.2d 689, 695 (11th Cir. 1984); *see also HIH Marine Servs., Inc. v. Fraser*, 211 F.3d 1359, 1362 (11th Cir. 2000) ("It is well-settled that the marine insurance doctrine of *uberrimae fidei* is the controlling law of this circuit."). *Uberrimae fidei* reflects "an enlightened moral policy" based upon the presumption that "the party [—12—] procuring insurance, is not . . . in possession of any facts, material to the risk which he does not disclose." *McLanahan v. Universal Ins. Co.*, 26 U.S. 170, 185, 7 L. Ed. 98 (1828). Indeed, "[i]t is the duty of the [insured] to place the underwriter in the same situation as himself." *Sun Mut. Ins. Co. v. Ocean Ins. Co.*, 107 U.S. 485, 510–11, 1 S. Ct. 582, 600, 27 L. Ed. 337 (1883) (quotation marks omitted). And from duty springs obligation: an insured must "fully and voluntarily disclose to the insurer all facts material to a calculation of the insurance risk." *Fraser*, 211 F.3d at 1362. To decide whether a fact is material, we inquire whether it could "possibly influence the mind of a prudent and intelligent insurer in determining whether he would accept the risk." *Kilpatrick Marine Piling v. Fireman's Fund Ins. Co.*, 795 F.2d 940, 942–43 (11th Cir. 1986). In this way, we have clarified, materiality is a concept "broadly defined." *Fraser*, 211 F.3d at 1363–64.

---

[6] The United States Constitution, Article III, § 2, cl. 1, provides in pertinent part: "The judicial Power shall extend . . . to all Cases of admiralty and maritime Jurisdiction . . . ." Congress has endowed federal district courts with "original jurisdiction, exclusive of the courts of the States, of: (1) Any civil case of admiralty or maritime jurisdiction . . . ." 28 U.S.C. § 1333. [—11—] In reading these two provisions, the Supreme Court has concluded that if a contract constitutes a "maritime contract"—an inquiry that turns on "the nature and character of the contract" and whether "it has reference to maritime service or maritime transactions"—it falls within the ambit of federal jurisdiction. *Norfolk S. Ry. Co. v. Kirby*, 543 U.S. 14, 24, 125 S. Ct. 385, 393, 160 L. Ed. 2d 283 (2004) (quotation marks omitted); *see also id.* at 23, 125 S. Ct. at 392 ("Our authority to make decisional law for the interpretation of maritime contracts stems from the Constitution's grant of admiralty jurisdiction to federal courts."). The insurance policy we consider here, without doubt, qualifies as a maritime contract. *Ins. Co. v. Dunham*, 78 U.S. 1,

33–34, 20 L. Ed. 90 (1870). The District Court properly exercised its jurisdiction as a result. We have jurisdiction over the appeal pursuant to 28 U.S.C. § 1291.

An insured who conceals or misrepresents a material fact commits "manifest fraud, which avoids the policy." *McLanahan*, 26 U.S. at 185. That holds true regardless of whether the misrepresentation is "[willful] or accidental, or result[s] from mistake, negligence or voluntary ignorance." *Steelmet*, 747 F.2d at 695 (quotation marks omitted). Commonsense dictates such an approach— "the law has placed the burden of good faith disclosure with the person in the best position to know all the facts: the insured." *Fraser*, 211 F.3d at 1363. [—13—]

The duty of utmost good faith will thus render this insurance policy void ab initio if (1) O'Neill made a misrepresentation to AIG and (2) that misrepresentation was material. "Mixed questions of law and fact, such as questions of materiality, . . . involve assessments peculiarly within the province of the trier of fact and hence are reviewable under the clearly erroneous rule." *Lucas v. Fla. Power & Light Co.*, 765 F.2d 1039, 1040–41 (11th Cir. 1985).[7] "A finding is 'clearly erroneous' when although there is evidence to support it, the reviewing court on the entire evidence is left with the definite and firm conviction that a mistake has been committed." *United States v. U.S. Gypsum Co.*, 333 U.S. 364, 395, 68 S. Ct. 525, 542, 92 L. Ed. 746 (1948).

2.

The District Court determined that O'Neill misrepresented the purchase price on his application for insurance. We cannot say this finding was clearly erroneous.

Elementary mathematics explains why. O'Neill paid $1.575 million for the *Bryemere*, plus the trade of another vessel valued at $700,000, for a total cost of $2.275 million. Anticipating the cost of future repairs following the *Bryemere*'s [—14—] purchase,

O'Neill negotiated a $150,000 adjustment downward in the price, for an adjusted sale price of $2.125 million. This figure is reflected in the closing statement for the vessel and is not disputed by the parties. Instead of providing that number, however, O'Neill's insurance application lists the purchase price at $2.35 million, a $225,000 misrepresentation.

But O'Neill objects to this calculation. He says we should include in the purchase price an additional $225,000 for the repairs AIG required him to make as a prerequisite for obtaining insurance. Adding $225,000 on to the adjusted sale price of $2.125 million, O'Neill contends, means the true purchase price of the *Bryemere* was accurately reflected in his insurance application at $2.35 million.[8]

As the District Court noted, however, O'Neill had already obtained a $150,000 reduction in the purchase price in anticipation of having to fund the repairs recommend by the Price survey report. So O'Neill wants to have it both ways: he wants to benefit from negotiating a lower price, but he does not want that lower price to appear on the insurance application, presumably so he can benefit from an increase in the value of the insurance policy. After all, adding the cost of intended repairs to the actual purchase price would inflate the value of the unrepaired vessel. Underwriters use the purchase price to determine the hull value [—15—] at the time the policy issues. If the purchase price were inflated to account for intended repairs, the true value of the hull at the time of purchase would be skewed.

O'Neill offers one additional point for us to consider. Relying on state contract law, he argues that the term "purchase price" on the insurance application was ambiguous and therefore should be interpreted in favor of the insured. Purchase price is not an ambiguous term. It simply means the value given in return for an item. But even assuming the term is ambiguous, it matters not. The federal maritime doctrine of *uberrimae fidei*—not

---

[7] The parties dispute whether a material-misrepresentation claim under the doctrine of *uberrimae fidei* must be pleaded with particularity. *See* Fed. R. Civ. P. 9(b). We need not reach a decision on that question, however, to decide this case, which comes to us on appeal from a bench trial.

[8] The parties have stipulated that O'Neill paid $225,000 to fund the repairs recommended by the Price survey report.

state contract law—governs this dispute, and it provides no refuge in claiming ambiguity. *See Steelmet*, 747 F.2d at 695 (noting that a misrepresentation, even if it is a result of "mistake, accident, or forgetfulness, is attended with the rigorous consequences that the policy never attaches and is void" (quotation marks omitted)).

3.

The District Court proceeded to hold that this misrepresentation was material and thus voided the policy. The District Court did not clearly err in so holding.

Our circuit has stressed that questions of materiality must be evaluated from the perspective of a reasonable insurer. We ask whether a fact could "possibly influence the mind of a prudent and intelligent insurer in determining whether he [—16—] would accept the risk." *Kilpatrick*, 795 F.2d at 942–43; *see also* Black's Law Dictionary 670 (9th ed. 2009) (defining a material fact as "[a] fact that is significant or essential to the issue or matter at hand").

Under that formulation, the District Court could have found that O'Neill's misrepresentation of the *Bryemere*'s purchase price was material. O'Neill misrepresented the price of the vessel by almost a quarter-million dollars. The District Court heard testimony indicating that a vessel's purchase price would hold sway over the mind of an insurer when determining whether to assume the underwriting risk. For example, underwriters Sean Blue and Susan Bonner testified that insurance companies routinely rely on the vessel's purchase price in determining coverage limits for a given vessel and in determining the amount of coverage provided under a mortgage clause.[9] This

---

[9] The District Court heard the following exchange at trial between Bonner and counsel for AIG:

> Q: What is the relationship when you're writing a breach of warrantee [sic] coverage between the purchase price and the amount of the loan coverage you're willing to write?

makes good business sense: the [—17—] vessel's purchase price, after all, "provides an objective measure of the vessel's worth." *N.H. Ins. Co. v. C'Est Moi, Inc.*, 519 F.3d 937, 939 (9th Cir. 2008).

In fact, our circuit has concluded, in an unpublished opinion, that the misrepresentation of a vessel's purchase price has the potential to be material so as to void an insurance policy under the duty of utmost good faith. *Markel Am. Ins. Co. v. Nordarse*, 297 F. App'x 852, 853 (11th Cir. 2008) (per curiam) (unpublished) (affirming the grant of summary judgment in favor of an insurer in light of a $54,000 misrepresentation in purchase price on a vessel worth, at most, $126,000).[10]

> A: Our guideline is about 80 percent. We will accept an amount about 80 percent or less.
>
> Q: 80 percent of what?
>
> A: The loan versus the total price of the vessel.
>
> Q: So the loan [coverage] is 80 percent of the purchase price?
>
> A: Yes.

[10] Other circuits appear to have held that a misrepresentation of the purchase price is material as a matter of law. *See, e.g., AGF Marine Aviation & Transp. v. Cassin*, 544 F.3d 255, 265 (3d Cir. 2008) ("[W]hen a marine insurer asks for the purchase price, it is a fact material to the risk, the misrepresentation of which violates *uberrimae fidei*."); *N.H. Ins. Co. v. C'Est Moi, Inc.*, 519 F.3d 937, 939–40 (9th Cir. 2008) ("[W]hen a marine insurance application specifically asks for the purchase price, the insured may not substitute, without a clear explanation, the present market value for the actual purchase price. . . . An insured is not free to substitute his own subjective evaluation of worth for what the insurance company sought to obtain, namely a purchase price that can be presumed to be objective because it was arrived at through arm's length negotiations between parties with opposing interests." (citation omitted) (quotation marks omitted)). Our circuit's approach in this area has been—and continues to be—that the materiality of a misrepresentation is a question for the factfinder "that can be decided as a matter of law if reasonable minds could not differ on the question." *Woods v. Indep. Fire Ins. Co.*, 749

The District Court did not clearly err in its determination that O'Neill committed a material misrepresentation rendering void ab initio his insurance [—18—] policy with AIG.[11] As a result, we need not—and do not—consider O'Neill's arguments regarding the District Court's determination that the policy was also void for O'Neill's misrepresentation of his prior loss history. *See id.* at 853 n.5 ("The district court found that only one misrepresentation is necessary . . . to void the policy, and that therefore it need not consider the other three alleged misrepresentations. We agree." (citation omitted)).

B.

BOA claims that the District Court erred in finding that BOA was not covered under the terms of the insurance policy's standard mortgage clause. BOA also says that the District Court should not have reached this issue in the first place because it was outside the scope of the pleadings and the pretrial stipulation.

F.2d 1493, 1496 (11th Cir. 1985) (quotation marks omitted); *see generally Kilpatrick Marine Piling v. Fireman's Fund Ins. Co.*, 795 F.2d 940 (11th Cir. 1986) (articulating this proposition in the context of *uberrimae fidei*).

[11] At oral argument, counsel for O'Neill cited two cases—*Underwriters at Lloyd's v. Cole*, 959 F.2d 241 (9th Cir. 1992) (unpublished), and *Kilpatrick Marine Piling v. Fireman's Fund Ins. Co.*, 795 F.2d 940 (11th Cir. 1986)—for the proposition that courts have found misrepresentations of a vessel's purchase price immaterial. But *Cole*, an unpublished opinion, antedates the Ninth Circuit's more recent treatment of materiality under the doctrine of *uberrimae fidei*. *C'Est Moi, Inc.*, 519 F.3d at 939 ("The fact that the insurer has demanded answers to specific questions in an application for insurance is in itself usually sufficient to establish materiality as a matter of law." (quotation marks omitted)). And *Kilpatrick* merely reaffirms that materiality is a question for the factfinder, one that is due deference on appeal. 795 F.2d at 943 ("Since we cannot say, as a matter of law, . . . that reasonable persons would not differ on the question whether the omitted facts were material, we decline to disregard the jury's finding."). Counsel's reliance on those cases, therefore, is misplaced.

In contrast to O'Neill's dispute, there is no judicially established federal admiralty rule governing the formation and the interpretation of a standard [—19—] mortgage clause. As such, we turn to state law. *Wilburn Boat Co.*, 348 U.S. at 320–21, 75 S. Ct. at 370, 373–74. The District Court concluded, and the parties do not currently dispute, that Pennsylvania law should guide our analysis.

1.

BOA believes that in considering the validity of the standard mortgage clause, the District Court permitted trial-by-ambush because that issue was outside the scope of the pleadings and the pretrial stipulation. To be sure, we have held that "parties are bound by their stipulations and a pretrial stipulation frames the issues for trial." *G.I.C. Corp. v. United States*, 121 F.3d 1447, 1450 (11th Cir. 1997). But we have also cautioned that "[w]e are not inclined to disturb the district court's interpretation of a stipulation agreed upon by the parties during pretrial proceedings and approved by the court." *Risher v. United States*, 465 F.2d 1, 5 (5th Cir. 1972);[12] *see also W. Peninsular Title Co. v. Palm Beach Cnty.*, 41 F.3d 1490, 1493 (11th Cir. 1995) (per curiam) ("[W]e owe great deference to the trial judge's interpretation and enforcement of pretrial stipulations.").

BOA's characterization of the proceedings below is simply unsupported by the record. The pretrial stipulation agreed to by all of the parties raises the very [—20—] question the District Court considered. Under the heading "A Concise Statement of Issues of Law which remain for Determination by the Court," the parties framed the issue as follows: "Notwithstanding any alleged acts or omissions of O'Neill, or flaws in the *Bryemere*, whether [BOA] is nonetheless covered under the terms of the mortgagee clause." So drafted, it is difficult to imagine how the pretrial stipulation could not have put BOA on notice that the extent of its rights under the

---

[12] In *Bonner v. City of Pritchard*, 661 F.2d 1206 (11th Cir. 1981) (en banc), we adopted as binding precedent all decisions of the former Fifth Circuit prior to October 1, 1981. *Id.* at 1209.

standard mortgage clause was one of the subjects to be litigated at trial. The District Court did not abuse its discretion in ruling on this issue.

2.

BOA goes on to argue that it can find refuge under the insurance policy's standard mortgage clause, O'Neill's misrepresentation aside. The text of that clause reads:

It is understood and agreed that in the interest of the Mortgagee(s) $1,976,000, shall not be impaired or invalidated by any act or omission, or neglect of the mortgagor, owner, master, agent or crew of the vessel(s) insured by this policy, or by failure to comply with any warranty or condition over what the Mortgagee has no control.

a.

We construe the terms of an insurance policy in accord with their plain meaning. *E.g.*, *Steuart v. McChesney*, 444 A.2d 659, 661 (Pa. 1982). The clause at issue here purports to protect BOA's interest, as a mortgagee, in the loan on the *Bryemere*. Pennsylvania law recognizes two types of mortgage clauses, both of [—21—] which safeguard a mortgagee's interest in the event of a loss, but which differ vastly in the level of protection they afford.

The first is an "open" or "simple" mortgage clause. A simple mortgage clause "places the mortgagee . . . in the shoes of the insured" such that the mortgagee "is simply a party appointed to receive the insurance proceeds to the extent of its interest, and its right to recovery is no greater than the right of the insured." *Cardwell v. Chrysler Fin. Corp.*, 804 A.2d 18, 24 (Pa. Super. Ct. 2002). As a result, the mortgagee "is subject to such defenses as the insurer may have against the mortgagor." *Id.* So when an insured-mortgagor's misconduct bars recovery under the policy, that misconduct will bar recovery by the mortgagee as well.

The second is a "union" or "standard" mortgage clause. A standard mortgage clause protects the mortgagee so that "the insurance [policy] shall not be invalidated by any act or neglect of the mortgagor or owner of the property." *Gallatin Fuels, Inc. v. Westchester Fire Ins. Co.*, 244 F. App'x 424, 429 (3d Cir. 2007) (unpublished) (quotation marks omitted) (applying Pennsylvania law). Unlike a simple mortgage clause, a standard mortgage clause "provides more coverage for the mortgagee . . . because the insurance policy expressly indicates that any act or neglect by the insured will not invalidate coverage." *Cardwell*, 804 A.2d at 24. [—22—]

An examination of the policy's plain language makes abundantly clear that, under Pennsylvania law, the clause can be fairly characterized as a standard mortgage clause. The clause explicitly and unambiguously protects BOA's interest in the loan on the *Bryemere* even if the underlying insurance policy is "impaired or invalidated by any act or omission, or neglect of the mortgagor." *See Cardwell*, 804 A.2d at 24 ("If the clause contains such language as to indicate that coverage of the mortgagee . . . will not be invalidated by the acts or omissions of the insured, it is a standard loss payable clause.").

Having identified a standard mortgage clause, we must determine what effect such a clause has, if any, on the relationship between BOA and AIG under the policy. "Where a policy is issued to the owner and a [standard] mortgagee clause is attached, the [insurance] company is, in effect, making two contracts. First, it is agreeing to indemnify the owner for the loss of the property and, second, it is insuring the creditor's security for his debt." *Freystown Mut. Fire Ins. Co. v. Whited*, 41 Pa. D. & C. 605, 609 (Ct. Com. Pl. 1941). This means that "a standard mortgagee clause . . . creates a separate, distinct and independent contract of insurance in favor of [the] mortgagee." *Guarantee Trust & Safe Deposit Co. v. Home Mut. Fire Ins. Co.*, 117 A.2d 824, 825 (Pa. Super. Ct. 1955).

For this reason, a standard mortgage clause "is unaffected by the misrepresentations or false statements of the mortgagor." 4 Steven Plitt et al., [—23—] Couch on Insurance 3d § 65:65 (2011). And more still, "[a] standard mortgage clause has been held effective to protect the interest of the mortgagee even though the policy was itself void as to the mortgagor ab initio." *Id.* § 65:50.

As a result, although O'Neill's misrepresentation rendered the policy void ab initio as to him, BOA's fate under the insurance policy does not necessarily rise or fall with the propriety of O'Neill's conduct. To evaluate BOA's rights under the policy, then, we must look instead to basic principles governing the standard mortgage clause under Pennsylvania law.

b.

The District Court determined that the mortgage clause does not cover BOA under the insurance policy. "We review conclusions of law made by a district judge following a bench trial *de novo*." *Renteria-Marin v. Ag-Mart Produce, Inc.*, 537 F.3d 1321, 1324 (11th Cir. 2008).

The District Court properly regarded this case as sui generis. That is because we are confronted with a scenario in which the named insured is neither the owner of the property insured by the policy nor the mortgagor on the loan for which the property serves as collateral. In what appears to be a case of first impression, we must decide what rights—if any—BOA maintains amid these circumstances. [—24—]

Were O'Neill the owner of the vessel and the mortgagor on the loan, our answer would be quite straightforward: under Pennsylvania law, BOA would, at the least, have the potential for coverage, O'Neill's misrepresentation notwithstanding. *See supra* part III.B.2.a. There is no dispute that O'Neill is the named insured. But O'Neill does not own the vessel—Carolina does. And O'Neill is not the mortgagor on the loan—Carolina is.

Yet the assumption undergirding the reasoning of the case law in this area is that "mortgagor" is synonymous with "named insured." *E.g., Overholt v. Reliance Ins. Co.*, 179 A. 554, 556 (Pa. 1935) ("The so-called

standard mortgage clause . . . creates in favor of the mortgagee a contract of insurance separate, distinct, and independent from that constituted between the *mortgagor* and *the insuring company* by the other provisions of the policy." (emphasis added)); *Willits v. Camden Fire Ins. Ass'n*, 189 A. 559, 561 (Pa. Super. Ct. 1937) (noting that a standard mortgage clause protects the mortgagee against conduct by "the *insured mortgagor or owner*" (emphasis added)); *see also, e.g., Guarantee Trust & Safe Deposit Co. v. Home Mut. Fire Ins. Co.*, 117 A.2d 824 (Pa. Super. Ct. 1955) (discussing a standard mortgage clause on a policy where the named insured was also the mortgagor); *Abbottsford Bldg. & Loan Ass'n v. William Penn Fire Ins. Co.*, 197 A. 504 (Pa. Super Ct. 1938) (same); *Risha v. Farmers Fire Ins. Agency*, 56 Pa. D. & C.4th 194 (Ct. Com. Pl. 2001) (same); *Benchoff v. W. Mut. Fire Ins.* [—25—] *Co.*, 8 Pa. D. & C.2d 471 (Ct. Com. Pl. 1954) (same). That assumption does not hold here. Carolina, a corporate entity, is the mortgagor but—critically, in our view—is not the named insured on the policy.

The difference between O'Neill and Carolina is no mere technicality. The corporate form matters: even though O'Neill is Carolina's sole shareholder, "the general rule is that a corporation shall be regarded as an independent entity even if its stock is owned entirely by one person." *Lumax Indus., Inc. v. Aultman*, 669 A.2d 893, 895 (Pa. 1995). Moreover, "property of a limited liability company is owned by the company itself rather than nominally or otherwise by the members." 15 Pa. Cons. Stat. Ann. § 8923 cmt. 1994.

To be sure, Pennsylvania courts have long held that an insurance policy "is on the insured's interest in the property, not the property itself." *Mut. Benefit Ins. Co. v. Goschenhoppen Mut. Ins. Co.*, 572 A.2d 1275, 1277 (Pa. Super. Ct. 1990). And we have no doubt that O'Neill possesses an insurable interest in the *Bryemere*, even if he does not hold legal title to the vessel. *See Luchansky v. Farmers Fire Ins. Co.*, 515 A.2d 598, 599 (Pa. Super. Ct. 1986) ("The general rule is that anyone has an insurable interest who derives pecuniary benefit or advantage from the preservation or continued existence of the property or who will suffer pecuniary loss from its destruction."). But that does not change the fact that the entire logic of the standard mortgage clause—protection for the mortgagee from acts or [—26—] omissions by the mortgagor—unravels when the mortgagor is not the named insured under the very policy purporting to insure the mortgagee's interest. *Cf.* 4 Steven Plitt et al., Couch on Insurance 3d § 65:8 (2011) (explaining that a standard mortgage clause protects the mortgagee "against loss from any act or neglect of the *mortgagor or owner* so that it shall not defeat the insurance so far as the interest of the mortgagee is concerned" (emphasis added)). Indeed, the District Court rightly noted that "the mortgagee's interest clause clearly relies on the presumption that the mortgagor is . . . the named insured . . . ."

So it bears emphasis that AIG and Carolina never entered into an insurance contract at all. O'Neill signed the mortgage in his capacity as managing member of Carolina; the insurance policy, by contrast, is in O'Neill's name alone. For this reason, the District Court made the factual determination that O'Neill acted on his own behalf—not on behalf of Carolina LLC—in procuring the insurance policy.[13]

The mortgage clause, moreover, was part and parcel of the deal BOA struck with Carolina, and BOA ran the risk that Carolina would err in how it obtained [—27—]

coverage. BOA was in the best position to take care that the two parties central to the proper formation of a standard mortgage clause—the named insured and the mortgagor—aligned so as to protect its interest in the loan.[14] But they did not. Accordingly, BOA cannot rely on the independent contractual status ordinarily conferred upon the standard mortgage clause by Pennsylvania law.

To hold otherwise would render the plain language of the clause internally incoherent. By its terms, the clause protects BOA from five different actors whose conduct might impair or invalidate the insurance policy: the mortgagor, the owner, the master, an agent, or the crew of the *Bryemere*. In this case, O'Neill is the relevant actor, but the mortgage clause appears to afford BOA no protection from his behavior, which rendered the policy void ab initio. Carolina is the mortgagor and owner. The District Court found, and BOA does not contest, that the record contains no evidence to indicate that O'Neill acted as either the master or crew member of the vessel in obtaining the policy. For the clause's plain language to [—28—] protect BOA from O'Neill's misrepresentation, we would have to reach the puzzling conclusion that O'Neill, in procuring the insurance policy, acted not to safeguard his own insurable interest, but rather as an "agent" of the *Bryemere*, a vessel that cannot be an "insured" in the first place. *E.g.*, *In re Gorman's Estate*, 184 A. 86, 87 (Pa. 1936) ("The [property] itself is not insured; the

---

[13] BOA argues that O'Neill acted as Carolina's agent in obtaining the policy. On this record, we are not left with the definite and firm conviction that the District Court's factual finding to the contrary is clearly erroneous. The District Court's determination is supported by the fact that the insurance application lacks any mention of Carolina or O'Neill's role as managing member of Carolina. More still, the insurance application stands in stark contrast to the mortgage, which O'Neill *did* sign in his capacity as Carolina's managing member. That Carolina had an obligation to obtain mortgagee insurance does not necessarily mean that O'Neill was acting on behalf of Carolina when he obtained the policy, much less establish that the District Court's finding constituted clear error.

---

[14] Consider the evidence indicating that BOA recognized this incongruity and requested a change in the insurance policy to remedy it. *See supra* part I.C.2. Indeed, BOA was likely aware that O'Neill and Carolina were separate entities, demonstrated by the fact that BOA, as a condition of Carolina's loan, required O'Neill to serve as guarantor. BOA's request for a change in the named insured was never communicated to AIG, who produced a final policy with O'Neill as the named insured and who did not learn about the existence of Carolina until years after the policy issued. All this suggests that BOA knew or had reason to know that O'Neill and Carolina were legally distinct and knew or had reason to know that AIG had made a mistake in drafting the policy as a result. But BOA appears to have never successfully alerted AIG to this critical error.

indemnity is provided for the insured and for his interest in the property.").[15]

In sum, an analysis of Pennsylvania law and the insurance policy's plain language reveals a fundamental assumption underlying the standard mortgage clause: that the mortgagor and the named insured are one and the same. This assumption was not satisfied here. As a result, the District Court correctly concluded that BOA is not covered under the policy.[16] [—29—]

IV.

For these reasons, we AFFIRM the judgment of the District Court.

(Reporter's Note: Concurring opinion follows on p. 654).

---

[15] Perhaps, under different circumstances, the appropriate remedy in a case such as this would have been for one of the litigants to ask the court to exercise its equitable discretion in order to reform the contract in accord with the intent of the parties. Restatement (Second) of Contracts § 155. We can only speculate, however, as to whether AIG would have issued the same insurance policy had it known the vessel was in fact owned by Carolina, not O'Neill. In fact, the evidence indicates that AIG may not have become aware that Carolina held title to the vessel until some two years after the issuance of the policy.

[16] The parties in this case have expended considerable energy in their briefs debating the District Court's factual findings and legal conclusions regarding communications exchanged between King, Foulds, Bonner, and two employees of Beacon, O'Neill's mortgage broker, prior to the issuance of the insurance policy. We have no reason to delve into this line of argument, because we affirm the District Court on a different ground: that both Pennsylvania law and the plain language of this policy's mortgage clause require the mortgagor to be the named insured. As the District Court explained, "the mortgagee's interest clause clearly relies on the presumption that the mortgagor is . . . the named insured . . . ."

[—30—] DuBOSE, District Judge, concurring in the judgment:

I concur fully with the majority's opinion that O'Neill cannot recover under the AIG policy. As to BOA, I also agree with the majority's opinion that the District Court did not abuse its discretion in ruling on the validity of the mortgage clause.

I concur in the judgment only as to the determination that BOA cannot recover under the policy. I would affirm based on the District Court's determination that in view of BOA's unique involvement with the procurement of insurance, no contract was formed in favor of BOA. This is because BOA rejected the offer of insurance by requesting that the insured's name be changed from O'Neill to Carolina.

I write to take exception to two of the majority's determinations as it relates to BOA's claim. First, the majority determined that in order for a mortgage clause to be valid, Pennsylvania law requires that an owner or mortgagor be the named insured. It is true that when discussing mortgage clauses, Pennsylvania courts have used the terms insured, mortgagor and owner interchangeably. However, under the facts of the cited cases, the terms were interchangeable. I do not agree that the interchangeable use of owner and insured in Pennsylvania law is a basis [—31—] for holding that an insured must be the owner or mortgagor of the collateral to have a valid mortgagee clause included in the policy.[1]

Second, the majority determined that the policy's plain language requires that the insured be the mortgagor/owner. The basis for this determination was because none of the five actors named in the mortgagee clause (from whose conduct the mortgagee is protected), was the named insured.[2] Thus, the majority concludes that the mortgagee clause would be rendered internally incoherent because the clause would not provide protection to the mortgagee from the acts of the insured.

I do not construe the mortgagee clause to require that the insured be the mortgagor/owner. It should be noted that the mortgage clause also provides that the mortgagee's interest is not invalidated "by failure to comply with any warranty or condition over what the Mortgagee has no control." (D.C. Doc. 478-1 at 23). [—32—] This phrase is not modified by reference to specific actors, but certainly would include the insured. Thus, if O'Neill failed to meet a condition of the policy over which the Mortgagee had no control, then the Mortgagee would be protected.[3]

---

[1] There are conceivable instances, which have not been addressed in Pennsylvania law, where it would be appropriate for a non-owner of the collateral to seek protection for the mortgagee. Such an instance occurred in this case. The loan agreement with BOA was executed by O'Neill (individually) as a co-borrower. (D.C. Doc. 477-1 at 27-30). The duty to obtain property insurance on the vessel and to insure the interests of AIG was found in the loan agreement and applied to both O'Neill and Carolina. (*Id.* at 28 ("You or yours means each borrower.... You agree to have physical damage insurance ... which covers both interests...")). Thus O'Neill, as a borrower, had a duty and a financial interest in securing insurance that protected the mortgagee's interest in the collateral.

[2] Although the District Court determined that O'Neill was an agent of the vessel, it was also determined that O'Neill was not acting as an agent when he procured the policy at issue.

[3] The "conditions" are defined to include the "AIG Private Client Group Yacht wording". (D.C. Doc. 478-1 at 23). Looking to the policy, the general conditions are found at pages 18-21, and include that the policy is void if inaccurate or incomplete information is provided. (478-1 at 20).

United States Court of Appeals
for the Eleventh Circuit

No. 14-14325

CARMOUCHE
VS.
TAMBORLEE MANAGEMENT, INC.

Appeal from the United States District Court for the
Southern District of Florida

Decided: June 15, 2015

Citation: 789 F.3d 1201, 3 Adm. R. 655 (11th Cir. 2015).

Before PRYOR, CARNES, and SILER,* Circuit Judges.

*Honorable Eugene E. Siler, Jr., United States
Circuit Judge for the Sixth Circuit, sitting by designation.

[—1—] PRYOR, Circuit Judge: [—2—]

This appeal requires us to decide whether the district court had general personal jurisdiction over Tamborlee Management, Inc., a Panama corporation that provides shore excursions for tourists in Belize. After Tawana Carmouche was injured during a shore excursion operated by Tamborlee in Belize, she sued Tamborlee for negligence in the Southern District of Florida. Tamborlee moved to dismiss Carmouche's complaint for lack of personal jurisdiction, and the district court granted the motion after allowing the parties to take jurisdictional discovery. Because Tamborlee's activities in Florida are not "so 'continuous and systematic' as to render [it] essentially at home" there, *Goodyear Dunlop Tires Operations, S.A. v. Brown*, 564 U.S. _, 131 S. Ct. 2846, 2851 (2011) (quoting *Int'l Shoe Co. v. State of Wash., Office of Unemployment Comp. & Placement*, 326 U.S. 310, 317, 66 S. Ct. 154, 159 (1945)), we affirm.

I. BACKGROUND

In November 2012, Carmouche, a passenger on a cruise operated by Carnival Corporation, was injured during a shore excursion operated by Tamborlee in Belize. Carmouche sued Carnival and Tamborlee for negligence in the Southern District of Florida. Tamborlee moved to dismiss Carmouche's complaint for lack of personal jurisdiction, and the district court granted Carmouche leave to take jurisdictional discovery. After jurisdictional discovery, Tamborlee renewed its motion to dismiss for lack of personal jurisdiction. [—3—]

Tamborlee is a corporation registered in Panama that provides shore excursions for tourists in Belize. Tamborlee has never operated a shore excursion in Florida, advertised to potential customers in Florida, or been incorporated or licensed to do business in Florida. Tamborlee's connections with Florida include insurance policies with several Florida companies, a bank account with Citibank that is handled by a department in Miami, and membership in the Florida Caribbean Cruise Association, a non-profit trade organization.

In 2005, Tamborlee entered into an agreement with Carnival Corporation to provide shore excursions for Carnival passengers in Belize. The initial contract between Tamborlee and Carnival provided that "[Tamborlee] consents to the personal jurisdiction over it and to the venue of the courts serving the Southern District of Florida in the event of any lawsuit to which CARNIVAL is a party and which is related to, in connection with, arising from or involving the Shore Excursion or the terms of this Agreement." The contract also listed a post-office box in Key West, Florida, as Tamborlee's "principal place of business." In December 2005, Tamborlee and Carnival executed a contract with the same terms as the initial contract, including the same forum-selection clause and the same Key West post-office box listed as Tamborlee's "principal place of business."

Also in 2005, Tamborlee filed a UCC financing statement with the Florida Secretary of State. The statement concerned the financing of a vessel named [—4—] "Belize Dream." One section of the statement lists a Belize mailing address for Tamborlee, but another section lists a Key West address next to Tamborlee's name. The Key West address listed on the financing statement is different from the Key West post-office box listed in the Carnival contracts.

Tamborlee filed a declaration of its co-founder, William Mackenzie, that the inclusion of the Key West post-office box in the contracts with Carnival was "entirely in error," that the address "has never belonged to or even been associated with Tamborlee, its owners, officers, representatives, agents or employees," that "Tamborlee has never used this P.O. Box for any purpose," and that the address "belonged to an entity which was owned or affiliated with" Peter Norquoy, an initial investor in Tamborlee. Mackenzie further asserted that the different Key West address listed in the 2005 financing statement never belonged to Tamborlee. Tamborlee also submitted insurance contracts, contracts with other cruise lines, and e-mails between employees of Tamborlee and Carnival that listed Panama and Belize addresses for Tamborlee.

The district court granted Tamborlee's motion to dismiss. Although "Tamborlee ... presented evidence that the [Key West post-office box] was placed in the [Carnival] agreement in error," the district court concluded that even if it "were to accept that the Key West post[-]office box was a Tamborlee mailing address, this is insufficient support for personal jurisdiction." [—5—]

II. STANDARD OF REVIEW

We review *de novo* the decision of a district court to dismiss a complaint for lack of personal jurisdiction. *Fraser v. Smith*, 594 F.3d 842, 846 (11th Cir. 2010).

III. DISCUSSION

"A federal court sitting in diversity undertakes a two-step inquiry in determining whether personal jurisdiction exists: the exercise of jurisdiction must (1) be appropriate under the state long-arm statute and (2) not violate the Due Process Clause of the Fourteenth Amendment to the United States Constitution." *United Techs. Corp. v. Mazer*, 556 F.3d 1260, 1274 (11th Cir. 2009). A defendant can be subject to personal jurisdiction under Florida's long-arm statute in two ways: first, section 48.193(1)(a) lists acts that subject a defendant to *specific* personal jurisdiction—that is, jurisdiction over suits that arise out of or relate to a defendant's contacts with Florida, Fla. Stat. § 48.193(1)(a); and second, section 48.193(2) provides that Florida courts may exercise *general* personal jurisdiction—that is, jurisdiction over any claims against a defendant, whether or not they involve the defendant's activities in Florida—if the defendant engages in "substantial and not isolated activity" in Florida, *id.* § 48.193(2).

Because Carmouche does not argue that the events that gave rise to her suit confer specific personal jurisdiction over Tamborlee, we need only consider whether the district court had general jurisdiction over Tamborlee under section [—6—] 48.193(2). And "[t]he reach of [section 48.193(2)] extends to the limits on personal jurisdiction imposed by the Due Process Clause of the Fourteenth Amendment." *Fraser*, 594 F.3d at 846. So, to determine whether the district court had general jurisdiction over Tamborlee under section 48.193(2), we "need only determine whether the district court's exercise of jurisdiction over [Tamborlee] would exceed constitutional bounds." *Id.*

"A court may assert general jurisdiction over foreign (sister-state or foreign-country) corporations," without offending due process "when their affiliations with the State are so 'continuous and systematic' as to render them essentially at home in the forum State." *Goodyear*, 131 S. Ct. at 2851 (quoting *Int'l Shoe Co.*, 326 U.S. at 317, 66 S. Ct. at 159). "[O]nly a limited set of affiliations with a forum will render a defendant amenable to all-purpose jurisdiction there." *Daimler AG v. Bauman*, 571 U.S. _, 134 S. Ct. 746, 760 (2014). A corporation's place of incorporation and its principal place of business are "paradigm all-purpose forums." *Id.* And "a corporation's operations in a forum other than its formal place of incorporation or principal place of business" will be "so substantial and of such a nature as to render the corporation at home in that State" only in "exceptional" cases. *Id.* at 761 n.19.

Tamborlee's connections with Florida are not "so 'continuous and systematic' as to render [it] essentially at home" there. *Goodyear*, 131 S. Ct. at [—7—] 2851 (quoting *Int'l Shoe Co.*, 326 U.S. at 317, 66 S. Ct. at 159). If we accept all of Carmouche's allegations as true, Tamborlee's connections with Florida are limited to having a Florida bank account and two Florida addresses, one of which is a post-office box, purchasing insurance from Florida companies, filing a financing statement with the Florida Secretary of State, joining a non-profit trade organization based in Florida, and consenting to the jurisdiction of the Southern District of Florida for all lawsuits arising out of its agreements with Carnival. These connections are not "so substantial" as to make this one those "exceptional" cases in which a foreign corporation is "at home" in a forum other than its place of incorporation or principal place of business, *Daimler AG*, 134 S. Ct. at 761 n.19.

The only "exceptional" case the Supreme Court has identified in which a court exercised general personal jurisdiction over a foreign corporation without offending due process is *Perkins v. Benguet Consol. Min. Co.*, 342 U.S. 437, 72 S. Ct. 413 (1952), but that decision is distinguishable. The defendant in *Perkins* was a Philippines mining company that ceased its mining operations during the Japanese occupation of the Philippines in World War II. *Id.*, 342 U.S. at 448, 72 S. Ct. at 419. The president of the company moved to Ohio, where he kept an office and oversaw the work of the company. *Id.* The Supreme Court held that Ohio courts could exercise general jurisdiction over the company without offending due process. *Id.* The Supreme Court later explained that in *Perkins*, [—8—] "Ohio was the corporation's principal, if temporary, place of business," *Keeton v. Hustler Magazine, Inc.*, 465 U.S. 770, 779 n.11, 104 S. Ct. 1473, 1481 n.11 (1984), and that "[g]iven the wartime circumstances, Ohio could be considered a surrogate for the place of incorporation or head office," *Daimler AG*, 134 S. Ct. at 756 n.8 (internal quotation marks and citation omitted). This record does not suggest and Carmouche does not contend that Tamborlee ever established its principal place of business in Florida.

The Supreme Court has held that general personal jurisdiction was absent in similar circumstances. In *Helicopteros Nacionales de Colombia, S.A. v. Hall*, the Supreme Court held that a Texas court could not exercise general personal jurisdiction over a Colombian corporation consistent with due process, even though the corporation had a bank account in New York that accepted checks drawn on a Houston bank, sent its chief executive officer to Texas to negotiate a contract, purchased eighty percent of its helicopter fleet from Texas, and sent personnel to Texas for training. 466 U.S. 408, 416, 104 S. Ct. 1868, 1873 (1984). And in *Daimler AG*, the Court held that California courts could not exercise general personal jurisdiction over a German company with a wholly-owned subsidiary that did business in California. 134 S. Ct. 746. The Court explained that California courts could not exercise general personal jurisdiction over the parent company even if the subsidiary's contacts with California were "imputable" to the [—9—] parent. *Id.* at 760. The Court reached this conclusion even though the company's subsidiary was the largest supplier of luxury vehicles to the California market and accounted for 2.4% of the parent's worldwide sales. *Id.* at 752.

We too have held that general personal jurisdiction was absent in a similar circumstance. In *Fraser*, this Court held that Florida courts could not exercise general personal jurisdiction over a commercial tour operator organized under the laws of the Turks and Caicos Islands. 594 F.3d at 844, 847. We reached this conclusion even though the tour operator maintained a website accessible from Florida, advertised in several publications circulated in the United States, including the Miami Herald, procured liability insurance through a Florida insurance agent, purchased about half of its boats in Florida, and sent employees and representatives to Florida for training and to promote its services. *Id.* at 844–45.

Carmouche is not a party to the agreements between Tamborlee and Carnival, and she does not attempt to enforce the forum-selection clauses in those agreements as a third-party beneficiary. Carmouche instead argues that the forum-selection clauses represent a connection Tamborlee has with Florida that we must consider in our jurisdictional analysis. But we are unpersuaded that Tamborlee's contracts with Carnival are sufficient to subject it to general personal jurisdiction in Florida. [—10—]

A foreign corporation cannot be subject to general jurisdiction in a forum unless the corporation's activities in the forum closely approximate the activities that ordinarily characterize a corporation's place of incorporation or principal place of business. And Tamborlee's activities in Florida do not satisfy that standard. Carmouche has produced no evidence that any office Tamborlee might have had in Florida played a significant role in its operations. And Tamborlee's remaining activities in Florida are not meaningfully different from the activities of the defendants in *Helicopteros*, *Daimler AG*, and *Fraser*. Accordingly, the district court did not have general personal jurisdiction over Tamborlee.

IV. CONCLUSION

We **AFFIRM** the order of the district court dismissing Carmouche's complaint for lack of personal jurisdiction.

United States Court of Appeals
for the Eleventh Circuit

No. 13-15858

SORRELS

VS.

NCL (BAHAMAS) LTD.

Appeals from the United States District Court for the Southern District of Florida

Decided: August 4, 2015

Citation: 796 F.3d 1275, 3 Adm. R. 659 (11th Cir. 2015).

Before **PRYOR** and **JORDAN**, Circuit Judges, and **JONES**,* District Judge.

*Honorable Steve C. Jones, United States District Judge for the Northern District of Georgia, sitting by designation.

[—1—] JORDAN, Circuit Judge: [—2—]

In slip and fall cases involving an allegedly dangerous or defective surface, the question of liability sometimes turns on (or is at least informed by) the surface's coefficient of friction (COF), which is, in layman's terms, "the degree of slip resistance." *Mihailovich v. Laatsch*, 359 F.3d 892, 896, 921 n.2 (7th Cir. 2004). *See also Shorter Oxford English Dictionary* 1035 (5th ed. 2002) (defining COF as "the ratio between the force necessary to move one surface horizontally over another and the normal force each surface exerts on the other"). "The higher the [COF], the less slippery the [surface] w[ill] be." *Mihailovich*, 359 F.3d at 921 n.2.

Evidence concerning a surface's COF is generally presented through the testimony of an expert witness, who opines on the appropriate COF industry standard and on whether the surface in question meets that standard. *See, e.g., Rosenfeld v. Oceania Cruises, Inc.*, 654 F.3d 1190, 1193–94 (11th Cir. 2011) (ceramic tile floor in cruise ship); *Great Am. Ins. Co. v. Cutrer*, 298 F.2d 79, 80–81 (5th Cir. 1962) (sidewalk); *McNeilly v. Greenbrier Hotel Corp.*, 16 F. Supp. 3d 733, 735–36 (S.D.W. Va. 2014) (hotel bathtub); *Frazza v. United States*, 529 F. Supp. 2d 61, 69–70 (D.D.C. 2008) (vinyl tile floor in White House).

While on a cruise in 2012, Teresita Sorrels slipped on the pool deck of NCL's *Norwegian Sky*—which was wet from rain—and fractured her wrist. She and her husband sued NCL for damages, alleging negligence. To support their [—3—] claims, Mr. and Mrs. Sorrels sought to present expert testimony concerning the COF of the pool deck of the *Norwegian Sky*, as well as publications which, according to their expert, set the COF standards applicable to the pool decks of cruise ships. The district court excluded all of the expert testimony and publications submitted by Mr. and Mrs. Sorrels with respect to the COF, and granted summary judgment in favor of NCL.

After review of the record and the parties' briefs, and with the benefit of oral argument, we conclude that the district court properly excluded some of the expert's proposed opinions, but erred in striking all of the expert testimony and publications concerning the COF. We therefore vacate the summary judgment in favor of NCL.[1]

I

In the early morning hours of April 14, 2012, Mrs. Sorrels exited the lounge of the *Norwegian Sky* and made her way onto one of the adjacent exterior pool decks. The deck was wet from rain. After walking approximately 100 feet on the deck, Mrs. Sorrels slipped and fractured her wrist. [—4—]

Mr. and Mrs. Sorrels sued NCL for negligence under maritime law, which governs the liability of a cruise ship for a passenger's slip and fall. *See Everett v. Carnival Cruise Lines*, 912 F.2d 1355, 1358 (11th Cir. 1990). Under maritime law, the owner of a ship in navigable waters owes passengers a "duty of reasonable care" under the circumstances. *See Kermarec v. Campagnie Generale Transatlantique*, 358 U.S. 625, 632 (1959);

---

[1] The district court also entered an order taxing costs in favor of NCL. Mr. and Mrs. Sorrels separately appealed from that order, *see* D.E. 111, and we granted the parties' joint motion to consolidate the two appeals. Because we vacate the district court's summary judgment order, we vacate the award of costs. *See Howard v. Roadway Exp., Inc.*, 726 F.2d 1529, 1536 (11th Cir. 1984).

Gibboney v. Wright, 517 F.2d 1054, 1059 (5th Cir. 1975). To prevail on their negligence claim, therefore, Mr. and Mrs. Sorrels had to prove "that (1) [NCL] had a duty to protect [Mrs. Sorrels] from a particular injury [i.e., her slip and fall]; (2) [NCL] breached that duty; (3) the breach actually and proximately caused [Mrs. Sorrels'] injury; and (4) [Mrs. Sorrels] suffered actual harm." *Franza v. Royal Caribbean Cruises, Ltd.*, 772 F.3d 1225, 1253, 2 Adm. R. 582, 603 (11th Cir. 2014) (internal quotation marks and citation omitted).[2]

To help establish the duty and breach elements of their negligence claims, Mr. and Mrs. Sorrels had Dr. Ronald Zollo, a civil engineer, conduct COF testing on the deck. The testing by Dr. Zollo (and by NCL's own expert) took place approximately 520 days after Ms. Sorrels' accident. Dr. Zollo—who performed his tests following a rainfall—reported that wet testing produced a COF range from 0.70 on the high end to 0.14 on the low end. The average value for all wet testing was 0.45. In addition to conducting on-site COF tests, Dr. Zollo also reviewed [—5—] video of Ms. Sorrels' accident, as well as Ms. Sorrels' deposition testimony and other documents relevant to the litigation.

Dr. Zollo opined that a COF of 0.45 is "below minimum standard values that have long been accepted as required in order to classify a walkway surface as slip-resistant." D.E. 60-1 at 3. According to Dr. Zollo, the American Society for Testing and Materials (ASTM), the Occupational Safety and Health Administration (OSHA), the Federal Register, and the Hospital Research Bureau set the minimum COF value for passenger walkways at 0.50. *See id.* Dr. Zollo further reported that, pursuant to § 11.12.1.2 of ASTM F1166-07 (entitled "Standard Practice for Human Engineering Design for Marine Systems, Equipment and Facilities"), walkways on ships "shall have a non-skid surface sufficient to provide a [COF] of 0.6 or higher measured when the surface is wet." *Id.*

Based on his investigation and the COF testing, Dr. Zollo rendered a number of opinions. First, at the time the deck was tested, it did not meet the minimum COF standard for passenger walkways under § 11.12.1.2 of ASTM F1166-07. Second, based on other reported slip and fall incidents that occurred aboard the *Norwegian Sky*, NCL knew or should have known that the condition of the deck in question posed an unreasonable risk to passengers when it was wet. Third, due to the "wide range of friction resistance along the walkway[,]" the deck "trap[ped] individuals via a false sense of security[.]" Fourth, even if NCL had posted [—6—] warning signs about the deck, they would have been inadequate to warn passengers of the potential "hidden" danger. *See id.* at 3–4.

The district court granted NCL's motion to strike the testimony of Dr. Zollo and the publications he submitted in support of the industry COF standard. The district court ruled that Dr. Zollo was qualified to testify as an expert with regard to the slip resistance of the pool deck of the *Norwegian Sky, see* D.E. 93 at 8–9, as well as "(1) individuals' mental and physical reactions to surfaces with varying slip resistances and (2) the necessity and adequacy of warnings concerning such surfaces." *Id.* at 9. But the district court concluded that Dr. Zollo's opinions were not based on reliable methods. *Id.* With respect to Dr. Zollo's "false sense of security" theory, the district court held that Dr. Zollo's testimony was unreliable because he had not tested the COF of the deck along the path Ms. Sorrels traveled before she slipped. *Id.* at 9–10. The district court also excluded Dr. Zollo's testimony as to the COF results obtained from the area where Ms. Sorrels slipped because the tests were conducted "nearly a year and a half after [the] accident." *Id.* at 10. The district court believed that Mr. and Ms. Sorrels had failed to show "that the same conditions existed on the deck at the time [she] fell." *Id.* With respect to the ATSM standard Dr. Zollo cited in opining that 0.6 was the minimum acceptable COF for the deck, the district court ruled that this standard was applicable only to crew members aboard ships. *Id.* at 11. [—7—]

---

[2] We discuss the maritime negligence standard in more detail in Part III, which analyzes the district court's grant of summary judgment in favor of NCL.

The district court also granted summary judgment in favor of NCL. Having excluded Dr. Zollo's testimony and opinions, the district court concluded that the other evidence presented by Mr. and Mrs. Sorrels failed to create an issue of fact as to whether NCL had created a dangerous condition on the deck by failing to properly maintain it. First, although Mr. and Mrs. Sorrels had submitted evidence of 22 other slip and fall accidents over a four-year period on teakwood flooring in public areas of the *Norwegian Sky*, those accidents were not "substantially similar" under cases like *Tran v. Toyota Motor Corp.*, 420 F.3d 1310, 1316 (11th Cir. 2005), and *Heath v. Suzuki Motor Corp.*, 126 F.3d 1391, 1396 (11th Cir. 1997). None of those other accidents, the district court noted, occurred where Mrs. Sorrels had fallen. *See* D.E. 93 at 15–17. Second, although Solange Winifred, an NCL restaurant employee on the *Norwegian Sky*, testified that the ship's deck department would sometimes post signs warning that decks could be slippery when wet, "she admitted that she did not actually know whether those signs were posted because she worked in the restaurant." *Id.* at 18.

II

"[We] review[ ] the district court's decision to exclude expert testimony under Federal Rule of Evidence 702 for abuse of discretion." *United States v. Paul*, 175 F.3d 906, 909 (11th Cir. 1999). A district court abuses it discretion when it makes a clear error in judgment or applies an incorrect legal standard. *See* [—8—] *SunAmerica Corp. v. Sun Life Assur. Co. of Canada*, 77 F.3d 1325, 1333 (11th Cir. 1996). Where a portion of the proffered expert testimony is reliable, wholesale exclusion can constitute an abuse of discretion. *See, e.g.*, *United Fire & Cas. Co. v. Whirlpool Corp.*, 704 F.3d 1338, 1341–42 (11th Cir. 2013) (holding that wholesale exclusion of expert testimony constituted an abuse of discretion and reversing as to one of the expert's opinions).

In determining the admissibility of expert testimony under Rule 702, courts analyze three basic requirements: the expert's qualifications; the reliability of the testimony; and the extent to which the testimony will be helpful to the trier of fact. *See United States v. Frazier*, 387 F.3d 1244, 1260 (11th Cir. 2004) (en banc). Through the application of these three requirements, a district court acts as a "gatekeeper" with respect to the admissibility of expert testimony. *See id.* "The objective of [this gatekeeping] requirement is to ensure the reliability . . . of expert testimony." *Kumho Tire Co. v. Carmichael*, 526 U.S. 137, 152 (1999).

NCL does not challenge Dr. Zollo's qualifications, and we have held that expert testimony relating to the COF of a flooring surface can be helpful to a jury in a slip and fall case. *See Rosenfeld*, 654 F.3d at 1193 ("A qualified expert who uses reliable testing methodology may testify as to the safety of a defendant's choice of flooring, determined by the surface's coefficient of friction."). This case turns, therefore, on the reliability of Dr. Zollo's opinions. [—9—]

The Supreme Court has identified four factors to guide district courts in their assessment of the reliability of expert testimony:

> (1) whether the expert's methodology has been tested or is capable of being tested; (2) whether the theory or technique used by the expert has been subjected to peer review and publication; (3) whether there is a known or potential error rate of the methodology; and (4) whether the technique has been generally accepted in the relevant scientific community.

United Fire & Cas., 704 F.3d at 1341 (citing *Daubert v. Merrell Dow Pharm., Inc.*, 509 U.S. 579, 593–94 (1993)).

A

We begin with ASTM F1166-07, one of the publications Dr. Zollo relied on for his opinion of the industry COF standard. As we have previously held, "[e]vidence of custom within a particular industry, group, or organization is admissible as bearing on the standard of care in determining negligence." *Muncie Aviation Corp. v. Party Doll Fleet, Inc.*, 519 F.2d 1178,

1180 (5th Cir. 1975). "Compliance or non-compliance with such custom, though not conclusive on the issue of negligence, is one of the factors the trier of fact may consider in applying the standard of care." *Id.* at 1180–81.

Entitled "Standard Practice for Human Engineering Design for Marine Systems, Equipment, and Facilities," ASTM F1166-07 "provides ergonomic design criteria from a human-machine perspective for the design and construction of maritime vessels and structures[.]" ASTM F1166-07 at § 1.1. In relevant part, [—10—] it specifies that "[w]alkways, passageways, decks and all other walking surfaces shall have a nonskid surface sufficient to provide a coefficient of friction (COF) of 0.6 or higher measured when the surface is wet." *Id.* at § 11.12.1.2.

On its face, § 11.12.1.2 applies to the pool deck of the *Norwegian Sky*. The district court, however, held that this standard did "not govern cruise-ship passenger decks" because it only discussed general safety standards for "**workers** aboard ships and d[id] not address the appropriate standards for passenger areas on cruise ships." D.E. 93 at 11 (emphasis in original). In so ruling, the district court relied on another section of ATSM F1166-07, which reads as follows: "The criteria contained within this practice shall be applied to the design and construction of all hardware and software within a ship or maritime structure that the human crew members come in contact in any manner for operation, habitability, and maintenance purposes." ATSM F1166-07 at § 1.2.

The district court abused its discretion. *See Sun Life*, 77 F.3d at 1333. On a cruise ship like the *Norwegian Sky,* there are numerous areas traversed by both crew members and passengers, including the pool decks. Even if they are not enjoying the amenities, crew members come into contact with pool decks for things like "operation" (e.g., bringing drinks to passengers) and "maintenance" (e.g., cleaning the pool or making repairs to chairs and tables), as described in § 1.2. As a result, in such commonly traversed areas the COF standard set forth in § [—11—] 11.12.1.2 may apply. A deck constructed of a single material

(here, teakwood) cannot be designed to meet two different COF standards—one for passengers and one for crew members—at the same time. The fact that Ms. Sorrels was a passenger, rather than a crew member, did not necessarily make § 11.12.1.2 inapplicable.[3]

One other point merits a brief discussion. At oral argument, counsel for NCL argued that the COF standard from the ASTM does not apply because it was promulgated after the *Norwegian Sky* was built. We decline to consider this argument because NCL did not press it below, the district court did not address it, and NCL failed to present it in its appellate brief. *See, e.g., Marek v. Singletary*, 62 F.3d 1295, 1298, 1301 n.2 (11th Cir. 1995) (issues not briefed are considered abandoned). Should NCL make this argument on remand, the district court may want to consider cases like *Keller v. United States*, 38 F.3d 16, 26 (1st Cir. 1994) (holding that district court did not err in finding that ASTM standard for fixed ladder safety possessed some probative value in determining industry safety practices, even though standard was promulgated after accident). [—12—]

B

The district court provided a second reason for excluding Dr. Zollo's proposed testimony with respect to the COF of the area of the deck where Ms. Sorrels slipped. Because "[Dr.] Zollo conducted his slip-resistance tests nearly a year and a half after [the] accident," the district court concluded that Mr. and Mrs. Sorrels had not shown that "the same conditions existed on the deck at the time [Mrs. Sorrels] fell." D.E. 93 at 10. The district court also noted that the surface of one of the planks Dr. Zollo tested had a "slimy" substance on it, which may or may not have been present when Ms. Sorrels slipped. It

---

[3] The district court did not abuse its discretion in excluding the COF standards from OSHA and the Federal Register, as Dr. Zollo was unable to explain how they applied. With respect to the standard promulgated by Carnival, a rival cruise line, we think it is best to allow the district court to take a look at that standard on remand in light of the portions of Dr. Zollo's testimony that are admissible.

further explained that Dr. Zollo had stated in his deposition that the problem with the deck related to maintenance, and not construction. *See id.*

Dr. Zollo reported that the COF of the deck at the time he tested it in wet conditions fell below what he believed to be the minimum acceptable COF for cruise-ship passenger decks. *See* D.E. 60-1 at 3 ("the deck surface in its present condition does not qualify as suitably slip resistant"). He did not opine that the deck at the time of Ms. Sorrels' accident was below the minimum acceptable COF. Notably, NCL did not urge that the delay in testing was a basis for excluding the testimony or opinions of Dr. Zollo, and therefore did not make any claim that the time between the accident and the testing adversely affected the validity of the tests. That was not surprising given that NCL's own expert, David Wills, tested [—13—] the pool deck at the same time as Dr. Zollo and used the same measuring equipment and testing protocol employed by Dr. Zollo. *See* D.E. 57-3; D.E. 66 at 3–4.

In our view, the district court abused its discretion by improperly applying the governing legal standard to the record before it. The "substantial similarity" test—a test found in various evidentiary standards—usually governs when a party seeks to introduce an out-of-court experiment to recreate a critical event or incident. *See, e.g., Bish v. Emp'rs Liab. Assurance Co.,* 236 F.2d 62, 70 (5th Cir. 1956); *United States v. Gaskell,* 985 F.2d 1056, 1060 (11th Cir. 1993); *Burchfield v. CSX Transp., Inc.,* 636 F.3d 1330, 1336–37 (11th Cir. 2011). For example, in *Barnes v. General Motors Corp.,* 547 F.2d 275 (5th Cir. 1977), a design defect case involving a Z-28 Camaro with engine mounts, the jury rendered a verdict in favor of the plaintiff. We reversed because the district court had improperly admitted evidence of a test performed by the plaintiff's expert on a different Z-28 vehicle without engine mounts; that test, we said, was conducted under "significantly different circumstances." *Id.* at 277.

Assuming without deciding that the "substantial similarity" test applied to the COF measurements taken by Dr. Zollo, the district court erred. To the extent there was any evidence concerning the similarity of the deck at the time of testing, all of that evidence was contrary to the district court's finding. For starters, both [—14—] experts, Dr. Zollo and Mr. Wills, testified that the wet condition of the pool deck when tested was substantially similar to its condition at the time of the accident. *See* Deposition of David Wills, D.E. 66-6 at 17 ("The condition that I created by doing the wet test by the pouring of the water . . . on the deck is very similar to the condition that is present after rainfall."); Deposition of Ronald Zollo, D.E. 88-3 at 214 ("Yes, I did have similar conditions. . . . Wet conditions are similar."). And an NCL representative, Jane Kilgour, testified that the deck itself had not been changed since Mrs. Sorrels' accident. *See* Deposition of Jane Kilgour, D.E. 66-6 at 16 ("Q: Has the teak deck been changed in any fashion on Deck 11 between 2009 and the present? A: No."). Such testimony constituted sufficient evidence of "substantial similarity" to allow admission. *See Buscaglia v. United States,* 25 F.3d 530, 533–34 (7th Cir. 1994) (that COF testing was conducted on tile from replacement stock, and not on the tile on which the plaintiff fell, went to weight and not admissibility); *Sparks v. Gilley Trucking Co.,* 992 F.2d 50, 54 (4th Cir. 1993) (whether officer properly performed COF test on road "goes more to the weight to be attached to his opinion than to its admissibility").

We have long held, moreover, that a delay in viewing or inspecting the place where an accident took place normally goes to weight and not to admissibility. Our decision in *F.W. Woolworth Co. v. Seckinger,* 125 F.2d 97 (5th Cir. 1942), is instructive. In that case, a patron who fell at an F.W. Woolworth store claimed that [—15—] her fall was caused by a defective condition in the floor. One of the witnesses at trial testified as to the condition of the floor 45 days after the accident. When the jury rendered a verdict in favor of the patron, Woolworth appealed. We affirmed, rejecting Woolworth's argument that the witness should not have been allowed to testify as to the condition of the floor:

The testimony relating to the condition of the floor a month and a half after the accident occurred was evidential of its earlier condition. There is no evidence in this case that the condition of the floor had undergone any material change in the months immediately following the accident. Furthermore, the defective condition of the floor complained of as causing the injury was shown to result from wear and decay, rather than from any abnormality or unusual circumstance of a temporary nature. Where the condition is of such character that a brief lapse of time would not affect it materially, the subsequent existence of the condition may give rise to an inference that it previously existed.

Id. at 98.

Although *Seckinger* involved a lay witness, we do not see why its rationale should not apply to expert witnesses, particularly where, as here, there is evidence that the deck on which Mrs. Sorrels fell had not changed in any material way since the accident. Any issues concerning the 520-day delay, or the one "slimy" plank, go to the weight, and not the admissibility, of Dr. Zollo's testimony. *Cf. Hurst v. United States*, 882 F.2d 306, 311 (8th Cir. 1989) (upholding admission of river hydraulics expert on cause of flood even though he had visited the site of the flood only once, and that one visit was two years after the flood: "Any weaknesses in the [—16—] factual underpinnings of [the expert's] opinion go to the weight and credibility of his testimony, not to its admissibility."). Cross-examination and the presentation of contrary evidence "are the traditional and appropriate means of attacking shaky but admissible evidence." *Daubert*, 509 U.S. at 596.

We recognize that the district court also relied on Rule 403 to exclude Dr. Zollo's testimony and opinions concerning the COF of the area of the deck where Mrs. Sorrels slipped. *See* D.E. 93 at 13 n.8. But we cannot affirm on this basis. First, the district court's Rule 403 balancing was based in part on a belief that Dr. Zollo's testimony had minimal probative value, and that belief was in turn based on rulings we have found to be erroneous. Second, to the extent the district court was concerned about the jury giving significant weight to Dr. Zollo's opinion about the applicable standard of care, that concern might not have been warranted given what we have held with respect to the standard of care. *See Muncie Aviation*, 519 F.2d at 1180–81.

There is a difference between unfairly prejudicial evidence, which may be excluded under Rule 403, and evidence that is "simply adverse to [an] opposing party." *United States v. 0.161 Acres of Land*, 837 F.2d 1036, 1041 (11th Cir. 1988) (internal quotation marks and citation omitted). Rule 403 calls for the exclusion of the former, not the latter. We leave it to the district court to consider [—17—] Rule 403 on remand given what we have said about the admissibility of portions of Dr. Zollo's expert testimony.

C

The district court also excluded Dr. Zollo's proposed testimony that "[t]he subject conditions will trap individuals via a false sense of security based on the wide range of friction resistance along the walkway." D.E. 60-1 at 4. As to this ruling, the district court was correct.

Dr. Zollo's theory was essentially that, because the COF values in the area he tested (the area where Ms. Sorrels slipped) ranged from 0.70 to 0.14, the same range of values can be expected across the entire deck surface. In other words, someone could walk across the deck without experiencing any instability, and then suddenly, step on an area of the deck where the COF drops significantly. And so, presumably, one would feel secure until one is not secure.

As the district court pointed out, there is a significant problem with Dr. Zollo's opinion as to this purported "false sense of security." And that problem is that Dr. Zollo did not perform any COF tests along the path Ms. Sorrels traveled to determine whether the COF values along that path varied to the same degree as the values obtained from the area Dr. Zollo actually tested. *See* D.E. 93 at 9–10. That Dr. Zollo saw a video of Mrs. Sorrels walking along the deck just before her fall does not give him the ability to opine on the COF measurements of the portions of [—18—] the deck he failed to test. Moreover, Dr. Zollo could not cure the deficiency in his methodology by merely walking along the same path that Mrs. Sorrels covered and saying that he did not feel he was going to slip. Dr. Zollo's subjective physical and mental perceptions are not the sort of reliable methodology Rule 702 demands. *See United Fire & Cas.*, 704 F.3d at 1341.

At bottom, Mr. and Mrs. Sorrels argue that Dr. Zollo's testimony is reliable because Dr. Zollo says so. But "'[t]he [district] court's gatekeeping function requires more than simply taking the expert's word for it.'" *Frazier*, 387 F.3d at 1261 (quoting advisory committee's note to Rule 702). And "nothing in either *Daubert* or the Federal Rules of Evidence requires a district court to admit opinion evidence . . . by the *ipse dixit* of the expert." *Gen. Elec. Co. v. Joiner*, 522 U.S. 136, 146 (1997). The district court correctly ruled that Dr. Zollo's "false sense of security" theory was unreliable.

III

We now turn to the district court's grant of summary judgment in favor of NCL, which is "subject to plenary review." *Harris v. Liberty Cmty. Mgmt., Inc.*, 702 F.3d 1298, 1301 (11th Cir. 2012). Generally speaking, we "will affirm if, after construing the evidence in the light most favorable to the non-moving party, we find that no genuine issue of material fact exists and the moving party is entitled to [—19—] judgment as a matter of law." *Alvarez v. Royal Atl. Developers, Inc.*, 610 F.3d 1253, 1263–64 (11th Cir. 2010).

A

Mr. and Mrs. Sorrels argued that NCL created a dangerous condition by failing to properly maintain the pool deck where Mrs. Sorrels slipped and by failing to warn passengers of the danger. The district court ruled that, without Dr. Zollo's testimony, the evidence submitted by Mr. and Mrs. Sorrels was insufficient to survive summary judgment. We vacate the summary judgment in favor of NCL and remand for the district court to apply the Rule 56 standards anew.

In this circuit, the maritime standard of reasonable care usually requires that the cruise ship operator have actual or constructive knowledge of the risk-creating condition. "[T]he benchmark against which a shipowner's behavior must be measured is ordinary reasonable care under the circumstances, a standard which requires, as a prerequisite to imposing liability, that the carrier have had actual or constructive notice of the risk-creating condition, at least where . . . the menace is one commonly encountered on land and not clearly linked to nautical adventure." *Keefe v. Bahama Cruise Line, Inc.*, 867 F.2d 1318, 1322 (11th Cir. 1989) ("BCL's liability thus hinges on whether it knew or should have known about the treacherous wet spot."). [—20—]

The district court ruled, however, that where, as here, the claim is that the ship owner itself created the dangerous condition, a plaintiff need not show that the owner had notice of the alleged condition. *See* D.E. 93 at 4 (citing cases such as *Long v. Celebrity Cruises, Inc.*, 982 F. Supp. 2d 1313, 1316 (S.D. Fla. 2013), and *McDonough v. Celebrity Cruises, Inc.*, 64 F. Supp. 2d 259, 264 (S.D.N.Y. 1999)). NCL does not take issue with this standard on appeal, so for purposes of this case we will apply that standard without passing on its correctness. *Cf. Pogue v. Great Atl. & Pac. Tea Co.*, 242 F.2d 575, 581 (5th Cir. 1975) (noting that, under Florida law, "the creator of the dangerous condition is charged with notice of the danger caused by his own creation"). On remand, the district court should analyze whether the admissible portions of Dr. Zollo's testimony and related evidence (including the evidence concerning the industry COF standard) are enough to allow a jury to determine whether NCL created a dangerous condition.

B

In case NCL's knowledge (actual or constructive) becomes an issue, we address the evidence submitted by Mr. and Mrs. Sorrels in an attempt to establish such knowledge. That evidence consisted of allegedly similar slip and fall incidents, and testimony by an NCL employee concerning the posting of warning signs. [—21—]

Mr. and Mrs. Sorrels introduced evidence of 22 other slip and fall incidents on teakwood flooring in public areas of the *Norwegian Sky* over a four-year period. The district court, applying another of our "substantial similarity" doctrines, *see, e.g., Heath v. Suzuki Motor Corp.*, 126 F.3d 1391, 1396, 1397 n.12 (11th Cir. 1997) (explaining that "before evidence of prior accidents or occurrences is admitted into evidence, the proponent of such evidence must show that conditions substantially similar to the occurrence cause the prior accidents"), found that none of the 22 incidents could be considered. *See* D.E. 93 at 15–17. First, none of them occurred where Mrs. Sorrels fell. Second, the liquids that the other passengers slipped on differed—most involved unknown wet substances—and many of the incident reports noted that there was no indication of rainwater, the liquid that supposedly helped cause Mrs. Sorrels' fall. Indeed, only three of the 22 passengers reported slipping on rainwater, and of those three, one was wearing high heels and another was wearing worn sandals. Third, in some of the other incidents there were other factors involved. For example, three passengers slipped while playing table tennis and another (a 12-year old) fell while chasing someone around the pool.

The "substantial similarity" doctrine does not require identical circumstances, and allows for some play in the joints depending on the scenario presented and the desired use of the evidence. For example, in *Borden, Inc. v.* [—22—] *Florida East Coast Railway Co.*, 772 F.2d 750 (11th Cir. 1985), an FEC train went off the track and damaged a warehouse owned by Borden. The reason the train derailed was that some young men had tampered with the track's signaling and switching system, causing the train to move from the main track to a short spur track. Borden sought to introduce evidence that the vandalism was foreseeable to FEC because of a previous tampering incident at a different location on the same track some five and a half months earlier. The district court excluded the evidence, but we reversed with the following explanation:

> The conditions surrounding the two incidents were similar enough to allow the jury to draw a reasonable inference concerning FEC's ability to foresee this type of vandalism and its results. The procedure used to reverse the track switch and disable the signaling system was identical in both incidents. . . . The incidents involved identical FEC siding switches located on the same track just six-tenths of a mile from one another. Although the results of the two incidents were dissimilar, this difference is insubstantial in considering the issue of the foreseeability of this type of vandalism.

Id. at 755.

Nevertheless, we affirm the district court's ruling with respect to the 22 incidents. The district court acted within its discretion given that Dr. Zollo, who opined about the allegedly defective and dangerous COF measurement in the area where Mrs. Sorrels fell, had not done COF testing at the other locations where there were accidents; that Dr. Zollo's "false sense of security" opinion was [—23—] properly excluded; and that only three of the other passengers reported slipping on rainwater (and two of those three were wearing either high heels or worn sandals).

The last piece of evidence concerning the notice issue came from Ms. Winifred, an NCL employee who worked in a restaurant on the *Norwegian Sky* adjacent to the area where Mrs. Sorrels slipped. The district court concluded that Ms. Winifred's testimony did not help establish that a dangerous condition existed on the pool deck where Mrs. Sorrels fell—or that NCL knew of such a condition—because Ms. Winifred admitted that she did not know whether warning signs were actually posted. *See* D.E. 93 at 18.

The testimony of Ms. Winifred was relevant, however, and went to the issue of NCL's knowledge that the pool deck could be slippery when wet. Ms. Winifred explained at her deposition that the ship's deck department would sometimes post warning signs on the pool deck after it had rained, and that she had been told to post warning signs in the restaurant whenever there was water or some other liquid on the floor of the restaurant because it was known to her supervisors that the teak floor could be slippery when wet. *See* D.E. 78-1 at 5–6; D.E. 66-6 at 105–07. The same goes for the testimony of Milan Rai, an NCL security guard. He testified, **[—24—]** consistently with Ms. Winifred, that he had seen signs posted on the deck when it rained.[4]

Neither Ms. Winifred, Mr. Rai, nor Ms. Kilgour could recall whether signs were posted on the night of Ms. Sorrels' accident. *See* D.E. 66-6 at 102 (Ms. Winifred); *id.* at 111 (Mr. Rai); *id* at 109–10 (Ms. Kilgour). But the issue is not whether NCL violated any of its own internal policies and procedures by not posting warning signs. Rather, the issue is whether NCL had actual or constructive knowledge that the pool deck where Mrs. Sorrels fell could be slippery (and therefore dangerous) when wet, and whether it negligently failed to post a warning sign after the rain that preceded Mrs. Sorrels' accident. *See Borden*, 772 F.2d at 755. *Cf. Burrell v. Fleming*, 109 F. 489, 492 (5th Cir. 1901) (Texas law: "But, knowing that [the trimming holes in the ship] were in this condition [i.e., without coaming or railings], and in a dark place, a proper care for the safety of others invited aboard ship would require those in charge of the ship to give notice of the danger, or to have the doors that led to the danger

securely closed."). The testimony of Ms. Winifred and Mr. Rai—that warning signs were sometimes posted on the pool deck after rain—viewed in the light most favorable to Ms. Sorrels, is enough to withstand summary judgment as to notice. **[—25—]**

We note, as well, that Ms. Sorrels testified that barring "barricades, or something to that effect," she assumed the deck was safe to walk on, despite the fact that it was wet. *See* D.E. 66-6 at 103. A reasonable inference from Ms. Sorrels' testimony is that warning signs had not been posted on the night in question.

IV

We affirm in part and reverse in part the district court's evidentiary rulings, vacate the grant of summary judgment and the award of costs in favor of NCL, and remand for further proceedings consistent with this opinion.

AFFIRMED IN PART, REVERSED IN PART, AND REMANDED.

---

[4] The record before us is missing pages 17–18 of Mr. Rai's deposition transcript. *See* D.E. 66-6 at 111–12. The parties, however, have represented that Mr. Rai testified that he had sometimes seen warning signs posted on the deck after it had rained. *See* D.E. 66 at 2 (citing Mr. Rai's deposition testimony at pages 16–19); Appellee's Br. at 40 n.7 (citing Mr. Rai's deposition testimony at pages 17–18).

United States Court of Appeals
for the Eleventh Circuit

No. 14-14838

WORLD WIDE SUPPLY OÜ
vs.
QUAIL CRUISES SHIP MANAGEMENT

Appeal from the United States District Court for the
Southern District of Florida

Decided: September 30, 2015

Citation: 802 F.3d 1255, 3 Adm. R. 668 (11th Cir. 2015).

Before **TJOFLAT**, **WILSON**, and **CARNES**, Circuit Judges.

[—2—] PER CURIAM:

This appeal concerns an attachment of property made pursuant to Supplemental Admiralty Rule B. The money at issue arose from the legal settlement of a dispute over the purchase of a cruise ship featured on ABC Television Network's long-running series, *The Love Boat*. The plaintiff below, and appellant here, has advanced a novel interpretation of Rule B. The district court was unpersuaded, as are we. Accordingly, we affirm the court's order vacating the attachment.

I. BACKGROUND

This appeal has a complicated background, involving multiple lawsuits in federal district courts, Florida state court, and a Spanish bankruptcy court. The common denominator of these suits is Quail Cruises Ship Management ("Quail"), from which multiple parties, including participants in this appeal, have tried to collect money that they believe Quail owes them. [—3—]

Plaintiff–Appellant World Wide Supply OÜ ("Plaintiff") entered into a contract with Quail for Plaintiff to supply provisions for the M/V Gemini, a vessel owned by Jewel Owner Ltd. ("Jewel"). When Quail stopped making payments to Plaintiff for those provisions, Plaintiff sought a prejudgment attachment of Quail's property to recover the unpaid €123,122.28 balance. Specifically, on January

29, 2014, Plaintiff filed in the district court below an emergency motion for a Rule B attachment of what it contended to be Quail property: a sum of money Quail was to receive from Agencia de Viagens CVC Turlimitada ("Viagens"), pursuant to a settlement agreement between the two. It is that attachment, and its subsequent vacation by the district court below, that gives rise to the present appeal.

Years before, Quail had sued Viagens in the Southern District of Florida "for fraud based on the purchase of what was, at one point, the boat . . . that appeared in the show, The Love Boat." In an unrelated lawsuit, ongoing at the time of the Quail–Viagens suit, Quail and Jewel agreed to a settlement under which any recovery, up to €3,395,519.45, from Quail's suit against Viagens would be paid to Jewel to settle its unrelated claim. Despite this agreement with Jewel, on November 30, 2011, Quail finalized with Viagens a secret settlement agreement whereby Viagens would pay $5,000,000 to Quail's parent corporation, Quail Travel, which was then in bankruptcy proceedings in Spain. Of course, if kept undisclosed, this would mean that Jewel would be cheated out of the approximate [—4—] €3.4 million to which it was entitled under its own settlement with Quail. But learning of the secret agreement between Quail and Viagens, Jewel filed a motion to intervene in the Quail–Viagens suit and also filed a petition in the Circuit Court of Miami-Dade County against Quail and Viagens to prevent any transfer of the settlement proceeds, asserting theories of constructive trust and equitable lien.

Meanwhile, Hainan Cruise Enterprise, S.A. ("Hainan"), which had prevailed against Quail in yet another lawsuit in the Southern District of Florida, obtained a writ of garnishment against Viagens under Rule B, seeking to recover its own judgment from this same, now not-so-secret, $5,000,000 settlement agreement.

At this point, Quail Travel filed for Chapter 15 bankruptcy in the Southern District of Florida and claimed, as its own property, this same $5,000,000 "secret" settlement fund that

Quail had promised to Jewel and that Hainan now claimed. Thus, there were three parties with claims to the settlement funds that Viagens was to pay to Quail: Jewel, Hainan, and Quail Travel. The district court overseeing Quail Travel's bankruptcy proceedings determined that Quail and Quail Travel each held an undivided 50% interest in the settlement proceeds. Quail's $2,500,000 portion, the district court ruled, was subject to Jewel's constructive trust and Hainan's Rule B attachment.

In compliance with that order, Quail, Jewel, Hainan, and Viagens verbally agreed to a settlement, under which Viagens would transfer Quail's $2,500,000 [—5—] share of the settlement to a trust fund account held by Quail's counsel, Holland & Knight. Holland & Knight would, in turn, disburse $1,500,000 to Hainan and $1,000,000 to Jewel. Viagens' transfer to Holland & Knight was to be made in two equal installments made 30 days apart; Holland & Knight was to distribute each installment to Hainan and Jewel after it had been received.

On January 3, 2014, the first installment was made, with Viagens transferring $1,250,000 to Holland & Knight, after which Holland & Knight distributed $500,000 to Jewel and $750,000 to Hainan. However, just before the second transfer by Viagens, on January 29, 2014, Plaintiff filed the above-referenced emergency motion to attach and garnish the funds that were about to be transferred in the second distribution. Representing Plaintiff in this action was Moore & Company, P.A., which had also represented Viagens in the Quail–Viagens lawsuit and had represented Viagens in the distribution of the settlement funds as recently as one week before filing the emergency motion on behalf of Plaintiff. In Plaintiff's view, once Holland & Knight received the funds that had been attached in Hainan's Rule B motion, the funds were no longer protected by the Rule B attachment because, under Rule B(3)(a), the funds had to either remain "in the garnishee's hands or [be] paid into the registry of the court." Having left Viagens' hands, Plaintiff argued, the funds

would become subject to Plaintiff's own new Rule B attachment. [—6—]

In opposition to Plaintiff's motion, Jewel and Hainan ("Appellees") and Holland & Knight raised various arguments. First, they argued that the funds Plaintiff was attempting to attach were still subject to Hainan's prior Rule B attachment and Jewel's constructive trust. Second, they argued that Plaintiff's "emergency" motion represented no emergency at all because Plaintiff's counsel had served as counsel for Viagens during the negotiations leading to the verbal settlement, and therefore was well aware of when and how the funds would be transferred. Plaintiff therefore had been dishonest in its representations to the district court in support of its Rule B attachment. They similarly argued that Plaintiff, because of this knowledge, should have intervened earlier in the proceedings, rather than wait until the eleventh hour to manufacture an emergency. Finally, Appellees argued that Quail's interest was only in receiving the $2,500,000 owed to it from Viagens and it had no claim on any funds that had already been transferred to third parties, including the funds being held by Holland & Knight.

After hearing from the parties, a magistrate judge issued a report and recommendation suggesting that Plaintiff's Rule B attachment should be vacated. The district court adopted the magistrate judge's report and recommendation, giving three key reasons in support of its decision to vacate Plaintiff's attachment. First, the court held, Plaintiff was relying on a narrow, unpersuasive reading of [—7—] Rule B(3)(a), under which an attachment was lost as soon as the *res* left the hands of the garnishee or the court's registry. Second, the motion was not an "emergency," as Plaintiff had characterized it, because Moore & Company had just represented Viagens in the secret settlement negotiations and therefore knew exactly what was planned and when the distributions would take place. Third, the language in the settlement agreement pertaining to the transfer and disbursement of the funds did not leave those funds open to attachment. Quite simply, the funds were no longer the property of Quail at the time Plaintiff sought to attach them. Thus, Plaintiff's attachment was invalid and must be vacated.

Plaintiff had argued in its objections to the magistrate judge's report and recommendation that its interpretation of Rule B(3)(a) was not too broad. For the most part, Plaintiff admitted that money does not become subject to a new attachment simply because it has left the garnishee's hands. Nonetheless, Plaintiff argued, the money does become available for a new attachment if it is sent to "a third party non-garnishee found in this District and the property remains that of the debtor." But, as the district court noted, Plaintiff failed to object to the magistrate judge's finding that the money was no longer the property of debtor Quail at the time that Plaintiff sought to attach the funds. Because Plaintiff failed to contest that finding in its objections to the report and recommendations, and it was not [—8—] clearly erroneous, the district court accepted the findings and rejected Plaintiff's argument.

The district court issued its order vacating Plaintiff's Rule B attachment on September 23, 2014, and Plaintiff filed this appeal from that order.

II. MOTION TO DISMISS AS MOOT

After the filing of this appeal, Jewel and Hainan filed a joint motion to dismiss Plaintiff's appeal as moot, asserting that once the district court vacated Plaintiff's Rule B attachment of the funds, Holland & Knight distributed those funds to Jewel and Hainan, who then transferred them out of the district through their ordinary course of business. Plaintiff had made no request that the funds be held pending the outcome of the appeal, and no court had ordered that the status quo be maintained. Because the funds were no longer in the district,[1] Appellees argued that the district court lacked *in personam* jurisdiction over Quail, and thus the question

whether the district court erred in vacating Plaintiff's Rule B attachment was moot.

Plaintiff countered that, with a Rule B attachment, *in personam* jurisdiction existed over the defendant—as opposed to *in rem* jurisdiction over the *res* itself—and therefore the fact that the property had left the district did not moot the appeal [—9—] because the district court would again have personal jurisdiction over Quail if the attachment were reinstated. Plaintiff further argued that the removal of the money from the district was premature because Hainan and Jewel were required to wait 14 days following the entry of judgment, which they had not done.[2] *See* Fed. R. Civ. P. 62(a).

"If events that occur subsequent to the filing of a lawsuit or an appeal deprive the court of the ability to give the plaintiff or appellant meaningful relief, then the case is moot and must be dismissed." *Al Najjar v. Ashcroft*, 273 F.3d 1330, 1336 (11th Cir. 2001). "The burden of establishing mootness rests with the party seeking dismissal." *Beta Upsilon Chi Upsilon Ch. at the Univ. of Fla. v. Machen*, 586 F.3d 908, 916 (11th Cir. 2009).

Rule B attachments are known as "quasi-in-rem" proceedings, because they are not actions directly against the *res* as a fictitious person, as is the case in *in rem* actions, but are actions against a party who is not personally present in the district but whose property is present. The Fifth Circuit has explained Rule B attachments, as follows:

An *in personam* admiralty or maritime claim is instituted by a complaint which may contain a prayer for process to attach the defendant's property found within the district. Whenever property is attached any person claiming an interest therein is entitled to a prompt hearing at which the plaintiff is required to furnish evidence [—10—] supporting the attachment or other appropriate relief. It is sometimes inaccurately stated that the writ of

---

[1] Jewel and Hainan provided affidavits to support their assertion that the funds had indeed left the district.

[2] Hainan and Jewel have not responded to this last argument.

attachment gives the district court *quasi-in-rem* jurisdiction over the defendant. A more precise understanding is that a good-faith allegation in the complaint that the *res* is present within the geographical jurisdiction of the court is *the* jurisdictional fact which gives the court *in personam* jurisdiction over the defendant purported to own the *res*.

Great Prize, S.A. v. Mariner Shipping Party, Ltd., 967 F.2d 157, 159 (5th Cir. 1992) (footnotes omitted).

Whether the subsequent departure of the *res* from a district in which it was originally present thereby deprives the court of jurisdiction is a question that is not entirely settled. Generally, however, "[s]tasis is not a . . . prerequisite to the maintenance of jurisdiction. Jurisdiction over the person survives a change in circumstances . . . ." *Republic Nat'l Bank of Miami v. United States*, 506 U.S. 80, 88 (1992). Noting that a civil forfeiture proceeding under 21 U.S.C. § 881 should "conform as near as may be to proceedings in admiralty," the Supreme Court has held that an appeal in an *in rem* forfeiture action is not mooted, and "the Court of Appeals is not divested of jurisdiction, by the prevailing party's transfer of the res from the district." *Id.* at 84, 88–89. Other circuits have applied this holding to Rule B attachments, determining that the departure of the attached *res* does not destroy jurisdiction. *See Stevedoring Servs. of Am. v. Ancora Transp., N.V.*, 59 F.3d 879, 882 (9th Cir. 1995) ("We read . . . the Court's holding to eliminate any requirement on a party seeking to institute a maritime attachment to obtain a stay [—11—] or post a *supersedeas* bond to preserve the district court's jurisdiction over the garnished funds while it appealed the release of the garnished funds."); *Vitol, S.A. v. Primerose Shipping Co., Ltd.*, 708 F.3d 527, 540–41, 1 Adm. R. 106, 114-15 (4th Cir. 2013) (same); *see also* 2 Thomas J. Schoenbaum, Admiralty and Maritime Law § 21-2, at 521 (5th ed. 2011) ("Even if the *res* is released [in a Rule B attachment action], the court retains jurisdiction.").

Therefore, even though this Court has not directly confronted the question of whether the *Republic National Bank of Miami* principle extends to Rule B attachments, the above persuasive authority leads us to assume that a Rule B attachment is not mooted simply by the fact that the *res* has left the district. Indeed, even in a maritime *in rem* action, where the action is directly against the *res*, the departure of the *res* from the district does not necessarily moot the case. *Republic Nat'l Bank of Miami*, 506 U.S. at 84 ("[T]he Government relies on what it describes as a settled admiralty principle: that jurisdiction over an *in rem* forfeiture proceeding depends upon continued control of the res. We, however, find no such established rule in our cases."); *see also United States v. One Lear Jet Aircraft, Serial No. 35A-280, Registration No. YN-BVO*, 836 F.2d 1571, 1579 (11th Cir. 1988) (en banc) (Vance, J., dissenting) ("As the doctrine of personification of the ship loses force, so should the rules which rest on it. Among the many such rules which courts have begun to jettison is the rule that the [—12—] presence of the *res* within the jurisdiction of the court is an absolute prerequisite to the court's jurisdiction." (citations omitted)).[3]

Rather, the departure of the *res* moots the case only if further proceedings would be "useless," and as the Supreme Court made clear, the "enforceability of judgments" does not "depend[] absolutely upon the continuous presence of the res in the district." *Republic Nat'l Bank of Miami*, 506 U.S. at 87–88. The purpose of a Rule B attachment, as the Second Circuit has explained, is two-fold: "first, to gain jurisdiction over an absent defendant; and second, to assure satisfaction of a

---

[3] The majority of this Court in *One Lear Jet* held that in an *in rem* forfeiture action jurisdiction was lost because the *res* was removed from the district after the district court's final judgment, but before the appeal was heard. 836 F.2d at 1573 ("Where an appellant fails to file a stay of judgment or a supersedeas bond, and the *res* is removed from the court's territorial jurisdiction, the appellate court does not have *in rem* jurisdiction."). One of our subsequent applications of that holding, however, was reversed by the Supreme Court in *Republic National Bank of Miami*, which cited Judge Vance's *One Lear Jet* dissent approvingly. *See Republic Nat'l Bank of Miami*, 506 U.S. at 83–84, 88.

judgment." *Aqua Stoli Shipping Ltd. v. Gardner Smith Pty Ltd.*, 460 F.3d 434, 437–38 (2d Cir. 2006), *overruled on other grounds by Shipping Corp. of India Ltd. v. Jaldh: Overseas Pty Ltd.*, 585 F.3d 58 (2d Cir. 2009). If an absconding *res* does not necessarily undermine the enforceability of a judgment, nor revoke the court's personal jurisdiction over the defendant, then mootness does not result. This interpretation, moreover, makes good sense, because it removes an incentive for defendants or garnishees to remove the *res* from the district. *See Stevedoring Servs. of Am.*, 59 F.3d at 882–83 ("Maintaining a continuous-control requirement [—13—] in *quasi in rem* proceedings would preserve an advantage for prevailing parties eliminated and criticized in the *in rem* context, the opportunity to shield a district court victory from review.").

It is apparent that a favorable judgment for Plaintiff on this appeal would not be a "useless" judgment for precisely the reason that Plaintiff articulates. It would allow Plaintiff to maintain the district court's personal jurisdiction over Quail because Plaintiff would then arguably have a valid Rule B attachment. *See Puerto Rico Ports Auth. v. BARGE KATY-B, O.N. 606665*, 427 F.3d 93, 102 (1st Cir. 2005) (pertaining to *in rem* action but indicating that the departure of the *res* did not deprive court of jurisdiction because a favorable judgment "could serve as a basis either for re-arresting the barge at any American port or for an in personam action against the barge's owner."). Should Plaintiff subsequently succeed in an action against Quail for the unpaid balance on the provisions it provided, the fact that it might not immediately be able to execute the judgment does not make such a judgment useless, because Plaintiff could seek to enforce it in another district where Quail could be found. *See Republic Nat'l Bank of Miami*, 506 U.S. at 87–88.

Thus, Appellees have not established mootness, and their motion to dismiss the appeal for mootness is **DENIED**. We thus proceed to the merits of the appeal. [—14—]

III. STANDARD OF REVIEW

We review a district court's order vacating a maritime attachment for abuse of discretion. *See Shipping Corp. of India Ltd. v. Jaldhi Overseas Pte Ltd.*, 585 F.3d 58, 66 (2d Cir. 2009). A district court abuses its discretion if it fails to apply the proper legal standard or follow proper procedures in reaching its determination, or if it makes a finding of fact that is clearly erroneous. *Ass'n of Disabled Americans v. Neptune Designs, Inc.*, 469 F.3d 1357, 1359 (11th Cir. 2006).

IV. WAS THE RULE B ATTACHMENT PROPERLY VACATED?

Under Rule B:

> If a defendant is not found within the district when a verified complaint praying for attachment and the affidavit required by Rule B(1)(b) are filed, a verified complaint may contain a prayer for process to attach the defendant's tangible or intangible personal property—up to the amount sued for—in the hands of garnishees named in the process.

Fed. R. Civ. P. B(1)(a); *see also Dresdner Bank AG v. M/V OLYMPIA VOYAGER*, 463 F.3d 1233, 1238 (11th Cir. 2006). Rule B therefore requires, as a precondition to its application, that the defendant not be present in the district, but that the defendant's property must be present there. Process is then served on the person in possession of the property, who becomes the garnishee. Fed. R. Civ. P. B(1)(a). That garnishee has certain responsibilities:

> The garnishee shall serve an answer, together with answers to any interrogatories served with the complaint, within 21 days after service [—15—] of process upon the garnishee. Interrogatories to the garnishee may be served with the complaint without leave of court. If the garnishee refuses or neglects to answer on oath as to the debts, credits, or effects of the defendant in the garnishee's hands, or any

interrogatories concerning such debts, credits, and effects that may be propounded by the plaintiff, the court may award compulsory process against the garnishee. *If the garnishee admits any debts, credits, or effects, they shall be held in the garnishee's hands or paid into the registry of the court, and shall be held in either case <u>subject to the further order of the court</u>.*

Fed. R. Civ. P. B(3)(a) (emphases added).

Plaintiff's argument that its attachment was improperly vacated comes down to its reading of the last sentence of Rule B(3)(a). Plaintiff contends that this sentence opens a window for its own Rule B attachment because the settlement funds were neither deposited into the district court's registry nor, once Viagens had transferred the funds to Holland & Knight, a non-garnishee, held by the garnishee. Moreover, according to Hainan's motion to release the funds, they were to remain the "property of Quail" throughout the process. In short, Plaintiff argues that when it sought the writ of attachment, the funds were still Quail's property and were held in the district by a party that was not a garnishee. Because this was contrary to the command of Rule B(3)(a), Hainan's writ of attachment lapsed and Plaintiff contends it could then seek its own Rule B attachment.

In their joint response, Appellees argue that the funds were not the property of Quail—they were being held in trust for Hainan and Jewel—and therefore they [—16—] were not available for attachment by Plaintiff. Appellees further argue that the funds remained under the authority of federal courts during the two-stage disbursement process and that the Hainan Rule B attachment was never vacated.

Plaintiff cites no authority in support of its position that, under these conditions, a Rule B attachment lapses or a party may assert a new Rule B attachment. Nor can this Court find any legal support for this novel view. The text of Rule B(3)(a) nowhere says that an attachment lapses if the court orders the *res*

transferred to a non-garnishee for distribution to the ultimate recipients. Moreover, although the text of Rule B(3)(a) does state that the funds should be held in the court's registry or by the garnishee, it immediately afterwards says that that is "subject to the further order of the court." That is precisely what was done here, with Viagens holding the funds until the court ordered them distributed, first to Holland & Knight, then to Hainan and Jewel. Plaintiff's reading of Rule B(3)(a) therefore holds no water, either as a stand-alone interpretation or as applied to this case.

Further, the record undermines Plaintiff's factual characterization of the case. In its motion to the district court, Hainan stated:

Hainan does not wish to dismiss the subject action until it has received full payment of the portion it is due under the Chapter 15 settlement. [Viagens] does not wish to violate the Federal Attachments and therefore will not commence any of the transfers outlined above without authority from this Honorable Court. Accordingly, the parties [—17—] have agreed and hereby request that the Court issue an Order authorizing [Viagens] to initiate the transfer outlined above notwithstanding the Federal Attachments.

Thus, Hainan proposed that "[u]pon Hainan's receipt of full payment of its portion of the $2.5 Million that is the property of Quail . . . , this action shall be dismissed with prejudice . . . ." The district court signed Hainan's proposed draft order, which stated:

2. [Viagens] will transfer $2.5 million that is the property of Quail . . . to the [Holland & Knight] Account.

3. [Viagens] will transfer $2.5 million that is the property of Quail Travel to the Quail Travel Account.

4. Upon Hainan's receipt of the full payment of its portion of the $2.5 million that is the property of Quail . . . , the parties shall forthwith file a stipulation of dismissal with

prejudice, with each party to bear its own attorney's fees and costs.

It is clear that, in context, the reference to "the property of Quail" is meant to distinguish the $2,500,000 earmarked for Hainan and Jewel from the same amount of money that was to go to Quail Travel. There is no plausible rationale for Plaintiff's interpretation that Hainan wanted to make sure that the funds remained Quail's property throughout the process.

For these reasons, we conclude that the Hainan Rule B attachment remained in effect until after the receipt of the funds by Hainan and Jewel. Contrary to Plaintiff's assertions, it is irrelevant that the funds were transferred to non- [—18—] garnishee Holland & Knight for disbursement because the Hainan Rule B attachment remained in effect until the funds had been received by Hainan and until the parties thereafter filed their stipulation of dismissal with prejudice.

V. CONCLUSION

The district court did not err in vacating Plaintiff's Rule B attachment because the funds Plaintiff sought to attach were at that time still subject to the prior Hainan Rule B attachment.

AFFIRMED.

United States Court of Appeals for the District of Columbia Circuit

United States Court of Appeals
for the District of Columbia Circuit

No. 13-3032

UNITED STATES
vs.
MIRANDA

Appeals from the United States District Court for the
District of Columbia

Decided: March 20, 2015

Citation: 780 F.3d 1185, 3 Adm. R. 676 (D.C. Cir. 2015).

Before SRINIVASAN, Circuit Judge, and EDWARDS
and SENTELLE, Senior Circuit Judges.

[—2—] SRINIVASAN, Circuit Judge:

Luis Alberto Munoz Miranda and Francisco Jose Valderrama Carvajal, citizens of Colombia, pleaded guilty to drug conspiracy charges under the Maritime Drug Law Enforcement Act (MDLEA). They contend on appeal that the MDLEA is unconstitutional as applied to their conduct, that the MDLEA fails to reach extra-territorially to encompass their conduct in Colombia, and that the facts in the record fail to support acceptance of their guilty pleas. We reject their challenges and affirm their convictions.

Appellants waived all but one of the arguments they now raise when they entered pleas of guilty without reserving any right to appeal their convictions. With respect to their remaining claim, concerning whether vessels used by the drug conspiracy were "subject to the jurisdiction of the United States" within the meaning of the MDLEA, that issue implicates the district court's subject-matter jurisdiction and thus could not be waived by appellants' guilty pleas. On the merits of the issue, however, appellants' statements of stipulated facts fully support the district court's conclusion that the relevant vessels were subject to the jurisdiction of the United States.

I.

On April 23, 2010, a federal grand jury indicted Munoz Miranda and Valderrama Carvajal, along with others not before us on appeal, for participating in an international drug smuggling conspiracy in violation of the MDLEA, 46 U.S.C. [—3—] §§ 70501 et seq. The indictment charged appellants with conspiring to distribute a controlled substance on board "vessel[s] subject to the jurisdiction of the United States." Id. § 70503(a)(1). The drug smuggling operation used "go-fast" boats (small boats capable of traveling undetected and at high speeds) to move drugs from Colombia to various Central American countries. From 2006 to 2010, the smuggling organization transported large quantities of drugs in numerous shipments.

Neither Munoz Miranda nor Valderrama Carvajal planned to, or did, leave Colombia in furtherance of the conspiracy. Valderrama Carvajal served as an organizer of the smuggling operations, and Munoz Miranda provided logistical support. In 2011, Colombian officials arrested Munoz Miranda and Valderrama Carvajal. They were extradited to the United States shortly thereafter.

In the district court, Munoz Miranda and Valderrama Carvajal moved to dismiss their indictments on a number of grounds. They claimed that the ships used by the conspiracy did not satisfy the statutory definition of vessels "subject to the jurisdiction of the United States," 46 U.S.C. § 70502(c), because the ships were in Colombian waters at the time of capture. Appellants further contended that, because their conspiratorial acts did not take place on board any vessel, the MDLEA does not reach their conduct. They also challenged the constitutionality of the MDLEA on two grounds, claiming (i) that Congress lacks Article I authority to criminalize their extraterritorial conduct, and (ii) that applying the statute against them without demonstrating a nexus to the United States violates their due process rights. On October 11, 2012, the district court orally denied appellants' motions to dismiss. [—4—]

The next day, appellants moved to enter guilty pleas under Federal Rule of Criminal Procedure 11. Each appellant executed an unconditional guilty plea agreement that did not "reserve[] in writing the right to have an appellate court review an adverse determination of a specified pretrial motion." Fed. R. Crim. P. 11(a)(2). Appellants entered joint statements of stipulated facts in support of their respective guilty pleas. They both stipulated that, from 2006-2010, they were "co-conspirator[s] in a drug trafficking organization which . . . transported narcotics from Colombia on stateless go-fast vessels through international waters." J.A. 93, 128.

Appellants' statements of stipulated facts also differed in certain respects. Munoz Miranda identified one particular shipment as an example of the conspiracy's use of stateless vessels to transport drugs: a shipment intended to travel from Colombia to Honduras "on board a go-fast boat" that was "not registered in Colombia and did not fly a Colombian flag." J.A. 94. That shipment never left Colombia because it was stolen before it could be moved. Valderrama Carvajal identified the same shipment as an example of the conspiracy's actions, and also described a second shipment as an additional example. The latter shipment departed Colombia on board a go-fast boat that "was not registered in Colombia or any other nation, and contained no registration identification." J.A. 129. Colombian authorities intercepted that vessel when it ran aground on Roncador Island, a remote Colombian island in the Caribbean Sea.

At their plea hearing, appellants confirmed that they knowingly and voluntarily entered pleas of guilty and waived any right to appeal. On October 12, 2012, the district court accepted both guilty pleas based on appellants' joint statements of stipulated facts. But before their sentencing could take [—5—] place, appellants filed a joint motion for reconsideration of their original motions to dismiss.

On February 20, 2013, the district court issued an opinion denying reconsideration and memorializing the reasons for its oral denial of the original motions to dismiss. The court first explained that, as established by appellants' factual stipulations, the two vessels identified as examples of the conspiracy's use of stateless boats—the vessel intercepted off of Roncador Island and the vessel intended to transport the stolen shipment—were both "without nationality" under the MDLEA's definition and thus were "subject to the jurisdiction of the United States." 46 U.S.C. § 70502(c)(1), (d). With respect to the extraterritorial reach of the statute, the court held that the MDLEA's conspiracy provision applies extraterritorially to encompass appellants' conduct. Finally, the court determined that the MDLEA, as applied to appellants, was a valid exercise of Congress's authority to define and punish "Felonies committed on the high Seas," U.S. Const. art. I, § 8, cl. 10, and that the MDLEA's extraterritorial application worked no infringement of appellants' due process rights.

II.

Munoz Miranda and Valderrama Carvajal appeal the district court's denial of their motions to dismiss and their related joint motion for reconsideration, as well as their judgments of conviction. Appellants raise both constitutional and statutory claims.

For each of appellants' arguments, we must first determine whether appellants' unconditional guilty pleas waived their right to appeal the issue. "It is well settled that a voluntary and intelligent plea of guilty made by an accused person, who has been advised by competent counsel, may not be collaterally [—6—] attacked." *Bousley v. United States*, 523 U.S. 614, 621 (1998) (internal quotation marks omitted). A defendant who pleads guilty can do so conditionally, reserving the ability to raise particular challenges on appeal. *See* Fed. R. Crim. P. 11(a)(2). Here, though, appellants entered unconditional guilty pleas, thereby waiving all challenges amenable to waiver. *See United States v. Delgado-Garcia*, 374 F.3d 1337, 1341 (D.C. Cir. 2004). Appellants therefore make no claim that their guilty pleas reserved their ability to press the arguments they now present.

Appellants instead contend that their arguments are immune from waiver. "There are two recognized exceptions" to the rule that an unconditional guilty plea waives a "defendant['s] claims of error on appeal." *Id.* First, a challenge to the district court's subject-matter jurisdiction—to the court's power to hear a given case—can never be waived or forfeited. *See Arbaugh v. Y & H Corp.*, 546 U.S. 500, 514 (2006); *United States v. Cotton*, 535 U.S. 625, 630 (2002); *Delgado-Garcia*, 374 F.3d at 1341. Second, certain constitutional challenges asserting a "right not to be haled into court at all" cannot be waived through a guilty plea. *Blackledge v. Perry*, 417 U.S. 21, 31 (1974); *see also Menna v. New York*, 423 U.S. 61, 62 (1975) (per curiam); *Delgado-Garcia*, 374 F.3d at 1341.

Appellants contend that either the subject-matter jurisdiction exception or the so-called *Blackledge/Menna* exception insulates each of their arguments from waiver. For the most part, we disagree. With regard to all but one of appellants' claims, we find that appellants' unconditional guilty pleas effected a waiver. One of their arguments, however, goes to the district court's subject-matter jurisdiction and cannot be waived: the argument that the vessels in question are not "subject to the jurisdiction of the United [—7—] States" within the meaning of the MDLEA. 46 U.S.C. § 70502(c). While we thus reach the merits of that issue, we conclude, contrary to appellants' argument, that the vessels are in fact "subject to the jurisdiction of the United States."

A.

Appellants contend that the MDLEA is unconstitutional as applied to their conduct in two respects. First, appellants argue that Congress lacks power under the High Seas Clause of Article I to criminalize their actions in furtherance of the charged conspiracy because their conduct did not itself take place on the high seas. *See* U.S. Const. art. I, § 8, cl. 10 (granting Congress authority to "define and punish . . . Felonies committed on the high Seas"). Second, appellants contend that application of the MDLEA to their extraterritorial conduct violates their Fifth

Amendment due process rights in the absence of a demonstrated nexus between their actions and the United States. *Cf. United States v. Ali*, 718 F.3d 929, 943 (D.C. Cir. 2013) (noting that "this Circuit has yet to speak definitively" on whether "due process may impose limits on a criminal law's extraterritorial application"). We do not reach the merits of those claims because we conclude they were waived by appellants' unconditional guilty pleas.

Appellants contend that their constitutional challenges fall within the subject-matter jurisdiction exception to waiver. We disagree. While appellants point to decisions from our sister circuits holding that certain *facial* challenges to the constitutionality of a statute implicate subject-matter jurisdiction, *see, e.g., United States v. Saac*, 632 F.3d 1203, 1208 (11th Cir. 2011), those decisions do not address whether *as-applied* constitutional challenges can be waived, *see United States v. Phillips*, 645 F.3d 859, 863 (7th Cir. 2011). Article III vests federal courts with authority to decide cases "arising [—8—] under . . . the Laws of the United States," U.S. Const. art. III, § 2, cl. 1, and Congress has granted the district courts general subject-matter jurisdiction over "all offenses against the laws of the United States" under 18 U.S.C. § 3231. Appellants do not dispute that the MDLEA was validly enacted and that it constitutes a "law[] of the United States" for purposes of 18 U.S.C. § 3231. They instead argue that application of the MDLEA to their particular conduct offends the Constitution in two ways. But those arguments do not call into question the district court's subject-matter jurisdiction over this case pursuant to Article III and 18 U.S.C. § 3231.

Our decision in *Delgado-Garcia* is controlling on this score. There, the defendants raised precisely the same due process challenge pressed by appellants here, contending that their convictions violated the Fifth Amendment because the government "did not prove a 'nexus' between [their] conduct and the United States," which "they claim[ed] the Fifth Amendment's due process clause requires." *Delgado-Garcia*, 374 F.3d at 1341. We held that the defendants had waived that constitutional claim by entering unconditional guilty pleas, and we rejected the defendants' argument that their challenge fell within the subject-matter jurisdiction exception to the waiver rule. *Id.* at 1342. The defendants' "Fifth Amendment claim," we explained, "is irrelevant to the court's Article III subject matter jurisdiction. The Constitution by its terms leaves it solely to Congress to allocate that power by statute, and there is no claim in this case that this jurisdictional grant is somehow independently unconstitutional." *Id.*

That conclusion governs the resolution of appellants' parallel Fifth Amendment claim here. And there is no reason to reach any different conclusion with respect to appellants' as-applied challenge concerning Congress's Article I authority under the High Seas Clause. For both challenges, the question [—9—] whether the MDLEA can be constitutionally applied to appellants' conduct is a merits question within the district court's authority to decide, not an antecedent question going to the district court's subject-matter jurisdiction over the case.

It is equally clear that the *Blackledge/Menna* exception fails to immunize appellants' constitutional claims from waiver. Together, *Blackledge* and *Menna* stand for the proposition that certain constitutional challenges are immune from waiver regardless of whether they raise issues of subject-matter jurisdiction. In *Blackledge*, the Court held that a due process challenge arising from repetitive, vindictive prosecution for the same crime could not be waived by guilty plea in a situation in which the alleged violation was apparent on the face of the indictment. 417 U.S. at 30. In *Menna*, the Court reached the same conclusion in the context of a double jeopardy challenge to an "indictment [that] was facially duplicative of [an] earlier offense of which the defendant had been convicted and sentenced." *United States v. Broce*, 488 U.S. 563, 575 (1989) (describing *Menna*); *see Menna*, 423 U.S. at 62-63 & n.2. *Blackledge* and *Menna* involved circumstances in which the defendant claimed a constitutional "right not to be haled into court at all" as opposed to asserting a "deprivation

of constitutional rights that occurred prior to the entry of the guilty plea." *Blackledge*, 417 U.S. at 30 (internal quotation marks omitted); *see Broce*, 488 U.S. at 574; *Delgado-Garcia*, 374 F.3d at 1342-43.

Appellants contend that their due process and Article I challenges fall within the *Blackledge/Menna* exception. Once again, our decision in *Delgado-Garcia* forecloses their argument. We held there that the *Blackledge/Menna* exception did not encompass the same due process claim advanced by appellants here. Such a challenge "is a claim that the due process clause limits the substantive reach of the [—10—] conduct elements" of the statute that the defendants were charged with violating, "not a claim that the court lacks the power to bring them to court at all." 374 F.3d at 1343. As a result, "[e]ven if the prosecution of [the defendants] violated the Fifth Amendment for this reason, [they] would still need to come to 'court to answer the charge brought against' them." *Id.* (quoting *Blackledge*, 417 U.S. at 30).

That conclusion not only governs appellants' parallel due process claim, but it also applies to appellants' Article I challenge. The latter argument amounts to a contention that the High Seas Clause "limits the substantive reach of the conduct elements" of the MDLEA. *Id.* Even if application of the MDLEA to appellants' conduct exceeded the legislative power granted by the High Seas Clause, they "would still need to come to 'court to answer the charge brought against' them." *Id.* (quoting *Blackledge*, 417 U.S. at 30). In *Blackledge* and *Menna*, by contrast, the very act of haling the defendants into court completed the constitutional violation. We therefore conclude that neither of appellants' constitutional claims qualify for the *Blackledge/Menna* exception. As a result, appellants cannot raise those claims in this court.

B.

In addition to their constitutional claims, appellants raise two arguments under the terms of the MDLEA. First, they contend that the MDLEA's conspiracy provision, 46 U.S.C.

§ 70506(b), does not apply extraterritorially to encompass their charged conduct in Colombia. Because the *Blackledge/Menna* exception applies only to constitutional challenges, appellants can avoid waiver only if their statutory argument goes to the subject-matter jurisdiction of the court. *See Menna*, 423 U.S. at 62 ("Where the State is precluded by *the United States Constitution* from haling a defendant into [—11—] court on a charge, federal law requires that a conviction on that charge be set aside even if the conviction was entered pursuant to a counseled plea of guilty." (emphasis added)).

The extraterritorial reach of a statute ordinarily presents a merits question, not a jurisdictional question. The Supreme Court's decision in *Morrison v. National Australia Bank Ltd.*, 561 U.S. 247 (2010), is illustrative. That case addressed whether § 10(b) of the Securities Exchange Act of 1934, 15 U.S.C. § 78j(b), reaches extraterritorially to cover misconduct in connection with securities traded on foreign exchanges. The Court concluded that the statute failed to encompass the alleged misconduct, but the Court first held that the question of the statute's extraterritorial reach is not an issue of subject-matter jurisdiction. *Id.* at 253-54. "[T]o ask what conduct § 10(b) reaches," the Court explained, "is to ask what conduct § 10(b) prohibits, which is a merits question." *Id.* at 254. "Subject-matter jurisdiction, by contrast, refers to a tribunal's power to hear a case." *Id.* (internal quotation marks omitted). The district court in *Morrison* thus had subject-matter jurisdiction "to adjudicate the question whether § 10(b) applies to [the defendant's] conduct." *Id.*

Appellants identify no reason for any different conclusion here. Just as in *Morrison*, to ask "what conduct [the MDLEA] reaches is to ask what conduct [the MDLEA] prohibits, which is a merits question," not a question of subject-matter jurisdiction. *Id.* Nothing in the terms of the MDLEA suggests any intention by Congress to depart from that ordinary understanding. The district court therefore had jurisdiction "to adjudicate the question whether [the MDLEA] applies to [appellants'] conduct." *Id.* It follows that the subject-matter

jurisdiction exception affords appellants no relief from the waiver rule for unconditional guilty pleas. [—12—]

C.

In their second claim under the statute, appellants contend that their charged offenses did not involve "vessel[s] subject to the jurisdiction of the United States" as defined by the MDLEA. 46 U.S.C. § 70502(c). Unlike appellants' other arguments, this one, we conclude, goes to the district court's subject-matter jurisdiction. Appellants therefore may raise (and we must address) the issue notwithstanding their entry of unconditional guilty pleas. On the merits, we affirm the district court's conclusion that the relevant vessels qualify as "subject to the jurisdiction of the United States." *Id.*

1.

The MDLEA prohibits manufacturing, distributing, or possessing with intent to distribute drugs "on board" (i) a "vessel of the United States," (ii) a "vessel subject to the jurisdiction of the United States," or (iii) "any vessel if the [defendant] is a citizen of the United States or a resident alien of the United States." 46 U.S.C. § 70503(a). The charges against appellants solely involve the second category. The statute's definition of "vessel[s] subject to the jurisdiction of the United States" encompasses certain non-United States vessels, including "vessel[s] without nationality." *Id.* § 70502(c)(1)(A).

The MDLEA prescribes that, in cases involving "vessels subject to the jurisdiction of the United States," the question whether the vessels at issue qualify as "subject to the jurisdiction of the United States" is a threshold question to be resolved by the district court, not a question for the jury: "Jurisdiction of the United States with respect to a vessel subject to this chapter is not an element of an offense. Jurisdictional issues arising under this chapter are preliminary [—13—] questions of law to be determined solely by the trial judge." 46 U.S.C. § 70504(a). If the "preliminary question" whether the vessels in issue are "subject to the jurisdiction of the United States" goes to the district court's subject-matter jurisdiction, it is immune from waiver.

The courts of appeals that have addressed the issue disagree on whether United States jurisdiction over a vessel under § 70504(a) presents a question of subject-matter jurisdiction. The Eleventh Circuit understands the MDLEA's "on board a vessel subject to the jurisdiction of the United States" requirement to be a "congressionally imposed limit on courts' subject matter jurisdiction, akin to the amount-in-controversy requirement contained in 28 U.S.C. § 1332." *United States v. De La Garza*, 516 F.3d 1266, 1271 (11th Cir. 2008); *see United States v. Tinoco*, 304 F.3d 1088, 1107 (11th Cir. 2002). The Fifth Circuit agrees. *See United States v. Bustos-Useche*, 273 F.3d 622, 626 (5th Cir. 2001). The First Circuit has reached the opposite conclusion, holding that Congress used the term "jurisdiction" in § 70504(a) "loosely" to "describe its own assertion of authority to regulate," as it does "whenever it fixes an 'affects interstate commerce' or 'involved a federally insured bank' as a condition of the crime." *United States v. Gonzalez*, 311 F.3d 440, 443 (1st Cir. 2002). Such issues, the First Circuit reasoned, "have nothing whatever to do with the subject matter jurisdiction of the federal district court," but instead "are routine questions as to the reach and application of a criminal statute." *Id.*

We agree with the Fifth and Eleventh Circuits and conclude that, under § 70504(a), the question whether a vessel is "subject to the jurisdiction of the United States" is a matter of subject-matter jurisdiction. In a series of decisions, the Supreme Court has addressed whether a threshold statutory [—14—] condition like § 70504(a) speaks to the district courts' subject-matter jurisdiction. *See Henderson ex rel. Henderson v. Shinseki*, 131 S. Ct. 1197 (2011); *Reed Elsevier, Inc. v. Muchnick*, 559 U.S. 154 (2010); *Arbaugh*, 546 U.S. 500; *Eberhart v. United States*, 546 U.S. 12 (2005) (per curiam). Those decisions contemplate "a 'readily administrable bright line' rule for deciding such questions." *Henderson*, 131 S. Ct. at 1203 (quoting

Arbaugh, 546 U.S. at 515-16). "If the Legislature clearly states that a threshold limitation on a statute's scope shall count as jurisdictional, then courts will be duly instructed and will not be left to wrestle with the issue." *Arbaugh*, 546 U.S. at 515-16 (footnote omitted). "But when Congress does not rank a statutory limitation on coverage as jurisdictional, courts should treat the restriction as nonjurisdictional in character." *Id.* at 516.

That approach indicates that the question whether a vessel is "subject to the jurisdiction of the United States" goes to subject-matter jurisdiction. The issue is framed as a "threshold limitation on [the] statute's scope," and "the Legislature clearly state[d] that" it should "count as jurisdictional." *Arbaugh*, 546 U.S. at 515. Congress prescribed that the "[j]urisdiction of the United States with respect to a vessel" is a "[j]urisdictional issue[]." 46 U.S.C. § 70504(a). Congress also deemed that "jurisdictional issue" to be a "preliminary question[] of law . . . determined solely by the trial judge." *Id.* The "preliminary question" set out in § 70504(a) thus operates precisely in the nature of a condition on subject-matter jurisdiction: subject-matter jurisdiction presents a question of law for resolution by the court, and courts have an "obligation to determine whether subject-matter jurisdiction exists" as a preliminary matter. *Arbaugh*, 546 U.S. at 514. Congress not only specified that the "jurisdiction of the United States with respect to a vessel" is a threshold question determined by the court, but also that it is "not an [—15—] element of the offense," 46 U.S.C. § 70504(a), fortifying its jurisdictional character. *See Arbaugh*, 546 U.S. at 514 (distinguishing statutory conditions that function as "element[s] of a claim" from those that go to subject-matter jurisdiction, and explaining that courts resolve the latter whereas juries resolve the former).

In addition, "context . . . is relevant to whether a statute ranks a requirement as jurisdictional," *Reed Elsevier*, 559 U.S. at 168, and here, the context of § 70504(a) strongly suggests a requirement of subject-matter jurisdiction. To understand why, it is important first to recognize that "[b]randing a rule as going to a court's subject-matter jurisdiction" is "of considerable practical importance for judges and litigants." *Henderson*, 131 S. Ct. at 1202. If the "jurisdiction of the United States with respect to a vessel" presents a requirement of subject-matter jurisdiction, the requirement would be immune from waiver or forfeiture by a defendant, and courts would bear an independent obligation in every case—and at every level of appellate review—to assure its satisfaction, regardless of whether a party were to raise it. *See id.*; *Arbaugh*, 546 U.S. at 514. On the other hand, if the requirement is non-jurisdictional, a court could forgo addressing it unless it is timely advanced by a party, and a defendant could either forfeit the issue by overlooking it or waive it by electing not to press it. *See Henderson*, 131 S. Ct. at 1202; *Arbaugh*, 546 U.S. at 514.

Those practical considerations ordinarily weigh in favor of construing a threshold statutory condition to be non-jurisdictional. *See Henderson*, 131 S. Ct. at 1202. Here, however, there are strong reasons to conclude that Congress intended the "jurisdiction of the United States with respect to a vessel" to be non-waivable and non-forfeitable by a defendant and to be independently confirmed by courts regardless of [—16—] whether it is raised. In particular, Congress made the requirement a jurisdictional one in order to minimize the extent to which the MDLEA's application might otherwise cause friction with foreign nations.

The MDLEA defines certain non-United States vessels as "subject to the jurisdiction of the United States," including a "vessel without nationality," a "vessel registered in a foreign nation if that nation has consented or waived objection to the enforcement of United States law by the United States," or a "vessel in the territorial waters of a foreign nation if the nation consents to the enforcement of United States law by the United States." 46 U.S.C. § 70502(c)(1)(A), (C), (E). With respect to the first of those categories, the statute in turn defines a "vessel without nationality" to include a "vessel aboard which the master or individual in charge makes a claim of registry

that is denied by the nation whose registry is claimed," and a "vessel aboard which the master or individual in charge makes a claim of registry and for which the claimed nation of registry does not affirmatively and unequivocally assert that the vessel is of its nationality." *Id.* § 70502(d)(1)(A), (C). The MDLEA goes on to set forth certain methods for ascertaining the "[c]onsent or waiver of objection by a foreign nation to the enforcement of United States law by the United States," or the "response of a foreign nation to a claim of registry." *Id.* § 70502(c)(2), (d)(2). In short, a foreign nation's "consent," "waiver," or "response" plays a central role in determining whether a vessel is "subject to the jurisdiction of the United States" under the MDLEA.

In that setting, it is eminently understandable why Congress would want the "[j]urisdiction of the United States with respect to a vessel," *id.* § 70504(a), to be insulated from waiver or forfeiture by a defendant, and would also want courts in every case—and at every level of review—to assure that the [—17—] requirement is satisfied. The requirement aims to protect the interests of foreign nations, not merely the interests of the defendant. It therefore is not a requirement that the defendant alone can waive by choice or forfeit by inadvertence. If a defendant could waive or forfeit the requirement regardless of the interests of a foreign nation whose prerogatives may be directly at stake, application of the MDLEA could engender considerable tensions in foreign relations.

Suppose, for instance, that a defendant wishes to plead guilty and thus has no desire to dispute that a vessel is "subject to the jurisdiction of the United States," even though the vessel is "registered in a foreign nation" and "that nation has [not] consented or waived objection to the enforcement of United States law by the United States." *Id.* § 70502(c)(1)(C). Or suppose that, in the same circumstances, the defendant inadvertently fails to raise the issue in the district court. If a court were to decline to address the issue on the theory that the defendant had waived or forfeited any objection, application of the MDLEA could cause substantial discord with a foreign nation. Congress guarded against that risk by rendering the "jurisdiction of the United States over a vessel" a condition on subject-matter jurisdiction, thereby obligating courts to examine the matter regardless of whether a defendant presses or preserves it. *Compare Cotton*, 535 U.S. at 629-31 (holding that a defendant's protection against defective indictments is waivable by the defendant and thus does not affect subject-matter jurisdiction).

Notably, Congress demonstrated the same sensitivity to the interests of affected foreign sovereigns in another provision of the MDLEA—enacted contemporaneously with § 70504(a), *see* Pub. L. 104-324, 110 Stat. 3901 (1996)—under which a defendant lacks "standing to raise a claim of failure to comply with international law as a basis for a defense" because the [—18—] defense "may be made only by a foreign nation." 46 U.S.C. § 70505. Under § 70504(a), similarly, a foreign nation's stake in the application of the MDLEA in cases involving a non-United States vessel asserted to be subject to United States jurisdiction means that a defendant effectively lacks "standing" to waive or forfeit the issue of United States jurisdiction over the vessel. Congress, moreover, cabined the jurisdictional inquiry to MDLEA cases in which foreign relations issues would most likely arise—*viz.*, cases involving non-United States "vessels subject to the jurisdiction of the United States," as opposed to cases involving "vessels of the United States" or defendants who are United States citizens or resident aliens. *See id.* §§ 70503(a), 70504(a). In the latter situations, the determination whether the vessel is "of the United States" or the defendant is a United States citizen or resident alien would go to an element of the offense, and so would be subject to waiver by a defendant who enters an unconditional guilty plea.

The government, relying on the First Circuit's divided decision in *Gonzalez*, argues that the term "jurisdiction" in § 70504(a) refers to the legislative "jurisdiction" of Congress in the sense of a so-called "jurisdictional element," not to the subject-matter jurisdiction of the federal courts. The government observes that § 70504(a) speaks in terms of the "jurisdiction of the United States," rather than—as with other statutes that define subject-matter jurisdiction—the jurisdiction of the "district courts." *E.g.*, 18 U.S.C. § 3231; 28 U.S.C. §§ 1331, 1332. For several reasons, we are unpersuaded by the government's argument.

First, the government fails to account for the strong reasons to understand § 70504(a) to establish a requirement of subject-matter jurisdiction as a means of protecting the interests of foreign sovereigns. Construing § 70504(a) only to [—19—] pertain to Congress's legislative "jurisdiction," for the reasons explained, would potentially give rise to foreign relations concerns in the application of the MDLEA. It is entirely understandable that Congress would define the subject-matter jurisdiction of district courts in a manner sensitive to the interests of another sovereign. *Cf.* 18 U.S.C. § 1152 (establishing an exception from general jurisdiction over federal crimes in certain circumstances for "offenses committed by one Indian against . . . another Indian" or by an Indian "in the Indian country who has been punished by the local law of the tribe"); 28 U.S.C. § 1604 (Foreign Sovereign Immunities Act).

In addition, when Congress establishes a so-called "jurisdictional element" addressing the reach of its legislative authority, Congress does not use the term "jurisdiction" in the statute. *See, e.g.*, 18 U.S.C. § 656 (criminalizing certain conduct by an individual who is "an officer, director, agent or employee of, or connected in any capacity with any Federal Reserve bank"); *id.* § 922(q)(2)(A) (making it "unlawful for any individual knowingly to possess a firearm that has moved in or that otherwise affects interstate or foreign commerce at a place that the individual knows . . . is a school zone"). Rather, "jurisdictional element" is a "colloquialism" used by "[l]awyers and judges." *Hugi v. United States*, 164 F.3d 378, 380 (7th Cir. 1999).

Statutes that establish "jurisdictional elements" not only contain no use of the term "jurisdiction," but, consistent with the description "jurisdictional *element*," treat the relevant condition as an element of the offense to be found by a jury. In that sense, "proof of [a jurisdictional element] is no different from proof of any other element of a federal crime." *Id.* at 381. By contrast, § 70504(a) specifically provides that the "jurisdiction of the United States with respect to a vessel" is [—20—] *not* an element of the offense and is to be determined by the court rather than by the jury, signifying that Congress did not intend to establish a "jurisdictional element." To be sure, allocation of the issue to the court rather than the jury gives rise to a possible Sixth Amendment claim (regardless of whether the issue goes to subject-matter jurisdiction), *see Gonzalez*, 311 F.3d at 444, but appellants raise no such claim here.

Additionally, a provision's "placement within" the statute can "indicat[e] that Congress wanted that provision to be treated as having jurisdictional attributes." *Henderson*, 131 S. Ct. at 1205; *see also Reed Elsevier*, 559 U.S. at 164-65; *Arbaugh*, 546 U.S. at 514-15. The placement of § 70504(a) reinforces that it pertains to the subject-matter jurisdiction of district courts rather than the legislative "jurisdiction" of Congress. Congress situated § 70504(a) within a provision addressing, per its title, "Jurisdiction and venue." 46 U.S.C. § 70504; *see INS v. Nat'l Cent. for Immigrants' Rights, Inc.*, 502 U.S. 183, 189 (1991) ("[T]he title of a statue or section can aid in resolving an ambiguity in the legislation's text."). The subject of "venue," addressed in § 70504(b), by nature speaks to the authority of a district court to hear a case. The subject of "jurisdiction," addressed in § 70504(a), is best understood likewise to address the authority of district courts to hear a case rather than Congress's own authority to regulate. In other instances in which Congress uses the term "jurisdiction and venue," the statute indisputably pertains to the jurisdiction of the courts. *See, e.g.*, 7 U.S.C. § 941; 29 U.S.C. § 1370; 40 U.S.C. § 123. Congress did the same in § 70504.

That is particularly evident in light of the history of § 70504. Before 2006, the language

of § 70504(a) addressing jurisdiction and the language of § 70504(b) addressing venue were combined in one statutory subsection. *See* 46 App. U.S.C. § 1903(f) (2000). The provision read: [—21—]

Any person who violates this section shall be tried in the United States district court at the point of entry where that person enters the United States, or in the United States District Court of the District of Columbia. Jurisdiction of the United States with respect to vessels subject to this chapter is not an element of any offense. All jurisdictional issues arising under this chapter are preliminary questions of law to be determined solely by the trial judge.

Id. That entire provision, including the references to "jurisdiction," self-evidently concerned the authority of district courts, not the legislative authority of Congress.

In 2006, Congress relocated the MDLEA, and in doing so separated what was § 1903(f) into two neighboring subsections within the new § 70504, without any material change to the text. There is no reason to conclude that Congress, despite making no relevant adjustment to the text, meant to fundamentally transform the "jurisdictional" portion so that it now speaks to legislative rather than judicial authority. *See* H.R. Rep. 109-170, at 2 (2005) ("The purpose of H.R. 1442 is to complete the codification of title 46 . . . . It does so by reorganizing and restating the laws currently in the appendix to title 46. It codifies existing law rather than creating new law."). Rather, both halves of a provision addressing "jurisdiction and venue" continue to pertain to the authority of courts.

For those reasons, we conclude that § 70504(a) relates to the subject-matter jurisdiction of the district courts. Appellants' entry of unconditional guilty pleas thus could not waive the question whether the pertinent vessels are "subject to [—22—] the jurisdiction of the United States" within the meaning of the MDLEA.

2.

Proceeding to the merits, we reject appellants' argument that the vessels described in their stipulated facts were not "subject to the jurisdiction of the United States." The district court concluded that appellants' charged conduct involved "vessels without nationality," one type of vessel "subject to the jurisdiction of the United States." 46 U.S.C. § 70502(c)(1)(A). While we review de novo the district court's legal conclusion that the vessels in this case meet the statutory definition, we review any predicate factual determinations for clear error. *See Herbert v. Nat'l Acad. of Scis.*, 974 F.2d 192, 197 (D.C. Cir. 1992). We find no error—clear or otherwise—in the district court's decision.

There is no basis for overturning the district court's finding that appellants were both involved with "vessels without nationality." In their factual stipulations, each appellant acknowledged that he "was a co-conspirator in a drug trafficking organization which, from in or about 2006 and continuing until August 25, 2010, transported narcotics from Colombia on *stateless* go-fast vessels through international waters to other countries." J.A. 93, 128 (emphasis added). Appellants do not dispute that "stateless" vessels are vessels "without nationality."

Additionally, appellants each gave a "particular" example of the conspiracy's plans to transport drugs from Colombia on board "stateless" vessels. J.A. 94, 129. Munoz Miranda stipulated that, "[i]n particular," he and others "planned to transport more than 500 grams of cocaine on board a go-fast boat leaving from the north coast of Colombia" in November 2006, and further stipulated that the "boat was not registered in [—23—] Colombia and did not fly a Colombian flag." J.A. 93-94. Valderrama Carvajal identified the same example, and also described an additional example that involved a "go-fast boat" that "did not fly a flag, was not registered in Colombia or any other nation, and contained no registration identification." J.A. 128-29. "No one in the crew, including the captain, claimed that the go-fast boat was registered in Colombia." J.A. 129. Those stipulations gave the district court an ample basis for its determination that appellants' conspiratorial acts involved "vessels without nationality."

Appellants contend that neither of the vessels highlighted as examples in their factual stipulations can count as "vessels without nationality" because both boats were in Colombian waters when captured. According to appellants, a vessel is "without nationality" only when on the high seas, and it ceases to qualify as stateless when within any nation's—here, Colombia's—territorial waters. The district court correctly rejected that argument. The statute describes "vessels without nationality" in a manner that makes no reference to the situs of a vessel when seized. *See* 46 U.S.C. § 70502(d)(1). Instead, the statute contains three nonexclusive examples of "vessels without nationality," each of which turns on the "registry" of the vessel. *Id.* § 70502(d)(1)(A)-(C). That is consistent with the general understanding of a stateless vessel under international law. *See United States v. Rosero*, 42 F.3d 166, 171 (3d Cir. 1994) ("Under international law, '[s]hips have the nationality of the State whose flag they are entitled to fly.'") (quoting Convention on the High Seas of 1958, 13 U.S.T. 2312, T.I.A.S. No. 5200, art. 5(1)). If a vessel in fact ventured in and out of statelessness depending on where it happened to be located when seized, the statute would create a perverse incentive for vessels to race to a foreign nation's territorial waters before submitting to interdiction. Congress established no such regime under the MDLEA, and the vessels [—24—] in this case thus qualify as "without nationality" even though they were located in Colombian waters when seized.

* * * * *

For the foregoing reasons, we affirm the district court's denial of appellants' motions to dismiss and for reconsideration. We also affirm the district court's acceptance of appellants' guilty pleas.

So ordered.

United States Court of Appeals
for the District of Columbia Circuit

No. 13-1250

TURLOCK IRRIGATION DIST.
vs.
FEDERAL ENERGY REGULATORY COMM'N

On Petitions for Review of Orders of the Federal
Energy Regulatory Commission

Decided: May 15, 2015

Citation: 786 F.3d 18, 3 Adm. R. 687 (D.C. Cir. 2015).

Before **PILLARD,** Circuit Judge, and **SILBERMAN** and
SENTELLE, Senior Circuit Judges.

[—2—] **SENTELLE,** Senior Circuit Judge:

In the proceeding under review, the Federal Energy Regulatory Commission determined that La Grange Hydroelectric Project ("Project") fell within the mandatory licensing provisions of the Federal Power Act, 16 U.S.C. § 817(1), for three independent reasons, which we will discuss more fully below. The owners of the Project, Turlock Irrigation District and Modesto Irrigation District (collectively, "Districts") petition for review of FERC's order, *Turlock Irrigation Dist. & Modesto Irrigation Dist., Order on Rehearing, Clarifying Intervention Status, and Denying Stay Pending Judicial Review*, 144 FERC ¶ 61,051 (July 19, 2013), contending that the Project does not fall within FERC's licensing jurisdiction. The Tuolumne River Trust and other conservation groups (collectively, "Trust") petition for review of FERC's order, arguing that FERC erred by not finding that it [—3—] had licensing jurisdiction for four reasons instead of three. For the reasons set forth more fully below, we conclude that FERC's jurisdictional determinations were supported by substantial evidence and deny the Districts' petition for review. We dismiss the Trust's petition as it raises no justiciable case or controversy.

BACKGROUND

Between 1891 and 1893, the Districts constructed the regional La Grange facility, which consisted of a dam at River Mile[1] ("RM") 52.2 of the Tuolumne River, impounding the waters of the river and creating a reservoir for the purpose of irrigating river valley farmland. See Appendix 1 for a map of the region. In 1924, the Districts expanded the facility and its purpose by the construction of the La Grange Powerhouse for the production of hydroelectricity. The Powerhouse was comprised of a smaller unit with two 500 kilowatt generators, and a larger unit with a 3750 kilowatt generator. In 1989, Turlock replaced the Powerhouse's turbines and generating units.

In June 2011, FERC received an inquiry from the National Marine Fisheries Service concerning the status of the theretofore unlicensed La Grange Hydroelectric Project. In response to the inquiry, Commission staff undertook a review of the Project to determine whether it is subject to the Commission's mandatory licensing jurisdiction under the Federal Power Act ("FPA"). *Turlock Irrigation Dist. & Modesto Irrigation Dist.*, 141 FERC ¶ 62,211 (Dec. 19, 2012). FERC provided notice to the Districts and other interested parties of its pending jurisdictional determination. On December 19, 2012, the Director of the Division of Hydropower Administration and Compliance issued an order determining that the Project did require licensure within [—4—] the jurisdiction of the Commission under the FPA and ordered the Districts to proceed to come into compliance with the requirements of licensure. *Id.* In the decision, the Director concluded that the licensure was required under three governing provisions of 16 U.S.C. § 817(1): the Project was (1) located on a navigable water of the United States, (2) occupied public lands of the United States, or (3) if the stream were not navigable, it was in any event one over which Congress had jurisdiction under its authority to regulate commerce. Thereafter, the

---

[1] River Miles are measured from the mouth of a river (RM 0).

Districts and the Trust petitioned the Commission for rehearing of the staff-level decision. The Districts argued that the Project was not within the licensure provisions of the FPA. The Trust contended that the Director's opinion erred in not assigning a fourth reason for imposing the licensing requirement: the Trust argued that the Project required licensure because it formed a complete unit of development with the Don Pedro Project, a neighboring federally licensed hydroelectric project. The Commission ruled against the Districts on all three grounds of their appeal. It further concluded that it need not determine whether the fourth ground asserted by the Trust was applicable, as it would not change the result in any event. The Districts and the Trust now petition this court for review of the Commission's order. For the reasons set forth below, we deny the petition of the Districts and dismiss the petition of the Trust.

ANALYSIS

The Federal Power Act renders unlawful the unlicensed construction, operation, or maintenance of any "dam, water conduit, reservoir, power house, or other works incidental thereto across, along, or in" any waters meeting statutory criteria. More specifically, and as relevant here, such licensure is required where the impounded waters are "navigable waters of the United States, or upon any part of the public lands or reservations of the United States . . . or . . . over which Congress [—5—] has jurisdiction under its authority to regulate commerce with foreign nations and among the several States . . . ." 16 U.S.C. § 817(1). The Commission found the Tuolumne River to be covered by all three of the quoted criteria. The Trust argues that while the Commission reached the right result that the Project is required to be licensed, it should have ordered that the Project be licensed as part of a single unit with another hydroelectric project, the Don Pedro Project, 2.6 miles upstream from the La Grange Project.

I. *The Trust's Petition*

Before determining the merits of the cause, we must first satisfy ourselves that we have jurisdiction. One element of jurisdiction is standing. There is no question that the Districts have standing to bring their current petition. They are entities regulated by the order under review, and the relief prayed would alleviate the harm asserted. They allege, and it is evident, that the acts of the Commission have caused the injury of which they complain, that is, that they must submit to licensure. It is equally evident that the relief sought in the current litigation, the vacating of the Commission's order, would alleviate that harm. The same is not true of the Trust.

The Trust seeks to have the Project made subject to the licensure requirements of the FPA. The Commission entered an order declaring that the Project is subject to the licensing requirements of the FPA. The Trust does not seek to have the court change the decision, but only asks the court to tell the Commission that it should do so for four reasons instead of three. Unlike Becket, the Trust does not speak of "do[ing] the right deed for the wrong reason." T.S. Eliot, Murder in the Cathedral, Act 1. Rather, it accuses the Commission of doing the right thing for too few reasons. This does not establish standing. Because standing "is an essential and unchanging part [—6—] of the case-or-controversy requirement of Article III," *Lujan v. Defenders of Wildlife*, 504 U.S. 555, 560 (1992), the Trust must establish it has standing before we may exercise jurisdiction over its claims, *County of Delaware, Pa. v. Department of Transp.*, 554 F.3d 143, 147 (D.C. Cir. 2009).

It is well established "that the irreducible constitutional minimum of standing contains three elements." *Lujan*, 504 U.S. at 560. "To establish constitutional standing, a petitioner must show an actual or imminent injury in fact, fairly traceable to the challenged agency action, that will likely be redressed by a favorable decision." *Exxon Mobil Corp. v. FERC*, 571 F.3d 1208, 1219 (D.C. Cir. 2009). An injury in fact is "an invasion of a legally protected interest which is (a) concrete and particularized, and (b) actual or imminent, not conjectural or hypothetical." *Lujan*, 504 U.S. at 560 (quotations and citations omitted).

The Trust did not suffer an injury in fact because the Trust received exactly what it sought. FERC accepted some of the jurisdictional theories advanced by the Trust, and found that the La Grange Project was required to be licensed. The Trust argues that it is aggrieved because FERC's refusal to license La Grange and the Don Pedro Project in a single proceeding doubles the cost the Trust must bear in order to actively participate in both licensing proceedings, and frustrates the creation of a coordinated fish passage through the two dams, thus resulting in a decline to the fish population. This decline in fish population, they argue, reduces the number of tourists who come to observe the spawning salmon, thus reducing the money the Trust will make from guided tours.

Neither of the Trust's asserted injuries satisfies the constitutional requirement of injury in fact. We have previously recognized that the expenditure of resources on advocacy is not a cognizable Article III injury. *See Center for Law and Educ. v. Department of Educ.*, 396 F.3d 1152, 1162 n.4 (D.C. Cir. 2005) [—7—] ("[T]o hold that a lobbyist/advocacy group had standing to challenge government policy with no injury other than injury to its advocacy would eviscerate standing doctrine's actual injury requirement." (citing *Sierra Club v. Morton*, 405 U.S. 727, 739–40 (1972))). This is true whether the advocacy takes place through litigation or administrative proceedings. *See Nat'l Ass'n of Home Builders v. EPA*, 667 F.3d 6, 12 (D.C. Cir. 2011) (concluding that time and money spent "submitting comments to the EPA" and "testifying before the United States Senate" does not suffice to establish an injury in fact). "The mere fact that an organization redirects some of its resources to litigation and legal counseling in response to actions or inactions of another party is insufficient to impart standing upon the organization." *Nat'l Taxpayers Union, Inc. v. U.S.*, 68 F.3d 1428, 1434 (D.C. Cir. 1995) (quotations and citation omitted). The Trust's decision to expend more of its resources by participating in both Don Pedro's and La Grange's licensing proceedings is the type of alleged harm that we have repeatedly held does not qualify as an injury in fact.

The Trust, relying on this Court's decision in *Equal Rights Center v. Post Properties, Inc.*, argues that if a "defendant's allegedly wrongful action prompts an organization to 'increase[] the resources [it] must devote to programs independent of its suit,' . . . the organization has shown an injury in fact." 633 F.3d 1136, 1138 (D.C. Cir. 2011) (quoting *Spann v. Colonial Village, Inc.*, 899 F.2d 24, 27 (D.C. Cir. 1990)). But *Equal Rights Center* is inapposite. As we noted in that case, an organization must allege that the defendant's conduct "perceptibly impaired" the organization's ability to provide services in order to establish injury in fact. 633 F.3d at 1138–39 (citing *Havens Realty Corp. v. Coleman*, 455 U.S. 363, 378–79 (1982)). The Trust does not allege impairment of its ability to provide services, only impairment of its advocacy. As we noted above, this will not suffice. [—8—]

The Trust's second asserted injury, a decline in tourism revenue, is also insufficient to satisfy the injury in fact requirement. It is purely conjectural. The Trust theorizes that if La Grange and Don Pedro are not licensed in a single proceeding, then the two projects will not have a coordinated fish passage, which will lead to a decline in the fish population, potentially reducing the number of tourists to the river and, consequently, the amount of money the Trust will make off of tourism. "This theory stacks speculation upon hypothetical upon speculation, which does not establish an 'actual or imminent' injury." *New York Regional Interconnect*, 634 F.3d at 587. We may reject as overly speculative the Trust's assumption regarding the future behavior of third parties. *See Crete Carrier Corp. v. EPA*, 363 F.3d 490, 494 (D.C. Cir. 2004).

Moreover, the Trust's prediction that separate licensing proceedings will result in the lack of a coordinated fish passage hypothesizes as to the outcome of future legal proceedings, and is thus "too speculative to invoke the jurisdiction of an Art[icle] III Court." *Platte River Whooping Crane Critical Habitat Maintenance Trust v. FERC*, 962 F.2d 27, 35 (D.C. Cir. 1992) (quoting *Whitmore v. Arkansas*, 495 U.S. 149, 157 (1990)). The record before us does not establish that FERC cannot coordinate fish passage between La Grange and Don Pedro despite separate licensing. *See* Nov. 14, 2014 FERC 28(j) Letter and attachment at 2, 7–8. Indeed, FERC suggested at oral argument that it intended to do so. Oral Arg. Rec. at 30:50–32:05, 33:25–34:00. The FPA empowers FERC to formulate comprehensive plans for, among other things, "enhancement of fish and wildlife." 16 U.S.C. § 803(a)(1). On this record, it is wholly speculative to suggest that separate licensing will lead to an uncoordinated fish passage.

The Trust also seeks to proceed under associational standing, arguing that a decline in fish population will diminish its members' ongoing use and enjoyment of the river for fly fishing. To establish standing as an association, the Trust must [—9—] demonstrate that at least one of its members meets the three element test set forth in *Lujan. See NO Gas Pipeline v. FERC*, 756 F.3d 764, 767 (D.C. Cir. 2014). However, the notion that a lack of a coordinated fish passage will lead to a decline in the fish population which in turn will lead to a decrease in tourism is doubly speculative, and thus cannot be the basis for an injury in fact for either the Trust or its members. As noted above, we need not accept the Trust's assertion that fish passage will not be coordinated. Moreover, we have repeatedly held that litigants cannot establish an Article III injury based on the "independent action[s] of some third party not before th[is] court." *Florida Audubon Soc. v. Bentsen*, 94 F.3d 658, 670 (D.C. Cir. 1996) (en banc) (quoting *Simon v. E. Ky. Welfare Rights Org.*, 426 U.S. 26, 42 (1976)). This is because "predictions of future events (especially future actions taken by third parties)" are too speculative to support a claim of standing. *United Transp. Union v. ICC*, 891 F.2d 908, 912 (D.C. Cir. 1989). The Trust's theory of standing rests upon unsupported presumptions regarding fish population, and guesswork about what future

tourists *might* do. This is insufficient to support a claim of standing.

Because the Trust has failed to establish standing either for itself or on behalf of its members, we dismiss its petition for lack of jurisdiction.

II. *The Petition of the Districts*

As suggested above, our jurisdiction to entertain the petition of the Districts is unquestionable, and we therefore will proceed to determine whether their allegations merit relief. They do not. The Districts argue that FERC acted arbitrarily and capriciously and without substantial evidence in making its determination that the Tuolumne River was navigable, that the reservoir was upon public land to the United States, and that even if the stream were not navigable, it was nonetheless one over which Congress had jurisdiction under its authority to [—10—] regulate commerce. We disagree as to all three jurisdictional findings.

When reviewing FERC's hydroelectric licensing decisions, "[w]e defer to the agency's expertise . . . so long as its decision is supported by 'substantial evidence' in the record and reached by 'reasoned decisionmaking,' including an examination of the relevant data and a reasoned explanation supported by a stated connection between the facts found and the choice made." *U.S. Dept. of Interior v. FERC*, 952 F.2d 538, 543 (D.C. Cir. 1992) (quoting *Electricity Consumers Resource Council v. FERC*, 747 F.2d 1511, 1513 (D.C. Cir. 1984)). If supported by substantial evidence, FERC's findings of fact are conclusive. *See Consolidated Hydro, Inc. v. FERC*, 968 F.2d 1258, 1261 (D.C. Cir. 1992) (citing 16 U.S.C. § 825*l*(b)). Moreover, "we are particularly reluctant to interfere with the agency's reasoned judgments" when its orders "involve complex scientific or technical questions." *NRG Power Marketing, LLC v. FERC*, 718 F.3d 947, 953 (D.C. Cir. 2013) (quoting *B&J Oil & Gas v. FERC*, 353 F.3d 71, 76 (D.C. Cir. 2004)).

A. Navigability Determination

The Districts first challenge FERC's finding that La Grange is located on a navigable water of the United States. The Districts argue that FERC's navigability finding is not supported by substantial evidence. They also argue that FERC failed to present credible evidence of the potential commercial use to which the Tuolumne River may be put. We disagree, and conclude that FERC reasonably found that the Tuolumne River is suitable for use in interstate commerce, and that this finding was supported by substantial evidence.

Under the FPA, navigable waters are defined as:

> [T]hose parts of streams . . . which either in their natural or improved condition notwithstanding interruptions between the navigable parts of such streams or waters by falls, [—11—] shallows, or rapids compelling land carriage, are used or suitable for use for the transportation of persons or property in interstate or foreign commerce.

16 U.S.C. § 796(8). A waterway is navigable within that definition if "(1) it *presently* is being used or is suitable for use, or (2) it has been used or was suitable for use in the *past*, or (3) it could be made suitable for use in the *future* by reasonable improvements." *Rochester Gas & Elec. Corp. v. Federal Power Commission*, 344 F.2d 594, 596 (2d Cir. 1965) (emphases in original); *see also FPL Energy Maine Hydro LLC v. FERC*, 287 F.3d 1151, 1155 (D.C. Cir. 2002) (same). "Navigability can be established based on any of these three requirements; each alone is sufficient." *FPL Energy*, 287 F.3d at 1155. In making the determination of navigability of the Tuolumne, FERC relied on evidence bearing on each of the three.

As to the present navigability, the Commission found that the Tuolumne River is presently navigable from its confluence with the navigable San Joaquin River at least to the La Grange Project tailrace—the channel carrying water away from the powerhouse— and with a short portage to the base of the La Grange Dam at RM 52.2. *Turlock Irrigation Dist.*, 144 FERC ¶ 61,051 P 34. The evidence supporting this finding included a declaration submitted by the Trust reporting the experience of a kayaker who had navigated the waters from a point approximately 1.5 miles downstream of the La Grange Dam to the base of the Dam. Additionally, the Commission relied on evidence from the California Department of Fish and Game to the effect that the Department's employees have traveled upstream to an area of the river just below the powerhouse.

We have previously found "evidence of recreational use," as well as evidence of "'[a]ny similar personal or private use not involving recreation,'" relevant to establishing a river's "'suitability for commercial navigation.'" *FPL Energy*, 287 [—12—] F.3d at 1157 (quoting *Kennebec Water District*, 88 FERC ¶ 61,118, 61,304 (July 28, 1999)). As the Supreme Court has recognized, "personal or private use by boats demonstrates the availability of the stream for the simpler types of commercial navigation." *U.S. v. Appalachian Elec. Power Co.*, 311 U.S. 377, 416 (1940).

The governmental boat use provides sufficient evidence that the River is currently navigable. The evidence in the record establishes that between October 2011 and January 2012, California DFG crews conducted weekly salmon surveys, generally traveling upstream to RM 51.5, and at times as far as RM 51.9, a point upstream of the Project's tailrace. Joint Appendix 358–60. This evidence of weekly trips is more substantial than the evidence of boating we found sufficient in *FPL Energy*. 287 F.3d at 1159 (concluding that "[three] test canoe trips provide sufficient evidence that the Stream is navigable"); *see also Montana Power Co. v. Federal Power Commission*, 185 F.2d 491, 493–94 (D.C. Cir. 1950) (concluding that use of the river by "several steamboats" was sufficient to support a navigability finding).

The Districts contend that FERC was required to demonstrate "that the river between the Powerhouse and Dam" was navigable. Districts' Br. 12. We disagree. The FPA does not require FERC to show that the river is navigable *"through* the La Grange site," Districts' Reply Br. 5 (emphasis added), only that some part of the project is located on navigable waters, *see* 16 U.S.C. § 817(1) (requiring licensing if the "dam, water conduit, reservoir, power house, or *other works incidental thereto,*" are located "in any of the navigable waters of the United States" (emphasis added)). The tailrace is one of the project works that make up the La Grange Project. *See* Report of Turlock Irrigation District to FERC on the La Grange Project at 1 (Oct. 11, 2011), Joint Appendix 72 (listing the tailrace as part of the La Grange Project); *see also* 16 U.S.C. § 796(12) (defining "project works" as the "physical structures of a [—13—] project"). Therefore, FERC need only show that the river up to the tailrace is navigable in order to assert jurisdiction over the La Grange Project. *See, e.g., Sheldon Jackson College,* 54 FERC ¶ 61,263, 61,763–61,764 (Mar. 8, 1991) (licensing required where only a hydroelectric project's tailrace was located on navigable waters).

The Commission also found that the Tuolumne was navigable in the past at least up to the falls where the La Grange Dam is now located. This finding was based on an 1850 *Stockton Times* article, which stated that during the winter of 1849, gold seekers used whale boats to travel up the Tuolumne River as far as Jacksonville, a town located 20 miles upstream of the La Grange Dam. The Commission also relied upon an 1851 finding by the California legislature that the Tuolumne was navigable up to the "foot of the rapids" that then existed at the present day site of the La Grange Dam. *Turlock Irrigation Dist.,* 144 FERC ¶ 61,051, PP 57–64.

The Districts argue that the 1850 newspaper article FERC used to establish that whaleboats traveled up the Tuolumne River is unreliable as it conflicts with the Districts' expert report discussing the physical characteristics of the River in 1850. They also argue that FERC's reliance on the 1851 findings of the California legislature that the Tuolumne River was navigable up to the "foot of the rapids" was misplaced because "[s]tate law is not determinative of navigability under federal law," *State of Wisconsin v. Federal Power Commission,* 214 F.2d 334, 336–37 (7th Cir. 1954), and because the California legislature later changed its findings and moved the head of navigation downstream.

In disputing the reliability of the 1850 newspaper article, the Districts rely on the expert report of their historian, which states that based on "the falls at La Grange, the river gradient, upstream falls or rapids and the topography of the river canyon [—14—] that would have made portaging extremely difficult . . . it seems safe to conclude that navigation by whale boats *above* La Grange was virtually impossible." Report of Dr. Alan Paterson at 12, Joint Appendix 302 (emphasis added). As we stated above, FERC need only show that the river was navigable up to the Project's tailrace. Accordingly, the Districts' contention that the river above the falls was non-navigable does not undermine FERC's conclusion that the river was navigable in the past up to the La Grange Dam. *See Turlock Irrig. Dist.,* 144 FERC ¶ 61,051 P 60 ("[I]t is sufficient to find, as we do here, that the river was navigable in the past at least up to the falls, where the La Grange Dam is now located.").

The Districts are correct that the 1851 findings of the California legislature are not determinative of navigability under federal law. *See Brewer-Elliott Oil & Gas Co. v. U.S.,* 260 U.S. 77, 87 (1922) ("[T]he navigability of the stream is not a local question for the state tribunals to settle."). Indeed, fundamental to our system of government is the notion that the laws of the United States "form the supreme law of the land, 'anything in the constitution or laws of any state to the contrary notwithstanding.'" *M'Culloch v. Maryland,* 17 U.S. (4 Wheat.) 316, 406 (1819) (quoting U.S. CONST. art. VI, cl. 2). But this point is not dispositive, as nothing prevents FERC from citing state navigability determinations as evidence of the historic navigability of a river for federal law purposes. Nor does evidence that the California legislature later amended its determination defeat a finding of navigability. "When once found to be navigable, a waterway remains so." *Appalachian Elec. Power Co.*, 311 U.S. at 408.

FERC's evidence of historic navigability is not overwhelming. Nor is it so compelling as to completely foreclose any argument that the River was non-navigable. But evidence of past navigability need not be large to sustain a finding of navigability. *See id.* at 416. When viewed as a whole, the evidence is sufficient to support FERC's finding that **[—15—]** the River was used in the past up to the falls where La Grange is now located.

Lastly, the Districts argue that FERC failed to present credible evidence of the potential commercial use to which the Tuolumne River may be put. This argument also fails. We have previously rejected the notion that "FERC's navigability test was flawed because FERC failed to identify the possible commercial use to which the Stream may be put." *FPL Energy*, 287 F.3d at 1158. As we explained, "[t]he test is whether the waterway is presently 'suitable for use for the transportation of persons or property in interstate or foreign commerce,' not whether the waterway is presently suitable for a specific type of commercial activity named by FERC and approved of by an opposing party." *Id.* (quoting 16 U.S.C. § 796(8)).

To uphold FERC's navigability determination, "we need only find that the evidence on which the finding is based is substantial." *FPL Energy*, 287 F.3d at 1160. The "substantial evidence" standard "requires more than a scintilla, but can be satisfied by something less than a preponderance of the evidence." *Id.* We conclude that FERC's evidence of actual use in the past, together with current use of the Tuolumne River by California DFG crews, constitutes substantial evidence supporting FERC's finding that La Grange is located on a navigable water of the United States.

B. *Federal Lands Determination*

The Districts take issue with FERC's determination that the La Grange Reservoir extends onto federal lands. The Districts argue that FERC acted arbitrarily by ignoring

their water level gradient analysis, which purported to show that the reservoir ended about 5,300 feet upstream of the dam, short of federal lands. They also argue that FERC's attempt to calculate the precise point where the reservoir ends disregards the practical limitations of the data, namely that the results of FERC's **[—16—]** backwater analysis can have no better than a 0.5 to 1.0 foot degree of accuracy. We reject both arguments, and hold that FERC properly relied on the results of its backwater analysis to conclude that the La Grange reservoir extends onto federal lands.

The FPA requires licensure of a hydroelectric plant if its "dam, water conduit, reservoir, power house, or other works incidental thereto" are located "upon any part of the public lands or reservations of the United States." 16 U.S.C. § 817(1). The Commission found that the La Grange reservoir extends onto federal lands located approximately 5,800 feet upstream of the La Grange Dam. To support this determination, the Commission relied upon its backwater analysis, as well as a contour analysis submitted by the National Marine Fisheries Service.

Contrary to the Districts' arguments, FERC also considered the Districts' water level gradient analysis when making its federal lands determination. It found the results "misleading." *Turlock Irrig. Dist.*, 141 FERC ¶ 62,211 P 31. As FERC explained in its order, the Districts' analysis "assumes that reservoir water surface gradients generally appear flat and uniform, whereas river gradients in steeper areas appear higher and follow the river bed." *Id.* However, because reservoirs are influenced by the terrain, they can have a gradient such that their surface level varies, depending on where it is measured. *Id.* Accordingly, FERC found that focusing on the gradient of the water surface elevation "can lead to incorrect conclusions about the extent of the reservoir." *Id.*

Instead, FERC relied on the results of its backwater analysis to determine whether the La Grange reservoir extends onto federal lands. FERC has previously defined "backwater" as "the amount the depth of flow has been increased by an obstruction such as a dam." *Turlock Irrig. Dist.*, 141 FERC ¶ 62,211 P 28. (citing *Public Utility Dist. No. 1 of Pend Oreille* [—17—] *County, Washington*, 77 FERC ¶ 61,146, 61,543 n.11 (Nov. 13, 1996)). Under this definition, the upstream extent of the reservoir is the point where the depth of the river for "with-dam" and "without-dam" conditions are equal. *Turlock Irrig. Dist.*, 141 FERC ¶ 62,211 P 28. When performing this analysis, FERC calculates the depth for "with-dam" and "without-dam" conditions, plots the data as two lines on a graph, and then, relying on "eye observation," determines the point of tangency, *i.e.*, the point where the two lines meet. *Turlock Irrig. Dist.*, 144 FERC ¶ 61,051 P 76. This point denotes the end of the reservoir. *Id.*

Both FERC and the Districts used this method to determine the end point of the reservoir, and their calculations regarding the depth of the river for "with-dam" and "without-dam" conditions were the same. *Compare* Joint Appendix 175–79 (the Districts' calculations), *with* Joint Appendix 421–27 (FERC's calculations). FERC and the Districts differed, however, in their interpretation of this data. The Districts interpreted the data as suggesting that the reservoir ended somewhere around 5,300 feet, before the federal lands boundary. FERC found that the Reservoir extended more than 11,300 feet upstream of the La Grange Dam, reaching BLM land. FERC opined that this discrepancy in interpretation was a result of the graphs upon which the Districts relied:

> The Districts reach a different conclusion because they plot their results on smaller graphs with a more compressed scale and use thicker lines to depict the with-dam and without-dam conditions. This makes the two lines appear to converge at a point somewhere between 4,700 and 5,300 feet upstream of the La Grange Dam, downstream of the BLM land boundary. [FERC] [s]taff, using slightly larger graphs with a less compressed scale and thinner lines, determined the correct point of tangency as occurring much

farther upstream, more than 11,300 feet upstream of the La [—18—] Grange Dam, and well upstream of the BLM boundary. . . . . Staff used the same method as the Districts, but its graphs showed the results more clearly.

Turlock Irrig. Dist., 144 FERC ¶ 61,051 P 77.

The Districts frame their arguments as objections to the techniques or models employed by FERC, but they are actually objecting to FERC's interpretation of the data. The Districts complain that FERC's interpretation of the data is erroneous because it ignores the 0.5 to 1.0 foot degree of accuracy limitation inherent in any backwater analysis. They assert that "[a]pplying this degree of accuracy, the upstream end of the La Grange Reservoir would extend no further than 5,400 ft upstream of the La Grange Dam." Districts' Request for Rehearing at 23 (Jan. 18, 2013). Without more, such conclusory statements do not provide sufficient evidence for us to overturn FERC's interpretation.

The Districts nowhere identify a methodology for taking the degree of accuracy into account. In fact, in their 34-page request for rehearing, the Districts devote only two sentences to this issue, neither of which explains how FERC ought to adjust its interpretation of the data based on the degree of accuracy. Despite this lack of explanation, the Districts ask us to overturn FERC's determination. This we will not do. "We are reluctant to interfere with an agency's choice of methodology so long as it is not irrational." *California v. Watt*, 668 F.2d 1290, 1320 (D.C. Cir. 1981). In the absence of evidence establishing that FERC's interpretation was erroneous, we reject the Districts' argument that FERC acted arbitrarily in its interpretation of the backwater analysis.

However, even if we were to disregard FERC's interpretation of the backwater analysis, we could still sustain FERC's conclusion that the reservoir extends onto BLM land based on the contour analysis survey performed by the National Marine Fisheries Service. FERC often relies on contour lines to [—19—] determine the length of a reservoir. *See* 18 C.F.R. § 4.41(h)(2)(i)(A)(1) (contour lines are the "preferred method" for describing project boundaries); Districts' Request for Rehearing at 25, Joint Appendix 452 ("A brief sampling of other licenses shows that the Commission often uses a contour line for establishing a reservoir's upstream boundary."). In this case, the Fisheries Service used a contour elevation projected from the La Grange Dam's spillway crest elevation of 296.46 feet mean sea level to demonstrate that the La Grange Reservoir extends onto BLM land. FERC found that this analysis "conclusively demonstrate[s] that the La Grange Reservoir occupies federal lands." *Turlock Irrig. Dist.*, 144 FERC ¶ 61,051 P 86.

The Districts argue that the Fisheries Service's analysis was flawed because it used the spillway crest elevation of 296.46 feet mean sea level as the normal maximum surface elevation, as opposed to using the level at which the Districts normally operate La Grange. FERC rejected this argument, noting that the "normal maximum surface elevation of a reservoir is typically defined as the crest of the dam or spillway." *Turlock Irrig. Dist.*, 144 FERC ¶ 61,051 P 85. "[B]ecause the top of the [La Grange Dam] is almost entirely a spillway," the spillway crest defines the reservoir's normal maximum surface elevation, "not some lower elevation that a project operator may choose to maintain for operational reasons." *Turlock Irrig. Dist.*, 141 FERC ¶ 62,211 P 32 n.64. This conclusion is consistent with FERC's data documenting the elevation of the reservoir between the years 2009 and 2011, *Turlock Irrig. Dist.*, 144 FERC ¶ 61,051 P 85 n.119, as well as the Districts' backwater analysis, which used 296.46 feet mean sea level as the normal water surface elevation, Joint Appendix 158.

"[W]hen agency orders involve complex scientific or technical questions . . . we are particularly reluctant to interfere with the agency's reasoned judgments." *B&J Oil and Gas*, 353 F.3d at 76. Where, as in this case, the agency has "examined the [—20—] relevant data and has articulated an adequate explanation for its action," we will defer to the agency's decision. *City of Waukesha v. EPA*,

320 F.3d 228, 247 (D.C. Cir. 2003) (quotations and citation omitted).

C. *Commerce Clause Determination*

Finally, the Districts challenge FERC's finding that the La Grange Project is subject to FERC's mandatory licensing jurisdiction based on Congress's "authority to regulate commerce with foreign nations and among the several States." 16 U.S.C. § 817(1). In order to assert jurisdiction based on Congress's Commerce Clause authority, FERC must find that the project (1) is located on Commerce Clause waters, (2) affects interstate commerce, and (3) was "constructed" or enlarged after 1935. *See L.S. Starrett Co. v. FERC*, 650 F.3d 19, 23 (1st Cir. 2011) (citing 16 U.S.C. § 817(1)). FERC interprets "construction" as any increase in a project's generating capacity, *i.e.*, an increase in either the installed capacity or actual capacity of a project. *See id.* at 27 (upholding FERC's interpretation of "construction"). The installed capacity is the "maximum potential generating capacity of a turbine generator," whereas the actual capacity is the "measured capacity upon installation, which is affected by various site conditions." *Id.* at 21 n.3.

FERC found that La Grange is located on Commerce Clause waters, that the Project affects interstate commerce through its connection to the interstate electrical grid, and that the Project's generating capacity increased in 1989 when the Districts replaced the Powerhouse's turbines and generating units. FERC relied upon an engineering report submitted by the Districts to support these findings. *Turlock Irrig. Dist.*, 144 FERC ¶ 61,051, PP 87–103.

The Districts do not dispute that the Project is located on Commerce Clause waters and affects interstate commerce. Instead, they challenge FERC's finding that "post-1935 [—21—] construction . . . occurred when the Project's generating capacity increased in 1989." *Id.* at P 87. Before we address the Districts' specific challenges, however, some background is necessary.

A hydroelectric project generates energy using a turbine, which converts flowing water to mechanical power, and a generator, which converts the mechanical power to electric energy. *Id.* at PP 90–91. With unlicensed projects, FERC determines whether there has been an increase in the generating capacity of a project by looking to whether the project's "installed capacity" has increased. The "installed capacity" of a unit is the lesser of the rating output of the unit's generator, determined by looking at the nameplate or manufacturer's rating, or the unit's turbine. *Id.* at PP 91–92.

FERC determined that La Grange's original generators were rated at 1,000 kW and 3,750 kW, for a combined total of 4,750 kW, while the replacement generators were rated at 1,231 kW and 3,693 kW, for a combined total of 4,924 kW. *Id.* at PP 94–95. Because the combined rated output of the replacement generators was 174 kW higher than the combined rated output of the original generators, FERC concluded that the 1989 rehabilitation increased La Grange's installed capacity, and thus, La Grange required licensure. *Id.* at PP 95–103.

The Districts present three arguments for overturning FERC's determination. First, the Districts argue that FERC never demonstrated that 4,750 kW was the correct pre-rehabilitation rating for the old generators. Second, the Districts assert that FERC erred in comparing the generating capacity of the new turbines to the generating capacity of the generators. Such an "apples to oranges" analysis, they argue, is flawed because it assumes the generators are 100 percent efficient, instead of taking into account the "standard efficiency factor" of the generators. Lastly, the Districts argue that even if FERC's finding was correct, FERC abused its discretion in asserting [—22—] jurisdiction over such a de minimis increase in generating capacity. All three of the Districts' arguments lack merit.

First, FERC adequately demonstrated that 4,750 kW was the correct pre-rehabilitation rating for the old generators. FERC based the 4,750 kW number on an engineering report prepared by the Districts' contractor, Bechtel ("Bechtel Report"), and submitted to FERC by the Districts. The Bechtel Report notes that La Grange is made up of two turbine generator units, a smaller unit "with two-500 kW generators coupled to each side," and a larger unit "with one directly coupled 3750-kW Allis-Chalmers generator." Joint Appendix 103.

The Districts contend that the Bechtel Report never explicitly refers to those ratings as the nameplate or manufacturer's rating, and thus, they reason, it was arbitrary for FERC to rely on those ratings as if they were the nameplate rating. Conspicuously absent from the Districts' brief is an alternative explanation for the ratings listed in the Bechtel Report. The Districts never explain what those ratings refer to, or why Bechtel would provide ratings other than the nameplate rating. The Districts note that because the original units were taken from another site, the generators' capacity "may have been different from what may have been stated on the units." Districts' Br. 26. However, speculation as to the actual capacity of the generators is irrelevant to a determination of the rated output of the generators. *See L.S. Starrett Co.*, 650 F.3d at 21 n.3 (noting difference between installed capacity and actual capacity). In the absence of proof to the contrary, it was reasonable for FERC to assume that the ratings listed in the Bechtel Report were the manufacturer's ratings for the generators.

Second, the Districts argue that FERC erred by comparing the generating capacity of the old generators to the generating capacity of the new turbines rather than the new generators—an erroneous "apples to oranges" comparison, in the Districts' [—23—] view. This argument fails. FERC's analysis followed standard industry practice and was based on the information the Districts provided. The chart upon which FERC relied to find the rated output of the new generators listed the capacity of the new units (pairs of turbines and generators) in kilowatts, the standard expression of generator capacity, and horsepower, the standard expression of turbine capacity. Joint Appendix 108; *see*

Districts' Rehearing Request at 29, Joint Appendix 456 (noting that "[t]urbines are rated as horsepower," and "[g]enerator capacity is . . . rated as kilowatt output"). FERC's comparison of the old generators to the new generators rests on FERC's finding that the kilowatt values in the chart reflected the capacity of the generators, while the horsepower values reflected the capacity of the turbines. *Turlock Irrig. Dist.*, 144 FERC ¶ 61,051 PP 96–98. That finding is reasonable in light of standard unit-labeling practice. The Districts argue that this finding is wrong, as evidenced by the fact that the kilowatt figures and the horsepower figures match when horsepower is converted to kilowatts. The Districts emphasize that generator capacity cannot actually match turbine capacity because no generator is 100 percent efficient, and that the figures FERC used thus must not be generator figures at all, but are alternate expressions of turbine capacity in kilowatts and horsepower. However, "[s]tandard engineering practice . . . require[s]" that a generator's capacity be matched to the capacity of a turbine. Report of Turlock Irrigation District to FERC on the La Grange Project at 8 (Oct. 11, 2011), Joint Appendix 79; *Turlock Irrig. Dist.*, 144 FERC ¶ 61,051 P 90 ("[T]he rated output of a generator is chosen to match the output of the turbine . . . ." (citing *Engineering and Design, Hydropower*, at 5-20, *Department of the Army, Corps of Engineers, Engineer Manual* EM1110-2-1701 (Dec. 31, 1985))). The fact that the turbine and generator figures were reported as matching therefore appears unsurprising. The Districts failed to provide any clearer or better data requiring a contrary conclusion. Thus, it was [—24—] reasonable for FERC to assume that the kilowatt values in the chart reflected the capacity of the new generators.

Lastly, we reject the Districts' argument the FERC should have declined to exercise jurisdiction over La Grange because the increase in generating capacity was minimal. FERC contends that it does not have the discretion to decline to exercise jurisdiction over a hydroelectric project that meets the statutory requirements. We need not go that far to resolve this issue. It is sufficient to find,

as we do here, that FERC did not abuse its discretion in asserting jurisdiction over the La Grange Project on the basis of post-1935 construction that resulted in an increase in generating capacity of 174 kW. *See L.S. Starrett Co.*, 650 F.3d at 21–22 (affirming FERC's assertion of jurisdiction over a project that increased in generating capacity by 86 kW).

CONCLUSION

For the reasons stated above, we deny the Districts' petition for review because we conclude that FERC's jurisdictional determinations were supported by substantial evidence, and reached by reasoned decisionmaking. We dismiss the Trust's petition for review for lack of jurisdiction.

So ordered.

United States Court of Appeals
for the District of Columbia Circuit

No. 13-3107

UNITED STATES
vs.
BALLESTAS

Appeal from the United States District Court for the District of Columbia

Decided: July 28, 2015

Citation: 795 F.3d 138, 3 Adm. R. 698 (D.C. Cir. 2015).

Before **GARLAND**, Chief Judge, and **SRINIVASAN** and **WILKINS**, Circuit Judges.

[—2—] SRINIVASAN, Circuit Judge:

Javier Eduardo Juan Ballestas, a Colombian citizen, was indicted under the Maritime Drug Law Enforcement Act (MDLEA) and extradited to the United States for prosecution. Ballestas pleaded guilty to a charge of conspiracy to distribute drugs "on board . . . a vessel subject to the jurisdiction of the United States," in violation of the MDLEA. 46 U.S.C. §§ 70503(a), 70506(b). He reserved the right to bring an appeal on certain issues, including whether the MDLEA's conspiracy provision reaches extraterritorially to encompass his charged conduct in Colombia, and whether the application of the MDLEA against him violates the Due Process Clause of the Fifth Amendment because of the absence of an adequate nexus between his conduct and the United States. Because we are unpersuaded by Ballestas's arguments on those and other issues, we affirm.

I.

A long-term investigation conducted by United States and Colombian officials uncovered an international drug-trafficking operation based in Colombia. The organization used stateless vessels to transport large quantities of cocaine from Colombia through international waters, ultimately destined for the United States. Email and phone surveillance revealed that Ballestas supported the organization's drug smuggling activities.

He provided maps and law enforcement reports purporting to reveal the location of United States, Colombian, and other nations' air and maritime forces in the vicinity of the Caribbean Sea at specific times. Vessels engaged in trafficking runs used those reports to evade detection and capture.

Between May 2008 and September 2010, law enforcement agents seized or attempted to seize eight of the organization's cocaine shipments. Intercepted [—3—] communications linked Ballestas to at least four of the seized shipments, which together accounted for thousands of kilograms of seized cocaine.

The government sought indictment of Ballestas and six co-conspirators for violating the MDLEA, 46 U.S.C. §§ 70501 *et seq.* The MDLEA provides that an "individual may not knowingly or intentionally manufacture or distribute, or possess with intent to manufacture or distribute, a controlled substance on board . . . a vessel subject to the jurisdiction of the United States," *id.* § 70503(a), or attempt or conspire to do the same, *id.* § 70506(b). The statute defines a "vessel subject to the jurisdiction of the United States" to include "vessel[s] without nationality." *Id.* § 70502(c)(1)(A). *See generally United States v. Miranda*, 780 F.3d 1185, 3 Adm. R. 676 (D.C. Cir. 2015).

In February, 2011, a federal grand jury returned an indictment charging Ballestas with conspiring to distribute drugs "on board . . . a vessel subject to the jurisdiction of the United States" in violation of the MDLEA. *See* 46 U.S.C. §§ 70503(a), 70506(b). Ballestas was arrested in Colombia and extradited to the United States to stand trial.

In September, 2012, Ballestas filed a motion to dismiss the indictment. He contended that the MDLEA's conspiracy provision did not extend extraterritorially to reach individuals (like Ballestas) who never came "on board" the relevant vessels. *Id.* § 70503(a). Ballestas also argued that applying the MDLEA against him violated the Due Process Clause because of the absence of a nexus between his conduct and the United States.

In response to Ballestas's motion, the government proffered facts supporting the conspiracy charge. Two boats [—4—] in particular, the government submitted, supported Ballestas's prosecution under the MDLEA for conspiring to distribute drugs on board a vessel without nationality. First, a boat intercepted in international waters near Panama on March 3, 2010, displayed no visible flag and held no valid registration. Second, another boat, seized in Panamanian waters on March 11, 2010, similarly had no flag or registration. Officials observed the vessel in international waters, pursued the vessel into Panamanian waters, and then seized it. According to the government's proffer, Ballestas provided assistance with the cocaine shipments aboard both of those vessels.

Several months after responding to the motion to dismiss, the government informed Ballestas that the crew members apprehended during the March 3rd seizure had been charged and convicted under the MDLEA in the Middle District of Florida. The government provided Ballestas with the docket number and name of that case.

In February 2013, the district court denied Ballestas's motion to dismiss the indictment. The court concluded that the conspiracy provision of the MDLEA applied extraterritorially to Ballestas's actions in Colombia. Physical presence "on board" a vessel, the district court held, is not an essential element of a conspiracy offense under the MDLEA. The court further held that the vessels apprehended on March 3rd and 11th qualified as stateless vessels "subject to the jurisdiction of the United States." 46 U.S.C. § 70502(c)(1). In addition, the court rejected Ballestas's due process challenge, finding that there is no requirement to show a nexus to the United States when the alleged crimes involve stateless vessels.

Ballestas sought reconsideration of the district court's denial of his motion to dismiss. He argued that certain [—5—] intervening decisions undermined the court's extra-territoriality and due process holdings. The district court denied the motion for reconsideration, and, shortly thereafter, Ballestas pleaded guilty to a superseding information. In connection with Ballestas's sentence, the superseding information omitted certain drug quantity specifications that had appeared in the indictment in order to avoid triggering a ten-year mandatory minimum term of imprisonment.

Ballestas's plea agreement reserved his right to appeal "the specific and limited issue" of the denial of his motion to dismiss and motion for reconsideration. App. 192. The agreement also preserved his right to appeal his sentence on the grounds that it "exceeds the maximum permitted by statute or results from an upward departure from the guideline range established by the Court at sentencing." *Id.* at 193. In connection with his plea agreement, Ballestas and the government entered a joint statement of stipulated facts. Those facts established Ballestas's awareness of and involvement with the vessel interdicted on March 3rd and also established that the vessel was "without nationality" and therefore subject to the jurisdiction of the United States. *Id.* at 181-82. The district court accepted Ballestas's plea after conducting a colloquy in accordance with Federal Rule of Criminal Procedure 11.

In November 2013, the district court calculated Ballestas's sentencing guidelines range to be seventy to eighty-seven months based on the quantity of drugs stipulated to have been recovered from the March 3rd vessel. The court sentenced Ballestas to a below-guidelines sentence of sixty-four months of imprisonment followed by three years of supervised release. Ballestas now appeals, challenging the denial of his motion to dismiss, the denial of his motion for reconsideration, and his sentence. [—6—]

II.

A.

Ballestas first contends that the MDLEA's conspiracy provision does not apply extraterritorially to reach his conduct in Colombia. We disagree.

The MDLEA's conspiracy provision, 46 U.S.C. § 70506(b), provides that a "person attempting or conspiring to violate section 70503 of this title is subject to the same penalties as provided for violating section 70503." The underlying substantive offense set forth in § 70503 prohibits "knowingly or intentionally manufactur[ing] or distribut[ing], or possess[ing] with intent to distribute, a controlled substance on board," *inter alia*, "a vessel subject to the jurisdiction of the United States," *id.* § 70503(a), which includes "a vessel without nationality," *id.* § 70502(c)(1)(A).

In arguing that the MDLEA's conspiracy provision fails to reach extraterritorially, Ballestas relies on two canons of statutory interpretation. First, he invokes the presumption against extraterritoriality, which dictates that, "[w]hen a statute gives no clear indication of an extraterritorial application, it has none." *Morrison v. Nat'l Austl. Bank Ltd.*, 561 U.S. 247, 255 (2010). Second, he relies on the so-called *Charming Betsy* canon, which takes its name from a decision in which the Supreme Court explained that "an act of Congress ought never to be construed to violate the law of nations if any other possible construction remains." *Murray v. Schooner Charming Betsy*, 6 U.S. (2 Cranch) 64, 118 (1804).

Each of those "principle[s]," however, "represents a canon of construction, or a presumption about a statute's [—7—] meaning, rather than a limit upon Congress's power to legislate." *Morrison*, 561 U.S. at 255. Thus, notwithstanding the presumption against extraterritoriality, a statute will be construed to apply extraterritorially if Congress gives a "clear indication" of that intention. *Id.* With regard to the *Charming Betsy* canon, similarly, if "a statute makes plain Congress's intent," a court "must enforce the intent of Congress irrespective of whether the statute conforms to customary international law." *United States v. Yousef*, 327 F.3d 56, 93 (2d Cir. 2003). After all, "Congress is not bound by international law," so "it may legislate with respect to conduct outside the United States, in excess of the limits posed by international law." *Id.* at 86.

Here, the extraterritorial reach of the MDLEA's substantive prohibitions is clear. Section 70503(b), entitled "extension beyond territorial jurisdiction," provides that § 70503(a), which sets forth the substantive prohibitions, "applies even though the act is committed outside the territorial jurisdiction of the United States." 46 U.S.C. § 70503(b). That straightforward expression of extraterritorial application settles the extraterritorial reach of § 70503(a).

Ballestas, however, attempts to draw a line between the extraterritorial reach of the MDLEA's substantive offense in § 70503(a) and the reach of the MDLEA's conspiracy offense in § 70506(b). He relies on the understanding that, "[w]hen a statute provides for some extraterritorial application, the presumption against extraterritoriality operates to limit that provision to its terms." *Kiobel v. Royal Dutch Petroleum Co.*, 133 S. Ct. 1659, 1667 (2013) (quoting *Morrison*, 561 U.S. at 265). In Ballestas's view, the MDLEA's extraterritorial application therefore should be confined to the substantive prohibitions set forth in § 70503(a), and should not extend to [—8—] conspiracy (or attempt) to commit those substantive crimes under § 70506. We are unpersuaded.

Under the presumption against extraterritoriality, the extraterritorial reach of a particular provision will not necessarily be imputed to an entire statute. But in the particular context of "an ancillary offense like aiding and abetting or conspiracy," we have held that, "[g]enerally, the extraterritorial reach of [the] ancillary offense . . . is coterminous with that of the underlying criminal statute." *United States v. Ali*, 718 F.3d 929, 939 (D.C. Cir. 2013). As a result, "when the underlying criminal statute's extraterritorial reach is unquestionable, the presumption [against extraterritoriality] is rebutted with equal force" for ancillary offenses in the same statute. *Id.*; *see United States v. Hill*, 279 F.3d 731, 739 (9th Cir. 2002). Here, because the substantive offense established in § 70503(a) applies extraterritorially, we conclude that conspiracy to commit that substantive offense under § 70506 also has extraterritorial reach. And with the extraterritorial reach of the conspiracy provision clearly established, we have no occasion to apply the *Charming Betsy* canon.

Our decision in *United States v. Ali* is highly instructive. Ali faced two sets of conspiracy charges. First, he was charged under the blanket conspiracy statute, 18 U.S.C. § 371, with conspiracy to commit piracy. The generic conspiracy provision, we observed, lacks affirmative indication of an intention to reach extraterritorially. Because the provision is "ambiguous as to [its] application abroad," we applied the *Charming Betsy* canon to determine whether extraterritorial application would be consistent with the law of nations. *Ali*, 718 F.3d at 935; *see Kiobel*, 133 S. Ct. at 1664-65. Ali was also charged with conspiracy to commit hostage taking under the Hostage Taking Act, 18 U.S.C. § 1203. Like the [—9—] MDLEA, the Hostage Taking Act specifically provides for its extraterritorial application, and it also criminalizes conspiracy in the same statute. *Id.* § 1203(a). Because the Hostage Taking Act made clear its extraterritorial reach, and because that understanding applied to the Act's conspiracy prohibition, we declined to apply the *Charming Betsy* canon. *Ali*, 718 F.3d at 943.

We follow the same course here with respect to the MDLEA. To be sure, the Hostage Taking Act's prohibition against conspiracy appears in the same statutory subsection as the underlying substantive offense, 18 U.S.C. § 1203(a), whereas the MDLEA codifies its conspiracy prohibition in a separate statutory section, 46 U.S.C. § 70506(b). But we view that to be a distinction without a difference.

Our conclusion that the MDLEA's conspiracy provision applies extraterritorially is consistent with Congress's purpose in enacting it. As the Senate Report for the MDLEA explains, Congress sought to address concerns about difficulties encountered in prosecuting persons involved with shipments of drugs to the United States on vessels, both with respect to the crew on board and others associated with the enterprise. Before the MDLEA's enactment, when the Coast Guard seized illegal drug shipments, the government could not "prosecute the crew *or others involved in the smuggling operation*" in the absence of often elusive evidence that the drugs were destined for the United States. S. Rep. No. 96-855, at 2 (1980), *reprinted in* U.S.C.C.A.N. 2785, 2786 (July 16, 1980) (emphasis added). In light of the obstacles to successful prosecution in the United States, the Coast Guard's drug interdiction efforts had "little deterrent effect on the crews *or the trafficking organizations.*" *Id.* (emphasis added). [—10—]

Recognizing that "trafficking in controlled substances aboard vessels is a serious international problem, is universally condemned, and presents a specific threat to the security and societal well-being of the United States," 46 U.S.C. § 70501, Congress enacted the MDLEA to enhance the government's ability to prosecute members of drug trafficking organizations. Giving the MDLEA's conspiracy provision the construction suggested by Ballestas would effectively inoculate many members of such organizations—including organizations targeting the United States—against prosecution. Drug kingpins and other conspirators who facilitate and assist in carrying out trafficking schemes would fall beyond the reach of the statute, compromising the overriding intent of Congress in enacting it. Those considerations reinforce our conclusion that the MDLEA's conspiracy provision reaches Ballestas's extraterritorial conduct in this case.

B.

Ballestas next argues that, even if the MDLEA's conspiracy provision applies extraterritorially, his particular conduct is still beyond the statute's reach. The MDLEA's substantive provision criminalizes the manufacture, distribution, or possession of a controlled substance "on board" a covered vessel. 46 U.S.C. § 70503(a). That language, Ballestas claims, imposes an express limitation on the scope of the MDLEA's extraterritorial application. The qualifying phrase "on board," according to Ballestas, means that the MDLEA should apply extraterritorially only when a person's charged conduct took place on board a covered vessel.

At the outset, we note that, under the interpretation Ballestas urges us to adopt, the conspiracy and attempt [—11—] prohibition contained in § 70506(b) would seemingly do little practical work. Under his interpretation, § 70506(b) would reach individuals conspiring or attempting to violate § 70503 only if their conduct took place while physically "on board vessels" covered by the statute. But it is unclear whether someone could conspire or attempt to violate § 70503(a) while "on board a vessel" without simultaneously violating the substantive prohibition itself. If a person on a covered vessel knows that drugs destined for distribution are on the vessel and has played a role in the trafficking enterprise (as would be the case in a conspiracy or attempt prosecution), that person might well also have committed the underlying substantive offense by "possess[ing]" (at least constructively), with intent to distribute, "a controlled substance on board" the vessel. 46 U.S.C. § 70503(a).

In any event, we need not definitively decide in this case whether, or to what extent, the phrase "on board a vessel" might limit the extraterritorial application of the MDLEA. Regardless, Ballestas's conduct would still fall within the statute's exterritorial reach. It is a well-established principle of conspiracy law that "the overt act of one partner in a crime is attributable to all." *Pinkerton v. United States*, 328 U.S. 640, 647 (1946). And "[a]s long as a substantive offense was done in furtherance of the conspiracy, and was reasonably foreseeable as a 'necessary or natural consequence of the unlawful agreement,' then a conspirator will be held vicariously liable for the offense committed by his or her co-conspirators." *United States v. Washington*, 106 F.3d 983, 1012 (D.C. Cir. 1997). Those settled principles apply to Ballestas.

The stipulated facts establish, first, that criminal conduct took place "on board" vessels covered by the MDLEA, and second, that the criminal conduct is attributable to Ballestas as [—12—] a co-conspirator. Ballestas

stipulated to his involvement in a drug trafficking organization that regularly transported drugs on board vessels traveling over the high seas. App. 179-80. In particular, Ballestas stipulated to his awareness that the organization transported approximately 1500 kilograms of cocaine on board a vessel apprehended by the United States Coast Guard on or about March 3, 2010. *Id.* at 181. The overt acts of other conspirators on board the March 3rd vessel are therefore attributable to Ballestas, satisfying any "on board a vessel" requirement that might arguably circumscribe the MDLEA's extraterritorial application.

III.

Ballestas next challenges Congress's authority to criminalize his actions under the Define and Punish Clause, U.S. Const. art. I, § 8, cl. 10. That clause grants Congress the authority "[t]o define and punish Piracies and Felonies committed on the high Seas, and Offenses against the Law of Nations." The clause encompasses three distinct powers: (i) to define and punish piracy; (ii) to define and punish felonies committed on the high seas; and (iii) to define and punish offenses against the Law of Nations. *See United States v. Smith*, 18 U.S. (5 Wheat.) 153, 158-59 (1820). In defending Congress's constitutional authority to apply the MDLEA in the circumstances of this case, the government relies solely on Congress's power under the Felonies Clause, *i.e.*, its power to define and punish felonies committed on the high seas. We agree that the Felonies Clause grants Congress authority to criminalize Ballestas's conduct.

Ballestas's argument relies in substantial part on the Eleventh Circuit's decision in *United States v. Bellaizac-Hurtado*, 700 F.3d 1245 (11th Cir. 2012). In that case, Panamanian officials apprehended the defendants on board a [—13—] stateless vessel in Panamanian waters. Panama consented to the prosecution of the defendants in the United States, but the Eleventh Circuit found that the application of the MDLEA to the defendants' conduct lay beyond Congress's constitutional authority. Critically, however, the government in *Bellaizac-Hurtado* relied solely on the Law of Nations Clause to support the constitutionality of the MDLEA's application. Responding to the government's argument, the Eleventh Circuit held that "drug trafficking is not a violation of customary international law and, as a result, falls outside the power of Congress under the [Law of Nations] Clause." *Id.* at 1249. *Bellaizac-Hurtado* did not address whether any alternative source of congressional authority—such as the Felonies Clause—could serve to criminalize the defendants' conduct. *Id.* at 1258. In fact, the court observed that "all of the [other] appeals in which we have considered the constitutionality of [drug trafficking] laws involved conduct on the high seas," and those convictions were upheld "as an exercise of [Congress's] power under the Felonies Clause." *Id.* at 1257. Because the government in this case defends Congress's authority under the Felonies Clause, not the Law of Nations Clause, *Bellaizac-Hurtado* is of little assistance to Ballestas.

In assessing whether the Felonies Clause grants Congress the power to criminalize Ballestas's behavior, we again rely on the established principles of conspiracy law set forth above. As discussed, "the overt act of one partner in a crime is attributable to all," *Pinkerton*, 328 U.S. at 647, as long as the act "was done in furtherance of the conspiracy, and was reasonably foreseeable as a 'necessary or natural consequence of the unlawful agreement,'" *Washington*, 106 F.3d at 1011 (quoting *Pinkerton*, 328 U.S. at 647-48). Here, the stipulated facts establish that Ballestas's co-conspirators committed felonious acts on the high seas, and also that those acts are [—14—] directly attributable to him. Ballestas acknowledged that one of the drug trafficking organization's vessels was apprehended on March 3, 2010, carrying approximately 1500 kilograms of cocaine. App. 181. He further acknowledged that the vessel had "traveled through the high seas." *Id.* As an admitted co-conspirator of the crew members, the acts of the crew—committed on the high seas—are attributable to Ballestas. The Felonies Clause therefore provides Congress with authority to "punish" Ballestas for his role in that conspiracy.

IV.

We next consider Ballestas's argument that the application of the MDLEA in his case violated the Due Process Clause because the government failed to demonstrate a nexus between his actions abroad and the United States. Our circuit has yet to decide "whether the Constitution limits the extraterritorial exercise of federal criminal jurisdiction." *Ali*, 718 F.3d at 943-44. Several other courts of appeals, though, have found that the Due Process Clause imposes limits on the extraterritorial application of federal criminal laws. *See, e.g., United States v. Brehm*, 691 F.3d 547, 552-54 (4th Cir. 2012); *United States v. Ibarguen-Mosquera*, 634 F.3d 1370, 1378-79 (11th Cir. 2011). Those courts generally require a showing of "sufficient nexus between the defendant and the United States, so that . . . application [of the law] would not be arbitrary or fundamentally unfair." *United States v. Davis*, 905 F.2d 245, 248-49 (9th Cir. 1990) (citation omitted).

Just as in *Ali*, we need not definitively resolve whether the Due Process Clause constrains the extraterritorial application of federal criminal laws. Even assuming the existence of a due process limitation, the extraterritorial [—15—] application of the MDLEA in this case would not run afoul of it. As we observed in *Ali*, nexus with the United States merely serves as a "proxy for due process" requirements. *Ali*, 718 F.3d at 944. "The 'ultimate question'" under the Due Process Clause is not nexus, but is "whether 'application of the statute to the defendant [would] be arbitrary or fundamentally unfair.'" *Id.* (quoting *United States v. Juda*, 46 F.3d 961, 967 (9th Cir. 1995)). There is no arbitrariness or fundamental unfairness in the circumstances of this case.

Again, Ballestas's factual stipulations establish that he was part of an international drug smuggling organization that used stateless vessels to transport drugs across the high seas, bound ultimately for the United States. The conduct to which Ballestas pleaded guilty involved obtaining and selling reports and maps "indicat[ing] where *U.S.*, Colombian and other countries' . . . maritime assets were operating in the Caribbean Sea on a particular day." App. 180 (emphasis added). He stipulated to his knowledge that his co-conspirators used the maps to "plan the best route to be taken by the cocaine-laden vessels so as to avoid detection by maritime and law enforcement authorities," including, specifically, United States authorities. *Id.* Those admissions establish that application of a United States drug trafficking law (the MDLEA) to Ballestas was neither arbitrary nor fundamentally unfair.

V.

Ballestas claims that the district court erred in accepting the government's allegations as true when the court denied his motion to dismiss the indictment. In denying the motion, the district court relied on the "the Government['s] proffer[] that the vessel seized on March 3rd, 2010, was a vessel without nationality" (and thus a vessel subject to the jurisdiction of [—16—] the United States). App. 76. In Ballestas's view, the court could not deny his motion without requiring the introduction of evidence on whether the vessel in fact was subject to the jurisdiction of the United States and presenting that issue to the jury for proof beyond a reasonable doubt.

Ballestas's argument fundamentally misperceives the nature of a motion to dismiss an indictment. Because a court's "use[] [of] its supervisory power to dismiss an indictment . . . directly encroaches upon the fundamental role of the grand jury," dismissal is granted only in unusual circumstances. *Whitehouse v. U.S. Dist. Court*, 53 F.3d 1349, 1360 (1st Cir. 1995) (citing *Bank of Nova Scotia v. United States*, 487 U.S. 250, 263 (1988)). An "indictment's main purpose is 'to inform the defendant of the nature of the accusation against him.'" *United States v. Hitt*, 249 F.3d 1010, 1016 (D.C. Cir. 2001) (quoting *Russell v. United States*, 396 U.S. 749, 767 (1962)). It therefore need only contain "a plain, concise, and definite written statement of the essential facts constituting the offense charged." Fed. R. Crim. P. 7(c). When considering a motion to dismiss an indictment, a court assumes the truth of those factual allegations. *See Boyce Motor Lines v. United States*, 342 U.S. 337,

343 n.16 (1952). Consequently, the district court did not err when it assumed the truth of the government's proffered facts in denying Ballestas's motion, including with regard to whether the pertinent vessel was subject to the jurisdiction of the United States.

VI.

Ballestas next argues that the government violated its constitutional obligation to disclose exculpatory evidence under *Brady v. Maryland*, 373 U.S. 83 (1963). According to Ballestas, the government waited too long to notify him of a [—17—] related trial that took place in the Middle District of Florida in 2010. That trial involved the prosecution of the crew members apprehended during the seizure of the vessel on March 3, 2010. Instead of disclosing the existence of the Florida prosecution at Ballestas's first appearance before the district court in February 2012, it appears that the government waited until December to notify Ballestas of the Florida proceeding. That delay, Ballestas contends, prevented him from gaining access to several documents that he thinks would have strengthened his case. The government argues that we should not reach the merits of Ballestas's *Brady* claim because he waived any *Brady* argument when he entered a guilty plea. *See United States v. Ruiz*, 536 U.S. 622, 628 (2002). We need not resolve the government's waiver argument, however, because we conclude that no constitutional violation took place in any event.

To succeed on the merits of his *Brady* claim, Ballestas must show that (i) the government suppressed evidence; and (ii) the evidence was favorable and material. *See Strickler v. Greene*, 527 U.S. 263, 281-82 (1999). Ballestas's claim fails at the first step. When a defendant challenges the government's alleged delay in disclosure of exculpatory evidence, "the defendant must show a reasonable probability that an earlier disclosure would have changed the trial's result." *United States v. Dean*, 55 F.3d 640, 663 (D.C. Cir. 1995). If a "defendant receives exculpatory evidence 'in time to make effective use of it,' a new trial is, in most cases, not warranted." *Id.* (quoting *United States v. Paxson*, 861 F.2d 730, 737 (D.C. Cir. 1988)).

Here, the government alerted Ballestas to the existence of the Florida prosecution by December 2012. Additionally, the government around that time disclosed to Ballestas law enforcement materials containing information about the [—18—] March 2010 vessel seizures. Those materials included the precise Coast Guard declaration Ballestas now claims is *Brady* material. Although the disclosures came after Ballestas had submitted briefing on his motion to dismiss, they occurred three months before the district court ruled on the motion and nine months before Ballestas entered his guilty plea. Ballestas therefore had ample time to "make effective use" of any information from the Florida trial in support of his motion to dismiss and in deciding whether to enter a plea of guilty. Consequently, Ballestas has not shown a "reasonable probability" that earlier disclosure of the Coast Guard declaration would have made any difference. *Id.*

Ballestas separately suggests that the government should have pointed Ballestas to a habeas petition filed by one of the Florida defendants—Victor M. Ballestero Linares. That petition included an affidavit by Linares, which Ballestas maintains would have been helpful to his case. But Linares's affidavit was listed under the criminal docket number disclosed to Ballestas by the government in December 2012. Because Ballestas had access to that affidavit "in time to make effective use of it," he cannot show that the government suppressed the document. *Paxson*, 861 F.2d at 737.

VII.

Finally, Ballestas challenges the sentence imposed by the district court. He claims that the MDLEA does not give the district court authority to consider conduct beyond the activity that took place on board the vessel seized on March 3, 2010—the only vessel specifically identified in the factual stipulations as having traveled through the high seas.. Appellant Br. 42-43. As an initial matter, the nature of Ballestas's argument is unclear. His guilty plea laid out the guideline calculations supported by the stipulated facts and [—19—] concluded that "the Defendant's Total Offense Level would be 27/Criminal History Category I or a Guidelines range of 70 to 87 months." App. 188. That guidelines range was based solely on the drug amount recovered from the vessel seized on March 3rd. *See id.* at 186-88. While the district court considered other conduct in ultimately selecting a sentence within (or, actually, below) that range, courts enjoy substantial discretion to consider a wide range of factors when imposing a sentence following calculation of the guidelines range. *See* 18 U.S.C. § 3553.

In any event, Ballestas's guilty plea waived his right to appeal his sentence except insofar as "the sentence exceeds the maximum permitted by statute or results from an upward departure from the guideline range established by the Court at sentencing." App. 192. Ballestas cannot succeed in challenging his sentence on either of the two grounds he preserved. His guilty plea laid out the guidelines calculations supported by the stipulated facts, arriving at a guidelines range of seventy to eighty-seven months of imprisonment based on the amount of drugs recovered from the March 3rd vessel. *Id.* at 188. The district court ultimately sentenced him to a below-guidelines sentence of sixty-four months. Ballestas therefore has no basis for appealing his sentence on the ground that it "results from an upward departure from the guideline range established by the [district court]." *Id.* at 192. Additionally, because the MDLEA allows for a maximum sentence of twenty years of imprisonment for the charged conduct, *see* 46 U.S.C. § 70506(a); 21 U.S.C. § 960(b)(3), Ballestas likewise has no basis for challenging his sixty-four month sentence on the ground that it "exceeds the maximum permitted by statute." App. 192. [—20—]

* * * * *

For the foregoing reasons, we reject Ballestas's challenges and affirm the judgment of the district court.

So ordered.

United States Court of Appeals
for the District of Columbia Circuit

No. 14-5203

WATERVALE MARINE CO.
vs.
UNITED STATES DEP'T OF HOMELAND SECURITY

Appeal from the United States District Court for the
District of Columbia

Decided: December 15, 2015

Citation: 807 F.3d 325, 3 Adm. R. 707 (D.C. Cir. 2015).

Before **GRIFFITH** and **SRINIVASAN**, Circuit Judges, and
SILBERMAN, Senior Circuit Judge.

[—2—] SILBERMAN, Senior Circuit Judge:

This case presents the question whether the Secretary of the Department of Homeland Security—acting through the Coast Guard—may impose certain conditions (nonfinancial in nature) upon the release of ships suspected of violating the Act to Prevent Pollution from Ships.

Ship owners appeal from the district court's holding that the case is nonjusticiable. We disagree as to justiciability, but affirm on other grounds.

I.

The Act is a federal statute passed to implement various environmental obligations that the United States assumed when it entered into the International Convention for the Prevention of Pollution from Ships. *See* 33 U.S.C. § 1901(a)(4). The goal of the treaty and its implementing legislation is to eliminate the intentional pollution of the oceans by "oil and other harmful substances," as well as minimize "accidental discharge of such substances." *See Wilmina Shipping AS v. U.S. Dep't of Homeland Sec.*, 934 F.Supp.2d 1, 6 (D.D.C. 2013) (citations omitted).

The Secretary of the Department of Homeland Security is authorized "to administer and enforce" the Convention and to [—3—] "prescribe any necessary or desired regulations to carry out" its requirements. 33 U.S.C. § 1903(a), (c)(1).[1] It is "unlawful to act in violation of the" Convention "or the regulations issued thereunder." 33 U.S.C. § 1907(a). Knowingly violating the law may give rise to both criminal and civil liability.

General authority to grant departure clearance to foreign-flagged ships is in Customs. *See* 46 U.S.C. § 60105(b). But a specific provision of the Act deals with the enforcement of the Convention:

> If any ship subject to the [Convention]…is liable for a fine or civil penalty under this section, or if reasonable cause exists to believe that the ship, its owner, operator, or person in charge may be subject to a fine or civil penalty under this section, the Secretary of the Treasury [now DHS], upon request of the Secretary [of DHS], shall refuse or revoke the clearance required by section 60105 of Title 46. Clearance may be granted upon the filing of a bond or other surety satisfactory to the Secretary [of DHS].

33 U.S.C. § 1908(e). Both references to the Secretary now refer to the Secretary of Homeland Security who supervises both Customs and the Coast Guard, but in accordance with regulations, Customs maintains authority to clear a vessel *unless* the Coast Guard requests otherwise, and it is the Coast Guard that has authority to accept a bond. [—4—]

Appellants own and operate two foreign-flagged vessels: the M/V AGIOS EMILIANOS and the M/V STELLAR WIND. Each periodically docks at U.S. ports, in the course of its oceangoing business, to load or offload cargo. In the spring of 2011, the Coast Guard began receiving whistleblower complaints asserting violations of the Act. Specifically, it was claimed that the appellants' vessels had falsified the oil record books required of all vessels when traveling over international

---

[1] The authority to grant clearance, originally vested in the Secretary of the Treasury, was subsequently transferred to the Secretary of Homeland Security, and then further delegated to Customs. *See* 68 Fed. Reg. 28323 (May 23, 2003).

waters and docking at U.S. ports. Upon initial investigation stemming from the complaints, the Coast Guard determined that it had reasonable cause to believe that the vessels' operators had committed violations of the Act. Therefore the Coast Guard ordered Customs to withhold departure clearance.[2] The vessels were held for investigation for differing lengths of time, ranging from a couple of days to over a month.

As the district court noted, the vessels were eventually released, but not until appellants had both posted a bond *and* executed a "Security Agreement." These agreements were required by the Coast Guard as a condition of release of the vessels. They were designed to allow the government to later prosecute its case if merited. As such, these agreements include several terms above and beyond the posting of a typical financial bond. They called for the vessel owners and operators to pay wages, housing, and transportation costs to crew members who remain in the jurisdiction, as well as facilitate their travel to court appearances, to encourage crew members to cooperate with the government's investigation, to help the government serve subpoenas on foreign crew members located outside of the United States, to waive objections to both *in personam* and *in rem* jurisdiction, and to enter an appearance in federal district court. After their release, the vessel owners initiated an [—5—] administrative appeal with the Coast Guard to challenge the validity of the Security Agreements.

Meanwhile, the Coast Guard proceeded with its criminal prosecutions. Ultimately, the management associated with the AGIOS EMILIANOS and STELLAR WIND pled guilty, and admitted to intentionally bypassing mandatory anti-pollution equipment on board and discharging oil waste directly into the waterways. Some among the crew on both ships had rerouted oily water around required water-oil separators and sludge incinerators, discharging it directly into the ocean. Those discharges were then hidden from the mandatory oil records book, and false entries that the environmental protection equipment was being used were made.

Appellants, having failed in all administrative appeals, challenge the nonfinancial Security Agreements that the Coast Guard demanded before granting departure clearance as beyond the Coast Guard's statutory authority. The district court ruled for the government, stating that the matter of conditional departure clearance was committed to the Coast Guard's discretion by law. The court did observe that the final sentence of § 1908(e), describing a "bond or other surety," might well be limited to purely financial terms. But the court was of the view that the language stating that "clearance may be granted upon the filing of a bond or other surety satisfactory to the Secretary" gave the Department (the Coast Guard) unreviewable discretion, and therefore the court had no standards by which to judge the claim. [—6—]

II.

Appellants challenge the district court's holding on several grounds. Of course, they insist that the case is reviewable; that there are judicially acceptable standards to apply. Then, proceeding to the merits, appellants assert that only Customs—not the Coast Guard—has authority to withhold a ship's clearance. And although the Coast Guard can require a bond (or other surety), it may not demand any nonfinancial conditions as part of the bond.[3]

---

[2] The AGIOS EMILIANOS and STELLAR WIND were held at ports in Louisiana.

[3] Appellants claim that the Coast Guard could have used several other techniques to accomplish what it sought by way of the Security Agreements. *See* 18 U.S.C. § 3144 (authority to secure testimony of material witnesses); Fed. R. Crim. P. 15 (authority to take depositions of witnesses); 14 U.S.C. § 89(a) (warrantless search, seizure, and arrest authority); Fed. R. Crim. P. 6 (grand jury powers); 28 U.S.C. § 1821; 28 C.F.R. Part 21 (authorizing and implementing procedures to pay transportation, lodging and other expenses to secure witness testimony). But, they claim, such measures are not permissible under § 1908(e).

The government reiterates its position before the district court; that we lack jurisdiction because the Coast Guard has unreviewable discretion to accept or reject a bond, and thereby prevent a ship's departure. Moreover before us, for the first time, appellants' standing is challenged and it is further claimed that the cases are moot. Turning to the surety, the government contends that the Coast Guard can insist on the nonfinancial conditions it imposed because such conditions are within the meaning of the terms "bond or other surety." Indeed, it is argued that such conditions are commonly included in bonds. (The government's brief boldly so asserts, but no examples nor dictionary definitions are cited, which is a novel approach to brief writing.) [—7—]

The government explains why the Coast Guard insisted on the nonfinancial conditions in these cases. It asserts—and appellants agree—that the financial terms of a bond referred to in the Act cover the ultimate liability of a ship owner, which can be determined only after a legal proceeding, either civil or criminal. In other words, nothing prevents the ship, after posting the bond, from sailing away. And if the government lacks sufficient evidence to present in court without the ship and its crew, the ship owner's liability disappears.

* * *

We have little doubt as to our jurisdiction. Appellants clearly have standing, and the case is not moot, even if the ships have sailed. The government contends that the agreements have no ongoing legal effect. Apparently this is because the plea agreements were reached by some appellants in the interim between the filing of the original complaint and this appeal. But the government overlooks that two of the appellants never pled to, nor were they, as yet, charged with a crime. It also ignores the fact that Security Agreements with two of the parties have no expiration date at all, and even for those Security Agreements with a duration provision, language releasing the parties has not been clearly triggered. Finally, the government disregards the point that even the criminal

pleas that were reached do not foreclose the government's ability to seek further civil penalties, as allowed under the Act.

Nor do we agree with the government and the district court that the Coast Guard's discretion is unreviewable. Although the Coast Guard may have wide discretion as to the *amount* of the bond it requires (we doubt that even that is totally unreviewable) there is no reason to believe that the legal question presented—whether the Coast Guard can impose nonfinancial conditions—is not suitable for judicial review. [—8—]

On the other hand, appellants' lengthy discussion of the respective roles of the Coast Guard and Customs seems rather academic. After all, both entities are in the same Department under the common supervision of the Secretary of Homeland Security. In any event, it is clearly the Coast Guard under the Secretary's regulations that has the authority granted by the Secretary to "request" that Customs "refuse" clearance.[4]

Which brings us to the main issue in the case; whether the Coast Guard may require the nonfinancial conditions. Appellants point to the legislative history indicating that Congress intended a bond or other surety to cover *only* financial liability for penalties imposed in civil or criminal proceedings. *See* H.R. No. 96-1224, *reprinted in* 1980 U.S.C.C.A.N. 4849. The government does not contest the House Report on which appellant relies, instead focusing on the phrase "satisfactory to the Secretary" as giving the Coast Guard broader authority. We find it unnecessary to decide the scope of the term "bond or other surety" because the first sentence of section 1908(e) gives the Coast Guard the requisite authority. It states that "[i]f any ship subject to the [Convention]…is liable for a fine or civil penalty…or if reasonable cause exists to believe that the ship…may be subject to a fine or civil penalty [Customs]…upon request of the Secretary [the Coast Guard]…shall refuse…clearance," and as such it clearly provides authority in the Coast Guard to simply hold the ship in port

---

[4] *See* 19 C.F.R. §§ 4.60a, 4.66a, 4.66c(a).

until legal proceedings are completed.[5] [—9—]

The nonfinancial conditions can, therefore, be thought of as simply the *quid pro quo* for allowing ships to depart. It is not necessary to consider whether those conditions are legitimately a part of "a bond or other surety" because they could be required independently of a bond. Although the Act *authorizes* the Secretary (Coast Guard) to request clearance of a ship if a bond is satisfactory, the Coast Guard is not required to accept a bond. (Here we agree with the district court that the words "may" and "satisfactory" are significant.) Indeed, as we understand the government, a financial bond, given its limited use, is ordinarily not satisfactory, so the Coast Guard need not accept bonds without accompanying nonfinancial conditions.

We note that another statutory section provides a ship owner with a cause of action for the government's unreasonable delay in granting departure clearance.[6] We need not consider whether the reasonableness of nonfinancial conditions is also subject to challenge because in the cases before us appellants have not asserted that the nonfinancial conditions are unreasonable.

Accordingly, we must assume that holding the ships and crew until a civil or criminal proceeding was completed was reasonable.

And since the Coast Guard can hold the ship for [—10—] such a purpose, it seems to follow that the Coast Guard can agree to notify Customs to release the ship only upon condition that a civil or criminal proceeding would not be jeopardized.

* * *

For the above reasons, we affirm the district court's judgment.

So ordered.

(Reporter's Note: Concurring opinion, in part, and concurring in the judgment, follows on p. 711).

---

[5] Our concurring colleague suggests that we are bypassing the text and resorting to our own reasoning. We concede we are reasoning, but we are focusing on the meaning and necessary implication of the first sentence of section 1908(e), which of course is textual analysis. The concurrence does not directly dispute that in the absence of the second [—9—] sentence of 1908(e), the first sentence would give the Coast Guard the requisite authority for the Security Agreements.

Nor do we understand why our own interpretation gives the Coast Guard any more authority than does our colleague's interpretation. After all, the concurrence contends that a "bond or other surety" can include *any* nonfinancial condition—lasting presumably indefinitely—so long as it is secured by a pot of money and labeled a bond.

[6] *See* 33 U.S.C. § 1904(h).

[—1—] **GRIFFITH,** Circuit Judge, concurring in part and concurring in the judgment:

The majority is correct that section 1908(e) authorizes the Coast Guard to accept a *quid* in return for the *quo* of releasing the ship. That *quid* is a "bond or other surety." 33 U.S.C. § 1908(e). Rather than find that the Security Agreements in this case qualify as a "bond or other surety," however, the majority bypasses the text of the statute and resorts to its own reasoning: the greater power granted by the statute to hold the ship must surely include the lesser power to condition its release. And as a matter of logic, that seems right. However, nothing in the text expressly authorizes such a broad, free-floating *quid pro quo* authority. Unlike the majority, I would not decide whether such authority exists by implication. Instead, I would affirm the judgment of the district court on the narrower ground provided by the text of the statute: a "bond or other surety"—the *quid* provided by Congress—includes the Security Agreements in this case.

As the majority recognizes, Congress has given the Coast Guard wide discretion in setting the conditions of a bond or other surety. My point is only that such discretion comes from an explicit statutory grant allowing the Coast Guard to accept a "bond or other surety." Apart from that authority, nothing in the express language of the statute permits a *quid pro quo* exchange and ignoring the phrase "bond or other surety" renders that provision superfluous.

Once a ship's clearance has been refused or revoked, the statute authorizes the granting of clearance "upon the filing of a bond or other surety satisfactory to the Secretary." 33 U.S.C. § 1908(e). Because the phrase "bond or other surety" is not qualified or defined, the phrase must be given its "ordinary meaning," *Taniguchi v. Kan Pac. Saipan, Ltd.,* 132 S. Ct. 1997, 2002 (2012), which includes both financial and [—2—] non-financial conditions. A bond, for example, is simply a "written promise to pay money *or do some act* if certain circumstances occur or a certain time elapses." BLACK'S LAW DICTIONARY (10th ed. 2014) (emphasis added); *see also* MERRIAM-WEBSTER UNABRIDGED DICTIONARY (online ed. 2015)

(defining "bond" as "a usually formal written agreement by which a person undertakes to perform *a certain act* (such as to appear in court or fulfill the obligations of a contract) or abstain from performing *an act* (such as committing a crime) with the condition that failure to perform or abstain will obligate the person . . . to pay a sum of money" (emphasis added)). A surety is similarly broad: a "formal assurance," especially "a pledge, bond, guarantee, or security given for the fulfillment of an undertaking." BLACK'S LAW DICTIONARY (10th ed. 2014); *see also* MERRIAM-WEBSTER UNABRIDGED DICTIONARY (online ed. 2015) (defining "surety" as "a pledge or other formal engagement given for the fulfillment of an undertaking").

These definitions demonstrate that both bonds and sureties are general contractual devices used to assure performance of some act. The text of the statute nowhere limits these ordinary meanings to financial conditions alone.

The cardinal rule of statutory construction—that the legislature says in a statute what it means and means what it says—cautions against overlooking the text and relying instead on what a court might think is an unstated principle that informs the provision. *See Conn. Nat'l Bank v. Germain,* 503 U.S. 249, 253-54 (1992). Reading the statute for what it says, the Security Agreements comfortably fit within the authorization to demand a "bond or other surety" in exchange for the release of the ship. Each Agreement requires the ship owner to post a "Surety Bond" to "ensure performance of [—3—] th[e] Agreement" and the payment of any fines or penalties. To perform the Agreement, the ship owner must waive objections to jurisdiction and assist in the investigation, for example by paying for lodging and meals for the crew to remain in the United States. The United States may keep the bond amount not only if it secures a judgment against the owner, but also if the owner "fail[s] to waive objections to jurisdiction as required by this Agreement." And it may keep a certain portion of the bond amount if the ship owner materially breaches the Agreement's other conditions. Thus, as with any bond or surety, the Agreements bind the ship owners "to perform [ ] certain act[s]"—waive objections to jurisdiction and assist in the investigation—"with the condition that failure to perform . . . will obligate the [ship owners] . . . to pay a sum of money." Merriam-Webster Unabridged Dictionary (online ed. 2015) (defining "bond").

The appellants challenge this reading of the statute, arguing that a phrase in the legislative history shows the Coast Guard lacks the power to impose non-financial conditions for the release of a ship:

> *To assure payment of any fine or civil penalties* that might be incurred upon completion of criminal proceedings or civil penalty actions, the Secretary of the Treasury is required to refuse or revoke clearance to any ship upon request of the Secretary of Transportation. However, clearance may be granted upon the filing of a bond or other satisfactory surety.

H.R. Rep. No. 96-1224, at 17 (1980), *reprinted in* 1980 U.S.C.C.A.N. 4849, 4864 (emphasis added). According to the appellants, "[t]o assure payment of any fine or civil penalties" [—4—] means that the bond or surety must be limited to covering the payment of a fine. Leaving to one side the debate about the value of legislative history in statutory interpretation, *see Samantar v. Yousuf*, 560 U.S. 305, 326-27 (2010) (Scalia, J., concurring in the judgment), we have consistently held that where the statutory text is clear, "[t]he plain meaning of legislation should be conclusive" unless it "compels an odd result." *Engine Mfrs. Ass'n v. EPA*, 88 F.3d 1075, 1088 (D.C. Cir. 1996) (internal quotation marks omitted); *Nat'l Pub. Radio, Inc. v. FCC*, 254 F.3d 226, 231 (D.C. Cir. 2001). Here, nothing odd results from imposing conditions that assist the United States in its prosecution of violations of the Act to Prevent Pollution from Ships. We would be stepping beyond the bounds of the judicial role were we to disregard the text of the statute based on a phrase in a House Report.

In any event, the appellants make too much of this phrase. The language from the House Report upon which the appellants rely does not limit a bond or other surety to financial conditions. Instead, it offers that one purpose of section 1908(e) is to make sure that fines are paid. But any likelihood of obtaining a fine vanishes if the United States cannot secure the conditions included in the Security Agreements here. For instance, if ship owners do not waive objections to jurisdiction, the United States may lack jurisdiction to prosecute them after granting clearance. No prosecution means no fine, in which case the United States must return the bond amount to the ship owners. Recognizing this problem, the appellants conceded at oral argument that a "bond or other surety" could, at a minimum, contain an obligation to waive objections to jurisdiction. Appellants then suggested a new line between non-financial conditions that are jurisdictional and those that are not. But that line, like the [—5—] distinction the appellants urge between financial and other conditions, has no basis in the text of the statute.

For these reasons, I would affirm the judgment of the district court on the ground that the Security Agreements are the type of "bond or other surety" that the statute's plain text authorizes the Coast Guard to accept in exchange for the release of the ship.

United States Court of Appeals for the District of Columbia Circuit

No. 14-1044

ADENARIWO

vs.

FEDERAL MARITIME COMM'N

On Petition for Review of an Order of the Federal Maritime Commission

Decided: December 15, 2015

Citation: 808 F.3d 74, 3 Adm. R. 713 (D.C. Cir. 2015).

Before **HENDERSON**, Circuit Judge, and **EDWARDS** and **SENTELLE**, Senior Circuit Judges.

[—2—] **SENTELLE**, Senior Circuit Judge:

Petitioner Adebisi Adenariwo petitions for review of two Federal Maritime Commission decisions relating to the loss of concrete masonry equipment shipped from the United States to Nigeria in two separate shipping containers. Transportation of the equipment was organized and carried out by BDP International (BDP) and Zim Integrated Shipping, Ltd. (Zim). Adenariwo filed with the Commission two identical complaints against Zim and BDP, alleging that they had engaged in unreasonable practices when handling the equipment, in violation of Section 10(d)(1) of the Shipping Act of 1984, 46 U.S.C. § 41102(c). The Commission dismissed Adenariwo's claims as to the equipment in the first container, but awarded Adenariwo reduced reparations for the loss of the equipment in the second container. Because we conclude that Adenariwo's petition for review of the Commission's decision relating to the first container was untimely under the Hobbs Act, 28 U.S.C. §§ 2342(3)(B), 2344, we dismiss the portions of his petition relating to that container for lack of jurisdiction. Because we conclude that the Commission improperly reduced Adenariwo's award for the loss of the equipment in the second container, we vacate the decision relating to that container and remand for award of the full amount supported by the record without mitigation and permitted under 46 C.F.R. § 502.301(b). [—3—]

I. BACKGROUND

A. Facts

Adenariwo is the owner and principal of MacBride Nigeria, Ltd. (MacBride), a producer of concrete masonry products in Lagos, Nigeria. In 2008, MacBride purchased equipment from Nethamer Ltd., a U.S.-based company. BDP, a licensed freight forwarder, arranged for the transportation of the equipment from the U.S. to Nigeria by Zim, a vessel-operating common carrier. Zim shipped the equipment to Nigeria in two containers. The first shipment (Container 1) arrived in Nigeria on or around April 17, 2008, but because of errors in the bill of lading, not the fault of MacBride, it was not released to MacBride and demurrage fees began to accrue. The second container (Container 2) arrived one month later, but LANSAL, Zim's agent, refused to release it until MacBride paid the outstanding demurrage fees for Container 1. As a result, demurrage fees began to accrue on Container 2 as well. Ultimately, Nigerian Customs officials seized both containers and the equipment was auctioned off.

B. Administrative and Federal Court Proceedings

On May 3, 2011, Adenariwo filed two separate but identical complaints—Informal Docket Nos. 1920(I) and 1921(I)—against BDP and Zim for informal adjudication under subpart S of the Commission's Rules of Practice and Procedure. See 46 C.F.R. §§ 502.301-305. The complaints allege that BDP and Zim violated Section 10(d)(1) of the Shipping Act of 1984, 46 U.S.C. § 41102(c), by engaging in unreasonable practices when handling the concrete masonry equipment. While Adenariwo alleges that he suffered a loss of $240,606 per container, he chose to pursue his claims through the informal adjudication process, which is limited to [—4—] claims of $50,000 or less. See 46 C.F.R. § 502.301(b). Thus, Adenariwo sought a total of $100,000 or $50,000 per container.

Pursuant to the Commission's Rules, a settlement officer was appointed to handle both informal dockets. On May 26, 2011, for purposes of clarity, the settlement officer deemed Informal Docket No. 1920(I) to seek reparations for Container 1 and Informal Docket No. 1921(I) to seek reparations for Container 2. The settlement officer also ordered that the dockets be consolidated, but stated that the consolidation would not affect Adenariwo's requested relief.

On April 18, 2012, the settlement officer issued a decision and order dismissing the claim relating to Container 1 for failure to timely file the complaint within the Shipping Act's three year statute of limitations, *see* 46 U.S.C. § 41301(a), and ordering Adenariwo to obtain a valid assignment from MacBride of the Container 2 claim in Informal Docket No. 1921(I). Adenariwo timely filed a petition for reconsideration of the settlement officer's decision to dismiss Informal Docket No. 1920(I), which the settlement officer denied. In another decision issued that same day, the settlement officer also determined that (1) MacBride had assigned its claims to Adenariwo and (2) Zim had violated Section 10(d)(1) of the Shipping Act by refusing to release Container 2 because of the unpaid demurrage fees from Container 1. *See Adebisi A. Adenariwo v. BDP Int'l, Zim Integrated Shipping, Ltd. and Its Agent (LANSAL) et al.,* Informal Dkt. No. 1921(I), at 8-11 (F.M.C. Mar. 7, 2013). The settlement officer awarded Adenariwo reparations in the amount of $18,308.94 for the loss of the equipment in Container 2, but denied Adenariwo the remainder of his requested relief finding that he could have mitigated his losses by paying the demurrage fees on the two [—5—] containers, thereby securing the release of the equipment in Container 2. *Id.* at 11-16.

Pursuant to the Commission's rules governing informal adjudications, the Commission has discretionary authority to review a settlement officer's decision. *See* 46 C.F.R. § 502.304(g). On March 22, 2013, the Commission declined to review the settlement officer's decision not to reconsider the dismissal of Informal Docket No. 1920(I), stating that the decision was "administratively final." On April 10, 2013, the Commission determined that it would

review the settlement officer's decision relating to Informal Docket No. 1921(I). On August 2, 2013, Adenariwo filed a complaint with the U.S. District Court for the District of Columbia seeking review of the Commission's decisions in Informal Docket Nos. 1920(I) and 1921(I). The district court dismissed the case, finding that it lacked subject-matter jurisdiction and observing that the settlement officer's decision regarding Informal Docket No. 1921(I) was not ripe for review because it was still under the Commission's consideration. *See MacBride Nig. Ltd. (Adebisi Adenariwo) v. FMC,* Civ. No. 13-1201, 2013 WL 6175823 (D.D.C. Nov. 26, 2013). On February 20, 2014, the Commission issued an order affirming the settlement officer's decision in Informal Docket No. 1921(I). *See Adebisi Adenariwo v. BDP Int'l, Zim Integrated Shipping, Ltd. and Its Agent (LANSAL) et al.,* Informal Dkt. No. 1921(I) (F.M.C. Feb. 20, 2014). Adenariwo filed his petition for review of the Commission's decisions with this Court on March 21, 2014.

II. ANALYSIS

Before this Court, Adenariwo contends that the settlement officer abused her discretion in dismissing his Container 1 claim on statute of limitation grounds and [—6—] improperly applied mitigation principles when she calculated Adenariwo's reparations award for the loss of the equipment in Container 2. The Commission asserts that this Court lacks jurisdiction to hear Adenariwo's challenge to the dismissal of his Container 1 claim and that if this Court has jurisdiction, the settlement officer properly dismissed the Container 1 claim because it was barred by the Shipping Act's three year statute of limitations. As to the award of damages, the Commission argues that the settlement officer properly applied principles of mitigation in reducing Adenariwo's award.

A. Jurisdiction

Our jurisdiction over this matter derives from 28 U.S.C. § 2342(3)(B). That statute provides that courts of appeals have jurisdiction to review "all rules, regulations, or *final* orders, of . . . the Federal Maritime

Commission issued pursuant to [listed statutes]." (emphasis added). Under the Commission's regulations, a settlement officer's decision is considered a *final* order, "unless, within thirty [] days from the date of service of the decision, the Commission exercises its discretionary right to review the decision." 46 C.F.R. § 502.304(g). Petitions for review of final agency action must be filed within 60 days after the entry of the order under review. *See* 28 U.S.C. § 2344.

Whether an administrative decision is final is determined not "by the administrative agency's characterization of its action, but rather by a realistic assessment of the nature and effect of the order sought to be reviewed." *Fidelity Television, Inc. v. FCC*, 502 F.2d 443, 448 (D.C. Cir. 1974). "[T]he relevant considerations in determining finality are whether the process of administrative decisionmaking has reached a stage where judicial review will not disrupt the [—7—] orderly process of adjudication and whether rights or obligations have been determined or legal consequences will flow from the agency action." *Blue Ridge Envtl. Def. League v. Nuclear Regulatory Comm'n*, 668 F.3d 747, 753 (D.C. Cir. 2012) (quoting *Port of Bos. Marine Terminal Ass'n v. Rederiaktiebolaget Transatlantic*, 400 U.S. 62, 71 (1970)); *see also Bennett v. Spear*, 520 U.S. 154, 177-78 (1997) (addressing the requirement of finality under the Administrative Procedure Act, 5 U.S.C. § 704, and explaining that to be "final" an action "must mark the 'consummation' of the agency's decisionmaking process" and "be one by which 'rights or obligations had been determined,' or from which 'legal consequences will flow'"). An agency order is final for purposes of 28 U.S.C. § 2342 "if it imposes an obligation, denies a right, or fixes some legal relationship, usually at the consummation of an administrative process." *Natural Res. Def. Council, Inc. v. U.S. Nuclear Regulatory Comm'n*, 680 F.2d 810, 815 (D.C. Cir. 1982) (internal quotation marks and citation omitted).

The Commission argues that the settlement officer's decision to dismiss Informal Docket No. 1920(I) became final on March 22, 2013—the day the Commission issued its notice declining to review that decision—and, therefore, this Court does not have jurisdiction because Adenariwo waited more than a year to file his petition for review. Although the dockets were initially consolidated, the Commission contends that they were later severed. When the Commission declined review of the settlement officer's decision to reconsider the dismissal of Informal Docket No. 1920(I), the settlement officer's decision became final and the clock started ticking.

Adenariwo argues that the settlement officer's decision to dismiss Informal Docket No. 1920(I) did not become final until February 20, 2014—the day the Commission affirmed [—8—] the settlement officer's decision relating to Informal Docket No. 1921(I). Because he filed his petition for review on March 21, 2014, less than 60 days later, this Court has jurisdiction to review the portions of the petition addressing Container 1. According to Adenariwo, his Container 1 and Container 2 claims were "one controversy," Pet.'s Reply Br. at 13, and, therefore, the clock did not start ticking on his Container 1 claim until his Container 2 claim had also been resolved. Because we agree with the Commission that the settlement officer's decision to dismiss Informal Docket No. 1920(I) became final on March 22, 2013, we must dismiss the portion of the petition relating to Container 1.

When the settlement officer received two identical complaints, she probably could have dismissed one of them thereby limiting Adenariwo to a possible recovery of $50,000. Instead, the settlement officer treated the two containers as two separate claims and assigned one container to each informal docket. By doing so, the settlement officer allowed Adenariwo to seek a total of $100,000 in reparations. She also consolidated Informal Docket Nos. 1920(I) and 1921(I) in order to move the claims forward more efficiently. On April 18, 2012, in a single decision, the settlement officer dismissed Informal Docket No. 1920(I) and requested more information about the claim in Informal Docket No. 1921(I). This was the last time the two claims were addressed together.

On March 7, 2013, the settlement officer issued two separate decisions, one denying Adenariwo's petition for reconsideration of her decision to dismiss Informal Docket No. 1920(I) and one awarding him reparations in Informal Docket No. 1921(I). In doing so, the settlement officer effectively severed the two cases. This is evident from the manner in which the cases proceeded. The Commission addressed whether it would exercise its discretionary right to [—9—] review the settlement officer's decisions separately. The Commission released a notice that it would not review the decision in Informal Docket No. 1920(I) on March 22, 2013. It released a separate notice that it would review the decision in Informal Docket No. 1921(I) on April 10, 2013.

The Commission's March 22, 2013 notice not to review was the "consummation" of the informal adjudication process for Informal Docket No. 1920(I). See Natural Res. Def. Council, Inc., 680 F.2d at 815. At that point, the settlement officer's decision to dismiss Informal Docket No. 1920(I) became final pursuant to the regulations governing informal adjudications, see 46 C.F.R. § 502.304(g), and neither the Commission nor the settlement officer could take further action. The Commission's decision not to review determined, for administrative purposes, the rights and obligations of Adenariwo and Zim vis-à-vis the equipment in Container 1. See Blue Ridge, 668 F.3d at 753. Adenariwo's only recourse was to challenge the Commission's decision in a federal court of appeals within 60 days of the Commission's notice declining to exercise its right to review. Because Adenariwo did not file his petition for review within that time period, we lack jurisdiction to review the portion of his petition relating to Container 1 and Informal Docket No. 1920(I). Accordingly, the petition is dismissed as to Docket 1920(I).

B. Mitigation of Damages – Informal Docket No. 1921(I)

It is undisputed that this Court has jurisdiction over the claims related to the second container and adjudicated in Informal Docket No. 1921(I). As to that docket number,

petitioner alleges that the settlement officer, as affirmed by the Commission, erred in reducing the award in this docket number for failure to mitigate damages. Failure to mitigate damages is an affirmative defense, on which the party [—10—] opposing the award of damages bears the burden of proof. See Tri County Indus., Inc. v. District of Columbia, 200 F.3d 836, 840 (D.C. Cir. 2000); Lennon v. U.S. Theatre Corp., 920 F.2d 996, 1000 (D.C. Cir. 1990). Mitigation requires a party to take reasonable steps after it has been injured to prevent further damage from occurring. See 1 D. Dobbs, Law of Remedies § 3.9, at 380-81 (2d ed. 1993). Adenariwo contends that the Commission "applied a legally untenable interpretation of mitigation of damages principles" when it affirmed the settlement officer's reduction of Adenariwo's award for the loss of the equipment in Container 2. Pet.'s Br. at 18. We agree.

In her March 7, 2013 decision, the settlement officer found that it was not only unreasonable but also unlawful for Zim to condition the release of Container 2 on payment of the demurrage fees for Container 1. However, in calculating the damages that Zim owed Adenariwo for the loss of the equipment in Container 2, the settlement officer concluded that, once it became clear that Zim was not going to release Container 2 without receiving payment for the demurrage fees on both containers, it would have been reasonable for Adenariwo to mitigate his damages by paying those fees. The settlement officer found that, as of August 21, 2008, it was apparent that Container 2 would not be released without payment of the demurrage fees. At that time, the demurrage fees totaled $13,192.94. Accordingly, the settlement officer awarded Adenariwo reparations in the amount of $18,308.94 plus interest, consisting of the $13,192.94 he could have paid to secure release of Container 2, and $5,116.00 for a refund on the contract because Zim failed to secure delivery of the goods.

The settlement officer's decision leads to absurd and unjust results. Under the settlement officer's reasoning, a [—11—] wrongdoer, such as Zim, can set unlawful conditions for the release of an injured party's property and have the damages it owes the injured party reduced if the injured party cannot or does not meet those unlawful conditions. The settlement officer and the Commission would have this Court punish Adenariwo for not doing the very thing the law says he should not have to do. The Commission conceded at oral argument that it had not identified any case in which a court endorsed such a view of mitigation. *See* Oral Arg. Recording 12:12–12:49.

Mitigation does not allow a wrongdoer to shift the cost of its malfeasance to the injured party. *See Shea-S&M Ball v. Massman-Kiewit-Early*, 606 F.2d 1245, 1249-50 (D.C. Cir. 1979) (plaintiff was not required to mitigate damages by constructing a dike when the defendant had breached its contractual duties by failing to control water overflow and could just have easily built a dike itself); *see also Welke v. City of Davenport*, 309 N.W.2d 450, 453 (Iowa 1981) (rejecting contention that a plaintiff's damages could be reduced when a tortfeasor illegally seized chattels and plaintiff did not try to reclaim the chattels by paying a fee and storage charge). Instead, classic examples of mitigation—*e.g.*, procuring a substitute, repairing harm that would otherwise cause consequential losses—involve the injured party taking beneficial steps to prevent *further* damages. *See* 1 D. Dobbs, Law of Remedies § 3.9, at 381 (observing that mitigation generally applies to consequential damages and citing common forms of mitigating damages); *Shea-S&M Ball*, 606 F.2d at 1249 ("[T]he law does not permit an injured party to stand idly by, accumulating damages, when certain obvious, reasonable steps, if taken, would [] greatly reduce[] the damages . . . ."). [—12—]

Moreover, we have held that mitigation of damages is inapplicable when the defendant has acted unlawfully and has the primary responsibility and an equal opportunity to perform an act that it knows will avoid damages. *See Shea-S&M Ball*, 606 F.2d at 1249, *supra*; *see also* 1 D. Dobbs, Law of Remedies § 3.9, at 384 ("If, after he has committed a tort or breached a contract, the defendant had an equal and continuing opportunity to minimize damages he has

caused, and at a cost no greater than would be required of the plaintiff, the grounds for reducing [the defendant's] liability seem doubtful."). Here, Zim had an equal, if not greater, opportunity to prevent the equipment in Container 2 from being auctioned off and it had the primary responsibility of doing so. It is also fair to assume that, as a vessel-operating common carrier, Zim knew the potential consequences of its refusal to release Container 2.

We conclude that mitigation is inapplicable to the facts of this case and therefore Adenariwo should be awarded the full amount supported by the evidence, without mitigation. We therefore remand the petition for the entry of an award by the Commission in favor of petitioner in the full amount of his unmitigated damages, together with such interest and costs as may be legally appropriate.

III. CONCLUSION

We dismiss the portions of the petition relating to Container 1 (Informal Docket No. 1920(I)) for lack of jurisdiction. We vacate the Commission's February 20, 2014 decision relating to Container 2 (Informal Docket No. 1921(I)) insofar as the award ordered mitigation of damages. We remand the Commission's order for further proceedings consistent with this opinion.

So ordered.

This page intentionally left blank

Tables of Authority

This page intentionally left blank

Table of Cases

This page intentionally left blank

TABLE OF CASES[1]

A

---

[1] Cases named solely after ships, *see. e.g., The Pennsylvania*, 86 U.S. (19 Wall.) 125 (1873), are alphabetized under the letter "T." Cases where the United States is the plaintiff are alphabetized by defendant under the letter "U."

B

C

D

E

F

G

H

I

J

K

L

M

N

O

P

Q

R

S

T

U

V

W

X

Y

Z

This page intentionally left blank

Table of Statutes and Rules

This page intentionally left blank

TABLE OF STATUTES AND RULES [1]

TREATIES/INTERNATIONAL

FEDERAL

CONSTITUTION

---

[1] As cited in the opinions reported.

MISCELLANEOUS

STATUTES

RULES

REGULATIONS

STATE

Index

This page intentionally left blank

INDEX

A

B

C

D

G

L

N

O

P

Q

R

S

W

Y

This page intentionally left blank

www.ingramcontent.com/pod-product-compliance
Lightning Source LLC
Chambersburg PA
CBHW081207220326
41598CB00037B/6703